THE OXFORD
COMPANION TO THE
Garden

THE OXFORD COMPANION TO THE

Garden

Edited by Patrick Taylor

OXFORD
UNIVERSITY PRESS

OXFORD
UNIVERSITY PRESS

Great Clarendon Street, Oxford OX2 6DP

Oxford University Press is a department of the University of Oxford.
It furthers the University's objective of excellence in research, scholarship,
and education by publishing worldwide in

Oxford New York

Auckland Cape Town Dar es Salaam Hong Kong Karachi
Kuala Lumpur Madrid Melbourne Mexico City Nairobi
New Delhi Shanghai Taipei Toronto

With offices in

Argentina Austria Brazil Chile Czech Republic France Greece
Guatemala Hungary Italy Japan Poland Portugal Singapore
South Korea Switzerland Thailand Turkey Ukraine Vietnam

Oxford is a registered trademark of Oxford University Press
in the UK and in certain other countries

Published in the United States
by Oxford University Press Inc., New York

British Library Cataloguing in Publication Data

Data available

Library of Congress Cataloging in Publication Data

Data available

Typeset by Alliance Interactive Technology,
Pondicherry, India
Printed in Italy
on acid-free paper by
Lito-Terrazzi srl
Florence

ISBN 0-19-866255-6   978-0-19-866255-6

1 3 5 7 9 10 8 6 4 2

Contents

Introduction &
Acknowledgements

*T*he *Oxford Companion to Gardens* (1986) was a pioneer book of its time. Its consultant editors, Sir Geoffrey Jellicoe and Susan Jellicoe, and its executive editors, Patrick Goode and Michael Lancaster, gathered together, from an international team of authors, precious information about the world's gardens and those who made them. It was a book that all with a serious interest in gardens and their history needed to have on their shelves. Anyone following in the path of that formidable team must do so with both trepidation and due modesty.

In what way does this new *Oxford Companion to the Garden*, apart from its slight change of title, differ from its predecessor? The single largest factor influencing this new *Companion* is, simply, the passage of time. Since 1986, the world has become smaller and more accessible. People interested in gardens will travel great distances, relatively easily, to see the places that interest them. Eastern Europe has been transformed, China and parts of the Middle East are now open to visitors, the Soviet Union has been dismantled, and the unification of Germany has opened many eyes to the great richness of the German contribution to garden design. New problems and anxieties, of a quite exceptional kind, have arisen. Climate change, or global warming as it is sometimes, perhaps rather too cosily, called, is seen to have profound implications for gardens. The genetic modification of plants presents to some the charming prospect of blue roses or magenta daffodils, but to others the terrifying prospect of a man-made genie possibly playing irrevocable havoc with the natural order of things. The science of herbicides and pesticides has in recent times been transformed, and organic, or generally more nature-friendly gardening, instead of being of marginal interest, has become a central one. The scope of man-made landscapes has been expanded to include land art.

In the present book, it has been our intention to give a clear idea of the sort of gardens made in those countries in which gardening has been a significant ingredient of the culture, and to cover those in which it looms less large but is nonetheless of great interest. Countries like Britain, France, and Italy must be at the centre of such an account because of the remarkable number of notable gardens they have created and for their international influence on garden design. We regard the USA as of special importance because of its great cultural diversity, its widely ranging climates, and a flora of such bewildering riches that no one has yet described it in detail. Public parks, the great estate gardens, gardens with exceptional collections of plants, community gardens, drylands gardens, and public gardens are found in great numbers; yet, partly because of the immense size of the country, exceptional gardens are not as well or as widely known as they would be in a smaller, more densely populous country.

In this new *Companion* we have put greater emphasis on the gardens themselves—not at the expense of their history, to which we pay due attention, but because we believe that only by experiencing a garden's essence and appreciating its beauty can its importance be understood. Most of the gardens described here are open to the public (indicated by the symbol [⊛] immediately after the garden's name). We have much extended the coverage of the gardens of certain countries. In the case of the USA there is a fourfold increase in the number of gardens described, providing a better view of their wide-ranging nature. In the case of other countries, such as France, it was felt that there was too much emphasis on the past (the result, perhaps, of having an outstanding garden historian, Kenneth Woodbridge, whose speciality was the 17th century, about which he was deeply learned). France has a fascinating recent history as well; furthermore, a 20th-century curiosity such as the Maison Picassiette has things to say about the French creative genius that Versailles will not teach you. We also reached the conclusion that the whole garden atmosphere of certain great cities could best be captured if they were treated as historical entities. Thus we devote major entries to the parks, gardens, and landscapes of London, New York, and Paris, and less extensive ones to Bucharest, Melbourne, Sydney, and Vienna.

As well as providing information about notable gardens, the book offers a convenient source of valuable material about garden designers; the history of gardening in different parts of the world; influential ideas in gardening; scientific developments that influence gardening, such as herbicides, pesticides, the genetic modification of plants, and climate change; important groups of garden plants; and many other aspects of the art, craft, and theory of gardening. We consider such matters as the aesthetics of gardens, the work of notable garden designers, the use of water in gardens, plant nomenclature, and the conservation and restoration of gardens. We consider all kinds of gardens, private and public. Kitchen gardens, flower gardens, meadow gardens, deer parks, gravel gardens, wild gardens, knot gardens, and the secret gardens of the Italian Renaissance are all described. In addition to these subjects we have ranged more widely into such territories as the history of beekeeping and gardens, the history of garden visiting, photography and gardens, the mysterious world of land art, and the use of fireworks as garden ornaments. All garden owners know that gardening is good for them and we have explored this most important aspect of gardening with entries on the design of hospital grounds, on gardens for disabled people, on the worldwide phenomenon of allotments (or community gardens as they are called in North America), and on the spirit of place. Although this new *Companion* is for the most part newly commissioned from garden experts across the world, we have retained perennially valuable entries by all the consultant and executive editors of the first book, as well as those by exceptional contributors such as the late Maggie Keswick, whose writings on Chinese gardens are retained largely without alteration.

No kind of book is more dependent on a collaborative effort than this. At Oxford University Press, Michael Cox commissioned the book, Pam Coote (who had worked on the original garden *Companion*) supervised its gestation, and Wendy Tuckey (followed by Jo Spillane) managed the computer input and communications with the contributors. They did all this with the greatest friendliness and efficiency, making a task that at times seemed onerous much less so. When the text was complete, an additional team—Rebecca Collins, Edwin Pritchard, and Jackie Pritchard—went through it with eagle eyes, immensely to its benefit. Carrie Hickman and Helen Nash expertly researched the illustrations and Nick Clarke designed the book most handsomely. In the final stages John Mackrell skilfully monitored proof reading and production.

We were able to recruit a valuable group of advisory editors who were very helpful in the planning of the book and in providing advice as it developed. I am most grateful to them all but I should like in particular to thank Frank Cabot, who planned the US coverage and put us in touch with admirable contributors, and Jan Woudstra who, with his marvellous range of international contacts and more youthful point of view, added a precious dimension. The advisory editors were of the greatest help in tracking down contributors. It is on the quality of their texts that the success of such a book as this obviously depends. To all the admirable garden scholars who give the book its flavour I extend my warmest thanks. One of the greatest benefits of working on this book has been that it has opened new perspectives and put me in touch with garden scholars all over the world. Of all the world's learned communities that of garden historians, and other experts in garden matters, must be one of the friendliest and most agreeable. For all sorts of additional help I should also like to thank Gábor Alföldy, Michel Baridon, Dr Sonia Berjman, Richard Bisgrove, Professor Gordon Campbell, Ethan Carr, Patrick Chassé, Edward Fawcett, Dr Gert Gröning, Alison Hardie, Hugh Johnson, David Lambert, Pilar San Pio, Christine Reid, Elizabeth Barlow Rogers, Aurélia Rostaing, John Sales, Dr Uwe Schneider, Dr Christopher Thacker, William Warren, Elisabeth Whittle, and Frances Wood.

Lurking in the background, once again, has been my wife Caroline. Throughout the evolution of the book she has been ready with excellent advice, cups of coffee, and delicious meals. All love and thanks to her.

PATRICK TAYLOR

Somerset
2005

Editorial Team

General Editor

Patrick Taylor is a well-known garden writer and lecturer. He was born in France and educated in Scotland. On leaving university he went into publishing. A practical interest in gardening, and a move to Somerset in 1977, encouraged an interest in garden history. He began writing on gardens and photographing them for magazines and newspapers, among them *The Garden* (the journal of the Royal Horticultural Society), *Gardens Illustrated* (for which he wrote a monthly column for eight years), and the *Sunday Telegraph*. Since his first book (*Planting in Patterns*, 1989) he has written fifteen books specializing in gardens and garden design but occasionally writing about plants (such as *Gardening with Roses*, 1995, and *Gardening with Bulbs*, 1996). His *Gardener's Guide to Britain* (1992) has been through eight editions and his *The Gardens of France* (1998) was described by *Country Life* as the 'easily the best garden guide to France available'. His most recent books are *The Gardens of Britain and Ireland* (2003) and *The Wirtz Gardens* (2004). He is a member of the Library Committee of the Royal Horticultural Society and has been a committee member of the Avon Gardens Trust and chairman of the Somerset and Avon National Council for the Conservation of Plants and Gardens.

Advisory Editors

Francis H. Cabot is a gardener, plantsman, and author. He is the creator of two outstanding North American gardens—at Les Quatre Vents in the province of Québec and Stonecrop in New York State—both of which are open to the public. He founded the Garden Conservancy, which is devoted to the preservation of exceptional private gardens in North America, and has served as chairman of the New York Botanical Garden. His book *The Greater Perfection* (2001), which describes the making of the garden at Les Quatre Vents, won an American Horticultural Society National Book Award in 2002. He is the recipient of many awards among them the Gold Veitch Memorial Medal of the Royal Horticultural Society in 2001.

Dr Brent Elliott is librarian and archivist to the Royal Horticultural Society and the author of many books, among them *Victorian Gardens* (1986), *Flora: An Illustrated History of the Garden Flower* (2001), and *The Royal Horticultural Society: A History 1804–2004* (2004). He was awarded the Gold Veitch Memorial Medal of the Royal Horticultural Society in 1993.

Penelope Hobhouse is a garden historian and garden designer who has worked in Europe, Australia, and the USA. Well known as a lecturer she is also a prolific and wide-ranging author. Among her many books are *Plants in Garden History* (1992), *Gardens of Italy* (1998), *The Story of Gardening* (2002), and *Gardens of Persia* (2003). With her husband Professor John Malins she restored the Arts and Crafts garden at Tintinhull House. She was awarded the Victoria Medal of Honour by the Royal Horticultural Society in 1996 and in 1999 she received the Lifetime Achievement Award of the Guild of Garden Writers.

Sir Roy Strong is an art historian, historian, author, gardener, and garden consultant who was director of the National Portrait Gallery from 1967 to 1973 and of the Victoria and Albert Museum from 1974 to 1987. In 1980 he was awarded the Shakespeare Prize for an outstanding contribution to the Anglo-Saxon cultural heritage of Europe. His books on *The Renaissance Garden in England* (1979), *Royal Gardens* (1992), and *The Artist and the Garden* (2000) are among the very few works of garden history also read by historians. Sir Roy is president of the Garden History Society. The garden he made in collaboration with his wife at The Laskett is one of the most ambitious and original formal gardens made in England since the Second World War.

Dr Jan Woudstra is a landscape architect and historian who studied at Frederiksoord (the Netherlands), the Royal Botanic Gardens, Kew, and at the University of York. As a landscape consultant he worked on the restoration of Chiswick House grounds and the reconstruction of the Privy Garden at Hampton Court Palace that was completed with his own practice EDA Environmental Design Associates in 1995. He has taught at the 'Conservation of Historic Parks and Gardens' course, now renamed 'Landscape Conservation and Change', at the Architectural Association School of Architecture in London since 1988. Since 1995 he has taught landscape architecture and history at the University of Sheffield. From 1998 to 2003 he was editor of *Garden History*, the journal of the Garden History Society.

Contributors

(in A–Z order by initials)

AB Allen Bush is the North American manager of Jelitto Perennial Seeds in Louisville, Kentucky.

AJ Anna Jakobsson is a Swedish landscape architect and garden historian teaching garden history and conservation in the department of landscape planning, Swedish University of Agriculture, Alnarp (Sweden).

AK Alenka Kolsek is a landscape architect who is an adviser on conservation of the landscape and historic gardens at the Institute for the Protection of Cultural Heritage of Slovenia. She is the author of numerous conservation studies, articles, and essays about Slovene garden architecture.

AKl Dr Axel Klausmeier studied history of art and medieval and modern history at the universities of Bochum, Munich, and Berlin. His MA thesis deals with the landscape park at Wörlitz, his Ph.D. focuses on English architecture of the 18th century. Between 1999 and 2001 he worked for the Foundation of Prussian Castles and Gardens in Potsdam in the field of garden conservation. Subsequent work has been in the field of conservation. Since 2001 he has been assistant professor at the department of architectural conservation at the Brandenburg University of Technology in Cottbus.

AKS Katherine Swift is a gardener and writer. Her garden at Morville Hall in Shropshire (England) (National Trust) is noted for its collection of old roses.

AL Annemarie Lund is a Danish landscape architect who studied at the Royal Veterinary and Agricultural University (Frederiksberg) where she was later an assistant professor in the department of landscape architecture. She has been the Danish delegate in the International Federation of Landscape Architects since 1995. She has been the editor of *Landskab*, the Danish journal for garden and landscape planning, since 1983 and is the author of *Danmarks Havekunst III* (2002) and *Guide to Danish Landscape Architecture* (1997) and co-author, with Sven-Ingvar Andersson, of *Landscape Art in Denmark* (1990).

AM Dr Andrea Massiah is a scientist on the staff of Horticulture Research International at East Malling (England).

AP Professor Attilio Petruccioli is dean and professor of landscape architecture at the Polytechnic of Bari (Italy) and is a specialist in Islamic and Indian architecture and urbanism.

APa Andreas Pahl became an apprentice gardener at the Großer Tiergarten and other major historic gardens in Berlin where he studied landscape architecture between 1992 and 1996. On the staff of the Foundation of Prussian Castles and Gardens Berlin-Brandenburg he worked as head gardener on Pfaueninsel and in Schlosspark Klein-Glienicke between 1997 and 2000. In 2000 he became head gardener of Branitz Park in Cottbus.

AS Adelheid Schönborn studied landscape architecture at the Fachhochschule Weihenstephan (Germany) and worked in the studio of Pietro Porcinai in Florence. She founded her own practice in Munich in 1970. She sits on several committees, among them Arbeitskreis Historische Gärten, Deutsche Gesellschaft für Landschaftspflege und Gartenkultur (DGGL), ICOMOS—IFLA, and the International Dendrology Society.

ASG Assen Gasharov studied landscape architecture at the University of Forestry in Sofia (Bulgaria) and later founded the landscape architecture practice Smart Ltd. in Bulgaria. After studies in environmental change and management at Oxford University he is now practising as an environmental consultant in Bath (England). Since 2002 he has been a consultant to ESD Ltd. (UK) on sustainable development and climate change.

AWL Andrew Lawson is an English garden photographer who has also written books on gardening. His own garden in Oxfordshire, England, decorated with sculptures by his wife Briony, is regularly open.

BA Barbara Abbs is a freelance English garden writer and author of *A Guide to the Gardens of the Netherlands and Belgium* (1999).

BBA Barbara Blossom Ashmun has a plant-packed garden in two-thirds of an acre in Portland, Oregon, USA. She is the author of six books including *Garden Retreats: Creating an Outdoor Sanctuary* (2000) and *Married to my Garden* (2003).

BBOŠ Dr Bojana Bojanic Obad Ščitaroci trained as an architect in Zagreb, Croatia. She is a freelance researcher and an author of several books and studies and of numerous projects of landscape design and town planning. She has interest in the field of the conservation of traditional architecture and of historic gardens and parks.

BE Dr Brent Elliott, Advisory Editor, see description above.

BH Dr Beatrix Hajós was born in Mallnitz, Carinthia, but since 1965 has lived in Vienna where she is an independent art historian and author. Among her books are *Die Schönbrunner Schlossgärten—Eine topografische Kulturgeschichte* (The Gardens of Schönbrunn—A Topographical History, 1995) and *Schönbrunner Statuen 1773–1780—Ein neues Rom in Wien* (The Statues of Schönbrunn 1773-1780—A New Rome in Vienna, 2004).

BM Dr Bernd Modrow is head of the gardens department and deputy director of the State of Hesse Palaces and Gardens Administration, Germany.

CCT Christopher Taylor is a landscape historian. He was head of archaeological survey for the Royal Commission on the Historical Monuments of England. Among his numerous books on archaeology and landscape history are *The Archaeology of Gardens* (1983) and *Parks and Gardens of Britain* (1998).

CEB Charles E. Beveridge is series editor of the Papers of Frederick Law Olmsted, department of history, American University, Washington, DC. He is the author, with the photographer Paul Rocheleau, of *Frederick Law Olmsted: Designing the American Landscape* (1998).

CMC Christopher M. Cochrane is the secretary of the National Bonsai Foundation (USA) and president of the Potomac Viewing Stone Group. His interests include bonsai, suiseki, and Asian aesthetics. He contributes regularly to the *Viewing Stone Mail List*, the *National Bonsai Foundation Bulletin*, and the North American Bonsai Federation newsletter.

CMK Claire King teaches in the department of soil science, University of Reading (England).

CMR Christine Reid is an Australian writer specializing in the social and cultural history of gardens, and designed landscapes, both historic and contemporary. Based in Melbourne, she contributes to many publications in Australia, Canada, and the UK.

CO Carole Ottesen is an American garden writer and photographer, currently associate editor of the *American Gardener* magazine published by the American Horticultural Society. She is the author of several books on gardening and has contributed to many magazines, among them *Martha Stewart Living*, *Garden Design*, and *Fine Gardening*.

CR Camilla Rosengren is a Finnish landscape architect with a special interest in historic and contemporary gardens.

C-ZC Chen Cong-Zhou was an architect and well-known expert in Chinese ancient architecture and classical gardening. He was a professor at Tongji University, Shanghai, China. He was the author of *On Chinese Gardens* (1984).

DAB Diana Armstrong Bell is a member of the Landscape Institute and founded Armstrong Bell Landscape Design in 1984. She has won a number of international design competitions, including Parco Certosa, Milan, Italy. She is a visiting lecturer at University of Greenwich (England) and Inchbald School of Design and has lectured at the Politecnico di Milano and the Italian Association of Landscape Architects.

DBK Brian Knox is a stockbroker, painter, and architects' client. He is the author of *The Architecture of Prague and Bohemia* (1962/5) and *The Architecture of Poland* (1971).

DCS David C. Streatfield is professor of landscape architecture, urban design, and adjunct professor of architecture, University of Washington, USA. A garden and landscape historian, he is the author of numerous articles and of *California Gardens: Creating a New Eden* (1994).

D-HL Li De-Hua is a Chinese architect and expert on Chinese gardens. He contributed to Patrick Goode and Michael Lancaster's *The Oxford Companion to Gardens* (1986).

DI Dorothée Imbert is an associate professor in landscape architecture at the Harvard Design School (USA), where she teaches design and history. She is currently finishing a book on Jean Canneel-Claes.

DMO Denise Otis is an independent American historian, writer, and editor. For many years editor of *House & Garden* (USA) she is a contributing editor to *Garden Design* and the author of *Grounds for Pleasure: Four Centuries of the American Garden* (2002).

DPMcC Professor Donal McCracken is dean of the faculty of humanities, development, and social sciences and a senior professor of history at the University of Casual-Natal (South Africa).

EBR Elizabeth Barlow Rogers is a senior fellow and the founder of garden history and landscape studies at the Bard Graduate Center for Studies in the Decorative Arts, Design, and Culture (New York). A resident of New York City since 1964, she is the first person to hold the title 'Central Park Administrator', a new parks department position created by Mayor Edward I. Koch in 1979. In an effort to bring citizen support to the restoration and renewed management of Central Park, she helped found the Central Park Conservancy in 1980 and was subsequently elected president of the new public–private partnership. Of her several books the most recent is *Landscape Design: A Cultural and Architectural History* (2001).

EC Ethne Clarke, a Chicago-born American who lived in England for many years, is a garden historian, lecturer, and award-winning author. She is based in Des Moines, Iowa, where she is creating an urban prairie garden, and is the garden editor of *Traditional Home* magazine.

ECa Ethan Carr is an assistant professor in the department of landscape architecture and regional planning at the University of Massachusetts, Amherst, and a visiting professor at the Bard Graduate Center in New York. He has worked in both private and public sector design offices, and his book *Wilderness by Design: Landscape Architecture and the National Park Service* won an American Society of Landscape Architects Honor Award in 1998.

ED Eleanor Dwight teaches literature and, currently, a course 'Great Books, Great Gardens' at the garden history and landscape studies program at the Bard Graduate Center in New York City. She has contributed articles and essays on literature, travel, and gardens to scholarly and popular publications. She is the author of *Edith Wharton: An Extraordinary Life* (1994).

EEC Dr Eva Crane was director of the International Bee Research Association from 1949 to 1983, and is an authority on the science and history of bees and beekeeping. Her most recent book was *The World History of Beekeeping and Honey Hunting* (1999).

FH Florence Hopper was an American who from 1950 lived in the Netherlands where she developed a scholarly interest in the history of Dutch gardens. She was the author of several contributions to journals and symposia.

FL Professor Frieder Luz is professor of landscape architecture at the University of Applied Sciences, Weihenstephan (Germany). She studied landscape architecture at Weihenstephan and, as a Fulbright Scholar, she also studied in the department of applied behavioral sciences at the University of California, Davis.

GA Gábor Alföldy is a landscape architect and garden historian. As the head of gardens of the Hungarian National Board for the management of state-owned historic properties (Budapest), he controls the conservation of many historic parks in Hungary. His research covers the history of parks and gardens as well as the works of designers in Hungary and in the Carpathian Basin. He has given his name to a number of books and articles as editor, contributor, or author.

GAJ Sir Geoffrey Jellicoe was an English garden designer, working in collaboration with his wife Susan Jellicoe. He was the joint author, with his wife, of *The Landscape of Man* (1974) and consultant editor to *The Oxford Companion to Gardens* (1986).

GC Professor Gordon Campbell is professor of Renaissance literature at the University of Leicester (England). Among his many books is *The Oxford Dictionary of the Renaissance* (2003).

GG Dr Gert Gröning is professor of urban horticulture and landscape architecture and executive director of the Institute for History and Theory of Design, faculty of design, architecture programme, Berlin University of the Arts (Germany). His main fields of interest are history and theory of garden and landscape architecture, social science aspects of open space planning and design of open spaces. He has been, since 1985, editor with Ulfert Herlyn of the book series Arbeiten zur sozialwissenschaftlich orientierten Freiraumplanung (Studies in Social Science Oriented Open Space Planning), 14 volumes to date (2005). He is on the international editorial boards of the journals *Landscape Research*, *Garden History*, and the *Journal of the Japanese Society of People–Plant Relationships*. He is the author of numerous publications (some 250) in various professional books and journals.

GH Dr Géza Hajós was born in Budapest, became an art historian and since 1965 has worked in Vienna at the Federal Office of Historic Monuments (*Bundesdenkmalamt*). Since 1986 he has been head of the historic gardens department in this institution. He lectures on garden history at Graz University and in 1991 founded the Österreichische Gesellschaft für Historische Gärten (Austrian Garden History Society) of which he is general secretary. He is on the editorial board of the journal *Die Gartenkunst*. He has written widely on garden history specializing in the theory and practice of conservation. His most important book is *Romantische Gärten der Aufklärung—Englische Landschaftskultur des 18. Jahrhunderts in und um Wien* (Romantic Gardens of the Enlightenment—English Garden Culture of the 18th Century in and about Vienna, 1989).

GL Georgina Livingston is a landscape architect. She contributed to Patrick Goode and Michael Lancaster's *The Oxford Companion to Gardens* (1986).

GMD Guilherme Mazza Dourado is an architect and landscape historian with a master's degree from the University of São Paulo. His *Landscape Sights* (1997) is a survey on contemporary landscape architecture in Brazil.

GSC Gordon Sydney Collier is a garden consultant and freelance horticultural writer in New Zealand with a special interest in woodland plants. He is the author of *The New Zealanders' Garden* (with Julian Matthews) (1985) and *Gordon Collier's Titoki Point* (1993).

GW Georgette Weir is a freelance writer and editor living in New York.

G-ZW Wu Guang-Zu is an expert on Chinese gardens and was a contributor to Patrick Goode and Michael Lancaster's *The Oxford Companion to Gardens* (1986).

HB Hugh Bilborough, formerly of Ethel Wormald College of Further Education, Liverpool, was a contributor to Patrick Goode and Michael Lancaster's *The Oxford Companion to Gardens* (1986).

HFO Dr Henry Oakeley is an amateur orchid grower, president of the Orchid Society of Great Britain, chairman of the Royal Horticultural Society Orchid Committee, and a trustee of the World Orchid Conference Trust.

HFvE Helmut Fritz van Emden is emeritus professor of horticulture, University of Reading (England). He taught pest control in agriculture/horticulture for over forty years and has published over 170 scientific articles and ten books, most recently (with M. W. Service) *Pest and Vector Control* (2004). He is past president of the Royal Entomological Society and the Association of Applied Biologists.

HG Heino Grunert studied landscape architecture at the University of Hanover (Germany). After working in private practice, he joined the urban parks department in Hamburg in 1993 and is now responsible for historic gardens and parks throughout Hamburg.

HGÜ Dr Harri Günther is a former garden director at Potsdam-Sanssouci. He contributed to Patrick Goode and Michael Lancaster's *The Oxford Companion to Gardens* (1986).

HH Henrik Hass is a landscape architect who trained at the Technical University of Dresden (Germany).

HHS Hatsy Shields lives and gardens in New England writes about design, gardens, and travel for various US publications including *Atlantic Monthly*, the New York Times' *Sophisticated Traveler* magazine, *Horticulture*, and *House Beautiful*.

HJ Hugh Johnson is an English writer on wine, trees, and gardens. Among his books are *The Principles of Gardening* (1979) and *The International Book of Trees* (rev. edn. 1993).

HM Heike Mortell is a landscape architect who works at the National Institute for Protection and Conservation of Historic Heritage, Saxony-Anhalt, Germany.

HN Hanka Naumann works in the field of the preservation of historic gardens in the Parks and Recreation Office, Leipzig (Germany).

HNo Henry Noltie works at the Royal Botanic Garden, Edinburgh, where he specializes in the taxonomy of Sino-Himalayan monocotyledons and the history of Indian botany. He has written two volumes of the *Flora of Bhutan* and numerous associated scientific papers and is currently working on the botanical drawings commissioned from Indian artists by Scottish surgeons working for the East India Company in the first half of the 19th century.

HS Hugo Segawa is an architect, associate professor at the University of São Paulo, Brazil. He is the author of *Ao amor do público: jardins no Brasil* (1996), a history of public gardens in Brazil from the 16th to early 20th century.

HW Helen Whitehouse is a senior assistant keeper in the department of antiquities in the Ashmolean Museum, Oxford. She has published extensively on images of Egypt in Roman and European art.

IB Dr Iwona Binkowska is an art historian specializing in the history of Silesian parks, urban green space, and gardens. She is keeper of the graphics department, Wrocław University Library (Poland) and a lecturer at Panstwowa Wyzsza Szkola Zawodowa (National Vocational College of Higher Education) in Sulechow.

ITL Irma Lounatvuori has been senior curator at the Finnish National Board of Antiquities, department of monuments and sites, since 1971. Her research subjects include rural architecture, manor houses, and historic gardens. She has published on interior design, gardens, and dwelling houses of the 18th century.

JA Jost Albert trained as a nursery gardener, and studied landscape architecture at the University of Hanover, majoring in garden history. Since 1995 he has been a garden historian in the Bayerische Schlösserverwaltung in Munich.

JB John Baines is professor of Egyptology, University of Oxford. Among his research interests are Egyptian art and the elite exploitation of the Egyptian landscape.

JBr Jane Brown is an English writer specializing in landscape and garden history. Among her particular interests are Edwin Lutyens and Gertrude Jekyll, V. Sackville-West, Lanning Roper, and Beatrix Farrand, on all of whom she has written books.

JBW James B. Watson is director of publications at the American Orchid Society, where he has been editor and art director of *Orchids*, the society's monthly membership magazine, since 1991.

JBy Dr John Byrom is honorary fellow and former director of the University of Edinburgh master of landscape architecture programme.

JEMS Jo Ellen Meyers Sharp has been writing about gardening since 1989. She is a regional director of the Garden Writers Association (in America) and co-author of *The Indiana Gardener's Guide*.

JF-W Jane Fearnley-Whittingstall studied landscape architecture and is a garden designer in England. She is the author of *Peonies—The Imperial Flower* (1999), *The Garden—An English Love Affair* (2003), *Rose Gardens, their History and Design* (1989), *Ivies* (1992), and *Gardening Made Easy* (1995).

JKM Dr Judith K. Major is a landscape historian and a professor of architecture at the School of Architecture and Urban Design at the University of Kansas, USA.

JM Jochen Martz is a landscape architect and garden historian. He studied landscape architecture at the Munich University of Technology in Weihenstephan and later worked at the Arnold Arboretum (USA) and carried out research on the gardens of the Imperial Court Castle (Hofburg) in Vienna.

JMo Joan Morgan trained as a biochemist but has for many years studied the history of fruit, with a particular interest in pomology.

JRC James R. Cothran is a landscape architect, urban planner, and garden historian. He serves as an adjunct professor at both the University of Georgia and Georgia State University, teaching graduate courses on America's historic gardens and landscapes. A fellow in the American Society of Landscape Architects, Cothran is the author of *Gardens of Historic Charleston* (1995) and *Gardens and Historic Plants of the Antebellum South* (2003).

JS Jens Scheffler studied landscape architecture at the Dresden University of Technology (Germany) and history and art of garden design and preservation of historic gardens. Since 2003 he has been scientific assistant to the Saxonian State Palaces, Castles, and Gardens.

JSa John Sales was gardens adviser and head of gardens to the National Trust (England) from 1972 to 1997 where he pioneered systematic historical surveys of parks and gardens. Since retiring he has been a gardens consultant, writer, and judge at the Chelsea and Hampton Court Flower Shows.

JSB Julia S. Bachrach is an American preservationist and historian for the Chicago Park District. She is author of the book *The City in a Garden: A Photographic History of Chicago's Parks* (2001).

JSu John Sutton's first article on a horticultural topic was published in 1954 since when he has contributed to many reference works. He is the author of *The Gardeners' Guide to Growing Salvias* (2004) and *The Plantfinder's Guide to Daisies* (2001). He was a senior lecturer at Pershore College (England) for twenty years, and has subsequently established himself as a commentator on new plant introductions in the horticultural trade press.

JW Dr Jan Woudstra, Advisory Editor, see description above.

KASW Kenneth Woodbridge was a garden historian with a particular interest in French gardens and in the history of Stourhead garden. He was the author of *The Stourhead Landscape*

(1971) and *Princely Gardens: The Origins and Development of the French Formal Style* (1986).

KF Kirsty Fergusson is an English garden writer and journalist based in France.

KFr Kathrin Franz trained as a landscape gardener in the park of Dresden-Pillnitz and studied landscape architecture at the Technical University of Dresden. In 1991 she established her own practice in Leipzig specializing in historic gardens. She has been responsible for the design and the redesign of numerous projects in central Germany, especially parks, cemeteries, and city squares in Saxony and Saxony-Anhalt. She has written numerous articles on landscape gardens in professional journals. She is a member of the working group for historical gardens of the German Society for Garden Architecture and Landscape Studies e.V.

KG Kurt Grübl trained as a landscape architect at the Fachhochschule Weihenstephan (Germany) and since 1996 has been on the staff of the Bavarian Administration of State Palaces, Gardens, and Lakes.

KK Katherine H. Kerin runs her own landscape design practice, using her training from both Cornell University (USA), where she received a master's degree in landscape architecture, and Stonecrop Gardens, where she obtained a Certificate in Practical Horticulture. She spent six years in the field of historic preservation, including a stint at the Garden Conservancy in Cold Spring, New York. She lives along the Hudson river in New York State and remains actively involved in the ongoing restoration of a nearby garden designed by Beatrix Farrand, a project she spearheaded as a graduate student.

KR Keith Rushforth is an English author who has written ten books on trees and woody plants—from conifers to flowering shrubs. He is a chartered forester and arboricultural consultant and has made a score of plant hunting expeditions to countries from Bhutan to Vietnam.

KT Kenneth Thompson is a plant ecologist and senior lecturer in the department of animal and plant sciences at the University of Sheffield, England. He has written over 100 articles in scientific journals and is a keen gardener. He writes a regular column on the science of gardening for *Organic Gardening* magazine.

LCJ Leila Jones is a freelance writer in the USA. She is the author of many magazine articles on gardens, design, and travel.

LJD L. J. Drake is chairman of Cambridgeshire Gardens Trust; a trustee of Moggerhanger Park,

Bedfordshire (laid out by Humphry Repton, 1796); author *The Gardens of Cambridgeshire—A Gazetteer* (2002); president of the Plant Heritage Group, London; and holds a National Collection of *Aquilegia*.

LM Dr Longin Majdecki was a distinguished landscape architect living in Poland who contributed to Patrick Goode and Michael Lancaster's *The Oxford Companion to Gardens* (1986).

LTC Lois Taylor Clarke was for more than twenty years a feature writer and garden columnist on the staff of the *Honolulu Star-Bulletin*. Now retired, she is active in the Garden Club of Honolulu and is a trustee of the Honolulu Botanical Gardens.

LTT Lorenza Tovar de Teresa trained as a biologist in Mexico City and is now a researcher and restorer of historic gardens. She works at the National Institution for Anthropology and History (INAH) on the researching, planning, and execution of gardens which currently include the San Diego Fort, Acapulco, and the convent of El Carmen, Mexico City. She has contributed articles to the journal *Arqueología mexicana*.

MA Maria Auböck is a practising Austrian landscape architect specializing in the design of public spaces and in conservation.

MC Dr Maureen Carroll is senior lecturer in Roman archaeology at the University of Sheffield (England). She has published widely on ancient Greek and Roman gardens, and excavated Roman gardens in Britain, Germany, and Italy, most recently in Pompeii.

MC-C Maggie Campbell-Culver is a historian of plants and gardens and a lecturer and broadcaster. She was responsible for the restoration of the garden at Mount Edgcumbe (England) between 1982 and 1996. She is the author of *The Origin of Plants* (2001) and *John Evelyn—Man of Trees* (2006).

ME Mette Eggen trained as a landscape architect at the Agricultural University of Norway and received an MA in architecture from the IoAAS (Institute of Advanced Architectural Studies), University of York (England). She is a member of the Norwegian association of landscape architects. She was an associate professor at the Agricultural University until 1999 and now works as an adviser at the Directorate for Cultural Heritage, Oslo, dealing mainly with the cultural environment and historic gardens.

MH Marjorie Harris is one of Canada's leading garden writers, the author of numerous garden books of which her most recent is *Botanica North America* (2004).

MHay Maunu Häyrynen is professor of landscape studies at the University of Turku (Finland). He has special interests in the history of Finnish gardens, urban parks, and popular landscape imagery.

MK Maggie Keswick was the author of a pioneer book on *The Chinese Garden* (1978) and, with her husband Charles Jencks, maker of the remarkable garden at Portrack (Scotland).

MLL Michael Lancaster was an English landscape architect and author who also taught at the University of Greenwich (London). He was joint executive editor (with Patrick Goode) of *The Oxford Companion to Gardens* (1986).

MM Marta Iris Montero is an Argentinian architect and landscaper designer. She was a disciple of Roberto Burle Marx and later worked with him as a partner from 1972 to 1994. Since 1993 she has designed a number of major projects in Buenos Aires, where she now lives. She is the author of the book *Burle Marx, the Lyrical Landscape* (1997; 2nd edn. 2001).

MMM Dr Margita Marion Meyer is a landscape architect and adviser for historic gardens in Schleswig-Holstein at the state Office for the Preservation of Monuments at Kiel. She is a member of the German Academy for Urban Development and Landscape Planning (DASL), the German Society for the Art of Garden and the Culture of Landscape (DGGL) and the National Association for the Research and Preservation of Orangeries. She is the editor, with Adrian von Buttlar, of *Historische Gärten in Schleswig-Holstein* (1996).

MOŠ Mladen Obad Ščitaroci is a professor of landscape architecture and of history of town planning at the faculty of Architecture, University of Zagreb, Croatia. He is the author of ten books and of numerous projects of landscape design and town planning.

MPK Marc Keane is a practising landscape architect, writer, and educator based in Ithaca, NY. He lived in Kyoto, Japan, for nearly twenty years and is now a visiting scholar at Cornell University (USA). He is the author of *Japanese Garden Design* (1996).

MR Michael Rohde trained as a landscape architect at the University of Hanover (Germany) where, since 1994, he has worked at the Institute for Greenspace Planning and Garden Architecture, teaching and researching on the history of open space planning, concentrating on garden heritage conservation. Since 1996 he has been editor of the 'Biographien europäischer Gartenkünstler' in 'Stadt + Grün'. He has advised on the conservation of many historic gardens and is the author of several books.

MS Michael Seiler is a German garden historian.

MSt Manfred Stephan is a landscape architect working for the Bayerische Verwaltung der Staatlichen Schlösser, Gärten und Seen, Munich.

MV Marta A. Viveros studied architecture at P. Universidad Católica de Chile in 1956 and since 1960 has practised as a landscape architect. Since 1973 she has been professor in the College of Fine Arts of P. Universidad Católica de Chile and, from 1989, first head of the graduate program in landscape architecture. She has lectured widely on landscape architecture, in particular 20th-century landscape architecture design in Chile. She has written numerous articles and books on Chilean landscape architecture. Between 1986 and 2002 she was president of the Chilean chapter of IFLA (International Federation of Landscape Architects).

MWRS Michael Symes is a garden historian based at Birkbeck, University of London, where he runs a programme including an MA in the subject. He has written a number of books including *Garden Sculpture* (1996) and *A Glossary of Garden History* (1993). His particular interest is in 18th-century gardens, British and continental.

NK Noel Kingsbury has worked as a nurseryman and garden designer in England. He is chiefly known as a writer and lecturer with a particular interest in contemporary nature-inspired planting design and in the culture and politics of the garden.

NT Neil Thomson was brought up in Sri Lanka and is now a landscape architect practising in London.

PB Patrick Bowe is a garden designer and historian practising in Dublin. He has written and contributed to many books among which are *Irish Gardens and Demesnes from 1830* (with Edward Malins, 1980), *A History of Gardening in Ireland* (with Keith Lamb, 1995), and *Gardens of the Roman World* (2004).

PC Patrick Chassé earned a master of landscape architecture degree from Harvard Graduate School of Design, after a BS in biology, graduate studies in botany, and an M. Ed. in environmental education. As a practising landscape architect he specializes in historic landscapes, reconstruction of natural plant communities, and design of new gardens, from Mt. Desert Island, Maine, to Istanbul. He lectures in the Landscape Institute of the Arnold Arboretum, Harvard University, at the New York Botanical Garden, and at botanic gardens and symposia across the country. He is a leader of efforts to preserve Beatrix Farrand's last home and garden, in Maine, and has recently been appointed the first curator of landscape at the Isabella Stewart Gardner Museum, in Boston. He is currently working on a book on moss culture.

PD Page Dickey is a garden writer, lecturer, and designer. Among her books are *Duck Hill Journal: A Year in a Country Garden* (1991) and *Breaking Ground* (1997). She has written on garden design for many periodicals, and lectures and teaches at the New York Botanical Garden.

PF Petra Friedrich is head of the preservation of historic gardens in the Park and Recreation Office, Leipzig, Germany.

PFi Dr Peter Fibich is a German landscape architect and garden historian.

PG Patrick Goode was author/executive editor for *The Oxford Companion to Gardens* (1986) and is author/executive editor for *The Oxford Companion to Architecture* (forthcoming).

PGr Pierre Grimal was professor of Latin literature at the Sorbonne and a member of the Institute. He wrote a great number of historical and archaeological studies on Rome. His best-known work is *The Dictionary of Classical Mythology* (1986).

PH Peter Hayden is an English garden historian (and former chairman of the Garden History Society) with a particular interest in Russian gardens. He has written numerous scholarly articles and several books. His most recent book is *Russian Parks and Gardens* (2005).

PHo Penelope Hobhouse, Advisory Editor, see description above.

PP Pauline M. Pears is head of information, HDRA—the organic organization (England), and technical editor of its periodical the *Organic Way*.

PRJ Preben Jakobsen is a Danish landscape architect. He worked as a nurseryman and studied at Kew and at the Danish Royal Academy of Fine Arts where he studied landscape architecture. He has spent much of his professional career in England practising as a landscape architect and also teaching.

PT Patrick Taylor, General Editor, see description above.

PW Penelope Walker works in publishing, and writes articles about the history of beekeeping. She is curator of the International Bee Research Association Register of Bee Boles and Other Beekeeping Structures and is currently setting up a database for the 1,200 records.

PWo Paul Wolterbeek works at the Boyce Thompson Arboretum (Arizona, USA) as the volunteer programme coordinator, and is also responsible for public and press relations.

RD Ray Desmond is an author, librarian, and garden historian. He was chief librarian and archivist at the Royal Botanic Gardens, Kew, and deputy keeper at the British Library. He has been chairman of the Garden History Society. Among his many books are the *Bibliography of British Gardens* (1984) and *Kew: The History of the Royal Botanic Gardens* (1995).

RF Dr Roland Fox works in the department of agriculture and horticulture at The University of Reading (England) as a lecturer in plant pathology. At present he is a lecturer in crop protection in the School of Plant Sciences. His research activities encompass the diagnosis of plant pathogens, improving the methods of controlling soil-borne diseases of plants (particularly honey fungus root rot). He has written many scientific papers. Dr Fox is the author of *Principles of Diagnostic Techniques in Plant Pathology* (1993), *The Gardener's Book of Pests and Diseases* (2001), and *Armillaria Root Rot: Biology and Control of Honey Fungus* (2000).

RG Roger Grounds is an English garden designer, a pioneer of ornamental grass gardening, and the author of *The Plantfinder's Guide to Ornamental Grasses* (1998).

RH Rainer Herzog studied garden design at the Humboldt University of Berlin (Germany) and landscape architecture at the Technical University of Dresden. From 1976 to 1983 he was director of Großsedlitz and from 1986 to 1990 worked at the Wilhelma (Stuttgart). Since July 1990 he has been deputy director of the garden department of the Bavarian Administration of State Palaces, Gardens, and Lakes.

RJ Rosamund Johnson worked at the Morris Arboretum (Pennsylvania) and Holden Arboretum (Ohio) before joining the English National Council for the Conservation of Plants and Gardens (NCCPG) as plant conservation officer in April 2001.

RJB Richard Bisgrove is senior lecturer in the centre for horticulture and landscape at the University of Reading (England). He is a fellow of the Institute of Horticulture and serves on the Editorial Advisory Board of the institute. For many years a member of the Council and Conservation Committee of the Garden History Society, he is also on the Gardens Panel of the National Trust and a consultant on the restoration and management of historic gardens. He has written many books on garden design and garden history, among them *The National Trust Book of the English Garden* (1990) and *The Gardens of Gertrude Jekyll* (1992).

author of several books, with a particular interest in Switzerland.

WB **Wojciech Bałus** is professor of art history at the Jagiellonian University in Cracow, Poland, specializing in art theory, history of architecture, painting, and garden art of the 19th century.

WFJ Professor emerita **W. F. Jashemski** is a retired professor of ancient history at the University of Maryland (USA). She is the author of many books including the monumental *The Gardens of Pompeii, Herculaneum, and the Villas Destroyed by Vesuvius* (1979).

WGW **George Waters** made three gardens in England between 1953 and 1972. He was a founding member of the Garden History Society. In California in 1975 he helped launch the magazine *Pacific Horticulture* of which he was editor for twenty-two years.

WLD **William Lake Douglas** is an American landscape architect and writer. He is the author of *Garden Design* (1984) and *Hillside Gardening: Evaluating the Site, Designing Views, Planting Slopes* (1987).

WLW **William Warren**, American by birth, has lived in Thailand since 1960. For thirty years he taught English at Chulalongkorn University. He is author of several books about tropical gardens and gardening, among them *Balinese Gardens* (1995).

X-WL **Luo Xiao-Wei**, architect and distinguished expert on world architecture, is a professor of architecture at Tongji University, Shanghai, China.

Thematic Index

List of Colour Plates

Note to the Reader

This book is designed for ease of use but the following notes may be of help to the reader.

Thematic Index The list of entries under major topics which appears at the front of the book (see pp. xix–xxvi) offers an alternative means of accessing the material in the *Companion*. It allows the reader to see at a glance all headwords relating to a particular subject.

[⊛] Symbol In individual garden entries, this symbol placed after the headword indicates a garden open to the public at the time of writing.

Alphabetical arrangement Entries are arranged in letter-by-letter alphabetical order up to the first punctuation (if any) in the headword with the exception that St is ordered as though spelt 'saint' and Mc is ordered as though spelt 'mac'.

Cross-references are denoted by small capitals and indicate the entry headword to which attention is being directed. Cross-references appear only where reference is likely to amplify or increase understanding of the entry being read and they are not given automatically merely to indicate that a separate entry can be found. Cross-references are given more freely to draw attention to entries on individual gardens, people, garden styles; foreign terms related to gardens; and certain specialist English terms.

Plant names Scientific names of plants conform to those listed in the *Royal Horticultural Society Plant Finder*. Genus and species names are given in italic and the cultivar name or names (if any) are given in single quotes, for example *Hydrangea serrata* 'Bluebird'.

Bibliography At the end of certain entries references provide guidance to further reading. In addition there is an extensive Select Bibliography at the back of the book (see pp. 531–8).

The Select Index at the back of the book lists gardens, people, themes, and features which are mentioned in the course of other entries but which do not have an entry of their own. In addition a few references are given that add to the information on some subjects which have their own headword.

Readers' comments   Every effort has been made to ensure that the information in the text is accurate. Readers are invited to call attention to any minor errors or inconsistencies that they discover, by writing to:

Patrick Taylor, *Oxford Companion to the Garden*, c/o Reference Department, Academic Division, Oxford University Press, Great Clarendon Street, Oxford, OX2 6DP.

Aalto, Alvar

(1898–1976), Finnish architect, designer, and artist. In addition to being one of the greatest architects of the modern movement, Aalto made notable contributions to garden and landscape design. His wife Aino Marsio-Aalto (1894–1949) collaborated with him on much of his design work as well as working on her own account on glassware, furniture, and interiors. Aalto was an intuitive designer, and the private house Villa Mairea (in which his wife and Paul OLSSON participated) demonstrates his ability to fuse the house and garden with nature. His stylization of contours in close proximity to the Maison Louis Carré, Bazoches, France (1956–8), and the earlier grass steps as an integral part of the design for Säynätsalo town hall (1950–2, in collaboration with Paul Olsson) bear evidence of this concept in landscape terms. Aalto laid out campuses at the Helsinki University of Technology (Otaniemi) and at the University of Jyväskylä. The experimental house at Muuratsalo (1953) was for him both work and play; here he used a combination of sculptural walls and brick patterns which have since been a source of inspiration for many Scandinavian landscape architects.   PRJ/MHay

Abbotsbury Subtropical Gardens ⊛

Abbotsbury, Dorset, England, owe their special atmosphere to a remarkable microclimate. The garden is very close to the sea, which in this part of the coast is very deep and has a pronounced warming effect on the atmosphere. The garden, of 8 hectares/20 acres, was made by the Fox-Strangways family (earls of Ilchester), who built a house here in the late 18th century. They later returned to their main residence of Melbury House when the new house was burnt down in 1913, but its walled garden was kept up and is still owned by the family. In the early 19th century the 3rd Earl of Ilchester enclosed the land surrounding the garden and planted shelter belts. His son, the 4th Earl, was a distinguished plantsman who introduced many exotics, among them tender shrubs such as *Citronella mucronata* from Chile and *Photinia nussia* from the Himalayas (the genus *Photinia* was originally *Stranvaesia*, the Latinization of Strangways). The woodland outside the walled garden, in particular the protected valley garden to the west, was greatly enriched with trees in the 19th century. Several plantings survive, among them splendid *Cupressus macrocarpa*, *Pinus radiata*, and a magnificent Caucasian wing nut (*Pterocarya fraxinifolia*). East of the walled garden a stream was dammed to form fine water gardens. By the end of the 19th century over 5,000 species were cultivated, making it an outstanding private collection of exotics. In the 20th century the garden has been excellently maintained, with further enrichment of the collection.   PT

Abelin, Rudolf

(1864–1961), one of Sweden's most prominent ambassadors for the garden's classic values and expressions, being at the same time both modern and progressive. He committed himself to the benefits and the economically profitable produce of gardens (fruit and nut growing), to their aesthetic organization and arrangement (designs and consultative advice for 35 Swedish estates), as well as to reforming horticultural education. Between 1900 and 1915 he published ten books on gardening. His influential *Den mindre trädgården: en bok för täppan och torpet* (The Smaller Garden: A Book for the Plot and the Cottage) appeared in four editions between 1902 and 1932). Norrviken, an estate in the north-western part of Skåne by the sea, became Abelin's primary mission in life between 1906 and 1941. The grounds illustrate Abelin's entire horticultural achievement. Here his aims were both aesthetic and educational—to create an exemplary garden that would also serve as a training ground for country estate gardeners. He laid out a variety of gardens, within the garden, in the great historical styles: a French garden with a pool and a mile-long perspective, a medieval-style building, a Renaissance garden, a Japanese-style garden, a half-English, half-Italian, rose and rhododendron parterre, a large natural park, a cemetery, and a small oriental garden.   KL

KOLBJÖRN WAREN, 'Rudolf Abelin (1864–1961)', in *Svensk Trädgårdskonst under fyrahundra år* (2000).

Abercrombie, John

(1726–1806), Scottish gardener and author born at Prestonpans, East Lothian, who worked at Kew gardens (SEE ROYAL BOTANIC GARDENS, KEW) and established his own nursery at Hackney in the 1760s. Author of *Every Man his Own Gardener* (1767), under the name Thomas Mawe, which had been printed in 23 editions by 1829. Among his fourteen other books was *The Gardener's Pocket Journal* (1789) of which the last continued to be published for more than 50 years after his death. Abercrombie's importance as a writer was that the information contained in his books came from his own deep experience of growing plants.   PT

Aberglasney ⊛

Llangathen, Carmarthenshire, Wales, has an ancient and mysterious history. In the 15th century it was probably the home of Rhydderch ap Rhys whose fame was sung by the 15th-century bard Lewis Glyn Cothi: 'He has a proud hall, a fortress made bright by whitewash, and encompassing it all around nine green gardens. Orchard trees and crooked vines, young oaks reaching up to the skies.' In 1995 a trust was established to acquire the house and garden of 4 hectares/10 acres, both of which were in an advanced state of dereliction and have now been restored. A striking arcaded court, surrounded by a raised walk, probably dates from the early 17th century. As part of the restoration a lawn was laid out in the court with a parterre-like pattern of shaped beds. A tunnel of yews north-west of the house, about which extravagant claims for its antiquity have been made, probably dates from the early 19th century. In the upper garden is an oval pattern of concentric herbaceous borders designed by Penelope HOBHOUSE and, in the lower garden, formal box-hedged kitchen gardens were designed by Hal Moggridge (b. 1936). East of the house a finely planted woodland garden leads to Bishop Rudd's Walk, named after a 16th-century bishop who possibly lived here from c.1600. The walk reveals views of the countryside, in particular of the landscape surrounding Grongar Hill celebrated by the topographical poet John Dyer (1699–1757). His description of the hill and its setting influenced picturesque landscapers later in the 18th century.   PT

PENNY DAVID, *A Garden Lost in Time* (1999).

Abkhazi Garden ⊛

Victoria, British Columbia, Canada, is a rare Canadian private garden open to the public.

Prince Nicholas (1899–1987) and Princess Peggy Abkhazi (1902–94) lost each other in prison camps during the Second World War, met again, and married in 1946. They built this very personal garden on its extraordinary site and worked together on it for 40 years. In 2000, the Land Conservancy of British Columbia snatched it from the clutches of a developer and turned it into a public park. The garden features Garry oaks (*Quercus garryana*), ornamental evergreens, 100-year-old rhododendrons, rock and alpine plants, naturalized bulbs, and superb examples of Japanese maples and weeping conifers. The 0.5-hectare/1 acre site contains the original summer house perched on top of the huge and dramatic outcropping of glaciated rock which dominates the site. The garden is a study in contrasts between the gigantic rock—some parts left deliberately bare, others planted with alpines and evergreens, others dammed up to create reflecting pools—and the lower part of the property which contains deeper soil where a rhododendron copse and a woodland garden thrive. The garden is a unique blend of Californian and Chinese garden styles. John Wade (1914–97), the California architect who designed the summer house, felt that buildings and gardens should relate cohesively one to the other, and Peggy Abkhazi, strongly influenced by Chinese gardens from years of living in Shanghai, was as interested in foliage and texture as flowers. As a result, the forms and materials were carefully chosen to reflect the amazing landscape's natural rhythm.   MH

Acelain Ranch ⊛

Buenos Aires province, Argentina, has an area of 12,000 hectares/29,654 acres of which the designed landscape amounts to 700 hectares/1,730 acres. Today it is a tourist ranch with game hunting and extensive plantations of pines, eucalyptus, and oaks (among them the North American *Quercus imbricaria*). Acelain means 'broken field', which was the name of the house in Guipúzcoa (Spain) originally owned by the Larreta family who made the ranch. It is one of the most perfect examples of Argentine *estancia* gardens, of the kind owned by aristocratic and cultivated families. It was the country estate of the writer and diplomat Enrique Larreta (1873–1961), who never lost his love for Spain. The original garden was laid out in 1906 by the German designer Hermann Böttrich (1871–1944) in an informal English style. Larreta himself remodelled it in 1917, turning the garden into a Hispanic Islamic one, the character preserved when a new house was built in 1924, designed by the local architect Martín Noel (1888–1963) in his typical neo-Spanish style. The house and the garden were inspired by the ALHAMBRA: the enclosed garden, for example, is modelled on the Patio de la Acequia in the GENERALIFE. The house is on a raised site with an axis descending by means of terraces, stairs, and ponds reflecting the surroundings to a lake with an area of 70 hectares/173 acres. Lines of Chinese weeping cypress (*Cupressus funebris*), flowering plants on a cliff, the foliage of contrasting colours, and the wild deer in the park are unforgettable.   SLB

Achabal,

Anantnag (Islamabad), Kashmir, lies to the south-east of Srinagar, where the Vale of Kashmir dies out against the mountains. The site is that of an ancient spring, Akshavala, which pours out with great force at the foot of the hills. The quality of the water was remarked upon in contemporary records, and no other Mughal garden retains a water feature of such power and volume. The great waterfall at the top of the garden, once lit from behind by lamps, broadens out below in a succession of pools filled with fountains. An island pavilion, reached by causeways, is set in the first pool; beyond, the water passes under the main pavilion, continues down two side CHADARS to yet another level, and thence to the river.

On either side of the garden two more canals carry a rushing flow of water cascading down tall water chutes and then running nearly level with the ground. Great plane trees surround the heart of the garden, and solid stone platforms (*chabutras*) are set at intervals among them. To one side is a *hummum* or bath. The existing pavilions are of later date, set on the old Mughal bases. François BERNIER records that the garden was once full of fruit trees: 'Apples, Pears, Prunes, Apricocks and Cherries'. The design (*c*.1620) is attributed primarily to the Empress Nūr Jahān, wife of Jahāngīr. The garden is currently in a good state of repair and the natural abundance of the water has preserved its original character to a remarkable degree.   SMH

Acosta, Carmen de la Fundación Rodríguez ⊛

Granada, Andalusia, Spain, a rare art deco house and garden created by the artist José Rodríguez Acosta (d. 1941) between 1914 and 1920. The site, on the precipitous slopes of Alhambra hill, commands magnificent views. The white stucco house, a cascade of cubist shapes, rises at the highest point with the gardens terraced below. Italian cypresses soar from the terraces along which run ALLÉES of clipped cypress hedges and arches. The occasional simple pool, square or round, is let into the paving and fine works of statuary enliven focal points. Vertiginous views from one terrace to another provide constant visual excitement. This is the essence of the garden— the contrast between the rational, functionalist house and the drama of the site. The word *carmen* is a Granadan one, meaning both house and villa. Many of the best examples of this tradition are those in the old town of Granada— the Albaicín—of strongly Islamic inspiration. Here, however, Acosta took this venerable tradition and made a radical new *carmen* of dazzling 20th-century character. The few flowering plants here seem a slightly meretricious intrusion.   PT

Adam, Robert

(1728–92), Scottish architect, son of William ADAM. One of the most prolific, successful, and distinguished architects of his day, chiefly practising in England but also designing notable houses in Scotland and a few in Ireland. He designed many garden buildings and also had a hand in landscape design. At Kedleston Hall (Derbyshire), as he wrote to his brother John in 1760, he had 'the intire Manadgment of [the] grounds . . . with full powers as to Temples, Bridges, Seats and Cascades'. A lake, great bridge and cascade, and exquisite lakeside FISHING HOUSE survive at Kedleston which is now owned by the National Trust. Among other gardens open to the public which contain excellent surviving garden buildings by Adam are Alnwick Castle (Northumberland), Audley End (Essex), BOWOOD, Croome Court (Worcestershire), Osterley Park (Middlesex), and the ROYAL BOTANIC GARDEN, EDINBURGH.

PT

Adam, William

(1689–1748), Scottish architect and garden designer born in Kirkcaldy. His sons John and Robert ADAM also became architects and extended the family business, resoundingly, into England. Adam laid out grand patterns of avenues and intricate wildernesses with occasional informal ingredients—he wrote that 'the risings and fallings of ground are to be humoured and generally make the greatest beautys in Gardens'. It seems likely that he designed, from 1722, the great formal terraces at CASTLE KENNEDY. At ARNISTON HOUSE (from 1726) Adam designed both the house and its pleasure grounds which, although essentially formal, with a great parterre, also borrowed the picturesque landscape of the rocky crag of Arthur's Seat. He designed gardens for his own estate at Blair Adam (Kinross-shire, from 1733), Cally (Kircudbrightshire, from 1742), Hopetoun House (West Lothian, from 1720), Newliston (West Lothian, from 1720), and several others. At HAMILTON PALACE in 1732 he designed Chatelherault, an extraordinary garden building, as an avenue eyecatcher, combining kennels, banqueting house, and menagerie—recently finely restored.   PT

Adelsnäs ⊛

Östergötland, Sweden, on an isthmus in Lake Bysjön, mentioned from the 16th century, became the country's only *baroni* (barony) established in 1783 by King Gustav III. From 1764 it was owned by the Adelswärd family. Originally comprising a *corps-de-logis* with four wings and traditionally regular gardens, a large English-style park, full of oaks, was laid out between 1800 and 1852, covering the whole peninsula, lake, and adjacent land. The present ARTS AND CRAFTS-inspired house (1916–20), park, and gardens is the result of a collaboration of several architects, supervised by the owner Theodor Adelswärd (1860–1929) and architect Isak Gustaf Clason (1859–1930). A rotunda (1860, 1912–1914), Badhus (bathhouse) (1921), tomb, and other park buildings are by Clason. Other ornamental buildings (including a HERMITAGE) are by Rudolf ABELIN, a formal kitchen garden by Edvard Glaesel (1858–1915), terraces by Edward White (1873–1952), a sunken garden by Ester Claesson (1884–1931) and additional designs by Gunnar ASPLUND. Adelsnäs is a Swedish variation of the Arts and Crafts idea, a neoclassical project of strong forms, considered to be one of the finest examples of modern English gardens in Sweden.   KL

ANNA LINDELL, *Adelsnäs: när parken berättar* (1999).

Adriana, Villa. See HADRIAN'S VILLA.

aesthetics of the garden.

Different cultures, and different people, have radically different views of what constitutes beauty in gardens. Much of the theory of garden beauty is taken up with a discussion of the relationship between art and nature. In the 11th-century Japanese book SAKUTEIKI ways of evoking nature, and respecting it, are held to be essential to garden making. In a wonderfully opinionated book, *L'Homme et ses jardins* (1975), Jacques Benoist-Méchin firmly laid down the law. Only six cultures, he explained, sought to express in their gardens the highest conception of happiness—the Chinese, Japanese, Persian, Arabic, Tuscan, and French. The English are explicitly excluded because their pursuit of nature, and refusal to consider any style that might raise gardens to the level of works of art, he argued, means that their gardens will always fall far short of true beauty. Imitations of nature in the English style, he wrote, are pseudo-gardens. Benoist-Méchin followed here the opinion of his compatriot Antoine Chrysostome Quatremère de Quincy (1755–

1849). In his *Essai sur la nature et l'imitation dans les beaux-arts* (Essay on Nature and Imitation in the Fine Arts) (1823) Quatremère de Quincy argued that imitation was the goal of all fine arts and thus, the irregular landscape garden could not be a fine art because it was composed of nature itself. G. W. F. Hegel (1770–1831) in his posthumous *Lecture on Aesthetics* (1835) argues that gardens are either architectonic in their design or they create a natural ambience. The latter, especially when decorated with 'Chinese pagodas, Turkish mosques, Swiss chalets, bridges, hermitages and such like', 'offers nothing to the eye which touches the infinite, it possesses no soul which speaks to our own'. Hegel believed that the architectonic garden had its own intrinsic rather than merely imitative character and that the 'architectonic principle found its most perfect expression in the art of the French garden'. However, this is not a view shared by all French gardeners. The Marquis de GIRARDIN despised 'Le majestueux ennui de la symétrie' (the majestic boredom of symmetry).

Many gardeners find the highest degree of happiness in the activity of gardening. The source of their happiness comes from the relationship with growing plants and the pleasure in seeing them flourish, together with the notion of the garden as a retreat from the nastier aspects of life outside it. The garden as a retreat, a microcosm over which one has substantial control, has long been an attractive prospect. It is part of the appeal of the *villeggiatura* (withdrawing to a country residence) which PLINY THE YOUNGER enjoyed in his Tuscan villa which he loved for its advantages over urban life—'there is no need for a toga, the neighbours do not come to call, it is always quiet and peaceful' (*Epistles*). The restorative powers of the rural life have been repeatedly sung: 'Horticulture and life in the country are, according to many learned people, the most *delightful*, the most *advantageous* and the *healthiest*, yes oftentimes also the most *blessed* life that one could wish for the person who is not bound by his profession to the town,' wrote Jan van der GROEN in his gardening manual, *Den Nederlandtsen hovenier* (1669). The beauty of gardens seen in this way is to do with the kind of life with which they are associated rather than with their appearance. The notion of the garden as a private sanctuary was precisely the opposite of a new kind of garden that appeared in Western Europe from the 16th century. The garden as status symbol—to proclaim wealth or political power—introduced a novel aspect of garden design. Henry VIII's HAMPTON COURT PALACE, Nicolas Fouquet's VAUX-LE-VICOMTE, Louis XIV's VERSAILLES, and William III's Het Loo went beyond aesthetics in the pursuit of

self-advertisement. Eighteenth-century England landscaping often had the effect of promoting the importance or wealth of the client and sometimes of artificially magnifying it. Long views from the house, with the boundaries concealed by naturalistic belts of trees, gave the impression of vast acres. Humphry REPTON liked to lay out the drive through a gentleman's park so that it followed a most indirect route to the house, thus giving the impression that the park was larger than it was.

The relationship between the garden and its site has been emphasized by many writers on garden design. A.-J. DEZALLIER D'ARGENVILLE in his *La Théorie et la pratique du jardinage* (1709) wrote, 'the greatest Skill in the right ordering of a Garden is, thoroughly to understand, and consider the natural Advantages and Defects of the Place; to make use of the one, and to redress the other' (English translation, *The Theory and Practice of Gardening*, 1712). Any skilful garden designer will, of course, recognize the natural beauties of a site and respect them in his layout. Designers of genius may discern unexpected charms and opportunities. Humphry Repton, when laying out the grounds of the industrialist Benjamin Gott at Armley in Yorkshire from 1809, made the great Gott mill building the focal point of a vista. Repton especially admired it at night when it presented 'a most splendid illumination of gas light'.

Garden aesthetics in the early 21st century present a dizzying eclecticism. The naturalistic tendency in planting, in one form or another, is one of the few styles that has achieved international prominence (see NATURALISTIC PLANTING). In the USA prairie planting and an emphasis on the use of native plants is a major theme. In Canada at Les QUATRE VENTS Frank CABOT has made a strongly eclectic garden with, at its heart, naturalistic plantings of both natives and exotics disposed in an exquiste natural setting. The interest of Gilles CLÉMENT in the way wild plants naturally colonize wasteland has introduced an unexpected atmosphere in French gardens more used to the rigours of the *jardin à la française*. At the Parc André Citroën in Paris (see PARIS PARKS AND GARDENS) Clément shows how this style of planting may work very well even in the context of a highly structured public park. Piet Oudolf (b. 1945), in his own garden in the Netherlands and for his many international commissions, uses naturalistic planting in the context of bold borders. Ecology and aesthetics seem to coincide with the recognition that plants from similar habitats, even though they may come from different parts of the world, associate well visually. In England Beth CHATTO has displayed this vividly. On the whole, the characteristic style of garden aesthetics in Britain is one of nostalgia—looking back to the abundant borders and pristine lawns of the age of Gertrude JEKYLL. In Spain, which has produced no garden designers of special note in recent times, the dazzling figure of Fernando CARUNCHO has drawn on the ancient theme of man's relationship with nature to create a new classicism which inspired his astonishing minimalist FERME ORNÉE at the Mas de les Voltes in Catalonia in which fields of olives, vines, and wheat assume a marvellously decorative role.

The ingredients of a garden that give pleasure to the owner, or to the visitor, are often regarded as beneath the lofty views of garden aesthetics. Yet almost anyone who enjoys gardens will relish the scent of garden plants: the varied scents of roses, the tropical luxuriance of some lilies (such as *Lilium speciosum*, especially on a warm, humid summer's evening), the vividly fresh citrus smell of the foliage of lemon verbena (*Aloysia triphylla*), the murkier but savoury whiff of rosemary, and many others. Gertrude Jekyll loved to flank an entrance with plants with aromatic foliage so that the passer-by would brush against them to release a delicious scent. COLOUR THEORY and its impact on garden aesthetics is a slippery subject to deal with. There is no doubt, however, that bursts of colour give great pleasure to gardeners, and a well-filled herbaceous border, almost regardless of niceties of design or good taste, will elicit cries of delight from garden visitors. The productive orderliness of the KITCHEN GARDEN, with regular rows of vegetables and beautifully espaliered or shaped fruit trees, is a sight that few will fail to find pleasurable. The simpler pleasure of entering the cool flickering shade of an avenue on a stifling summer's day is an experience to be relished. Some of these pleasures will be experienced as part of a sense of general well-being without its precise source being identified. The greatest gardens of the Italian Renaissance, such as the Villa LANTE, strike many visitors as simply marvellous places to be in. You can read about harmony, the skilful articulation of levels, the subtle revealing of views of the countryside. You can experience for yourself the beauty and inventivess of the stonework, the splashing of water from cascades or fountains and the delicious shade of the oriental plane trees. All these must be among the ingredients that make the place remarkably beautiful—but it is experienced as a totality rather than as a series of events. See also PLACE, THE SPIRIT OF.   PT

Aislabie, John

(1670–1742), English politician, landowner, and landscaper born near York who inherited the STUDLEY ROYAL estate near Ripon, North Yorkshire. Aislabie became a Member of Parliament in 1695 and was Chancellor of the Exchequer from 1718 until 1720 when the South Sea Company, in which he was criminally involved, collapsed. After imprisonment in the Tower of London he retired to his Yorkshire estate where he completed the laying out in the valley of the river Skell of one of the most remarkable landscape gardens of its day.   PT

Aislabie, William

(1700–81), English landowner and landscaper, son of John AISLABIE. He added to the STUDLEY ROYAL landscape between 1730 and 1750, in particular by acquiring the Cistercian Fountains Abbey, whose beautiful ruins he wove into the landscape as its triumphant conclusion. He created his own sublime landscape, enlivened by buildings of Gothic character, streams, and cascades, not far from Studley Royal in the precipitous valley of the river Ure at Hackfall. Aislabie also had an estate at Kirkby Fleetham (North Yorkshire). Arthur Young described it in 1771 as 'one of the seats of *William Aislabie*, Esq; of *Studley*, and the grounds greatly ornamented by him' (*A Six Month Tour of the North of England*, 1771). The house was connected to the village by a 1.6-km/1-mile viewing terrace which Young described: 'the edge of it planted, and temples, etc., built at those points which command the best views.' This little-known garden, of which nothing survives, sounds remarkably similar to the other North Yorkshire viewing terraces at DUNCOMBE PARK and RIEVAULX.   PT

Aiton, William (1731–93) and William Townsend

(1766–1849) Father and son gardeners, botanists, and plantsmen. The elder Aiton was born at Hamilton in Scotland and, from 1754, worked at CHELSEA PHYSIC GARDEN under Philip MILLER. He was recruited by the 3rd Earl of Bute to work for the Princess Augusta at Kew (which became the ROYAL BOTANIC GARDENS, KEW) where he became head gardener in 1784 and latterly also worked as 'Gardener to His Majesty' for King George III who had bought the adjoining estate. At Kew he was the chief author of the plant catalogue *Hortus Kewensis* (1789), which lists the 5,600 plants grown in the gardens at that time. Dates of plant introductions, and the names of their introducers where known, were given, making it a key source. Aiton was given expert botanical advice for the catalogue by Daniel Solander (1733–82) and Jonas Dryander (1748–1810), who organized the herbarium at Kew for Sir Joseph BANKS. The younger Aiton succeeded his father as head gardener at Kew in 1793 on his father's death. He was the author of a second edition of *Hortus Kewensis* (1810–13), the catalogue of plants grown at Kew, now listing over 11,000 species. He designed new gardens for Brighton Pavilion (Sussex), Buckingham Palace (London), and WINDSOR CASTLE. He was put in charge of the royal gardens at St James's Palace and Kensington Palace (see LONDON PARKS AND GARDENS) and became director general of royal gardens to George IV.   PT

RAY DESMOND, *Kew: The History of the Royal Botanic Gardens* (1995).

Ajuda Botanic Garden ✿

Lisbon, Portugal, was founded in 1768 by the Marquês de Pombal. Its terraced layout, parterres, and fine statuary all belong to the 18th century. The position is high and airy, with fine views over the rooftops to the Tagus. On the upper terrace a very large number of order beds (see BOTANIC GARDEN) contain the systematic collection. Here, too, is a group of distinguished trees: a superb spreading specimen of the dragon tree, *Dracaena draco*, native to Madeira, an *Araucaria bidwillii*, and a beautiful Moreton Bay fig (*Ficus macrophylla*). A grand balustraded double staircase with a statue of a Roman soldier in a niche leads down to the central terrace, which is laid out in the form of two parterres. Between them is an elaborate fountain pool whose fountain is richly decorated with seahorses, toads, serpents, and exotic birds. Segmental beds surrounding it are edged in box with clipped mounds of *Pittosporum tobira* at the apex of each segment. In the scalloped pool are thickets of papyrus (*Cyperus papyrus*) and yellow irises (*Iris pseudacorus*). The parterres, each of which has a large central circular pool, are divided into lozenge-shaped beds hedged in box which is cut at different levels, rising towards the centre of the parterre. Mounds of box or myrtle mark the corners. The west-facing terraced wall is garlanded with both white and yellow Banksian roses. William BECKFORD saw the garden when it was quite new and admired the 'airy groves' and 'marble balustrades of shining whiteness … I have never seen balustrades better hewn or chiselled.'   PT

WILLIAM BECKFORD, *The Journal of William Beckford in Portugal and Spain 1787–88* (1954).

Akbar

(1542–1605), 3rd Mughal Emperor (1556–1605), became the greatest of the Mughals, extending his empire to cover more than half of India. Renowned for his valour and statesmanship, he was also a prolific builder, a patron of literature and painting, and an active sportsman. Major works of his reign were the fort at Agra and the city of Fatehpur Sikri. He also built the fort of Hari Parbat, at Srinagar, Kashmir, commanding the views of Lake Dal. His conquest of Kashmir in 1586 was of the greatest significance to later garden design, for it provided superb opportunities for his successors, with ample water, brilliant sunshine, and a fertile soil. He once called it his private garden. His interest in gardens included the importation of trees and flowers to Agra, and their subsequent care. He also commissioned much road building and tree planting. A vivid picture of his reign is provided by the *Akbar-nama* and the *Ain-i-Akbari*, prepared on his instructions by Abu-'l-Fazl. His policies of religious and racial tolerance, his employment of Rajput craftsmen, and his marriages to Rajput wives gave rise to new concepts in design, resulting in a fusion of Indo-Islamic art.   SMH

Alberti, Leon Battista

(1404–1472), Italian humanist polymath. His importance for garden design arises not so much from his architecture as from his seminal architectural treatise *De Re Aedificatoria Libri X* (Ten Books on Architecture), which was completed by 1452 (when he presented it to Pope Nicholas V) and published in 1485. In Book 5, which is devoted to private houses, there is a section on villas (5. 14–18), and Alberti returns to the subject in Book 9, in which he applies his concept of architectural beauty to villas (9. 2–4).

In Alberti's view, suburban and country villas should be sited on hilltops for reasons of visibility to strangers, security, attractive views, and cooling breezes. They should be cheerful and welcoming in character, and so not fortified. Rooms and exterior elevations should observe the proportions of ancient buildings. Loggias are recommended, whether attached to the house or free standing in the gardens. Villa gardens, he argued, should be decorated with vases, grottoes, and topiary (using box and scented evergreen herbs), like the gardens of classical antiquity.

These precepts were implemented so exactly in the Villa QUARACCHI that its design has been attributed to Alberti. His treatise subsequently exercised a profound influence on many Italian Renaissance gardens, and also on garden design in France and the Netherlands.   GC

Alcázar, Real ⊛

Seville, Andalusia, Spain. The Real Alcázar has its origins in a stronghold built in the 9th century by Abd al-Rahman II but this in turn may possibly have been built on the foundations of a Roman praetorium. The castellated external walls that guard the estate preserve a military character to this day. The first garden known here was a kitchen garden, but under the Muslims and after the Christian Reconquest in the 13th century a series of gardens, made by Muslims, was laid out, many of which survive to make this one of the most interesting and attractive gardens in Spain. To the historian, and to the visitor, it presents a bewildering sequence of spaces and buildings. The earliest parts of the garden to survive are those to the west, close to the palace buildings, and to the south. The palace has outstanding enclosed patios some of which, such as the Patio de Yeso, with its large pool, date from the 12th century. The Palacio del Rey Don Pedro was built in the 1360s after the Castilian Reconquest of Seville. It is built in a refined intermingling of Islamic and Christian elements (the style known as *mudéjar*). The Patio del Léon and the Patio de las Doncellas are contemporary with the finest patios of the ALHAMBRA and yield nothing to them in beauty. The Patio de las Doncellas was given Renaissance details in the mid 16th century.

In the heart of the gardens, to the south of the palace buildings, is the Jardín de Alcoba (Garden of the Alcove). This had a Muslim pavilion, or *al-qubba* (from which the word alcove is derived), which was rebuilt in the 1540s for the Emperor Charles V, known today as the Pabellón (pavilion) de Carlos V. The elegant arcaded building has an interior with superb 16th-century AZULEJOS. The garden here spreads out all about, with straight or curved paths often hedged in myrtle and shaded by great palms linking its various parts. These provide an anthology of garden styles of many kinds. The former kitchen garden (El Retiro) was converted into a garden with the flavour of a public park in the 20th century. A 19th-century English garden (Jardín Inglés) has paths winding among groves of shrubs and trees. The 16th-century Ladies' Garden (Jardín de las Damas) was redesigned in the 17th century with eight hedged compartments and splendid fountains. In the centre is the Fuente de la Neptuna with a bronze figure of Neptune (after GIAMBOLOGNA) rising above a white marble basin and, at the end, the noble rusticated Fuente de la Fama (Fountain of Fame). The Jardín del Estanque (Pool Garden) has a large cistern converted into an open pool in the 16th century with, on one side, an arcaded screen of rocaille work crowned with a pediment and finials. At the centre of the pool is a bronze figure of Mercury standing on an elaborate plinth with cherubs, water spouts, and masks. Throughout the garden are fine trees, many palms, cypresses, and citrus plants, but also such exotics as *Chorisia speciosa*, *Melia azedarach*, *Simmondsia chinensis*, and several large *Magnolia grandiflora*. In the mid 14th century, when Seville was conquered by Castile, the Alcázar became a Castilian royal palace, and it remains to this day a royal residence (and may be closed when the monarch visits).   PT
JUAN CARLOS HERNÁNDEZ NÚÑEZ and ALFREDO J. MORALES, *The Royal Palace of Seville* (1999).

Alcsút ⊛

(also known as Alesútdoboz) Habsburg Park, Fejér county, Hungary. Construction began on the residence of the Hungarian line of the Habsburg dynasty in 1819, at the instruction of Palatine Joseph. The grounds were probably designed by Karl Tost (1789–1852), who had learned his craft at SCHÖNBRUNN and was the creator and head gardener of the Palatine's landscape garden at MARGITSZIGET, Budapest. Although the terrain was treeless and barren, by the middle of the 1820s with its hills, lake, GLORIETTE, its Roman bathhouse, and the little pavilion of the children's garden, the park at Alcsút became one of the most beautiful landscape gardens in Hungary. The Palatine, himself an expert gardener, generated the improvement of the whole estate. The park, neglected after the Revolution of 1848–9, was after the Compromise of 1867 comprehensively extended to *c*.40 hectares/100 acres and improved by Archduke Joseph, the Palatine's son and himself a trained and enthusiastic botanist, on the basis of designs by, and under the direction of, landscape gardener Vilmos JÁMBOR. Jámbor further enhanced the variety of the grounds with the inclusion of small hills and valleys. He made use of the given resources—and of the water output of Vilmos Zsigmondy's artesian well—to enlarge the lake, creating an island in the middle, as well as adding a waterfall, a bear's and eagle's house, and enriching the already varied flora with exotic plants. In 1872 a huge palm house was built to designs by the architect Miklós Ybl (1814–91) accompanied by substantial horticultural development. The inventory of flora in the park was recorded by the Archduke himself, and published in 1892. In this he lists almost 1,000 woody taxa, but the collection of bulbous and other herbaceous plants was also considerable, as was the rich variety of greenhouse plants. The palace was burnt down during the Second World War and later dismantled, together with the greenhouses. The gardens, however, have survived largely unscathed.   GA

Aldobrandini, Villa ⊛

Frascati, Lazio, Italy. One of the most important of the late Renaissance villas, and one of the earliest to embrace the baroque style, the Villa Aldobrandini was given to Cardinal Pietro Aldobrandini by his uncle Pope Clement VIII in 1598. Built in the foothills of the Alban Hills overlooking the Roman Campagna at Frascati, already a popular venue for *villeggiatura* (withdrawing to a country residence), it was remodelled by Giacomo della Porta (1537–1602), Carlo Moderno (*c*.1556–1629), and subsequently Giovanni Fontana (1540–1614). The introduction of water from the Modara Springs on Monte Algido in 1603 made it possible to introduce the impressive cascade and water theatre. Behind the villa a hemispherical courtyard, the Water Theatre, is framed by a wall ornamented with Ionic pilasters and niches, centred on the Fountain of Atlas, shown holding up the world. Shaded by the back of the villa the chambers in the base of the NYMPHAEUM are a cool refuge, flanking the great cascade, which descends from between two rustic garlanded columns, the Pillars of Hercules. Higher up above the water ladder an avenue of holm oaks leads into the oak and chestnut woods. John EVELYN visited in 1645 and found the villa 'one of the most delicious places I ever beheld for its situation, elegance, plentiful water, groves, ascents and prospects' (*Diary of John Evelyn*).   PHo

Aleksandria ⊛

Byelaya Tserkov, Ukraine, was the romantic setting for Count Branicki's palace, Dedinyets, laid out between the late 18th century and 1850. Near the palace in the eastern part of the park were parterres, sculpture, pavilions, fountains, pools with cascades, and decorative bridges. Beyond this formality the site sloped steeply down to the river Ros. The western part of the park was mainly natural oak woodland. Work in the park virtually ceased with the emancipation of serfdom in 1861, and great damage was caused in the 20th century during the civil war and the German occupation. Impressive restoration of the park buildings and the landscape began in the 1950s, and new landscaping was undertaken. Particularly attractive on the slope down to the river Ros is the Great Glade with a remarkable variety of fine trees, a seasonal carpet of wild flowers, the Echo Colonnade, and an artificial ruin with a pool and cascade.   PH

Alfabia ⊛

Buñola, Mallorca, Spain, standing in the hills above Palma, was the country house of the Muslim governor of Mallorca. When Mallorca was reconquered by Don Jaime I, Count of Aragon, in 1229 such estates as Alfabia were given to Don Jaime's supporters. Alfabia is what in Mallorca is called a *son*, a manor house at the heart of an agricultural estate. There is a plentiful water supply here, as there usually is in any Muslim garden. The garden here is terraced, and falling water in one form or another is one of its chief ingredients. A pair of statues of somnolent crouching lions looks down a shallow staircase inlaid with fine pebbles which descends through an avenue of palm trees with on each side a stepped rill glistening in the shade. A remarkable 17th-century pergola swathed in vines has a metal framework supported on bold octagonal stone columns. On the low wall between the columns there are from time to time carved stone vases with jets which give a fine spray of water. The water falls onto the path, which is surfaced with pebbles laid out in decorative criss-cross patterns which gleam with the sprinkling of water. At a lower level is an orange garden and, mounted on a wall, a baroque fountain with water splashing down into two basins. An avenue of plane trees (*Platanus* × *hispanica*) leads up to Alfabia and the cobbled courtyard that leads to the entrance of the house.   PT

Alhambra ⊛

Granada, Andalusia, Spain. The Alhambra is a marvellous ornament on the eastern edge of the city of Granada. A heterogeneous group of buildings rises high on a hill which commands fine views back towards the old city of Granada, the Albaicín, and far out into the countryside, dominated by the mountains of the Sierra Nevada whose peaks, as often as not, are shrouded in snow. The buildings themselves, and, in particular, the exquisite patios enclosed by them, must delight any visitor. However, exactly what these buildings are and how they assumed their present appearance is a story that is hard to unravel and many fanciful interpretations of them have been presented.

The Alhambra was the creation of the Muslim occupiers of Spain from the 9th century when they built a citadel (or *Qasaba*) on the western point of the Alhambra hill. Granada remained a Muslim stronghold longer than any other place in Spain—Muslims were expelled only in 1492. The buildings we see today (with the exception of Charles V's Renaissance palace added in the early 16th century) were built by the Muslim occupiers at different times over a span of five centuries, with the bulk of them no earlier than the early 14th century. After the Christian reconquest of Spain (the *Reconquista*) the Alhambra became a royal palace but later declined, and very little was heard of it until the 19th century. When the Venetian ambassador Andrea Navagiero visited Granada in 1524 he left a description of the Alhambra and GENERALIFE (*Viaggio fatto in Spagna, 1524–1526*). In the Patio de los Arrayanes (Myrtle Patio) he noted, on either side of the canal, espaliered myrtles and a few orange trees. He praised the 'magnificent garden' and water features of the Generalife which he thought 'the most beautiful thing I have seen in Spain'. This is a rare early description to give any detail of the Alhambra.

The whole site of the Alhambra occupies an area of 14 hectares/35 acres. The buildings we see have suffered much damage (part of them being blown up by the French army in the Peninsular War, 1808-14) and much restoration, in particular during the 19th century. Nineteenth-century visitors, too, had the habit of lopping off any decorative part of the buildings that caught their fancy. Murray's *Handbook to Spain* (1912) refers to 'the vulgar and rather disgusting habit of cutting names and tearing off pieces of plaster and tiles from the Alhambra'. It seems likely that, following on from the early citadel, the site developed as a *madina* (town), which it is called in Arab records, and that a series of palaces were built—new ones sometimes encroaching on old ones. Robert Irwin in the book cited below suggests that these palaces may have started as rural villas, conveniently close to the Sierra Nevada where an enclosed hunting park was established from the early 13th century. The earliest palace to survive at least in part is the Partal Palace which dates from the first years of the 14th century. The inward-facing façade of the building is in the form of a loggia, with five noble arches, surmounted by filigree work, overlooking a serene pool. A portico in the shape of a square tower (the Torre de la Damas—the Ladies' Tower) rises high above the building and from its small windows are views over the Albaicín and the mountains to the north. To the west of the Partal Palace are the two most famous, and beautiful, patios of the Alhambra. The Patio de los Leones (Court of Lions), dating from the late 14th century, has at its centre a fountain in the form of a stone basin and water jet supported by twelve stone lions each spouting water. Four rills run to the fountain, each leading from the colonnaded rooms that surround it, quartering the patio. The pale arcades with slender columns and intricate stuccowork that line the patio are exquisitely beautiful. Its present calmly introspective character (or as calm and introspective as the crush of visitors will allow), however, dates from modern times. Robert Irwin points out that in the 14th century it was 'gaudily painted in blue and gold and other colours' and 'brilliant carpets and hangings' decorated the patio. It is believed, too, that there was a sunken garden here, bright with flowers and orange trees, with the fountain rising above its centre. A German visitor, Hieronymus Münzer, saw the patio in 1494 and described it as being paved in marble. Close to the Patio de los Leones is the Patio de Arrayanes (Myrtle Patio) dating from the 14th century. This is a long rectangular space with a slender canal running down the centre with at each end a circular basin with a water jet. Modern hedges of clipped myrtle flank the canal. A richly decorated colonnade spans each end of the patio, and the lower part of the wall behind is decorated with AZULEJOS. A smaller patio to one side (Cuarto Dorado), which probably formed the entrance to the 14th-century Comares Palace, has an especially beautiful pool. Hexagonal in shape, it has a slightly raised fluted basin whose central jet causes concentric ripples to radiate outwards.

The Alhambra, whatever its origins or purpose, seems always to seduce the visitor with its sequence of sometimes surprising spaces, shade and light, calm or gurgling water, graceful architecture and wonderful carved stucco, and sudden views of the Sierra Nevada or of the Albaicín. The garden purist may wince at the potted pelargoniums but historical correctness in gardens is rarely in itself a source of beauty or charm. Besides, very little is known of the gardens that existed here. Indeed, is it reasonable at all to think of the Alhambra as any kind of garden? The only early reference to it as such is that of Andrea Navagiero cited above. By the time J. C. LOUDON described it in his *Encyclopaedia of Gardening* (1822) its fame seemed sketchy at the best. He referred to it as 'the remains of a reputed Moorish garden'. He describes its hilltop site 'with wood cut into quarters by straight and winding walks, and interspersed with fountains. . . . Several of these fountains, and many of the walks were formed by Charles V.' Apart from the 'palace' and 'certain venerable cypresses', 'no other part can with certainty be traced to the days of the moorish kings'. The renown of the Alhambra, and indeed its very reputation as a garden, seems a very modern one. It is also the subject of much romantic myth making, especially in the 19th-century writings of Washington Irving. Even without the myths, however, it remains a most beguiling place. The book cited below, short as it is, is the most valuable single work on its subject. It is strongly opinionated but its opinions are supported by evidence and it has an excellent critical bibliography.   PT
ROBERT IRWIN, *The Alhambra* (2004).

Ali Qapu ⊛
Isfahan, Iran. Built by Shah Abbas I as his palace at the beginning of the 17th century, the Ali Qapu or Lofty Gateway in Isfahan overlooks the great *maidan* (esplanade), known as the *naqsh-e Jahan*an or Mirror of the World. From 1598 Shah Abbas transformed Isfahan into the Safavid capital of Persia. The palace marked the entrance to the complex of stables, harem, and royal gardens, which, shaded by plane trees, and alive with water tanks, channels, and fountains, provided a cool royal retreat. Beyond lay the famous CHAHAR BAGH AVENUE. Rising six storeys high the Ali Qapu comprised administrative offices, besides containing the Shah's domestic quarters on the top two floors. Built like an airy cube, the palace draws inspiration from 14th-century Timurid tented pavilions rather than the more solid tradition of Sasanian or Seljuk architecture, reflected in Safavid religious constructions. A lofty open porch on the third level, supported by eighteen slender tree trunks, allowed the Shah to overlook activities in the square below—such as reviews of troops, horsemanship, and polo matches, besides being visible to his subjects. Here feasts for ambassadors and courtiers were held around the central marble basin into which, with water raised by oxen, fountains played.
PHo

allée,
in ordinary everyday French, signifies a passage between walls or a walk between two rows of trees. In the garden context it implies a formal walk designed for sauntering. It was an essential ingredient of French baroque gardens of the 17th century, often leading off the chief axis of the garden layout and linking subsidiary incidents. The *allée* could be lined with topiary pieces, in particular of yew, with hedges (often of hornbeam or lime), or enclosed in a tunnel of pleached trees. The surface of the *allée* was usually of raked sand, fine gravel, or shorn turf.
PT

Allegri Arvedi, Villa ⊛
Cuzzano, Verona, Italy. The 17th-century garden at Allegri Arvedi remains as it was originally conceived in front of the villa built by G. B. Bianchi in 1656 at the foot of a wooded hillside. A *broderie* PARTERRE of low-clipped box in swirling French-style arabesques punctuated by clipped box shapes set in gravel surround a simple circular pool. Amazingly dendrochronology has proved that the topiary box plants date to the 17th century before the Arvedi family bought the property. At one end of the terrace a *stanzone* (shelter for overwintering citrus plants) houses two grottoes encrusted with *pietra spugnosa* stalactites. The dramatic parterre lies below the villa from which views incorporate the outer landscape of fields and distant hills. The villa was bought by Giovanni Antonio Arvedi in 1824.

It is part of a working farm, the approach lined with persimmon trees and vineyards. Engravings of the garden by Montalegre were published by Volkammer in 1714.   PHo

Allerton Garden ⊛
Lawai Valley, Kauai, Hawaii, USA, is one of five National Tropical Botanical Gardens, chartered in 1964 by an act of the United States Congress. Located near the popular resort area of Poipu, Allerton Garden occupies about 32 hectares/80 acres of land first developed in the mid 1800s. Queen Emma, wife of King Kamehameha IV, had a retreat built on the bluff overlooking Lawai Bay and planted lavender bougainvillea (*Bougainvillea spectabilis*) that still spills down the cliff. The property was acquired in 1938 by Robert Allerton and his son John Gregg Allerton who transformed the site into a series of garden rooms. Their design used the placing of rocks, sculpture, and gravity-fed pools and fountains, as well as hundreds of species of plants, to create a magical landscape. The Diana Fountain, for example, features a U-shaped reflecting pool with a stone sculpture of the goddess Diana at one end and an Italianate pavilion at the other. Planting includes Java plum (*Syzygium cumini*), tamarind (*Tamarindus indica*), and the welcome shade of graceful monkeypod trees (*Samanea saman*). The Mermaid Fountain is created on a downhill slope and is first visible from above through the foliage of several trees. A 39-m/126-ft waterway flows by gravity through the garden in a curved path among stands of bamboo (*Bambusa vulgaris*) and oak-leafed fig (*Ficus montana*). Bronze mermaids standing at each end of the stream give the garden its name. *Lawai*, the Hawaiian name of the valley, is translated as valley of plenty, and the garden offers an abundance of beauty.   LTC

allotment.
Allotments are the English manifestation of an international movement, widespread in Europe (see KLEINGÄRTEN), of gardens not attached to houses to provide space for urban dwellers to grow vegetables and fruit or to have small pleasure gardens. In England the allotment is almost always used for kitchen gardening, the pleasure garden being much more unusual. Historically several influences have fostered the existence of allotments. The 16th-century and 18th-century enclosures of common land, which passed into the ownership of large landowners, deprived many people of the right to cultivate small plots. The Industrial Revolution and the resulting expansion of towns stimulated the search for out-of-town space for urban dwellers to garden. In Birmingham the Westbourne Road Town

gardens were established in the 18th century and by 1831 J. C. LOUDON noted that there were 2,000 such gardens, some of which survive. The midlands were a pioneer area for such gardens. Hill Close gardens (Warwick), dating from the 19th century, were complete small gardens—with lawns, flower beds, kitchen gardens, and ornamental summer houses, each enclosed in hedges to give an air of autonomous privacy. By 1998 they were derelict but have been rescued and restored, with some of the original summer houses and plantings surviving, by a group of dedicated volunteers.

By the end of the 19th century the need for allotments was recognized in law, with the passing of an Act of Parliament in 1887 obliging all local authorities to provide allotments where there was a demand. This was confirmed in the Small Holdings and Allotments Act of 1908 and is still in force. In the 20th century the two world wars, and resulting shortage of food, stimulated the desire for allotments. During the First World War the number of allotments rose from 600,000 in 1914 to 1,500,000 in 1918, encouraged by the 'Every-man-a-gardener' campaign. In the Second World War the 'Dig for Victory' campaign found new space for allotments in public parks and other novel sites. The traditional allotment has an area of 10 poles. The pole is a slightly variable square measure equivalent to 27.75 sq. m/272.25 sq. ft. Thus, the allotment would have an area of 277.5 sq. m/2,925 sq. ft. Such an area was reckoned to to provide enough to feed a family of four for a year. However, the area of allotments is variable, especially on privately owned land.

Late in the 20th century ecological anxieties, and the quality of mass-produced fruit and vegetables, encouraged a new wave of interest, often among organic gardeners. The demand for allotments has fluctuated but has never entirely evaporated and the right to have them has been tenaciously protected. However, much of the old land for allotments was privately owned and has been sold for other purposes. The same is true of land owned by local authorities and in the past dedicated to allotments. Privately owned allotments still survive—in the grounds of the Bishop's Palace of Wells Cathedral (Somerset) are allotments enclosed in ancient walls which benefit from one of the loveliest settings in the country. Many people see the allotment as the restitution of rights withdrawn from them by the privatization of common land in the enclosures.

In the USA and Canada allotments are called community gardens and have their origins in the early 20th century, in particular in the First World War. These may be groups of individual plots or whole gardens cultivated in a cooperative, communal way, and they may be both productive and ornamental. The American Community Garden Association (ACGA), founded in 1979, gives advice to those setting up community gardens and disseminates information among members. The North American term 'community garden' has proved attractive to gardeners in Britain who regard the term allotment as having an institutional air—a privilege handed out from on high rather than a right—far removed from popular community spirit which can be such an attractive feature of such gardens. The book cited below contains moving descriptions of the spirit of cooperation, friendliness, and disinterested kindliness among very different kinds of people that can flourish among allotment holders. Something of this impulse is enshrined in the objectives of the National Society of Allotments and Leisure Gardening (NSALG, founded in 1901), which are 'to help all enjoy the recreation of gardening and so promote their health, recreation and community fellowship'.   PT

DAVID CROUCH and COLIN WARD, *The Allotment: Its Landscape and Culture* (1988; new edn. 1997).

Alnarp ⊛

Scania, Lomma, Sweden. A park of about 20 hectares/49 acres, around the palace of Alnarp (1859–62) by the Danish architect Ferdinand Meldahl (1827–1908). The park has its origin in the woods of Alnarp, dating from 1457, Sweden's only remaining forest of elm (*Ulmus glabra*). The park was created 1870–2 under supervision of head gardener Carl Ludwig Siemers (1798–1878) and Professor Hjalmar Nathorst (1821–99). It is designed as a botanic woodland garden in a landscape style, with plantations in clearings. The park and gardens, indeed the whole estate, may be thought of as a blending of education and aesthetics, with agriculture, forestry, and horticulture united on a single site. It was inspired by, among others, the pomologist Olof Eneroth (1825–81). Today Alnarp is a part of SLU, the Swedish University of Agricultural Sciences, serving education in plant knowledge (with more than 2,000 taxa of woody plants), with experimental fields, a landscape laboratory, and it also serves as a park for recreation.   KL

Alphand, Jean Charles Adolphe

(1817–91), a French engineer and landscape designer with a great influence on the design of new parks associated with the redevelopment of Paris under Georges-Eugène HAUSSMANN. Between 1855 and 1870 Alphand was chief engineer in the Services des Promenades et Plantations in Paris working closely with the city's head gardener Jean-Pierre BARILLET-DESCHAMPS. Among the parks with which he was especially involved were the Bois de Boulogne (from 1855), the Bois de Vincennes (from 1857), Parc Monceau (1861), Montsouris (1865), and Buttes-Chaumont (1865–7). From 1871 to 1891 Alphand was *directeur des travaux de Paris*. The results of the transformation of Paris under Haussmann may be seen in Alphand's *Les Promenades de Paris* (1867–73). His *L'Art des jardins* (1886), written in collaboration with Baron Ernouf, sets out his aesthetic principles. See also PARIS PARKS AND GARDENS.   PT

Alpine garden. See ROCK GARDEN.

Altamont Garden ⊛

County Carlow, Ireland, was laid out in the 20th century as the setting for a mid 18th-century country house, but the site goes back at least to the 16th century. In 1923 the estate of 16 hectares/40 acres was leased to Feilding Lecky Watson who later purchased it. The acid soil and relatively mild climate were perfect for the cultivation of the flowering shrubs in which he was especially interested. Through his friendship with the director of the NATIONAL BOTANIC GARDENS at GLASNEVIN in Dublin, Sir Frederick Moore, Watson had seeds of many newly introduced plants, in particular rhododendrons. Watson's daughter Corona took charge of the garden after her father's death in 1943 and continued the work he had initiated. The ornamental heart of the garden is a lake linked to the house by a walk which leads between mixed borders and pairs of old Irish yews which curve over to form arches. The banks of the lake are richly planted with trees, in particular conifers, and with flowering shrubs. Walks about the lake reveal shifting views across its surface and lead deeper into the woodland that edges it on one side where the ground slopes down to the river Slane. Here are fine trees, a bog garden of Robinsonian (see ROBINSON, WILLIAM) character, and many old rhododendrons. A walk skirting the garden makes the most of marvellous views of the rural scenery and of the Wicklow Hills. With skilful planting and planned walks Altamont makes the most of a beautiful site.   PT

Alton Towers ⊛

Staffordshire, England, is an estate of rare eccentricity and extravagance covering an area of 135 hectares/333 acres. From 1810 Charles Talbot, 15th Earl of Staffordshire, built an extraordinary house of wild Gothic character to the designs of several architects the chief of whom were Thomas Allason (1790–1852) and

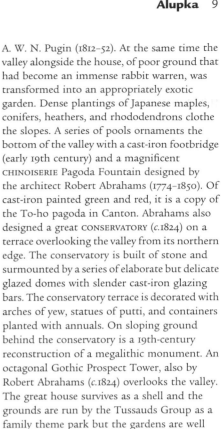

A. W. N. Pugin (1812–52). At the same time the valley alongside the house, of poor ground that had become an immense rabbit warren, was transformed into an appropriately exotic garden. Dense plantings of Japanese maples, conifers, heathers, and rhododendrons clothe the slopes. A series of pools ornaments the bottom of the valley with a cast-iron footbridge (early 19th century) and a magnificent CHINOISERIE Pagoda Fountain designed by the architect Robert Abrahams (1774–1850). Of cast-iron painted green and red, it is a copy of the To-ho pagoda in Canton. Abrahams also designed a great CONSERVATORY (*c.*1824) on a terrace overlooking the valley from its northern edge. The conservatory is built of stone and surmounted by a series of elaborate but delicate glazed domes with slender cast-iron glazing bars. The conservatory terrace is decorated with arches of yew, statues of putti, and containers planted with annuals. On sloping ground behind the conservatory is a 19th-century reconstruction of a megalithic monument. An octagonal Gothic Prospect Tower, also by Robert Abrahams (*c.*1824) overlooks the valley. The great house survives as a shell and the grounds are run by the Tussauds Group as a family theme park but the gardens are well cared for. PT

Alupka ⊕

Crimea, Ukraine, is spectacularly situated between the mountains and the Black Sea. Edward Blore (1787–1879) designed the palace for Count Mikhail Vorontsov without visiting Russia. Another English architect, William Hunt, supervised the work (1830s) and probably laid out the impressive terrace garden in front of the palace, where marble fountains, clipped box, and flowering plants are dominated by three pairs of magnificent marble lions from the studio of Francesco Bonanni. The rose Countess Vorontsov still flourishes in the garden. A series of further terraces with fountains and flowering shrubs and trees descends to the sea. Two very large magnolias on the second terrace were ordered for Count Vorontsov in 1829 by the director of the Nikitsky Botanical Garden from Wagner's nursery in Riga after originating in the Hackney nursery of Conrad LODDIGES.

The upper park (40 hectares/99 acres) behind the palace is a fine example of picturesque landscaping by the German gardener Karl Kebach. Preparation involved the removal of a vast quantity of rock; the introduction of many tons of black earth from the Ukraine and fertile soil from mountain pastures; and the diverting of mountain streams to feed watercourses with cascades. A winding path from the palace leads under leafy shade past

The Pagoda Fountain at **Alton Towers** designed by Robert Abrahams.

moss-covered rocks, grottoes, streams, and waterfalls and eventually reaches an open glade with magnificent trees—pines, cedars, and cypresses. And then three further glades all with exceptional trees—Italian, Mexican, and Crimean pines, cedars of Lebanon, planes, chestnuts, cypresses, sequoias, silver firs, and cork oaks.   PH

Alves Park, Rodrigues (Woodland Park) ✣

Belém, Pará state, Brazil, was decreed on paper by provincial government legislation in 1870, but only in 1883 was it effectively created when the local government used it as a solution to occupying vacant land then located at the city's edge. The occupation of these new areas was carried out according to the sanitary policies of urban planning at the time. In 1903 it was restored and reinaugurated by the mayor of the time, Antônio José de Lemos (1843–1913), an administrator whose plan was to create a system of woodland parks and public squares for the city in the period from 1898 to 1911. The park covers a rectangular area of approximately 15 hectares/38 acres, today completely surrounded by the city, with an imposing entrance from Avenida Almirante Barroso. At the beginning of the 20th century it was the biggest public garden in the city, and despite the transformations and losses over its 100-year history it is still an important landmark, forming a natural reserve of Amazon vegetation. Divided into four quadrilaterals crossed by curving lines, its focal point is a central lake creating a scene typical of Brazilian gardens of the turn of the century, with amenities such as ponds, waterfalls, islands, footbridges, rotundas, grottoes, pavilions, and enclosures for birds and animals typical of the Amazon as well as areas for gymnastic exercise. The park was restored in 1995, when the opportunity was taken to recreate its *belle époque* splendour.   HS

> HUGO SEGAWA, *Ao amor do público: jardins no Brasil* (For the Love of the Public: Gardens in Brazil) (1996).
>
> SILVIO SOARES MACEDO and FRANCINE GRAMACHO SAKATA, *Brazilian Urban Parks* (2002).

Amber ✣

Rajasthan, India, capital of the Katchawa Rajput, situated on high ground in a strategic position overlooking the road to Delhi. The settlement is surrounded by two artificial lakes created in the 15th century to provide water for the city. Two gardens—the Dilaram Bagh and the Kesar Kyari—were laid out along the shores of the lower lake, called Lake Maotha. The first is divided into two sections: a panoramic garden (recently restored) in the form of a

CHAHAR BAGH on the lake shore, punctuated by four pavilions, two on each of the main axes; and a garden in the shape of a trapezoid with a pavilion at the centre, located 12 m/39 ft below the first. The two sections are linked by a waterfall. The second is a semi-hanging structure in the middle of the lake, below the palace and a short distance from the monumental waterworks. It is laid out along two terraces, in the form of flowering parterres, that descend to the lake on three sides, and is reminiscent of ISOLA BELLA on Lake Maggiore in Italy. The upper terrace towards the entrance is a pure *chahar bagh*, where the points of intersection between the different levels and the axes are marked by red sandstone *chini khanas* (walled enclosures, one of whose walls is an open arcade, whose interior has niches (for candles) and a fountain). In the Diwan-i Khass courtyard of the palace is a garden with a parterre on a plan that recalls Shāh Jahān's (1628–58) ANGURI BAGH in Agra fortress.
AP

Ambras ✣

Innsbruck, Tyrol, Austria. The park of Ambras Palace, which dates from the Middle Ages with Renaissance alterations, is in three parts: the Keuchengarten (Kitchen Garden) in front of the Spanischer Saal dates from the 16th and 19th centuries, the Wildpark (Deer Park) dates from the 16th century, and the Landschaftspark (Landscape Park) from the 19th. In Ambras traces can still be found today of the humanist concept of the tripartite garden world— pleasure garden, *boschetto* (see BOSCO), and *selvatico* (see GIARDINO SEGRETO). Archduke Ferdinand II of Habsburg, Prince of the Tyrol from 1564 to 1595, was well educated and also had a garden on the Italian model laid out near his Innsbruck residence (site of the Hofgarten) between 1566 and 1572. He amassed an extensive library, including gardening books, and a chamber of curiosities, and had as a young man been instructed in the garden arts in Prague, and visited his married sisters in Mantua and Florence. The Ambras gardens are extensively praised in a description by Stephanus Pighius in 1574. The Keuchengarten today still includes the relics of the Ballhaus, the Bacchusgrotte, and a terrace with a tower from the period of its creation. In the deer park is an artificial waterfall dating from the 16th century. Between 1856 and 1862 under the governorship of Archduke Karl Ludwig the Keuchengarten was enriched with an ornamental pool and a 20-hectare/49-acre landscape park laid out. In 1997 a replica border was recreated in the Keuchengarten based on a drawing by Hans Puechfeldner (author of three books on gardening, active in

Prague 1592–4, a pupil of Vredeman de VRIES).
GH

American garden.

The discovery of the riches of North American plants in the 18th century sparked a fashion among British and Irish gardeners for 'American gardens' which were simply collections of American plants, in particular trees and shrubs. Through Peter COLLINSON and John BARTRAM of Philadelphia large numbers of new plants came to England. From the 1730s Lord Petre at Thorndon Hall (Essex) received many of these exotics from Collinson. Collinson wrote to Bartram in 1741 that 'Last year Ld petre planted out about ten Thousand Americans'. He is referring here to trees and shrubs, which, he said, Lord Petre was very skilful at intermingling with more familiar exotics to produce striking variations of foliage and bark. The Duke of Richmond at Goodwood (West Sussex) also received seeds from Bartram from 1741 and established an American Grove, noted for its magnolias. Because American plants were largely ericaceous, American gardens came to mean any ericaceous bed of shrubs and trees regardless of their origin. As late as 1813 Humphry REPTON laid out an American Garden at Ashridge (Middlesex) for the Earl of Bridgwater. At Tullynally Castle (County Westmeath, Ireland) Maria Edgeworth in 1834 saw 'the most beautiful American garden'. American gardens were still being made at the time of the exploration of the Pacific north-west coast in the mid 19th century, which brought new and spectacular conifers to Britain, but the PINETUM became the favourite manner of displaying them.   PT

Amerongen, Kasteel ✣

Amerongen, Utrecht, the Netherlands, situated at the edge of the Utrecht range of hills by the river Rhine. It occupied a strategic position from the Middle Ages onwards. The house, destroyed a number of times during its history, takes its Dutch classicist form from a rebuilding after having been burned down by the French in 1673. Proposals for grand formal gardens produced for Godard Adriaan Baron van Reede and his son Godard, the 1st Earl of Athlone, at the end of the 17th century were only partially executed, due to the low-lying land being subject to flooding. However in 1696 a canal was dug and a long vista created from the house to a distant hill, by demolition of Kasteel Lievendaal. During the 18th century the separately moated gardens continued to display baroque features of PARTERRES and BOSQUETS while respecting the irregular sized squares. Early 19th-century alterations of the various quarters in landscape style were undone again by the landscape architect Hugo POORTMAN. From 1887 onwards he restored formal features, including *broderie* work (see PARTERRE) and *plates-bandes* (see BORDER) with shaped trees. An orangery with a rose and flower garden, a playhouse, and bandstand were also added. Sold to a foundation in 1977, a restoration scheme of the late 1980s continues to retain the 17th-century character and features while respecting later additions.   JW

H. TROMP, 'Kasteel Amerongen: een beheersplan van de Stichting P.H.B. voor de tuinen van Kasteel Amerongen', *Kasteel Amerongen Bulletin*, No. 9 (1987).

Ammanati, Bartolomeo

(1511–92), Italian sculptor and architect. Many of his finest sculptures are tombs in the style of Michelangelo, but Ammanati also used his skills as a sculptor and architect for fountains designed for urban and garden settings. In 1555 he received a commission from Duke Cosimo I de' Medici to build a *fountain of Juno* for the Sala Grande of the Palazzo Vecchio in Florence. In the event, the fountain was instead installed in the garden at PRATOLINO, where it was praised by Michelangelo as 'una bella fantasia'; the fountain figures are now in the Bargello. His work for Duke Cosimo's garden at the MEDICI Villa at Castello includes the bronze *Hercules and Antaeus* (1559–60) for Niccolò Tribolo's Fountain of Hercules and the bronze giant representing the Apennines standing shivering in the pond on the highest terrace. Ammanati's best-known sculpture is the Fountain of Neptune (*c*.1560–75) in the Piazza della Signoria in Florence.   GC

Ammann, Gustav

(1885–1955), one of the most famous Swiss garden architects. Born in Zurich, he had a shaping influence on the development of Swiss landscape architecture. Between 1901 and 1903 he learnt the gardener's craft in the reputable Froebels Erben landscape gardening company in Zurich, and from 1905 till 1911 studied at the Kunstgewerbe- und Handwerkerschule in Magdeburg, Germany, and worked in the offices of notable German landscape architects, among them Leberecht MIGGE in Hamburg. Ammann was senior garden architect with Otto Froebels Erben from 1911 until the company was wound up in 1933. In 1934 he set up his own office in Zurich and worked with many leading modern architects including Richard Neutra (1892–1970). Among his most important projects were the Neubühl housing development in Zurich (1929–30), the Allenmoos (1939) and Letzigraben (1949) public baths in Zurich, and numerous other Swiss projects in a moderate modern style. Amman

was responsible for the garden architecture of the ZÜGA 1933 garden exhibition and the Landi Swiss garden exhibition in 1939. In numerous articles and his book *Blühende Gärten* (1955) he was a shaping influence on the discussion of garden theory. Among other posts he was a founder member of the association of Swiss landscape architects (Bund Schweizer Gartenarchitekten, BSG) and secretary general of the International Federation of Landscape Architects (IFLA). See also AMMANN-PARK.   UW

Ammann-Park ⊛

Canton of Zurich, Switzerland, planted in 1942 on an area of 0.3 hectare/0.75 acre by the garden architect Gustav AMMANN, is today one of the best-preserved early 1940s parks in Switzerland. In 1939 the director of the Bührle & Co. machine tools factory commissioned the architect Robert Winkler (1898–1973) to design a building in the Oerlikon industrial area of Zurich to serve as a 'welfare house'—a place of rest and recreation for workers and staff during their work breaks. The attached park was planned by Ammann and laid out under his direction in 1942–3. Amman's aim was to offer pleasant, 'natural' garden scenes in the domestic garden style that would take one's mind off the industrial daily grind and evoke affectionate memories of the holiday landscapes of Ticino. On a sloping, cleverly modelled area to the south of the building he devised a modest but varied park in contemporary style with many winding granite-paved paths and groups of loosely spaced trees and shrubs. Ammann's design, with its plantings of woodland and river valley plants and the flora of southern Switzerland, has a varied, in places Mediterranean, charm. The central visual focus of the park with its many carefully designed sitting places is a small garden pond with round stepping stones, surrounded by contrasting large- and small-leafed plantings. A free-standing female nude figure close by completes the evocative, intimate atmosphere by the water. Through his skilful use of rustic pergolas with climbing plants as screens and creators of spaces Ammann created a variety of secluded spaces that continue to invite workers, local residents, and interested visitors to linger in the park. The historically important, well-maintained grounds were placed under a conservation order in 1993 and today complement the ensemble of four new parks the city district built in the former Zurich-Oerlikon industrial area.   UW

Amsterdam Bos ⊛

Amsterdam, Noord-Holland, the Netherlands, is, with its 660 hectares/1,630 acres, one of the largest 20th-century public parks. It was

innovative in its concept, avoiding the words 'park' and 'garden', because these had become associated with the bourgeoisie. Since it emerged from a proud socialist city, it attempted to redefine parks for the common man as *bos*—woodland. This was to serve for the recreation of Amsterdam citizens, to enable the experience of the beauty of nature, healthy exercise, and freedom to roam in 'merciful' silence. While agreement for it was reached in 1928 it took until 1934 to finalize a plan. Produced by Cor van Eesteren (1897–88) and Jakoba Mulder (1900–88), who together also prepared the General Development Plan for Amsterdam in 1935, the Bos formed a crucial element in the green space strategy of the city. While functionalist objectives guided the design, it sought a new formal language without clichés. As a result there is an absence of any monumentality and symmetry, and the design follows a natural progression of flowing spaces with informal boundaries, creating a coherent whole. The dominating feature within this is an Olympic-size rowing canal, while there are bathing and paddling pools, a viewing mound, an open-air theatre, and good facilities for horses and cycling.   JW

J. T. BALK, *Een kruiwagen vol bomen: verleden en heden van het Amsterdamse bos* (1979).

SERGIO POLANO, 'The Bos Park, Amsterdam and urban development in Holland', in Monique Mosser and George Teyssot, *The History of Garden Design: The Western Tradition from the Renaissance to the Present Day* (1990).

Ancy-le-Franc, Château d' ⊛

Yonne, France, built in the mid 16th century for Antoine de Clermont to the designs of Sebastiano Serlio. A drawing of *c*.1576 by DU CERCEAU shows the moated chateau at the head of a walled rectangular garden with twelve rectangular beds, a BOSQUET, and corner pavilions. The estate became derelict by the 17th century, but later in the century it was restored with a new garden in the style of LE NÔTRE with PARTERRES *de broderie*, PATTE D'OIE, and fountains. In the 18th century an octagonal pavilion was built on an island in a lake and it survives today, a fine eyecatcher closing a vista from a lawn edged with sweet chestnuts.   PT

Andersen, Jeppe Aagaard

(b. 1952), Danish landscape architect. Vice-president of the International Federation of Landscape Architects (IFLA) from 2002, he has taken part in many competitions for parks, plazas, and waterfronts in Denmark and abroad. Significant works are gardens at Holstebro Courthouse (1991), HERNING CITY HALL SQUARE, the plaza by the Old Dock Warehouse in Copenhagen (1996–8), the waterfront project Sundsparken in Malmö, Sweden (2001), and from 1998 landscape planning for the town of Ørestaden. Strict, minimalistic geometry with squares, circles, and diagonals based on central features of the building and its surroundings is used, but it is not wholly symmetrical. Although the design is modern, LE NÔTRE is seen as an main ideal and many of the basic and traditional elements of garden art, such as ALLÉES and QUINCUNXES, are incorporated.   AL

Andersson, Sven-Ingvar

(b. 1927), landscape architect, born and educated in Sweden. From 1963 to 1994 he was professor at the Royal Danish Academy of Fine Arts, School of Architecture, Copenhagen, succeeding C. Th. SØRENSEN. Early works in Sweden consisted mainly of private gardens and housing projects, including the courtyard gardens for the Archive for Decorative Art in Lund (1958) and the town hall square in Höganäs (1961) where light and water were used. With a team of architects and city planners he has won several important competitions and designed parks and plazas all over Europe: for example Karlsplatz, Vienna (1971), Parc de la Villette, Paris (1982), Tête Défense, Paris, (1986), and MUSEUMPLEIN, Amsterdam (1992). In Sweden he was inspired by Sven HERMELIN, Holger BLOM, and Ulla Molin, and in Denmark by C. Th. SØRENSEN. He has written several books, with Steen Høyer: *C. Th. Sørensen— Landscape Modernist* (2001, from the Danish edn. 1993). In many projects ovals and ellipses are used, as in Karlsplatz and Parc de la Villette, but also in recent plazas at Helsingborg and Malmö, Sweden. Andersson has a clear idea of how to restore gardens, and he has worked on several: the manor garden Frederiksdal in Helsingborg (1965) and the romantic garden of Sophienholm in Kgs. Lyngby (1969), the Damsgård rococo garden, Bergen (1983), and the Tycho Brahe Renaissance garden at URANIBORG (1992). In Ronneby Brunnspark in Sweden (1987) two special gardens were made—a scented garden with a huge pergola and a Swedish-Japanese garden. Andersson uses the fewest possible materials with the richest variations in detail, an approach also seen in the garden of his holiday house in Skania.   AL

André, Édouard

(1840–1911), French garden designer and author associated between 1860 and 1868 with ALPHAND and BARILLET-DESCHAMPS in the landscaping of new parks laid out as part of Haussmann's transformation of Paris (see PARIS PARKS AND GARDENS). André worked widely in Europe and also in America. He was commissioned, jointly with Lewis Hornblower, to design SEFTON PARK

in England which was completed in 1872. It introduced to Britain André's characteristic bold pattern of ellipses and circles and his technique of mounding to conceal paths. He also worked in the Netherlands at Kasteel WELDAM; in Lithuania at Palanga; and in Luxembourg. Apart from his work on parks he also laid out historicizing designs in gardens in France such as the Château de Caradeuc (Ille-et-Vilaine) and the Château de la Treyne (Lot). One of his most attractive surviving gardens is the ROSERAIE DE L'HAŸ-LES-ROSES. André's book *L'Art des jardins: traité général de la composition des parcs et jardins* (1879), with its vigorous historical feeling, was particularly influential on the design of public parks. In this book he spells out his belief in the virtues of the composite style of garden design in which art and nature, architecture and landscape, are happily intermingled. In 1890 he was appointed to the chair of landscape architecture at the École d'Horticulture in Versailles (now the École Nationale Supérieure d'Horticulture).   PT

Androuet Du Cerceau, Jacques.

See DU CERCEAU, JACQUES ANDROUET.

Anet, Château d' ⊛

Anet, Eure-et-Loire, France, built between 1547 and 1552 for Diane de Poitiers to the designs of Philibert de L'ORME—one of the finest French Renaissance buildings. De L'Orme also designed an ORANGERY overlooking its own walled garden. Nothing survives of this, and only fragments of the other gardens seen in DU CERCEAU's engraving—a magnificent ensemble of ornate parterres in a galleried enclosure to the north of the chateau. Later in the 16th century the earliest known PARTERRE *de broderie* was designed for Anet by Claude Mollet (see MOLLET, ANDRÉ) whose father Jacques Mollet worked here with Étienne Dupérac. The Renaissance garden was swept away by a giant baroque scheme, probably by Claude DESGOTS, in the 1680s. Some of the magnificent Renaissance buildings survive at Anet, including de L'Orme's superb domed chapel, but the garden may only be seen in the imagination.   PT

Anglesey Abbey ⊛

Cambridgeshire, England, was laid out from 1930 by Huttleston Broughton, 1st Lord Fairhaven. There had been an Augustinian abbey here and some of the monastic buildings survive, although the present house is largely 20th century. The flat site, of 40 hectares/100 acres, still has the occasional trace of monastic fish ponds. Huttleston Broughton designed a garden of a great originality, with something of the spirit of an 18th-century landscape garden

but dominated by giant formal avenues which quarter the site. An 18th-century park would have depended on changes of level but that is not possible here. Broughton saw that the chief way to animate the scene was to introduce the vertical emphasis of trees. The Coronation Avenue, planted in 1937 to celebrate the coronation of George VI, is a quadruple alignment of horse chestnuts 400 m/1,400 ft long forming the chief axis of the garden. Subsidiary avenues or walks of holm oaks (*Quercus ilex*), horse chestnuts, limes, or yews march across the land on three sides of the house. An outstanding collection of sculptures and architectural fragments is deployed among the trees. Close to the house are formal gardens enclosed in yew hedges or beech hedges with excellent borders. Since 1966 the estate has belonged to the NATIONAL TRUST which, starting in 1998, has laid out an admirable winter garden to the east of the house. Here winding walks pass between skilful plantings of trees, shrubs, bulbs and perennials chosen for ornamental bark, winter blossom, or striking foliage.   PT

Anguri Bagh ⊛

Agra, Uttar Pradesh, India, literally 'grape garden', is situated within the harem of the Agra fortress to the east of the Diwan-i Khass. Completely exposed to the sun and closed on three sides by white marble walls, it once gave access to the pavilion of the princesses. The difference in ground level between the Diwan-i Khass enclosure and the garden is signalled by a waterfall with a *chini khana* (see AMBER). This is a stone garden and the only vegetation is four small parterres arranged like a CHAHAR BAGH. The layout of the parterres, with beds for the different flowers, recalls the pieces of a puzzle, and is similar to that of the Diwan-i Khass of the Rajput palace at Amber in Rajasthan. In the days of Shāh Jahān there was a small stone pergola decorated with a lattice-work of emeralds and rubies, representing vine leaves as they turn from green to red, from which the name of the garden probably derives.   AP

S. CROWE and S. HAYWOOD, *The Gardens of Mughul India* (1972).

E. B. MOYNIHAN (ed.), *Paradise as a Garden in Persia and Mughal India* (1979).

Anhalt-Dessau, Franz, Prince of

(1740–1817), gifted German landowner who with the help of German craftsmen laid out his extensive estates in accordance with English ideas and impressions gained on his travels. Careful consideration was given to agriculture, forestry, and horticulture. From 1764 over a period of 50 years he and his gardeners J. G. Schoch and J. F. EYSERBECK created the Gartenreich (Garden Kingdom) (see DESSAU-WÖRLITZ GARTENREICH), covering *c*.150 sq. km/90 sq. miles and containing a number of parks, which was much admired by his own contemporaries.

The landscape of the Gartenreich was given a park like character, emphasized by farm buildings in classical forms, without detriment to the economic aspects of the estate. Anhalt brought the neo-Gothic style to the Continent through his connection with Strawberry Hill (see WALPOLE, HORACE) in his Gotisches Haus at Wörlitz.

From 1765 he worked on the Wörlitz Park (see DESSAU-WÖRLITZ GARTENREICH), one of the earliest landscape gardens on the Continent, and on the Luisium (see DESSAU-WÖRLITZ GARTENREICH). In 1777 he built the hermitage of Sieglitzerberg (42 hectares/104 acres) on the high banks of the Elbe; this had affinities with STOURHEAD, with a small Schloss (1777), a Roman burial tower (1779-80), statues, vases, and gatehouses, all integrated in an 'ordered natural setting'. At Oranienbaum (see DESSAU-WÖRLITZ GARTENREICH) he created a Chinese garden and buildings in the CHINOISERIE style. He had a decisive influence on the planning of the Georgium Park which is wrongly attributed to J. F. Eyserbeck.   HGÜ

Anlan Yuan,
China, lies in the small town of Haining, now called Yanguan, 40 km/24 miles north-east of Hangzhou in Zhejiang province. When built by Chen Yujiao between 1573 and 1620, on the site of a ruined garden owned in the Southern Song dynasty by the Prince of Anhua, it covered only 2 hectares/5 acres, but in 1733 one of his descendants doubled its size. The garden was given the name Yu Yuan, then later Suichu Yuan. On four of his six journeys south of Changjiang (Yangtze river) between 1751 and 1784, the Qianlong Emperor made this garden his temporary palace, and in 1762 gave it its name Anlan which, since the sea is quite near, literally means Calming the Waves. In his preface to a *Book of Poems*, the owner of the garden describes it modestly as 'quiet and tastefully laid out, simple and unsophisticated . . . [with] only some water surfaces, bamboos and rocks'. During the two decades of intermittent imperial visits, however, it became increasingly elaborate, was enlarged to *c*.6 hectares/15 acres, and acquired at least 30 new groups of buildings—among them twelve *lou* (see CHINA), unique in Chinese garden planning. Though the garden thus lost its Ming simplicity, literary men of the time—and the Emperor himself—still praised in poetry its naturalness and the delicious fragrance of its plum trees. And in

1764 the Emperor commissioned a replica of Anlan Yuan bearing the same name, in the YUANMING YUAN near Beijing. Today nothing remains of either except a few scattered rocks and mounds.   C-ZC/MK

Annes Grove ✿
Castletownroche, County Cork, Republic of Ireland, has a garden of 16 hectares/40 acres dominated by its site. Here is the mild climate of southern Ireland and a fine natural landscape with an escarpment overlooking the picturesquely looping river Awbeg. The house was built on the escarpment above the river in the 18th century for the Grove family, and later in the century a Grove heiress married an Annesley, in which family the estate remains today. A fine walled garden was built at the same time as the house, probably intended originally as a protected orchard. In the 19th century it was laid out as pleasure gardens and it retains its period character. A double walk of box-hedged circular beds of lupins of this period runs down one side of the garden. Here, too, are mixed borders along an axial path, distinguished flowering shrubs such as hoherias and magnolias, and a mount with a 19th-century lattice-work summer house shrouded in escallonia and fuchsias. In 1907 Richard Grove Annesley started to make a new garden outside the walled garden. He was one of several distinguished Irish garden makers who subscribed to the plant collecting expeditions of Frank Kingdon WARD and other collectors in the 1920s and 1930s. The slopes of the valley are planted with dogwoods, scarlet-flowered *Embothrium coccineum*, *Luma apiculata*, magnolias, and rhododendrons. Mossy paths lead down through the trees and shrubs to meadows along the river whose banks are thick with *Gunnera manicata*, Himalayan primulas, *Lysichiton americanus*, and stately *Cercidiphyllum japonicum*.   PT

Annevoie, Château d' ✿
Annevoie-Rouillon, Namur, Belgium. The gardens of Annevoie, with an area of 14 hectares/34.5 acres, are among the finest water gardens in Europe. A variety of features, influenced by 16th-century Italy, 17th-century France, and the English landscape garden, are laid out in a wooded valley well supplied with water. Tall clipped hedges contrast with mature beeches and oaks. Fountains and cascades work continuously from the natural pressure of the water, much stored in the Grand Canal above the garden, and jets of water over 6 m/20 ft high shoot constantly into the air. The estate was acquired by the Montpelliers, a family of ironmasters, in 1696 but it was only when Charles-Alexis de Montpellier inherited the

property 50 years later that the garden was created. He had done the grand tour and returned inspired by the Villa d'ESTE and VERSAILLES and sensible to the possibilities of his own site with its springs and streams. Le Buffet was one of the earliest features to be constructed, in 1760. Small jets in a symmetrical pattern emerge from a terraced grass slope, cascading into a narrow rill. The jets are irregularly sited to produce an accentuated perspective and to lead the eye along the vista. La Grande Allée provides another vista, leading via L'Artichaut, a circular pool with a crown of jets, to a statue of Minerva. Parallel to this is the small canal and parallel again, a *miroir d'eau* (literally 'water mirror', a large symmetrical expanse of water often placed to reflect a great house or ornamental building). Water glides into the small canal over a three-tiered cascade with scalloped edges, creating subtle patterns. At right angles to the *miroir d'eau* is Neptune's Grotto. There is an English cascade, a French cascade, below, an octagonal pool with a single 'gravity-defying jet', and beyond, the spectacular Peacock Fountain, with arching semicircular sprays. The statues of Neptune and of the four seasons in the Grande Allée are made of cast iron, a reminder of the source of the family's wealth. Annevoie is currently the subject of an ambitious restoration programme designed to recreate the romantic and baroque appearance it had at the beginning of the 19th century.   BA

BARBARA ABBS, 'Belgian reflections', *The Garden*, Vol. 124 (Mar. 1999).

annuals and bedding plants.
Annuals are some of the most colourful and easily grown of all garden plants. The diverse range of species covers many plant habits, textures, colours, and fragrances, making them adaptable to most garden situations. Annuals by their very nature have a short life cycle and many bloom in profusion throughout the summer and continue right through to the autumn, making them a valuable addition to the garden. Annuals are frequently used as bedding plants but not all bedding plants are annuals. In climates such as that of the British Isles perennials or shrubs like *Plectranthus*, *Dahlia*, *Salvia patens*, *Heliotropium arborescens*, and *Pelargonium* are not sufficiently hardy to withstand the winter climate and are bedded out only when the weather is mild enough. True annual species are those that are sown, germinate, and grow to maturity in one season. Once they have flowered they set seed and die. Annuals can be divided into three groups. The first, hardy annuals, are those that can stand some frost and may be sown *in situ* in the early spring and some in the autumn. Examples of

these are such species as *Calendula, Clarkia, Eschscholzia,* and *Nigella.* The second group are the half-hardy annuals, which are species that are not frost hardy and need to be sown in the early spring and raised under glass. These are then grown on under protection and hardened off before being planted out in the open ground once the danger of frost has passed. Examples of these are species such as *Ageratum, Callistephus, Impatiens, Lobelia,* and *Tagetes.* The third group is the tender annuals. The species in this group need the most protection of all and are best grown under glass in pots and containers throughout their growing season. Examples of species in this group are: *Calceolaria, Cuphea, Cobaea,* and *Schizanthus.*

Diversity of annual species

Annuals grown in gardens today come from many different habitats. *Clarkia, Eschscholzia, Limnanthes,* and *Nemophila* are Californian natives. South Africa is home to a very wide range of species including *Lobelia, Gazania, Mesembryanthemum,* and *Osteospermum.* Mexico and Central America are home to *Cosmos, Salvia, Tagetes,* and *Verbena,* and further south, in Chile, *Calceolaria, Mimulus, Salpiglossis,* and *Schizanthus* are to be found. Many of the annual members of the daisy family (Compositae) came from Australia such as *Helichrysum,* and China is home to such species as *Callistephus* and *Dianthus.*

History

The dates of the introductions of many annuals and bedding plants into Britain have been lost in time, but some are very ancient. With selection over the years to suit modern gardens some are also quite different from their ancestors growing in their wild habitats. For example the pot marigold *Calendula* was known in Roman times and was probably single flowered and distributed throughout the Roman Empire. Almost all other species are much more recent introductions. A surprisingly early introduction is that of the begonia, which was brought from the Americas in the 17th century by the French priest-botanist Charles Plumier (1646–1706). It was the subject of much hybridization, and today well over 600 varieties are still available from British nurseries. A well-documented early introduction of an annual is the sweet pea, *Lathyrus odoratus.* The species is native to Sicily and a monk called Father Cupani sent the original seed to Robert Uvedale of Enfield, England, in 1699; it was available commercially by the early 18th century. It was not until Victorian times that Henry Eckford began breeding sweet peas and he extended the range available. In 1901 William Unwin of Histon noticed a larger-flowered variety among Henry

Eckford's varieties named 'Prima Donna'; at the same time this sport was also noticed by Silas Cole, the gardener to Earl Spencer. He named this sport 'Countess Spencer', which is the origin of the strain of Spencer sweet peas which have been the dominant varieties in modern times. The edging lobelia (*L. erinus*), a tender perennial, was brought from South Africa in 1752 and its value as a bedding plant was recognized by Joseph PAXTON at CHATSWORTH in 1839. In many cultivars it remains a very popular bedding plant today. Dahlias were introduced into Europe from Mexico in 1789 via the ROYAL BOTANIC GARDEN (MADRID). Early forms were completely single and in the 19th century many types were crossed and selected and these form the basis of the dahlia we grow today. Their heyday was in the late 19th century when well over 400 varieties were offered for sale. The Californian poppy, *Eschscholzia,* was named on its discovery in California in 1820 after the physician and naturalist Johann Friedrich Eschscholz (1793–1831) and collected in 1825 during an expedition by David DOUGLAS, who introduced it to Europe. The 19th century saw an explosion of new introductions as bedding schemes became universally fashionable.

Uses for annuals in the garden

Annuals are so diverse that they can be used in many situations and, despite their relatively short life, can have great impact. In a newly established garden they are especially valuable, providing a colourful display while the newly planted perennials or shrubs are becoming established. Later on in the garden's life they are invaluable to fill gaps in established borders where plants may have died or need to be cut back.

One of the most interesting and rewarding parts of gardening is raising plants from seed. Some of the direct sown hardy annuals represent excellent value for money and with careful selection of varieties can transform a garden and give colour all season long. Species such as *Calendula, Centaurea, Clarkia, Lavatera, Linum,* and *Papaver* are excellent for this purpose. Flowering annuals lend themselves to fine colour effects and may be used to great effect in contrast with annuals of distinguished and striking foliage such as *Zea mays* (sweetcorn), *Amaranthus* species, or *Ricinus communis.* Such architectural plants can also give a focal point and height to an annual border.

Bedding schemes of annuals, disposed in crisply formal patterns, are still the flowering mainstays of municipal parks planting in many countries. Less formal arrangements, often using direct sown hardy annuals distributed in a naturalistic fashion, have become fashionable

in recent years. Annuals can also be very useful when sown or planted in herbaceous borders to create highlights of colour amongst the more permanent plantings. They retain their popularity as a valuable plant to cultivate in containers. Patio pots, hanging baskets, flower pouches, and window boxes are ideal for growing colourful displays of species such as *Lobelia, Begonia, Impatiens, Petunia,* and *Verbena.* Climbing species such as *Ipomoea, Lathyrus,* and *Tropaeolum* are also excellent for growing up fences and trellises. The use of annuals as cut flowers and for drying has become popular, using such species as *Antirrhinum, Centaurea, Callistephus, Limonium, Rudbeckia,* and *Lathyrus.*

Trends

Over the past 50 years considerable developments have been made in annuals as bedding plants. Plant breeders have created a wide range of new varieties by selection and hybridization, in particular with a view to breeding varieties of compact habit to suit the smaller gardens of today. New flower colours and types have also been created that are earlier flowering and more floriferous, thereby extending the season. In the 1950s and 1960s most gardeners raised their own plants at home. Bedding displays of annuals tended to be very formal in style. *Alyssum* and *Lobelia* were used for edging, and such species as *Tagetes, Salvia,* and *Antirrhinum* were at the height of their popularity. Hardy annuals were very popular and many individual colours of *Clarkia* and cornflower were available, whereas today most of these are available only in mixed colours. Since the 1970s and 1980s, with the great increase in garden centres, it has became much commoner to buy annuals rather than raise them oneself. The range of varieties available has expanded immensely and in the early 21st century there has been a boom in buying bedding plants by mail order, as plugs or small plants ready to pot on or plant out in the garden. Taste in colour has changed, with pastel colours becoming more fashionable from the 1990s. More attention to specific colour effects is also noticeable—most seed companies list mixtures of hardy annuals by colour. Over the past twenty years seed quality and packaging have improved considerably. This has been brought about by better storage techniques, and most retail seeds are now sold in foil sachets, impervious to moisture and therefore much prolonging the life of the seeds. Other technologies such as seed mats, seed tapes, and pelleted seed have been developed to make it easier to raise plants from seed. Seed companies continue to explore all kinds of improvements, both in the range and quality of plants available and in their ease and convenience of cultivation. Breeding new colours for particular species remains a constant quest. In New Zealand, for example, exciting work is being carried out in breeding sweet peas in an attempt to introduce the gene for yellow flowers from other species into *Lathyrus odoratus*.   TH

Ansouis, Château d' ⊛

Vaucluse, France. The site goes back to the Middle Ages, commanding a grand position overlooking the valley of the river Aigue close to the Luberon mountains. From the 12th century it has belonged to the Sabran family. The present chateau is largely 17th century and of the same date is a series of grand terraced gardens laid out on three sides of the chateau. Each is planted with a formal pattern of clipped box of strongly architectural character. No date is known for the garden but it has a distinctly Italianate atmosphere and immense charm.
PT

Antoine, Franz the elder (1768–1834) and Franz the younger

(1815–86), Austrian gardeners, descendants of a family of gardeners from Lothringen (today France). The elder Antoine was a playmate of the young Emperor Franz I/II who was himself a gardener. In 1800 the elder Antoine was, like his father before him, appointed head gardener at the castle in Vienna, which included the emperors' private collection of succulents and later also of pelargoniums, which were both among the largest in Europe. He published the book *Abbildung von 51 Pfirsichgattungen* (1821) with numerous outstanding illustrations of peaches. In 1847 the younger Antoine also became head gardener at the castle in Vienna where he redesigned the gardens in the style of the English landscape garden, using the experience from his two-year journey through the important gardens of Western Europe, including England. His admired book *Der Wintergarten in der Kaiserlichen Königlichen Hofburg zu Wien* (1852) contains splendid plates of his illusionistic landscape redesign of the interior of the conservatory. In 1865 he was appointed garden director. An internationally known botanist, he raised an extensive collection of bromeliads and published the work *Phyto-Iconographie der Bromeliaceen des K. K. Hofburggartens* (1884–6, uncompleted).   JM

Antony House ⊛

Torpoint, Cornwall, England, was built in the early 18th century for Sir William Carew possibly to the designs of James Gibbs (1682–1754). A formal garden to the north-west of the house was made at this time but it does not survive. In 1792 Reginald Pole Carew consulted Humphry REPTON, who produced a Red Book of recommendations in the same year. The landscape at Antony harmoniously incorporates features of different periods, many of them of the 20th century. The house faces northwards across a great lawn towards the estuary of the Lynher river. To one side of the house are magnificent yew hedges and topiary which is echoed by a large cone-shaped water feature by the sculptor William Pye (b. 1938). Concealed behind the hedges are a fine summer flower garden and a knot garden with patterns of clipped hedges of box and germander (*Teucrium* × *lucidrys*). To the north-west, in a former WILDERNESS, an 18th-century bathhouse draws its water from the estuary. At the centre of the lawn to the north of the house is a single magnificent ornament, an American black walnut (*Juglans nigra*), possibly planted in the 18th century. Beyond it lies woodland through which, on Repton's recommendation, was cut a PATTE D'OIE of rides revealing three vistas of the shimmering water of the estuary. The house and garden (10 hectares/25 acres) has belonged to the NATIONAL TRUST since 1961 but the woodland garden (40 hectares/100 acres), with fine shrubs and excellent modern sculptures, still belongs to the Pole Carew family.   PT

Anuradhapura Gardens ⊛

Sri Lanka. Although probably first settled in the 5th century BC the major development of Anuradhapura dates from the planned growth of the city under King Pandukabhaya (308–275 BC) when the city reached a size of some 4,000 hectares/9,880 acres. He laid out flower gardens along the Kadamba (Malwatte Oya) river, built massive city walls with great gates facing the cardinal points, and created a large garden, the Mahamegha, planted with fruit trees and flowering shrubs. In the Mahamegha was planted the sacred bo-tree (Tree of Wisdom) which survives today 2,300 years later, an object of great veneration. The tree was planted as a sapling from the *Ficus religiosa* beneath which the Gautama Buddha himself attained enlightenment. Today the tree is supported by iron crutches surrounded by a special platform, a Bodhighara. Its leaves are said to provide the shape from which Sri Lanka's dagobas (dome-shaped monuments containing Buddhist relics) are designed. Saplings have been planted outside other temples throughout the island and as far away as Burma. The original gardens were under the care of monks of the Great Monastery, but the tree has been under the hereditary custodianship of just one family throughout its life.

Royal pleasure gardens covering 16 hectares/40 acres still exist by the Tisa Wewa tank.

Through their length are scattered great boulders, many of which were capped with summer houses. Rock pools with fine reliefs of elephants lead to the 3rd-century rock temple of Isurumuniva. Two perfect monks' bathing ponds (Kuttam Pokuna) dating from the 3rd century can be seen to the north, water entering the pools through beautifully carved gargoyles.
NT

Apremont, Parc Floral d' ⊛

Apremont-sur-Allier, Cher, France. This is an unusual type of French garden—a flower garden strongly influenced by the English tradition of cottage gardens. It was made from 1971 in a former meadow by Gilles de Brissac, who had been inspired by visits to England. The site is an attractive one, 4 hectares/10 acres on the edge of an exceptionally pretty village. The garden successfully juggles different styles, with open lawns, a cascade, a dashing Chinese bridge and pergola over a stream, and a Turkish kiosk; and fine trees enliven the landscape. Ornamental rockwork of oriental character decorates the banks of a lake and evergreens are clipped in *à la japonaise*. Fine borders in the English style are contrasted with passages of formality. A border of alliums, alstroemerias, *Eremurus* species, hardy geraniums, peonies, and poppies is backed by a monumental hornbeam hedge in which giant buttresses are crowned with clipped spheres. A tunnel arbour veiled with white wisteria passes between two mixed borders, and a row of soaring obelisks of hornbeam makes a dramatic backdrop to a border filled with white-flowered plants. This exuberance of flowers seems to have inspired other inhabitants of the village, whose main street, lined with handsome old houses, is profusely decorated with planting.   PT

Aranjuez ⊛

Madrid, Spain. Aranjuez became a royal estate in the 16th century during the reign of Philip II, who saw it as a place of recreation close to the banks of the river Tagus in the wild Castilian plain south of Madrid. An anonymous painting c.1630 in the Prado shows a bird's-eye view of the estate. The Renaissance palace and its long loggia stands at the centre of giant avenues running deep into the surrounding countryside. Behind the palace is a sweeping curve of water and, close to the river banks, a star-shaped pattern of eight avenues converging on a single point. If the date of this painting is correct this was a remarkably *avant-garde* garden of its time—a large-scale formal garden of a kind not seen elsewhere in Europe until the latter part of the 17th century. Against the palace's southern façade, which survives from the 16th century, there remains an enclosed garden, an Italian Renaissance GIARDINO SEGRETO overlaid with *mudéjar* style (post-Reconquest Muslim work). Two other similar gardens are found on the north and eastern façades of the palace. There rare survivals, dating from the late 16th century, appear to have been the royal privy gardens of their time. One has been restored in recent times, with a parterre of box and fruit trees. Also in the 16th century a tributary of the Tagus, the Ontígola, was dammed to form a lake. This, made to provide a permanent source of water for fountains and pools in the garden, was later turned to ornamental purposes, with mock naval battles fought there and islands with hedges built in it.

On the northern side of the palace a canal, spanned by a bridge dated 1733, separates the palace from the Jardín de la Isla (garden of the island) which is built on an island in the Tagus. This garden was made in the late 16th century and it is not known what form it originally took. Elements survive from the 17th century—a MIRADOR on the river banks, fountains of Apollo and of Hercules—but the garden as it is today dates almost entirely from the 18th century and later. A plan of the garden by Cuéllar, dated 1737, shows it laid out as a grid of paths and enclosures of formidable complexity. Today something of this complexity survives—the garden presents a labyrinthine scene of walks lined with trees and hedges decorated from time to time with pools, fountains, statuary, and stone benches. A path is lined with water jets to surprise passers-by; these *burladores*, as they are called in Spanish, are in the tradition of Italian GIOCHI D'ACQUA.

The Jardín del Príncipe (Prince's Garden) is a large 18th-century woodland park on the banks of the Tagus made for Charles IV (formerly Prince of Asturias) between 1789 and 1808. Earlier features were incorporated—pavilions, a kitchen garden, and a stone jetty (with sentry boxes)—in what became a late 18th-century picturesque garden with a lake and temple, a pagoda, and shady walks. There is an element of the FERME ORNÉE, too, in an ornamental Casa de Labrador (Workman's Cottage) which has its own garden. A modern museum displays the pleasure boats which the royal family used for river excursions.   PT

arboretum.

A collection of trees as a particular type of garden makes its appearance in the 19th century. J. C. LOUDON's *Arboretum et Fruticetum Britannicum* (1838) seems to be the first printed use of the word, and in this book Loudon refers to 'collecting trees from a distance . . . to assemble them in one plantation or arboretum'. There are several ways of laying out such a collection but the governing principle is either aesthetic or taxonomic. There is also the fundamental consideration of the original habitat of the plants and the appropriateness of the site for their cultivation. In the 19th-century arboretum at WESTONBIRT in England the Holfords laid out a PATTE D'OIE of avenues of which the central avenue, with trees of contrasting shapes, forms the heart of the arboretum today. The spaces between the avenues were used to plant groups of smaller ornamental trees to vary the scale of the planting. Here, too, they also grouped trees specifically to make the best of autumn colours to form glades of a particular character. The Arboretum National des BARRES in France, founded in 1866 by the great VILMORIN family of plant collectors and nurserymen, groups plants taxonomically, by country of origin, and, in the park that surrounds the house, on purely ornamental grounds. However, even within the more scientifically arranged parts of the arboretum it is hard to resist an opportunity to make an attractive arrangement. Later arboreta, often allied to botanic gardens, often prefer a scientific arrangement. At the John F. KENNEDY ARBORETUM in Ireland trees are grouped either by place of origin or by genus. But in the latter part trees are often carefully placed—to form attractive groups, disposed in glades, lining walks—and sometimes sightlines are arranged to focus on some particularly fine specimen. In the 19th century, when there was a strong impulse to combine recreation and education, arboreta were often combined as public parks. The DERBY ARBORETUM, designed by J. C. Loudon in 1840, was of this tradition, combining fine design and well-displayed specimens. The same is true of the ARNOLD ARBORETUM in the USA, which was founded in 1872 as a public park that was also a place of learning. Many arboreta do not cater for the interests of gardeners. The UNITED STATES NATIONAL ARBORETUM, founded in 1927 in Washington DC has a programme of breeding garden plants, and since its foundation it has introduced more than 650 cultivars into commerce in the USA. One of the most successful modern arboreta is the KALMTHOUT ARBORETUM in Belgium. The site was the former premises of a firm of nurserymen and was rich in good 19th-century trees, especially conifers. It was bought by George and Robert de Belder in 1952 and the latter's wife, Jelena de Belder, had a strong influence on the planting. Apart from the old trees the site is an uninteresting one but Jelena de Belder showed great skill in grouping plants—trees, shrubs, and often interesting underplantings of herbaceous perennials—and keeping open long sightlines which lure the visitor on. Kalmthout firmly acknowledges that the beauty of plants is at least as significant as their scientific importance.   PT

arbour,

a leafy sitting place or retreat, with ornamental plants trained over a framework; a very ancient garden feature. The word BOWER has similar connotations. An Egyptian tomb painting of the 12th century BC depicts something of the sort. Arbours existed in late medieval gardens in Western Europe—Boccaccio's *Decameron* (1349-51) describes 'alleys . . . embowered with trellises of vines'—but modern ideas of them derive largely from the Renaissance. The HYPNEROTOMACHIA POLIPHILI (1499) shows a domed bower and tunnel arbours of the kind that became common in RENAISSANCE GARDENS. In British gardens of ARTS AND CRAFTS style in the late 19th and early 20th centuries arbours and tunnel arbours became fashionable once again. At HESTERCOMBE, for example, Edwin LUTYENS and Gertrude JEKYLL devised an elegant arbour with a canopy of pleached wych elm (*Ulmus glabra*) which may still be seen.   PT

archaeology of gardens.

The discipline of archaeology has grown from antiquarian beginnings in the 16th century into a complex subject that encompasses a broad range of techniques including excavation, field and geophysical survey, aerial photography, and various palaeoecological methods, as well as historical research. Garden archaeology has mirrored this growth, albeit more slowly. Archaeologists and garden historians have been tardy in appreciating the value of archaeology for the understanding of gardens, and the relatively crude nature of early excavations prevented the recognition of much evidence of gardening activity.

Excavation

Gardens associated with the ancient civilizations of the Mediterranean and the Near and Middle East began to be revealed by excavation in the second half of the 19th century. However, as these excavations concentrated on the more obvious and apparently more important structures, such as palaces, villas, and temples, rather than on their gardens, the sites of the latter were often interpreted as courtyards or open spaces not worth examining. The courtyards of the late 2nd-millennium BC Hittite temples at Boghazköy in Turkey, excavated in the 1930s, or the stone figures and stone stack found at Ishigami in JAPAN, subsequently interpreted as being from a 7th-century Buddhist garden, illustrate this. Some excavations in the 1920s and 1930s examined the sites of gardens, but the standards of excavation meant that only well-built structures were revealed. Even so, terraces, watercourses, steps, and paths were identified and this evidence, together with contemporary descriptions, frescoes, and inscriptions, enabled archaeologists to begin to understand the framework of many actual or presumed ancient gardens. Amongst the most notable were the excavations at Ur in Iraq, where terraces on the Ziggurat were interpreted as gardens, at PASARGADAE, in Iran, where the stone pools and watercourses of the 6th-century BC garden were revealed, and at the Thracian city of Seuthopolis, in Bulgaria, where a drainage system within a courtyard was presumed to be part of a garden substructure.

The decades between the two world wars also saw excavation directed at recovering information on gardens at sites such as KIRBY HALL in Northamptonshire (England), and at Jamestown, Virginia (USA). However, the primary aim of many of these excavation was restoration, and this, combined with the relatively crude excavation techniques, meant that little more than paths, boundaries, and associated buildings were discovered. The subsequent planting arrangements were based on historical sources rather than on archaeological evidence.

The explosion in the amount of archaeological work since 1945, together with greatly improved excavation methods, the application of new scientific techniques, and the growing interest in garden history, has resulted in many research- and restoration-led excavations. The excavation of former gardens is now regarded as a proper study and its value to garden history is beginning to be appreciated.

Amongst the most important excavations since 1960 have been those at POMPEII, Italy, where over 450 gardens, including those of major villas, have been examined, and the first-century AD Roman palace at Fishbourne (see BRITISH ISLES), Sussex, England, where the arrangement of a Mediterranean-style garden was revealed. Other important sites are the late 17th-century Privy Garden at HAMPTON COURT PALACE, London, England, the excavations at which have made possible a full and accurate restoration, and the gardens at Colonial WILLIAMSBURG, Virginia, USA, which have also been fully restored. Other smaller but methodologically valuable excavations in England include those on an 18th-century town house garden at Bath, the 1830s garden at Audley End House, Essex, where the original flower beds were found, and the mid 19th-century garden belonging to Charles Darwin at Down House, Kent, where, again, the positions of the original beds were established.

Palaeoecology

The role of palaeoecological and other scientific techniques in garden archaeology has grown in value as excavation methods have improved. It is now possible to recover details of the botanical content of former gardens as well as of their soils. Not all of these techniques have been wholly successful. For example, the fact that pollen can be carried by wind over considerable distances and that it is virtually impossible to distinguish the pollen of hybrids and cultivars from their wild species has limited the value of pollen analysis to garden history. The excavations at Aberdour Castle, Scotland, demonstrated this. The pollen recovered there was largely that of weeds of cultivation and of cereals from the adjacent farmland. On the other hand the study of carbonized or waterlogged plant remains and of phytoliths or silica faunal remains, which tend to stay close to where the source plant died or was disposed of, has proved to have greater potential, as work at the Tucker Garden at Williamsburg and at Thomas JEFFERSON's garden at MONTICELLO, both in Virginia, USA, has demonstrated.

The analysis of macrofossils from soils and rubbish pits is now another common practice. Examination of pits in a late medieval town garden at Hull, Yorkshire, England, led to the identification of an extensive range of fruits, flowers, herbs, and vegetables. The bones of fish, birds, and small mammals have also been studied and the analysis of molluscs especially has produced valuable results. This is demonstrated at the garden of the Villa of Livia, Rome, where the species of molluscs found in the 1996–9 excavations suggested that the central area of the garden was an open space, that the snail *Rumina decollata* could have been used as a biological pest control agent, and that seashells were used as fertilizer. The chemical and physical examination of garden soils has also been of great value at sites such as Pompeii and Fishbourne (Sussex). At the latter, the addition of chalk to the soil, perhaps to increase its pH, was noted.

Other archaeological studies have involved the recording of the foundations of garden buildings such as the 16th-century Banqueting House at NONSUCH PALACE, the Eagle House and Pavilion of 1738–42 at PAINSWICK HOUSE, and various 18th-century structures at PAINSHILL, all in England. Work has also been carried out in Britain and the USA on the classification and chronology of types of garden equipment, including flowerpots.

Analytical field archaeology

An entirely different form of garden archaeology developed from the largely British tradition of analytical fieldwork. The study of upstanding earthen remains (earthworks) of prehistoric, Roman, and medieval settlements, field systems, and burial mounds by detailed surface examination and survey has always been an important aspect of British archaeology. The earthwork remains of abandoned gardens were first recognized in the late 19th century and by the 1920s were being surveyed and published. But it was not until the 1960s that it was realized how many abandoned gardens might exist in Britain. Many hundreds have been recorded and many more must still await discovery. Most of them are of 16th- or 17th-century date and usually have their structural details preserved as grass-covered earthworks. Others have been flattened and are visible as crop or soil marks on aerial photographs. They usually represent relatively short-lived gardens abandoned soon after construction because their associated houses became redundant or fashions changed. Amongst the best are the terraces, ponds, flower beds, and prospect mounds laid out in the 1590s by Sir Christopher Hatton at Holdenby, Northamptonshire, and the similar remains of the early 17th century created for Sir Baptist Hicks at Chipping Campden, Gloucestershire. Even more spectacular are the traces of lakes, canals, and water gardens designed in the contemporary French style between 1683 and 1709 for Lord Montagu at Boughton House, Northamptonshire. Perhaps more important are the many small and ill-documented remains of gardens created by minor landowners, some of which have evidence of considerable changes. At Stainfield, Lincolnshire, there were three completely different gardens, ranging in date from the 16th to the 18th century, and superimposed on one another.

Detailed surveys of 18th- and 19th-century landscaped parks have revealed the considerable earth moving involved in their construction. At the otherwise undistinguished 18th-century Chippenham Park, Cambridgeshire, the soil dredged from the lake was reused as tree mounds. Elsewhere, studies of the distribution and age of parkland trees have shown that the 'instant' creation of some parks was achieved by the incorporation of existing hedgerow trees into the new landscapes. Since 1970 other fieldwork has discovered former medieval gardens. Some, such as those at Tintagel, Cornwall, and at Nettleham, Lincolnshire, confirm the traditional picture of medieval gardens as small, enclosed areas with intricate paths and beds. But others, as at Linton, Cambridgeshire, indicate that elaborate water gardens existed.

A notable advance in British garden archaeology since the 1980s has been the recognition of extensive designed landscapes created around castles, manor houses, and even monasteries between the 12th and 15th centuries. These are characterized by the archaeological remains of lakes, ponds, and drives, often associated with deer parks and laid out to create vistas. The most elaborate is at Bodiam Castle, Sussex, of 1380, and others include the site of the great Mere at Kenilworth Castle, Warwickshire, and the lake and ponds at Leeds Castle, Kent. Paintings and documents indicate that such landscapes also existed in continental Europe but no archaeological evidence corroborates them.   CCT

Archbishop's Garden,

Bratislava (formerly Pozsony), Slovakia. The most important late Renaissance garden of Hungary was the Archbishop's Garden in Pozsony (the capital of the Hungarian kingdom in the 17th and 18th centuries, today capital of Slovakia). Its founder was Archbishop Ferenc Forgách, who erected fountains and planted an orchard in 1614. Between 1642 and 1663, Archbishop György Lippay remodelled most of the garden as an outstanding Renaissance ornamental garden. Thanks to Lippay's Italian connections, the garden showed a direct Italian influence. A series of etchings from 1663 by Mauritz Lang shows the structure and details of the finished garden, with 24 quadrangular compartments and an orchard divided by crossing BERCEAUX, and an orangery garden (*Hortus Italicus*). There was a fish pond with an equestrian statue of St George and a labyrinth beside the palace. Two fountains and two sundials stood in the compartments next to the palace. Three important constructions were placed against the rear garden wall: a grotto with various playful waterworks surmounted by a BELVEDERE at the end of the central axis; a ruinlike hermitage with statues of St Jerome and other saints; and 'Mount Parnassus' surmounted by a Pegasus and with figures of Apollo and the Muses at the corners. In addition to this the garden had a unique collection of botanical rarities. In his comprehensive three-volume work titled *Posoni kert* (The Garden at Pozsony), inspired by this garden, the Archbishop's brother János Lippai listed more than 150 species of flowers. Between 1707 and 1715, in the time of Archbishop Prinz Christian August von Sachsen, and around 1730, in that of Archbishop Imre Esterházy, the garden was substantially redesigned in the baroque style with elaborate PARTERRES *de broderie*. Today only the statue of St George remains in the courtyard.   GA

GÉZA GALAVICS, 'Pictorial representation of the gardens of Hungary—part I: 17th century', in *Történeti kertek—kertművészet és műemlékvédelem.* (Historic Gardens in and around Hungary) (2000).

JÁNOS STIRLING, *Magyar reneszánsz kertművészet a XVI–XVII. században* (Hungarian Renaissance Gardens in the 16th–17th Centuries) (1996).

Archer, Thomas

(*c*.1668–1743), English architect, country gentleman, and Member of Parliament from Warwickshire. Between 1691 and 1695 he travelled in Europe, to the Low Countries, Germany, Austria, and, in particular, Italy, where he fell under the spell of baroque architecture. He designed churches, country and town houses, and garden buildings. Among the latter are the Cascade House (1702) at CHATSWORTH and the splendid domed garden pavilion (1709–11) for WREST PARK.   PT

Argenville, Antoine-Joseph Dezallier d'.

see DEZALLIER D'ARGENVILLE, ANTOINE-JOSEPH.

Århus Concert Hall Park ✿

Århus, Denmark. Sven HANSEN's park around the Concert Hall, built 1979–82 by architects Kjær (b. 1924) and Richter (1925–98), consists of two grass-covered plateaux linked by a terraced slope. The spectacular glass-enclosed part of the building, the large mirror basin, and the central garden are located on the higher plateau, while the visually heavier parts of the building are situated at the back, on the lower plateau. An amphitheatre forms part of the slope's terraces. The clearly defined, large area in front is laid out as a parterre garden which is asymmetrical, yet classical, without being overbearing. Patterns of clipped yew stand out as a dark-green snowflake-shaped volume with small flower gardens, trellis-work, and water features, crossed by functionally laid out diagonal paths. The garden contains azaleas ranging in colour from white to the darkest red. Trellis-work is planted with clematis, wisteria, or laburnum, and in the centres are small fountains.   AL

Århus University ✿

Århus, Denmark. After winning a competition in 1931, architects Kay Fisker (1893–1965), C. F. Møller (1898–1988), and Povl Stegmann (1888–1944), with C. Th. SØRENSEN as the landscape architect, built this university 1933–47. The hilly area had a ravine with a stream in the centre and small lakes at the bottom. The proposal kept the ravine clear and placed the buildings at the edges, away from the hollow. Closely trimmed ivy clothes the simple yellow brick buildings. In time, Århus University became a modern campus situated in an open pastoral landscape with full-crowned, broad oaks. The university's main building lies on the north, transverse to the ravine. The difference in the terrain is accommodated by a large, gently curved retaining wall, from which the steps of an amphitheatre protrude at right angles. On the other side, the steps run right into the hill, and seen from above, this open-air THEATRE covers only one-quarter of a circle. Like each of Sørensen's other open-air theatres, in Boeslunde, Roskilde, Bellahøj, and Slagelse, this example has its own geometry, determined by the site. The university buildings and grounds have been continually expanded, but without compromising the original concept.   AL

Arizona-Sonora Desert Museum ✿

Tucson, Arizona, USA, is a botanical garden as well as a zoo and natural history museum, created in 1952, celebrating the flora and fauna of the Sonora Desert. Of North America's four major deserts, the Sonora Desert has the highest rainfall, of 5–10 cm/2–4 in annually, resulting in a richness of plant, bird, and animal life. The museum, which is set in a breathtaking landscape of columnar saguaro cactuses (*Carnegiea gigantea*) and mountain views in the Avra valley, maintains 3.2 km/2 miles of   ▶

Colour plates

The central lake and Princes Lawn at the **Royal Botanic Gardens, Melbourne**, Australia

Garden and **loggia** at the 15th-century Palazzo Piccolomini, Italy

Harold Peto's Italianate terraced garden at **Iford Manor**, England

A raked sand or 'dry garden' (***karesansui***) at Zuiho-in, Kyoto, Japan

paths crossing 8.5 hectares/21 acres of varied desert habitat with 1,200 species of plants and 300 animal species on display. A walk-through aviary of the seven species of native hummingbirds and the colourful desert annuals that attract them, and a display garden of pollinators and their floral partners, are two of the highlights of the Desert Museum. By encouraging an understanding and appreciation of the Sonora Desert, the museum's goal is to inspire visitors to live more in harmony with the natural world.   PD

Arkadia ⊛

near Łowicz, Poland, one of the most magnificent landscape gardens, laid out for Helena Radziwiłł (1753–1821) not far from her residence at Nieborów. The work at Arkadia was begun in 1777, to continue uninterruptedly until the early 19th century. Its main designer was Szymon Bogumił ZUG, but later Henryk Ittar (c.1773–1850) was also active here. The garden was laid out on a long and rather narrow plot with the Łupia river flowing through it, in the northern part dammed up into an elongated pond with an island. The principal structure is the classicist Temple of Diana (Zug, 1783), standing by the pond. Zug also built the High Priest's Sanctuary (1783), an irregular artificial ruin with a tower, with Gothic and Renaissance fragments set into the walls, the Roman Aqueduct (1784), serving as a bridge over the cascade, and the Gothic House above the Sibyl's Grotto (1795–8). It was to Ittar that Arkadia owed its Circus and the Tomb of Illusions (early 19th century, not surviving). Arkadia was Helena Radziwiłł's retreat, which is confirmed by the Italian inscription 'm'inolvo altrui par ritrovar ma stessa' (I leave others to find myself) over the entrance to the Temple of Diana. This seclusion was to provide an escape to the pastoral land of eternal bliss. However, already in antiquity the inevitability of death had become an inherent part of the Arcadian myth. This theme appeared in Arkadia in a conventional form on the Poplar Island, raised in imitation of its namesake at ERMENONVILLE. There is also the tomb of St Cecilia inscribed 'et in arcadia ego'. The death of the Princess's daughters made her strongly accentuate the inevitable fact of departing from this world. The Tomb of Illusions became a real grave containing the ashes of the dead, its very name attesting to a departure from the sentimental vision of death. The garden is preserved in a very good condition. It is now a branch of the National Museum in Warsaw.   WB

Arkhangelskoye ⊛

Moscow, Russia, was the home of the Golitsyns in the 18th century and of the Yusupovs from 1810 until 1917. The late 18th-century classical palace by Charles de Guerne (b. 1748) was built at the top of a slope running down to the river Moskva, with exceptional views of picturesque meadows and woodland beyond. The two garden terraces by Giacomo Trombaro (1742–1838) are copiously ornamented with statues and vases, while the stone stairways lead down to a vast TAPIS VERT, a formal representation of the Russian meadow, flanked by avenues of limes and extending to the river. 'Natural' landscaping might have been expected at this period rather than the retention of the lines of earlier formality. Among the architectural features in the park are an attractive small tea house, a monument to Pushkin, and a colonnaded mausoleum (1916) built in vain for Prince Yusupov.   PH

Arley Hall ⊛

Northwich, Cheshire, England, is at the heart of an ancient estate, owned by the Warburton family from the 12th century. The park was landscaped in the 1760s and 1780s by William EMES, who built a HA-HA separating it from the PLEASURE GROUNDS which cover an area of 4.8 hectares/12 acres. Formal gardens were laid out in the 18th century of which walls and a garden alcove survive. From 1832 to 1845 the house was rebuilt in neo-Jacobean style and there was much work in the garden shortly afterwards. W. A. NESFIELD designed a parterre in 1846 but this was removed in 1940. By far the most important development was the laying out of a pair of herbaceous borders c.1851. These are usually considered the first example of herbaceous borders in England. They were laid out on either side of a grass walk descending from the 18th-century alcove and backed with yew edges ornamented with topiary and buttresses to divide the space. A series of watercolours painted in 1889 by George Samuel Elgood show the borders in their heyday and much resembling their appearance today. Gertrude JEKYLL came here in 1900 and admired 'the grandly grown borders of hardy flowers' and 'the garden's comfortable walls of living greenery'. The planting in the borders today has perhaps more carefully contrived colour schemes but in spirit remains true to the original plantings. Among 20th-century additions to the gardens are a splendid avenue of clipped holm oak (Quercus ilex) and lively ornamental planting in the walled former kitchen garden.   PT

Arniston House ⊛

Gorebridge, Midlothian, Scotland, is a great mansion by William ADAM built from 1726 for Robert Dundas in a designed landscape of 426 hectares/1,052 acres. Adam also laid out the grounds with a parterre and a pattern of avenues and rides. One of the avenues BORROWED the landscape of the craggy escarpment of Arthur's Seat 20 km/12 miles away. Only traces of this formal scheme remain—the alignments of some avenues and an urn which stood originally at the centre of a formal WILDERNESS. Most of the detail was swept away when the grounds were landscaped by Thomas WHITE the elder in 1791. A painting by Alexander Nasmyth c.1800 shows the effects of this work with the house framed in trees and set in open parkland. A walled garden, built in the 1760s, incorporates a grand gateway with carved stonework from the Renaissance Parliament Hall in Edinburgh destroyed in 1808.   PT

Arnold Arboretum ⊛

Jamaica Plain, Massachusetts, USA, was established in 1872 on 55.4 hectares/137 acres of land just outside Boston given to Harvard University, and is the oldest public ARBORETUM in America. It was conceived as both a public park and a scientific arboretum, organized as a collection of exotic and indigenous trees, shrubs, and herbaceous plants that would grow in the north temperate climate of eastern Massachusetts. Charles Sprague SARGENT was the first director, and moulded the design and mission of the arboretum as it stands today. Frederick Law OLMSTED was commissioned to lay out the landscape, incorporating it into a larger series of parks he designed for the Boston park system—called the 'Emerald Necklace'. The initial arboretum design was synoptic in its arrangement of the collections, after the taxonomic organizations of Bentham and Hooker, but the plants within each group were also arranged in pleasing naturalistic aesthetic masses and specimens. Plantings were heaviest in the late 1880s and 1890s, when tens of thousands of plants were added each year. Beatrix Jones (later Beatrix FARRAND) was apprenticed to Professor Sargent during this period, capitalizing on his vast botanical knowledge and the ongoing design and horticulture of the new collections. Plant collecting, especially in Asia, became an important part of the arboretum's charge. Ernest H. WILSON, most famous of the Arnold Arboretum's collectors, brought back hundreds of Chinese plants for the collections, including the beloved dove tree Davidia involucrata and the paperbark maple Acer griseum. Many such plants have been introduced from here to the public for garden use. Plant collecting in Asia continues to the present, with significant finds in pharmacologically active species. Research in many other aspects of botany, from molecular systematics to plant pathology, remains an important scientific mission.

The Arnold Arboretum now consists of 107 hectares/265 acres of rolling land, covered with meadows, woodlands, and shrub masses in a naturalistic GARDENESQUE style. Views of Boston's skyline can be had from the highest points, yet the valleys and dells provide green enclosures seemingly far from any city. It is treasured as a park by the local community, and the greater public flocks there to observe seasonal blooming of famous collections, such as the lilacs—one of the two largest collections in the hemisphere—and to view special horticultural collections such as bonsai and penjing—among the oldest in North America. Of special interest are the strong collections of *Fagus* (beech), *Lonicera* (honeysuckle), *Magnolia*, *Malus* (crab apple), *Quercus* (oak), *Rhododendron*, and *Syringa* (lilac). A favourite walk is the Chinese Walk, lined with plants brought to America by E. H. Wilson. The living collections include more than 4,500 botanical and horticultural taxa, and a HERBARIUM collection holds more than 5 million specimens—an invaluable reference for students and scholars. An extensive library and the archive of invaluable photographs and other documents illustrate the history of horticulture and botany in America. The education programme features a wide array of botanical, horticultural, design, and landscape history courses, connecting to the greater world of plants and landscapes.   PC

artist and the garden, the

The Middle Ages

The representation of actual gardens is a Renaissance phenomenon which stemmed from the new impulse to record the surface externals of the natural world. That was made possible by the new optical principles of depiction, resulting from the reordering of a picture's surface according to the rules of aerial and scientific perspective. As gardens became symbols of ownership and manifestations of secular power the interest in depicting them accelerated. But the Renaissance drew on various existing traditions. The first was biblical: representations of the Garden of EDEN, the garden of Gethsemane, and paradise. All of these oft depicted scenes could include elements of contemporary garden design. Fra Angelico's vision of paradise in the convent of San Marco, Florence (after 1437), for example, depicts a late medieval flowery mead. To these we can add, in the later Middle Ages, paintings of the Virgin in the HORTUS CONCLUSUS, an iconographic motif the result of associating her symbolically with the garden of the Song of

Solomon. Into this walled or hedged enclosure would be gathered flowers and artefacts symbolic of her, like the rose, the lily, and the fountain. A famous instance is Stefan Lochner's *Madonna in the Rose Arbour* (*c*.1440) (Wallraf-Richartz Museum, Cologne). Fifteenth-century Flemish pictures of the Virgin and Child also often include a garden in the background, clearly recording reality.

There was equally a secular tradition. One was of representations of the months or the four seasons. In the case of the former, often features of books of hours, there would be a garden for April or May, and in that of the latter a garden would appear for spring. Both April and June in the *Très Riches Heures* (Musée de Condé, Chantilly, MS 65) illuminated for Jean, Duc de Berry by Pol de Limbourg and his brothers (*c*.1409-16) incorporate some of the earliest glimpses of actual medieval gardens. Fifteenth-century Flemish manuscripts are a rich source for these images which, with the advent of printing, pass into the repertory of the engraver, giving us an abundance of records of late 16th- and early 17th-century gardens of the northern Renaissance.

Medieval romances, above all the celebrated *Roman de la Rose* (13th century), called for illuminations of gardens of another sort, those for amatory dalliance, as arenas for music, lovemaking, and the dance. One the most famous of these is in the British Library (*c*.1485, MS Harley 4425). These in turn are complemented by illuminated copies of Pietro de' CRESCENZI's *Liber Ruralium Commodorum* (1305), the first serious medieval treatise on the PLEASURE GARDEN, which was frequently illuminated and thus delineated late medieval gardens. By the close of the Middle Ages occasional records of what must be actual gardens also begin to appear in illuminations of princely persons like René of Anjou or the dukes of Burgundy.

Renaissance

The garden as it developed through the 16th century in its Renaissance phase was increasingly a manifestation of secular power, of the taming of nature by art in the service of the prince. This inaugurated new uses of the garden in art. One was their appearance in portraits. The garden of Whitehall Palace (see LONDON PARKS AND GARDENS), laid out in the 1530s, is depicted in the background of a family group of Henry VIII (*c*.1545, Royal Collection), an early instance of a steady stream until, in the 18th century and the advent of the landscape style, the sitters are literally placed into their own garden. These pictures celebrate ownership and are connected in turn with the development of both cartography and the view

picture. Maps become increasingly valuable sources for garden layout and as they cross into the 17th century they begin occasionally to include views of gardens. In the Netherlands this gave birth to a new genre, plans of the house and garden surrounded by vignette views of both. A seminal work was the engraving of Constantine Huygens's estate of HOFWIJCK (1656). This had successors in the Netherlands and also later in England in the series from the 1730s and 1740s by John Rocque which recorded the innovative gardens of Richmond, CHISWICK, Esher, and CLAREMONT.

The aerial view picture proper begins in Italy with one of the garden of Villa d'ESTE, TIVOLI, a fresco on its walls dated 1565 by Girolamo Muziano and pupils (*c*.1568) followed by those of the Villa LANTE and Villa FARNESE at CAPRAROLA, and both frescoes in the Palazzina Gambara at Lante (1574-8). To them can be added the celebrated series by Giusto UTENS of the various Medici villas (1599, Museo Topografico, Florence). These are the founts of the aerial view which was to find its most influential expression in Étienne Dupérac's engraving of the Villa d'Este (1573). This was to influence garden iconography throughout Europe for two centuries and was to be the iconographic source for such famous engraved records of gardens as Salomon de CAUS's HORTUS PALATINUS (1620), Isaac de CAUS's WILTON *Garden* (*c*.1645-6), and those in Jan Kip's *Nouveau Théâtre de la Grande Bretagne* (1716), recording the great houses and gardens of late Stuart England.

From the middle of the 17th century onwards suites of engravings would be printed devoted to various parts of a single garden either as separate sheets or in book form. These were not aerial views but ones from ground level recording the experience of the visitor on foot. Stefano della Bella's series of six of the Medici garden at PRATOLINO from the 1620s are the forebears of this new format. They were followed in France by 22 engravings of Liancourt (1654), nineteen of Cardinal Richelieu's RUEIL (1661), and fourteen of LE NÔTRE's VAUX-LE-VICOMTE (*c*.1665) by Israel Silvestre who had worked with della Bella. Their successors were to be the glut of engravings depicting the gardens of Louis XIV and his rival William III which formed part of the propaganda war waged through the closing decades of the 17th century. These found their imitators in Germany where there was an equal desire to get into print the mini-Versailles created at the various princely courts. These in their turn led on to sets of paintings of a particular garden as seen from various viewpoints, like those of CHISWICK by Peter Andreas Rysbrack (*c*.1728-1732) (mainly

Devonshire Collection), of Hartwell House by Balthasar Nebot (*c*.1737) (Buckingham County Museum, Aylesbury), and of CLAREMONT (*c*.1750) (private collection). To those can be added Thomas Robins's records of many of England's rococo gardens in the 1740s and 1750s and Jacques Rigaud's views of STOWE (1733-4) which were engraved. Finally come Paul Sandby's engravings of Kew in Sir William CHAMBERS's *Gardens and Buildings at Kew in Surrey* (1763).

Parallel series recorded the great gardens of 18th-century France such as L. Carrogis (CARMONTELLE), *Jardin de Monceau* (1779), G.-L. LE ROUGE, *Jardins anglo-chinois à la mode* (1776-85), and A. L. J. Laborde, *Description des nouveaux jardins de la France . . .* (1808-15). France also produced two artists who responded to the garden in their art, Hubert ROBERT, who recorded the ruined gardens of Renaissance Italy, going on to paint those of Versailles and later becoming *dessinateur des jardins du roi* in 1778. Two of his most famous garden pictures record the gardens of Versailles after the disastrous storm of 1774 (Musée National du Château, Versailles).The second was Jean Honoré Fragonard (1732-1806), who studied with Robert in Italy and equally responded to gardens in his work, capturing to the full the Enlightenment's highly romantic response to nature.

The Romantic movement and after

With the advent of the cult of sensibility as a desirable human quality and the arrival of the Romantic movement the garden shifts away from being an attribute of power and display, becoming instead a reflection of man's sensitivity to the world of nature. The spread of the landscape style too virtually dissolved the boundary between what was clearly a painting of a garden and what was a painting of a landscape. This can be traced in the work of Richard Wilson (1713/14-82) in, for example, his views of Wilton (*c*.1758-9, Earl of Pembroke and the Trustees of the Wilton House Trust), or in pictures like John Constable's (1776-1837) *View of the Grounds of Wivenhoe Park, Essex* (National Gallery of Art, Washington).

As the 19th century progressed artists responded to the advent of small middle-class gardens and also to the new municipal parks. New graphic methods beyond etching and engraving precipitated a vast explosion in illustrated garden books and magazines. Techniques such as lithography allowed artists to represent tonal qualities in addition to line, and colour replaced black and white. But by 1900 garden photography had already reached a perfection in the work of the photographer Charles Latham (see PHOTOGRAPHY AND GARDENS) for *Country Life* (1897 onwards) in a manner that was to release artists from the necessity of recording as against interpreting gardens.

Gardens returned as subject matter as the 19th century drew to its close in the work of two groups of artists. The first was a group of late nineteenth-century English watercolourists headed by George Samuel Elgood (1851-1943), Ernest Arthur Rowe (1862-1922), and Beatrice Parsons (1870-1955). Together they formed a golden age of English garden painting which coincided with the eras of William ROBINSON and Gertrude JEKYLL. These painters glorified the English formal garden as it re-emerged in the decades before 1914. Equally the idyll of the cottage garden was celebrated by artists such as Arthur Claude Strachan (1865-*c*.1935) and Helen Allingham (1848-1946). To them can be added the work of book illustrators such as Kate Greenaway (1846-1901) and Walter Crane (1845-1915) whose graphic work contributed to this celebration of the 'olde worlde' English garden with its topiary, knot and herb gardens, nut walks, arbours, pergolas, and orchards, all abundant with old English flowers—roses, daisies, poppies, lavender, honeysuckle, lilies, and primroses. Thanks to the new colour printing processes the work of all these artists was available in a steady stream of publications devoted to gardens.

The impressionists were, in sharp contrast, not such *petits maîtres* but epitomized a revolution in painting. In their work they tried to recreate the sensation that light produces as it becomes optical perception. Their *plein air* technique was ideally suited to recording the expansion in flower varieties of the period, the advent of greenhouses and conservatories, and the role of the garden as a setting for middle-class social interplay in scenes like the picnic, the walk, or tea in the garden. All of these subjects recur in the pictures of Édouard Manet (1832-83), Pierre Auguste Renoir (1841-1919), Camille Pissarro (1830-1903), Berthe Morisot (1841-95), and Claude Monet (1840-1926). In the case of Monet his celebrated garden at GIVERNY became a major subject, the inspiration over a long period of time for a whole series of canvases capturing every nuance of light and shade and the passage of the seasons, making him arguably the greatest of all artists in the garden. The most famous of these canvases are the long series of *Water Lilies* (Orangerie, Paris) which he painted over and over again, the largest and most important of which were begun in 1916. Monet died in 1926, by which time PHOTOGRAPHY had long released painting from the burden of the topographical tradition, leaving that to the camera and, later, film and video. These artists have had no sucessors in late 20th-century art, whose prime focus was the urban industrial and commercial world together with responding to the impact of two world wars and the ecological problems of the universe.   RS

VIRGINIA TUTTLE CLAYTON, *Gardens on Paper* (1990).
ANDREW CLAYTON-PAYNE, *Victorian Flower Gardens* (1988).
PENELOPE HOBHOUSE and CHRISTOPHER WOOD, *Painted Gardens* (1988).
ROY STRONG, *The Artist and the Garden* (2000).

Arts and Crafts movement.

The Arts and Crafts movement in Britain was a rebellion against industrialization and an attempt to return to vernacular traditions. Its most fertile period was between the end of the 19th century and the beginning of the First World War. The name has its origins in the Arts and Crafts Exhibition Society which was founded by the Art Workers' Guild in 1888. William Morris (1834-96), in the examples of his own craftsmanship in furniture, textiles, and wallpapers, and in his polemical writings on all manner of subjects, was one of the most influential figures in the movement. As a socialist he saw the traditional crafts of the Middle Ages as having been destroyed by the mass production and relentless capitalism of his own time. He regarded the whole setting in which people lived as important for their well-being, especially important in an increasingly industrialized society. He wrote in 1895 in *The Quest* (the journal of the Birmingham Guild of Handicraft): 'Gardens, both private and public, are positive necessities if the citizens are to live reasonable and healthy lives in body and mind.' In gardens the Arts and Crafts movement achieved its most complete expression in the work of Sir Edwin LUTYENS and Gertrude JEKYLL. Lutyens's inventiveness in the use of vernacular materials and his brilliant articulation of levels and enclosures was perfectly complemented by Jekyll's profound knowledge of plants and sensitivity to the atmosphere of the garden. Many other architects practised in the same tradition and made the period one of the most fertile in the history of British garden design. They had in common the principle, on which Morris had insisted, that house and garden should be a continuum. As far as gardens were concerned this was a revolution largely executed by architects. Among the most distinguished examples of the work of Arts and Crafts architects are Sir Robert LORIMER at Earlshall (Fife); Charles Rennie Mackintosh (1868-1928) at The Hill House (Dunbartonshire); Francis Inigo THOMAS at Chantmarle (Dorset) and ATHELHAMPTON; and C. F. A. Voysey (1857-1941) at New Place (Surrey). Lesser-known architects also produced admirable work. One of the most attractive was M. H. Baillie Scott (1865–1945) who designed smaller houses and gardens, including some of those in Hampstead Garden Suburb (London). Blackwell, the house and garden he designed in Cumbria overlooking Windermere, has recently been finely restored and is open to the public. At Rodmarton Manor (Gloucestershire) the Cotswold architect Ernest Barnsley (1863–1926) created the apotheosis of the Arts and Crafts house and garden, started in 1909 but, because of the war, completed only in 1926. The rambling stone house is set in a garden of terraces, yew hedges, topiary, paved paths, and secret passages. The timber for the house was felled on the estate and wherever possible craftsmen from the village were used in its building. The Arts and Crafts influence is strongly present in two of the most influential English gardens of the 20th century—HIDCOTE MANOR and SISSINGHURST CASTLE. This style of gardening, with a pattern of enclosures and boisterous planting schemes, has remained the most pervasive influence on British gardens right into the 21st century.   PT

> WENDY HITCHMOUGH, *Arts and Crafts Gardens* (1997).
>
> FIONA MACCARTHY, *William Morris* (1994).

Asakura Villa Remains ⚘

Fukui prefecture, Japan, along with those of the Shūrinji Temple in Shiga prefecture and the KITABATAKE VILLA GARDEN in Mie prefecture, are noted for their rockwork, which exemplifies that done by provincial lords during the Muromachi period (1333–1568). Asakura Toshikage (1428–81) took control of Echizen province (at present Fukui prefecture) in 1471 and moved his seat of power to Ichijōdani, where five generations of the Asakura family continued to live until they were destroyed by Oda Nobunaga (1534–82) in 1573. The Asakuras, who were known for their interest in cosmopolitan culture, often entertained cultural figures from the capital, Kyoto, and the gardeners who worked on the Asakura Villa may also have come from there. The remains of several gardens can be found throughout the valley, the most striking of which is at the Suwa villa, built just four years before the annihilation of the Asakuras by Nobunaga. The garden centres on a small pond and powerful arrangement of large rocks, including one 4 m/ 13 ft tall. Although no physical evidence remains, it is recorded that the fences of that garden were gilded and the doors inlaid with polished crystal, a striking contrast to the lichen-patinaed atmosphere found at present.
MPK

Ashland Hollow,

Hockessin, Delaware, USA, the 6.9-hectare/17-acre private garden of Mr and Mrs William H. Frederick Jr., occupies a narrow, steep-sided stream valley. From 1965 the owner, the landscape architect William H. Frederick Jr. developed fourteen sub-gardens, home to some 1,000 plant taxa. These include a winter garden, a stream valley garden, and a swimming pool garden around an 1850s spring house. Meandering paths allow the visitor to stroll from a house that bridges a stream through all-season gardens as well as those with short-lived but spectacular displays such as the quince hillside and the old shrub rose garden.   CO

Asplund, Gunnar

(1885–1940), Sweden's leading architect during the period between the two world wars. He is known less for his buildings than for his remarkable ability to integrate them with their sites and with the design of the landscape itself. A supreme example is the Forest Cemetery (Skogskyrko-gorden), Enskede, near Stockholm. This was the subject of a competition and subsequent commissions, implemented by Asplund and his partner Sigurd Lewerentz between 1917 and 1940. In it they have transformed a nondescript site of old gravel pits and pinewoods, bounded by roads and a railway, into one of the finest landscapes of the 20th century. The grandeur of the great earth sculpture enclosing the processional way up to the cross is reminiscent of Capability BROWN; it balances perfectly the intimacy of the pine forests which accommodate the graves, cemetery, and crematorium buildings.   MLL

Athelhampton ⚘

near Dorchester, Dorset, England, has one of the finest ARTS AND CRAFTS gardens. The house, on a 6-hectare/15-acre site, was built in the 15th century and changed hands many times. In 1891, by then derelict, it was bought by Alfred Cart de Fontaine who commissioned a new garden from Francis Inigo THOMAS. Thomas laid out a series of enclosures with refined architectural detail extending from the south façade of the house. A garden door leads into a spacious rectangular walled garden with a lawn and a long axial pool with scalloped ends leading down its centre which 'catches the reflection of the house' as Thomas intended. A cross-vista leads to other enclosures, the first of which is the exquisite Corona Garden, circular in plan with a central fountain pool. The crest of the walls that enclose it is decorated with concave sweeps of stone decorated with finials in the shape of obelisks. Quadrant beds line the walls and gateways lead to other parts of the garden. The sunken garden has a lawn with a pool

surrounded by ten monumental yew pyramids. This, beautiful as it is, does not correspond to Thomas's original intentions. A *Country Life* photograph of 1909 shows a rather fussy pattern of zigzag beds between the yews. These have been removed, leaving no ornament but the pool and the giant yews. A raised balustraded walk, with a pretty pavilion at each end, overlooks the sunken garden. Thomas's harmonious yet sprightly design is a masterpiece.   PT

Attiret, Jean-Denis

(1702–68), French artist who studied in Rome and became a Jesuit who went to China for the order in 1737. He was admired by the Emperor Ch'ien Lung who appointed him painter to the Emperor. He wrote a letter to a friend describing the Emperor's gardens which was published in English in an abbreviated version in 1752 under the title *A Particular Account of the Emperor of China's Gardens near Pekin*. In it he described 'All the risings and hills . . . sprinkled with trees. The sides of canals, or lesser streams, are not faced with smooth stone . . . but look rude and rustic, with different pieces of rock . . . In some parts the water is wide, in others narrow; here it serpentizes, and there spreads away.' Much of what he described was close to the ideas of the 18th-century English landscapers and perhaps explains in part the French tendency to call the English 18th-century park UN JARDIN ANGLO-CHINOIS.   PT

Attre, Château d' ⚘

Attre (Brugelette), Hainaut, Belgium, completed in 1752 by the Count of Gomegnies. Flanked by two fine curved pavilions in Louis XVI style, the building is completely open to view from the highway. An axis begins on the far side of the road between two Italian marble columns, continues over a small bridge flanked by two more columns, and over an immaculate TAPIS VERT. This classically simple design by A. Coutant dates from 1909 and replaced the original *cour d'honneur* (the chief, and usually grandest, entrance court to a house). Behind the château the mood changes from clarity and order to the mysterious and the sublime in the picturesque 17-hectare/42-acre landscape park, laid out in the 1780s. Set in a landscape of carefully constructed dramatic scenery and wild vegetation are five FABRIQUES designed to create a mood of awe and terror. Le pilori is a relic of pre-Revolutionary times where bigamists, liars, or prostitutes would be pelted with rubbish. Further along are the ruins of a 10th-century Norman keep, once the residence of a bandit called Vignou who, pretending to be a hermit, robbed and murdered his visitors. The third feature is the Swiss Chalet set on a small mound; this was built in the 19th century as a place of quiet retreat. In the undergrowth there are lakes and rock grottoes. The most famous feature is Le Rocher, an artificial rock, 24 m/78 ft high, with a tower on top, built of huge blocks of stone. Its paths are not for the faint hearted. In front is a dramatic drop down to a hollow with more rocks and mysterious openings overhung with ferns, leading to a labyrinth underneath. It is possible to enter the grottoes there and pass from one side to the other, if one has the courage. The planned restoration of this feature, including the underground fountains, should make it less fearsome. A path through the woods emerges by the Pavillon des Bains. The four columns on the front come from the Abbey of Cambron which was destroyed during the French Revolution. The building is tiny, with a circular staircase and large marble pedestals with *hauts reliefs*.   BA

MARCUS BINNEY, 'Château d'Attre, Hainaut', *Country Life*, 11 Jan. 1973.

Augustusburg

Brühl, Germany, was the favourite residence of the Elector and Archbishop of Cologne Clemens August von Wittelsbach (1700–61). In 1725, Clemens August commissioned the Westphalian master builder Johann Conrad Schlaun to build on the ruins of a medieval moated castle. However, from 1728 onwards, the Bavarian court master builder François de Cuvilliés was responsible for turning Augustusburg into one of the most outstanding residences of its time. The building process took more than 40 years and it was only the Archbishop's successor who saw the completion in 1768. By bringing together architecture, ornamentation, painting, and horticulture, a comprehensive work of art was created, and today Augustusburg is one of the finest examples of the rococo period in Germany. In 1984 UNESCO added Augustusburg, the nearby hunting lodge Falkenlust, and the palace gardens to the World Heritage List. Dominique GIRARD created the baroque garden from 1728 in the French style. Girard, a pupil of André LE NÔTRE, had previously also worked on the gardens at NYMPHENBURG and SCHLEIßHEIM as well as at the BELVEDERE in Vienna. The main feature of the park is the impressive sunken parterre. The middle axis stretches beyond a pond, which forms the boundary of the PARTERRE *de broderie* and continues far into the grounds. Avenues of lime trees frame the magnificent parterre, which was reconstructed twice (1934–5 by Georg Potente and after the Second World War in 1947) in accordance with the original design. Apart from the parterre, the garden and

surrounding woodlands were redesigned by Peter Joseph LENNÉ in the 1840s when a railway line was built across part of the park. Lenné created a landscape park intermingling densely wooded areas and open spaces combined with great vistas. These woodlands, which today still provide pleasant walks, resemble an English landscape park. Both Augustusburg and Falkenlust were severely damaged during the Second World War but have been extensively restored. For many decades after 1949, Augustusburg was used for official functions by the German President and government.   AK

WILFRIED HANSMANN and GISBERT KNOPP, *Die Schlösser Augustusburg und Falkenlust in Brühl* (2002).

Aulanko (Karlberg) Park

Hämeenlinna, Finland, was created by Colonel Hugo Standertskiöld (1844–1931) between 1883 and 1910 on a site of 70 hectares/200 acres. The area consisted of farmland and an ancient hillfort covered by coniferous forest. The Swedish gardener brothers Karl and Erik Zätterlöf contributed to its design. A number of picturesque buildings were built, of which a crenellated mock castle, a grotto, a neo-Gothic Temple of Happiness, and two ornamental ponds—one adorned by a neo-Gothic wooden pavilion—remain. Quantities of exotic tree species were planted, of which a row of *Salix* 'Sibirica' by the lake as well as *Larix sibirica* and *Abies sibirica* in the woodland survive. In 1906, a National Romantic granite lookout tower was designed on the hilltop overlooking a forested lake landscape. From it a long flight of stone steps descended to the lake shore below, ending beside another grotto housing the *Bear Family* sculptural ensemble. Thus the park became divided into two different parts, of which one has the flavour of a public park with carpet bedding, cast-iron fountains, and sculpture as well as tree-lined walks. The other part exemplifies an exceptional attempt towards a Finnish national garden style. The city of Hämeenlinna purchased the estate in 1926. The woodland park was designated as a nature conservation area in 1930, and has since been maintained by the Forest Research Institute. In 1938 a 19th-century wooden house which had been burnt down was replaced by a functionalist hotel building. Today, a golf course dominates the hotel surroundings.

MHay

Aurangzīb

(1618–1707), 6th Mughal Emperor (1658–1707), deposed his father SHĀH JAHĀN and embarked upon a long reign of almost incessant war and religious controversy. A complete contrast to his predecessors, deeply religious and with little

interest in the arts, his achievements were of buildings rather than gardens. Notable works were the Badshahi mosque at Lahore, the Moti Masjid in the RED FORT at Delhi, and a great external gateway to the same fort. He set up his southern capital at Aurungabad, and two gardens here are linked with his name, the Mausoleum of Rābi 'a-ud-Daurāni, and the Pan Chakki watermill. From his reign, however, date some of the most complete accounts both of the Mughal gardens and of Kashmir, by European writers such as François BERNIER and Jean-Baptiste Tavernier.

Together with a decline in the arts, Aurangzīb's policies of repression led to tensions within his empire, which contributed to its decline under his successors and its eventual disappearance under British rule.

SMH

Australia.

The history of gardening in Australia chronicles a 200-year journey from the first European settlement in the singularly strange environment at Sydney Cove to the present day where gardens of all forms celebrate diversity, experimentation, and adaptation. Sir Joseph BANKS is arguably the founder of gardening in Australia. His voyage of discovery with James Cook in 1770, when he collected thousands of plant seeds and specimens, provided the basis of his interest in New South Wales. 'Of plants in general . . . many of these possess properties which might be useful for physical and economic properties which we were not able to investigate,' wrote Banks (quoted in Sir Joseph HOOKER (ed.), *Some Account of That Part of New Holland Known as New South Wales*, 1896). Banks's influential report led to the British government to the idea of establishing an agrarian settlement using convict labour. Subsequently Banks advised the first governor, Captain Arthur Phillip, on economical plants for the First Fleet: seeds and plants from England, Rio de Janeiro, and the Cape of Good Hope. These plants and seed, essential for survival, were grown on what is now the site of the Sydney Botanic Gardens. While the earliest settlers were concerned with growing something to *eat*, from the outset, exotic ornamental plants were also transported as seeds, cuttings, bulbs, and growing specimens from all the ports where ships called that were bound for Australia. Tough survivors of the long sea voyages came from Mauritius, Brazil, the Cape, and India. Cool climate plants, from oaks to primroses, represented England and 'home' in the collective memory. Early settlers sought to recreate the cottage gardens of memory with mixed outcomes.

By the 1830s, the rich in New South Wales were making large gardens—the Macarthurs at

CAMDEN PARK, the Macleays at ELIZABETH BAY, the Rouses at Rouse Hill—using both imported and native plants. In this decade in New South Wales and Tasmania, the 'garden' is perceived as an Arcadian ideal with a Greek Revival house as the centrepiece of a romantic landscape with clumps of trees, grassy meadows, and grazing cattle. Only a handful of these early colonial gardens survive, especially in the environs of Sydney where the pressures of urban development have been greatest. These gardens have also been victim to the climate and soils of the region, neither of which could be described as suited to European garden flora. However, in Tasmania, the second Australian settlement, a more benign climate allowed success with introduced plants. Hawthorn hedges still line the quiet roadsides and oaks mark the driveways to Georgian-style houses. The remaining European-style gardens created by these early settlers in both colonies are reflections of their social and climatic history and echo the memories of a land left behind.

By the 1870s, retreating to the hills became fashionable. Just as the British Raj moved up to the fresh air of Simla to escape the heat of the Indian plains, so too did the colonial governors in Australia. Mount Macedon in Victoria and Mount Wilson in New South Wales have surviving examples of these hill station gardens; viceregal parties also retreated to the NSW Southern Highlands, escaping Sydney's summer humidity. Amid the misty fern gullies and beneath the majestic mountain ash (*Eucalyptus regnans*), exotic plants, especially rhododendrons, camellias, and azaleas, flourished in the cool breezes. Gradually simple timber cottages in the bush gave way to quite grand houses and gardens, embraced by green lawns, mossy steps, and deciduous trees. Victoria in the 1850s had been the golden magnet for prospectors worldwide, following the discovery of extensive gold fields. Miners created simple cottage gardens in bush settlements, bringing plants with them across the seas; conifers from the Pacific west coast, *Pinus radiata* and *Cupressus macrocarpa*, are among the many that have thrived. Following the gold rush, a number of exceptional botanic and private gardens were created from pastoral and gold rush wealth.

The legacy of landscape designer William GUILFOYLE in the 19th and early 20th centuries is paramount. He created a series of grand gardens for his private clients, the wealthy and influential of Melbourne and Victoria's Western District, of which MAWALLOK is a superb example. This was in addition to his masterpiece, the successful remodelling of Melbourne's BOTANIC GARDENS, where he was director 1873-1901.

From Australian bush to garden

In early gardens, Australian plants were seldom used, except where they provided useful residual plant backdrops, as at Camden Park and VAUCLUSE HOUSE. But gradually, the Australian bush and the beauty of native flowers exerted a stronger appeal. Kings Park, a bushland area in the heart of Perth, was declared a national park in 1878; a year later, the Royal National Park, on the coast south of Sydney, came into existence. In the following 125 years, many thousands of hectares (including World Heritage Sites) have been set aside; they have become the treasured 'gardens' of the nation. Architect Walter Burley Griffin (1876-1937), winner of the design competition to create the new federal capital in Canberra in 1912, became an enthusiastic advocate of the Australian bush. Griffin and his wife Marion Mahony (1871-1961) developed Castlecrag, a Sydney suburb, in the natural bushland on the shores of Sydney Harbour in the 1920s. Their aim was to make the houses blend unobtrusively into the environment; no red roofs and no fences were permitted.

Environmental issues also became preoccupations of Edna WALLING, Australia's most significant and prolific garden designer. Walling, English born, arrived in Australia *c.*1914, and her early gardens show the undoubted influence of Gertrude JEKYLL. For three decades, Walling designed gardens with a harmonious synthesis of the formal and natural; her work encompassed city and country gardens. At first her plant palette consisted almost entirely of exotics, but gradually she became more enthusiastic about the beauties of Australian plants. She was one of the early advocates of native plants in gardens and parks and in *The Australian Roadside* (1937) promoted the sole use of indigenous plants on Australian highways. She communicated her knowledge and enthusiasm to a wide readership. Her ideas and techniques were a great influence on her associates such as Glen Wilson and Ellis Stones in creating the naturalistic landscapes of bush gardens. *Designing Bush Gardens* and *More about Bush Gardens* (1966 and 1967) by Australian plant devotees Betty Maloney and Jean Walker, in Sydney, expand on Walling's themes of earlier decades. In Eltham, in outer Melbourne, Gordon Ford's bush gardens are classics of the genre. Perhaps surprisingly, gardens of Australian wildflowers are largely a Western Australian phenomenon, a reflection of the outstanding and extraordinary flora of that state. By definition, one would assume that gardens with Australian plants would be the essence of Australian gardening. The country is noted for its rich and diverse flora, with more than 25,000 native species and a huge range of garden hybrids and cultivars. But, paradoxically, the growing of native plants in Australian suburban gardens has been fraught with difficulties. Problems with propagation, scale of plants (for example, the eucalypt described as small may, with an increase in water, grow to 20 m/70 ft), the specific needs of indigenous plants, and a lack of understanding of their life cycles have led to disenchantment. It was a prevalent but uninformed belief in the 1960s and 1970s that the native garden was a low-maintenance garden. Triumphs and failures were common as enthusiasm failed to match horticultural knowledge. However, specific Australian plants, such as grevilleas and kangaroo paws (*Anigozanthus*), are beginning to be found in a traditional garden idiom. Many of the native grasses and plants with rushlike foliage are now used in formal private gardens, street plantings, and on highway verges.

Suburbia

While the ethos of the bush with its open spaces, blue horizons, distinctive perfumes, and constantly surprising flora is still a vivid reality, most Australian gardeners live in suburbia in the 21st century. One hundred years ago, Australian cities and suburbs began to expand; the quarter-acre block became standard. The availability of reticulated water, the hose, and lawnmower significantly affected garden making; vast areas of neatly trimmed grass were possible for everyone. The concurrent advent of tough imported grasses from South Africa— couch (*Agropyron repens*), buffalo (*Stenotaphrum secundatum*), and kikuyu (*Pennisetum clandestinum*)—were lauded and grew just as vigorously as they do today. American influences in Australia in the inter-war period were disseminated from Hollywood. The popular Californian bungalow-style home featured a lawn of couch or buffalo grass. Clipped privet or cypress hedge was planted at the street edge; typical plantings included jacaranda, acacia, and citrus—lemon, orange, and grapefruit. The back garden probably also had a lemon tree, a shed, clothes line, and vegetable garden. Above all, the garden contained roses; standard roses grown either side of the path to admire as one walked to the front door.

Roses

Australians' enthusiasm for roses has not abated. Except in the tropics, roses thrive in Australia. From the earliest days of settlement roses are mentioned in the list of European plants brought to Australia, and by the mid 19th century were grown in abundance. For example, in 1857 John Rule of Melbourne lists many roses in his sale catalogue, among them, the tea rose 'Devoniensis' (still grown in gardens today); nurseryman George Smith of Ballarat in 1862 suggests that the cottage gardener buy half a dozen good varieties of roses. Cemeteries throughout Australia are still sources of long-forgotten roses. Interestingly, at the turn of the century, in 1903, local authorities such as C. Bogue Luffman (who was principal at Burnley, the newly founded horticultural college in Melbourne where Edna Walling trained) suggested that Australian gardeners include in their libraries *Roses for English Gardens* (1902) by Gertrude Jekyll and Edward Mawley. In the 1920s and 1930s, favourite roses, according to newspaper polls of the time, included 'Mme Abel Chatenay', 'Lady Hillingdon', and 'Frau Karl Druschki'; also on the list were 'Sunny South' and 'Lorraine Lee', bred in Australia by Alister Clark (1864–1949). Clark, inspired by his love of roses, aimed to breed them to suit Australia's hot dry conditions and to flower through the year. His roses, bred for the garden and not the show bench, have a character all their own; 'Nancy Hayward' and 'Lorraine Lee' are among his finest. Clark's roses went into eclipse after his death; recent research has revealed many of them surviving in private gardens for 50 years or more, the ultimate proof of Clark's breeding success. Rose shows, rose festivals, and rose gardens continue to attract visitors; heritage rose societies hold biennial conferences; rose-swathed trellises, arbours, and pergolas in gardens remain eternally fashionable, even if the roses grown have been in and out of fashion. Early in the 20th century, the popular choice would have been 'Dorothy Perkins' (1901), 'American Pillar' (1902), and 'Paul's Scarlet Climber' (1916). Today Australian gardeners might choose 'Wedding Day', 'Graham Thomas', or 'Gold Bunny'. Roses remain ever popular with eight million plants sold each year. However, in a climate of clear skies and year-round sunshine, most Australians now want their gardens to be places of leisure. The beauty of the suburban lawn is no longer top priority and the backyard is remarkably changed; the swimming pool and barbecue area have taken over. In inner city town houses and apartments, the garden has become an extension of the living room, with decorative paving and water features as the focus and minimal emphasis on plants. Garden commentators bemoan the ubiquitous plantings of city developers—the overuse of a limited palette of plants, such as Manchurian pears (*Pyrus ussuriensis*), *Camellia sasanqua*, standard 'Iceberg' roses, and box hedging. Automated sprinkler systems and air-conditioning mean a retreat to the hills is no longer necessary. But people are still growing vegetables; heirloom varieties of tomatoes are popular, as are all forms of coloured lettuce, and the traditional northern hemisphere beauties of spring bulbs and autumn colours still excite Australian gardeners.

Gardening media

The rich diversity of gardening ideas, from the strictly utilitarian to the superbly ornamental, is well illustrated in the abundance of printed material available from early colonial times. The emphasis ranges from practical manuals (*The Farm and Garden*, published in South Australia, 1859) to catalogues of vegetables (*The Wreath: A Gardeners' Manual for the Climate of Tasmania*, published in 1855) to *The Home: An Australian Quarterly*, popular in the 1920s, featuring the best in design ideas and appealing to the aspiring home and garden maker. Magazines such as *Your Garden*, appealing to both the practical and aspiring gardener for more than 50 years, reflect the social changes. Today, a plethora of lifestyle and homemaker magazines feature sections on home gardens, gardening columns, and inspirational ideas. Popular 'infotainment' television shows attract millions of viewers each week. Gardening and gardening know-how is a minor part of these lifestyle entertainment programmes, which feature celebrity gardeners and quick make-overs for backyards.

Garden shows continue to draw crowds; country people flock to support the local daffodil or dahlia show; Tulip Time in the New South Wales Southern Highlands, after 40 years, still attracts thousands of visitors. On a grander scale, the Melbourne International Flower and Garden Show, held in April each year, is a showcase for the nursery industry and landscape designers with more than 20,000 visitors annually.

Australia's Open Garden Scheme

Although there has been a long tradition in Australia of opening private gardens for charity, the first organized scheme began in 1987 when distinguished English garden owner and author Rosemary VEREY launched Victoria's Garden Scheme. Modelled initially on Britain's National Gardens Scheme, the venture was so successful that five years later Australia's Open Garden Scheme had evolved. Since that time, the scheme has steadily expanded into all states and territories, showcasing an enormous number of gardens: from 63 in 1987 to more than 800 each year, attracting many thousands of visitors. The scheme is a non-profit organization; the aim is simply to promote the knowledge and pleasure of gardens and gardening. Its annual guidebook is a veritable garden tour from inner city gardens to country landscapes, celebrating Australia's different regions and climates. Across the country, on the same weekend, an organic farm, a heritage garden with familiar European flora, a garden with brilliant tropical foliage, or a garden under snow could all be open to visitors.

Australian Garden History Society

Founded in 1980, the Australian Garden History Society is committed to conservation of significant cultural landscapes and historic gardens. Branches exist in all states; activities range from working bees to lectures and visits to historic properties; a monthly journal and annual conference inform members. Both Australia's Open Garden Scheme and the Australian Garden History Society celebrate Australian gardening achievements.

Australian garden style

In the early 21st century, it is fair to suggest that no one style characterises or dominates Australian gardening. Within the country's extensive boundaries, eclecticism and adaptation are the key characteristics of Australians' gardens. With seven or more wildly varying climate zones, gardeners across Australia have different priorities. In Brisbane, summer humidity dictates plant choices; in Melbourne, February's hot northerly winds from the continent's interior are an annual trial; Perth's sandy soils make gardening difficult and in Adelaide, increasing water salinity is the gardeners' problem. In Darwin, restoring a garden after a cyclone is a distinct possibility. In poet Dorothea McKellar's words: in 'the land of droughts and flooding rains', water is the most crucial word in the gardeners' dictionary: how much water is available and when. Gardeners in the second driest continent are slowly coming to terms with the country's climate and terrain. Wherever they live, Australian gardeners understand the true character of their environment—those indefinable and unique conditions of sparkling clarity of light and sense of space.　CMR

Austria.

Austria's rich cultural tradition offers a wide range of examples of garden art and landscape architecture influenced by designers and botanists from northern Italy, southern Germany, and the Balkans, who stimulated a local interpretation of their own stylistic tendencies. In addition, the natural landscape and its variety of landforms, climate zones, and vegetation offered great potential for garden making. The western part of the country, the Alpine region, is characterized by primary rock and limestone and alpine vegetation like *Picea abies*, *Pinus nigra* var. *austriaca*, and *Larix decidua*. The eastern part is situated along the Danube valley and stretches into the plains in the eastern provinces around Vienna. The vegetation here is dominated by decidous trees like beech and maple (*Acer campestre*, *A. pseudoplatanus*, and *A. platanoides*) and expands southwards towards Lake Neusiedl, characterized by the pannonic climate. In all *c*.3,100 native plants are found of which *c*.80 species (notably alpines) are endemic. Extremes of hot and cold are found in Austria—with a maximum temperature of 38 °C/100 °F and a minimum of –20 °C/–4 °F.

There is early evidence of gardening in Austria. Some archaeological sites, such as Hallstatt's salt mines, show signs of early Celtic or Avaric settlements and trade routes.

Since the beginning of Roman settlements *c*.186 BC in the southern parts of the country, in particular in Carinthia and up to the Danube valley, vineyards and gardens have been documented, for example at the archaeological site in Carnuntum. In the Middle Ages horticulture was concentrated in monasteries, such as Klosterneuburg near Vienna, castles, and certain garden sites within the walled cities. Through trade routes and the return of the Crusaders, new plants were introduced from the Near East in this period.

Among the few sites surviving from Renaissance times are the partially reconstructed Keuchengarten at AMBRAS Castle in the Tyrol, Schallaburg in Lower Austria, and Neugebäude in Vienna. The great botanist Carolus CLUSIUS worked at Neugebäude from 1573 to 1576. An important event in the 16th century was the arrival of TULIPS brought to Vienna from Constantinople in 1554 by Ogier Ghiselin de Busbecq, Ferdinand I's ambassador to Suleiman the Magnificent. The influence of the Renaissance is seen in the remarkable early 17th-century grottoes at HELLBRUNN. It is also seen in the garden at Ambras. As a result of the Turkish wars in 1527 and 1683 and the Thirty Years War between 1618 and 1648, the eastern provinces were sacked and most of the garden sites were destroyed. Following the rebuilding of the country in the late 17th century, baroque garden art evolved under the influence of Dutch botanists, Italian and French garden artists like Jean Trehet (d. after 1754) at SCHÖNBRUNN, and 'fontainiers' like Dominique GIRARD. Many of the garden sites of major private estates, monasteries, and city squares retain their baroque character to the present day. The first large park to be laid out in the English style was Neuwaldeg (1766) by Duke Moritz Lacy, who had been to England and visited BLENHEIM and STOWE. By the turn of the 18th century the English landscape park was widely influential—for example at the royal park in LAXENBURG to the south or the Pötzleinsdorfer Park (1799) to the north of

Vienna. A garden such as Schönbrunn showed every garden fashion of the 18th century—baroque at the beginning, followed by rococo and an English-style landscape park at the end.

From the early 19th century public parks were an important aspect of Austrian garden design. The Volksgarten in Vienna was opened in 1823. The VIENNA RINGSTRAßE and its attendant parks were laid out from the mid 19th century. In the late 19th century several parks were laid out—Türkenschanz Park in Vienna or the City Park in Graz as well as in the provinces of Salzburg, Carinthia, and Upper Austria. A little later, as a result of the Viennese zoning laws, the Vienna Woods were protected in 1905. During the Viennese Secession era (1883-1935), garden art flourished—villa gardens were seen as essential parts of domestic life, urban parks were considered vital parts of city life. The ALLOTMENT movement reached its peak due to economic hardships after the fall of the Austro-Hungarian monarchy and the First World War. By then the projects of council flats included landscaped housing areas like the Karl-Marx Hof in Vienna.

In the 20th century landscape architects were hired to deal with projects for the preservation of the natural landscape and for the landscaping of such works as dams, highways, and railway tracks. The Third Reich left the country sites and urban parks damaged and the profession of garden design devastated. Subsequently the task was to repair damage and develop new parks. In the 1950s new housing estates were built and recreation areas included bathing facilities on the banks of the Danube like the Gänsehäufl in Vienna or at the lakes and touristic resort areas in the mountain ranges of the Tyrol, Salzburg, or Semmering. Urban projects like pedestrian areas, international garden shows, the landscape design of the Danube Island, and the Marchfeld Channel were important projects of the last third of the 20th century. More recently new parks have been created for thermal spas in Styria, the Tyrol, and Lower Austria. In cities, landscape design's current themes include the restoration of historic gardens, reclaiming urban sites (such as the creation of parks near traffic hubs), the laying out of green spaces in housing estates, office blocks, and government centres.

The conservation of landscape and of historic gardens has gained importance. Each of the nine Austrian provinces has its own law for the protection of nature and, for the whole of the republic, there is the federal law for protection of monuments in effect which includes the protection of 57 historical garden estates.   MA

Aveleda, Quinta de ✺

near Paredes, Porto, Portugal, a wine-growing estate, dating from the late 19th century, producing well-known Vinho Verde. The garden has a romantic flavour with, particularly in the woodland, picturesque detail. The entrance drive runs as straight as an arrow through woodland to the house. The drive is lined on either side with ramparts of azaleas—pale salmon pink, cream, or rusty red—underplanted with silver dead nettle (*Lamium*), ferns, irises, and Solomon's seal (*Polygonatum odoratum*). A cross-vista leads through the woods to where a rustic stone bridge leads over to an ivy-shrouded island in a lake. At the end of the lake a cast-iron bridge leads to a second island with a charmingly eccentric cottage *orné* (a picturesque rustic cottage designed as a landscape ornament) with rustic wood-encrusted walls, thatched roof, and veranda. The interior has a table whose top is made of coiled rope and a bench in the shape of a boat with crossed oars forming its back. The coved ceiling is decorated with china creatures—a toad, fish, crocodile, terrapin, and eagle. Paths wind through the woods planted with swathes of azaleas. A carved stone shrine to the Virgin in neo-Renaissance style has obelisks and gables. A stone mask gushes water into a basin which feeds a zigzag rill. An impeccable lawn, with a large ball of clipped box at each corner, is surrounded by deep borders of azaleas.   PT

avenue.

The word originally meant an approach but has assumed the meaning of alignments of trees, usually flanking the entrance to a country house. John Evelyn seems to have been the first person to have used the word in its modern meaning in his diary for 25 August 1654 on his visit to Sir Christopher Hatton's great house Kirby Hall in Northamptonshire—'built *à la moderne*; the garden and stables agreeable, but the avenue was ungraceful and the seate naked'. The principle of the avenue, however, is far more ancient than our modern word. In his book *Mediaeval Gardens* (1981) John Harvey describes alignments of elms leading to the west front of Wells Cathedral (Somerset, England) in the 13th century. In the 17th century the avenue became an essential ornament of gardens in Britain, France, and the Low Countries. Johannes Kip's and Leonard KNYFF's *Britannia Illustrata* (1707) depicts several English estates whose gardens chiefly date from the late 17th century. Almost all of them show avenues, often used as a way of projecting into the surrounding landscape the linear formalities of the garden. Three engravings of Badminton in Gloucestershire show a vast pattern of avenues radiating in all directions from the house with patterns of intersecting avenues. In the Low Countries in this period the avenue was ubiquitous. Jan van der GROEN's *Den Nederlandtsen hovenier* (1669—reprinted nine times by 1721), a great influence on the garden taste of his time, sings the praises of avenues of elms, oaks, and poplars both as a protection from the wind and as a way of introducing desirable order into the wild landscape. Apart from their use in the designed landscape they were also frequently planted flanking canals, as may still be seen today very widely in Belgium and the Netherlands. John EVELYN's *Sylva* (1664), of great influence in Britain, recommended the common lime (*Tilia* × *europaea*) as 'the choice and universally acceptable tree' for avenues but English elms (*Ulmus minor* var. *vulgaris*) were also acceptable. The common lime had the advantage for avenues of being among the tallest broad-leafed trees yet remarkably resistant to strong winds. It was not propagated in England in Evelyn's time and he recommended the Low Countries as a source. In France avenues were commonly used in 17th-century gardens. At the Château de BALLEROY in Normandy an avenue (replanted in modern times with silver limes, *Tilia tomentosa*) extends from the *cour d'honneur* (see ATTRE, CHÂTEAU D') to run along the village high street. André Mollet's *Le Jardin de plaisir* (1651) states that the most important embellishment for a royal house is 'a double or triple avenue, either of female elms or of limes (which are the two species which we consider the best for this purpose)'. This avenue should be aligned with the centre of the entrance front of the chateau with the parterres, BOSQUETS, PALISSADES, and so on behind it. This, in a simplified form, is exactly what may be seen at the Château de COURANCES, although the splendid double avenue of planes was planted in 1782.   PT

> SARAH CROUCH, 'The practice of avenue planting in the seventeenth and eighteenth centuries', *Garden History*, Vol. 20: No. 2 (1992).

aviary.

In the Italian Renaissance 'No garden was complete without aviaries and fishponds', wrote Claudia Lazzaro in *The Italian Renaissance Garden* (1990). There were aviaries in the Villa GIULIA in the 1550s and Utens's painting of 1599 of the Villa MEDICI (Pratolino) shows a leafy aviary in the garden. In the 16th-century Villa LANTE a pair of aviaries were part of the pattern of the garden. Birds were regarded as intrinsically beautiful and interesting creatures but also their song was thought to be an ornament of the garden's atmosphere. Aviaries appeared in French gardens influenced by Italian examples. Jacques BOYCEAU DE LA BARAUDERIE's *Traité du jardinage* (1638) considered that 'Les vollières donneront aux jardins un embellissement fort divers' (Aviaries will embellish gardens in many different ways). He praised the beauty of birdsong but also remarked on the pleasure of being able to study birds' behaviour close up. Aviaries were occasionally found in 18th-century English landscape gardens—Capability BROWN designed one for Melton Constable (Norfolk). In the 19th century, with the introduction of many new exotic birds, aviaries were built in numerous gardens. Gabriel Thouin's pattern book *Plans raisonnés de toutes les espèces de jardins* (1820) illustrated a design for one. They were often seen in 19th-century public parks in France and England—an especially decorative Gothic example, modelled on Pisa Cathedral, still stands in Cannizaro Park (London) and a pretty CHINOISERIE example may still be seen at the Parc du THABOR in Brittany. In the same period there was a craze for them in private gardens—an outstanding one, built in 1889, may be seen at WADDESDON MANOR complete with magnificent brilliantly coloured birds.   PT

Avrig Park

(also known as Freck, Felek, and Bruckenthal Park) ✤ near Sibiu county, Romania. Described by contemporaries as the 'Eden of Transylvania', the summer palace and its garden were created for Baron Samuel von Bruckenthal, governor of the Transylvanian principality around 1768. Placed on the top of a steep slope on the banks of the river Olt, the formal gardens have a symmetrical structure divided into terraces. Long, spectacular stairs and a fountain were placed in the line of the central avenue. Two orangeries were built beside the symmetrical ornamental compartments in the kitchen garden. In 1780, Bruckenthal created a landscape garden around the formal parts with a grotto, a dairy, and a neoclassical bathhouse. A long avenue of spruces was planted across the main axis in the second half of the 19th century and a Swiss Cottage was built in the same period. Some formal parts were probably redesigned around 1900. In the 1870s, when the Bruckenthal family died out, the estate was bequeathed to the Protestant grammar school of nearby Sibiu. Today the house operates as a sanatorium, and the gardens are in need of restoration. The 16-hectare/40-acre park is the only remaining example of a baroque garden in present-day Romania. The Bruckenthal Foundation is endeavouring to restore its former splendour.   GA

Ayazmo Park ✤

Stara Zagora, Bulgaria, dominates the northern side of the city, covering a hillside of 380 hectares/940 acres and displaying a rich diversity of vegetation. In 1895, Bishop Metodi Kusev initiated the afforestation of the bare, rocky, and arid Fool's Hill to create a marvellous ARBORETUM. Over 27 years he struggled to raise money for the cause and introduced exotic trees and shrubs from southern Europe, Asia, and North America. The favourable climatic conditions coupled with intensive irrigation, in a unique ecological experiment, turned the wilderness into a densely planted park. More than 150 common and ornamental species are found, among them cypresses, cedars, pines, maples, oaks, and many fruit trees. The harmonious layout, made by amateur designers, provides endless paths through woodland with intimate groves and specimen trees, and leading across meadows. Park attractions were introduced, including an open-air theatre, an observatory, a sports complex, and several children's playgrounds. The small zoo, however, appears to be the prime sightseeing spot.   ASG

Ayrlies ✤

Whitford, Auckland, New Zealand, a garden of 4 hectares/10 acres, was started in 1964 by its owners, Beverley and the late Malcolm McConnell. The site was bare, exposed to the elements, and poised on a gently undulating hillside facing north across the sea to the young volcanic cone of Rangitoto. The McConnells adopted a naturalistic style and, in the garden's formative years, vast quantities of soil were moved to create a series of ponds and waterways where a range of aquatic and marginal plants including the spectacular *Colocasia* 'Lime Fizz' make luxuriant growth. A newer feature is a large rock and water garden where indigenous New Zealand plants such as the diminutive southern gunneras are displayed. The mild maritime climate permits tropical and cool climate plants to be grown in close proximity. You can look down on the magnificent foliage of *Cecropia peltata* and *Schizolobium parahybum* growing alongside Abyssinian bananas (*Ensete ventricosum*) and vireya rhododendrons, then walk a short distance and find yourself amongst a riot of old roses, clematis, and associated plants.

For a private garden (in New Zealand) Ayrlies is unusual not only for its size and its use of themed colour over large areas, but also for its excellence of maintenance and extensive plant collections. Near the house grey foliage plants mingle with yellow, lime green, and lemon-coloured flowers where a giant furcraea is a dramatic centrepiece and where tropical palms, aloes, agaves, and yuccas feature around a naturalistic swimming pool.

Nearby the exotic blue-flowered climber *Petrea volubilis* makes a spectacular display in summer. Beyond the swimming pool lies an informal border where hot colours and bold foliage plants predominate and where the new, Auckland-bred *Dahlia* 'Ayrlies' with bright red flowers displayed over finely cut bronze foliage can be seen. On the other side of the house the garden falls to a large pond, the steep slopes planted with rhododendron, azaleas, and small shrubs. The garden links through massed plantings of liquidambars to a 16-hectare/40-acre wetland habitat recently formed for birds and water life—the McConnells' unique contribution to conservation.   GSC

azulejo

is the Portuguese and Spanish for a glazed, frequently polychrome, tile of a kind which has formed part of the decorative scheme for both architecture and gardens since at least the 15th century. The word is derived from the Arabic *al-zulaich* and it was Muslims, who had learned the craft of glazing ceramics from the Chinese, who introduced *azulejos* to Granada in the 13th century. Throughout Portugal they are part of the street scene—frequently used to embellish the façades of houses of even the most modest kind, a tradition extending into recent times. They appear, also, as often prettily decorated plaques indicating street names. In great houses from the 16th-century onwards they are used as wall decoration, often disposed to form pictorial panels—fine examples are to be seen in Portugal at the PALÁCIO NACIONAL DE SINTRA. In Lisbon the Museu do Azulejo, housed in a magnificent baroque convent, Madre de Deus, displays a superb representative collection of *azulejos* of every kind and period. In Spain the Real ALCÁZAR in Seville has exceptional examples of *azulejos* in both the palace and garden. The outstanding examples in the palace are the Renaissance pictorial tiles with portraits of Spanish monarchs designed by Cristóbal de Augusta in 1575 for the Capilla del Palacio Gótico. In the Jardín de la Alcoba (Garden of the Alcove) is an elegant arcaded summer house, the Pabellón de Carlos V, built between 1543 and 1546 on the site of a *qubba* (pavilion) dating from the Islamic period. Its interior has a fountain pool and walls covered in *azulejos* by Diego and Juan Pulido. This is a rarity, for the garden use of *azulejos* in Spain dates largely from a much more modern period. In the 20th century their use was much stimulated by the Parque MARÍA LUISA in Seville, designed from 1918 by J. C. N. FORESTIER who used *azulejos* prolifically to decorate plinths of statues, the backs of garden seats, and the walls of raised pools.

In Portugal the outstanding use of *azulejos* may be seen at the Palácio FRONTEIRA in Lisbon. Here the terracing of the formal gardens laid out at the end of the 17th century is embellished with a feast of *azulejos*. The climax of the scheme is a series of huge portraits of the Marques de Fronteira and his fellow officers mounted on prancing horses filling arched panels that rise above a great water tank. Throughout the garden niches, retaining walls, the backs of benches, and the entrance to a grotto are decorated with a virtuoso display of *azulejos*. At the royal Palácio de QUELUZ close to Lisbon the palace has, in the 'Corridor of Sleeves', superb pictorial *azulejos* designed by Francisco Jorge da Costa and put into place in 1784. In the garden is a walled ornamental canal, used by the royal family to take jaunts in small boats, which is lavishly decorated with *azulejos*. These were made between 1756 (when João Antunues was paid to lay about 50,000 tiles) and *c.*1775 when Manuel da Costa Rosado painted *azulejos* for the canal. In shades of pale blue and lemon yellow they depict mythological, nautical, and hunting scenes.   PT

Babelsberg ⊗

Brandenburg, Potsdam, Germany. In the course of his efforts for the improvement of the Isle of Potsdam Peter Joseph LENNÉ wanted to complete the eastern part of the area. In 1833 he drew up the first plan for the future Emperor Wilhelm I, and this was partly executed. Karl Friedrich SCHINKEL designed the neo-Gothic Schloss (1833–4). The court gardener Kindermann carried out the technical work on the garden. Work ceased in 1838 because of financial problems, and PÜCKLER-MUSKAU took over the work in 1843. In 1845 running water was artificially brought by a steam engine to the top of Babelsberg hill. Now the vegetation could grow luxuriantly, and fountains and lakes of various sizes were created which greatly enliven the park. The very undulating terrain harmonizes with the calm waters of the river Havel. Between the Schloss and the Havel is the much-admired Bowling Green, joined on the western side by a pleasure ground (reconstructed in 1977) with flower beds enclosed by tiles. The Lenné-Höhe, a lookout point towards Potsdam, marked the park boundary until 1841; from 1871 this was emphasized by the addition of the Berlin Gerichtslaube (a Gothic market cross). Scattered oak trees, some trained to grow into bushy shapes, and tall trees which serve to direct the eye, characterize the park.

Further paths were laid down to facilitate exploration of the area around Potsdam and of particular buildings; skilful use of the terrain and careful planting of individual trees or groups of trees result in a highly picturesque landscape. Individual buildings aid the creation and enjoyment of landscape scenes: the Kleines Schloss on the Havel (1841–2), kitchen buildings, the Flatow tower (1853), the Court Nursery (1862–3), and the Victoria Column; at the entrances to the park stand gatehouses modelled on English lodges. The 13 hectares/32 acres of the park beneath the castle had been occupied and destroyed between 1961 and 1990 by the Berlin wall and are now restored.

H.GÜ/MS

Bābur

(b. 1483), 1st Mughal Emperor (1508–30), a descendant of both Genghis Khan and Timūr Leng, was, throughout a lifetime of incessant and successful warfare, devoted to the making of gardens and the cultivation of the arts. At the age of 14, he briefly captured Samarkand, and remained much influenced throughout his life by its splendours. In 1504 he became ruler of Kabul, Afghanistan, styling himself Emperor in 1508. Here he began to lay out gardens, and to develop the love of trees, fruit, and flowers that absorbed him all his life. After a period of comparative peace, Bābur's invasions of India began in 1518, and in 1526 he was proclaimed Emperor in Delhi. Kabul he regarded always as his home, but his life lay henceforward in India. In conditions less appealing to him than those in Kabul, he and his followers laid out a series of splendid sites, mainly along the banks of the river Jumna in Agra. Of these, the RAM BAGH, Zahara Bagh, and Dehra Bagh have been attributed to Bābur himself. Water was first controlled to provide wells, reservoirs, and aqueducts, and the gardens, in a climate of dust, heat, and humidity, evolved as enclosed paradises.

Bābur's own memoirs, the *Bābur-nama* (translated into English by A. P. Beveridge, 1922), included vivid and detailed accounts of the construction of his gardens and their planting. He was buried temporarily in one of his gardens in Agra, but later, as he had wished, in Bagh-i-Bābur Shah at Kabul, overlooking his favourite views.　SMH

Babylon, the Hanging Gardens of,

one of the Seven Wonders of the World in late classical sources. Until recently no archaeological or Babylonian textual support could be found for their location and features, a lack which gave rise to many and varied speculations. Recently, however, it has been shown that the tradition was based on a garden built by the Assyrian King Sennacherib (704–681 BC) at Nineveh, for Nineveh and Babylon were confused by biblical, classical, and later writers, likewise Assyrian Sennacherib and Babylonian Nebuchadnezzar II were telescoped and confused.

The garden was set into an artificial hill beside the palace, and was constructed and laid out to imitate a natural hilly landscape with trees and running water. The shape and dimensions were similar to those of a Greek theatre. Running water from mountains 50 km/30 miles away was brought into the garden along an aqueduct halfway up the slope, so that stone vaults supported the upper part of the garden. The top levels of the garden consisted of an open, pillared walkway with a roof constructed like a narrow field planted with trees, so that one walked beneath the roots. Water was brought up to the top level by means of cast bronze screws encased in cylinders, whose invention has often been attributed to Archimedes, many centuries later. Pavilions with Ionic pillars stood in the garden, and there was probably a recreational lake at the lowest level. Details in an inscription of Sennacherib, combined with two depictions of the garden on contemporary palace relief sculpture, match the descriptive details given by much later, classical writers. Sennacherib called the palace with its garden 'a wonder for all peoples', anticipating the later tradition. Although the garden cannot now be located with precision, Sennacherib's inscription makes it clear that his south-west palace was adjacent, allowing the deduction that the slope looked out over the river Khosr, probably roughly south-west facing, with a view towards the southern part of Nineveh and the Tigris valley. Information about plants is lacking in detail, but two types of rather stereotypical trees are shown, haphazardly planted as if by chance.

The supposition that Nineveh was totally destroyed in 612 BC has been disproved by archaeological evidence, and by a better understanding of the textual tradition. The technological skills required for providing water along the aqueduct and through the screws, together with the pillared walkway with trees above, explain why the garden counted as a world wonder.　SDa　⊃ page 30

Bacalhôa, Quinta da ⊗

Aceitão, near Setúbal, Portugal. In the 15th century the estate belonged to Alonso de Albuquerque whose illegitimate son, Braz de Albuquerque, laid out a new garden in the early years of the 16th century. He had visited Italy in 1521 and there is certainly something Italianate in the garden he made. In the use of AZULEJOS and in the garden's great water tank he also showed the influence of Islamic gardens. The huge rectangular water tank is overlooked by a building which runs the whole length of one side, the Casa do Fresco (Cool House). It is elegantly arcaded to form a loggia where it faces the tank, breaking out into pyramid-roofed pavilions at each end and at the centre. The interior has a series of rooms decorated with *azulejos* going back to the early 16th century. A loggia of the house overlooks a four-part parterre with a tiered fountain rising from a scalloped pool at the centre. The planting of the parterre is a pattern of clipped box scrolls edged in hedges which break out into topiary. This is a modern arrangement and it is not known what the original planting was. A long walk, backed by a high wall, leads to the water tank. Along the wall is a raised bed faced in *azulejos* into which benches are set from time to time, also inlaid with *azulejos*. The garden designer Russell PAGE saw the Quinta da Bacalhôa between the wars when it was derelict but he recognized the quality of the place. He wrote, 'For sheer boldness and simplicity of plan and the striking use of whitewash and coloured tiles this garden, though now sadly neglected, is one of the most striking in all European garden art' ('Some Portuguese gardens', *Landscape & Garden*, Vol. 2: No. 3 (1935)). The estate was acquired in the 1960s by an enterprising American, Mrs Scoville, who restored it and began to make excellent wine. Today it is owned by one of Portugal's largest winemaking firms, JP Vinhos. PT

Backhouse, James

(1794–1869), English plant collector who acquired, with his brother Thomas, the Friars' Garden nursery in York in 1816. From 1831 to 1838 James travelled in Australia, as a Quaker missionary and plant collector, sending plants back to Thomas 'to test their hardiness in England'. James's account of his visit to the Australian colonies was published in 1843. William Hooker (see HOOKER, SIR JOSEPH DALTON) (then director at Kew) honoured James Backhouse in 1845 by naming a genus *Backhousia*, evergreen trees and shrubs belonging to the myrtle family and native to Australia. *Backhousia citriodora*, commonly known as lemon ironwood, is one of the most delightful of the world's many plants with lemon fragrance.

CMR

Bacon, Francis, 1st Baron Verulam and Viscount St Albans

(1561–1626), English statesman, philosopher, essayist, and gardener. His essay 'Of gardens' (1625)—'God *Almightie* first Planted a *Garden*. And indeed, it is the Purest of Humane pleasures. It is the Greatest Refreshment to the Spirits of Man'—is one of the most eloquent statements on the delights of gardening. His taste in gardening looked forward and backward. He disapproved of knot gardens ('You may see as good Sights, many times, in Tarts'), loved plants, relished 'a *Natural wildernesse*', but also enjoyed the formality of alleys, arbours, cascades, and fountains. He also enjoyed 'a *Mount* . . . to looke abroad into the Fields', an early reference to the charms of drawing in the surrounding landscape. Bacon inherited the family estate at Gorhambury (Hertfordshire) in 1601 and in 1608 gave 'directions of a plott to be made to turn ye pond yard into a place of pleasure'. In this he was inspired by the activities of his cousin Robert Cecil at HATFIELD HOUSE in the same county. The author John Aubrey saw Bacon's garden in 1656 long after Bacon's death and left a detailed description of it. He was greatly struck by a triple avenue leading to the house whose central avenue was so broad that 'three coaches may passe abreast'. He noted that the avenues were planted with a very wide range of trees—chestnut (*Castanea sativa*), beech, elm, hornbeam, service tree (*Sorbus domestica*), and 'Spanish-ash' (presumably a *Fraxinus* species). The pond yard garden was 1.6 hectares/4 acres in area and at its centre was a square pool clasped by four L-shaped pools. On a square island in the central pool was 'a curious banquetting-house of Roman architecture'. Aubrey noticed that pools under water were decorated with coloured pebbles.   PT

Bad Muskau ⊛

Saxony, Germany. Approximately 41 km/25 miles north of the city of Görlitz lies the park

---

Visualization of the **Hanging Gardens of Babylon** by the archaeologist Stephanie Dalley.

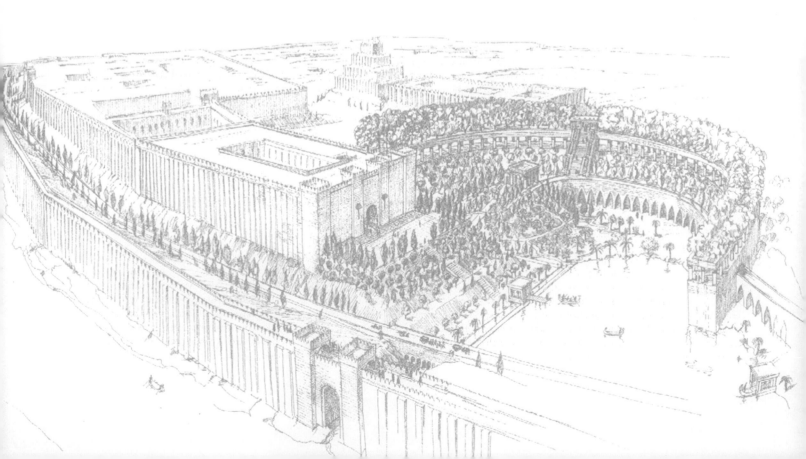

of Muskau, which was begun in 1811 by one of the most talented and influential German garden designers of the 19th century, the eccentric Prince Hermann of PÜCKLER-MUSKAU. Through his lavish work *Andeutungen über Landschaftsgärtnerei* (Hints on Landscape Gardening, 1834) Pückler exerted a considerable influence on contemporary garden design and documented a great amount of his work at Muskau. Pückler, who was strongly influenced by Humphry REPTON, created a vast landscape park which covers a total of c.830 hectares/2,050 acres, most of which lies in Poland today. After Muskau was sold due to financial difficulties in 1845 and Pückler had moved to his second family seat at BRANITZ, the park was completed by several other garden designers, one of whom was Eduard PETZOLD. The park consists of the following sections: the Schlosspark, Badepark, and Bergpark on the German side as well as the Unterpark, the Arboretum (1824), and the Braunsdorfer Felder on the Polish side. The layout of Muskau is characterized by hilly sections beside the flat meadows of the river Neisse, a great number of old trees (beeches, oaks, and limes), undulations, woodland and fields, garden buildings (of which several have been destroyed), and long vistas that connect picturesque scenes. Sixteen bridges and viaducts once connected the various parts. Pückler took great care to integrate the beauty of the landscape into his overall design, but also 'helped nature', e.g. by channelling a narrow, artificial tributary of the river Neisse (Hermannsneisse) into the lake around the palace. Skilfully constructed embankments appear as if they were perfectly natural. The park was severely damaged in 1945 and has been carefully reconstructed and restored since the 1950s. During the 1980s and 1990s, the collaboration to restore the park on both sides of the Neisse was intensified and an outstanding job creation programme in both Germany and Poland is helping to restore great parts of the park, albeit mainly in Poland. As a result the park was inscribed on the World Heritage List in 2004.   AK

Bagatelle, Château de.
See PARIS PARKS AND GARDENS.

Bagh-e Delgosha ⊛
Shiraz, Iran. Although famous as a garden during Safavid times (1502–1736) and possibly dating to the 11th century, the Bagh-e Delgosha (Garden of Heart's Ease) is now much reduced in size, having suffered from flooding and earthquakes through the centuries. Lying to the north-east of the main avenue in Shiraz, it was first restored by the Regent Karim Khan Zand in the 18th century but in 1845 came into the possession of a member of the Qavam ol-Molk family (now known as the Qavam-Shirazi) who used the Bagh-e Delgosha as a winter residence. Today the central water channel, originally fed by its own *qanat* (underground water conduit), is still flanked by orange trees as described by earlier travellers. Date palms, pomegranates, bushes of double yellow jasmine, walnut trees, and weeping mulberries, all traditional garden plants in the south of Persia, augment the scheme.   PHo

Bagh-e Doulatabad ⊛
Yazd, Iran, was created in the second half of the 18th century by Mohammad Taqi Khan, a governor of the town. The Doulatabad garden depended on water brought from the Shirkuh mountains by *qanats* (underground water conduits). With Yazd, surrounded by desert on the Iranian plateau, having the hottest summers in Iran, water features were limited to one outside octagonal pool with five interior pools cooled by breezes captured by a high wind tower (*badjir*) fanning cold air into basement rooms. A winter pavilion faced south down a widely spaced avenue of pines and cypresses, while the summer pavilion was shaded by a cypress grove. The walled enclosure, extending to 3 hectares/7.5 acres, was always a productive one with orchards of pomegranates and a vineyard, still evident today. The garden (2005) is currently under restoration.   PHo

Bagh-e Eram ⊛
Shiraz, Iran. This mainly 19th-century garden, with an area of 23 hectares/57.5 acres and now the University Botanic Garden, has origins in the Seljuk period (11th–12th centuries). Laid out in traditional CHAHAR BAGH or 'fourfold' style, with verdant orange groves flanking axial and cross-axial waterways and alleys of tall cypress and stately pines, the garden is luxuriantly planted with Judas trees, lilacs, rose bushes (including Banksian roses), wisteria, and other exotics. Scented Brompton and Virginia stocks grow in pale terracotta pots, artistically arranged in colour schemes by the gardeners. Nightingales, emblems of Shiraz and of poetic imagery, still sing in the trees. The Qajar pavilion, overlooking a square reflecting tank at the top of the garden, was built by Mohammad Hassan, a famous Shirazi architect of the mid 19th century. Thirty rooms on two storeys are tiled with quotations from the poetry of Hāfeiz.   PHo

Bagh-e Fin ⊛
Kashan, Iran. The walled Fin Garden, outside the city of Kashan, is the most beautiful in Iran and the best preserved, with 400-year-old cypresses towering over bubbling water channels lined with turquoise tiles. The garden has always been ascribed to the great Shah Abbas but its 17th-century date is often queried as records affirm Shah Tahmasp visited here in the early 16th century. It seems the oasis garden, fed by water brought by underground *qanat* (conduit) from the distant mountains, may well have had a longer history, but it was Shah Abbas who built a new royal dwelling in the garden and probably enriched the rills with tiling. Qajar restorations and a late 19th-century pavilion do nothing to mar the effects. The water, stored in a great reservoir outside the walls, still works by gravity. Shade from the trees makes growing roses, always a tradition here, almost impossible today, but delicately scented rose-water is sold in the kiosk in the centre of the garden.   PHo

Bagh-e Golshan ⊛
Tabas, province of Yasd, Iran. The Bagh-e Golshan (8 hectares/20 acres) is in one of the most remote towns of Iran on the central Iranian plateau 600 m/2,000 ft above sea level between the great salt deserts of Dasht-i-Kavir and Dasht-i-Lut. Although its major monuments were devastated by an earthquake in 1978, Tabas still retains its 18th-century garden, laid out on a slope in standard Persian style with a series of low terraces and rushing cascades, ample water coming from a series of natural springs. The original pavilion was destroyed in the earthquake but the garden, its outer walls now restored, suffered little. In the benign climate and with ample water, the garden is intensely romantic, vibrant with scents and birdsong. It overflows with both traditional trees—cypresses, date palms, citrus groves, pomegranates, jasmine, and Judas trees—but is augmented with Australian eucalypts, the grey-leaved *Populus euphratica*, cycads, roses, and hollyhocks, all cared for by cheerful, skilled gardeners. It is paradise on earth, well worth the seven-hour desert drive. Today the garden belongs to the town.   PHo

Bagh-e Shahzadeh ⊛
Mahan, Iran, is situated in the desert south-east of Mahan and backed by distant snow-capped mountains from which water comes by *qanat* (underground conduit) to a vast cistern outside the garden walls. The Bagh-e Shahzadeh, also known as the Farman Farma or Prince's Garden, although dating only to the 1880s, expresses the true spirit of a traditional Persian oasis garden. Constructed by Naser ud-Douleh, governor of Kerman, the walled enclosure has a central layout of cascades, pools, and fountains flanked by orchards of pear trees, citrus, walnuts, and pomegranate. Today the ruined summer pavilion looks up the restored

waterway, in which fountains sparkle in the sunlight, its edges shaded by tall cypresses. A few roses struggle to perform. The governor's residence at the top (now a restaurant) is glimpsed through a mist of water jets.   PHo

Bagh-e Takht,

Shiraz, Iran. The Bagh-e Takht, the Garden of the Throne, with its legendary seven terraces, lay at the foot of a rocky hillside in the northern edge of Shiraz. Covering an area of 1.4 hectares/ 3.5 acres when first constructed in the 11th century, its site has been built over recently by a modern hotel complex. The Takht may well be the garden described by the French jeweller Jean-Baptiste Tavernier during his Persian travels in 1639. He called it the Bagh-e Ferdous. 'It is full of fruit trees and roses in abundance. At the end of the garden stands a great piece of Building and below a large pool affords it water' (*Six Voyages . . . through Turkey and Persia and the East Indies*, 1678). Today the pool is dry and little remains of past glory.   PHo

Bagh-i Wafa,

Kabul, Afghanistan, the Garden of Fidelity, was the favourite garden of the 1st Mughal Emperor BĀBUR and is described in his memoirs. It was divided into the four plots of the classic CHAHAR BAGH with running water and a reservoir. Here the Emperor had imported and planted such trees as citron, orange, plantain, and pomegranate, together with sugar cane. A later painting of the Mughal school shows Bābur directing the construction of this garden. He was able to visit it during a pause in his campaigns, and to enjoy it in its full maturity. His reference to the mildness of the climate, and the nature of the vegetation itself, suggest that it was not in the town of Kabul, but at a lower and milder altitude. There are the remains of a garden on the Mughal pattern lower down near the river Kabul at Nimla near Jelalabad, but no firm identification of the site can be made.   SMH

Balaine, Arboretum de ⊛

Allier, France, founded in 1804 by Aglaë Adanson, who came to Balaine at the age of 30, and whose father Michel Adanson had worked in Louis XV's botanic garden at the Petit Trianon (see VERSAILLES, CHÂTEAU DE). The soil is mostly acid here and, at an altitude of 228 m/ 750 ft, the climate is far from benign—the winter temperature frequently descends to -15 ˚C/5 ˚F and has been known to go as low as -20 ˚C/-2 ˚F. This part of France, however, is famous for the remarkable oak forest of the Tronçais, planted in the 17th century as a source of timber for the French navy and to this day the source of very expensive timber for barrels

for winemaking. No one, however, had ever planted in these parts the great range of exotics which the young Mademoiselle Adanson built up, so she was largely navigating without a map. She drained the land, forming attractive winding streams, and in an area of 21 hectares/ 52 acres built up a very large collection of woody plants. She arranged the plants with skill in the style of a *parc à l'anglaise* and from early on recognized the possibilities of sheltering less hardy species in woodland glades. Today, with over 1,200 species of trees and shrubs, and much decorative underplanting of herbaceous perennials, it is one of the largest and most attractive arboreta in France. A nursery based at the arboretum sells an excellent range of woody plants.   PT

Balbianello, Villa del ⊛

Lake Como, Italy. The ravishing setting of villa and casino on the Lavedo Point thrusting out into Lake Como, combined with arrival via a romantic watergate, sets the scene for this immaculately kept garden, where holm oaks and plane trees are pruned to an exceptional standard. The site allows views down the three branches of the lake fronting the promontory of Serbelloni. The first villa was built in 1540 but was later moved inland because of danger of flooding. In 1787 the property was acquired by Cardinal Durini who in 1790 erected the elegant airy CASINO with loggia, today garlanded with *Ficus pumila* and flanked by a library and music room. The property now belongs to the Fondo per l'Ambiente Italiano, so its future is assured.   PHo

Balchik, Palace of ⊛

Balchik, Bulgaria, named 'the quiet nest', built on a serene site of 36 hectares/90 acres on the Black Sea coast by Queen Maria of Romania between 1924 and 1936. The palace is composed of several villas, a chapel, and a Roman bath, designed by Italian architects in various styles, predominantly Orthodox and oriental. The dynamic topography of the park gave its creator, the French garden designer Jules Janine (1879-1936), scope to lay out terraces, thematic gardens, and intimate corners interconnected by stairs and archways. The rare abundance of springs was used to form canals and cascades. With a strongly geometrical layout, the park boasts cobble paths, pergolas, ponds, and walls, some of distinct Muslim patterns, and a variety of materials. Most striking however is the collection of ornamental plants—over 200 species of trees and shrubs, 500 flower varieties, and 600 cacti species—arranged in the magnificent Garden of Allah, Blue Wave Garden, and Lilium Alley, all decorated with amphorae and other earthenware pots. Since

the early 1950s the park has been managed by Sofia University Botanical Gardens.   ASG

Bali.

The Indonesian island of Bali emerged from the sea in a series of volcanic explosions 2-3 million years ago. This turbulent beginning is responsible for the remarkable diversity of topography that can be found in its relatively small area, consisting of just 5,500 sq. kms/3,150 sq. miles, which ranges from volcanic peaks and valleys to lowland plains and arid coasts, with numerous rivers and streams. The extraordinarily fertile soil in higher areas supports a rich abundance of jungle trees, *kebun*, or home gardens, and rice, the staple food, grown in terraced fields that create spectacular vistas. Mount Agung, at over 3,000 m/9,842 ft the tallest volcano, dominates the island's scenery, as well as much of its ritual life.

Unlike the rest of Indonesia, which has the largest Muslim population of any country, Bali is Hindu and its culture and garden development also followed a different path. Traditional gardens are rather sparse, with one or two trees, an expanse of bare packed earth, and sometimes a few flowering shrubs. Temple and palace gardens are more complex, with elaborate water features—ponds, fountains, and moats—and ornate structures made of stone. Temple gardens usually contain a *waringin*, or banyan, tree (*Ficus beghalensis*), believed to be the abode of spirits and, indeed, often the original reason for building a temple or shrine. The most famous temple garden is Pura Taman Ayun, while perhaps the most beautiful of the remaining palaces is that of the former kings of Klungkung, where the outstanding feature is a *bale kambang*, or 'floating pavilion', surrounded by an artificial lake full of water lilies. Both are located in the hills near Ubud, an area preferred by the Balinese, who rarely built either palaces or temples near the sea.

More contemporary garden designs came with the discovery of Bali by international travellers. Dutch colonial rule reached the island at the beginning of the 20th century with a series of violent encounters, in one of which the royal families committed mass suicide rather than surrender to the invaders. Thereafter, however, the Dutch tended to leave Bali more or less alone, allowing its people to continue using their own language and customs and encouraging their traditional arts. Bali's legendary reputation as a tropical paradise arose from the enthusiasm of a small number of outsiders in the late 1920s and 1930s, among them writers, painters, and anthropologists. Some of them settled for lengthy periods on the island, mostly near the sea at Sanur but also in the cultural centre of

Ubud. The popular author Vicki Baum, for example, wrote a novel, *A Tale from Bali*, about the Dutch occupation; the Mexican-born painter Miguel Covarrubias produced another one with alluring illustrations; the German Walter Spies became both a painter and a choreographer; and the anthropologist Margaret Mead wrote about its complex society. Such works extolled the beauty of Balinese scenery, its abundance of artistic activity, and prepared the way for the age of mass tourism which arrived in the 1960s when air travel made the island more readily accessible.

Aside from those in the temples, nearly all the best gardens today were created in this later period and reflect contemporary styles of tropical design. Bali has an estimated 4,500 native species, though the great majority of trees and shrubs seen in gardens were introduced fairly recently, some by the Dutch from the great botanical garden at Bogor, on Java, many others by private growers and landscape designers. Made Wijaya, or Michael White as he was known in his native Australia, who has lived in Bali since 1975, has been responsible for a number of notable creations, including the extensive garden of the Bali Hyatt Hotel in Sanur, the Four Seasons Hotel on the Bukit Peninsula, and his own house, the Villa Bebek, near Sanur.

Gardening conditions vary in different parts of the island. Thanks to its natural setting in the hills, with dramatic ravines, rivers and streams, waterfalls, and the most scenic of Bali's terraced rice fields, Ubud has some of the most beautiful creations. Walter Spies's former home at Campuan, 'Where Two Rivers Meet,' now a boutique hotel, consists of a number of bungalows on a hillside, planted with ferns, gingers, *Dracaena*, palms, and other jungle-type specimens; water flows down from one level to another, eventually to a river at the bottom of the ravine. A more recent garden is that of Linda Garland, an interior decorator who has made her home in Bali; it has numerous species of bamboo and has been subtly landscaped to blend naturally into neighbouring rice fields. Just north of Ubud is Begawan Giri, which began as a private holiday home and is now a collection of villas for rent by the affluent. To the already luxuriant landscape, which includes a holy spring believed to have magical powers, designers Karl Princic and John Pettigrew added numerous other ornamentals, among them heliconias, gingers, hibiscus, anthuriums, orchids, and giant maidenhair ferns.

At Sanur on the sea coast, notable gardens include Batujimba, a private estate with well-tended lawns contrasting with densely planted beds and vine-draped walls of coral stone;

Taman Mertasari (Garden of Holy Water Essence), which has several Balinese-style houses and a large lotus pond in which several of the property's original coconut palms grow on islands; Made Wijaya's Villa Bebak, a traditional arrangement of courtyards that offer both privacy and a sense of surprise; and the Bali Hyatt Hotel, which covers some 15 hectares/36 acres on the sea and contains over 500 different species of trees, shrubs, and decorative ground covers.

A different sort of terrain prevails in the southernmost extremity of the island along Jimbaran Bay and the Bukit peninsula. The soil is sandy, lime based, and arid, hardly ideal for luxuriant planting. Yet several superb gardens have been created here through the use of such drought-resistant plants as bougainvillea, agave, adenium, pandanus, and plumeria and also by bringing in topsoil for less hardy specimens. Made Wijaya, together with Ir Ngurah Aetawa, Dewar Sedana, and Drs Nyoman Miyoga, designed the 22-hectare/55-acre gardens of the Four Seasons resort at Jimburan, laid out like a series of seven villages. Another impressive garden, covering 40 acres, surrounds the Grand Hyatt at Nusa Dua. This was designed by Tong, Clark, and McClelvey, a Honolulu-based firm, executed on site by local designer Indo Sekar, and was inspired by Balinese palaces with numerous water features and courtyards.   WLW

Ballenstedt Palace ⊛
Ballenstedt, Quedlinburg, Saxony-Anhalt, Germany. The park at Ballenstedt represents one of the last examples of the œuvre of the landscape architect P. J. LENNÉ, combining the informal style with elements of the formal garden. Today the estate consists of the old palace with a theatre, a northern terrace, a formal garden with water axis, and a landscape garden with three ponds and a mill. Originally an 11th-century monastery, the palace building was used after major reconstructions in 1748 as permanent residence of the Anhalt-Bernburg princedom. A formal kitchen garden at the bottom of the almost bare castle hill had been the only garden when first works to embellish the surroundings started in the middle of the 18th century. The area was planted with trees and shrubs and made accessible. Several castles were erected nearby, serving as eyecatchers. The park already gave the impression of a romantic landscape decorated with numerous features, such as various small buildings and seats, when the changes by Lenné in the 1850s and 1860s took place. An impressive cascading water axis was constructed, being an example of the use of patterns found in the Italian Renaissance garden. After a period of neglect at the end of

the 19th century Ballenstedt Park was municipalized in 1922. During the Second World War it suffered from a considerable loss of sculptures. In 1950 after its listing as a historic monument reconstruction works began, which continue to the present day.
HM/HH

Balleroy, Château de ⊛
Calvados, France, built between 1616 and 1636 for Jean de Choisy to the designs of François MANSART, one of his earliest works. The village was laid out at the same time and its main street, to the east of the chateau, today lined with pollarded limes, forms an avenue leading to it—doubtless designed by Mansart himself. The effect for the visitor approaching from this direction is especially splendid, for the road rises and falls, and the chateau is suddenly revealed in the distance from the crest of a hill. In the chateau's forecourt is a pair of 17th-century style PARTERRES *de broderie*, the work of Achille DUCHÊNE in 1934. Old woodland, chiefly of beech and oaks, presses in behind the chateau forming a wild background to its suave elegance.   PT

Balze, Villa Le ⊛
Fiesole, near Florence, Italy, was built between 1912 and 1913 by the English architect Cecil PINSENT for the American philosopher Charles Augustus Strong. Both the villa and its integrated garden are a masterpiece of spatial organization, proportion, and planning, to rival Michelozzo's adjacent Villa MEDICI, a 15th-century engineering feat poised on the same steep slope. On a narrow ledge of the cliff (*balze* means cliffs), Pinsent constructed the villa and linear garden in a series of interior and exterior compartments allowing long views to give a feeling of penetration, each space glimpsed in turn from the preceding 'room'. Dramatic panoramic views over the valley of the Arno and Florence are revealed as carefully chosen surprises. The garden merges gently into a wood, below which sun-loving rosemary, *Cistus*, and other native plants fall down the hillside. At the back of the house Pinsent added an elaborate 17th-century-style dripping grotto in tufa stone and shells, framed by staircases, one of which led to the original entrance from the Fiesole lane.   PHo

Bambouseraie de Prafrance ⊛
Anduze, Gard, France, was started in the 1850s by a traveller and amateur botanist, Eugène Mazel, who became fascinated by bamboos. He built up a collection but ran into financial difficulties in 1890. The estate changed hands more than once but was taken over in recent times by the Crouzet family, who also run a

nursery on the site. With deep alluvial soil, a Mediterranean climate, and a relatively high rainfall of 1,100 mm/44 in (supplemented by irrigation canals) the conditions are very favourable for the cultivation of bamboos, of which almost 200 species and cultivars may be seen. Although other plants are grown here, in particular Asiatic shrubs and trees (some of which go back to Mazel's time), it is the great stands of bamboos that give the landscape its rare character. Some of these grow to immense height—*Phyllostachys edulis* can reach a height of 27 m/87 ft. In addition to the garden, which covers an area of 34 hectares/84 acres, and nursery there is a shop which sells an extraordinary selection of objects made from bamboo. Visitors to the Bambouseraie may also be interested to know that Anduze is also a centre of pottery craftsmanship. The firm of Les Enfants de Boisset has been making garden pots since the 17th century when they were supplied to VERSAILLES.   PT

Bampfylde, Coplestone Warre

(1720–91), English landowner, soldier, landscaper, and artist. In 1750 he inherited the HESTERCOMBE estate in Somerset where his mother's family, the Warres, had lived since 1391. He created a landscape park in the picturesque valley—'a rural sequestered vale' as the traveller Arthur Young described it in 1771. He was a friend of Sir Charles Kemeys Tynte of Halswell (Somerset) and Henry Hoare II of STOURHEAD, with both of whom he shared a passion for landscaping. He was much admired by another landscaper, William SHENSTONE, who wrote of him, his 'fortune, person, figure and accomplishments can hardly leave him long unnoticed in any place where he resides'. His watercolour paintings of his own park at Hestercombe and of Stourhead are valuable contemporary records.   PT

Bancroft, Ruth, Garden ⊗

Walnut Creek, California, USA, the life's collection and garden refuge of Ruth Bancroft. Located on a section of a former ranch, the garden covers 1.6 hectares/2.4 acres and was started in the early 1950s, with an urge for collecting succulents. Plants from other arid zones found their way here. The collection, mostly in pots, was transferred to garden plantings in 1972 when a walnut orchard died and left a space to be planted. Mrs Bancroft, trained as an architect, has created a composition of rich colours and textures with help and support from nurseryman Lester Hawkins, friends, and family. The collection of cactus, succulents, shrubs, and trees native to Africa, Australia, California, Chile, and Mexico, was introduced as small (4.5 l/1 gal or less)

potted specimens, but now they enclose and populate the garden as mature specimens. The garden is naturalistic in style and bold in the use of exotic plants. African aloes, haworthias, and gasterias are featured components of the colourful array of succulents. Pines and mesquite (*Prosopis* species) trees form the main canopy sheltering the garden. Concern about this remarkable garden's future led the GARDEN CONSERVANCY, a new non-profit organization, to set up a local group to operate and maintain the garden. The Ruth Bancroft Garden was the Conservancy's first such project, and it now stands as a model for preservation of other private gardens in communities across America. The new Ruth Bancroft Garden organization operates the garden for the public, with Ruth Bancroft *in situ*.   PC

bandstand.

As an ornamental and ingeniously practical garden building the bandstand was a universal feature of 19th-century, and later, public parks in Britain. Its essence is a raised platform with a roof which both protected the band from rain and, more importantly, served as a kind of sounding board which magnified the music. As often as not it was built with a cast-iron superstructure and a high-pitched circular or polygonal roof. The first cast-iron bandstand was made in 1861 by Captain Francis Fowke of the Royal Engineers for the Royal Horticultural Society Gardens in South Kensington—an elegant structure with a roof of oriental character. However, the principle was anticipated before 1751 by a two-storey brick pavilion in Vauxhall Gardens (see PLEASURE GARDEN) with the band playing in the upper storey. Although many 19th-century bandstands have been lost, many also remain and are still used for musical performances.
                                                          PT

HAZEL CONWAY, 'The Royal Horticultural Society Bandstand mystery—or, what happened to the first cast-iron bandstands', *Garden History*, Vol. 29: No. 2 (2001).

Bánffy Palace.

See BONȚIDA.

Banister, John

(*c*.1650–1692), American missionary plant collector. Born in Gloucester, he received his BA Oxford in 1671, and three years later Bishop COMPTON sent him as Anglican minister to the West Indies and later to Virginia. He was a competent botanist and developed into an enthusiastic plant collector. By 1680 Banister had completed the first study of American plants, the catalogue of which appeared in Revd John Ray's (1627–1705) three-volume *Historia*

Plantarum (1686–1704). Banister collected material also for the newly opened CHELSEA PHYSIC GARDEN and OXFORD BOTANIC GARDEN. He proved to have a good eye for potential garden plants, discovering and introducing to cultivation the first magnolia *Magnolia virginiana* (Sweet bay), *Dicentra cucullaria* (Dutchman's breeches), the Scarlet oak (*Quercus coccinea*), and the beautiful *Liquidambar styraciflua*. Banister died in May 1692 while collecting plants on the banks of the Roanoke river in Virginia.   MC-C

Banks, Sir Joseph

(1743–1820), English scientific patron, distinguished botanist. Joseph Banks came from a wealthy Lincolnshire family. At Oxford University he was frustrated that no botanical lectures were available, so he arranged for the eminent botanist Israel Lyons (1739–75) to lecture. Banks was elected Fellow of the Royal Society in 1761 and five years later undertook a journey to Newfoundland. In 1768 with influence from Lord Sandwich (1718–92), First Lord of the Admiralty, he sailed as botanist accompanying Captain James Cook (1728–79) on the *Endeavour*. Sailing to Tahiti to record the Transit of Venus and later voyaging and discovering New Zealand and Australia, his companions were Dr Daniel Solander (1733–82), a pupil of Linnaeus and later Banks's librarian, and Sydney Parkinson (*c*.1745–1771) the natural history draughtsman, who died during the voyage. After three years the *Endeavour* returned in triumph with some 1,500 Antipodean plants. The following year Banks made his last expedition, returning from Iceland with specimens of lava which were incorporated in the rock garden at CHELSEA PHYSIC GARDEN. He became honorary director of Kew and in 1778, president of the Royal Society, holding both posts until his death in 1820.

Banks's single-minded but pragmatic approach to scientific discovery dominated the botanical world for almost 50 years. He was perhaps the first person to understand the universality of the natural world, and in 1781 was knighted for his services to science. Banks's global vision decided him to dispatch Kew trained gardeners to collect plants from overseas. They included Francis Masson (1741–1806) to the Cape, William Kerr (d. 1814) to China, Archibald Menzies (1754–1842) the surgeon-botanist who explored the western shores of America onboard the *Discovery* (1790–5) and Peter Good (d. 1803) who accompanied Matthew Flinders (1774–1814) on the circumnavigation of Australia. Banks too was responsible for planning the Tahitian breadfruit (*Artocarpus altilis*) voyage of Captain Bligh (1754–1817) and its subsequent second ▶

entirely successful voyage to the West Indies. In 1804 Banks with six friends formed what eventually became the ROYAL HORTICULTURAL SOCIETY. During his travels he made only two plant introductions (from Newfoundland) but his horticultural legacy is remembered in the naming of the *Banksia* genus of Australia.

MC-C

Bankshaven,

Newnan, Georgia, USA, located approximately an hour's drive south of Atlanta, is the estate home of William C. Banks Jr. Bankshaven features extensive landscape grounds and a *c.*1828 federal-style house designed by New England-born architect-builder Daniel Pratt of Temple, New Hampshire. In 1968, this imposing structure was moved from Jones County, Georgia, to its present location. The Pratt house replaced an original Tudor Revival structure built in the 1920s by Mr and Mrs William Banks Sr. Bankshaven, as it is now known, includes a variety of formal and informal gardens designed by noted landscape architect William C. Pauley (1893–1995), Georgia's first professionally licensed landscape architect. Development of the gardens and

grounds was initiated in 1928 under the direction of William Banks Sr. and was continued under the direction of his son, William C. Banks Jr. Today, the property exhibits a variety of landscape styles and themes which include: an informal entrance drive and arrival court situated in a woodland setting; a grassy terrace on the south side of the house that sweeps past a ha-ha wall to a small spring-fed lake that dates back to Civil War times; a box-bordered parterre and maze with a Gothic-styled gazebo; a formal garden east of the house with a cast-iron fountain bordered by boxwood and colourful flower beds; a large walled garden designed for the display of roses, seasonal flowers, and bulbs; and a secluded swimming pool with a Victorian-style pool house and pavilion. Bankshaven remains in the ownership of William Banks as a private residence.   JRC

Banmu Yuan,

Beijing, China, was once described as 'the most beautiful Chinese garden in Peking', but its fame rests also on that of its owners and the fine art collections they gathered there. Said to have been built *c.*1680 by Li Yu, a well-known dramatist, poet, and essayist, for an official in the Ministry of Construction, it lies off Huangmi hutong near the north-east corner of the Forbidden City, and still contains a 'false mountain' of rocks supposedly composed by Li himself. Banmu means Half Acre, a modest name in keeping with the one Li Yu chose for his own Peking home: 'The Garden Small as a Mustard Seed' (Jiezi Yuan). In the early 19th century, after many ownership changes, a high Manchu official named Linqing heard of Banmu Yuan while drinking tea in the Mustard Seed garden. Though he had to wait 30 years to acquire it, in 1840 he began to restore the estate, added to its art and rock collection, and eventually left an intimate record of it in his woodcut-illustrated diaries. Today the garden still has much that was built in Linqing's time: in plan the most interesting feature is the pavilion shaped like a Greek cross that stands on a rocky isle dividing the Pond of Rippling Jade. The characters for this name, encouraging an optimistic interpretation of murky grey-green city water, were once cut into one of the edging rocks. To the south a hexagonal pavilion on a rocky mound overlooks the whole garden, with its zigzag *lang* (see CHINA) gallery connecting halls and study rooms to the east and, to the west, Li Yu's old rockery of yellow stones from the Yongning mountains near the Western Imperial Tombs. Though small, Banmu Yuan is significant as perhaps still the finest example of an old Beijing garden, and for the strangely unchanging atmosphere it preserves.   C-ZC/MK

Banqiao,

Taibei, Taiwan, Republic of China, has long been the most famous private compound on the large and subtropical island of Taiwan. This garden in the suburbs of Taibei was built between 1888 and 1893 by Lin Weiyuan, a minor official in the Qing government and a member of an immensely successful merchant family who had moved there, four generations earlier, from Fujian province on the mainland.

The garden, covering *c.*1.6 hectares/4 acres north-east of the family courtyards, uniquely combined the rockeries, ponds, and clustered buildings of southern Chinese gardens with European-influenced axial planning and flower beds. It was composed of four building groups, including a banqueting hall, guest houses, and the master's study, mostly connected by open *lang* (see CHINA) corridors. An irregular-shaped Pond of the Tree Shadows lay between them and an artificial rockery which rose in swooping curves along the boundary wall. For viewing the garden by moonlight, a pavilion set in the lake was built with a flat roof, something rare in China. Although it was neglected for years after the Japanese occupation (1895–1945), extremely detailed plans and reconstructions, which give an excellent idea of the garden, have been made for its proposed restoration.

D-HL/MK

Barbarigo Pizzoni Ardemani, Villa ⊕

Valsanzibio, near Padua, Italy. This unique late 17th-century garden, with water as its central theme, is laid out in the valley amphitheatre below the villa backed by the Euganean Hills south of Padua. Planned on two axes with hedged alleys, water canals, a box-tree maze, and a rabbit island (the Garena), the garden was originally approached by water through the imposing baroque Portale de Diana, which marks the ancient landing stage for arrivals from Venice. Through its central archway a series of fish ponds flanked by statues and linked by cascades set in rustic rockwork are glimpsed to create the east–west axis. Avenues of clipped evergreens backed by cypresses and pine trees on the cross-axis link the water features with the villa and stretch up the hillsides providing a leafy background to statues of mythological figures. From 1669 an earlier 17th-century garden was 'improved' by Antonio Barbarigo, a Venetian procurator, until his death in 1702. His extensive iconographical landscape was designed to represent the Garden of Eden as a rural oasis, in contrast to the struggle of contemporary political life. The garden has been admirably restored by Prince Pizzoni Ardemani.   PHo

Barillet-Deschamps, Jean-Pierre

(1824–73). Barillet-Deschamps came to a slightly shadowy prominence as head gardener between 1855 and 1869 under Jean Charles Adolphe ALPHAND in HAUSSMANN's transformation of Paris. Haussmann himself, in his *Mémoires* (1893), refers somewhat disparagingly to 'ce pauvre Barillet-Deschamps . . . avec ces grandes qualités et ses petits défauts' (that poor Barillet-Deschamps . . . with his great qualities and minor faults). The qualities that Haussmann admired were Barillet-Deschamps's skills at laying out undulating lawns interspersed with groups of trees and shrubs and mounds of evergreens enlivened with flowering plants. Among his faults were 'un certain abus de détails et un peu trop d'allées' (a certain weakness in details and rather too many paths). He worked in particular on the Bois de Boulogne (after 1855) (see PARIS PARKS AND GARDENS) where his skill in creating an undulating terrain enlivened a very flat site, especially at the Jardin d'Acclimatation (1859–60) in the Bois de Boulogne; and in the Bois de Vincennes (1860–5) he laid out lakes, streams, and winding paths; at the Parc des Buttes-Chaumont (1864–7), for an especially complex site, with an immense range of ingredients, all his talents were required. Shortly after he left Paris and, with the help of Haussmann's recommendation, acquired a job with the viceroy of Egypt, Ismail Pacha, but, as Haussmann wrote, 'il ne put supporter cette transplantation, et mourut promptement à son nouveau poste' (he could not stand the change and shortly died in his new position).

PT

Barnsley House ⊕

near Cirencester, Gloucestershire, England, is a 17th-century village house with a garden made by Rosemary VEREY which influenced a generation of gardeners. Rosemary Verey and her husband came to live at Barnsley in 1951 and, strongly influenced by her knowledge of garden history, she started to make a garden on the irregular, slightly undulating 1.6-hectare/4-acre site. She never made a master plan for the garden, which evolved gradually over a long period. Nonetheless she established a bold pattern which provided a flexible framework for planting. South and south-east of the house she laid out a series of formal gardens which take their cue from the house. On the other side of the house, across broad lawns, she made the Wilderness, in effect a miniature arboretum with shrubs. The formal garden has strong axes. From the garden door of the house an avenue of Irish yews runs along a paved path planted with rock roses (*Helianthemum* cvs.). A grass walk forms a cross-axis with a parallel lime and laburnum walk. The latter, underplanted with red 'Apeldoorn' tulips in May followed by the purple drumsticks of *Allium hollandicum* in June when the laburnums flower, became one of the most photographed scenes in any English garden of its time. An ornamental kitchen garden inspired many imitations. Throughout the garden lively design was matched by brilliant planting and sculptures and garden buildings were woven into the scene. Mrs Verey died in 2001 and the house has now become a hotel. PT

baroque gardens.

The term baroque embraces several nuances of meaning which make it admirably useful, in a vague sort of way, to convey notions of drama (even theatricality), splendour, muscular vigour, monumentalism, and movement. Sometimes it is thought of as a sturdier form of ROCOCO which, in itself, is scarcely possible accurately to define. The *Oxford English Dictionary* says that the term is applied in particular 'to a florid style of architectural decoration which arose in Italy in the late Renaissance and became prevalent in Europe during the 18th century'. *Baedeker's Central Italy & Rome* (5th edn. 1877) refers to 'the degenerated Renaissance known as Baroque . . . An undoubted vigour in the disposition of detail, a feeling for vastness and pomp, together with an internal decoration which spared neither colour nor costly material to secure an effect of dazzling splendour.' Allen Weiss in *Mirrors of Infinity: The French Formal Garden and 17th-Century Metaphsyics* (1995) finds the term ambiguous but associates it with impermanence and movement as opposed to the harmony and immutability of the Italian Renaissance. He quotes the sculptor BERNINI as saying, 'A man is never so similar to himself as when he is in movement.' Bernini's bust of Louis XIV (1665) shows a man apparently turning sharply to his right, waves of hair tumbling vigorously about his face and shoulders; his clothing seems to be swept as though by a violent wind. The gardens of Louis XIV's era, in particular those of André LE NÔTRE are characterized by vastness, drama, splendour, and movement. At VERSAILLES the chief axis of the garden, focused on the royal apartments at the centre of the chateau, divides the PARTERRE d'Eau, descends a slope past the Parterre de Latone, runs serenely along the TAPIS VERT, and is then continued by the Grand Canal, which seems to run to the horizon beyond which, for all we know, the axis could run for ever. An exactly similar effect is achieved at VAUX-LE-VICOMTE. At both Versailles and Vaux-le-Vicomte the chief axis is interrupted, but not broken, by the cross-axis of a canal which only serves to emphasize its insuperable nature. In contrast to the central axis both these gardens have a patchwork of BOSQUETS and parterres spreading out on each side. These garden spaces imply movement, as does the swirling pattern of the *parterres de broderie* so often found in French gardens of this kind. There is movement, too, in the fountains to which so much importance was attached at Versailles.

Other French gardens of the late 17th century, and continuing into the 18th century, share the qualities we associate with the baroque. Gardens of baroque character dominated European garden taste in the late 17th century and continued well into the 18th century. In England gardens were made in this tradition but none survives and none has been recreated. At Badminton (Gloucestershire), as displayed in KIP's engraving in *Britannia Illustrata* (1707), not only was the house pierced by a central axis extending deep into the landscape at either end but many other avenues radiated out from the pleasure grounds. The Kip engraving shows parterres, pools, fountains, and gargantuan intricately clipped *bosquets*. The gardens of CHATSWORTH seen in Kip's engraving are of similar style, except here is a sequence of parallel axes extending the lineaments of the garden into the greater landscape. These gardens were laid out by George LONDON and Henry WISE in the late 17th century. In the Netherlands Daniel Stoopendaal's bird's-eye view (1699) of Heemstede (near Utrecht) shows a layout of Versailles-like ambitions. Het LOO, although on a much smaller scale, has many parallels with Versailles, not least the Herculean imagery which was William III's riposte to the Apollonian imagery of Louis XIV. Baroque gardens were made in Germany at the Großer Garten, HERRENHAUSEN (1680), and at SCHLEIßHEIM (1715–17). In Spain at La GRANJA (from 1721) an elaborate French-inspired baroque garden was laid out. NAGYCENK (from 1750) in Hungary showed the baroque style in a modest compass of only 9 hectares/22 acres, and at FERTŐD (formerly Eszterháza) (from 1764) the spirit of Versailles is eloquently expressed. A precursor to all these, and the first garden in which the baroque character is plainly seen, is the Villa ALDOBRANDINI created in the early 17th century. Here drama, movement, and splendour are evoked with typical Italian brio.

PT

Barragán, Luis

(1902–88), Mexican architect and garden designer born in Guadalajara. After training as an engineer he travelled in Spain and France where, as an independent scholar, he studied architecture and gardens, attending lectures by Le Corbusier in Paris. He established an architectural pratice, at first in Guadalajara but from 1936 in Mexico City. Barragán was deeply influenced by modernist architecture but there was also a profound spiritual dimension to his work. At the huge housing development of PEDREGAL DE SAN ANGEL (1945–53) he created houses and luxuriantly planted gardens which lead into the existing dramatic scenery of lava. Bold rockwork, wild planting, leaping fountains, and serene spaces mediate between nature and artifice. Barragán had the humility to recognize at Pedregal that the natural landscape was of much greater beauty than anything a landscape designer could do. His Plaza del Bebedero de los Caballos (Plaza of the Horse Trough—he was a devoted horseman) in Las Arboledas, Mexico (1958–62), vividly displays the quality of his work to create a powerful sense of place with bold and simple means. The trough is a raised canal, with water trickling over its lip on either side. The plaza is shaded by great eucalyptus trees and, contrasting with serene white walls, one of which soars high among the trees, is a horizontal wall of intense blue. Free-standing walls, sometimes surfaced in stucco and often painted a bold colour, appeared in many of his designs. Barragán was awarded the Pritzker Architecture Prize in 1980. In his acceptance speech he spoke of the garden designer collaborating with nature: 'In a beautiful garden, the majesty of nature is ever present, but nature reduced to human proportions and this transformed into the most efficient haven against the agressiveness of contemporary life.' He valued solitude and silence, believing that 'silence sings'.   PT

Barres, Arboretum National des ⊕

Nogent-sur-Vernisson, Loiret, France. The estate was bought in 1821 by Philippe André de VILMORIN of the notable family of plantsmen and nurserymen. He and his descendants built up a collection of woody plants which is today one of the finest in France. The area of 35 hectares/86 acres given over to the ARBORETUM today is only a small part of a large estate which also includes an agricultural lycée and, housed in the chateau, the IFN (Inventaire Forestier National—national forestry inventory which lists and describes all woodland in France, *département* by *département*). The arboretum contains around 2,700 species with large collections of firs, pines, maples, and oaks. The Fruticetum Vilmorinianum, of shrubs and ornamental trees, has exceptional collections of some genera—150 species of thorn (*Crataegus*), for example. As a collection of noble old

specimens, and of many rarities, the arboretum is of great distinction.   PT

Barron, William

(1805–91), English gardener and garden designer. He became gardener to the Earl of Harrington at ELVASTON CASTLE in 1830, where he created a garden divided into compartments by hedges, each centred on a different style or feature. In order to make a garden that was instantly mature, he became his period's greatest expert at the transplanting of mature trees. On the Earl's death in 1851, the garden at Elvaston was opened to the public, and immediately created a fashion for architectural topiary in England. Barron established a nursery firm that lasted into the 20th century, both designing gardens and transplanting trees. His greatest notoriety in transplanting was achieved in 1880, when he moved the 800-year-old Buckland yew to the further end of the churchyard. In 1852 he published a book on his techniques, *The British Winter Garden*; one of his transplanting machines is preserved at Kew. As a landscape designer his most famous commissions in his later years were Locke Park, Barnsley, and Abbey Park, Leicester.   BE

Barry, Sir Charles

(1795–1860), English architect and garden designer. He became known in the 1830s for his introduction of Italianate domestic architecture into England, with a series of important country house commissions. In 1836 he was commissioned to build the new Houses of Parliament, and was knighted on their completion in 1852; this work resulted in a change of style, as he turned progressively to Tudor architecture as his model. As a garden designer Barry was most important for his country house gardens, modelled on Renaissance gardens he had seen in Italy on the grand tour in the 1820s. The first of these, Trentham, Staffordshire (1840), had a notoriously flat site, and Barry created three large shallow terraces descending to the lakeside balustrades and loggias. He intended also to terrace the islands in the Trentham lake to create miniature versions of ISOLA BELLA, but was overruled by his clients. In subsequent gardens—HAREWOOD; CLIVEDEN; SHRUBLAND PARK—he was able to use hillside sites for imposing terraces; at Shrubland his terraces were connected by a massive staircase, the slope on either side sown with tree seeds left to grow untrained, to give the effect of an overgrown Renaissance garden. Gardeners approved of Barry because he left details of planting to the head gardeners, and his gardens were regularly commended and offered as models in the

gardening press; by the 1850s the Italian garden in Barry's manner was becoming the major fashion in Victorian garden design, and continued until the end of the century.   BE

Barth, Erwin

(1864–1933), German landscape architect who was an outstanding personality in his profession in the first third of the 20th century. Barth's most famous work before the Second World War was the design for the open space along the Marlistraße in Lübeck where he created a number of vantage points from which visitors could enjoy picturesque views of the city. From 1912 to 1925 Barth was head of the municipal parks department in the city of Charlottenburg, which became incorporated into Berlin in 1920. There he created a series of outstanding public spaces, such as Brixplatz, Karolingerplatz, and many others. Barth excelled with his designs for the people's park Jungfernheide (Virgin's Heath) in Charlottenburg, which he started in 1922. As head of the parks department of Great-Berlin he popularized paddling pools in Berlin, including them when such city squares as Arkonaplatz (1926), Boxhagener Platz (1929), Traveplatz (1929), and others were redesigned. From 1920 Barth served as a lecturer in garden art at the faculty of architecture at the Technical University Charlottenburg in Berlin becoming, in 1927, an honorary professor. In 1929 he received the first chair for garden art in Germany, established at the Agricultural University Berlin. Mounting National Socialist pressure and the fear of losing his sight led him to commit suicide in July 1933.
   GG

Bartram, John

(1699–1777), American botanist and plant collector, born in Pennsylvania of a Quaker family. Although self-educated Bartram was considered by LINNAEUS 'the best natural botanist in the world'. In 1728 he began making a collection of American flora on his farm near Philadelphia. His exploratory and plant collecting travels took him through the unexplored regions of the eastern seaboard of America. Bartram's enthusiasm came to the attention of Peter COLLINSON in London, who was keen to grow and distribute new introductions from America. Bartram agreed to send regular consignments of seeds, and occasionally live material, for subscribers to receive via Collinson. European horticulture benefited by about 200 different species from their 40-year association.

By 1740 John Bartram's reputation as an expert botanist was acknowledged on both sides of the Atlantic. He corresponded with

leading botanists including Philip MILLER and Johann Jakob Dillenius (1687–1747), the German botanist who became first Sherardian professor of botany at Oxford University. In 1748 Bartram met the Finnish colleague of Linnaeus, Pehr Kalm (1715–79), who had been commissioned by the Swedish government to report on the continent's natural resources. At the age of 66 John Bartram was appointed by George III 'American Botanist to the King of England'; contemporaneously his *An Account of East Florida, with a Journal* was published. It was on his last expedition to Georgia, undertaken with his son William, that he discovered on the banks of the Altamaha river an almost unique tree, *Franklinia altamaha*, the single-species genus which has not been found in the wild since then. See also HISTORIC BARTRAM'S GARDEN.
MC-C

Bartram, William

(1739–1823), naturalist and writer interested in America's native flora, the only son of John BARTRAM. At the age of 14 he first accompanied his father on an exploratory journey and in 1765 travelled with him to Florida. William became a natural history draughtsman and assisted by Peter COLLINSON in London undertook commissions. One patron was the Quaker plantsman Doctor John Fothergill (1712–80), who supported Bartram's plant hunting for four years (1773–7). The result, *Travels through North and South Carolina, Georgia, East and West Florida*, was published fourteen years later following the War of Independence. It was widely read and in Britain poets and writers of the Romantic movement were influenced by the work. The American Indians, with whom Bartram enjoyed good relations, named him Puc-Puggy, 'The Flower Hunter'. Making no further journeys, Bartram continued to develop the 'botanic garden' begun by his father, publishing in 1784 a catalogue of *American Trees, Shrubs and Herbacious [sic] Plants.*   MC-C

Bartram's Garden. See HISTORIC BARTRAM'S GARDEN.

Bastie d'Urfé, La ⊛

Saint-Étienne-le-Molard, Loire, France, an estate going back to the Middle Ages with a fine Renaissance house built in the 1550s for Claude d'Urfé, a diplomat in the service of Henri II. Between 1549 and 1551 d'Urfé had been posted to Rome as ambassador to the Holy See, and his French estate is full of Italian character. He built an arcaded loggia and a superlative vaulted grotto inlaid with shells and pebbles and decorated with a figure of Neptune. Outside, a formal garden has an eight-part

arrangement of lawns with, at its centre, a pavilion with pairs of Ionic columns which also dates from the 16th century.   PT

Bauer, Walter

(1912–94), Swedish landscape architect and artist. He is perhaps best known for his reconstruction work on historic parks and gardens, notably the baroque garden at DROTTNINGHOLM from Nicodemus TESSIN THE YOUNGER's drawing, the park at GUNNEBO CASTLE, Mölndal, from Carl Wilhelm Carberg's drawings of c.1780, the Botanic Gardens in UPPSALA from a plan by Carl HÅRLEMANN, and also gardens at FORSMARKS BRUK and Leufsta Bruk, both in Uppland. Following a period with the Stockholm parks department, he started his own practice in 1946, undertaking work in the Middle East and India as well as in Denmark. He wrote widely in the professional press and taught at the technical high schools in Helsinki and Stockholm, and the Art Academy in Stockholm. In 1981 he collaborated in the exhibition *Fredrik Magnus Piper and the Romantic Park*, and had an exhibition of his own drawings and watercolours at the Art Academy in 1985. He was awarded the Gustav-Adolf Medal in 1978 and the Prince Eugen Medal in 1984.   PRJ/PT

Bayou Bend ⊛

Houston, Texas, USA, the former home of Houston philanthropist and collector Ima Hogg (1882–1975), was built in 1928, designed by Houston architect John Staub and Houston landscape architects Ruth London, and later Pat Fleming. Today Bayou Bend is part of the Houston Museum of Fine Arts, featuring Hogg's collection of American furniture and decorative arts in a house museum setting, but the 5.6 hectares/14 acres of landscaped garden rooms are its real tour de force. The River Oaks neighbourhood, of which Bayou Bend is the centrepiece, would eventually include homes with landscape designs by Ellen Shipman, the Olmsted Brothers, and other east coast designers, but Bayou Bend's architecture and landscaped gardens are emblematic of the best of the Gulf South region and specifically of Texas. Hogg had very specific ideas and interests concerning landscape, and used Bayou Bend as a laboratory in which to explore her passion for the native plants of the Texas countryside alongside her interest in classical design, stimulated by her grand tour of Europe as a young adult. She devoted much of her life to bringing together a personal collection of the best of design, from American furnishings and decorative arts to landscape design with a distinctly regional character. The garden's plan takes advantage of the bluff above the Buffalo

Bayou floodplain, and its principal feature is the Diana Terrace, incorporating existing native hardwoods into a formal series of terraces terminating in a fountain and pool backed by a sculpture of the goddess Diana. Other Italian sculptures punctuate the flanking garden rooms.   SLT

Bayreuth, Eremitage. See EREMITAGE (BAYREUTH).

Beaton, Donald

(1802–63), horticultural journalist. He was born into a Gaelic-speaking Highland family, learning English only in his twenties. While gardener at Haffield House, Herefordshire, he was launched on a journalistic career in J. C. LOUDON's *Gardener's Magazine*. He became famous as the head gardener of SHRUBLAND PARK, where his experiments in ornamental bedding were described in his weekly articles in the *Cottage Gardener* and its successor the *Journal of Horticulture*. Probably the leading horticultural journalist of the generation after J. C. Loudon's death, Beaton had an immense influence on colour schemes for the mid-century garden, as well as being a pioneer breeder of bedding plants, especially pelargoniums. In 1852 he retired from Shrubland Park, whose garden was then redesigned by Charles BARRY, leaving Beaton's maze as his only surviving garden feature. Beaton spent his last years in Surbiton, where an admirer provided him with an experimental garden that served as the source for his later articles.   BE

Beckford, William

(1760–1844), English art collector, connoisseur, and writer who travelled widely, in particular in France, Germany, Italy, and Portugal. From 1796 he built an extraordinary house, FONTHILL ABBEY, designed by James Wyatt (1746–1813), whose most notable feature was a spirelike tower 80 m/276 ft high. At Fonthill he occupied himself with gardening, although precisely what he did there is conjectural. The picture is made more complicated by the fact that Beckford's father, also William and usually known as Alderman Beckford, had made gardens for the house at Fonthill which preceded the Abbey. Alderman Beckford was making grottoes at Fonthill designed by Joseph Lane (1717–84) of Tisbury soon after buying the estate in 1745. Of William Beckford's gardening activities at Fonthill his most recent biographer, Dr Timothy Mowl, is dismissive. Elsewhere he seems to have achieved more. From 1794 to 1809 Beckford leased a house in Portugal, MONSERRATE at Sintra, where he made a picturesque garden of rills, a cascade, and

Gothic garden buildings some of which survive today. In 1822 when Beckford sold Fonthill he went to live in Lansdown Crescent in Bath. Behind the house, on land sloping up Lansdown Hill, he built a Moorish kiosk and beyond it Beckford's Ride, a planned walk with meadows of wild flowers, pools, a rockery, a grotto tunnel shrubbery, and an arboretum of exotic conifers. At the summit of the hill he built, by 1828, Lansdown Tower designed by Henry Goodridge, close to which is Beckford's tomb.   PT

Timothy Mowl, *William Beckford* (1998).

bedding plants.
See annuals and bedding plants.

Bedgebury National Pinetum ⊛
near Cranbrook, Kent, England, is established on a fine undulating site of 121 hectares/300 acres in a broad valley enlivened with streams and lakes. There had been a private pinetum here, established in the 19th century for Bedgebury Manor. In 1924 the Forestry Commission in conjunction with the royal botanic garden at Kew started to develop the site to form a comprehensive collection of conifers from temperate climates. It was laid out by William Dallimore, a specialist in conifers on the staff at Kew. The design is skilfully contrived both to take advantage of the landscape and to group trees so that they may be studied in systematic fashion. Some trees are grouped by place of origin—America, China, or Japan for example. Others are grouped by genus and these are often carefully arranged into categories. Pines, for example, are grouped together but they are also grouped according to their key diagnostic feature, those with two, three, or five needles. Some trees are planted in sites particularly favourable for their cultivation—swamp cypresses (*Taxodium distichum*) on the banks of the lake or cedars which require drier sites on sloping ground. Five National Collections are held here: of *Taxus*, *Juniperus*, *Thuja*, × *Cupressocyparis*, and *Chamaecyparis lawsoniana* cultivars. Apart from the conifers flowering shrubs (especially rhododendrons) and deciduous trees ornament the landscape. The autumn colours are very beautiful and there is the additional interest in that season of a remarkable range of fungi. See also conifers; pinetum.   PT

Beeckestijn ⊛
Velsen-Zuid, Noord-Holland, the Netherlands, is part of a complex of country estates that also includes Waterland and Velserbeek. First recorded in 1380, the early development is rather obscure before Jan Trip Jr. bought it from his father in 1719. He altered the house and ornamented the garden with a formal pond and statuary, but also carried out extensive planting, leading to the conclusion that he was probably responsible for the principal baroque layout. During successive generations the estate was further embellished according to the fashion of the time. A survey by the architect J. G. michael of 1772 prepared for the owner Jacob Boreel shows a largely surviving baroque layout with later features. The groves contained winding and serpentine paths, in a manner reminiscent of what was being proposed by Batty langley in England conveyed to the Netherlands in the translation of Philip miller's *Gardeners Dictionary* (1731). A number of follies, a Corinthian arch, a gardener's cottage in the shape of a Gothic chapel and hermitage, probably all date from Boreel's ownership. By 1952 when the Boreel family sold the property to Velsen Council the estate had been neglected. From 1953 to 1963 the grounds were restored on the basis of Michael's survey, but the original vegetable garden became a rose, flower, and herb garden. Statuary was introduced from other sources. In 1959 the buildings were restored as well, and became an annexe for the Rijksmuseum Amsterdam in 1969. In 1994 a new management strategy was conceived by Buro Albers Adviezen, resulting in further research. In 1996 inconclusive archaeology was followed by conjectural reconstruction work, once again based on the Michael survey.   JW

beekeeping and gardens.
An enclosed garden has been closely connected with beekeeping since early times, and nowadays many hobby beekeepers throughout the world keep a few hives in their gardens, where the bees can forage on nearby flowers. In the 700s bc the ruler of Assyria said that he brought bees down from the mountains, and he and his gardeners knew how to deal with the honey and wax. In ancient Rome the garden was regarded as the best place for hives because they were protected from wind, farm animals, and thieves; the hives should face south or south-east. From the 16th century onwards, beekeeping books gave similar advice, and some authors suggested plants to grow for bees. In *The Feminine Monarchie* (1609), Charles Butler wrote that if there were many hives a special area should be set aside, but for a few, 'your Garden of Hearbs and Flowers will serve'. He advised that hives should be within sight of the house so that swarms could be watched for. In the gardens of large houses the hives were often put near the vegetable garden or orchard, and in cottagers' gardens they were usually near the house, and might be looked after by the housewife. J. C. loudon even published designs for labourers' cottages with adjoining shelters for hives. From the 17th century, observation hives allowed the beekeeper to watch his bees at work; John evelyn had one in his garden in 1654.

Modern hives are weatherproof, but certain types used until the late 18th century needed protection in wet, windy regions. Some beekeepers in north-west Europe built special protective structures, many of which still survive in gardens. The most common is a row of small recesses (bee boles), each for one hive (skep), in a garden wall; there are good examples in the gardens of packwood house and heligan. Alternatively, several hives might be put in an open-fronted roofed bee shelter, or in a bee house. In the latter, the hives were kept inside, and the bees flew out through holes in the walls. In a large garden the bee house might be an ornamental feature. Many of these three types of protective structure are part of listed buildings.

Bees collect nectar and pollen from flowers within their flight range (about 3 km/1.8 miles), and in the hive they convert nectar into honey which they store in the combs. The protein-rich pollen is fed to the young bees. A garden with plants suitable for bees therefore contains herbs, shrubs, and trees which flower successively and provide nectar and/or pollen. However, not all flower species are attractive to bees, and generally double-flowered cultivars are not useful to them. From the gardener's point of view, foraging bees are welcome because they are good pollinators and their presence can increase yield and quality of fruit and seed plants. In addition, the activities of the bees can be watched and enjoyed. However, the beekeeper has to site hives carefully to reduce the risk of people being stung.   PW/EEC

Beervelde, Park ⊛
Beervelde, Lochristi, Oost Vlaanderen, Belgium, designed in 1873 for Count Charles de Kerchove de Denterghem. As president of the Ghent Floralies (flower show) the Count was involved with the burgeoning horticultural trade of the region and the 20-hectare/50-acre park was planned as a showcase. A fine avenue leads to a wooded landscape park—azaleas, rhododendrons, and lily of the valley make it ravishing in May during a plant fair. The family continues the tradition of supporting the horticultural trade and the park is the venue for important plant fairs each May and October. Sweeps of lawn are bounded by a winding river, crossed by picturesque bridges. A 19th-century pavilion and a pergola planted with wisteria overlook a serpentine lake. The woodland contains American and European oaks, *Hamamelis* species, and of particular note is

a collection of Ghent hybrid azaleas, increasing each year as old varieties are rediscovered.   BA

Beihai Park ✿

Beijing, China, is located north-east of the Forbidden City in the centre of Beijing; with a name that, literally translated, means North Sea, this is the oldest and largest park in the Chinese capital. It was first recorded under the Liao dynasty in the 10th century as the site of the Precious Islet Imperial Lodge. In 1179, under the Jin dynasty (on the outskirts of whose capital Zhongdu it then lay), the land was dredged and an artificial hill called Qionghua (the Isle of Fine Jade) was made from the earth. On it was built the Guanhan dian or Hall in the Moon Palace, and the whole became part of a great villa—the Daning gong—which was used for short royal visits. When in the early 13th century Zhongdu was destroyed, the Daning gong was left undamaged and in 1260, when Kublai Khan began to build his new city of Dadu on the same site, he made as its centre the Qionghua Islet, reshaped, renamed the Ten Thousand Year Hill, and planted with evergreens and rocks of lapis lazuli. Marco Polo described its 'trees and rocks alike . . . as green as green can be . . . no other colour to be seen'. Under Kublai the lake was renamed Taiyi or Pool of Heavenly Water, and further palaces—later destroyed by the first Ming Emperor—were built on its east and west banks. Under the Ming and Qing emperors, still more buildings were added and since the middle of the 17th century the 36-m/118-ft high White Dagoba, a Tibetan-style tower shaped like a fat-bellied bottle, has added its commanding silhouette to the top of the island. Today, nearly all of the buildings below it, including the elegant double-storeyed walkway that runs for 30 m/98 ft along the north shore of the island, date from the time of the Qianlong Emperor in the 18th century.

More than half of the park's present 67 hectares/165 acres is made up of water. At its centre, the isle of the White Dagoba, with the Eternal Peace Temple and the Propitious Clouds Tower on its southern slope, is linked to the main entrance on the shore by a wide bridge of white marble. In summer the lake here is completely covered by the blue-green umbrella leaves of lotus rising to make a new vegetable surface more than a metre above the water. Nearby massive grey walls rise around the terrace of the so-called Round City with its temple hall and magnificent white-barked pines overlooking the lake. From here wide paths lead away around the lake shore to many different building complexes, halls, and artificial hills (*jiashan*) with hollows and grottoes said to be made of rocks salvaged from the imperial garden GENYUE of the Song dynasty. Remarkable among all these are the Five Dragon Pavilions built out on zigzag causeways over the water, and the splendid Yuan-dynasty Nine Dragon Screen made of multicoloured glazed bricks. A number of small, walled gardens-within-the-garden are also spread along the lake shores, among them the Tranquil Heart Studio or Jingxinzhai, renovated in 1982 and considered among the best of Beijing's old courtyard gardens.

Beihai is a large public park much used by the people of Beijing. For students of gardening it is significant for the delicate play of contrast between its open areas of park and lake, and the enclosed, more intensely landscaped 'little sceneries' scattered along the shores.   G-ZW/MK

Beijing,

Hebei province, China. Settled from prehistoric times, the site of Beijing (formerly known in the West as Peking) already supported a town under the Zhou and Qin dynasties (*c*.1027–206 BC). In the 12th century it became the Jurched Tartars' capital, with imperial gardens watered by the Lianhuachi pool, and Kublai Khan made it his Great Capital (Dadu) in 1261. Between its double walls he kept many kinds of deer, ermine, and squirrels, while Marco Polo described also Kublai's great lake and river and the artificial Green Hill thick with trees transplanted there, fully grown, on the backs of elephants. In 1403 when the Yongle Emperor of the Ming again made Beijing the capital, he greatly increased the lake-parks, BEIHAI, ZHONGHAI, and Nanhai. Later, despite the dry climate, gardens were still flourishing under the Qing emperors within the city (BANMU YUAN, JING SHAN), inside the imperial palace (Yuhua Yuan; QIANLONG GARDEN; Zhongshan Park), and in the suburbs (YIHE YUAN; YUANMING YUAN; CHANGCHUNYUAN). In the Western Hills beyond the city, monasteries and private villas took advantage of the forested landscape to 'borrow views' (see JIE JING). As well as these, Qing princes and aristocrats built a number of grand palaces with gardens around the Houhai, or back lakes, in the city, some of which still exist today and are open to the public.

In general these northern gardens are stiffer and more formal than those of the Jiangnan region and the south; often their pools are edged with cut stone rather than irregular lake rock; and their *lang* (see CHINA) galleries run in straight lines and at right angles instead of in the irregular zigzags familiar from Suzhou. At the Xiangshan hotel in the Fragrant Hills outside Beijing, a new garden using rocks from the Stone Forest at Kunming has recently (1981) been made along traditional lines. It includes a 'wine-cup stream' in the style of the Qing dynasty cut into the stone floor-slabs of a bridge in memory of the famous poetry-writing competition at the LANTING. An impressive programme of tree planting under the People's Republic (see also NANJING) has helped lessen the effect of dust storms and wind, and several public parks with small lakes have been made in the city. Among famous buildings set in their own parks are the Temple of Heaven, with splendid ancient junipers, and the Ming tombs set in hills on the outskirts of the city. Beyond the Great Wall lies the Qing imperial park and palace BISHU SHANZHUANG.   MK

Bélanger, François-Joseph

(1744–1818), French architect and landscape designer practising in and around Paris, the designer of many distinguished houses. His most notable surviving garden building is the Bagatelle (see PARIS PARKS AND GARDENS) on the edge of the Bois de Boulogne built in 1777 for the Comte d'Artois. From 1784 he worked on the landscape at MÉRÉVILLE. In the 1780s he designed remarkable garden buildings for the Folie SAINT-JAMES where his client, the Baron Saint-James, is said to have told him, 'Build whatever you like, provided that it is expensive.' There was a tunnel grotto, much picturesque rockwork, a lake, cascade, many bridges, and exquisite buildings—chinoiserie, Gothic, and Moorish. Saint-James was bankrupted by 1787 and nothing survives of the astonishing garden he created. Bélanger designed the interior (1777) of Saint-James's town house, 12 Place Vendôme, which survives intact.   PT

BERND H. DAMS and ANDREW ZEGA, *Pleasure Pavilions and Follies in the Gardens of the Ancien Régime* (1995).

Belgiojoso, Villa

(Villa Reale) ✿ Milan, Italy. The neoclassical villa, which now houses the Gallery of Modern Art, was designed by Leopold Pollack in 1790–3 and the garden laid out under the influence of the French baroque, although it was soon turned by Villoresi into a romantic landscape park, with a serpentine lake. It was described by Ercole Silva in his treatise on Italian gardens written in 1801.   PHo

Belgium.

The climate of Belgium is temperate maritime, with average summer temperatures of between 19 °C/66 °F in the centre and 14 °C/57 °F in the Ardennes; and average winter temperatures of 3 °C/37 °F on the coast and –1 °C in the

Ardennes. The annual rainfall is 750–1,000 mm (30–40 in). There are about 1,500 species of flowering plants native to Belgium, and 35 species of fern and 730 liverworts, hornworts, and mosses. Botanists divide Belgium into two, European Atlantic to the north of a line along the Sambre–Meuse valleys and Middle European to the south, then subdivide in the north into maritime, a continuous 8–17-km/5–10-m wide band of sand dunes and polders along the coast, the flat Flanders plain, the Campine, a marshy and woody region crossed by canals, and the fertile Brabant region. Subdivisions in the south are Mosan, the forested hills of Ardennais, and Lorrain.

Belgium did not exist as a state until 1830 after being ruled by Austria, Spain, France, and the United Provinces (now the Netherlands). These changes frequently affected garden design, as can be seen vividly at MARIEMONT. In 1384 Philip the Bold of Burgundy became ruler of Flanders. The first documented gardens were created under Burgundian rule, which lasted until 1477 when Mary of Burgundy married Maximilian of Austria, and the Low Countries became part of the Habsburg Empire. At ENGHIEN a park attached to a *château fort* was first enclosed between 1390 and 1433. By 1475 a farm had been constructed, gardens laid out, and the first water systems built.

Sixteenth century

Following the reign of Philip the Good (1419–67) and the expansion of the Burgundian Empire in Belgium, a flourishing court developed in Brussels. The gardens attached to the Brussels court were mainly wooded; like Enghien, much of the ground was a game park, but soon a flower garden with a loggia, a jousting field, and a menagerie were added, open to a selected public. A more private area, initially an orchard, was altered in 1520. Emperor Charles V planted trees to form ALLÉES and arbours and decorated it with fountains. In 1550 the Emperor'sister Mary of Hungary had Italian terraced gardens built at Mariemont. Rembert DODOENS published his herbal in 1554, dedicating it to Mary. It mentions 1,060 plants and owed much to Leonhart Fuchs's *De Historia Stirpium* translated into Flemish in Belgium in 1543. African marigolds were grown at this time, being replanted each year. In 1581, the Antwerp printer Christophe Plantijn printed in L'OBEL's *Plantarum seu Stirpium Icones*—drawings of plants which had been engraved for the works of Dodoens, CLUSIUS, and L'Obel. The first garden pattern book which depicted the garden as an art form, *Hortorum Viridariorumque Elegantes et Multi Plicis Formae* by Hans Vredeman de VRIES, was published in Antwerp in 1583. His PARTERRES *de pièces coupés* were perfectly designed to display the newly introduced exotic plants.

Seventeenth century

Shortly before his death in 1598, Philip II had given the Netherlands to his daughter Isabella when she married her cousin Archduke Albert of Austria, already stadtholder of the Spanish Netherlands. The gardens at Mariemont were altered to a Spanish style. In the same period at ENGHIEN, Charles d'Arenberg was developing his garden, ordering flower seeds—impatiens, nasturtium, and *Mirabilis jalapa*—from Matteo Caccini (*c*.1573-1640), a Florentine dealer in rare plants. At the beginning of the 17th century Salomon de CAUS added rock and shell grottoes and ornamental waterworks. In 1610 the painter Rubens moved to the Wapper in Antwerp, where the reconstructed garden at RUBENSHUIS has separate trellised plots, topiary, and arbours found in the designs of Vredeman de Vries. Twenty years later, still under Isabella's regency, Philippe-Charles d'Arenberg created the elaborate Renaissance garden at Enghien. Simpler and perhaps more representative was the garden at the castle of Tilleghem. An illustration from 1641 shows the garden detached from the house, with parterres, some plain, others more elaborate, round a central fountain. The moated castle at Diepesteyn, illustrated in 1694, has a walled garden outside the moat, with a pavilion against the wall and eight decorative parterres arranged symmetrically around a central arbour.

Eighteenth century

During the second half of the 17th century the country was reduced to provincial status as Louis XIV tried to exert control over the Spanish Netherlands. Architectural activity stagnated and it is not until the 18th century when the Spanish Netherlands passed to Austria that there was a revival of agriculture and garden making. In 1720 the gardens of the Abbaye de la Cambre in Brussels were laid out in a flight of terraces. In the middle of the century at BELŒIL Prince Claude Lamoral de Ligne laid out a classical garden, while at Mariemont Charles of Lorraine altered the gardens to a French classical style with a central *allée* with fine parterres on both sides at the back of the chateau, and in the park, an ornamental *bassin* (formal pool) and *charmilles* (hedges, typically of *charme* (hornbeam)). The garden at ANNEVOIE with its French, Italian, and English influences dates from the same decade, as does the terraced garden at FREŸR, which is firmly French in its symmetry. Plantsmanship continued to flourish. A botanic garden was laid out at Leuven in 1738, and in the same year a book on auricula cultivation was sold in Brussels. By 1766 Charles-Joseph de Ligne was adding English landscape features to the garden at Belœil, although formal gardens were still being made several years later; for example, the Prince Bishop of Liège laid out a formal garden as well as a landscape park at his castle at HEX, and the BRUSSELS PARK, which replaced the Brussels Court gardens, dates from as late as 1774–83. The garden at ATTRE (1780) with its FABRIQUES is an example of the picturesque as is the Royal Estate at Laeken. The baroque garden created between 1690 and 1709 at the Alden Biesen in Limburg was joined by a JARDIN ANGLAIS complete with a Temple to Minerva.

Nineteenth century

The French Revolution ended Austrian rule and Belgium became a battlefield. The Prince de Ligne left his beloved Belœil and never returned. After the fall of Napoleon, the Congress of Vienna united the Austrian Netherlands and Holland into the kingdom of the Netherlands under William I from 1815 to 1830. During this short period William had built the orangery at the Royal Palace of LAEKEN, founded the Liège botanic garden, and showed a keen interest in the Society for Agriculture and Botany, founded in Ghent in 1808. Ghent rapidly became a centre of horticulture, noted for the growing of rhododendrons and azaleas, which it still is. The first *Azalea indica* (today *Rhododendron indicum*) was introduced around 1818 and the first hybrid, known as *Azalea mortieriana*, was produced by Pierre Mortier in 1825, crossing several North American species. The first Ghent azaleas were crosses between his hybrids and the hardy *Azalea pontica* (today *Rhododendron luteum*).

The Ghent flower show, the Floralies, went from success to success. In 1839 the great decennial exhibitions began. Azaleas were joined by camellias and begonias in popularity. By 1838, it has been said, around 35,000,000 tuberous begonias were transplanted in Ghent each year. In eastern Flanders alone there were 511 specialist growers of begonias. Fruit growing was another area in which Belgians had long been expert. A horticulturist from Tournai, Joseph Gabriel Cornille, published in 1784 one of the earliest catalogues of fruit trees. Jean Baptiste van Mons (1765-1842) was a fruit breeder who discovered how to transport scions overseas and in spring 1834 more than 300 varieties of Flemish pears were introduced to the USA. Pierre-Joseph Esperen (1780-1847) produced Josephine de Malines while Charles-Louis Durondeau produced Beurre Durondeau in 1811. There was a Royal Commission of Pomology which published its *Annales* 1853-60. The Leuven botanic garden was recreated in 1821 and became the property of the town in 1835. The herb garden at Antwerp was laid out in 1825, and a year later the Botanic Garden at Brussels was founded. In 1830, Belgium finally became an independent state and elected Leopold of Saxe Coburg as King. That same year Mariemont underwent another transformation, becoming a landscape park with a collection of rare trees. Schools of Horticulture were founded at Vilvoorde and at Gendbrugge-lez-Gand in 1849. The latter offered public lectures on the pruning of fruit trees. In the latter half of the 19th century, dendrology and silviculture expanded. The Rond-chêne landscape park (Liège) was planted, and KALMTHOUT nursery founded. The garden of the Provincial School of Horticulture at Tournai, with its walled fruit garden, rockery, and order beds (see BOTANIC GARDEN), and the Agricultural College arboretum at Gembloux were started. Two influential journals were published during this period: *La Belgique horticole*, in Liège, 1851–85 and *La Revue d'horticulture belge*, in Ghent, 1875–1914. Alongside growing urbanization and industrialization, and assisted by the enormous wealth of Leopold II (1865–1909) from the Congo, there was an increase in municipal parks and woodlands. Formal gardens surrounding the Museum of Africa at Tervuren were designed for the 1897 International Exhibition with the Tervuren arboretum following in 1902. In Brussels, the Bois de la Cambre had been designed by the landscape architect Edouard Keilig in 1862. This was soon joined by the Park of Laeken, the Colonial Garden, the Parc Leopold, and the Parc Cinquantenaire. In 1867 Keilig designed the Stadspark at Antwerp. Parks were created at Namur, the Parc Louise-Marie in 1878, and the Park de Chapeau in 1882. In Ghent the Parc de la Citadelle was laid out, now dominated by the Palais des Floralies. The royal greenhouses at Laeken were extended, setting a fashion for 'winter gardens' filled with exotic plants. In 1900 the Ghent University Botanic Garden was laid out, as, shortly after, was the aboretum at Gedinne.

Twentieth century

Horticulture suffered a great deal in the 1914–18 war. The 18th Ghent Floralies did not take place until 1923. Jules Buyssens, the landscape architect of the city of Brussels, restored the gardens at the Abbaye de la Cambre in 1930 and contributed to the 1935 Brussels Exhibition. Buyssens also laid out the garden at Hof ter Saksen at Beveren. The Second World War was equally devastating with the Floralies suspended until 1950; subsequently it has been staged every five years. Around the middle of the century several notable arboreta were

planted or extended including BOKRIJK, Kalmthout, and Hemelrijk by Jelena de Belder, Wespelaar and HERKENRODE by the Spoelberch family, and later the less well-known but delightful Hof ter Saksen. The noticeable enthusiasm for dendrology continues today with some fine collections in modest private gardens like those of Dr A. De Clercq in Nevele and M. B. Choteau's Arboretum du Centre at Binche. Buyssens's famous pupil René Pechère (d. 2003) is described as eclectic, with a tendency to formality and attention to detail (*Oxford Companion to Gardens*, 1986). Pechère, author, bibliophile, and distinguished landscape designer, designed many public spaces including Mont des Arts, Erasmus' house, Park Tenbosch, SENEFFE, the VAN BUUREN MUSEUM, and the old Jardin Botanique in Brussels, and restored the 17th-century POTAGER at Écaussines-Lalaing.

Clipped evergreens, hedges, and blocks of greenery creating a strong architectural framework to a bold planting are to be found in private gardens designed by Andre van Wassenhove, Piet Beckaert, Piet Blankaert, and on a larger scale and more internationally by Jacques WIRTZ and his sons Martin and Peter as well as in many owner-designed gardens. A love of new and rare plants is frequently balanced by a strong sense of design.

Ghent hybrid azaleas had fallen out of favour in their homeland but latterly a collection has been reassembled through the dedication of Léon de Clerq, Count Renaud de Kerchove de Denterghem, and Albert de Raedt. The collection, which includes hybrids reintroduced from SHEFFIELD PARK in England, can be seen at the Park BEERVELDE.

In recent years municipal parks and woodlands like the Forêt des Soignes and the Domein Lippensgoed have been joined by 'leisure parks' designed for millions of visitors. Walibi, Wegimont, and Meli Park although landscaped have more in common with earlier places of entertainment like Tivoli and Vauxhall.   BA

Bellevue Botanical Garden ⊕

Bellevue, Washington, USA, has been open to the public since 1992, and consists of 15 hectares/36 acres of display gardens, woodlands, meadows, and wetlands. Highlights include Perennial Borders, Waterwise Garden, Yao Japanese Garden, Alpine Rock Garden, Native Plant Garden, and summer displays of dahlias, fuchsias, container gardens, and hanging baskets. The Visitor Center was originally a Paul Kirk-designed home owned by Calhoun and Harriet Shorts, who deeded their property to the city of Bellevue in 1984. The city owns and manages the garden together with

dedicated community groups, such as the Bellevue Botanical Garden Society, the Northwest Perennial Alliance, the Eastside Fuchsia Society, and Eastlake Washington District of Garden Clubs. A master plan was designed by landscape architect Iain Robertson (b. 1948).

The Perennial Border, designed by Glenn Withey, Charles Price, Bob Lilly, and Carrie Becker of the Northwest Perennial Alliance, and installed by volunteers, is the jewel in the crown. Mixed borders layering choice trees, shrubs, perennials, vines, and bulbs for all seasons demonstrate inspiring, sophisticated colour schemes—cerise and gold; yellow, black, and blue; hot border; variegated and saturated. Memorable plants include *Catalpa bignonioides* 'Aurea', *Robinia pseudoacacia* 'Frisia', *Cotinus* 'Royal Cloak', *Hydrangea serrata* 'Preziosa', and *Berberis thunbergii* 'Atropurpurea'. The hillside site demonstrates how to garden on a slope, while capitalizing on dramatic views, with plants often flowering at eye level. A footpath traverses the backbone of the garden affording visitors an Alice-in-Wonderland experience, in which they are surrounded by dazzling colour and scent.   BBA

Belœil, Château de ⊕

Belœil, Hainaut, Belgium, the seat of the Ligne family since the 11th century. The present building is a copy of one built in 1538, embellished in the 17th century, but destroyed by fire in 1900. The gardens were laid out in the French style in the 18th century by Prince Claude-Lamoral II de Ligne, with either Jean-Baptiste Bergé or Jean-Michel Chevotet (1698–1772). The main axis is on a monumental scale—a 457-m/1,500-ft long lake begins immediately behind the chateau leading into a grand perspective which extends for 3 km/2 miles. On either side of the lake is a sequence of green enclosures. To the east, the first is Le Bassin Vert or BOULINGRIN followed by a rose garden, play area, and a goldfish pond in the centre of a newly planted BERCEAU and an oval pool. The final section here is Les Miroirs, four still reflecting rectangular pools. Behind these enclosures is the 600-m/2,000-ft long path, L'Allée du Doyen, with hedges 6 m/20 ft high. Between the walk and the hedges is a narrow stream, Rieu d'Amour, the creation of Prince Charles-Joseph de Ligne, who inherited Belœil in 1766 and added some naturalistic elements in the fashionable English style. As well as the sinuous rill, there is an English garden, now known as the deer park, with a Temple to Morpheus and a copy of the ruined temple to the Sibyl at Tivoli, which was laid out with the help of F.-J. BÉLANGER. At the end of the lake is a fine statue of Neptune flanked by reclining figures of Aeolus and Aquilon, and spirited seahorses. Returning along the west side, a QUINCUNX of copper beeches is followed by more BOSQUETS flanked by an avenue of oaks. In Le Cloître double hedges of hornbeam enclose a rectangular pool and Le Bassin des Dames is surrounded by impressive hornbeam tunnels. A cross-axis leads to a Temple of Pomona in the POTAGER, and close to the chateau is Le Bassin aux Glaces, a reflecting pool surrounded by an arbour. BA

PRINCE CHARLES-JOSEPH DE LIGNE, *Coup d'œil sur Belœil* (1795), trans. as *Coup d'Œil at Belœil and a Great Number of European Gardens* (1991).

Belon, Pierre

(1517–64), French naturalist, plant hunter, and writer born near Le Mans, who studied medicine in Paris and became interested in natural history. His botanical enthusiasm brought him to the attention of Cardinal de Tournon, who became Belon's patron, enabling him to travel widely in pursuit of his studies. He became particularly interested in trees and in 1545 received the gift of a plum tree from the Venetian master gardener Aloisio. Between 1546 and 1549 he toured the Middle East, beginning in Crete where he discovered the pink-flowered *Paeonia clusii*. The account of his journey described local flora, unknown in Western Europe, and the accurate recording of the plants (and animals) he saw contributed to the study of botanical nomenclature. Receiving a pension from Charles IX, Belon lived in the Château de Madrid in the Bois du Boulogne, near where in 1564 he was murdered by a footpad. MC-C

Belsay Hall ⊕

Belsay, Northumberland, England, was built for Sir Charles Monck to his own designs between 1807 and 1817. Monck had changed his name from Middleton (his maternal grandfather's name) in 1799 in order to inherit from his mother's family. The Middletons had lived here since at least the 13th century and built a castle in the 14th century, of which the remains survive to ornament the landscape. The hall is set in gardens of 12 hectares/30 acres and the old castle looks out over a park of 275 hectares/679 acres which was landscaped in the mid 18th century. The chief ornament of the hall garden is a remarkable picturesque ravine-like quarry from which the stone for the hall was taken. It lies between the hall and the old castle, with vertiginous cliffs of rough-hewn stone flanking a passage which widens and narrows. Mosses, ferns, and liverworts cling to the stone and Monck planted the verges of the walk with rhododendrons, Chusan palms (*Trachycarpus fortunei*), the great lily

Cardiocrinum giganteum, and such ornamental trees as *Aralia elata* and *Cercidiphyllum japonicum*. The ravine leads gently uphill and ends with views of the castle across a meadow. A decorative terrace garden runs along the south side of the hall from which there are views over a garden of rhododendrons punctuated by Irish yews. In the park (which is not visitable) is a Gothic FERME ORNÉE, Bantam Folly, built in 1757 to act as an eyecatcher from the castle. PT

belvedere.

The Italian word means simply a place from which there is a beautiful view. In English it seems at first to have had an architectural use—part of a house from which there is a view. In the context of gardens it has come to mean an ornamental building which commands an especially fine view and which is usually, in itself, an eyecatcher. A.-J. DEZALLIER D'ARGENVILLE's *La Théorie et la pratique du jardinage* (1709) describes belvederes (or 'dawn pavilions') as stone pavilions on the edges of the park or of a raised turf terrace commanding views. PT

Belvedere ⊛

Vienna, Austria. The gardens of the Belvedere Palace in Vienna are 'among the finest Baroque al fresco creations in Europe' (Dieter Hennebo). The gently sloping site was of restricted dimensions, and so in the years between 1700 and 1723 architect Johann Lukas von HILDEBRANDT, master *fontainier* Dominique GIRARD, and head gardener Anton Zinner created a garden full of incident, where the common elements of baroque garden art were presented in condensed, concise form. The original intentions were limited to the Lower Belvedere including the residence of Prince Eugene of Savoy, but later the idea arose of erecting a temple of honour and the arts on the hill above, which became the Upper Belvedere. Thus one could read this garden from two poles: from above (the Field Marshal's triumphal prospect of the Vienna hills, scene of his first successes against the Turks in 1683), and from below (the mythological path from the Underworld to the Olympus of Apollo as represented by the fountain and cascade figures). The Lower Belvedere includes the BOSQUET area with BOULINGRINS, hedged CABINETS, and ALLÉES, against which the sunken middle PARTERRE and upper *broderie* parterre stand out, interrupted by the Triton Fountain. The row of Hermes pillars lining the side of the gardens, and the statues directly in front of the façade of the Upper Belvedere, no longer exist. The spatial features were complemented by the Prince's private garden (Kammergarten), the orangery directly accessible from his quarters, an aviary at the far end of the Kammergarten,

the menagerie to one side of the Upper Belvedere, and a large glasshouse beside the Ehrenhof. The upper southern entrance to the entire garden, with an imposing iron gate, is laid out as a water parterre, dominated by a large pond and enclosed by *allées* of several rows. After a period of neglect, around 1850 the gardens were renovated in neo-baroque style by the painter Peter Krafft, statues moved from the parapet of the orangery to the central axis of the *bosquet* area, and the Hermes pillars replaced with sphinxes. Just before the First World War, when the Belvedere was the residence of heir to the throne Franz Ferdinand, the *cour d'honneur* (Teichhof; see ATTRE, CHÂTEAU D') was redesigned in *Jugendstil* by court gardener Anton UMLAUFT. GH

Belvedere ⊛

Weimar, Germany. The estate extends over the ranges of the Eichenleite hills to the south-east of Weimar, covering an area of 42 hectares/104 acres. In 1724 Duke Ernst August commissioned J. A. Richter to build a hunting lodge which was converted into a French-inspired stately summer residence in 1728. The layout of a network of avenues in the shape of a star, with the manor house at their meeting point, served mainly hunting purposes. Likewise, animal enclosures were fitted into the avenue network in the immediate surroundings of the manor house. A horseshoe-shaped orangery, built by G. H. Krohne between 1739 and 1753, completed the ensemble. During the reign of Duchess Anna Amalia new paths and sitting places in the early landscape style were added to the axial layout of avenues from 1758 onwards. Under her son Carl August the park remained unaltered except for the Hortus Belvedereanus, a botanical garden for scientific research that was added to the orangery section 1780–1820. By 1820 the garden, designed with Goethe's active involvement, boasted a collection of some 7,900 species.

Between 1815 and 1830, under Carl Friedrich and Maria Pavlovna, the ducal gardener family Sckell converted the park into a post-classical romantic landscape by adding such features as the Rosenlaube (Rose Arbour) in 1815, Mooshütte (Moss Hut) in 1817, Viergelehrtenplatz (Four Scholars Square) with the busts of Goethe, Schiller, Herder, and Wieland in 1818, Rosenberceau (Rose Tunnel) 1821–3, and the Obelisk and Schneckenberg (Snail Hill) 1822–23. As a souvenir of the garden of the Tsar's family at PAVLOVSK, Maria Pavlovna's home, the Russian Garden was built in 1823, extended later with a hedge theatre in 1823 and a maze in 1843. This layout, in essence, survives today. From 1974 to 1978 preservation and reconstruction work was carried out on the landscape park and between 1978 and 1982 and again in 2004 the Russian Garden was reconstructed. Currently, the orangery is being restored and the Hortus Belvedereanus returned to its layout of the 1820s.   USc

Belvedere Court. See VATICAN GARDENS.

Belvoir Park ⊛

Canton of Zurich, Switzerland, was created at the beginning of the 19th century by the prosperous merchant Heinrich Escher Zollikofer (1776–1853) and is still today one of the finest rural-style villa gardens in Zurich. In the first half of the 19th century merchants and entrepreneurs in Zurich developed an enthusiasm for English-style landscape gardens. Belvoir Park was one of the largest landscape gardens in the region. Zollikofer, who had as a young man amassed a considerable fortune in North America and was known as 'Amerika-Escher', in 1826 purchased Wyssenbühl, a hill covered in vines adjoining Lake Zurich. He had the crown of the hill removed and used the material to fill the marshy edge of the lake, planting it with exotic trees and shrubs, some of them from America. On the hilltop site with its glorious prospect of the lake a classical-style villa was built between 1826 and 1831, with a landscape park of sweeping lawns, pleasure grounds, and flower beds laid out before it. Zollikofer lived here with his family and devoted himself to study of the natural sciences and the care of his estate, which he named Belvoir. After the suicide of his granddaughter Lydia the family fortune was transferred to the Gottfried Keller Stiftung (foundation) and the park was intended to be built on to increase the capital. A citizens' campaign managed, however, to purchase the park from the foundation and open it to the public, and in 1901 Zurich City Council took it over. The grounds have been continually altered since their establishment: access to the lakeside had already been blocked by construction of the railway line in the 19th century, around 1.1 hectares/3 acres of the park were sold off as building land, and the first Swiss garden exhibition, G|59, merged the grounds with the neighbouring Schneeligut estate. In the mid 1980s an iris garden was planted and has become a special attraction in the flowering season from March to July.   UW

bench. See SEAT.

Benrath ⊛

Düsseldorf, Germany. In 1756 Elector Karl Theodor von Pfalz-Sulzbach (1724–99) commissioned the architect and park designer Nicolas de Pigage (1723–96), who had already designed the park at SCHWETZINGEN, to build a new Schloss and park in the existing grounds at Benrath. Pigage designed a typical *maison de plaisance*, a building consisting of a central block with two semicircular wings arranged around part of a great pool. Thus the building is set back from the former main approach and today's busy road. Due to major restoration work during the past few years the formal layout of the original design can once again be easily discerned. The French garden with its principal axis is to the east of the house. Water played an important role in Pigage's design, in the form of a canal joined on the western side to the major BOSQUET. While twisting paths run through the *bosquet*, which once also contained *salles de verdure* (see CABINET) at the points of intersection, the *bosquet* itself is encircled by a narrow canal. The square ground plan is divided into a star-shaped pattern and hedged avenues provide access to the park, the overall size of which is approximately 61 hectares/151 acres. An exhibition about the history of gardening is on permanent display in one of the wings of the Schloss.   AK

INGE ZACHER, *Schloß und Park Benrath in Düsseldorf* (1998).

Bentinck, Hans Willem (William), **1st Earl of Portland**

(1649–1709), Dutch statesman whose career began when he became page to William, Prince of Orange (later stadtholder and William III of England). He became William's closest friend and adviser on many different matters, including gardens, for which he acted as the King's superintendent—supervising work in both the Netherlands and England as well as visiting France to inspect gardens on the King's behalf. In 1698 Bentinck took George LONDON to France where they met de La QUINTINIE and asked LE NÔTRE to make designs for the Maestricht Garden at WINDSOR CASTLE. Le Nôtre, by that time too old to travel to England, sent his great-nephew Claude DESGOTS, whose plan for the garden was never executed. In 1675 Bentinck bought the ZORGVLIET estate, whose garden he altered with advice from Johan Maurits van NASSAU-SIEGEN. Late in his life, in 1706, Bentinck acquired the estate of Bulstrode (Buckinghamshire) where he laid out new gardens, possibly with the help of Henry WISE and Claude Desgots, only traces of which survive today.   PT

Berbie, Palais de la ⊛

Albi, Tarn, France, the 13th-century former archiepiscopal palace of Albi which today houses paintings by Albi's most famous artist, Henri de Toulouse-Lautrec. The palace stands on the banks of the river Tarn with walks along its ramparts which are shaded by arbours of grapevines and wisteria. Below, towards the palace, is a sunken garden with a dazzling parterre. At its centre is a circle of clipped box with a swirling pattern of annuals and on each side fan shapes of clipped box swerve outwards. The box has rounded edges and the patterns ressemble those of a plump eiderdown. Narrow beds of annuals, usually pink and white, edge the parterre. There was a garden on this site in the 17th century but the present garden must date from the early 20th century. It is a charming sight, a sprightly modern evocation of 17th-century ideas.   PT

berceau.

The French word *berceau* has a cluster of meanings to do with cradles and bowers. Its specialist garden sense is also varied. It can be a simple arch, or niche, of trellis-work, or a series of arches on which plants are trained to form a continuous tunnel ARBOUR. These were common features in French 17th-century gardens and those influenced by them. At HET LOO the Queen's Garden had an extraordinary pattern of tunnel *berceaux* designed by Daniel MAROT. These, originally of box, have been reinstated, in a form not quite as elaborate as the original, with hornbeam trained over an arched wooden framework. In the great ornamental POTAGER at VILLANDRY *berceaux* of a different kind are placed at the meeting points of walks. These, on the angle, are trellis-work alcoves enclosing benches and lavishly swathed in climbing roses.   PT

Berlin Botanic Garden ⊛

Berlin-Dahlem, Berlin, Germany, was founded in 1893, laid out by the botanists Ignatz Urban and Adolph Engler (1844–1930) and the architect Alfred Koerner, and opened in 1903 on a site of 43 hectares/106 acres. It contains one of the most outstanding collections of plants in Europe (about 22,000 different species). Being the successor of the old botanic garden in Berlin-Schöneberg (founded in 1679), the new botanic garden had the traditional features of a botanic garden of that time— a systematic department, an arboretum, biological and pharmacological departments, a huge plant house (finished in 1907) with tropical and subtropical plants, and finally a building for the Botanic Museum (finished in 1906). The grounds are arranged like a landscape park with an artificial lake in the arboretum as well as meadows and woodland areas with winding paths and seats to enjoy the scenery. The symmetrically laid out plant houses (the main plant house is 60 m/200 ft long, 30 m/100 ft wide, and 30 m/100 ft high) are surrounded by a so-called Italian Garden, which is arranged formally with hedges, rhythmically planted evergreens, and flower borders; the plant houses display Mediterranean and tropical plants as well as plants from arid regions (especially cacti). The most spectacular part of the garden is the vast plant geographic department, in which Engler arranged plants of the northern hemisphere, reaching from Central Europe, the Iberian Peninsula, south-east Europe, and Scandinavia to Siberia, East Asia, and North America. Plants from South Africa and Mexico are displayed in pots only in summer. Following patriotic interests Engler also included indigenous (*einheimische*) plant collections, which were arranged like a map of selected popular German regions, reaching from the Alps in Bavaria to the heaths and marshes of Lower Saxony and the dunes of the North Sea. The collections of the Berlin Botanic Garden significantly influenced the education of German gardeners, in particular because the Royal College of Gardening (Königliche Gärtnerlehranstalt) was reopened in 1903 in its immediate neighbourhood. The garden as well as the buildings and the collections were heavily damaged during the Second World War but have been completely restored and reconstructed. They have belonged to the Freie Universität Berlin since 1995.   US

BERNHARD ZEPERNICK and ELSE-MARIE KARLSSON, *Berlins Botanischer Garten* (1979).

Berlin Tiergarten. See TIERGARTEN.

Bernheim ✺

Clermont, Kentucky, USA, is a 5,666-hectare/ 14,000-acre research forest and arboretum, with one of the most comprehensive holly (*Ilex*) collections (700 taxa) in the world. The Olmsted Firm of Brookline, Massachusetts, founded by Frederick Law OLMSTED, designed the site plan that was adopted in 1935, and includes a 101-hectare/250-acre landscaped arboretum at the entrance. First opened to the public in 1950, Bernheim features over 5,000 taxa in its arboretum, most planted by Clarence 'Buddy' Hubbuch (1930–2000), with especially good dogwoods (*Cornus*) and crab apples (*Malus*). 58 km/35 miles of hiking trails criss-cross Bernheim's meadows and wooded knolls. Bernheim was founded by German immigrant Issac W. Bernheim (1848–1945), a peddler of 'Yankee' notions who settled in Kentucky after his horse died. With his brother, Bernheim established a distillery and produced the successful I. W. Harper bourbon whiskey brand. In 1928 he began purchasing land and donated it the following year to a foundation bearing his name. Between 1929 and 1947, restoration of the worn-out forest and farmland was begun with the owner's intention for the land 'to be

developed and forever maintained . . . for the people of Kentucky, and their friends, as a place to further their love of the beautiful in nature and in art'. A new visitors' centre above the scenic Cedar Lakes is designed to be one of the most environmentally friendly buildings in the USA, incorporating such energy-saving features as passive solar, geothermal elements, and a green roof. As a gesture to the founder of this unique place, recycled whiskey barrels were among the construction materials used.

AB

Bernier, François

(1625–88), French author, physician, and traveller whose vivid descriptions of what he saw in India and Kashmir in the 17th century contain precious early accounts of gardens. They were published in 1699 as *Voyages contenant la description des états du Grand Mogol* (Travels Containing a Description of the Estates of the Great Moghul). He saw the notable gardens of Kashmir—ACHABAL, SHALAMAR BAGH, and Vernag—and the RED FORT and TAJ MAHAL in India. He saw Kashmir as 'a fertile and highly cultivated garden . . . meadows and vineyards, fields of rice, wheat, hemp, saffron and many sorts of vegetables . . . intermingled with water, rivulets, canals and several small lakes, vary the enchanting scene' (*Travels in the Moghul Empire*, 1914).   PT

Bernini, Gianlorenzo

(1598–1680), Italian sculptor, architect, and painter, primarily valued as the greatest sculptor of 17th-century Europe. Although he never designed a garden, Bernini did design urban landscapes that have many features associated with gardens. He worked principally in Rome, where he enjoyed the patronage of a long succession of popes. Bernini's most important architectural design was St Peter's Square (Piazza San Pietro, 1656–67). He demolished the existing medieval and Renaissance buildings and laid out a huge oval with its axis parallel to the façade of the basilica; the oval was centred on the Egyptian OBELISK that had been placed in the square in 1586. The piazza was then framed with two huge curved free-standing colonnades, each consisting of four rows of Doric columns. Although this is a ceremonial space rather than a garden, its layout is indebted to current practice in garden design.   GC

Bertiz, Jardín del Señorío de ✺

Bertizarana, near Pamplona, Navarra, Spain. The ancient manor (*señorío*) dates from the 15th century. The soil here is acid and the rainfall is very high. The present garden, laid out in the 19th century, is a characteristic period piece

with the fashionable conifers of the day such as *Araucaria araucana*, *Cedrus atlantica*, and *Sequoiadendron giganteum* providing a fine backdrop to flowering shrubs, in particular camellias and rhododendrons. Over 120 woody species are displayed in a picturesque setting with the river Bidasoa flowing through the grounds enlivened with grottoes, cascades, and pools. Thickets of bamboos and mature swamp cypresses (*Taxodium distichum*) date from the garden's original layout. The garden extends into natural Atlantic broadleaf woodland that is also a nature reserve with marked byways.

PT

Betlér. See BETLIAR, ANDRÁSSY PARK.

Betliar (Hungarian: Betlér), Andrássy Park ✺

near Roznava, Slovakia. The creation of one of Hungary's most important landscape gardens started at the turn of the 18th and 19th centuries during the ownership of Count Lipót Andrássy. From this early period survives a rotunda (originally a library) and the Freemasons' Pavilion. The latter, standing on an island, is decorated with wall paintings and various masonic symbols. The Count continued the construction of the park in between 1810 and the 1820s, supposedly with the help of Heinrich NEBBIEN. Joseph Bergmann, whose plans are known from 1823, created the aqueduct with a huge waterfall. Remnants of a medieval ('Bosnian') castle also became an important feature of the park. In the late 19th century the park was substantially remodelled and extended in the time of Manó Andrássy with the creation of a lake, a menagerie (a mock ruin), a Hermes Grotto, and a Japanese Bridge as well as with the planting of a great number of exotic plants. Around 1900, in the time of his son, a formal pleasure ground in front of the house with a tennis court and a small Chinese Pavilion were created. The 81-hectare/200-acre park, with its long vistas and surviving features, is one of the best preserved historic gardens in present day Slovakia and a World Heritage Site.

GA

MARTIN KRIAK, *Prírodný Park v Betliari* (1982).
JÓZSEF SISA, 'Landscape gardening in Hungary and its English connections', *Acta Historiae Artium*, No. 35 (1990–2).

Bettoni, Villa ✺

Lake Garda, Lombardy, Italy. The gardens of the 18th-century lakeside Villa Bettoni, on terraces above the road at its rear, were designed by Amerigo Pierallini between 1764 and 1768 with an impressive display of elegant ramps and staircases, housing grottoes and statues in niches, the latter by Locatelli. A simple set piece, the garden takes the shape of an amphitheatre criss-crossed by architectural detail. The terraces, designed for lemon cultivation, ascend the hillside from which there is a fine view across the lake, the garden continuing more naturalistically to the higher slopes. A view from the lake reveals villa and gardens backed by the mountains.   PHo

Betz, Château de,

Oise, France, in the 18th century the home of Marie-Christine de Brignole, Princesse de Monaco, who was the mistress of Louis-Joseph de Bourbon, Prince de Condé, who lived nearby at CHANTILLY. In this romantic place, with the chateau on an island in the river Grivette, a gentleman landscaper, the Duc d'Harcourt, aided by Hubert ROBERT, laid out from 1780 a phantasmagoric landscape richly decorated with numerous FABRIQUES. Stylistically these were a heady mixture of Roman, Gothic, oriental, and druidical inspiration. The Vallée des Tombeaux (Vale of Tombs) was a sombre walk of evergreens—cedars and pines—ornamented with tombstones, some dating from the Middle Ages. These came from the Cimetière des Innocents, the most ancient cemetery in Paris (founded by the 12th century), which was suppressed in 1786. The surviving Temple of Friendship, designed by Jean-François Leroy, is an Ionic building with an austere interior decorated with Jean-Baptiste Pigalle's (1714–85) figure of *Love and Friendship*. At the Revolution the Princesse de Monaco left the estate, and subsequently the chateau and landscape fared badly and by the early 19th century they were derelict. The estate today is firmly private—it has belonged in recent times to King Hassan II of Morocco.   PT

Biddulph Grange ⊛

near Stoke-on-Trent, Staffordshire, England, is one of the most remarkable and original gardens of its time. In 1840 James Bateman came to live here with his wife Maria. Bateman from a tender age was fascinated by orchids and in his twenties built up a collection. From 1837 (when he was 26) to 1843 he published *Orchidaceae of Mexico and Guatemala* which Wilfrid Blunt's and W. T. Stearn's *The Art of Botanical Illustration* (1994) describes as 'probably the finest, and certainly the largest botanical book ever produced with lithographic plates'. Bateman had a taste for the exotic and at Biddulph he gave it full rein. On a site of 6 hectares/15 acres he laid out a garden of a kind that had never been seen before. His wife came from a distinguished family of gardeners, the Egerton-Warburtons, and in 1847 Bateman met Edward Cooke, an artist and gardener. Cooke was also the son-in-law of one of the most

notable nurserymen of the period, George Loddiges, whose nursery at Hackney was in its day the greatest collection of commercially available plants in the world (see LODDIGES, JOACHIM CONRAD). Bateman with his wife and Edward Cooke laid out a garden which intermingled some of the rediscovered formality of their day with ideas of startling strangeness. Close to the house the sloping ground is terraced in Italianate style. Formal walks lead down past groves of rhododendrons to a lake. A dark tunnel leads to an unknown destination, suddenly revealing a Chinese temple and bridge painted in brilliant colours with Japanese maples reflected in the water. A stone temple, Egypt, is guarded by sphinxes and monumental yew shapes. A dahlia walk leads to a solemn avenue of deodars and Wellingtonias penetrating woodland. The estate at Biddulph was sold in 1871 and the house destroyed by fire a little later. It was rebuilt and became a hospital in 1923, after which the grounds were neglected and, increasingly, vandalized. In 1988 it was acquired by NATIONAL TRUST which launched a successful appeal for funds to restore the garden, which has been done with brilliant success.   PT

PETER HAYDEN, *Biddulph Grange* (1989).

Biebrich, Schloßpark ⊛

Wiesbaden, Hesse, Germany. Maximilian von Welsch (1671–1745) had a summer residence with a 3-hectare/7-acre formal garden and orangery erected here between 1701 and 1721. After 1745 it was redesigned by Joachim Stengl (1694–1787) as a three-wing palace for Prince Karl von Nassau-Usingen (1718–75). From 1817 the baroque garden was reshaped as a landscape garden and extended to 35 hectares/86 acres to plans by Friedrich Ludwig von SCKELL for Duke Wilhelm von Nassau (1816–39); the extensive main ALLÉE and two lesser *allées* in front of the east and west wings were retained from the original baroque design. The dominant feature of the landscape park is the Wiesenthal valley, running north to south and bordered by trees and shrubs. At the end of the Dicke Allee the Mosburg castle ruins were reworked after 1804 by Karl Florian Goetz as a neo-Gothic castle. Landscaping by Sckell to the west of the Mosburg created a pond and gentle hills planted with groves of indigenous trees. The natural courses of the Mosbach and Nachtigallenbach streams enliven the aesthetically pleasing landscape. Paths following the 'line of beauty' lead through the park and, like the belt walk, offer many views and sightlines. The Pomologischer Garten is an orchard where rare varieties of apple are propagated.   BM

Bijhouwer, Jan T. P.

(1898–1974), Dutch professor of garden and landscape architecture. Following his training as a botanist, he assisted in educating garden designers and helped the emerging profession to deal with both large-scale landscape projects and gardens. He became the leading academic, teaching at universities in Wageningen and Delft. Finding inspiration for landscape design in Dutch landscape painting and in local semi-natural landscapes, he developed his ideas on this basis. His interest in how landscapes were used and worked ensured adaptation of functionalist ideas that are best appreciated in his studies of traditional Dutch farmyards and in the planning of new ones for the Noordoostpolder. These designs show the dichotomy between tradition and modernism that was so typical for the majority of new development in the Netherlands. In his garden planning he was primarily concerned to create space that was usable, of the right scale and proportion, while promoting planting design according to phytogeographical principles.

JW

Biltmore House ⊛

Asheville, North Carolina, USA, most magnificent among America's Gilded Age properties, sits on a bluff in the Appalachian foothills looking west over river valleys and rising forests to distant mountains. Commissioned by George W. Vanderbilt (1862–1914) to echo the splendour of Loire valley chateaux, the turreted and towered 250-room stone mansion, designed by Richard Morris Hunt (1828–95), soars four storeys, boasts 65 fireplaces, and is surrounded by 100 hectares/250 acres of designed landscape. Upon completion, Vanderbilt, a 33-year-old bachelor, welcomed his first guests on Christmas Eve 1895, after six years of construction with as many as 1,000 workers on the job. He married three years later and today one of his great-grandsons, William Cecil Jr., manages the historically important and beautifully preserved property, a commercial operation open to the public. Laid out by Frederick Law OLMSTED, this breathtaking site, including formal gardens that give way to descending meandering walks, woodlands, and meadows, itself fits into a larger area of 3,239 hectares/8,000 acres of managed forestland. When Olmsted took on the project in the late 1800s, productive, sustained timbering was an innovative concept in the USA, involving selective thinning and replanting. Biltmore has since served as a national model for responsible forestry. Driving up the winding 5-km/3-mile approach road, visitors immediately glimpse Olmsted's genius for surprise and naturalistic planting. We seem to be enclosed in the deepest forest, crossing chiselled ravines, flanked by lush native rhododendrons, laurels, and clethra, or peering into sunny glades of sourwoods (*Oxydendrum arboreum*) and flowering abelia. Then, without warning, a full view of the glorious ersatz chateau opens beyond a forecourt of perfect, level lawn ornamented by an enormous fountain and lined by double rows of tulip trees. To the east, a pillared temple crowns a grassy hilltop. The scene is stunning but even so withholds the next drama. Not until one walks through the mansion or steps onto the southern terraces are the mountains or descending gardens revealed. The grand scale of the gardens perfectly complements the ambitious architecture. Visitors today, as a century ago, stroll from the dignified, hemlock-hedged Italian pool garden adjacent to the house, along a path among unusual trees and shrubs, many grown from cuttings from the ARNOLD ARBORETUM, like Japanese stewartia, winter jasmine, and Yoshino cherry. The shrub garden leads into a 1.6-hectare/4-acre walled garden, intricately laid out in geometric beds planted in a progression of seasonal colour, a profusion of bulbs, roses, phlox, and tender annuals. Orchids, bananas, palms, and citrus trees flourish in a glass-ceilinged conservatory and its three connected greenhouses. By this point Olmsted itches for wilderness. Rustic trails circle engineered ponds, follow a flood-controlled creek, and zigzag across a meadow planted in wildflowers. Reshaped and replanted, the land is convincingly natural, a beautiful, rugged hike. Olmsted's last great landscape, the Biltmore gardens were overseen for 60 years by estate superintendent Chauncey Beadle, an avid plant hunter. In 1940 Beadle donated his collection of 3,000 azaleas to Biltmore, enhancing an 8-hectare/20-acre azalea garden, the ascending return to the house, a perfumed pink cloud in bloom.   HSS

Bingerden, Huis ✿

Angerlo, Gelderland, the Netherlands. The old house was burned down in 1945 at the end of the war. The losses included the archive, and as a result historiography of the estate is scant. Dating back to the Middle Ages, the estate was bought by an ancestor of the present owners in 1660. After 1789 a formal layout was altered into the landscape style with winding walks. The German landscape architect J. P. Posth (1763–1831) was responsible for some of the alterations that involved the shaping of the formal canals surrounding the gardens into a more sinuous river-like appearance. The spoil was used to make a viewing mound. In 1868 W. Baron van Heeckeren van Kell initiated further

improvements, employing the German landscape architect Eduard PETZOLD. After the wartime destruction the architect E. A. Canneman rebuilt the house for the van Weede-van Heeckeren van Kell family in 1958. Since 1980 its owners, and particularly Eugénie van Weede, have initiated a revival of the gardens, restoring them in places and adapting other areas to new uses. Of particular note is the planting of the formal and children's gardens near the house and of the kitchen garden.   JW

J. BOLONJE, 'Het Huis Bingerden te Angerlo (Gld.)', *Jaarboek Centraal Bureau voor Genealogie*, No. 13 (1959), No. 14 (1960).

Birkenhead Park ✿

Birkenhead, Merseyside, England, was the first public park financed with public money in Britain. The 90-hectare/222-acre site lies on formerly marshy land in the Wirral. It was laid out between 1843 and 1847 by Joseph PAXTON, who ingeniously solved the problem of the waterlogged ground by draining the water into two lakes whose spoil was mounded up to make the park's distinctive landforms. The banks of the lakes are edged with mounds planted with trees, greatly enlivening the otherwise flat site, and both have wooded islands. Paxton laid out a sinuous carriage drive, Park Drive, about the park's perimeter, edged with a pedestrian path and planted with belts and clumps of trees. A network of pedestrian paths led from the carriage drive to the centre of the park. Paxton also made plans for new houses ringing the park to be built in informal groups, providing income to defray the costs of the park. These were not completed exactly according to his proposals. Frederick Law OLMSTED visited Birkenhead Park in 1850 soon after it was opened to the public and is said to have been inspired by it for his design of Central Park in New York (see NEW YORK CITY PARKS AND GARDENS). Paxton's layout, in particular the pattern of paths and much of the original planting, substantially survives but some park buildings have been lost and others added not entirely in sympathy with the character of the place. It remains nonetheless one of the finest public parks in the country.   PT

Birmingham Botanical Gardens ✿

Birmingham, England, were founded by the Birmingham Botanical and Horticultural Society in 1831 and opened to the public in 1832. The society wanted to make an ornamental garden with an arboretum and scientific order beds (see BOTANIC GARDEN). In addition it was thought that produce from fruit and vegetable gardens, to cover more than a third of the site, could contribute towards the running costs of the gardens. The 6-hectare/16-acre site was laid

out by J. C. LOUDON, who devised a remarkable design that made excellent use of the sloping site. The centrepiece of his plan, occupying the north-west corner of the site, was to have been an extraordinary circular glasshouse of visionary design, enclosing an area of 0.70 hectares/1.75 acres and shaped like either a giant doughnut or a great dome with a spiral walk. This was rejected by the society as too expensive and a range of much simpler glasshouses was built, with additions later in the century and much rebuilding in the late 20th century. Loudon's swooping pattern of paths, following the contours of the ground, survives but the area set aside for fruit and vegetables was disposed of in 1844. Today, with its BANDSTAND, brilliant bedding schemes, aviary of exotic birds, and period gardens, Birmingham Botanical Gardens has more the character of a public park. An attractive little garden is laid out with plants introduced by E. H. WILSON, who served as an apprentice here from 1893 to 1897.   PT

MELANIE LOUISE SIMO, *Loudon and the Landscape* (1988).

Birr Castle ✿

County Offaly, Republic of Ireland, has been owned by the Parsons family (latterly earls of Rosse) since the early 17th century. The Parsons rebuilt an ancient castle, introduced magnificent new interiors in the 18th century, and in the early 19th century, in the time of Sir Lawrence Parsons (later 3rd Earl of Rosse), who was a friend of the Gothic novelist Maria Edgeworth, the house was thoroughly Gothicized, making a picturesque ornament in the landscape rising up above the banks of the river Camcor. There was a formal garden here in the 17th century with a maze and an ALLÉE of box of which remarkable old plants, said to be part of the 17th-century scheme, may still be seen. In the 18th century Sir William Parsons made a landscape park, creating a lake on the marshy ground early in the 19th century. The site is too flat to make an interesting park and there is no rising ground from which to admire the lake. In the 1840s the 3rd Earl erected a building to house a telescope, then the largest in the world, immediately in front of the house and matching it, in Gothic style. It makes a landscape ornament that is curious rather than beautiful. The 3rd Earl was a learned astronomer who in 1845 was the first to observe the spiral shape of nebulae. In 1995 his descendant, the 7th Earl, had the attractive idea of celebrating the 150th anniversary of the discovery by laying out a spiral walk of lime trees (*Tilia cordata*) close to the observatory. From the early 20th century the family became keen plant collectors and sponsored expeditions by George FORREST, Augustine HENRY, E. H. WILSON, and others. Their acquisitions are found in many parts of the demesne—for example, some superb old magnolias are planted along the river walks—but the greatest concentration is in the arboretum on the far side of the lake. The 5th Earl, before the First World War, made a terrace below the castle to command views of the river and made walks along the river banks which are planted with trees and flowering shrubs. Quite close to the castle there is a cascade and the river is spanned by an elegant metal suspension bridge built in 1826, a remarkably early date for such a building. In 1935 the 6th Earl married Anne Messel of the family that owned Nymans (Sussex, England), and together they made a great formal walled garden to one side of the castle, close to the site of the 17th-century formal garden. Part of the garden is enclosed in cloisters of clipped hornbeam with 'windows' cut into them to frame views of the gardens within. Here are herbaceous borders, a parterre of box made of a pattern of Rs, rose beds full of 19th-century cultivars, and a yew *allée* which leads to an arbour of roses. The designed landscape at Birr covers an area of 49 hectares/120 acres and is one of the most varied and attractive gardens in Ireland.   PT

Bishop's Close.
See ELK ROCK, GARDEN OF THE BISHOP'S CLOSE.

Bishu shanzhuang ⊛
Chengde, Hebei province, China, is located beyond the Great Wall 260 km/156 miles north-east of Beijing; this Mountain Retreat to Escape the Heat is the largest imperial garden remaining in China today. Also known as the Rehe (formerly spelt Jehol) xinggong or Hot River Summer Palace, its boundary wall winds and falls some 10 km/6 miles around a group of natural hills that rise in the centre of a valley. Outside the park, in the foothills of the surrounding rim of mountains, eight great Outer Temples in Mongolian, Tibetan, and traditional Chinese styles are visible above the river and, with a strange geological formation—the Club Peak, shaped by the elements into a gigantic pestle silhouetted on the horizon—contribute dramatic borrowed views to the garden (JIE JING). This, and the genial climate, first impressed the Kangxi Emperor of the Qing when he toured the region in the early years of his reign. Construction of the park started in 1703 and continued on a large scale for 87 years. Both the Kangxi and Qianlong emperors personally gave inscriptions for 36 scenes; and from 1711 the Qing emperors regularly moved their courts there in summer so that it became an important political centre.

The park covers 1,400 hectares/3,458 acres, four-fifths of it hilly and the rest low lying, with lakes drawn from the hot spring. The emperors dwelt and held temporary court in several palace complexes near the main entrance. One group, with Songhezhai (the Pine and Crane Hall) as its main structure, was the Empress Dowager's; the others are the Eastern Palace, where in summer operas were staged for the court on a large, covered stage (destroyed by fire in 1945), and Wanhuo songfeng or Valley of Soughing Pines, used as a studio. Within the principal palace, the main building—Danbojing chendian or Hall of Simplicity and Sincerity—is built of nanmu, a highly prized aromatic hardwood, with carvings of bats and scrolls on its ceiling and partitions. The imperial boudoir, poetically named Refreshing with Mists and Ripples, lies behind it. The whole palace area is formally planned with straight, covered walkways linking a succession of finely proportioned halls and courtyards enclosed by walls and planted with old pine trees. The effect, calm and ageless, is unique in China, and the simplicity and elegance of the architecture harmonize agreeably with the natural landscape.

The park beyond is in three parts: lakes, lowland, and mountains. The lakes lie in the south-east but north of the palace. Dotted here and there with small islands, they are crossed by willow-planted dykes and surrounded by embankments and low hills. At the southern end is the Midlake Pavilion and, in the centre, an island called As you Wish, on which stand several clustered towers and *tings* (see CHINA) known as Moon White and Water Tunes. This is where the emperors and their families came on moonlit nights to celebrate the serenity of the lake. Another tall building, Misty Rain on the Heliotrope Islet, was modelled after its namesake in the South Lake of Jiaxing, Zhejiang province, and used for viewing the lake on misty days. In the east, on the islet Golden Hill, an octagonal three-storeyed building was built in imitation of the God's Chamber in the Golden Hill Temple at Zhenjiang, Jiangsu province. A stele ,engraved with the characters 'Rehe Spring', and several pavilions with the high surrounding hills beyond, are reflected across the water.

Further north is a grassy plain known as the Garden of Ten Thousand Trees, once a deer park. Here the Qianlong Emperor (1736–95) entertained Mongolian princes and the Banchan Lama VI of Tibet to imperial picnics, and received Lord Macartney, Britain's first envoy to China. The Library Wenjinge, in the western part of the lowland, is a replica of the famous Tianyige, at Ningbo, Zhejiang province. Two great collections, *Gujin tushu jicheng*

(Collected Works, Ancient and Contemporary) and the *Siku quanshu* (Four Vaults of Classics), were once among other treasures in this library. On the other side of the flatland stands the Pagoda of Buddha's Remains, a version of the Glazed Tower in the Temple of Gratitude at Nanjing, destroyed in 1851, and the Pagoda of Six Harmonies, built in 1163. The western part, covering most of the Resort, is made up of natural hills with the ruins of over 40 garden structures scattered among them. Recently a few of them—the Pavilion of Viewing Southern Hill Deep in Snow, Sunset at Club Peak, and the Pavilion Facing Clouds and Hills Around—have been rebuilt.

Bishu shanzhuang is exceptional among imperial gardens for the elegant simplicity of its palace buildings, unusual in the Qing dynasty, and the combination of this with the lyric grace of China's landscape tradition south of the Changjiang (formerly Yangtze river). Above all, however, it is the changing effects of seasonal mist and clear northern light on the borrowed scenery of the surrounding hills and temples that make it exceptional.   G-ZW/MK

Bjerkebæk,
Lillehammer, Oppland, Norway, is today a part of the Maihaugen Museum. The novelist Sigrid Undset (1882–1949), who won the Nobel Prize for Literature 1928, acquired the property in 1921 after her success with *Kristin Lavransdatter I*. With love and understanding of plants and gardens, always present in her writing, she created the 0.2-hectare/0.5-acre garden in a former paddock with birch woodland and a small creek which she developed. Inspired by traditional and formal gardens, she laid out the main garden with hardy roses and perennials, fruit trees, a kitchen garden, and planted a drystone wall. At the back she made a rock garden for alpine plants. During the Nazi occupation she fled the country and stayed in the USA while the property was used by the occupying forces. The aim of the restoration plan by Marit Brandtsegg (b. 1959) of the landscape architects Feste Lillehammer is to return the garden to its pre-war state and many of Sigrid Undset's favourite plants have been replanted. When the visitors' centre is built, the garden will be open to the public.
ME

METTE EGGEN, 'Husfruen til Bjerkebæk', in E. Conradi et al., *Gjennom hageporten* (2000).

Blaikie, Thomas
(1750–1838), Scottish botanist and gardener who carried out a pioneer plant hunting expedition to the Swiss Alps for Dr John Fothergill and Dr William Pitcairn in 1775. In 1776 he went to work in France for the Comte d'Artois at Bagatelle

(see PARIS PARKS AND GARDENS) where he helped to design the garden the remains of which may be seen today, and later for the Duc de Chartres (later Duc d'Orléans), at the Jardin de Monceau (see PARIS PARKS AND GARDENS). He remained in France during the Revolution but his career was destroyed—J. C. LOUDON's *Encyclopaedia of Gardening* (1822) records that 'the Directory employed him to plant the Tuileries with potatoes, and never paid him'. His memoirs, published in 1931 under the title *Diary of a Scotch Gardener*, well worth reading today, have splendid accounts of Blaikie's explosive relationship with the Comte d'Artois at Bagatelle where he sulked, thinking himself underappreciated.   PT

Blaise Castle and Hamlet ⊛

Henbury, Bristol, England, are on land that was originally part of the Henbury Manor estate. It was bought in 1762 by Thomas Farr who in 1766 commissioned a sham castle from the architect Robert Mylne (1733-1811). Triangular in plan, with a castellated round tower at each corner, it rises high on a wooded eminence. It is one of the few identifiable gardens mentioned by Jane Austen. Isabella Thorpe in *Northanger Abbey* (1818) claimed that it was 'the finest place in England; worth going fifty miles any time to see'. In 1795 a new owner, John Scandrett Harford, consulted Humphry REPTON and a Red Book was made the same year. It proposed a vertiginous and very circuitous new drive winding through a steep valley: 'I cannot describe those numberless beauties which may be brought before the eye in succession by the windings of a road, or the contrast of ascending and descending thro' a deep ravine of rich hanging woods.' Repton built a castellated Gothic lodge at the head of the new drive which was ornamented on the way with a Woodman's Cottage with smoke rising decoratively from its chimney. The Red Book is on view in Blaise Castle House. In the early 19th century John NASH was called in to design Blaise Village, a picturesque group of busily vernacular estate cottages grouped about a mock village green—a delightful sight.   PT

STEWART HARDING and DAVID LAMBERT, *Parks and Gardens of Avon* (1994).

Blankenburg ⊛

near Quedlinburg, Saxony-Anhalt, Germany. The ensemble consists of the Large and the Small Palace with an adjoining park including a pond, a conservatory, a terrace garden with an enclosed Orange and Melon Garden, the Berggarten (Hill Garden), a pheasantry, and a large deer park. A 17th-century terraced garden marked the starting point of the ensemble. At the beginning of the 18th century a baroque

residence, the Large Palace, was erected. The spacious orangery built nearby, called the Small Palace, was reconstructed as a summer palace after the abandonment of its original use. A terraced pleasure garden south of it included water basins and stairs, which led to a Neptune's Grotto and the Melon Garden. These features probably date from the first half of the 18th century when the estate was owned by the Duke of Brunswig Luneberg. Together with the flanking terraces they form the spine of the baroque ensemble to which the terraced Berggarten still forms a background. The courtyard with a recently restored central water basin in front of the conservatory, a half-timbered building next to the Small Palace, is called the Orange Place because of its former use as display area for potted plants. The nearby pheasantry was designed in the 18th century as a formal garden in which pheasants were kept. It had been in different use for the last 200 years (latterly as allotment gardens since 1950) before it was reconstructed a few years ago. Improvements under Prince Albrecht of Prussia at the end of the 19th century failed to halt the garden's deterioration and reduction. Irrevocable changes affected parts of it after the Second World War—large parts of the park became wild, other parts were used for public green spaces, and houses and a recreation home were built in the park. Since the 1970s careful reconstruction works of the remainder have been carried out.   HM/HH

Blenheim Palace ⊛

Woodstock, Oxfordshire, England, was built to celebrate the military triumphs of the Duke of Marlborough over Louis XIV. Designed by John VANBRUGH and built between 1705 and 1716, it was completed by Nicholas HAWKSMOOR between 1722 and 1725. On the estate is the site of Woodstock Manor, originally an Anglo-Saxon hunting lodge. In the 12th century it was a palace of Henry II, who entertained his mistress Rosamund Clifford here and built a garden, possibly inspired by the romance of Tristan and Isolde, with a well as centrepiece. According to the architectural historian Sir Howard Colvin, Henry's water garden was possibly influenced by water gardens in Sicily with which his court had close connections. The well, now called Everswell, still exists. The old manor, by then ruinous, still existed in the first Duke of Marlborough's time and Vanbrugh lived in it while working on the palace—it stood immediately to the north of the site of the new palace. He was so taken with its picturesque charms that he tried unsuccessfully to persuade the Duchess of Marlborough to retain it as a landscape ornament but it was demolished in 1723. A garden for the new palace, known as the

Military Garden, was laid out by Henry WISE, Queen Anne's royal gardener, as the palace was being built. South of the house and enclosed in giant walls with military bastions, it was connected axially with the house and disposed symmetrically. Planted entirely with evergreens—bay, box, holly, and yew—it was rectilinear in plan except for serpentine walks on either side. All this disappeared after 1764 when Capability BROWN was called in. He flooded the valley of the river Glyme to create a great serpentine lake, nipped in at the centre to retain the noble bridge designed by Vanbrugh. Brown landscaped the grounds, with turf running up to the palace walls, and planted belts of trees about the park's boundary. To the north of Vanbrugh's bridge he left a great avenue (since replanted more than once) at the bottom of which stands a Column of Victory designed by Lord Herbert and built between 1727 and 1730. Boswell and Johnson visited Blenheim in 1776 and, while admiring 'the genius of Brown', Boswell said to Johnson 'You and I, Sir, have, I think, seen together the extremes of what can be seen in Britain—the wild rough island of Mull, and Blenheim Park'. In the early 20th century new formal gardens were made below the palace walls designed by Achille DUCHÊNE, the French neoclassical garden designer. The Italian Garden, completed in 1910, lies immediately to the east of the palace, with four PARTERRES *de broderie* about a central circular fountain pool decorated with a bronze by Waldo Storey of a naked nymph holding aloft a ducal coronet. The Water Terraces, west of the palace and completed in 1930, are in two parts. The upper terrace has scalloped pools and fountains framed in parterres with scrolls of box. The chief ornament on the lower terrace is a small version of Bernini's fountain in the Piazza Navona in Rome flanked by winged sphinxes. From this terrace are handsome views westwards over the lake.   PT

Bloedel Reserve ⊛

Bainbridge Island, Washington State, USA, is a 61-hectare/150-acre site benefiting from Puget Sound's mild, moist climate. Once owned by Prentice and Virginia Bloedel, it combines their vision and the genius of landscape architect Thomas CHURCH, who guided the design of nearly 28 hectares/70 acres of developed landscape from the 1950s to the 1970s. In the early 1960s Fujitaro Kubota (1879-1973) designed the tranquil Japanese-style garden with beautiful stone pathways and tori gate (originally designed to purify the soul at the entrance to a Shinto shrine). More than half the property is dense north-west forest of Douglas fir, western red cedar, and hemlock, with an understorey of ferns and mosses, undisturbed except for trails. Remaining areas have been cultivated into gardens, ponds, and a waterfall that dovetail gracefully into the natural setting. The overall atmosphere is serene, inspiring reverence and awe for nature, with a hushed beauty interrupted only by birdsong and footfalls. Highlights of the developed gardens include the rectangular Reflection Pool, surrounded by clipped Irish yew hedges, a study in geometry that contrasts with the forest; the Bird Sanctuary, where geese, swans, and blue herons shelter; and the Rhododendron Glen, carpeted with hardy cyclamen. The original home, now the visitors' centre, is an elegant French country house designed by J. Lister Holmes (d. 1986) in 1931. Surrounded by formal plantings, including a magnificent copper beech (*Fagus sylvatica* Atropurpurea Group) and katsura tree (*Cercidiphyllum japonicum*), the centre enjoys views of Port Madison Bay and Seattle on clear days.   BBA

Blom, Holger

(1906–96), Swedish architect and director of the parks department in Stockholm from 1938 to 1971. During his time in office, he devised and implemented an extensive programme of renovation and construction of public spaces in the Swedish capital. The parks were designed in the modern style, which in Sweden was called functionalism. By content, everyday values, and social use it was very different from the decorative stroll parks of the late 19th century. As for form, the surrounding countryside landscape was used as inspiration. The new movement was later labelled the Stockholm School of Park Design. Blom also became known as an active debater in urban design issues in which he argued for parks as constitutional parts of the city itself. When the IFLA (International Federation of Landscape Architects) had its world congress in Stockholm 1952, Blom had the opportunity to display his achievements to colleagues from all over the world.   TA

Blomfield, Sir Reginald

(1856–1942), English architect, garden designer, and author. His book *The Formal Garden in England* (1892), written in collaboration with Francis Inigo THOMAS, was a trumpet blast in support of the style of architectural garden which he himself designed, and an attack on Robinsonian natural gardening (see ROBINSON, WILLIAM). Gardens, or parts of gardens, designed by him survive at: Brocklesby Park (Lincolnshire), Caythorpe Court (Lincolnshire), Chequers (Buckinghamshire), GODINTON HOUSE (Kent—his finest garden, very well restored in the late 20th century), Heathfield

Park (East Sussex), Moundsmere Manor (Hampshire), Sulgrave Manor (Northamptonshire), and Waldershare Park (Kent).   PT

Boboli Gardens ✿

Florence, Italy. Created and altered over four centuries, the Boboli Gardens in Florence represent layers of garden history. Begun in 1549 by Duke Cosimo I and his wife Eleonora of Toledo, after the acquisition of the Pitti Palace from the Pitti family, the initial stage of the garden was the work of Niccolò TRIBOLO, who had already designed the Villa MEDICI (Castello) for the Duke. His main contribution was to plant the 'natural' amphitheatre (formed by the old sandstone quarry which had provided stone for the palace) on an axis with the centre of the Pitti Palace at the base of the Belvedere Hill. It was terraced and formally heavily planted with evergreen oaks, bay laurel, and viburnums as portrayed in the lunette (in the topographical museum in Florence) painted by Giusto UTENS in 1599, the regular rows providing the Tuscan *ragnaia* for catching small birds. Davide Fortini and Giorgio Vasari (1511–74) continued Tribolo's work after his death in 1550 until 1561, when Bartolomeo AMMANATI took over, improving buildings and garden to complete Tribolo's original design in 1579. Under Duke Francesco I, Bernardo Buontalenti (1536–1606) was employed to create the Grotta Grande. GIAMBOLOGNA's granite Fountain of Oceanus (later moved to the Isolotto) is first documented in front of the *teatro di verdura* (green THEATRE) in 1577. Under Cosimo II (Grand Duke from 1609 to 1621), the garden was enlarged as far as the original walls erected during the wars against Siena. The garden, bounded by the city walls to the east and on the west by the city, now stretched down a long cypress avenue to the north, the Viale dei Cipressi, decorated with statues, towards the new oval Isolotto Basin, where, on an island, a lemon and flower garden was created between 1614 and 1619 by the architect Giulio Parigi (1571–1635). The green amphitheatre was also transformed by Parigi by order of Grand Duke Ferdinand II between 1630 and 1634, his son Alfonso Parigi (1606–56) completing the transformation in 1637. The trees were removed to build a stone auditorium with concentric steps where an audience could sit to view performances. One of the first spectacles was to celebrate Ferdinand's marriage to Vittoria della Rovere. The woods were extended to the east with extensive alleys and three labyrinths which were destroyed in 1834 for a new carriage drive, while winding paths through the woods gave a more naturalistic air. A garden of rare plants, an aviary, a fish pond, and a menagerie were

introduced under Cosimo III, besides the Garden of the Cavaliers. During the 18th century under the Lorraine dynasty, other buildings were added to the garden: the Kaffehaus (1775), the Limonaia (1777–8), and the Palazzina della Meridiana started in 1776.

The Boboli Gardens are still distinguished by a number of important statues by Giambologna, in particular the Fontana dell'Oceano created in 1574–7 but moved to the Isolotto by Parigi. Other famous sculptures include the *Nano Morgante* by Valerio Cioli (1529–99), a naked fat dwarf riding a tortoise, supposedly an allegory of laziness and wisdom. Two *Prigionieri Daci* (Dacian prisoners) date from the 3rd century AD. The Grotto di Madama was commissioned by Eleonora of Toledo and constructed between 1553 and 1555 by Davide Fortini and Marco del Tasso, and decorated with tufa stone and sculpture by Baccio Bandinelli (1493-1560), with paintings by Bachiacca (1494-1552) in the dome. The pavement is by Santi Buglione. Around the grotto the Medici grew an orchard of dwarf fruit, many of the trees being grafted on quince. The more famous Grotto del Buontalenti (recently under restoration), begun in 1557 and completed between 1583 and 1593 by Ammanati and Bernardo Buontalenti, is more complex, representing the world of ancient mythology and the forces of nature. In 1587 its façade was decorated by Giovanni del Tadda with rustic figures. Inside a series of stalactites and tufa sculptures represented the myth of Deucalion and Pyrrha and surrounding walls had frescoes by Bernardino Poccetti. In the third room there is a marble statue of Venus by Giambologna. Water drops and jets cool the air. Recently, under Dottore Giorgio Galleti, the gardens and grottoes have been under restoration, with hedges cut back to original heights and a programme of replanting, especially of the Isolotto with old rose species. In front of the Limonaia, where the Medici had their collections of rare citrus, beds edged with low box are planted with historic 16th-century flowers. High hedges and tunnels of holm oak, bay laurel, *Phillyrea*, *Rhamnus*, myrtle, and laurustinus define the pathways and provide dark shady walks.   PHo

FRANCESCO GURRIERI and JUDITH CHATFIELD, *Boboli Gardens* (1972).   ➲ page 51

Bodnant Garden ✿

Conwy, Wales, is a garden in which distinctive styles of British gardening are finely intermingled. The site is very beautiful, 32 hectares/80 acres in north Wales on wooded slopes above the river Conwy, with views to the mountains of Snowdonia. Henry Pochin bought the estate in 1874 and soon realized the gardening possibilites. South-west of the house the river Hiraethlyn flows swiftly through a sheltered ravine where in the 1870s and 1880s Pochin planted many conifers, some of which survive today to provide a splendid background to the large numbers of flowering shrubs which ornament this part of the garden, the Dell. Pochin was also responsible for a delightful and much admired feature at Bodant, the laburnum tunnel. A broad walk curves beneath a wide metal framework on which are trained the branches of *Laburnum* × *watereri* 'Vossii' which has especially long racemes, which in late May or June hang down from the roof inside the tunnel creating an extraordinary effect. Between the trunks on each side Welsh poppies (*Meconopsis cambrica*), ferns, and mosses lavishly cover drystone walls behind which are plantings of brilliantly coloured spring-flowering azaleas. Pochin's daughter Laura, who had married Charles McLaren, inherited the estate in 1905. McLaren, a barrister and MP, was made a peer in 1911 taking the title Lord Aberconway. Their son, the 2nd Lord

Aberconway, added immensely to the garden. He was a great plant collector, subscribing to the expeditions of Harold Comber, George FORREST, Frank Kingdon WARD, and others. He was especially interested in magnolias and rhododendrons of which there are magnificent examples in the garden today—the magnolias on lawns south and south-west of the house and rhododendrons spectacularly clothing the slopes of the Hiraethlyn. Immediately to the west of the house, where the land slopes down steeply towards the Hiraethlyn valley, Aberconway built grand terraces. Close to the house is a magnificent old *Arbutus* × *andrachnoides*, planted in 1906, and a formal rose garden overlooking a croquet terrace below which ornamental gardens descend the slope. The Lily Terrace, with a great lily pool, is overshadowed by two great cedars, a cedar of Lebanon and a blue Atlas cedar. Curving steps, enclosed in a trellis-work pergola shrouded with roses, lead down to the Canal Terrace where an elegant 18th-century pavilion, the Pin Mill, is reflected in the canal with, facing it at

the far end, a raised turf terrace with a William KENT garden bench and hedges of yew. Bodnant is an excellent example of a particularly British kind of garden, made by generations of cultivated gardeners and plantsmen, taking an intense interest in their garden and having the means to make it as good as they possibly could. Although owned by the NATIONAL TRUST since 1949 the garden has continued to be supervised by the Aberconways, with three generations of the Puddle family as head gardeners. This, despite the very large numbers of visitors it receives, has allowed Bodnant to preserve the atmosphere of a private estate.   PT

Bodysgallen Hall ⊛
near Llandudno, Conwy, Wales, stands on a rocky promontory, with views of the Conwy valley and of Snowdonia, and was thought once

---

Plan of the **Boboli Gardens** from H. Inigo Triggs's *The Art of Garden Design in Italy* (1906) based on Varcellini's plan of 1780.

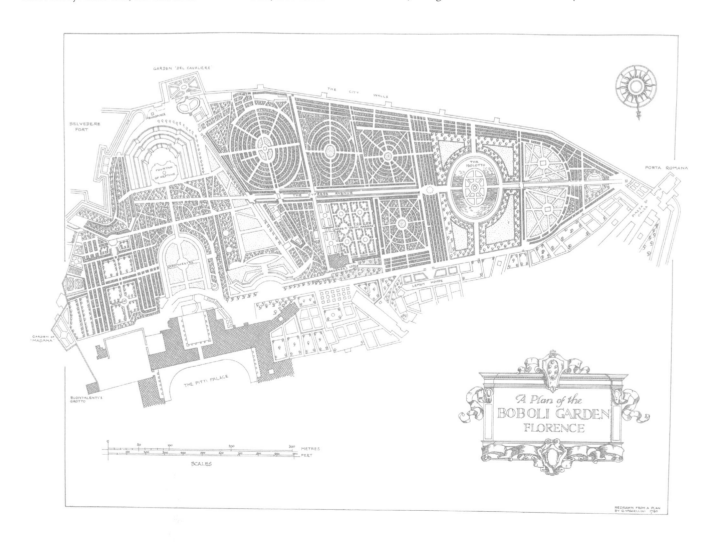

to have been a lookout for Conwy Castle. The house dates from the early 17th century and was built for the Mostyn family. The terraced and walled gardens are of ancient origin and could well be the same date as the house. They have been restored in recent times when the house became a hotel. An elaborate box parterre, formal rose garden, and splendid topiary are disposed on the terraces—all of recent planting but with period charm.   PT

Boer, Wim

(1922–2000), Dutch landscape architect and professor of garden and landscape architecture at the Technical University in Delft whose main interest was in urban green space. His unpublished book on garden design emphasizes the significance of gardens in the wider context of the city and the environment in general. His designs follow modernist principles; the garden became an extension of the house, designed with the spatial continuity of the De Stijl movement with uncompromising modern materials in a well-structured sequence of mostly rectangular spaces. The planting was naturalistic in approach and softened the harsh geometry with both exotic and native plants.   JW

Bogoroditsk Park ✿

near Tula, Russia, was created by Andrei Timofeyevich Bolotov (1738–1833), a prolific and influential Russian writer on agriculture with a special interest in gardening. Influenced by the writings of C. C. L. HIRSCHFELD, he rejected the artificiality of the French formal garden and advocated the landscape style, but he was anxious that Russian parks should have their own national character rather than imitate English models. He took nature as his guide, with the Russian climate a controlling factor, and he used native Russian trees and plants.

After being appointed steward at Bogoroditsk, the estate of Alexei Bobrinsky (1762–1813, illegitimate son of Catherine the Great and Count Grigorii Orlov), Bolotov was presented with a great opportunity to put his ideas into practice. The palace—facing the town across a large stretch of water—and church were both by I. E. Starov (1743–1808), whose plan for a small formal park was rejected. The site was promising with steep slopes and gullies but without water. Bolotov found a source about 2 km/1.25 miles away and the water was channelled to feed a newly created system of interconnected pools, cascades, and waterfalls. Two hundred serfs were available, and while some moved earth to reshape the landscape, others fetched saplings—birch, aspen, oak, lime, maple, rowan, bird cherry, ash, willow, spindle tree, and honeysuckle—from nearby woodlands

and planted them in the park. Wild flowering plants were also brought in. Architectural features included a rotunda, a pavilion, and an obelisk, while a steep sandstone slope was laid bare and carved to appear as a ruined castle with cavelike interiors.   PH

Bogstad Mansion ✿

Oslo, Norway, once one of the largest estates in Norway, was sold in 1954 to the city of Oslo with forests, fields, and a lake. The 18th-century buildings, surrounded by a park of 130 hectares/320 acres, today are a museum. The cultivated merchant Peder Anker, later Prime Minister, bought Bogstad in 1772. Having seen the new landscape style in gardening on his European grand tour he sent his head gardener on a study trip to England. On the gardener's return the formal garden at Bogstad was extended in the 1780s by a landscape park, the first of its kind in Norway. At the lakeside south-west of the mansion the park was laid out with serpentine paths and ponds and long vistas across the water.

Contemporary paintings show three pavilions, of which only the fishing pavilion exists today. A large number of foreign plants were introduced in the park, but only few have survived, e.g. spiked rampion (*Phyteuma spicatum*) and white wood-rush (*Luzula luzuloides*) in the lawn. Among the oldest trees are the white spruce (*Abies alba*), Siberian pine (*Pinus cembra*), and the Weymouth pine (*Pinus strobus*). The vegetation today consists mainly of indigenous trees (birch, ash) and common park species (elm, lime, horse chestnut, and lilacs).
ME

MADELEINE VON ESSEN and KNUT LANGELAND, *Parken og hagen på Bogstad: til nytte og behag* (2002).

Bois de Boulogne.

See PARIS PARKS AND GARDENS.

Bokrijk Arboretum ✿

Bokrijk, Genk, Limburg, Belgium, is today part of a major tourist attraction, Park Midden Limburg. The domain had belonged to the Abbey of Herkenrode until 1791 and later was privately owned, the present castle being built in 1896 in the 'Meuse Renaissance' style. The province acquired the estate and in 1950 started the ARBORETUM which has an area of 12 hectares/30 acres and is at some distance from the main tourist attractions. The trees are planted in systematic order beds (see BOTANIC GARDEN) as well as naturalistically as if in a landscape park. Three thousand species of woody plants are grown, with extensive collections of ilex, malus, and bamboo. It is particularly well known for its conifers, which have now reached majestic proportions—here is the place to see the

Leyland cypress (× *Cupressocyparis leylandii*) grown to its magnificent best as well as a good collection of *Chamaecyparis* species. Acers, birches, and beeches are also well represented. There is a fine *Acer* × *zoeschense* 'Anna', *A. cissifolium. A. platanoides* 'Globosum', and good specimens of *Fagus sylvatica rotundifolia*, *F.s.* var. *heterophylla* 'Aspleniifolia', and *F.s.* 'Dawyck'. Among flowering trees and shrubs are witch hazels, magnolias, and viburnums, and in acid, fen areas, vacciniums, and other ericaceous plants. The estate of Bokrijk also contains an Open Air Museum with reconstructed old buildings, a new herb garden, several restaurants, playgrounds, a nature reserve, and marked footpaths through the surrounding woods. Near the castle is a large rose garden.
BA

Bologna, Giovanni da. See GIAMBOLOGNA.

Bomarzo

(Sacro Bosco) ✿ near Viterbo, Lazio, Italy, was defined by Gustav René Hocke in *Manierismus in der Literatur* (1963) as an 'intellectual and aesthetic Arcadia of terror'. The Sacred Wood at Bomarzo, also called the Parco dei Mostri, is a unique 16th-century park bearing no relationship to contemporary Renaissance garden architecture, although it marches with the original garden of the Palazzo Orsini laid out in traditional geometry. It was created for Vicino Orsini by Annibal Caro (1507–66) from 1552. It is a strange and grotesque assembly of mythical, literary, and heraldic symbols, carved in stone, lurking in woodland. Their iconography and symbolism still remain baffling to historians. The fantastic lichen-covered stone creatures, inducing feelings of horror and of beauty, may have been inspired by Torquato Tasso's (1544–95) *Amadigi* and *Floridante* (from *Gerusalemme liberata*) or taken from Ariosto's *Orlando furioso* (1516). Here are an elephant with a towering howdah, a dragon fending off lions, a giant gaping mouth carved out of the hill inside which is a banqueting hall, a turtle surmounted by Fortuna, a giant Neptune (or Father Tiber), and a Pegasus fountain, besides a carving of an upside-down figure being torn apart by his legs. An inscription carved in tufa on the ogre's mouth reads 'lasciate ogni pensieri voi che entrate' (abandon every thought you who enter)—a fitting invitation to a journey of nightmares.
PHo

Bom Jesus do Monte ✿

near Braga, Portugal. The church of Bom Jesus do Monte ('good Jesus of the hill'), of dashing baroque style, rises high on its wooded hill. Below it a cascade of stairs plummets down the steep slope. It dates from 1723 but work on it, of one kind or another, continued until the end of the century. The unforgettable feature is the staircase itself and the decorative devices that enrich it. It links a series of landings—the steps dividing above and below each landing to approach it or leave it from either side to form a dazzling zigzag. The whitewashed retaining walls, following the descending slope, bristle with ornament—obelisks, finials, and statues. References are made to the Old Testament—a statue of Noah with a sheep, quotations from Deuteronomy or Ecclesiastes. Some of the statuary is sprightly and amusing—monkeys or peacocks flanking a fountain—but others are more macabre—the mask of a woman out of whose eyes water gushes. Each landing has a floor of a mosaic pattern of stone with a fountain set into its retaining wall. The walls flanking the landings are decorated with topiary—a base of clipped box out of which rise a clipped mound of camellia and spheres of box. At the bottom of the staircase is a pair of stone columns with a spiral runnel curling about down which a serpent pours water. At the head of the staircase, below the walls of the church, is a curious picturesque garden. A double staircase links two levels and bedding schemes with curling patterns are disposed about it. Just north of the church is an exotic MIRADOR which rises above a GROTTO, copiously endowed with stalactites and stalagmites, which stands on the edge of a pool.   PT

bonsai

is the horticultural practice and art of growing plants in containers to suggest a natural scene or the abstract beauty of a tree in miniature. The Japanese word is literally a *sai* (planting) in a *bon* (pot or tray). Bonsai are most often recognized as the miniature of an idealized tree in nature. Grown in free-draining containers using coarse soil mix to promote root health, bonsai may be made from a wide variety of trees or shrubs. While some tropical plants can be grown indoors, most traditional bonsai are grown outdoors. They require judicious watering, feeding, and occasional root pruning.

The bonsai designer simplifies the structure of a full-sized tree in miniature to suggest age, stability, and elegance. Mature species have compact rounded tops and lower branches that are horizontal or angled downward. The trunk should rise with taper from a buttress of exposed roots radiating around its base. Branches are positioned to support horizontal 'clouds' of foliage. The illusion of an old tree requires that tree parts be proportional. Plants chosen should have small leaves or needles that will reduce in size with training. Branches on the lowest part of an upright bonsai should be

both the largest in diameter and the longest. Shortening the height of the plant makes the girth of the trunk appear larger. Depending on the characteristics of the plant, bonsai may be trained into several distinct styles including straight or curved upright trunk, slanting trunk, literati, rock-clinging, twin-trunk, forest, cascade, or semi-cascade. The designer's eye and the plant's inherent characteristics determine which style is best suited.

Bonsai have seasonal features. Early blooming Japanese apricots (*Prunus mume*) are appreciated for withered, gnarled trunks contrasting with buds and flowers that can withstand snow. Winterberry (*Ilex serrata*) bonsai are attractive for their bare silhouette and bright-red berries. Symbolic of the New Year, Japanese black pines (*Pinus thunbergii*) are enhanced by deeply fissured bark that recalls long life. *Stewartia monadelpha* and Japanese beeches (*Fagus crenata*) are displayed for their striking smooth bark when bare, though beech also may be displayed for coppery leaves remaining in winter. Satsuki azaleas (*Rhododendron* 'Satsuki' (EA)) are grown for flower display as well as treelike form. Japanese maples (*Acer palmatum*) are highly regarded for autumn leaf colour.

The famous Chinese recluse scholar Tao Qian (d. 427) grew potted wild chrysanthemums, but their appreciation as bonsai is inconclusive. The earliest illustration of bonsai was discovered in the Chinese tomb of Prince Zhang Huai, who died in 706. Artistic potted trees continued to be cultivated in China as documented by literati scholars in the Tang, Song, Yuan, and Ming periods (618–1644). Chinese artistic potted trees are referred to as penjing (tray scenery). Knowledge of cultivating miniature trees reached Japan from China. The earliest record of Japanese bonsai is illustrated in a scroll dated 1195. Along with scrolls from the 14th century, it relates bonsai to the practice of Zen. Bonsai cultivation was an elite taste, and its shapes suggested either highly articulated classical forms or reference to metaphysical, contemplative landscapes. In 17th-century China and Japan, peace and prosperity expanded the clientele for artistic potted trees. Commercial production satisfied regional fashions. Peace in China was short-lived, however, and penjing practice declined after the first quarter of the 19th century. In modern China, regional styles have been revived adopting many styling and plant varieties. The 'Clip and Grow Method' developed around 1900 is considered among the most artistic in developing natural tree forms and competes with techniques of styling using palm-leaf fibres or wire for branch placement. Beginning in the 1960s, use of flat stone trays to display

miniature landscapes improved the display of cliff faces and the interplay of water and shorelines. In Japan of the Edo era (1600–1868), a passion for growing plants and commercialization resulted in popularity for a variety of potted flowering trees, trees with variegated foliage, and more showy pots. The artistic literati maintained interest in Chinese styles and pots which were sparse and elegant. In the Meiji period (1868–1912) the Emperor promoted bonsai as a Japanese art. By the 1890s, interest in Chinese styles of trees and pots declined. Low rimmed pots better expressed individual trees standing in the landscape. The first large Western exhibit of Japanese bonsai was held in London in 1909, but only since the Second World War has it been widely practised in the West. Modern Chinese and Western bonsai influence are growing. Today, worldwide, this rich history has evolved into a rewarding hobby and venerable profession.

CMC

DEBORAH KORESHOFF, *Bonsai: Its Art, Science, History and Philosophy* (1984).
HIDEO MARUSHIMA, 'The history of bonsai', in *Classic Bonsai of Japan* (1989).

Bonţida (in Hungarian Bonchida), Bánffy Park ⊕ Bontida, Romania. The castle and park, known as the 'Versailles of Transylvania', are among the most important monuments of the region. The palace was built for the Bánffy family, who played a crucial role throughout the history of Transylvania. The castle with four towers, one on each corner, was built on the side of the river Szamos in the 1660s, on the site of a 15th-century fortification. The castle was greatly enlarged and redesigned as a stately palace in baroque style richly decorated with statues around 1750 by Count Dénes Bánffy. The lavish park was built at the same time, designed by Austrian gardener Johann Christian Erras from Marchegg. The structure of the 170-hectare/ 380-acre garden was defined by the four straight avenues, each over 2.5 km/1.5 miles long, which radiated out from a bridge over a canal west of the house.

One of the first large-scale baroque garden compositions of Transylvania, this garden was laid out around the same time as the West Hungarian garden of Eszterháza (see FERTŐD), which was to have a similar PATTE D'OIE pattern of avenues. The outer part of the park was used as a game reserve with hunting lodges and grottoes and a hothouse was built in 1776–83, designed by Johann Eberhard Blaumann.

In the 1830s the park was turned into a landscape garden by Count József Bánffy who also rebuilt parts of the palace in the Gothic style. Trees close to the palace were felled, winding pathways took the place of straight avenues, with clumps of trees and flower beds between them. The designer was Samuel Hermann, whose designs also included a fisherman's hut, a Schweitzerei (ornamental dairy), a Temple of Solitude, a GLORIETTE, a Temple of Pan, fountains, a pavilion, a hermitage, a botanic garden, an obelisk, and a sundial. A map dating from 1831 shows that Hermann's schemes were, at least in part, carried out. A pleasure ground was created on the western side of the palace in the middle of the 19th century. The garden's layout remained unchanged until the First World War, and it was preserved as a possession of the Bánffy family after 1920 when Transylvania was annexed to Romania. After 1945, the building was looted, part of it collapsed, and almost every tree in the park was felled. Thus, Bonţida is a representative example of the fate of many Transylvanian country houses and parks. However, conservation of the ruined house has recently been started within the framework of an international project.   GA

BIRÒ, JÒZSEF, *A bonczhidai Bánffy-kastély* (Bánffy Palace at Bonchida) (1935).

border.

The border has a long history, evolving gently before it assumed its full splendour in late 19th-century England. At its most straightforward the border is a strip-shaped bed planted with flowers—the *plate-bande* of French baroque gardens of the 17th century. Although *plate-bande* means literally 'flat strip', the surface was often mounded along its axis, rising to a crest (*dos de carpe*—'carp's back') or rounded (*dos d'âne*—'donkey's back'), which allowed the decorative planting to rise in prominence. An early version of the *plate-bande* may be seen in the designs for PARTERRES in André Mollet's *Le Jardin de plaisir* (1651). Something of this sort was used to frame the *parterres de broderie* in the garden at Het LOO in the Netherlands in the late 1680s and exactly reinstated (with its *dos d'âne*) in the splendid recreation carried out from 1970. Late 17th-century illustrations and plans show that these ornamental strips were planted in a thoroughly regimented fashion, with a regular arrangement of small clipped usually evergreen shrubs interspersed with flowering plants disposed as individual specimens. In the restored late 17th-century Privy Garden at HAMPTON COURT PALACE (in which Daniel MAROT, who also worked at Het Loo, probably had a hand) the *plate-bandes* were the subject of much research. The repertory of plants used in the Privy Garden included yew, variegated holly, *Phillyrea angustifolia*, and *Rhamnus alaternus*, all of which would have been clipped. Among flowering plants were several kinds of bulbs, among them daffodils, hyacinths, irises,

and tulips. Annuals and herbaceous perennials would also have been used. The *plate-bande* may be regarded as a prototype of the modern border but in one regard it was essentially different—it was subservient to some larger decorative scheme rather than being a feature in itself.

The first borders in England in the modern sense are generally considered to be those at ARLEY HALL in Cheshire, laid out in the mid 19th century and still surviving. However, by this time there had for many years been much experimenting and theorizing about the art of the border. Some of the late 18th-century shrub borders described by Mark Laird in *The Flowering of the Landscape Garden* (1999) display an intriguing intermediate form of border, with something of the regimentation of the *plate-bande* but also an incipient blowsiness. These borders were much deeper than the *plate-bande* and introduced the idea of ranging plants in size, with the tallest at the back. According to Sir William CHAMBERS's *Dissertation on Oriental Gardening* (1772) this gradation of size was characteristic of Chinese planting. 'They avoid all sudden transitions', he wrote, 'both with regard to dimension and colour.' Nathaniel Swinden's *Beauties of Flora Display'd* (1778) shows a circular bed with concentric circles of plants, rising in height towards the middle, 'meeting nearly in a point at the centre'. Swinden was also interested in colour, specifying that 'not two flowers of the same colour . . . [be] seen together'. Although, as Mark Laird shows, there was much discussion of leaf colour in 18th-century landscaping and laying out of shrubberies, flower colour, of much importance to the aesthetics of the border, was less debated. Sir William Chambers's reference to the Chinese use of colour is especially interesting in relation to the history of the border. Chambers writes of the Chinese 'varying their tints, by easy gradations, from white, straw colour, purple and incarnate, to the deepest blues, and most brilliant crimsons and scarlets'. By the time J. C. LOUDON wrote his *Encyclopaedia of Gardening* (1822) there was a very large repertory of plants regarded as 'border flowers' and the principle of grading by size and paying attention to colour was firmly established. Loudon prints a very elaborate table listing herbaceous perennials by colour and height for each month in the flowering year, from February to October. Similar tables are shown for bulbs, biennials, hardy annuals, and half-hardy annuals.

The heyday of the border spanned the late 19th and early 20th centuries. Gertrude JEKYLL, with her artist's eye for colour and shape, and her profound knowledge of plants and practical horticulture, was its most consummate practitioner. Her book *Colour Schemes for the*

Flower Garden (1908) shows precisely the effects she sought to achieve. In Britain the design of borders was deeply influenced by her example at gardens like CRATHES CASTLE (from 1926), HIDCOTE MANOR (from 1907), and SISSINGHURST CASTLE (from 1930), in particular in the use of colour theming, not always accurately reflecting Jekyll's ideas. The management of a Jekyll herbaceous border, with its fastidious regimen of staking, division, and constant titivation, depends on a large and highly trained garden staff. Jekyll's theory of border drifts illustrates the sort of effects she sought to achieve. Drifts were long swathes of plantings of a single kind, arranged in sweeping parallels, often at an oblique angle to the axis of the border. Different species or varieties were juxtaposed so that, as soon as one drift was past its flowering best, it could be cut back, allowing the adjacent drifts to billow outwards to conceal the gap. In modern times the true herbaceous border has become a rarity, having been superseded by the mixed border, with woody and herbaceous plants intermingled, which, although still needing much attention, is not as labour intensive as the true herbaceous border. Christopher LLOYD's Long Border at GREAT DIXTER shows the multifarious possibilities of the mixed border. The true herbaceous borders designed by Graham Stuart THOMAS in 1969 for the National Trust at CLIVEDEN are a rare late 20th-century exercise in the grand manner. The borders are planted in bold clumps, with restricted colour schemes—'One border has got no pinks, mauves or purples, the other has got no oranges, reds or yellows; and that, I think, is the way to do gardens', as Thomas wrote. Although such grand arrangements are a rarity today, the border is still a universal feature in early 21st-century British gardens. In most gardens, however, it is not the canvas for some eloquent Jekyllesque arrangement of form and colour, rather a frame for a jumble of plants.   PT

Borghese, Villa ⊛

Rome, Italy. Situated just outside the Porta Pinciana, the villa and huge garden, begun in 1608 for Cardinal Scipione Borghese, was originally laid out by D. Savino, G. Rainaldi (1570–1655), and G. Fontana (1540–1614), and was the first of the great Roman parks in which the actual building, designed by the Flemish architect Giovanni Vasanzio (d. 1622) for the Cardinal's collection of antique sculpture (today the Galleria Borghese), was subordinate to the surrounding garden and woods. It seems that in creating the complex Cardinal Borghese was inspired by HADRIAN'S VILLA at Tivoli. The Casino Nobile, the core of the estate, was flanked by two intimate walled gardens for rare flowers and espaliered citrus and an aviary by Rainaldi. The outer grounds were divided into three areas. The first, closest to the casino, was wooded, consisting of compartments laid out in geometric form to make avenues edged with clipped hedges decorated with antique statues, herms, fountains, columns, and seats, the whole anticipating French developments during the later 17th century. The second enclosure was a hunting park with two loggias for entertaining and the third was a less regular layout of hills, woods, and glades with two spectacular *ragnaia* for bird trapping. Towards the end of the 18th century Prince Marcantonio Borghese enlarged the estate and with his sons, Camillo and Francesco, introduced the English-style Giardino del Lago, with a Temple of Aesculapius designed by Asprucci, while other architects added the Casino Fountain and the Casina dell'Orologio, all under the supervision of the Scottish painter Jacob Moore. Further extensions were made after 1822. The park passed to the state in 1901 and is now administered by the Municipality of Rome. An engraving by G. B. Falda in *Li giardini di Roma* (c.1683) shows the complex still in its geometric form, while a description written in 1700 by D. Monelatici gives more detail. Balustrades in front of the CASINO were acquired by Viscount Astor in 1896 and now decorate the terraces at CLIVEDEN. The park and inner walled gardens are currently under restoration.   PHo

borrowed landscape.
What is visible beyond the confines of a garden is often a vital part of its atmosphere. In Japanese garden aesthetics, as SHAKKEI, it assumed great importance, as it did also in China as JIE JING. To open up a view of something beautiful—a glimpse of a church steeple or a finely composed piece of landscape—is in itself to extend the scope of a garden. The most exciting examples, however, are those which make a strong connection between what is outside the garden and what is inside it. The Scottish 17th-century architect and garden designer Sir William BRUCE in two of his most notable gardens borrowed the landscape in brilliant fashion. At Balcaskie (Fife, c.1668–74) he laid out a strongly axial garden, centred on the house, connecting a series of terraces sloping down towards the Firth of Forth. The axis is precisely centred on a curious hump-backed island, the Bass Rock, 21 km/13 miles away. At KINROSS HOUSE, a little later, he designed another axial layout connecting house and garden. The axis pierces the house and leads down a gentle slope to an opening and wrought-iron gate in the garden wall which frames the ruins of Loch Leven

Castle standing on an island in the loch beyond. Bruce made a further connection between inside and outside. Above the gateway, finely carved in stone, is an urn containing several species of fish all of which are identifiable as freshwater species found in the loch. In the 17th and 18th centuries the HA-HA allowed uninterrupted views of the landscape beyond the pleasure garden. The tradition of the borrowed landscape has continuing currency. At Plas BRONDANW the peaks of Snowdon and Cnicht are centred on axial walks. In very different circumstances a similar effect is achieved in the late 20th-century garden at the OLD VICARAGE, EAST RUSTON, where in the flat landscape of east Norfolk distant church spires have been drawn in as eyecatchers.   PT

bosco.
The Italian word means a wood but in the context of gardens, from the Renaissance, it assumed more specific meaning. In the 15th-century HYPNEROTOMACHIA POLIPHILI the hero has to traverse the Hercynian Forest to reach his goal of Cytherea. Perilous journeys of this kind are frequently found in classical literature and something of this perilous flavour may be found in the Renaissance *bosco*. From the 16th century the *bosco* was a more or less formal wooded garden, decorated with buildings or ornaments. The *Sacro Bosco* (sacred wood) of BOMARZO is of this kind, with much irregularity in its undulating site. The 17th-century *bosco* at the Villa CETINALE, with its imposing arched entrances, seems at first to be simple woodland, but it is decorated from time to time with curious stone creatures emerging from the ground and with shrines beside paths. Ligustri's late 16th-century engraving of the Villa LANTE shows, to one side of the formal garden, a *bosco* with straight walks through the woods, pools, a maze, and a central CASINO. UTENS's painting (1598) of the Villa PRATOLINO depicts a *bosco* of great elaboration spread out on either side of a central walk. Dense woods of regularly spaced trees are pierced by numerous straight walks with occasional clearings and statues placed either as eyecatchers at the end of walks or to mark a junction. A *bosco* of this kind is close in spirit to the formal wildernesses of 17th- and early 18th-century England.   PT

Bosque, El ⊛
Béjar, Castilla y Léon, Spain. In the 16th century the estate of El Bosque was embellished with a new house—the *palacete* (small palace)—and a chapel overlooking a large pool. It was built in 1567 for the Duke of Béjar, Francisco de Zúñiga y Sotomajor, at the heart of an estate with an enclosed hunting park and ornamental

gardens. About the pool were stone fountains of Renaissance character, some of which survive. On an island in the pool is a curious metal pavilion like a bandstand which must date from the 19th century. Stone steps lead down to a lower garden, which is watered by a rill linked to the upper pool, with winding paths lined with box hedges and fountains. One of these, built into a wall and bearing the Duke's arms, is provided with water jets to sprinkle the unwary. The Renaissance character of the garden is overlaid with an air of 19th-century melancholy, much of it derived from the mature Wellingtonias (*Sequoiadendron giganteum*) that shade it.   PT

bosquet.
The French word means literally a small wood or clump of trees, deriving from the Italian *boschetto*, the diminutive of BOSCO. In the context of the garden it is first recorded in France in 1572 at the famous early Renaissance Château de GAILLON in a document which mentions the making of new bosquets—'troys petitz bocquetz plantez de boys qui seront partiz en trois, lesd. bocquetz estans faictz en forme de pallissade' (three small *bosquets* planted with trees, the said *bosquets* being made in the form of a PALISSADE) (Document of 1572 in the Archives Nationales quoted by Michel Conan in *Dictionnaire historique de l'art des jardins*, no date). In the 17th century the *bosquet* was an essential element in the decorative repertoire of the French baroque garden. It was a formal planting of trees, usually a square, crossed by a formal pattern of walks with the trees lining the walks cut into a *palissade*. The trees recommended by André MOLLET are hornbeams, privet, or phillyrea which he describes in detail in his *Le Jardin de plaisir* (1651). The *bosquet* could be substantial in size—one of which he gives a plan is 40 *toises* square (a *toise* was 2 m/6.5 ft). The more complicated designs could have interior compartments (CABINETS) decorated with a statue or a single tree at the centre. The *cabinets* might also been lined with flower beds *trois pieds* (1 m/3.75 ft) wide. Mollet recommends planting all sorts of small trees behind the *palissades* to encourage the presence of birds to form 'une volière naturelle . . . beaucoup plus agréable que l'artificielle' (a natural aviary . . . far more attractive than an artificial one). Chapter VI of A.-J. DEZALLIER D'ARGENVILLE's *La Théorie et la pratique du jardinage* (1709) is devoted to *bosquets* and spells out their different types in detail.   PT

botanical illustration.
The drawing and painting of plants so they may be accurately identified demands a rigorous academic approach combined with great

artistic talent. Their accurate representation began as a necessity for teaching the identification of plants. Some of the earliest images appear on Minoan wall paintings and frescoes of *c.*1750-1500 BC where both the madonna lily (*Lilium candidum*) and saffron crocus (*Crocus sativus*) are clearly identifiable. One hundred years later, on the Egyptian tomb of Tuthmosis III at the Temple of Karnak, a group of 275 bas-relief plants may be seen, including the pomegranate (*Punica granatum*) and the dragon arum (*Dracunculus vulgaris*), both recorded as being collected from Syria.

It was during the 1st century AD that the Greek physician DIOSCORIDES wrote his book *De Materia Medica* in which he concentrates on medicinal herbs. The earliest copies of this influential work were probably not illustrated, but there is a manuscript dating from *c.*512 housed in the Austrian National Library in Vienna, known as the *Codex Vindobonensis*, which contains nearly 400 full-page watercolour paintings of identifiable plants. There is no confusion as to what they are, all seem clearly and boldly painted from life, and many of the names Dioscorides gave to the plants are still in use today. This great pharmacological work was soon translated into Latin, and throughout the coming centuries both the text and the illustrations were copied, plagiarized, and added to. Most early herbals emanated from around the eastern Mediterranean and were often plagiarized. One written by Apuleius Platonicus during the 6th or early 7th century may be singled out, as it was translated *c.*1050 into Anglo-Saxon. Its importance lies not in its information or painting but that it appears to be the earliest vernacular translation from Latin into any language of such a document.

The European monasteries were the original source and inspiration of the style of painting from the 10th to the 13th centuries, but during the 14th century a more naturalistic approach emanated from Tuscany, spreading throughout Europe, and was reflected in the floral detail. This style was taken to greater heights by Jean Bourdichon (1457-*c.*1521), born in Tours, who trained first as an artist and later learnt botany. He was court painter successively to three kings of France from *c.*1483 until his death in Lyon in 1521, painting portraits and religious subjects, but the work for which he is renowned belongs to the then fashionable idea of painting botanically correct and beautiful floral borders around religious or devotional manuscripts. Ten of these precious books survive, the most exquisite being the *c.*1508 *Book of Hours* made for Anne (1476-1514), Duchess of Brittany and Queen to both Charles VIII and later Louis XII. Some 340 native plants of Touraine are portrayed in gouache in the tiny gilded rectangles, each one given its French and Latin name, and their identity helps to show the range of plants then being grown.

Existing side by side with botanical painting since at least the 1400s was the art of the woodcut, a more stolid and by its nature less refined ideal for illustrating plants. It was however a useful method for illustration in the early printed herbals and often appeared as a black and white line drawing with the background cut away. The wood blocks were nearly always crude copies of much earlier classical drawings. In 1530-6 the three-volume *Herbarum Vivae Eicones* (Living Portrait of Plants) was published in Strasbourg, written by the botanist Otto BRUNFELS, who employed the artist Hans Weiditz (Latinized to Johannes Guidictius) to illustrate the work. The resulting woodcuts are some of the finest ever achieved, and it can be seen that the artist drew direct from nature with all the concomitant hazards of insect damage, torn leaf, or drooping flower head. A few of his original drawings survive and are now housed in the University Botanic Institute at Berne.

By the middle of the 16th century the first botanic gardens were being created in Italy, where interest in medicinal plants was such that it stimulated Italian artists to record the flora accurately and scientifically. The decline of using the woodcut for botanical illustration had now begun and slowly plants were being depicted not just for their identification and usefulness but also for their intrinsic beauty. This new approach coincided with the beginnings of world exploration, when as a result of the exotic flora from foreign lands introduced into Europe, plants were eagerly painted by court painters for their royal patrons. Collections of paintings were being bound together to form florilegia—a word coined during the 17th century. One of the earliest of these was *Le Jardin du roy très chrestien Henry IV* of 1608 whose author, Pierre Vallet, was both the draughtsman and engraver of the 75 flowers illustrated from the French royal gardens. Naturalistic and engaging, they were originally intended to be used as embroidery patterns, the whole being dedicated to Marie de Médicis, the consort of Henri IV (1533-1610). From the celebrated de Passe engraving family of Utrecht came *Hortus Floridus* (1614) compiled by Crispin de Passe (b. *c.*1590) and comprising some 200 images, its multilingual texts in French and English appearing almost immediately. It was widely copied and the plate details may be traced in one instance over 100 years later when Sir John Hill, an apothecary and owner of a botanic garden in Bayswater, used them in his book *Eden* (1757).

All over Europe collections of natural history, flora, fauna, and curios were being gathered together and displayed and sometimes recorded, both native and foreign objects being considered worthy of attention. In Blois Gaston d'Orléans, brother of Louis XIII, engaged an artist, Nicholas Robert (1614-85), to record his collection, and it is from these botanical drawings that a stupendous collection has been amassed. There were 70 volumes of them by 1767; now there are 100, the whole collection being housed in the library of the Muséum National d'Histoire Naturelle, Paris. Known as the *Vélins du Muséum* they are an astounding record of both botanical art and science. An early contributor to the *vélins* (vellums) was Claude Aubriet (1655-1742)—remembered in the species *Aubrieta*—following his journey to the Levant with Joseph Pitton de TOURNEFORT, as, at a later date, was Pierre-Joseph Redouté (1759-1841), who contributed over 500 paintings.

In Holland the floriferous oil paintings of the 17th and 18th centuries, while not strictly botanical illustrations, nonetheless contribute to our knowledge about plants, even though the voluptuously filled vases could not have all been in flower at the same time. One of the artists was Jan van Huysum (1682-1749), whose younger brother Jacobus (*c.*1687-1740) worked in Britain on illustrating two books, John Martyn's *Historia Plantarum Rariorum* (1728-36) and *Catalogus Plantarum* (1730), for the Society of Gardeners (*fl. c.*1720-*c.*1727). A German artist of great merit who first trained as a gardener was Georg Dionysius Ehret (1708-70), who settled in Britain, marrying at 30 the sister-in-law of Philip MILLER, curator of the Chelsea Physic Garden. Ehret painted the new introductions arriving, particularly from America, his paintings being both stylish and accurate. Ehret also had great finesse as an engraver: for his own book, *Plantae et Papiliones Rariores* (Rare Plants and Butterflies) (1748-59), he prepared his drawings for engraving and colouring. Teaching both drawing and botany, he was for several decades influential in the botanical life of Europe.

Teaching was one of the talents of James Sowerby (1757-1822), a botanical artist and engraver who wrote *Easy Introduction to Drawing Flowers According to Nature* (1788). His prodigious output included 25,000 watercolours, of which 3,000 were engraved, for the 36 volumes of *English Botany* (1790-1814) and he also engraved the drawings of the Austrian Ferdinand Bauer (1760-1826) for *Flora Graeca* (10 volumes, 1806-40). Bauer had first travelled to Australia with Matthew Flinders recording the flora and later engraving and colouring the plates illustrating them. He was also responsible for the execution of the paintings for the two-volume *Description of Genus Pinus* (1803) for Aylmer Bourke Lambert (1761–1842), vice-president of the Linnean Society of London. Francis Bauer (1758–1840), Ferdinand's brother, also had a rare botanical talent and settled in England under the patronage of Sir Joseph BANKS, where he became royal artist in residence at Kew.

The royal patronage of the Empress Joséphine Bonaparte (1763–1814) for Pierre-Joseph Redouté's paintings, particularly the representations of roses, helped ensure his artistic pre-eminence; he was known as the 'Raphael of Flowers' and the 'Rembrandt of Roses', and although the prints of his work are endlessly reproduced, the paintings exude a serenity and seem to capture the essence of the flower.

In Britain, the history of botanical illustration was being taken forward by the botanist and publisher William Curtis (1746–99), who in 1787 founded *Curtis's Botanical Magazine* illustrating and describing *the Most Ornamental Foreign Plants, Cultivated in the Open Ground, the Green-House and the Stove*. Despite various financial and other vicissitudes its publication continues and it is now the oldest illustrated periodical in the world. During a long period in the 19th century its artist was Walter Hood Fitch (1817–92), who drew over 2,700 plates between 1834 and 1877. He had come to the notice of Sir William Hooker, then professor of botany at Glasgow, and when Sir William came south to the ROYAL BOTANIC GARDENS, KEW, in 1841, he insisted that the artist came too. Fitch was a meticulous draughtsman, and a most talented engraver, illustrating many of the sketches made by Joseph HOOKER during his travels in the Himalayas in 1847. Hooker believed he could seize 'the natural characters of plants'. Fitch's industry also led him to make over 1,000 wood engravings for George Bentham's *Handbook of British Flora* (1858).

The technical advances in printing and reproduction from the middle of the 19th century altered the perception of botanical illustration. The development of lithography, and the founding of the Photographic Society in 1853, threatened to cast aside the artistic botanical skills of illustrating the floral world. Yet botanical talent continued to flourish, and a slow change was taking place. From earliest times the artists were almost without exception men, but gradually women took over their role. One of the earliest and most remarkable was Lilian Snelling (1879–1952), who was engaged by the ROYAL BOTANIC GARDEN, EDINBURGH 1916–21 as botanical artist and then, from 1922 and for the next 30 years, was the principal illustrator for *Curtis's Botanical Magazine*. Another early woman artist was Stella Ross-Craig (b. 1906), who undertook, among much work at Royal Botanic Garden, Kew, to create 1,286 black and white images to illustrate the *Drawings of British Plants* issued in 32 parts between 1948 and 1973. Margaret Mee (1909–88), who specialized in Amazonian flora, lived for many years in Brazil where she began her painting career at the Instituto de Botanic in São Paulo. In 1986 the Jill Smythies Award for botanical painting was instituted by the Linnean Society of London. By 2002 there had been fifteen awards, of which only four recipients were men. The previous year, also in Britain, the Society of Botanical Artists had been formed, the instigator and first president being Suzanne Lucas, whereby highly esteemed artists including Royal Horticultural Society gold and silver-gilt award winners were invited to create a focus of botanical art and keep alive the tradition of artistic excellence. Ten years later, in 1995, a similar organization was established in America. In the 21st century the art of botanical painting and drawing is still considered to be the best way of illustrating a plant's character and is the format that most botanists prefer to use in the identification of new plants.   MC-C

botanic garden.

The scientific study of plants started as soon as gardeners began to examine plants and their behaviour in detail and must therefore have had its origins with the first gardens. The garden specifically devoted to botanical research, however, is usually thought of as an introduction of the Italian Renaissance, but there is evidence that Muslims in early medieval Spain had botanic gardens. The first botanic gardens in Europe are considered to be those that were founded at PISA (*c*.1543), PADUA (1545), and Florence a little later. However, John Harvey in *Mediaeval Gardens* (1981) points out that Islamic Spain had 'scientific botanical gardens' at Toledo and Seville founded in the 11th century by Ibn Wafid. One of the directors of the garden at Toledo, Ibn Bassal, wrote the *Book of Agriculture* (*c*.1080) which, despite its name, is chiefly about gardening and shows the scope of the author's botanical knowledge. Furthermore, outside Europe, the very early study of plants of medicinal value in such cultures as those of China and Egypt certainly involved gardens, at least part of whose purpose was botanical. The physic gardens of ancient Rome and Greece, too, had a strong botanical emphasis. In Europe soon after the founding of the botanic gardens of the Italian Renaissance similar gardens were started in other countries. In Germany a botanic garden was founded at Leipzig in 1580; in the Netherlands the Hortus Botanicus at the University of LEIDEN was founded in 1592 (with Carolus CLUSIUS as its first *Praefectus horti*); in France the JARDIN DES PLANTES was founded at Montpellier in 1593 and the Jardin Royal des Plantes Médicinales (later Jardin des Plantes; see PARIS PARKS AND GARDENS) was founded in Paris in 1635; in England the OXFORD BOTANIC GARDEN was founded (as a 'phiseck garden') in 1623 and the CHELSEA PHYSIC GARDEN in 1670; in Scotland the ROYAL BOTANIC GARDEN in Edinburgh was founded in 1670 (as the university garden of medicinal plants). Remarkably, the first botanic garden in the Americas was founded *c*.1642, in the city of Recife, Brazil.

With the Linnaean revolution in taxonomy and nomenclature in the 18th century it became the practice to arrange plants for botanic study according to their families and genera, in 'order' or 'systematic' beds, so that they could be studied in taxonomic context. The characteristic pattern is of a series of parallel beds containing plants arranged as individual specimens. Such arrangements are still found in botanic gardens and are as valuable to the gardener as they are to the botanist. A group of species of, for example, the genus *Paeonia*—such as may be seen today at Kew—is a marvellous and instructive sight. Early botanic gardens were laid out with a pattern of small beds. The botanic garden at Padua, for example, is laid out in a giant circle divided into a symetrical pattern of an immense number of small beds each of which was planted with a single species of plant. This is an attractive way of focusing attention on the characteristics of a particular plant, and creates an ornamental pattern, but does not have the analytical rigour of later 'order beds'. The 18th century saw the founding of perhaps the single most influential botanic garden of all, the ROYAL BOTANIC GARDENS, KEW. In India the CALCUTTA BOTANIC GARDEN was founded in 1786. Initially specializing in the study of economic plants, it became under the directorship of William Roxburgh from 1793 a centre for the study of the floras of India and of South-East Asia. A few other notable gardens, such as the ROYAL BOTANIC GARDEN, MADRID (founded 1755), date from the 18th century but it was not generally a great period for the founding of new botanic gardens.

The involvement of botanic gardens with plants of economic value has been crucial in the development of, in particular, the economies of tropical countries. On the island of Mauritius, near Port Louis, the charmingly named garden Pamplemousses (grapefruit) was laid out in 1735 and became one of the first botanic gardens in the tropics; it was involved in the introduction of cinnamon, nutmeg, and pepper. It later played an important role in the development of the cultivation of sugar canes in Mauritius. The garden survives today under the name Sir Seewoosagur Ramgoolam Botanical Gardens. A botanic garden was founded on the Caribbean island of St Vincent in 1764. The *Bounty*, under Captain Bligh, was sailing for St Vincent with a cargo of breadfruit trees, to provide cheap food for slaves, when the famous mutiny took place in 1787. In the 19th century Kew was at the heart of a distribution network of economic plants—receiving seeds and specimens, propagating them, and sending them all over the world. Cork oaks (*Quercus suber*) were sent to the Punjab and Vallonea oaks (*Quercus ithaburensis*) to the Cape. Varieties of pineapple were widely distributed by Kew, one of which became so popular it was named the 'Kew pine'. The Queensland nut (*Macadamia ternifolia*) was sent to India, Singapore, South Africa, and the West Indies. Kew took a role in advising countries on the best crops and on the wisdom of polyculture to guard against the dangers of a single crop failure. Kew's involvement in the gathering, propagation, and dissemination of the various species of trees that yield rubber is an epic richly described in Ray Desmond's *Kew: The History of the Royal Botanic Gardens* (1995). As a result the three major rubber trees indigenous to South America were introduced to the East and the rubber industries of Malaya, Ceylon (Sri Lanka), and several other countries.

The 19th century was one of the greatest periods for the founding of new botanic gardens, especially in the New World, where they added immensely to the repertory of worldwide botanical studies. Most of them, too, were gardens which informed the public both about the botanical heritage of their own countries as well as that of the rest of the world. In Australia the Sydney Botanic Garden was founded in 1813 and the ROYAL BOTANIC GARDENS, MELBOURNE was founded in 1853. Both are distinguished landscapes whose collections, among other things, give a vivid notion of the exceptional riches of the Australian flora. CHRISTCHURCH BOTANIC GARDEN was founded in New Zealand in the 1860s. In the USA the first botanic garden was the MISSOURI BOTANICAL GARDEN, opened to the public in 1859. Today it is a beautifully kept public garden, displaying huge numbers of plants, but it also has a vast HERBARIUM (with 5.3 million specimens), a continuing programme of research into plants of the tropical rainforests, and a Center for Plant Conservation which, in the late 20th century, with the destruction or depletion of many habitats, became a major subject of botanical studies. The NEW YORK BOTANICAL GARDEN (founded in 1889) is a model of its kind, with a diversely attractive landscape (including the wonderfully attractive Enid A. Haupt Conservatory), a magnificent collection of plants, and the largest herbarium of North American species in the world. One of the most

valuable aspects of some botanic gardens in the United States, apart from their general roles as places of scientific study and as public gardens, is the particular emphasis on plants of their own particular region. The HUNTINGTON BOTANICAL GARDEN (founded 1925) displays, among much else, a remarkable collection of drylands plants with over 5,000 species in a finely landscaped setting. Apart from their botanical value such displays also have a powerful influence on garden taste, for they emphasize the full scope of the repertory of plants suitable for a particular climate. The SANTA BARBARA BOTANIC GARDEN (founded in 1939) specializes in Californian natives many of which are disposed in naturalistic settings with a backdrop of real nature—the Santa Ynez mountains. The founding of botanic gardens thus continued into the 20th century. South Africa's KIRSTENBOSCH NATIONAL BOTANIC GARDEN, founded in 1913 but with 17th-century features, is an exceptional example. In Canada the Montréal Botanical Garden was founded in in 1931. New botanic gardens continued to be started in Europe. One of the most attractive, and unusual, is the Jardin Botanique Alpin du Lautaret, near Briançon in the Hautes-Alpes of France, which was founded in 1899. At an altitude of over 2,000 m/6,562 ft, it displays over 2,000 species of alpine plants, indigenous and exotic, in a magnificent Alpine setting. Visitors are offered refreshment—water from a nearby glacier.

Today the *International Directory of Botanical Gardens* (4th ed. 1983) describes 798 gardens throughout the world. The best botanic gardens in recent times have combined their scientific work with a desire to inform and delight the public. They have also assumed a new role, that of the conservation of plants whose habitats are threatened. In some cases botanic gardens have propagated such plants and helped to reintroduce communities of them in the wild. Many botanic gardens, too, may give advice on conserving plant habitats. An intriguing development is that the pharmacological study of plants, which has become a major part of the work of many modern botanic gardens, has taken them back to their ancient roots in the world of physic gardens.   PT

Bothmar Castle ⊛

Malans, Canton of Graubünden, Switzerland. Dating from the 18th century, the palace grounds of Bothmar are among the best-preserved baroque gardens in Switzerland. The cordial relations of the Graubünden aristocracy with foreign courts was one reason that the French garden arts flourished here in the 18th century. Situated on an eminence above the

village of Malans, the nucleus of Bothmar Castle dates from the 16th century, while its wings with their decorations were erected in the course of the 18th century. Since 1760 the castle has been in the possession of the Salis-Seewis line; the building with its two wings and the copse of yews on the hill of Malans stands as a symbol of aristocratic ascendance. Between the residence, with its neighbouring tenant's house, and the gardener's house lies the impressive baroque garden, probably dating from 1740–50, but the name of its creator is not known. The inscription over the archway on the main axis of the garden is dedicated to the renewer of the castle and the artistically rich grounds, Gubert Abraham von Salis de Bothmar. As the main axis of the baroque garden is not aligned with that of the castle one must assume that the garden was a later addition to the castle. Massive box topiary spheres and closely clipped hedges lead down through three terraces to a central fountain pool, whose slim column of water adds the sound of splashing water. Irises, azaleas, and roses flower in the geometric box hedge compartments; the closely planted box topiary creates narrow spaces so that the garden as a whole feels rather like a maze. Many of the earlier, Renaissance, garden elements were retained in the new garden layout. A BOSQUET of yew and *Thuja occidentalis* to the north-west provides a marked contrast to the architecturally conceived garden with its pronounced horizontal and vertical lines in the French baroque style. This garden, in which nature and architecture are closely intertwined, set against the magnificent Alpine backdrop, exerts a unique enchantment on the visitor.

UW

Bouchout, Domaine de ⊛

Meise, Vlaams Brabant, Belgium, the home of the National Botanic Garden of Belgium, a scientific institute with a herbarium, researchers, and impressive publications. The 92-hectare/227-acre estate, mainly laid out as an English-style landscape park, is an attractive area of lawns, avenues, and clumps of forest trees. The castle, originally a defensive fortress, was remodelled in the 17th century but burnt down in 1944—only the orangery survives. Gardens in the Italian Renaissance style became a romantic park in the 19th century and the state acquired the domain in 1938; the Botanic Garden moved there from Brussels shortly afterwards. An enormous complex of greenhouses, the Plant Palace, contains a splendid collection of tropical and subtropical plants with houses devoted to the flora of Africa, the Americas, Australia, and Asia laid out as naturalistic landscapes. Two houses are devoted to useful plants and another, the

Victoria house, has a fine *Victoria amazonica*. A renovation programme of the thirteen houses open to the public is under way. The outdoor collections include Chinese maples and oaks, a new peony and camellia garden, a pinetum, a fruticetum, a herbetum, and a garden of medicinal plants. The fruticetum includes magnolias, eleagnus, hamamelis, and aralias. In the herbetum perennial plants are divided into sub-families in a half-hexagon around an elegant cast-iron greenhouse designed by Alphonse Balat (1818–1905) in 1853.

BA

boulingrin,

a Gallicization, dating from 1664, of the English bowling green, a tribute to the great admiration held by the French for the perfection of fine LAWNS seen in England. A.-J. DEZALLIER D'ARGENVILLE's *La Théorie et la pratique du jardinage* (1709) devotes a whole chapter to the subject, defining it as a lawn, assuming different forms, but with no connotation of

bowling—indeed he specifically rejects the notion. His *boulingrins* were highly ornamental patterned lawns characterized by *renfoncements* (depressions) or *glacis* (chamfering) which introduced a subtle three-dimensional effect.

PT

Boutcher, William

(d. 1738), Scottish nurseryman and garden designer. He worked for the Duke of Argyll at Inveraray Castle (Argyll) *c.*1721 where he both supplied plants and advised on the design of the landscape. He worked in a similar capacity for the Earl of Stair at the great new garden at CASTLE KENNEDY *c.*1722. According to the work cited below, 'His designs were strictly formal with a ruthless application of the ruler and setsquare which made his proposed area of "Naturall Wood" at the bottom of the park at Kilkerran, Ayrshire, of 1721 quite exceptional and unexpected.' Boutcher's son, also called William (d. *c.*1780), followed his father as a nurseryman, with premises at Comely Bank,

Edinburgh. He was the author of *A Treatise on Forest-Trees* (1775) which many regarded as the best 18th-century book on its subject, and it retains much of its value today.   PT

A. A. TAIT, *The Landscape Garden in Scotland 1735–1835* (1980).

bower.

The earliest definition, from 1534, of the word given by the *Oxford English Dictionary* is 'A shady recess, or arbour'. It has another meaning, too. The garden made for his mistress Rosamund by Henry II at Woodstock Manor was known as 'Rosamund's Bower'. J. C. Loudon's *Encyclopaedia of Gardening* (1822) gives the etymology as 'Saxon for parlor' and defines the garden use of bower as 'an arbor of trees'. It is a word with a cosy-sounding, cottagey ring to

---

Plans for ***boulingrins*** in A.-J. Dezallier d'Argenville's *La Théorie et la pratique du jardinage* (1709).

it but it does not seem to denote anything sufficiently distinct from ARBOUR to be of much value.   PT

Bowood ⊕

Calne, Wiltshire, England, has one of the most beguiling of Capability BROWN's landscapes. The estate at Bowood is very ancient; part of it was a royal deer park in the Middle Ages. It was bought in 1754 by the 1st Earl of Shelburne, whose son, later the 1st Marquess of Lansdowne, rebuilt the house to the designs of Robert ADAM. From 1761 Capability Brown worked on the landscape, flooding the valley east of the house by damming a stream and creating a long serpentine lake backed by woodland. On the far side of the house from the lake Brown laid out woodland planting on an undulating site where Adam designed a family MAUSOLEUM. In the 1780s a fine naturalistic cascade was added to the woodland by Brown's lake to the design of Charles Hamilton of PAINSHILL. In the cliffs to one side of the cascade are grottoes made by Josiah Lane, who also designed a Hermit's Cave overlooking the lake. In the mid 19th century a PINETUM was planted by the 3rd Marquess, who also made formal gardens designed by Sir Robert Smirke (in 1818) and by George Kennedy (in 1851). From 1854 rhododendrons were planted in the Mausoleum wood which now has an excellent collection of both species and the showier cultivars. The view back towards the house from the Mausoleum, revealed by openings cut in the woods, is magnificent. Adam's house was demolished in 1955, the family moving into outhouses, but the grounds of 40 hectares/100 acres survive in excellent state.   PT

box.

There are around 70 species of box (*Buxus*), all evergreen shrubs and trees, with a wide distribution in Africa, Central America, Asia, the Caribbean, and Europe. From the gardening point of view, for those who live in a temperate climate, the most valuable species is common box, *B. sempervirens*, although the Asian box, *B. microphylla*, also has its merits. Common box has been used in gardens since ancient times—in Sumerian, Egyptian, and ancient Roman gardens, for example. Islamic gardens, including those in Spain, used box for hedging. In Italian Renaissance gardens box was a valuable ingredient and has remained so in European gardens ever since. In French gardens of the 17th century it was considered the best plant for the elaborate arabesques of PARTERRES *de broderie*.

It is a very variable plant, with at least 50 cultivars available in British nurseries, and the type itself is variable both in leaf shape (from

quite narrow and pointed to rounded) and in the shade of foliage colour which ranges from deep emerald to glaucous. In habit it ranges from the distinctly prostrate (in the cultivar *B.s.* 'Prostrata') to the truly columnar (in the cultivar *B.s.* 'Graham Blandy', formerly known as *B.s.* 'Greenpeace'). The vigorous *B.s.* 'Handsworthensis' has large, rounded leaves with a distinct blue cast to them and a generally upright, although scarcely columnar, habit of growth. Many cultivars with variegated leaves exist. *B.s.* 'Aureovariegata' (syn. *B.s.* 'Aurea') has rather oval leaves marked with golden yellow stripes. *B.s.* 'Argenteovariegata') (syn. *B.s.* 'Argentea') has slender leaves edged in pale silvery yellow, making an ethereal and elegant if rather artificial looking plant. *B.s.* 'Elegantissima' is similar, with creamy white-margined foliage, and naturally forms a compact and shapely bush. The very small-leafed and smaller growing cultivar *B.s.* 'Suffruticosa', dwarf box, is one of the oldest cultivars and has long been used in France and Britain for low hedging in kitchen gardens.

It is the common box, and its slight clonal variations, however, that is overwhelmingly the most valuable sort. It has fine sparkling foliage, attractively catching the light especially when wet, is long lived, easy to propagate, takes clipping very well, and is generally trouble free (but see below). Many gardeners love the slightly foxy smell of the foliage, especially noticeable when freshly clipped. It is not often seen as an unclipped shrub but freely grown in this way it has its charms. The resulting more open growth gives the plant greater movement, causing it to sparkle attractively, seen at its best in light shade. It can live for a very long time and old clipped plants take on marvellous character. At POWIS CASTLE an ancient undulating hedge has risen to a height of well over 5 m/16 ft. For topiary and hedging in formal gardens common box is the most valuable of plants and garden designers have used it with relish. Old box hedges sometimes (unlike those of yew, *Taxus baccata*) do not respond well to being cut hard back. The garden designer Jacques WIRTZ, in his own garden near Antwerp, refashioned the old neglected box hedges in his kitchen garden by gradually shaping them into billowing mounds running along the paths. Old apple trees, the bottom of whose trunks have been submerged in the box, rise above the hedge from time to time.

The Asiatic *B. microphylla*, used in gardens in Japan since the Middle Ages, is also an excellent garden plant. It is slow growing, forming a dense, twiggy plant, and some cultivars, such as *B.m.* 'Green Pillow', assume an attractive natural cushion shape. *B.m.* var. *japonica* (of which there are also prettily variegated forms) is

the rather larger form particularly seen in Japanese gardens. Closely related is *B. sinica*, which was formerly considered a form of *B. microphylla*. The Balearic box, *B. balearica*, is less hardy but will flourish in temperate maritime climates such as most of the British Isles. It is one of the largest species and will form a handsome small tree up to 10 m/35 ft. The largest collection of species and varieties of box is held at the UNITED STATES NATIONAL ARBORETUM.

At the end of the 20th century box in many gardens in Britain suffered from a blight caused by a new fungus, *Cylindrocladium buxicola*, which is thought to have been introduced from the Netherlands. It seems to flourish in humid conditions, causing foliage to discolour and die. It affects all varieties of common box and also such species as *B. microphylla* and *B. sinica*. It seems to spread with ease, with the spore of diseased fallen leaves being transmitted by muddy boots or even the paws of animals. No fungicide is available to gardeners. The cultivar *B. microphylla* 'Faulkner' is said to be particularly resistant to infection.   PT

B. HENRICOT, A. PEREZ-SIERRA, and C. PRIOR, 'A new blight disease on Buxus in the UK caused by the fungus Cylindrocladium', *Plant Pathology*, Vol. 49: No. 6 (2000).

Boyceau de La Barauderie, Jacques

(d. *c*.1633), from 1602 a courtier to Henri IV, whom he advised on gardening matters and, under Louis XIII, *intendant des jardins*. His posthumous book *Traité du jardinage selon les raisons de la nature et de l'art* (1638), looks forward to some of the ideas of BAROQUE gardening from a Renaissance viewpoint. The third section of his book, on laying out the garden, emphasizes the virtues of variety—curved lines and polygons may be intermingled with straight lines and quadrilaterals. A hilly site ('un terrain montueux') may be preferable to a level one. It has the virtue of allowing a vantage point from which to look down on the whole pattern of a garden. He pays much attention to planting and praises the ornamental possibilities of the POTAGER. A PARTERRE may intermingle useful and ornamental plants.   PT

Boyce Thompson Arboretum ⊕

Superior, Arizona, USA, was founded in 1926 by mining engineer William Boyce Thompson 'to instill in people an appreciation for plants'. Since 1965 it has been a botanical research department of the University of Arizona's College of Agriculture and a little later became an Arizona State Park. Arizona's oldest botanic garden displays 3,200 desert plants, native and exotic, in an area of 130 hectares/320 acres in an exceptional natural setting with massive volcanic rock formations and Picket Post Mountain towering above. Three kilometres/2 miles of paths take the visitor through collections of indigenous Sonoran and Chihuahuan desert plants, an extensive cactus garden, riparian areas, a hummingbird and butterfly garden, an Australian forest, and herb and rose gardens. Among the most striking plants here is the great native saguaro cactus, *Carnegiea gigantea*, which will grow to a height of 16 m/53 ft, and whose white blossom is the state flower of Arizona. The Curandero/Sonoran Desert Trail describes traditional herbal medicines of the Sonoran Desert (*curanderos* are traditional healers in Mexican culture). Also open to the public are greenhouses with cacti and succulents that otherwise would succumb to winter cold at this 732-m/2,400-ft elevation; indeed, it snows on occasion even in the Sonoran Desert. The Smith Interpretive Center, between the display greenhouses, has exhibits on plants and local history and a Demonstration Garden offers tips and examples of water-efficient landscaping design. More than 200 bird and 72 terrestrial species have been observed in the area—Ayer Lake and Queen Creek on the Main Trail are particularly rich in wildlife.   PWo

Boye, Georg

(1906–72), Danish landscape architect, vice-president of the International Federation of Landscape Architects (IFLA) from 1954 to 1956. He was actively involved in establishing the Landscape Institute at the Royal Veterinary and Agricultural University and from 1963 to 1972 was professor there. In the 1930s he worked at the Park Administration in Århus, latterly with C. Th. SØRENSEN. His own practice from 1943 ranged from private gardens to green spaces around large housing projects estates, hospitals, and schools. For many years he was landscape architect for the state mental hospitals and institutions for the mentally handicapped. He had an everlasting interest in geometrical forms shaped by pruned hedges—hexagonal forms are fundamental in the cemetery in Næstved (1948) and also in the Memorial Park in HERNING (1947) where the six hexagonal flower gardens are framed with clipped hornbeam. Other well-known projects include gardens for the Television House in Gladsaxe (1960) and the ministerial buildings on Slotsholmen, in Copenhagen (1962). He published the books *Anlægsgartneri* (Landscape Gardening) (1959) and *Havekunsten i kulturhistorisk belysning* (Garden Art from a Cultural Historic Viewpoint) (1972).   AL

Boyle, Richard.

See BURLINGTON, 3RD EARL OF.

Bozzolo, Il (Villa della Porta) ⊕

Lake Maggiore, Italy. One of the first villas and gardens to be taken over by Fondo per l'Ambiente Italiano, Il Bozzolo has a dramatic situation in a verdant valley of the Alpine foothills. Although constructed in the 17th century in dramatic Roman style with a central perspective traversing a terraced hillside, unusually the villa is not aligned with the garden but set to the side, allowing passers-by to appreciate the uninterrupted view of garden and landscape. The vista soars up across five small terraces, designed for lemon pots, and opens out into an octagonal grassy space, enclosed by a low wall and surrounded by sparsely planted cypresses. A monumental fountain, flanked by stairways, marks the topmost centre of the grass, leading the eye upward through a cypress-lined avenue which cuts through the dense woods. The original architect of this remarkable garden is unknown, although it remained in the della Porta family from its conception until taken over and admirably restored by Fondo per l'Ambiente Italiano in 1989.   PHo

Bradley-Hole, Christopher

(b. 1951), English architect and garden designer, the most significant proponent of minimalist gardens in late 20th- and early 21st-century Britain. Bradley-Hole's disillusionment with the bureaucratic restrictions that were interfering with his work as an architect in the 1980s propelled him into garden design where the philosophy that underpinned his architecture could be explored in comparative freedom outdoors. Classical proportion, a sense of order, and an abhorrence of arbitrary ornamentation, characteristics in Bradley-Hole's architectural work, have been translated into his garden design. His use of the golden section to divide space in the planning of a garden is crucial for creating harmony through proportion. His gardens are rigorously minimalist but far from bland—they are full of colour, pattern, texture, and detail, but by drawing well-defined spaces and cleverly juxtaposing materials they impart an overall feeling of simplicity. This simplicity is not achieved at the expense of excitement, energy, and atmosphere, from small city roof gardens and his Chelsea Flower Show gardens, to larger projects in the English countryside. Unlike other minimalists, who eschew planting as unnecessary ornamentation, Bradley-Hole uses plants to reinforce the theme running through a garden. Amongst the uncompromisingly modern framework of polished limestone, steel, and glass at his Chelsea Flower Show Mediterranean Garden for the *Daily Telegraph* in 2000, irises, vines, sages, and fennel were not

so much decoration as essential elements. Old-fashioned roses, alliums, and aquilegias reinforced the voluptuously romantic theme in his 2004 Paradise Garden for HH Sheikh Zayed Bin Sultan Al-Nahyan. His attendance at the 1995 Perennial Symposium at Kew informed Bradley-Hole's lavish use of perennials and ornamental grasses, which are incorporated into his large-scale planting schemes in impressive quantities, creating loose but linked patterns. The random patterns of his planting inject asymmetry within a rigidly geometric framework. Metal-edged square grids that are visible in March but almost impenetrable by August when the impressionistic planting is building up to an autumn crescendo are a feature in many of his country projects. The space between the blocks adds fluidity to the planting and the repetitive use of geometry provides a settled backbone in lean months. He frequently contrasts his densely planted perennial matrices with impeccable circular lawns ringed in taller meadow grasses, such as in the Oxfordshire garden at Crockmore House. In a large Sussex garden a two-tier stone amphitheatre encircles a lawn, with a narrow gap drawing the eye like a laser beam into the distant countryside. At Bury Court (Surrey) for John Coke he has replaced perennials with still water in one of the squares, imparting a similar contrast. The strong sense of space and place, clean lines, and purity of form which he finds so exhilarating in the work of Charles BRIDGEMAN, Sir Geoffrey JELLICOE, Le Corbusier, and Tadao Ando is abundantly evident in Bradley-Hole's work. His work likewise informs the diploma students to whom he teaches landscape design at the Royal Botanic Gardens, Kew, and the wider public through his book *The Minimalist Garden* (1999).   TC

Bragança, Parco dos Duques de ⊕

Terreiro do Paco, Vila Viçosa, Portugal. The ancient estate belonged to the royal family of Bragança whose first King, João IV, was born here in 1604. The garden presents a series of decorative interludes of different periods and styles. The gardens, dating from the 16th century onwards, were originally entirely enclosed in walls but many of these were later removed. The kitchen garden is one of the oldest parts with a great pergola of vines and roses trained on stucco pillars and wooden crossbeams. The Jardim das Damas (Ladies' Garden) dates from the 18th century but the present planting is modern. A four-part parterre has at its centre a scalloped fountain pool. Scrollwork beds of clipped box are decorated with box cones. But these are traces only of what had been an immensely elaborate garden of which many

17th-century descriptions survive and a survey plan of 1845 shows a layout of great complexity.   PT

Bramante, Donato

(1443/4–1514), Italian architect, engineer, and painter. He left his native Urbino for Lombardy in 1472, and settled in Milan, where he worked until the French conquest of 1499. His standing as an architect is based on the buildings of his years in Rome (1500–14), particularly the Tempietto. His principal accomplishment in garden design is the Belvedere Court (Cortile del Belvedere), a vast extension to the Vatican Palace on which work began in 1505 (see VATICAN GARDENS).

The Belvedere Court as it now stands represents Bramante's design as modified by Pirro LIGORIO during construction (c.1565) and subsequently altered by Domenico Fontana (1587–8). Bramante's original plan survives in several early accounts, notably the Codex Coner now in Sir John Soane's Museum in London. The courtyard was designed to link St Peter's with the Villa Belvedere (which no longer exists) some 300 m/984 ft to the north, and was to incorporate the villa's outdoor sculpture museum (completed 1506; remodelled 1773).

The court was bisected in 1587 by the Vatican Library built by Fontana, so what is now the Giardino della Pigna was originally the northern end of an unbroken court which ascended in three vast terraces. The lowest terrace was designed as a theatre, and led by a straight staircase to the middle terrace, where there was a NYMPHAEUM. Ramps on either side of the nymphaeum led to the highest terrace, which concluded with a semicircular exedra that led up a flight of steps to the sculpture garden. Bramante also built the spiral staircase ramp in a tower near the sculpture garden.

The other important work of garden architecture now associated with Bramante is the nymphaeum (now in a ruined state) outside the Colonna palace of Genazzano. This structure was designed both as a bathhouse and as a pavilion from which an audience could watch performances and spectacles in the lake below. The recent attribution of the nymphaeum to Bramante is based on stylistic considerations rather than documentary evidence, but is nonetheless compelling. If the attribution were confirmed, it would mean that late in his career Bramante was willing to introduce new proportions into his deployment of the Doric order.   GC

Bramham Park ⊕

Wetherby, West Yorkshire, England, has a garden that is a rare survival—a great formal layout of 250 hectares/617 acres dating from the period 1698 to 1713. Most English formal gardens of this kind were lost in the landscaping craze in the later part of the 18th century. Robert Benson inherited the estate in 1677 and, probably influenced by what he had seen on a grand tour of France and Italy, started to lay out the grounds in 1698. The house was rebuilt at the same time, probably to Benson's own design. It is possible that the Bath architect John Wood the elder (c.1705–1754), in the 1720s, was associated with the landscape design. Benson animated the gently undulating site with a formidable network of beech-hedged rides. A giant axis runs south-east from the façade of the house with, close to it, a temple by James PAINE (c.1753) and, at its far end, a noble columned Ionic temple and, standing at the centre of nine radiating rides, a great obelisk. A second axial vista, almost parallel to the first, lies to the south-west. But one of the charms of the landscape is that there is no regular pattern, rides dart off at an angle, sometimes enlivened by a canal, a water garden, a giant urn, or an ornamental building. One, to the south-west of the house, leads to a bastion on the garden's boundary with grand views of the rural landscape. Still owned by Benson's descendants, the Lane Foxes, the garden is finely kept.   PT

Brandt, G. N.

(1878–1945), eminent Danish landscape architect. He was educated as a gardener, and after apprenticeship, around 1900, he worked in England, France, and Germany. From 1914 to his death he developed parks and cemeteries in Gentofte Municipality where, from the 1920s, he was parks director. He both mastered the craftsmanship and highly strengthened the profession by writing and teaching as associate professor 1924–41 at the Royal Danish Academy of Fine Arts, School of Architecture, Copenhagen. Brandt called himself a gardener although he designed and carried out a large number of projects, formal as well as informal, and worked with elements from the man-made landscape—orchards, meadows, forests. But he retained many formal elements in his designs. In the June garden at Svastika in Rungsted (1926) yellow and white flowers were placed in square and rectangular planting beds with equal width grass walks between. His own neoclassicist garden in Ordrup (from 1914), today a public garden adjacent to Ordrup Churchyard, has a sequence of five clearly defined spaces, not without similarities to the plan of Villa GAMBERAIA. Brandt also followed the principles of such English garden designers as William ROBINSON, Edwin LUTYENS, and Gertrude JEKYLL. He paid particular attention to the relationship between the architectural elements of the garden and the natural ecologically appropriate elements—strips of grass with wildflowers, grass walks flanked by informal hedges, and stone walls with plants growing in the cracks. His work includes the renovation of the garden at Marienlyst Palace in Elsinore (1919), the neoclassicist Hellerup Coastal Park with perennial gardens and a rose garden (1912–18), Ordrup Cemetery (1919–30), the Solbakken allotment gardens in Elsinore (1935), the flower garden in TIVOLI, roof gardens on the Radio Building (1943), and the outstanding MARIEBJERG CEMETERY.   AL

Branitz ⊕

Cottbus, Germany. After selling the Muskau (see BAD MUSKAU) estate in 1845, Prince PÜCKLER-MUSKAU withdrew to Branitz, his father's estate, near the city of Cottbus. The landscaped park can be divided into a very intensively landscaped inner park of roughly 100 hectares/247 acres and a so-called outer park of about 500 hectares/1,235 acres, the latter of which was designed in the style of a FERME ORNÉE. In contrast to the park in Muskau where Pückler was able skilfully to make use of the natural spaces, the challenge of Branitz was to turn a plain agrarian landscape into a diverse and highly individual landscaped park. Branitz is considered Pückler's final work and signifies at the same time the final stage in the development of landscape gardens in Germany. While Pückler's landscaping of the outer park essentially is restricted to the skilful composition of forest, meadow, and arable land and their ornaments, the landscaping within the inner park is much more elaborate. A row of artificially created hills as well as waterways alternate with accentuated tree plantings. In the succession of different images and the increasing intensity of the landscape design from the outer park towards the residence, Humphry REPTON's zoning concept becomes apparent. On the east side of the inner park is the meadow-of-the-smithy (Schmiedewiese) with a neo-Gothic gatehouse that also served as a smithy. Immediately surrounding the residence is the pleasure ground that contains a large number of sculptures as well as ornamental flower beds. It was originally confined by an iron fence, along with several special gardens and a pergola. Several lakes characterize the area west of the residence; the reed lake (Schilfsee), in particular, constructed in 1857–8, clearly shows Pückler's signature. The accompanying picturesque and naturalistic rows of hills were built from the excavation material of the lakes. The pyramid level forms the western closure of the inner park. It contains two earthen pyramids, the park's special features. One is the land pyramid, constructed in 1863 and built originally as a step pyramid, together with the so-called water pyramid, which contains Pückler's grave and is situated in the middle of a lake (Tumulussee). After Pückler's death, garden inspector Christoph Bleyer completed the landscape work of the park.   APa

HELMUT RIPPL, *Der Parkschöpfer* (1995).

Branklyn ⊕

Dundee Road, Perth, Scotland, is a small garden, 0.7 hectares/1.75 acres, in the eastern suburbs of Perth. Here, from 1920, John and Dorothy Renton made a fastidious plantsman's garden taking every advantage of the acid soil and fairly high rainfall. On a gently sloping site they made paths following the contours which were planted with azaleas, daphnes, magnolias, maples, and rhododendrons. The underplanting makes exquisite use of the herbaceous plants that thrive so well here. Here are beautiful erythroniums, fritillaries, Himalayan meconopsis, primulas, and trilliums. This dazzling and unexpected spectacle is now owned by the National Trust for Scotland.   PT

Brazil.

South America's largest country, with an area of over 8.5 million sq. km/5.1 million sq. miles, straddles the neo-tropical vegetation zone, and has a climate that ranges from relative cold in the south, where snow is not unknown, to the intense droughts of the north-east. It is home to countless geological and geo-morphological formations with ecosystems of enormous richness and diversity, including the Amazon (57% of which is located within Brazil), the Pantanal wetlands, the Atlantic Rain Forest, and vegetation zones such as the *caatinga* scrubland and the transitional *cerrado* savannah. The Amazon alone has around 80,000 plant species and some 30 million animal species (including insects).

The exuberance of the tropics was already part of the European collective subconscious in the 16th century: the American continent was where Thomas More located his mythological lost paradise *Utopia* (1516). After 1500, Brazil became part of Portugal's overseas dominions, the only non-Spanish colony in the Americas in their first 150 years of European colonization. It was nevertheless neither the Portuguese nor the Spanish who first carried out scientific studies on the nature of the New World. In the period 1637 to 1644, Johan Maurits van NASSAU-SIEGEN established a Dutch colony in Recife (Pernambuco state), bringing with him several naturalists who carried out extensive research on the flora, fauna, and geography, as well as making astronomical and meteorological observations. Among the first pictorial records of the American landscape are the paintings of Franz Post (1612–80), Albert Ekhout (*c*.1610–*c*.1665), and Zacharias Wagener (1614–88). Within this spirit of naturalistic curiosity, Nassau created the first botanical garden in the Americas in around 1642, in the city of Recife.

The creation of Brazil's first public garden, Rio de Janeiro's Passeio Público, was commissioned by the Viceroy Dom Luís de Vasconcelos (1740-1807) and carried out between 1779 and 1783, with its design attributed to Valentim da Fonseca e Silva (1745?-1813). Its achievement was prior to or contemporaneous with various European public gardens and is representative of a peculiarly Iberian-American style of public garden that flourished throughout the 18th century. Although its original design was remodelled in 1862, Rio de Janeiro's Passeio Público is the only public garden still extant from Brazil's colonial period.

Portuguese interest in Brazilian botany would gain systematic form at the end of the 18th century, when physiocracy inspired the Portuguese crown to commission research on the identification of colonial plants believed to be of economic value. In 1796 a Botanical Garden was commissioned for Belém in the Brazilian Amazon region, not a huge distance from the Botanical Garden in Cayenne, set up shortly before by the French in their colony of Guiana. A royal decree of 1798 ordered the governors of the colonial provinces of Pernambuco, Bahia, Minas Gerais, and São Paulo to create botanical gardens along the lines of those of Belém, although without success.

With the transferral of the Portuguese court to Brazil due to Napoleon's advance on Portugal, the Prince-Regent, Dom João (the future King Dom João VI of Portugal), in 1808 commissioned the Botanical Gardens of Rio de Janeiro, the second to be commissioned by the Portuguese and the only one to survive to the present. As a counterbalance to Rio de Janeiro, the Botanical Garden of Olinda was created in 1811, although soon to disappear. Only after Brazil's independence in 1822 were further botanical gardens created in Ouro Preto and São Paulo, both in 1825.

An emblematic figure in Brazilian landscaping of the 19th century was Auguste François Marie Glaziou (1833-1906), a French civil engineer and botanist who worked in Brazil from 1858 to 1897, first as director of forests and gardens and then as director of parks and gardens for the imperial court in Rio de Janeiro. Responsible for the remodelling of the gardens of the Quinta da Boa Vista (1874-8), his principal achievement was the landscape design for the Campo de Santana (1873-80, now the Praça da República), which followed the aesthetic fashions prevalent in France at the end of the 19th century. The recognition given Brazilian flora and its introduction into the public gardens of Rio de Janeiro was one of Glaziou's most important contributions.

The turn of the 20th century was marked by the recognition of the importance of vegetation in urban space as a health factor. The consolidation of urban planning as a discipline in this period meant recognition for the importance of green areas in cities. The system of parks and gardens established by mayor Antônio José de Lemos (1843-1913) in the city of Belém, between 1898 and 1911, was one of the most successful in this period (see ALVES PARK, RODRIGUES). In the design of the new capital of Minas Gerais state, Belo Horizonte, in 1895, urban planner Aarão Reis (1853-1936) reserved an area of 54 hectares/158 acres for the Municipal Park. For the city of São Paulo, the French urban planner Joseph-Antoine Bouvard (1840-1920) in 1911 proposed the creation of two large garden areas: Anhangabaú Park and Várzea do Carmo Park (later D. Pedro II Park). The last of the great urban parks of this generation was the Redenção Park, in Porto Alegre, designed by French planner Alfred Agache (1875-1959) and inaugurated in 1935.

The GARDEN CITY concept was introduced to Brazil by one of its creators, Barry Parker (1867-1941), who in 1918 and 1919 worked in São Paulo and designed the neighbourhoods of Jardim América, Pacembu, and City Lapa. The plan for the new capital of Goiás state, Goiânia, designed in 1933 by Attilio Correia Lima (1901-43) bore witness to the influence of the garden city model.

Brazil's most important landscape designer was Roberto BURLE MARX, one of the creators of a modern landscape design language for the 20th century almost unparalleled in the world, which exploited the tropical regions' wealth of vegetation diversity, and created a peculiar aesthetic linked to modern art and a precursor of environmentalism, long before this became fashionable in the last quarter of the 20th century. Among his principal achievements is the Parque del Este in Caracas (1957-61), Venezuela, covering an area of 70 hectares/173 acres, and FLAMENGO PARK in Rio de Janeiro (1961-5), composing an area of 120 hectares/296 acres and one of Brazil's most significant urban parks. Burle Marx was also responsible for the landscaping of various sectors of Brasília (starting in 1960). The country's new capital, designed by Lucio Costa (1902-98), was to be the realization of the concept of the *ville verte* preached by Le Corbusier. The landscaping treatment given the shoreline of Copacabana beach (1970) became a model for interventions in urban shoreline areas, with similar projects appearing in various Brazilian coastal cities. The country house of Santo Antônio da Bica, now renamed SÍTIO ROBERTO BURLE MARX, which he began work on in 1949, was the landscape architect's home, studio, and experimental plant nursery, where he brought together and cultivated a vast collection of plants gathered on his botanical expeditions around South America.

Roberto Burle Marx was the instigator of a special current of thinking in landscaping in Brazil. Fernando Chacel (b. 1931) is today one of the most recognized of this current. In São Paulo, the landscaping course set up by Roberto Coelho Cardozo (b. 1923) in the Architecture and Urban Planning Faculty at the University of São Paulo in the 1950s was responsible for turning out several important landscape designers, such as Rosa Grena Kliass (b. 1932) and Miranda Martinelli Magnoli (b. 1932). Both Chacel and Cardozo are among the pioneers in defining the parameters in interventions causing great environmental impact, such as in the hydroelectric projects set up by Centrais Elétricas de São Paulo (CESP) in the 1970s. The designs of Cardozo, who worked with Garrett ECKBO in California, and Octavio Augusto Teixeira Mendes (1907–88), who studied landscape architecture at Columbia University, bear witness to a certain American influence in landscaping in Brazil. Teixeira Mendes was responsible for the landscaping of the Anchieta Highway (1948) linking São Paulo to the coastal city of Santos, as well as the Carmo (1951) and Ibirapuera Parks (1954) in São Paulo.

Starting in 1971, when architect Jaime Lerner (b. 1937) became mayor, the southern city of Curitiba began to implement a system of parks that encouraged not only an increase in the city's green spaces but also their functional linkage to the city's urban drainage and flood control systems. The parks of Barigüi, Barreirinha, and São Lourenço were among the first initiatives, continued in the 1990s with the implementation of public amenities such as Pedreira Park, the Botanical Gardens, the Bosque Zaninelli woodland park, and the Parque dos Tropeiros, among others, resulting, according to official figures, in an area of 54 sq. m/176 sq. ft of green space per inhabitant, an amount surpassed only by the pilot project for Brasília.   HS

Brécy, Château de ⊕

Saint-Gabriel-Brécy, Calvados, France, dates from the early years of the 17th century and has been attributed to François MANSART. It was built for Jacques Le Bas, a relation of Jean de Choisy for whom Mansart had designed the Château de BALLEROY nearby. The garden, enclosed in fine stone walls, lies behind the house and ascends in a series of five gentle terraces as it extends from the house. The lowest terrace has a pair of PARTERRES de broderie of a simple pattern of box scrolls, and the upper terraces, becoming wider as they rise, have lawns and topiary. Everywhere there is finely carved stone ornament—crouching lions, urns, pilasters on the walls, and garlands of flowers and fruit. Central steps link the terraces and are aligned with a noble wrought-iron gateway flanked by decorative piers and urns which pierces the wall at the back of the final terrace. Brécy has a secret air, hidden away behind woods in a thoroughly rural setting. The quality of the architecture, of both house and garden, comes as an enchanting surprise.
PT

Breidablikk ⊕

Stavanger, Rogaland, Norway, is a well-preserved 19th-century villa with period interiors, outhouses, and garden. The 0.2-hectare/0.5-acre property is today a museum. The house was built in 1882 for a shipowner, designed by the architect Henrik Nissen (1848–1915) in the Swiss style with pseudo-Gothic details and painted in characteristic natural colours. The garden was laid out by the landscape gardener Poul Holst Poulsson (1834–1915) in a Victorian style with serpentine gravel walks. Poulsson was known to use exotic trees and shrubs in his garden designs and introduced the monkey-puzzle (*Araucaria araucana*) to Norway. Today the Breidablikk garden is in a mature state with large trees and shrubberies of great diversity in colours, shapes, and heights. Among the trees are both clipped and free-growing beeches, two monkey-puzzles, hollies, yews, and a range of rhododendrons.
ME

PER TH. GRIMNES and HEIDI URTEGAARD, *Trehusbyen Stavanger: grønn veileder* (1998).

Bremen-Osterholz, Cemetery ⊕

Bremen, Germany. This was laid out in 1910 to the designs of the Berlin architect Franz Seeck (1874–1944) and the garden architect Paul Freye (1896–1958) as the first cemetery of the German cemetery reform movement. Its inauguration took place in 1920. Laid out on a site of 79.5 hectares/196 acres it consists of long ALLÉES of different species of deciduous trees, symmetrically disposed squares, and smaller units, subdivided by hedges, which make easier orientation within the wide space. The architectural centre of the cemetery is a chapel with a vestibule and a cupola in the shape of the Panthéon, with extended wings on each side. A unique element is the artificial canals surrounding and subdividing the whole area. Whereas earlier cemeteries in Germany were dominated by a simple grid in order to give as much room as possible, or used landscape design elements (e.g. Ohlsdorf cemetery in Hamburg (see OHLSDORFER FRIEDHOF)), the Osterholz cemetery for the first time in Germany was based on a system of geometric-architectural balanced spaces, terraces, and slopes, a pattern of straight *allées* and rhythmic hedges and trees, in order to give a harmonious artistic impression. After the Second World War several memorial cemeteries for victims of the German concentration camps and the Bremen bombing were integrated within the cemetery space. It was enlarged in 1948 by the garden director Erich Ahlers, with an area of about 30 hectares/74 acres, by using landscape elements; a last enlargement was executed from 1972 onwards.   US

GERT GRÖNING and UWE SCHNEIDER, 'Anfänge der Friedhofsreformbewegung . . .', in *Vom Reichsausschuss zur Arbeitsgemeinschaft Friedhof und Denkmal* (2002).
UTA MÜLLER-GLASSL and FRANK GLASSL, *Friedhöfe in Bremen: Osterholz* (1995).

Bremen Rhododendronpark ⊕

Bremen, Germany, was founded in 1936 with an area of about 16 hectares/40 acres by the city of Bremen. On the site of former country house parks it was designed by the Bremen garden designer and garden director Richard Homann (1899–1963) and was planted with the help of Johann Berg (1902–67), who later became the park director. Its landscaped grounds with slightly curved paths and irregularly shaped ponds contain about 1,680 species and varieties of rhododendron and about 970 species and varieties of azalea, and it is among the most important collections of these plants worldwide. From 1939 onwards the Botanic Garden of Bremen, which was originally located in the city of Bremen, moved to the Rhododendronpark on a site of 3.2 hectares/8 acres. With the enlargement of this garden, which was completed in 1951 under the Bremen garden director Erich Ahlers, Homann planned to concentrate on indigenous plant formations of the north-western regions of Germany, thus demonstrating regional and national tendencies in the field of garden culture. In 1972 the Wilhelm-Kaisen-Haus was built for tropical and subtropical rhododendrons and the Azalea-Museum, a plant house for Indian azaleas, was opened in 1980. The whole area covers about 46.5 hectares/115 acres. See also RHODODENDRONS.   US

EBERHARD PÜHL, *Wegweiser durch den Botanischen Garten und Rhododendron-Park Bremen* (1994).

Brenthurst Garden, The

Johannesburg, South Africa, lies on the Parktown Ridge. This private estate of the Oppenheimer family is one of the finest gardens in South Africa. Originally the great house and garden, dating from 1904, was called Marienhof and was the home of the gold mining magnate Sir Drummond Chaplin. Later it was maintained by Consolidated Goldfields of South Africa. The house was designed by Sir Herbert Baker (1862–1946), who commented, 'The site favoured the design of a beautiful garden with terraces, pergolas, waterpools, and a natural rock-garden in the lichened rocks on which the house stood.' Much work was carried out on the Brenthurst garden in the latter half of the 20th century by Harry and Bridget Oppenheimer. South Africa's premier landscape designer, Joane Pim (1904–74), was employed to help with the task. The result was a major transformation with large numbers of indigenous South African plants being introduced. Today the Brenthurst garden has display houses, nurseries, a rose garden, an orchid collection, a water garden, various ponds, and a fine collection of interesting sculpures. The site is also the home of the famous Brenthurst Library. DPMcC

Brenzone, Villa

Lake Garda, Italy. Built on the promontory of San Vigilio in the middle of the 16th century, Villa Brenzone is attributed to the architect Michele Sanmicheli (1484–1559). It was built for the well-known philosopher and lawyer Agostino Brenzone, a connoisseur of classical literature and culture, who wrote a treatise on the joys of solitary life. The square villa sits on the lake shore, its garden laid out formally to one side (now reduced to lawn panels), still preserved in its original shape, decorated with ancient and modern statues—many of them busts of Roman emperors with Latin inscriptions reminiscent of the Temple of British Worthies at STOWE—enclosed in a circle of dark cypresses. Alternating light and shadow, lemon trees, bay laurel and myrtle bushes, and a pergola overlooking the lake completes the simple garden. Famous during the 16th century for the beauty of the site and the reputation of its owner, the garden welcomed visitors with an inscription: 'honour in this sanctuary the best and highest God, to drink the cup that will quench your thirst . . . to fill your hands with boughs, flowers and fruit' before returning to 'the town and duty'. PHo

bridge.

In the Heian period of Japan (794–1185) water gardens made notable use of magnificent bridges. Straight, or gently arched, they were painted the brilliant vermilion so familiar to Western gardeners in CHINOISERIE and japonaiserie gardens. No gardens survive from this period but they are richly documented in paintings, writings, and the evidence of archaeological excavations. At the opposite stylistic extreme to these elegant and sophisticated designs are the bridges of single rough slabs of stone found in Zen Buddhist gardens such as DAISENIN in Kyoto (c.1513) where the bridge passes over a river of raked gravel. Bridges played an important part in Chinese gardens. The semicircular 'moon' bridge, with the circle completed by its reflection in the calm water below, proved especially attractive to Western gardeners and is also found in Japanese gardens.

In Western gardens one of the most remarkable uses of bridges is shown in Giusto UTENS's painting of 1599 of the Villa Medici at PRATOLINO of which very little survives today. Utens shows, descending the steep slope to one side of the villa, an extraordinary sequence of irregular pools and cascades which are crossed by bridges of various designs. Although water was used with wonderful inventiveness in gardens of the Italian Renaissance bridges are rare. A curious Italian influence in England is that of the Palladian bridge, an elegant covered bridge of which a drawing by PALLADIO survives; the original was supposedly built of wood. There are three such bridges—at WILTON HOUSE (1737, designed by the 9th Earl of Pembroke and Roger Morris), STOWE (1745, possibly by James Gibbs), and PRIOR PARK (1750). Of the three that at Prior Park is by far the best placed in the landscape, spanning the neck of a lake in a wooded combe. In Russia Catherine the Great built a copy of the Wilton bridge at TSARSKOE SELO. In the English 18th-century landscape park, with its interest in drives and approaches to the house, the bridge assumed great importance. At Kedleston Hall in Derbyshire Robert ADAM, who also designed the landscape, designed a noble three-arched bridge (1769–70) to carry the drive across a stream which feeds a lake, with a splendid cascade below. In this flat and naturally uneventful site Adam's bridge introduces excitement and drama. In the park at Kenwood House in London an 18th-century white-painted sham bridge was reflected in the dark waters of the lake. Humphry REPTON, who was consulted about the landscape, thought it 'an object beneath the dignity of Kenwood' and proposed removing it. It happily survives, in a recreated version. In the 21st century garden bridges tend, rather tamely, towards the styles of the past. PT

Bridgeman, Charles

(d. 1738), English landscape designer who was an important influence in the transition in the early 18th century from formal garden to the informal landscape style. J. C. LOUDON in his *Encyclopaedia of Gardening* (1822) referred to him as one 'who established the modern style'. Despite his importance remarkably little is known about him and no layout by him survives to show exactly what sort of gardens he designed. Among his most important gardens were BLENHEIM PALACE (from 1709); STOWE in 1716 where he collaborated with VANBRUGH, with whom he also worked at Eastbury (Dorset) and CLAREMONT (where his turf amphitheatre has been restored); and WIMPOLE (c.1720 to 1724). He was appointed royal gardener to George II in 1728. Bridgeman worked at Stowe in collaboration with John Vanbrugh for ten years, until 1726. The 1739 engraved plan of the gardens at Stowe shows the result of their work. The layout is strongly axial, centred on the house, and full of formal devices, but it is far from symmetrical and there are informal touches: Vanbrugh's Temple of Sleep was set in a wilderness of winding walks and, on the other side of the chief axis, the Elysian Fields, with its buildings of the 1730s by William Kent, is a prototype of landscape informality. Horace Walpole found 'strait walks and high clipped hedges' in Bridgeman's work but 'the rest he diversified by wilderness, and with loose groves of oak'. PT

PETER WILLIS, *Charles Bridgeman and the English Landscape Garden* (rev. ed. 2002).

Brighton Royal Pavilion.

See ROYAL PAVILION.

Brihuega, Royal Cloth Factory Garden

Castilla y Léon, Spain. The cloth factory is a remarkable, and beautiful, survival of an 18th-century industrial building. Completed in 1783 to the designs of Manuel de Villegas the building is circular in plan. The factory fell on hard times and was closed in the early 19th century. In the mid 19th century it was bought by private owners who laid out a garden, only 0.4 hectare/1 acre in area, to one side of the curving wall of the factory. It occupies the site of a former drying yard of the factory. Running along one side is a double colonnade of clipped cypresses beyond which the land falls away and there are grand views of the valley of the river Tajuña. The garden is divided into an irregular pattern of beds hedged in box which breaks out into topiary from time to time. Arches of cypress span the paths and billowing trees of Chusan palm (*Trachycarpus fortunei*) rise up. Hexagonal aviaries have roofs like Prussian helmets and a fountain pool burbles in the shade. The picturesque, intimate garden contrasts with the distinguished but austere architecture of the factory and the wild views of the landscape in the valley below.   PT

Brissago Islands ⊗
Brissago, Canton of Ticino, Switzerland, two islands on Lake Maggiore, of which the larger (2.5 hectares/6.2 acres) was transformed into an exotic island of flowers in the 19th century. Today it is the botanical garden of the Canton of Ticino. Both islands lie near Porto Ronco, almost in the centre of Lake Maggiore, and are blessed with a mild climate; the average temperature over the year is 12.8 °C/54.5 °F. The park on the larger of the two islands, Isola di San Pancrazio, owes its design to the Russian Baroness Antoinetta Saint-Léger, who acquired both islands in around 1885 and took up residence here. The Baroness not only pursued a cultivated life but also introduced a multitude of rare subtropical plants that thrived on the island, planted in groups according to their origins. In 1927 the impoverished Baroness sold both islands to Max Emden, an affluent Hamburg merchant who built the villa which stands today, an island palace in the Tuscan style, and added the harbour and Roman baths. He also had the plantings renewed and extended the botanical garden. After his death in 1940 the island lay unused until, in 1949, both Brissago islands were purchased jointly by the Canton of Ticino, the municipalities of Ascona, Brissago, and Ronco sopra Ascona, the Swiss homeland conservation association, and the Pro Natura organization. The smaller island, Isola di Sant' Apollinare, is closed to the public but Isola di San Pancrazio opened in 1950 as the botanical gardens of the Canton of Ticino and attracts over 100,000 visitors each year. The island climate is so exceptionally mild that only a few plants have to spend the winter months in glasshouses and indoors. Plants of subtropical origins can be cultivated outdoors; the park is thus the northernmost European mainland location for all-year-round growth of these species and today contains over 1,600 different species, many of which are to be found nowhere else in Switzerland.   UW

British Columbia, University of, Botanical Gardens ⊗
Vancouver, British Columbia, Canada, the oldest university botanic garden in Canada. Established by British Columbia's first provincial botanist, John Davidson (1878–1970), in 1916, it had a collection of 900 species. By the 1930s the garden had numerous significant plant collections, as well as a fine selection of native and exotic trees in the campus arboretum. Sadly, these original collections were lost or integrated when the gardens were

established on their present site in 1968. Today the 44-hectare/110-acre site boasts of over 8,000 varieties of plants in approximately 12,000 living accessions with major rhododendron, maple, magnolia, and clematis collections. It has the best alpine garden in the country with a collection of alpine flora from around the world with the necessary variety of habitats. The Nitobe Memorial Garden is considered among the top five Japanese gardens located outside Japan. The garden contains combinations of trees and shrubs imported from Japan as well as natives that underwent the traditional Japanese style of training and pruning. A 4-hectare/10-acre coastal forest provides the chance to appreciate native British Columbia flora. Some of its best-loved plants include *Penstemon* 'Purple Haze', *Vaccinium ovatum* 'Thunderbird', and *Arctostaphylos* 'Vancouver Jade'. The David C. Lam Asian Garden with one of the largest rhododendron collections on the continent features plants from Tibet, Japan, Korea, China, and Manchuria, and is a tranquil respite from the openness of the rest of the garden.   MH

British Embassy, Bangkok,
Thailand. The existing British Embassy was built in the mid 1920s in a large park adjoining the LURSAK GARDEN of which it was once a part. Over the years it has been very well planted and maintained by successive members of the British Foreign Service, with occasional advice from outsiders like the late M. R. Pimsai Amranand. The most distinctive features of the embassy compound are its spacious lawns and its numerous mature, well-shaped trees, among them rain trees (*Samanea saman*), yellow flame (*Peltophorum pterocarpum*), angsana (*Pterocarpus indicus*), and flamboyant (*Delonix regia*). In the 1980s a new chancery was added at the end of a rectangular lake along the north side, bordered by enormous rain trees. The main problem for the designer, Maurice Lee, was to achieve a sense of openness and continuity of the garden while controlling both access and some angles of view. The resulting structure is a hollow square of three storeys with an open side towards the lake at the ground and first-floor levels. The central courtyard is planted with low ground cover such as *Calathea*, *Maranta*, *Philodendron*, and ferns, and at the next scale with bold heliconias, alpinias, and other ginger species. The floor of the courtyard is paved with large slabs of natural laterite and planted intermediately with a broad-leafed grass.
    MLL/WLW

British Isles.
The topography of the British Isles is varied but never extreme. The mountain ranges, although they may be vital ingredients in fine landscape,

rise to no very dramatic peaks—Ben Nevis (1,343 m/4,406 ft) in the western highlands of Scotland is the highest mountain. Snowdon (1,085 m/3,560 ft) in the northern Cambrian Mountains is the highest in Wales; Carrantuohill (1,050 m/3,445 ft) in County Kerry is the highest in Ireland; and Scafell Pike (978 m/3,208 ft) in the Lake District is the highest in England. The temperate, maritime climate, together with the pronounced effect of the North Atlantic Drift of the Gulf Stream, allows the cultivation of an astonishing range of garden plants. The North Atlantic Drift brings warm water from the Gulf of Mexico to bathe the western coasts of Ireland and Britain. This has a striking effect on the minimum temperatures on, or close to, these coasts, regardless of their degree of latitude. With the further protection of coves or valleys many sites enjoy a virtually frost-free climate. A garden such as INVEREWE, for example, on the north-west coast of Scotland, grows many tender southern hemisphere plants but lies on the same latitude, 58° N, as Labrador or Leningrad. The range of temperatures experienced in the British Isles is not very great. The average minimum January   ▸

Colour plates

The walled **Bagh-e Fin**, Persia, with its 400-year-old cypresses dates from at least the 17th century

The Bassin de Latone at **Versailles**, France

Roman mosaics and peristyle water garden at **Conimbriga**, Portugal

An elephant with a castellated howdah in the 16th-century garden of **Bomarzo**, Italy

An obelisk in memory of Frederik V in the 18th-century garden of **Fredensborg** Palace, Denmark

temperature in the south-east (London) is 2 °C/
35.6 °F and the average maximum is 6 °F/42.8
°F; in the north-east (Lerwick in the Shetland
Islands) the corresponding figures are 1 °C/33.8
°F and 5 °C/41 °F. In the month of August they
are as follows: (London) minimum 13 °C/55 °F,
maximum 21 °C/70 °F; (Lerwick) minimum 10
°C/50 °F and maximum 14 °C/57 °F. Rainfall,
however, varies strikingly, with average annual
rainfall in the wettest parts of the west coast of
Scotland and Ireland of over 2,500 mm/100 in;
but in the dryest parts, Essex in south-eastern
England, only 500 mm/20 in. The range of
rainfall corresponds, at its driest, to Santa
Barbara in southern California and at its
wettest to parts of the Himalayas. The variation
in rainfall and sunshine has a greater effect on
the repertory of plants in gardens than the
variation in temperature. The east and south-
east coast of Britain, with its lower rainfall and
longer hours of sunshine, allows the cultivation
of many Mediterranean plants which will not
flourish on the wetter, although milder, west
coast. The possibility of growing a wide range of
plants from a very diverse range of habitats has
had a profound influence on garden styles
throughout the British Isles. The indigenous
flora is not extensive, with around 1,300
flowering plants of which about 30 are trees. In
fact virtually all these 'native' plants are
reintroductions after the last ice age and only
around sixteen British natives are endemic. The
temperate climate, and a horticultural tradition
that has usually ignored boundaries, make it
sensible to treat the history of gardening in the
British Isles as an entity, although striking
regional variations will be noted. The very
large number of ancient estates that survive,
often with designed landscapes that are
beautiful and historically interesting, is one of
the most remarkable features of the region.
Long periods of political stability, the system of
primogeniture, under which the eldest son
inherits a landed estate, and a dislike of
violent change are some of the factors that
explain this.

Roman occupation.
Romans invaded Britain in 43 AD and remained
until the middle of the 5th century. Although
they invaded as far as Scotland and Wales it was
England, in particular the south, that was most
heavily Romanized. A very large number of sites
have been excavated but our knowledge of the
kinds of gardens the Romans made here is
sparse. At Fishbourne (Sussex) a palatial Roman
villa with fine mosaic pavements has been
excavated since its discovery in 1961. Dating
from the 1st century, this was the residence of a
very wealthy man who has been possibly
indentified as Tiberius Claudius Cogidubnus, a

local ruler who had assisted the Romans. He
had a great garden in the form of a rectangular
space enclosed in a colonnaded courtyard.
Archaeological evidence revealed a pattern of
paths edged with beds in which hedges were
almost certainly planted. It seems plain, too,
that this garden had fountains and pools—the
remains of water mains encircling the garden
were found as well as fragments of marble
basins. There is also evidence that a more
naturalistic garden, with a stream and
informally planted shrubs and trees, was laid
out south of the formal garden. Parts of the
garden at Fishbourne have been reinstated,
including a patterned box hedge. There is also a
representative collection of plants known to
have been used in Roman gardens in England.
The Romans introduced such plants as
rosemary (*Rosmarinus officinalis*), myrtle (*Myrtus
communis*), lavender (*Lavandula stoechas*), sweet
bay (*Laurus nobilis*), wormwood (*Artemisia
absinthium*), and many others. All these, hardy in
the south of England, would not be dependably
hardy in the north. After the departure of the
Romans in the 5th century most of their
settlements were abandoned and the sites of
Roman houses were very rarely used for later
dwellings. It is unlikely that the plants they
introduced would have survived but some, in
particular culinary plants, may have done. It is
even less likely that any Roman tradition of
garden design would have been continued.
Thus, although there was a very large Roman
presence in England and gardens were certainly
made, it cannot be said that the Romans
influenced the development of English
gardens. After the 5th century, until the
establishment of monasteries in the Middle
Ages, nothing is known about gardens in the
British Isles.

The Middle Ages.
It is possible to speak of gardens in the Middle
Ages only in the most fragmentary way. There is
no surviving detailed description of any
medieval garden in the British Isles and no
picture of any identifiable garden remains. The
most vivid notions of the appearance of gardens
of this time come from the very end of the
period in question, from the Flemish
miniatures of the late 15th century. The
Domesday Book, compiled in 1085-6, mentions
gardens only very occasionally, and in these
instances the gardens are of modest size and are
mentioned only in the context of productivity—
with entries typically reading '41 cottagers, who
pay 40s. a year for their gardens'. The greatest
influence on gardening, and indeed on every
branch of learning, between the collapse of the
Roman Empire and the Renaissance came from
the monasteries. The Benedictine order,

founded in the 6th century, which established
itself throughout the British Isles, attached
great importance to manual labour and self-
sufficiency so that agriculture and horticulture
were at its heart. At the Benedictine monastery
of ST GALL in Switzerland, named after a 7th-
century Irish hermit, a plan was drawn up in the
9th century showing the ideal monastic
community. It clearly shows the importance of
gardens in monasteries at this time. A PHYSIC
GARDEN is spread out by the physician's house, a
larger area is devoted to eighteen rectangular
beds of herbs and vegetables, and fruit trees are
planted in rows in the cemetery. The plan lists
plants which are largely culinary but roses,
irises, and lilies were also grown. The layout of
the gardens, with axial walks and symmetrical
arrangements, shows a pattern of gardening
which has never gone out of fashion and retains
its currency to this day. The Cistercian order,
founded in the 11th century, had the greatest
presence in the British Isles. It was founded in
an attempt to return to the original principles
of the Benedictine order which, it was felt, had
lost its way. Like the Benedictines the
Cistercians emphasized the importance of
labour and self-sufficiency, in addition they
regarded remote sites as most appropriate for
the monastic life. Benedictine houses were
autonomous, owing authority only to the Pope.
Cistercians, however, were answerable to the
General Chapter which met annually at Cîteaux
in Burgundy. The Cistercians, thus, had the
opportunity to disseminate information, which
would surely have included information about
gardening, among their many houses. By the
13th century there were 75 Cistercian abbeys in
Britain and 26 nunneries. The remains of
several Cistercian abbeys are still to be seen
throughout the British Isles. The sites tell us
little about horticulture but the ruins have
assumed the role of exquisite landscape
ornaments. Tintern Abbey in Wales, Rievaulx
and Fountains in North Yorkshire, Deer Abbey
in Aberdeenshire, and Jerpoint in County
Kilkenny remain places of extraordinary
atmosphere.

Of royal gardens in the British Isles nothing
is known before the Norman Conquest (1066).
At Woodstock Manor (Oxfordshire) Henry I
enclosed a park and had a menagerie in the early
12th century and later in the same century
Henry II laid out a maze and a very early water
garden (see MEDIEVAL GARDENS). At WINDSOR
CASTLE there was a 'King's herbary' within the
castle's curtain walls by the late 12th century
and in 1246 an ornamental garden was laid out
outside the walls. At Manorbier Castle
(Pembrokeshire) Gerald of Wales grew fruit
trees and had a vineyard in the 12th century—it
was described in 1188 as having 'a noble pool of

deep waters and a very beautiful orchard by it, shut in by a wood of hazels on a rocky eminence'. Deer parks, associated with royal estates or with those of the aristocracy, were known before the Norman Conquest, after which they became much more numerous. In many cases the old deer park was subsumed into an 18th-century landscape park. Knowledge of Scottish royal gardens, or of any others, in this period is very sparse indeed. At STIRLING CASTLE a park was enclosed under William I in the 12th century and by the 15th century there were gardens below the castle ramparts on its western side. Some princes of the Church in England had notable gardens in the Middle Ages. Cawood Palace (Yorkshire), a palace of the archbishopric of York, had a substantial 13th-century garden which had the unusual feature of three long parallel pools, one of which survives today. The Bishop of Ely at Somersham Palace (Cambridgeshire) had a very large moated garden with lakes dating from the 13th or 14th century whose layout is clearly visible as a pattern of cropmarks in an aerial photograph shown in Christopher Taylor's *Parks and Gardens of Britain: A Landscape History from the Air* (1998). What little is known about Irish gardens in the Middle Ages is largely limited to monastic houses. A tantalizing exception is the Earl of Norfolk's manor of Old Ross (County Wexford) which in the 13th century had a courtyard garden, a dovecote, beehives, an orchard, and a deer park paled in oak. As in England, deer parks were enclosed, certainly by the beginning of the 13th century.

We know that gardens in this period had lawns, orchards, vineyards, kitchen gardens, and PLEASURE GROUNDS (*viridarium, virgultum,* or *viretum*—'a green place . . . merry with green trees'). For the most part they were not extensive and were usually protected by walls, and the range of plants grown is fairly well established. A list written by Alexander Neckam, dating from the late 12th century, lists about 140 species. These are mostly edible or useful plants but among many ornamentals are box (*Buxus sempervirens*), wild daffodil (*Narcissus pseudonarcissus*), Christmas rose (*Helleborus niger*), purple iris (*I. germanica*), madonna lily (*Lilium candidum*), *Viola odorata,* and *Rosa gallica.* More surprising are exotic fruit trees—date palms (*Phoenix dactylifera*), oranges, and lemons. John Harvey in his *Mediaeval Gardens* (1981) points out that these, all easily raised from seed, would have been grown as pot plants. By the end of the 14th century, the Dominican friar Henry Daniel cultivated 252 herbaceous plants in his garden at Stepney (London). Two manuscripts by him, in 15th-century copies, survive in the British Library—*De Re Herbaria* and *De Arboribus.* He was plainly botanically

learned but even more interesting from a garden point of view is his frequent response to the beauty of plants—*Iris germanica* is 'wonder fair to sight' and *Geranium sanguineum* is 'delightful to look on'.

The Tudor age

The first Tudor monarch was Henry VII, who came to the throne in 1485, and the last was Elizabeth I, who died in 1603. In 1587 William Harrison, Dean of Windsor, in his *Description of England* (1587) wrote that gardens had so improved 'within these forty years' that 'in comparison with their present, the ancient gardens were but dunghills and laystows [open drains]'. Harrison also notes the exotics which had been appearing in gardens—'I have seen capers, oranges and lemons, and heard of wild olives growing here, besides other strange trees brought here from afar whose names I know not.' In this period the evidence of the appearance of gardens—from books, paintings and drawings, and contemporary descriptions—is far richer than for earlier periods. Furthermore, much of the fabric of gardens survives. HELMINGHAM HALL (Suffolk) gives a vivid foretaste of Tudor splendour as the Middle Ages drew to a close. With its crenellated gables and diaper patterns of brick it was started in 1487 for John Tollemache whose descendants have lived here ever since. Although the detail of the garden, in particular the beautiful planting, is entirely 20th century the moated house, its moated garden, and setting at the heart of a deer park with Tudor oak trees is one of the most complete ensembles of the early Tudor period in the country. Descriptions of known gardens also provide precious detail of the appearance of gardens. At Thornbury Castle near Bristol (which still survives) the 3rd Duke of Buckingham made a great garden *c.*1511. His gardener was 'diligent in making knots', a contemporary description reports, and 'On the south side . . . is a proper garden, and above the same a goodly gallery . . . On the east side of the castle . . . is a large and goodly garden to walk in, closed with high walls embattled . . . a large and goodly orchard [is] full of newly grafted fruit trees well laden with fruit, many roses and other pleasures; and in the same orchard . . . are other goodly alleys.' At HAMPTON COURT from 1514 Thomas Wolsey built a palatial house with a garden 'embanked with benches to sit and take my rest; | The knots so enknotted it cannot be expressed, | With arbours and alleys so pleasant and so *dulce,* | The pestilent airs with flavours to repulse.' The activities of the royal family, and those close to it, are central to gardening in the Tudor period. Henry VIII took over Hampton Court from Thomas Wolsey in 1525 and made a new

garden—the results are seen in Anthony van den Wyngaerde's view of the palace drawn in 1558. It shows the Privy Garden, with heraldic beasts mounted on columns, the Mount Garden with a domed arbour, and the Pond Garden, with rectangular fish ponds outlined with heraldic beasts. We also know that there were many sundials and that beds were edged with rails painted green and white. At Whitehall Palace (which had also belonged previously to Wolsey) Henry VIII had a garden of similar splendour, also decorated with heraldic beasts, of which some of the sumptuous detail is seen in a painting of him and his family of *c.*1545.

Queen Elizabeth's favourite Robert Dudley, Earl of Leicester, made a great garden at Kenilworth Castle (Warwickshire), where he received the Queen and a masque was performed in her honour. A visitor described the garden in 1575: 'Beautified with many delectable, fresh, and umbragious bowerz, arberz, seatz, and walks that with great art, cost, and diligens wear very pleasantlie appointed.' THEOBALDS PARK, laid out between 1575 and 1585 for William Cecil, was an especially large garden: the Great Garden alone was 2.8 hectares/7 acres in area and had nine knots, each with a white marble fountain at the centre. A garden of princely magnificence was that made by Lord Lumley at NONSUCH PALACE towards the end of the 16th century, a rare English exercise in an elaborate mannerist garden of Italian character. One of the most extraordinary survivals from the Elizabethan period is Lyveden New Bield (Northamptonshire). Here, from 1596, Sir Thomas Tresham built a great banqueting house at the heart of an elaborate water garden with an orchard to one side. Tresham was a Catholic and the banqueting house was rich in Christian symbolism, of the Trinity and the Passion. Tresham was persecuted because of his religion and his banqueting house was never used and the garden not completed, but its beautiful shell remains, rising triumphantly on its moated site with the earthworks and two canals surviving. An unusually complete gentry house of the period, MONTACUTE HOUSE, also dating from the 1590s, retains the pattern of its Tudor courts and much ornamental stonework of the period, including a pair of gazebos and elaborately enriched garden walls.

In Wales, at RAGLAN CASTLE, the 3rd Earl of Worcester made a new garden from 1549 with substantial terraces and a lake, and later added a terrace walk with busts of Roman emperors and a water PARTERRE. Tudor terraces survive, too, at the 15th-century Plas Machen (Gwent) with a long fish pond in the valley below the house. There were formal gardens by the end of the 16th century at Carew Castle (Gwent), CHIRK

CASTLE (Clwyd), and St Donat's Castle (Glamorgan). At St Donat's the layout of the Tudor garden, with terraces and a handsome 16th-century gateway, may still be seen. St Fagans Castle (Glamorgan)—more a manor house than castle—built between 1586 and 1596, preserves the pattern of enclosures of an elaborate garden of the same date and has been finely restored in recent times. Of Scottish gardens in the Tudor period virtually nothing is known. There were certainly great royal palaces, such as the substantially surviving Renaissance FALKLAND PALACE where it is known that there was a park and woodland in the 16th century. It is unlikely that such a sophisticated house would have been without a garden to match. In Ireland we have glimpses only of the state of gardening in the 16th century, which was a most troubled time. Sir Walter Raleigh (1552–1618), in his garden at Myrtle Grove in Youghal (County Cork), is said to have grown the first potato in Ireland, the first myrtle, and tobacco. It is said that when smoking a pipe in his garden a maid, fearing that he was on fire, threw a bucket of water over him. Myrtle Grove still exists and has an ancient yew said to date from the 16th century. In England many estates of the gentry rather than the aristocracy survive with eloquent remains of Tudor gardens. Gawsworth Hall (Cheshire) has a very large walled garden with 16th-century walls, a raised walk, and the site of a canal. Chilton Hall (Suffolk) has a 16th-century garden whose castellated brick walls have arched recesses. Melford Hall (Suffolk), rebuilt in the mid 16th century, possesses an exquisite octagonal summer house, each façade crowned with a pointed gable. The owner was an influential lawyer, Sir William Cordell, who in 1578 received Queen Elizabeth whose retinue included '200 young gentlemen cladde alle in whyte velvet, and 300 of the graver sort apparrelled in black velvet coates . . . with 1,500 servyng men all on horsebacke'.

Far more is known about garden plants in the Tudor period than ever before and with the printing of the first books on plants and gardening a new era in garden knowledge began. William TURNER's *A New Herball* (1551) and Lyte's translation of DODOENS's *Crüÿdeboeck, A Nievve Herball* (1578), were influential plant books of the time. By the end of the period the repertory of plants had increased enormously in the 200 years since Henry Daniel's time. John GERARD the herbalist, who also managed William Cecil's garden at Theobalds, grew in his own garden at Holborn (London) an immense range of plants which he listed in his *Catalogus Arborum, Fruticum ac Plantarum . . . in Horto Johannis Gerardi* (1596) which described 1,033 plants. This is thought to

be the first catalogue of a single garden's plants ever published. His *Herball* (1597), derivative and defective though it may be, was a major event in horticultural publishing. Thomas HILL's *A Most Briefe and Pleasaunte Treatyse* (1563), the first English practical gardening manual to be published, is subtitled 'howe to dress, sowe, and set a Garden'. This went through several editions, as did his posthumous *The Gardeners Labyrinth* (1577), which appeared under the punning pseudonym of Didymus Mountaine. Here, with its designs for knot gardens and sprightly evocation of the pleasures of gardening ('delectable sightes and fragrant flowers'), we have a vivid idea of the garden as a source of delight. It is plain, too, that Hill was writing for a readership of gardeners who had only modest gardens. Thomas Tusser's *Hundred Good Points of Husbandry* (1557) contains a calendar of gardening activities, chiefly concerned with vegetables and herbs, of exactly the sort found in modern garden manuals. With an amusing commentary in rhyming couplets ('In March and in April, from morning to night, | In sowing and setting, good housewives delight') Tusser paints a lively picture of the productive 16th-century garden.

In the Tudor period there appears a type of gardener which became influential in British garden history—the amateur connoisseur of plants. At Syon Park (near London) the Duke of Somerset recruited the botanist William Turner as his physician. With Turner's help a botanical garden was established at Syon and here Turner wrote his book *The Names of Herbs* (1548) which is dedicated to the Duke. Edward, 11th Baron Zouche (c.1156–1625) (whose guardian when he was a child was William Cecil (later Lord Burghley) of Theobalds), became acquainted with the botanist Carolus CLUSIUS and had a garden at Hackney (London) in the late 16th century. This garden was managed by the great French botanist Mathias de L'OBEL (whose name is remembered in the genus *Lobelia*) and became a gathering place for plantsmen. Here Lord Zouche grew many exotics, in particular from Turkey. He later made another garden at Bramshill (Hampshire) where, although the garden does not survive, a room in the house is decorated with 150 panels bearing paintings of plants apparently taken from woodcuts that illustrated L'Obel's books.

The 17th century
The 17th century falls into two strikingly different halves separated by the immense upheaval of the Civil War between 1642 and 1649 when Charles I was executed followed by the Commonwealth which lasted until 1660 when Charles II (who had fled to France in 1651) was restored to the throne. In terms of garden

history the first period marks the end of Renaissance influence, with a flourish of Franco-Italian grotto making and water gardens, and the second sees a resurgence in national confidence, a boom in building and in gardens, and the arrival of a new kind of French influence, that of the BAROQUE GARDEN. The garden at HATFIELD HOUSE belongs emphatically to pre-Civil War Britain. Robert Cecil, William Cecil's son, exchanged the estate of Theobalds for the royal estate of Hatfield where from 1607 he built a new house and, as the house was being built, embarked on a new garden laid out under the supervision of Mountain Jennings, who had been gardener at Theobalds. Also working here, from 1610, was John TRADESCANT the elder, who was charged with acquiring plants many of which came from the Low Countries and from France. In 1611 there is a record of the acquisition of 'two fyg trees in an other basket called the whit fygs with manye other Rare shrubs given me by Master Robyns'—this refers to Jean ROBIN, royal gardener in France to Henri III. Hatfield had a great collection of plants at this time. Among fruit trees were apples, apricots, cherries, medlars, nectarines, oranges, peaches, pears, and pomegranates. Among ornamental plants there were cypresses, *Daphne mezereum*, myrtles, oleanders, and countless smaller plants, among them anemones, fritillaries, hepaticas, irises, narcissi, pinks, tulips, and much else. In around 1611 Salomon de CAUS made a formal diamond-shaped lake with an island and banqueting house with grottoes on two corners and a pavilion on a third. This was seen in 1663 by a French visitor, Samuel Sorbière, who described 'a small River, which as it were forms the Compartiments of a large *Parterre*, and rises and secretly loses itself in an Hundred Places, and whose banks are all Lined or Boarded'. He also describes an elaborate garden with fountains and terraces on the site of today's East Garden and adds 'from [the] Terrass you have a prospect of the great Water Parterre'. De Caus, who was in England from 1607 to 1613, also made gardens for the Queen, Anne of Denmark, both at Somerset House (London) and at Greenwich Palace (London). At Somerset House he made Mount Parnassus, a mountain-like grotto with waterworks. This was described by a German visitor, J. W. Neumayr (who was travelling with the Duke of Saxony), in 1613: 'the mountain or rock is made of sea-stones, all sorts of mussels, snails, and other curious plants put together: all kinds of herbs and flowers grow out of the rock which are a great pleasure to behold. On the side facing the palace it is made like a cavern. Inside it sit the Muses, and have all sorts of instruments in [their] hands. Uppermost at the top stands Pegasus, a golden horse with wings.' At Greenwich, also visited by Neumayr, there was a pool and 'a large fountain . . . [and] a female figure gives water out of a cornucopia . . . gilded all over'. Here, too, was an elaborate grotto/aviary with a great number of birds flying around inside and 'a figure, half a woman and half a horse . . . made from shells and mussels'. These decorative fantasies reflect a Renaissance love of magic and mystery far from the stately formality that was to dominate garden making at the end of the 17th century. In contrast to the imaginative delights of such gardens was the foundation in 1621 of Oxford Botanic Garden, the first university botanic garden in the British Isles—the botanic garden at Edinburgh, later the Royal Botanic Garden, was not founded until 1670. The Oxford Botanic Garden, apart from its scientific importance, was also unusually finely laid out, enclosed in noble stone walls and with magnificent architectural gateways. It was founded at the instigation of Henry, Earl of Danby, whose brother Sir John Danvers had notable gardens at Chelsea House (London) and at Lavington (Wiltshire). His garden at Chelsea of c.1624 was in the Italian style and is seen in a Kip engraving in *Britannia Illustrata* (1707). The diarist and antiquary John Aubrey described the garden—'At the four corners of the garden . . . are low pavilions of brick . . . fir and pine trees, shumacs, and the quarters all filled with some rare plant or other. The long gravel walks surrounding it were bordered with hyssop and several sorts of thyme. There were boscages of lilac and philadelphus.' Aubrey mentioned a charming detail: '[Danvers] was wont on fine mornings in the summer to brush his beaver hat on the hyssop and thyme, which did perfume it with its natural essence and would last a morning or longer.' The GROTTO craze continued with an exceptional example, filled with watery symbolism, at WOBURN ABBEY designed before 1627 by Isaac de CAUS—nephew or brother of Salomon—for Lucy Harington, Countess of Bedford. He too designed the great new formal garden at WILTON HOUSE. A more modest grotto was made c.1630 at Enstone (Oxfordshire) by Thomas Bushell (1594-1674), who discovered a natural cave, hung with stalactites, and converted it into an ornamental grotto with jets to squirt water at visitors in the old Renaissance tradition. Bushell devised many other water devices—a hedge of water, a spout imitating the song of a nightingale, a vertical column of water 4 m/14 ft high balancing a ball on the top, and much else. Charles I visited it in 1634 and 1636. In the 1650s John Evelyn laid out his formal garden at SAYES COURT showing the influence of both Italian and French gardens. The 17th century before the Civil War was a flourishing period for the

study of plants. We have noted the founding of the Oxford Botanic Garden. The activities of the Tradescants were a powerful stimulus to plantsmanship in the period. At their garden in Lambeth (London) they gathered together a collection of around 1,500 species, among them their own introductions. The American *Robinia pseudoacacia* introduced by the elder Tradescant before 1629 had, according to John Parkinson's *Theatrum Botanicum* (1649), by 1640 grown 'to be a very great tree, and of an exceeding height'.

In the latter part of the 17th century the French influence on gardens was stimulated by the work of André MOLLET. In St James's Park (London) c.1661 he laid out a PATTE D'OIE of avenues with a giant canal running along the central avenue. Even more spectacular avenues were planted at Badminton House (Gloucestershire) before the end of the century. Here they criss-cross the great estate to form dizzying patterns in the landscape. Several of these alignments and some of the original trees still survive. Such large-scale landscape design was a new feature in English gardens. At Boughton (Northamptonshire) from 1685 a somewhat shady Dutch gardener, van den Meulen, planted great avenues of limes extending from the house deep into the surrounding landscape. The illustrations in Knyff and Kip's *Britannia Illustrata* (1707) give poignant evidence of the explosion of formal garden making in the last 40 years of the 17th century. Over 60 English estates are depicted and virtually all of them show new layouts of the period. Some of these were among the most elaborate and magnificent English gardens ever made. None survives (although many of the houses do) and none has ever been restored to its original appearance—the cost of maintenance alone of many such gardens would be beyond the purse of any conservation organization. The layout designed in the 1690s by George LONDON and Henry WISE for Badminton House had many PARTERRES, pools, fountains, and formal groves. Its culmination was a group of four gigantic blocks of hedging clipped into mazelike patterns. Its design was powerfully axial and the axes were aligned with avenues extending the formality into the surrounding landscape. At CHATSWORTH from 1688 London and Wise designed a garden with some similarity to that at Badminton but here, in addition, there were sumptuous *parterres de broderie* and a vast canal made by diverting the water of the river Derwent. A garden that has been attributed to George London on stylistic grounds is New Park (Surrey). Laid out for the Earl of Rochester, it was one of the most remarkable gardens of its period. The site, on the slopes of the Thames valley at Petersham,

presented rare possibilities. The grounds were terraced, with parterres and pools, and immense formal walks extending the terraces. On the upper slopes there was an expanse of wilderness, criss-crossed with ALLÉES, with a MOUNT at its highest point. This last is the only part of the garden to survive and is now part of Richmond Park. It is interesting to note that this magnificent landscape, conceived on a giant scale, was the setting for a relatively modest house. Most of the gardens shown in *Britannia Illustrata* are for great country houses but a tantalizing few are for much smaller, and sometimes urban, houses. Sir William Blackett's house within the city walls of Newcastle upon Tyne had a delightfully intricate but appropriately small-scale garden. The house of the Pierrepont family in Nottingham had a rectangular garden with eight quadripartite beds edged in topiary, four with circles at the centre and four with diamond shapes. A garden of modest size but of major significance in the late 17th century was LEVENS HALL, laid out by a Frenchman and using, for the first time in England, a French invention—the HA-HA, which was in the 18th century to become an essential device of the landscape park.

The 17th century was a period of great interest for Scottish gardens. EDZELL CASTLE is the earliest dated garden in the country—its walls are decorated with a plaque bearing the arms of its maker, David Lindsay, and the date 1604. The surviving garden walls, with niches for planting and stone panels of the planetary deities, the liberal arts and cardinal virtues, and a summer house, give a vivid impression of the Scottish decorative sense that has appeared repeatedly in its gardens. In the 1630s a great terraced garden was laid out at DRUMMOND CASTLE which survives today in a Victorianized form. At about the same time, by 1633, the King's Knot was laid out at STIRLING CASTLE. Towards the end of the 17th century there was a flurry of garden activity. At PITMEDDEN in 1675 Sir Alexander Seton laid out a garden whose walls, pavilions, and staircase survive today. Sir William BRUCE at his own houses of Balcaskie (Fife) c.1670 and KINROSS in the 1680s designed remarkable gardens with dominant axial vistas which ingeniously draw in the BORROWED LANDSCAPE. Both of these survive in excellent state. A great formal walled garden was made before 1685 for the Gray family (earls of Tweeddale) at Yester House (East Lothian). A series of paintings of that date by an unknown artist shows a group of hedged rectangular beds with topiary, patterned beds, statues, and a central fountain pool. Outside the walled garden was an ornate pavilion at the head of a cascade leading down to a canal and an elaborate mount whose slopes are decorated with a maze. Beyond the pleasure gardens avenues marched across the landscape. Traces of avenue aligments survive today but nothing of the formal gardens which were obliterated when the grounds were landscaped after 1752. A very attractive terraced garden of the late 17th century survives in rather dishevelled state at Barncluith (Lanarkshire). On the banks of the river Avon five terraces were made which were described in James Macky's *A Journey through Scotland* (1723) as being ornamented with 'walks and grottoes all of them filled with large evergreens in the shape of beasts or birds'. It was plain that the terraces also had the purpose of displaying fine views of the wooded valley. A modest merchant's town house with the grandiose name of CULROSS PALACE, built in the late 16th and 17th centuries on the banks of the river Forth, has a precipitous terraced garden which in the late 20th century was restored and divided into rectilinear beds planted with fruit, vegetables, and flowers of the period, with crushed shell walks and a tunnel of pleached mulberry and grapevines. This skilful reconstruction gives a charming idea of a modest garden layout of its period.

An outstanding plantsman's garden was made in Wales during the Commonwealth by Sir Thomas Hanmer (1612–78), a friend of John Evelyn who had advised on the planting of Sayes Court. Hanmer lived at Bettisfield (Clwyd) and his garden, according to the nurseryman, florist, and author John Rea (d. 1681), had 'an incomparable' collection of garden plants. During the Commonwealth Hanmer wrote his *Garden Book* which was published only in 1933. It contains much detail of how a garden was laid out in the 1650s and a wealth of information on the cultivation of the flowers that particularly interested Hanmer, among them anemones, auriculas, carnations, narcissi, and tulips. At Llanerch Hall (Clwyd) c.1660 an outstanding terraced garden was made by Mutton Davies on his return from a visit to Italy. Only traces of it survive today but it is magnificently displayed in a painting of c.1662 showing a series of descending enclosures ornamented with topiary, fountains, staircases, pavilions, and fine gateways to a circular garden at the bottom of the slope enclosed in concentric rings of topiary with at its centre a circular pool and a statue of Neptune. The garden originally had Italianate GIOCHI D'ACQUA. A visitor in the 18th century, Philip Yorke of Erddig, saw a sundial with a surprise water jet and the inscription 'Alas! My friend, time soon will overtake you; And if you do not cry, by G–d I'll make you.' Of a similar date are the remarkable surviving terraces at POWIS CASTLE where some of the 17th-century yews survive, too, now grown to giant size.

In Ireland one of the greatest of all early 17th-century estates was Portlumna (County Galway) where c.1618 the 4th Earl of Clanricarde built a magnificent Renaissance castle. It had fine gardens of arbours, a grotto, walks, parterre, fountain pools, and waterfalls. Clanricarde was a friend of Sir John Danvers whose gardens at Chelsea House are said to have influenced Portlumna. The castle was gutted by fire in 1826 but the noble shell survives and in recent times formal gardens have been reinstated. Overlooked by castellated towers they show a pattern of paths radiating out from a circular lawn and segmental lawns and beds. An unusually complete early 17th-century garden survives at LISMORE CASTLE. Here the 1st Earl of Cork laid out a great terraced walled garden with castellations and pavilions. Thomas Dinely described it in *A Voyage through the Kingdom of Ireland* (written in 1681, published 1870) as 'extremely pleasant, being on the side of the mountain overlooking the whole town . . . with walks one above another . . . the uppermost walk had also a spring at the end thereof, whiche it is said the Earle of Cork intended to supply fountains with belowe, to form delightful throws of water'. At the beginning of the 17th century Sir Francis Chichester at Belfast Castle (County Antrim) had a garden with a bowling green, cherry garden, apple garden, and arbours, and walks which ran down to a river, a tributary of the river Lagan. There is record of a payment to 'women gathering Violatts in ye fields to sett in the Gardens'. Antrim Castle (County Antrim) had a notable garden in the 17th century in the Anglo-Dutch style with canals, cascades, hornbeam hedges, a parterre, and a formal wilderness. Mrs Delany saw it in a state of decay in 1758 and wrote that it 'was reckoned a fine one forty years ago—high hedges and long narrow walks'. An extraordinary formal garden of the late 17th century, largely intact today, was laid out at KILLRUDDERY in the 1680s by a Frenchman named Bonet, about whom nothing else is known. With its great canals and intimate hedged BOSQUETS it has a thoroughly French air.

The publishing of books on gardening and on plants flourished in the 17th century. William Lawson's *A New Orchard and Garden* (1618) is of special interest for its section on 'the Country Housewifes Garden for herbes of common use', the first time women gardeners specifically had been addressed. Lawson's practical manual of gardening had the everyday gardener in mind and was plainly written from practical experience. It also recognizes the delights and recreational values of gardening, particularly praising the orchard as a place for busy people 'to renue and refresh their senses, and to call home their over-wearied spirits'. John PARKINSON's *Paradisi in Sole Paradisus Terrestris* (1629), describing the flower garden, kitchen garden, and orchard, is rich in first-hand plantsmanship, and many of the plants described (almost 1,000, mostly exotics) were grown in the author's own garden in Long Acre (London). Parkinson's much less known *Theatrum Botanicum: The Theater of Plants* (1649) is a herbal describing almost 4,000 plants. John EVELYN's *Sylva* (1664), 'a discourse of forest trees' was to have a great influence on tree planting from both the economic and ornamental point of view—by 1729 it had appeared in five ever expanding editions. John Rea's *Flora: seu, de Florum Cultura* (1665) was a flower book for the amateur gardener of a very modern kind, intended 'to acquaint the unskilful with such Rules and apt Forms, as may be fit for the planting and disposing of the best Flowers . . . [so that] every person of any capacity may be enabled thereby to be his own Gardener'. Rea gives advice on laying out a flower garden and gives a good idea of the repertory of plants available in his time. In 1683 was published the first Scottish book on gardening, John Reid's *The Scots Gard'ner*. This sturdily practical book, 'published for the Climate of Scotland', gives occasional glimpses of something more pleasurable. He explains that pleasure gardens should 'be divided into walkes and plots, with a Bordure round each plot, and at the corner of each may be a holly or some such train'd up, some Pyramidal, others Spherical'. He conjures up a pretty picture of the kitchen garden whose walks may be hedged in 'Thyme, Lavendar, Hyssop, Rue, &c.' or, even more decoratively, with 'Parsly, Strawberries, Violets, July-flowers [Gilly flowers, that is carnations]'. In the plant world a major development was the founding of the Brompton Park Nursery in 1681. The founders were Roger Looker, Moses Cook, John Field, and George LONDON and they quickly built up a large stock. In having the involvement of a major garden designer, George London, the nursery was able to sell plants for several of the most notable gardens of the day. This was by no means the first nursery in the British Isles but it had more influence, and was more intimately linked with the most lucrative market, than any before it.

The 18th century

It is easy, and misleading, to think of the 18th century overwhelmingly in terms of the landscape park. It is true that the work of Capability BROWN, and those practising in his style, was extremely fashionable. Furthermore, the informal landscape park is the only garden style of the British Isles that was of international influence, as influential in its time as were the French gardens designed in the style of LE NÔTRE in the previous century. The historical circumstances which produced the landscape park are of particular importance. In England the 18th century was one of the greatest periods of enclosures, by which common land passed into private ownership—1,214,574 hectares/3,000,000 acres of land were enclosed in this time—and the landscape park, relatively cheap to lay out and extremely cheap to maintain, presented itself as a particularly attractive way of embellishing an estate. Such parks, largely an English phenomenon, were certainly very visible, but formal gardens continued to be made throughout the British Isles and such formal features as avenues very often survived landscaping. In the early years of the 18th century London and Wise continued to be active and the somewhat enigmatic figure of Charles BRIDGEMAN intermingled the formal and informal in gardens such as STOWE. In some estates the two traditions lived happily together—ERDDIG had both a large walled early 18th-century formal garden on one side of the house and a landscape park, designed by William EMES c.1760, on the other side. At ROUSHAM much of Charles Bridgeman's early 18th-century formal layout was retained when William KENT set out a much more modern, indeed avant-garde, layout in the late 1730s. There is a tendency in garden history to seek heroic figures as the progenitors of great developments but the truth is that changes take place gradually—almost everything important in gardening takes place slowly. William Kent was regarded as a great innovator by Horace Walpole—'he leaped the fence and saw that all nature was a garden'. But the chief method of drawing in the landscape, the sunken fence or ha-ha, had been used by others before Kent—by Beaumont at LEVENS HALL, VANBRUGH at CLAREMONT, and Bridgeman at Stowe—and the idea of opening up views of the country beyond the garden was done, with bastions in the park wall, at BRAMHAM PARK, in the very early 18th century. Furthermore, the notion of the borrowed landscape, as we have seen, was well understood by Sir William Bruce in Scotland in the late 17th century.

The 18th century is best understood as a swirling mass of influences and tendencies, some more novel than others. A minor, but delightful and surviving garden that illustrates the mixture of idioms of some 18th-century gardens is Goldney House (Bristol). The Quaker Goldneys were pioneer industrialists who founded the Coalbrookdale cast-iron works. Thomas Goldney rebuilt his house in 1720 and embellished the garden with cast-iron railings and gates—probably the first ever to be used in a garden. His son made a three-chambered shell GROTTO and by the 1760s the garden had a canal, a Gothic prospect tower, a viewing terrace, and, most remarkably, a beam engine which pumped water to a cascade in the grotto. Many of the most remarkable and attractive gardens do not fit easily into the garden historian's paradigms. At Corby Castle (Cumbria), for example, between 1709 and 1739, Thomas Howard laid out a garden of great originality. Corby is on the banks of the river Eden and Thomas made a garden of Edenic character inspired by Milton's *Paradise Lost* which describes 'Eden's lofty banks' as a 'steep wilderness; whose hairie sides / With thicket overgrown, grottesque and wilde'. Howard made planned walks along the river bank with a grotto, temple, cascade, and figure of Polyphemus. Not all large-scale landscapes were informal. A garden such as Bramham Park, using its giant beech *allées* to animate a vast area and later on placing temples and other ornaments as eyecatchers, mixes influences of the 17th century with those of the 18th-century landscape park. Lord Bathurst's immense landscape at CIRENCESTER PARK, laid out in the 1730s and surviving largely intact, is on a similar scale, with an avenue 8 km/5 miles long. It was conceived as both a fine landscape and as a profitable timber business and is run in exactly the same way today. A garden such as STOURHEAD, laid out by a gentleman amateur, Henry Hoare II, in the 1740s, is one of the most dazzling and attractive gardens of its period. It was often thought of as the *beau idéal* of its time, yet it is a far from characteristic example. It was conceived as a single self-contained entity—a surprise in the landscape not a setting for a house. At Stourhead the landscape garden is at some distance from the house and not visible from it. The garden at Stowe, laid out from 1713 to the 1750s, drew on a series of garden designers who reflected the changing styles of their times—Sir John Vanbrugh, Charles Bridgeman, William Kent, and Capability Brown. It is stylistically far more heterogeneous than Stourhead and on a much grander scale—500 hectares/1,235 acres as opposed to the 16 hectares/40 acres of Stourhead. Humphry REPTON, whose first garden designs date from the late 1780s, marked a transitional stage in garden style. His clients were frequently of much more modest circumstances than the dukes for whom Capability Brown often worked. Some of the detail of Repton's gardens—such as the children's garden and flowery terrace at ENDSLEIGH HOUSE—looks forward to the Victorian era. Repton was modern in another way, too. He was the first professional garden designer to describe his working practices, in *Sketches and Hints on Landscape Gardening* (1795).

Garden history tends to emphasize the intriguing byways of 18th-century English garden design—the FERME ORNÉE, the rococo gardens associated with Thomas Robins, or extremes of the picturesque such as Richard Payne KNIGHT's Downton Castle (Shropshire)—yet none of these represents a major style of the period. Until quite recently, on the other hand, the flower garden, which flourished in the 18th century, was not given its just prominence. Throughout the 18th century the nursery trade flourished and groves of flowering shrubs were a common feature. Smart new terraced houses in the rapidly expanding towns invariably had their own walled gardens. Todd Longstaffe-Gowan's *The London Town Garden 1740–1840* (2001) illustrates the great variety of ornamental urban gardens and describes the full horticultural infrastructure required to support them. In Bath (Somerset) the 'Georgian Garden' is a late 20th-century reconstruction of such a garden based on meticulous archaeological evidence and laid out with period planting—with mixed borders and fruit trees espaliered against the enclosing walls.

The early 18th century in Wales produced gardens of exceptional interest. Leeswood Hall (Clwyd) was built c.1724-6 for George Wynne, who commissioned a garden from Stephen SWITZER. Switzer laid out lawns close to the house, blocks of woodland through which vistas were opened, a turf amphitheatre, and a mount crowned with stone alcove seats. Only traces of this garden survive today. At the GNOLL (Glamorgan) Humphry Mackworth, a copper smelter, in the 1720s with the help of the garden designer Thomas Greening (1684-1757) enlivened a wooded valley with a great pool close to the house and a fine formal cascade, multi-tiered and descending a gentle slope. Shapes of stone were placed in the cascade to produce different forms and sounds of splashing water. Some time later, in the 1740s, he made a cascade of completely different character at the head of the valley. Here the cascade is naturalistic, descending 55 m/180 ft in a series of falls and running through the woods in a naturalistic rocky stream. Walks linked the two cascades, with the occasional rustic building enlivening the progress. William EMES, practising in the Brownian style, laid out several Welsh parks, among them CHIRK CASTLE, Erddig, Penrice Castle (Glamorgan), and Gregynog (Powys). Wales is rich in the picturesque scenery which 18th-century landscapers found especially attractive. In their day PIERCEFIELD (laid out from the 1750s) and HAFOD (from 1783) were among the most notable landscapes in Britain and attractive fragments of both survive.

The naturalistic landscape park was never an important feature of Scottish estates and formal gardens continued to be laid out in the 18th century. At CASTLE KENNEDY a rare formal landscape garden on the grand scale was laid out from 1722, possible to the designs of William ADAM. Adam certainly designed the elaborate gardens in 1720 at Taymouth Castle (Perthshire) with *pattes d'oie* of avenues and parterres, and *c.*1726 at ARNISTON HOUSE (Midlothian) he made a layout in similar style. At PENICUIK HOUSE from the 1720s Sir John CLERK planted trees on the grand scale, over 300,000 of them, some of which were arranged in avenues. But he also built picturesque landscape buildings—Hurley Cave (a tunnel grotto) and a machicolated watch tower. The 2nd Duke of Atholl at Blair Castle (Perthshire) in the 1740s and 1750s made a garden of parterres and avenues which was illustrated in Georges-Louis LE ROUGE's *Jardins anglo-chinois* (1785). Something of the atmosphere of the English landscape park was caught at Dunkeld House where in the 1780s the Duke of Atholl built grottoes on the river bank, the HERMITAGE overlooking a cascade, and Ossian's Cave, a rustic cavern. The exquisite PINEAPPLE built in 1761 at Dunmore is an example of a particularly fertile period of ornamental garden buildings in Scotland. William Adam's Chatelherault (1732) at HAMILTON PALACE, Robert ADAM's temple-like tea pavilion at Auchincruive (1778, Ayrshire), and the Whim, a Gothic eyecatcher at Blair Castle (1762, Perthshire) are a few examples only of a tradition that produced many prospect towers, mausoleums, grottoes, obelisks, dovecotes (doocots in Scotland) that enlivened the 18th-century Scottish landscape. Thomas WHITE, father and son, were the great practitioners of the Brownian style in Scotland but, in all, they designed no more than 40 gardens.

In Ireland formal gardens were still being made at the beginning of the 18th century. For the great Palladian mansion of Castletown House (*c.*1722) a great *patte d'oie* of avenues was made. The ancient estate of the Fitzgeralds at Carton (County Kildare) had by *c.*1730 been divided by patterns of avenues and rides, and fine formal gardens lay about the house. A simple semicircular forecourt would scarcely have prepared visitors for the complexity of what lay behind the house—beds framed by topiary, canals, wildernesses, and rides through groves. At Howth Castle (County Dublin) in the 1730s an elaborate pattern of rides through woodland was laid out—surviving giant beech hedges may be part of that scheme. The 1st Earl of Limerick at Tollymore planted the first

ARBORETUM in Ireland and a little later, in the 1770s, embellished his demesne with a rustic hermitage, Gothic bridge, barbican, and a barn built like a Gothic chapel all of which may have been designed by Thomas WRIGHT who visited Ireland in the 1750s. The Irish garden designer John Sutherland practised in the style of Capability Brown. At Derrymore House (County Armagh) his work was described in 1803 by Sir Charles Coote: 'The very fine improvements . . . show the correct and elegant taste of Mr Sutherland.' He particularly praised the elaborate cottage *orné* (1776; a picturesque rustic cottage designed as a garden ornament)—'the most elegant summer lodge I have ever seen'. Sutherland also designed landscapes at Slane Castle (County Meath), Rockingham (County Roscommon), and Gracefield Lodge (County Laois). A little later, in the 1790s, at Kilfane Glen (County Kilkenny) another cottage *orné* (now beautifully reconstructed) was built as part of a picturesque landscape in a wooded valley. An important event was the founding in 1795 of the NATIONAL BOTANIC GARDENS at Glasnevin.

A novel development in the 18th century was the opening of houses and gardens to the public. Stourhead received visitors by the 1750s, in 1760 Chatsworth was open regularly, and BLENHEIM and Woburn Abbey were opening by 1790. Already there was sometimes a need to control visitors and at Chiswick House tickets had to be applied for beforehand and it was stipulated that 'They that would have tickets are desired not to bring children'. At HAFOD in the late 18th century Thomas Johnes had a hotel built to receive visitors. Many estates, although they may not have had regular opening times, were amenable to requests to visit.

Publishing of gardening books flourished in the 18th century—around 600 new titles on horticulture and botany were published, about six times the number in the previous century. An important influence on garden design in the early years of the century was *The Theory and Practice of Gardening* (1712), John James's translation of A.-J. DEZALLIER D'ARGENVILLE's *La Théorie et la pratique du jardinage* (1709). This gives a detailed description of laying out gardens in the style of Le Nôtre but it also offers a glimpse of the future—the first description in English of the ha-ha. Thomas Fairchild's *The City Gardener* (1722) met the needs of a new and growing market. Philip MILLER's *The Gardeners Dictionary* (1731) was one of the most infuential reference books of plants. Its revised editions trace the great increase in available garden plants. By the time of the 6th edition (1768) Miller was able to write that the number of plants cultivated in England 'are more than double those which were here when the first

edition of this book was published'. The theoretical writings of Joseph Addison, Alexander POPE, Stephen Switzer, Richard Payne Knight, and Uvedale PRICE have been much discussed by garden historians but their impact on the way people gardened is hard to assess. Thomas WHATELY's *Observations on Modern Gardening* (1770) was a pioneer—in effect the first guide to important gardens ever published. John ABERCROMBIE's astonishing series of practical gardening manuals—on fruit growing, kitchen gardening, growing mushrooms, sylviculture, and much else—met a receptive readership. His *Every Man his own Gardener* (1767) was in its 34th printing by 1848.

The 19th century

The 19th century was the busiest period in the history of gardening in the British Isles. Stylistically it is by far the most varied period of British garden history. Landscape parks continued to be laid out, reproduction 'period' gardens in several styles were designed, a taste for rockeries developed, the herbaceous border was invented (at ARLEY HALL *c.*1851), the woodland garden made its appearance, and Robinsonian (see ROBINSON, WILLIAM) wild gardening had a strong influence. Gardening became a leisure occupation of a huge number of people whose interest was fostered by an outpouring of books and periodicals. Municipal public parks provided places of recreation in which visitors could also learn about plants and gardening. Fashionable garden style was largely dominated by historicizing schemes evoking, often with a characteristic Victorian boisterousness, the styles of the past. Trentham Park (Staffordshire)—'the Versailles of the Midlands'—may be taken as the epitome of a certain 19th-century attitude to garden making. Belonging to the Levesons (later Leveson-Gower and dukes of Sutherland) since the early 16th century, the old house was transformed in the 1830s and 1840s into an Italianate palace by the architect Sir Charles BARRY, who laid out a garden in keeping with it, profusely furnished with balustraded terracing, golden yew topiary, statues, pools, fountains, parterres, and pavilions. Old houses were often garnished with new gardens which sought to create what was thought of as an appropriate period style. For the Jacobean Gawthorpe Hall (Lancashire) Barry designed a 'Jacobean' garden *c.*1849 which, with its shaped beds, mounded carpet bedding, and plumes of *Cordyline australis* (introduced in 1823) could scarcely look more 19th century. W. A. NESFIELD was one of the most prolific practitioners of the historicist style, especially skilful at designing flamboyant parterres. Historicizing gardens of this kind were also made in Ireland, of which Killarney House (County Kerry) was a good example. Laid out by J. D. Sedding (1838–91) after 1872 it was a terraced garden with a fan-shaped parterre, colonnade of topiary, and heraldic arms worked in clipped box. At POWERSCOURT in the 1840s Daniel Robertson remodelled existing 18th-century terraced gardens with Victorian exuberance. A similar transformation was made in Scotland for Drummond Castle where from 1820 Lewis Kennedy, possibly with advice from Sir Charles Barry, refashioned 17th-century terraces. In around 1850 Sir Charles Barry worked at Dunrobin Castle (Sutherland), where he designed two parterre gardens to be viewed from the castle terraces. In Wales W. E. Nesfield (1835–88) designed a terraced 'Venetian'-style garden in 1873 at Kinmel Mark (Clwyd) with yew topiary and a great central pool with a tiered fountain. He showed his versatility in also designing a swirling box 'Dutch' parterre at about the same time for Bodrhyddan (Clwyd).

Glasshouses of every kind, ornamental and productive, were a vital part of the 19th-century garden. Heated glasshouses were used to cultivate tender fruit and to raise annuals for the bedding schemes which decorated so many of the formal schemes of the day. Such schemes were detested by William Robinson, a dominant figure in the late 19th century who vigorously challenged artificialities of this kind and the prevailing architectural style of gardening. His *The Wild Garden* (1870) and *The English Flower Garden* (1883) are essential texts in the history of British plantsmanship. Plantsmanship and architecture were not, however, irreconcilable. Robinson's colleague Gertrude JEKYLL, who shared many of his beliefs, achieved her greatest distinction in the plantings she executed for the strongly architectural layouts of Edwin LUTYENS. Indeed this style of gardening may be regarded, with the 18th-century landscape park, as the only truly distinctive garden style produced in Britain. The ARTS AND CRAFTS style of gardening, intermingling vernacular architecture with subtle planting, was one that had influence throughout the British Isles.

In suitable sites throughout the British Isles the woodland garden, often called the Robinsonian garden in Ireland, was introduced in the 19th century. In England notable examples were made in Cornwall at Glendurgan (from the 1820s), HELIGAN (from *c*.1820), Penjerrick (from the 1840s), and TREBAH (from 1842). In Scotland INVEREWE, one of the most remarkable of all woodland gardens, was started in 1862, and Arduaine (Argyll) in the 1890s. In Ireland among the notable Robinsonian gardens are Derreen (County Kerry) (from 1866) and MOUNT USHER (after 1868), and the tradition continued into the 20th

century with gardens such as ANNES GROVE. The north-west coast of Wales provided suitable sites for woodland gardens of which BODNANT (started in the 1880s) and the Gwyllt woodland garden (today part of the PORTMEIRION estate) (started in the 1850s) are fine examples. Taste for rhododendrons which became such an important ingredient of these gardens was given great impetus by the plant collecting in the Himalayas of J. D. HOOKER. His account of his discoveries, *The Rhododendrons of Sikkim-Himalaya* (1849–51), revealed to gardeners the riches of the Himalayan rhododendrons. By the end of the century, with the work of E. H. WILSON, the hunt for Himalayan plants was in full cry. The 19th century was a great period for the planting of conifers and the many new introductions, in particular from the north-west Pacific coast of North America, were often gathered together in a pinetum.

The number of books published in the course of the century was so great that no bibliography of them has ever been completed. There was an outpouring of gardening periodicals, many of them aimed at a wide readership of which the *Gardeners' Chronicle* (from 1841) was probably the most influential. They ranged from the specialist (such as the *Florist and Pomologist*, from 1862) to the overtly populist (*Gossip for the Garden*, from 1856). Book publishing for a mass readership was born in the 19th century. The remarkable J. C. LOUDON and Jane Loudon published a series of books which struck a deep chord with gardeners. Loudon's immense *Encyclopaedia of Gardening* (1822), describing every aspect of his subject, remains one of the most remarkable reference books ever written. William Robinson was the great figure at the end of the century. His *The English Flower Garden* (1883) was in its seventh printing by the end of the century and continued to be reprinted in the 20th century. The repertory of plants it recommended still exerts a strong influence on garden taste. Gertrude Jekyll, although she wrote many articles, and contributed the section on 'Colour in the Flower Garden' in *The English Flower Garden*, published only one book in the 19th century, *Wood & Garden* (1899). An eloquent book setting out the principles of the architectural garden, with many examples of historic gardens, was *The Formal Garden in England* (1892) by Reginald BLOMFIELD and F. Inigo THOMAS.

The 20th and 21st centuries
The two world wars were the greatest influence on gardening in the British Isles in the 20th century. The intensive gardening practised by gardeners such as Gertrude Jekyll, requiring a highly trained and numerous garden staff, did not survive the Second World War. Nor did the

great tradition of the municipal public parks which suffered bomb damage and neglect in the Second World War and suffered even more grievously in the 1980s when so many municipal parks departments (with their precious apprenticeship schemes) were liquidated and their maintenance put out to 'competitive tendering' (that is to say, the cheapest won). In the early part of the century the greatest stylistic influence was that of the Arts and Crafts movement. Many of the gardens produced at this time, especially those of Edwin Lutyens, Harold PETO, and Francis Inigo Thomas, remain among the most beautiful of the century. There has been no truly distinctive and widely influential garden style in the British Isles to supersede it. Although Britain received refugees from the Bauhaus, and notable International Modern houses were built between the wars, the modernist garden never caught the public imagination. Landscape architects of the post-Second World War period, such as Sir Geoffrey JELLICOE, Brenda COLVIN, and Dame Sylvia CROWE, were all touched by the ideas of modernism but the landscaping of nuclear power stations, motorways, and new towns has not built up a body of work that many people enjoy. Sir Geoffrey Jellicoe's charmingly idiosyncratic and richly atmospheric gardens at SHUTE HOUSE or SUTTON PLACE, both of which draw deeply on the past, strike deeper chords than his roof garden for Harvey's Department Store in Guildford (Surrey). It is a matter of some puzzlement, too, that Sir Frederick Gibberd should be the designer both of the unappetizing Harlow New Town and of his own strikingly attractive garden (GIBBERD GARDEN). In the late 20th century several notable garden designers were also influential garden writers, among them John Brookes, Penelope HOBHOUSE, Arabella Lennox-Boyd, and Rosemary VEREY. All were knowledgeable about plants, practised in a more or less classical tradition, and were much to the taste of the time. The same could be said about two of the finest gardener-writers of the period, Christopher LLOYD and Graham Stuart THOMAS.

By the end of the 20th century throughout the British Isles garden taste was in thrall to the past. The work of Ian Hamilton FINLAY and Charles Jencks (b. 1939), dazzling though it is, seems to have spawned no disciples. In 1927 the National Gardens Scheme was founded, arranging the opening of private gardens to the public in England and Wales to raise money for charities (the separate Scotland's Gardens Scheme does the same). The thousands of gardens that have been opened have been deeply influential on garden taste, reinforcing an essentially conservative tendency. Gardens in the ownership of the NATIONAL TRUST have shown the same inclination. No new garden, as opposed to a reconstructed period garden, had ever been laid out in a National Trust garden until 2003 when Arne Maynard was commissioned to design a new garden for Dyrham Park (Gloucestershire). Conservation and concerns about the environment were essential ingredients of the gardening mood in the late 20th century. The GARDEN HISTORY SOCIETY was founded in 1965, followed in 1974 by its invaluable *Journal*, and stimulated interest in the horticultural past. The NATIONAL COUNCIL FOR THE CONSERVATION OF PLANTS AND GARDENS (which is entirely to do with plants rather than gardens) was founded in 1978 and has, with its network of National Collections of garden plants, carried out valuable work. The *Plant Finder* (now the *RHS Plant Finder*) first appeared in 1987 and has, by informing the public of commercial sources of sometimes very rare plants, greatly contributed to the cause of garden plant conservation. The listing of historic parks and gardens, started by English Heritage and continued in Wales by CADW and in Scotland by Historic Scotland and the Countryside Commission, confers no protection in law but directs that any planning applications that might affect such sites should be considered particularly carefully. The possibility of global warming causing a radical and long-term change in climate (see CLIMATE CHANGE) made some gardeners turn their attention to sustainability and to natural communities of plants of the sort recommended, for different reasons, 100 years previously by William Robinson. This revival of interest in naturalistic planting was perhaps the only distinctive style of British gardens at the end of the 20th century.

At the beginning of the 21st century, in 2001, the EDEN PROJECT was opened to the public. It combines exciting architecture, a mission to educate the public about the plight of plants, landscaping, and a mammoth tourist attraction (although it claims to be not so much 'a destination as a place in the heart'). It became another, albeit immensely successful, example of the garden planned for visitors. Unlike the 19th-century public gardens (which were always free) the Eden Project is a commercial venture in the sense that it raises money for the charitable foundation that owns it (entrance for adults in 2004 was £10 a head; compared, say, with the £7 entrance fee for SISSINGHURST CASTLE). Visiting gardens and home gardening are both very popular leisure activities throughout the British Isles. The media coverage of gardening through television, radio, and publishing (books, newspapers, and magazines) is intensive, wide ranging, and of high quality. Television coverage, although often at peak viewing times, does not attract the mass viewership which is common, for example, for major sporting events. It tends to have a practical emphasis, concentrating on plants and planting rather than on garden aesthetics. The most influential gardening programme is probably the BBC's weekly *Gardeners' World*, which was founded in 1968. Its sequence of presenters—Percy Thrower, Geoff Hamilton, Alan Titchmarsh, and Monty Don—have all been knowledgeable gardeners and skilful presenters. In recent years there have been occasional worthwhile attempts to address garden historical subjects, in particular historically based restoration of distinguished gardens. The BBC radio programme *Gardeners' Question Time*, launched in 1947 as *How Does your Garden Grow?*, is one of the longest running programmes on any subject. The profession of gardening is beset by low pay and unsatisfactory working conditions and there is also anxiety about the quality of training in some quarters. However, the training of gardeners at places like the Royal Botanic Gardens at Kew, and at Wisley, maintains very high standards. The Royal Horticultural Society (RHS), with 360,000 members by 2004, four display gardens, a lively journal (*The Garden*), regular shows, and a stream of influential publications is a valuable source of information and inspiration. Some interesting garden designers of a younger generation, such as Christopher BRADLEY-HOLE, Dan Pearson, Tom Stuart-Smith, and Kim Wilkie, have introduced a sprightly new atmosphere in garden design, but little of their work is to be seen in public places. The nursery trade remains very diverse and more plants are commercially available than ever before—British gardening is still largely dominated by a love of plants.

Vernacular gardens.

Garden history usually ignores the commonest, and most popular, kind of garden—the lovingly tended, ordinary garden which many of the readers of this book possess and cherish and which is the surest indicator of the horticultural health of a country. Gardens of this sort, bringing their owners into regular contact with plants, supplying vegetables more delicious than any to be bought in a shop, and creating an intimate microcosm in which the gardener may be lord of all he surveys, remain of fundamental importance to those living in the British Isles. Such gardens have existed for a very long time—far longer than history can tell—but details of how they were laid out and planted are hard to come by. They are the silent majority of British and Irish horticulture. Fashionable gardeners feverishly scan the pages of glossy magazines and follow the advice of media gardeners while vernacular gardeners build on the ancient wisdom and taste of generations of gardeners. One of the great values of the National Gardens Scheme is that many of the thousands of gardens which it makes open to the public belong to this vernacular tradition, so, if we cannot know its history, we can at least experience its magic. See also VERNACULAR GARDENS. PT

Brodick Castle ⊛

Isle of Arran, Scotland, was given to James Hamilton by his cousin King James IV in 1503. Rebuilt in the 17th century and in the 19th century, the castle occupies a dramatic site looking westwards across the Firth of Clyde. Nothing is known of the garden until 1710 when a walled kitchen garden was built. The garden today is largely the work of the Duchess of Montrose (a granddaughter of the 10th Duke of Hamilton) from 1919. The climate, affected by the Gulf Stream Drift, is very mild here, the rainfall is high, and the soil is acid—the perfect conditions for a woodland garden. This was the great period of discoveries in the Himalayas and the Duchess made plantings of such newly introduced rhododendrons as *R. giganteum* (introduced by George FORREST in 1919), *R. macabeanum*, and *R. magnificum* (Frank Kingdon WARD in 1920 and 1931). Ornamental trees such as acer, nothofagus, and sorbus provide a handsome background and there is much underplanting of *Gunnera manicata*, meconopsis, and Asiatic primulas. The 18th-century walled garden, divided into three, has been turned into an ornamental garden with mixed borders, a circular flower garden, and roses on trellis-work. Close to the sea is a rustic Bavarian gazebo built *c*.1848 by the 11th Duke for his wife Princess Marie of Baden with a magnificent ceiling decorated with pine cones and patterns of larch wood. Since 1958 the castle and its 24 hectares/60 acres of gardens have belonged to the National Trust for Scotland. PT

Brodsworth Hall ⊛

near Doncaster, South Yorkshire, is an unusual example of a distinguished house and garden from an unfashionable period, the 1860s. The house was built, replacing an 18th-century house, in neoclassical style for Charles Thellusson, possibly to the designs of a London architect, Philip Wilkinson. A new garden of an appropriate kind was made at the same time with fine turf terraces and flights of steps south and west of the house. An Italian sculptor, G. M. Casentini, made the beautiful white marble urns and figures of whippets on the terraces and other sculptures in the garden. The entrance to the house, on the east side, leads under old cedars of Lebanon (from an earlier garden) past evergreen shrubberies with female figures. To the west a flower garden has a grand tiered fountain pool (also by Casentini) flanked by monkey-puzzles and surrounded by shaped beds filled with annuals cut into a lawn. To the west, on the site of a quarry, is the Grove, a garden of romantic character in contrast to the classical restraint of the house's surroundings. Here is a pets' cemetery, a rare terraced fernery, and an elegant 18th-century pavilion (the Target House) standing at the end of the archery lawn. Behind it an iron pergola festooned in roses curves among box-edged beds of shrub roses. The house and garden (of 6 hectares/15 acres) were given in 1990 to English Heritage. Now finely restored, inside and out, it is an unusual, and delightful, ensemble of its period.   PT

Brondanw, Plas ⊛
Penrhyndeudraeth, Gwynedd, Wales, is a rare, unclassifiable garden of great beauty. The estate was given to the architect Clough WILLIAMS-ELLIS by his father in 1908, when he was 25. The 17th-century stone house was divided when he came here, and occupied by seven families. He gradually restored the house and made a garden, chiefly in the 1920s and 1930s. He recognized, as all good garden designers do, the particular virtues of his site—here is a spectacularly beautiful setting, with giant views of the Snowdonia landscape. This single fact determined the kind of garden he made. On a sloping site below the house a series of yew-hedged compartments is tricked out with charming architectural conceits and ornaments. The main axis is kept open with Snowdon borrowed as an eyecatcher, rising above yew topiary to the east. A view of another mountain, Cnicht, is revealed more surreptitiously, a surprise revelation through a CLAIRE-VOIE. There are plants in the garden but they are as nothing in relation to the green architecture, the ornaments, and the natural setting. A garden of wilder character lies on the wooded hills behind the house. A path leads through the woods, past a corrugated iron pavilion painted turquoise and gold and a terrifying vertiginous quarry to a field of grazing sheep. Here, on the top of a hill, is a castellated stone lookout tower built in 1915—partly defensive, 'to repel the expected German invasion', and chiefly ornamental, to give a magnificent panorama of Snowdonia.   PT

Brooklyn Botanic Garden ⊛
Brooklyn, New York, USA, is a miracle of land reclamation. Built on 16 hectares/39 acres of ash dump and filled land in 1910 it has evolved into a 21-hectare/52-acre botanic garden with remarkable collections, gardens, scientific research, and educational programmes. The first gardens developed were the Native Flora Garden, the Children's Garden, the Japanese Hill-and-Pond Garden, and the Rock Garden. Along with a magnolia collection, the substantial Cranford Rose Garden, the 'Kwanzan' Cherry Esplanade, a Fragrance Garden, the modern Steinhardt Conservatory, a Palm House, and other plantings, these form a densely packed horticultural oasis in New York city. The scientific mission for research, collecting, and plant hybridization, and the drive for public education have been strong throughout the development of this institution. Major collections, like the Cranford Rose Garden—said to be the most comprehensive rose collection in the USA—draw plant enthusiasts from afar, and the local home gardener can find information and inspiration in demonstration gardens and gardening workshops. The designed gardens also offer grand spaces on a public scale, like the dramatic Cherry Esplanade in early May. The world's more tender flora can also be found here, in desert and tropical collections in the new Steinhardt Conservatory. The most widely known image of a garden here is of the vermilion tori (see BLOEDEL RESERVE) arch emerging from the water in the classic Japanese Hill-and-Pond Garden—built in 1915 and recently restored. The Brooklyn Botanic Garden condenses the world of plants to fit the plan.   PC

Brown, Lancelot 'Capability'
(1716–83), English landscape designer and architect, born in Kirkharle, Northumberland, the most successful, and arguably the greatest, landscape gardener of his day. He was known as 'Capability' from his ability to realize the capabilities of a landscape. Very famous in his day, and in demand by owners of many of the noble estates, his reputation had started to decline by the early 20th century. This was chiefly as a result of the polemics of those who had rediscovered the delights of the formal, architectural garden of which Brown was regarded as the chief destroyer. His fame was reinstated by such writers as Christopher Hussey and, above all, Dorothy Stroud, his biographer, in the 1950s and 1960s. More recently garden historians like David Jacques and Tom Williamson have emphasized the fact that Brown was one only of many 18th-century landscape designers, such as William EMES, Adam Mickle (c.1730–1809), Nathaniel Richmond (1724–84), and Richard WOODS, whose work and achievements are only beginning to come into focus. Some of these designers started their career with Brown. Recent research, too, has emphasized that Brown was by no means a one-man band. He depended on a large group of people to supervise the execution of his schemes and he may be thought of as among the first garden designers to have something resembling a professional practice.

The success of Brown's career comes from his own rare talents and the time in which he happened to live. It was a period of great prosperity and one of the chief signs of wealth was the increase in size of landed estates. The 18th century, as W. G. Hoskins describes in *The Making of the English Landscape* (1955), was the great age of parliamentary enclosures of open fields and waste land—almost 1,214,574 hectares/ 3,000,000 acres were enclosed, that is to say passed into private ownership. Hoskins prints a map showing the greatest concentrations of enclosures in England which overlaps eerily with the map of Brown's commissions shown by Dorothy Stroud in *Capability Brown* (new edn. 1975). At the peak of his very busy career, in the 1760s and 1770s, he was astonishingly successful, with an average annual turnover of £15,000 (around £1,000,000 today). In addition to his landscape designing he also undertook architectural design, for houses as well as garden buildings. Throughout his career he worked on designs for over 200 estates, between 1741 (STOWE) and 1782 (Stourton House, Yorkshire). Ann Bermingham in *Landscape and Ideology* (1986) makes the suggestion that the naturalistic style of the Brownian park was especially attractive to landowners anxious about the naturalness of the means by which they had acquired their rolling acres.

The usual description of Brown's characteristic work amounts almost to a cliché—the park surrounded by belts of trees, clumps of trees in the open landscape, and a lake in the middle ground, usually formed by damming a stream and often of serpentine form so as to resemble a river. Very little is known about either the theory or practice of his craft. He left no theoretical writings and the few snippets of information we possess are anecdotal. The writer Hannah More, for example, bumped into Brown at HAMPTON COURT and recorded a memorable conversation in which Brown 'compared his art to literary composition. "Now *there*", said he, pointing his finger, "I make a comma, and there" pointing to another spot, "where a more decided turn is proper, I make a colon; at another part, where an interruption is desirable to break the view, a parenthesis; now a full stop, and then I begin another subject." ' He published no account of his aesthetics or his working methods but tantalizing evidence survives in miscellaneous correspondence. In recent years it has been pointed out that Brown also took great interest in the PLEASURE GROUNDS of an estate as well as the park. He often designed more or less flowery shrubberies close to the house (as he did, for example, in the pleasure grounds of PETWORTH). His work was not universally admired in his time—the architect and garden designer Sir William CHAMBERS criticized his landscapes in 1772 because they 'differ very little from common fields, so closely is nature copied in most of them'. Richard Payne KNIGHT, the apostle of the picturesque, memorably dubbed him as the 'genius of the bare and bald'. Humphry REPTON, who followed in his footsteps, criticized 'that fondness for levelling, so prevalent in all Brown's workmen: every hillock by them is lowered, and every hollow filled to produce a level surface.'

Much of the research into Brown's career and work has been concerned with circumstantial matters, with delving in archives (such as they are) rather than examining what is visible in his landscapes. Only recently has there been a close study of his surviving works to try and explain what he actually did. Tom Williamson's article on Brown's work at CHATSWORTH in the issue of *Garden History* cited below shows Brown going about his business with much greater subtlety than has previously been recognized, especially with regard to viewpoints and approaches. Many of Brown's landscapes survive in greater or lesser states of dishevelment. Among his most atmospheric and attractive works open to the public are BOWOOD, HAREWOOD, and Petworth. These have great charm, but how do we know to what extent they correspond to Brown's intentions? In one of the very few documents in which Brown discusses his ideas, in a letter to the Reverend Thomas Dyer in 1775, he describes what is needed to design landscape: 'a perfect knowledge of the country and the objects in it, whether natural or artificial, and infinite delicacy in the planting etc., so much Beauty depending on the size of trees and the colour of their leaves to produce the effect of light and shade'. Brown was a designer of great subtlety and until more work has been done in the field we are not in a position to assess his genius at its full worth.   PT

'Lancelot Brown (1716–1783) and the Landscape Park', special issue of *Garden History*, Vol. 29: No. 1 (2001).
DOROTHY STROUD, *Capability Brown* (1950; new edn. 1975).

Browne, Sir Thomas

(1605–82), English doctor and author. His curious book *The Garden of Cyrus* (1658) has the subtitle 'The Quincunciall, Lozenge, or Net-work Plantations of the Ancients, Artificially, Naturally, Mystically Considered'. Browne discusses the history of ancient gardens, starting with Eden, and proceeds to analyse the QUINCUNX as first described by Xenophanes 'in his gallant plantation at *Sardis*'. The quincunx was a way of planting trees in regular patterns of five, like the 'Cinque-point of a dye'. Browne discerns the pattern of the quincunx in architecture, the cutting of gems, the battle order of the Roman army, and much else.   PT

Brownlow Hill,

New South Wales, Australia, was the Macleay family's country estate near Camden, managed by Alexander Macleay's younger son George after 1827. The house, the property of the Downes family since 1858, sits on a levelled shale knoll with dramatic views of the surrounding countryside and fertile river flats. The approach is via a driveway bordered by clipped box and overhung with large Chinese elms (*Ulmus parvifolia*); a low stone wall, set with urns, near the entrance gates acts as an edge to an elegant lily pond. This scene is charmingly depicted in W. Hardy Wilson's *Old Colonial Architecture in New South Wales and Tasmania* (1924). The drive ends in a broad carriage sweep in front of the house, which is surrounded by thick plantings including many *Araucaria* species. The back garden, as the Downeses describe it, is made up of lawn, pathways, and flower beds cut in geometric patterns and filled with old-fashioned roses and flowering perennials. A fine sundial is inscribed 'George Macleay Esq. 1836' and beyond is an aviary, a curious little building with arched openings. Garden historians have highlighted how Macleay, *c*.1840, incorporated many fashionable landscaping devices of the time; in particular, the remarkable similarity between elements of the garden at Brownlow Hill and J. C. LOUDON's view of Mrs Lawrence's 'Italian walk' and 'French parterre' in *The Suburban Gardener and Villa Companion* (1838). Today Brownlow Hill is regarded as one of Australia's finest examples of the GARDENESQUE style.   CMR

Bruce, Sir William

(*c*.1630–1710), Scottish architect and garden designer born at Blairhall in Perthshire. A royalist, he travelled to the Low Countries where Charles II lived in exile and was involved in plans for his restoration. There is no evidence that he visited France but it seems likely for, especially in his garden designs, there is a strongly French flavour to his work. He was appointed surveyor-general and overseer of the King's buildings in Scotland in 1671, an appointment he held until 1678. In this period he was working on the reconstruction of the palace of Holyroodhouse. At Balcaskie (Fife, *c*.1668–74) and KINROSS (1686–93) he built houses of exceptional interest garnished with dazzling gardens of much originality, both of which survive. Both gardens were conceived as extensions of the house, disposed about the same axis, which was focused on some distant external object (the Bass Rock and Loch Leven Castle respectively). In England his only known surviving works are the gateways at HAM HOUSE built in 1671 and 1675 for the Countess of Dysart (later Duchess of Lauderdale). It is not known whether he had any connection with the formal gardens at Ham House which were being made at this time, but it is possible. Bruce is a very attractive and intriguing figure, perhaps more original as a garden designer than as an architect. But he remains shadowy; very little is known of the details of his life.   PT

HUBERT FENWICK, *Architect Royal* (1970).

Bruckenthal Park. See AVRIG PARK.

Brühl Park ⊗

Wettingen, Canton of Aargau, Switzerland, was designed as a public park in 1984 by Dieter Kienast (1945–98) and marks the transition from naturalistic garden design to modern landscape architecture. In the early 1980s the municipality of Wettingen commissioned the landscape architecture partnership of Stöckli and Kienast to plan and construct a modest urban park. Dieter Kienast took on its design, which was influenced by the 1920s German *Volkspark*, offering as many possible uses and ways in which the community could identify with the park as possible. The centre of the park is marked by a slightly sunken lawn enclosed by striking grassed pyramids, a design motif borrowed by Kienast from the famous 'Poets' Garden' designed by Swiss garden architect Ernst Cramer (1898–1980) in 1959 for the first Swiss garden exhibition, G|59 in Zurich. Like Cramer, Kienast sought an abstract interpretation rather than an imitation of nature. The abstract, artificial turf pyramids offer a crisp formal contrast with the natural foothills of the Jura mountains in the distance. A carefully tended arrangement of trellis-work with roses and precisely trimmed geometrical hedges around a circular pond create pleasant spaces in which to linger. The contrast between freely growing and architectural forms is particularly explicit at the centre of the park: the ensemble of hedges contrasts with the rather mysterious atmosphere of the adjacent little wood with its sculptures by Eduard Spörri. While the southern border of the park is delineated by an avenue of limes, the principal borders and the ends of its axes are marked by large Lombardy poplars. This conversion of the former football fields beside Wettingen town hall into a modern, architecturally conceived urban park signalled the transition from the ecological imperative in 1970s natural garden design to the aesthetic principle in Swiss landscape architecture of the 1980s and 1990s, with Dieter Kienast as its principal protagonist. UW

Brühlpark ⊛

Quedlinburg, Saxony-Anhalt, Germany, which is south of the palace, has been part of the gardens of the former religious establishment in Quedlinburg since the 16th century. A convent for ladies of rank (*Damenstift*) was founded at Quedlinburg in AD 936 by Emperor Otto I. Brühl was a very popular leisure spot and it belonged to the St Wipeti monastery until the Reformation. Under the Abbess Anna Dorothea Herzogin von Sachsen-Weimar, Brühl was designed on artistic garden principles in 1685. It included a square courtyard and an axial cross planted with lime trees which was aligned with the palace and large abbey garden. Abbess Anna Amalie, Princess of Prussia, commissioned the addition of a diagonal boulevard of trees. Towards the end of the 18th century, the Abbess Sophie Albertine, Princess of Sweden, commissioned plantings and paths in the new English landscape style in the east meadow adjacent to Brühl. The Prussian King, Friedrich Wilhelm III, gave Brühl to the town in 1817 following the closure of the religious establishment. It was gradually extended and developed into a 30-hectare/74-acre park. In 1831, a monument was built for the town's famous son, the poet Friedrich Gottlieb Klopstock. Karl Friedrich SCHINKEL designed it and the bronze bust came from Christian Friedrich Tieck (1776–1851). Two famous garden designers in succession were involved in planning the garden. In 1866/7, Eduard PETZOLD provided an expert report and three drafts for the redesign of Brühl. In 1900, the director of gardens for Magdeburg, J. G. SCHOCH, presented a further design. Nevertheless, neither of the plans was fully executed. The park and part of the monastery garden are owned by the town of Quedlinburg, which plans to redevelop them. KFr

URSULA GRÄFIN ZU DOHNA, *Die Gärten Friedrichs des Großen und seiner Geschwister* (2000).

ANTON FIEGE and KATHRIN FRANZ, 'Der Brühlpark in Quedlinburg' and MARGIT REITZAMMER, 'Die Lustgärten in Quedlinburg', in *Fülle des Schönen: Gartenlandschaft Harz* (2002).

Brunfels, Otto

(1489–1534), physician, born near Mainz. After some years as a Carthusian monk, he became a Lutheran convert and ultimately the town physician of Berne, where he died. The first part of his *Herbarum Vivae Eicones* was published in Strasbourg in 1530, followed by a second in 1532, and a third in 1536, a book that marked the beginning of the greatest century in the production of printed herbals. A German translation followed in 1532–7. Although he encouraged his artist Hans Weiditz to draw plants from nature, demanding 'new and really lifelike figures', Brunfels himself was still more interested in those with a good pedigree in classical literature, especially DIOSCORIDES. He seems never to have realized that different regions have different native plants, although some are common to many countries. He even wanted to segregate the plants known only by vernacular names into a mere appendix. The artist seems to have rebelled, for he drew what he liked, regardless of the status of the plant, turning the book into a high point in the development of BOTANICAL ILLUSTRATION. SRa

Brunswick Park ⊛

Dolná Krupá (formerly Alsókorompa), near Trnava, western Slovakia. The country house of the Brunswick family had a baroque garden in the 18th century. There were 30 large coffee trees mentioned in the orangery in 1783. In the 1790s Count József Brunswick had his house redesigned by architect József Tallherr who also drew plans for various structures—a Chinese pavilion and a GLORIETTE, for the new sentimental (rococo) garden. In 1812 Heinrich NEBBIEN became the manager of the estate. He redesigned the whole area (c. 114 hectares/282 acres) as a park. The improvements were most intensive before 1814 but continued until 1825. A map of 1822 shows the final layout, similar in structure to BROWN's landscapes with spacious meadows, clumps of trees, and a serpentine lake. The colourful plantations, shrubberies, however, made it more various, and a grotto (with a dancing area on top), a bathhouse, and statues added to this variety. Special features were 'salons'—enclosures surrounded by trees of different species ('poplar salon', 'linden square', 'cedar room', 'elm square', and so on). Distant parts of the park contained an extended vineyard and arable fields. In the late 19th century, the vegetation was enriched with many exotic species and conifers. Today the estate is much reduced in area and is in need of conservation. GA

GÉZA GALAVICS, *Magyarországi angolkertek* (Landscape Gardens in Hungary) (1999).

JANA ŠULCOVÁ, *Tri kapitoly zo stavebných dejín kaštiel'a v Dolnej Krupej. Ars* (1996).

Brussels Park ⊛

rue royale, Brussels, Belgium, with its statues, ranks of mature trees and broad paths, was the last great formal park to be created in Belgium in the 18th century. This large public square, 13 hectares/32 acres in extent and today somewhat dull, was designed and laid out by Barnabé Guimard (1731–1805) between 1774 and 1787 in the French style. Three straight ALLÉES radiate in a PATTE D'OIE, from a large circular *bassin* (a formal pool) and fountain surrounded by ivy and busts of Roman emperors. The central path was designed with a perspective view beyond the park, which now ends at the royal palace in one direction and the parliament building in the other. The views along the two diagonal *allées* also continue beyond the perimeter, one down to the Place Royale, the other, less clear, between a wing of the royal palace and the Palace of the Academies. There are two cross-*allées* both with perspectives that extend into the streets beyond and a hornbeam-edged walk all round the park. In between these straight paths edged with formal rows of trees are small BOSQUETS. There is a small theatre and Vauxhall, an area of cafés and shops, dating from 1783. BA

Bruun, Andreas

(b. 1936), Danish landscape architect who has designed open spaces around large building schemes as well as private gardens. His book *Danske Haver i Dag* (Modern Danish Gardens) (1971) clearly demonstrates the Danish preoccupation with geometrical forms, and shows Danish private gardens from the 1960s. Among them are several by Bruun, in Bagsværd (1962) and Kgs. Lyngby (1960). They are characterized by articulated forms, knowledge of craftsmanship and nuanced planting design with clipped and carefully selected plant forms. Also more recent private gardens in Lund (1967) and Køge (1987) as well as cemeteries in Greve (1984) and Jyllinge (1987) and the renovations of G. N. BRANDT's Historical Botanical Gardens (1996) in Vordingborg and at the Karen Blixen Museum, in Rungsted, reflect his impeccable craftsmanship. AL

Buçaco, Mata Nacional de ⊛

Luso, Portugal. The great walled forest of Buçaco was the estate of Carmelites from 1630 to 1834. With an area of 110 hectares/271 acres it has a wild character with waymarked paths leading the visitor through woodland of great beauty and interest. At the heart of the wood, built on the site of the convent, is a former hunting lodge of the late 19th century, now a luxury hotel. It is built in the immensely elaborate neo-Manueline style, wriggling with lavish carved stone ornament. It overlooks a sunken parterre of box compartments filled with *Stachys byzantina*. Rose beds rise on the banks above and a pergola runs along a terraced walk. It is swathed with *Wisteria floribunda* which is hard pruned so that it has formed substantial ancient trunks covered in moss. Behind the pergola is a grove of camellias and magnolias and, above a goldfish pool, a beautiful old Morinda spruce (*Picea smithiana*). This is as formal as the garden gets—ramparts of trees press in all about and moss-covered walks lead up vertiginous walks. The Via Sacra is a long winding walk with small stone houses decorated with strips of rocaille work each housing a sculpture of the Stations of the Cross visible, faintly illuminated by a skylight, through a grille in the door. The planting is almost entirely naturalistic of a wild kind but occasionally producing effects of great artistry. A long, damp curving walk of giant tree ferns (*Dicksonia antarctica*), for example, is lavishly edged with arum lilies (*Zantedeschia aethiopica*) glowing in the shade. Close to the main drive a grand formal cascade emerges from the woods. The water falls over rustic rockwork and flights of steps lead up either side. At its lowest point it is shaded by a beautiful and rarely seen American ash *Fraxinus pennsylvanica*. Good trees are found throughout the woods. The garden is famous for its old stands of Buçaco cedar (*Cupressus lusitanica*), and many other species of conifer flourish in the mild, moist climate. Here are good specimens of Moreton Bay pine (*Araucaria bidwillii*), Mexican pine (*Pinus patula*), Indian pine (*Pinus roxburghii*), and many others. There are around 700 species of woody plants cultivated, by no means a large collection in a climate that would allow an immense range. The beauty of the place is that the trees are often fine specimens and they are encountered in the context of a wild and lovely woodland setting. PT

Bucharest city parks ⊛

Romania. The spacious Romanian capital is rich in public parks, leafy avenues, and scattered lakes. The first public park, *Cișmigiu*, was laid out by the German landscape gardener Carl F. W. Meyer, who was called to Bucharest to create a People's Park in the 1830s. He drained marshland, created lakes with islands, meadows with clumps of trees, and laid out drives and paths. Meyer planted more than 30,000 trees and shrubs, and placed pavilions to enjoy the main viewpoints of the city and the park. Later alterations have included the eclectic work of the German architect F. von Rebhuhn in 1910. Today long rows of clipped lime trees, yew hedges, rose gardens, and box-edged beds filled with seasonal bedding provide a basic structure. Some recently landscaped areas such as a

circular lawn decorated with busts of Romanian writers enhance the stylistic diversity of the 16-hectare/40-acre park. *Kiseleff Garden* (14 hectares/35 acres), also designed by Meyer, with its triple lime avenue, was the most elegant promenade of the capital in the 19th century. *Cotroceni Park* (17 hectares/42 acres), was laid out in the 19th century around a monastery, later the residence of King Ferdinand I and his English wife Queen Mary. In 1874 part of the park was given to the relocated *Botanic Garden of Bucharest University*, and its new layout was completed in 1891 by the Belgian L. Fuchs. That part of the park which still belonged to the royal residence was redesigned by F. von Rebhuhn towards the end of the 19th century and later on by the French Julius Janine with flower-filled terraces, pergolas, and balustrades. During the 1920s, the greatest public park of Bucharest, *Herăstrău* (198 hectares/495 acres)—then called Parcul Carol after King Charles—was constructed after the plans of French designer Pinnard for an international exhibition. The enormous park still retains the form of a natural landscape of water and islands planted with willows and poplars. It houses an open-air village museum and an annual flower show. *Park of Liberty* (Parcul Libertatii), a great park (49 hectares/123 acres) in the southern part of the city, was created by the important French designer E. Redont in the early 20th century. GA

Buda Royal Castle Gardens ⊛

Budapest, Hungary. No documents remain from medieval times concerning the area of the Hungarian capital's royal palace, though we can presume that as early as the 14th century the side of the hill or the space between the fortified walls may have been home to some kind of garden. The first surviving written records, from the age of King Matthias (reigned 1456–90), already describe a Renaissance garden, with a labyrinth, an aviary, gymnasium, and various other constructions. During the Turkish occupation (1541-1686), and finally during the siege of Buda, the gardens were completely destroyed. The new palace constructed in place of the ruins was surrounded by small baroque gardens between the castle walls. In 1765-6 architect Franz Anton Hillebrandt and Adrian van Steckhoven, head gardener at SCHÖNBRUNN, designed parts of the gardens. Between 1790 and 1800 a larger-scale landscape garden was created outside the castle walls, on the south-east side of the hill, with a hermitage and mock ruins, using remains of the medieval castle, one of which was the Gothicized Dutch Peasant House. In the first half of the 19th century, thanks to Palatine Joseph's love of gardens and the work of head gardener Antal Tost, the

Castle Gardens finally became worthy of the royal residence. The plant inventory recorded in 1826 lists 2,440 species and varieties. In the course of the siege of the palace in 1849 the garden was damaged, but it was renovated in the 1850s. During Franz Joseph's reign, from the 1870s until the turn of the 20th century, the garden was continually improved with new work for Queen Elisabeth (the Castle Gardens bazaar on the bank of the Danube, a new 'Hungarian' peasant house, a winter garden, a grand flight of steps), statues, fountains, a grotto with a rockery, and neo-baroque parterres near the palace. The reconstruction was largely the work of Hungarian architects and landscape gardeners—Miklós Ybl, Alajos Hauszmann, Keresztély ILSEMANN, Ármin PECZ JR., and Nándor Witzel—but Anton UMLAUFT, director of the Imperial Gardens of Schönbrunn, also completed designs for it. Around 1900, alongside the work on the landscape garden, emphasis was also placed on the cultivation of ornamental plants: in the first half of the 20th century the garden, with 30 new glasshouses, became famous for its improved orchid hybrids. The parks and flower gardens, evolving ever since the 18th century, were—like the palace itself—completely destroyed by Second World War bombing. On the site of the former royal gardens there now stands a modern public park, built in the 1960s. GA

Buen Retiro ⊛

Madrid, Spain. From 1629, in the reign of Philip IV, an immense and elaborate new royal palace was built on what was then the edge of Madrid. A bird's-eye view painting of the estate by Jusepe Leonardo (d. 1652) shows that the palace was set in vast gardens. These were laid out by an Italian, Cosimo Lotti, who had worked on the BOBOLI Gardens. Behind the palace was a star-shaped pattern of eight ALLÉES, known as the Octagon, sweeping through woods. The *allées* were enclosed in trellis-work which was intertwined with quinces, roses, and mulberries. Scattered in the grounds were several hermitages which were by no means of exlusively religious significance—some had their own ornamental gardens and were used for grand picnics. A very large pool was overlooked by pavilions and traversed by ornamental boats (including Venetian gondolas) which also sailed up the canals that led into it. In its day Buen Retiro was as busy with royal amusements as VERSAILLES would become later in the century. In the early 18th century there were proposals to refashion the garden in the French style and Robert de Cotte, who thought the existing gardens were 'monotonous and lacking in perspective', made plans which were never executed. In the late 18th century, under Charles III, a royal cemetery, a school of gardening, and a royal china factory were opened in the grounds. In the Peninsular War the estate suffered grievously and the royal china factory was blown up by Wellington. Today a small part only of the palace survives and is an army museum. The gardens have become a public park with a fine parterre, a large and elegant 19th-century glasshouse, many fountain pools, a rose garden, and much fine tree planting. An equestrian statue of Alfonso XII (reigned 1874–85) and colonnade overlooks the great pool. Many paths are still edged with irrigation rills of Islamic character and the octagonal pool of Philip IV's time survives.   PT

Bühler, Denis (1811–90) and Eugène

(1822–1907), French garden designers who often worked together, noted chiefly for the design of public parks. Parc de la TÊTE D'OR in Lyon designed before 1857 is the Bühlers' masterpiece—III hectares/274 acres with a 16-hectare/40-acre lake and fine groups of trees and shrubs, the whole laced with winding walks. In Béziers (Hérault) Le Plateau des Poètes (1863–7) is a miniature Parisian park (4 hectares/10 acres) with a lake and swooping carriage drives in the style of BARILLET-DESCHAMPS. The Bühlers sometimes laid out historicizing parterres in the context of a parklike setting as at the 1865 design for Parc du THABOR. Occasionally they restored period schemes as at Azay-le-Ferron (Indre) where they refashioned a 17th-century garden in 1870. At Kerguéhennec (Morbihan) in 1872 they laid out a park rich in exotic trees which today serves as a modern sculpture park.   PT

Buitenhof,

The Hague, Zuid-Holland, the Netherlands, is an example of one of the gardens designed on pure geometric principles which appeared in Renaissance Europe at the end of the 16th and early 17th centuries. Imbued with iconography inspired by cosmology, astronomy, and astrology, they were mainly compositions of squares and circles. Established by Prince Maurits, the garden at Buitenhof was completed by his brother Frederik Hendrik in 1625 and consisted of two circular bowers within two adjoining squares, connected by a pavilion. The arrangement was contrived within a walled space and there were arbours in the corner positions. Designed by Jacques de Gheyn II (1565–1629), the separate bowers and arbours were planted with beech, while there was a box-lined parterre and a basin in the centre of each circle, surrounded with eight

bronze vases. This garden was demolished in the early 18th century, while during the 20th century the site served mainly as a car park, which has recently been replaced with buildings of the Dutch parliament.   JW

VANESSA BEZEMER SELLERS, *Courtly Gardens in Holland 1600–1650: The House of Orange and the Hortus Batavus* (2001).

bulbous plants

have in common the ability to store food and water so that they may survive periods in which neither may be available. A bulb proper is a form of the base of a plant's leaves which have become swollen to provide means of storing water and food. If you cut across a bulb, a tulip for example, you will see the concentric layers of leaf of which it is composed. Alliums, fritillaries, some lilies, narcissus, and tulips are bulbs. Corms are underground fleshy stems which provide sustenance for one season's growth only, a new corm being formed above its parent. Crocosmias, colchicums, crocus, and gladiolus are examples of corms. Rhizomes are swollen stems growing horizontally underground or half submerged, such as some bamboos, several species of iris, and some lilies. Tubers are swollen roots or stems either totally submerged or growing close to the surface of the grounds. The potato is one of the best-known tubers but many ornamentals are also, including some anemones, dahlias, some corydalis, and cyclamen. Some genera, generally pure herbaceous perennials, also have tuberous species, such as *Geranium tuberosum* and *Thalictrum tuberosum*.

Bulbous plants vary in their mode of reproducing, sometimes showing more than one means of doing so. The pretty but alarmingly invasive *Allium roseum*, for example, forms undergound bulbils and also aerial ones, formed at the base of flowers, which fall when fully ripe and rapidly colonize the surrounding ground. *Allium pyrenaicum*, on the other hand, forms a clump, which may be divided in the same way as any herbaceous perennial. Tulips are propagated by seed or by offsets from a mature bulb, but garden cultivars are usually sterile, and the only means of propagation is by gathering offsets. The same is true of fritillaries, of which there are few cultivars such as the varieties of *Fritillaria imperialis*, but most of which are species. Many tubers, like cyclamen, seed themselves but others, like potatoes, form new tubers underground.

Bulbous plants are one of the essential groups of garden plants and have been used in gardens of many kinds for as long as gardens have been made. The madonna lily (*Lilium candidum*) is depicted in Egyptian pottery dating from 1750 BC. They may be used in many

different styles of garden. In gardens of the Italian Renaissance a large repertory of bulbous plants was grown—asphodel (*Asphodelus ramosus*), cyclamen, lily of the valley (*Convallaria majalis*), narcissus (especially the jonquil, *N. jonquilla*). Sixteenth-century Turkish gardens consumed bulbs in vast quantities. Sultan Selim II (who reigned from 1566 to 1574) ordered tulips in quantities as great as 50,000 to plant in the royal gardens. In 17th-century Dutch gardens single specimens of *Fritillaria imperialis* or of tulips were displayed in narrow mounded *plate-bandes* (see BORDER). English gardens of this period and the early 18th century (such as the Privy Garden at HAMPTON COURT) used bulbs in the same way. In the late 17th century in France they were used lavishly as part of the movable decor of parterres at the Grand Trianon (see VERSAILLES, CHÂTEAU DE) and at MARLY. Prophets of wild gardening, such as William ROBINSON, found them to be ideal plants, naturalizing easily and suitable for many different sites. In *The Wild Garden* (1870) he recommended all sorts of naturalistic schemes—pools of winter aconite or spring snowflower (*Leucojum vernum*) under deciduous trees and intermingled small and larger plants such as *Narcissus jonquila* rising out of a sea of *Anemone apeninna*.

In modern home gardens bulbous plants remain popular. No garden is too small to allow room for groups of cyclamen, snowdrops, or tulips. In the smallest of town courtyards many bulbous plants may be cultivated in containers or window boxes. In larger gardens they are a valuable ingredient of naturalistic meadow gardens in which anemones, erythroniums, fritillaries, lilies, and narcissi are often seen at their best. In northern hemisphere gardens bulbous plants are too easily thought of as essentially an ornament of the spring. In fact, there is no month of the year in which one species or another does not flower. Summer months are rich in all sorts of decorative species, many of them native to South Africa, the greatest source in the world of bulbous plants. This is the season of statuesque crinums, eremurus, eucomis, kniphofias, lilies, tulbaghias, watsonias, and much else. In woodland gardens of acid soil the superb Himalayan *Cardiocrinum giganteum*, soaring to a height of over 3 m/10 ft and flaunting sweetly scented trumpet flowers, is one of the most spectacular of garden plants. Later in the season come the pink or white flowers of *Cyclamen hederifolium*, colchicums, autumn crocuses, and the delicate white flowers of the tender *Zephyranthes candida*. In the winter aconites (*Eranthis hyemalis*), *Cyclamen coum*, and snowdrops are plants of which no gardener ever tires.

The flowers of many bulbous plants are so dazzlingly attractive that their other qualities are easy to overlook. Their foliage is often wonderfully ornamental. The glistening marbled leaves of *Arum italicum* subsp. *italicum* 'Marmoratum' bring life to a damp and shady corner. The foliage of *Cyclamen hederifolium*, ivy shaped and subtly patterned, is at least as ornamental as the flowers. The filigree, and often glaucous, foliage of many corydalis species is beautiful—the intricately dissected fronds of *C. cheilanthifolia* the most decorative of all. Many bulbous plants have striking structural character. The emphatic punctuation marks of the taller alliums such as *A. rosenbachianum*, rising 90 cm/36 in high, give crisp structure to a busy border. Several of the asphodels have emphatic shapely presence of which *A. aestivus*, with its 1.2-m/4-ft high candelabra of white flowers, is an outstanding example. Bulbous plants provide some of the best of garden scents. The white recurved trumpets of *Lilum speciosum* fill the air with the scent of the tropics, as does *L. regale*. Not all gardeners enjoy the foxy whiff of *Fritillaria imperialis* but others think of it as the quintessential smell of spring. Some scents are puzzling without being agreeable. E. A. Bowles could never make up his mind whether the smell of the foliage of *Nectaroscordum siculum* resembled a gas leak or a new mackintosh. There can be no disagreement, though, about the pure, sweet scent of lily of the valley (*Convallaria majalis*).   PT

Bulgaria

Climate
Centrally located in the Balkan Peninsula, Bulgaria has a temperate transitional-continental climate with four distinctive seasons. The southernmost parts enjoy warm Mediterranean influence, while the Black Sea softens the coastline climate in the east. Typically, winters are cold (down to -15 °C/5 °F) with a durable snow cover and summers are hot (up to 35 °C/95 °F) with occasional rain. Wet cool springs and autumns ensure proper vegetative periods. Abundant mountain ranges (up to 2,900 m/9,500 ft) seriously modify local weather patterns as in higher altitudes temperatures drop and precipitation increases. The Balkan Mountains span the length of the country and divide it laterally into northern and southern, while the Rila, Pirin, and Rodopi Mountains form a considerable south-western massif.

Flora
Determined by diverse climatic, relief, and soil conditions the country's vascular flora displays significant richness with more than 3,800 species of 886 genera and 153 families. The specific geographical position has allowed the distribution of Central European, Mediterranean, Orientaloturanic, Pontic, Steppe, and Pannonian floristic elements. The families richest in species are Asteraceae (464 spp.), Fabaceae (287 spp.), and Poaceae (316 spp.), followed by Rosaceae, Caryophyllaceae, and Brassicaceae. A total of 8% of the flora are endemic to Bulgaria—170 species and 100 subspecies.

Antiquity and the Middle Ages
A clear need for and appreciation of garden aesthetics can be traced in all the various cultures which left their footprint on the land that is Bulgaria today. A multitude of remains show skilful incorporation of gardens into the space and functions of ancient settlements. The Thracian town of Seuthopolis (4th century BC) had dwellings organized around colonnaded inner courts with primitive drainage systems and rich vegetation. The Greek polises along the Black Sea coast have defined ritual and residential gardens. An excavated villa in Razgrad from the Roman period, probably owned by a wealthy landlord, exhibits a large rectangular atrium (25 × 25 m/80 × 80 ft), paved in marble slabs. After the Bulgarian state was established in 681 the feudal social order created early examples of ornamental gardens within great city walls. In the capital Preslav during the First Kingdom's golden age, palaces and churches stood amidst tastefully arranged gardens. The reign of Tsar Simeon I in the early 10th century saw significant progress in all arts, including landscaping with achievements equalling those of Byzantium and Persia. During the Second Bulgarian Kingdom (12th–14th centuries), the new capital Veliko Tarnovo, situated on two majestic hills—Tzarevets and Trapezitsa—boasted elaborated gardens on several terraces. The steep topography was skilfully subdued to the designs of architects, harmoniously uniting nature with the built environment. This was also the case of many monasteries of the time, strategically located in hidden, protected sites, where the inner courtyards with paved walks, fountains, and trees visually flowed outwards to the wild forests of Silva Bulgariae. The Turkish occupation, which began in 1396, did not make any contribution to garden art but in fact significantly retarded most aspects of Bulgaria's cultural development for centuries.

Bulgarian national revival (18th–19th centuries)
After nearly 300 years of oppression and economic decay, a new social stratum was formed in the second half of the 18th century as a result of craftsmanship and trade. Still under the Ottoman Empire, several progressive Bulgarian towns, particularly those in the Balkan Mountain foothills, gained economic and cultural momentum, which was also reflected in the functional and aesthetic organization of public and private spaces. Traditionally protected behind high stone walls, individual building plots began to relate spatially with their surroundings. This pertained mostly to the front gardens and courtyards of schools and churches, which opened onto the street and became clearly representative. Most characteristic of the period, however, is the family house courtyard phenomenon, developed particularly in the towns of Koprivshtitza, Karlovo, Trjavna, Kotel, and Gabrovo. These relatively small (0.1–0.2 hectares/0.3–0.5 acres) enclosed gardens of irregular shapes and asymmetrical composition synthesized the whole private and working life of the residents. They were essentially the only place of private freedom, which explains the huge diversity of creative layouts and exceptional maintenance. The unity of space is embodied in the gentle transition from the house through the *chardak* (veranda) to the courtyard, also reiterated by the vine-embraced pergola, extending from the porch. Originally, these courtyards consisted of a single multifunctional space with the house at the far end from the street. A cobble-paved area for rest and receiving guests was usually coupled with a tidy, colourful flower garden, flanked by rows of box shrubs and flowers in pots. Low wooden fences and paved walks gave structure to the plot and separated the orchard and vegetable garden. A stone drinking fountain and a well implied water presence and emphasized the relationship between style and utility. A remarkable sense of proportion, in relation to the human scale, was achieved in all elements. Their organization also mirrored the cultural symbolism—a single large tree (chestnut, walnut, or pear) would dominate the skyline, giving protection to the courtyard. Later on, around 1850, the increasing importance of social standing led to the establishment of two distinctive court spaces: the front garden, for more public activities, and the back garden for domestic activities. Significant regional differences based on the local topography can be observed. The low-lying towns of Karlovo and Koprivshtitza feature larger, elongated, rectangular courtyards, usually on one or two levels. In contrast, the mountainous settlements (Kotel, Zheravna) have smaller, compact, and terraced gardens. The courtyards of monasteries further represent the strong link between natural surroundings and garden layout. Creating a whole miniature universe

using local materials, these courtyards also incorporate the characteristics of place such as rocks, woods, and rivers. Rila, Bachkovo, Trojan, and Rojen monasteries feature typical cobble walks, solitary holy plants (vine, fig, or cypress trees), colourful herbal plots, and stone drinking fountains.

Bulgarian independence (post-1878)

The nation's liberation from the Ottoman Empire after the 1877–8 Russian-Turkish War gave a new impetus for garden architecture. At that time, public green spaces were absent in most Bulgarian cities and it was the new capital, Sofia, which first established its City Garden (1878) in front of the former Turkish town hall. The beginning of structured urban planning saw many cities designating public parks. Their huge popularity for socializing and recreation stimulated increasingly sophisticated layouts, for which foreign landscape architects were invited from around Europe such as Daniel Neff (1843-1900), Josef Fray (1873-1953), and Anton Kraus (1870-1958). They introduced the types of design then fashionable across 19th-century Western Europe including eclecticism of baroque geometry and English landscape style. This was coupled with the introduction of many new ornamental exotics, which hugely enriched the appearance of parks. The first public gardens were centrally located, often adjacent to city squares and town halls, and were regarded with pride—the city gardens of Plovdiv (Knjaz Dondukov's and Prince's gardens, 1880), Sevlievo (1887), Veliko Tarnovo (1891), Pleven (1904), and Rousse (1906). Then, larger peripheral parks were created, blending in the surrounding topography and allowing more scope for original design—KING BORIS'S GARDEN (1882), AYAZMO PARK (1895), the MARITIME PARKS of Varna (1894) and Bourgas (1910), and the DANUBIAN GARDENS of Vidin (1902) and Rousse (1920). The first botanical gardens and zoos also appeared around the 1890s.

Another major feature of the period was the creation of several royal palace gardens throughout the country to serve the new monarchs' needs. They combined fine design and elaborate planting of large areas, again the work of foreign landscape architects. EVKSINOGRAD PALACE (1881) on the Black Sea coast developed as a characteristic example of a summer residence with a fine layout and an admirable plant collection. Vrana Palace (1890), just outside Sofia, had the character of a nature park with flowing landscapes and long vistas. King Ferdinand's (1887-1917) obsession with plants made both parks into outstanding botanical collections. Likewise, Krichim Estate (1906), close to Plovdiv, initially intended as a royal game park, was handsomely decorated

with various tree and shrub species. Later on, BALCHIK PALACE (1924) appeared as an intimate ornamental garden estate, most famous for its cacti collection.

Socialist era (post-1945)

During the post-war decades, the rapid urbanization and overstated social values brought about a new wave of public city gardens and parks, often of larger scale, modern aesthetics, and utilitarian character. Many existing parks were also extended to accommodate additional public amenities and increased visitor numbers. All projects were based on centralized long-term planning and design methodologies with defined requirements. Common elements include open-air theatres, sports and children's playgrounds, and reading corners, appropriately isolated by vegetation. Parks were also classified according to their predominant features into hydro, forestry, memorial, sports, or exhibition ones. The recognizable influence of Russian ideas can be seen in many of these parks—especially in the monumental axes and grand sculptural symbolism. Sofia alone acquired several large prominent parks, among which are South Park and West Park, providing diverse functions and amenities—quiet and busy zones, representative and informal areas, and a variety of open and enclosed spaces. A 1980s inner city redevelopment resulted in a splendid central garden in front of the National Palace of Culture, with well-planned amenities and boasting a wide marble-paved main promenade with an imposing system of cascading fountains. Several government complexes sprang up around the capital in the 1970s—Bojana and Bankja are typical of these. They both demonstrate skilful treatment of space, with formal and informal components, and high ornamental achievements.

An important arena for landscape architecture in the last 40 years has been the seaside resorts, where whole complexes have been landscaped along the Black Sea coast. The resorts of Albena, Golden Sands, and Sunny Beach deserve special mention with their skilful layout, dynamic structure, and diverse planting. Similarly, spa resort towns, such as SANDANSKI and Hisarja, developed good recreation parks. Memorial parks, often joined with forestry parks, also had growing popularity because of their out-of-city location and combined a formal rectilinear style with natural woody paths—such as those in Plovdiv, Pleven, and Lovech.

Private gardens were virtually non-existent during this period since the ruling political system almost completely abolished private property.

The period as a whole is marked by the work of exclusively Bulgarian landscape architects, among whom particular contributions have been made by Professor Rashko Robev, Professor Delcho Sugarev, Professor Krastan Karakashev, and Professor Jordan Kuleliev. Since 1951, the University of Forestry in Sofia has run the only landscape architecture course in the country, teaching up to master's degree level.   ASG

Buonaccorsi, Giardino ✿

Potenza Picena, Marche, Italy. A perfectly preserved garden, standing on the crest of a hill overlooking the Adriatic Sea, the Giardino Buonaccorsi, dating to the 17th and 18th centuries, is laid out in a series of terraces. Although still owned by the original Buonaccorsi family there is no record of the architect. A painting in the house dating to the middle of the 18th century shows the layout of stars and diamond-shaped parterres almost exactly as they have survived into the 20th century. In Georgina Masson's *Italian Gardens* (1961) she suggests that Andrea Vici may have had a hand in the design. Surrounded by sheltering woodland, five terraces provide space for the GIARDINO SEGRETO, BERCEAUX, grottoes, aviaries, potted citrus plants, and espaliered lemon trees on the wall. The original stone edging still marks out the flower bed patterns. The third terrace was originally planned as a sheltered walk. Below, an orangery, walled orchard, and vegetable gardens complete the picture. This is a remarkable survival of an isolated garden.   PHo

Burke, Edmund

(1729-97), Irish philosopher, statesman, and author best known for his many writings on political matters of his time. To garden historians he is of interest for his book *A Philosophical Enquiry into the Origin of our Ideas of the Sublime and Beautiful* (published anonymously in 1756). His ideas of the sublime were seized upon by garden theorists such as Richard Payne KNIGHT and Uvedale PRICE, who saw them as justification for a wild and picturesque landscape. Burke wrote, 'Whatever is fitted in any sort to excite the ideas of pain, and danger, that is to say, whatever is in any sort terrible . . . is a source of the sublime; that is, it is productive of the strongest emotion of which the mind is capable of feeling.' Although of absorbing interest to garden theorists it is unlikely that these ideas had any profound influence on the character of gardens.   PT

Burle Marx, Roberto

(1909-94), Brazilian artist, plantsman, and   ▶

garden designer who introduced the art of the landscape garden to Brazil and established the idea of the contemporary garden. He undertook over 2,000 projects in differing regions of the world, the majority of these being in Brazil. Parks such as the FLAMENGO, Largo de Carioca, or Petrobras had an impact upon the development of Rio de Janeiro. Self-taught, he went to Berlin in 1928, and was involved in European avant-garde movements of the time. On his return he studied fine art in Rio de Janeiro, at a time when architecture was inspired by rationalism and Brazil's artists and intellectuals aligned themselves with the modernist movement.

The most widely recognized element of his style is the application of graphic form in the design of his gardens; however, his originality came both from a unique working method, and from the creation of a style that complemented his surroundings. The flora of Brazil, some 50,000 species, was at that time little known and undervalued. Assisted by teams of architects, geographers, and botanists, Burle Marx set out to make an inventory of the plants of the virgin rainforest. He collected all manner of seeds and plants, which he then cultivated in

Colour plates

The Rousseau Island at **Wörlitz**, Germany, inspired by the island tomb of Rousseau at Ermenonville

Harold Peto's water garden at Buscot Park, England

Parterre de broderie at the Palais de la Berbie, France.

20th-century naturalistic planting of herbaceous perennials at **Westpark**, Germany

his 80-hectare/198-acre estate, sítio ROBERTO BURLE MARX. He discovered over twenty new species, and collected over 3,000 species from the families Araceae, Amaranthaceae, Bromeliaceae, Musaceae, Orchidaceae, and Velloziaceae. These were chosen for use in his work, not only because they were the best adapted to local conditions, but also in order to demonstrate fully the expressive qualities of tropical vegetation. He was greatly admired by his clients, and also, by creating a demand for these in the market, ensured that growers cultivated native plants.

His inspiration when designing gardens came from the landscape around him, its light and its shapes; he also incorporated elements of local craftsmanship, and stimulated an interest in the older pre-Columbian, African, and colonial styles. He thus created a new idiom and a new palette in horticulture. His journeys around the world were tremendously influential. Thus, alongside native species, he grew exotic plants from similar ecosystems. He was of the belief that a well-ordered garden, with its own individual essence, was the best way of reconciling the opposites of architecture and nature. His style inspired disciples, both in America and in Europe. He gained renown with the Paseo de Copacabana (Rio de Janeiro, Brazil) and the spectacular green spaces of Brasilia, alongside the town planning of Lucio Costa and Oscar Niemeyer, which was awarded a gold medal by the French Architectural Academy.

A tireless worker, he integrated elements of song, art, and sculpture into his gardens. To his landscape gardening he applied the basic essentials of artistic composition—contrast, analogy, and rhythm. His flower beds took on organic forms, with dense masses of herbaceous perennials of the same species, emphasizing colours and repeating textures. He recognized that garden design differed from all other art forms in the transitory and ephemeral nature of plants. From the detail of his floral layouts, to the giant parks such as that at Mangabeiras (235 hectares/580 acres, in Belo Horizonte, Brazil), every one of his creations shows a desire for synthesis, to display the plants to their full potential and to make the ensemble as accessible as possible. He also warned continuously of the dangers of growing deforestation, lobbying for the creation of educational plant reserves in the various phytogeographic regions of Brazil. In his lifetime he donated his assets to the state. Today the Burle Marx Foundation continues his work of conservation and education.   MM

Burlington, Richard Boyle, 3rd Earl of (1694–1753), English connoisseur and

gentleman architect who played a vital role in the Palladian revival in the early 18th century, befriending and inspiring artists, garden designers, and writers. He designed his own rural villa in the exquisite form of CHISWICK HOUSE (1727–9) loosely inspired by PALLADIO's Villa Rotonda. His travels to Italy in 1715 and 1719 enabled him to study Palladio's buildings at first hand and he made a collection of drawings by Palladio. He created a remarkable garden at Chiswick House, with some involvement by William KENT. At his East Yorkshire estate of Londesborough Park Burlington laid out a new garden between 1728 and 1732 with the help of Thomas Knowlton (1692–1781). This was an essentially formal garden but with traces of informality, in winding walks through woodland. Avenues of oaks and walnuts survive from this time.

PT

Busch, John

(1730–95), German nurseryman (originally Johann Busch) from Hanover who came to England in the 1740s. By 1756 he was living in Hackney (London) where he rented land to start a small nursery. He supplied plants to the Princess Augusta's garden (which became the ROYAL BOTANIC GARDEN, KEW), corresponded with John BARTRAM and had seeds from Peter COLLINSON. In 1771 he went to Russia where he was appointed imperial head gardener to Catherine the Great, for whom he worked on the gardens at Kolomenskoe (near Moscow), Pulkovo (near St Petersburg), and TSARSKOE SELO. He possibly collaborated with Charles CAMERON, who married his daughter Catherine, on landscape designs. John Busch's son Joseph Busch (1760–1838) took over as imperial gardener on his father's return to England in 1789. John Busch's nursery in Hackney was the foundation of the great nursery started by Conrad LODDIGES.   PT

DAVID SOLMAN, *Loddiges of Hackney* (1995).

Buscot Park ✻

Faringdon, Oxfordshire, England, is a late Georgian house built for Edward Loveden Townsend. The site is much older, going back at least to the 16th century. A park was made in the 18th century, with a lake. The 8-hectare/20-acre garden, however, apart from some 19th-century terracing, is entirely of the 20th century. Between 1904 and 1913 Harold PETO was employed by the 1st Lord Faringdon to make a new garden and to improve the approaches to the house. East of the house Peto cut a great axis through the woods leading to the west side of a lake. The central part of this axis is composed of a virtuoso Italianate water garden with a narrow rill descending a gentle slope which occasionally widens into pools and narrows, tumbles down cascades, and is crossed by ornamental bridges. Grass paths on either side are punctuated by Irish yews and backed with box hedges. On the far bank of the lake a classical temple aligned with the water garden draws the eye. The woodland to the south is crossed by 20th-century rides and avenues. The 18th-century walled kitchen garden was turned to ornamental purposes in the late 20th century with walks of pleached hop hornbeam (*Ostrya carpinifolia*) and Judas trees (*Cercis siliquastrum*) designed by Tim Rees (*fl.* late 20th century). In the former melon ground Peter Coats (1910–90) designed double mixed borders of a yellow and blue colour scheme. The estate was given to the NATIONAL TRUST in 1948.   PT

Butterstream Garden ⊛

Trim, County Meath, Republic of Ireland, is the creation of Jim Reynolds, who has been a great influence in a renaissance of interest in gardening in Ireland in the late 20th century. The garden, then of 1.75 hectares/4 acres, was started in the 1970s, originally inspired by the 'irrational desire to possess a few roses'. The garden soon outstripped this modest ambition and now presents a sequence of skilfully contrived compartments of varied character and lively planting. The site, of 3 hectares/8 acres today, is flat and its only natural attraction is an old stream which forms a boundary to the chief part of the garden. The stream is crossed by a charmingly sketchy Gothic bridge, with pointed arches, finials, and gentle castellation. The banks of the stream are planted with ash and sycamore and among them astilbes, ferns, hostas, Himalayan meconopsis, and primulas. A formal pool garden is hidden in woodland, with a pillared pavilion overlooking a rectangular water lily pool surrounded by spirals of clipped box and giant lollipops of clipped sweet bay in containers. The most recent addition to the garden is a pair of classical pavilions with Palladian windows which overlook a pair of parallel canals ornamented with urns and obelisks and avenues of limes. A miniature woodland garden lies about the spreading branches of a katsura tree (*Cercidiphyllum japonicum*) underplanted with ferns, hellebores, orchids, and other choice ornamentals relishing the cool shade. Nearby, giant herbaceous borders display contrasting exuberance.   PT

Buttes-Chaumont, Parc des.

See PARIS PARKS AND GARDENS.

Byōdōin ⊛

Kyoto prefecture, Japan, the Retreat of Non-Discrimination, is an independent temple of the Tendai sect of Buddhism located just south of Kyoto city in Uji city. The Phoenix Hall, Hōōdō (Amida Buddha hall), and pond garden remain in their general disposition from the mid-Heian period (794–1185) and comprise one of the few extant examples of what is known as a Pure Land garden (see JAPAN).

The property was the site of aristocratic country villas from at least the mid-9th century but was developed as a temple by Fujiwara no Yorimichi (992–1074) in 1052. The year is significant because, according to Japanese Buddhist calendars, it was the first year of *mappō*, the Age of the End of Law, believed to be a time of ruination for Buddhist practice and upheaval on earth. The end-of-epoch mentality that prevailed at that time was the impetus for the construction of many Pure Land temples where prayers for salvation could be made to Amida Buddha.

In the original form, the temple was approached from the east and would have been first seen to the west as one crossed the Uji river. Having crossed the river, and arrived at a small viewing hall on the east side of the pond, one could have seen, dimly, the face of the enshrined Amida statue across the garden's lotus pond, within the dark temple hall (symbolizing Amida's Pure Land, which was said to lie in a western place). A dyke now divides the river from the pond garden, changing this approach.

The garden, which covers about 2 hectares/5 acres, is presently undergoing a thorough restoration, and a modern museum hall has been built nearby to describe the history of the temple. Byōdōin is listed by UNESCO as a World Heritage Site.   MPK

cabinet.

The French term *cabinet* is defined by Michel Conan in his *Dictionnaire historique de l'art des jardins* as an 'Endroit couvert de verdure qui permet de trouver un peu d'intimité dans un jardin' (place covered in greenery where a little intimacy may be found in a garden). It was often found in French gardens of the 17th and 18th centuries. It was sometimes an additional hedged enclosure within a BOSQUET, containing a decorative surprise—a statue, pool, or parterre. The phrase *cabinet de verdure*, meaning green room, is also found. A.-J. DEZALLIER D'ARGENVILLE's *La Théorie et pratique du jardinage* (1709) explains that a *cabinet* may also form an enclosure within, or at the end of, a tunnel BERCEAU. *Salle de verdure* or *salon de verdure* are terms similar to *cabinet*   PT

Cabot, Francis H.

(b. 1925), American gardener, plantsman (especially alpines), and author. Frank Cabot has made two remarkable North American gardens—at Les QUATRE VENTS in the province of Québec and STONECROP in New York State. He founded the GARDEN CONSERVANCY which is devoted to the preservation of exceptional private gardens in North America and has served as chairman of the NEW YORK BOTANICAL GARDEN. His own account of the garden at Les Quatre Vents, published as *The Greater Perfection* (2001), is one of the best books ever written about the making of a garden by its creator. As a benign and knowledgeable *éminence grise* in North American horticulture Frank Cabot has done much to promote high standards in the art and craft of gardening. He is the recipient of many awards.   PT

Caerhays Castle ⊕

near Gorran, Cornwall, England, is a Gothic castellated building, built for J. B. Trevanion *c.*1808 to the designs of John NASH. It occupies a magnificent position, at the head of a broad combe which runs down to the sea. The estate was bought in 1854 by Michael Williams, a Cornish mine owner whose descendants still own it. The Williams family became one of the outstanding Cornish plant collecting dynasties, creating a woodland garden of exceptional flowering shrubs. J. C. Williams had the greatest impact on the garden, from the late 19th century. He recognized that the protected site, warmed by the Gulf Stream Drift, with high rainfall and acid soil, was perfect for the Asiatic exotics he wanted to collect. Sponsoring the plant collecting expeditions of men like E. H. WILSON he built up one of the best collections of camellias, magnolias, and rhododendrons in a 40-hectare/100-acre site of unusual beauty.
                                                        PT

Calcutta Botanic Garden ⊕

Calcutta, India. Known since 1950 as the Indian Botanic Garden, throughout the 19th, and for much of the 20th century, this was one of the great botanic gardens of the world. Sadly, the garden is now in a state of seemingly terminal decline, held to ransom by militant trade unions; its layout, largely dating from Sir George King's remodelling of the 1870s, survives, but many of its spectacular radiating lakes are choked with weed and scarcely distinguishable from terra firma. Other highlights include the great banyan tree (*Ficus benghalensis*) planted in 1783, now forming a copse over 400 m/1,400 ft in circumference; a handsome domed 19th-century palm house, its net roof a living curtain of creepers; and a fine collection of monuments to the early botanist-surgeons who founded the Botanic Garden of the Honourable East India Company and nurtured it as the Royal Botanic Garden Calcutta.

Colonel Robert Kyd (military secretary to the Bengal government) founded the garden in 1786 on a virgin site of about 20 hectares/50 acres on the right bank of the Hooghly river at Sibpur near Calcutta. Despite periodic flooding (and susceptibility to cyclones), it remained on this site, eventually extending to over 121 hectares/300 acres. The initial aim was to grow economic plants to help overcome famines, but under the patronage of the East India Company it rapidly acquired an additional scientific agenda and was an important base for the exploration of the floras of India and South-East Asia, notably under Kyd's successor William Roxburgh, who ran the garden from 1793 to 1813 and greatly developed it. Succession of the early superintendents was never simple, but in 1814 Nathaniel WALLICH, a Danish surgeon working for the EIC, took over temporarily, remaining there with interruptions until 1846. Other great names in Indian botany, all surgeons, were superintendents for varying periods: Francis Buchanan (1814), William Griffith (1842–4), Hugh Falconer (1846–55), Thomas Thomson (1855–61), and Thomas Anderson (1861–9).

Griffith, who took over during one of Wallich's furloughs, caused consternation by turning it into a 'botanical laboratory', adopting a Candollean planting scheme (with plants arranged in 'order beds' according to the classification of plant families devised by the Swiss botanist Auguste Pyramus de Candolle (1778–1841)), symptomatic of perennial arguments over the roles of art and science in the function and design of botanic gardens.

Possibly the greatest director was Sir George King (1871–97) who, as we have seen, redesigned the garden, but also built the herbarium (1882), and established the once important scientific journal, the *Annals of the Royal Botanic Garden Calcutta*. Although in British hands until 1947, the first Indian director, Kalipada Biswas, had been appointed in 1937. Since 1963 the garden has been administered by the Botanical Survey of India (of which King was first director in 1891), whose headquarters it is, but there is currently little linkage between the herbarium and garden, with almost no plants labelled except the most glaringly obvious; the geographical planting scheme started by David Prain in 1904 is thus apparent only from the garden plan on a painted noticeboard, the single piece of interpretative matter available to the visitor.   HNo

Cambridge University Botanic Garden ⊕

Cambridge, Cambridgeshire, England. The 16-hectare/40-acre garden was founded in 1831 by Professor J. S. Henslow, the Regius professor of botany, and opened to the public in 1846. The site is flat but today is much enlivened by many mature trees, some dating from the founding of the garden. Among these are specimens of the Austrian pine (*Pinus nigra*) which Henslow planted to show natural variations within a single species. Henslow's favourite pupil was Charles Darwin whose study of the formation of species was first kindled in the botanic garden. A large collection of different species of lime (*Tilia*), examples of native species of rowan (*Sorbus*), and the oldest specimen of

Wellingtonia (*Sequoiadendron giganteum*) in the country give the landscape of the garden great character. Here are over 10,000 species, including many tender plants housed in a range of glasshouses. Two rock gardens show the very different kinds of plants from limestone habitats and ericaceous plants growing in sandstone. Three National Collections are kept: shrubby species of *Lonicera*, hardy geraniums, and tulips. Systematic, or 'order' beds, with plants arranged according to botanical family, date from the foundation of the garden and now display 1,600 hardy plants. A collection of British native species has a stretch of Cambridgeshire hedgerow showing its characteristic range of plants. The glasshouses contain around 3,000 species of tender plants from temperate, humid tropical, and alpine habitats and there is an unusual collection of non-flowering plants such as ferns, liverworts, and mosses.   PT

Cambridge University college gardens ⊗

Cambridge, Cambridgeshire, England, are a vital part of the university landscape. A unique and prominent feature is the green space of the Backs, a stretch of land behind those colleges which back onto the river Cam in the centre of the town, between St John's College to the north and Queens' College to the south. The Backs were originally simply those spaces behind the college buildings which were gradually planted up or laid out in one way or another. An engraving by Samuel and Nathaniel Buck of 1743 shows the landscape as it had then evolved. King's College and Trinity College had lawns flanked with formal rows of trees running down to the river—Trinity with an elegant domed pavilion on its bank. St John's had a romantic style of woodland planting running down to the river along whose banks the college had at this time laid out planned walks to take in its beauties. The land on the far side of the river, where modern Queen's Road is, was then a rural landscape. Two major landscaping schemes, neither of them executed, threatened a fundamental change of character for the Backs. An engraving of King's College in 1741 by James Essex shows a great formal garden between the Gibbs building and the river which is continued on the west side of the Cam where a vast formal basin is carved out of the river bank, with a domed temple at its head and walks and multiple rows of trees on each side. Charles BRIDGEMAN had Cambridge associations and this design is not dissimilar to his style, but he had died three years before the date of the engraving. At all events, the scheme was never executed. Later in the 18th century Capability

BROWN was consulted by St John's College, around 1772. A little later, in 1779, Brown on his own initiative submitted to the university a comprehensive plan for landscaping the Backs. He suggested widening the river, to give it more the air of a serpentine lake, with two narrow islands, with clumps of trees planted on its banks; and, west of the river, the land was to be laid out like a gentleman's park, with clumps and perimeter belts of trees. Apart from the immense cost of the scheme there was the probably insuperable difficulty of securing the cooperation of the individual colleges, jealous of their independence. A further, and intriguing, problem of a theoretical kind was that it was thought that Brown's scheme failed to distinguish 'between a nobleman's pleasure ground, and a spot to be adopted to the health and exercise of students'. The Backs today, where they run along the western bank of the Cam, present an informal landscape of paths, lawns, and trees. This forms a handsome foreground to views of the great college buildings some of which, seen across their own expansive greensward, do resemble some nobleman's country seat rather than a seat of learning, as Brown's critics feared.

The individual colleges possess gardens of varied character. Christ's College has an unusual garden of the first half of the 18th century with a bathing pool overlooked by a loggia-like summer house. A series of 18th-century busts of college luminaries, such as John Milton, decorates the garden. All this, a rare survival, had originally been part of an ornamental formal WILDERNESS. Clare College preserves a rare axial vista dating from the 17th century, linking the college courts east of the Cam with a bridge and a straight walk across the Backs to fine wrought-iron gates on Queen's Road. More surprisingly, it has remarkable 20th-century gardens. From 1947 Professor Nevill Willmer, who had a particular interest in the science of colour perception, laid out a series of colour-themed borders between the river and Queen's Road. Firmly set in a framework of yew hedges, with an ornamental pool and soaring cypresses, it is one of the best Cambridge gardens. King's College has little by way of a garden. The simple formality of the garden on the Backs seen in the Bucks' print was transformed in the early 19th century into meadow-like informality, with grazing cattle. The view of King's chapel and the neighbouring Gibbs building from the Backs, with its foreground of trees and meadow, one of the loveliest in Cambridge, has the Arcadian atmosphere that Brown sought in his proposal for the landscaping of the Backs. St John's College consulted Capability Brown in 1772 and as a result the Fellows' Garden (usually known

as The Wilderness) by the river was changed from austere 17th-century formality into an intimate and leafy landscape. A former bowling green was enlarged and densely planted about with trees—very much the scene that is visible today. Far more modern, but effective in their colourful way, are the mixed borders that run along the Gothic screen of New Court—a thoroughly 19th-century spectacle. Newnham College, removed from the crowded historic centre of Cambridge, had enough space to make one of the best of Cambridge gardens, with room to plant a notable collection of trees. Unlike the older colleges, too, garden and buildings could be planned together. The college buildings, designed by Basil Champneys, were started in 1875 and their landscaped surroundings which followed shortly after, built by James BACKHOUSE and Co., give the atmosphere of a self-contained campus. The buildings look across spacious lawns, with groups and specimens of trees, and a harmonious pattern of paths linking the buildings. Trinity College has more garden history than existing gardens of note. The largely late 16th-century Great Court has at its centre a superlative Elizabethan fountain, octagonal with a dome supported on columns. In the 17th century, as depicted in Loggan's *Cantabrigia Illustrata* (1690), there were formal gardens on either side of Great Gate, one of which was supposedly used by Isaac Newton when he was a Fellow of the college. An apple tree stands here, said to be propagated from the tree at Newton's childhood home of Woolsthorpe Manor in Lincolnshire which inspired his theory of gravity.   PT

RONALD GRAY, *Cambridge Gardens* (1984).

Camden Park,

New South Wales, Australia, was, from 1820 onwards, home to pioneer horticulturist and plant breeder William Macarthur (1800–82) and his brother James (1798–1867), sons of renowned pastoralists John and Elizabeth Macarthur. In 1817, after two years in Europe, William and James, with their father, returned to Australia bringing with them an extensive collection of plants including fruit trees, grapevines, and others new to the colony, including cork oak (*Quercus suber*), and *Rosa chinensis*. From this date the Camden estate, managed by William and James, became widely known for its ornamental and experimental gardens— particularly the orchards and vineyards with innovative irrigation—surrounding a notable two-storeyed sandstone house by architect John Verge (1782–1861) built 1832–4. From 1843 William Macarthur issued Camden Park nursery catalogues highlighting his collections of camellias, grapes, olives, and other imported exotics, then dispatching plants to nurseries and private growers in New South Wales, Victoria, Tasmania, and South Australia. These catalogues have become a significant source of information on plants available in the colony during this period. Macarthur's profuse correspondence, papers, and plans document his unique contribution to Australian garden history and ensure Camden Park's status as a significant site in Australian horticulture.

CMR

camellia house.

The common camellia, *C. japonica*, was introduced to Britain in the early 18th century but until the late 19th century it was thought not to be hardy in the open and was cultivated in glasshouses. J. C. LOUDON's *Encyclopaedia of Gardening* (1822) says that 'Camellias have the best effect, and are grown to most advantage in a house entirely devoted to them'. A superb surviving camellia house is to be seen in Scotland at Culzean Castle (Ayrshire) built in 1818 in lively Gothic style and probably designed by James Donaldson. By the 7th edition of William ROBINSON's *The Flower Garden* (1898) it was recognized that the camellia would flourish out of doors, flowering profusely in the south of England, especially near the coast. Camellias were always grown out of doors in Portugal, which seems to have introduced them as early as the 16th century, and immense old specimens survive in gardens in northern Portugal.   PT

Cameron, Charles

(*c.*1743–1812), Scottish architect and landscape architect, probably born in London, where he was apprenticed to his father, a member of the Carpenters' Company, and studied architecture under Isaac Ware. His deep interest in the forms of classical antiquity led him to Rome, and the publication of *The Baths of Rome* (1772) earned him an international reputation. He went to Russia in 1779, where he was to work as decorator, architect, and landscape architect for Catherine the Great, to whom he represented himself as a Jacobite aristocrat, and his achievement and influence there in the field of park and garden architecture were quite exceptional. At TSARSKOE SELO he built a remarkable suite of rooms and baths, lavishly redolent of ancient Rome, which delighted Catherine, some distinguished park buildings, and a small town with a cathedral which could be viewed from the park. At PAVLOVSK he designed the palace, the formal gardens around it, and landscaped a large area of the park, which Loudon attributed to Capability BROWN. When Catherine died Cameron was dismissed by Paul I, but he was re-employed by Alexander I and designed some notable buildings as

architect-in-chief to the Admiralty. Through an advertisement in the *Edinburgh Evening Courant* in 1784, Cameron had recruited 73 Scottish craftsmen to work under him at Tsarskoe Selo.Two of them were to earn considerable distinction in Russia, William Hastie (*c.*1755–1832) as architect and town planner, Adam Menelaws (1763–1831) as architect and landscape architect.   PH

Campbell, Colen

(1676–1729), Scottish architect. A nephew of the laird of Cawdor Castle, he began life as a lawyer but became an architect and worked on several estates with notable gardens. Campbell was a key influence in the early 18th-century English taste for Palladian architecture, publishing the three-volume work *Vitruvius Britannicus* (1715, 1717, and 1725) which sang the praises of the 'antique simplicity' of PALLADIO and Inigo JONES (as distinct from the 'affected and licentious' baroque) and illustrated many neo-Palladian projects. At Wanstead House (Essex) Campbell built (1714–20) the first great neo-Palladian country house, for the banker Sir Richard Child. He designed the house at STOURHEAD (*c.*1720–4) in Wiltshire, Houghton Hall (1722–35) in Norfolk, and the Palladian stables and, probably, the banqueting house at STUDLEY ROYAL in Yorkshire (*c.*1729). One of his prettiest surviving houses is Ebberston Hall (North Yorkshire, originally Ebberston Lodge, 1718) which has a rare water garden attributed to Stephen SWITZER. Mereworth Castle (Kent, 1722–5) is a dazzling version of Palladio's Villa Rotonda. His Great Room, a garden house, was built in 1724 for Edmund Waller's HALL BARN but was destroyed by fire in the 19th century.

PT

Campen, Jacob van

(1595–1657), Dutch painter and architect. After his training as a painter, this self-taught architect led the development of a new style that became known as Dutch classicism and also influenced garden design. This movement, distinguished by its plinths, pilasters, and pediments in symmetrical façades, reached its maturity in the Mauritshuis, The Hague (1633), designed for Johan Maurits van NASSAU-SIEGEN. It was a free-standing town house on an awkward site that did not fully allow the classical proportions to be continued in the gardens and which necessitated a grotto to negotiate an obtuse angle. Van Campen's theories of classical proportions for gardens are most obvious in HOFWIJCK where from 1639 he advised Contantijn HUYGENS, and which uses the Vitruvian human figure as a basis for the proportions. The classical garden at Elswout (1642) is attributed to him, and in the 1650s he

worked at CLEVES for Johan Maurits where he designed a classical EXEDRA above the amphitheatre.   JW

Campo, Casa de ⊛

Madrid, Spain. A 17th-century painting (in the National Museum of Archaeology in Madrid) by an unknown artist shows a bird's-eye view of the estate. The house, with a loggia, overlooks a pattern of parterres, each square with nine square beds and a central fountain pool. In the woods to one side is glimpsed a grand tiered fountain and facing the house is an equestrian statue on a plinth. House and garden as seen in the painting date from the time of Philip II (reigned 1556–98), for whom the house was a hunting box at the centre of a great hunting ground. The painting is one of the most complete views we have of a Spanish garden of its period. Today nothing survives of house and garden—but the equestrian figure (of Philip II) by GIAMBOLOGNA is now displayed in the Plaza Mayor in Madrid. The estate today is a wild and very large public park with an area of 1,700 hectares/4,199 acres.   PT

Canada.

The origin of Canadian gardening is thousands of years old. By the time Europeans came in the 15th century, this was not virgin territory. There had been a form of agriculture for millennia, the forests and prairies were controlled by burning, and every aspect of every useful plant was employed. Different nations cultivated plots of the 'three sisters'—corn, squash, and beans—edged with sunflowers (*Helianthus annua*) and tobacco (*Nicotiana tabaccum*). Women of the Pacific coast cared for camas (*Camassia quamash*) as a food crop and a trading tool. All were protected by invisible lines of property known to each family and respected by them. This seemingly unorganized form of gardening was alien to the Europeans who came laden with horticultural baggage. Their honey bees escaped the minute they got off their ships, changing the ecology in ways still unknown. Many of their beloved garden plants (as well as weeds) nudged out native species, and the wholesale felling of trees from east to west degraded this fragile landscape with a speed previously unknown.

Canada's climate seems to be either extremely hot or extremely cold. Parts of the Boreal Forest (a 360-km/600-mile wide band from Newfoundland in the east to Alaska in the west) have only 90 frost-free days annually; the semi-arid Prairie climate is prone to severe drought; the west coast rainforest is dripping wet a good deal of the year; and to the far north temperatures drop to –35 ˚C/–31 ˚F in winter. As settlers found out, however, they could grow an astounding range of plants because of the fertile soil and the long, brilliant summer days.

All through the 16th century botanist-priests such as the Jesuits of New France tested plants to send back home. In fact, the first Canadian flora, *Canadensium Plantarum Historia* by Jacques-Philippe Cornut (*c.*1606–51) was based on plants in the Jardin des Plantes in Paris (see PARIS PARKS AND GARDENS). But by the 18th century every expedition had a botanist. David DOUGLAS, alone, sent back 245 North American plants.

As the country became more domesticated, a familiar garden pattern was established: a POTAGER with house surrounded by foundation shrubs and trees for shade and warmth. What most people wanted were views: views of the water, of the trees, the land and mountains in the distance. Picturesque Canada was ever at their doorsteps and what little conscious design there was took advantage of the surroundings. By the late 18th century the English tradition of the country manor with PICTURESQUE elements became a symbol of prosperity. Catharine Parr Traill (1802–99) in her books extolled the picturesque, and gardens of the wealthy such as RIDEAU HALL exemplified the Canadian version of this concept. The average town garden, however, was simply grass and a couple of shrubs until the fad for Victorian bedding out took over. This huge demand for seeds actually helped develop the nursery industry. But as experience demonstrated, they looked pretty awful in a climate with five months of winter. This awareness eventually led to a more NATURALISTIC form of gardening by the turn of the century.

The railways which scooped millions of acres of public lands for their rights of way began a 70-year tradition of railway gardens. They were intended to clean up the mess left by construction, draw settlers into the west, and show the folks how to garden here. In the 1940s they shipped 10,000 packets of seed to over 200 gardens. By the 1960s, most were parking lots.

Gardening had a moral purpose: improved public spaces have a happy populace. The Macdonald movement was designed to get the children interested in the soil. It faded, but never quite into oblivion as Canada flung itself into Victory Gardens in the 1940s to eke out the rationed food supply. Back to Earthers started allotment plots during the 1970s; and with the 1990s, the greening of the schoolyards (so busily cemented over in the 1960s) became a national passion. In 1995, Communities in Bloom was established to beautify towns, conserve the urban forest, and educate the populace to be more environmentally aware. It now has over 100 participants often spearheaded by the local horticultural society.

The first Horticultural Society was established in 1834 in Kingston, Ontario, and soon spread across the country taking on public projects such as the planting of street trees. The Public Parks Act passed in 1883; and by 1897, the Act to Encourage the Planting and Growing of Trees for streets lanes and highways came into law. This all coincided with the City Beautiful movement with its grandiose plans for parks and street tree plantings

Until 1874, parks were confined to CEMETERIES and the homes of the wealthy. But in that year, F. L. OLMSTED was invited to design Montréal's Mount Royal Park. His protégé Frederick G. Todd (1876–1948) went on to design a number of parks from coast to coast including Winnipeg's Assiniboine Park; plans for the national capital in Ottawa (not done); and Wascana Park for the new capital of Saskatchewan in 1905. British landscape architect Thomas MAWSON designed its elaborate formal hedges and flower beds and began to influence the way Canadian gardens looked, as did Howard Dunnington-Grubb (1881–1965) and several other English-trained designers who gave Toronto's smart areas their own formal style in the 1950s and 1960s.

By then the nursery trade was big business. Its first boost came in 1830 when Chauncey Beadle (1823–1905) started a nursery in St Catharines, Ontario. His son Delos W. Beadle (1866–1950) became the first editor of *Canadian Horticulturalists* (founded in 1878). He also wrote the first all-Canadian gardening book, *Canadian Fruit, Flower and Kitchen Garden*, published in 1872. From this time on, hybridizers abounded, giving Canada its first genuine garden revolution. The search was on for ever hardier plants. After the First World War, the Dominion Experimental Farms System (established in 1889) led the way in ornamental research and breeding. Guided first by William Saunders (1836–1914) (who developed Marquis wheat); and then by W. T. Macoun (1869–1933), who established a system of arboreta, the system introduced hundreds of hardy plants for the trade. Isabella Preston (1881–1965) became known for hybridizing lilies and lilacs in Ottawa. In Manitoba Frank Skinner (1882–1967) developed more than 200 hybrids (roses such as 'Agnes' and 'Adelaide Hoodless' were famous). By the 1990s there were dozens of first-rate nurseries growing their own and importing rare and unusual plants.

In 1970, *The Chatelaine Gardening Book* by Lois Wilson (1908–93) was almost the only Canadian gardening book. But the second major revolution came in the early 1990s, when lavish books based on the more spectacular gardens of the country were produced. This became a veritable flood by the new century. Writers developed their own style instead of aping the British, as did the gardeners who sensibly stuck to working with their regional problems to create a look of their own. Eighty per cent of the population now claims to have some interest in gardening. A movement towards conservation and restoration of native habitats is increasingly important to this public. They support two national magazines (*Gardening Life* and *Canadian Gardening*) as well as dozens of regional ones.

BOTANICAL GARDENS—the first established in 1836 in Halifax (which survives as a public park)—today number 80. There are several excellent schools of garden design and six universities confer landscape architecture degrees. Gardeners in Canada are a horticulturally literate group who have created superb private gardens in every region of the country including the far north where, it was once said, nothing will grow.   MH

canal.

The garden canal is in essence a rectangular pool, longer than it is wide, but there are many possible variations. In the earliest known gardens, in the Near East, water was especially important. In early Egyptian gardens canals, arranged in elaborate patterns, were used to preserve water, and in the gardens of Mesopotamia and Persia ingenious forms of canals were common, for both irrigation and ornament. The same was true in ancient ROMAN GARDENS. HADRIAN'S VILLA (2nd century AD) had several canals one of which, in the Piazza d'Oro, had underground channels and sluices supplying water both to another canal and to irrigate the beds about it. In Mughal and Islamic gardens the canal was a universal feature.

In Italian Renaissance gardens, although water was brilliantly used in pools, fountains, rills, and cascades, the canal never found favour. In French 17th-century gardens, however, the canal assumed central importance, as a key structural element, not merely an incidental ornament. The immense cross-shaped Grand Canal at VERSAILLES forms part of the garden's central axis as well as linking features to each side. André LE NÔTRE explored the canal's possibilities in other gardens, in particular at CHANTILLY and VAUX-LE-VICOMTE. In English gardens of the late 17th and early 18th centuries the canal, for example at CHATSWORTH and HAMPTON COURT PALACE, was often a major feature of the layout. In late 20th- and early 21st-century gardens, usually on a small scale, it has been used inventively by garden designers in many countries.   PT

Canberra,

Australia, was created in the early 20th century specifically as the nation's capital, American Walter Burley Griffin (1876-1937) having won the design competition for the city in 1912. Griffin's vision of Canberra as an ideal city is a synthesis of both the City Beautiful and GARDEN CITY movements. Symmetry and geometry linking the natural features of hills, mountains, and water are major themes in Canberra's design. However, it has been argued recently by landscape architects that, while the city acknowledges Griffin's legacy (the lake that links the design is named after him), much of the formality and geometry of Griffin's original design has been eroded. The parliamentary triangle is the critical node in Griffin's plan. Many of the buildings in this area—Parliament House, the High Court, the National Library, and the Australian National Gallery—have been constructed with landscape an integral part of their design. Griffin and Charles Weston (1866-1935), who planned the early plantings in the city 1913-26, were advocates of Australian native plants and embraced the concept of planting native trees as well as exotic species. As a result, Canberra's avenues, streets, and highways are lined with plantations featuring a magnificent selection of Australian native and exotic trees. Contrast in planting style is also evident in such examples as the formal rows of trees lining the highly symbolic Anzac Parade leading to the massive Australian War Memorial; informality is the key to the planting of indigenous species in the Sculpture Garden at the Australian National Gallery where the sculpture is displayed in fifteen garden rooms with seasonal themes.

Landscape architect Richard Clough (b. 1921), following Griffin's plan for a great artificial lake, carefully related this feature to Canberra's existing natural and man-made landscape, which became more obvious as the lake filled in the 1960s. Dame Sylvia CROWE designed the major lake shore precinct, Commonwealth Park. The Australian National Botanic Gardens on the slopes of Black Mountain offer opportunities for exploring a fine collection of Australian flora while the Garden of Australian Dreams at the National Museum of Australia's entrance, opened in 2001 and designed by Richard Weller (b. 1963) and Vladimir Sitta (b. 1950), is a challenging, thought-provoking space. From the snowy peaks of the Brindabella Ranges on the horizon to the golden pastures of summer or the rich autumn tints reflected in the lake, the beauty of nature is celebrated in Canberra, fulfilling Griffin's vision.   CMR

Cane, Percy

(1881-1976), English garden designer practising in a simplified form of ARTS AND CRAFTS style. Arthur Hellyer summed up the two characteristic features of his work: 'a mainly classical use of stonework . . . the other, for want of a better term, I call the slightly formalised woodland glade.' Among gardens that open to the public his work may be seen at DARTINGTON HALL and FALKLAND PALACE. At the first he laid out dramatic but subtle flights of

---

Perelle's engraving (c.1685) of the **canal** at Chantilly seen from the *vertugadin*.

steps, with bold associated planting, for an ancient terraced garden. At Falkland, for the historic setting of a Scottish royal palace, he designed a great border and a series of island beds. Cane was a very successful professional designer, winning many medals at the Chelsea Flower Show, and securing prestigious commissions (such as designing gardens for the Emperor Haile Selassie at the palace in Addis Ababa). He was a designer who planned bold effects and those that have survived have very much stood the test of time.   PT

Canglangting ⊛

Jiangsu province, China, in the south of the city of Suzhou dates back to the 10th century. Later, in 1044, a noted poet, Su Zimei, built for himself a garden on the old site, naming it Canglangting or the Pavilion of the Dark Blue Waves, after an ancient saying which counsels acceptance of the vicissitudes of life: 'When times are good I wash my ribbons of office in the waters of the Canglang river—when times are bad, my feet.' Later again, the garden belonged to General Han Shizong, a national hero in the Southern Song dynasty (1127–79). What survive are the remains of successive reconstructions made during the Qing dynasty (1644–1911).

The layout of the garden is unique in Suzhou in that a hill, rather than a pond, lies at its centre. Its entrance is across a bridge, slightly zigzag, above a wide canal. In the gatehouse, there is a rare portrait engraved on a stone by the Buddhist monk Ji Feng (or Fang) at the end of the last century, showing the garden as it was in 1884—it is almost unchanged today. Beyond the gate one faces immediately an earthy artificial hill, embellished with yellow rocks in the east and Taihu (the rock most prized for artificial 'mountains') rocks in the west, which occupies the whole width of the garden. This is the highest of the artificial hills in Suzhou; the Canglang pavilion (unfortunately rebuilt in concrete) on its top gives its name to the garden. Covered *lang* (see CHINA) galleries dotted with small pavilions and halls surround the hill and open *lou chuang* (see CHINA) windows allow views of the canal to become part of the garden. There are several structures south of the hill, one of which is the double-storeyed Kanshanlou, which literally means Seeing Mountains since it draws into the garden distant views (JIE JING) of the hills beyond the southern suburbs.

D-HL/MK

Canneel-Claes, Jean

(1909–1989), Belgian landscape architect who remains an emblematic figure in the definition of modernist landscape architecture. The first garden architect to graduate from the Decorative Arts School of La Cambre in 1931, where he also studied urbanism and architecture, Canneel actively promoted the connection between house, garden, and city. Throughout the 1930s he refined his view for a contemporary, democratic, and productive garden while collaborating with Belgian modernist architects such as Louis de Koninck and Huib Hoste. He expanded his garden idiom to the public landscape of the 1939 Exposition of Water in Liège. During the German occupation he joined the urbanism section of the Agency for the Restoration of the Nation where he contributed to the reconstruction of cities and the design of cemeteries, before emigrating to Belgian Congo as a planner in 1950 for a few years.

Canneel's own residence in Auderghem (1931) best illustrated the interconnection between modernist architecture and landscape. The result of a two-year process with an initial proposal by Le Corbusier (1929) and a final design by De Koninck, the house opened up to the south and Canneel's 'functionalist garden'. Canneel visually and functionally balanced the interior volumes with a graphic and spatial composition of implied outdoor rooms allowing for solar exposure, leisure, and physical exercise. In the 1930s gardens, Canneel proposed a system of ingredients—modular paving, sandbox, wading pool, flower and vegetable beds, fruit trees, and sunbathing lawn—adjusted to the demands of the client and the characteristics of the site. Thus the van de Putte (1932), Danhier (1933), Fouarge (1935), and Heeremans (1937) gardens reflected contemporary aesthetics, met the requirements of modern life with minimal cost and upkeep, and expressed a concern for views, topography, and existing vegetation.

Although Canneel's remained a singular voice in Belgian landscape architecture—set apart from those of contemporaries René Pechère and René Latinne—it found an echo in the opinions of Christopher TUNNARD in England. Following the first International Congress of Garden Architects held in Paris in 1937, Canneel and Tunnard founded the Association Internationale des Architectes de Jardins Modernistes (AIAJM). The AIAJM manifesto called for the exchange of ideas among garden designers of all nationalities and their collaboration with architects, urbanists, and artists. The Second World War prevented the association's ideals from developing, but Canneel's ambition to establish the landscape architecture profession within a contemporary design world and an international discourse endured, as witnessed in the founding of the International Federation of Landscape Architects (IFLA) a decade later.   DI

DOROTHÉE IMBERT, *Defining Modernism: Jean Canneel-Claes Belgian Landscape Architect* (forthcoming).

Canon, Château de ⊛

Mézidon, Calvados, France, a garden of unique charm, deftly intermingling ingredients of different periods and styles. The estate was inherited in 1768 by a cultivated lawyer, Jean-Baptiste Jacques Élie de Beaumont, with a particular taste for gardens. Among his distinguished friends was Horace WALPOLE (with whom he visited STOWE and KEW) who excited his interest in 18th-century English gardens. Another friend was Voltaire, whose garden of formal pools and walks, informal woods ('bois très irréguliers', he called them), undulations, kitchen garden, meadows, and fruit trees was much to Élie de Beaumont's taste. Voltaire loved both 'le peigné et le sauvage' (the combed and the wild). Élie de Beaumont remodelled the house, giving it an Italianate character especially on its west side where it overlooks a *miroir d'eau* (dating from 1730; see ANNEVOIE, CHÂTEAU D') on whose banks white marble busts raised on plinths gaze back towards the chateau. Woodland presses in on either side of the pool pierced by a long north-south path, lined with lime trees and vestiges of an old box hedge, cutting across the garden. At its southern end is the Temple de la Pleureuse (1783), a simple pedimented temple built in memory of Élie de Beaumont's wife. At the northern end of the walk is a building of very different character, an open-work Chinese kiosk, painted ox-blood red and brought here by Élie de Beaumont from the Château des Ternes (as were the fine wrought-iron gates opening onto the *cour d'honneur* (see ATTRE, CHÂTEAU D')). The kiosk faces into the woods and, on the other side, it gives views over a boundary stream to pastures and woodland. Winding paths, leading off the central walk, thread the enveloping woods. Within the woods are BOSQUETS and a garden of streams and a cascade as the setting for the picturesque remains of the 17th-century Château Béranger. In the north-east corner of the garden is one of the most unusual features of the estate, the *chartreuses*. This is a series of walled enclosures linked by an axial walk piercing a series of arched openings. Originally designed as a fruit garden, it is today chiefly used for ornamental purposes, with colourful herbaceous planting lining the paths and, at the head of the garden, a gleaming white marble figure of Pomona, clasping her cornucopia, rising in late summer from a sea of pink dahlias. *Chartreuses* are usually taken to mean ornamental pavilions—the use of the word to mean enclosed fruit gardens seems unique to Canon. The entrance

façade of the chateau is more modest than that of the garden front. Here, too, are handsome busts on plinths but also, to one side, is the stable yard, built in this position by Élie de Beaumont. An avenue of lime trees, extending eastwards from the *cour d'honneur*, fixes chateau and garden firmly in its larger setting.   PT
ALAIN DE MÉZERAC, *Le Château de Canon* (1992).

Cantonal School of Gardening.
See OECHSBERG HORTICULTURAL COLLEGE.

Capponi, Villa ⊛
Arcetri, Florence, Italy. Although frequently changing hands over three centuries the Villa Capponi has been fortunate in its owners. Originally in 1572 belonging to Gino do Lodovico Capponi, its gardens, a series of walled enclosures relating to the house, have been mainly 18th-century additions. The first garden lay before the house giving views to the north over Florence and the Arno valley; the second was directly below on the next level. Edged by tall walls with rococo curvilinear decoration and ornamented with terracotta urns, they retain their 18th-century flavour. In 1882 Lady Elizabeth Scott added two external loggias, and in the early 20th century a new garden was attached on the south. Cecil PINSENT worked at Capponi in 1935 adding a further swimming pool garden hidden by tall cypress hedges.   PHo

Capricho de la Alameda de Osuna, El.
See OSUNA, EL CAPRICHO DE LA ALAMEDA DE.

Carlotta, Villa ⊛
Lake Como, Italy. The 18th-century villa on the northern shores of Lake Como combines a formal layout around the immediate villa with an English-style woodland garden made after 1843, devoted to interesting trees and shrubs, in botanical interest far beyond the usual colourful rhododendrons and azaleas typical of the lakeside gardens. In the favourable climate lemon arbours, scented akebia, twining jasmine, roses, tall camellia hedges, and formal flower beds with bedding out make the formal garden beautiful. It was built in 1745 as a wedding gift to Carlotta, Duchess of Saxe-Meiningen, who began the landscape garden. Today a dell of tree ferns, palm trees, Japanese maples, cork oaks, and giant magnolias revels in the mild microclimate to make a semi-tropical jungle effect.   PHo

Carmen de la Fundación Rodriguez Acosta.
See ACOSTA, CARMEN DE LA FUNDACIÓN RODRIGUEZ.

Carmen de los Martires.
See MARTIRES, CARMEN DE LOS.

Carmontelle, Louis Carrogis
(1717–1806), French artist, born Louis Carrogis, who assumed the name Carmontelle. His most famous work was for the Duc de Chartres for whom in the 1770s he designed a garden, the Jardin de Monceau, in the village of Monceau outside Paris. Its remains may be seen today in the Parisian Parc Monceau (see PARIS PARKS AND GARDENS). Carmontelle's particular skill owed more to the theatre than to horticulture—he devised many FABRIQUES in heterogeneous styles giving the garden the atmosphere of an ephemeral stage set. Carmontelle also painted a series of panoramas of imaginary rural scenery on transparent paper which could be illuminated from behind and unrolled to give the impression of a shifting scene. Carmontelle's booklet *Le Jardin de Monceau* (1779) expresses his philosophy: 'The true art is to know how to hold the attention of strollers by the variety of objects, without which they will seek in the open countryside that which they lack in the garden, the illusion of liberty.'
PT

carpet bedding
was a Victorian invention, using low plants of uniform size or which could be clipped to create carpet-like bedding schemes of abstract patterns, coats of arms, initials, and the like. Plants typically used were tender annuals such as *Alternanthera* and *Iresine*; succulents like *Echeveria* or *Sempervivum*. It was the foliage of the succulents that was regarded as ornamental; the flowering stems were often carefully removed. Carpet bedding should be distinguished from other forms of patterned bedding schemes in which plants of very different sizes are used. Its inventor was John Fleming, the head gardener at CLIVEDEN in Buckinghamshire in 1868. In the late 20th and early 21st centuries there has been a minor renaissance of carpet bedding. This has involved either the re-creation of historic schemes, such as the charming panels at the Victorian pleasure garden at Cragside in Northumberland, or, much more interestingly, completely new designs. At WADDESDON MANOR in Buckinghamshire the artist John Hubbard was commissioned in 1999 to design carpet bedding for the Millennium. Using traditional plants he devised sweeping abstract veils of colour of striking beauty. Each year a new design is commissioned from a different artist.
PT

Carton,
Maynooth, County Kildare, Republic of Ireland, had one of the most remarkable early formal gardens in Ireland. The estate had belonged to the FitzGerald family (late dukes of Leinster) from the 12th century. The estate was leased to the Talbot family who in the 17th century laid out a garden in elaborate French baroque style. A painting attributed to William van der Hagen and dating from around 1730 shows a semicircular entrance forecourt from which a PATTE D'OIE of avenues radiates outwards. Behind the house, enclosed in avenues, is a giant rectilinear layout on an axis centred on the house. The design is not as symmetrical as a French garden of this date would have been but is plainly influenced by that tradition. In 1739 an astonishing obelisk known as Conolly's folly, which still survives, was built on the margin of the Carton estate linking the landscape with that of neighbouring Castletown. Possibly designed by Richard Castle (1695–1751), the obelisk is mounted on a series of huge arches, a dramatic if slightly ungainly sight. After 1747 the formal garden was gradually dismantled to be replaced by a Brownian landscape, which is depicted in a painting of 1776 by Thomas Roberts. In the 1740s Emilia, 1st Duchess of Leinster, made an exquisite garden house whose interior is lavishly decorated with shellwork, mirrors, mother of pearl, and patterns of pine cones. In the 19th century new formal gardens were made and these survive. Today, golf courses have been made in the demesne and the house is a clubhouse.   PT

Caruncho, Fernando
(b. 1957). The contemporary private garden is enjoying a considerable revival in Spain in the 21st century, a phenomenon due almost entirely to the impact of the Spanish-born, Madrid-based designer Fernando Caruncho. Caruncho studied philosophy at the University of Madrid and his fascination with pre-Socratic Greek philosophy awakened a deep curiosity about the relationship between man and the natural world which translated itself into a preoccupation with garden design. The best gardens, he felt, acted as portals to a lost and innocent world where man understood his position in the universe, conversing on an intuitive and intimate level with the hidden mainspring of the world. Caruncho prefers to express himself in the language of philosophy, yet his thinking is permeated by a profound respect for theology, believing the origins of garden making to have been formed within a religious context. As early as 1979 the young philosophy graduate found himself responsible for the design of a small private garden on the outskirts of Madrid for a house by the Viennese modernist Richard Neutra (1892–1970). This

first garden set the scene for what was to follow: simple geometric forms, with frequent references to grid patterns, glassy water, and clean, light-filled spaces delineated by dense evergreen planting. While the overall impression is of minimalist modernism, inspiration from sources as diverse as Islam, Zen, and European classicism is clearly in evidence.

Following a formal training in landscape design at the University of Madrid, Caruncho continued to develop his personal idiom, creating gardens in Spain and, more recently, for private clients in France and the United States. In 1999 he designed the garden for the Spanish Embassy in Tokyo. His public commissions are much fewer, but include the grounds of the Clinica Teknon in Barcelona, an interior courtyard for the University of Deusto in Bilbao, and a new, elevated section of the ROYAL BOTANIC GARDEN, MADRID. His use of light is one of the most remarkable features of his work. Light, he believes, makes the language of geometry intelligible. The reflective surfaces of water, pale stone paths, and walls washed in tawny ferrous sulphate, combined with glossy mounds of clipped escallonia or box, are much in evidence. The decorative use of colour is shunned, as in Caruncho's construct it serves only to distract from the essential truth disclosed by light, which is why he uses a very limited palette of flowering plants. One of his best-known gardens, the Mas de les Voltes in Catalonia, contains a vast rectangular parterre planted entirely with wheat and punctuated with columnar cypresses. Closer to the house, olives, cypresses, and vines fill the terraces above a grid of four square pools bisected by broad grass paths. The strong reflected light, clear water and the handful of plants—vines, olives, wheat—on which Mediterranean civilization grew and the cypresses which gave shelter and shade locate Caruncho's gardens firmly within the cultural context of southern Europe. The universality of the language his gardens speak is evident in the growing demand for his work around the world.   KF

Casa de Mateus. See MATEUS, CASA.

Casa de Pilatos. See PILATOS, CASA DE.

Casa de Serralves. See SERRALVES, PARQUE DE.

cascade.
The waterfall, or cascade, is a garden feature that has been interpreted in many different ways. In Islamic gardens the movement and sound of water was a much esteemed part of the atmosphere. The cascades were gentle falls of

water linking different levels such as the stepped rill in the Estanque del Mirador and the water chute falling to the pool in the Patio de Arrayanes in the ALHAMBRA. Italian Renaissance gardens used water with greater exuberance. The Villa d'ESTE, made from 1559, is the most outstanding celebration of water. The Oval Fountain has a great veil of water, behind which you may walk, and which falls from a balustraded walk into a pool below. The Fountain of Rome, which only partly survives, has a cascade of a very different kind—a series of naturalistic falls over boulders. In French 17th-century gardens the cascade was occasionally used with dramatic effect. At Saint-Cloud on the edge of Paris Antoine Le Pautre (d. 1679) designed a monumental Grande Cascade which was built between 1664 and 1665 and, in a slightly modified form, is one of the few parts of the 17th-century garden to survive. At SCEAUX André LE NÔTRE from 1673 laid out the ground with a grandiose double cascade falling down to an octagonal pool. English gardens of the late 17th and early 18th century often had formal cascades influenced by the French example. At CHATSWORTH a Frenchman, Monsieur Grillet, designed a 24-step cascade, with falls of slightly different heights to vary the sound, completed in 1696. At the GNOLL ESTATE at Neath in Glamorgan a copper smelter, Sir Humphry Mackworth, used the water from his industrial activities to make two memorable cascades. One, made in the 1720s, is in the French tradition—a formal cascade descending a gentle slope in a series of shallow falls, with different shapes of stone beneath the falls to create patterns of splashing. In the 1740s he made a second cascade of entirely different character. At the head of a wooded valley, where a stream gushes out of a bank, Mackworth created a majestic informal cascade, a series of plummeting falls with a total drop of 55 m/180 ft which curves through a rocky ravine. Both cascades survive in what is now a public park. The cascade of an informal character is often found in English 18th-century landscape parks. It was a convenient way of linking two lakes, which were often formed by damming a stream. The cascade could be combined with a bridge. In the 1970s Sir Geoffrey JELLICOE designed for SHUTE HOUSE a cascade whose four falls are interrupted by V-shaped pieces of metal. In theory, the greater number of 'V' shapes the higher the pitch of the sound of falling water. It was Jellicoe's hope that the sound of the four falls would produce a harmonic chord which, for unknown reasons, was never achieved. In the late 20th century outstanding cascades have been made in the USA. At the McIntyre garden (California, 1961) Lawrence HALPRIN designed a minimalist Mughal-inspired garden with a

fountain pool leading to a stepped cascade and rills of exquisite refinement. For the Portland Open Space Sequence (Oregon, 1961–8) Halprin showed himself to be the master of cascades in a different idiom—here the water tumbles explosively over man-made cliffs. Paley Park in Manhattan is a miniature public park (1965–8) designed by Zion & Breen whose chief feature is a high wall of water, falling like a curtain, which both cools the air and subdues the street noise.
PT

Caserta. See REALE, PALAZZO.

casino.
An ornamental pavilion originating in Italian Renaissance gardens. Outstanding examples at the 16th-century Villa LANTE are two loggia-like buildings on the uppermost terrace, echoing in more modest form the twin *palazzine* (miniature palaces) on the lower level. Sir William CHAMBERS's *casino* (1758–76) at Marino House in Ireland is a beautiful 18th-century example.   PT

CLAUDIA LAZZARO, *The Italian Renaissance Garden* (1990).

Cassan, Pavillon de ✲
L'Isle-Adam, Val d'Oise, France, all that remains of a notable late 18th-century picturesque garden. It was the creation of Pierre-Jacques Bergeret de Grancourt who in 1778 inherited a great fortune from his father, a tax farmer. Grancourt laid out a vast landscape park about an artificial lake, ornamented with many FABRIQUES, of which a beautiful CHINOISERIE pavilion is the only survivor. It is suggested that the designer was the artist Jean Honoré Fragonard, who accompanied the Grancourts, father and son, on the grand tour, but there is no hard evidence. Beautifully restored in recent times, it is one of the finest chinoiserie garden buildings in France. The octagonal pavilion has a double swooping roof with fretted architraves and a ravishing interior decorated with panels of trailing branches, birds, and flowers painted in pale orange and smoky blue. It is raised up on a monumental vaulted stone base.   PT

Cassiobury Park,
Watford, Hertfordshire, England, was in the Middle Ages part of the monastic estate of St Albans. At the dissolution of the monasteries it was acquired by Sir Richard Morrison from whose family it passed by marriage to the Capel family, later earls of Essex. A new house was built in the 1670s to the designs of Hugh May (1621–84) and a garden was laid out by Moses Cook (*fl.* late 17th century) and George LONDON. The garden is shown in a KIP engraving in *Britannia Illustrata* (1707) with a single parterre

by the entrance couryard and pair of parterres and pools to one side of the house and in the surrounding landscape an elaborate pattern of avenues. Aligned with the house and parterres a double avenue pierces woodland and ends in a giant circular clearing. John EVELYN saw the garden shortly after it was completed and wrote, 'The gardens at Cassiobury are very rare, and cannot be otherwise, having so skilful an artist as Mr Cook to govern them.' In 1720 Charles BRIDGEMAN, according to Horace WALPOLE, 'laid out the Wood', but it is not known what exactly he did. In 1795 the Grand Union Canal was built across the park and in around 1801 Humphry REPTON made proposals for the landscape which resulted in the remains of Cook and London's formal groves becoming informal. Later earls of Essex sold land for development and the house was demolished in 1927. Today there are golf courses and a public park on the site.   PT

Castelo Branco: Jardim dos Bispos

(Bishops' Palace garden) ✤ Beira Baixa, Portugal. The palace of the bishops of Guarda dates back to the 16th century. The garden was made in the early 18th century for Bishop Dom João de Mendonça. Dates on statues in the garden of 1725 and 1726 give the date when it was put into place. At its heart, overlooked by the palace walls, is a gigantic parterre with round fountain pools at the centre and in each corner. The beds, of which there are 24, are edged with box with wriggling patterns of box hedges within the compartments and monumental rounded shapes of topiary rising above at regular intervals. Roses are planted in some of the compartments with statues of saints, and other ornaments, among them. Statues of Spanish kings are half-sized to symbolize the Portuguese contempt for their former overlords whom they had finally ousted in 1668. On the far side of the parterre, at a higher level, is a narrow rectangular water tank with three crowns on plinths running down the centre. Behind it is a curiously shaped garden with a triangular pool in which slightly raised beds edged in stone are planted with flowers to form sweeping arabesques of colour on the surface of the pool. A second, much larger, water tank to one side of the parterre is ornamented with stone balustrades. In the past the tank was decorated with AZULEJOS, stone masks, and pebble inlays but little trace of these survives today.   PT

Castle Howard ✤

near York, Yorkshire, England, stands in grounds of 1,240 hectares/3,062 acres part of which constitutes one of the largest designed landscapes in the British Isles. The house was designed by Sir John VANBRUGH, with the help of Nicholas HAWKSMOOR, for Charles Howard, 3rd Earl of Carlisle. Work started in 1699 but was still incomplete at Vanbrugh's death in 1726. Although Vanbrugh designed some of the ornamental buildings in the landscape, and it is established that he was often involved in the design of the settings for his houses, it seems that at Castle Howard there was never any predetermined plan which united house and setting. According to Charles Saumarez Smith's *The Building of Castle Howard* (1990) the landscape developed in a haphazard fashion. George LONDON had made proposals as early as 1699, involving the destruction of a beautiful old beech wood, Ray Wood, close to the site of the new house, which were rejected, although London later supplied plants for the garden. However, from 1705 there was activity in Ray Wood, with references in the accounts to a 'New Garden in Wray Wood' and bills for statues and pedestals. In the 1720s visitors reported statues, a rockwork fountain, waterfalls, summer houses, and winding walks among the old trees in Ray Wood. This sounds very much like a precursor of the 18th-century landscape garden and many garden historians have described it as such. Many of the ingredients of Ray Wood are those of formal gardens of its time but it is the winding walks, the irregular disposition of ornamental incidents, the maintaining of the ancient trees, and the views of the surrounding countryside that make it novel. In *Ichnographia Rustica* (1718) Stephen SWITZER describes Ray Wood where 'Nature is ruly imitated, if not excell'd, and from which the Ingenious may draw the best of their Schemes in Natural and Rural Gardening'. Also at this time great buildings were being planned for the greater landscape, remarkably similar in effect to those of the later landscape parks. In 1714 Vanbrugh designed an obelisk (30 m/100 ft high) west of the house to stand on a north-south avenue and indicate the entrance avenue eastwards to the house. At the southern end of the north-south avenue Vanbrugh designed in 1719 a monumental entrance arch, precisely aligned on the obelisk, and surmounted by a pyramid. East of the house, on the edge of Ray Wood, Vanbrugh designed a Temple of the Four Winds which was built between 1724 and 1728. Later on Hawksmoor also designed buildings in the landscape—a pyramid to the south of the house in 1728 and, most spectacularly, a great mausoleum in the park east of the house completed in 1729. This last was so loved by Horace Walpole that he wrote that it 'would tempt one to be buried alive'. Today the giant landscape remains ornamented by its great buildings. The fine remains of a formal garden by W. A. NESFIELD spread out south of the house and there is a good modern rose garden. Ray Wood still has serpentine paths but is now enlivened by a remarkable collection of trees and shrubs built up with the advice of James Russell since 1975.   PT

CHARLES SAUMAREZ SMITH, *The Building of Castle Howard* (1990).

Castle Kennedy ✤

near Stranraer, Wigtownshire, Scotland, has a vast designed landscape extending to over 900 hectares/2,223 acres. The position of the chief parts of the gardens is very beautiful, a broad undulating strip of land between two lochs, the Black Loch (also known as Loch Crindil) and the White Loch (or Loch of Inch). There are two castles here, one at each end of the strip. The 15th-century castle of the Kennedy family was burnt out in 1716 and its picturesque ruins rise up at the southern end of the strip. At the opposite end, in a wooded hollow, is Lochinch Castle, built in Scottish baronial style in the 1860s for the Dalrymple family (earls of Stair) who had acquired the estate in 1677. Between 1722 and 1750 a new garden was made for the 2nd Earl of Stair, a soldier who had risen to the rank of field marshal in the Marlborough campaigns and was ambassador to the French court in 1715. It seems likely that the gardens were designed by the architect William ADAM who also designed gardens for the Earl of Stair at Newliston, his estate near Edinburgh. It is also possible that they were designed by the nurseryman William BOUTCHER about whom very little is known. At all events, a garden was made even though there was no house on the estate and the family had to rent a house elsewhere. The land was shaped into a series of banks, mounds, and terraces some of which were named after Lord Stair's military exploits, such as Mount Marlborough and Dettingen Avenue. Such large-scale shaping of the land was unprecedented although, knowing Lord Stair's French connection, it is tempting to seek some influence there, but it is wholly unlike French gardens of the early 18th century. The gardens became famous in their day—a visitor described them in 1744 as 'one of the most charmingest places ever I saw'. By the end of the 18th century they had become neglected and were restored and replanted in 1840 under the supervision of J. C. LOUDON. There was much new planting in the garden at this time, in particular of newly introduced exotics such as monkey-puzzles (*Araucaria araucana*) and *Rhododendron arboreum*. The garden today retains the early 18th-century terracing and mounds which extend on the slopes about the 18th-century Round Pond, a 0.8-hectare/2-acre formal pool which is now enclosed in thickets of rhododendrons. The 19th-century overlay, which includes a splendid if intermittently wind-damaged avenue of monkey-puzzles, makes a striking contrast to the austere 18th-century gardens. Among the flowering shrubs are fine camellias, embothriums, eucryphias, magnolias, and many rhododendrons. Below the ruins of the old castle is a walled garden built in around 1607 which still has the remains of summer houses of the same period built into two corners. Double borders, laid out in the late 20th century, decorate the garden.   PT

Castlewellan National Arboretum ⊛
Castlewellan, County Down, Northern Ireland. The Annesley family bought the Castlewellan estate in 1741 and lived in a farmhouse until they built the present baronial mansion in 1856 to the designs of William Burn (1789–1870). In 1740 William Annesley built a brick-walled kitchen garden which in the 19th century became richly planted pleasure grounds with glasshouses. William, the 4th Earl Annesley, transformed the gardens in the 19th century, introducing a flood of new plants. Among these were the fashionable conifers of the day, in particular those, like the Wellingtonia (*Sequoiadendron giganteum*), from the newly explored Pacific north-west coast of America. Later in the century the 5th Earl added immensely to the collection which became one of the finest collections of trees and shrubs in Ireland. The climate here, quite close to the sea, is generally benign but in the bitter winter of 1895–6 over 1,000 species were killed. Today, the collection is once again enormous. The old walled garden, now named the Annesley Garden, is a treasure trove of rare species enlivened by a pair of fine borders and a noble tiered Italian fountain. Tender plants like the Madeiran *Echium pininana* sow themselves here and the lovely Himalayan *Cornus capitata* thrives. Outside the walled garden is a woodland garden of azaleas, camellias, and rhododendrons among old beech and oak. The banks of the lake are planted with deciduous trees chosen for the splendour of their autumn colour. The demesne, covering an area of 460 hectares/1,136 acres, has been a National Forest Park since 1969.   PT

Castries, Château de ⊛
Castries, Hérault, France, a medieval castle rebuilt in the 17th century for René Gaspard de Lacroix (later Marquis de Castries) who became governor of Montpellier. The small garden is sometimes attributed to André LE NÔTRE although there is no hard evidence, nor does an attribution on the basis of style seem convincing when one sees the site as it is today. A PARTERRE *de broderie* planted with box is laid out on a terrace (laid out in 1930 but apparently based on the original design) and a second parterre has two circular fountain pools. On the ground below the terrace is a large circular pool and an avenue. In 1670 an aqueduct was built, attributed to the engineer of the Canal du Midi, Pierre-Paul Riquet, bringing water from Fontgrand, 7 km/4 m away, to irrigate the chateau gardens.   PT

Catesby, Mark
(1682–1749), plant collector, naturalist, and artist born in Suffolk. His interest in natural history was encouraged by Revd John Ray (1686–1704). At the age of 30 Catesby visited Virginia from where he collected and dispatched seeds to Bishop COMPTON and Thomas FAIRCHILD. Two years later in 1714 he travelled to Jamaica where he again returned with plant material and a growing reputation as an authority on American natural history. Consequently, in 1722, a syndicate of patrons supported his plant collecting to the Carolinas and Bahamas for four years. Travelling out Catesby took with him European plant material to distribute to his American friends. He returned with extensive collections of plants and animals, and these, with his notes and drawings, formed the basis of his pioneering two-volume *Natural History of Carolina, Florida, and the Bahama Islands* (1730–47).   MC-C

Caus, Isaac de
(b. *c.*1590), French Huguenot architect, engineer, maker of automata, and designer of grottoes, younger brother of Salomon de CAUS. He worked at Whitehall Palace (London), Moor Park (Hertfordshire), WILTON HOUSE (his masterpiece), and WOBURN ABBEY. The grotto he designed for Woburn Abbey, completed before 1627, survives in remarkably complete state—a very rare survival from this period. At Wilton fragments only of another grotto remain. In 1638 he designed a house and garden for Richard Boyle, 1st Earl of Cork, in Dorset, of which nothing is known.   PT

Caus, Salomon de
(*c.*1576–1626) French Huguenot author, garden designer, and hydraulic engineer, elder brother of Isaac de CAUS. A specialist in elaborate waterworks, he worked on several gardens in England, most notably at Greenwich Palace (London), HATFIELD HOUSE, Richmond Palace (Surrey), and Somerset House (London). Around 1600 he worked at Brussels for the Archduke Albert where he built shellwork grottoes, with waterworks and automata, and renovated the 16th-century garden at Brussels Court. He was the author of *La Perspective avec les raisons des ombres et miroirs* (1612) and *Les Raisons des forces mouvantes* (1615). In 1613 he went to work on the HORTUS PALATINUS at Heidelberg where he was in charge of both the buildings and the gardens, illustrated in his book *Hortus Palatinus* (1620).   PT

Celle, Parco ⊛
Santomato di Pistoia, Tuscany, Italy. A 17th-century villa and garden complex built by Cardinal Carlo Agostino Fabroni was extended as a romantic landscape from 1818 by the architect Gambini under Count Caselli, who installed a naturalistic lake, island, and temple, a waterfall and rustic bridge, and an Egyptian monument. A neo-Gothic Temple of the Spring was built by Ferdinando Marini. Owned by Giuliano Gori since 1969 it has proved the perfect setting for modern sculpture. Amongst the displays are a labyrinth by Robert Morris, an *anfiteatro* by Beverley Pepper (b. 1924), two pieces of a gigantic head transfixed by the arrows of Hercules and Apollo and variations by Fausto Melotti (1901–86), and a group of geometric metal sculptures rising from the lake.   PHo

Celsa, Castello di ⊛
Siena, Tuscany, Italy. The 16th-century garden, probably designed by the great Sienese architect Baldassare Peruzzi (1481–1537), has disappeared, overlaid by a formal parterre today displaying the Aldobrandini coat of arms in a box pattern, leaving only the elegant circular chapel as a record of the architect's work. Seventeenth-century designs for imposing gateways and a new pool mark the transition from fortress to villa. In the same century a semicircular balustraded NYMPHAEUM was erected on the wood's edge, its site at the top of a steep ascent marked by rides cut through the oak woods, as a PATTE D'OIE. As Georgina Masson points out in *Italian Gardens* (1961), the rides were not only ornamental but made it easier to capture the numerous bandits who lurked in the thick woods. Cypress hedges, clipped into trim swags, line the approach through a meadow of wildflowers.   PHo

cemetery.
The burial of the dead in some special place is a very ancient practice, extending far into prehistoric times. In the Christian tradition the church, and later the churchyard—consecrated ground—was in the past the usual place of burial. The word cemetery, derived from the Greek for a dormitory, originally had the meaning of a churchyard but, with the laying out of burial grounds not attached to a church, the term cemetery acquired a new meaning. The impulse to find a substitute for churchyards came in the 19th century when the expanding urban population, and anxieties about public health, led to the creation of cemeteries on

spacious new sites often in the suburbs of towns or entirely outside them. The great period for the laying out of cemeteries of this kind was the first half of the 19th century. Their atmosphere was carefully considered, with practicalities, landscape aesthetics, and the emotions of the bereaved taken into consideration and often skilfully interwoven.

In France in 1804 a law was passed which forbade burials within the city of Paris. In the same year the city acquired an estate which had belonged to the Jesuits in which Father François de La Chaise had lived in the 17th century. The cemetery of Père Lachaise (see PARIS PARKS AND GARDENS) designed c.1810 by Alexandre-Théodore Brongniart (1739–1813) was built on the site and conceived as a picturesque landscape enlivened by ornamental buildings. Its later extension, and overcrowding in the original section, has caused the loss of some of its original Arcadian character but it contains exceptionally fine monuments. In Britain the first cemeteries of the modern kind were a little later. Their character and appearance were subtly contrived—of Highgate Cemetery (1839, London) the *Lady's Newspaper* (1850) wrote, 'In such a place the aspect of death is softened'. There was also an occasional anxiety about social class. Of London Road Cemetery (1845, Coventry), designed by Sir Joseph PAXTON, a contemporary wrote that it had 'more the air of a gentleman's park than a city of the dead' (quoted in *London Road Cemetery*, c.1994). In 1828 the Necropolis was opened in Glasgow designed by David Mylne on a dramatic hilltop, and it later acquired superb monuments commemorating the Glasgow great and good. The Dean Cemetery (1845) in Edinburgh on the banks of the Water of Leith had as its site the pleasure grounds of the 17th-century Dean House. It retains much of its 19th-century planting of holly and yew and weeping forms of ash, cherry, and oak. Trees were an important ingredient of the Abney Park Cemetery (1840, Hackney, London) and were supplied by the great local nurseryman George Loddiges (see LODDIGES, JOACHIM CONRAD). In the USA a pioneer cemetery with a rural setting was MOUNT AUBURN which dates from 1831 and has a fine collection of trees. LEXINGTON CEMETERY, opened in 1849, was founded after an outbreak of cholera and has the character of an arboretum with a notable collection of trees native to the southern states. One of the best-known 20th-century cemeteries is the Forest Lawn Memorial Park Cemetery founded in 1917 at Glendale, California. These lavishly designed grounds, with an area of 121 hectares/300 acres, were ornamented with decorative buildings, including several non-denominational chapels, including the 'Wee Kirk o' the Heather'. Today,

with several branches, the original Forest Lawn at Glendale is notable for the monuments of many figures from the golden age of Hollywood. The novelist Evelyn Waugh was so taken with its 'unsurpassed glories' (as he called them) that he wrote a novel, *The Loved One* (1948), in which it is cheerfully satirized as 'Whispering Glades'. With the great increase in cremation extensive cemetery grounds are not laid out as frequently as they were in the 19th century. New cemeteries tend towards austerity—a far cry from the splendours of the generously conceived 19th-century landscapes. The major English crematorium, at Golders Green (London), was laid out in 1902. Originally it had a pergola designed by William ROBINSON and, although the landscaping today is scarcely exciting, it contains many excellent monuments, among them the Philipson Memorial designed by Sir Edwin LUTYENS in 1938.   PT

Central Park.

See NEW YORK CITY PARKS AND GARDENS; OLMSTED, FREDERICK LAW.

Cerceau, Jacques Androuet du.

See DU CERCEAU, JACQUES ANDROUET.

Cerro Santa Lucia, Parque del ⊛

Santiago de Chile, Chile, with an area of 3.76 hectares/9.2 acres in the heart of the city. It was presented as a public park by Benjamin Vicuña Mackenna to the city of Santiago in 1875. The layout includes two defensive terraces built by the Spanish conquistador Pedro de Valdivia in 1542. The transformation of the Santa Lucia Hill, a barren site turned into a substantial park, was initiated in 1872 at the same time as the most ambitious plan for the modernizing of Santiago that had ever been undertaken to that date. Vicuña Mackenna, then the regional governor, was a man with varied abilities and interests as a politician, social reformer, writer, and historian. He travelled extensively through Europe and the United States, always taking notice of the advanced urban experiences in those places. The ambitious project included garden pavilions, a restaurant, a chapel, and the first historical museum to be established in Chile. The creation of the Santa Lucia Promenade was the first of a series of initiatives for the public use of the hills which are such a feature of the site. In 1936 Oscar Prager finished a project for the southern slope of the hill which descends to the Alameda, one of the most important streets in the layout of Santiago. The gardens he laid out, with descending ramps and stairs, stand in great contrast to the picturesque paths and grottoes of Vicuña Mackenna's plan.

Native trees intermingled with Mediterranean flora cover the rocky slopes.   MV

Cetinale, Villa Chigi ⊛

Soviceville, Tuscany, Italy. In the 17th century the villa, originally not much more than a farmhouse set among extensive oak woods and arable land south-west of Siena, was expanded to become a symbol of the power and prestige of the Sienese banking family of Chigi. Cardinal Flavio Chigi, nephew of the Chigi Pope, Alexander VII (1655–77), retired there and employed the Roman architect Carlo Fontana (1638–1714) to add an imposing double marble staircase to the west façade and to embellish the garden with a walled grass ALLÉE, the width of the staircase, which leads the eye between brick gate piers, framed by copies of 15th-century Romanian statues. The alley narrows up a gentle slope to widen at the base of a steep wooded hill into a semicircular 'theatre' lined with busts. Today cypresses flank the steps that lead upwards to the Hermitage, or Romitorio, finished by Fontana in 1713. The Cardinal, anxious to atone for his profligate youth, also created a penitentiary Thebaïd in the adjacent woods, with green rides cutting through the dark mysterious BOSCO following a series of votive chapels decorated with frescoes representing the Seven Sorrows of the Virgin. An avenue of clipped ilex leads from the east face of the villa across a ravine to a massive statue of Hercules.

The original approach from Siena was from the west following the contours at the base of the hermitage hill, to allow a first view of the main façade, but today visitors come through the village and enter through the 19th-century Italian garden where lemons in pots, clipped Portugal laurel, and evergreen viburnums sit between statues by Giuseppe Mazzuoli (1644–1725). Since 1976 Cetinale has been the property of Lord Lambton and Clare Ward. Showing total respect for Fontana's original design, chapel, clock tower, stonework, and terraces have been repaired, the Thebaïd cleared of undergrowth, and, most recently, the Hermitage (or Romitorio) sensitively restored. A flower garden below the south side of the villa, started by the English mother of a Chigi marquis in the early 20th century, has been expanded to make one of the most successful 'English' gardens in Italy. With axial paths and arbours, roses, peonies, irises, and perennials weave a rich exciting scented pattern, overlooked by a giant wisteria which drapes the villa. A further project by Lord Lambton includes extending the 17th-century garden, never completed by Fontana, below the green *allée*. Formal walks of clipped box and ilex enclose garden 'rooms' where fruit trees are

sculptures, walkways, and the castle on top of the hill. An expanse of natural forest on Grasshopper Hill (Cerro del Chapulín) is densely planted with, among other trees, *Taxodium mucronatum*. From the pre-Hispanic period until the 19th century springs at Chapultepec supplied water for the inhabitants of Mexico.   SAO/LTT

Charleston ⊛

near Firle, Lewes, East Sussex, England, is a 17th-century country house discovered in 1916 by Leonard and Virginia Woolf where Vanessa Bell, Duncan Grant, and David Garnett lived, in various permutations, over the years. It became the country seat of the Bloomsbury group and remains a most vivid introduction to their ideas and way of life. The old walled garden was taken over in the 1920s by Roger Fry who had a special interest in gardening. He laid out the gravel paths, box hedging, and ebullient borders which are garnished with all manner of decoration—a terrace inlaid with broken china, masks gazing from the walls, and a Venus lurking under an apple tree. Outside the walled garden a duck pond is overlooked by statues by Quentin Bell, a reclining but levitating woman, a torso made of carved bricks, and a concrete Pomona. The interior of the house, with original furniture, books, and painted panelling and furniture, adds to one's understanding of Bloomsbury, and there are lovely elevated views of the garden. It is the ensemble, house, contents, and garden, that gives Charleston its interest and charm—the perfect introduction to the Bloomsbury spirit.
PT

QUENTIN BELL and VIRGINIA NICHOLSON, *Charleston: A Bloomsbury House and Garden* (2003).

Charlottenburg ⊛

Berlin, Germany. The Elector Friedrich III of Brandenburg, who was crowned the first King of Prussia (as Friedrich I) at Königsberg in 1701, built the Schloss (1695 onwards), which at the time was still known as Lietzenburg, for his wife Sophie Charlotte, the daughter of the Electress Sophie of Hanover who had laid out the famous garden at HERRENHAUSEN. Like her mother, Sophie Charlotte was a close friend of the philosopher Leibniz and was known as 'the philosophical Queen'.

The large baroque garden was laid out on Sophie Charlotte's instructions by Siméon Godeau, a disciple of LE NÔTRE, and is the first example of the French style in northern Germany. A large *bassin* (formal pool), fed from the river edging the garden on two sides, was constructed at the end of the unusual large parterre, which was flanked by avenues laid out in rows of four; beyond the parterre on the west side were BOSQUETS. Many statues stood on the terrace in front of the Schloss and in front of the orangery at the side of the main building. Charlottenburg, which at the time stood outside the gates of Berlin, was the favourite summer residence of Friedrich and Sophie Charlotte, who enjoyed the view into the surrounding countryside from the Schloss over the TAPIS VERT and through a wide cutting in the woods.

Under Friedrich Wilhelm II (1786–97) and Friedrich Wilhelm III (1797–1840) the garden was transformed in landscape style, largely by Peter Joseph LENNÉ; the parterre was completely rearranged and the *bassin* naturalized as a lake.

There are three outstanding buildings in the park: the belvedere, built under Friedrich Wilhelm II by the architect C. G. Langhans, which today houses a collection of porcelain; the mausoleum, built as a temple to a design of Heinrich Gentz by Friedrich Wilhelm III after the death of his wife Luise; and the pavilion designed by SCHINKEL, built by Friedrich Wilhelm III in the eastern part of the garden as a continuation of the terrace. Both the Schloss and the garden suffered extensive damage in the Second World War, but the Schloss has been completely restored. The restoration followed the conception of the Lenné garden, except the parterre and the western *bosquets*, which were reconstructed to baroque designs.
UD/MS

Chase Garden ⊛

Orting, Washington, USA, was developed by Ione and Emmott Chase from 1962 onwards in an area of 1.82 hectares/4.5 acres, and constitutes an exceptional example of a modern north-west garden. The garden is arranged as a series of zones attesting to the owners' interests in traditional Japanese garden design traditions and Pacific north-west flora. The owners hauled in large rocks from the Puyallup river, collected seed from the local forest, and propagated native plants. A curving drive through stands of second growth trees leads to the single-storey house, inspired by Japanese buildings, sited at the top of a steep bank and commanding a sweeping view of Mount Rainier. The modernist entrance garden was designed by Rex Zumwalt and installed by the owners. Two small reflecting pools, narrow decking, and a dry stream bed in an area of pea-gravel evoke a Japanese KARESANSUI garden. A deep porch at one end of the house overlooks a large sloping meadow. This is a poetic evocation of an Alpine meadow and its large irregular beds are filled with drifts of geraniums, hypericums, iberis, dianthus, phlox, dragon's blood, veronica, helianthemum, and alpine plants. Specimen maples and a grove of aspens frame the view toward Mount Rainier. A stand of second growth Douglas firs, cedars, and hemlocks was retained and complemented with an understorey of native shrubs with snowdrops, false Solomon seal (*Smilacina racemosa*), wild ginger (*Asarum canadense*), fawn lily (*Erythronium californicum*), trilliums, and other low-growing native plants.   DCS

Chasma Shahi ⊛

Srinagar, Kashmir. Built in 1632, the garden is veined by a waterway that springs from a natural source in the highest pavilion, symbolizing a grotto and laid out on three terraces along the slopes. The waterway passes under a second Kashmiri-style pavilion resting on a 6-m/20-ft high retaining wall, and flows down a slide (*mahepusht*) on the lowest terrace, from which one has an exceptional view of Lake Dal. The trees are not original and somewhat recall an Italian garden, while the Mughal contribution is related to the architecture and hydraulic works. The flower garden, mainly of lilacs, is noteworthy, and has fruit trees on the lower terrace near the entrance.   AP

S. CROWE and S. HAYWOOD, *The Gardens of Mughul India* (1972).

E. B. MOYNIHAN (ed.), *Paradise as a Garden in Persia and Mughal India* (1979).

C. M. VILLIERS STUART, *Gardens of the Great Mughals* (1913).

Chateaubriand, Maison de ⊛

Châtenay-Malabry, Hauts-de-Seine, France. The statesman and writer François-René Vicomte de Chateaubriand came to live here, which he renamed La Vallée aux Loups (Wolf Valley), in 1807 and remained (usually spending the winters in Paris) until 1818 when, to his intense regret, debts forced him to sell. In his *Mémoires d'outre-tombe* (published in its entirety only in 1902) he described his passionate affection for the estate, especially for the trees which he had planted. Of his pines, firs, larches, and cedars he wrote in his *Mémoires*, 'je les connais tous par leurs noms, comme mes enfants: c'est ma famille, je n'en ai pas d'autre, j'espère mourir auprès d'elle' (I know them all by their names, like my children: it is my family, I have no other, I hope to die beside it). He planted many other trees—catalpas, cedars of Lebanon, magnolias, and tulip trees—and cared for them meticulously. The house faces down a broad valley with lawns and trees encircled by a gravel walk. On one side is a curious 18th-century building which Chateaubriand used as his writing room and named the Tour Velleda. The finest trees surviving from Chateaubriand's time are some superb cedars of Lebanon. This unspoilt and atmospheric place has charm intermingled with melancholy.   PT

Chatsworth ⊛

Bakewell, Derbyshire, England, was acquired by the Cavendish family (later dukes of Devonshire) in the 16th century. In the late 17th and early 18th centuries the house and garden were transformed for the 1st and 2nd Dukes into an estate of ducal splendour. The house was rebuilt by William Talman and Thomas ARCHER and by 1690 George LONDON had designed a new parterre and a little later Henry WISE also designed a parterre. By 1696 a great formal cascade designed by a Frenchman, Monsieur Grillet, had been laid out east of the house. The KIP engraving of Chatsworth in *Britannia Illustrata* (1707) shows one of the most elaborate English gardens of its date. The London and Wise parterres spread out close to the house with, on the slightly rising ground to the east, a dazzling array of formal gardens. A long canal between the house and the river Derwent, and avenues in all directions, extend the garden's axes into the greater landscape. From 1755 this great scheme began to be undone by Capability BROWN. A painting by William Marlow of *c.*1760 shows the house set in a naturalistic landscape with the river widened, and its banks on the house side graded. A little later, by 1764, a noble three-arched bridge by James PAINE had been built to take the drive over the river. In 1826 Joseph PAXTON came to work at Chatsworth as head gardener at a salary of £70 (around £2,500 today) plus a cottage. Paxton, working with Sir Jeffry Wyattville, restored formal terraced gardens close to the house, in particular the West Terrace with its topiary of gold and common box. Paxton also added a PINETUM in 1829 and in 1835 an ARBORETUM with over 1,500 species of trees. One of Paxton's great interests was glasshouses and he introduced several at Chatsworth, some of which were for growing cucumbers, grapes, peaches, and pineapples. Increasingly, tender ornamental exotics, such as orchids, were grown and glasshouses were needed for them. In 1836 the foundations were laid for the Great Conservatory, designed by Paxton in association with Decimus Burton (1800–81). This, the largest glasshouse in Britain in its day, housed a tropical garden and was 0.3 hectare/0.75 acre in area. Charles Darwin visited it in 1845 and wrote, 'more wonderfully like tropical nature than I could have conceived possible—Art beats nature altogether here'. Its stoves consumed 300 tons of coal a year, more than was needed to heat Chatsworth House. The Great Conservatory was demolished in 1920. There was much garden activity in the late 20th century with a new rose garden in front of a 1690s conservatory, double rows of pleached limes flanking the canal south of the house, CRINKLE-CRANKLE beech hedges planted by the 11th Duke and Duchess in 1953, and much new planting. The garden shows features ranging from a 16th-century banqueting house to fine modern sculptures by artists such as Angela Conner. Today, with 40 hectares/100 acres of finely kept garden, Chatsworth is one of the best-run and most attractive estates open to the public in the country.   PT

The Duchess of Devonshire, *The Garden at Chatsworth* (1999).

Johannes Kip's engraving of the gardens at **Chatsworth** from *Britannia Illustrata* (1707).

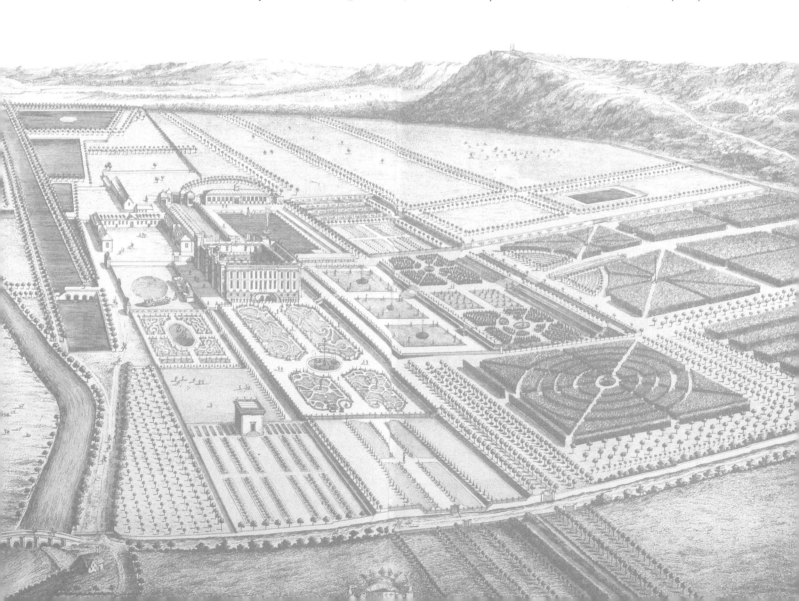

Chatto, Beth

(b. 1923), English author, gardener, and nurserywoman who made her garden and nursery in Essex, BETH CHATTO GARDENS, a mecca for gardeners seeking good plants and an understanding of how to use them in their gardens. Between 1977 and 1986 her exhibits won a gold medal every year at Chelsea. This was partly because of the quality and interest of her plants but also because of the seductive, and at that time novel, way in which they were displayed—in naturalistic groups as though snatched from the ground moments before. Among her excellent books are *The Dry Garden* (1978), *The Damp Garden* (1982), and *Beth Chatto's Gravel Garden* (2000). She popularized many good plants and taught a generation of gardeners to attach more importance to the sites of their plants. For her, gardening is more than merely a hobby: 'The dedication and devotion needed, and the response from plants, provides both solace and inspiration, supportive through many crises that inevitably come in the course of life.' PT

Chatto, Beth, Gardens ⊛

Elmstead Market, Colchester, Essex, England, started in 1967, combining a commercial plant nursery and gardens in which the plants sold could be seen performing. The primacy of a plant's site rules both nursery and gardens. In the nursery plants are grouped according to the site they prefer. The gardens provide two radically different kinds of site. The first was made by constructing a series of pools out of a drainage ditch shaded by old alders, oaks, and willows. Here Beth Chatto was gradually able to make a garden in which shade- and moisture-loving plants would flourish. About the edges of the pools are communities of ferns, *Gunnera tinctoria*, *Iris sibirica*, *Lysichiton americanus*, and Himalayan primulas. In 1991 a second garden was made, a gravel garden which would have no artificial irrigation, depending only on rainfall, which in these parts, at around 50 cm/20 in per annum, is the lowest in Britain. Here she planted naturalistic drifts of alliums, *Artemisia*, cistus, grasses, lavenders, and lilies in lavish profusion, with many plants allowed to self-seed. The principle throughout the gardens is that plants should always be chosen for their site. But there is also an aesthetic point—that plants coming from similar natural habitats not only flourish together but also look well together. PT

Chaumont-sur-Loire, Château de ⊛

Chaumont-sur-Loire, Loir-et-Cher, France. The site goes back to the 10th century when the Comte de Blois built a lookout tower commanding the river. The present chateau, which has had many owners, is largely of the 15th and 16th centuries with later additions. Nothing is known of the early garden history of Chaumont before Henri DUCHÊNE laid out a *parc à l'anglaise* in around 1900. Since 1992 Chaumont has organized the annual Festival International des Jardins which takes place from May to October. A site designed by Jacques WIRTZ has 30 spaces enclosed in beech hedges, each of an area of 240 sq. m/2,350 sq. ft, in which garden designers are invited to submit designs in accordance with an annual theme. The theme for 2004 was 'Vive le chaos: ordre et désordre au jardin' (long live chaos: order and disorder in the garden) and earlier themes have included 'MOSAÏCULTURE', 'erotism in the garden', and 'weeds in the garden'. The maximum budget for each garden is 12,000 euros. At the end of each festival the gardens are usually destroyed although, exceptionally, a particularly successful one may be kept. The prevailing spirit of the exhibits is one of innovation, youthful exuberance, and perhaps a touch of *épater le bourgeois*. As a way of refreshing ideas about garden design it is an attractive and salutary influence. PT

Cheere, John

(1709-87), English sculptor and maker of garden statuary who took over the Hyde Park (London) business of the van Nost family (see NOST, JOHN VAN) in 1737. Cheere became the most prolific caster of lead garden ornaments of his time. By 1751 he had taken over two other statuary yards in the Hyde Park area. He supplied ornaments to many notable gardens of the day—among them BOWOOD, CASTLE HOWARD, HAMPTON COURT PALACE, STOURHEAD, and WILTON. One of the largest surviving groups of Cheere figures still in the garden for which they were made may be seen at QUELUZ in Portugal. Towards the latter part of the 18th century, with the craze for landscape parks, the demand for statuary dwindled. PT

JOHN DAVIS, *Antique Garden Ornament* (1991).

Chehel Sotun ⊛

Isfahan, Iran. Although originally part of the garden complex behind the ALI QAPU PALACE, the Chehel Sotun Palace (the Forty Columns) and garden layout were not completed until the reign of Shah Abbas II (1641-68). The building was restored after a fire in 1706. The name derives from the projecting *talar* (hall) in front of the building, supported by twenty carved plane tree columns, which when mirrored in the long pool, seem to be 40. A smaller marble basin, filled by spouts from stone lions supporting the columns, lies under the wooden roof. A typical construction derived from Timurid open plan pavilions, this Safavid palace has a minimum of weight-bearing walls, with building and garden flowing together. It was described in some detail by Sir John Chardin, the 17th-century Anglo-French traveller, as 'the largest and most lavish' of the buildings in the royal enclosure (*Voyages en Perse*, 1811). Although the water rill around the pavilion is now dry, the main tank still survives and alleys of elms and plane trees provide welcome shade in the garden. The interior rooms have become part of a museum with the restored Safavid frescoes on display. PHo

Chelsea Physic Garden ⊛

London, England, was founded in 1673 by the Society of Apothecaries for the cultivation of medicinal plants—after OXFORD BOTANIC GARDEN the second oldest botanic garden in Britain. Hans SLOANE, who bought the manor of Chelsea in 1712, granted the society a perpetual lease on the 1.6-hectare/4-acre site in 1722 at a fixed annual rent of £5 provided that it was 'kept up and maintained by the Company as a physick garden'. The garden is still owned and maintained by the society. An engraving by John Haynes shows the garden in 1751 in its heyday: an irregular plan divided by a central walk with a statue of Sir Hans Sloane (as he then was) by Michael Rysbrack at its centre. The garden was laid out in a four-part arrangement with two wildernesses 'where many kinds of trees grow' with winding paths, a pool with cedars of Lebanon on each corner, and rows of order beds (see BOTANIC GARDEN). Philip MILLER had been appointed gardener in 1722, remaining here until 1770 during which time he reigned over the garden's greatest period. Other distinguished botanists worked here, among them William Forsyth, William Curtis, and Robert FORTUNE. In the 19th century the garden began to lose its importance but in the late 20th century it underwent a renaissance. Today the garden is well maintained and presents a charming oasis in its walled seclusion by the river Thames. Its garden of ethnobotany, the first in the country, reflects a renewed interest in natural medicine. PT

Chenonceaux, Château de ⊛

Bléré, Indre-et-Loire, France. The site goes back to the 13th century but the present chateau, apart from a 15th-century donjon (the Tour des Marques), dates entirely from the 16th century. It is a delightful building whose charm is increased by its position jutting out into the river Cher. It is extended by a galleried bridge designed by Philibert de L'ORME and built 1556-9 shortly after the estate was given to

Diane de Poitiers by her lover Henri II. From 1551 Diane de Poitiers had a new garden laid out on a raised rectangular platform, 1 hectare/2.5 acres in area, surrounded by a moat to the north-east of the chateau. A drawing by DU CERCEAU shows the garden divided into four by ALLÉES of trees, with each quarter further divided into six rectangular beds. The detailed planting is uncertain but records show the purchase of many fruit trees at this time, as well as such ornamentals as lilies, musk roses, and violets, and part of the garden was given over to vegetables. Du Cerceau's drawing also shows a long approach avenue from the north, which records show was planted with elms and evergreen oaks. It is aligned with the chateau and bridge and the axis is continued on the south bank of the river, where it is flanked by two square gardens divided into rectilinear patterns. This axis, and indeed traces of the garden on the south bank, is visible in a modern aerial photograph. Today, the site of Diane de Poitiers's garden survives, but the space is divided in an entirely different way and the topiary of clipped yew, *broderie* (see PARTERRE) of santolina, and the use of bedding plants owes more to 20th-century municipal planting than to the Renaissance. West of the chateau forecourt the site of a garden made by Catherine de Médicis, after 1559, has a rather simpler modern layout with a central circular pool and segments of lawns edged in narrow beds.   PT

Cheval, Palais Idéal du Facteur ⊛
Hauterives, Ardèche, France, the creation between 1879 and 1912 of Joseph-Ferdinand Cheval, the village postman (*facteur*), who made an extraordinary grotto-like garden building of cement encrusted with masks of strange animals, plants, writhing snakes, figures in niches, snarling monsters, and much else. The architecture is busy with crenellated towers, buttresses, archways, finials, pillars, and richly worked cornices, and all manner of inscriptions are worked into the building, many of a religious import. The effect is unforgettable if not exactly beautiful. It was loved by the surrealists but others may feel they are intruding on a private dreamlike world—like trespassing on a psychoanalytic session.
PT

Chèvreloup, Arboretum de ⊛
Le Chesnay, Yvelines, France. This has its origins in the *plaine de Chèvreloup*, land to the north of the Domaine de VERSAILLES bought by Louis XIV in 1699. At first it was used as a farm and there was a reservoir, which still survives, in which to accumulate water from Marly for the Grand Canal at Versailles. The original

enclosing walls built by Louis XIV also survive. Louis XV made a botanic garden at the Trianon advised by the botanist Bernard de Jussieu, who also planted trees at Chèvreloup. A beautiful *Sophora japonica* planted by him in 1747 was destroyed in the great storm of December 1999 when 1,700 mature trees in the arboretum were lost. The land at Chèvreloup was given to the Muséum National de l'Histoire Naturelle in 1927, but plans to develop the arboretum were interrupted by the Second World War, and it was not until the 1960s that the arboretum assumed its modern character. The area of the arboretum is 200 hectares/494 acres which is divided into three. The largest section (120 hectares/300 acres) groups hardy trees and shrubs by region of origin with some very large collections—500 species from China, 700 from the USA, and 160 from Japan and Korea. In all there are 2,700 taxa of woody plants. Many species are rare or threatened such as *Abies chensiensis* (from China), *Prumnopitys andina* (from Chile), and *Abies nebrodensis* (Sicily). Large glasshouses protect a very wide range of tropical plants, over 5,000 taxa, from both arid and humid habitats. The third department, Production Horticole, is responsible for the propagation of ornamental plants for the public gardens at the Jardin des Plantes (see PARIS PARKS AND GARDENS). The site of Chèvreloup is a fine one, high and airy, with a handsomely undulating terrain.   PT

Chicago Botanic Garden ⊛
Glencoe, Illinois, USA, situated in 156 hectares/385 acres north of the city, was created by the Chicago Horticultural Society in 1965, and opened to the public in 1972 as a permanent site for plant collections, research, and education, with an emphasis on suitability to the growing conditions of the mid-western United States. The mid-west has a challenging climate, with temperatures ranging from a maximum of 40 °C/104 °F to a minimum of -33 °C/-27 °F, relatively little snow cover, and an abundance of wind over mostly flat terrain. The soil for the most part is heavy clay and alkaline. One of the botanic garden's focuses is to acquire genetically superior plants for the mid-western USA; and its collections are representative of plants found in an analogous climate band worldwide.

The garden's property is unusual for its large amount of water. Display gardens are set on a series of islands in lakes created by the Skokie river. Experiments and research in waterside planting help to educate the public, a valuable resource in the mid-west, celebrated for its abundance of magnificent lakes. Also of special note among the native habitats at the garden

are a 40-hectare/100-acre oak woodland and a 6-hectare/15-acre prairie. Woodland of white oak (*Quercus alba*) was once common in north-eastern Illinois; it now appears only in small patches. The demonstration prairie with its tall grasses and brilliant summer flowers is a magical sample of the habitat that once covered much of Illinois, and now has almost disappeared.   PD

Chicago parks.
In 1837, Chicago's nascent government adopted the motto *Urbs en horto*. This Latin phrase meaning *City in a Garden* proved to be prophetic. Then little more than a muddy village on the edge of the prairie, Chicago went on to establish many of the nation's premier parks and green spaces. In 1849, developer and civic booster John S. Wright envisioned 'a magnificent chain of parks and parkways' encircling the city that have not their equal in the world (reprinted in *Chicago City Manual*, 1914). Wright's idea began taking shape in 1869 when the Illinois legislature established three separate park commissions. The South, West, and Lincoln Park Commissions each created its own portion of a unified park and boulevard system resulting in a legacy of significant and influential green spaces. Frederick Law OLMSTED and Calvert Vaux laid out the magnificent South Park, now known as Washington and Jackson Parks and the Midway Plaisance. The 427-hectare/1,055-acre site still contains shadowy lagoons, winding paths, open meadows, and remnants of the 1893 World's Columbian Exposition, on which Olmsted collaborated with architect and planner Daniel H. Burnham (1846–1912). In 1905, the Olmsted brothers continued building upon their father's tradition, designing fourteen revolutionary south-side parks to provide breathing spaces and social services to the city's growing immigrant community.

Architect and engineer William Le Baron Jenney (1832–1907) developed plans for the city's west-side parks—Humboldt, Garfield, and Douglas. The West Park Commission could only build small phased improvements and Jenney's plans were never fully executed. In 1905, during a period of reform, newly appointed West Park system superintendent Jens JENSEN began making impressive large-scale improvements to the parks. Between 1912 and 1920, Jensen, now considered the doyen of prairie-style landscapes, created his masterpiece—Columbus Park. Jensen created a 58-hectare/144-acre idealized prairie landscape of native trees and shrubs, stepping stone paths, meandering waterway, and waterfalls with walls of stratified limestone. In recent years, Columbus Park

work, while the mention of 'concealed vistas' begins to suggest an increasingly sophisticated handling of nature, both within and beyond the garden wall. From now on, the garden is less a borrowing of nature than an interpretation, an illusion conveyed by skilful manipulation of space and form. From the 5th century Buddhism, gradually spreading into China from the west, also began to affect men's thinking, and Buddhist monasteries set among the hills enhanced the association of nature with spirituality. The example of Vimlakirti also affected gardens. As a householder who achieved Buddhahood by 'remaining unmoved in the midst of movement', he reinforced the indigenous Confucian tradition (so unlike that of Europe's celibate priests) of a married elite—whose gardens were thus used for family parties as well as for contemplation.

In the Tang dynasty (618–907) all this found its perfect—and lasting—expression in the country estate of Wang Wei, a poet, painter, calligrapher, and musician who was himself a devout Buddhist. The scroll painting and poems he kept of his WANG CHUAN VILLA, endlessly copied and recopied down the years, made its gentle hills, its river, and various pavilions bowered in trees some of the best known in the history of Chinese country retreats. Its atmosphere of tranquillity and cultivated scholarship was one which, the modern historian Wango Weng says, 'every Chinese scholar since would like to recreate around him'.

Petromania
Tang gardeners also took another well-established interest to a new level, as well-known public figures, like Niu Sengju and Li Deyu, competed in collecting rare and strangely shaped stones. These they displayed in their gardens in groups or, if they were especially fine, as commanding objects on stands or plinths. Since the Han dynasty, large garden rockeries (*jia shan*)—like the stone cave 'over 200 paces long' in Xiao Yi's Liang dynasty (907–23) garden—had occasionally been recorded, but the unique Chinese passion for collecting and displaying unusual *single* stones (*shi feng*) both big and small, in gardens and on scholars' desks, seems to have taken hold particularly from the Tang. By contrast, the Japanese were to develop a more disinterested attitude and prefer stones of simpler, less extravagant shapes. Later, the Song Emperor Zhaoji (1101–1126) in his garden Genyue, the calligrapher Mi Fei, who bowed to his finest stone and personified it with the honorary title of 'Elder brother', and the Qing dynasty owner of the Banmu Yuan, with its special pavilion to house his collection, all became famous for their love

of stones. From the Song dynasty onwards, no garden was complete without rocks, and in SUZHOU people would 'move houses and rebuild walls to display them'. This southern city, later to surpass all others in the number and standing of its scholars and gardens, had already recorded a famous garden belonging to Ku Pichang in the 4th century. By the 5th century, 'all' of its people were said to 'pile rocks and channel water, plant trees and dig grottoes, and in a short time it all flourishes and looks natural'. During the Five Dynasties period after the fall of Tang, the Wu and Yu kingdoms around Suzhou, by avoiding civil war, became the richest provinces in China. The son of Qian Liu (who ruled them from his capital at Hangzhou) built many terraces and ponds while in charge at Suzhou, and aristocrats and officials followed his lead—among them his General Sun Chengyou who made a garden where the CANGLANGTING now stands.

Golden age of gardens
It is, however, the Song dynasty that is often nostalgically seen as China's golden age of gardens, perhaps because so many were in cities and open to the public on festivals and holidays. But, perhaps also because the standard of achievement under the Song is so extraordinary in all the arts (and particularly in the related area of landscape painting), it seems that gardens too, though only descriptions remain of them (see LUOYANG MINGYUANJI), must have reached a unique level of refinement. Under the following Yuan dynasty private gardens continued to flourish because old families, loyal to the conquered Song, refused to take active political part in the new Mongol government. From this dynasty we have still the name of the Shizilin garden in Suzhou, which, though unrecognizably altered since, was first made by the Yuan painter Ni Zan. By the time the Ming dynasty returned a Chinese emperor to the throne in 1368, the Confucian ideal of the retired scholar-without-portfolio had acquired new strength and, since the Ming was a repressive dynasty, it continued to be acceptable for a gentleman to devote his time, with like-minded friends, to the cultivation of his spiritual, literary, and artistic life in the elegant setting of an urban garden. Men like Wen Cheng-ming developed into major poets, painters, calligraphers, and gardeners while calling themselves amateurs, with only brief and usually unsatisfactory excursions into public office. The Zhouzheng Yuan, partly designed by Wen, still exists, though much changed from the garden he recorded in verse and little paintings soon after its making. But even more important perhaps, for preserving and recording Ming tradition, is the treatise on

gardening *Yuan ye* (Garden Tempering), published in 1634 and the most comprehensive in Chinese. The author states firmly that 'in garden design there are principles but no fixed formulae' and his work aims to teach through suggestion and example rather than by rules. Other important books with chapters on gardening (see LI YU), which continued to classify and regularize the tradition of garden design, also appeared under the Ming and Qing.

In fact, from the mid 16th century private garden making flourished as never before in Beijing, many towns and cities of Jiangnan, and later in Guangzhou (Canton) and the south, and families of master craftsmen in the art of 'piling mountains' grew famous. Though the gardens of the capital seem more stiff and formal than the lyrically graceful southern gardens of Suzhou, the similarity of design in gardens as far apart as Beijing and Taipei is more remarkable than the differences. Those who commissioned them were now sometimes successful merchants as well as gentlemen scholars, and in 1865 Yuan Xuelan described how 'members of rich families compete to embellish pools and pavilions . . . In Spring they open their gardens and people wander in to admire, staying till the moon is full.' Certainly some of these gardens were rather vulgar interpretations of the tradition, built more for praise than personal pleasure, and rather better on lavish general effect than in refinement of detail. Today, the gardens which remain, though they cover a wide range—from Qing imperial parks (like Yihe Yuan) to the private gardens of merchants (like Li Yuan) or of scholars (like WANGSHI YUAN)—have all been greatly altered and restored during their usually long histories. Mostly, after the wars and revolutions of the last 150 years in China, they are urban gardens hidden, except for the topmost branches of their trees, behind high white walls in the midst of cities. The most famous of all are in Suzhou, and, just as it is possible to trace the rise and fall of dynasties by the building and destruction of imperial parks, so the poignant histories of these old private retreats—endlessly neglected, sold or gambled away, rescued, rebuilt, and sold again—reveal the instability of traditional Chinese society.

For foreigners unused to the tradition such a garden may be at first confusing, but it is hardly surprising if a quick tour leads to visual indigestion. Made to be savoured over a lifetime, like Pan En's YU YUAN in Shanghai, they often took a lifetime to make, while for a woman with bound feet in old China, her family garden (if she was lucky enough to have one) might be the sum total of her universe.

The making of a Chinese garden

For the garden maker this is a task that requires not only individual skill and imagination but serious consideration of *feng shui* principles, and a tradition that supports the suspension of disbelief. 'The question of reality will not bother the visitor', says the modern historian Chuin Tung, 'as long as he ceases to be in the *garden* and begins to live in the *painting*.' Just as the connoisseur of painting unwinds a landscape scroll from right to left, and sees the hills and valleys rise and fall around the little human figures travelling through it, so a garden should unfold a series of linked views around the visitor as he strolls along its three-dimensional paths. But the scrolls are linear and the gardens enclosed, and to make the most of each successive vista the garden maker creates a labyrinth, in which available space is layered by gateways and subdivided by walls that wind among the trees and rocks with the regular undulations of sea snakes or dragons. Each garden is a composition of courtyards, some large, some small, some disappearing round corners, some open ended, some cul-de-sacs, some fitted together like pieces of a puzzle. And the visitor is led on through them, not only by pebble-patterned pathways (*luan shi pu di*) and open doorways (*di xue*), but by the constant suggestion of something new and delightful half revealed through the latticed windows (*lou chuang*) or above the walls (*yun qiang*) of the next enclosure.

Rocks and water form the structure of these gardens, then architecture, and only then trees, shrubs, and flowers; for the Chinese word for landscape (*shanshui*) means 'hills and waters' and, while in English we speak of 'planting' a garden, a common phrase for garden making in China translates literally as 'piling rocks and digging ponds'. The two elements are inseparable. Rocks are not only built up into 'false mountains' (*jia shan*) or used singly, like pieces of sculpture (*shi feng*), in the garden, but also represent 'the bony structure of the earth'; as the 'masculine' (*yang*) element—hard, rough, and unmoving—they must, in the Chinese phrase, 'harmonize' with the soft, reflective *yin* of water. *Yin* and *yang*, the two elemental forces which the Chinese see lying behind all creation, are also quite consciously balanced out in the garden as high places lead to low, open to closed, shady to sunny, and wide to narrow, in a finely tuned patterning of opposites. In practice the effect can be almost magical. By leading him on through twisting galleries (*lang*) or over bridges (*qu qiao*), by allowing the glimpse of a distant roof (*lou*; *ge*; *fang*; *xie*; *xuan*), or an end vista (*dui jing*), by turning him back or suggesting a momentary pause (*ting*; *mei ren kao*), or by 'borrowing a view' (*jie jing*; *Ji Chang Yuan*; *Sui Yuan*) beyond the garden wall, the Chinese designer manages so to confuse the visitor that the space of his little garden seems to extend indefinitely.

Trees, shrubs, flowers

Planting increases this layering of space. Obviously there are great regional differences between, for example, plants in a Beijing garden with its dry climate and extreme variations of temperature, and those of the subtropical south, but no garden is complete without the 'Three Friends of Winter'—pine, plum, and bamboo. All old and especially twisted trees, like the junipers in the Yuhua Yuan, are valued for their age and dignity, as are fruit trees—crab apples, persimmon, and peach in Beijing, loquat and kumquat as well as flowering cherries further south. A great many plants, especially *Wisteria sinensis* in Jiangnan, lilacs in the Yi He Yuan, and all the languorous frangipanis of the south, are chosen for their scent, but few for their horticultural novelty.

In fact, though China has one of the richest natural floras in the world, the Chinese do not appreciate plants for their rarity but rather for their accumulated symbolic and literary associations. Among others the lotus, which in summer makes a new, swaying, blue-green surface some 1.2 m/4 ft above the level of garden pools, symbolizes the Buddhist soul rising, in the words of the 11th-century Zhou Tunyi, 'without contamination from the mud, reposing modestly above the clear water, hollow inside and straight without'. Bamboo, which bends with the wind but does not break, suggests an honourable man, and the orchid a true gentleman because it scents a room so subtly nobody notices it until he leaves. The peach, hallowed by centuries of cultivation, lore, and legend, still promises fecundity and immortality; the peony wealth and elegance. Under the Song, peony growing became almost a national obsession, with Luoyang the greatest centre. Today they are mostly grown in raised beds to make a short but dazzling seasonal display. Chrysanthemums, the symbol of autumn, and probably the oldest cultivated flower in China, are grown in pots and set along garden *lang* or formally on the terraces (*tai*) of grander halls (*bian*; *ting*), while pengjing, the Chinese bonsai, tended in special courtyards of their own within the garden, are brought into halls and pavilions to decorate stands and tables often silhouetted in open *lou chang* window frames. There are, however, no open areas of grass. A cultivated Chinese, visiting England in the 1920s, wondered about the appeal of 'a mown and bordered lawn which, while no doubt of interest to a cow, offers nothing to the intellect of a human being'. The Chinese are rice growers, and to them cows can only suggest (if anything) hordes of barbarian cattle raisers riding to plunder peaceful Chinese settlements. In China it is water, not grass, that is the peaceful, contemplative element in a landscape, and at the heart of every garden lies a smooth but rock-bordered pool overhung by latticed balconies from which the visitor can lean out to 'catch the moon in the palm of his hand' on summer nights.

A lawn is also undeniably mindless and a Chinese garden, while a place to 'refresh the heart' by contact with nature, has also to engage the intellect. All the arts come together in the garden—which needs a painter not only to design it, but to appreciate it too, a poet to immortalize it, and a calligrapher to write it down. As far as possible, all these accomplishments were combined in each garden visitor, who, using the *nom de plume* that absolved him from the formalities of life outside, would write poetry with the aid of a little yellow wine, in pleasant competition with his friends or family. These poems, engraved on stone tablets and let into the garden walls, record—from perhaps 50 or 100 years ago—the same sights and sounds that still surround a visitor today. Thus, a Chinese garden gradually acquires an extra dimension over time, while the names of halls and the couplets chosen for tablets (*bian*) on each side of pavilions—names drawn from earlier poems or literary works known to everyone in that highly cultivated society—make another link with great men of the past.

Chinese gardens were not, however, the holy places of hushed reverence this might suggest. Though the intellectual pleasures they offered might seem austere—and the formally arranged furniture of garden pavilions, though elegant, was, in modern terms, decidedly uncomfortable—unlike the gardens of Japan, they can accommodate without violation a wide variety of human activities, from family festivals to amorous assignations. The Chinese garden, though it reveals a profound and serious view of the world and man's place in it, is above all a sensuous delight, and full of joy and laughter as well as peaceful contemplation.

MK

Architecture in the Chinese garden

Architecture plays a pivotal role in the structural layout and form of the garden, as well as its function and imagery. The garden spaces are formed by architectural elements, and living spaces within the garden are often defined as discrete structures or terraces, all interconnected by complex patterns of circulation on the horizontal plane. The resulting garden is more complex and seemingly more expansive for the visual and spatial manipulations employed, thanks to a number of artistic and theatrical devices wrought in three dimensions.

Traditional residential architecture, with its Confucian hierarchical organization, tends to be condensed in plan and axially arranged by functional and family social order. Many family compounds existed without the benefit of a distinct garden space, except for small courtyards off studies and other private quarters of the residence. Pleasure gardens were too large to fit within the framework of the house, and were usually annexed on contiguous parcels of land, often exceeding the size of the main house compound.

Classical gardens, both urban and rural, are carefully circumscribed by walls, fences (in more rural settings), and buildings. Of these, walls—sometimes called 'cloud walls' for their role as a landscape backdrop—are the most significant structural and architectural element in defining the Chinese garden. They provide dense dividers between and around garden spaces. Views of neighbouring gardens are sometimes 'borrowed' through lattice-work windows, further heightening the illusion of contiguous garden rooms. The variety of portals and windows piercing the walls is unlimited. Shapes, both geometric and symbolic, frame views into and out of the garden rooms—adding layers of allusion to the landscape scene. The 'moon gate' is perhaps the form most associated by Westerners with the Chinese garden—and the most imitated abroad. Other popular forms include plum blossom, gourd, leaf, vase, jar, and peach. Windows through walls, in a similar range of shapes, can either be open or grilled with ceramic or plaster traceries of geometric or symbolic forms. These 'tracery windows' pierce the wall with light, and allow glimpses to and from adjacent spaces. Outside walls of neighbouring buildings are often incorporated in the perimeter wall of a garden, creating a certain mystery about how many buildings make up the garden. Internal walls further subdivide spaces and create a maze of garden courtyards and buildings to be explored.

In these courtyards are located garden pavilions and structures in great variety, each with a particular seasonal or ceremonial use, and each with its own poetic and visual identity. Pavilions serve as both social spaces within the garden and focal or decorative elements to be enjoyed from other points in the garden. Both prospect and refuge are served by these structures, in a rich variety of styles and materials.

The typology of garden structures is based on function, shape, size, and type of construction.

Distinctions are made between buildings constructed of round timbers and those built from rectangular beams. The size of the structure, in area, in the number of bays or sections, in the number of rooms, and the number of storeys, is part of building taxonomy. The style of roof, whether hipped or a simple gable, and its detailing, are important elements of a building's character. Symbolic building forms, such as fan-shape or doubled coins, and buildings that mimic other pleasure structures, such as boats, add allusion and richness to the architectural expression of the garden. Poetic naming of pavilions, like the 'Moon Appearing and Breeze Coming Pavilion' in the Wang Shih Yuan, Suzhou, and the 'Embroidered Silk Pavilion' in the Zhouzheng Yuan, Suzhou, tie the garden into literary, philosophical, and historical underpinnings of Chinese culture.

Terminology for architectural garden features is complicated by differences in local usage and common synonyms and homonyms. Some of the more significant garden structures include the following:

bian is a calligraphic title panel, hung on a pavilion.

da ting is the main hall or most significant garden building.

fang is an inner chamber or room, separated from a main room.

fang (or *fong*) is a boat pavilion or 'landboat' shaped like a boat, usually built in or beside the water.

ge is a building open on four sides, hip roofed, and often two storeyed.

guan is a guest house 'lodging' or study.

jiu jia liang is a nine-pillared structure.

juan is a porchlike extension for a small building.

lang is a covered walkway or gallery.

lou is a 'tower' of more than one storey.

louchuang is a lattice window.

men lou is an imposing tower built above the main gate.

meirenkao is a seat-balustrade in a kiosk or a walkway.

qi jia liang is a seven-pillared structure.

qiao is a bridge.

qulang is a winding walkway.

tai is a terrace or balustraded platform.

tang is a main hall built with round timbers.

ting is an open kiosk or resting place, built with squared beams, and highly variable in plan—geometric through figurative. Another variation is half a *ting* form, built against a wall.

wu jia liang is a five-pillared structure.

xie is a waterside pavilion, often sited partly over water.

xi tai is a stage for entertainments in the garden.

xuan is a carriage-like building or gallery, elevated in siting.

yan is a 'penthouse' building, built against a cliff.

yuanyan ting is a 'mandarin duck hall', partitioned into two spaces.

yunqiang is a 'cloud wall' or garden wall.

zhai is a secluded pavilion for study or contemplation.

Within the garden, the mountain and water landscape unfolds, surrounding, embracing, and sometimes supporting pavilions and other structures. The bridges, covered walkways, and arbours interconnect sections of the garden, while also serving as transparent structural dividers within the spaces. Combined with the surface paths, steps, and terraces, the effect is a labyrinthian circulation through the garden—thereby expanding the perceived size and complexity of the whole. The covered walkways wind through the garden, and can be doubled with a centre wall, or stacked into a two-storey corridor. The low walls flanking these walkways serve as seats as well as subtle partitions in the garden, shifting the viewer's path and aspect. The garden visitor is thus guided through a seemingly random itinerary of experiences.

PC

Chinampas ⊕

Xochimilco, Mexico City, Mexico. A highly productive agricultural system developed around 1265 to increase the available arable land by encroaching on the lakes of Chalco and Xochimilco that surrounded Tenochtitlán, capital of the Aztec Empire. Between AD 1400 and 1521, they reached their maximum extent and productiveness, becoming major suppliers of agricultural products and flowers to Tenochtitlán. The word Chinampa derives from the Nahuatl (Aztec language) *chinamitl* meaning 'reed fence' and *pan* meaning 'over the'. Chinampas were built in the water close to the lake banks by marking an area of up to 100 m/330 ft × 8 m/26 ft with stakes interwoven with dead reeds to form an underwater fence. The enclosed space was filled with alternate layers of rock, aquatic vegetation, natural waste, and lake bottom soil, which create a very rich soil. Rising above the water level by up to 0.6 m/2 ft, they protect the crops from seasonal flooding. *Ahuejote* (*Salix bonplandiana*) trees were planted along the edges to secure the enclosed earth to the lake bed and prevent erosion. Maize, beans, squash, chillies, marigold, and dahlias were the main crops. Canals were left between each Chinampa to transport workers and produce. Today there is a small network of

canals and artificial islands that attract thousands of visitors who tour the canals in *trajineras* (punts) and buy medicinal herbs, shrubs, and ornamental flowers that are still cultivated here such as dahlias, begonias, and poinsettia (*Euphorbia pulcherrima*). Xochimilco was declared a World Heritage Site in 1987.
SAO/LTT

Chinese gardens abroad
are a relatively recent phenomenon. From the 18th-century fascination of Europeans with the unusual charms of Chinese gardens, real and imagined, ideas and impressions were freely incorporated into Western gardens, often under a title of 'Chinese'. The fashion for CHINOISERIE and the exotic ornamentation of architecture and garden swept Europe and its colonies, leaving a trail of rockeries, pagodas, and tracery balustrades around the world. The increasing accuracy of information brought back to the West by architects and artists refined European impressions of Chinese garden arts, but the effect in garden emulation was still well shy of authentic re-creation.

With increasing ease of transportation in the 20th century, garden makers were able to travel to China and East Asia and bring back plants, furnishings, images, and first-hand impressions of both private and imperial Chinese gardens.

Although 'Chinese' gardens in the West from this period still tended to exhibit ornamental use of Chinese features and furnishings, rather than a true Chinese conceptual framework, a few stand out as having true insight into the spatial proportions and functioning of a Chinese garden. The American landscape architect Fletcher STEELE travelled to China in 1934, as did his client Mabel Choate (see NAUMKEAG) in 1935, and subsequently a small 'Chinese Garden' was added to the property. It is a walled courtyard garden with a borrowed view of the mountains and not a true *shan shui* ('mountains and water') landscape garden, but its proportions, architecture, and livability are plausibly Chinese. Other designers, such as Beatrix FARRAND, created hybrid gardens incorporating some of the strongest concepts of Eastern and Western traditions. SEAL HARBOR (the Abby Aldrich Rockefeller Garden) in Maine, USA, designed in 1926 for Mr and Mrs John D. Rockefeller Jr., stands as a prime example of a balanced meeting of East and West in a garden.

Although there has been a modern tradition in Europe and the Americas for importing Japanese designers to create Japanese-style gardens abroad, no such impetus has existed for Chinese gardens—until the last quarter of the twentieth century. The new thirst for Chinese gardens is not only for authenticity of design,

but also for authenticity of execution. These facsimile gardens are re-creations of private gardens from the classical period of Chinese garden design, during the Ming and Qing dynasties. They are designed in China by professional architects and craftsmen who are involved in the restoration of historic gardens there, mostly in the Suzhou area. Much of the garden architecture is prefabricated in China, and the building materials for both garden and structures are assembled and shipped to the host country. A team of Chinese designers and craftsmen accompanies the materials to the predesignated garden site and fabricates the entire garden, from walls and pavilions, to rockeries, Taihu stones (the rock most highly prized for artificial 'mountains'), and plantings. The effect is in some ways more real than a Suzhou garden, given the newness of material and the crispness of new construction. The spatial relationships and the livability of the garden are conveyed in ways that no photograph or publication can match. The visitor's understanding of the whole garden expression is profoundly enhanced.

The first true facsimile Chinese garden to set this trend was created for the Metropolitan Museum of Art in New York, at the behest of Mrs Vincent Astor. A full-scale prototype was built in Suzhou, now open there under the name East Garden, before shipping and constructing the garden in New York in 1981. The garden is a single courtyard, modelled after the courtyard and study, called the Late Spring Studio, of the Wang Shi Yuan garden in Suzhou. The courtyard, a modest 14 m × 5.4 m/ 45 ft × 17 ft in size, is mostly paved and contains rockeries, planting beds, Taihu stones, a half pavilion, and a covered walkway. Despite its severity and sparse plantings, this garden has stimulated great interest in traditional Chinese garden design, an interest that has spread and deepened throughout North America.

Since that initial foray into Chinese design and construction of traditional gardens abroad, several dozen gardens have been constructed throughout the world by the two primary government-sanctioned Chinese landscape design companies. Many of these gardens were constructed under the concept of cultural exchange or friendship, sometimes as a direct result of a 'sister city' relationship with a Chinese municipality—as in Sydney, Australia. Some are constructed as a cultural asset for a local community of Chinese immigrants, and others—like the proposed garden in Tacoma, Washington, USA—are built as a bridge of reconciliation between alienated communities. Although Asian gardens share some common roots, they differ as much as they are alike. The construction of Chinese gardens in Singapore,

Japan, and other Pacific nations helps to contrast and compare garden traditions within Asia.

Canada boasts the first true Chinese landscape gardens, larger and more complex than the single court gardens, in Vancouver and in Montréal. Germany is the Chinese garden centre of Europe, with gardens in Berlin, Frankfurt, Munich, Stuttgart, Düsseldorf, and other cities. The United States continues to add new, and larger, gardens to its collection, with significant garden complexes opened in Staten Island, New York, and Portland, Oregon, and more in the planning stages.

The most ambitious Chinese garden re-creation being planned is for the HUNTINGTON BOTANICAL GARDENS, in San Marino, California. The garden will cover 4.85 hectares/12 acres with a lake, a stream, four clusters of courtyards and pavilions (identified with the four seasons), five collection gardens, numerous bridges, and a landscape setting more spacious and verdant than any of its urban predecessors around the world. The scale of this garden may even outshine that of traditional gardens being constructed within China. The classical garden is a strong cultural touchstone there, and new gardens in traditional styles outnumber those with more modern or 'international' inspiration. These new gardens at home and abroad continue the tradition of reinvention within the classical vocabulary and palette, and shun slavish copying. This model could well be emulated by other cultures in the conservation and adaptation of historic landscapes. PC

chinoiserie,
a French word, dating from the early 19th century, to denote something influenced by the Chinese style. It may also carry a slightly pejorative meaning, as something with a false air of Chinese-ness. A taste for things from China has had a profound influence on the art of gardens and on decorative arts. The stories of Marco Polo's travels to China in the 13th century, however fictitious they may be, fired the imagination. In the 17th century trading links with China opened up a new phase in the study of Chinese artefacts. The first East India Company ship visited China in 1637 but no formal trading links were established until 1685 when the Manchu Emperor opened ports to foreign trade. From 1695 the export of Chinese armorial porcelain, to Britain, France, the Netherlands, Portugal, and Sweden, organized by private traders not by the various East India companies, encouraged a taste for Chinese crafts. The first instance of Chinese taste in the European garden is often claimed to be the Trianon de Porcelaine at VERSAILLES. Designed by Louis Le Vau in 1670, this group of buildings

was only slightly Chinese. The exterior walls were surfaced in blue and white Delftware of supposedly Chinese style, and the elaborate roofs of the buildings swarmed with china vases and painted sculptures of birds. The Trianon de Porcelaine was demolished in 1687 to make way for the Trianon de Marbre which stands today on its site (see VERSAILLES). Apart from the isolated Chinese pavilion of the Trèfle at Lunéville (Meurthe-et-Moselle), designed shortly after 1738, most French examples are much later, such as the Pagode de CHANTELOUP (1775), the magnificent Maison Chinoise at the DÉSERT DE RETZ, a pagoda at RAMBOUILLET (c.1780), and the Chinese Pavilion at CASSAN (L'Isle-Adam) (1787). In England Sir William TEMPLE's *Upon the Gardens of Epicurus* (1692) described the Chinese way of laying out grounds, an irregular style 'without any Order or Disposition of Parts'. Whether this influenced the English 18th-century informal style of landscape park it is hard to prove. However, buildings in the Chinese style were an occasional ingredient in the new landscape. William KENT made designs for Chinese temples in the 1730s but none was built. At Shugborough in Staffordshire a Chinese pavilion was built in 1748 and may still be seen, based on a sketch of a building seen in China for George Anson whose brother owned Shugborough. Sir William CHAMBERS certainly encouraged a taste for China. At KEW Chambers designed a Chinese pavilion, the House of Confucius (1749), and his beautiful Pagoda (1761–2) which was very widely admired. In 1772 Chambers designed a most unusual Chinese Temple/Bridge at Amesbury Hall (now Amesbury Abbey) in Wiltshire, spanning a tributary of the river Avon. This was no doubt the rebuilding of a much earlier Chinese building mentioned in a letter of 1750: 'Saw the Duke of Queensberry's: a Chinese House and Bridge'.

By the end of the 18th century chinoiserie as an influence on garden taste was scarcely fashionable in England but was still strong in France. A French source, the writings of the Jesuit Jean Denis ATTIRET, had, as early as 1743, included a detailed account of the pleasure gardens at Yuanming Yuan. These writings aroused great interest in Europe but any influence on French gardens was felt only much later. Of the twenty volumes of engravings by GEORGES-LOUIS LE ROUGE, *Détails des nouveaux jardins à la mode* (1774–89), ten are devoted to *le style anglo-chinois* (see JARDIN ANGLAIS). A few isolated instances of Chinese-style buildings in English gardens in the 19th century include two outstanding examples: Sir Jeffry Wyatville's exquisite Fishing Temple (c.1825) for VIRGINIA WATER and the Pagoda Fountain (1827) designed

by the architect Robert Abrahams at ALTON TOWERS. In other European countries there is a scattering of examples of fine chinoiserie garden buildings. A particularly fine Chinese house was built at the Swedish royal palace of DROTTNINGHOLM between 1753 and 1763. In Germany, at Frederick the Great's SANSSOUCI, a Chinese tea house was built between 1754 and 1756. The Esterházy estates in Hungary at CSÁKVÁR and at TATA both had Chinese pavilions. Examples of whole gardens laid out in the Chinese style are numerous and are described under the CHINESE GARDENS ABROAD.

PT

Chirk Castle ⊕

Chirk, Clwyd, Wales, was built in the 13th century. The Myddelton family came here in 1595 and owned the estate until it was transferred to the NATIONAL TRUST in 1981. The medieval deer park was landscaped by William EMES in the 1760s and 1770s and is today ornamented with magnificent wrought-iron gates (1712–19) by Robert and John Davies. In the late 19th century topiary yew hedges were planted about the castle which have now assumed a dramatically monumental character. Here is a rose garden of Edwardian character and deep mixed borders descending a slope with fine views.   PT

Chiswick House ⊕

Chiswick, London, England, was built for the 3rd Earl of BURLINGTON between 1727 and 1729. Burlington designed the house himself and made it one of the most attractive and influential of Palladian houses. It was connected by a wing early in the 18th century to a Jacobean manor house which was demolished in 1788. The garden which Burlington made was a distillation of the advanced garden taste of his time. By 1733 it showed a mixture of formality and informality contained in a firmly axial arrangement. Behind the house a walk led across a formal grove at the end of which a PATTE D'OIE of ALLÉES radiated, each with its terminal decorative building—the Bagnio, the Domed Building, and the Rustic House (only the last survives). Between the avenues winding walks led through a WILDERNESS with a bowling green. A Doric column stood at the centre of five walks; an orange tree garden was overlooked by an Ionic Temple (which survives) designed by Burlington. An informal stretch of water forms the garden's south-western boundary—beyond it in 1733 were wildernesses with zigzag and winding paths with at their centre an antique obelisk which Burlington acquired from the Arundel collection (a copy of it survives today). Today, with some fine statuary and urns, beautiful old cedars of Lebanon, and Chiswick

House itself triumphantly restored, it is a delightful place to visit. Some restoration has been done in the garden but much more is needed. It is ironic that the 19th-century walled garden to the east, which was laid out as an 'Italian Garden' by Lewis Kennedy (1789–c.1840), is the best-kept part of the estate. With its glasshouse of c.1811 by Samuel Ware, dapper bedding schemes, mop-headed acacias, and Coade stone urns it presents a pretty picture of 19th-century taste.   PT

JOHN HARRIS, *The Palladian Revival: Lord Burlington, his Villa and Garden at Chiswick* (1994).

Choroszcz ⊕

near Bialystok, Poland. This baroque summer residence on the *entre cour et jardin* (between courtyard and garden) scheme was commissioned by Hetman Jan Klemens Branicki. The palace was erected in 1725–59; the garden was laid out in 1748–52 by unknown French garden designers. Following the example of VAUX-LE-VICOMTE, the palace was sited on an island. It was preceded by a *cour d'honneur* (see ATTRE, CHÂTEAU D') with pavilions, outbuildings, and guardhouses in symmetrical disposition. An arrangement of two canals intersecting at right angles, modelled on VERSAILLES, extended into a deer park which is divided by radiating ALLÉES. The main axis ended in a mound on the top of which there was a pavilion surrounded by trellis-work. The transverse canal was closed at one end by a sculpture of Diana and at the other by a Chinese pavilion today partly destroyed. In the immediate vicinity of the palace there were ornamental parterres. The palace, badly damaged during the First World War (1915), was rebuilt and the park restored after the Second World War.   WB

Christchurch Botanic Garden ⊕

Christchurch, New Zealand, holds a fine collections of plants and extends over 40 hectares/99 acres containing herbaceous borders, rose gardens, conservatories, ponds, extensive lawns, and woodland. The garden is itself embraced by Hagley Park, a 56-hectare/144-acre green oasis in the centre of the city, a city where one-third of the land is devoted to recreation. Christchurch has strong ties with England from whence its early settlers began to arrive in 1850, so it is not surprising that many of the plants grown are exotic. The scale of the great tree-studded lawns and woodlands is unparalleled and the river Avon which winds around the boundaries adds further to the illusion of 'home'. Queen Victoria sent four acorns to New Zealand on the death of her husband, Prince Albert, and one of the resulting seedlings, known as the Prince Albert Edward oak, was planted here in 1863. Another notable tree is a madrona (*Arbutus menziesii*), one of the finest in cultivation. There is a large assembly of native plants centred on the Cockayne Memorial Garden including fine collections of shrubs and forest trees and also small understorey trees such as *Schefflera digitata* (a member of the ivy family) and rangiora (*Brachyglotis repanda*). *Dicksonia squarrosa* with its distinctive skirt of spent fronds is one of many tree ferns. A notable plant in the alpine garden is *Lepidothamnus laxifolius,* the smallest conifer known. Dr Leonard Cockayne (1855–1934) was a pioneering New Zealand botanist and plant ecologist.   GSC

Church, Thomas

(1902–78), American landscape architect and pioneer of what later became known as the 'California style'. He evolved an original approach to the problems of 20th-century garden design, transcending both the Beaux-Arts-inspired formalism previously dominant in the United States, and the picturesque manner usually seen as the only alternative. After education at Berkeley and Harvard in the Beaux-Arts tradition, he began his practice in California in 1930, having already rejected this tradition in theory (along with Dan KILEY, James Rose, and Garrett ECKBO).

Faced with the challenge of small irregular plots and steep hillside sites, his response—asymmetrical plans, raised planting beds, seat walls, bridges, paving, and broad timber decks—established an entirely new vocabulary of garden design. In these he responded positively to the needs of modern life—especially to the increasing use of garden space by families living in smaller houses and the need for low-maintenance gardens. He made a place in the landscape for the motor car; and realized that as the modern house evolved with walls of glass the garden had to become a functional extension of the house, an outdoor living room.

During the early 1930s most of his work consisted of small gardens in the San Francisco area. He began to experiment with angular forms giving the illusion of greater size—the most innovative and widely known example being the Sullivan Garden (San Francisco, 1937), where the longer arm of an L-shaped path covers two-thirds of the diagonal of a rectangular site.

In 1937 he made his second visit to Europe. In Finland he met Alvar Aalto, whose architecture and glassware inspired him to adopt more relaxed, informal, and organic garden plans with curvilinear forms. This new approach was first realized in two garden designs for the Golden Gate exhibition (1939). The central axis was finally abandoned in favour of a multiplicity of viewpoints and the use of asymmetrical lines to create greater apparent dimensions to the site. His justification for this new style was essentially functional rather than aesthetic.

Between 1939 and 1949 he produced a wide variety of gardens for numerous clients throughout California, including one of the most famous 20th-century gardens in the world, the El NOVILLERO garden at Sonoma (1947–9). Designed on a hilltop encircled by mature oaks and overlooking the Sonoma valley, the garden extends visually to the countryside beyond. The kidney-shaped swimming pool and the edges of the paving echo the rolling hills and winding salt marshes of the valley.

Although Church undertook public commissions during the war years and after, the small residential garden continued to be his dominant concern until a serious illness in 1976. By this time he had been responsible for over 4,000 residential gardens and projects. His first book, *Gardens are for People* (1955), affirms his view of the garden as a work of art—a composition in form and space, but one which must emerge from the needs of the client and the nature of the site. Major Californian figures, such as Eckbo, Lawrence HALPRIN, and Robert Royston, were considerably influenced by his example.   GL

Cicogna Mozzoni, Villa ✿

Bisuschio, Lombardy, Italy. Originally a hunting lodge, this is one of the rare 16th-century villas in Lombardy, with views towards Lake Lugano. Villa Cicogna Mozzoni, transformed into a country villa by Ascanio Mozzoni between 1530 and 1560, is built into a steep hillside, with magnificent garden rooms on three levels. The entrance is through an arcaded courtyard frescoed with trellis-work of fruit and flowers by the contemporary Campi brothers from Cremona, opening out into a walled garden with cool fish ponds, a NYMPHAEUM, and a GROTTO. After 1592 the architectural garden was further embellished by Agiola Mozzoni and her husband Count Gianpietro Cicogna. The upper garden, 17th century in origin, is reached directly from the *piano nobile*, the entrance framing a spectacular water staircase, originally flanked with cypresses, which flows from a small pavilion at the top. The water came originally from a spring but today is recirculated by an electric pump. A broad grass walk runs along the north side of the villa and above the lower garden, allowing views to Lake Lugano and the countryside. In the 18th century the woods were turned into a naturalistic English park. The villa still belongs to the original family. The important garden, now under the protection of the Fondo per l'Ambiente Italiano, is being slowly restored.   PHo

Cimbrone, Villa ✿

Ravello, Campania, Italy. The villa was built by Ernest Beckett (later Lord Grimthorpe) in 1904 on the cliffs in Ravello, named after a rock jutting out into the sea on the Amalfi coastline. Although only a ruin when acquired, the foundations dated to the 12th century. The villa was designed for Lord Grimthorpe with Moorish embellishments by the local tailor from Ravello, Nicola Mansi, to hint at the Arabian-Norman architecture of the 11th and 12th centuries typical of Sicily and southern Italy. The dramatic central axis of this eclectic garden leads along a wisteria-clad pergola to the distant Temple of Ceres and busts along the terrace, 300 m/1,000 ft above the sea, revealing incomparable views. Formal side gardens, a rose garden, bright bedding out of Edwardian taste, a pink garden, and an Arabian garden are all overhung with umbrella pines, while plane trees, cypresses, and olives mix with exotic palms, cycads, phormiums, and yucca. Informal paths wander through the lower woodland. In contrast, wildflowers—euphorbias, asphodels, sea squills, Algerian irises, scented violets, anemones, giant fennel, and, in shade, cyclamen and acanthus—provide a relaxed air and add considerable charm. Lord Grimthorpe died in 1917 but the family retained the villa until 1960 when it was acquired by Marco Willeumier, the owner of the local Palumbo Hotel.   PHo

Ciołek, Gerard

(1909–69), Polish architect, landscape architect, and garden historian, professor at the polytechnics in Warsaw and Cracow. In Cracow he held the chair of town planning (1951) and established the chair of landscape planning (1963). He introduced to Poland the theory and practice of the conservation of historic gardens. As a result of his inspiration many gardens were conserved, among them ARKADIA, Łańcut, ŁAZIENKI, Nieborów, Pieskowa Skała, Pszczyna, PUŁAWY, Rogalin, and WILANÓW. He made a study of the history of Polish garden art. Only a part of his researches were published in his books *Ogrody polskie* (Polish Gardens) (1954) and *Materiały do słownika twórców ogrodów polskich* (Materials for a Dictionary of Polish Garden Creators, with B. Plapis (1968)). The majority of his manuscripts (archival research, inventories) and photographs are preserved in Warsaw (Teki Ciołka in Krajowy Ośrodek Badań i Dokumentacji Zabytków).   WB

Cirencester Park ⊛

Cirencester, Gloucestershire, England, was laid out in the early 18th century by Allen Bathurst (from 1712 Lord Bathurst) who, from 1718, had the help of his friend Alexander POPE. In 1716 Bathurst bought the manor of Sapperton, some 8 km/5 miles to the west of Cirencester, and planted an avenue linking the two places which remains, the longest avenue in England. Pope made several visits and recorded the atmosphere of his meetings in a letter in 1718: '[I] talk tender sentiments with Lord B. or draw Plans for Houses and Gardens, open Avenues, cut Glades, plant Firrs, contrive water-works, all very fine & beautiful in our own imagination.' Between 1722 and 1732 Alfred's Hall was built, the earliest known Gothic garden building in England. Among other garden buildings are the Hexagon (*c.*1736), Pope's Seat (*c.*1736), and Queen Anne's Column (1741). Bathurst had a taste for avenues whereas Pope inclined more to 'the amiable Simplicity of unadorned Nature' rather than 'the nicer Scenes of Art' (essay in *The Guardian*, 1713). A pattern of rides through woodland was laid out, focused on BORROWED LANDSCAPE (such as church spires), buildings, and monuments, and meeting occasionally at rond-points (circular spaces from which paths radiate). This pattern of activity continued until Bathurst's death in 1775 when such a linear approach to landscape, already old fashioned when he started, had become desperately unfashionable. Bathurst's intentions were not exclusively ornamental, for behind the avenues timber was grown for profit, which the estate, still belonging to the Bathurst family, continues to do today. With an area of 971 hectares/2,400 acres Cirencester Park is one of the finest and most attractive surviving parks of its period. PT

cisterns and water tanks.

Ancient Roman and Islamic gardens had cisterns used to store water and sometimes connected to irrigation channels or, in the case of Islamic gardens, to an ornamental rill. Pliny the younger in the 1st century AD described a cistern in his garden used to store water which flowed into a basin which served as a table, with dishes disposed about its margins. Smaller dishes floated in the water which presumably served to keep them cool. At Abd al-Rahman's estate at Almeria in Andalusia in the 11th century there was an elaborate system of connected cisterns which supplied water to the gardens and the residence. The most beautiful example of a cistern, as an integral part of a garden design, is that at the 17th-century Palácio FRONTEIRA in Lisbon which is enclosed in staircases and a terrace walk, the whole exquisitely decorated with pictorial tiles. Late 17th- or 18th-century lead cisterns, with decorative moulded patterns and often with a date and the owner's initials, originally used for collecting rainwater, are found in many old English gardens. Cisterns were a vital part of the kitchen garden, and in glasshouses they held water that would be of the right temperature to water plants under protection. PT

CITES.

See CONVENTION ON INTERNATIONAL TRADE IN ENDANGERED SPECIES OF WILD FAUNA AND FLORA.

Citroën, Parc André.

See PARIS PARKS AND GARDENS.

claire voie.

A French term meaning literally 'clear way' and signifying an opening in an enclosure allowing

Alfred's Hall at **Cirencester Park** shown in an etching (*c.*1725) by Thomas Robins.

one to see beyond it. It was much used in French 17th-century gardens and those influenced by them. A.-J. DEZALLIER D'ARGENVILLE in his *La Théorie et la pratique du jardinage* (1709) describes the use of 'grills . . . essential in enfilades of ALLÉES to extend the view'. At the late 17th-century garden of WESTBURY COURT grilles are let into the garden's boundary wall allowing views into the garden from what was then a busy thoroughfare.   PT

Claremont ⊛

Esher, Surrey, England, was bought by the architect Sir John VANBRUGH *c.*1710, 'the situation being singularly Romantick' as he recorded at the time. He almost immediately sold it to Sir Thomas Pelham-Holles, later Duke of Newcastle, for whom Vanbrugh rebuilt the house and designed a castellated BELVEDERE. In 1716 Charles BRIDGEMAN, with whom Vanbrugh worked on several gardens, came to work on the garden and built a great turf amphitheatre overlooking a formal circular pool. In 1729 the Duke of Newcastle called in William KENT who introduced a serpentine HA-HA, where Bridgeman had a wall and bastions, and remodelled the formal pool so that it resembled a naturalistic lake, with an island at the centre planted with trees and the New House, a classical pavilion. On the southern bank of the lake, where it is fed by a stream, he introduced a cascade. In the 1760s the cascade was turned into a massive rustic grotto, possibly by Josiah and Joseph Lane, who were working nearby at PAINSHILL at the time. The Duke of Newcastle died in 1768 and the estate was bought by Lord Clive. Capability BROWN rebuilt Vanbrugh's house and worked on the grounds, obliterating Bridgeman's amphitheatre with trees. After Clive's death the estate passed through many hands, the house becoming a school and the estate being broken up. The NATIONAL TRUST bought the pleasure grounds in 1949 and started to restore them in 1975. Huge amounts of clearing of undergrowth was done, trees replanted, and Bridgeman's amphitheatre reinstated. Kent's pavilion still stands on its island, the grotto survives, and Vanbrugh's belvedere rises on its hill beyond the pleasure grounds' boundary.   PT

Clausholm ⊛

Randers, Denmark. The sharply sloping terrain which falls 20 m/70 ft from the home farm inspired a terraced garden of Italian character in 1723, planned by architect J. C. KRIEGER for King Frederik IV (1671–1730). The fine main building, built in 1693 for chancellor C. Rewentlow, stands on a little embankment. This early Danish baroque complex follows the same main axis, with a symmetrical group of buildings continuing in a long linden avenue towards the north. The plans for the original cascades that ran down three terraces, 8 m/28 ft wide with 3-m/10-ft slopes, were probably designed by N. TESSIN the younger. The cascades were reinterpreted in the 1970s by C. Th. SØRENSEN in the form of a narrow rivulet, with octagonal pools with bowl fountains at the foot of the slope.   AL

Clearing, The ⊛

Ellison Bay, Door County, Wisconsin, USA. The Clearing, on a site of 52.5 hectares/129 acres, was founded in 1935 as an educational centre by Jens JENSEN. This working farm of clearings within forested land lies on a level bench above layered limestone cliffs on the inner side of the Door County peninsula on Lake Michigan. Jensen acquired the land between 1919 and 1935 for a summer home. Inspired by Danish Folk Schools, The Clearing was established to provide outdoor instruction on the local ecology, soils, flora, and fauna. Students divided the day between instruction and working the land. All the designed features were intended to heighten the experience of being in nature. Modest stone buildings, designed by Hugh Garden (1873–1961), are sited close to a large clearing. The main building was sited to catch views of the rising sun and a western clearing provides views of the setting sun. The small Cliff House, perched on a ledge above the steep cliffs, provides a more protected and intimate place for viewing storms and sunsets. Close to the Cliff House is a Council Ring overlooking Green Bay, which is used for storytelling, music, and dance with a central fire pit. Council Rings figured prominently in Jensen's public parks as representations of democratic communities. Jensen's deep love for the prairies and the native landscapes of the mid-west is reflected in his consistent use of native plants as shown in the rock garden close to the main building.   DCS

ROBERT E. GRESE, *Jens Jensen: Maker of Natural Parks and Gardens* (1992).

Clément, Gilles

(b. 1943), French garden designer and author trained at the École Nationale Supérieure du Paysage at Versailles, graduating in 1969. In a series of influential books he has set down his beliefs in the importance of ecology, the charms of *friche* (fallow land) when spontaneously colonized by plants, and his admiration for shifting communities of plants (*Le Jardin en mouvement* is the title of one of his books, published in 2000) which is nature's way of designing a garden. His work may be seen in several gardens open to the public: the Parc André Citroën (Paris; see PARIS PARKS AND GARDENS), the Parc Matisse (Lille), the Château de Blois, the Arche de la Défense (Paris), and LE RAYOL. In his most recent book (*La Sagesse du jardinier*, 2004) he writes, 'Regarder, pourrait bien être le plus juste façon de jardiner demain' (looking could well be the best way of gardening in the future).   PT

Clerk, Sir John

(1676–1755), of Penycuik, Scottish poet, garden maker, and garden theorist. His rather ponderous unpublished poem 'The Country Seat' (1727) shows an advanced taste for informal gardens—'Nature requires the Gardiners helping Hand, / Yet never force her with unkindly art.' Like Alexander POPE, he believed in the importance of the genius of the place—'Gardens must always some Proportion bear / To e'vry kind of Structure which they grace.' He put his ideas into practice at the family estate of PENICUIK and made a further garden at Mavisbank (Midlothian) as a setting for the Palladian villa (1724–39) which he designed in association with William ADAM. In a picturesque valley of the river Esk Sir John made an ancient tumulus the chief feature of his landscape, connecting it with the garden by hedged walks leading to its summit. The house was gutted by fire in 1973 and now, derelict and forlorn, presents one of the saddest sights in Scotland.   PT

Cleveland Botanical Garden ⊛

Cleveland, Ohio, USA, has maintained a commitment to botanical education since its inception in 1930 as a small garden library. Initially named the Garden Center of Cleveland and housed in an ageing boathouse, the non-profit centre moved to its current 4-hectare/10-acre location in 1966, and unveiled its most magnificent feature in 2003, a crystal-peaked conservatory containing more than 350 exotic plant species and 50 species of animals, interpreted within the context of two ecosystems: Madagascar's spiny desert and the cloud forest of Costa Rica. The semi-arid desert biome includes the largest collection of mature baobab trees (*Adansonia rubrostipa* and *Adansonia za*) in North America, cliffs sprouting vibrant yellow, pink, and purple blooms, and a pair of Oustalet's chameleons (*Furcifer oustaleti*) roaming among the euphorbias, pachypodiums, and aloes. In the misty Costa Rican replica, epiphytes crowd the branches of palm, black olive, avocado, and fig trees, birds and more than 200 butterflies flutter freely, and an elevated footbridge provides a view of the orchid-adorned canopy and ginger and heliconia plants below. Outside, the garden's focus on teaching is evident in the diversity and restrained scale of the displays. Along with a herb garden featuring more than 300 species and a rose garden topping 50 varieties, there are Japanese, woodland, topiary, and horticultural therapy gardens, as well as six theme gardens that change biennially. Perhaps the most exemplary of all is the children's garden, replete with a tree house, dwarf forests, scrounger garden, hand-painted signs, and a maze.   LCJ

Cleves

(Kleve), North Rhine-Westphalia, Germany. The first experiment in Germany of integrating parks and gardens with a city was conducted here between 1647 and 1678 by Johan Maurits van NASSAU-SIEGEN, while serving as stadtholder to the Elector of Brandenburg. Combining Dutch and Italian ideal forms with German monumentalism, Johan Maurits created, in the hilly surrounds, five unique complexes of parks or classical landscapes and gardens linked to the city by a network of avenues. Baroque in concept and mannerist in detail, each had a distinctive character which bore his personal stamp and each embodied the arts, the sciences, nature, and horticulture as well as affording pleasure and meditation. Equally unique were the various trophies erected throughout as focal points.

Connected to the Nassauer Allée (1653), planted with lime trees from the Netherlands, was the Freudenberg (c.1650) containing pleasure gardens, animal parks, and fish ponds. The New Deer Park encompassed the amphitheatre garden of Springenberg (1652–7) conceived by Jacob van CAMPEN, and the Sternberg (1656) whose radiating avenues led far into the distance. The intimate Prinzenhof pleasure gardens (c.1670) had a hedged rond-point (see CIRENCESTER PARK) as central motif and a wilderness along a steep slope where nature was given free rein. In emulation of the Romans, Johan Maurits placed his tomb along a road at Bergental (1670–8), his final creation, where he spent his last days in a hermitage. In an Arcadian setting, the tomb was flanked by a brick EXEDRA adorned with grottoes, urns, and Roman antiquities in niches and it was linked to the park by one arm of a PATTE D'OIE.   FH

climate change.

On a geological timescale the world's climate has oscillated incessantly between long periods of extreme cold and millennia of higher temperatures. During the last ice age 40,000–50,000 years ago (the period of cave paintings in southern France and Spain), lowered sea levels allowed migrations across land bridges and narrowed water channels from Asia to North America and Australia. Between 5,000 and

3,000 BC the climate was wetter and 1–3 °C warmer than today. Elephant, rhinoceros, and giraffe roamed over a green Sahara. By 2,600 BC these had disappeared as desert conditions extended across the landscape. It is highly probable that the advances of civilizations in Egypt, Mesopotamia, India, and China in the 3rd millennium BC were all stimulated by the need to feed an increasing population in a deteriorating climate. In the last 4,000 years, the period in which human activities have included the making of gardens, there has been no discernible long-term change in climate, with mean temperatures more-or-less constant at 0–0.5 °C below present temperatures, though this simple picture masks short-term fluctuations. Between 500 and 200 BC the mean temperature dropped by 1 °C and there were further mini ice ages AD 400–900 and AD 1550–1850. In the warm interval between these last two cold periods summer temperatures in Europe were 1 °C warmer than at present. This coincides with the period of great cathedral building in Europe and the extension of vine cultivation into northern Britain. During this period of relative stability in climate each culture has made gardens which respond to the climate of the region: the enclosed, water-filled oases of Hispano-Moorish gardens, the more expansive gardens of Italy with their shaded BOSCHI and cooling cascades, or the expansive greensward of the English landscape garden with its subtle perspectives derived from the misty atmosphere.

Throughout history humans have been affected by climate change. In the 20th century, though, it became apparent that the climate might be affected by human activity. In the last third of the 20th century, in particular, what seemed to be a continuous stream of devastating storms, floods, and droughts led to concerns that the climate may be changing and the suspicion that much of that change may be attributable to human activities, especially the production of carbon dioxide (from the burning of fossil fuels) and other 'greenhouse gases' which act as an insulating blanket around the globe. Global temperature has been increasing since the beginning of the Industrial Revolution and this temperature increase parallels the production of carbon dioxide and other greenhouse gases in the atmosphere. The most recent report of the UK Climate Impact Programme (UKCIP 2002) suggests that the global temperature may increase by 2–4 °C by the end of the 21st century, a rate unprecedented in climate history. Extreme weather events associated with the El Niño temperature patterns in the Pacific Ocean are already increasing from once in ten years to once in four. Another impact of global warming

is the expansion of water in the oceans and sea-level rise. On a global level this rise is anticipated to be 20–30 cm/8–12 in by the end of the 21st century although, in northern Europe, especially, the effect is complicated by changes in land level as the land surface continues to rebound after the retreat of the last ice sheets. In more detailed modelling of the UK climate likely outcomes are temperature increases of 2–4 °C, with summer temperatures rising more rapidly than winter temperatures and temperatures in the south-east rising more rapidly than those in the north-west. Temperature extremes are also expected to increase with once-in-a-decade highs of 42 °C compared with the current 35 °C. Winter rainfall will increase by 10–30% while summer rainfall is expected to decrease by 30–50%, depending on the scenario and region. The overall impact will be an increase in the occurrence of hot dry summers and warmer, wet winters with more of the rain falling as intense storms. In private gardens, where change and the challenge of growing plants on the edge of their hardiness are part of the excitement of gardening, climate change over the next century will have both advantages and disadvantages. In temperate zones climate change should permit a wider range of more exotic and more exciting plants to be grown, and should produce a more favourable climate for the enjoyment of gardens, apart from occasional extremes of temperature. Hotter and drier summers will result in brown lawns and perhaps, if water becomes strictly rationed, the replacement of lawns by gravel, decking, or drought-tolerant ground cover plants. In areas of Mediterranean climate, summer temperatures will become too high for human comfort and for plant survival especially if restrictions on water use are imposed. Desert landscapes and 'xeriscape gardening' may spread. In heritage gardens, especially those in which historic plant collections determine the significance of the garden, major difficulties may be anticipated in conserving the essential elements of the garden. Centuries-old trees will increasingly be stressed by high summer temperatures and drought, and will therefore be more prone to succumb to increasing storms. Lawns, the essential centrepiece of the landscape garden, may grow through the winter but become brown for progressively longer periods each summer. The plant vocabulary of beds and borders will necessarily change. Lakes and ponds will be subject to irregular water supply, to increased pollution as soil organic matter breaks down more rapidly at higher temperatures, and to damaging algal blooms. The difficulties of predicting climate change and of differentiating between climate change and short-term weather fluctuation should not be underestimated, but there is an expanding body of evidence to suggest that the world is warming up and that the most important reason for that warming is the increased output of greenhouse gases by the developed world. Temperature changes of the scale anticipated and over enormously longer time-spans have had profound effects on human activity in the past. Given not only the scale but the pace of change anticipated for the 21st century, climate change could be the most important factor in determining the fate of humankind. RJB

climbing plants.

Plants which, in the wild, scramble through trees and shrubs, scale cliffs, or tumble down banks, can, in gardens, be trained against walls and fences, over pergolas, arches, and arbours, or on pillars and posts. The degree of support needed depends to a great extent on the plant's method of climbing.

Climbers fall into three broad categories. Some, notably roses, hoist themselves up by grappling the host plant with sharp, hooked thorns. With initial help, large rambler roses such as the sweet-scented 'Paul's Himalayan Musk', 'Francis E. Lester', and 'Wedding Day' can scale small trees and cascade from the crown. They are used in this way to great effect in old orchards. Smaller varieties of rambler and climbing rose should be tied securely to a frame of horizontal wires or a trellis, arch, tripod, or pergola.

The second category of climbing plants are self-supporting, clinging, in their native habitats, to tree trunks or rock faces using aerial roots (for example, *Hedera helix* and other ivies, *Hydrangea anomala* subsp. *petiolaris*) or tiny suction pads, like *Parthenocissus quinquefolia* (Virginia creeper), and *P. henryana*. The third category twine, attaching themselves by means of twisting stems (*Lonicera* spp.), tendrils (*Vitis vinifera* and other vines, and sweet peas), or leaf stalks (*Clematis* spp.). Twiners need the support of other plants, or trellis or wire mesh. Once they have taken hold they do not need tying in but benefit from being coaxed in the right direction, to prevent an unsightly tangle.

Plants trained over structures of stone, brick, timber, metal, plastic, or a combination of these materials, can have various functions in the garden, in both formal and informal situations. They may be used as decorative barriers to divide one part of the garden from another; they can camouflage sheds, walls, tree stumps, or other unsightly features; and they can be grown for their own sake, to display attractive foliage, flowers, or fruit.

In hot climates, pergolas, tunnels, and arbours provide essential shade in the heat of the day. An early example (2nd century BC) is shown in a Roman mosaic, now in the Museo Nazionale Archeologico, Palestrina, Italy. It shows a scene on the river Nile in Egypt, with a wide arch of bamboo trellis covered in grapevines. Under the arch are two broad, low seats where several picnickers and musicians recline. The river flows between them, under the centre of the arch. Later, medieval manuscripts showed vines and roses on trellis fences, arbours, and tunnels. The effect can be seen in Sylvia Landsberg's re-creation of Queen Eleanor's Garden at Winchester. The choice of roses available at that time was limited to Alba and Gallica roses, valued for the beauty and fragrance of their flowers, and the sweet-brier, *Rosa rubiginosa*, with its apple-scented leaves. Other sweet-scent climbers used in medieval and Tudor gardens were the native *Lonicera periclymenum* and *L. caprifolium* (two forms of honeysuckle, or woodbine), and jasmine. *Clematis cirrhosa* (virgin's bower, 1596), *C. flammula* (1590), and *C. viticella* (1569) would all have been known to Tudor gardeners. With the introduction from Brazil in 1609 of the almost evergreen *Passiflora caerulea*, flowering from June through September, of *Campsis radicans*, the spectacular trumpet vine (from the southeast United States, 1640), also flowering in late summer, and the true Virginia creeper (*Parthenocissus quinquefolia*) with its flaming autumn colour, the season of interest provided by climbers was greatly extended.

One of the most successful and enduringly popular of all climbers in Europe and the USA has been wisteria or glycine. It grows rapidly, the stems twining clockwise, corkscrew fashion, to embrace whatever is offered as support. *Wisteria sinensis* was introduced from China in 1816, and the Japanese species *Wisteria floribunda* came to Holland in 1856. Wisteria is easy to please, with only two special requirements: one is a sunny site, the other, plenty of space in which to develop. The branches can reach as far as 36 m/120 ft on each side of the main stem, and will easily cover the frontage of a large house, or a substantial pergola. Even when such generous space can be provided, firm pruning is needed to control the growth and encourage flowering. Other climbers frequently crammed into too small a space include *Parthenocissus* and *Vitis* species, *Clematis montana*, and the famous *Rosa filipes* 'Kiftsgate' which, at KIFTSGATE COURT in Gloucestershire, smothers two large mature beech trees. When choosing climbing plants it is as well to check their eventual height and spread. It is also important to choose plants that will thrive in the aspect provided for them, a north-facing wall being the hardest.

Plants for a north aspect include clematis varieties, *Aristolochia macrophylla*, *Hydrangea anomala* subsp. *petiolaris*, jasmines, *Lonicera* × *Americana*, and several shrubs which, although not climbing plants, are often trained against a wall, including *Euonymus fortunei*, *Garrya elliptica*, and most pyracanthas. For any aspect, including north, ivy offers an enormous variety of leaf shapes and colours. *Hedera canariensis* and *H. colchica* have large leaves, plain in some forms, variegated in others, and there are hundreds of forms of *Hedera helix*, the native European ivy. It is not true that ivy damages trees, although the weight of ivy in the upper branches of a mature tree does make it more vulnerable to wind damage. On house walls ivy can be beneficial, providing weather protection and insulation.

Ivies are also invaluable as ground cover in shady situations. Irish ivy, *Hedera hibernica*, actually prefers to creep along the ground rather than to go upwards. There are other climbing plants that, in the wild, grow horizontally and downwards as well as up, sprawling along the ground and cascading down slopes. *Jasminum nudiflorum* and *Rosa wichurana*, for example, prefer to go down rather than up, and can usefully provide ground cover on banks or on level ground.

For a formal effect, climbers are sometimes grafted or trained to form standard 'trees' on single stems. Rambler roses grafted as weeping standards, honeysuckle, and wisteria are all effective when used in this way. JF-W

Clingendael ❀

Wassenaar, Zuid-Holland, the Netherlands, is situated in the inner dune area near The Hague; the name refers to *clingen* (dunes) and *dalen* (valleys). In 1591 Philips I Doublet bought a 16th-century farm, which was passed onto Philips II Doublet, brother-in-law of Constantijn HUYGENS, who made improvements. His son Philips III Doublet married Constantijn's daughter and maintained contacts with her brother the mathematician Christiaan Huygens, who lived in Paris 1663–81. From 1680, acting as his own architect, he modernized the gardens inspired by French examples, with advice from others within the circle of Stadtholder William III. An extensive, virtually symmetrical baroque layout surrounded by canals and with ponds, it included various compartmented gardens surrounded by high hedges. The estate was acquired by the van Brienen van de Groote Lindt family in 1759, who owned it until 1954. No major improvements, however, appear to have taken place until the 19th century. In 1838 J. D. ZOCHER Jr. transformed the gardens in the landscape style, which were further extended in

1851 by L. P. ZOCHER and by Eduard PETZOLD in 1888. The latter improvements included a rosarium and were partially supervised by Leonard A. SPRINGER who was also responsible for some of the detailing. Further additions took place in *c.*1915 for M. M. Baroness van Brienen with a JAPANESE GARDEN designed by Theo J. Dinn. While the baroque structure is still recognizable today these later additions have enriched the character, which now is informal and mature. It has been open as a public park since 1955.   JW

> WYBE KUITERT, 'Japonaiserie in London and The Hague: a history of the Japanese gardens at Shepherd's Bush (1910) and Clingendael (*c.*1915)', *Garden History*, Vol. 30: No. 2 (2002).

Cliveden ⊛

Taplow, Buckinghamshire, England, was completed in 1677 for the 2nd Duke of Buckingham to the designs of William Winde (d. 1722) on a great terrace with magnificent views over the Thames valley. This house was destroyed by fire in 1745, and its successor in 1849, when the present house was built by Sir Charles Barry for the 2nd Duke of Sutherland, completed in 1851. In 1893 the estate was bought by William Waldorf Astor, later 1st Viscount Astor, whose descendants gave it to the NATIONAL TRUST in 1942. The gardens could scarcely be more eclectic, with ingredients of every period. Winde's terrace is arcaded, like a noble Italian Renaissance garden, overlooking an immense apron of lawn above the Thames. Here is a 19th-century parterre on the grand scale, a version of what had been designed in 1713 by Claude DESGOTS. In the early 18th century there was much work in the garden. Charles BRIDGEMAN laid out a turf amphitheatre in 1723 and Giacomo Leoni (*c.*1686–1746) designed the Blenheim Pavilion nearby *c.*1735. Lord Astor laid out the curious Long Garden, with *commedia dell'arte* statues and serpentine hedges. He also introduced marvellous antiquities in many parts of the garden and commissioned Thomas Waldo Story's Fountain of Love in the entrance drive. A garden by Sir Geoffrey JELLICOE of *c.*1960 was redesigned with herbaceous borders by Isabelle van Groeningen (b. 1935) in 2001. Graham Stuart THOMAS laid out magnificent new herbaceous borders in the entrance forecourt in 1969.   PT

cloche.

The word is French for a bell but it came to mean, in French and English, a bell-shaped glass cover used to warm the earth or to protect young or tender plants. First used in France *c.*1600 it was not known in England before 1629, when John PARKINSON referred to it in *Paradisi*

in Sole Paradisus Terrestris—'Greate hollow glasses like unto bell heads'. The term is used loosely today to indicate any form of portable light, but the bell shape has the great aerodynamic advantage of being difficult to blow over.   PT

Cloisters, The ⊛

New York, USA, a branch of the Metropolitan Museum of Art created in 1938 to house the museum's medieval art collection. It consists of a cluster of monastic buildings set high on the Palisades overlooking the Hudson river. Within these recreated medieval buildings are three cloistered gardens known for their serenity and charm. Each of them is a patterned enclosure within columned arcades planted with the flowers and herbs celebrated in medieval literature and tapestries. Four old quince trees surround an Italian well-head in the Bonnefont Cloister Herb Garden, where 250 species of plants cultivated in the Middle Ages are arranged according to their use—medicinal, culinary, as fragrance, dyes, or pesticides. The Cuxa Cloister surrounds a garth, or enclosed yard, with quadrants featuring fruit trees and fragrant flowers. The Trie Cloister Garden is a gathering of the flora depicted in the remarkable 15th-century Unicorn tapestries displayed within the Cloister walls. The arcades of the three gardens are glazed in winter and filled with pots of rosemary, jasmine, bay, and citrus, as well as madonna lilies, grape hyacinths, crocuses, and narcissus.   PD

Clotilde, Santa ⊛

near Lloret de Mar, Catalonia, Spain. The Costa Brava became a fashionable place to live, or to have a holiday home, in the early 20th century. This estate was acquired in 1927 by Dr Raúl Roviralta who commissioned a garden from María Rubío i Tudurí (b. 1891) who was director of public gardens in Barcelona. The site, on a cliff overlooking the Mediterranean, is extraordinarily beautiful. Tudurí made the most of the site by fashioning a pared-down vision of an Italian Renaissance garden with a touch of austere art deco modernism. The esplanade facing the house is dominated by a fountain pool and a quartet of monumental cypresses clipped into dumpy columns, each forming the background to a 17th-century white marble statue. From the esplanade a long stepped vista lined with Italian cypresses (*Cupressus sempervirens*) plummets down towards the sea. Fine statuary of many periods is skilfully disposed—often on plinths covered in clipped ivy. Ivy is also trimmed against the risers of steps. Small hedged enclosures and sitting places punctuate the garden. At Santa Clotilde the designer has recognized the power

and beauty of the site and concentrated on revealing its essence in the most subtle way.
                                                        PT

Cluj (in Hungarian Kolozsvár) **Botanic Garden** ⊛

Cluj Napoca, Romania. The philanthropic Count Imre Mikó founded the Transylvanian Museum Association in 1859. At the same time, he bestowed his neoclassical manor and its garden upon the association. The 7-hectare/17-acre landscape garden had been laid out by the Bethlen family. The newly founded Franz Joseph University hired the garden from the association in 1873 and transformed a collection of plants into a systematic botanic garden, supervised by the director Ágost Kanitz and head gardener Lajos Walz. Rockeries and hothouses were added to the garden by directors Gyula Istvánffy (1896–1900) and Aladár Richter between 1900 and 1913, but its territory was much reduced by new university buildings. A bigger piece of ground was bought to the south of the town in 1910, but the laying out of a new garden and the transplanting of plants was started as late as 1919, under the directorship of Alexandru Borza, by Kornél ▶

Colour plates

The garden of the **Villa Il Roseto** at Fiesole, Italy, designed in the 1960s by Pietro Porcinai

The 18th-century grotto of Diana in the picturesque **Sanspareil Rock Garden**, Germany

A glimpse of **Jichang Yuan**, China. A 16th-century Ming garden, known as the Garden of Ecstasy, it was destroyed in the 19th century and meticulously rebuilt

The entrance to the **kitchen garden** at Somerleyton Hall, England

Gärtler. A rose garden with 600 species, a spectacular JAPANESE GARDEN, a palm house, and six more hothouses were built on a 12-hectare/30-acre slope. Apart from displaying natural local plant associations, the garden also contains a remarkable taxonomic collection as well as show gardens of herbs and kitchen plants. Both the old Museum Garden and the new Botanic Garden are open to visitors today.
GA

ALBERT FEKETE, *Kolozsvári kertek* (Gardens of Cluj) (2004).

Cluj (in Hungarian Kolozsvár)
Promenade ⊛

Cluj Napoca, Romania. The first public park of Transylvania, this garden was created on a marshy piece of land on the north-western side of Cluj (Kolozsvár), by the river Someş (Szamos) at the beginning of the 19th century. It soon became a popular walking area after it was opened to the public in 1812. The channelled river bed and its surroundings were laid out to the designs of a French engineer named Hochard. Along the triple avenue running through the middle of the park landscape gardens were created later on by Samuel Hermann, designer of the landscape park at BONŢIDA, for which many trees were brought. A lake was created around 1866 to the designs of Antal Kagerbauer with an island. A CASINO on its banks with an ornate fountain and a music pavilion are later additions of the 1890s. With these, the lake and its surroundings became the new centre of the park. More land was acquired until, by 1917, the promenade's territory had extended to 18 hectares/45 acres. The park continued to grow after the Second World War but today it has lost much of its former unity and character, although its basic structure has been preserved.   GA

Clusius, Carolus

(Charles de L'Écluse) (1526-1609), botanist and traveller born in Arras, Flanders (now France). Clusius became a doctor and botanist, a true Renaissance figure fluent in eight languages. Over 25 years (1550-c.1575) he undertook expeditions throughout Europe discovering species of narcissi and iris in Spain and Portugal, *Primula auricula* in Hungary, and *Scabiosa atropurpurea* in Austria, which he sent to John GERARD. Clusius became prefect of the imperial gardens in Vienna (1573-7) which gave him the entrée to the exotic flora of the Levant and Turkey. It is introductions from those regions, which included anemones, ranunculus, and hyacinth species, the crown imperial (*Fritillaria imperialis*), and, most interestingly of all, the garden TULIP, for which he is justly remembered. Clusius received the tulip from

Ogier Ghiselin de Busbecq (1522-91), the ambassador at Constantinople, who like Clusius was an enthusiast for the flowers he saw. Clusius' introductions soon enabled gardeners to create quite different designs. From Sir Francis Drake (c.1540-1596) he learnt about world flora following the circumnavigation (1578-80). By 1587 Clusius was garden adviser in Frankfurt, and still growing and dispatching new plants, in particular the tulip, around Europe. In the Low Countries he introduced the potato. In 1593 Clusius became *horti praefectus* at Leiden University with responsibility to develop a new botanic garden (see LEIDEN BOTANICAL GARDEN), a post he amply fulfilled. Today his influence is still recognized in the Dutch bulb industry. Clusius was the first horticulturalist to attempt to classify European flora. The account of his botanical travels is contained in three books, the last being written in 1601, *Opera Omnia Rariorum Plantarum Historia*.   MC-C

Cockerell, Samuel Pepys

(1753-1827), English architect whose country houses at Daylesford (Gloucestershire, 1788-93) and SEZINCOTE both show orientalist details. Both houses were built for Indian 'nabobs', the latter for his brother Sir Charles Cockerell. At Sezincote he designed an extraordinary curving conservatory in Mughal style. Humphry REPTON worked at Sezincote and in his designs for the ROYAL PAVILION at Brighton must have been influenced by the house.   PT

Cogels Park ⊛

Schoten, Belgium, is a public park designed by Jacques WIRTZ in 1970. In the grounds of a country house, now engulfed by suburban sprawl, Wirtz used existing features, including excellent mature trees, to make a public amenity of beguiling character. At its heart is a serpentine lake, which was already in place. Irregular sweeping lawns penetrate the enclosing woodland and scattered in the park are several mysterious pyramids built of old stone paving setts. In an urban setting of notable anonymity Wirtz has created a park with a true sense of place. It shows his characteristic virtues of making the best of existing features and adding his own tactful but distinctive mark.   PT

Coimbra Botanic Garden ⊛

Coimbra, Portugal, was founded in 1772-4 and is, after AJUDA BOTANIC GARDEN, the oldest in the country. It forms part of the department of botany of Coimbra University and is dedicated to botanical research but it is also a well-designed and outstandingly attractive public amenity. Enclosed in fine stone walls, at its

centre is a sunken garden, the Quadrado Central, to which a grand double staircase descends on each side. A circular pool with a triple-tiered fountain stands in the middle with concentric beds edged in box and decorated with topiary cones of clipped privet (*Ligustrum japonicum*). The beds are planted with trees and shrubs most of which would be familiar to gardeners from Western Europe—flowering cherries, Japanese maples, oleanders, *Prunus cerasifera* 'Pissardii', and waves of agapanthus. Much more exotic plants, however, are nearby. On the terrace above are some species of the Myrtaceae family, *Eugenia foetida* and *Angophora intermedia*. The Myrtaceae are a major interest of the garden which also displays over 50 species of eucalyptus, some of which are now magnificent mature specimens, among them a noble *E. cornuta*. A collection of plants native to the Canary Islands and Madeira includes many species rarely seen in mainland European gardens such as the laurel *Apollonia barbujana* from Tenerife. An upper terrace gives grand views over trees at the lower level some of which are exceptional specimens of familiar trees (like *Koelreuteria paniculata*) but others are much less familiar, like the handsome monotypic evergreen *Lagunaria patersonii*. At the end of the terrace, in the shade of two *Ginkgo biloba*, is a statue of the botanist Félix Avelar Brotero who became director of the garden in 1791. From this point is a view over a jungle of palms, bananas, and tender ferns. Coimbra displays remarkable plants in a fine setting but has also retained the sympathetic character of a public garden.   PT

cold frame.

A wooden or brick enclosure with a sloping glazed roof, traditionally sloping towards the south, which may be removed or hinged upwards. It is used to give protection to help germinate seeds, or to protect seedlings or young plants, gradually increasing ventilation until they are hardened off and ready to be planted in their permanent position. Brick walls, providing much better insulation, are considered superior. In substantial old kitchen gardens there is often found an area called the frameyard which would have several cold frames but also heated frames (often using fermenting fresh manure) for plants such as melons needing more warmth than the climate will provide. An excellent example of a frameyard in action may be seen in the superbly restored Edwardian kitchen garden at West Dean in West Sussex.   PT

Collinson, Peter

(1694-1768), English Quaker and plant collector who introduced many North American plants into English gardens. He lived all his life in and around London where the family business was that of wholesale woollen drapers. The firm had strong connections with the North American colonies which, later, proved of great benefit to his horticultural activities. Collinson was elected a Fellow of the Royal Society in 1728, and about the same time was in correspondence with a remarkable botanist, John BARTRAM the Derbyshire Quaker, who had settled in Pennsylvania. Collinson's gardens at Peckham and later at Mill Hill (now Mill Hill School) were planted with some of his introductions. He enthusiastically supported Philip MILLER at the CHELSEA PHYSIC GARDEN and others, by supplying plants and seeds he was sent from the New World. The diligence of the partnership between Bartram and Collinson resulted in about 200 new plants being introduced into Britain. MC-C

Colombière, Parc de la ⊛

Dijon, Côte-d'Or, France. The site dates from 1649 when Louis de Bourbon, Prince de Condé (le Grand Condé), bought the estate on the banks of the river Ouche. His grandson, the Duc d'Enghien, laid out an extraordinary formal garden between 1682 and 1685 designed by LE NÔTRE, who sent his pupil Antoine de Maerle to execute the scheme. From a central rond-point (see CIRENCESTER PARK) sixteen ALLÉES, eight of them broad and the rest narrower, radiated out. Their outer extremities were linked by an octagonal *allée* and along the bank of the river were PARTERRES *en broderie*. Most unusually, on the margin of a plan dated 1682, there are details of plants—yew, spruce, lilacs, honeysuckle, and sunflowers. In 1683 10,000 hornbeams were planted, 500 box plants, and 100 limes, and in the two subsequent years 8,000 hornbeams, 200 lilacs, 140 spruce, and 140 yews. The central part of the design, within the octagon, consisted of groves of trees with lawns and ornamental plantings beyond it. From the moment of its completion the garden was open to the citizens of Dijon. In the 20th century the park, now owned by the town of Dijon, was well cared for. The 17th-century Temple d'Amour has been replaced, thousands of trees replanted, and the original pattern of *allées* resurfaced. Henry James described it in his *A Little Tour in France* (1883): 'a dear old place . . . alleys and rond-points, in which everything balances.'

PT

MARIE-CLAUDE PASCAL, *Jardins historiques de Dijon* (1996).

Colombières, Jardin des ⊛

Menton, Alpes-Maritimes, France, the creation of Ferdinand Bac (1859–1952) a French humorous artist, writer, inveterate traveller, and amateur garden designer. From 1919 he was asked to design the garden of Émile Ladan-Bockairy on the precipitous slopes above Menton. Bac loved FABRIQUES, 'ces ponctuations lapidaires', he called them, and filled the landscape with such features as a pergola bridge, rotunda, obelisk, viewing platforms, and Homer's Garden with its atrium and pool. In each he wanted to evoke 'un lieu ravissant, parfumé et silencieux' (a ravishing place, scented and silent). He always respected the natural rocky landscape and was less

Plan of the **Parc de la Colombière** (*c*.1682).

interested in flowers than in trees, in particular the Italian cypress (*Cupressus sempervirens*) whose soaring shapes enlivened the garden. He regarded it, rather than the fashionable date palms, as the natural tree of the Riviera landscape. His books *Les Colombières, ses jardins et ces décors* (1925) and *L'Âme du jardin* (1926) give an idea of his garden philosophy.   PT

Colonial Williamsburg.

See WILLIAMSBURG.

colour theory.

John Ruskin thought that 'colour is the most sacred element of all things'. There has been much writing on the theory of colour in painting but early discussions of colour in relation to gardens are rare. Sir Henry Wotton (1568-1639) in his *The Elements of Architecture* (1624) describes Sir Henry Fanshaw's garden in which 'hee did so precisely examine the *tinctures*, and *seasons* of his flowres, that in their *setting*, the *inwardest* of those which were to come up at the same time, should be alwayes a little *darker* than the *outmost*, and to serve them for a kind of gentle *shadow*, like a piece not of *Nature*, but of *Arte*'. That is an unusually sophisticated discussion of colour in the garden. In the 18th century colour is discussed more frequently but, like much 18th-century garden theorizing, there was perhaps rather less putting into practice of the ideas described. Landscape gardeners of the period, like Capability BROWN, took an interest in the different colours of trees, and shrubberies of flowering plants were becoming fashionable.

It is not until the 19th century, when the idea of the BORDER was fully developed, that colour was debated thoroughly. By the time Gertrude JEKYLL published *Colour Schemes for the Flower Garden* (1908) her ideas on the subject were fully worked out. In gardening in Britain, where colour theory seems to have the greatest infuence, it is Gertrude Jekyll's ideas, whether acknowledged or not, that have had the widest currency. She describes gardens 'in which some special colouring dominates' such as her own grey border. But she warns against the danger of taking monochrome arrangements too far, pointing out that, for example, 'a blue garden, for beauty's sake, may be hungering for a group of white Lilies, or for something of the palest lemon-yellow'. She believed that 'the business of a blue garden . . . [was] to be beautiful first, and then just as blue as may be consistent with being beautiful'. She explains that 'any experienced colourist knows that the blues will be more telling—more purely blue—by the juxtaposition of rightly placed complementary colour'. The idea of juxtaposing complementary colours was integral to

Gertrude Jekyll's ideas. She also believed that the proper deployment of colour could help to make 'living pictures of plant beauty', as she explained in an article called 'Colour sequences' in the *Journal* of the Royal Horticultural Society in 1929. She describes a border 60 m/200 ft long which starts with pale pink, blue, yellow, and white, followed by stronger yellow 'and passing on to deep orange and rich mahogany, and so coming to a culminating glory of the strongest scarlet, tempered with rich but softer reds'. She then explains how 'the progression of colour . . . recedes' until it comes to the further end where there is the 'quiet harmony of lavender and purple and tender pink, with a whole setting of grey and silvery foliage'. Gertrude Jekyll's American contemporary, Louise Beebe Wilder, shared many of her beliefs. In her *Colour in my Garden* (1918) she meticulously describes the colours of different plants in different seasons and makes suggestions of combinations. She is not prescriptive—she explains why she herself has found certain arrangements effective. She, like Gertrude Jekyll, strongly believed in the effect one colour can have upon another—'a single scarlet Poppy will kindle into life a whole sea of dim blue Campanulas'.

Sylvia CROWE's *Garden Design* (1958) has been among the most influential late 20th-century textbooks for garden designers. In this book she describes three ways of using colour: the Italian way, with the occasional high note of colour in a largely monotone composition; to imitate the natural harmonies of nature; or to treat colours as the artist does, to paint a picture. She does not explain what she means by the first of these. The second, she says, resembles the planting of an old hayfield, in which the sometimes brilliant colours of wildflowers are dotted about in the grass and not 'separated out into beds or solid drifts'. She says that this randomness is the essence of cottage garden planting. The last of her categories is surely the hardest to achieve—difficult enough for the artist working with unchanging colours, but how much more difficult for the gardener whose palette is so ephemeral. Even the colour of conifers varies strongly according to season, as does the foliage of many other evergreens. Thus, a really subtle and well-calculated effect will often be fleeting. The architecture of a garden, its spatial ingredients, on the other hand—the division of spaces and the sequence of events—is permanent. It will, of course, vary in different lights and seasons, but its essence will remain strongly present. One of the great beauties of the gardens made jointly by Edwin LUTYENS and Gertrude Jekyll is that in winter the harmonious spaces, shifts of level, and exquisite architectural detail are revealed in their full splendour without the distraction of

plants. Equally, without the pattern of spaces, frames, and different viewpoints that Lutyens's designs provided, how beautiful would the planting alone have been? Is there any garden in the world widely recognized as great in which deliberately deployed colour is the source of its distinction?

In the late 20th century there was a rediscovered interest in colour. This was partly prompted by a nostalgia for Jekyllesque gardens which was nourished by an outpouring of reprints of her books after 1982 when they went out of copyright. Initially this resulted in a taste for subdued borders of grey and silver slightly enlivened with pale blue and lilac. Later in the 20th century William ROBINSON's taste for explosive 'subtropical' combinations of form and colour was rediscovered. Arrangements of cannas, bananas, dahlias, and ricinus—until recently desperately unfashionable plants— appeared in many English gardens in the last twenty years of the 20th century. The impetus here, however, seems to have been a desire for the bright shock of brilliant colour rather than as part of any more carefully worked out scheme.   PT

Columella, Lucius Junius Moderatus

(1st century AD), Roman landowner whose agricultural manual *De Re Rustica* (*c.* AD 60) also contains, in Book 10, precious information on the practice of Roman gardening, written in verse in homage to VIRGIL. Witty, even occasionally funny, this is rich in horticultural advice, both practical and aesthetic—it gives advice on laying out the garden and also describes the beauties of several flowers. Book 11 is more prosaic (and written in prose) and concentrates on practicalities with particular advice on the kitchen garden. *De Re Rustica* was plundered by many subsequent garden writers.
PT

Colvin, Brenda

(1897-1981), English landscape architect, garden designer, and author, designer of both private gardens and large-scale industrial landscapes. She helped found in 1929 the Institute of Landscape Architects (originally called the British Association of Garden Architects) of which she became president in 1951. Two of her largest surviving landscapes are those at Aldershot Military Town (Surrey) and Gale Common (Yorkshire). She also worked on private gardens, among them Sutton Courtenay Manor House (Oxfordshire) for the Hon. David Astor, where she transformed Norah Lindsay's flower garden into a landscape of sweeping lawns, trees, and long views. She also designed private gardens at Burwarton House (Shropshire) and Woodhall Park

(Hertfordshire). She wrote *Land and Landscape* (1948), which became a standard textbook, *Trees for Town* (1947), and a collection of poetry, *Wonder in a World* (1977). PT

compost.

Composting is a natural means of processing animal manures, and garden and kitchen waste of organic origin, before they are returned to the land. Recycling organic wastes to maintain and build soil fertility is an ancient art, still practised by gardeners today. It is a keystone of organic gardening—both maintaining soil fertility, and avoiding the environmental pollution that results from bonfires and landfill.

The composting process converts organic waste into compost—a dark-coloured, friable soil-like material. Compost can be dug into the soil, or applied as a surface mulch, to build and maintain soil structure, biological activity, and fertility. Its nutritional value will depend on the materials used to make compost, and the proportion of nutrients lost in the composting process. Research has shown that compost can help combat soil-borne pests and diseases, and that plants grown in composted soil may be less attractive to pests. Compost is also a useful ingredient in home-made potting mixes. A new development is the huge growth in the use of composting as a means of reducing the volume of putrescible waste going to landfill sites. Across the world, governments are actively promoting both home, and larger commercial-scale, composting.

The ingredients of a compost heap have remained very similar over the centuries. Anything that once lived could be composted, though some materials, such as contaminated wastes, are best avoided. Heat, and the intense biological activity, can deal with many pests, diseases and weed seeds—but particularly persistent problems, such as clubroot, eelworm, or bulbils of oxalis, are best avoided. Local legislation may restrict what can be composted, or where a heap can be located. In nature, plant and animal debris decomposes where it falls; composting simply harnesses this natural process in a tidier fashion, to give a useful end product. The creatures involved in the process include bacteria, fungi, and other micro-organisms; also macro-organisms such as worms, woodlice, and springtails. All appear naturally and do not have to be added.

The basic principles of compost making are few. Weeds, grass mowings, and other organic wastes are stacked up in a free-standing heap or in a compost box. For a good end product, a mixture of tough (carbon rich) and less fibrous (nitrogen rich) wastes is essential. Such materials are sometimes known as 'browns' and 'greens' respectively. Scientifically speaking, the carbon to nitrogen ratio should be around 25/30 : 1, though on a garden scale there is no need to be that precise. The only other essentials are water and air in the right proportions. Some gardeners like to add a compost 'activator' to help the process. There is no need to use an activator if a mix of different types of material is being composted; any nitrogen-rich material that rots quickly (such as grass mowings or comfrey leaves) will get the process started. However, some gardeners find that herbal mixtures or activators containing micro-organisms are useful.

The speed of the composting process, and the quality of the end product, can be adjusted by the detail, the way in which everything is put together. Although a free-standing heap can be used to make compost, generally some form of compost box or container is used. Compost bins are typically made of plastic (preferably recycled) or wood. The volume should be no less than 350 litres. Sturdy construction, solid sides, a lid or cover of some sort, and no base are other important features. For the quickest composting, a compost heap should be assembled at one go. Tough and bulky materials are chopped or shredded; dry items are watered as the heap is built. Different materials may be added in layers—but a mixture of ingredients is probably more effective. Within a few days the activity of the decomposition organisms will have raised the temperature of the heap. Temperatures of up to 70 °C/158 °F can be achieved. Thermophyllic bacteria, actinomycetes, and fungi are involved at this stage. The heat kills weed seeds and pathogens, and further speeds up the process of decay. After a few days more the temperature will fall, as the declining air supply in the heap slows the activity of the aerobic bacteria. If the compost heap is dismantled, the ingredients mixed, then the heap rebuilt, heating up will start again (though to lesser heights) as air has been replaced. The cycle of heating and turning can be repeated several times until the easily decomposable materials have run out. At this stage the process slows down. Bacteria and fungi that prefer lower temperatures will move in to start work on the tougher ingredients. The final stages of decomposition are carried out by larger creatures such as mites, springtails, and worms. Using this method, compost can be made in around 30 days.

A slower system, where the compost heap is built piecemeal rather than in one batch, is more appropriate for most gardeners. Suitable materials are added to a heap as they become available, still paying attention to a balance of 'browns' and 'greens', and air and moisture. Heating may or may not be noticeable, depending on the volume of material added at one time. After 6-12 months a new heap can be started, and the old one left to finish composting for another few months. Finished compost at the bottom of the heap can be removed at this stage.

Useful compost can also be made from vegetable waste alone, using a system called worm composting. A colony of compost worms (usually *Eisenia foetida*) is kept in a plastic or wooden 'worm bin' and fed a regular supply of fruit and vegetable scraps. They will gradually convert the waste into worm compost (which is in fact worm manure). Fruit and vegetable scraps and waste household paper can also be combined to make compost. This system, named 'High Fibre' composting by its inventor Peter Harper of the Centre for Alternative Technology in Wales, was designed to recycle two common household wastes. Waste paper—cartons, paper bags, kitchen paper and the like, but not newspaper and quality flat paper that can be recycled in other ways—and vegetable and fruit scraps are added, in equal quantities, to a compost bin, as they become available. Worms, woodlice, ants, and other micro-invertebrate decomposers are the main players in this system of composting. The composting process is slow to start while the population of decomposers builds up. After six months or so finished compost can be removed from the bottom of the heap.

Composting is set to continue to be a valuable process, reducing waste disposal problems and producing a valuable end product for gardens and farms alike, for many more centuries. PP

Compton, Henry,

(1632-1713) Bishop of London, plant collector, and sponsor of plant collecting expeditions. He gardened at Fulham Palace which became in his day one of the most notable plant collections in the country. His gardener at Fulham Palace was George LONDON, who founded the Brompton Park Nursery in 1821 which distributed many of Compton's plants. Stephen SWITZER wrote of him in *Ichnographia Rustica* (1718): '[he] was one of the first that encouraged the importation, raising, and increase of exoticks . . . He had above 1000 species of exotick plants in his stoves and gardens.' Compton was especially interested in North American plants (his see extended to the American colonies), receiving seed from John Banister's and Mark CATESBY's expeditions to America. The American endemic shrub *Comptonia peregrina* is named after him. PT

Compton Acres ⊛

Poole, Dorset, England, was started by Thomas

William Simpson just after the First World War when he built a clifftop house with magnificent views. The mild climate and acid soil allowed him to grow the tender flowering shrubs that interested him. After the Second World War the house was demolished and the gardens were turned into a tourist attraction. Today they present a bustling array of themed gardens which range from the outstandingly good (the JAPANESE GARDEN, built in 1920 by Japanese craftsmen) to the mediocre. The Italian Garden, with a huge rectangular lily pool, fountains, and statuary, is finely designed but let down by poor detail. The position is still marvellous and there remain many excellent plants.   PT

Concepción, Hacienda de la ✿

near Málaga, Andalusia, Spain. Also known as the Finca de la Concepción, the garden has its origins in the 19th century when the estate was owned by Jorge Loring Oyarzabel (1822–1900) and Amalia Heredia Livermore (1830–1902). Both the children of wealthy businessmen in Málaga, they built a fine house, filled it with precious objects (especially archaeological artefacts), and began to make a garden. The site must have been especially attractive to them for it is said to have been that of a Roman villa. After their death the estate was occupied during the Civil War and fell into dereliction, and since 1990 it has belonged to the city of Málaga which has been restoring it. The beauty of the garden comes partly from the excellent collection of plants—in particular mature specimens of tender trees—and partly from its jungle-like profusion suffused in spring with the scent of *Pittosporum japonica*. Very large specimens of the rubber tree (*Ficus elastica*), Norfolk Island pine (*Araucaria heterophylla*), and Chilean wine palm (*Jubaea chilensis*) rise above shrubs like *Sparmannia africana* and cycads among the brilliant flowers of clivias and strelitzias. A water garden with a pool (on which black swans used to be seen), cascade, and rills is under restoration. A large pergola draped with wisteria was used by the Oyarzabels for alfresco feasts.   PT

> RUTH BROWNLOW, 'A world of plants on the Andalucían coast', *Historic Gardens Review*, No. 13 (2004).

conifers.

At the end of the last ice age Britain was blessed with a very poor woody flora, including about 35 different tree species and perhaps three times as many woody shrub species. Of the trees, only five were evergreen and three of these conifers. Scots pine (*Pinus sylvestris*) was the tallest of these, growing to 30 m or so on sheltered sites. Yew (*Taxus baccata*) is rarely as tall as 20 m/98 ft but much longer-lived, and juniper (*Juniperus communis*) occasionally grows to 8 m/26 ft, but often prostrate (the other evergreen trees are holly, *Ilex aquifolium*, and box, *Buxus sempervirens*). Scots pine in particular is a relict of the arcto-tertiary flora, occurring on the lands north of the ancient Tethys sea from Scotland, Spain, and Norway in the west nearly to the Pacific Ocean in north-east China. It quickly colonized bare glacial sands but was out-competed on the better soils which formed. The wet Atlantic period, around the first 500 years AD, saw it drowned out on poorly drained soils, such as those which developed into Irish peat bogs, and its useful timber probably caused its elimination from sandy soils, such as the Surrey heaths, by the 14th century—except of course in Scotland. Yew survived much better, partly because it can coppice (grow again if cut down), but also because it tolerates dense shade and the red fleshy part of the fruit is eaten by birds, badgers, and other discerning animals and the seeds spread. Also yew developed religious connections, which is why many of the oldest yew trees are in historic religious sites, now often with churches dating from the Saxon period.

The setting when people started planting gardens was a grave paucity of evergreen foliage and this spurred our early plant hunting. We have no record of conifer introductions as living plants before the 16th century—we know the Romans brought stone pine nuts (seeds of *Pinus pinea*) over, but to eat; if they grew any they left no record. Evergreens, of which conifers are par excellence, are invaluable for providing lasting shelter and screening, as well as a backcloth against which to admire other plants in season. The first conifer to have been introduced in modern times is Norway spruce, *Picea abies*, which came in sometime around the year 1500. Actually it was here before: the most recent natural report is a fossil from Cheshire dated as 54,000 BC. At its best it is a lovely tree, but most of the genus are more attractive. Norway spruce is found in the main mountain ranges of Europe, extending into Scandinavia, including eastern Norway. Modern uses include as a Christmas tree, for which it is hopelessly inappropriate, losing the needles at the first whiff of a mince pie in a modern home.

The European silver fir, *Abies alba*, soon followed, coming here in the early 17th century when James VI of Scotland ascended the English throne as James I, and incidentally reintroduced Scots pine into England. *Abies alba* is well suited to the moister western parts and is mainly seen in the west country where it naturally regenerates. Both *Picea abies* and *Abies alba* are geographically the closest members of their genera, with excellent timbers. However, both have suffered from insects brought in on related species. Also introduced from Europe in James's reign is the European larch, *Larix decidua*, again widely planted as a timber tree but deciduous, giving excellent bright green new foliage in spring and glorious autumn colour, with a winter tracery of golden yellow twigs.

These three were all introduced as timber trees but perhaps the most important introduction in this period was the cedar of Lebanon, *Cedrus libani*. This first saw our shores in 1638, with one survivor from that time. It was widely used in large landscaping schemes for its attractive shape and foliage—although when Capability BROWN first employed it he only knew trees perhaps fifteen years old. At this age it is a narrow upright tree, quite unlike the majestic spreading specimens two or three hundred years old that we can enjoy today. Also, unlike the other early arrivals from our nearer neighbours, this one actually does quite well here and is the best cedar if you can wait a century or so. For the less patient, or for those less confident of their longevity, Atlas cedar (*Cedrus atlantica*) with its (frequently) silvery blue foliage and deodar cedar (*Cedrus deodara*), both introduced in the 19th century, are better—although deodar cedar should be replaced every twenty years or so, as young trees are so much more shapely. The 1700s saw several of the North American conifers introduced, with the Weymouth pine, *Pinus strobus*, being the most successful. Eastern white cedar, *Thuja occidentalis*, had actually come in in the 1500s but like its compatriots from the eastern half of the continent is not well suited to our climate. The most enduring conifer at this time was the ginkgo or maidenhair tree, *Ginkgo biloba*. Virtually unchanged for the past 200 million years, this tree also came home when reintroduced in 1754. The 'young' tree at Kew is from this introduction, and probably still in the first half of its lifespan. As a garden tree, it is spectacular for the brilliant golden autumn colour, but is deciduous. It is the first tree of note to come from the eastern hemisphere.

The early years of the 19th century saw a massive increase in introductions. Perhaps the oddest was the monkey-puzzle, *Araucaria araucana*, from Chile. It was first collected by Archibald Menzies in 1795 but the main introduction was in 1839. Again, this was not really something new—the genus was found in both the northern and southern hemispheres until wiped out in the north at the same time as the dinosaurs—truly a tree for Jurassic parks, and suburban front gardens. Although a well-formed tree retaining its branches down to the ground is a majestic sight, it really looks better in groups. Also, where both male and female trees are planted, you get (if the squirrels don't get them first) the seeds, which are edible raw but delectable roasted like chestnuts. Of greater impact, though, were the many trees from western North America. David DOUGLAS was sent by the newly formed Horticultural Society (now the Royal Horticultural Society) to find and collect plants in western North America in the 1820s. At the time a single collection Douglas made—introducing the flowering currant *Ribes sanguineum*—paid for the entire trip but it was his conifer collections which sparked lasting interest. The fast growth of trees like the ubiquitous Sitka spruce (*Picea sitchensis*) and the nearly as common Douglas fir, *Pseudotsuga menziesii*, neither first found by Douglas but both introduced by him, has had the most dramatic impact upon our scenery and they are widely planted in forestry. The success and paradoxically also the rarity of these Douglas introductions led to the formation of the Oregon Society, a group of like-minded Scottish landowners who clubbed together to send John Jeffrey into Oregon in the 1850s. He introduced *Pinus jeffreyi*. Around the same the towering redwood, *Sequoia sempervirens*, and the Wellingtonia, *Sequoiadendron giganteum*, arrived. These two are more used in parks, or avenues, with Wellingtonia frequently forming the tallest tree. However, two more beautiful trees from this area are the western red cedar, *Thuja plicata*, whose foliage is delightfully scented, and the western hemlock, *Tsuga heterophylla*, whose habit as a young tree surpasses all others. Mention has to be made of the Lawson cypress, *Chamaecyparis lawsoniana*, which has given many different forms; also of the blue spruce, *Picea pungens*, although this is apt to become scruffy due to needle loss. The best American spruce only just made it in in 1897—Brewer spruce, *Picea breweriana*, with its level branches festooned with hanging branchlets.

The 19th century also saw many conifers from eastern Asia, such as Japanese cedar, *Cryptomeria japonica*, and Veitch fir, *Abies veitchii*, but perhaps the very best of these is the lacebark pine, *Pinus bungeana*, whose bark peels to reveal layers of creamy white, pinkish green, and purple. The blue pine, *Pinus wallichiana*, came to our shores from the Himalayas and some of the missing European trees were also introduced, especially the Serbian spruce, *Picea omorika*, Caucasian spruce, *Picea orientalis*, and Nordmann fir, *Abies nordmanniana*—fast becoming the Christmas tree of discernment.

The main contribution to conifers in Britain made during the 20th century was from China. WILSON and FORREST collected spruces such as Sargent spruce, *Picea brachytyla*, and Lijiang spruce, *Picea likiangensis*, but perhaps the pearl of their introductions is the silver firs they found—Wilson finding the slow growing and early coning Korean fir, *Abies koreana*, Forrest the taller growing species which bears his name, *Abies forrestii*. However, the most significant introduction was the discovery and arrival of the dawn redwood, *Metasequoia glyptostroboides*, in the 1940s. Fossils show that it was here before. This makes a fast-growing tree, excellent on both wet or normal soils and capable of growing in a foot of permanent water. It has a neat crown shape, attractive summer foliage, and brilliant autumn colour. Yes, it is one of the deciduous conifers. What was that point about our need for evergreens spurring our search for new trees? KR

Conimbriga ⊛

near Coimbra, Portugal, was a great Roman city dating largely from the 3rd century AD. It has been only partially excavated but the wealth of what has been revealed gives a vivid notion of its splendours. Superb mosaics including a maze with a minotaur at its centre and flowerpots were discovered, but of much the greatest garden significance was the peristyle garden of a grand villa. The truncated brick columns of the peristyle surround a rectangular pool in which a symmetrical pattern of intricately shaped raised beds edged in stone is planted with irises. All about the edge, close to the columns, very fine spouts direct jets of water arching into the pool. The walk surrounding the peristyle, with lavish geometric mosaics, remains in place. Nothing is known of the original planting but the surviving layout and its elaborate water is one of the finest Roman gardens of which substantial evidence remains. PT

conservation of garden plants.

The UK native flora is relatively sparse; however our climate is ideal for growing plants from a remarkable range of geographical locations. Plant introductions to the UK, particularly over the last 2,000 years, have reflected a history of invasions, occupations, exploration, scientific research, and gardening. Britain also has a remarkable history of expert horticulturalists and great plant breeders. This fascination with plants and gardening has resulted in one of the most diverse garden floras in the world. This is becoming increasingly recognized as both a scientific and a cultural asset that should be documented and conserved. For most of history conservation of garden plants has been a slightly haphazard affair with plants being collected and exchanged between gardeners. The pink, *Dianthus* 'Pheasant's Eye', has survived in this fashion from the 17th century, with gardeners propagating it from cuttings to retain its unique patterning for hundreds of years. Monastic gardens, cottage gardens, and the great estate gardens all had a role to play by growing plants, collecting them, and passing them around.

The preservation of gardens has been very important in the conservation of garden plants, providing a reservoir waiting to be discovered. The beginning of a serious movement for the conservation of landscapes and gardens emerged when the study of the history of the garden became a subject in its own right in the middle of the 20th century. In the 1980s, a national record of historic parks and gardens was initiated. English Heritage established this record, known as the *Register of Parks and Gardens of Special Historic Interest in England*, which now contains nearly 1,450 sites. The formation of the NATIONAL TRUST in 1895 and of the National Trust for Scotland in 1931 are noteworthy, both now managing a number of historic gardens and the plants within them. Concern about the loss of garden plants began to be expressed at the end of the 19th century; Gertrude JEKYLL talked of plants that had 'passed out of cultivation or can only rarely be heard of'. The emergence in 1804 of an organization established 'for the improvement of horticulture' was to provide garden plants with a champion. Initially called the Horticultural Society of London, it became the ROYAL HORTICULTURAL SOCIETY, or RHS, in 1861. It now holds more than 67,500 plants in its collections representing just under 30,000 different kinds of plants.

Real concern, which would lead to an organized attempt to conserve garden plants, first took shape in the staff tearoom at the RHS Garden at WISLEY. This was often a meeting point for horticultural luminaries such as Graham THOMAS when visiting the garden. Ongoing discussions between colleagues were stimulated into action by the decision of Hillier's Nurseries radically to reduce their catalogue list, a decision that many nurseries had to make in the economic climate of the time. Christopher Brickell, the then director of the RHS Garden Wisley, organized a conference in 1978 with delegates attending from over 100 organizations. This conference led to the formation of the NATIONAL COUNCIL FOR THE CONSERVATION OF PLANTS AND GARDENS, (NCCPG) and its main conservation endeavour, the National Plant Collections® scheme. The NCCPG has been the template for other garden plant conservation organizations around the world, including Le Conservatoire des Collections Végétales Spécialisées (CCVS) in France and the Ornamental Plant Collections Association (OPCA) in Australia. There is now a Swedish national programme to ensure the diversity of cultivated plants called Programmet för Odlad Mångfald (POM) and in 1999 the Ornamental Plant Germplasm Center was set up in Ohio, USA, to conserve and nurture the world's wealth of herbaceous ornamental plant diversity.

Gardens also have a role to play in the conservation of wild plants, particularly for plants that are at risk or even are extinct in their natural habitat. An example would be *Echinocactus grusonii*, the golden barrel cactus. This native of Mexico now has nearly no native habitat remaining; the construction of a large dam has left only a small wild population on the steep slopes above the reservoir. The Mexican government allowed an extensive salvage operation before the valley was flooded. It is a very popular plant for amenity plantings in the desert parts of the USA. Another plant that is dependent on gardens for its survival is *Franklinia alatamaha*. First seen by botanists William and John BARTRAM by the Altamaha river in Georgia in 1765, William later gathered seeds. It has not been seen in the wild since 1803; however literally thousands exist in cultivation. Traditionally conservation of wild plants out of their natural habitats has been a function of botanic gardens. In more recent years the value of plants in private and public gardens has been recognized. *Berberidopsis corallina* is a climber endemic to Chile that has only 22 known populations, some of which are of less than ten plants. A survey of the material in gardens has shown that a surprisingly good genetic diversity has been retained from the single introduction into the UK. In 1991 the International Conifer Conservation Programme (ICCP) based at the ROYAL BOTANIC GARDEN, EDINBURGH was established and has since developed a network of over 100 'Safe Sites' across the country where a broad genetic base of threatened conifers can be grown. The ICCP has shown that conservation collections can be incorporated into public gardens and private estates. Recently the value of the knowledge that private collectors, gardeners, and horticulturists have is being better recognized as an important resource for the conservation of plants in the wild. Being able to propagate and successfully grow a plant can be vital to conserving it.

The development of international plant conservation programmes as a result of the 1992 Convention on Biological Diversity is leading to greater coordination of the efforts between organizations such as the RHS, the NCCPG, the National Trusts, and botanic gardens. There is also potential for coordination of efforts at an international level in the future. The increase in the use of information technology is going to be the key to identifying what plants are protected, where they are, and saving the vital information associated with them.   RJ

conservation of gardens.

The conservation of gardens (including designed landscape parks) should be a continuous process, not only reflecting the way they are relentlessly changing and decaying but also taking account of their constant growth and development. Garden conservation involves guiding dynamic biological systems as well as repairing buildings and other artefacts. Conservation is not the same as restoration, re-creation, or adaptation but may well need to employ all these and other strategies to ensure a garden's survival. Nor does conservation rule out innovation provided that the proposed changes respect and enrich the site's meaning and value. The principal aims of conservation should be to reveal and enhance these qualities while consistently repairing and renewing the garden's structure and content.

Conservation history
British gardeners and designers have often looked backward, and abroad, for inspiration in making new gardens and redeveloping established layouts. This has usually entailed the free adaptation of styles and ideas from other countries and former times, transformed to meet contemporary values and requirements, often strongly influenced by newly introduced exotic plants. The comparative stability of British land ownership, at least since the 18th century, led many families towards a conservative approach to their gardens, which successive generations have extended, refashioned, and enriched rather than entirely destroyed and reconstructed. This has endowed Britain with the greatest diversity (and density) of significant historic gardens in the world, a unique palimpsest of styles and exotic plants. But the 20th-century decline of the country house also put gardens and parks in peril, a dilemma met in part by the National Trust Act of 1937. Along with great country houses, gardens and parks were accepted 'for preservation', but it was not until 1947 that, with the acquisition of HIDCOTE, the NATIONAL TRUST began to conserve gardens in their own right. Any objective approach to conserving gardens because of their special histories, features, and qualities developed only slowly, at first through the National Trust's experience of managing and showing gardens. As garden visiting became popular, and more and more private gardens were opened, so interest in their origins, designs, and plantings developed along with a burgeoning national interest in recreational gardening. This growing fascination with garden history led to the formation of the GARDEN HISTORY SOCIETY in 1965 and the elevation of the subject in the realms of academic study and research. The history of gardens and the challenge of their conservation were given a much higher profile in the 1970s with a major exhibition at the Victoria and Albert Museum, which finally established these subjects in the national consciousness. The concept of the historic garden was introduced into legislation through the Town and Country Amenities Act 1974, which covered grant aid but not protection against alteration or destruction. Using criteria agreed with ICOMOS and the Historic Buildings Council, the Garden History Society drew up the beginnings of a national inventory based on the existing historic importance of the garden or park. Each garden was either the work of a famous designer, representative of a style of gardening, an integral part of the setting of an historic building, or associated with famous people or events.

Conservation planning
Although there had already been notable attempts at historicist re-creation and restoration of gardens in the 1960s and 1970s such as Moseley Old Hall (Staffordshire), WESTBURY COURT, HESTERCOMBE, and HAM HOUSE, purposeful conservation planning began in effect with the publication by the National Trust of *The Conservation of the Garden at Stourhead* (1978), which set out to provide a framework for a century of management, restoration, adaptation, and renewal, based upon full studies of the history of the place and its plants. The Stourhead plan was an important milestone which emphasized the need for comparable conservation plans for other historic gardens based upon a full knowledge of the place, for which few possessed the resources or the expertise. Nevertheless in the late 1970s the National Trust began to commission research reports on selected properties aimed at integrating precise surveys of physical features—topographical, architectural, horticultural, and archaeological—with exhaustive documentary research and local enquiry at, for example, WIMPOLE HALL and Osterley Park (Middlesex). The latter being at the time managed by the Royal Parks, this was instrumental in inspiring them to commission similar historic surveys of all the central Royal Parks (see LONDON PARKS AND GARDENS).

A new profession of historic garden and landscape survey had been born, leading directly to the emergence of long-term plans for the management and conservation of historic parks and gardens. Expertise in survey and research of this kind covering land, buildings, water, ornament, plants, and history is now well perfected but needs to be supplemented by research into the biological and horticultural processes that have contributed to the distinctiveness of the place. Funding has always been a constraint for an inevitably expensive and labour-intensive process, and well-researched management (conservation) plans were produced only in small numbers before the late 1980s. Founded following the National Heritage Act 1983, English Heritage was charged with producing an official national *Register of Parks and Gardens of Special Historic Interest in England*, putting historic gardens and parks alongside historic buildings as important elements of the national heritage. Incorporating the unofficial lists of the Garden History Society, English Heritage created a system of grading, matching that for historic buildings. Although no new controls were applied, the system serves to alert planners, owners, and statutory bodies to the historic significance of gardens and the need to protect them. The 1987 Great Storm caused severe damage in the south and east of England and gave rise to English Heritage grants for listed gardens for restoration and renewal, which were made dependent on the production of, at least basic, 'management (conservation) plans' based on the history of the place. More than anything else these grants and subsequent tied financial assistance for gardens and parks brought the value of serious long-term conservation planning to the attention of owners and managers. Equally importantly it allowed for the development of expertise in survey, research, analysis, and conservation planning.

Significance

Conservation has to do with assessing the full value and meaning of what exists and arranging as far as possible for these qualities and features to be retained for the future. These may be, in the broadest sense, predominantly historic but the site will have acquired other significant values and interest, sometimes by intention but often by chance. 'Conservation is about negotiating the transition from past to future in such a way as to secure the transfer of maximum significance' (A. Holland and K. Rawles, 'Values in conservation', *ECOS*, Vol. 14: No. 1, June 1993). Although written with nature conservation in mind this definition holds good for most fields of conservation but begs the question as to what is meant by 'significance'. In this context it can be defined as distinctive value, special importance, unique quality, particular merit.

As well as significance being related to history, design, and the garden's structure and

planting, significant values can be aesthetic, educational, recreational, social, cultural, architectural, horticultural, biological, and environmental. In gardens significance is likely to involve processes—development and decay; systems of upkeep and renewal; distinctive methods of production; traditional skills vital to the place. Significance also embraces less tangible qualities of character, ethos, and meaning which depend upon subjective perceptions that will vary between locals, visitors, and specialists according to their familiarity with the place, their knowledge of it, and their own background and interests. Nonetheless these perceptions are significant considerations in conservation planning.

Statement of significance

Any plan for the conservation of a garden or park should begin with a clear and concise statement of significance covering the whole spectrum of its importance and potential. For historic gardens this would be based on comprehensive physical (including architectural, horticultural, and archaeological) surveys of what exists combined with exhaustive historical research leading to a full report incorporating chronology, design history, planting, buildings, archaeology, and analysis. But the report should also take account of the other values and qualities outlined above and cover potential—i.e. for restoration, adaptation, innovation, education, recreation, nature conservation. For the sake of clarity and for management it is important to know in comparative terms the degree of significance of each of the factors identified. Although they are inevitably interdependent, it is useful to set them out in order of precedence because of the likelihood of occasional conflict, e.g. between the precise repair of a formal architectural feature and the preservation of wildlife habitat.

Conservation principles

Guiding principles for the long-term conservation and management of the garden should arise directly from the statement of significance combined with a realistic consideration of management constraints, which inevitably influence policy and govern strategy. Change of use and surroundings, funding constraints, the availability of skilled staff, and health and safety and planning legislation are important management imperatives which must be taken into account in setting out an achievable vision for the foreseeable future. These principles should set out concisely the policies and assumptions which would govern all important decisions—restoration, renewal, adaptation, innovation, management, staffing, standard of upkeep,

planting style, access, interpretation, nature conservation, etc. The principles should also take account of sensitive and fragile characteristics of the garden and embody policies for restraint and protection, especially in respect of access and interpretation.

Conservation and management plan

As with the principles of conservation, the long-term conservation and management plan should be formulated by, or in close consultation with, the managers and owners so that it would be realistic and 'owned' by them. Essentially it should set out an achievable vision, first for the place as a whole and then for each identifiable part of it, with strategies for achieving and sustaining these aims. With reference to the principles of conservation already decided, the conservation plan is best formulated by addressing the following consideration for the place as a whole and for each character area within it:

- historic precedent (particularly with regard to overlays);
- perceived ideal (aesthetic, horticultural, architectural, etc.);
- constraints (planning, resources, skills, fragility, etc.);
- opportunities (restoration, adaptation, enrichment, innovation, etc.);
- proposals (for the foreseeable future, in general, and for each character area).

The aim should be to indicate a clear course of action and to provide information for future owners and managers as to the motives and assumptions behind the plan, right or wrong. Subjective judgement, especially on aesthetic ideals, is both vital and inescapable. It should not be shirked but needs to be explained. Some policies and strategies for conservation may be best dealt with in general, for the place as a whole, e.g. access, circulation, interpretation, security, visitor facilities, restoration, nature conservation, staffing, training, planting policy, plant sources, rate of renewal, style of upkeep, etc. Others may be better dealt with under individual character areas. Proposals will be inevitably governed by resources and strongly influenced by any change of use of the house and estate, e.g. from private to institutional, and the garden, e.g. increased opening to visitors. The plan should explain the dilemmas created by these changes and the reasons for selecting the preferred options. Major proposals would need to be phased according to available funding but otherwise the proposals should be timeless in the sense of setting an achievable ideal, a permanent aspiration, described and illustrated as precisely as possible. In this respect it is important that style and standard of upkeep should be prescribed and provision made for renewal and reworking, probably on a cyclical basis. By far the most important single factor in the successful conservation of gardens is the regular employment of trained and motivated gardeners in sufficient numbers, properly equipped. Every conservation plan should include a strategy for the recruitment, retention, training, and development of gardeners with the appropriate blend of skills, judgement, and management ability. At the first Conservation Conference in 1968, Frank Clark, the first president of the Garden History Society, stressed the need to propagate the value of traditions expressed in the great gardens: 'The inheritance of a tradition confers both riches to an indigenous culture and responsibilities to the new generations that inherit it.'   JSa

conservatory.

A building with large, usually south-facing, windows used to protect tender plants. The word is first used with this meaning in John EVELYN's *Kalendarium Hortense* (1664). In *Elysium Britannicum*, on which Evelyn worked intermittently unto his death in 1706, he gives precise details of the size of his 'Conserve'—15 or 18 m/50 or 60 ft long by 7.4 m/24 ft high—'which for cold may be reduced to halfe'. He says that the south front should consist 'of a range of *Colomns* of the wreathed forme & adorned with foliage & *Corinthian* capitals'. He adds 'Such a Conserve did *Salomon de Cause* [i.e. DE CAUS] erect for the *Electors* Incomparable Gardens at Heidelburge'. Here Evelyn is referring to the HORTUS PALATINUS which was laid out *c.*1615. For Evelyn a conservatory was indistinguishable from a greenhouse, which was so named because it was used to protect tender evergreens. The conservatory was heated in winter, for which Evelyn recommended an ingenious external stove which would circulate air in the conservatory, providing both warmth and ventilation. J. C. LOUDON in his *Encyclopaedia of Gardening* (1822) defines a conservatory as a plant house 'on which the plants are grown in a bed or border without the use of pots'. This would distinguish it from an ORANGERY in which the citrus plants are cultivated in containers to allow them to be moved out of doors from late spring to early autumn as they have been, for example, at VERSAILLES since the 17th century. Loudon says that it is desirable in a conservatory 'that the roof, and even the glazed sides, should be removable in the summer' which allows the plants to be exposed to full light and air, so that instead of being 'etiolated and naked below' they develop 'a bushiness of form, closeness of foliage, and a vividness of colour' that they would otherwise lack.

One of the earliest surviving conservatories in Britain is at CHATSWORTH, built *c.*1690 and usually referred to as the greenhouse. Throughout the 18th century they were frequently built in gardens, both for their use and for their ornamental potential, and they continued to be built in the 19th century. An outstanding and curious example is the curved conservatory designed *c.*1805 by Samuel Pepys COCKERELL for SEZINCOTE with scalloped Mughal windows and ending in a beautiful octagonal pavilion. Until the early 19th century the glazing bars of the conservatory were wooden, supported in a sash window, but thin iron glazing bars allowed much more elaborate designs. At Syon Park (Greater London) Charles Fowler designed the magnificent Great Conservatory with a vast dome which was built between 1827 and 1830. In modern usage the conservatory is usually thought of as a glazed extension to a house in which to grow tender plants. These became very popular in Britain in the late 20th century partly because it was one of the few ways of extending a house without planning permission. Increasingly it became thought of as primarily a place for people to bask in the sun in which a few plants would also be tolerated.   PT

MAY WOODS and ARETE SWARTZ WARREN, *Glass Houses* (1988).

container.

Containers in which to grow plants have an ancient history. As an ornament in itself, and as a way of transporting a tender plant into the protection of a greenhouse, the container has played an important role in gardens. The earliest examples would probably have been used for practical purposes. In ancient Roman horticulture terracotta pots were used for rooting layered plants or for seedlings. Cato in *De Agri Cultura* (*On Agriculture, c.*169 BC) explains how, when the plant has formed roots, the pots may be cracked and planted straight into the soil. Archaeologists have excavated pots of the kind described by Cato in positions which show they were used in the way he describes. Surviving pots have holes in the base, presumably both for drainage and to allow roots to grow through. In ancient Roman gardens, for example at Herculaneum and POMPEII, plant containers were disposed about a pool at the centre of an atrium. The use of pots for propagation is described in Theophrastus' *History of Plants*, which says they were used to propagate cedars and palms in Persia in the 4th century BC.

In illustrations of European gardens from the late Middle Ages containers are only occasionally seen. A drawing of *c.*1460 by the Master E.S. shows a loving couple on a turf seat on which there is also a castellated pot containing a small tree. A similar scene is depicted in a miniature from the *Roman de Renaud de Montauban* (*c.*1475) in which is seen a pot of carnations, then a recent introduction to northern Europe. Since the Renaissance containers, often of elaborate design, have been widely used. A Flemish painting of *c.*1525 shows a fine piece of topiary in a pot being transported in an early form of wheelbarrow. In Renaissance Italy potted plants are seen, in a distinctive pot-bellied shape, in Giusto UTENS's painting *c.*1599 of the Tuscan Villa Petraia. Here they are woven into the garden's design, used to mark the corners of parterres or arranged along the crest of a wall. In French 17th-century gardens containers had various purposes. Louis Liger's *La Nouvelle Maison rustique ou économie générale de tous les biens de campagne* (1700) emphasizes that ' containers of flowers should be disposed symmetrically in parterres, to one side, along terraces . . . raised on slopes or on stone plinths'. A particular form of container was the 17th-century *caisse de Versailles*, the Versailles box, a square wooden container standing on legs. The sides were hinged so that the box could be opened to give access to the metal liner which contained the plant. Boxes of this sort were commonly used in 17th-century gardens in France both for ornamental purposes as well as for allowing the easy transport of tender plants, in particular citrus plants, in and out of a glasshouse. Brackets on each side of the box would allow wooden staves to be inserted horizontally so that two men could carry a large *caisse* with its plant. At the orangery in VERSAILLES, where some of the citrus plants are very old and large, the *caisses* are still used for this purpose. Today the citrus, and other tender plants, are disposed higgledy-piggledy on the esplanade outside the orangery. In the 17th century, as seen in Jean Cotelle's painting of 1693, they were beautifully arranged in patterns. The orangery also used the distinctive goblet-shaped glazed Pots d'Anduze, made in the 17th century by a firm in Anduze called Les Enfants de Boisset which still exists and still makes exactly the same kind of pot. Flowerpots were used in immense numbers for the Trianon garden at Versailles. Plants for bedding schemes were kept in pots so that they could be quickly planted out, pot and all, completely to change the appearance of a parterre. According to Pierre-André Lablaude in *The Gardens of Versailles* (1995) 2 million pots were used in this way.

In the 19th century, with all kinds of historicizing garden styles in fashion, there was a flourishing renewal of interest in containers, many of them made in period styles and cast in iron. These were often planted up with summer bedding plants, in particular with pelargoniums. Brent Elliott in his *Victorian Gardens* (1986) describes a fashion for 'winter bedding' in which evergreens in pots were planted straight into beds. An engraving of a winter bedding scheme at Heckfield Place shows a giant urn brimming with plants surrounded by shaped beds. In the 20th century containers have found favour in different ways. In English gardens it became fashionable to use old 'coppers', originally used for washing clothes, as plant containers. Vita Sackville-West at SISSINGHURST CASTLE was a pioneer and hers may still be seen in the Cottage Garden there. Old lead CISTERNS, originally made for gathering rainwater, have also been used as planters. In modern times the use of containers has become common in pedestrianized inner-city areas. These, alas, are frequently of poor quality, typically made of moulded vandal-proof concrete in a sweeping shape or, in many ways even less attractive, copies of period styles looking very unconvincing in concrete. In private gardens modern Tuscan terracotta pots, hand thrown and of fine quality, are occasionally seen, but these are very expensive and mass-produced industrial pots are much commoner. In England one craftsman, Philip Thomasson, has been making containers out of a modern version of Coade stone which has a hard surface and can be moulded with very crisp detailing. This has been used to make simple pots of graceful shape, often of very large size, as well as exactly faithful reproductions of old designs. Not all period reproductions have had such happy outcomes. Plastic copies of Tuscan lemon pots are a sad sight but fibreglass reproductions of lead containers are fairly close to the original and have the great advantage of being light. In everyday gardening the beautiful old hand-thrown terracotta flowerpots have been replaced by unlovely plastic pots which, however, have the advantage of being moisture retentive and far more durable. Furthermore, they are often square in section, fitting neatly into trays and making them far more economical of space.   PT

Convention on International Trade in Endangered Species of Wild Fauna and Flora

(CITES), established in 1975 to supervise the traffic in animals and plants at risk in the wild. It is based on an agreement between governments of those countries supporting the principles adopted by CITES—by 2003 164 countries were signatories of the convention. The essential principles are that any trade in species should be sustainable and should not damage habitats. CITES lists endangered plants and animals under three categories: (I) those threatened with extinction; (II) those that will become threatened with extinction unless trade is controlled; and (III) those endangered in one country which seeks the cooperation of other countries to limit trade. Around 28,000 plants were listed in 2004, the species most at risk being those of very high commercial value—such as mahogany (*Swietenia macrophylla*) from Central and South America where forests have declined spectacularly between the 1950s and the 1990s. Many garden plants are also endangered. In a country like Turkey (which is a signatory), for example, the great richness of indigenous plants, particularly bulbs, of special horticultural interest made the flora vulnerable. Among plants of garden interest that are endangered are *Sternbergia lutea*, several species of snowdrop, and no less than 30 species, or forms, of cyclamen. All listed plants exported, re-exported, or imported between signatories of the Convention have to be licensed by CITES.   PT

Copijn, Hendrik

(1842–1923), Dutch landscape architect, the son of a nurseryman, who made a speciality of large landscapes and public spaces and had a particular knowledge of trees. Between 1860 (Blookerpark) and 1922 (the beautiful 18th-century estate of Vollenhoven, both in the province of Utrecht), he worked on a large number of estates and was active in the transforming of former city defences into public parks at the end of the 19th century. Among the most notable gardens on which he worked are those at the Kasteel de HAAR from 1894 and MENKEMABORG where, in parthership with his son Lodewijk Wilhelmus Copijn (1878–1945), he restored the gardens from 1921. The son continued the family business until the outbreak of the Second World War and worked on several fine gardens, among them the Pinetum Blijdenstein (Noord-Holland, 1929) and Berg en Bos (Apeldoorn, 1932).   PT

Corsini, Palazzo ⊛

Florence, Italy. The palazzo was purchased by Filippo Corsini in 1621 from the Acciaiuoli family, the palazzo and rare late Renaissance town garden with loggia having been started by Bernardo Buontalenti (1536–1608). Fillipo and Maddalena Corsini employed the architect Gherado Silvani to complete the project in baroque style, with geometric beds, and an 'avenue' of statues and lemons in pots. Using false perspective Silvani placed the statues on pedestals at progressively decreasing heights to give the illusion of greater distance. During the 19th century the garden was partly remodelled so that wooded areas, in the romantic style of a *giardino inglese* (see JARDIN ANGLAIS), with a small lake, framed the main parterres. Hedges of bay laurel and evergreen viburnums line the paths in the BOSCO with underplanting of periwinkle and acanthus. Recently restored by Oliva di Collobiano, with authentic 17th-century planting in the parterres, the garden contains some interesting shrubs and trees, including a Chinese bead tree (*Melia azedarach*) and specimen *Poncirus trifoliata* in the flower beds, besides 115 tortoises.   PH0

Cothay Manor ⊛

near Wellington, Somerset, England is a remarkably unchanged late medieval house. Nothing is known of any early gardens here and the history of the garden as it is today is entirely 20th century. The estate was bought in 1925 by Colonel Reginald Cooper, a retired diplomat, connoisseur of country houses, and friend of Harold Nicolson of SISSINGHURST, Lawrence JOHNSTON of HIDCOTE, and Norah Lindsay of Sutton Courtenay Manor. He formed the habit of buying fine houses in distress, restoring them, and making a garden. At Cothay he laid out a strong axial walk of yew hedges with compartments leading off, each opening in the hedge marked by piers of clipped yew. In 1993 the estate, then much neglected, was bought by Alastair and Mary-Anne Robb who restored the fine yew hedges, relaid paths, removed clutter, and introduced much distinguished new planting. Existing enclosures were replanted, such as the fine entrance forecourt with its colour scheme of orange, yellow, and red and a garden of white and silver off the yew walk. An entirely new garden is a walk of mop-headed acacias (*Robinia pseudoacacia* 'Umbraculifera') underplanted with lavish drifts of 'White Triumphator' tulips and catmint. Along the wooded banks of an outlet of the river Tone is a garden of wilder character, with shade- and moisture-loving plants by the water's edge. This is an old-fashioned garden for an old-fashioned place and shows the continuing liveliness of the tradition of the garden of compartments filled with good planting.   PT

cottage garden.

The idea of the cottage garden is essentially late Victorian in its origins but it had its greatest influence on English garden design in the 20th century. The notion of cottage life that gave rise to the idea had a heavy dose of Victorian sentimentality. Several late 19th-century artists painted views of gardens which sum up the cottage garden essence. Artists such as Helen Allingham (1848–1926), G. S. Elgood (1851–1943), Lilian Stannard (1877–1944), and several others of this time painted ripe borders, soaring hollyhocks, billowing topiary, and arbours of roses, all as often as not bathed in the golden light of a late summer's afternoon. The gardens they painted were usually those of the middle and upper classes who certainly did not live in cottages. The air of lavish, fairly uncontrived floriferousness of their gardens was, however, close to the true cottage spirit. Gertrude JEKYLL saw the charms of cottage gardens and of old-fashioned flowers (on which she wrote an article in *Black's Gardening Dictionary*, 1928). She liked the word 'old', writing about old roses and designing gardens 'on old-fashioned lines'. She loved the whole pattern of traditional country life and wrote about it in *Old West Surrey: Some Notes and Memories* (1904).

The two world wars had a dramatic effect on the economics of gardening in England. Until the Second World War it was usual for the middle classes to have at least one gardener, as well as a cook and a maid. After the war the numbers of such people declined steeply and increasingly gardens were maintained by their owners with occasional help from jobbing gardeners. In this context the laissez-faire approach to gardening suggested by the cottage garden was both attractive and, above all, affordable. It was Margery FISH at East Lambrook Manor who, no doubt unwittingly, codified the cottage garden style. She and her husband bought 'a poor battered old house' in Somerset in 1937 and in *We Made a Garden* (1956) she described 'the modest and unpretentious . . . cottage garden' she made 'with crooked paths and unexpected corners'. Her garden was not undesigned; it was made according to firmly held principles. It should (like that of a Renaissance villa) be 'as much part of the house as possible'. It should have 'bones', structural planting of evergreens to give the garden permanent interest. It should have a lawn to give 'a feeling of space and restfulness'. In a long series of later books she described the plants she grew, some of them from the hedgerows, like natural forms of primrose (*Primula veris*), catmint, peonies, hardy geraniums, and *Stachys byzantina*. With the much increased wealth in the late 20th century the appeal of cottage gardening dwindled. A cottage was perfectly desirable but it was no longer a house in which you lived, it was where you spent weekends. Your garden might still be influenced by Gertrude Jekyll but only in so far as it had colour-themed borders and was filled with old shrub roses.   PT

Cottesbrooke Hall ✤

near Northampton, Northamptonshire, England, is a fine early 18th-century house in flat country with long views over the rural landscape. The spire of Brixworth church 5 km/ 3 m away across parkland south-east of the house is drawn into the park as an eyecatcher. The gardens as they are today are entirely of the 20th century. The architect Robert Weir Schultz (1860–1951) designed a sunken courtyard garden with a pool and pergola, and a long paved terrace walk between mixed borders and overshadowed by old cedars of Lebanon. A pair of 18th-century gates lead to pleached limes and a statue of a gladiator. A statue walk with yew hedges has four fine statues by Peter SCHEEMAKERS originally in the Temple of Ancient Virtue at STOWE and bought in the Stowe sale of 1938. South of the house, which was originally the entrance façade, a new garden surrounded by wrought-iron railings was laid out in 1937 by Sir Geoffrey JELLICOE in the form of a quadripartite parterre, with topiary shapes of common and golden yew disposed among lead statues, beds of 'Iceberg' roses, and tubs of agapanthus. This is not the highly intellectual Jellicoe of late years, rather a pitch-perfect and decorative response to the gentlemanly sobriety of the site.   PT

Courances, Château de ✤

Milly-la-Forêt, Essonne, France, an estate that goes back to the 14th century. The chateau was largely rebuilt in the 17th century for Claude Gallard with 18th-century additions. In the middle of the 17th century a garden was laid out, possibly to the designs of Jean Le Nôtre (c.1575–1655), the father of André LE NÔTRE. This is essentially the remarkably beautiful garden which is visible today. The entrance drive runs along an avenue of plane trees (planted in 1782) flanked by canals and this axis is continued on the far side of the moated chateau. A pair of PARTERRES *de broderie* on the moated garden opens the vista on this side and continues with a broad grassy walk and a long canal piercing woodland to end in a circular pool overlooked by a figure of Hercules. The woods on each side, rich in mature trees, are laced with ALLÉES, and to the west are further canals and pools. The garden is also notable for cascades. By the 19th century the garden was in decay but in the 1870s was restored to its 17th-century character by Jean de Ganay with the help of Achille DUCHÊNE. Walks through the woods, the solemn reflections of great trees in placid water, the occasional splashing of a waterfall, and long views back towards the chateau give the greatest pleasure.   PT

Courson, Château de ✤

Courson-Montcloup, Essonne, France, essentially a 17th-century remodelling of an earlier and more modest house. There were formal gardens *à la française* associated with the 17th-century rebuilding, but all this was swept away in the early 19th century when Napoleon's cousin, the Duc de Padoue, lived here. Many of the fine surviving trees in the park date from this time. Later in the century the BÜHLER brothers made a great lake and carried out more tree planting, and in the 20th century the planting has been further enriched. Since 1982 Courson has been the home of the Journées des Plantes, a festival of gardening with nurseries selling plants and all sorts of garden-related events which takes place twice a year, in May and October. Even without this lively event Courson deserves to be better known for its serene park and fine planting.   PT

Court van der Voort, Pieter de La

(1664–1739), Dutch cloth merchant, art patron, and gardener. His father Pieter de La Court was at the forefront of hothouse technology and in 1658 grew the first pineapple at Meerburg near Zoeterwoude. The son is best known for his gardening treatise *Byzondere aenmerkingen over het aenleggen van pragtige en gemeene landhuizen, lusthoven, plantagien en aenklevende cieraeden . . .* (1737) (Particular Remarks on the Layout of Beautiful and Common Country Houses, Pleasure Gardens, Plantations, and Associated Ornaments) (1737), which was translated into both French (1750) and German (1758). It was the first treatise in Dutch to provide a theoretical basis for garden design. It also addressed various practical issues, including the cultivation of plants, propagation, and stove and hothouse technology, the latter presumably embodying the knowledge held within the family.   JW

Cranborne Manor ✤

Cranborne, Dorset, England, was in the 13th century a royal hunting lodge in Cranborne Chase. In the early 17th century the manor was granted by Elizabeth I to Robert Cecil, 1st Earl of Salisbury, who also owned HATFIELD HOUSE. The house was rebuilt between 1608 and 1612 with much Renaissance detailing, including an elegant LOGGIA, in a style suitable for the royal entertaining which Cecil had to undertake. The Cecils' gardener at Hatfield, John TRADESCANT the elder, also worked at Cranborne where in 1610 he was planting trees. Garden walls were being built, including those of an orchard which the agent Thomas Hooper said was 'the fittest place for apricocke and such lyke'. A 17th-century estate map shows formal gardens of which some of the axes survive today. The present garden in its detail dates from 1954 when the present Dowager Marchioness of Salisbury (then Lady Cranborne) came to live here. She is a skilled practical gardener who is also learned in garden history. The gardens she made are wholly appropriate to the site in terms of atmosphere and historical inspiration. West of the house there survives a 17th-century mount which is now the centrepiece of a pattern of beds edged in box and Irish yews and planted with shrub roses. To the south-east of the house is an enfilade of enclosed gardens—a knot garden of herbs, a pair of grand mixed borders, and a four-part garden of roses and herbs.   PT

Crarae Gardens ⊛

Crarae, Argyll, Scotland, occupy a site which has been used to create a wild woodland garden of great distinction. On the north-west bank of Loch Fyne the Crarae burn flows through a rocky and precipitous glen on whose banks the garden was laid out. The woodland garden has its origins in trees planted c.1800 by Crawford Tait and ornamental gardening was first done in 1912 by Lady Campbell who was an aunt of Reginald FARRER the plant hunter, alpine plant expert, and author. The soil is acid and the climate is fairly mild but with high annual rainfall of 185 cm/75 in. These conditions are excellent for the trees and shrubs which are the garden's chief beauty. Conifers do notably well here and in 1932 Sir George Campbell planted up 90 plots of different conifers which have grown to great size. In the woodland garden, with the ravine running across it, are trees such as cercidiphyllum, eucalyptus, maples, nothofagus, poplars, rowans (*Sorbus* species), and styrax. The flowering shrubs include camellias, disanthus (notable for its autumn colour), drimys, magnolias, osmanthus, pieris, and rhododendrons. These are the great ornaments of the landscape here but there are also attractive plantings of Himalayan meconopsis and of primulas. There are in all 51 hectares/126 acres here and despite the exotic planting the garden at Crarae seems completely harmonious with the landscape that surrounds it, of which delicious views of Loch Fyne to the east and the mountains to the west open out repeatedly. Since 2002 Crarae has belonged to the National Trust for Scotland.   PT

Crathes Castle ⊛

near Banchory, Kincardineshire, Scotland, was built between 1553 and 1596 for Alexander Burnett whose family had lived here since the 13th century. By the 17th century there was a notable garden here made by Thomas Burnett who, a contemporary wrote, 'subdued the genius of the place, for by planting firs and other trees of many kinds [he] has covered the forbidding crags . . . laid it out with gardens and clothed it with pleasance'. The gardens today are chiefly laid out in a large walled and hedged enclosure, 2.8 hectares/7 acres in area,

on two levels to the east of the castle. This layout dates from the early 18th century; the magnificent yew hedges, ornamented with swirling topiary, survive from that time. The ornamental planting within, however, is almost entirely 20th century, although there were notable borders here in the late 19th century which Gertrude JEKYLL saw and wrote about admiringly in *Some English Gardens* (1904). The present gardens were the inspiration from 1926 of Sir Robert Burnett and his wife Sybil. Influenced by Gertrude Jekyll and by Lawrence JOHNSTON of HIDCOTE whom they knew, they laid out a garden in which colour, firm structure, and a sequence of enclosures determined the atmosphere. Borders of orange and yellow, monumental blocks of clipped yew, hidden borders of white and silver, a gold garden, and a pair of fortissimo mixed borders (with the castle as an eyecatcher rising above) are skilfully deployed. The Burnett family gave the Crathes estate to the National Trust for Scotland in 1952.   PT

Crescenzi, Pietro de'

(1230–1305), born in Bologna where he studied natural history, law, and medicine. When living on his farm near Bologna he wrote, between 1299 and 1305, the *Liber Ruralium Commodorum* which was rapidly translated into French, German, Italian, and Polish. The book draws on the writings of earlier authors such as the Romans Cato (234–149) and Varro (116–27 BC) but shows originality in his discussion of pleasure gardens. He divides these into three sizes: small gardens with herbs and flowers, rather larger gardens with an orchard and trellis arbour, and princely gardens which had a hunting park.   PT

crinkle-crankle wall.

The term dates from the 16th century but its application to a kind of wall is 18th-century. Usually built of brick, it is a wall that curves back and forth, or zigzags, regularly along its length. It is found in gardens of the Netherlands (where it is known as a *slange muur*—snaking wall) and in England chiefly in East Anglia, where the Dutch influence was strong largely because of Dutch engineers coming to drain the fens and work in other watery parts. Most of the surviving examples in England date from the late 18th and early 19th centuries. The crinkle-crankle design has the structural advantage that a great length of wall may be built without the need for piers or buttresses; it also has an advantage of cost, for the wall can be made much thinner, even with only a single course of bricks. It is found in kitchen gardens and, in particular, in fruit gardens, where the concavities were thought to

protect fruit trees, especially the earliest flowering kinds like pears. However, it is also claimed that the shape of the walls causes buffets of wind which may damage the plants. J. C. LOUDON's *Encyclopaedia of Gardening* (1822) finds no practical merit in them as an aid to fruit growing. At Wroxall Abbey in Warwickshire, where Sir Christopher Wren lived until his death in 1716, is a remarkable wall with lobe-shaped alcoves designed to shelter fruit trees—probably designed by Wren. This is not exactly a crinkle-crankle wall but it looks very much like a prototype.   PT

Crowe, Dame Sylvia

(1901–97), English garden designer, landscape architect, and author. She was president of the Landscape Institute from 1957 to 1959 and helped to found the International Federation of Landscape Architects (IFLA) of which she became acting president. She worked on the landscaping of new towns at Basildon (Berskhire), Harlow (Essex, with Sir Frederick Gibberd), Warrington (Cheshire), and Washington (Tyne and Wear) and was employed by the Central Electricity Generating Board to landscape the setting of the nuclear power station at Trawsfynydd in Snowdonia. As Landscape Consultant to the Forestry Commission in 1964 she put into practice her belief that 'Aesthetic and ecological principles are inseparable, certainly in afforestation' and was instrumental in adopting mixed plantings of broad-leafed and coniferous trees and abandoning the blanket planting of regimented conifers which had had such a disastrous effect on the landscape. Her book *Garden Design* (1958) remains of great value. Its first words are 'Gardens are the link between men and the world in which they live' and she eloquently explores this fundamental theme in relation to gardens of every kind.   PT

Csákvar ⊛

(Esterházy Park) Fejér County, Hungary. Count János Esterházy made this the centre of his estates in 1777, and immediately set about the construction of his palace and its grounds. It was almost certainly Isidore Canevale (Ganneval), who redesigned the Augarten in Vienna, the Imperial Gardens in LAXENBURG and possibly another Esterházy garden at the nearby TATA, who was the first creator of this transitional-style 'English' garden. The garden was soon extended to a larger scale park by Franz Stautenrauss. Although the style was irregular, the system of viewlines began by following the example set by the Eszterháza estate (see FERTŐD) of the princely line of the family, though some parts—the 'English' garden, the Star Avenue behind it, the pheasantry, and the so-called '*Allée* Forest'—deviated from it substantially. In the course of the 1780s and 1790s a number of structures—partly the work of stage-designer Pietro Rivetti—were constructed in the park, including a Turkish pavilion, a Dutch peasant house, a hermitage, an Indian hut, a pyramid and Egyptian house, a Chinese GLORIETTE, a grotto, a military tent, the Anna *hameau* (hamlet; named after the Countess), temples of Diana and Apollo, mock ruins, a sundial, and the Gessner House (imitation mill). The mock ruins—like those in the garden at Tata—were built using stones from the ruins of the medieval abbey at nearby Vértesszentkereszt. Most of the garden's constructions were erected to celebrate family occasions. In 1800 the estate was inherited by Count Miklós Esterházy, who had the park redesigned by Ferdinand Zart as a larger-scale, picturesque landscape garden. Some of the buildings had already disappeared in the 19th century, while others were destroyed after the Second World War, when the park was divided. A garden that was once one of Hungary's largest and most richly endowed with ornamental structures still awaits renovation.   GA

Csáky Gardens. See HODKOVCE.

Culross Palace ⊛
Culross, Fife, Scotland, is a 17th-century merchant's house at the centre of a wonderful enclave of finely preserved village houses close to the banks of the river Forth. The house was well restored by the National Trust for Scotland which also recreated a period garden on the terraced slopes in the walled enclosure behind it. Here are regimented raised beds of period fruit, herbs, ornamentals, and vegetables. A wooden tunnel arbour is festooned with pleached mulberries and trained vines, and paths are surfaced in crushed shells. It is both delightful and convincing—a most unusual authentic re-creation of a vernacular garden of its time.   PT

Cunningham, Allan
(1791–1839), English plant collector, who became a gardener at Kew in 1808 and was one of the many collectors sent by Sir Joseph BANKS to unexplored parts of the world. Cunningham arrived in New South Wales (1816) at a time when inland and coastal exploration of colonial Australia was intensifying. He travelled inland

in 1817 with explorer John Oxley, collecting about 450 plant species, all unknown to science. Cunningham made several journeys around Australia (1817–22) in the survey ship *Mermaid*, always sending his enormous collections of seed and bulbs to Kew. In 1831 Cunningham was offered the post of colonial botanist. He declined the position and his younger brother Richard (1793–1835) was appointed, arriving in 1833. However, Richard was killed during a surveying trip down the Darling river in 1835. Allan then accepted the post of colonial botanist, returning to Australia in 1837 where he died in 1839. The majestic Moreton Bay pine, *Araucaria cunninghamii*, and other plants, commemorate Cunningham's pioneering work.   CMR

Cura, Huerto del ⊛
Elche, near Alicante, Spain. *Huerto* is the Spanish for 'market garden', 'kitchen garden', or 'orchard', and *cura* means 'priest'. The most extraordinary feature of the Huerto del Cura is a grove of date palms, *Phoenix dactylifera*, a native of North Africa and western Asia. These were thought to have been brought here by the Phoenicians and have become naturalized. The oldest specimens are around 250 years old and today there are thousands of trees in the grove, or El Palmeral, as it is called. To one side of the Palmeral is the Huerto proper in which exotic fruit trees—among them bananas, citrus plants, jujubes (*Zizyphus jujuba*), and pomegranates—have been cultivated since at least the Middle Ages. There is also a modern garden of cacti.
PT

Cuseni, Casa,
Taormina, Sicily, Italy, built by the Englishman Robert Kitson in 1907. The garden, on a steep slope overlooking the sea and Mount Etna, with a series of architectural terraces, has a distinctive English atmosphere given by the range of interesting plants, with great advantage having been taken of the favourable microclimate. The garden is essentially formal with a series of geometric rooms on flat terraces, joined by steep steps and ramps, many decorated with pebble mosaic patterns and old tiles from Tunisia. On one terrace a small basin with dripping water is backed by rococo decoration, and other walls are stencilled with caricatures of the owner and his builder. On the highest terrace above the house a swimming pool, framed with wisteria, reflects Mount Etna

on its surface. Kitson probably designed the house and garden himself, and it is a fine example of how Italianate architectural motifs can combine with the English love of plants to produce a small masterpiece. Plants reflect a 100-year-old taste for collecting: a citrus orchard, almond trees in early spring, seeding *Geranium maderense*, tender echiums, and jasmine flourish, with snowdrops and cyclamen in the shady corners. Today this beautiful garden with incomparable views is maintained by Robert Kitson's niece Daphne Phelps.   PHo

cutting garden.
The cutting garden is a part of the garden set aside for the cultivation of flowers for use in the house. It is mentioned in Olivier de Serres's *Le Théâtre d'agriculture et mesnage des champs* (1600) where 'Fleurs pour le jardin bouquetier' (flowers for the cutting garden) are described, among them pinks, peonies, and tulips. J. C. LOUDON's *Encyclopaedia of Gardening* (1822) does not mention the cutting garden specifically but says that flowers should be gathered 'only from the reserve-garden' to avoid disfiguring the plants in the main borders and compartments. Great gardens of the past, in particular in the late 19th and early 20th centuries, required quantities of flowers to decorate the rooms of the house. In the VATICAN GARDENS a cutting garden is cultivated to provide altar flowers. In modern times some of the plants grown may be chosen specifically to meet the needs of the flower arranger. It is not only flowers that are of interest here but seed-heads of striking shape, or ornamental foliage. The cultivation of such a garden is no different from any other part of the flower garden as regards soil, exposure, nourishment, and watering. In the cutting garden, however, plants may be disposed in spaced rows of a single species or variety which makes it much easier to devise support for those plants that need it. Few gardens open to the public show cutting gardens in action. At Priorwood Garden in Melrose in Scotland there is a garden devoted to 'everlasting flowers' with around 200 varieties of flowers of different types suitable for drying. In the USA gardens exist where customers may cut their own flowers, such as the Cutting Garden at Sequim (Washington State) which has an area of 8 hectares/20 acres.   PT

Cuzzano, Villa. See ALLEGRI ARVEDI, VILLA.

D

Daigo-ji. See SANBÔIN.

dairy.
The dairy is a building rarely treated in an ornamental way in gardens but a few examples are of exceptional beauty and interest. In French late 17th-century and 18th-century gardens the dairy was recognized as a possible form of decorative pavilion. One of the earliest was that built between 1689 and 1694 to the designs of Jules HARDOUIN-MANSART for the Prince de Condé at CHANTILLY. Antoine-Nicolas Dezallier d'Argenville described it in his *Voyage pittoresque aux environs de Paris* (1762) as having 'a vaulted, circular drawing room built of fine white stone and paved with marble'. In the Hameau at VERSAILLES Richard Mique designed a Laiterie de la Reine (Queen's Dairy) for Marie-Antoinette that was built between 1784 and 1786, a curious rustic building unexpectedly ornamented with grand white marble busts on columns between the windows—Diana, a shepherd, a shepherdess, and a faun. This juxtaposition of the Arcadian rustic with the smoothly classical is at the heart of the idea of the ornamental dairy. The Laiterie de la Reine at RAMBOUILLET is the most magnificent dairy of all and one of the outstanding French garden buildings. A grand neoclassical building, with two chambers and a grotto, it was designed by Jacques-Jean Thévenin and built in 1785.

Outside France ornamental dairies are rare and tend to be primarily functional, and even when decorative are rarely in a position of prominence. A pretty example is at KILLRUDDERY in Ireland where a late 19th-century octagonal dairy has stained-glass windows, Gothic tracery, and an interior with decorative tiles. It is also provided with a veranda, presumably made to overlook the mid-Victorian garden which is laid out below it. At Belvoir Castle in Leicestershire is a Gothic dairy dating from the mid 19th century and said to have been designed by the Duchess of Rutland. A typically unemphatic but charming dairy is the 19th-century thatched building with a rustic porch at Conock Manor in Wiltshire which has something of the atmosphere of the FERME ORNÉE. The mysterious Ladies of Llangollen at Plas Newydd in Clwyd (Wales), who in the late 18th century sought a life of rustic simplicity, arranged a planned walk which took in the beauties of the farm, including the dairy. A rare example of the truly swagger dairy in England is at WOBURN ABBEY in Bedfordshire where Henry Holland designed a CHINOISERIE dairy of the greatest splendour (between 1787 and 1802). An exceptional early 20th-century example in Scotland is John Kinross's superb Gothic dairy, vaulted and surfaced with different kinds of sumptuous marble, at Manderston in Berwickshire.   PT

Daisenin ✤
Kyoto city, Japan, the Retreat of the Great Sages, founded in 1509 by Kogaku Sōkō (also Shūkō, 1465–1548), is a sub-temple of Daitokuji, a temple of the Rinzai sect of Zen Buddhism located in north-central Kyoto. The garden of note lies at the north-east corner of the main hall, *hōjō*, and is just slightly more than 100 sq. m/328 sq. ft in size. It was built in the dry landscape garden style (see KARESANSUI) and can be understood as a three-dimensional re-creation of an ink landscape painting.

The stone arrangement at the corner of the garden depicts a waterfall crashing down through a series of mountains and flowing out into a broad, calm river. The water is expressed with white sand and the mountains with thin, blue-stone boulders (*aoishi*, chlorite schist) set upright, one behind the next. To the right and left of the waterfall are, respectively, a crane and a tortoise isle, Taoist symbols of longevity. The isles are made with granite boulders from the mountains north of Kyoto and the blue-stone for the waterfall comes from the island of Shikoku. This difference in material, as well as in the design of the rock arrangements, leads to the hypothesis that the garden may have been built in two stages; the first, under the direction of Sōkō, immediately after the main hall was built, and the second, in the late 16th century,

perhaps under the direction of Gyokuho Jōsō, head priest of the sub-temple Kōtōin. Jōsō was from the Mitsubuchi family who donated stones to Daisenin. There are also many records that attribute the garden to the painter Sōami (d. 1525) but are believed by most scholars to be apocryphal.   MPK

Dal. See LAKE DAL.

Dampierre, Château de ✤
Dampierre, Yvelines, France. This had been a manor house in the 13th century. In the early 16th century the estate belonged to Jean Duval, treasurer to François I, and by the end of the century, when Androuet DU CERCEAU illustrated it in *Les Plus Excellents Bastiments de France* (1576–79), it had a fine garden. The moated chateau looked southwards over six parterres enclosed in elaborate walls and pavilions and also moated. To the east a hedged enclosure on terra firma had 24 parterres, each of a different design. From 1682 all this was changed when the chateau was refashioned by Hardouin-Mansart and the gardens laid out by André LE NÔTRE for the Duc de Chevreuse. Le Nôtre greatly extended the existing pools and moats to make a dramatic watery landscape for the chateau. It overlooks rectilinear pools and lawns towards a balustraded pool where the land rises in a scalloped amphitheatre with a statue of the *Enlèvement d'Hélène* (1756) at its head. The chief canal extending away from the chateau ends in a charming PAVILION of dressed stone inlaid with tufa and putti playing with lions and dolphins on its parapet. In recent years a *parc floral* was planted at Dampierre but it is the Le Nôtre landscape for the great chateau and its equally beautiful outhouses that is of compelling attraction.   PT

Damsgård Mansion ✤
Bergen, Hordaland, Norway, is a small country house with gardens and park of 0.45 hectare/1.1 acre. Rebuilt in the rococo style in 1770, it is now a museum. The white-painted symmetrical building complex is situated on a hillside above the Bergen fjord, facing north, and the old lime avenue between the fjord and the mansion is partly intact. The gardens and park were restored 1985–9 based on a plan by Sven-Ingvar ANDERSSON. Two small gardens are situated at either side of the main building, the formal pleasure garden to the east, the kitchen garden to the west with a pond for carp and another for duck. The gardens are enclosed on two sides by stone walls topped with tiles, on the third side by a wooden fence behind a row of clipped lime trees. In the pleasure garden the symmetrical parterre is divided into six compartments, planted with 18th-century

herbs and flowers, known from old herbaria of pharmaceutical plants from Bergen and collected by the department of botany, University of Bergen. In summer white-painted copies of the original wooden garden sculptures with mythological motifs adorn the gardens. Next to the mansion there is a miniature 19th-century landscape park with a grove of lime trees, a pond, and the dry bed of a stream crossed by a bridge.   ME

KNUT FÆGRI, DAGFINN MOE, PER MAGNUS JØRGENSEN, and SVEN-INGVAR ANDERSSON, 'Damsgård have', *Foreningen til norske Fortidsminnesmerkers Bevaring* (1989).

Danubian Gardens ⊛

Bulgaria, is the generic name for several riverside public parks in cities along the river Danube, most of which were laid out at the beginning of the 20th century. The river forms the country's northern border, and the first of three notable examples from west to east are the Danubian Gardens of Vidin. Established in 1902 on 10 hectares/25 acres, the park displays a neo-baroque character with a linear composition and skilfully designed vistas to the river. Their unique character stems from the adjacent medieval fortress of Baba Vida, rich vegetation (poplars, willows, ashes, and cedars), and architectural elements (fountains and sculptures). To the east, the Danubian Park of Rousse was created largely by the Czech landscape architect Richard Noivert (1905–48) in the 1920s and completed by Bulgarian designers in the 1970s. It has magnificent flower parterres and picturesque groups of planting. Peaceful corners and deep river perspectives are laid out in a harmonious landscape style. Further east is the Danubian Park of Silistra, dating back to 1870 with the construction of the CASINO, but furnished with a fountain, pergolas, and gazebos around 1900. Gradually extended and enriched, the park has charming rose plots and oak groves among ancient ruins in a site of 20 hectares/50 acres.   ASG

Darmstadt Prinz-Georg-Garten ⊛

Hesse, Germany, a walled garden in Darmstadt city centre named after Prince Georg Wilhelm von Hesse-Darmstadt (1722–82). In the 18th and 19th centuries it was the setting for less formal festivities that were not part of the court calendar. It is still apparent, from the way its main axes converge at a right angle, that Prinz-Georg-Garten evolved from two separate gardens. Under Landgrave Ernst Ludwig (1678–1739) the baroque Prinz-Georg-Palais was erected in 1710, its garden extending southwards in a fan shape to the boundary of the garden of General Johann-Rudolf von Pretlack (1667–1738), who in 1711 had the prettily

painted Gartenhaus erected. This survives to the present day and was restored in 2004. The gardens were combined in 1748. The grounds are laid out on a rectangular grid of paths, their intersections graced with fountains and sundials. One exceptional feature is the Nische pergola, reconstructed in 2004 as an eyecatcher at the head of the main axis. The parterre beds are planted according to historical examples alternately with decorative and edible plants propagated in the garden's own nursery, while the Orangerie and Orangeriegarten contain citrus trees and shrubs. The Orangeriegarten theatre is a *théâtre de verdure* (see THEATRE) built around 1779 with hedges of clipped beech (*Fagus sylvatica*). Restoration work on the garden began in 1995. The Nische, a TREILLAGE pavilion, as the southern visual focus on the main axis of the Palaisgarten, was restored in 2004 based on views by J. H. W. Tischbein (1751–1829).   BM

Dartington Hall ⊛

near Totnes, Devon, England, is a rare, unusually complete, medieval house dating largely from the late 14th century but on much older foundations. The estate was bought in 1925 by Leonard and Dorothy Elmhirst who were interested in new ideas about education and in stimulating the rural economy. They also took good advice about the gardens so that the hall today has one of the best and most attractive of landscape settings. H. Avray Tipping (1855–1933) advised from 1927, followed by Beatrix FARRAND and Percy CANE. The undulating and wooded site already had striking landforms with, below the hall, the Tournament Ground, a dramatic turfed terrace. It has been suggested that this dates from the Middle Ages but it is much more likely to be of 18th-century origin. Percy Cane designed superb broad flights of stairs leading down to it, one of them memorably flanked with great magnolias underplanted with azaleas. Beatrix Farrand laid out the hall's courtyard, with a sweep of flagged path, cobbles, and a lawn, giving it a collegiate air. She also laid out woodland walks on the slopes west of the Tournament Ground, lined with spring plants, camellias and rhododendrons. Overlooking the Tournament Ground on this side is a terrace walk with superb old sweet chestnuts (*Castanea sativa*) and a fine Henry Moore bronze of a reclining woman (1947). This is a garden of bold effects and excellent detail, in keeping with the magnificent hall and the noble natural landscape.   PT

David, Armand

(1826–1900), French missionary and naturalist. Born in the Pyrenees, with an early love of

natural history, David joined the Lazarist order, becoming a professor at their college in Italy, pursuing both theological and scientific studies. In 1861 Professor Henri Milne-Edwards (1800–85) of the Paris Muséum National d'Histoire Naturelle requested that a member of the order be sent to China to assist in scientific research, and David was chosen. He travelled to Peking (Beijing) in 1862 with a list of natural history requests and on arrival reported the opportunities to Paris, resulting in his release from missionary duties two years later to pursue research. For ten years he explored intensively in southern Mongolia, central China, and Tibet. This resulted in David, primarily an ornithologist, discovering some 3,500 new plant species, including *Pinus armandii*, *Clematis armandii*, *Davidia involucrata*, and *Magnolia dawsoniana*, and a deer, *Elaphurus davidianus*. Ill health forced his permanent return to France in 1874.   MC-C

Deepdene, The,

near Dorking, Surrey, England, in the 17th century the home of Charles Howard who laid out a garden in an amphitheatre in the valley (or dene) below the house. John Aubrey knew the garden in its 17th-century heyday and described 'cherry trees, myrtles etc. . . . a great many orange trees and syringas . . . 21 sorts of thyme . . . it is stored full of rare flowers, and choice plants.' Howard also made a grotto and laid out walks; Aubrey describes a tunnel piercing the hill 'through which as through a tube you have a vista over all the south part of Surrey and Sussex to the sea'. In the early 19th century The Deepdene was owned by Thomas Hope, described by J. C. LOUDON in his *Encyclopaedia of Gardening* (1822) as 'a man of great taste in all the fine arts, and eminently in architecture and gardening . . . the grounds . . . are highly romantic'. The house is long since demolished and little remains of the grounds.   PT

deer park.

Enclosed royal hunting parks, or 'forests', governed by special laws go back to Anglo-Saxon England. The term forest has in this context no necessary connotation of trees. Oliver Rackham in his *The History of the Countryside* (1986) gives the legal definition of a forest as a 'region in which the King (or other magnate) has the right to keep deer and make Forest Laws'. The 'other magnate' would refer to a great churchman or a powerful courtier. The Bishop of Durham, for example, had a deer park at Auckland Palace by the 13th century. The deer park of the Bishop's Palace in Wells is now turned over to grazing but it still provides a parklike setting of marvellous beauty for the exquisite ensemble of moated palace and cathedral. The chase was not merely sport, for venison was an important source of food and the deer parks were skilfully managed so that the population maintained appropriate numbers for the grazing available. The deer park, as a precursor of the landscape park, and as an ornament of the landscape in its own right, has had a profound influence on the appearance of the English landscape. There are innumerable examples of the sites of deer parks being transformed into landscape parks in the 18th century by Capability BROWN and others.

PT

Dég

(Festetics Park) ⊕ Fejér county, Hungary. One of the greatest landscape gardens in Hungary, this park shows traits of the BROWNIAN style. Its construction began in 1817 for Count Antal Festetics. Situated in a valley, at the meeting of three streams, the parkland extends over an area of 250 hectares/625 acres. Its designer is unknown. The magnificent neoclassical house, built around 1815, was designed by Mihály Pollack, the most significant Hungarian architect of the time. This building has become the focal point of the huge park and estate. It was built on the highest point of the valley, on the axis of the main road leading to the village, so its impressive portico was discernible from a long distance. The road itself was levelled, edged with trees, and diverted to a new track at the borders of the park. Viewed from the palace's garden front, the park stretches forth majestically, with a serpentine lake and the so-called Dutch house in its middle. The two churches in the village (the Roman Catholic one was designed by Pollack too) are also important features of the scenic view. Spacious clearings and long openings provided an open view to the furthest point of the park.

A neoclassical ORANGERY, designed by Pollack, was built on the edge of the park, in the vegetable garden. The ruinlike 'Antique Fountain' was placed near the house. The Dutch House, built in 1891 on the largest island in the lake, is the park's most important edifice. Members of the family were buried on a small mound in the south-west corner of the park. In the 1920s, a Rose Garden and a tennis court were created with a neoclassical pergola and a *broderie* 'pebble PARTERRE'. The reinforced concrete Gothic Pump House was built at the same time.

After the estate was expropriated by the state in 1945, the western part of the park was maintained by the forestry department. As a result, its original unity of structure disappeared. The palace's surroundings (an area of 28 hectares/70 acres), complete with the serpentine lake and garden buildings, have survived, however, one of the most impressive historic gardens of Hungary. Its conservation has already been started. GA

GÁBOR ALFÖLDY, *A dégi Festetics-kastélypark* (The Festetics Park at Dég) (in preparation 2005). JÖZSEF SISA, *The Festetics Mansion at Dég* (in preparation 2005).

De Haar. See HAAR, KASTEEL DE.

De Keukenhof. See KEUKENHOF, DE.

Delany, Mrs Mary
(1700–88), née Granville, artist, gardener, grotto maker, traveller, and writer who in 1731 went to live in Ireland where, in 1741, she married Dr Patrick Delany who was a connoisseur of gardens and knew Joseph Addison, Alexander POPE, and Jonathan Swift. Delany had made a garden of rococo decorativeness at his estate Delville on the edge of Dublin at Glasnevin. Mary Delany is a valuable source of descriptions of 18th-century Irish gardens—*The Autobiography and Correspondence of Mary Granville, Mrs Delany* was edited by Lady Llanover and published in 1861. In her seventies she started to make remarkable exquisitely fashioned paper collages of flowers, 'mosaicks' as she called them, of which there is a collection in the British Museum. PT

de la Vallée, Jean. See VALLÉE, JEAN DE LA.

Delavay, Jean Marie
(1834–95), French missionary to China who collected for the Muséum National d'Histoire Naturelle in Paris. Born in Haute-Savoie Delavay was sent as a missionary to China in 1867, to Guangdong province in south-east China and later to Yunnan in the north-west, where he remained for the rest of his life, dying in its capital Kunming. He was a tireless and inveterate explorer and an avid plant collector. Over the years he sent back to the Muséum some 200,000 dried specimens including around 1,500 new species, among them specimens of new genera. Many of the packages which he sent back remained unopened at the Muséum for many years due to lack of resources. Delavay's discoveries included *Meconopsis betonicifolia* (syn. *M. baileyi*), later introduced to Britain by George FORREST. Among the plants that he introduced were *Primula vinciflora*, *Paeonia lutea*, and *Osmanthus delavayi*, of which he sent the first seeds to Maurice de Vilmorin in 1890. MC-C

de L'Orme, Philibert.
See L'ORME, PHILIBERT DE.

De Menkemaborg. See MENKEMABORG, DE.

Demidoff, Villa. See PRATOLINO, VILLA.

Denmans ⊕
Fontwell, West Sussex, England, belongs to the garden designer John Brookes (b. 1933) who inherited an existing layout from his predecessor, Mrs Robinson, but has very much put his stamp on it. On a flat site of 1.4 hectares/3.5 acres he has made a garden of very independent character. There is an easy flow of events with very few straight lines and none of the formal devices such as box hedges, knot gardens, pleached lime walks, and so on which became so ubiquitous (sometimes monotonously so) in English gardens of the late 20th century. Brookes allows the plants to do the talking, contrasting their character or colour or, as in the case of a little grove of silver birches, eliciting the essential beauty of a single species. A drift of gravel, like a flowing river, ambles across the garden with scatterings of sometimes self-sown plants. The walls of an enclosed garden are smothered in plants and its rectangular shape hidden by thickets of plants threaded by a winding path. PT

Denmark.
The Danish landscape can be described as a gently undulating agricultural landscape, varied and mild, dotted with small deciduous forests, watercourses, and lakes. The climate is temperate. Some of the oldest architectural additions to the landscape are entombments, for example dolmens and passage graves from c.2000 BC, and later, the distinctive domed barrows of the Bronze Age, from 1500 to 500 BC. The three Viking fortifications from c.1000, Trelleborg in Slagelse, Fyrkat in Hobro, and Aggersborg in Aggersund, are unique. We know only a little about the oldest Danish gardens. Medieval gardens were mainly laid out as simple, cruciform cloister gardens and had a functional purpose. In Scandinavia, these cloister gardens were mostly found at Benedictine and Cistercian monasteries, and the first known gardener in Denmark was Abbot Vilhelm of Eskildsø and Æbelholt (1127–1203). The Renaissance garden arrived in Denmark from Italy in the mid-16th century, and Hans Raszmussøn Block, an expert on herbs, published the first book on Danish gardens, *Horticultura Danica*, in 1647. The astronomer Tycho Brahe's (1546–1601) manor, Uraniborg Observatory, and Renaissance gardens on the island of Hven were laid out in 1581 (see URANIBORG), and Christian IV (1577–1648) began to lay out the Renaissance King's Gardens in Copenhagen in 1606. In ▶

the 1690s, a distinctive Italianate terraced garden unparalleled in Denmark was laid out at CLAUSHOLM. Splendid 17th-century larger-scale gardens are FREDERIKSBERG, FREDENSBORG PALACE, and FREDERIKSBORG CASTLE. In the late 1760s the English landscape garden, already in the form of a romantic garden, began to gain ground in Denmark. The period's gardens were often conceived by educated amateurs, LISELUND being considered the finest example. The concept of landscape gardener began to gain ground, through the work of such men as J. L. Mansa (1740–1820) and Rudolph Rothe (1802–77). The romantic style spread quickly since it could also be used in smaller spaces, and parsons and schoolteachers laid out model gardens. In the 1800s societies for the beautification of cities often took the initiative to lay out parks. The parks laid out on Copenhagen's former ramparts, including the TIVOLI GARDENS and many parks in provincial cities, are fine examples of these new meeting places for the middle classes. They were dominated by winding paths that skirted groups of exotic trees, laburnums, and lilacs. Henry August FLINDT worked with both public parks and manor gardens, at Clausholm,

Colour plates

A 'Dutch house' overlooks the lake in the early 19th-century landscape park at **Dég**, Hungary

Statue of the Wine Harvest (1599–1608) by Valerio and Simone Cioli in the **Boboli Gardens**, Florence, Italy

Fallen camellia blossom at **Heligan**, England

Wangshi Yuan, China, is named Master of the Fishing Nets after its 12th-century creator who loved fishing

GLORUP, Egeskov, and Bregentved. Edvard Glæsel (1858–1915) has been called 'the last landscape gardener', since he was the link to the 'architectural garden style'. Erik Erstad-Jørgensen (1871–1945) also worked both architecturally and with an eye to the landscape. At the beginning of the 20th century gardens were often laid out in small plots, characteristically in courtyards at the centre of apartment blocks. G. N. BRANDT strongly influenced the development of the profession in Denmark with his designs at Ordrup Cemetery, Hellerup Coastal Park, and MARIEBJERG CEMETERY. Other landscape architects in this period were Peter Wad (1887–1944), Georg Georgsen (1893–1976), Aksel Andersen with MINDELUNDEN in Ryvangen, and C. Th. SØRENSEN, who established a strong tradition in the 1920s of creating varied, lavishly planted recreational areas with playgrounds and leisure facilities around housing developments. The famous 'Finger Plan' from 1947 ensured the establishment of green areas close to Copenhagen, and park directors in the 1930s and 1940s established an outer green belt around Copenhagen. Several landscape architects, such as C. Th. Sørensen, Sven HANSEN, and Georg BOYE, continued to experiment with geometrical shapes, most notably at NÆRUM ALLOTMENT GARDENS and at HERNING ART MUSEUM. Other projects, laid out quite simply but especially expressive because of their subtle planting, were designed by Aksel Andersen, Troels Erstad (1911–49), and Arne JACOBSEN. After the Second World War, housing construction, schools, universities such as SOUTHERN UNIVERSITY DENMARK in Odense and the TECHNICAL UNIVERSITY OF DENMARK, training centres, health-care and cultural institutions, and cemeteries involved landscape architect such as Sven Hansen and Sven-Ingvar ANDERSSON, Georg Boye, Eywin LANGKILDE, Inge and Jørgen VESTERHOLT, Edith and Ole NØRGÅRD, Agnete Muusfeldt (1918–91), and J. Palle SCHMIDT. Large recreational areas were established as Greater Copenhagen expanded: Vestskoven, Køge Bay Coastal Park, Hedeland, and STORE VEJLEÅ VALLEY with Kongsholm Park, Vallensbæk Moat, and Lake Herstedvester. Most projects carried out in recent decades have continued the 20th-century tradition of creating specific spaces in the landscape. But in recent years, landscape architects in Denmark, e.g. Jeppe Aagaard ANDERSEN and Stig L. Andersson, like their colleagues in the United States and southern Europe, have tended to be more spectacular. The social, public aspect appears to have moved into the background. Important exceptions are the many carefully planned courtyard renovations.   AL

Denver Botanic Gardens ⊛

Denver, Colorado, USA, is a tightly contained 23-hectare/57-acre garden oasis, with several satellite locations in the region, totalling 1,729 hectares/4,270 acres of plant and wildlife habitat. The mission 'to connect people with plants'—especially indigenous Rocky Mountain plants—began with the garden in 1951. Overcoming the challenge of little space, this oasis has now grown to include many gardens, including a modern Tropical Conservatory, a traditional JAPANESE GARDEN, a herb garden, a Children's Secret Path, home-demonstration gardens, a water garden, a fragrance garden, and a garden inspired by the art of Monet; and the Gardens of the World hold plants from Asia, Europe, Africa, Australia, and the tropics. One of the most intriguing exhibits is the dramatic Cloud Forest Tree, featuring orchids and other epiphytes, arrayed on a 12-m/40-ft wide tree replica, under glass. Conservation of water in gardening in this dry climate is an important subject in programmes and the demonstration gardens. The Denver Botanic Gardens are 1.6 km/1 mile above sea level, and indigenous plant communities of the desert, plains, mountain foothills, and alpine zones are displayed as part of plant conservation education and the Center for Plant Conservation, based here. The ethnobotany of plants important to the indigenous peoples of the region is the subject of a special garden. The 25,000-volume botanical and horticultural library is a valuable resource for the entire region. The City of Denver administers the Botanic Gardens as part of its parks programme.   PC

Derby Arboretum ⊛

Derby, Derbyshire, England, was opened to the public in 1840, the first public park in England. Its promoter was the mayor of Derby, Joseph Strutt, who gave the land and conceived the park as a place of both recreation and instruction—it 'should comprise a valuable collection of trees and shrubs (from around the world), so arranged and described as to offer the means of instruction to visitors'. The original site of 4 hectares/10 acres was extended by 3.5 hectares/8.5 acres in 1852 to accommodate recreational facilities. J. C. LOUDON designed the original park, laying out a pattern of winding paths and enlivening the flat site by building up mounded ground on each side of paths. This introduced spatial diversity and concealed the relatively modest size of the park. Furthermore, many of the trees and shrubs, of which there were over 800 species, were planted on these mounds, displaying them to great advantage. His design became famous and the arboretum was visited by A. J. DOWNING in 1850 and by Frederick Law OLMSTED in 1859. By the end of the 20th century Derby Arboretum, like many great urban parks in England, was neglected. A Heritage Lottery Fund award of £4,246,000 was made in 2002 and, with additional funding, a wholesale refurbishment was well under way in 2003.   PT

Desert Botanical Garden ⊛

Phoenix, Arizona, USA, is set in an arid valley landscape punctuated by the red rock buttes of Papago Park, and contains within its 20 hectares/50 acres one of the world's most complete collections of desert flora. Twenty thousand plants, representing almost 4,000 taxa in 133 plant families native to the south-west of the United States and to Central and South America, are displayed along desert trails and in exhibits. The garden is famous for its cacti, covering 1,300 different species, and its collection of agaves and yuccas. In early spring, after winter rainstorms, the botanic garden is alive with hummingbirds, taking advantage of the vivid flowering of the desert plants. A fascinating 1.2-hectare/3-acre exhibit, 'Plants and People of the Sonoran Desert', demonstrates how Native Americans for centuries depended upon the plants in their desert environment. Ocotillo (*Fouquieria splendens*) was used as living fences; the woody ribs of the saguaro cactus (*Carnegiea gigantea*), combined with grass, mud, and ocotillos, were used in building dome-shaped houses; the fleshy fruits of prickly pear (*Opuntia*) were eaten raw and made into syrup and jelly. The garden shows in detail how the native plants interact with the animals and birds of the desert as well, to the fascination of visiting children as well as adults. The precept of the Botanical Garden, formed by a group of valley citizens in 1939, was to encourage an appreciation and understanding of the world's arid-land plants, with a particular emphasis on the succulents and the native flora of south-western United States.   PD

Désert de Retz, Le ⊛

Chambourcy, Yvelines, France, the creation of François Nicholas Henri Racine de Monville between 1774 and 1789. Monville bought a deserted estate in the forest of Marly in 1774 and a little later also acquired the ruined 13th-century parish church which he admired as a picturesque adornment of the landscape. Monville himself laid out the grounds and designed many remarkable ornamental buildings with the help of the architect François Barbier (who had to sue Monville for his fees). The most complete view of the garden in its heyday is contained in a map and engravings of it published in Book 13 of *Détails des nouveaux jardins à la mode* (1785) by Georges

LE ROUGE. The map shows an area of 38 hectares/95 acres with winding walks, informal groves of trees, a stream, two lakes, and numerous FABRIQUES, seventeen in all, identified in a key. The entrance to the garden was a grotto enshrouded with trees and decorated with two figures of satyrs, made of tin, clasping flaming torches. The most curious building, which substantially survives, was the Colonne Détruite (Ruined Column), built to resemble the truncated remains of a gigantic fluted column in whose interior Monville made a four-storey apartment, some of whose rooms were illuminated by apparent cracks in the stone. Access to the several rooms, some of them oval in plan, was by a magnificent central spiral staircase. There were six storeys in all, including two subterranean cellars. A Chinese house (which partly survived into the 20th century) was built overlooking a small CHINOISERIE pavilion, the whole set in their own garden with a thatched cottage and a wriggling stream with islands, entered by gateways of Chinese character. An orangery in the Chinese garden was crowned with a curious tower like a prototype for the Eiffel Tower. A columned rotunda was dedicated to Pan, a Tartar tent stood on an island in a lake, and an ICEHOUSE appeared in the form of a great PYRAMID (now restored) between tall columnar poplars. An obelisk made of tin but painted to resemble stone overlooked the *métairie* (smallholding), a mixture of themes creating a sort of Egyptian FERME ORNÉE. In its day the Désert was notable, and visited by many notable people, among them Thomas JEFFERSON in 1786—of the Colonne Détruite he said, 'How grand the idea excited by the remains of such a column.' After the Revolution Monville sold the estate, which was looted by revolutionaries. It changed hands several times, but by the early 20th century the landscape was decaying; however, in 1939 it was listed as a Monument Historique. The Désert was rediscovered in the 20th century—the surrealists, unsurprisingly, found it much to their taste. Cyril Connolly visited it in 1945 and 'fell hopelessly in love with the place', and at that time the Colonne Détruite was inhabited by goats which Connolly saw 'clattering up the beautifully undulating spiral staircase'. In 1983 the estate was acquired by Olivier Choppin de Janvry and Jean-Marc Heftler who embarked on a restoration plan. Now partly restored as a result of their devotion and energy it is the best surviving example of a group of extravagantly picturesque gardens (such as MÉRÉVILLE and the FOLIE SAINT JAMES) made in the dying days of the *ancien régime*.   PT

DIANA KETCHAM, *Le Désert de Retz* (1994).

⊃ page 133

Desgots, Claude

(d. 1732), French gardener and garden designer, a great-nephew of André LE NÔTRE. Desgots came from a dynasty of gardeners—his father Pierre was *jardinier ordinaire du roi* under Louis XIV and both his grandfather and great-uncle were gardeners at the Tuileries (see PARIS PARKS AND GARDENS). He worked at VERSAILLES and in 1688 succeeded his father at the Tuileries. Of his garden design work in France his joint project with Le Nôtre for Denis Tallon at the Château d'Issy in the 1680s was probably his greatest work, destroyed during the siege of Paris in 1871. He was the intermediary on behalf of Le Nôtre for a proposed garden in England at Greenwich Park (London) which was never made. Desgots himself designed two English projects neither of which was completed: the Maestricht garden in 1700 at WINDSOR CASTLE and a parterre for the Earl of Orkney at CLIVEDEN *c.*1713.   PT

DOMINIQUE GARRIGUES, *Jardins et jardiniers de Versailles au grand siècle* (2001).

Dessau-Wörlitz Gartenreich ⊛

Wörlitz, Germany. The Dessau-Wörlitz Gartenreich (Garden Realm), a declared Unesco World Heritage Site, is regarded, as the citation reads, as an 'outstanding example of the application of the philosophical principles of the Age of the Enlightenment to the design of a landscape that integrates art, education, and economy in a harmonious whole'. Today it spreads over an area of 150 sq. km/57.6 sq. miles, about one quarter of its original size. Being 25 km/15 miles in width, it is the largest and one of the earliest parks of this type in continental Europe. Its origins trace back to the sovereign Leopold III Friedrich Franz von ANHALT-DESSAU, who was inspired by advanced English farming methods and the desire to beautify nature, which he had studied in his travels in England and now wanted to adopt. Six parks, forming part of a landscape conceived as both decorative as well as useful, constitute an extraordinary work of art as well as an outstanding example of the philosophical principles of the enlightenment translated into the language of the landscape.

Luisium Palace

The palace and park form one of the jewels of the Dessau-Wörlitz Garden Realm. It was designed by F. W. von Erdmannsdorff in 1774 for Princess Luise of Anhalt-Dessau as a garden retreat. The park is divided into two by an axial path and a transverse way crosses the western part of the park leading to the Luisium Palace, which stands on a gentle rising hill. The southern garden is made accessible by a Palladian bridge over an extended lake which is decorated with a well, a GROTTO, and an alcove seat. The eastern part of the park with its regular path layout indicates its former use as an orchard. A neo-Gothic garden house overlooks this scene and an orangery is a feature of the farmyard. A gate in classical style flanked by neo-Gothic gatehouses serves as access to the garden from the east. Three hunting tracks, extending into the landscape, connect the ensemble to its surroundings.

Mosigkau Palace and Park

Probably the best-preserved rococo ensemble in this part of Germany, the Mosigkau Palace and Park were created a few years after the sovereign Leopold III Friedrich Franz of Anhalt-Dessau purchased the estate in 1742 as a present for his daughter Anna Wilhelmine. The ensemble consists of a regular layout south of the three-winged palace building with a rococo garden in the south-west corner and a more informal area north of it. A long ALLÉE which leads from north towards the palace ends at the *cour d'honneur* (see ATTRE, CHATEAU D') in front of the palace. Behind the palace traces of a parterre can still be made out although its arbours and hedges are gone. The whole ensemble reflects the French principles of landscape design as propagated by A.-J. DEZALLIER D'ARGENVILLE. An axial path leads from the palace's central hall southwards into the garden, starting from a semicircular forecourt. The flanking PARTERRES *de broderie*, with flower beds on each side and sunken lawn, are hardly visible today. Two orangeries mark the southern entrance to the garden with, to one side, a rococo garden with a small pond, and a bowling alley, a labyrinth, and garden enclosed by hedges with an octagonal tea house in the middle. The English Hill, a modest elevation densely planted with trees, forms a background to the garden and bears witness to a new taste for the picturesque. The transformation of parts of the park into a landscape garden and the planting of fruit and mulberry trees are much later changes.

Oranienbaum town and park

Situated close to Wörlitz, Oranienbaum is considered a fine and rare example of baroque town planning and garden design in Germany. It was named in 1673 after Princess Henriette Catharina of Nassau-Oranien. In 1709 the ensemble of the palace and outhouses was completed—buildings and their enclosing park reflect a Dutch influence. A bird's-eye view reveals the baroque design of the whole layout with the chief axis leading from the palace to a deer park. A stone bridge connects the palace's inner court with a *parterre* and the main features of a maze to the south are still visible. The symmetrically placed Island Garden represents an unique example of an Anglo-Chinese style garden laid out before 1800, which is still in good condition. Narrow paths, bridges, and canals shape the landscape and a Chinese tea house and a pagoda serve as architectural points of emphasis. The PAGODA, still acting as viewpoint, was inspired by descriptions by the English architect William CHAMBERS of the pagoda he designed for Kew Gardens (see ROYAL BOTANIC GARDENS, KEW). West of both compartments, intersected by the main axis and structured by straight paths, the deer park stretches out. One of the longest orangeries in Europe, built between 1812 and 1818 in classical style, is situated on the south edge of the park.

Wörlitz Gardens

The earliest German landscape garden, Wörlitz Gardens, is the most famous part of the Dessau-Wörlitz Garden Realm and regarded as its culmination. The gardens consist of several parts—the Palace Garden, Neumarks Garden, Schochs Garden, and Neue Anlage (New Gardens). No less than nineteen different bridges ornamenting the landscape provide a pattern book of bridge engineering. Numerous

---

Engraving of the ruined column at the **Désert de Retz** from Georges Le Rouge's *Détails des nouveaux jardins à la mode* (1785).

Vue Perspective de la Colonne

features in the park reflect admiration for ancient Greece and Rome. Monuments, paths, and vistas link the park with its surrounding landscape and no fence bars the way for visitors.

The palace (called the Landhaus), on the site of a former hunting lodge, was built between 1769 and 1773 to the designs of F. W. von Erdmannsdorff (1736–1800). Like most of the buildings in the Wörlitz Gardens it is an early example of the new-born classicism in German architecture. Virtually the only feature to survive of the old formal Palace Garden is an avenue of limes. In the landscape park that succeeded it the English Seat (1765) was the first garden building to be erected. A rotunda (1789/90), modelled on the Temple of Vesta at Tivoli, was used as a Jewish synagogue—in the tradition of the ideals of the Enlightenment. Designs for the garden were made as the palace was being built. However, floods in the 1770s caused a revision in the designs—declivities which had filled with water were retained as lakes, and the earthworks of damaged dykes were integrated into the landscape.

Neumarks Garden is located to the west of the Palace Garden. It is enclosed by dykes, which determine the pattern of paths, and is divided into two by a narrow turfed axis. It is separated from the road by the Eisenhart, a wall made of iron ore, serving as the foundations for two pavilions which were originally a library and a collection of South Sea art (both collections have been moved). An avenue of poplars, on the western edge of the garden, leads to the Rousseau Island, a copy of the one at ERMENONVILLE where Rousseau was buried. In the labyrinth, which covers a substantial part of the garden, the baroque idea of an amusing and playful garden feature is challenged by features of a more serious character—such as a glade decorated with busts of the philosophers J. K. Lavater (1741–1801) and C. F. Gellert (1715–69).

The Schochs Garden to the north is connected to Neumarks Garden by ferries via the so-called Rose Island. Here is the Gothic House, Leopold III's island retreat where he also kept a collection of art. On the banks of the lake the NYMPHAEUM is another example of a classical reference at Wörlitz. Schochs Garden includes a grove of Diana, a vineyard, and several sculptures. Five different bridges give access to the adjacent parts of the park, with, to the north-west, the Flora Garden dominated by a Temple of Flora (1796–8). A Temple of Venus (1794–7) ornaments the nearby Luise Valley with its man-made ornamental cliff. A HERMITAGE serves as a sitting place among the numerous garden features. A dyke, planted with oaks and fruit trees, encloses the garden to the north where, in a part of the garden called Weidenhager, there is a lake named the Nymphs' Bath.

The eastern part of the park, the Neue Anlage, shows a marked influence of Capability BROWN. Its chief ornament, the Große Walloch Lake with two islands, is connected to Wörlitz Lake by two canals. The nearby Pantheon (1794–7), as well as an Italian peasant's house, makes reference to the Italian landscape. From the Pantheon a path leads to the Stein, an island which intermingles different Mediterranean landscapes even including a working copy of Vesuvius which can be made to spit fire. The Villa Hamilton (1791–4) is the island's chief architectural ornament. Flights of stairs, several temples, grottoes, a Roman Bath, and a columbarium are further references to the glories of classical culture.   HM/HH

MICHAEL STÜRMER, URSULA BODE, and THOMAS WEISS, *For the Friends of Nature and Art* (1997).

De Voorst. See VOORST, DE.

de Vries, Hans Vredeman.
see VRIES, HANS VREDEMAN DE.

De Wiersse. See WIERSSE, DE.

Dezallier d'Argenville, Antoine-Joseph
(1680–1765), French courtier, natural historian, artist, and influential garden theorist. He was a sufficiently distinguished scientist to be appointed to the Royal Society in 1750. As a garden theorist he had great influence as a commentator on the baroque gardens of France. His book *La Théorie et la pratique du jardinage* (1709) is in effect both a practical and theoretical manual to the French baroque garden. It was printed four times during the author's lifetime. Although he is essentially describing the world of LE NÔTRE only one garden by the latter, SCEAUX, is included. Translated into English as *The Theory and Practice of Gardening* (1712) it was influential on English garden design. His son Antoine-Nicolas Dezallier d'Argenville was the author of *Voyage pittoresque des environs de Paris ou description des maisons royales, châteaux et autres lieux de plaisance, situés à quinze lieues aux environs de cette ville* (1762), a valuable account of the architecture of the Île-de-France.   PT

Dig ⊛
Dig, Rajasthan, India, in the district of Bharatpur, was constructed during the 17th century by the Jat (1722–68). The builders combined the system of the Jal Mahal (water palace) with the formal plan of the Mughal garden. The complex is composed of a large CHAHAR BAGH closed off on two sides by two great basins, the Gopal-sagar and the Rup-sagar. At the ends of the four arms formed by the routes and water canals are four pavilions, or *baradari*, two of which, the Kesav Bhawan and the Gopal Bhawan, face the water. Each pavilion possesses dignity without having an imposing character, favouring a unity and harmony between the architecture and the garden. On the south side are the residential buildings, among which are the Purana Mahal and the Suraj Bhawan, as well as the noteworthy artificial reservoir placed high up to feed the entire garden and the fountains with descending water, serviced by two long ramps. The garden parterres, located on a lower level, are surrounded by flagged footpaths, connected to the pavilions by ramps. Numerous water jets rise from the canal and the central tank. The layout of the plants recalls a Mughal order of planting, even if we recognize the characteristics of an Indian moonlight garden.
    AP

M. C. JOSHI, *Dig* (1971).

Dillon Garden, The ⊛
Sandford Road, Dublin, Ireland, a rare, very distinguished private city garden that opens to the public. The genius of the place is Helen Dillon who came to live in this handsome Georgian house in 1972. The garden is divided in two, a sliver at the front and a walled enclosure behind, with a total area of 0.3 hectare/0.75 acre. There was no garden to speak of when she came and she was a novice gardener. The garden she made has become an inspiration to Irish gardeners and to the many visitors who come from other countries to admire what she has done. The secrets of her success are threefold: she made a garden perfectly suited to the site; she filled it with finely chosen plants; and she maintains it to perfectionist standards. The front garden, with an oblique gravel walk to the front door, is informal but with crisply clipped shapes of holly and silver pear and small beds by the steps alive with arisaemas, celmisias, orchids, and the other small and difficult plants she grows so well. The garden behind is dominated by a central canal of Islamic character flanked by strips of grass and fortissimo mixed borders—chiefly red on one side, blue on the other, but both given order by much plant repetition. Paths lead about the perimeter of the garden with decorative episodes and wonderful, frequently rare, plants at every turn.   PT

Dioscorides
was a Greek physician living in Cilicia (a southern region of modern Turkey) in the 1st

century AD who compiled what was then the most comprehensive herbal in existence, describing aromatic, culinary, and medicinal plants, which was translated into Latin in the 6th century AD, under the title *De Materia Medica*, and circulated widely in Europe in this form. The oldest surviving manuscript of the almost complete text is the *Codex Vindobonensis* (also known as the *Codex Aniciae Julianae*—it belonged to the Byzantine princess Juliana Anicia who died *c.* AD 527) held in the Austrian National Library in Vienna where it has been since the 16th century. Dating from before AD 512 this extraordinarily rare survival is finely illustrated. The first printed herbals in the 16th century drew on Dioscorides just as he himself must have taken material from manuscript herbals compiled before his time.   PT

disabled people, gardens for.

The idea of making gardens accessible to those who are wheelchair bound, or whose mobility is restricted less severely, and of extending the garden's attractions to include features that can be enjoyed by those who are blind, or have less severe sight impairment, was a major development of the late 20th century. In England the Disabled Persons Act of 1970 obliged gardens (and other amenities) open to the public to provide facilities for disabled people. Major gardens in many countries, even when there has been no legislation, recognize the need for such facilities. A garden such as the ROYAL BOTANIC GARDENS, KEW, provides free parking bays for disabled people, free wheelchairs at all entrances, and a large-print map of the gardens for sight-impaired people. Long before this, however, research had been carried out into the very different, but no less important, matter of advising disabled people of ways in which they may tend their own gardens. Designing tools that may be used by those who suffer from arthritis and planning raised beds that would be accessible to people in wheelchairs were among the vital considerations that were examined. The English organization Thrive is a national horticultural charity that exists 'to enable disadvantaged, disabled and older people to participate fully in the social and economic life of the community'. A mixture of permanent staff and volunteers run programmes at their various Garden Projects for clients who are usually referred to them from the local social services departments. Many national organizations pay attention to the needs of disabled people. The NATIONAL TRUST, for example, produces a booklet containing information for visitors with disabilities.

Gardens, or parts of gardens, planned specifically for blind people are found in many countries. In Canada L'Institut National Canadien pour les Aveugles (INCA) has advice on laying out gardens for blind people, with scented gardens and beds of plants with tactile foliage placed at a height which allows them to be touched. In the USA the Oral Hull Park (Sandy, Oregon) is a Five Senses Garden which includes signs in braille, plenty of birdlife, cascades and fountains, scented and tactile gardens. It also has a large trout pool in which people are encouraged to guddle for fish. San Antonio Botanical Gardens (Texas) has a garden for the blind specializing in Texan natives. In India the M. S. Swaminathan Research Foundation made a remarkable 'touch and smell' garden at Chennai (formerly Madras) specifically intended for blind children. All signage is in braille and plants are chosen for their scented or tactile qualities. Gardens for blind people are found in botanic gardens in South Africa—at both KIRSTENBOSCH (with a Braille Trail) and DURBAN. An outstanding 20th-century garden designer, Leandro Silva Delgado (b. 1930), designed a garden for blind people and discovered much about scent, texture, and sound that influenced the designs he made for gardens for people who were not disabled.

The swiftly expanding subject of horticultural therapy has as its goal to harness the therapeutic values of gardens and gardening to the benefit of people disabled in many different ways. This aspect of the powers of gardens and gardening has been long recognized. William Lawson in his *A New Orchard and Garden* (1623) described the psychological benefits of gardening to garden owners: 'to renue and refresh their senses, and to call home their overwearied spirits.' In England in the 19th century gardens were considered an important part of hospital design. The Manchester Royal Hospital for the Insane, opened in 1849, had 'spacious grounds for husbandry, and gardening, and exercise'. There were originally 12 hectares/30 acres of meadow, 4.5 hectares/11 acres of arable land, 1 hectare /2.5 acres of kitchen garden, and 2 hectares/5 acres of flower garden. A model dairy farm provided milk for the asylum and patients were encouraged to work in the gardens or farm. The benefits of gardens and gardening today are well understood. The American Horticultural Therapy Association encourages 'the practice of horticulture as therapy to improve human well-being'. Horticultural therapy in the USA had been found to be valuable in the treatment of war veterans in the 1940s and 1950s. Organizations giving information about, and carrying out research in, horticultural therapy exist in many countries—the Horticultural Therapy Association of Victoria (Australia), the Canadian Horticultural Therapy Association and Gardening Horticulture Therapy (UK).   PT

disease control.

Plant diseases vary greatly in their severity and some are so mild as to be of no consequence. Some, like the tulip breaking virus (see TULIPS), even add to the aesthetic value of ornamental plants. Fossil records show that the causes of diseases, pathogens, have been around for millions of years. In ancient and even medieval times most disease control practices were rooted in mysticism and superstition. In the Bible Amos considered plant disease epidemics as Jehovah's retribution on sinners. The Romans created two gods for rusts, Robigo and Robigus, but they were found to be ineffectual. The Romans also believed in spontaneous generation—some life forms were thought to arise spontaneously from decaying matter. Despite this, some Roman gardening practices, like the rotation of crops and soaking seeds in brine to control disease, were surprisingly advanced and were eventually rediscovered later.

In the 17th and 18th centuries scientists made many discoveries about plant disease. Spores of fungi were observed under compound microscopes. Although pathogens were associated with plant diseases, they were still believed to be created spontaneously. In 1802, the copper sulphate added to fungal spores was found to be fungicidal and subsequently sulphur and lime sulphur were used as fungicides by gardeners. In other contexts the value of sulphur had long been understood—in Roman times it was collected from volcanoes as a disinfectant. In Ireland between 1844 and 1845 ignorance of the cause of the potato famine resulted in widespread death and migration. After the cause of late blight had been found, Anton de Bary revealed *Phytophthora infestans* as its pathogen in 1853 leading to the era of disease control. By 1866 gardeners were substituting copper sulphate for sulphur. After Louis Pasteur's germ theory overturned the theory of spontaneous generation, Robert Koch postulated rules to establish the cause of disease. In 1879, downy mildew of grape was introduced into Europe on American rootstocks, spreading rapidly threatening ruin. Then in 1882 a mixture of copper sulphate and lime, concocted to deter grape thieves, was found effective. Known as Bordeaux mixture by 1885, it stimulated the chemical revolution, not only rescuing the European vineyards, but also becoming a favourite fungicide in the garden. Gardeners also treated seeds with hot water and steam was being pioneered to control soil pathogens in glasshouses.

At the start of the 20th century copper fungicides were widely used and formalin was used as a soil fungicide to control damping-off of seedlings. Formaldehyde and chlorophenol-mercury were introduced to control seed-borne diseases. The breeding of disease-resistant plants rapidly increased. Organic sulphur-containing dithiocarbamate fungicides became widely used from the 1930s. Nonetheless the far more toxic arsenic and mercury formulations were regularly applied until the 1960s. By 1931, the concepts of biological control became scientifically acceptable. Around this time carbon disulphide was pioneered as a soil fumigant. During the 1940s several organic protectant fungicides and antibiotics were established. Hence traditional disease control practices used in the garden such as sanitation and crop rotation became considered outdated now that consumers insisted on produce without blemishes.

In the 1960s, shortly after the first synthetic systemic fungicides were introduced, Rachel Carson's book *Silent Spring* (1962) turned public opinion against pesticides, as several of the insecticides used then were found to be harmful to wildlife. Biological control became established. John Rishbeth at Cambridge inoculated pine stumps with the fungus *Phlebiopsis gigantea* to protect against its root pathogen *Heterobasidion annosum*. Biological control of crown gall by *Agrobacterium radiobacter* was investigated and the cause of suppressive soils was discovered, leading to a better understanding of competition. Soil solarization was pioneered by horticulturalists and is increasingly used in sunny climates to reduce soil diseases without the need for chemicals. Increasing environmental awareness in the 1990s led to phasing out of ozone-depleting substances like the soil fumigant methyl bromide in horticulture. Attempts are being made to replace it by integrated pest management such as growing mustard and other green manures which decompose to release substances acting like biological soil fumigants.

At present the choice of conventional fungicides available to home gardeners is much more limited than in the 1990s as many have been replaced on grounds of safety, efficiency, or lack of adequate environmental data. Since the providing of environmental data costs in the range of £400,000–£800,000 per product, less profitable but occasionally effective compounds are often no longer available. Among these are those based on tar oils. Some active ingredients in products to control rose black spot, rust, and powdery mildew have had to be changed. There is also now a legal obligation to adhere to all of the instructions printed on the pesticide container, including dilutions, plants to be treated, and number of applications permitted. As a result many gardeners are again more tolerant of the blemishes and reduced yields caused by disease. Other environmentally sensitive techniques have been adopted. Rose leaves with black spot are removed and burnt with any that have fallen. Disease is encouraged if roses and lawn grass are wet during the night, so gardeners should not water them late in the afternoon. Powdery mildew can be avoided by not growing plants in a shady position. Gardeners face a challenge; fortunately the solution is in tune with the advent of informality in the garden. Maybe there will even be a place for pathogens?   RF

Dodoens, Rembert

(1517–85), Flemish botanist and physician who was born in Malines and died in Leiden. His herbal *Crüÿdeboeck* was published in 1554. An English translation (based on the French translation by Carolus CLUSIUS), *A Nievve Herball*, was made by Henry Lyte and published in 1578 with two more editions in the 16th century. Dodoens's collected botanical works, *Stirpium Historiae Pemptades Sex*, was published in 1581. Dodoens became court physician to the Emperor Maximilian II at Vienna in 1574 and ended his career as professor of medicine at Leiden University.   PT

Doe Run Farm ⊛

Coatsville, Pennsylvania, USA. The 81-hectare/200-acre private estate of Sir John Thouron and the late Esther du Pont Lady Thouron includes 6 hectares/15 acres of gardens that comprise one of the finest collections of rare and unusual perennials in the United States. Formerly known as Glencoe, Doe Run Farm evolved from the early 1950s, when it was a horse farm with an apple orchard, to its present splendour, a feat that earned Sir John Thouron the Local Horticulture Award from the American Horticultural Society in 1995. Four greenhouses supply seed-grown plants for series of garden beds and islands, each leading to a new vista of garden-to-come. A semicircle of stone steps, housing a collection of rock garden treasures such as native American penstemons and campanulas, descends from the main house. Double borders, backed by a hedge of fine-textured hemlock (*Tsuga canadensis*), flank a broad stone path to a sunken garden, at its peak in July when tall pink and blue *Delphinium* 'Pacific Giant' bloom. A new folly garden of weeping and dwarf evergreens is a memorial to the owner's late sister. Fine specimens grace the estate including an orange trumpet vine (*Campsis radicans*) taller than the house and

a splendid weeping beech (*Fagus sylvatica* 'Pendula') with a small doorway cut through cascading branches. In the cool, shady interior a rustic twig chair invites rest and contemplation. The fabled BOSQUET of red-stemmed Japanese willows (*Salix alba* subsp. *vitellina* 'Britzensis') has recently been replaced with healthy new ones.   CO

Donald M. Kendall Sculpture Gardens.

See KENDALL, DONALD M., SCULPTURE GARDENS.

Doria Pamphili, Villa ⊛

Rome, Italy. The 17th-century gardens of the Villa Doria Pamphili beyond the Janiculum Hill were originally designed as a large park with an intimate small formal garden around the CASINO. The small building constructed for the powerful Donna Olympia Maidalchini by her admirer Camillo Pamphili looks over a scrolled French-style parterre, the GIARDINO SEGRETO, fringed by lemon trees in pots. Originally mostly vineyards planted between 1644 and 1652, the garden was redesigned by Alessandro Algardi (1602–54) and a landscape painter Giovan Francesco Grimaldi in 1650 with formal avenues and rides resembling those of the park at the Villa BORGHESE. An engraving by G. B. Falda (*Le fontane di Roma*, 1691) shows a Fountain of Venus by Ferrabosco and a snail fountain by BERNINI set in the retaining wall below the building. After 1793 Prince Andrea Doria, the new owner, under the influence of his English wife Mary Talbot, was to destroy all hints of formality in the park, adding lakes and ornamental pools, softening the baroque effects. By 1850 straight lines of avenues and rides were further obliterated by G. B. Busiri Vici to create a more pastoral landscape. Before selling the villa and park to the state in 1963 the Doria replaced all the fountains with copies, taking the originals with them. Many earlier features such as a Doric temple, and the fountains of Regina and of the Tritons hidden under the umbrella pines, still remain to be discovered. The park inspired paintings by Corot and de Camp.   PHo

Doria Principe, Palazzo ⊛

Genoa, Liguria, Italy. The palace was built for the Genoese Admiral Andrea Doria (1468–1560), founder of the Republic of Genoa, by an unknown architect before 1543, with three terraces added by Giovanni Angelo Montorsoli (c. 1507–1563) who also laid out extensive gardens, containing fountains, parterres, and pergolas, stretching down towards the sea. A focal point of the garden was a large statue of Neptune later replaced by Taddeo Carlone's marble fountain *Neptune on a Sea Chariot*, on the lower level, which still remains, although the garden has almost disappeared with new highways cutting it in half. From the 16th to the 18th century the gardens were the settings for celebrations and entertainments.   PHo

Dornava ⊕

Ptuj, Slovenia. The manor of the most important baroque ensemble in Slovenia was owned by the counts of Attems, a powerful aristocratic family in Styria. Josef Tadeus Count of Attems (d. 1772) remodelled the original hunting lodge as a manor with ornamented façades, illusionistic frescoes, and a chapel 1753–5 to the designs of the Viennese architect Josef Hueber (1715–87). The axial garden layout consisted of an entrance ALLÉE leading to a front garden with citrus plants and lavish sculptural ornaments—allegories of the seasons, various figures, a heraldic gateway, and urns. An inner courtyard with varied enclosed gardens and onamental gateways had a BOSQUET on the banks of the river Pesnica. The most notable part, Neptune's Garden, contains a central water basin with a sculpture of Neptune and mythological creatures. The garden features two series of stone sculptures symmetrically disposed around the water basin and encircled with tall hornbeam topiary hedges forming a CABINET *de verdure*. The earlier series consist of twelve dwarf figures, caricatures of the estates of society, influenced by the Central European garden fashion of the early 18th century and the latter a group of six sages of antiquity. An adjacent parterre was laid out with a pair of symmetrical orangeries, an orchard, and finally an area of woodland with a PATTE D'OIE of *allées*. The citrus collection comprised around 200 trees of bitter and sweet oranges, with citrons and lemons. The complex has substantially decayed since the Second World War—only the manor and sculptural ornaments are preserved.   AK

Douglas, David

(1798–1834), Scottish plant collector in Pacific North America. Born in Perthshire, he was apprenticed aged 11 at Scone Palace near Perth, later joining the Botanic Gardens of Glasgow University in 1820, at the same time as William Hooker (see HOOKER, SIR JOSEPH DALTON) became Regius professor of botany. In 1823 he recommended Douglas to the Horticultural Society of London as a plant collector. Douglas travelled three times to the American continent for the society, the latter two journeys, made in 1824–27 and 1829–34 along the Pacific western coast, being the most significant. Douglas began botanizing at the estuary of the Columbia river and for two years explored the western side of the Rockies where he collected

many plants, some of which had been first described by surgeon Archibald Menzies (1754–1842) in 1792 voyaging with Captain George Vancouver (1758–98) aboard *The Discovery*. Douglas collected and introduced numerous species of conifers, including *Pinus lambertiana* and *Pseudotsuga menziesii*; later there were *Abies grandis*, *Cupressus macrocarpa*, *Pinus radiata*, *P. contorta*, and *Picea sitchensis*. Traversing the Rockies he journeyed to Hudson's Bay where he sailed for London in 1827. In 1829 Douglas explored California and further north into Canada, where in a canoeing accident he lost his journal and plants. Embarking for England in 1834 he landed at Hawaii, where walking alone in the hills he fell into a cattle pit and was gored to death. Over 200 horticultural introductions were made by Douglas, many of which have proved popular in cultivation including *Mahonia aquifolium*, *Garrya elliptica*, *Ribes sanguineum*, and several species of penstemons and lupins.   MC-C

WILLIAM MORWOOD, *Traveller in a Vanished Landscape* (1973).

dovecote.

The dovecote was an important part of the rural economy. Pigeons were a precious source of fresh meat, especially in winter, their feathers were used for pillows and eiderdowns, and their droppings were among the best of garden manures. In Britain dovecotes were introduced by the Normans and, to this day, the *pigeonnier* is even commoner in France than the dovecote is in Britain. A distinctive difference is, however, that in England the dovecote was often a valued garden ornament (for example at Lytes Cary in Somerset and ROUSHAM) whereas in France, decorative though it may be, it is usually strictly a part of the farmyard. In the Middle Ages the keeping of pigeons was restricted to the aristocracy (both lay and religious) and to substantial landowners. The fact that pigeons gathered their food far and wide was a source of discontent among the peasantry. In Scotland, where dovecotes are called doocots, there are many architecturally distinguished examples. One of the earliest dovecotes in Britain is at Manorbier Castle in Pembrokeshire, dating from the 12th century. The last examples of free-standing dovecotes date from the early 19th century. An outstanding example is the Gothic doocot at the House of PITMUIES with castellated towers and cruciform stained-glass windows. After that date they were usually incorporated, as a pigeon loft, into some other building.   PT

Downhill Castle ⊕

near Coleraine, County Londonderry, Northern Ireland, is the remains of a spectacular estate

built up in the 18th century by Frederick Augustus Hervey, 4th Earl of Bristol and Bishop of Derry, a compulsive collector and builder. The Earl Bishop had two other great estates—Ballyscullion, also in County Londonderry, which does not survive, and Ickworth in Suffolk which today belongs to the NATIONAL TRUST. The shell only of Downhill Castle survives, but nearby on the brink of a cliff overlooking the Atlantic is the Mussenden Temple, a superb rotunda dating from the 1780s designed, probably by Michael Shanahan, as a library and landscape ornament.   PT

Downing, Andrew Jackson

(1815–52), American landscape gardener, horticulturist, author, and editor. Downing's *A Treatise on the Theory and Practice of Landscape Gardening Adapted to North America* (1841) was the first book in the USA devoted exclusively to the subject, and *Fruits and Fruit-Trees of America* (1845) was recognized as the standard pomological work. As editor of the *Horticulturist* (1846–52), Downing wrote on a range of 'rural arts', and his *Cottage Residences* (1842) and *The Architecture of Country Houses* (1850) stressed that architectural beauty must be considered jointly with the beauty of the landscape. Downing lived his 36 years along New York's Hudson river valley, and this dramatic setting was a significant factor for the landscape gardener who promoted an American version of the British picturesque. The *Treatise* addressed landscape gardening as a fine art. Initially, Downing was particularly indebted to J. C. LOUDON's theory of imitation in landscape gardening, but he soon realized that the adoption of Loudon's notion that the natural style could be acknowledged as art only through the use of exotics made little practical or aesthetic sense. Revising for later editions (1844, 1849), Downing was influenced by Alison, REPTON, PRICE, and Ruskin; yet the *Treatise* remained a guide for country gentlemen in the creation of ideal homes and extensive pleasure grounds.

The new starting ground for American landscape gardening theory and practice rested more truly in the *Horticulturist*; one-quarter of Downing's 74 editorials specifically addressed landscape gardening and many did so peripherally. In 1850 Downing embarked on a trip abroad where he acquired a partner in the English architect Calvert Vaux and an understanding of the value of his country's native plants. This insight along with his growing practical experience effected a change in the *Horticulturist*. While still encouraging Americans to live a refined life, Downing increasingly advocated simplicity, frugality, and the use of indigenous vegetation. By selecting the finest native trees and recomposing the material into a more polished scene than could be found in nature, Americans could achieve Downing's ideal of the 'natural' style. Downing's practice prospered after the *Treatise* was published, yet with his papers lost only a short list of commissions has been verified. In 1851 Matthew Vassar engaged Downing to design several buildings and to improve the grounds with walks and drives at Springside in Poughkeepsie, New York. That same year, at the request of President Millard Fillmore, Downing designed the L-shaped area extending from the President's house along the Mall to the foot of Capitol Hill. The Public Grounds would have expressed on a grand scale what Downing considered the national style in landscape gardening—the 'natural' style. Downing was in the midst of supervising these improvements when he drowned in a Hudson river steamboat accident on 28 July 1852. Downing's most important legacy was as an author and editor, for he not only addressed the practical needs of Americans, he also convinced a great number of his countrymen and countrywomen of the value of beauty in daily life.   JKM

> JUDITH K. MAJOR, *To Live in the New World: A. J. Downing and American Landscape Gardening* (1997).

Dr Jordan Park. See JORDAN, DR, PARK.

Drottningholm ⊛

Lovön, Uppland, Sweden, has been the home of the Swedish royal family since 1982 and a popular public park since the 19th century. The palace was built from 1662 by Dowager Queen Hedvig Eleonora, to the designs of Nicodemus TESSIN the elder and Nicodemus TESSIN the younger. Drottningholm is famous for the harmony between the interiors and the gardens, with their richness of colours and forms and their iconographic programme. The gardens — orchard, kitchen garden, and deer park—date back to the reign of King Gustav Vasa (1496-1560) and King Johan III, though little is known about their original design and use. A highly decorated garden was established in the middle of the 17th century between the main building and Lake Mälaren during the ownership of the Chancellor Count Magnus Gabriel de La Gardie (1622-86). The surviving baroque garden was constructed from 1681 to 1720 following drawings by Tessin the younger, based on his father's designs, inspired by VAUX-LE-VICOMTE, with motifs from CHANTILLY, VERSAILLES, and MARLY. A terrace nearest the palace is followed by PARTERRES *de broderie*—partly by Johan HÅRLEMAN—fountains, water parterres, cascades, statues (bronzes by Hans Vredeman

de VRIES), and BOSQUETS. A large *bosquet*, Stjärnan (The Star), closes the axis. Double avenues of over 800 lime trees (*Tilia* spp.) frame the garden. A small intimate rococo garden with arbours, aviaries, clipped hedges, and horse chestnut avenues was created around the Chinese Pavilion (1753-63), west of the pleasure garden, by Carl Fredrik Adelcrantz (1716-96) for King Adolf Fredrik and Queen Louisa Ulrika in the 1750s. A landscape garden on the theme of a meandering channel with ponds and islands, clumps, and park buildings (notably a Gothic tower of 1792-3) and meadows grazed by sheep, based on designs by King Gustav III (1746-92) himself and Adelcrantz, was built north of the pleasure garden from 1778, later modified by the architect Fredrik Magnus PIPER.

The 19th century brought alterations to the grounds—the cascades were demolished and the parterres became lawns. Restoration started in the 1930s by the palace architect, Professor Ivar Tengbom (1878-1968), and Professor Nils G. Wollin (1892-1964). The most extensive restoration has been carried out by garden designer Walter BAUER in the years 1950-69, whose contributions are like a modernistic interpretation of the baroque. Continuing restoration includes the renewal of lime avenues (1989-2014) and replanting of box framing the former *parterres de broderie* (1999). The grounds were designated as a World Heritage Site in 1991.   KL

Drummond Castle ⊛

near Crieff, Perthshire, Scotland, was built in the late 15th century for the 1st Lord Drummond. In the early 17th century the 2nd Earl of Perth reworked the castle and on the steep slope below it laid out a terraced garden of Renaissance character. Nothing is known in detail of this garden but a magnificent polyhedral tower sundial designed by John Mylne III *c.*1630 survives at the centre of the garden. It is known, too, that an extensive formal layout beyond the garden was planted at this time and the park was extended in the 18th century from which period fine trees survive. The great event in the garden's history was the re-creation of a formal garden on the 17th-century terraces in the early 19th century. J. C. LOUDON's *Encyclopaedia of Gardening* (1822) refers to it—'the grounds highly improved by the present owner, assisted by his ingenious steward, Lewis Kennedy'. Queen Victoria visited it in 1842 and thought the garden 'really very fine, with terraces, like an old French garden'. It is this garden, with much replanting and amendments, that is seen today. The view of it from the castle forecourt, suddenly revealed as you approach the steps, is one of the most memorable of garden scenes. Below lies a giant

parterre with a central axial walk and the pattern of a huge St Andrew's cross. Fan-shaped or triangular brilliantly planted flower beds radiate out among a profusion of clipped shapes of copper beech, holly, purple-leafed plum (*Prunus cerasifera* 'Pissardii'), and yew (both common and golden). The beds are edged in box and planted with a mixture of bedding, herbaceous perennials, and massed roses. Fine urns and statuary decorate the garden, and the occasional architectural fragment, such as a grand 18th-century decorated gate from GRIMSTHORPE CASTLE which is also owned by the family. The central axis is continued beyond the wall where it pierces the woodland. This must have been an axis established in the landscape planting of the 17th century. Seen from above the parterre has a very different character from that which is experienced when walking the paths. From above it seems so regular but the ground is rather undulating and the overall pattern seems much less crisply defined.   PT

Dubrovnik Renaissance gardens ⊛

Dubrovnik county, Croatia, are a specific type of European garden influenced by the Renaissance and created from the 15th century to the 18th century. These were the product of a fusion of Italian Renaissance ideas with the specific characteristics of the Dubrovnik area. There was a medieval tradition of gardens in Dubrovnik, in harmony with country life and agriculture. Town planning also existed in the Middle Ages and there was a town plan of Dubrovnik as early as 1272. The influence of the Renaissance was particularly strong in the case of villas. Although some villas with gardens were built in the 15th century the majority date from the 16th century (after the earthquake of 1520). We do not know who the designers and builders of the gardens were, but the ground plan is typically geometrical, generally rectangular. Villa and garden were decorated with stone walls, steps, terraces, belvederes, and pergolas. An axial and symmetrical composition is not always the rule. The vine PERGOLA is a traditional part of the Dubrovnik gardens from ancient times up to today and paths, covered with pergolas, divided the gardens into a few rectangular or square compartments. Garden furniture and ornaments, always made of stone, consisted of benches, seats, tables, fountains, urns, and vases. Water is used sparingly: small fountains located in niches in walls, water channels in the walls of terraces, and fish ponds filled with sea water. Plants, including the orange tree, lemon tree, lime tree, dog rose, vine, and aromatic herbs, generally reflected the utilitarian purpose of the gardens. Their delightfulness originates from the fragrance and appearance of plants such as myrtle, sweet bay, rosemary, Mediterranean cypress, jasmine, oleander, rose, lily, carnation, and violet. The gardens are on a hillside and generally quite small, mostly about 0.5 hectare/1.2 acres. There are about twenty preserved gardens today, out of about 300 once upon a time. See also TRSTENO GARDEN AND ARBORETUM. MOŠ/BBOŠ

MLADEN OBAD ŠĆITAROCI, 'The Renaissance gardens of the Dubrovnik area, Croatia', *Garden History*, Vol. 24: No. 2 (1996).

Du Cerceau, Jacques Androuet

(c.1515–c.1586), French Huguenot architect and engraver whose two volumes on *Les Plus Excellents Bastiments de France* (1576 and 1579) are a precious document in the history of the Renaissance garden in France. Meticulous engravings show the house and its designed setting and Du Cerceau's text always gives details of the topography, the house and the garden with its ornaments and buildings. It is especially valuable for the information on such estates as ANET, GAILLON or the remarkable Château de Madrid in the Bois de Boulogne (see PARIS PARKS AND GARDENS) which no longer exist or only partly survive. His earlier two *Livres d'architecture* (1559 and 1561) are also of historic importance. The first is the earliest printed handbook of architecture by a Frenchman. The second is rich in designs for garden ornaments and buildings showing the characteristic French style of his time. Du Cerceau's sons both became architects: Jacques, who was also an engraver, was superintendent of the royal buildings until 1594 and designed the Hôtel Sully and Hôtel de Mayenne in Paris, and a notable garden building, the Pavillon de Flore, in the Tuileries gardens (see PARIS PARKS AND GARDENS); Baptiste designed the Pont Neuf in Paris. PT

Duchêne, Henri (1841–1902) and his son Achille

(1866–1947), French garden designers who practised chiefly together. They were influential in the rediscovery of the French baroque garden of the 17th century which in many cases had been superseded by parks in the tradition of the JARDIN À L'ANGLAISE. At many notable estates, such as the Château de CHAMPS and VAUX-LE-VICOMTE, they recreated 17th-century layouts when almost nothing of the original design survived. Achille Duchêne extended the scope of their work by designing original compositions intermingling the influences of the Italian Renaissance with the *jardin à la française*, as at BLENHEIM PALACE. In all, the partnership achieved 380 projects in Argentina, Australia, Britain, France, Russia, and the USA.

Their reinterpretations of the gardens of LE NÔTRE were seen through 19th-century eyes. For example, the texture of the parterres was much more uniform and carpet-like, resembling 19th-century municipal MOSAÏCULTURE more than authentic LE NÔTRE designs. The 17th-century engravings of Israel Silvestre of Vaux-le-Vicomte, for example, show much shaggier planting in parterres than the Duchênes would have thought appropriate. Authentic restoration or re-creation is, in the end, always an impossibility. The Duchênes opened a door on an almost forgotten world but it is curious that their pioneer work has not been followed by greater authenticity. PT

MONIQUE MOSSER, 'Henri and Achille Duchêne and the reinvention of Le Nôtre', in Monique Mosser and Georges Teyssot (eds.), *The History of Garden Design* (1991).

Dueñas, Palacio de las,

Seville, Spain. The great house was built in the 15th century by the Pinedas family on the site of a former convent (*dueñas* means sisters) and today belongs to the Duke of Alba. The house, in the centre of Seville, is surrounded by gardens and the whole estate enclosed in walls. From noble wrought-iron gates a central path hedged in myrtle leads to the chief patio enclosed in double height cloisters. The *mudéjar* style—Muslim work produced after the Reconquest—is seen at its best here with tall arches, slender columns, and intricate filigree stucco. At the centre of the patio an octagonal pool is decorated with AZULEJOS and brims with arum lilies (*Zantedeschia aethiopica*). Date palms shade the patio and box-edged beds are filled with clivias. The external walls of the house are draped with climbers—the sweetly scented double white *Rosa banksiae* var. *banksiae*, *Bignonia capreolata*, bougainvillea, and *Solanum jasminoides*. Paths of fine gravel often hedged with *Euonymus fortunei*, whose gleaming leaves sparkle in the shade, lead among densely planted beds with a profusion of hibiscus, oranges and lemons, loquats (*Eriobotrya japonica*), a spreading coral tree (*Erythrina crista-galli*), and the beautiful *Xanthoceras sorbifolium*. An ancient CISTERN provides water for the garden and an octagonal raised pool, whose walls are covered in lozenge-patterned *azulejos*, stands at the meeting point of paths. Shade, sweet scents, brilliant flowers, filtered sunlight, and an unexpected rural calm dominate the garden and provide a wonderful setting for the stately house. PT

Dule Yuan,

China. The fame of this 11th-century Garden of Pleasure in Solitude rests on a collection of

poems written about it by its maker, the great historian of the Northern Song dynasty, Sima Guang (1019–89). At one time Prime Minister and leader of a conservative faction, he later suffered such setbacks that he retired from active politics to the old capital city of Luoyang in Henan province and devoted himself to history and his garden. Compared to other gardens of the time described in *Luoyang mingyuanji* (The Famous Gardens of Luoyang), it was a modest retreat with beds of herbs, wooden fences, and thatched pavilions, lying in the southern part of the city and separate from his house. A 'fisherman's hut' was made of tree bamboos planted in a ring and then bent over and tied together at the tips. However, the historian also collected a library of some 5,000 volumes in the Book Reading Hall where, he says in his preface, he took 'the sages as his teachers and the many virtuous men [of antiquity] as his friends: if his resolve was weary and his body exhausted, he took a rod and caught fish, held up his sleeves and picked herbs . . . His eyes, lungs, feelings were all his own. What enjoyment could be greater than this?' His words inspired many later gardeners and artists, among them the Qing painter Qiu Ying (1510–51), whose long and exceptionally beautiful handscroll follows the historian's descriptions of his garden. C-ZC/MK

Dumaine, Jardin ⊕

Luçon, Vendée, France. One of the great glories of French horticulture is the range and quality of public parks. In the quiet town of Luçon the Jardin Dumaine is a particularly attractive example of the tradition. In the centre of the town, next to the Hôtel de Ville, this 4-hectare/10-acre garden had been the private property of Hyacinthe Dumaine who gave it to the town in 1895. The donation is celebrated at the garden's entrance by a bust of Dumaine standing on a plinth which rises from an intricate pattern of MOSAÏCULTURE. An octagonal lily pond has a tiered fountain decorated with bronze nymphs at whom bronze frogs spout water from below. *Caisses de Versailles* (see CONTAINER) are filled with palms, and blue-glazed urns standing on tall plinths are filled with pelargoniums. To one side an octagonal BANDSTAND has cast-iron balustrades and is capped with a high lantern. The heart of the park is shrouded with woodland with a lake at its centre. A tall jet of water erupts from the lake on whose banks are a grotto and rocaille work. On a flawless great lawn—the Grande Pelouse—are topiary animals finely fashioned of clipped and trained *Helichrysum petiolare*. Here too is a tableau of a scene from La Fontaine's fables, the Fox and the Grapes, intricately worked in different plants. An ALLÉE of yew clipped into pyramid shapes, dating from 1830, leads to a *théâtre de verdure* (green THEATRE). The garden is finely kept and much used by locals and passers-by. In July evenings it is lit with hundreds of Chinese lanterns and presents a charming and cheerfully decorative scene.   PT

Dumbarton Oaks ⊕

Washington, DC, USA, is the site of one of America's most celebrated gardens. It was designed by Beatrix FARRAND and created largely over a period of two decades, starting in 1922, in collaboration with its owner, Mildred Bliss. Dumbarton Oaks was the home of Mr and Mrs Robert Woods Bliss from 1920 to 1940, when they gave the house, grounds, and their extensive Byzantine and pre-Columbian art collection to Harvard University. Nonetheless, Mildred Bliss continued to oversee the garden until her death in 1969. It was Mrs Bliss's desire from the beginning to create a garden influenced by Italian, French, and English design, but with a unique sense of place and regard for appropriate plants. The 4-hectare/10-acre garden as we know it today is the culmination of Mrs Bliss's vision and Mrs Farrand's sense of scale, discerning eye for detail, and knowledge of plants. On ground dramatically sloping away from the Georgian brick house, Beatrix Farrand developed a series of terraces using stone, brick, and ironwork to enclose formal, intimate gardens near the house and lead to progressively more naturalistic areas beyond.

The great trees around the property are a notable feature today: native white oaks (*Quercus alba*), magnolias, a magnificently spreading katsura (*Cercidiphyllum japonicum*) near the garden entrance; an American beech (*Fagus grandifolia*)—its roots carpeted with blue scilla in spring—on the Beech Terrace; drifts of silver maples, flowering cherries, crab apples, and dogwoods. The gates, iron railings, seats, finials, and sculpture Beatrix Farrand designed for the garden are all remarkably distinctive, often ornamented with floral designs very much in the feeling of the ARTS AND CRAFTS MOVEMENT. The architectural features of the garden—walls, steps, pavements, balustrades, and pergolas, as well as garden furniture and ornamentation—play as important a role at Dumbarton Oaks as the plantings.

The 19th-century Orangery at the east end of the house, its interior walls covered with *Ficus pumila*, opens onto the Green Garden, an outdoor entertaining room dominated by a venerable black oak (*Quercus velutina*) and a view below to the elegant swimming pool and Crabapple Hill beyond. The 'horseshoe' steps leading down to the pool divide and curve around a small oval basin and fountain. The

largest of the terraces below the house contains the box-edged Rose Garden; below it the Fountain Terrace is planted with seasonal flowers. From here the garden lapses charmingly into informality with a meandering brick path through the woodland-like Melisande's Allee, carpeted with spring bulbs. This leads to Lover's Lane Pool and a small mossy amphitheatre.

Remarkably, with a few exceptions, most of the original design of the garden is still evident. The ornate Pebble Garden, which replaced the original tennis court, was created by Mrs Bliss and an associate of Beatrix Farrand's, Ruth Havey, after Mrs Farrand's death in 1959. The Ellipse, originally of boxwood, was planted in the 1960s with a double row of American hornbeam (*Carpinus caroliniana*) clipped into an aerial hedge. The Arbor Terrace, formerly a herb garden, is now a paved area for fragrant potted plants. Nevertheless, Dumbarton Oaks is the only major garden on the east coast, other than the Rockefeller Eyrie Garden on Mount Desert Island in Maine, to retain the character and details of Beatrix Farrand's design.   PD

Duncombe Park ⊕

Helmsley, North Yorkshire, England, was built for Thomas Duncombe to the designs of William Wakefield between *c.*1713 and *c.*1730. At the same time a great terrace 600 m/2,000 ft long was built above the wooded valley of the river Rye with picturesque views of the ruins of Helmsley Castle and of the river. At each end of the terrace is a temple—Ionic to the north (*c.*1730, possibly by Sir John VANBRUGH) and Tuscan to the south (*c.*1730, possibly by Sir Thomas Robinson)—and between them a figure of Father Time and a sundial by John van NOST. Duncombe's son, another Thomas, built the terrace at RIEVAULX.   PT

Dunedin Botanic Garden ⊕

Dunedin, New Zealand, established in 1863, was the first botanic garden in New Zealand. From the original site in the grounds of the university it soon moved to the present 28-hectare/69-acre location on two distinct levels; an extensive flat area comprising the Lower Garden, and an Upper Garden overlooking the central city. One of the first recorded trees was the 'Royal Oak' planted on 30 June 1863 to commemorate the marriage of the Prince of Wales (later Edward VII) to Princess Alexander. David Tannock was the first superintendent and a major influence for the next 40 years—his foremost project was the development of an area for rhododendrons in a mixed indigenous and exotics setting in the Upper Garden. This planting, The Dell, now covers 4 hectares/10

acres and, of the 3,500 specimens, 800 are species—many are of treelike proportions. Another of Tannock's important projects was the rock garden, one of the largest in the world. *Pachystegia insignis* (syn. *Olearia insignis*), *Heliohebe hulkeana*, and diverse hebe species are a few of the many native shrubs growing here. A peat garden in the Upper Garden is unique in New Zealand. The native plant collection is significant, being organized according to families, physical characteristics, or natural habitat. Within these groupings the divaricating plants are particularly fascinating. Nearby a boardwalk crosses a wetland area and there is a large collection of phormium selected by the Maori for their intrinsic values.   GSC

Durban Botanic Gardens ⊕

South Africa, is Africa's oldest surviving botanic gardens and Durban's oldest public institution. The Natal Agricultural and Horticultural Society founded it in 1849 when the British Colony of Natal was only seven years old. The garden was moved to its present site on the Berea ridge in 1851, where lion still roamed. Today the 14.5-hectare/36-acre municipal-run site is in the heart of Durban's upmarket residential area. In the early years of its existence, the Durban Botanic Gardens acted as the agricultural research station for the colony. The region's sugar industry owes much to the pioneering experiments carried on in the gardens on various varieties of cane. Tea, coffee, and cotton were also successes, but the subtropical climate was not suited to cinchona or rubber. The gardens were also a centre of the Victorian plant hunting craze that fired settler society. Many WARDIAN CASES filled with newly discovered plants from what is today KwaZulu-Natal were sent from here to KEW GARDENS or scientifically described in the gardens' Colonial Herbarium by John Medley Wood. Today the gardens have a combination of indigenous and exotic flora, with a fine collection of African, Indian, and American trees, an interesting bromeliad garden, an orchid house, a palm area, and a remarkable collection of South African cycads which includes the 'world's rarest plant', the cycad *Encephalartos woodii*.   DPMcC

Dyffryn ⊕

St Nicholas, Cardiff, Glamorgan, Wales, is a palatial country house designed for Sir John Cory by E. A. Lansdowne and built in the 1890s. There had been a 16th-century house on the site, with a small walled garden. Sir John's son Reginald, a learned plantsman, started to make a garden when the house was being built and, from 1906, collaborated with

Thomas MAWSON on an ambitious new layout. Recently restored, it is one of the most and interesting ARTS AND CRAFTS gardens in Britain. South of the house, beyond a terraced croquet lawn and a procession of Irish yews, an axial rill planted with water lilies runs across the Great Lawn. It opens out into a rectangular pool at the centre with a Chinese bronze fountain decorated with a dragon which came to the garden in the 1950s. To the south is a patchwork of enclosed gardens of varied character: the Pompeian Garden has colonnades festooned with wisteria and a raised fountain; the Lavender Garden is enclosed in yew with beds of lavender and roses; the Theatre Garden, with a stage and yew hedges, was originally planned to display a collection of bonsai. Informal passages of sweeping lawn have excellent trees, among them Japanese maples, and a background of shrub borders. There are 22 hectares/55 acres of garden at Dyffryn, rich in often attractive incident, but overall rather lacking coherence.   PT

E

East Ruston Old Vicarage.
See OLD VICARAGE.

Eckbo, Garrett
(1910–2000), American landscape architect and city planner, brought up in California, which later became the base for his extensive practice. He was a pioneer in modern landscape design, not only in relating it to modern art, but by his concept that gardens are for people, and for each individual in particular. His philosophy was presented in his book *The Landscape We See* (1969) (with co-authors Dean, Austin, and Williams) in which he emphasizes the complexities of domestic garden design, writing that 'Residential design is the most intricate, specialized, demanding, responsible, and frustrating field for designers.' His city planning projects, mostly in south-west Asia, have all been imbued with a similar sense of 'people'. Eckbo was long associated with the University of California at Berkeley, where he was professor emeritus. Among his numerous awards was the Medal of Honor (1975) of the American Society of Landscape Architects, of which he was a Fellow. GAJ/PT

MARC TREIB and DOROTHÉE IMBERT, *Garrett Eckbo: Modern Landscapes for Living* (1997).

Écluse, Charles de L'.
See CLUSIUS, CAROLUS.

Ecocathedraal, De ⊛
Mildam, Friesland, the Netherlands. This encompasses and highlights the theories of the artist and philosopher Louis Guillaume Le Roy (b. 1924). From the late 1960s onwards he proposed an ecologically sustainable society, proposing a creative counter-culture as an antidote to existing monocultural agriculture and the inhuman architecture of cities. This included the idea of recycling the waste of the modern consumer society in gardens, using this as a starting point for both creative and natural processes. These principles are displayed on a plot of land acquired for his studio. From the 1970s Le Roy has been recycling paving materials and building rubble to create the foundations of an eco-cathedral that is intended to develop over 1,000 years 'towards a climax endlessly in space and time, and is based on co-operation between people, plants and animals'. It is freely accessible and visitors are welcome to join Le Roy in the building process.

JW

ESTHER BOUKEMA and PHILIPPE VÉLEZ MCINTYRE, *Louis G. Le Roy: natuur, cultuur, fusie/Nature, Culture, Fusion* (2002).

ecology of the garden.
The term ecology was coined in 1866 by the German biologist Ernst Haeckel from the Greek *oikos* meaning 'house'. It is literally the study of living organisms 'at home' or, more formally, the distribution and abundance of living organisms, their habitats, and the interactions between them and their environment. Until quite recently, you would not normally have found the words 'garden' and 'ecology' in the same sentence. Even though a thriving discipline of 'urban ecology' has existed for many decades, its practitioners have tended to act as though gardens do not exist, focusing instead on derelict land and public open space such as parks and playing fields. Since around a quarter of the area of the average British city is private gardens, this may seem like a surprising omission. This neglect of gardens probably has two origins: first, simply the practical difficulties of studying gardens, i.e. their fragmented ownership and essentially private nature. Second, private gardens lie outside the normal sphere of government or local authority control.

A wider problem is the implicit belief that gardens are just too unnatural or artificial, or too dominated by alien plants, to have any ecology worth studying. In truth gardens are no less natural than most of Britain, which has been ploughed, fertilized, grazed, drained, hedged, mown, coppiced, and burnt for centuries. Much ordinary British countryside is occupied by foreign plants—wheat from Iraq, apples from Asia, and conifers from North America. In fact, in the 21st century the boundaries between agriculture, conservation, and gardening are increasingly blurred.

Modern interest in the ecology of British gardens can be traced to one woman: Jennifer Owen. Owen has spent half a lifetime documenting the wildlife of her quite ordinary suburban garden in Leicester, and in 1991 she published her book *The Ecology of a Garden: The First Fifteen Years*. To anyone reared on the conventional view of gardens as wildlife deserts, Owen's book was a revelation: her garden was clearly crammed with wildlife. Perhaps more surprising, to anyone who does not look beyond the bird table, was the nature of that wildlife. Owen documented over 2,000 species of animals and plants in her garden, but this list is far from exhaustive. She found 1,602 species of insects, but she never looked at many kinds, so there may have been over 8,000 species of insects in her garden. Nor were they all common—twenty species of parasitic wasps were new to Britain, and four were new to science. For its size, the invertebrate fauna of Owen's garden can stand comparison with many nature reserves. On the other hand, relatively few vertebrates turned up in her garden—just seven mammals, for example. In fact it was only by including a dead field vole, probably dropped by a passing kestrel, that she was able to get to seven. The live mammals (hedgehog, grey squirrel, wood mouse, house mouse, fox, and an unknown bat) in Owen's garden are the same six I see in my garden, and few urban gardeners are likely to add more than one or two to that list. The lesson is clear: gardens are rich in biodiversity, but most of it has either more than four legs or none at all.

Moreover, by observing over such a long period, Owen was able to go well beyond mere 'stamp collecting'. For example, she was able to show that *the* ladybird, the seven-spot, was far from the commonest species in her garden. Much more abundant in nearly every year was the two-spot ladybird. During her study, the best year by far for ladybirds was 1976. The hot, sunny weather of that year led initially to an explosion of ladybird numbers, but when most countryside became parched and brown as the drought continued, many migrated to the better-watered environment of private gardens.

Inspiring as Owen's work is, it applies to only a single garden. Clearly gardens have enormous wildlife potential, but what about the other 15 million gardens in Britain? Are they all as diverse as Owen's? Are some of them even better? And crucially, *why* are some gardens better than others? The Biodiversity in Urban Gardens in Sheffield (BUGS) project has recently attempted to answer these questions. The core of this project was a study of the invertebrate wildlife of 61 carefully chosen Sheffield gardens. Constraints of time and money meant that BUGS could not match the level of detail in Owen's study, but this was compensated by the ability to compare many very different gardens.

BUGS confirmed Owen's finding that gardens are rich in biodiversity, but it also showed that many common beliefs about garden wildlife are wrong. For example, that big gardens are better for wildlife than small ones, and gardens in the leafy suburbs are better than city-centre gardens. In fact both of these ideas are rooted in misconceptions about garden wildlife. Insects, spiders, and snails are quite unaware of distinctions of ownership. A hedge, from their perspective, is not a boundary, it is simply another piece of habitat. A fence is simply a place to hang a web, sunbathe, or search for prey. Similarly, garden wildlife is abundant in city gardens because that is exactly what it is: wildlife that is born, lives, and dies in gardens. If urban gardens contained only the last flotsam of a tide of wildlife that started out in the country, then garden wildlife would be very peculiar indeed (which it is not). Nor would a rather limited survey of Buckingham Palace gardens have found 895 species of insects and other invertebrates.

Perhaps most surprisingly, BUGS also found no evidence for the idea that native plants are better for wildlife. There are many reasons why this 'surprising' result is not so surprising after all, but here are just two. First, around three-quarters of the invertebrates in gardens do not depend directly on living plants, so have correspondingly little interest in where those plants come from. Pollinators *do* depend on plants, but also do not care about their origins—after all, nectar is nectar, and pollen is pollen. Coming to the minority of animals that actually eat plants, many gardeners are beguiled by the number of species that specialize in a few native trees—oak is the example usually cited by supporters of the 'native is best' view. But oak is really very unusual—most native plants (especially the less common ones) have few or no specialist herbivores. In reality most garden herbivores are quite catholic in their choice of food. In her garden, Jennifer Owen found that caterpillars of native moths ate more alien plants than native ones.

If native plants are not good for biodiversity, then what is? In a word—trees. Gardens with trees and large shrubs had more (and more diverse) wildlife than gardens with few or no trees. Many different animals, from millipedes to beetles, benefit from trees, first because trees simply provide more habitat to live in and more food to eat. Second, because trees provide the damp, shady conditions and leaf mould that

encourage a whole suite of animals that like such conditions, such as earthworms, slugs, snails, woodlice, springtails, and millipedes, plus the animals that eat them, such as centipedes, spiders, ground and rove beetles, and, ultimately, the birds, hedgehogs, and frogs that eat *them*.

In a separate study, the BUGS project looked at a few popular 'quick fixes' that are widely believed to enhance gardens as wildlife habitats. Many, such as ponds and log piles, were found to work as predicted, but some did not. You will be relieved to hear that growing nettles for butterfly larvae is a complete waste of time.

But there is more to garden ecology than wildlife abundance and diversity. Ecosystems (an ecosystem is the sum of all the interacting animal, plant, and microbial life in a habitat) also perform valuable services, keeping the planetary life-support system going, but the contribution of urban ecosystems is usually ignored. For example, official government figures on how much carbon dioxide is mopped up by vegetation ignore gardens completely. To take another example, consider the valuable service performed by the nation's compost heaps. The average Briton consumes about 2.2 kg/5 lb (fresh weight) of fresh fruit and vegetables per week. This is the amount that actually enters the house, and it seems reasonable to assume that about a quarter is waste, in the form of potato peelings, apple cores, banana skins, etc. Thus a household of two would accumulate over 1 kg/2.7 lb of waste every week from kitchen sources alone, while garden waste (e.g. weeds and lawn clippings) is probably at least the same again. If this material from all of Sheffield's 175,000 private gardens were composted, this would mean 18,200 tons per annum that did not need to be incinerated or dumped in landfill. In practice we have some way to go—fewer than one-third of Sheffield's gardens have compost heaps and the quantity of green waste in dustbins has come close to extinguishing Sheffield's waste incinerator on several occasions. An appreciation of garden ecology can have benefits beyond wildlife! See also HEEMPARK; NATURALISTIC PLANTING.   KT

Eden, Garden of.

The creation of the Garden of Eden is described in the second chapter of the Book of Genesis of the Authorized Version of the Holy Bible: 'And the Lord God planted a garden eastward in Eden; and there he put the man whom he had formed. And out of the ground made the Lord God to grow every tree that is pleasant to the sight and good for food . . . And a river went out of Eden to water the garden; and from thence it was parted, and became four heads.' Attempts to locate the historic site of Eden, and to

determine the date of its making, have not been successful. However, its symbolic value has been a potent influence in garden history. It is sometimes said that the four-part division of Islamic gardens, with cross-axial rills, was inspired by Eden. However, D. Fairchild Ruggles in *Gardens, Landscape, and Vision in the Palaces of Islamic Spain* (2000) argues that this 'garden symbolism (at least until the eleventh century) [is] environmental, economic, and political rather than explicitly paradisaic'.

The notion of the garden as a personal paradise is certainly one that many gardeners treasure. At Corby Castle on the river Eden in Cumbria Thomas Howard laid out a garden of wooded walks in the picturesque river valley between 1709 and 1739 making an explicit connection between his Eden and that of the Bible described in Milton's *Paradise Lost* (1667). The poet tells of Satan who 'to the border comes | Of *Eden* where delicious Paradise, | Now nearer, Crowns with her enclosure green, | As with a rural mound the champain head | Of a steep wilderness, whose hairie sides | With thicket overgrown, grottesque and wilde | Access deni'd'. Milton's Eden, with its 'umbrageous grots', 'shaggie hill', and 'steep glade', sounds like an early version of the more PICTURESQUE English 18th-century landscape garden. Milton, too, explicitly excludes the formalities of 'nice Art | In beds and curious knots' in favour of nature and the 'happy rural seat of various view'.   PT

Eden Project ⊕

St Austell, Cornwall, England, perhaps better thought of as a phenomenon than as a garden. The person who inspired it and had the vision, energy, and skill to make it happen is Tim Smit of HELIGAN. At the Eden Project he took a disused china clay pit in the desolate deserted industrial landscape north of St Austell and built a group of futuristic pleasure domes devoted to the celebration of plants. The domes, or biomes as they are called, designed by Nicholas Grimshaw and Partners, are very beautiful, hugging the chalk cliff of the pit. They house two controlled climates, a humid tropical zone and a dry Mediterranean climate. The first is splendidly landscaped with a waterfall, pool, and authentically jungly atmosphere, the second, sparser and less dramatic. Outside, the bowl of ground between the visitors' centre and the biomes is terraced, with sweeping varied plantings. In exhibits in the Visitors' Centre, and placards in the humid tropical biome, there is much encouragement to think about the depletion of plant resources and the wicked things that man is doing to the environment. The Eden Project cost £86,000,000, of which half was a Millennium

Commission award. It opened to the public in 2001 and in its first four years of opening it averaged 1,500,000 visitors per annum—far more paying visitors than any other garden in Britain. Many come to have a good time, others perhaps want to learn—both are possible. Some visitors are slightly unsettled by the hectoring gung-ho tone of some of the placards and captions.   PT

Edinburgh, Royal Botanic Garden.
See ROYAL BOTANIC GARDEN, EDINBURGH.

Edzell Castle ⊛
near Brechin, Angus, Scotland, was built in the 15th century for the Lindsay family (earls of Crawford) who had lived here since the 14th century. David Lindsay made a 'pleasaunce', or walled garden, which is dated 1604. Ochterlony's account of Forfarshire (1682) describes the gardens as 'far exceeding any new work of their times'. The walls are decorated with 21 relief carvings representing planetary deities, liberal arts, and cardinal virtues. Below each carving is a stone container, thought originally to have contained plantings representing the Lindsay heraldic colours. In one corner is a small banqueting house built into the walls. In the 1930s a parterre of box and roses was laid out at the centre, with the Lindsay motto, *Dum spiro spero* (as I breathe I hope), clipped in box. This is pretty enough but the real distinction of Edzell is the enclosure, carvings, and remarkable details.   PT

Egypt, ancient

Dynastic Period (c.2950–332 BC)
Egypt is the source of the world's oldest pictures of gardens and the location of an exceptionally long and seminal tradition of gardening. The basic type of garden was probably established by the Old Kingdom (c.2600–2150 BC) and greatly developed during the New Kingdom (c.1530–1070 BC).

Climate; origins
The country is temperate to subtropical and almost rainless, so that the annual inundation of the Nile was necessary for agriculture, allowing winter crops to be produced after the flood water receded, from roughly the middle of October. From the first, however, perennial irrigation and weeding of small areas must have been necessary in order to raise vegetables. The climate allows these to be grown virtually all year round, as was desirable with a largely cereal diet, and in the hot summer months the labour of watering and the production of delicate species was best shaded. Palms and fruit trees needed most attention in summer when the fruit ripened, and they provided shade; they

could be irrigated, or their roots could tap the ground water. Gardens also needed protection from unwanted flooding—although some encroachment is beneficial—and from the persistent winds. Settlements were generally on slightly elevated ground near the river, from which water could be drawn if a garden contained no pool, so that villages were naturally integrated with gardens. The pool was essential to all gardens of any size, being valued for its cool appearance, its plants, its provision of irrigation water, its attraction for birds, and its fish. In difficult locations pools or wells were dug out to extraordinary depths so that ground water could be reached. This pattern of gardening in or on the edge of settlements may go back far into prehistory, when food production was more horticultural than agricultural in scale. At a miniature scale, pools, plants, and a surrounding wall or courtyard are also essential to a house of quality, and remained so in the Middle Ages.

The general importance of gardens emerges in short 'biographies' of Old Kingdom high officials (c.2350–2150 BC) which describe an ideal life in stereotyped form. People say, 'I came from my town; I returned from my estate [typical journeys]; I built a house and set up doorways; I dug a pool and planted trees.' In this vision of estate life, pleasure is taken in observing agricultural work and watching or participating in agricultural or marsh pursuits. Nearer home, house, pool, and trees form the core of a garden; laying out a garden is integral to a full life. Vegetables, which were so important that professional growers were employed for people who lived in the desert and could not produce their own, are never mentioned in these texts. This shows that they had no great prestige, not that gardens did not contain them.

Gardens never left their origins behind entirely. None seems to have been exclusively ornamental: all produced at least fruit from trees and vines, as well as flowers for cutting. They were set among walls and buildings; layout was formal and geometric. The natural landscape was not imitated or 'domesticated', which is not surprising in a country that consists largely of the flat floodplain with its few trees and the almost plantless desert plateaux and mountains. Another important characteristic is the lack of ground cover. Bare, unirrigated earth surrounds and defines the plants, all of which must be irrigated and intensively weeded; where there is no irrigation, only deep-rooted trees and palms grow.

Representations and descriptions
The oldest indication of gardening is on one of the earliest preserved reliefs (c.3000 BC), which

shows an area crossed by waterways, in one part of which is a palm with an enclosure round its base to protect it against animals; this must be a 'specimen' plant rather than part of a grove, either in a building compound or in a settlement.

From the Old Kingdom no pictures of ornamental gardens are known. A few scenes show vegetable plots, some fruit trees, and pools. Everything here was used, including the lotus in the pool, the Egyptians' favourite flowers, which were cut in vast quantities, and the papyrus on the pool edge, which was also harvested. In detail these austere reliefs show elaborate chequerboard arrangements that optimize the watering of each small plant. These beds were laboriously irrigated from pots carried in pairs hanging from yokes. Some beds have been excavated at the Egyptian fortress of Mirgissa in the northern Sudan (c.1800); the squares had a side of c.45 cm/18 in and the complete plot was 13 m/43 ft square (a comparable system is in use today for the horticultural crops of Egyptian smallholders). The general design of a garden is implied in one relief where beds flank a central pool. This disposition suggests that real gardens were already arranged symmetrically, and were visually satisfying as well as productive.

The reliefs do not tell the whole story. Texts of the Old and Middle Kingdoms (2550–1640 BC), during which pictures show no real developments in garden design, refer to house plots of up to about a hectare, much of which would be orchard or garden. One of the oldest passages of continuous language celebrates the beauty of such an orchard. Others mentioning life at court refer to the *she* of the palace, which may be the pool, or garden, or both, suggesting that the king conducted business by a landscaped and colonnaded pool. A later cycle of stories (c.1600 BC) depicts King Snofru (c.2550 BC) boating on his 'pool', which is large enough to take a boat rowed by twenty beautiful women clad only in nets. Another story in the same papyrus shows a wife taking advantage of her husband's absence to invite her lover to spend a day in a pavilion in the garden (similar to the shelters used by the wealthy in the fields and marshes). When evening comes the lover goes for a swim in the pool, which later harbours a crocodile sent by the husband.

These texts tell us about associations of gardens but do not enable us to envisage them. A minimal pleasure garden is preserved in a model of c.2000 BC. A house portico with two rows of grand columns faces onto a small enclosure, more than half of which is filled with a pool, round whose edges are seven trees; there could have been flowers beside the pool. From the New Kingdom (c.1500–1250 BC) there are paintings of estate gardens. The earliest (c.1480 BC) includes a list of the trees, among them 73 sycamores, 31 perseas, 180 date palms, 120 dom palms (*Hyphaene thebaica*), 5 fig trees, 2 moringa trees, 12 grapevines, 5 pomegranate trees, 1 *Medemia argun* palm (now extinct in Egypt), 9 willows, tamarisks, and various unidentifiable species. Most of these plants bore fruit, but some may have been kept for other properties perhaps including, for the *Medemia argun*, rarity. The picture shows a wall enclosing a house with granaries, a pavilion, a pool, and rows of trees in no particular order—a productive estate that was also enjoyed as a garden. The lack of elaborate arrangement is compensated in later pictures, all of which show some planning.

The grandest of all these paintings belonged to the 'overseer of the plantation of [the god] Amun' of c.1400 BC, from which 'all sorts of plants' were presented to the King. The picture probably shows this 'plantation', which is approached from a quay, beside which is a row of trees in front of a large entrance like that of a temple in the enclosure wall. Inside are four pools, many stands of trees, a large area of grapevines, inner groups of trees surrounded by their own walls, two pavilions, a small temple with another pool and marsh plants beside it, and a house. The pools would have been distributed through the plantation for ease of irrigation, but they also create a set of areas centred on water rather than a massive field. This 'additive' design is in keeping with the formal spirit of all these gardens, which can also be seen here in the strictly symmetrical total layout—whether in reality or in the picture. Since this was the garden of a god, one is left wondering who was privileged to sit in its pavilions.

These large gardens would have contained flower beds, often next to the pools, but the beds are seldom depicted, perhaps because of problems of scale. Of the more than 100 species of garden plants known from Egypt, many were valued for their flowers, the most important being lotus (two species and later a third), papyrus for its umbels, cornflower, poppy, *Chrysanthemum coronarium*, and mandrake. Reliefs of the 7th–4th centuries BC show lilies (species uncertain) being harvested and pressed to make perfume. A number of herbs and spices were grown and valued both for their flowers and for flavour, medicinal purposes, and use in preservation and mummification; among these were dill, marjoram, rosemary, coriander, and cumin. It is uncertain whether vegetable gardens were separate from the formal tree gardens we know, or how far spices and flowers were grown in market garden style. Such gardens might be attached to the palace,

great temples, and major administrative institutions, but there was little 'market' for perishables, because in the non-money economy people mostly received them as part of their 'pay' or produced them for themselves. The definition of a parcel of land by reference to a cucumber patch in an inscription of the mid 1st millennium BC shows that some 'market' gardens could be local landmarks. More modest part-pleasure gardens probably continued to include a pool, trees, flowers, and vegetables.

Landscape design and temples

From before 2000 BC temples could be approached through groves of trees that both landscaped public spaces and acted as a transition to the inner areas, where many of the architectural elements were derived from plant forms, particularly aquatic plants, symbolizing the swamplike environment of the world at creation. For the Temple of Nebhepetre Mentuhotep at Deir el-Bahri in western Thebes (c.2000 BC), tree pits up to 10 m/33 ft deep were dug in the desert forecourt. Statues of the King were set up in the shade of the larger trees (*Ficus sycomorus*), and large separate flower beds were created. There was a similar scheme in front of the adjacent terraced Temple of Hatshepsut (c.1470 BC), where the trees were imported incense trees perhaps from Eritrea (probably *Boswellia* sp.), which would keep their resin perpetually available for the god (the introduction was a failure).

The most striking example of plants in a temple is a set of reliefs of many different species (mostly unidentifiable and quite a few of them clearly fictitious) with a large variety of birds in a court, often called the 'botanical garden', of the Temple of Karnak (c.1440 BC). These are said to be 'all sorts of plants and flowers which [King Thutmose III] brought' from campaigns to Syria and Palestine, although many Egyptian plants are also shown. The plants are presented as 'specimens' with detached fruits, and are probably offered to the god as a token of his beneficence in creating the world of nature. With the title of books on an oil-bearing plant (the *baq*, of uncertain identification) and the pomegranate (?) preserved from c.1360 BC, these reliefs constitute rare evidence for a 'plantsmanship' that may well have been widespread. From Graeco-Roman times come fragments of a herbal, written in Egyptian demotic and wholly within the indigenous tradition, that provide eloquent testimony for deep knowledge of plants.

In the 14th century BC the ceremonial capital, Thebes, was laid out on a grand scale with alleys of sphinxes up to 3 km/1.8 miles long linking temples; these were probably planted with trees, as later renewal programmes certainly were. An

enormous temple was built on the opposite, west bank of the Nile near a vast palace; an artificial harbour, 1 km × 2.5 km/0.6 miles × 1.5 miles in size, was excavated between the two. The outer parts of the temple contained plants, as surely did the palace, and the entire project was probably landscaped, the most colossal marriage of architecture and plants known from Egypt. In a text from the same area, the *maru* of Amun, a 'pleasure temple', is said to be the 'place of relaxation of [the god] . . . planted with all sorts of beautiful flowers. The primeval waters were in it at all times. It had more wine than water, like the rising of the inundation.' Thus flowers, vines, and pool, perhaps here the artificial harbour/lake, celebrated the god and re-established the world at the creation. The rising of the inundation was the annual sign of the renewal of nature.

Later New Kingdom developments

In c.1350 BC a spacious capital city was laid out at el-Amarna, 300 km/180 miles south of Cairo, on the low desert. Here the grander houses were arranged suburban fashion on large plots with surrounding walls, and had gardens whose construction and maintenance, in which soil and water had to be brought from a distance, were extremely laborious. Several significant innovations are visible. Some gardens abandoned the traditional, strictly formal layout in favour of looser schemes (known both from preserved remains and from pictures). There is also the first painting of the *shaduf*, a water-lifting device of great value in horticulture. Gardens invaded dwellings. In palaces some rooms were painted all over with plants, birds, and swamp life, and contained birdcages or nests. The rooms looked onto courtyards with pools and plants, so that distinctions between interior and exterior, dwelling and garden, were minimized. Even floors were painted with foliage and wildlife. The same tendency is visible in the *maru* of the god Aten, which consisted largely of water and plantations of trees.

The symbolism of gardens was important, especially for the afterlife. In the boating excursion quoted above, the King appears as the creator on the primeval waters and looks through the marsh to the solid land of the world. In the next world the dead drink from pools planted with palms. Some plants were identified with deities, such as the dom palm with Thoth, one of whose forms was as a baboon, the animal used to gather the dom fruits. Sycamores were fused with a goddess who was depicted holding out food offerings and libations to the deceased. Such scenes could be placed before a pool, creating a minimal, symbolic garden which may have luxuriant vegetation, in contrast with the plantless desert of real tombs. The landscape at the foot of the desert, near many tombs, often contained swamp and palms, and may have influenced this conception. A rather less garden-like belief is in the otherworldly 'fields of Earu', where the deceased cultivated a strip in an ideally luxuriant, watery landscape. Both these themes are frequent in the Ramessid period (c.1300-1070 BC), but real gardens are rarely depicted, although an example in the tomb of a chief temple gardener under Ramesses II (1279-1213 BC) testifies to his ability to afford such a memorial and to their importance.

The secular side of gardens now appears in a new type of text, the love poem. Like the adulterous couple in the story, the lovers meet in the garden, in this case without moral stigma. They wish to be close to the beloved and to be his or her beloved, or gardener. A character can be identified with a tree, or a tree can speak on behalf of the lovers, who meet in its shade or in a reed hut while it promises, if properly watered, to keep their secret. One of these poems, probably spoken by the pomegranate, includes information about the tree itself and self-praise of it, probably as indirect praise of the woman (in modern Egypt, the pomegranate can signify a woman's breast). These associations and literary types provide parallels for later periods and other cultures, from the Hebrew Bible on. Formal and orchard-like though the Egyptian garden is, it is the place of delectation, shade, and water that appears again and again in different times and places.

Graeco-Roman Period (332 BC–AD 641)

Although climate and the irrigation system ensured that the pattern of gardening remained substantially unchanged in this period, Ptolemaic rule brought a number of innovations; some of these were the result of direct royal influence, with Ptolemy II Philadelphus manifesting a personal and scientific interest in the trial cultivation of certain species. New crops and varieties were introduced—different strains of wheat, vines, garlic, and cabbage among them—and others previously known but not so widely exploited were now cultivated to meet the needs of the Greek settlers, who wanted the wine, olive oil, and types of vegetables familiar to them in their native country. Thus, Philadelphus' Minister of Finance, Apollonius, undertook the planting of large numbers of olive trees at Memphis and on his estate at Philadelphia in the Fayyum depression c.100 km/60 miles to the south-west; the latter area and the environs of Alexandria were singled out by Strabo as the two centres of

olive cultivation in Egypt in his *Geography* of the early Roman imperial period.

By firm administrative control and a policy of settlement on the land, particularly of military reservists, the new rulers increased the area under cultivation throughout the Nile valley; many new settlements like Philadelphia were created by the reclamation of land in the Fayyum, which was henceforward known for its horticultural richness, prolific in grain, pulses, fodder crops, and vegetables. It was also noted for its vineyards, another form of cultivation which gained increased importance in Ptolemaic times. The most celebrated viticultural area, however, was around Lake Mareotis, south of Alexandria, where a wine was produced that was esteemed throughout the Mediterranean world. Dotted with islands and fringed with settlements, the lake was also a resort for the people of Alexandria. Strabo records the popularity of boating parties among the tall thickets of the Egyptian bean—the pink-flowered Indian lotus *Nelumbo nucifera*, which had been introduced into Egypt in late dynastic times and to some extent supplanted the traditional blue and white *Nymphaea* lotuses. A more notorious resort was the town of Canopus, east of Alexandria, the site of an important temple, but also renowned for the licentious behaviour of its visitors. The wayside inns which lined the canal leading from Alexandria to Canopus, and likewise the summer villas on the shores and islands of Lake Mareotis, probably counted among their attractions gardens with water features, shade trees, and cool arbours.

In Alexandria itself, gardens formed part of the great public and royal building complexes, like the palaces of the Ptolemies, within whose confines Ptolemy II Philadelphus, curious to know more about animals as well as plants, created a zoo; later, the Roman Caesareum, the vast temple of the imperial cult, was described by Philo in the 1st century AD as containing 'walks and consecrated groves'. The larger private houses also had gardens at all periods—the Byzantine writer John Moschus, describing the city shortly before the Arab conquest, remarked on the *paradeisoi* (parks), belonging to the houses of the great in the centre. Centuries earlier Strabo had noted 'the many gardens and tombs' of the western Necropolis suburb; but such gardens were probably commercially exploited, to judge by contemporary evidence for tomb gardens to the east, which produced a high yield of fruit and vegetables and must have presented an orchard-like appearance. Throughout the country the emphasis was probably always on the productivity of gardens: a rare reference to an urban garden appears in the petition of a grammarian of the mid-3rd

century AD in the provincial city of Oxyrhynchus, requesting the grant of a productive and leasable orchard to supplement his meagre income. Exceptions to this productive aspect were the sacred temple groves, like that of acacia trees at Abydos and the grove of Osiris on Biga island next to Philae in the First Cataract, or occasional large estates with space for pleasure gardens. Most settlements would have consisted of a dense mass of housing and an adjacent area of cultivation, with sporadic trees and vegetation marking the course of river or canal, and domestic gardens confined to potted greenery beside doors or on roofs.

In all periods, all types of cultivation—market gardening in the city, crop raising in the fertile Delta and Fayyum, and the specialized industries such as papyrus growing, the flower trade, and the supply of scented flowers and aromatic products of certain trees as raw materials for the perfume trade in Alexandria—ultimately depended on the efficient working of the irrigation system. The mechanics of this were improved by the introduction of two water-lifting devices in addition to the *shaduf*: the Archimedes screw, and the waterwheel drawn by oxen. For agriculture and market gardening, an important body of evidence exists in the fragmentary documents recovered from certain sites, especially the Fayyum settlements; these have yielded copious information on landholding, types of crops, methods of cultivation, and the economics of farming. Rare evidence for the working conditions of a gardener is afforded by a document of the 3rd century AD purporting to be a contract between a lady garden owner and her prospective employee: he is to take charge of irrigation work, make the soil-carrying baskets after his day's work in the garden, and take his wages in produce or cash; the garden seems to be primarily a vineyard, and the owner imposes strict measures to prevent pilfering by the gardener.

For the visual appearance of gardens, there is little evidence from Egypt itself; they probably continued to be formal in character, defined by irrigation channels and dykes. Our best pictorial source is Roman mosaics and paintings, created to satisfy a foreign demand for pictures of the 'land of wonders'. In the Palestrina mosaic of c.125 BC, a procession of priests passes along the causeway outside a temple whose crenellated walls enclose a grove of trees, while elsewhere a drinking party is in progress beside a canal shaded by a vine-covered pergola; a Pompeian frieze of picnic and boating scenes includes a Canopus-type inn where a labourer works a screw, while ducks swim in neat basins outside the inn. Painted gardens of the kind found on walls elsewhere in the Roman world have not so far been discovered in Egypt, though an inscription of AD 219 may allude to both the planting and painting of a garden court in a shrine at Koptos, and bucolic scenes including a waterwheel pulled by oxen and a grove bounded by a fence with a sculpted herm were painted on the walls of an Alexandrian tomb. The Roman creation of Egyptianizing gardens implies the existence of prototypes in Egypt itself but is also related to an idealized concept of the country. Its temperate climate and extraordinary fertility and the mysterious phenomenon of the Nile flood always attracted admiration in the ancient world: Callixeinus of Rhodes, describing a midwinter banquet given by Philadelphus, related how the floor of the specially built pavilion was strewn with all kinds of flowers that were elsewhere rare or bloomed only briefly—such was the abundance of Egypt. To some extent, the country offered the ideal garden landscape, in which the hand of man apparently produced the maximum with the minimum of effort; in due course, the Roman iconography of the Nile, its canals, and gardens was adapted to Christian needs and came to depict the riverine paradise.   JB/HW

Ehemalige Abtei Seligenstadt ⊕

Hesse, Germany. The Benedictine abbey was founded in 828, probably deriving its layout from the ST GALL plan. Work began on a new baroque building and grounds in 1685 after the depredations of the Thirty Years War. During secularization the abbey became the property of the landgraves of Hesse-Darmstadt. Reconstruction of the buildings and garden has been in progress since 1982. In the Konventgarten to the south-east of the abbey church a geometrical parterre has been laid out in eight compartments, planted according to historical examples with vegetables, espaliered fruit, and herbs. The physic garden has been relaid next to the reconstructed pharmacy. Excavations made it possible to locate and reconstruct the Engelsgärtchen (dedicated to the Virgin Mary), the Thiergarten (where deer were kept), and the garden beside the abbot's quarters. An ORANGERY, built in 1757, is a rare survival of its date. It has also been possible to reconstruct domestic facilities of monastic life such as the stables, dovecote, beehives, cold rooms, well, and mill wheels. The monastery with its grounds has become an important cultural centre for the region.   BM

Eichbühl Cemetery ⊕

Zurich-Alstetten, Canton of Zurich, Switzerland, a modern CEMETERY conceived on strict architectural lines by Fred Eicher (b. 1927) and Ernst Graf (1909–62), completed in 1966 and regarded as one of the best cemeteries of its time. Its characteristic qualities are its conceptual formal simplicity and a sensitive dialogue with the surrounding landscape. It is among the most interesting 1960s cemeteries in Switzerland, not only because of its 'un-Swiss' generosity of extent—12.5 hectares/31 acres. Enormous population growth meant that the old cemetery was too small and the municipality announced a design competition for a new one. The winners, architects Hubacher and Studer in partnership with garden architects Graf and Eicher, executed the project between 1963 and 1966. Their design was based on the guiding principle of preserving the spaciousness of the existing rural situation by placing the grave plots and cemetery buildings in clearly defined units around a central meadow. The direct path layout and accentuation of the open landscape with geometrically positioned groups and rows of trees enhances the spacious character of the whole site, whose basic grid structure at first glance seems insensitive to the site. It is only with a visit to the cemetery that the sensitive approach to the location becomes apparent. The entrance is flanked by a relief formed of shotcrete (sprayed mortar) by sculptor Robert Lienhard (1919–89). This building material, whose use in garden architecture is hotly debated, was also used to model parts of the topography for grave areas and urn niches with solid walls. The laying-out hall, the central shelter, and the chapel are, in their powerful formal expression, excellently attuned to the ensemble as a whole. Large reflective pools emphasize the striking structures and bring light and an almost meditative calm into the central area of this remarkable cemetery.   UW

Eichstätt Bastion Garden ⊕

Eichstätt, Bavaria, Germany. In approximately 1600, Prince Bishop Johann Conrad von Gemmingen (reigned 1595–1612) commissioned the architect Elias Holl (1573–1646) to rebuild the Willibaldsburg, then the seat of the bishops of Eichstätt. Holl designed a complex of buildings which is today one of the best examples of the early baroque style in southern Germany. Gemmingen's main interest was however his garden and the collection of plants it contained, which included numerous botanical rarities. The garden in the vicinity of the castle was begun in 1592 by the Nuremberg doctor Joachim Camerarius (1534–98) and continued after his death by the pharmacist and botanist Basilius Besler (1561–1629), who also lived in Nuremberg. Little is known of its precise location and design. In 1613 Besler published the monumental collection of copperplate engravings, the *Hortus Eystettensis*, a florilegium consisting of 367 engravings and 1,084 individual illustrations of almost all the plants in the Eichstätt garden. The florilegium remains as an impressive record of the scope of this important early plant collection. During the Thirty Years War the Eichstätt Garden suffered considerable damage but was not entirely destroyed. It was only when the last gardener's post was eliminated in 1795 that the once famous botanical garden was abandoned and finally disappeared altogether. In the 1990s the plants illustrated in the *Hortus Eystettensis* were gradually reassembled in a new garden in the grounds of the Willibaldsburg in memory of Gemmingen's famous plant collection. In 1998 this educational garden, covering an area of 2,000 sq. m/6,560 sq. ft, was reopened under the name of the Bastion Garden. The individual beds are planted in the order in which they appear in the florilegium, based on their blooming season: the first bed is planted with spring flowers and the last with flowers that bloom in the winter. The plants on display in the Bastion Garden are primarily from botanical gardens, plant specialists, and private gardens in Germany and abroad.   JA

Eihōji ⊕

Gifu prefecture, Japan, is a temple of the Nanzenji branch of the Rinzai Zen sect of Buddhism founded by Musō Soseki (1275–1351) in 1313. The garden, which covers a little less than 1 hectare/2.47 acres, is representative of the Kamakura period (1185–1333) for which there are very few extant gardens. In the centre of the garden is a pond, named the Sleeping Dragon, which is crossed by a long, arched wooden bridge. At the high point of the arch is a roof and paired benches allowing the garden to be comfortably viewed from that venue. The bridge leads to a Buddhist Hall called Suigetsujō that enshrines the deity Kannon (Sanskrit: Avalokitesvara). The pond contains two small isles, one representing a crane and the other a tortoise (symbols of longevity), and is enclosed on one side by a natural, rocky precipice. The water cascading down the face of the precipice has been named the Sound of Buddha. As with many of the temples Musō was associated with, the garden most likely pre-dates the founding of the temple, dating from when the property was the estate of the Toki family. In the process of creating a temple Musō reworked the estate, adding Buddhist halls, perhaps the bridge, and giving Buddhist names to parts of the landscape.   MPK

Eisenstadt ⊕

Burgenland, Austria. The Eisenstadt palace gardens—still owned by the Esterházy royal family—are, along with LAXENBURG, among the most important English-style landscape parks in Austria (having been part of Hungary until the First World War). Between 1682 and 1683 there had been a large ornamental garden (*horto italico*) beside the palace. Baroque gardens were laid out between 1721 and 1734 by gardener Anton Zinner for Esterházy's consort Maria Octavia Gilleis. Renovations in rococo style were carried out around 1760 by Louis Nesle, known as Gervais, a Lotharingian garden artist who had previously played a leading role at SCHÖNBRUNN. The first remodelling in the English style was undertaken by court gardener Matthias Pölt between 1801 and 1806, and today's landscape structure was completed between 1807 and 1824 by Parisian architect Charles Moreau for Prince Nikolaus Esterházy II. The park was restored, with some new plantings of conifer species, by court gardener Anton UMLAUFT from 1898 for Prince Nikolaus IV. Its notable features are the Leopoldinentempel with its artificial GROTTO, a monopteros (see TEMPLE) by Moreau for the statue of Princess Leopoldine by Antonio Canova (*c.*1820), numerous pools, and the engine house providing water for the park (the first Watt steam engine in what was then Austria-Hungary). The Great Orangery was restored at the end of the 20th century—in the 19th century it had an exceptionally rich, and much admired, botanical collection.　GH

Ekaterintal

(Kadriorg) ✪ Tallinn, Estonia, is an outstanding baroque palace and park built in 1718 by Peter the Great for his Estonian wife Catherine I (d. 1727) to the plans of Niccolo Michetti. Mikhail Zemtsov (1688–1743) also worked here. The palace, externally well preserved, is situated outside the city on sloping ground near the sea and is the centre of the composition with formal gardens before and behind. The main avenues and the trees—predominantly chestnut, oak, and larch—have survived in the lower garden, but the parterres are much altered. According to a contemporary description, there were ten grass parterres with tulips, narcissi, carnations, and rose bushes in flower beds, and vases of flowers on wooden pedestals, The same account refers to eighteen semicircular summer houses, to the covered walks which flanked the garden, and to the canal which surrounded it on three sides. The upper garden was also laid out with grass parterres and flower beds with flanking covered walks. A week before his death in 1725 Peter instructed Zemtsov to install two fountains in the upper garden and two in the lower. Beyond the canal and to one side of the lower garden there is a large, rectangular ornamental pool

reminiscent of the similarly situated American Pool at Strelna, where Michetti also worked, and there are other compositional similarities between the two parks.　PH

Eleutherian Mills ✪

Wilmington, Delaware, USA, the 1803 Georgian-style mansion of gunpowder manufacturer Eleuthere Irenee du Pont, founder of the DuPont Company, is a part of the 93-hectare/230-acre Hagley Museum and Gardens. This working replica of an early manufacturing community features water-powered mills and workers' homes. The grounds of Hagley Museum support ten state champion trees, including a 350-year-old osage orange (*Maclura pomifera*), measuring 23.6 m /77 ft, and a 35-m/116-ft, 225-year-old sugar maple (*Acer saccharum*). Eleutherian Mills, furnished with antiques and memorabilia of the du Pont family, perches on a hill overlooking the Brandywine river and, in front of the mansion, the restoration of E. I. du Pont's French-style garden. Excavation of 0.8 hectare/2 acres, uncovered original paths and the locations of the original garden structures. A latticed summer house, a rose parterre, and supports for espaliered fruit trees have been reconstructed within an encircling orchard of fruit trees. Garden curator Peter Lindtner has restored the garden, documenting the kinds of plants in the original garden from household accounts and letters. Many plants were introduced by E. I. du Pont to America from the Jardin des Plantes in Paris (see PARIS PARKS AND GARDENS). Among these were oriental poppies (*Papaver orientale*), *Dianthus*, and Canterbury bells (*Campanula medium*). Each spring over 2,000 tulips bloom, followed by peach, pear, and apple trees, lilacs, and old roses. Other gardens at Hagley include an Italian ruin garden, an 1880s vegetable garden, and Louise du Pont Crowninshield's 1920s Renaissance Revival garden, located on a hillside below the mansion.　CO

Elizabeth Bay House ✪

New South Wales, Australia, is the most elegant and sophisticated house of the 1830s decade in New South Wales. The house, built by Alexander MACLEAY between 1835 and 1839, is an extraordinary example of early Australian craftsmanship, most evident in its cedar joinery and graceful cantilevered stone staircase. Today the house is in the care of the Historic Houses Trust of New South Wales, but Macleay's once renowned garden, dramatically sited on the shores of Sydney Harbour, has been sacrificed to urban development. However, it is possible on a walking tour to appreciate the layout of the former estate, particularly Macleay's use of the terrain. The house's siting on an axis with Clark

Island and the Heads (of Sydney harbour)—painted by Marianne North (1830–90) in 1881—was a significant aspect of the carefully stage-managed landscape and is still recognizable today. The lawn, now a public reserve, and adjacent shrubbery and garden terraces, formed the core of the Elizabeth Bay garden, with indigenous vegetation forming a dense border. Contrasts in terrain, vegetation, and formality were important elements of the design and experience of the estate. In 1835 Thomas Shepherd described the walks thus: 'At the extremity of this mowed-grass lawn, wood walks . . . commence, winding through thickets of trees naturally grouped among picturesque rocks. Here also rustic chairs and rustic caves are placed and the river [harbour] is seen from them through a rich foreground of natural trees and beautiful creepers' (*Lectures on Landscape Gardening*, 1836). Further remains of the garden's grandeur are found in a grotto complete with a finely carved classical niche, a retaining wall, and mature kauri (*Agathis australis*) and hoop pines (*Araucaria cunninghamii*) now in neighbouring gardens. A natural grotto shelter also remains as a reminder of a celebrated garden.　CMR

Elk Rock, Garden of the Bishop's Close ✪

Portland, Oregon, USA, developed by Peter and Laurie Kerr with the help of landscape architect John C. Olmsted and landscape designer Emanuel Tillman Mische. Born in Scotland, Kerr was a grain merchant who brought back plant treasures from overseas. He was also interested in native plants, using them throughout the garden. Kerr hired D. E. Lawrence to design a Scottish manor-style house, and Olmsted sited the house to take advantage of the glorious Mount Hood view. After Kerr's death in 1957, the house and garden were donated to the Episcopal Bishop of Oregon, with provisions for public access. This British landscape-style garden on 2.43 hectares/ 6 acres has many mature magnolias, including *Magnolia grandiflora*, *M. salicifolia*, and *M. delavayi*. Members of the witch hazel family (Hamamelidaceae) are numerous, including *Parrotia persica*, *Parrotiopsis jacquemontiana*, *Sycopsis sinensis*, *Hamamelis mollis*, and *Corylopsis pauciflora*. The area surrounding the house looks like a spacious park, with mature specimens of katsura (*Cercidiphyllum japonicum*), *Metasequoia glyptostroboides*, *Abies pinsapo* 'Glauca', and *Stewartia monodelpha*. Outlying trails reveal views of the Willamette river and snowcapped Mount Hood. Native plants include a grove of Oregon oak (*Quercus garryana*), *Garrya elliptica*, *Ribes sanguineum*, and carpets of *Erythronium grandiflorum*. The

Cascades, a waterfall area created in 1963 and redesigned in the 1970s by Kerr's daughter Jane Kerr Platt, features a grove of paperbark maple (*Acer griseum*), *Enkianthus campanulatus*, and *Fothergilla major* that turn flame red in the fall.

BBA

El Novillero. See NOVILLERO, EL.

Elswout ⊛

Overveen, Noord-Holland, the Netherlands, started as a formal layout in the 1630s which survived, with changes, until 1781 when the estate was acquired by Jacob Boreel. He employed J. G. MICHAËL to create a romantic landscape park. This made excellent use of the existing dune landscape: streams were widened in places to form ponds, embellished with fountains, and crossed by a Swiss bridge. Other features included a classical TEMPLE and woodland cave. After 1805 the gardens were improved and extended by the merchant family Willem Borski I, II, and III. The last demolished the existing house and built the present neo-baroque building, commencing alterations in the grounds according to 1883 designs by Eduard PETZOLD, which were partially carried out under the supervision of Leonard A. SPRINGER. Landscape works were halted however by Boreel's sudden death in 1884, after which the estate remained empty. There have been restoration proposals in 1948 by G. Bleeker, *c.*1960 by J. T. P. Bijhouwer, and in 1991 by Bureau B+B. JW

> H. W. M. VAN DER WIJCK, *De Nederlandse Buitenplaats: aspecten van ontwikkeling, bescherming en herstel* (1982).

Elvaston Castle ⊛

Elvaston, Derbyshire, England, dates from the 17th century but was made into a Gothic mansion in the early 19th century to the designs of James Wyatt (1746–1813). The 4th Earl of Harrington married an actress in 1831 and, as a result, felt the need to retire from society. With the help of his head gardener, William BARRON, he made a curious garden designed in part to celebrate the triumph of true love. Magnificent topiary, of both common and golden yew, was lavishly deployed and a Moorish Temple has a painting of the Earl kneeling before his wife. Walks lead through the woods on the banks of a lake decorated with picturesque rockwork. All this survives, one of the oddest landscapes in England. PT

Emes, William

(1730–1803), English landscape designer practising in a similar style to Capability BROWN but usually working for less grand clients and particularly active in the midlands. His work

survives at ARLEY HALL, Belton Hall (Lincolnshire), CHIRK CASTLE, Dudmaston Hall (Shropshire), ERDDIG, HAWKSTONE PARK, Sandon Park (Staffordshire), and Tixall Hall (Staffordshire). At Arley Hall in 1763 he laid out a great lawn south of the house separated from the park by a HA-HA. In 1785 he designed major work in the park—a tree belt and woodland, and the removal of hedges and fields to make a clean sweep down to a new lake. PT

Emirgan Park ⊛

near Istanbul, Turkey. To the north of Istanbul overlooking the Bosporus is the village of Emirgan, chosen as a favourite location by Sultan Murat IV (1623–40) for drinking and debauchery. Sited on a hill above the village, this 35-hectare/75-acre park has become famous for the tulip festivals held annually in April. Paths are lined with rows of cedars, umbrella pines, and weeping sophoras. Three Victorian Ottoman structures in this public park have been restored by the Turkish Touring and Automobile Club and are now used as cafés. The timber Yellow Kiosk in the style of a Ukrainian country house overlooks a pool with extensive rock formations and grotto all in reinforced concrete. The route to the White Kiosk, which stands amongst a formal pool and parterre garden, is lined with wide beds planted with tulips. LJD

Endsleigh House ⊛

near Tavistock, Devon, England, was originally a monastic estate belonging to Tavistock Abbey but it passed to the Russell family (later dukes of Bedford) in 1540 at the dissolution of the monasteries. The Russells built no house here until the early 19th century when the 6th Duke commissioned a fishing and shooting lodge, in the form of a grand cottage *orné* (see AVELEDA, QUINTA DE), from Sir Jeffry Wyatville (1766–1840). The site, overlooking the steep wooded valley of the river Tamar, is wonderfully beautiful. In 1814 Humphry REPTON produced a Red Book of proposals for the grounds. As a result a flowery terrace walk was built, extending from the house along the upper contour of the valley of which it has fine views. A cottage was built on the river bank on the far side as an eyecatcher—Repton liked such signs of life in the landscape. It is said, too, that he liked a wisp of smoke from the cottage chimney and preferred a fire to be lit even when it was unnecessary for warmth. In an angle of the house a children's garden was built, fan shaped with concentric and radial paths dividing the space into beds for flowers, and a central fountain and a pool for toy boats. Wyatville built other ornamental buildings and later in the 19th century an excellent collection of trees

was planted, largely in a valley behind the house. In recent years much restoration of the garden has been done, with the reinstatement of the terrace walk. The site of the children's garden is still visible but not its original layout. PT

Enghien, Château d' ⊛

Enghien, Hainaut, Belgium, arguably Belgium's most important historic garden site. The property of the dukes of Arenberg for over 300 years, it passed to the Baron Empain in 1913 and to the town of Enghien in 1986. Since then major restoration projects have been undertaken. The park was first enclosed between 1390 and 1433 by Pierre de Luxembourg; gardens and a hydraulic system were laid out in 1473–5. New gardens, a hunting park, and a wooded park were created between 1482 and 1523. In 1606 the domain of Enghien was sold by Henri IV to Charles d'Arenberg. Almost immediately d'Arenberg began to redesign the entrance gardens. He brought orange trees from Brussels, grafts from Paris, pines from Spain, and vines from Arenberg. However the main designs for the gardens, which were soon reputed to be the finest in Europe, were the work of his son Philippe-Charles (1593–1669), known as Père Charles, a Capuchin monk and an architect, from 1630, and his nephew Philippe-Francois, 1st Duke of Arenberg (1635–74). A series of seventeen etchings by Romain de Hooghe (*c.*1687) shows how fine they were, although what remains today scarcely evokes their Renaissance splendour. There were five enclosed gardens, a *parterre de fleurons* (with compartments in the shape of flowers) with four CABINETS or arbours, a flowery parterre with orange trees, a labyrinth, fountains, a grand canal, elaborate steps, and a pool in an amphitheatre. In 1731 after a period of change and neglect, 19,000 trees were planted, and in 1736 the Porte des Esclaves (Slave Gate) was moved from inside the park to its present position forming the entrance to the *cour d'honneur* (see ATTRE, CHÂTEAU D'). The 6th Duke (1779–1820) had a new chateau built which was seriously damaged by fire in 1786 and the buildings that remained became a hospital after the French Revolution. The chateau was demolished and the park transformed *c.*1803–5, and a new chateau was built on the site of the old orangery after 1913. Today the domain is approached through the Slave Gate. Beyond the stable block one of the five Renaissance gardens has been faithfully restored as have two remaining pavilions, the Chinese Pavilion (1656), the interior decorated with Chinese designs in coloured inlays, and the Painting Pavilion, which contains information about the restoration of the gardens. In the woodland beyond the 20th-century chateau, the Pavilion of the Seven Stars or Temple of Hercules (1656) at the centre of a series of converging ALLÉES has been restored. This heptagonal pavilion is set in a circular *miroir d'eau* (see ANNEVOIE, CHÂTEAU D') which reflects the Ionic colonnade. The seven *allées* are each bordered by trees of different species including oak, beech, and cherry. Much of the woodland which had become overgrown has been felled and replanted. There are several new gardens, one of dahlias, and one of medicinal plants to the left, past the *miroir d'eau*, and a rose garden with a long pergola planted with climbing roses.   BA

JANINE CHRISTIANY et al., 'Le Parc d'Enghien dans tous ses états', École d'Architecture de Versailles. Paper given at Enghien: Actes du Colloque du 22 septembre 2003.

England. See BRITISH ISLES.

Englischer Garten ⊛

Munich, Germany. On 13 August 1789, in the wake of the French Revolution, the Bavarian Elector Karl Theodor ordered the court hunting grounds on the Isar ('Hirschanger') to be remodelled 'for the use of the general public in your residential city of Munich'. On the initiative of the American Benjamin Thompson, who subsequently became Reichsgraf von Rumford, a garden for the use of the military had already been commenced in July 1789. Now the Elector extended this commission to 'the laying out of a public English garden'. In August 1789 Friedrich Ludwig von SCKELL was thus summoned to Munich to design the first section of the new garden. Under the supervision of Rumford, numerous footpaths, carriageways, and bridle paths were created, together with a round temple that was replaced in 1838 with the Stone Bench. In 1790 the Chinese Tower and the Chinese Tavern were built, in 1791 the neoclassical officers' dining hall (Rumford Hall). As a public park (*Volksgarten*), the English Garden in Munich represented an entirely new type of garden. It was intended for the public right from the beginning, designed, in the words of its initiator Rumford, 'to benefit not just one class of society, but the whole population'. From 1792 the English Garden was available to the people of Munich as a place of recreation. Rumford was succeeded by Reinhard Freiherr von Werneck who removed the military gardens, added the Kleinhesseloher See, and extended the garden considerably to the north (Hirschau). In 1804 Sckell became directly responsible for managing the English Garden, a post he held until his death in 1823. His magnificent concept for redesigning the

park incorporated spacious open areas, many different vistas, and a variety of vegetation, and the finished creation was a classical landscape garden. In 1824 a monument was erected to Sckell by the Kleinhesseloher See. The last building to be added was the Monopteros (see TEMPLE): commissioned by King Ludwig I, it was designed by the architect Leo von Klenze and built in 1836/7 on an artificial hill. Today the English Garden, with an area of 370 hectares/914 acres, is one of the largest inner city green areas in the world.   RH

THEODOR DOMBART, *Der Englische Garten zu München* (1972).

HANS LEHMBRUCH, 'So wirkte Sckell. Friedrich Ludwig von Sckell als Stadtplaner in München', *Die Gartenkunst*, Vol. 2 (2002).

English garden abroad.

Versions of the English garden are found in many countries and are often as remote from the original as are many of the countless 'Japanese' gardens found outside their native country. It is flattering to many English gardeners that in the 20th century the Japanese became so interested in English gardens, sending horticultural students to England to work in gardens and also making English-style gardens in Japan. Other kinds of English garden abroad also exist, in particular the gardens made by English people living in foreign countries and sometimes indulging a yearning for the borders and lawns of home. The English families that created the modern market for Port and Madeira made gardens, some of which survive, that are strongly nostalgic. The Blandys at the Quinta do PALHEIRO on the island of Madeira, for example, laid out mixed borders of English flavour but using tender exotics. In the 19th and early 20th centuries English families bought houses on the Mediterranean, especially in France and Italy, and although they would often use tender plants they would also plant the irises, phlox, and roses seen in every English border.

In the 18th century the English landscape garden became fashionable internationally and foreign connoisseurs came to England to see such prodigies as CLAREMONT, PAINSHILL, The LEASOWES, and STOWE and sometimes went home and attempted to do something similar. In addition, the writings of English garden theorists were widely read. Late in the 18th century Thomas WHATELY's *Observations on Modern Gardening* (1770) was taken as a guidebook to the English gardens worth seeing—within a year of its publication it had been translated into French. The *jardin anglais* is viewed in France as the polar opposite of the rational 17th-century garden, the *jardin à la française*. Gardens such as Racine de Monville's

DÉSERT DE RETZ and the Marquis de Girardin's ERMENONVILLE were plainly, explicitly or not, influenced by the English 18th-century landscape garden. The English garden also influenced taste among cultivated circles in the French provinces in gardens of more modest ambition. The delightful Château de CANON in Normandy has an 18th-century garden made by Élie de Beaumont, an Anglophile lawyer who was a friend of Horace WALPOLE. In the woodland is a long walk with, at one end, a classical temple and at the other a Chinese kiosk built on the very edge of the woodland and overlooking pastures with grazing cattle. The idea of real views of the rural landscape, as opposed to fantasy views of dairies or cottages, was a very English one. In Germany the ENGLISCHER GARTEN at Munich (1789) was the epitome of the English garden seen through German eyes, with its Chinese pagoda, naturalistic woodland, river with cascades, and classical buildings. At SCHÖNBUSCH F. L. von SCKELL, from 1785, laid out a convincingly English landscape park ornamented with charming rococo buildings.

In more recent times the English garden abroad has had a much diminished influence. Few English gardeners have large estates on the Mediterranean coast and, in any case, other styles of gardening have become more influential. It is now more widely recognized that the climate is the one ingredient of English gardens that is not easy to duplicate abroad and, to many people, not desirable. Working with the climate, and above all with plants suitable for the climate, is today a vital part of gardening. There was a time, for example, when gardens in southern California attempted English-style borders. Today drylands plants, naturalistically disposed, constitute the fashionable style of gardening. A herbaceous border in the great heat of the French Riviera is simply not possible. But in the north of France, where the climate is closer to that of England, English influences are still to be seen, particularly in the fairly recent popularity of herbaceous perennials. The English term 'mixed border' is used to denote what in England would be called a herbaceous border. The term is defined in Michel Conan's *Dictionnaire historique de l'art des jardins* (no date, but *c*.2000) as 'Massif de plantes herbacées vivaces formant une plate-bande en général le long d'un mur' (bank of herbaceous perennials forming a bed, usually along a wall). A garden like PLANTBESSIN in Normandy not only has borders of English inspiration but possesses a nursery which was amongst the first in France to specialize in herbaceous perennials. Interpretations of the English garden are sometimes less happy—at VERSAILLES in recent memory there used to be a JARDIN ANGLAIS which consisted of a woodland clearing with an impeccable lawn and a bed of totally French bedding schemes. PT

CHARLES QUEST-RITSON, *The English Garden Abroad* (1992).

Entsūji ⊛

Kyoto city, Japan, is a temple of the Rinzai sect of Zen Buddhism located amid low hills just north of Kyoto city. The site was originally developed by Emperor Gomizunoo (1596–1680) as his Hataeda Detached Palace, which he used intermittently before building the still extant Shugakuin Detached Palace. Gomizunoo moved his villa permanently to Shugakuin in the mid 1650s, and eventually founded a temple at the old Hataeda property in the late 1670s. He had discussed the idea of founding a temple with Chinese Zen priest Yinyuan Longqi (Japanese, Ingen Ryūki; 1592–1673), who came to Japan in 1654 and founded the Ōbaku sect of Zen Buddhism in Uji, south of Kyoto.

The main hall faces east onto a rectangular court of moss, about 600 sq. m/1,962 sq. ft in size, which holds about 40 low stones set in ranks depicting mountain ranges. Outside the garden, some kilometres to the east, can be seen a prominent mountain, Hiei-zan, the view to which is framed by a low clipped hedge, Japanese maples (*Acer palmatum*), and tall conifers (*Cryptomeria japonica* and *Chamaecyparis obtusa*). The artful capturing of the mountain scene by framing it is a classic example of the gardening technique known as 'borrowed scenery' (see SHAKKEI).

It is not known for certain when this garden was made but a clue rests with a large stone, called the Banda Stone, which is depicted in the centre of the garden in a guide to famous sites around Kyoto, *Shūi Miyako Meishō Zue* (1787). Yinyuan wrote a journal called *Records of the Banda Stone*, which implies that the garden was already in existence at the time it was an imperial villa. MPK

Eötvös Loránd University Botanical Gardens. See FÜVÉSZKERT.

Erddig ⊛

near Wrexham, Clwyd, Wales, is a late 17th-century house refashioned in the early 18th century. In 1733 the estate passed to Simon Yorke in whose family it remained until 1973 when it was given by Philip Yorke to the NATIONAL TRUST, with 810 hectares/2,000 acres. An engraving by Badeslade made in 1740 shows walled formal gardens behind the house, with a central walk aligned on a canal, the whole flanked by regular plantings. When these garden were being made a park was also laid

out, but this was largely transformed by William EMES between 1767 and 1789, with the removal of all formality, much tree planting, and planned walks in woodland. By the time the National Trust took over, the house was in decay, sheep grazed in the walled garden, and the park landscape was blemished by subsidence caused by coal mining. In a remarkable feat of restoration the trust recreated the walled formal gardens (the canal and an avenue of limes survived) and restored the parkland. This makes a harmonious setting for the house, but in many ways the most attractive features of the garden are of much later date. Immediately behind the house is an Edwardian garden of parterres with bedding schemes and a fountain set between two handsomely gabled outhouses. A Victorian flower garden leads between urns into woods of laurel and holly where there is an agreeably melancholy walk. PT

Eremitage ⊛

Arlesheim, Canton of Basle Land, Switzerland, took shape in the 18th century as the largest English-style landscape garden in Switzerland and as such is of exceptional significance in the history of Swiss garden art. The picturesque castle hill of Birseck with its cliffs, grottoes, and caves, the view of the mountains and of a stream in the valley below, with three fish ponds and two mills, offered a marvellous setting for laying out a romantic landscape garden. Canon Heinrich von Ligertz and his cousin Balbina von Andlau, wife of the last Sheriff of Birseck, are thought to have begun the garden in 1785. It was originally dedicated to the ideal of the unsullied landscape following the philosophy of Jean-Jacques ROUSSEAU, and intended to display the beauties of nature to advantage. The landscape setting of this park still has a very special charm. From its foundation until the destruction wrought by French troops in 1793 the gardens were enriched with numerous attractions and stylistically influenced by the rococo fashion. From 1810 to 1812 Conrad von Andlau and Heinrich von Ligertz reinstated the park and adorned it with new attractions, enhanced by the authentic ruined 13th-century castle of Birseck, where the chivalrous romanticism popular in the 19th century found a rich source of inspiration. Among the exceptional attractions were, however, numerous grottoes with different themes, made accessible through the construction of winding paths and steps and adorned with monuments and inscriptions. Today there is still a monument to the idyllic poet Salomon Gessner (1730–88) at the grotto bearing his name and, in the Proserpina Grotto, a statue in honour of Balbina von Andlau. A carousel and

playground were part of the plans from the beginning, for young people who, according to Rousseau, should learn from nature in the landscape garden. The centre of the park accentuates the hermit's retreat, regarded as the epitome of an unspoilt life in the midst of nature. In a bark-clad hut a wooden figure was installed, later replaced with a mechanically animated statue. The Eremitage is still today suffused with reverence for nature and natural philosophy (see also HERMITAGE). UW

Eremitage ⊛

Bayreuth, Germany. The Bayreuth Margrave Georg Wilhelm had the game preserve that had belonged to his father Christian Ernst converted into an Eremitage (hermitage). The summer palace designed by Johann David Räntz—today known as the Old Palace—was begun in 1715. In front of the banqueting hall of the four-wing complex there was originally a simple parterre and a cascade which flowed down the hillside to the river, the Roter Main. Paths wound through the wooded areas covering the slopes, and led on the northern slope to scattered hermits' huts. The Eremitage was designed by Margrave Georg Wilhelm as a place where he and his court could play at being hermits, imitating the simple life and following the rules of an order of hermits. In 1735 the Eremitage was given by Margrave Friedrich to his wife Wilhelmine who embarked on major alterations, starting with the enlargement of the Old Palace. The garden to the west of it was substantially altered and enlarged. New, self-contained garden areas such as the Lower Grotto, the New Palace with the Upper Grotto, and several hedged sections were created. Various park buildings were also added, most of them designed by the architect Joseph Saint-Pierre. After the death of the Margravine in 1758, and especially after the margravate came to an end in 1791, the elegant rococo garden was neglected. The transformation of the geometric garden areas 'into beautiful and useful meadows', already begun by Margrave Alexander in 1789, was continued under the administration of the Prussian government (1792 to 1807). In 1811 Bavaria acquired the former territory of the Margrave from Napoleon (as crown land). Today, as a result of comprehensive reconstruction work and continuous maintenance, the *c.*49-hectare/121-acre complex is once again complete with both its rococo and landscape elements. KG

Ermenonville ⊛

Aisne, France, was the estate of Louis-René, Marquis de GIRARDIN, who after inheriting in 1762 laid out a PICTURESQUE garden in the wooded valley of the river Launette. Girardin set down his philosophy of gardening in his *De la composition des paysages* (1777). Here he rejects regional styles—old gardens, new gardens, English gardens, Chinese gardens—he would only 'treat of ways of embellishing and enriching nature of which the various combinations are infinite and beyond classification and are appropriate for every period and every nation'. Girardin's ideas also embraced the principle of linking the useful and the beautiful, the essential spirit of the FERME ORNÉE. At Ermenonville he put these ideas into practice and the remains of his garden may be seen today. What remains, however, gives only a partial and slightly misleading picture of Girardin's landscape. The farm and farm labourers' cottages that were an important part of the landscape no longer exist and only part of the whole landscape survives. Girardin's *désert* was a wild and rock-strewn place with no ornaments, merely the occasional inscription and a pattern of paths leading through the wilderness. This was a favourite place of Girardin's friend Jean-Jacques ROUSSEAU, according with his love of untamed nature; he had a cabin here which still survives (although the land where the *désert* was is now in separate ownership). Rousseau spent much time at Ermenonville and died here, being buried on an island on the lake shrouded with poplars in a tomb of noble Roman character designed by Hubert ROBERT. Rousseau was much loved by revolutionaries and his mortal remains were moved to the Panthéon in Paris in 1794 although the tomb remains on the Île aux Peupliers. The exact influence of Rousseau on the garden at Ermenonville (which is often referred to as the Parc Jean-Jacques Rousseau) is not easy to discern. Although there are passages of fairly wild nature there were, and are, all sorts of FABRIQUES which are as unnatural as can be. Close to the chateau, to the north of the lake, Girardin introduced 'Dutch' features—a canal, brewery, watermill, and windmill none of which remains. Many *fabriques* erected by Girardin no longer survive—several temples, an obelisk, an altar to friendship, and a grotto for dreaming. Most of the surviving buildings and ornaments are on the slopes west and south-west of the lake. A rustic Dolmen, like the entrance to a druidic cave, stands inconspicuously among trees. A little beyond it is the Jeu d'Arc provided for Girardin's farm labourers to divert themselves with bows and arrows. In grass on the edge of a field (an Arcadian meadow in Girardin's time) is the Autel de la Rêverie (the altar for dreaming), a stubby stone column, with plain plinth and capital, inscribed with the words *A la Rêverie* (usually translated as 'to dreaming'; although the French word (from which the English 'rave' comes), also means

delirium, a notion of much attraction to some 18th-century romantics). Above the field is the most memorable of the surviving *fabriques*, the Temple de la Philosophie, attributed to Hubert Robert and based on the Temple of the Sibyl at Tivoli. Dedicated to Michel de MONTAIGNE, this half-rotunda of columns, built incomplete (for the work of philosophy is never complete), commemorates modern philosophers—Descartes, Newton, William Penn, Montesquieu, Voltaire, and Rousseau. The other surviving *fabriques* include memorials to an unknown suicide and to Mayer, a friend of Girardin's who died here; a rustic stone kiosk, a prehistoric cavern, and, in a grove close on the bank of the lake, the Table des Mères (Mothers' Table) surrounded by chairs. The walk about the banks of the lake, with pauses to admire buildings and magnificent mature trees, is immensely pleasurable.   PT

Eryldene ⊕

New South Wales, Australia, is a memorial to the creative collaboration in 1913 between patron Professor Eben Gowrie Waterhouse and architect William Hardy Wilson (1881-1955). Situated on Sydney's North Shore, the house, in the early colonial style with strong Georgian influence, is recognized today as the finest unaltered example of Hardy Wilson's domestic work while the garden, planned by Waterhouse, was designed as a sympathetic extension of the house in a series of rooms, each leading to the next, filled with trees, shrubs, and flowers. Superbly proportioned buildings designed by Hardy Wilson—a secluded study, a temple, a Chinese-inspired pavilion with lacquer red columns and a delightful shingled pigeon house—furnish the garden rooms and contribute to Eryldene's tranquil atmosphere. Camellias were a passion of Professor Waterhouse and Eryldene's extensive collection is considered Australia's most significant. A linguist by profession, Waterhouse became one of the world's foremost authorities on the camellia. He raised and named many popular varieties, founded Sydney's famous Camellia Grove nursery, and was president of the International Camellia Society. He was an authority on the history and nomenclature of early camellia cultivars. Hybrid camellias 'E. G. Waterhouse' and 'Margaret Waterhouse' are just two of the professor's successes that have remained popular with Australian gardeners since their introduction in 1954. Eryldene has remained virtually unchanged since it was built, giving it an important place in Australian architectural and horticultural history.   CMR

Escorial, El ⊕

Madrid, Spain. Philip II, who commissioned El

Escorial, wrote to his architect Juan de Herrera (1530-97), 'do not forget what I have told you: simplicity in the construction, severity in the whole, nobility without arrogance, majesty without ostentation'. Herrera at first worked as the assistant to Juan Bautista de Toledo (d. 1567), but on his death was in charge of the new buildings which were completed in 1583. The huge ensemble of palace, library, monastery, church, and mausoleum is marked by the taste of the two architects for *estilo desornamentado* (plain style). The notable gardens here are each associated with a particular building. The monastery (of San Lorenzo) has a square patio overlooked by double height cloisters. The garden, called the Patio de los Evangelistas (Court of the Evangelists), is unusual in following Christian symbolism. At its centre is a domed and pillared octagonal pavilion with statues in niches of the four evangelists each overlooking a square pool. In the 16th century there was an elaborate planting scheme here with medicinal plants and ornamentals. Today the space is divided into a pattern of twelve squares (like the twelve disciples) planted in box with hedges, clipped domes on each corner, and a knot pattern within. The Casita de Abajo (Lower Pavilion), to the south-east of the monastery, was built in 1772 for the Prince of Asturias (it is also known as the Casita del Príncipe) to the designs of Juan de Villanueva. This elegant TRIANON-like building, with magnificently decorated interiors, stands at the centre of a grove of oaks cut through with ALLÉES. A parterre has curving hedges of box and arches of clipped cypress, a fountain stands at the meeting point of *allées*, and climbing roses garland the garden walls. A large pool at the upper level provides water for the garden and here are rose beds and a curved terrace. The Casita de Arriba (Upper Pavilion), a simple neoclassical building, has a high and airy site. It also was designed in the late 18th century by Villanueva as a rural retreat for Charles III's son the Infante Don Gabriel—it is also known as the Casita del Infante. The garden is terraced, with parterres and fountains. From one of the terraces, with stone table and chairs, are fine views back towards the Escorial monastery whose towers rise above the trees. Nineteenth-century plantings of conifers, among them some very large Wellingtonias (*Sequoiadendron giganteum*) which frame the *casita*, add a more sombre note.   PT

Este, Villa d'

(Como), Cernobbio, Lombardy, Italy. The villa and garden have a view over Lake Como. Built in 1568 by the architect Pellegrino Tibaldi (1527-96), known as Pellegrino, as a private residence for Cardinal Tolomeo Gallio (he also built Villa

BALBIANELLO for the Cardinal), the villa was exceptional with outstanding gardens containing a double water staircase flanked by cypresses leading to a NYMPHAEUM set to the side of the villa, allowing an uninterrupted view from the lake. Other architectural motifs were only completed over the centuries. After Cardinal Gallio's death the villa fell into the hands of the Jesuits and then became the property of the Marchese Bartolomeo Calderata for his wife Vittoria Peluso, a famous dancer, who built the strange mock fortifications to honour her husband, one of Napoleon's generals. Bought by Caroline of Brunswick, the neglected wife of the English King George IV, in 1815, the Villa d'Este was renamed and the garden restored in contemporary taste. The Queen's Pavilion built in 1860 was named in her honour. The Villa d'Este has been a luxury hotel since 1873.   PHo

Este, Villa d'

(Tivoli) ⊕ Tivoli, Lazio, Italy. Pirro LIGORIO made a new design for Ippolito d'Este, son of Alfonso I Duke of Ferrara and Lucrezia Borgia, remodelling the old Franciscan monastery and garden at Tivoli between 1551 and 1572. The garden's supreme achievement was its skilful use of water, using hydraulic experts to contrive ingenious and spectacular fountains which still blast the mind today with a roar of rushing water, huge jets, and murmuring tinkles. Giovanni Alberi Galvani supervised the construction of masonry steps, fountains, and fish ponds. The garden itself was laid out in a series of narrow terraces, linked by steps and ramps, around a central axis on the steep slopes below the villa, its iconographical features dedicated to Hercules, identified with Cardinal d'Este, the symbol of power, and Hippolytus, symbol of chastity, creating one of the most complex examples of Roman mannerism (originally unfolding from the approach at the bottom of the garden). Terraces flattened out towards the bottom of the slope to contain tranquil fish ponds, orchards, and covered BERCEAUX. Ligorio derived inspiration from classical ruins, in particular from HADRIAN'S VILLA nearby. The famous waterworks include the vast Organ Fountain (completed in 1641), the Owl Fountain, and the Walk of a Hundred Fountains, based on the hydraulic theories of Hero of Alexandria (c. AD 100). Recently completely restored, the Villa d'Este is a bewildering world of sparking spray and rushing water.   PHo

Esterházy Park. See CSÁKVAR.

Estufa Fria ⊕

Lisbon, Portugal, is in a corner of the Parque Eduardo VII, the largest public park in Lisbon (named after the English King Edward VII who, as Prince of Wales, was a popular visitor to Portugal). The Estufa Fria, which means 'cool greenhouse', was built in the 1930s on the site of a south-facing quarry. The dramatic stony walls remain and the space has been roofed with laths of wood to provide an environment of cool shade. Paths zigzag up the cliffs giving views over dense exotic planting. Maidenhair ferns (*Adiantum venustum*) have colonized the stonework and grotto-like hollows are occupied by doves whose cooing adds to the atmosphere of the place. Here are substantial trees such as the Belmore sentry palm (*Howea belmoreana*) from the South Pacific and thickets of perennials like *Strelitzia nicolai*. The terrestrial and epiphytic fern *Asplenium bulbiferum* has established itself and large tree ferns of several different species seem entirely at home rising over naturalistic pools. In a fine collection of succulents some specimens (such as the *Cereus uruguaynus*) have grown to fearsome size. These exotic plants, many of them unfamiliar to European visitors, in an authentically shady jungle-like setting have dramatic presence.   PT

Eszterháza. See FERTŐD.

Evelyn, John

(1620–1706), English author, scientist (Fellow of the Royal Society), gardener, garden designer, and arboriculturist. His book *Sylva* (1664)—'A discourse of forest-trees, and the propagation of timber in his majestie's dominions'—emerged from research conducted by the Royal Society into the cultivation of trees, prompted by the government's desire to provide timber for naval vessels (the title of the book changed to *Silva* in 1706). In around 1657 he began a never completed gardening encyclopedia, *Elysium Britannicum*, of which part, *Kalendarium Hortense*, was published, at first as a supplement to *Sylva* and later as an independent volume; his account of salads, *Acetaria*, also from the *Elysium*, was published in the same way. Another part of *Elysium Britannicum*, 'Pomona, or an appendix concerning fruit-trees, in relation to cider', was also included in the first edition of *Sylva*. *Sylva* went into four editions in Evelyn's lifetime and was produced in a posthumous edition, expanded by Alexander Hunter, in 1786 which itself was reprinted four times. It was by far the most influential book on arboriculture of its time and introduced to many landowners the notion of both growing a much-needed and lucrative crop and beautifying the landscape. Evelyn translated an influential book on kitchen gardening, Jean-Baptiste de La QUINTINIE's *Instructions pour les jardins fruitiers et potagers* (1690), which appeared in English as *The Compleat Gard'ner* (1699). The complete text of *Elysium Britannicum* (or as much of it as was completed) was published, in an extraordinary variorum edition, for the first time in 2001. Evelyn's diaries, covering the years 1641–1705, that is, almost all of his adult life, are a vivid account of historical events, people met, and gardens visited (in Italy and France as well as in England), seen through the eyes of a marvellously well-informed and observant man. In recent years it has been said that some of his garden descriptions have been borrowed, unacknowledged, from other writers. He was a practical gardener both at his family house of Wotton (near Dorking in Surrey) and later at his own estate of SAYES COURT. Of the first, made from 1650 onwards, which survives in part and has recently been restored, he wrote in his diary, 'I should speake much of the Gardens, Fountaines and Groves that adorne it were they not as generally knowne to be amongst the most natural & most magnificent that England afforded.' In 1671 Evelyn advised Lord Arlington at Euston Park (Suffolk) 'about ordering his plantations of firs, elmes, limes, etc. up his parke, and in all other places and avenues'. In about 1674 he designed a garden for Henry Howard (later 6th Duke of Norfolk) at Albury Park (Surrey) with two giant terraces 400 m/1,400 ft long and a *crypta*—a tunnel which pierces the hill behind the terraces—all of which survive.   PT

Evksinograd Palace ⊕

Varna, Bulgaria, stretches along a 3-km/1.8-mile Black Sea coastline strip north of the city in dramatic landscapes. The palace was a royal summer residence, commissioned by Knjaz Alexander Batenberg from the Austrian architect Victor Rumpelmayer (*fl.* 1870s) in 1881. The imposing building in 18th-century French style is centrally situated in a large and beautiful park (55 hectares/135 acres) of fine layout and planted with rare exotic plants. Completed mostly in the 1880s–1890s, the park acquired its Mediterranean character initially under the German landscape architect Eduard PETZOLD, succeeded by the French Édouard ANDRÉ. Picturesque terraces and skilfully composed groups of plants open deep perspectives and magnificent clifftop views to the sea. By 1912, the most imposing part—an elegant French-style *parterre* with the Fountain of Neptune in the middle—featured large clipped shapes of yew and box trees, as well as rows of palm trees in containers. It harmoniously flowed out into the parts of the park in the English landscape style where extensive woodland was planted. A very large collection of exotic trees and shrubs was formed by the succeeding monarch, King Ferdinand, who also built greenhouses for the tropical plants. In 1921, the park became a branch of the Royal Botanical Gardens. During the last 50 years Evksinograd Palace has been a government centre for events and recreation, with health, spa, and entertainment facilities. The palace takes pride, also, in its cellar of locally produced wines.   ASG

exedra.
The original Greek meaning of the term was a kind of open portico of a gymnasium (a place for teaching athletics) or palaestra (a place of public education) in which discussions could take place. It later came to mean a bench against a semicircular wall. In Roman gardens it denoted a room open on one side but screened by a peristyle, either attached to a house or serving as a free-standing garden pavilion. In 18th-century gardens it signified a free-standing semicircular wall, usually elaborately decorated, with a seat below. At CHISWICK HOUSE in the early 18th century William Kent designed an exedra in the form of a yew hedge with niches for statues. At PAINSWICK there is a Gothic filigree exedra, a reconstruction of an 18th-century original.   PT

eyecatcher.
An ornament or ornamental building in some prominent and carefully chosen position in a garden layout, for example on the horizon or serving as the focal point of an avenue or of some other vista. It is a common feature of 17th-century French gardens and of 18th-century English landscape parks. At VAUX-LE-VICOMTE a copy of the Farnese Hercules is an eyecatcher at the highest point of the central vista. At

BRAMHAM PARK the chief vista from the house, in relatively flat ground, ends in an OBELISK at the centre of a pattern of radiating rides, and on the rising ground in front of the house a huge urn on a plinth acts as an eyecatcher where rides meet. These are grand examples in large gardens but the principle of the eyecatcher may be used effectively in small gardens to direct the gaze.
PT

Eyrignac, Manoir d' ⊛
Salignac-Eyvignes, Dordogne, France, an intricate formal garden for a pretty 17th-century stone manor house. It was made from 1960 by the owner of the house, Gilles Sermadiras, an amateur gardener. Here is an avenue of curved buttresses of hornbeam supported by columns of yew, a pared-down box parterre spiced with Italian cypresses, much topiary, and skilfully deployed vistas. Visits are by guided groups only and your guide may tell you what are the best features to photograph. The greatest attraction of Eyrignac is the quality of the impeccable maintenance, for the design, ingenious though it may be, is rather soulless.   PT

Eyserbeck, Johann August
(1762–1801), German garden designer, the son of J. Friedrich EYSERBECK (see below). After an apprenticeship at Oranienbaum (see DESSAU-WÖRLITZ GARTENREICH), he was employed at Leipzig and in the GROßER GARTEN in Dresden. He was summoned by the successor of Friedrich II of Prussia to SANSSOUCI, where his main contribution was to make alterations in the sentimental manner around the Neues Palais and to introduce the landscape style. In c.1786-7 he drew up plans for the NEUER

GARTEN at Potsdam: an early sentimental park laid out on the banks of the Heiliger See, and divided into charming gardens with Chinese and especially Egyptian façade structures. In 1786, also, he may have been involved in the Schlosspark Belvedere, TIERGARTEN. From 1788 he was court gardener at CHARLOTTENBURG near Berlin, and was responsible for the modernization of the baroque garden. He influenced the style of estate parks in Brandenburg by his advice and plans.   H GÜ

Eyserbeck, Johann Friedrich
(1734–1818), German garden designer. After a prolonged stay in the Netherlands and England from 1762 to 1817, he became court gardener in the Luisium near Dessau (see DESSAU-WÖRLITZ GARTENREICH). In c.1774 he redesigned the 14-hectare/35 acre park to specifications by Prince Franz of Anhalt, although he also drew up his own plans; in 1775 he laid out the 14-hectare/35-acre pleasure garden at Dessau to a regular design reminiscent of the ancient form of the hippodrome. From 1777 he advised on and partly executed the building of the hermitage of Sieglitzerberg. The plan for the Georgium in the Dessau-Wörlitz area, hitherto attributed to Eyserbeck, was probably drawn up by D. Klewitz and Prince Franz of Anhalt. Originally a park of 13.5 sq. km/8 sq. miles, it included the landscaped meadows on the banks of the Elbe; today it covers 20.5 hectares/61 acres, with the classical Schloss (1784), Ionic Monopteros (see TEMPLE), Roman ruins, and other small buildings. Eyserbeck had great influence on undertakings to improve the countryside and on horticulture, especially fruit growing.
HGÜ

fabrique.

A French term for a decorative garden building, originally used by landscape artists to describe such buildings in their paintings but later borrowed by garden designers in 18th-century France. Jean Morel in his *Théorie des jardins* (1776) describes *fabriques* as 'all those constructions which human ingenuity adds to nature for the embellishment of gardens'. There is no exact English equivalent, for the French term embraces both ornaments (urns, obelisks, monuments) and types of buildings (tents, temples, bridges), but the way in which *fabriques* may be used in the landscape and the kinds of meanings with which they may be imbued are exactly the same in France and England. In the Folie de Chartres (1773) at Monceau (see PARIS PARKS AND GARDENS) CARMONTELLE believed that *fabriques* were essentially impermanent and could be used to modify the atmosphere of a landscape; they could be changed 'like the stage sets at the Opéra'. In other gardens permanence and impermanence could be combined in a single building. The Ruined Column (1781) at the DÉSERT DE RETZ is a multi-purpose *fabrique*. It is the remains of a column of the Doric order, evoking the classical world. But it has an interior, a whole house in which its builder, Racine de Monville, lived. It also has intense mystery, for the column is 15 m/50 ft in diameter, and if it were part of a temple the building would be 120 m/400 ft high. In many 18th-century gardens exotic *fabriques*—a Turkish TENT, an Egyptian PYRAMID, a Chinese PAGODA— were made to seem even more exotic by being set in a naturalistic landscape.   PT

Fagervik Ironworks ⊛

Inkoo, south-west Finland, is one of several 17th-century ironworks on the southern coast. Prosperity resulting from the exclusive right to produce sheet iron enabled the enlightened owners to create a garden that was unique so far north. A typical 18th-century FERME ORNÉE, the garden is among the oldest in Finland and has an unbroken history. Its oldest parts are the mid 18th-century formal garden and the orchard. The first ORANGERY was built around 1760 as part of a geometrical garden. Later, a picturesque landscape garden was created on a slope rising up to a cliff. It was inspired by the 1783-4 grand tour of Fagervik's owner, Mikael Hisinger, to gardens of Central Europe. Dating from that same period, a large landscape park north of the actual ironworks area is set against a backdrop of rocks, woodland, and lake. Footpaths lead the visitor to a labyrinth, a HERMITAGE, and a delicately proportioned Chinese pavilion standing on a rock in the lake. This pavilion, the only one of its kind in Finland, has connections to the Chinese pavilions designed in Sweden by Fredrik Magnus PIPER and Carl Råbergh. Fagervik's landscape park is the foremost Finnish representative of English garden art. Many details have disappeared, but the basic idea and design remain. Restoration of the park and the neo-Gothic conservatory for orchids, camellias, and exotic fruits is under way.   ITL

Fairchild, Thomas

(1667-1729), London nurseryman who began as a cloth worker but from the beginning of his apprenticeship also gardened. Employed in 1690 at Hoxton, London, then a centre of the nursery business, he purchased a nursery and remained there for the rest of his life. Elected freeman of the Gardeners' Company in 1704, Fairchild developed an interest in growing the new introductions, particularly the material collected by Mark CATESBY in America and sent to Philip MILLER. A practical gardener, interested in scientific research, Fairchild experimented in hybridization, producing the first artificial hybrid between *Dianthus caryophyllus* (carnation) and *D. barbatus* (sweet william). The flowers resembled a sweet william, but were larger and red, but the seeds proved infertile and the plant became known as 'Fairchild's Mule'. He corresponded with LINNAEUS and read papers on his experiments to the Royal Society. His *The City Gardener* (1722) is a detailed guide to gardening in the city of London. In 1725, with Philip Miller and Robert Furber (*c*.1674-1756), he helped found the London Society of Gardeners.   MC-C

MICHAEL LEAPMAN, *The Ingenious Mr Fairchild* (2000).

Fairchild Tropical Garden ⊛

Coral Gables, Florida, USA. A short distance due south of downtown Miami, the garden was founded in 1938 by Robert H. Montgomery (1872-1953), a businessman with a love of plant collecting. He named the garden to honour his friend, the eminent botanical explorer David Fairchild (1869-1954), who had retired to Miami in the mid 1930s. The 34-hectare/83-acre garden was designed by William Lyman Phillips (1885-1966), a student of Frederick Law OLMSTED at Harvard and subsequently a partner in the Olmsted firm. He was a pioneer in the use of tropical plants and became the foremost landscape designer in Florida, laying out several of south Florida's public parks and countless public housing projects, hospitals, cemeteries, airports, roads, highways, private gardens, and college campuses. His masterpiece was the Fairchild Tropical Garden. Begun and opened to the public in 1938, the garden was conceived as a showcase for tropical plants growing in a natural environment. While aesthetically rewarding, the garden fulfils an important role in the documentation and display of tropical botanical specimens. Its collections showcase palms, cycads, fruit trees, vines, and flowering trees and shrubs. The majority of the plant material has been collected in the wild. The palm collection includes more than 400 species of 193 genera and is a haven for many of the world's endangered plants. The cycad collection is among the world's most diverse with approximately 200 species. A collection of special interest is that of 450 species and cultivars of tropical fruit such as canistel (*Pouteria campechiana*), jackfruit (*Artocarpus heterophyllus*), mango, mamey sapote (*Pouteria sapota*), and lychee. With more than 100 endangered and rare species, Fairchild is committed to the propagation, reintroduction, and nurture of seedlings.   HSS

Falkland Palace ⊛

Falkland, Fife, Scotland, is one of the finest Renaissance houses in Scotland, started in the late 15th century for James IV, but the first castle recorded here dates from 1120. There were gardens by the 15th century when the accounts show gardeners' wages. James V was married to Madeleine de Valois who caused French masons to come here in 1537, which resulted in superb carved stonework. Charles I laid out a new garden in 1628 with 'sundials and pillars'. Charles II was the last monarch to stay here—in 1654 it was burnt out by Cromwell's army. The palace was restored in the late 19th century for the 3rd Marquess of Bute, and between 1946 and 1952 Percy CANE laid out new gardens. Instead of attempting any historicist exercise Cane designed a strongly planted garden in which the beautiful palace has pride of place. On the level ground below he laid out six large island beds planted with trees and shrubs underplanted with herbaceous perennials. Where they are adjacent to each other the beds have curved edges, with winding turf paths between them. Where they face the straight edges of the enclosing space, however, they too have straight sides. A great border, 180 m/590 ft long, running along the old stone wall, has pale colours at each end becoming richer towards the centre, where they explode into hot reds, yellows, and oranges. Cane's bold and dramatic design, in an area of 2.8 hectares/7 acres, provides a fine setting for the palace.   PT

Fantaisie Palace ⊛

Donndorf, near Bayreuth, Germany, is today the location of the Fantaisie Palace Garden Museum, which opened in 2000 and is the first of its kind in Germany. Here the history of garden design in the period from the 17th to the 19th century is vividly portrayed in all its various aspects. Numerous original exhibits, including garden sculptures, paintings and drawings, porcelain and faience, garden plans and garden models, gardener's apprenticeship certificates, garden furniture, and garden tools show how garden design developed, particularly in south Germany. The palace was begun in 1763 and completed under Duchess Elisabeth Friederike Sophie von Württemberg, daughter of Margravine Wilhelmine von Bayreuth (see EREMITAGE; SANSPAREIL) and niece of Frederick the Great of Prussia (see SANSSOUCI). By 1780 Elisabeth Friederike Sophie had created a varied formal garden divided into small sections with a pavilion, cascade, and Neptune Fountain. In 1770 she officially named her property 'Fantaisie'. Between 1793 and 1795 Duchess Friederike Dorothee Sophie von Württemberg extended the complex in the style of a sentimental landscape garden with architectural features (catacomb, pillar of harmony, straw hut). And finally, from 1839 to 1881, it was enlarged again by Duke Alexander von Württemberg in the mixed or eclectic style, and acquired landscape park sections with exotic trees, a pond with a fisherman's cottage, a terraced vineyard, sculptures, fountain pools, and flower beds. The approximately 17-hectare/42-acre palace park harmoniously combines original design elements from the three relevant phases of development in the rococo, the sentimental landscape, and the mixed style.
RH

Farnese, Palazzo ⊛

Caprarola, Lazio, Italy. The pentagonal fortress palace of Caprarola, begun by Baldassare Peruzzi (1481–1536) and Antonio da Sangallo the younger (1485–1546), and completed by Jacopo Barozzi da VIGNOLA for Cardinal Alessandro Farnese from 1557, stands at the top of the town, dominating the view looking towards Rome. The work was completed by Giacomo del Duca (c.1520–1604) and Girolamo Rainaldi (1570–1655) in 1620. Two square walled gardens, the Winter Garden and Summer Garden, further subdivided into four compartments, project from each side of the palace, leaving a wedge shape in between. They are connected by bridges to the palace. Originally fruit trees and flowers were planted in the beds today distorted by overgrown hedges of box, holly, and cherry laurel and a few camellias. From the Summer Garden terrace a path leads 400 m/1,300 ft through woods of holm oak, chestnuts, beech, and pines to da Vignola's masterpiece, the Casino del Piacere (House of Pleasure) of 1560 and a GIARDINO SEGRETO glimpsed beyond two stepped ramps down the centre of which a long runnel (*catena d'acqua*) tumbles through a series of small basins cut in the shape of dolphins. The ramp leads to water giants guarding a pool from which curved steps lead to the simple box parterre, defined by herms, below the *casino*. A 'theatre' of flowers beyond created by Rainaldi in the 17th century is in need of restoration with authentic plants. The palazzo and gardens are owned by the Italian state.   PHo

Farrand, Beatrix

(1872–1959), American landscape gardener and founder member of the American Society of Landscape Architects (1899). Her early life was divided between New York city, where she was born, and her family's summer home, Reef Point at Bar Harbor on Mount Desert Island in Maine. This beautiful sea-girt landscape with its rich natural and cultivated flora was her inspiration and she had taken charge of Reef Point's extensive garden by the time she was 17. She had to educate herself to landscape gardening, travelling to study European and English gardens, taking instruction in surveying and technical drawing, and attending botany lectures at the ARNOLD ARBORETUM. She always acknowledged her debt to Professor Charles Sprague SARGENT and his wife Mary, a botanical artist, who introduced her to Frederick Law OLMSTED and took her to see his works in progress, notably the Chicago 1893 Exposition and Biltmore in Maryland. At the outset of her career she gave an interview to the *New York Sun* in 1897, speaking with a breezy confidence of her technical approach, and how she was draining a 10-hectare/25-acre swamp,

transforming a 16-hectare/40-acre forest plot into a 'pleasing grove', laying out a cemetery, planting private gardens in Bar Harbor, and designing and planting the entrance to Tuxedo Park, a resort development in upstate New York.

She was tall and elegant and always beautifully dressed, but every inch an accomplished, innovative, and hard-working professional. Between 1897 and 1949 she amassed at least 200 commissions which included a garden for the White House (1913), long-term consultancies on campus landscapes (Yale, Chicago, Oberlin, and others), and her gardens for DUMBARTON OAKS and DARTINGTON HALL. Her 'Plant Book for Dumbarton Oaks' (ed. McGuire, 1980) remains a model management plan. In the 1920s she had offices in New York, Bar Harbor, New Haven, and San Marino (California), where her husband Max Farrand, whom she married in 1913, was director of the Huntington Library. In 1955 she gave her library, herbarium, and papers to the University of California (Berkeley) where they form the Reef Point Collection, along with Gertrude JEKYLL's drawings, which Farrand saved from destruction.   JB

JANE BROWN, *Beatrix: The Gardening Life of Beatrix Jones Farrand 1872–1959* (1995).

Farrer, Reginald

(1880–1920), plant collector and writer who, after Balliol College, Oxford, developed a precocious interest in alpine plants. He explored the Alps, then Japan, and in 1907 Ceylon (Sri Lanka), there becoming a Buddhist. His Japanese experience produced his first book, and in 1907 *My Rock Garden* was published, giving him the immediate reputation of an expert, followed successfully by three associated titles. In 1910 he conceived and began writing the two-volume encyclopedia *The English Rock Garden* (1919). China beckoned, and he made two journeys to the East, the first during 1914–16 with Kew-trained William Purdom (1880–1921), the second 1919–20 partly in the company of Euan Cox (1893–1977), the noted rhododendron collector and breeder. Two books resulted, *On the Eaves of the World* (2 vols., 1917) and *Rainbow Bridge* (1921), posthumously published following his death in Burma. Farrer's plant introductions are few but choice, and his writings illuminate his enthusiasm for alpine plants.   MC-C

NICOLA SHULMAN, *A Rage for Rock Gardening* (2001).

Fazenda Marambaia

(formerly the Odette Monteiro Residence), Correas, Rio de Janeiro state, Brazil, was a pivotal project in Roberto BURLE MARX's most creative phase. This private park in the Serra dos Órgãos mountain range was commissioned by Odette Monteiro and her husband Júlio in 1945. Some changes had been made to the original design by the time of its completion in 1947, decided on site by the landscape designer himself. By the mid 1980s, the property was falling into disrepair. In 1988, Burle Marx and Haruyoshi Ono were hired by the new owner to restore the gardens and suggest a new project that would maintain the ideas of the composition, but add several new plant species. In this work the landscape designer masterfully synthesized a plastic vocabulary that was to become characteristic of his mature work: the notable chromatic associations and the curved lines of his design. The 1947 plan used refined harmonies of analogous and contrasting colours in the spatial structuring. A counterpoint was established by three large groups of vegetation with foliage or blossoms of vibrant and lasting colours, giving the gardens a certain chromatic permanence, principally of yellows, oranges, and reds. By interpreting the chromatic experiments of William ROBINSON and Gertrude JEKYLL, and refining the way of working with the contrasting palettes of fauvism and surrealism, Burle Marx created a unique compositional syntax, in which the use of polychromatic colours and not just shades of green became a structural given and a protagonist in the creation of the gardens. Burle Marx showed a predilection for placing herbaceous plants, shrubs, or trees in homogeneous groups and, wherever possible, over large areas, thinking of their potential for chromatic change throughout the seasons—the colours of the leaves, blossoms, fruit, seeds, trunks, and branches. This was done avoiding to the maximum the use of bedding out as practised in European gardens of the 19th century. Burle Marx's idea of landscape was not based on the substitution or replanting of specimens, involving intensive horticultural work, but rather on the subtle comprehension and use of the vegetation's physiology and morphology.

GMD

GIULIO L. RIZZO (ed.), *Roberto Burle Marx: il giardino del novecento* (1992).
ROSSANA VACCARINO, 'The correspondence of time and instability: two gardens', in Rossana Vaccarino, *Roberto Burle Marx: Landscapes Reflected* (2000).

Felek. See AVRIG PARK.

fence.

The garden fence is not a feature of gardens that distinguished garden designers often have occasion to discuss. Distinguished gardens have for their boundaries fine walls of brick and stone, or noble hedges of yew or hornbeam. Humphry REPTON for his own cottage garden at Hare Street in Essex, which overlooked the village street, removed a pretty lattice-work fence, extended his flower-filled garden, and planted a hedge about the boundary. Yet fences can be beautiful and a vital part of the garden's character, such as the exquisitely patterned bamboo fences of Japanese gardens. Western gardens do not achieve this level of refinement but the picket fencing of New England gardens with their varied patterns, English fencing of hazel or willow hurdles, and elaborate rustic fencing of the Victorian period all have their beauty. In gardens surrounded by grazing land the fence is an obtrusive feature and its design is important. Post and wire fencing is business-like and charmless. In North America zigzag fencing of split cedar (*Thuja occidentalis*) rails often admirably suits the landscape on both sides of the fence.   PT

feng shui

is sometimes referred to as the Chinese version of geomancy which, though quite different, is the nearest Western equivalent to this ancient art. *Feng shui* (or *kan yu*) is actively practised today in Hong Kong, Taiwan, and expatriate Chinese communities round the world, although on the mainland of China it has not been encouraged by the People's Republic because of the superstitious element in its composition. In the latter part of the 20th century in the West it became fashionable, often in a much debased form, in several different contexts. In simple terms, the basic principle of *feng shui* is that streams or currents of 'vital spirit' or 'cosmic breath' (in China called *qi*) run through the earth according to its topography. These currents forcefully influence the fortunes of individuals and their descendants, depending on how they place their houses and—most importantly—their graves, in relation to the winds (*feng*), waters (*shui*), hills (*kan*), and valleys (*yu*) of the landscape in which they live.

Since changes to the landscape were thought actively to affect the flow of *qi*, a complex set of rules and principles was developed to guide men's building activities. By the 3rd century BC the biography of Qu Yuan, a *feng shui* expert, was already included in one of China's earliest literary works. Such experts came in time to advise not only on the siting of graves and buildings, but on remedial action (planting or cutting trees, digging ditches, relocating furniture, and hanging mirrors to deflect evil influences) if family fortunes seemed to be sliding.

Two main schools of practice exist today: one (originating in Jiangxi province) is based on the physical features—such as the shapes of hills, rocks, or trees—of a locality; the other (originating in Fujian province) on orientation (the Chinese invented the magnetic compass for geomantic use). However, for both schools the ideal dwelling should stand facing south, two-thirds of the way up a hill on dry ground, with lower, protective hills to the east and west. Water should gather in a pool below it forming a reservoir of benevolent influences, which might be carried away by a stream flowing too swiftly past the property. Since evil influences (*sha*) were thought to travel in straight lines, winding walls and roads which seem to follow the patterns of the landscape are preferred to straight ones, while in cities, no entrance should open at the end of a street or at a corner where the straight 'arrows' of evil might attack it from several directions at once. The masonry screens or 'spirit walls' built just inside Chinese courtyard entrances not only provide visual privacy for those who live inside, but deflect these arrows and protect the good fortunes of the family.

Not surprisingly, *feng shui* has had an important influence on garden layout. Before anything could be designed a *feng shui* practitioner checked the site, its surroundings, its balance of *yin* and *yang* forces, the flow and availability of water, and advised on the garden's orientation. Interestingly, of the four cardinal directions (east—the Green Dragon symbolizing spring, west—the White Tiger symbolizing autumn, south—the Crimson Bird symbolizing summer, and north—the Black Turtle symbolizing winter), it is the western that is considered most harmful: 'A garden may be built on the Green Dragon's head, but never on the mouth of the White Tiger.' Gardens ideally should be at the back or to the east of a house, and if the site was so limited that its garden had no alternative but to lie on the west, a gate was always opened in the east wall of the main residence to make another courtyard—or sometimes, as in the WANGSHI YUAN, even simply a corridor if space was tight—to the east; in the OU YUAN, the west garden is balanced by an east garden to counter the ill effects of the White Tiger's influence.

A garden is also always surrounded by a wall, which preserves its peace and holds the good influences of the site within its smooth enclosure. No large doors or low *lou chuang* (see CHINA), from which this accumulated vitality might leak away, are allowed in this boundary. Inside it, winding interior walls further concentrate good influences and these, like the spirit screens, add greatly to the intricate charm and seclusion of the garden. Old trees, repositories of *qi*, are valuable and preserved, while some gardens grow only trees and flowers—like magnolia, crab apple, peonies, and laurel—with names or features that suggest happiness and wealth. Water, also symbolizing wealth, is led gently through the garden landscape, and gathered in pools before the main pavilions. Its departure, often hidden by rockwork 'mountains', is made as inconspicuous as possible. In the late Qing period few caves were made in these artificial 'mountains' for fear that any evil influences overlooked in the garden's planning might accumulate in their open mouths.

Although over the centuries *feng shui* acquired a considerable weight of superstition, and some—and perhaps even much—of what goes on today in its practice seems unnecessary mumbo-jumbo, its basic tenets are not only endorsed by modern scientific ideas of physical and psychological well-being, but have been of great aesthetic value to China in the past.

X-WL/MK

ferme ornée.
The words, meaning 'ornamented farm', were first used by the garden theorist Stephen SWITZER in *Ichnographia Rustica* (1718). However, he had already introduced the idea of 'mixing the useful and profitable Parts of Gard'ning with the Pleasurable' in his *The Nobleman, Gentleman, and Gardener's Recreation* (1715) and subsequently used the expression 'ornamental farm' in the *Practical Husbandman* (1733). In *Ichnographia Rustica* Switzer describes the *ferme ornée* in the context of his ideas about 'rural and extensive Gardening', as opposed to 'the stiff Dutch way'. He describes Lord Bathurst's garden at Riskins 'lay'd out . . . upon the Plan of the *Ferme Ornée* and the Villa's of the Ancients'. In the garden 'the Lawns round about the House are for the feeding of Sheep'; 'there are . . . private Hedge-Rows or Walks round every field . . . [and] at every Angle [of the field] is a little piece of Wood in the form of a Labyrinth.' Switzer emphasizes the high standards of maintenance in his 'Farm-like Way of Gardening': 'the Lawns and Fields are kept free from Ragweed and Thistles, and the Turf well rolled in Spring, and all Mole-Hills and the Dunging of Cattle kept continually spread about.' This, claims Switzer, is the 'best Way of Gardening in the World, and such as the politest and best Genius of all Antiquity delighted in'. In France the *ferme ornée* is first mentioned in the 1774 edition of Claude-Henri Watelet's *Essai sur les jardins*. He describes 'verdure, shrubs and flowers . . . paths . . . edged in lawns and trees . . . crossing meadows of grazing cattle and leading to small buildings scattered haphazardly in the hedgerow'. By J. C. LOUDON's time the poetry seems to have been drained from the idea of the *ferme ornée*. His

Encyclopaedia of Gardening (1822) says that it differs from a 'common farm in having a better dwelling house' and hedges 'are allowed to grow wild and irregular and are bordered on each side by a broad green drive, and sometimes by a gravel walk and shrubs'. Among the most frequently mentioned *fermes ornées* in England are The LEASOWES, Richings Park (also known as Riskins, which was in Buckinghamshire), and WOBURN FARM. An interesting Irish example is LARCHILL in County Kildare which is difficult to date but was probably made in the early 19th century. It is, with The Leasowes, one of two surviving examples which is open to the public and, recently restored, Larchill is in far better condition. Although the subject was widely discussed in the 18th century, it seems that few *fermes ornées* were made but the notion of making farm buildings decorative, especially in the Gothic style, was widely influential.   PT

ferns, ferneries, and fernhouses.
There are about 12,000 species of fern, with many cultivars, among around 250 genera whose taxonomy has been a nomenclatural battlefield. They are distributed widely through the world, preferring temperate and damp climates. Exotic ferns were introduced to Western Europe from the 17th century but they were usually regarded as of only botanical interest. J. C. LOUDON's *Encyclopaedia of Gardening* (1822) describes only tender species of fern but later in the 19th century there was a passion for ferns which amounted to pteridomania. The interest in ferns was fostered by the fact that many were suitable for ROCK GARDENS, which became fashionable in the later 19th century, and for woodland gardens which were being created to house the exotic flowering shrubs which were being introduced in such quantities in the 19th century. Several books stimulated the interest, among them Shirley Hibberd's *The Fern Garden* (1869) and William Robinson's *The English Flower Garden* (1883), the best-selling gardening book of the late Victorian period, which has a chapter devoted to 'The hardy fern garden'. Both these authors were influential among owners of gardens of modest size. Gertrude Jekyll showed how versatile ferns were as garden plants. Her book *Wall, Water and Woodland Gardens* (1901) recommends *Asplenium*, *Cystopteris*, and *Woodsia* in walls and steps; *Blechnum*, *Onoclea*, and *Osmunda* for waterside planting; and *Athyrium*, *Polystichum*, and *Thelypteris* for woodland. The term fernery is used either for a part of the garden devoted to ferns or, confusingly, a glasshouse for tender species, which should more properly be termed a fernhouse. Nineteenth-century ferneries are found in many British gardens; among examples in

gardens open to the public are those at Kingston Lacy (Dorset), with yews providing shade, and beds raised on banks for close inspection of different species, and at FOTA ARBORETUM, which has a climate mild enough to allow tender tree ferns (*Dicksonia antarctica*) to flourish among the hardier species. The tree fern is a 19th-century introduction, from Australia, to Britain and is perfectly hardy in gardens in Cornwall and Ireland. At Derreen in County Kerry, where they were planted in 1900, there is a rare naturalized community looking completely at home in a suitably jungly setting. In the late 20th century tree ferns became fashionable garden plants in Britain, more often than not planted in microclimates quite unsuitable for them, requiring much laborious cosseting and never looking really happy. The fernhouse is a 19th-century development. An outstanding example is at Tatton Park (Cheshire), designed by Sir Joseph PAXTON and his son-in-law G. H. Stokes in about 1859 and planted with tree ferns in naturalistic rock-edged beds underplanted with drifts of *Agapanthus africanus*. At Ashridge Park (Hertfordshire) Matthew Digby Wyatt designed a grand neoclassical fernhouse which was built in 1864. An unusually fine Scottish fernhouse of *c*.1879 at Ascog Hall on the Isle of Bute was rescued from dereliction in 1997 and has been restocked with the advice of the Royal Botanic Garden, Edinburgh. Despite many years of neglect one fern survived from the original plantings, a specimen of the tropical *Todea barbara*.   PT

Ferrari, Villa ⊛
Stanjel, Slovenia, in the arid region of Karst near Trieste and the Adriatic Sea. Stanjel is a village with a 17th-century castle and church on a steep hill with medieval houses in a semicircular formation. The villa is located by the external castle wall and consists of a group of buildings around a central stone-built loggia with three arches, which were renovated between 1920 and 1935 by architect Max Fabiani (1865–1962) for the Ferrari family. In addition he designed a 26-hectare/64-acre garden in terraces, connected with staircases and steep paths. The garden combines the architectural tradition of Karst, Italian Renaissance gardens, 19th-century elements, and modernistic details. An important feature is the pergola of vines which follows the curve of the upper terrace, linking the villa with the landscape. A terrace with a greenhouse and flower beds is beneath the loggia, and the lowest level features a water basin with a miniature island, footbridge, a grotto fountain with a shell, and a pavilion on an icehouse. The architectural structure of the garden is still preserved, but the original

vegetation has mostly disappeared. It was originally a mixture of Mediterranean fruit trees, vines, exotic cypresses, yews, umbrella pines, Mediterranean pot plants, and various perennials. Plants in tubs—standard and rambling roses, citruses, oleanders, laurels, as well as pot herbs—were cultivated. The villa and its garden were supplied with rainwater gathered and distributed in an exceptional system of water tanks and pipes, which was mostly destroyed during the Second World War together with Fabiani's archive.

AK

STANE BERNIK et al., *20th Century Architecture: From Modernist to Contemporary*, Guide to Architecture (2002).
MARKO POZETTO, *Maks Fabiani, Vizije prostora* (1997).
—— *Maks Fabiani, Exhibition Catalogue* (1988).

Ferrell Gardens at Hills and Dales ⊕

La Grange, Georgia, USA, were begun in 1841 by Sara Coleman Ferrell (1817–1903), and today represent one of the oldest surviving parterre gardens in the American south. Located 116 km/ 70 miles south-west of Atlanta, Ferrell Gardens feature a series of terraces, intricate box-bordered parterres, and an ornamental grove. While tradition has it that the gardens in their earliest stage were laid out by Mrs Ferrell, it is believed that at some point in time a European itinerant landscape gardener was secured to develop an overall comprehensive plan. As Mrs Ferrell implemented the plan, various religious symbols were incorporated into the design as a testament to her belief that a garden should be a reflection of faith and religious piety. Included among these ecclesiastical icons are: a lyre, an organ, a bishop's chair, a collection plate, a cluster of grapes, and the motto 'God is Love'. Legend has it that the Ferrell property was spared by federal troops during the final days of the American Civil War (1861–5), because of the spiritual nature of Mrs Ferrell's beloved gardens. In 1912, the Ferrell estate was purchased by Fuller E. Callaway Sr. a respected business leader in the southern textile industry. Mr Callaway replaced the original Ferrell home with an imposing country house designed by the noted Atlanta architect Neil Reid. Built in an Italianate style, the house was sited and designed to complement the existing gardens. Today, Ferrell Gardens survive as one of the south's finest horticultural treasures.   JRC

Ferrières, Château de ⊕

Ferrières-en-Brie, Seine-et-Marne, France, bought by James de Rothschild in 1829, who in 1854 asked Joseph PAXTON to design a new chateau and a landscape setting for it. Much work had already been done on the landscape by Placide Massey in 1830 and in 1850 by Louis-Sulpice Varé and Pierre BARILLET-DESCHAMPS. Paxton's chief work on the landscape was to create a lake, with accompanying planting, behind the chateau. A paved terrace overlooks a formal arrangement of yew topiary, gravel walks, a pair of recumbent stone lions, and James de Rothschild's initials worked in carpet bedding. The long sinuous lake is framed in groups of trees through which vistas are revealed. Many of the 19th-century plantings survive, in particular such newly introduced conifers as *Sequoiadendron giganteum*, but these are intermingled with deciduous trees—fine limes, maples, oaks, and planes. Visitors today see only a small part of the designed landscape. In its heyday there was a great perimeter drive, and a sequence of avenues, of horse chestnuts or sweet chestnuts, divided the land. By the end of the 19th century the Ferrières estate was on a gigantic scale with 400 hectares/988 acres of park, 1,500 hectares/3,705 acres of agricultural land, and over 8,000 hectares/19,000 acres of woodland. In 1978 Guy de Rothschild gave the chateau and 150 hectares/370 acres of land, including the park, to the University of Paris.

PT

Fertőd (formerly Eszterháza) ⊕

Győr-Moson-Sopron county, Hungary. The golden age of the Hungarian Versailles was under Duke Miklós Esterházy I (Nicholas the Magnificent, succeeded 1762, died 1790). In the place of a small palace built by Anton Erhardt Martinelli in 1720 and its baroque garden, the work of Viennese garden designer Anton Zinner, the Duke created one of Central Europe's most significant residences in various stages, probably according to designs by Nicolaus Jacoby. In addition to its architectural and garden historical importance, it was the composer Joseph Haydn's position as court composer which brought it world renown. The structure of the *c.*300-hectare/*c.*740-acre park is determined by a PATTE D'OIE leading from the palace's ceremonial hall, which, passing the parterre, continues through the pleasure wood, the pheasantry, and the game park, leading in the direction of various points in the surroundings. The earlier PARTERRE *de broderie* was turned into a *parterre à l'angloise* decorated with statues, vases, and fountains around 1777, probably according to Jacoby's designs. Two cascades were constructed at the end of the parterre in 1784, while—from the 1760s—in the pleasure wood were temples of Diana and Apollo, of Fortune and Venus, a number of fountains, rose gardens, and a Chinese 'Bagatelle'. Following the death of Nicholas the Magnificent in 1790, the ducal court left the palace, which was abandoned for a century, and

the famous opera house, a number of other buildings, and a large part of the garden disappeared. Around 1900, however, Miklós Esterházy IV moved back into the palace. The grounds were reconstructed according to plans by Anton UMLAUFT, under the direction of ducal chief gardener Károly Hulesch, with the creation of a new parterre, privy gardens, a rose garden, and with some naturalistic parts, but their essential baroque layout remained. For the most part, the resulting neo-baroque and landscape park composition still stands today, and its renovation has begun.   GA

GÉZA GALAVICS, 'Eszterháza 18. századi ábrázolásai' (18th-Century Depictions of Eszterháza), *Ars Hungarica*, No. 1 (2000).
MIHÁLY MŐCSÉNYI, 'The epochs of Eszterháza', in Gábor Alföldy (ed.), *Principal Gardens of Hungary* (2001).

Festetics Park. See DÉG.

Filoli ⊕

Woodside, California, USA, was created between 1917 and 1921 on an estate of 50 hectares/125 acres, and is one of the finest estate gardens in the country. The estate was developed by William Bourn II, the owner of a gold mine, and the president and owner of the Spring Valley Water Company. Bourn selected the site because of its resemblance to English parkland with extensive groves of California live oaks, *Quercus agrifolia*. Captain George Vancouver had commented on the similarity in the late 18th century. The large brick Federal-style mansion was sited in a shallow valley facing the western flank of the wooded Santa Cruz Mountains. The garden was designed by Bruce Porter (1865–1955), a painter who was greatly influenced by the Pre-Raphaelites. Porter planted grey foliage trees such as Atlas cedars on the entrance drive near the house and olive trees within the gardens to tie his carefully structured formal spaces to the broader regional landscape with its greyish colours. Adjoining the house is a formal terrace, below which a large L-shaped terrace commands views north over the park. The garden is organized on a north–south axis which runs through one arm of the terrace, a large walled garden, a yew-lined walk through the kitchen and CUTTING GARDENS, and terminates in a semicircular belvedere with columns and chains wreathed in wisterias. A cross-axis passes through the other arm of the L-shaped terrace and a sunken water garden beside the main house terrace. The walled garden contains several subsidiary formal spaces, including an area reproducing a stained-glass window at Chartres cathedral, a tiered diagonal vista, and fluid areas planted with azaleas, camellias, and fruit trees. The

Plan of the garden at **Fertőd** (formerly Eszterháza) engraved by Marcus Weinmann (1784).

garden was remodelled in 1937 when the property changed hands. A swimming pool and bathing pavilion were added at the south end of the L-shaped terrace which was closed off from the park by a row of yew trees. An extensive collection of camellias and rhododendrons was created adjoining the walled garden. After the garden was given to the National Trust in 1976 the kitchen garden was converted into a series of display gardens with a knot garden using germander and cotton lavender.   DCS

Finland.

The climate of Finland is warmed by the Gulf Stream. The country belongs to the temperate coniferous—mixed forest zone with cold and wet winters. The mean temperature of the warmest month is no lower than 10 °C/50 °F and that of the coldest month no higher than –3 °C/27 °F, while the extremes in the Finnish interior may reach 35 °C/95 °F and –50 °C/–58 °F respectively. Along the Baltic coast, the differences in temperature are less drastic. Mean annual precipitation is between 600 mm/ 24 in and 700 mm/28 in, with much of the total falling as snow.

The landscape was shaped by the glaciations and is characterized by subtle small-scale variations but modest absolute height differences. The soils are shallow and the mostly granite or gneiss bedrock often laid bare. Glacial deposits form long ridges. There are more than 56,000 larger lake basins, and the Baltic coastline is fringed by an extensive archipelago. Owing to land upheaval, the coastline is constantly changing, more so in the west.

Forests cover more than two-thirds of Finland, lakes and farmland both a tenth. Vegetation is chiefly boreal, *Pinus sylvestris*, *Picea abies*, and *Betula pendula* and *B. pubescens* being the dominant forest species. The southern coast is hemiboreal, with *Quercus robur*, *Tilia cordata*, *Fraxinus excelsior*, and *Corylus avellana* growing naturally in places. Northern Lapland is subarctic. There are approximately 3,200 vascular plant taxa in Finland, of which some 900 may be considered indigenous species, 190 ancient exotics, and another 190 more recent, yet established exotics.

The first traces of gardening in Finland date back to the Middle Ages, when much of the present country belonged to Sweden. Most of the early gardens were small orchards, herb gardens, or vegetable patches, belonging to monasteries, castles, or individual burgesses. Only documentary evidence of them exists. In the 16th century, some Finnish noblemen started cultivating orchards on their estates. The garden of Duke John (1537–92), the future King Johan III of Sweden, at the castle of Turku

(Åbo) appears to have been a short-lived example of the northern Renaissance pleasure garden. Finland was almost left untouched by the baroque garden. Most documents suggest orchards and kitchen gardens, while nothing points at ambitious formal compositions. Yet a number of exotic ornamental flowering plants appear to have been commonly used by the end of the 17th century, many having medicinal uses as well.

After a bleak period of wars and cold weather, interest grew in ornamental gardens, garden literature, and plants during the late 18th century. The influence of the first university of Finland, Åbo Academy, and the disciples of Carolus LINNAEUS there, Pehr Kalm (1716–79) and Pehr Gadd (1727–97), was marked. Plant trials were performed. A formal, rectangular, and axial garden was advocated, combining utility gardening with aesthetic pleasure in the manner of French physiocratic gardens. This model was followed in the gardens of Lutheran rectories and lay landed estates. *Syringa vulgaris*, *Caragana arborescens*, and *Philadelphus pubescens* became common ornamental plants, while domestic broadleaves (see above) were used for tree planting. Ornamental features such as clipped hedges, arbours, simple parterres, and tree-lined alleys became common, as did pavilions and conservatories.

At the turn of the 19th century, the picturesque landscape garden or English park made its debut in Finland. It was first adopted by three groups: professors of Åbo Academy, parvenu owners of ironworks estates, and high-ranking landed gentry. Often an earlier formal garden was surrounded by a landscape garden, adorned by typical picturesque FABRIQUES, including CHINOISERIE. The surrounding lake or coast scenery was often incorporated into the composition (see FAGERVIK IRONWORKS; JOENSUU ESTATE PARK).

In 1809, Finland was ceded from Sweden to Russia. Although the stylistic models were still western, coming mostly from Sweden and Germany, a strong eastern influence could be marked in the garden plants of the 19th century. Still commonly used plants originating from or transmitted through the east are *Acer negundo*, *Malus baccata*, *Salix* 'Sibirica', as well as a number of poplars and ornamental shrubs. *Abies sibirica*, *Larix sibirica*, and *Pinus cembra* subsp. *sibirica* had been introduced earlier but now became fashionable in conifer groves and ALLÉES. Several important plant collections and the first market gardens and nurseries were established. Classicist garden buildings coexisted with Gothic, Swiss, and National Romantic styles (see AULANKO PARK).

The first surviving planted public walks of Finland date from the late 18th century and the

first public parks from the first half of the 19th century. Towards the end of the century, the bigger towns set out to establish municipal parks, the style corresponding to the German landscape garden (see KAIVOPUISTO PARK). Many of the first professional gardeners originated from Sweden. Bedding out was extensively used in both public and private gardens, and the repertory of ornamental plants expanded. More simplified nature or 'people's parks' were laid out in the outskirts, often at the waterfront, and also in smaller inland towns. State authorities planted gardens in connection with railway stations, canals, hospitals, and prisons. The first designed cemeteries were commissioned by Lutheran congregations. The choice of plants was remarkably widened by the onset of domestic market gardening from the mid 19th century onwards.

The first Finns to become trained garden architects were Paul OLSSON and Bengt Schalin (1889–1982), who brought from Germany the *Architekturgarten* style—skilfully adapting it to the uneven terrain and the climatic restrictions (see KULTARANTA GARDEN). Apart from prolific design activity, they also introduced new ornamental species, especially perennials, alpine plants, and a variety of ornamental shrubs. They and their followers moved on to functionalism during the 1930s, replacing formal axes, ornamental pools, topiary, and flowering walls with informal planting, undulating lawns, and irregular flagstone paths. Together they designed or redesigned a great proportion of Finnish estate and villa gardens, factory surroundings, and public parks in the pre-war era.

In town planning the first experiments with green zones were already made in the 1910s, then assuming the form of monumental formal compositions inspired by American reform parks and German *Volksparks*. After national independence was gained in 1917, the diversity of green spaces increased to include allotment gardens, 'park forests', and various sports facilities, allowing for a more informal treatment. Following the Second World War, the garden architect profession was replaced by that of landscape architect. The tasks evolved to include extensive green planning (see TAPIOLA GARDEN CITY). In 1967, the training of landscape architects began at the University of Helsinki's faculty of agricultural science. It was transferred to the Helsinki University of Technology's department of architecture in 1972. Garden designers are trained in two polytechnics.   MHay

Finlay, Ian Hamilton

(b. 1925), Scottish poet, publisher, sculptor, and garden maker, a rare multi-talented creator.

Born in Nassau (where his father is said to have made, and lost, a fortune bootlegging), he came to Scotland as a child, studied fleetingly at Glasgow Art School, served (rising to a sergeant) in the Royal Army Service Corps, became a shepherd and a farm labourer, and started to write and publish short stories in the 1950s. He founded, with Jessie McGuffie, the Wild Hawthorn Press in 1961 and the periodical *Poor.Old.Tired.Horse.* the following year. His writings, in which typography and pictorial ingredients have played a part, are sometimes referred to as 'concrete poetry'. At all events his muse is one that is at least as visual as it is aural and frequently hovering tantalizingly between the two. In 1966 he moved to Stonypath (Lanarkshire), an abandoned croft where he and his wife Sue started their garden, LITTLE SPARTA, which has become one of the most famous gardens of the late 20th and early 21st centuries. His own publications—rare, beautiful, and sought after—show an astonishingly original and yet accessible creativity. For a clear and comprehensive idea of his gardening activities there is no substitute for a visit to Little Sparta. In all his work he draws on a wide range of inspirations—the political philosophy of the French Revolution, Scottish fishing boats, Arcadian garden theories, Scottish vernacular jokes, and much else. Part of the public garden of Stockwood Park (Bedfordshire) is designed by him and shows his work at its most beguiling. Yves Abrioux's excellent and finely illustrated book *Ian Hamilton Finlay* (rev. edn. 1994), is a valuable source of information about all aspects of his career. Jessie Sheeler's *Little Sparta* (2003) is a good account of the garden.

PT

fireworks

were used on special occasions in Italian Renaissance gardens of the 16th century. At the Villa LANTE, when Pope Gregory XIII visited in 1578, there were fireworks in the form of dragons breathing flames. This seems to have been the earliest recorded use although a second, English, example follows closely after it in the 16th century, at Elvetham Hall in Hampshire. Roy Strong's *The Renaissance Garden in England* (1979) describes an entertainment arranged in 1591 by Lord Hertford for Elizabeth I to celebrate the defeat of the Spanish Armada. An emblematic garden was made with Elizabeth depicted as 'the moon goddess . . . who rules over the watery empire'. A lake had islands one of which was planted with trees like ships' masts, a second had a fort built by Neptune to defend England, and the third a mount 6 m/20 ft high encircled with privet symbolizing Spain: 'Yon ugly monster creeping from the South | To spoyle these blessed fields

of Albion'. This elaborate festival in honour of Elizabeth's great victory ended in 'a great firework display in which Neptune's fort vanquished the wicked monster mount'. Fireworks formed an important ingredient of the special displays arranged for festivals in gardens of the 17th and 18th centuries. At VERSAILLES immensely expensive fêtes were arranged to celebrate great events. In 1668, to celebrate the Treaty of Aix-la-Chapelle, feasting, drama, music, and a ball had their climax in a gigantic firework display with the King's monogram picked out in the sky. In German baroque gardens sumptuous firework displays were often organized in the gardens of great houses such as the palace in Dresden of Augustus the Strong, Elector of Saxony. Eighteenth-century Mughal gardens in India had elegant fireworks, much more refined than the excesses of France and Germany. In Green Park in London in 1749, to celebrate another treaty of Aix-la-Chapelle (which ended the War of the Austrian Succession), a firework display took place in conjunction with the first performance of Handel's *Music for the Royal Fireworks*—11,000 fireworks were let off, disposed on scaffolding 123 m/410 ft long and 34 m/114 ft high.   PT

GEORGE PLIMPTON, *Fireworks: A History and Celebration* (1984).

Fish, Margery

(1893-1969), English plantswoman, gardener, and author, creator of the garden at East Lambrook Manor (Somerset) from 1938 onwards. She took a special interest in curious forms of English native plants and devised an informal planting style in which to deploy them. She was the author of several books of which *We Made a Garden* (1956) gives a not always deliberately amusing account of the beginning of her gardening life with her husband Walter. Their joint gardening activities revealed hitherto unknown abysses of incompatibility—he loved large, bright flowers (dahlias the size of soup plates) and sabotaged some of her less showy plantings. Her other books such as *Gardening in the Shade* (1964) and *A Flower for Every Day* (1965) are still valuable and show her keenly observant eye for plants and deep practical knowledge of their behaviour in the garden. Generous with advice and plants, she inspired many novice gardeners and had a profound influence on vernacular garden taste in England in the second half of the 20th century.   PT

fishing house.

The fishing house, usually combined with a boathouse, is found in many English 18th-century gardens frequently occupying a

position of prominence in the landscape. Robert ADAM designed a beautiful fishing house (1770-2) for Kedleston Hall in Derbyshire where he also designed the park. Lower chambers gave room for boats and an upper room has a Venetian window from which a line could be cast into the lake. Its interior has fine plasterwork and a fishing scene painted by Francesco Zuccarelli. A most unusual CHINOISERIE fishing house, called The Quarters, stands overlooking a stream in the grounds of Alresford Hall (Essex). Built in 1765, it was painted by John Constable, 'the little fishing house'. At Tendring Hall (Suffolk), the Palladian Fishing Temple of *c*.1750, possibly by Sir Robert Taylor (1714-88), overlooks a canal originally stocked with trout. An example of fishing houses fully worked into the design of a garden is at STUDLEY ROYAL. Here John Aislabie in the 1720s, as part of his great water garden, built a weir on the river Skell flanked by a pair of square fishing houses with Palladian windows. They form splendid punctuation marks rising above the weir and its flanking balustrade. Their architect is unknown. The grandest of fishing houses is at Exton Park in Rutland. Fort Henry is an enchanting Gothic building by ▸

William Legg (1785-8), with castellations, pinnacles, and trefoils, on a lake. In Portugal at the Palácio de Marquês de POMBAL there is an especially beautiful late 18th-century Casa de Pesca with AZULEJOS and elaborate rococo plasterwork.   PT

Flamengo, Parque do ⊛

Rio de Janeiro, Rio de Janeiro state, Brazil, the most important urban shoreline park created in South America in the second half of the 20th century. The project was designed to preserve some of the most distinctive landscapes in the city of Rio de Janeiro, in an area reclaimed from the sea between the neighbourhoods of Glória and Flamengo and originally planned solely for road traffic. The state government entrusted the development of the landscaping to Roberto BURLE MARX, assisted by Luiz Emygdio de Mello Filho and Maria Augusta Costa Ribeiro, and the buildings and amenities to Affonso Eduardo Reidy, Jorge Machado Moreira, Hélio Mamede, Sérgio Bernardes, and Berta Leitchic. In 1962 the team completed the first draft of the park's plan. The occupation of the landfill site of around 120 hectares/300 acres was based on the premiss of not creating focuses of interest, but rather distributing groups of vegetation and various amenities along the whole strip of land. There were to be restaurants, sports amenities, playgrounds, an open area for flying model aeroplanes, a theatre, an aquarium, a bicycle path, and a system of paved walkways, in addition to restoration of the beaches for swimming. Dividing the park into eleven sectors, Burle Marx specified an enormous variety of shrubs, trees, and palms—over 240 different species from Brazil and other tropical regions—making for an experiment unprecedented in his professional career. The trees and palms were planted in homogeneous groups, according to landscaping and botanical criteria. Except for the grassed areas, there were to be no herbaceous plants in general defining the horizontal planes. The planting of the 16,250 specimens was carried out between 1962 and 1965, using various species that were little known to Brazilian urban landscaping, such as the trees *Bauhinia blakeana* ('pata-de-vaca'), *Calophyllum inophyllum* (apricot), and *Chorisia insignis* among others.   GMD

> MARTA ÍRIS MONTERO, *Burle Marx: paisajes líricos* (1997).
> VERA BEATRIZ SIQUEIRA, *Burle Marx* (2001).

Flindt, H. A.

(1822–1901), Danish landscape gardener who worked with more than 200 manor house gardens and parks in both Denmark and Sweden. After apprenticeship in several royal gardens he travelled to England, Scotland,

France, and Germany. In Copenhagen he planned the botanical gardens (1882) in connection with the other embankment parks such as the scenic Ørsteds Park (1876) with curving paths. He also made the plan for the Royal Danish Horticultural Society's Garden (1884). From *c.*1850 for over 40 years he redesigned the baroque gardens of manor houses and added English-style landscape parks at places such as GLORUP, Gavnø, Vallø, and Sanderumgård. In 1877 he succeeded Rudolph Rothe as chief inspector of the Danish royal gardens.   AL

florists' flowers.

The word florist only acquired its modern meaning, of a shop that sells cut flowers, in the late 19th century. It originally meant anyone who knew about and cultivated flowers because they were beautiful rather than merely useful. In the 17th century, when the word first appeared, florists in England were people who specialized in the cultivation of certain groups of decorative flowers. One of the nurserymen who supplied their needs was George Ricketts (or Rickets) of Hoxton, near London. John Rea's *Flora* (1665) describes the many tulips that 'may be had of Mr. Rickets of Ogesden near London . . . the best and most faithful florist now about London'. A copy of Rickett's catalogue of 1688 survives, listing many florist's flowers: there are several sorts of single and double anemones; of auriculas there are 'double of several sorts', 'strip'd, great varieties', and 'plain colours'; 'very many sorts' of carnations; and 'great varieties' of tulips. These, together with ranunculus (cultivars of *Ranunculus asiaticus*), were the chief interests of florists in the latter part of the 17th century. By the early 18th century groups of florists were formed, with annual feasts which later on became competitive shows. The 18th century saw an extraordinary increase in the nursery trade in Britain, much of it devoted to supplying florist's flowers. James Maddock's *The Florist's Directory* (1792) describes the cultivation of anemones, auriculas, carnations, hyacinths, pinks, polyanthus, ranunculus, and tulips. Maddock had a nursery at Walworth, near London, but was originally from Warrington in Lancashire—the north of England being a great centre of florists. The range of varieties cultivated at this time was gigantic—one nurseryman's list offered in 1769 1,110 different ranunculus cultivars priced between 5*d.* and 1*s.* (that is about £1.24 and £2.98 today) each. Whole collections were sold at bargain prices with, for example, 700 different sorts available for £12 10*s.* (around £747). There were 575 hyacinths of which the most expensive fetched astronomical prices—'Black Flora' was priced at £21 (around £1,254 today). The

fanatical interest in florist's flowers at this time is shown by the ranges of cultivars stocked—far greater than any nursery today would carry of any genus. The scale of the mania is shown in the publication of Richard Weston's *Botanicus Universalis et Hortulanus* (The Universal Botanist and Nurseryman) (4 vols., 1770-7). Weston reprinted many nurserymen's catalogues so that the 'florist may here indulge his utmost fancy in selecting from among all the minute varieties that are to be found in the French, Dutch, and Flemish flower-gardens'. In the early 19th century florist's flowers remained immensely popular. Thomas Hogg's *Practical Treatise on the Culture of the Carnation, Pink, Auricula, Polyanthus, Tulip and Other Flowers* (1820) was reprinted five times by 1839. In the 19th century societies were started specializing in particular florist's flowers—the National Carnation and Picotee Society (1850), the National Tulip Society (1849), and the National Auricula Society (1873). The number of different cultivars of florist's flowers is incalculable. Of carnations, it is estimated that by the 19th century there were thousands of cultivars. In the late 20th century there was an renaissance of interest in auriculas with old cultivars keenly sought and new ones flaunted.
                                                           PT

> JOHN HARVEY, *Early Nurserymen* (1974).
> BLANCHE HENREY, *British Botanical and Horticultural Literature before 1800* (1975).

flower garden.

To many gardeners, especially those in Britain, a garden is by definition a place of flowers. From the earliest times of garden making flowers must have been of absorbing interest to gardeners. In France Charles Estienne's *L'Agriculture et maison rustique* (1564) avowed, 'Ce qui est le plus plaisant et recreatif en la metairie Françoise, c'est le jardin à fleurs, tant pour la recreation du seigneur à qui appartient l'heritage, comme pour les ruches des mouches à miel' (that which is most agreeable and diverting in farming in France is the flower garden, as much for the recreation of the owner as for the hives of honey bees). Flower gardens were one of the wonders of the Renaissance, and the scientific study of plants, and connoisseurship of new exotics, were the foundations of flower gardening in Europe. In 1611 Philipp Hainhofer visited the great garden at EICHSTÄTT and recorded, 'Each of the eight gardens contained flowers from a different country; they varied in the beds and flowers, especially in the beautiful roses, lilies and tulips' (quoted in Nicolas Barker, *Hortus Eystettensis*, 1994). In simpler gardens writers such as William Lawson in *A New Orchard and Garden* (1618) leave no doubt as to the importance of flowers. In Lawson's orchard he had 'The Rose red, damaske, velvet, and double province Rose, the sweet muske Rose, double and single, the double and single white Rose. The faire and sweet senting Woodbine, double and single. Purple Cowslips and double Cowslips. Primrose double and single. The Violet nothing behinde the best, for smelling sweetly. And 1000 more will provoke your content.' However, the flower garden, as a part of the garden in which flowers are the chief ingredient, has a more particular connotation. The notion of the flower garden as an entity was certainly established in the 18th century. John ABERCROMBIE in his *Every Man his Own Gardener* (1767) recommends that the kitchen garden should be 'concealed by buildings or plantations, the flower-garden and pleasure-grounds should stand conspicuously attached to the family residence'. In William Mason's rather ponderous poem *The English Garden* (1772–81) he describes the kind of flower garden he laid out for Lord Harcourt at Nuneham Courtenay (Oxfordshire)—'So here did Art arrange her flow'ry groups | Irregular, yet not in

patches quaint, | But interpos'd between the wandering lines | Of shaven turf which twisted to the path.' Humphry REPTON later in his career introduced flower gardens in his designs close to the house—as he did at ENDSLEIGH HOUSE (from 1814). J. C. LOUDON in his *Encyclopaedia of Gardening* (1822) points out that flowers have long been cultivated among the fruit and vegetables of the KITCHEN GARDEN. However, he adds, 'in residences which aim at any degree of distinction the space within the walled garden is confined to the production of objects of domestic utility, while the culture of plants of ornament is displayed in the flower-garden or shrubbery'. By Loudon's time the flower garden was well established. In discussing the size of flower gardens he recommended they should be of one-fifth of the size of the kitchen garden. He warns about having too large a flower garden and quotes John ABERCROMBIE—'To cover twenty acres with mere flowering plants . . . would be puerile and ridiculous' (*The Practical Gardener's Companion*, 1816). The flower garden was an essential part of the 19th-century British garden whose

repertory of appropriate hardy plants was codified in William ROBINSON's *The English Flower Garden* (1883). Robinson emphasized the possibility in a temperate climate of having flower gardens that would bloom, or at least present handsome foliage or bark, in every season. In his chapter on the flower garden in winter he nonetheless finds many excellent flowering subjects—heathers, hellebores, *Iris unguicularis*, winter jasmine (*Jasminum nudiflorum*), winter sweet (*Chimonanthus praecox*), and much else. Robinson's view of the flower garden was that it is not merely a formal garden of flowers near the house—it could, in one form or another, be part of the ornamental scheme anywhere in the garden. By the time Gertrude JEKYLL wrote *Colour Schemes for the Flower Garden* (1908) the flower garden was the most intensively cultivated part of the ornamental garden. Miss Jekyll was writing at the height of the ARTS AND CRAFTS movement of

The **flower garden** shown in Crispin de Passe's *Hortus Floridus* (1615).

which she herself was an important protagonist. The Arts and Crafts movement, with its love of the architectural manipulation of space, inspired gardens of separate compartments which were ideal for flower gardens of different kinds. In many ways the flower garden in the context of a setting inspired by Arts and Crafts architects was the dominant style in 20th-century British gardens. It provided different sites, of sun and shade, that allowed a wide repertory of plants. Furthermore, the compartments enclosed in walls or hedges made the perfect setting for the colour-themed arrangements of which Gertude Jekyll was a pioneer. Gardens such as HIDCOTE MANOR (from 1907) and SISSINGHURST (from 1930) deployed flower gardens of very different atmospheres in an Arts and Crafts framework.

In gardens today most hobby gardeners would not think of the flower garden as something independent from the garden as a whole. In Britain it is a rare garden that has no border of flowers in a place of prominence. British garden designers in the late 20th century have emphasized the importance of flowering plants and of colour as central to garden taste. Flowering plants have assumed such importance in gardens generally that the flower garden in itself is scarcely known. However, some garden designers like to conceal a flower garden so that it forms no part of the chief layout. Jacques WIRTZ is a notable example of this tendency. He may lay out a flower parterre forming the entrance to a house, or have a concealed flower garden hidden behind hedges and suddenly revealed to the visitor. PT

Foce, Villa La

Chianciano Terme, Tuscany, Italy. A green oasis in the barren Sienese countryside, the Villa La Foce reflects the restoration undertaken by the Marchesa Origo (the English/American author Iris Origo) and her husband from the 1920s, when they bought the abandoned estate. Using the English architect Cecil PINSENT to alter and extend the villa, an old coaching inn, and to lay out the garden in Renaissance proportions, the Origos created one of the most important modern gardens in Italy. Pinsent perfectly understood his task. The garden is on a series of terraces, its plan most formal near the villa and becoming increasingly more naturalistic with native shrubs and flowers further from the house as garden merges into meadow and woodland. The centrepiece is the formal lemon garden, criss-crossed with high box hedges, overlooked by a summer house curtained with wisteria and a pergola, the surrounding beds rampant with English-style flower garden

plants, reflecting Iris Origo's background and interest in gardening. Next to the house an intimate hedged 'room' contains an oval pool. The pergola winds round the contours of the hill, continuing as a pathway to the chapel in the woods, where the Origos are buried. A steep *viale* (avenue) of cypresses leads up the hill from the house, sheltering cyclamen in spring. The last garden compartment made by Pinsent is the most formal, a sunken area with triangles of simple box hedging framed by cypresses, its only concession to flowers two vast evergreen magnolias. PHo

Foerster, Karl

(1874–1970), German nurseryman, plant breeder, and writer, whose achievements were honoured with numerous titles and medals, e.g. the honorary doctorate by the Humboldt-Universität Berlin (1950). His new perennial plant cultivars and his introduction of native and foreign perennials, ferns, and grasses as central space-creating components of the garden strongly influenced modern garden design in Germany. His breeding methods affected the work of horticulturalists such as Wilhelm Schacht, Richard Hansen, and Heinz Hagemann. After an apprenticeship in the SCHWERIN PALACE GARDENS (1889–91), studies at the Royal Gardeners' Training School in Wildpark-Potsdam, and six years of travel working in gardens and nursery firms in Germany and Italy, he established his own nursery in Berlin in 1903 and moved to Potsdam-Bornim in 1910/11. Here he developed his breeding method influenced by the theories and ideas of Charles Darwin and Johann Wolfgang von Goethe. By selection from an abundant number of seedlings, vegetative propagation, wild fertilization, and a five-year observation period and evaluation he aimed at enhancing the plants' strength and their value as garden plants. Besides promoting public gardens in different climatic regions for the testing and observation of new cultivars, e.g. the garden on the Freundschaftsinsel in Potsdam (1938–9), he promoted the design of artistic low-maintenance gardens by offering appropriate hardy plants. He opposed carpet bedding, but an affinity to the nature garden as described by Willy LANGE encouraged him to combine architectural and naturalistic garden styles. This is demonstrated in his own garden in Potsdam-Bornim and in works of the landscape architects Herta HAMMERBACHER and Hermann MATTERN with whom he founded a design studio in 1928. His popularity is also due to his lectures and highly emotive writings in numerous books (e.g. *Vom Blütengarten der Zukuft* (1917), *Blauer Schatz der Gärten* (1940), *Ferien vom Ach* (1962)). His articles were partly

published in the journal *Gartenschönheit* which he edited from 1920 until 1941. SD

SONJA DÜMPELMANN, *Karl Foerster: Vom großen Welt- und Gartenspiel* (2001).
EVA FOERSTER and GERHARD ROSTIN, *Ein Garten der Erinnerung: Leben und Wirken von Karl Foerster—dem großen Garten-Poeten und Staudenzüchter* (2001).

Folie Saint-James. See SAINT-JAMES, FOLIE.

folly.

The term is an unfortunate expression, with a pejorative ring to it. Folly, as a garden building of probably foolish purpose, in all likelihood covers many buildings which have a very definite role in the landscape—as an eyecatcher, a retreat or viewpoint, or simply as a graceful flourish on the horizon or in some other prominent place. Equally, many buildings termed 'folly' have a precise functional, poetic, or symbolic role. To create a building which has no purpose whatsoever, even inadvertent, would be a tricky undertaking. *The Oxford English Dictionary* defines a folly as 'A popular name for any costly structure considered to have shown folly in the builder' (but cf. Fr. *folie*, 'delight', 'favourite abode'). Barbara Jones, the author of the wonderful book *Follies & Grottoes* (1953), has difficulty in describing what she means by a folly. It cannot be described, she writes, as 'a useless building erected for ornament on a gentleman's estate' because garden temples could be described in exactly the same way. She says the folly is only built by rich men, is replete with 'some mood or emotion', is fragile, is often cheap and ephemeral, and is 'personal in a way no great architecture ever is'. None of this, alas, explains what a folly looks like. In French, according to Littré's *Dictionnaire le la langue française*, a *folie* 'Se dit de certaines maisons de plaisance, d'ordinaire avec l'idée qu'on y a fait de folles dépenses' (is applied to kinds of pleasure pavilion, usually with the implication that they have been madly expensive). The famous garden that the Baron Saint-James made at Neuilly from 1781 was designed by François-Joseph BÉLANGER who was told, 'Build whatever you like, provided that it is expensive.' The garden thus became known as the Folie SAINT-JAMES. *Folie* is used in everyday French to mean extravagance, without any pejorative sense, merely generosity. Some French garden historians connect the word *folie*, in relation to garden buildings, with the word *folié* which means foliate, or leafy. This type of garden building, they say, was a leafy arbour. Whatever the truth of that, the problem about the term folly as it is usually employed is that it makes too many assumptions about the motive of the builder. After all, what seems a mad extravagance to a suburban gardener in the 21st century might have been considered a perfectly reasonable expense to an 18th-century landscaper. As Alexander POPE wrote in his *Moral Essays*, 'Tis use alone that sanctifies Expense'. Conspicuous expenditure has rarely been more conspicuous than in the embellishment of the great landscape gardens. Rather than attempting to unravel the motives of the builder, and relative notions of extravagance or madness, it is probably safer to consider the use to which the building is put and its role in the designed landscape. It is at this point that the usefulness of the term 'folly' seems to melt away before one's eyes. It is hard to avoid the conclusion that any garden building described, often rather dismissively, as a 'folly' could be more precisely and usefully described in terms of its exact role or genre—as a banqueting house, column, EYECATCHER, GAZEBO, GROTTO, HERMITAGE, OBELISK, PAVILION, TEMPLE, or MAUSOLEUM.   PT

Folly Farm ✼

Sulhamstead, Berkshire, England, is an excellent place in which to see the genius of Sir Edwin LUTYENS in full flow. Between 1905 and 1906 he grafted onto a simple 17th-century farmhouse a dapper house of refined William and Mary character. A little later, from 1912, for a new client he added an entirely new house, connected on one side, in a muscular ARTS AND CRAFTS style. Suitable gardens were also laid out, with plantings by Gertrude JEKYLL. The south front of the William and Mary extension overlooks a canal pointing away from the house with, at its far end, a curved balustrade at a raised level. Simple and elegant, this perfectly suits the mood of the house. A great feature of the Arts and Crafts house is a cloistered pool clasped in a corner of the house. The house overlooks a garden in which Gertrude Jekyll planned a FLOWER GARDEN in the form of a parterre. A walk leads between yew hedges and an avenue of crab apples away from the formal garden. To one side, concealed behind high yew hedges, is a sunken rose garden with an octagonal lily pool at whose centre an island is planted with roses and lavender. The architectural detail of the formal gardens, and of a walled kitchen garden at a little distance of the house, is of exquisite quality. Lawrence Weaver in his *Houses and Garden by E. L. Lutyens* (1913) comments on Lutyens's perfectionism in small things so 'that even the vegetable racks in the scullery are more interesting than the fittings of many a library'. The same is true of the finely laid brick PATHS, steps, and walls of Folly Farm. Very little of the original planting survives, however, and much of the later planting is strongly out of sympathy.   PT

Fontaine, Jardins de la ✼

Nîmes, Gard, France, one of the finest and most enjoyable public gardens in France. Its origins are Roman—in honour of the Emperor Augustus (63 BC–AD 14) an Augusteum was built with a portico, a theatre, a Temple of Diana, and spring-fed pool from which water was canalized to a NYMPHAEUM. The site was abandoned in the Middle Ages—the Temple of Diana became a Benedictine chapel. Later on the industry of Nîmes depended on a plentiful water supply for the treatment of cloth (the word denim is thought to derive from *serge de Nîmes*). In the pursuit of water an archaeological excavation in the early 18th century discovered the Roman spring and the elaborate irrigation system connected with it. In the 1740s the engineer Jacques Philippe Mareschal was put in charge of restoring this water supply and also of transforming the site into a public park as an amenity for the growing population of the town. The garden as it is today is the result of Mareschal's work. The spring-fed pool and the site of the nymphaeum, both enclosed in stone balustrades and decorated with stone urns and statuary, are at the heart of the garden which is enclosed in iron railings with the original magnificent 18th-century wrought-iron gates. Statues and urns here, and elsewhere in the garden, are the work of Dominique Raché. The remains of the Temple of Diana stand on the western site of the garden and to the north a walk winds through woods of holm oak (*Quercus ilex*) and other evergreens to the Mont Cavalier, the source of the spring, which is crowned with a Roman tower, the Tour Magne. From these slopes the view to the south shows the Avenue Jean Jaurès precisely aligned on the garden sweeping southwards through the town—the whole a masterpiece of urban design that makes the most of a site of unique history.   PT

JEAN-MARIE PÉROUSE DE MONTCLOS (ed.), *Le Guide du patrimoine: Languedoc Roussillon* (1996).

Fontainebleau, Château de ✼

Fontainebleau, Seine-et-Marne, France, a royal dwelling since at least the 12th century. It was François I who established Fontainebleau as his chief residence in 1528, transforming a medieval castle into a Renaissance palace and making the first remarkable garden here of which much is visible today. VIGNOLA made bronze casts of classical statuary for the garden—the Apollo Belvedere, Ariadne, and Laocoön—all of which are now in the Louvre. Francesco Primaticcio (*c.*1504–1570) and Sebastiano Serlio (1475–*c.*1554) were also involved in the palace—a surviving rustic architectural grotto, the Grotte des Pins, was probably designed by them, possibly with Vignola's collaboration. Primaticcio also

painted a fresco for the Pavillon de Pomone which does not survive. Androuet DU CERCEAU's engraving in *Les Plus Excellents Bastiments de France* (1576), some time after François I's death, shows a long entrance avenue to the north, a quadripartite pattern of parterres to the south, and, at some distance to the north-east, more parterres edged with groves of trees. In the reign of Henri IV, from 1584, many changes were made. In the Étang (Pool) south of the chateau a garden was made jutting out into the water and supported on bastioned walls. Francini's engraving of 1614 shows the Étang surrounded on three sides by ALLÉES and elaborate patterns of gardens. Claude Mollet (see MOLLET, ANDRÉ, AND FAMILY) worked here from 1595 and from 1602 Alessandro FRANCINI was responsible for water and fountains. In 1609 a slender canal 1,145 m/3,756 ft long extended eastwards from the garden. In 1645 André LE NÔTRE came to work at Fontainebleau and in the enclosed courtyard of the Jardin de la Reine laid out PARTERRES *de broderie*. In 1660, east of the Étang, he designed an immense four-part *parterre de broderie* with a rectangular pool at its centre and a circular pool to its south. In the early 19th century ground to the west of the Étang was made into a *jardin à l'anglaise* which survives today in a much simplified form. Historically Fontainebleau is one of the most important of French gardens, with period features ranging from the 16th to the 19th centuries. In its present pared-down form, with no *broderie* in Le Nôtre's parterres, a slightly forlorn *jardin à l'anglaise*, and a general lack of decorative exuberance in keeping with the splendours of the chateau, it is not a very lovable place.   PT

Fontevraud, Abbaye de ✼

Fontevraud-L'Abbaye, Maine-et-Loire, France, founded in the 11th century to house two monastic communities, of men and women. The beautiful 12th-century abbey church survives, with the tombs of several members of the Plantagenet royal family, and other distinguished monastic buildings. A modern physic garden contains plants from Charlemagne's list of plants to be cultivated. A *hortulus*, or kitchen garden, close to the walls of the 12th-century kitchen building, has both culinary plants and those used for dyeing, brewing, fibres, and other useful purposes. The plants are not scrupulously of the period but the result, in a magnificent medieval setting, is delightful.   PT

Fonthill Abbey,

Wiltshire, England, was built from 1796 by William BECKFORD whose father, Alderman Beckford, had bought the ancient estate *c.*1736.

He enclosed almost 810 hectares/2,000 acres of ground in a high stone wall and started work on the existing garden. What exactly he did behind the wall was the subject of much speculation in his lifetime, as it has been since his death. It seems he made grottoes, designed by Josiah Lane (1753–1833), planted more than a million trees, and made an American Plantation on the banks of a lake. The Abbey collapsed, Beckford moved to Bath, and today little remains of the 18th-century landscape.   PT

TIMOTHY MOWL, *William Beckford* (1998).

Forestal Park ⊛

Santiago de Chile, Chile. To the east of the city, by the Mapocho river, Forestal Park was founded as the setting for the Fine Arts Museum constructed in 1910 to celebrate the First Century of Independence. It occupied a depression by the river bed left after the Tajamar defences were built against frequent flooding by ice melting off the nearby Andes range. The temperate climate of the central zone allowed acclimatization of tree species from the whole temperate world which were used to embellish the traditional patios, gardens, and parks designed by French, Irish, and English landscape designers. George Dubois designed the Parque Forestal on the banks of the Mapocho in a picturesque and naturalistic style inspired by English gardens, with plants imported from Europe and the north of Argentine. A romantic lake with balustrades has now disappeared, but the magnificent six rows of London planes (*Platanus × hispanica*) structure a promenade with views to the nearby Cerro San Cristobal Park. Little by little both sides of the river banks have been provided with other parks. In the 1930s, the German landscape architect Oscar Prager designed the Parque Providencia, introducing for the first time in Chile the country's native flora in a public park. In recent times a great impulse has been given to the creation of urban parks for the poorer sectors of the city.   MVL

Forestier, Jean-Claude Nicolas

(1861–1930), French engineer and garden designer who practised in an eclectic style intermingling the traditions of the informal landscape style and that of the *jardin régulier* with a touch of modernism. He was also vividly aware of the qualities of plants as Dorothée Imbert discusses in the book cited below. From 1887 he worked for the city of Paris, overlapping with the end of ALPHAND's career as *directeur des*

travaux de Paris and becoming *conservateur de promenades*. Here he was particularly involved with the city's acquisition of the Bagatelle estate (see PARIS PARKS AND GARDENS) in 1905 where he overlaid formal ingredients, including a rose garden, on an essentially 18th-century park. His work on the Champs-de-Mars (1908) leading up to the Eiffel Tower, in collaboration with J.-C. Formigé and J. Bouvard, with its

strong central axis flanking paths winding through groves, is a surviving example of Forestier's characteristic style. In addition to his work for the city of Paris Forestier also practised privately, advising on urban projects, often abroad (for example in New York and Mexico), and designing private gardens (among them the dazzling little terraced garden of the Casa del Rey Moro in Ronda, Spain). He

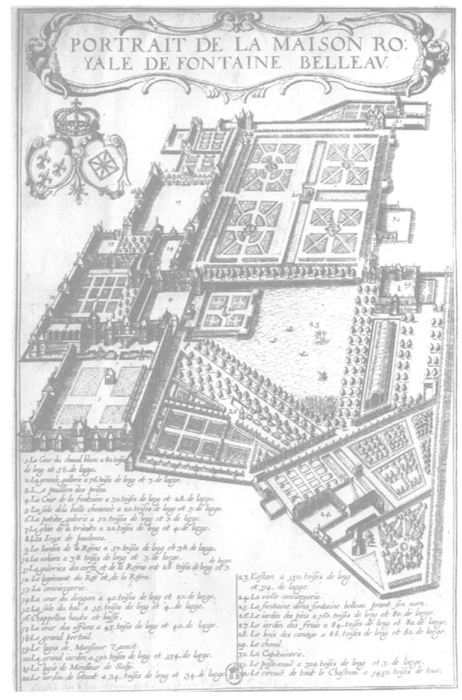

Bird's-eye view of **Fontainebleau** from an engraving by A. Francini (1614).

designed the Parque MARÍA LUISA in Seville (1911), a large public park whose rectilinear grid is softened by winding walks and enlivened with lively water features and brilliantly coloured tiles in the Muslim tradition. For the Parc Laribal in Barcelona (1916) Forestier copied the Patio de la Acequia in the GENERALIFE. Forestier was one of the most interesting, versatile, and accomplished garden designers of his time.   PT

> DOROTHÉE IMBERT, *The Modernist Garden in France* (1993).

Forest Lodge ⊗

South Australia, Australia, is a late Victorian house in the Gothic manner, complete with castellated octagonal tower. Mining entrepreneur John Bagot constructed the house of local stone in 1890. The elevated Adelaide Hills setting of house and garden offers some slight relief from the state capital's notorious summer heatwaves. To enhance the house, John Bagot laid out a garden within a typically Victorian framework of grottoes, bridges, and fountains. He visited Japan and returned to Australia with trees and varieties of camellias, introducing them to the colony. John's architect son Walter Bagot, on inheriting Forest Lodge, reworked the garden by introducing Mediterranean plants and the style of Renaissance Italy. He introduced formal vistas punctuated by dark green banks of cypress, imported urns and statuary, ceramic vases and terracotta pots, linking them in the manner of Italian gardens. Below the house, wide gravel walks meander between massed rhododendrons, and azaleas thrive beneath the tree canopy. Bagot's 19th-century conifer collection remains one of the finest in Australia, emphasizing the magnificence of the formal landscape. The unmistakable impression at Forest Lodge is of a shady and cool mountain retreat.   CMR

Forrest, George

(1873-1932), Scottish plant collector who, as a teenager, travelled to Australia and South Africa, and on returning to Edinburgh joined the staff of the herbarium of the ROYAL BOTANIC GARDEN. In 1904 his powers of endurance and organizational abilities brought him to the attention of A. K. Bulley (1861-1942) the nurseryman, who was creating a garden on the Wirral, and who engaged Forrest to collect suitable plants from western China. Over the following 28 years six journeys were undertaken by Forrest encompassing north-west China and Tibet. A remarkably successful plant collector, he maintained meticulous and systematic field notes, and was one of the few men to use native collectors. He sent home in excess of 30,000

botanical specimens, of which over 300 were new species of rhododendron. Forrest was supported by a number of patrons, including the Cornishman John Charles Williams of CAERHAYS CASTLE and the Rhododendron Society (founded 1915).   MC-C

Forsmarks Bruk ⊗

Uppland, Sweden, is an authentic mill village of the late 18th century. Forsmarks Bruk, meaning the mill at Forsmark, was built as a model community, a self-contained and self-supporting world. The single street gives shape to the village, being lined with houses, blacksmiths' forges, schools, and stores, with the church situated at one end and the manor at the other. Thus, the village reflects the outer world in a miniature scale. The manor was designed in the 1770s by Jean Eric Rehn (1717-93) and has at its south side a French parterre garden of the same date. On the other side is a garden in the style of an English landscape park, possibly the single best-known feature of Forsmark. It was probably designed by Johan Christian Ackermann (1738-1810), and built 1786-91. The park is contemporary with the royal parks of DROTTNINGHOLM and HAGA but considerably smaller and more intimate. The park uses three ponds as a point of departure, each connected to the larger mill pond. It is ornamented with a Hermitage, a Bark Temple, and the so-called Mirror Temple. During the 1960s the park was restored by landscape architect Walter BAUER. It is one of the best-preserved examples of the genre in Sweden.

TA

Fortune, Robert

(1812-80), Scottish plant collector in China and Japan who trained at the ROYAL BOTANIC GARDEN, EDINBURGH, before moving south to the (Royal) Horticultural Society Garden at Chiswick. Following the 1842 Treaty of Nanking (Nanjing) and the opening up of trade with China, Fortune was selected on the society's behalf to journey to China collecting plants. For three years from 1845 he visited the treaty ports along the coast purchasing material from gardens and nurseries. Subsequently he undertook two further expeditions on behalf of the Honourable East India Company collecting seed and tea plants which, with the help of the newly invented WARDIAN CASE, helped lay the foundation of the Indian tea industry. His fourth and last journey (1860-2) was mainly to Japan where he collected among others *Cryptomeria japonica* and *Dicentra spectabilis*. From China he introduced some 190 new plants including *Trachycarpus fortunei*.   MC-C

Fota Arboretum ⊗

Carrigtwohill, County Cork, Ireland, has a splendid site in the great estuary of the river Lee east of Cork. The proximity of the sea, warmed by the Gulf Stream Drift here, creates a particularly benign microclimate. The estate is very ancient, going back to the 12th century when it was owned by the de Barri family whose descendants remained here until the 20th century. The site is a flat one, indeed some of the land was reclaimed from the sea, with an area of 13 hectares/32 acres. The house was built in the 18th century as a hunting lodge but remodelled in elegant Regency fashion in the early 19th century. In the 19th century James Smith-Barry made formal terraced gardens close to the house with, in their heyday, parterres of elaborately shaped beds. These have gone today but the terraces, with lawns and fine stonework, survive and create a stately formal setting for the house. The walled former kitchen garden to one side of the house, now turned over to ornamental purposes, has been restored in recent years. An axial walk links the house with a lake whose banks are richly planted with trees. Here, and about the surrounding lawns, are excellent trees some of which date from early 19th-century plantings. Here are the tender Himalayan *Cornus capitata*, a spectacular Crimean pine (*Pinus nigra* var. *caramanica*), an *Arbutus menziesii*, and much else. A Victorian fernery has magnificent old trees of *Dicksonia antarctica*.   PT

Fountains Abbey. See STUDLEY ROYAL.

Four Seasons Resort ⊗

Chiang Mai, Thailand. Opened in 1994, this resort is located about 30 km/18 miles from Chiang Mai in a scenic valley. The extensive gardens, designed by the Bangkok-based Bensely Design Group, spill down a hillside and incorporate a number of terraced rice fields at the lower level; practical as well as picturesque, these are ploughed by a family of working water buffaloes owned by the hotel. Along with scattered flowering trees such as African tulip (*Spathodea campanulata*), jacaranda, flamboyant (*Delonix regia*), and *Plumeria*, as well as native trees already growing on the site, the lawns are planted with swirling masses of low-growing specimens to create patterns of colour reminiscent of the gardens of the Brazilian landscape architect Roberto BURLE MARX. Elsewhere, linking the resort's pavilions and other facilities, are massed beds of ornamental plants, among them elephant's ear (*Alocasia*), crinum lilies with both green and gold leaves, a *Heliconia* cultivar with dark red foliage, spider lily (*Hymenocallis littoralis*), spathiphullum, and sanseverias with both variegated and pure silver leaves. Flowering bananas, torch gingers (*Etlingera elatior*), bird's nest ferns, and stag horn ferns contribute to the jungle-like effect. In the cooler winter months some beds are planted with such temperate annuals as *Zinnia*, *Celosia*, and *Salvia*. WLW

France

With the Alps to the south-east, the Pyrenees to the south-west, and the mountains of the Massif Central at the centre and the Cévennes to the south, France has dramatic and varied natural scenery. The highest mountain, which is also the highest in Western Europe, is Mont Blanc (4,808 m/15,774 ft), and several peaks in the Pyrenees exceed 3,500 m/11,482 ft. The French coast is also striking diverse, with the Channel to the north, the Bay of Biscay to the west (with a pronounced effect of the Gulf Stream Drift), and the Mediterranean to the south. This diversity of geography and of microclimates is reflected in an exceptionally rich flora. There are around 4,900 native flowering plants and at least a further 1,000 introductions that have become naturalized. France is particularly well wooded, with an ancient tradition of woodland management. Much of the woodland, especially of the royal and aristocratic estates of the Île-de-France, but also in other parts of the country, is intact. The Forêt de Tronçais in central France, for example, was a natural oak forest (mostly *Quercus robur* but with a few *Q. petraea*) acquired by the Bourbon family in the 14th century. In 1528 it was confiscated by François I and remained royal property until 1788. In 1670 Colbert reorganized it to supply timber for Louis XIV's navy. Today, with an area of 10,500 hectares/25,935 acres, it has superb old trees and is one of the most important sources of wood for barrels for the vineyards of Bordeaux. Managed woodland in France is frequently a marvellous adornment of the landscape—often cared for with all the skills that the French bring to the training of fruit trees and the clipping of hedges in an ALLÉE.

The Romans occupied France most intensively in the east and south but we have only glimpses of the gardens they made. In the 5th century AD Sidonius Apollinarius, a Gallo-Roman living in Lyon, described a friend living near Nîmes who had 'secluded gardens which are like those that bloom on honey-bearing Hybla [Sicily] . . . among his violets, thyme, privet, serpyllum, casia, saffron, marigolds, narcissus, and blooms of hyacinth . . . or he may have chosen to rest in his mimic grotto on the edge of the hill'. Nîmes, founded by the Emperor Augustus in 16 BC, became one of the most populous cities in Roman France, and has a rare survival in the Jardins de la FONTAINE,

an 18th-century reworking of the Roman Augusteum that still retains some of the Roman fabric. To increase the water supply for the town, water was brought from Uzès, 50 km/30 miles away, crossing the river Gardon by a gigantic aqueduct at the Pont-du-Gard, one the greatest civil buildings to survive from the Roman Empire.

The Middle Ages

With the Hundred Years War, great dynastic upheavals, and an often fragmented nation, the Middle Ages was an exceptionally turbulent period in French history. Even at the end of the period, when Charles VIII came to the throne in 1483, France was not wholly united—Brittany and Navarre remained independent. Our knowledge of gardens in this period, as in other parts of Europe, is sketchy. However, they frequently appear in the poems of the troubadours, as often as not as the setting for an amorous encounter. They appear, too, in illustrations for the *Roman de la Rose* and in books of hours, such as the magnificent *Très Riches Heures* of the Duc de Berry. These, almost all dating from the 15th century, usually show unidentifiable, probably imaginary, gardens. At the very least they give clear evidence of how close gardens were to the creative consciousness of the Middle Ages, but those that show known gardens are especially valuable. *The Book of Hours of Isabella of Portugal* (c.1480) shows a garden made by King René of Anjou who, deposed from the kingdom of Sicily, had returned to his native France where he made several gardens. It is not known which of his gardens is depicted but it is sufficiently idiosyncratic to have the atmosphere of a real garden. The King is seen writing in a garden pavilion which overlooks a moated walled garden which has raised beds, tiered topiary, a hexagonal fountain, a turf seat, and paths paved in black and white chequerboard patterns. The monasteries were, as elsewhere in Europe, a profound influence on garden making. Although the cultivation of medicinal plants and food crops is usually emphasized monastic gardens were also planned to be places of beauty. Baudry, the Abbot of Bourgueil (Indre-et-Loire), who lived 1046–1130, described his own garden: 'I have a garden filled with scented flowers in which flourish roses, violets, thyme, crocus, lilies, narcissi and rosemary. Other flowers appear in their season so that at Bourgueil spring is perpetual. No sooner does one flower fade than another takes its place. I have a sweet-flowing stream to water my garden. Transparent waves splash over marble pebbles and lose themselves after thousands of detours in the middle of a meadow. When the sun's rays beat down I can shelter my weary

guests in agreeable shade. Bourgueil has a grove in which grow willows, sweet bay and myrtle, where the pear intermingles with olives, cherries or apples' (quoted in L. Berluchon's *Jardins de Touraine*, 1947). The Carthusian order, founded in the late 11th century at the Grande-Chartreuse in the French Alps, attached particular importance to gardens, with each cell having its own enclosure in which to cultivate plants. Pietro de' CRESCENZI was influential on French medieval gardens—his *Opus Ruralium Commodorum* was ordered to be translated by Charles V in 1373. Charles V's own garden at the Hôtel Saint-Pol (situated in what is today the Marais, Paris), with an area of 8 hectares/20 acres, was replanted in 1398. Part of it, the Jardin du Champ-au-Plâtre, was planted with quantities of vines, pears, apples, cherries, bay trees, roses, lilies, and irises. One of the most remarkable, and best-documented, French gardens of the Middle Ages was laid out at Hesdin (Pas-de-Calais) in the late 13th century for Comte Robert II d'Artois. On the banks of the river Ternoise was a hunting park with a banqueting house built on pilotis overlooking the river with lawns running down to the water. The poet Guillaume de Machaut (1310–77) in his poem *La Fontaine amoureuse* describes the garden at Hesdin mentioning in particular a fountain pool of marble and ivory with images of Venus, Paris, and Helen of Troy. There were also elaborate water features of the kind called GIOCHI D'ACQUA much later in Italian Renaissance gardens. Those at Hesdin were almost certainly made by Arab water engineers whom Robert d'Artois had met when he was King of Naples. They survived the Hundred Years War, which ended in 1453, and the banqueting hall is seen in a miniature of 1461 in Christine de Pisan's *Epistle of Othéa to Hector*. All were destroyed after a siege by the Emperor Charles V in 1553 and no trace of them survives today.

The Renaissance

In 1494 Charles VIII's army invaded Italy, reviving the Angevin claim to the kingdom of Naples. Some of those in the King's entourage studied Italian houses and gardens on the campaign and took Renaissance ideas back to France. The somewhat shadowy figure of Pacello de MERCOGLIANO, a Neapolitan priest who came back from Italy with the King, is mentioned in association with royal or noble estates which showed Renaissance influence. Nothing is known definitely about his work at the royal Château d'Amboise (Indre-et-Loire), which had a symmetrical arrangement of ten parterres and a central pavilion housing a fountain. In 1499 he was put in charge by Charles VIII of the gardens of the Château de

Blois (Loir-et-Cher) whose garden was similar to that of Amboise. The pavilion—the Pavillon d'Anne de Bretagne—still survives. Pacello de Mercogliano introduced at Blois the cultivation of oranges and lemons in containers. He advised on the new garden for the Château de GAILLON with its spectacular position high above the river Seine. Here a terraced garden, again with a pavilion (here containing an Italian marble fountain), was laid out between 1502 and 1509, with a series of square beds with flowers, fruit trees, or box and rosemary cut into figures—one depicted the arms of France. An extraordinary separate garden, Le Lydieu, on the boundary of the park, is seen in a 16th-century drawing by Androuet DU CERCEAU. An ornate moated banqueting house stands at the head of a canal at the other end of which is a HERMITAGE in the form of a rocky MOUNT. The latter, a feature of Renaissance gardens in Italy and England, was found in no other French garden of the 16th century. Italian influences acquired a dynastic dimension with the marriage in 1533 of Catherine de' Medici (the daughter of Lorenzo de' Medici), whose name was Gallicized to Catherine de Médicis, to Henri de Valois who became King Henri II. France was one of the first countries to show the influence of the HYPNEROTOMACHIA POLIPHILI which was translated into French—*Le Songe de Poliphile*—in 1546. A figure from a similarly fantastical world was the diversely skilful Bernard PALISSY—grotto maker, ceramicist, garden theorist, maker of automata, garden designer—an important figure in the background. The architect Philibert de L'ORME was a vital influence in bringing Renaissance architectural ideas to France. He studied in Italy in the 1530s and 1540 was appointed *architecte du roi* to Henri II. He worked at ANET, CHENONCEAUX, Montceaux-en-Brie (Seine-et-Marne), SAINT-GERMAIN-EN-LAYE, and the Tuileries (see PARIS PARKS AND GARDENS). At Montceaux and the Tuileries his patron was Catherine de Médicis, Henri II's queen. De L'Orme also sometimes designed the landscape setting for his houses, attaching particular importance to large expanses of water. Italian craftsmen and architects such as Sebastiano Serlio (1475–*c*.1554), Francesco Primaticcio (*c*.1504–1570) who painted murals at Fontainebleau, and Jacopo da VIGNOLA who cast statues for FONTAINEBLEAU. Renaissance notions took root quickly in royal circles but they were also influential in the provinces. At La BASTIE D'URFÉ in the 1540s Claude d'Urfé, a diplomat, made a garden directly influenced by what he had seen in Italy. The regular pattern of beds, spatial inventiveness, and the architectural character of French Renaissance gardens were translated, on an immensely grander scale, into the baroque gardens of the 17th century of which LE NÔTRE was the pre-eminent designer.

The 17th century

This is the period in which France's greatest contribution to garden art, the *jardin à la française*, was defined. The Château de BALLEROY designed by François MANSART in the 1620s is a foretaste of this style. The single most important ingredient of the 17th-century French garden, the PARTERRE, was described in several influential books of the period. Jacques BOYCEAU DE LA BARAUDERIE's *Traité du jardinage selon les raisons de la nature et de l'art* (1638), posthumously published, looked forward to a lavishly planted new style of parterre. By the time André Mollet published his *Le Jardin de plaisir* (1651) the language of the *jardin à la française* was fully formed and it was left to the genius of André Le Nôtre to exploit it at its most eloquent. Simultaneous with this stylistic development was the growth in the study, and collection, of plants. The first botanic garden had been founded in 1593, the JARDIN DES PLANTES at Montpellier, and in Paris the Jardin Royal des Plantes Médicinales (later Jardin des Plantes—see PARIS PARKS AND GARDENS) followed in 1623. It is estimated by Kenneth Woodbridge in *Princely Gardens* (1986) that the number of garden plants rose from around 150 in 1550 to 800 in 1669. Because modern reconstructions of 17th-century gardens, and surviving examples from the period, make little use of ornamental plants it is not widely understood how important these were to 17th-century French gardens. Dominique Garrigues in *Jardins et jardiniers de Versailles au grand siècle* (2001) documents in detail the gigantic quantities of plants consumed. In 1694 André Le Nôtre described the garden at Trianon 'which is always full of flowers which are changed in each season with pots and no dead leaf is ever seen nor any shrub that is not in flower . . . for which it is necessary to change more than 2,000,000 pots'. The plant needs of the various royal gardens were so great that a nursery, La Pépinière du Roule, was established in Paris in 1671 to the north-west of the Tuileries gardens (close to the present-day place Saint-Augustin—its site is commemorated in the street name rue de la Pépinière (nursery)). A map of *c*.1712 shows that it had over 50 substantial enclosures of plants. The English physician Martin Lister visited Roule in its heyday and met its superintendent Noël de Morlaix who told Lister that 'he had sent from hence to Marli [MARLY] alone, in four years time, eighteen Millions of Tulips and other Bulbous Flowers' (*A Journey to Paris in the Year 1698*, 1699). Roule, however, was not sufficient for the needs of the royal gardens and many plants were also bought from the commercial nurseries established in the faubourg Saint-Antoine to the east of the Bastille. With the making of VAUX-LE-VICOMTE in the 1650s and VERSAILLES in the 1660s great layouts in the style of Le Nôtre became the essential landscape of royal gardens and of courtiers, especially those involved in the financial management of France. However, the best-known examples of these gardens were largely confined to the region of Île-de-France which surrounds Paris. In the provinces, throughout France, versions of the *jardin à la française*, sometimes enterprisingly attributed to Le Nôtre, were laid out in the 17th century. Among the countless examples of such gardens are the following, all open to the public: Château de Marquessac (Dordogne), Château de CASTRIES (Hérault), Jardin de l'Évêché (Tarn), and Château de la Chaise (Rhône). For town gardens, in the provinces as well as in Paris, the *parterre de broderie*, or a simpler form of parterre, was a universally popular garden feature. Idiosyncratic 17th-century gardens were made in the provinces of which one of the most remarkable surviving examples is the Parc de la COLOMBIÈRE in Dijon which was designed in 1682 by Le Nôtre and opened to the public as soon as it was complete. The Château de BRÉCY in Normandy, with its modest size, exquisite stonework, and flight of rising terraces, is chamber music compared with the resounding symphonies of Le Nôtre. The Château de Foucaud in Gaillac (Tarn) also has terraces and a most unusual garden pavilion with bold columns to its corners, and has been turned in the 20th century into a municipal park. By the end of the century the *jardin à la française* was firmly established but it was also seen to be capable of lending itself to many interpretations.

The 18th century

The *jardin à la française* continued to be central to garden design in the 18th century—A.-J. DEZALLIER D'ARGENVILLE's *La Théorie et la pratique du jardinage*, which spelled out in great detail the principles of the 17th-century French garden, was published in 1709 and continued to be reprinted in the 18th century. It was taken as a pattern book of formal gardening. Another influential book in the same tradition was *De la distribution des maisons de plaisance* (1737) by Jacques-François Blondel (1705–74), which was faithful to the classical tradition of French garden design, with one exception. Blondel accepted the contrasting charms of distant glimpses of nature or even of picturesque disorder at the garden boundary. Well into the middle of the century great gardens continued to be laid out in the classical tradition, such as the Château de Menars (Loir-et-Cher) and the Château de Bellevue (Hauts-de-Seine), both belonging to Madame de Pompadour. Remarkable gardens were made influenced by the English landscape garden but, fashionable though they may have been, they were not numerous, and were chiefly confined to the latter part of the century and exclusively to the wealthiest and most fashionable classes. ERMENONVILLE in the 1760s, DÉSERT DE RETZ from 1774, MAUPERTHUIS in the 1770s, Folie SAINT-JAMES in the 1780s all showed an English influence but, with the Revolution hurrying near, were the last of their kind.

Georges-Louis LE ROUGE's *Détails des nouveaux jardins à la mode*, published in 21 parts between 1775 and 1789, was influential in the taste for picturesque gardens. Somewhat surprisingly the greatest impact of the English 18th-century park came in the following century when it inspired designers of public parks (such as Édouard ANDRÉ) and influenced the design of many 19th-century private gardens. In the 18th century there developed a minor tradition somewhat similar to that of the English FERME ORNÉE. Louis XV's chief minister, the Duc de Choiseul, at the Château de CHANTELOUP had a superb yard with a herd of Swiss cows for whose care a Swiss cowherd was imported. It was visited in 1787 by Arthur Young who admired 'a noble cow-house' and the 'very fine Swiss cows' which the Duke visited every day. He also noted 'the best built sheep-house I have ever seen in France' (*Travels during the Years 1787, 1788, and 1789*, 1792-4). The farmyard at the Château de Barbentane (Bouches-du-Rhône) in the 1760s was designed to be visited and admired. Doorways were inscribed with the names of whichever animals were housed within—'cochons', 'pigeons', 'poules', 'vaches', and so on. Farm buildings, if not designed for specifically ornamental purposes, were often sufficiently finely designed to associate harmoniously with the chateau. At RAMBOUILLET Louis XVI commissioned in 1786 a *ferme expérimentale* from the architect Jacques-Jean Thévenin which nobly decorates the landscape today. The Queen's Dairy at Rambouillet and the Hameau at Versailles, both made for Marie-Antoinette in the dying years of the *ancien régime*, also come close to the spirit of the *ferme ornée*.

Away from Paris and the royal court the 18th century was rich in idiosyncratic gardens of which the following all survive and all are visitable. The Château de MALLE in the early 18th century had a stately terraced garden enriched with a parade of statues. At the Château de Merville (Haute-Garonne) the Marquis de Chalvet-Rochemonteix in the mid 18th century laid out a labyrinthine grove of box hedges and oak trees. Of the same date is the Jardin

d'Albertas (Bouches-du-Rhône) which, with its theatrical terraces, *buffet d'eau* (a stepped cascade against a wall), mysterious statues, waterfall, and fountains, has an air of Italianate melancholy. The Château de la MIGNARDE (Bouches-du-Rhône), made by the son of a *pâtissier* from Aix-en-Provence, has a garden dating from the 1760s in which an airy grove of plane trees is animated with rows of statues and a terrace ornamented with mythological figures. The Château de CANON memorably intermingles axial geometry with an Arcadian atmosphere that has an English flavour. Distinguished precursors of the great tradition of public gardens in France date from the 18th century. The Jardins de la FONTAINE in Nîmes was a brilliant new public garden created in the 1740s based on a rare Roman site. At Bordeaux the Jardin Public was laid out in 1756, partly designed by Ange-Jacques Gabriel (1698-1782); its chief axis was aligned with the 18th-century street pattern.

The 19th century
Eclecticism ruled gardens in 19th-century France. The English landscape park continued as an influence, for both private and public gardens, but towards the end of the century, particularly in the person of Henri DUCHÊNE, there was a revival of interest in the *jardin à la française*. A late flowering of the picturesque tradition in the first years of the century was Frédéric Lemot's Arcadian riverside landscape at La GARENNE-LEMOT. There is something of the landscape park, too, at the Maison de CHATEAUBRIAND, but Chateaubriand's chief love here was for trees which he planted discerningly from 1807 and looked after (as he said) as though they were his own children. Joseph PAXTON's lake set in a park of fine trees at the Château de FERRIÈRES in the 1850s also looks back to 18th-century England while using the newly introduced conifers of the day. The century was a great period for the connoisseurship of plants. The Empress Joséphine's collection at MALMAISON from 1809, the great VILMORIN tree collection at BARRES founded in 1866, the outstanding rose garden at the ROSERAIE DE LA HAŸ-LES-ROSES laid out in the 1890s all testify to a passion for plants. In 1855 the botanist Gustave Thuret (1817-75) recognized the potential of the Côte d'Azur as a place to grow tender species. On the Cap d'Antibes he amassed a huge collection, especially of southern hemisphere plants, among them the first eucalyptus to be planted on the Riviera. His collection survives, as the Villa Thuret, since 1927 in the ownership of the Institut des Recherches Agronomiques. This was the great age of public parks which were laid out in greater numbers than ever before or

since. Haussmann's Paris (see PARIS PARKS AND GARDENS) was a profound influence in other parts of the country—every municipality needed a public park. Among many fine surviving examples outside Paris are the Square Darcy in Dijon (Côte d'Or, 1838-40), the Jardin Public at Coutances (Manche, 1854), the Parc de la TÊTE D'OR in Lyon (1856), the Parc Borély in Marseille (Bouches du Rhône, 1860), and the Parc du THABOR in Rennes (1865). A curiosity of the late 19th century is the garden at GIVERNY which Claude Monet made from 1883 and whose lily pool became, in his final years of painting, his favourite subject. Such private gardens must have been numerous in Monet's day but only in the case of Giverny, because of the fame of its owner, has it been thought worthwhile to recreate such a garden.

The 20th century and beyond
In the early part of the 20th century France, in particular Paris, was the most flourishing centre of art in the world. To a certain extent avant-garde attitudes of the visual arts were found in garden design, but surprisingly briefly and of very limited diffusion. It is surprising that the brilliant colours of the post-impressionists and the strong patterns of non-figurative artists had such little impact on garden design. The garden designer André VERA executed designs inspired by a pared-down version of the *jardin à la française* and his brother, the artist Paul Vera, made paintings of them with a strongly cubist atmosphere. J. C. N. FORESTIER retained a taste for the *jardin régulier* but this did not exclude romantic landscaping of an 18th-century English style—the two are happily intermingled in the Champs-de-Mars (Paris). The so-called cubist gardens of Gabriel GUEVREKIAN seemed to amount to no more than a two-dimensional pattern inspired by cubist painting. As the purpose of cubist painting was to try and display three dimensions on a two-dimensional surface it seems rather absurd to fail to recognize the presence of three dimensions which virtually all gardens display. The leading avant-garde architect, Le Corbusier (1887-1965), seems to have found no landscaper to devise modernist settings for his houses. At the famous Villa Savoye (1928-30) at Poissy open lawns and dotted trees formed the landscape setting and a terrace was adorned with blockish raised beds in a sea of square paving slabs. In a project for a house for Madame Meyer (1925) in Neuilly Le Corbusier's sketches show, filling a panoramic window, the Arcadian remains of the late 18th-century Folie Saint-James in the distance. Either borrowing an existing landscape, or adapting an earlier idiom to the taste of the time, garden designers in the great days of modernist design failed

to arrive at solutions which matched the power and originality of the architecture.

The taste for Japanese, and other Eastern-inspired, gardens was seen in France. From 1910 the banker Albert Kahn (1860–1940) at Boulogne-Billancourt (Hauts-de-Seine) laid out a refined Japanese garden, constructed by Japanese craftsmen, which survives today (now the Musée Albert-Kahn) in a slightly watered-down form. At Maulévrier (Maine-et-Loire) in the first years of the 20th century an architect, Alexandre Marcel, who had travelled widely in the East made a garden inspired by his travels. He created a sinuous lake, planted its banks with bamboos, ferns, mosses, spring-flowering trees, and Japanese maples, and introduced Japanese snow lanterns, copies of Khmer statuary, and a facsimile of a temple from Angkor-Wat. It survives today, well cared for and open to the public under the name Le Parc Oriental. At COURANCES, best known for its sublime 17th-century water garden, a Japanese tea garden was laid out before the First World War. More densely, and variously, planted than any true Japanese garden, it nonetheless has touches of japonaiserie in its cloud-clipped plants, serenely irregular pool, and island.

Although there seems to have been little influence on garden design from avant-garde art there are examples of gardens influencing art. Ferdinand Cheval's unique PALAIS IDÉAL was so esteemed by the surrealists that André Breton wrote a poem about it (in *Le Revolver à cheveux blancs*, 1932) and the Museum of Modern Art in New York included photographs of it in the major exhibition *Fantastic Art, Dada and Surrealism* (1936). The later Maison PICASSIETTE, created from 1938, was also esteemed by artists such as Jean Dubuffet as an example of populist *art brut* (raw art). Oddities, by definition, are not part of a tradition in so far as they are *sui generis* and most unlikely to have progeny. In the late 20th century highly original public gardens were laid out in Paris (see PARIS PARKS AND GARDENS) at the Parc André Citroën and the Parc de la Villette. At the Parc de la Villette (from 1983) Bernard Tschumi (b. 1944), in collaboration with many garden designers, laid out a heterogeneous, occasionally highly original, landscape whose very heterogeneity makes it almost inconspicuous in the context of the dazzling buildings that rise about and within it. The Parc André Citroën, designed by Gilles CLÉMENT and Alain Provost (b. 1938) and created from 1985, is less intellectualized and far more successful. An interesting and unexpected fashion in the late 20th century, of unknown origin, was the interest in laying out 'medieval' gardens of varying quality but sometimes in splendid medieval settings. The Abbey of

Eschau (Bas-Rhin) has a handsomely designed garden of medicinal plants. At the Abbey of Daoulas (Finistère) superb 12th-century buildings provide the background to finely laid out gardens of simples and ornamentals. The priory of Notre-Dame d'ORSAN, a modern garden inspired by medieval ideas and with authentic medieval buildings, is one of the exceptional examples of late 20th-century neo-medievalism.

In the late 20th century hobby gardening flourished in France. Since 1982 the rather smart and very well-run twice-yearly Journées des Plantes at COURSON much stimulated an interest in garden plants, particularly among the prosperous middle classes. The annual Festival International des Jardins at CHAUMONT-SUR-LOIRE since 1992 has displayed a wide range of new garden designs—sometimes outrageous, sometimes genuinely original, sometimes beautiful, and always stimulating. The French show an attractive disposition to embrace the avant-garde, at least as an idea. The late 20th century saw an outpouring of garden books, some of them plainly destined only for the coffee table but others of much greater consequence. France has long been a source of outstanding practical books on horticulture—Jean de La Quintinie's *Instruction pour les jardins fruitiers et potagers* (1690), an essential book on kitchen gardening in the 17th century, has its modern counterpart in the admirable *Le Jardin utile et gourmand* (ed. Patrick Mioulane, 2001). The best book on the training and clipping of plants, very much a French speciality, remains *L'Art de tailler les plantes* (9th edn. 1973) by Georges Truffaut and Pierre Hampe. In more recent times there has been an increase in the publishing of excellent garden historical works. Michel Baridon's very successful *Les Jardins* (1998) gathered much valuable scholarly material together for the common reader. *Jardins et jardiniers de Versailles au grand siècle* (2001) by Dominique Garrigues, drawing on a wealth of archival research, brilliantly illuminates the practice of gardening at Versailles. *Jardiner à Paris au temps des rois* (by several authors, 2003) made use of much unfamiliar documentation to tell the rich story of the capital's gardens before the Revolution. Practical and inspirational magazines are largely aimed at hobby gardeners but in 2004 a new scholarly journal of garden history, *Polia*, was initiated. Of the other media television shows little interest in gardening and newspapers almost none at all. An occasional exception is the august and happily unpredictable *Le Monde* which in 2004 ran an interview with Jean-Paul Pigeat, the founder of the Festival International des Jardins, and a series on the work of several modern French

garden designers. In the early 21st century gardening in France presents a lively scene. Hobby gardening has seen an increase in popularity in recent times. By 2004 it was estimated that 83% of French citizens have some kind of gardening space, if only a window box. In the five years between 1999 and 2004 the amount spent on gardening rose by 23% and increasing numbers of private gardens were opened to the public. It is still true, however, that the great importance of historic gardens is not sufficiently recognized. A very encouraging straw in the wind was the fact that in the summer of 2004 the Château de Versailles had 25 restoration projects for the chateau and its gardens running simultaneously with a total budget of 60 million euros. In the gardens this included the recreation of the Bosquet des Trois Fontaines and the Bosquet de l'Obélisque, the restoration of the orangery, the replanting of the Trianon park and the restoration of the Temple de l'Amour and the *rivière anglaise* (winding stream). PT

Francini family, a dynasty of Florentine hydraulic engineers who came to work in France at the turn of the 16th and 17th centuries and were involved with some of the most notable gardens of the day. In France the name was later Gallicized to Francine. Tommaso Francini (1571–1651), to whom the water-powered automata at PRATOLINO have been atributed, came to France c.1599, with his brother Alessandro, to work for Henri IV on the water features of the gardens at SAINT-GERMAN-EN-LAYE. Tommaso worked on the elaborate water supply for Marie de Médicis at the new gardens for the Luxembourg Palace (see PARIS PARKS AND GARDENS) and in collaboration with Clément Métezeau constructed the aqueduct which brought a water supply from Rungis—the foundation stone was laid by Louis XIII in 1613 and the aqueduct was completed in 1623. His work in the new gardens was so extensive that a house was built for Tommaso Francini nearby in 1613, possibly to his own design, and it may still be seen at 42 rue de l'Observatoire where it is still known as Maison des Fontainiers. Underneath it, still surviving, is the great reservoir built by Tommaso to store water from the aqueduct. Tommaso was also a gifted architect and designed the beautiful NYMPHAEUM at the Château de Wideville (Yvelines, 1635) for Claude de Bullion, Louis XIII's *surintendant de finances*. The rocaille grotto at RUEIL built for Richelieu may have been designed by the Francini brothers. Alessandro Francini (d. 1649) designed the Fontaine de Médicis for the Luxembourg gardens, which survives. Alessandro spent much of his life working on the gardens at FONTAINEBLEAU where from 1602 he was in charge of the fountains. Tommaso's sons, with thoroughly Gallicized names, François de Francine (1617–88) and Pierre de Francine (1621–86), both worked at Versailles where the water supply was, and remains, a perennial problem. In 1672 Louis XIV issued an *Ordre à observer pour les fontaines de Versailles* (order to be observed for the Versailles fountains) that 'they should play only in the presence of the king or of a person of rank'. The King was immensely envious of the great water gardens at CHANTILLY where, according to A.-J. DEZALLIER D'ARGENVILLE, the fountains played day and night. François was put in charge of water and fountains (*intendant des eaux et fontaines*) for the gardens in 1651. For the Grotto of Thetis, completed in 1668 but which does not survive, they brought water from the higher ground at Clagny which also provided water for some of the fountains of which there were 1,400 at the time of the Francine brothers. The interior of the grotto had sound effects of trickling water and a water-powered organ which imitated the twittering of birds. The last of the dynasty, the son of François, was Pierre François de Francine (1654–1720) who succeeded his father as *intendant des eaux et fontaines*.   PT

KENNETH WOODBRIDGE, *Princely Gardens* (1986).

Frankfurt Palmengarten.
See PALMENGARTEN.

Freck. See AVRIG PARK.

Fredensborg Palace Gardens ⊛
Fredensborg, Denmark. Around 1720 King Frederik IV (1671–1730) worked on large-scale gardens at FREDERIKSBORG and Frydenlund. An early plan *c.*1720 for the Fredensborg Palace gardens, attributed to J. C. KRIEGER, and perhaps inspired by the gardens at HAMPTON COURT, takes as its focal point the palace's garden façade. The fan-shaped garden, with a parterre and BOSQUET and a radius of *c.*140 m/ 470 ft, was laid out in front of the building, and, continuing this geometry, seven radiating avenues divided the deer park into six parts. In the late 1730s, the avenues were linked by concentric ring avenues. A spiral maze, pheasant garden, and an area where polecats and stoats hunted hares and rabbits were laid out between them. King Frederik V (1723–66) had the palace extended in the 1750s by architects N. Eigtved (1701–54) and L. de Thurah (1706–59). N.-H. Jardin's (1720–99) plan from the 1760s opened the central avenue into a broad TAPIS VERT, flanked by rows of trees and figures by the sculptor J. Wiedewelt (1731–1802). In 1764, the sculptor J. G. Grund (1733–96)

made sandstone figures for the Valley of the Norwegians, which lies in a hollow in the landscape as a flat circle surrounded by three concentric terraces lined with precisely placed trees. Palace gardeners J. L. Mansa (1740–1820) and Rothe (1802–77) made the garden more like an English landscape park, but since the 1970s, the park has been renovated following Jardin's 18th-century plan.   AL

Frederiksberg Gardens and Søndermarken ⊛
Copenhagen, Denmark. Frederiksberg Palace was built 1699–1703 for King Frederik IV (1671–1730). The original baroque garden was laid out *c.*1700, probably designed by engineering officer Hans Hendrick Scheel (1668–1738), and influenced by a plan by the Swede Nicodemus TESSIN the younger in 1697. Scheel's garden had a system of avenues around eight identical square BOSQUETS. The emphasis was on the palace's cross-axis, but the main axis was accentuated with four oval pools. In the 1720s, architect J. C. KRIEGER transformed the rise in the terrain to the plateau on which the palace stands to terraces planted with lime trees. On Søndermarken (South Field) avenues were planted *c.*1708 in a PATTE-D'OIE, radiating from the palace's entrance façade. From *c.*1800 the gardens were partly changed by palace gardener Peter Petersen (1754–1826) in the informal English manner. Winding canals and a lake were dug, and a Chinese pavilion on an island, and grottoes, bridges, pavilions, and gazebos, were built.   AL

Frederiksborg Castle Gardens ⊛
Hillerød, Denmark. In 1721, King Frederik IV (1671–1730) commissioned J. C. KRIEGER to create gardens for Frederiksborg Castle on the slope by the castle lake, combining an Italian terrace garden with a French baroque garden. The sloping site made it possible to create cascades flowing down the garden's central axis. The terrain was remodelled into four terraces with slopes bordered by lime trees. Seen from the castle, the terraces gives a deep perspective, and the effect was reinforced by reducing the height of the steps as the distance from the castle increases. The cascades were completed in 1725, but the accession of a new king, changes in taste, and problems with the structure led to their being abandoned just 40 years later. The axial cascade complex, 230 m/754 ft long, 4 m/ 16.5 ft wide, with a canal, seven waterfalls, and pools, was recreated in 1996, based on J. C. Krieger's plan, but using modern techniques and materials. On the lowest terrace, four PARTERRES *de broderie* were laid out with new monograms—of Frederik IV, Christian VI, Frederik V, and Margrethe II. A 19th-century

landscape garden lies west of the baroque garden.   AL

Freÿr, Jardins de ⊛
Freÿr (Hastiere), Namur, Belgium. The formal French-style gardens, covering an area of 10 hectares/25 acres, were laid out in the 18th century although the chateau was started in 1571. In 1759 the garden was divided into long terraces ascending the west bank of the Meuse and parallel to the river. A cross-axis encompassing a large oval pool on the second terrace and a cascade was created in the following year and then in 1774 a pretty pavilion, Frederic's Hall, was constructed to provide a focal point. It is from this pavilion that the best view of the garden is seen, although there is also a spectacular bird's-eye view from the cliff on the other side of the Meuse. The lowest terrace is in three parts: a parterre with four pools in two different styles, symmetrically arranged; an area of pleached limes which form enclosures around a central pool; finally, two long rectangular pools decorated with 33 ancient orange trees which came from the court of Stanislas Leczinsky at Nancy before 1740. The second terrace is laid out in eight ornate box parterres enclosed by tall hedges arranged round the central pool. A grass slope leads to the pavilion, divided from the rest of the garden by a railway line, the only alteration in the garden since the 18th century. Twenty-two statues by the Belgian sculptor Paul-Louis Cyffle (or Ciffle) (1724–1806), including copies of six that had been stolen, are to be replaced on the walls.   BA

Friberg, Per
(b. 1920), Swedish architect and landscape architect, working with projects from the larger scale of the residential areas and the power station landscapes to the smaller scale of private houses and gardens. Integrity and awareness of scale are words that can describe his work. The buildings communicate with the garden as well as with the surrounding landscape and the garden always communicates with the buildings in Per Friberg's work. Even more so, the larger landscape scale is communicating with the smaller scale, and vice versa. Friberg is well known for projects with cemeteries, in particular at Jakobsberg (1977), outside Stockholm, and Augerum (1980), Karlskrona. He takes great inspiration from historical gardens. At both Jakobsberg and Augerum he designed a path near a water chain, like the *catena d'acqua* in the Renaissance gardens of Italy. Friberg studied architecture and landscape architecture in Stockholm, Copenhagen, and at Harvard, and in 1950 he

started his own practice in Helsingborg. Five years later he moved to Bjärred and started a practice from where he is still working. In 1964 he was the first professor in Sweden of garden architecture and nature conservation at the Swedish University of Agriculture in Alnarp, where he taught for twenty years and still gives lectures. He has thereby influenced younger generations of landscape architects and the development of garden architecture in Sweden.

AJ

TORBJÖRN ANDERSSON, TOVE JONSTOIJ, and KJELL LUNDQUIST (eds.), *Svensk trädgårdskonst under fyrahundra år* (2000).
H. MILES, 'Swedish beauty', *Architectural Review* (1991).

Fronteira, Palácio ⊛

Lisbon, Portugal, built in the second half of the 17th century for Dom João Mascarenhas, Conde da Torre, who, in recognition of his part in the war against Spain, was awarded the title of Marquês de Fronteira in 1670. The garden, laid out as the house was being built, is one of the most important, and attractive, surviving Portuguese gardens of the 17th century. The house overlooks an immense rectilinear box parterre with fountains. The box has grown so as to leave only small gaps which are filled with modern roses, and rounded cones or mounds of clipped box rise above the level of the hedges. Lead figures on tall plinths punctuate the parterre which is surrounded by shallow terracing whose walls are marvellously decorated with pictorial AZULEJOS.

To one side of the parterre is one of the most marvellous of all garden scenes. A great rectangular water tank is backed by an arcaded wall and a raišed terrace walk to which grand balustraded flights of steps rise at each end of the water tank. The arches in the retaining wall are filled with lively figures, formed of *azulejos*, of cavalrymen riding to battle. A pavilion with a steep pyramidal roof stands at each end of the terrace whose wall is covered in sky blue *azulejos* and inset with niches containing marble busts of Portuguese kings. The niches are lined with textured lustre tiles and surrounded by blue and lustre tiles with pine cones in low relief. The pavilions overlook the formal gardens but one also has views outside them. It overlooks a

kitchen garden with lemon trees and loquats with, on the wooded hill above, a domed pavilion of baroque character.

From the west pavilion a passage leads through to a grotto pavilion whose interior, with white stone basins, is lavishly incrusted with rocaille work inset with fragments of blue and white Chinese porcelain with a dado of pictorial *azulejos*. In front of the grotto (whose exterior is also decorated with rocaille and porcelain) is an intricate, swirling water garden with scrollwork stone patterns. Dolphins ridden by boys spout water into the pool which is lined with *azulejos* showing fish frolicking through water. The formal garden in front of the pavilion, the Garden of Venus, has somewhat lost its formality. An elaborate star-shaped fountain pool survives but the definition of parterres has gone—waves of blue and white agapanthus now flow among Judas trees (*Cercis siliquastrum*). Close to the house a scalloped cistern is backed by a gabled wall decorated with rocaille work and with niches. A terrace walk runs along the wall of the house decorated with blue and white *azulejos* plaques depicting the arts and sciences. Between them are niches with fine marble figures on plinths with, above each one, a circular garland of fruit and foliage enclosing a relief bust. In the early years of the 21st century the gardens were not well cared for although they remained a delightful place to visit.   PT

Furukawa Garden ⊛

Tokyo, Japan, now a public park managed by Tokyo city, is the former reception hall of the Furukawa family, Meiji-period (1868–1912) copper mining magnates. The property was originally owned by the Mutsu family but came to the Furukawas when Furukawa Ichibe'e (1832–1903), founder of the Furukawa *zaibatsu* (financial conglomerate), adopted Mutsu Junkichi as his heir. The house and garden as they exist at present were the work of the third-generation Furukawa, Toranosuke (1887–1940), who hired Josiah Condor (1852–1920) to design a Western-style reception hall for the family. Condor was an English architect working in Japan designing a wide variety of buildings ranging from mansions for wealthy business

leaders to public halls and churches. Condor was also the author of *Landscape Gardening in Japan*, one of the first encyclopedic books on Japanese gardens written in English.

Adjoining the reception hall are terraced, western-style gardens laid out in a symmetrical geometric manner, including a well-known rose garden. The terraces step down to a pond garden designed in a traditional Japanese style by well-known Kyoto gardener, Ogawa Jihei (1869–1933). The garden centres on a large pond surrounded by tall broadleaf evergreen trees. The inclusion of both Western and Japanese-style gardens on the property, yet maintaining an almost complete separation of the two, is indicative of the sentiment of Meiji-period social attitudes and forms one of the salient features of this garden.   MPK

Füvészkert (Eötvös Loránd University Botanical Gardens) ⊛

Budapest, Hungary. The university's first botanical garden was founded by botany professor Jakob Winter in Nagyszombat (today Trnava, Slovakia) in 1771. The garden was transferred, together with the university, first to Buda, and then to Pest, where its first seed catalogue was published in 1788, with 1,656 species. From 1807 to 1817 its director was the noted Hungarian botanist Pál Kiatibel, and the number of seed types approached 4,000, while by 1830 (under the direction of Károly Haberle) it had reached 10,000. In 1847 the university purchased the Festetics Villa and garden in Pest, allowing the botanical garden to occupy one of the city's most important landscape gardens, which was embellished with a lake, mock ruins, and other spectacular elements. A palm house was built between 1863 and 1866, to be followed by the Victoria house, a number of greenhouses, and an alpine house. From 1894 to 1911 the garden was drastically reduced by the construction of the university hospital, and it remains in its truncated form today. After the destruction of the Second World War and the decades that followed, new collections were added from the 1960s to the 1980s, and the garden continues to maintain wide-ranging international connections to this day.

GA

Gaillon,

Eure, France, had one of the most celebrated Renaissance gardens, made by Cardinal Georges d'Amboise, Archbishop of Rouen, and minister of Louis XII (see MERCOGLIANO, PACELLO DA). The upper garden at Gaillon was made between 1502 and 1509, on a level terrace enclosed on one side by a gallery overlooking the valley of the Seine. It had a large wooden pavilion sheltering a marble fountain from Italy, and was divided into square beds, each planted differently with flowers, fruit trees, or box and rosemary cut into figures. One square had the arms of France made with small plants, another was in the form of a labyrinth. A unique feature was a private retreat in the park, known as Le Lidieu, with a chapel, a house, and a garden. After 1550 Cardinal de Bourbon extended it with a canal, a rock hermitage, and a sumptuous CASINO, the Maison Blanche, in High Renaissance mannerist style. At the same time a very much larger garden was made on the level ground below the upper garden. The gardens were redesigned by LE NÔTRE for Jacques Nicolas Colbert between 1691 and 1707. Only the terraced site of the upper garden now survives.   KASW

Galiana, Palacio de ⊛

Toledo, Spain. Toledo was occupied by Muslims from 711 to 1085. One of the great attractions was the alluvial soil of the Tagus, in a loop of which the city of Toledo was built. When the Venetian ambassador Andrea Navagiero visited Toledo in 1524 he left a description of the gardens and a Muslim palace. He found a great orchard, still irrigated by the Arabic *norias*—waterwheels used to draw water from the river. In the orchard he saw the ruins of a Muslim palace called Galiana—'The ruins show the palace to have been very fair and its site most peaceful' (*Viaggio fatto in Spagna, 1524-1526*). In the 11th century Toledo was an important independent Muslim state ruled from 1043 to 1075 by Al-Ma'mun. Al-Maqqari's *History of the Mohammedan Dynasties* (1840-3) describes a glass pavilion which Al-Ma'mun had built in a lake—water cascaded over the pavilion in which the King could sit 'without being touched by the water. He could also light wax candles if he wished.' Al-Ma'mun's palace of Galiana changed hands many times and is today privately owned. The buildings have been finely restored—their castellated towers a notable Toledo landmark. Impeccable new gardens of an ARTS AND CRAFTS character date from the 1960s.   PT

Gamberaia, Villa ⊛

Settignano, Tuscany, Italy. The 15th-century villa above Florence was purchased in 1718 by the Capponi family, who enlarged the villa, laid out fountains, added statues, constructed the GIARDINO SEGRETO opposite the house entrance, and created the long Bowling Alley leading to the NYMPHAEUM of Pan besides the lemon garden and *stanzone* (shelter for overwintering citrus plants) on a higher level. The main terrace was designed as a simple parterre with a rabbit island. In 1894 the property was bought by Princess Kashko Caterina Ghyka who, with her American friend Mrs Blood, totally altered the main terrace, creating four water panels edged with narrow flower beds, while maintaining the historic elements. On the east a semicircular pool was hedged by cypresses clipped into arches, the central arch revealing a view to the *duomo* of Florence in the valley below. The property passed to an American, Baroness Von Ketteler, in 1905. She, with advice from Cecil PINSENT, simplified the planting. Although Princess Ghyka's 'restoration' was criticized at the time for its lack of authenticity, the exquisite proportions, box hedging, and pillars of yew and reflecting water mirrors combine with its earlier Renaissance features to make Gamberaia a garden icon. In the early 1950s the property was purchased by Dottore Marcello Marchi who restored war damage. His family still maintain the garden to the highest standards.   PHo

garden city.

The social and intellectual origins of the garden city go back to the 18th and early 19th centuries when the Industrial Revolution in Europe prompted concern about the living conditions of workers. The French social theorist and utopian Charles Fourier (1772-1837) proposed the organization of society into self-sufficient communities of 1,800 people which he christened *phalanstères* (soon Anglicized to 'phalanstery'). *Phalanstères* were established but none succeeded. In 1783 at New Lanark (Lanarkshire, Scotland) the industrialist David Dale created a model village for workers in his cotton mill (the village survives and has recently been restored). This was taken over in 1800 by the Welsh social reformer Robert Owen, who was in touch with Fourier. In 1825 Owen set up a community on the lines of New Lanark at New Harmony (Indiana, USA) which was very short-lived and collapsed in 1837. Such communities were not merely disinterested attempts to house working people in decent accommodation—good living conditions produced healthy, and profitable, workers. The tradition of employers providing good housing for their workers produced many new 'model villages' in 19th-century England—at Salt's Mill (Bradford, Yorkshire) in 1853, at Bourneville (Birmingham) from 1879, and at Port Sunlight (Cheshire) from 1889.

The garden city was the invention of Ebenezer (later Sir Ebenezer) Howard (1850-1928), an English visionary social reformer and pioneer town planner. Howard was born in London but as a young man travelled widely, in particular to the USA and to France, and had admired the CHICAGO PARKS system and the tree-lined boulevards of Haussmann's Paris. In his book *Tomorrow* (1898) (republished as *Garden Cities of Tomorrow*, 1902) he proposed a self-supporting city in which the land would be held in common ownership. He saw land as the source of all wealth and its common ownership as fundamental to social equity. Howard also believed in the compatibility of science and religion and saw a harmonious community, in which the life of the town and that of the country were united in a new kind of city, as fundamental to human happiness. This community was referred to as Rurisville, Unionville, and, later and more attractively, as the Garden City. In *Tomorrow* he gives a plan of this ideal city. Circular in plan, it had at its centre a circular public park of 60 hectares/150 acres girdled by a continuous glass arcade and overlooked by municipal buildings. Radial boulevards extended outwards from the park and the residential quarter was laid out behind the municipal buildings. A circular 'grand avenue' behind the residential quarter formed a 'belt of green' separating it from the industrial outer ring of the city. The first garden city planned by Howard was Letchworth (Hertfordshire), which was founded in 1903. The layout was not as radical as Howard proposed in *Tomorrow*. Houses were built, in vernacular style, on curving streets linked by straight thoroughfares. Existing trees were preserved and houses had gardens at both front and back. Letchworth has been added to enormously since Howard's time but the broad residential streets, with mature planting, remain very attractive. Welwyn Garden City, also in Hertfordshire, was founded in 1920 with Howard's advice and follows the pattern of Letchworth. At Welwyn particular care was taken to preserve existing trees and hedgerows.

In the USA in 1837 the new city of Chicago (see CHICAGO PARKS) adopted as its motto *Urbs en horto* (City in a garden). The urban developer John S. Wright, from 1869, had the dream of 'a magnificent chain of parks and parkways' encircling the city 'that have not their equal in the world' and in the same year the parks began to take shape. In Australia the planning of CANBERRA in the early 20th century showed an enlightened attitude to landscaping. From the 19th century onwards landscaping, in particular the notion of the 'green belt', usually formed part of most urban planning. None of these, however, is quite the same as Howard's all embracing vision of the perfect city built on a new site and owned by the community. As is often the case with visionaries Howard was ridiculed in his lifetime (George Bernard Shaw called him 'Ebenezer the Garden City Geezer') but, despite the impracticalities of some of his theories, he was a great man. The author Lewis Mumford after visiting a house in Welwyn Garden City wrote, 'I have actually had a foot in utopia at one moment in my life' (M. R. Hughes (ed.), *Letters of Lewis Mumford and Frederic J. Osborn*, 1971). No city has ever been built in strict accordance with Howard's vision, but successful town planning, with well-conceived landscaping, in Europe and elsewhere, owes much to his inspiration. Had his influence been universal much of the meretricious squalor and ugliness of new city developments might have been avoided. Idealism may have its problems but so does the rapacity of commercial development.   PT

ROBERT BEEVERS, *The Garden City Utopia: A Biography of Ebenezer Howard* (1988).
PATRICK EYRES, 'Et in Utopia ego', *New Arcadian Journal*, Vol. 28: Winter/Spring (1988/9).

Garden Club of America,

founded in 1913 when the Garden Club of Philadelphia, then nine years old, invited eleven other clubs to create a national garden club. The club's original mission was 'to stimulate the knowledge and love of gardening among amateurs; to share the advantages of association through conference and correspondence in this country and abroad; to aid in protection of native plants and birds; and to encourage civic planting'. Since then the club's interests have expanded to include promoting environmentally correct ways not just of gardening but of improving the quality of life—whether it be working for safe fertilizers, pure drinking water, or the preservation of threatened prairies and marshes. Today there are 17,000 members based in communities all over America—from Hawaii to Maine. The GCA operates on the local and national levels. Members—almost all are women—meet regularly at 195 clubs in 40 states. They have lectures, organize flower shows, oversee civic beautification projects, encourage horticultural education in the community, and exchange information on their own gardens. The GCA president appoints chairs of committees and zone chairs who assemble national committees from local clubs in twelve geographical zones in the areas of horticulture, conservation, education, garden history, and flower arranging. They keep historic archives of American gardens, share botanical information, launch conservation projects, organize flower shows, back the saving of public lands and historic properties, and research environmental issues locally and nationwide. These GCA volunteers started their efforts in a world largely without cars, before power lawn mowers and widespread plant hybridization. Today improved technology not only makes gardening easier but enables the GCA's website and internet communication among members on important issues. At the same time the threats to the environment are far greater. The club's mission has been broadened as members focus their influence in an ever-growing range of work. They keep track of legislation and meet yearly for a three-day session in Washington to be briefed by Congress and to lobby for environment causes. The GCA has always been an important force in America on environmental and horticultural issues. During the world wars it put a tremendous effort into the production and preservation of food. Members canned, froze, and dehydrated home-grown vegetables, and sent seeds to England and Finland. The club initiated a campaign to ban billboards in 1919. And in the 1920s it started work to save the redwoods in northern California. The GCA remains an active institution today. The GCA Horticulture Committee publishes a newsletter of gardening advice for members and brochures for public distribution. This committee organizes seed and plant exchanges and distributes an invasive plant list. The National Affairs and Legislation Committee keeps watch on environmental legislation, working closely with the Conservation Committee in such areas as air quality and toxic substances, land use, and water and wetlands projects. The Garden History and Design Committee collects historic images—including slides and photographs documenting important American gardens. The club organizes an extensive scholarship programme, which offers financial aid for study in such areas as medicinal botany and landscape architecture.   ED

Garden Conservancy,

a national non-profit organization founded in 1989 by Francis CABOT which aims to preserve exceptional North American gardens as works of art that can be enjoyed by the public. It is the only national advocate for the preservation of exceptional American gardens as important and essential elements of the country's cultural heritage. The recognition by the conservancy of a garden as exceptional takes into consideration aesthetic, horticultural, and historical/cultural factors. The Garden Conservancy's rigorous selection process has helped establish it as an arbiter of national standards for horticultural and design excellence. Exceptional private gardens once known to a fortunate few have won wide recognition and appreciation as a result of the Garden Conservancy's sponsorship and assistance. The Ruth BANCROFT GARDEN, until 1989 the private domain of an outstanding garden artist, became the Garden Conservancy's inaugural project and now has a worldwide reputation as an exceptional example of dry garden beauty and sustainability. Ruth Bancroft's work of art, which inspired Cabot to create the Garden Conservancy, now has an established and growing infrastructure of staff, volunteers, and programmes that will sustain the garden beyond the lifetime of its creator. As it did with Ruth Bancroft, the Garden Conservancy achieves its goals primarily by working in collaboration with garden artists, their heirs or successors, and supporters. Typically, a local non-profit entity is established that assumes responsibility for preservation of a garden and its transformation and maintenance as a public resource. The conservancy contributes its assembled expertise in the areas of non-profit organization and management, fund-raising, law, landscape preservation, and horticulture to new, evolving, and already established gardens open to the public.

The ever-expanding list of gardens, which by the beginning of 2004 numbered more than 30, preserved with the assistance of the Garden Conservancy extends coast to coast and, in recent years, into Canada. It includes such important works of garden art as Beatrix FARRAND's Garland Farm (Maine) and Lockwood de Forest's VAL VERDE but also such rare landscapes as the gardens made by the inmates and officers of Alcatraz Island. Because the conservancy's particular focus is on helping gardens make the transition from private to public, its list of projects includes some gardens that continue as private residences and others that have become fully open to the public with regular visiting hours, research programmes, and educational offerings of their own. The work of the Garden Conservancy also includes advancing public appreciation of gardens and their cultural importance. Its largest educational effort is a national garden-visiting programme, called Open Days. Each year Open Days enlist hundreds of gardeners across the United States to open their private gardens to visitors. The programme was inaugurated in 1995 and has ushered hundreds of thousands of visitors through gardens that are normally strictly private. Other educational programmes include lectures, symposia, and garden-study tours.   GW

gardener, profession of.

J. C. LOUDON, in his *Encyclopaedia of Gardening* (1822), wrote, 'Very much of the comforts and pleasures which a private gentleman derives from his garden, and garden-scenery, depends on the qualifications of the gardener which he employs to manage them.' In ancient Roman gardens the *topiarius* was the person in charge of embellishing and caring for a garden—the profession is first mentioned in a letter from Cicero to his brother in 54 BC. Although the clipping of plants (see TOPIARY) may have formed part of his work, he was in charge of the *topia*, or place. It is evident that the *topiarius* was held in high esteem and the profession was mentioned in epitaphs on Roman gravestones. The importance of the qualities of the gardener is recognized in early books on gardening. In Jacques BOYCEAU DE LA BARAUDERIE's *Traité du jardinage* (1638) he says that we should choose a gardener with the same care with which we choose a garden plant: 'Or tout ainsi que nous choisissons pour notre jardin les arbres jeunes, la tige droite, de belle venue, bien appuyée de racine de tous costez, et de bonne race: prenons aussi un jeune garçon, de bonne nature, de bon esprit, fils d'un bon travailleur' ('For, just as we would choose for our garden young trees with a straight stem, of good origin, well provided with roots and of good stock: let us also take a young boy, of good nature, good wit, and the son of a good worker'). Boyceau de La Barauderie also thought that the young gardener should be taught to read and write

and to draw and paint, for his artistic gifts were as valuable as the purely horticultural. By the 17th century in Paris there was a guild of gardeners regulated by statutes, and the royal nursery of Roule (see PARIS PARKS AND GARDENS) organized a school of gardeners in the late 17th century. The status of the professional gardener, of whom André LE NÔTRE was the outstanding example, rose immensely in the reign of Louis XIV. Late in his reign, in 1713, a not very senior royal gardener, named Renard, was supplied with a suit of livery to undertake a visit to Spain on the King's behalf. In England the Worshipful Company of Gardeners was recognized by royal charter in 1605 but its origins go back to the 14th century. Royal gardeners in France, England, and Germany, in charge of very large and elaborate gardens, were the senior members of their profession. LE NÔTRE in France, Henry WISE in England, and P. J. LENNÉ in Germany combined the tasks of garden management and design to standards of the highest professionalism. Lenné, too, was one of the founders of the first garden school in Germany—the Königliche Gärtnerlehranstalt (Royal Garden College) in Berlin and Postdam in 1823. In 19th-century England the number of large gardens, sometimes belonging to newly rich families owing their fortunes to the Industrial Revolution, expanded enormously. Apart from running the pleasure grounds the head gardener was also in charge of the kitchen gardens which, for many households, were expected to produce all kinds of unseasonal fruit and vegetables. The great increases in new plants, and the introduction of new styles of gardening (such as tender bedding schemes), added new burdens to the head gardener. The flourishing of public, usually municipal, gardens in many European countries in the 19th century created a demand for professional gardeners of high quality. This was especially true in Germany where several garden schools were founded in the 19th century to meet the need (see GERMANY). In Britain municipal gardens also had a system of apprenticeship which provided excellent training for gardeners. This tradition continued well into the post-Second World War period but was profoundly weakened in the 1970s when local authorities found it economically impossible to fund their parks and gardens departments and the maintenance of public gardens was put out to 'competitive tendering'. In the 1990s the NATIONAL TRUST embarked on a scheme of modern apprenticeship in which school leavers spent three years learning the practice of gardening in Trust gardens supplemented by blocks of theoretical study at local colleges. Graduates earn an NVQ (National Vocational Qualification). The results have been excellent

but the cost is high—£40,000 for the three-year course.

Before the 19th century the names of English head gardeners in private non-royal service are rarely recorded. However, in that century professional gardeners flourished as never before and the head gardener achieved great status, having a profound influence on the garden in his care. Joseph PAXTON, who became head gardener at Chatsworth in 1826 (at the age of 23), may be regarded as the exemplar of the most successful professional gardener. To his horticultural and managerial skills he added great gifts as an architect and garden designer. By the age of 49, however, he was earning only £650 a year—the equivalent of around £33,000 in 2004. But the training of gardeners in Britain is well provided for. Excellent courses combining practical horticulture and botany are offered at the Royal Horticultural Society's garden at WISLEY and the ROYAL BOTANIC GARDENS, KEW. At Merrist Wood (Surrey) courses are run on garden design, horticulture, and landscaping. The National Trust for Scotland has its own School of Practical Gardening at Threave (Dumfriesshire). Many other regional schools offer courses in horticulture. However, despite great public interest in gardening, the status of the professional gardener is not high—not remotely as high as it was in the 19th century. No estate in the British Isles today has a head gardener comparable to Joseph Paxton and no one would regard a career in gardening as a way to the great wealth and social advancement that Paxton attained. The head gardener in charge of a great historic garden is not well paid—around £30,000 per annum seemed to be the maximum in 2004.   PT

gardenesque.

A term invented by J. C. LOUDON first used in *Gardener's Magazine* in 1832. Loudon wrote that 'there is such a character of art as the gardenesque, as well as the picturesque'. By this he intended that, instead of imitating nature, especially in its more picturesque manifestations, garden art could draw on its own intrinsic resources. With the growth of the urban population, and many middle-class gardeners looking for an aesthetic that would embrace small gardens, the gardenesque was the right idea at the right time. One of its principles was that individual plants, in particular trees and shrubs, should be planted unaccompanied so that their intrinsic virtues could be best displayed. The lonely monkey-puzzle (*Araucaria araucana*) or thicket of pampas grass (*Cortaderia selloana*) at the centre of a suburban lawn is perhaps the distillation of the gardenesque idea. Loudon believed that the juncture of the trunk of a tree with its root system was part of its beauty. Thus, he often planted trees (for example at the DERBY ARBORETUM) on mounds so that they were raised to a position of prominence and the upper part of the roots made visible.   PT

garden history.

'Why do we need a history of gardens?' asked John Dixon Hunt in *Perspectives on Garden Histories* (ed. Michel Conan, 1999). He answers his own question with the argument that we should have histories of gardens because gardens exist and they deserve a history just as various other subjects, perhaps less central to human life than gardens, have their histories (he cites clothes, ice cream, and luggage as subjects of recent historical books). He goes on to wonder why garden history lacks the rigorous methodology of other disciplines and hovers only on the margins of 'professional academic life'. In this regard it is possible that ice cream studies labour under the same handicaps. It is true, as Dixon Hunt acknowledges, that garden history has been almost entirely the preserve of the amateur—it is not a subject that has found a home in the modern university and it lacks the precise terminology of academic disciplines. Nonetheless, garden history has achieved much. Its methodological aimlessness has perhaps given it the freedom to explore the nooks and crannies which a more disciplined approach might have forbidden. Gardens, and gardening, are subjects too large and baggy to be easily caught in a conceptual framework. Garden history, to tell the story it seeks, needs to deal with a bewildering range of subjects—horticulture, botany, aesthetics, philosophy, social history, anthropology, and much else. The making of gardens is connected to so many aspects of life, and gardens themselves are infinitely various.

One of the pioneers of garden history was J. C. LOUDON, who showed a strongly political dimension in his views, not found again in British garden historical writing until far into the 20th century. In his *Encyclopaedia of Gardening* (1822) he gives the history of gardens in China, France, Germany, the Roman Empire, Russia, North America, with less comprehensive excursions to India, Persia, South America, and the British colonies. Here he is concerned to describe the kinds of gardens that each country made in different periods. Loudon, however, was not a mere writer of lists. He was also interested in 'gardening as affected by different forms of government, religions and states of society'. He thought that monarchies went in for show, republics for practicalities and a rather austere display. Louis XIV, he wrote, 'set the fashion not only in France but in Europe . . . but never, in all probability added a foot of ground to the garden of a single cottager, or placed an additional cabbage or potatoe on his table'. After the Revolution the French, Loudon noted, disapproved of the 'productions of forcing-houses, and the taste for double flowers'. He thought that those countries which had religions 'whose offices are accompanied by splendour and show' (like Italy) 'will be favorable to the culture of flowers and plants of ornament'. But countries (like his own Scotland) whose religion is 'founded in fear, and consequently gloomy and austere in its offices . . . cannot be said to encourage gardening'. Loudon thought that in 'Free states of society, where commerce is a leading pursuit, and property is irregularly distributed among all classes . . . gardening is likely to prosper in all its branches'. He thought that this had been the case in Holland and, in his own time, was true of Britain. Loudon was the first writer on gardens to formulate such patterns of influence.

Few historians in modern times have shown an interest in garden history and, on the whole, most garden historians have shown little interest in history at large. However, some books, with varying success, range more widely than formal accounts of the appearance of gardens. Keith Thomas's marvellous *Man and the Natural World* (1983) is a very rare example of a work of history which explores the landscape in a more general context. His discussion of 'cultivation or wilderness?', looking at the origins of the English landscape park and the taste for wild nature, brings out a richness of themes rare in garden historical writing. Simon Schama's *Landscape and Memory* (1995) bristles with sprightly inquisitiveness about mankind's relationship with landscape in many contexts and opens intriguing avenues of exploration. Allen S. Weiss's *Mirrors of Infinity* (1995), on the other hand, wrestles with the philosophical background to the French gardens in the 17th century, exploring the influence of Descartes and Pascal and, in the words of one reviewer, considering how such gardens are 'conceived historically as social and cultural symbolic space'. Such an enterprise will, on the whole, be more attractive to the denizens of academe than to the common reader. Tom Williamson's *Polite Landscapes: Gardens and Society in Eighteenth-Century England* (1995) discusses the English landscape park in a much wider economic, social, and political context than is usual. Michel Baridon in his *Les Jardins: paysagistes—jardiniers—poètes* (Gardens: Landscapers—Gardeners—Poets) (1998) addresses the gardening traditions of the world, paying much attention to the whole cultural background of gardens supported by quotations from a huge range of diverse reading. Baridon's very long book (over 1,200 pages), intended for a general readership, was in its fifth printing by 2000. Unlike most garden historical books intended for the general reader Baridon's is unsupported by colour plates—its few monochrome illustrations are relentlessly grey, in sharp contrast to the exceptionally lively text.

A particular interest in plants informs much English garden historical writing in recent times. A pioneer (amateur) garden historian of the late 20th century was John Harvey. He was the author of a remarkable history of European gardens in the Middle Ages (*Mediaeval Gardens*, 1981) and two deeply researched books on the English nursery trade—*Early Gardening Catalogues* (1972) and *Early Nurserymen* (1984). These two books cover the period in England from the 13th to the 19th century. They show a world of gardens in which plants are the chief interest and are revealing, too, in what they say about garden taste. The 18th century in England is sometimes described as being wholly in thrall to the landscape park. But this was the fashion among the more prosperous landed families. Immensely more numerous were the gardens of the less well off—and Harvey's books show that the 18th century was a period in which nurseries did a roaring trade in flowering plants of every kind—not merely the trees and shrubs demanded by the aristocratic patrons of Capability BROWN. *The Vanishing Garden: A Conservation Guide to Garden Plants* (1986) by Christopher Brickell and Fay Sharman does not sound like garden history at all. It turns out to be a detailed account of the introduction of plants to British gardens and the importance of conserving them. A characteristically English view of garden history throughout the world is seen in Penelope Hobhouse's *Plants in Garden History* (1992), which explores the trade in plants and their impact on the forms which gardens took. Her later book, *The History of Gardening* (2002), again covering the world's gardens, gives due prominence to the role of planting in garden design.

Garden history is a divided subject. Some academics, such as John Dixon Hunt, have made an attempt to establish it on a more academic footing. Many academics, on the other hand, regard it as a dilettante subject just as, in the past, art history was viewed with similar suspicion. Some art historians, however, have written admirable books which have found a wide general readership. Claudia Lazzaro's *The Italian Renaissance Garden* (1990) and Roy Strong's *The Renaissance Garden in England* (1979) and *The Artist and the Garden* (2000) please general readers without compromising scholarship. No university   ▶

offers a degree in garden history and most historians find it possible to do their work without referring to gardens. Garden history of an academic tone is uncongenial to many, possibly most, readers of books on gardening and lovers of gardens. On the other hand, vulgarization can produce horrible results. When television turns to garden history it sometimes presents it as a 'game show' in which there is a race against time to transform some historic site into what is thought to have been its pristine original state.

The value of garden history to students of landscape architecture, or of garden design, is another subject. It is hard to imagine any student of gardens or landscapes failing to be inspired and informed by the great designs of the past. In the hands of an excellent teacher the significance of such designs may be interpreted in ways that are invaluable to the student. The same is true of university courses in literature. However, the university does not necessarily have an immaculate record in guarding the great traditions. It is all too easy for the reputation of some writer to fall by the wayside because he or she does not conform to some critical theory. Some authors, loved by the

Colour plates

The *pigeonnier* reflected in the Lac des Cygnes at **Les Quatre Vents**, Quebec, Canada

The rose garden designed by **Graham Stuart Thomas** at Mottisfont Abbey, England

A characteristic **Jacques Wirtz** flourish–a late 20th-century mount of hornbeam and beech hedging in a garden near Antwerp, Belgium

Jacques Wirtz's own garden at Botermelk, Belgium, in which the old box **hedges** of a venerable kitchen garden have been clipped into billowing mounds

The 19th-century Great Palm House at **Schönbrunn**, Vienna, Austria

The baroque garden of the **Belvedere** Palace in Vienna, Austria

common reader (such as Anthony Trollope), are not taught in universities because they fail to present sufficient critical problems—they are too transparently enjoyable. It would be tragic to see garden history fall victim to such a curious belief or be overwhelmed by some fleetingly fashionable critical theory such as deconstructionism. Perhaps the great tradition of garden making and garden history is safer in the hands of the horticultural equivalent of the common reader.   PT

Garden History Society,
founded in England in 1965. A registered charity, its purpose is 'To promote the study of the history of gardening, landscape gardening and horticulture in all its aspects. To promote the protection and conservation of historic parks, gardens and designed landscapes, and to advise on their restoration. To encourage the structure for the creation of new parks, gardens and designed landscapes.' The society is supported by the subscriptions of its members who, by 2004, numbered 2,400. From 1973 it has published a journal, *Garden History*, which has done much to promote the aims of the society and to introduce a large number of people to the delights of garden history. The first editor of the journal was Dr Christopher Thacker. The journal metamorphosed from a periodical of charmingly amateur appearance, with typewritten text, to the present elegantly produced very professional publication, and the quality of information has never flagged. The early issues were rich in excellent and, to many people, unfamiliar material. The issue for Spring 1978, for example, had a pioneering article by Peter Hayden on BIDDULPH GRANGE—partly historical and partly a plea for its preservation—illustrated with photographs and a facsimile of the detailed catalogue of the sale of the Biddulph estate in 1871. This was typical of the early work of the society which, in 1983, led to its greatest achievement in the field of garden conservation. The society had, from the 1970s, floated the idea of listing historic parks and gardens in a way similar to the listing of architecture which was already in force. Under the National Heritage Act of 1983 English Heritage was empowered to compile a Register of Parks and Gardens of Special Historic Interest in England. Christopher Thacker was in charge of this and himself, between 1984 and 1988, inspected nearly 1,200 sites for the register. Listing in the register confers no protection of a site in law, but legislation was enacted which obliged local authorities to consult the Garden History Society about any planning application that affected a site on the register. The register was the first state-sponsored systematic listing in the world of any country's garden heritage

and is a key document in any research on English historic parks or gardens.

The activities of the society have also extended to organizing garden tours for members in different countries, immensely increasing knowledge of historic gardens in other countries. The editorial advisory board of *Garden History* in 2004 included garden historians from Germany, the Netherlands, Sweden, Italy, Australia, and USA. A society originally chiefly concerned with the gardens of its own country has much expanded its sphere of interest. *Garden History* publishes much international material and its Winter 2000 issue was entirely devoted to the Netherlands. Almost every notable English garden historian since the 1960s has been involved in the Garden History Society in one way or another, if only as a member. A group of enthusiastic, well-informed, and dedicated amateurs has had a profound influence on the course of garden history and the public awareness of the value of a country's garden heritage.   PT

Garden House, The ⊛
Buckland Monachorum, Devon, England, a garden laid out by a retired schoolmaster, Lionel Fortescue, from 1945 until his death in 1981. The setting on the edge of Dartmoor is wonderfully beautiful, a gently rolling landscape with plump hedgerows and distant prospects. The climate, however, is harsh and the most obvious place to make a garden was in the 16th-century walls of the remains of the Abbot of Buckland Abbey's house. This gives protection from the wind, but it is on a steep north-facing slope. Apparently undaunted Fortescue filled his garden with flowering shrubs—eucryphias, hoherias, magnolia, philadelphus, pieris, rhododendrons, and roses, all lavishly underplanted with bulbs and herbaceous perennials. An axial path on the lower slopes links two entrances, with great wisterias snaking along the old walls, and a pattern of paths, along or across the contours, gives crisp structure. Keith Wiley, who had worked with Fortescue, ran the garden after his death and has added immensely to it on land to the west of the house. Here are the sham ruins of a cottage smothered with cottage garden plants, a superb maple walk, a bank of creeping plants, and, as an eyecatcher at the end of a long walk, a miniature stonehenge.   PT

Garden in the Woods ⊛
Framingham, Massachusetts, USA, an 18-hectare/45-acre sanctuary of wildflowers indigenous to temperate North America, with an emphasis on the native flora of the north-east. The garden was developed over a period of

30 years by Will C. Curtis and Howard O. Stiles on a parcel of deciduous woodland purchased in 1930. The land provided them with a variety of plant habitats for their garden, from high ridges to low land, with stream, bog, and pond. In 1965, the two men transferred ownership of their creation to the New England Wildflower Society, the oldest plant conservation organization in the USA. Today, the society maintains the Garden in the Woods as its botanic headquarters, showcasing over 1,600 varieties of plants, including many rare and endangered species. Three miles of woodland trails are breathtaking in April and May with trout lilies (species of *Erythronium*), hepaticas, bloodroot (*Sanguinaria canadensis*), oconee bells (*Shortia galacifolia*), lady slippers (*Cypripedium* spp.), trilliums, and vast sweeps of native woodland phlox (*Phlox stolonifera*, *P. divaricata*) and foamflower (varieties of *Tiarella*), beneath flowering redbuds (*Cercis canadensis*) and shadblow (*Amelanchier* spp.). Native azaleas and dogwoods bloom later in spring with mountain laurel (*Kalmia latifolia*). Drifts of the scarlet cardinal flower (*Lobelia cardinalis*), blue gentians, and Turk's cap lilies (*Lilium superbum*) are highlights in summer. The naturalistic plantings of native flowers, shrubs, and trees are displayed, and labelled, in a number of different habitats: woodland, pine barren, western alpine, meadow, bog, and pond side. Two definitive books on growing and propagating native wildflowers, trees, and shrubs of the United States and Canada have been produced by the garden's nursery manager and propagator, William Cullina.

PD

Garden of Cosmic Speculation.
See PORTRACK HOUSE.

garden visiting.
Garden visiting is such a prominent aspect of mass tourism in the 21st century, chiefly in Europe and the USA, that it is easy to suppose that it is a modern phenomenon. In fact, certainly in Europe, it has a long and fascinating history, interesting not merely from the point of view of social history, and of fluctuations in garden taste, but also because so many garden visitors who have described their journeys were remarkable people.

From quite early on the need was seen to make some provision for garden visitors. When Louis XIII founded the Jardin Royal des Plantes Médicinales in Paris in 1626, which later became the Jardin des Plantes (see PARIS PARKS AND GARDENS), he allowed the provision of a seller of lemonade for the benefit of visitors who were admitted to the garden from 1640. In England in the 18th century the principle of allowing any

respectable person to visit a house and garden was widely recognized, part of the burden of *noblesse oblige*. The housekeeper was expected to be knowledgeable about the history of house and garden so that she could answer visitors' questions. By the 18th century comprehensive guides to the notable estates were published in Italy largely to satisfy the grand tour market. The first guide to a garden ever published in England was *A Description of the Gardens of Lord Viscount Cobham, at Stow in Buckinghamshire* in 1745. STOWE was the most visited English garden of its day welcoming visitors from all over Europe and elsewhere—Thomas JEFFERSON came in 1786 (he was critical—'The Corinthian arch has a very useless appearance'). By the early 19th century garden visiting in England was such a widely accepted pastime that the 6th Duke of Devonshire told his staff that the fountains were to be turned on at the request of any visitor, 'irrespective of social class'.

At different periods there were different especially compelling reasons for visiting gardens in certain countries. The Low Countries in the 17th century were a region of brilliant nurserymen and was seen as a great source of plants—John EVELYN in England recommended it as the best source of trees for avenues. France in the late 17th century had the irresistible allure of André LE NÔTRE's great baroque landscapes which became influential throughout Europe. For some reason it is not until the 19th century that the Islamic gardens of southern Spain began to be noticed by foreign visitors. The American writer Washington Irving was a pioneer devotee, spending three years in Spain from 1826 to 1829 and living on the ALHAMBRA hill in Granada. The English 18th-century landscape park was the object of the greatest fascination to visitors and it took the place of French baroque gardens as a widely adopted international style. But the single country to which all garden lovers were repeatedly drawn was Italy. The detailed history of garden visiting starts with the history of the modern garden, in Renaissance Italy.

Michel de MONTAIGNE, a man who took a discerning interest in everything of interest, visited Italy in 1580-1 and his *Journal du voyage en Italie* gives the most vivid descriptions of what he saw in such gardens as the Villa D'ESTE at Tivoli, the Villa PRATOLINO near Florence, the Villa FARNESE at Caprarola, and the Villa LANTE at Bagnaia. When Montaigne saw these gardens they were very recently completed—the oldest of them, the Villa d'Este, was started in 1559 and the latest, the Villa Farnese, was started in 1570. How different this is from the modern garden tourist who will be chiefly interested in gardens of the past—VERSAILLES, the Alhambra, MONTICELLO, or Het LOO. In the late 20th

century some of the most popular of gardens were reconstructions of period styles such as the Château de VILLANDRY, and GIVERNY, each of which attracts more than 400,000 visitors a year. Travellers in 16th-century Italy knew that the houses and gardens they visited were remarkable new things and immediately saw their point. When Montaigne visited the Villa Lante it was only twelve years old and already famous. Pope Gregory XIII had scrutinized the garden two years previously and found it 'exceedingly beautiful and delightful'. Sixteenth-century popes were knowledgeable about gardens and, besides, the Villa Lante was built by a cardinal. Montaigne was by no means the only foreign garden visitor in 16th-century Italy. The Scot Fynes Moryson, an indefatigable European traveller, visited Italy in 1594 and published an account of *An Itinerary Containing his Ten Years Travell* in which he describes several of the Italian gardens he saw. The German architect Heinrich Schickhardt lived in Florence in 1600 and visited the Villa Pratolino. All these reports of Italian gardens in their heyday are especially valuable to modern garden tourists for they are an indispensable aid in a proper understanding of the gardens. For example, the way in which the modern visitor approaches the Villa d'Este at Tivoli gives a false impression of the garden. For reasons of convenience, and what the modern tourism industry calls 'visitor flow', the garden is approached through the rooms of the *piano nobile* of the villa at the top of the terraces. In the past visitors would approach from the side through a covered passage—an arbour and then a pergola—from whose shade they would emerge to be dazzled by the garden façade of the villa suddenly, dramatically, revealed and the immense spread of astonishing gardens flowing down the slope before it. There are many other instances of the character of historic gardens being falsified for the convenience of tourists. In the case of many 18th-century English landscape parks, in which the manner of approaching the house was often treated with great subtlety, one-way routes for cars may obliterate this subtle notion. Both STOURHEAD and STUDLEY ROYAL suffer in this way, especially the latter.

The history of garden visiting in Italy is a long and busy one, reaching the height of its influence in the grand tour of the 18th century. By this time the gardens of the Renaissance were in decline and many grand tourists saw them in a state of neglect. This gave rise to a curious misapprehension about their character. When a garden is neglected the first thing to go is the detailed flower planting, with more long-lived plantings of hedges, topiary, and trees surviving. Thus it was supposed that the Italian

Renaissance gardener had no interest in flowering plants, which was quite wrong. The Renaissance was a brilliant period for the study of plants—botanic gardens, the earliest in Europe, were founded in PADUA and PISA in 1545 and 1544 respectively. Italy has remained the greatest of garden visiting countries—but almost entirely because of its historic gardens. It remains all too easy, in Henry James's words, to be seduced by 'that element of the rich and strange for the love of which one visits Italy'. James's friend and compatriot Edith Wharton was an especially observant visitor and wrote an excellent book, *Italian Villas and their Gardens* (1904). Later in the 20th century Georgina Masson's scholarly, original and finely written *Italian Gardens* (1961), by an Englishwoman living in Rome, stimulated a new wave of visitors.

Until the 20th century, and the advent of mass tourism, garden visiting was the pursuit of a cultivated, and prosperous, minority. Since the Second World War, however, it has immensely widened its appeal. The number of gardens accessible to visitors rises every year. Britain has by far the greatest number—well over 3,500 are listed in *Gardens of England and Wales Open for Charity* (known universally as the 'Yellow Book'). In France the most comprehensive guide, Michel Racine's *Jardins en France*, lists 850 'jardins remarquables'. In Germany Ronald Clark's *Gärten* includes 850 parks and gardens. In Belgium, a country with a population of 10,000,000, *Le Guide des jardins en Belgique* by Christine de Groote describes 350 gardens. In the United States of America there are, in relation to the population, relatively few gardens open to the public. Even so, *The National Geographic Guide to America's Public Gardens*, by Mary Zuazua Jenkins, finds 300 places to list, the great majority of them owned by institutions of one kind or another (it should be explained that in the USA a public garden is one that is open to the public and may be privately owned). A new phenomenon became apparent in the beginning of the 21st century— the making of gardens that are not public parks designed specifically to attract the public. The EDEN PROJECT, which opened to the public in 2001, was planned in great detail to receive very large numbers of visitors. Easily one of the largest items on its budget was the building of new roads connecting the garden to the public road system.

At the heart of this frenzied expansion of garden visiting lies an unhappy paradox. In the year 2000 the Alhambra received 2.2 million visits with, at the height of the summer, queues crawling painfully slowly through its serene patios. It was the visitors themselves that had become, by a very wide margin, the most strikingly visible feature. The Alhambra is open on every day of the year but a very disproportionate number of visitors come between Easter and the end of August. Other small gardens, with far fewer visitors than the Alhambra, like Monet's Giverny or Vita Sackville-West's and Harold Nicolson's SISSINGHURST CASTLE, undergo a horrible transformation when inundated with visitors. Apart from the impact on their atmosphere, the crush of visitors also has a decided impact on the fabric of the gardens—no path of finely mown turf can withstand the tread of 4,000 visitors a day. Russell PAGE in his *Education of a Gardener* (1962) describes the adjustments he made at Longleat (Wiltshire) to accommodate visitors. Paths had to be much wider to avoid congestion and garden features had to be big and bold because large numbers of visitors tend to move fairly fast and have no time to take in anything that requires close scrutiny. In Britain there is a curious phenomenon created by the NATIONAL TRUST. Now owning more than 100 gardens that open regularly to the public, the National Trust has created a certain homogenization of the garden visiting experience. There is the 'livery' of the Trust, its distinctive colour scheme; shops selling more or less identical goods through which visitors are usually forced, as the only exit route, when they leave; a café or restaurant selling very similar food. It is sometimes all too easy to have the impression that one is visiting a National Trust garden rather than an idiosyncratic work of art. But even in privately owned gardens these great numbers of visitors bring in their train increasing commercialization, with the need for car parks, lavatories, tea rooms, and shops to sell postcards and gifts. All this means that gardens have in their essence become, simply, something completely different, and, more often than not, something at odds with the impulse that created them. The refuge from the pressures of an overcrowded world, the setting for a life of cultivated *villeggiatura* (withdrawal to a country retreat), the place pervaded by harmony where nature and art hold sway, has become just another busy stopping point on the tourist's route. The historian Jacob Burckhardt, who died in 1897, was worried about the effect of photography on the study of architecture. Before photography students of architecture, amateur and professional, used to draw what they saw. Burckhardt noted that this meant, whatever the quality of the drawing, that the buildings at least had to be studied carefully—it made you look at them. He believed that photography would remove the need to look at one's subject—you could always scrutinize your picture when you got home. How far-sighted Burckhardt was, and how true his fear has become in the case of gardens. The hectic pace of the garden tour leaves no time to dwell on any part of the garden—best to snap it quickly and get on to the next.   PT

garden writing.

Styles of garden writing are as varied as gardens themselves. The site, the plants, the buildings and ornaments, and the history are all parts of the essential nature of a garden. In some gardens it is the owner, or ghosts of past owners, who may be the ruling spirit of the place. All these, however, may be meticulously described without evoking the actual experience of being in the garden. Being in a garden, willingly submitting to it, is an experience of a very personal and interior kind. Few garden writers attempt to describe it. Louis XIV was a garden writer of a pioneer kind whose approach, somewhat surprisingly, is as impersonal as could be. In his book *Manière de montrer les jardins de Versailles* (How to Display the Gardens at Versailles) he set down exactly how a visitor should proceed about the garden, with directions as to what should be seen and admired at every turn. The manuscript text (sometimes amended in the King's own hand) exists in six versions, with slight variations of the route, composed between 1689 and 1705, and it was never published in the King's lifetime. It is not in the slightest evocative, nor does it glory in kingly magnificence (the sun symbolism of the garden is not mentioned). It is a series of laconic snapshots of the garden's essential ingredients linked by a route that will best display their beauties. The *sens de la visite* (the visitor's route) is an important part of the atmosphere of many French gardens. Jacques-François Blondel writing about VERSAILLES in 1756 observed how quickly one runs out of ways of applauding its marvels and it is best for visitors to 'judge for themselves what art and intelligence can achieve when taken to the highest degree of perfection'. On the other hand Stendhal found that too much to admire was a rich diet and he found it easy to suffer from the 'ennui de l'admiration' (the tedium of admiring).

Pliny the younger's writings on his gardens in the 1st century AD are among the earliest in the West. But there is no European book on gardening remotely as ancient as the Japanese SAKUTEIKI (Record of Garden Making) dating from the 11th century and attributed to Tachibana no Toshitsuna. In European medieval writings there are all sorts of fleeting references to gardens. The cultivation of medicinal plants, or the science of agriculture, loomed much larger than any consideration of the aesthetics of gardens. It is significant that the first printed book in England devoted to gardening is *The Crafte of Graffynge and Plantynge of Trees* (*c*.1520) and other early books, such as William TURNER's *The Names of Herbes* (1548), are devoted to herbs. William Lawson's *A New Orchard and Garden* (1623) is largely a practical manual but it also recognizes the psychological benefits of gardening to garden owners: 'to renue and refresh their senses, and to call home their overwearied spirits.' Francis BACON, writing at almost exactly the same time, described the garden as 'the greatest refreshment to the spirits of man' in his essay 'Of Gardens' (1625) which remains one of the best descriptions of the delights of gardening and gardens.

Systematic descriptions of gardens are found in the 16th century with writers like Michel de MONTAIGNE, whose accounts of the Italian Renaissance gardens are detailed, lively, critical, and competitive (he finds PRATOLINO not as beautiful as the most beautiful houses in France). It is the richness of detail that is so striking in Montaigne, not merely of such obvious things as the architecture, automata, and the *giochi d'acqua* (water games) such as the 'seats which squirt water at your buttocks'. At the Villa MEDICI, Castello, he describes in detail a tunnel arbour 'woven very thickly of scented trees like cedars, cypress, oranges, lemons and olives, the branches so interwoven that it is easy to see that the sun, even at its height, would never pierce it'. John EVELYN in the 17th century wrote about some of the gardens visited by Montaigne and notes many of the same features but very rarely comments on planting. In about 1680 John Aubrey described Francis Bacon's garden at Gorhambury House in Hertfordshire with admirably vivid detail, from the mosaic patterns at the bottom of pools to the multifarious trees used in avenues ('viz. Elme, chestnut, beach, hornebeame, Spanish-ash, cervice-tree, & c.'). Aubrey is better known as the author of piercing portraits of his contemporaries rather than accounts of gardens but to his description of Francis Bacon's garden he brought the same skills as those he used to describe people—a careful scrutiny of what lay before him and sharp judgement of what was significant. Celia Fiennes (1662–1741) rode on horseback over much of England in the late 17th and early 18th centuries, a key period of English garden making, and described with panache what she saw. There is something of the journalist in her, pouncing with relish on the telling detail. The accuracy of her garden descriptions may be corroborated by comparing them with the KIP engravings which cover much of the same ground. In the 18th century much garden writing is more concerned with theory than

with practice. A notable exception is Philip MILLER's *Gardeners Dictionary* (1731), an immensely influential book of its time and the forerunner of many subsequent gardening reference books. By 1768 it was in its 8th edition and Miller noted the 'number of plants now cultivated in England are more than double those which were here when the first edition of this book was published'.

The 19th century was the greatest period of garden writing. J. C. LOUDON's *Encyclopaedia of Gardening* (1822), which covers everything from how to cultivate broad beans to the most notable gardens in Russia, is one of the greatest gardening books ever written. Loudon's style was serviceable rather than elegant but he wrote clearly, his curiosity was unlimited, and his energy astounding. He wrote another gigantic reference book, *Arboretum et Fruticetum Britannicum* (8 vols. 1838), several other books, and a huge quantity of journalism. At the other end of the century William ROBINSON occupies a similarly dominant position with his *The Wild Garden* (1870) and *The English Flower Garden* (1883) and, like Loudon, much journalism. Robinson's boisterous and sometimes pugnacious style won him many admirers (and a few enemies) and he had a profound influence on garden taste. Robinson's colleague Gertrude JEKYLL had an attractive, intimate style and her writings, always based on her own deep experience, decisively shaped the direction gardening took in the 20th century.

The outpouring of garden writing in the 20th and 21st centuries has been immense, in books, newspapers, and magazines. However, the great improvement in colour printing, and in the quality of garden photography, has resulted in an emphasis on 'picture-led' articles and books in which the quality of the text is of secondary importance. Equally, much of the information which earlier had been contained in books is now transmitted on television. Some garden writers are fine stylists but, increasingly, their craft is scarcely valued. Michael Pollan's *Second Nature: A Gardener's Education* (1991) is in the tradition of garden autobiographies, describing the author's struggle to make a garden in 'five acres of rocky intractable hillside' in Connecticut. But it is beautifully written and widens out into much broader perspectives than those of personal anecdote.   PT

Garenne-Lemot, La ⊛
Gétigné, Loire-Atlantique, France, the creation in the first quarter of the 19th century of Frédéric Lemot (d. 1827), a sculptor who had worked in Rome and was seduced by the picturesque beauties of the Sèvre valley. The nearby town of Clisson had been all but

destroyed in 1793 during the anti-republican war in the Vendée and Lemot, in collaboration with like-minded artists and architects, rebuilt it giving it an Italianate feel. He bought an estate on the other side of the river facing the town and started to lay out a romantic garden influenced by his sojourn in Italy. An Italianate villa was built facing south-west across the river. Lemot planted hundreds of trees, in particular poplars, and erected a series of ornamental buildings and monuments along a walk planned to take in the beauties of the river bank and views back towards Clisson. At the head of a rocky outcrop above the river he built the Temple of Vesta, copied from that at Tivoli. It was planned to have a naturalistic cascade plummeting down the rocks but this was never put into place. Along the path following the river are a tomb with the inscription *Et in Arcadia ego*, an aedicule (a columned niche with a pediment) of brick and stone, a grotto dedicated to Héloïse (the lover of Abelard), a rock celebrating Rousseau, and much else of a picturesque kind. Gustave Flaubert knew the garden and scoffed at it in *Par les champs et par les grèves* (1847)—Héloïse's grotto left him unmoved although he thought it might make a convenient dining room, with the river at hand to cool the wine.   PT

Garzoni, Villa ⊛
Collodi, Italy. One of a series of magnificent villas built into the foothills of the Apuan Alps east of Lucca, Garzoni has a spectacular baroque garden standing to the side of the villa, a steep hillside of terraces, stone and terracotta statues, and fountains overlooking an elaborate parterre. Originally an allegorical layout, its meaning lost over the centuries, it is still possible to identify certain features. At the top of the garden the statue of Fame blows a triumphant conch, lower down statues of the Serchio river of Lucca and the Florentine Arno frame a pool and descending cascade; a Grotto of Neptune is hidden between staircase ramps. On each narrow terrace a transverse alley leads off towards the villa hidden in woodland. One walk crosses a bridge over a ravine lined with gigantic bamboos. An old labyrinth has almost disappeared but the French-style parterre, surrounded by topiary hedges, with pools and gigantic water sprays has been restored with elaborate and gaudy planting, best appreciated from above.   PHo

Gatchina ⊛
Russia. The palace and park, 45 km/28 miles south-west of St Petersburg, belonged to Catherine the Great's favourite, Count Grigorii Orlov, from 1765 until his death in 1783. Catherine bought it for her son, Grand Duke

Paul, later Paul I. Paul wanted formality near the palace and in the 1790s the Private Garden was added featuring geometrically clipped trees, BOSQUETS, TREILLAGE, and a considerable collection of Italian statues and vases. Two other formal gardens were inspired by Dutch gardens. An octagonal basin, the Carp Pool, with a canal separated the formal areas from the park. There was also a formally laid out botanic garden (2.6 hectares/7 acres), but its appearance changed in the 19th century when oaks and limes were planted there.

Water is the main element in the park (143 hectares/388 acres), created by John BUSCH assisted by two other British gardeners, Charles Sparrow and James Hackett. Picturesque walks take the visitor along the banks of lakes, pools, and watercourses with islands, bridges, and other architectural features enhancing the scenery. The water is unusually clear at Gatchina, its mirror surfaces reflecting grey willows, dark green conifers, and the changing patterns of the sky.

A visit to the Prince de Condé's CHANTILLY in 1782 had greatly impressed the Grand Duke and the Grand Duchess, and a Sylvia, a Temple of Love, an Island of Love, and a small Birch House, made to look like a wood pile but with a luxuriously appointed interior, at Gatchina were echoes of Chantilly. When the Prince de Condé was a refugee after the French Revolution, Paul had the Priory Palace (architect N. A. Lvov, 1751–1803) built for him by the Black Lake—the Prince was Prior of the Sovereign Order of the Knights of Malta, of which Paul was Grand Master.

Gates led from the park into a game reserve (400 hectares/988 acres) where deer, wild boar, and bison were kept and hunted.   PH

gate.
The gate is a garden feature of the greatest versatility. Supported on a pair of grand piers, or encased in a turreted gatehouse, it may serve as a scene-setting flourish at the entrance to a garden. At the distant end of a path it makes an appetizing EYECATCHER. An ornamental gate of wrought iron or of railings may simultaneously draw attention to what lies beyond but, at the same time, coyly veil it. Gertrude Jekyll in *Garden Ornament* (1918) lays down the universal principle of choosing gates for gardens—'An honest relation must exist between the entry and what is entered.' A picket gate leading from the cottage garden into an orchard is entirely in harmony with the scene and so are the grandly exquisite late 17th-century wrought-iron gates by Jean Tijou masking the Privy Garden at HAMPTON COURT PALACE. Apart from its role as an eyecatcher or as a frame, the gate also influences the way in which a garden is

experienced. Giusto UTENS's painting of the Villa PETRAIA in the late 16th century shows a terrace below the front of the house with simple gates at each end leading to a flight of steps flanking a pool. The gates here form a temporary barrier, causing the visitor to stop and look—in this case over the whole garden spread out below—before continuing. Gates are not common in Italian Renaissance gardens and when they do appear they are used purposefully and in harmony with the garden's atmosphere. A gate may be used to signal a change in mood. At PACKWOOD HOUSE a pair of 18th-century wrought-iron gates supported on brick piers separates a flowery walled garden from an austere garden of monumental yew topiary. In Britain the great period of wrought-iron work was from the late 17th to the early 18th century. A superb example is the pair of wrought-iron gates at TREDEGAR HOUSE made by the Bristol blacksmiths William and Simon Edney between 1714 and 1718. They ornament a courtyard and originally opened a vista of a lime avenue. One of the finest blacksmiths of his time was Robert Davies (*fl.* early 18th century) of Wrexham, who probably supplied the beautiful wrought-iron gates for ERDDIG. Now at the end of the avenue in the formal garden, they were formerly part of the entrance courtyard. Working with his brother John, he made the gates at CHIRK CASTLE that now, painted an ethereal white, form the main entrance to the park. In the ARTS AND CRAFTS period in England architects paid special attention to gates. In 1897 C. F. A. Voysey designed a house and garden for the publisher Sir Algernon Methuen, New Place in Surrey, in which he planned every detail, including a wrought-iron gate with a bold pattern of stylized foliage. Robert Weir Schultz designed in 1903, for a 'Dutch' garden at Tylney Hall in Hampshire, a pair of magnificent wrought-iron gates with an intricate pattern of intertwined roses—although the garden is now a swimming pool the gates remain, and the house is now a hotel. A small house designed in cottagey character in 1912 by M. H. Baillie Scott (1865–1945) for a client in Cambridge has a front garden with a white-painted picket fence and gate precisely in keeping with the style of the house. In the late 20th century, at PORTRACK HOUSE, Charles Jencks commissioned a futuristic wrought-iron gate formed of Soliton waves (pulses of energy).

Gates do not need to be elaborate to play a powerful part in a garden's atmosphere. The garden designer Russell PAGE in his *The Education of a Gardener* (1962) describes the garden of a friend in Norfolk where a sequence of 'plain but well-designed . . . painted wood-railed gates' both enlivens and gives harmony to

a long axis linking a kitchen garden, paddock, and woodland on a flat site.   PT

Gaude, La ⊛
Les Pinchinats, Bouches-du-Rhône, France, built in the 18th century. It overlooks a terraced garden, possibly of the same date as the house but comprehensively restored after the Second World War. The house faces south over a moated mazelike box parterre with, beyond it, a second terrace with a lawn and a circular pool with a PATTE D'OIE of walks radiating from it. Finely kept, and in perfect keeping with the classical spirit of the house, it is a model garden of its kind.   PT

Gaudí, Antoni
(1852–1926), Spanish architect whose life was centred on Barcelona where great works by him may still be seen, some of them, like the church of the Sagrada Família, still dazzlingly incomplete. His meeting with Eusebi Güell I Bacigalupi, a cultivated textile tycoon, was crucial. It was probably through him that Güell was exposed to the influence of the English ARTS AND CRAFTS movement and the Pre-Raphaelites (he loved the poetry of Rossetti). His first commission for Güell, in 1883, was a hunting box at Sitges. His architecture shows an immensely wide range of influences—he relished strongly organic shapes, the brilliant colouring of ceramic tiles often contrasting with sturdy monumentalism. His Casa Batlló (Barcelona, 1904–6) intermingles exuberant decorativeness (he was a connoisseur of sculptural and sometimes brilliantly coloured chimney pots) with the exquisite, monastic austerity of white arched passages in the upper floor. Had he lived in the 18th century he would have been one of the busiest of designers of garden buildings. His orientalist Casa El Capricho (Santander, 1883–5), with its soaring minaret, is a house conceived as a wildly ornamental garden pavilion. At Santa Coloma de Cervelló, south of Barcelona, where his patron was Güell, Gaudí designed (1898–1917) a grotto-like crypt of intricately patterned vaulting—all that was completed of a projected church. His one great landscape, the Park GÜELL, shows what he could do as a garden designer. The terracing supported on organic columns, as natural as stalactites, is set against sparkling buildings of festive decorativeness.
  PT

gazebo.
A garden building, the word deriving from jokey Anglo-Latin for 'I shall look about'. Originally, in the 18th century, it was a turret, lantern, or some other vantage point in a building but it has come to mean an

ornamental building of slightly uncertain character, without the gravitas of a temple nor with the frivolity of something more whimsical. It carries undertones of cheerful if insubstantial and ephemeral prettiness, made of trellis, clapboarding, or rustic work.   PT

Generalife, El ⊛

Granada, Andalusia, Spain. The Generalife was built at the beginning of the 14th century on the slopes below the ALHAMBRA and at some distance from it. The word is supposedly derived from the Arabic *Janna al-'Arif*, meaning 'Garden of the Architect', but this is far from certain. It seems likely that the Generalife formed a kind of country house, a retreat for the Sultan from the busy life of the palaces of the Alhambra—in exactly the way that MARLY was regarded by Louis XIV. The atmosphere of the Generalife is quite different from that of the Alhambra. The Generalife is a relatively compact group of buildings, with a single substantial court, the Patio de la Acequia. It is emphatically in the country and there were probably orchards here and a park of wild animals. Originally there were two other palaces nearby but by 1524 when the Venetian ambassador Andrea Navagero described the 'magnificent garden' here, with myrtles and oranges (*Viaggio fatto in Spagna, 1524–1526*), the other palaces were derelict.

The Patio de la Acequia is one of the most photographed views of any garden. A long, slender canal is flanked by regular rows of water jets which arch over towards each other to form graceful plumes. Flower beds on either side are filled with orange trees and cypresses underplanted with smaller flowering plants. Raised walks give fine views down onto the patio with breezy miradors at its northern end and western side. The northern mirador stands above a pavilion which opens out where it faces the garden in a finely decorated loggia. In 1958 the Generalife was badly damaged by fire and the subsequent restoration revealed much about the original garden. Originally there were four beds here arranged like an elongated quadrant, with a long north–south axis and a short east–west axis, each aligned on a MIRADOR. The soil of planted beds was discovered at a much lower level than the surrounding paving. It seems that the original planting would have risen to the level of the paving—like a carpet. Also discovered was the original irrigation system which suggests that there may have been a pool in the west *mirador* linked to a central fountain where the axes intersected. The arching water jets that are seen today are not original. Water played an important part in the original garden at the Generalife. Andrea Navagiero particularly commented on it,

pointing out that some water jets could be controlled by a tap as a watery surprise to incautious visitors—exactly like the GIOCHI D'ACQUA of Italian Renaissance gardens. A water staircase to the east of the Generalife buildings may date from the 14th century. From the south the Generalife is approached by a sequence of gardens enclosed in sculpted hedges, with pools, fountains, and parterres laid out by the Granadan architect Francisco Prieto-Moreno after the Second World War. The long, patchy, and sometimes mysterious history of the Generalife has resulted in a place of potent and delightful if enigmatic atmosphere.   PT

D. FAIRCHILD RUGGLES, *Gardens, Landscape, and Vision in the Palaces of Islamic Spain* (2000).

genetic modification of plants.

At present, genetically modified (GM) plants are not grown commercially in the UK. Such plants are grown predominantly in North and South America and Asia, and include the major broad-acre commodity crops such as canola, cotton, soybean, and corn. Since its advent in the early 1980s, GM crop technology has advanced considerably and many hundreds of plant species can now be genetically modified.

GM plants are conventionally engineered by introducing one or more foreign genes into the recipient plant's own genetic material (the chromosomes), which resides within the nucleus of every cell. Conventionally, the new gene in turn introduces a coded protein that can give the plant an improved or new characteristic. To assist the process, it has also been found necessary to introduce an additional gene to enable the few genetically modified cells to be selected from among the millions of unaltered cells. This additional gene is commonly antibiotic or herbicide resistant, so that when an antibiotic or herbicide is introduced to the culture medium, the GM cells survive and the rest die. Each genetically engineered cell can then be regenerated, as with conventional vegetative plant propagation, into a fully mature plant (i.e. each cell is 'totipotent').

Although it was first adopted to engineer herbicide tolerance or pest resistance in commercial food crops, GM technology can equally well be applied to garden plants. Traits such as hardiness (tolerance to drought or cold), habit, flower characteristics, growth on particular soils, and improved pest and disease resistance can all be engineered. This has been made possible by the vast and accelerating increase in fundamental scientific knowledge of plant genetics, growth, development, and biochemical pathways over the last 40–50 years. Our knowledge of plant hormones and their role in development, for example, has led to

genes being used to alter plant architecture by means of hormone biosynthetic pathways. There is now a wealth of knowledge on *homeotic* genes that control all aspects of the flowering process and floral development. These genes can be used to alter flowering time, achieve repeat flowering, and alter the structure of the flower (creating double petals for example). Flower colour has been manipulated experimentally and successfully in *Petunia* and *Lisianthus* species by introducing genes which produce proteins that alter the biosynthesis of natural pigments, the flavonoids. Significant pests of garden plants, in particular container-grown plants, are weevils and beetle larvae which feed on the roots and can lead to the plant's death. The targeted and precise introduction of genes that make highly selective insecticidal proteins, such as those from the organically approved bacterium *Bacillus thuringiensis* (Bt), have been hugely beneficial in broad-acre agriculture (178 million hectares/440 million acres of GM crops—ten times the whole agricultural area of the UK—grown globally since 1996), as they are efficient at conferring pest resistance.

GM may therefore be used to bring about a significant improvement in garden plants, providing a powerful alternative to slow, imprecise, and unpredictable breeding methods. It also provides opportunities for new traits to be engineered by the addition of single genes sourced from plant species that would not have been viable in a conventional cross. Unlike 'traditional' breeding, in which a large number of complex undesirable genetic characteristics may be inherited along with the trait of interest, or the novel introduction of alien species with 30,000 foreign genes, GM offers precision. Perhaps the most important potential application of GM in garden plants lies in flower colour, for only GM has the potential to introduce unique and novel flower colours.

As with all new technologies, the potential risks, whether perceived or real, must be considered. GM plants producing foreign proteins, be they natural insecticides or proteins conferring antibiotic resistance, could have a real or theoretical impact on ecology, human health, or non-target organisms. A major concern is the presence of the foreign gene and its coded protein in pollen. In nature, it is possible for cross-pollination to occur between GM and non-GM plants that are closely related and sexually compatible. Numerous studies have been and are being carried out to assess pollen viability, pollen dispersal, and compatibility between related species, on a case-by-case basis. There is also a remote potential for novel proteins, which may be expressed in pollen, to be toxic or allergenic to non-target species. Large numbers of investigations have assessed any possible non-target effects of foreign protein-producing GM plants on insect biodiversity. So far, field trial results have indicated no significant risk.

With reference to antibiotic resistance selectable marker genes, one speculative concern has been that these genes could be transferred to mammalian gut bacteria following consumption of a GM plant food product. The notion that humans could, as a consequence, become resistant to the relevant antibiotic has been refuted since there is no scientific evidence from genomics studies to suggest that such horizontal gene transfer occurs *in vivo* (at least not in the last 600 million years). Indeed, we consume large amounts of foreign (plant) DNA (genes) every day in our food without any transfer to our intestinal microflora. It should also be noted that the statutory risk assessment of GM plants for open-field release is a rigorous process, far more stringent than any similar analysis required for 'conventionally' bred or imported exotic species. Most people are unaware that, for over 100 years, most of our food and ornamental crops have been bred using extremely artificial technologies such as embryo-rescue, colchicine-induced chromosome abnormalities, gamma-ray irradiation, and potent chemical mutagens (mustard gas) to increase the diversity of genetic traits for breeder selections. Most of these 'normal' events are lethal to the plant.

GM technology is constantly evolving and current developments largely focus on reducing any potential associated risks, no matter how unlikely. Antibiotic or herbicide resistance genes, used routinely in the past during the generation of GM plants, are usually superfluous in the final product, and strategies have been devised to eliminate them from the plant. This usually requires going through a sexual generation. Alternatively, biotechnologists employ cell-selection systems which do not rely on antibiotic resistance: for example, the metabolism of a rare sugar that the plant would only be able to use if a specific gene and its encoded enzyme were present.

In the first generations of GM plants, foreign protein(s) were expressed in all plant tissues ('constitutive expression'). It is now possible to control when, where, and to what degree foreign proteins are made throughout a plant. This is achieved by using what are termed 'promoters', which can be considered as genetic switches. These powerful tools ensure, for example, that insecticidal proteins targeted at soil-borne weevils will be made only in the roots. Thus, aerial regions of the plant will be free of insecticidal proteins and would pose minimal risk to non-target organisms, or as a food. Similarly, proteins affecting pigment biosynthesis could be made specifically in the petals.

Another significant advance in GM technology has been the recent breakthrough in what is called 'chloroplast transformation'. Rather than introduce foreign gene(s) into the plant's nuclear genetic material, as in conventional GM, gene(s) can be inserted into the far simpler genetic material of the chloroplast. Chloroplasts are found in all green plant cells and are responsible for generating energy and sugar from sunlight. One attraction of this technique is that chloroplasts are not present in pollen. This means that although novel plants created using chloroplast transformation are still GM, the pollen is GM free. Therefore any possible risks associated with GM pollen *per se*, or through out-crossing to close relatives, are eliminated.

There is no doubt that biotechnology and GM are well positioned to support, better target, and accelerate conventional breeding in the production of novel, added-value garden crops. Regrettably, the technology is unlikely to be adopted in Europe in the short-to-medium term as a consequence of well-organized activist propaganda campaigns which have created misunderstanding and anxiety among the public and politicians alike. Nevertheless, with ongoing refinements, demand for more interesting and unique plant characteristics, and reduced pesticide and fungicide inputs, the future still looks optimistic. AM

Genyue,

Henan province, China, was a vast man-made landscape built in 1117–23 during the time of the Song Emperor Zhaoji (posthumous name Huizong). It was located north-east of the capital Bian Liang, now the city of Kaifeng. The Emperor, a painter of considerable merit, was, it seems, personally involved in planning the park, but it was supervised by Liang Shicheng with several imperial commissioners working under him. One, a merchant Zhu Mian, became notorious for his pursuit of rare plants and rocks around Suzhou; another, Ling Bi, collected for the park some 1,500 km/900 miles away in south China. Originally named Phoenix Mountain, the garden's new name was made up of *yue* meaning high mountain, and *gen*, one of the Eight Trigrams—usually signifying mountain and the orientation north-east— in the ancient book of philosophy *Yi jing*. The name suggests that the park had some geomantic purpose beyond that of the Emperor's own personal pleasure (see FENG SHUI).

The perimeter of the park was *c*.5 km/3 miles, with water in the west and hills and rocky peaks in the east. Collections of bizarre and fantastic rocks spiralled out of these ridges which rose at their highest point to the Peak of Ten Thousand Years' Longevity with a pavilion at its top. From here the Emperor beheld what seemed a microcosm of the universe with city and park spread out 'as if lying on the palm of the hand'. All around 'peaks, caverns, mature trees and grasses' blended with nature 'as if it had all been here since creation' while islands embellished with palatial halls and gazebos lay along the waterways. Among innumerable buildings were the Red Sky Chamber, the Hall of the Flower with Green Sepals, a library, and a circular Pavilion for the Immortals. Unfortunately, the expense of building Genyue weakened an already tottering dynasty. Today nothing remains of it except two great monolithic rocks in the YU YUAN in Shanghai and the LIU YUAN in Suzhou, once supposedly chosen for the mountain of Genyue.

G-ZW/MK

Gerard, John

(1545–1612), English surgeon, botanist, and author born in Cheshire. Gerard worked for William Cecil, 1st Lord Burghley, as superintendent of his gardens in the Strand in London and at Theobalds in Hertfordshire. Gerard's own garden in Holborn, London, contained more than 1,000 species, of which he published a catalogue in 1596. A reprint of this was made in 1876 edited by B. D. Jackson, who described it as 'the first professedly complete catalogue of any one garden, either public or private, ever published'. In 1597 he published the book that made him famous, the *Herball*. Although there has been much debate about the origins of Gerard's information, and he certainly made howlers (such as claiming the potato came from Virginia), it stands today as an unrivalled account of the range of plants grown in England at the end of Queen Elizabeth I's reign. PT

BRENT ELLIOTT, '400 years of Gerard's *Herball*', *The Garden*, Vol. 122: Part II (1997).

Germany

Climate and characteristic topography

About 82 million people inhabit some 357,000 sq. km/138,000 sq. miles in Germany. The climate is maritime in the northern parts and in the west, and more continental in the eastern and southern parts. Vast low-lying lands characterize the north whereas mountains up to 1,500 m/4,921 ft are the most prominent features of central and southern Germany. A small ribbon of Alpine formations forms the border regions to Switzerland, Austria, and Italy in the south. Germany is a highly industrialized country where 87% of the population lives in urban areas.

Antiquity and the Middle Ages

Antiquity had a decisive influence on the development of medieval Western horticulture and agriculture. Classical writers on agriculture such as Marcus Terentius Varro (116–27 BC), COLUMELLA (1st century BC), and PLINY THE ELDER were absorbed into the medieval literature of gardening. In his book *De Rerum Naturae* (About Nature) which is believed to be the first on science in Germany, Hrabanus Maurus, the Abbot of Fulda monastery (784–856), embarked upon these earlier writings. The Capitulare de Villis vel Curtis Imperii (Rules for Imperial Estates and Courts), written about 800 during the reign of the Emperor Charlemagne, lists different species of vegetables, flowers, and herbs, many of them from the Mediterranean region. The poem *Hortulus* or *Liber de Cultura Hortorum* (Book about the Culture of Gardens), written after 842 by Walahfried Strabo, the Abbot at Reichenau monastery on an island in Lake Constance, is the most important source for early medieval garden culture in Germany. This poem not only gives an impression of the religious symbolism and significance of plants at that time, it also informs us about common gardening practices. Albertus Magnus (1193–1280), who was a monk, a bishop, and a professor, dealt with horticultural techniques and plant cultivation in his book *De Vegetalibus* (About Plants), around 1260. In a chapter about ornamental gardens (*viridaria*) he mentioned design features such as a fountain in the centre of a lawn, a turf bench, as well as a lawn with borders of herbs and flowers.

Garden culture in Germany in the 16th and early 17th centuries

During this period interest in botanical knowledge rose considerably in Germany. Between 1530 and 1600 about one dozen *Kräuterbücher* (herb books) were written which helped to establish botany as an independent science. The foundation of botanical gardens in Königsberg (1551), Leipzig (1580), and Heidelberg (1593) reflects this. The botanic garden at EICHSTÄTT became famous for its *Hortus Eystettensis*, a florilegium published in 1613. *Hausväterbücher* (husbandry books) which were typical from the 17th century onwards adopted a more practical approach to gardening and agriculture and aimed at the instruction of the middle classes in the knowledge of plants, gardening techniques, and garden design. The first of its kind in German appeared from 1591 to 1601 in Wittenberg as *Calendarium Oeconomicum et Perpetuum* (Economic Calendar). It was written jointly by Jakob and Johannes Cöler and was reprinted and revised about fourteen times. Meanwhile, the emerging middle classes in affluent cities such as Nuremberg, Augsburg, and Frankfurt am Main, as well as in Hamburg, Danzig, and Leipzig, developed a strong interest in gardening. The garden of Dr Laurentius Scholz in Breslau from 1585, and the garden (before 1641) of the mayor of Frankfurt, Johannes Schwindt, are examples which displayed lavish garden design. The first specialized treatise which dealt with pleasure gardens in Germany was published in 1597 as *Garten Ordnung* (Garden Order) by Johann Peschel. Compared with other treatises, such as *Hortorum Viridiarumque Elegantes et Multiplices Formae* (Elegant and Manifold Forms of Gardens) (1583) by Hans Vredemann de VRIES, Peschel's designs are simple. In the second half of the 16th century garden art bloomed and features such as parterres, arbours, BERCEAUX, fountains, fish ponds, mazes, grottoes, and sculptural programmes became common. Humanistic studies of antiquity, the discovery of new countries and the introduction of new plants, international exchange via commerce, and tours of the aristocracy to Italy and France began to shape the international perception of garden culture. Around 1570 the garden at the Stuttgart residence of Duke Christoph of Württemberg was considered the most beautiful garden in Germany. Although never finished, due to the Thirty Years War (1618–48), the HORTUS PALATINUS in Heidelberg (1615 onwards) was the most outstanding garden in the first half of the 17th century. It was designed by the French architect and engineer Salomon de CAUS, who describes the sophisticated features of this garden in his treatise *Hortus Palatinus* (1620). The Thirty Years War brought the prosperous period of garden art in the late Renaissance to an end. Reflecting upon the detrimental impacts of the war, the architect Joseph Furttenbach (1591–1667) nevertheless promoted the pleasures of gardens. In 1628 he published *Architectura Civilis*, in 1640 *Architectura Recreationis*, and in 1641 *Architectura Privata*. His designs recognize principles such as the close relationship between buildings and gardens and display an interest in a central axis which heralds the artistic period which followed.

Garden culture in Germany in the 17th and 18th centuries

After the Thirty Years War Germany slowly recovered. The more than 300 semi-independent states were only loosely united under the Habsburg emperors who resided in Vienna. The numerous courts built palaces and gardens which frequently took as example Louis XIV's VERSAILLES with its central axis and a tripartite layout of parterres, BOSQUETS, and formal woodland separated by canals, hedges, and alleys. HERRENHAUSEN, begun in 1666 under Duke Johann Friedrich, is a remarkable example, which had a partly French, partly Dutch garden layout in the time of Electress Sophie 1696–1714. NYMPHENBURG had a small baroque garden with a central axis which was extended under Max Emanuel of Bavaria from 1701 to the designs of Dominique GIRARD and the court gardener Joseph Effner, who had been sent to Paris to study landscape architecture. The garden of Schleißheim shows Dutch influences in its canals, whereas the central axis, the parterres, and *bosquets* reflect French designs. The layout derives from a design of 1700 by the Italian architect Enrico Zuccalli, which was modified by Dominique Girard from 1715 to 1717. French influences are predominant also in the gardens of AUGUSTUSBURG (1727–8). The gardens of CHARLOTTENBURG, executed from 1696 to 1699, were designed by the Huguenot Simon Godeau (1632–1711 or later), who introduced the classical French garden in the style of LE NÔTRE to Germany.

In some cases a spirit of absolutism demanded straight alleys and visual lines reaching far out from the immediate residential area into the surrounding countryside to other palaces and gardens, or to hunting lodges. In Dresden, Augustus the Strong (1670–1733) connected the castle and garden of Übigau, the Japanese Palais, PILLNITZ, as well as the gardens of the Zwinger in a kind of necklace along the Elbe river. Comparable examples can be found in Berlin and even earlier at CLEVES under Johan Maurits van Nassau-Siegen in the second half of the 17th century. Such ideas preceded *Landesverschönerung* (land embellishment) which became popular in the second half of the 18th century.

Treatises like *Erlustierende Augenweide* (Enjoyable Pleasures for the Eye) by Matthias Diesel (from 1717 to 1722) and Jean Baptiste Broebes's *Vues des palais et maisons de plaisance de sa majesté le roy de Prusse* from 1733 show the lavishness these gardens displayed in the baroque period. A.-J. DEZALLIER D'ARGENVILLE's *La Théorie et la pratique du jardinage* (1709), which was published in German in 1731, 1741, 1764, and 1769, demonstrates the importance of the French style of gardening for the 18th century. However, other ways of laying out gardens and their main features can be found in Germany in this period. The park of Carlsberg (or WILHELMSHÖHE), only partially executed to the design of Giovanni Francesco Guerniero (1701–18), was intended to incorporate the mountain of Wilhelmshöhe within a long cascade of water. Other plans were based on the central position of the castle, which was surrounded by the garden instead of having a main axis with a separate front and rear garden. Examples of this are the garden of Seehof near Bamberg (1693 onwards), Pillnitz (1720 onwards), and the GROßER GARTEN (1715 onwards). In some designs we find circular or elliptical forms for the arrangement of parterres and *bosquets*, for example at SCHWETZINGEN (1753–8). GROßSEDLITZ (1723 to 1727) is a highly individualistic design, a unique garden on steep slopes with long flights of steps, retaining walls, huge terraces, cascades, and varied buildings. Such gardens served for political display and spiritual enjoyment as well as physical pleasure.

Rococo gardens

The period refered to as rococo (1710–60) overlaps with the classical period of baroque garden art. Characteristics of this style are variety, intimacy, and the loosening of geometrical and architectonic values, resulting in dynamic, labyrinth-like structures. The ROCOCO GARDEN is thus unlike the classical French garden with its characteristics of grandeur, magnificence, and *dignité*. Another characteristic is the use of exotic or CHINOISERIE architecture found in gardens such as SANSSOUCI, Pillnitz, and VEITSHÖCHHEIM. Variety in the sense of the rococo implies a garden consisting of independent parts, decorated with extremely rich architectonic and sculptural features. An example is the garden of RHEINSBERG, which was extended from 1744 to 1778 under Prince Heinrich of Prussia as a collection of different garden designs, loosely connected along the lake of Grienerick. The gardens of Veitshöchheim were begun with a summer house and a small, longitudinal garden in 1702/3. From 1719, and finally from 1763 onwards, an independently designed garden was added. Small garden spaces with stylistically different buildings, pools, and a large number of sculptures are distributed within the complex of the second part. Another example of this kind of variety is the layout of La Solitude near Stuttgart, built by the Duke of Württemberg (1763 onwards).

Late 18th and 19th centuries: the landscape garden and picturesque style

Until the second half of the 18th century the tradition of the architectonic or regular style determined garden art in Germany, whereas in England the layout for gardens and parks had completely changed by this time. Germany followed this new style but with considerable delay. Between 1764 and 1815 Prince Leopold Friedrich von ANHALT-DESSAU made the first garden influenced by this English invention at his estate in WÖRLITZ. The huge park integrated the riverscape of the Elbe with adjoining lakes, and the softened lines of the parkland and agricultural areas in the tradition of a FERME ORNÉE with framed views. The fact that the house of Hanover also provided the sovereigns of England from 1714 onwards explains the early interest for the landscape style by some small courts in Lower Saxony. The gardens of Schwöbber by Otto II von Münchhausen (1763 onwards), the Hinübersche Garten in Hanover-Marienwerder by Jobst Anton von Hinüber (1774 onwards), and Harbke by Friedrich August von Veltheim (1760 onwards) are modest, but nevertheless important examples of this new English style.

A period of reflection on the nature of landscape gardening developed within a short time, which appears in the writings of outstanding poets such as Friedrich von Schiller (1759–1805) and Johann Wolfgang von Goethe (1749–1832). A large number of garden guides and treatises popularized landscape gardening. The most prominent are the five-volume *Theorie der Gartenkunst* (Theory of Garden Art) (1772–85) by C. C. L. HIRSCHFELD, and Johann Gottfried Grohmann's *Schöne Gartenkunst* (Beautiful Garden Art) (1798). Garden guides, such as Wilhelm Gottlieb Becker's *Das Seifersdorfer Thal* (1792), were influential. Becker described the landscaped valley near Seifersdorf, laid out from 1781 with 45 arrangements of sculptures and inscriptions evoking emotional scenes with literary and historical allusions. Court gardeners like the Sckells from Munich, the Köllners from Saarbrücken, as well as Peter Joseph LENNÉ from Potsdam went to England in order to study the new style. The same was true of sovereigns such as Count Ludwig of Nassau-Saarbrücken, Landgrave Friedrich II von Hessen, and Duke Karl Eugen von Württemberg who was in England in 1776 and created between 1776 and 1783 the landscaped park in Hohenheim (near Stuttgart). One of the most famous travellers was Hermann, Prince of PÜCKLER-MUSKAU who went to England in 1816, 1826–9, and again in 1851. His ideas for the layout of a park which he published as *Andeutungen über Landschaftsgärtnerei* (Hints on Landscape Gardening) (1834) reflected his practical experience with the design of his park at MUSKAU.

Garden culture in the 19th century

Lenné, the director of the royal Prussian gardens at Potsdam-Sanssouci, promoted the professionalization of landscape architecture in Germany. In 1822 he was one of the founders of the Verein zur Beförderung des Gartenbaues in den Königlich-Preussischen Staaten (Association for the Promotion of Horticulture in the Royal Prussian States) and participated in the foundation of the Königliche Gärtnerische Lehranstalt (Royal Horticultural College) at Wildpark near Potsdam in 1823. His most important layouts were executed at Potsdam (Sanssouci, Charlottenhof, Russian Colony) and in Berlin (Klein-Glienicke, PFAUENINSEL, and TIERGARTEN). The designs by Lenné, Pückler, and Friedrich Ludwig von SCKELL represented the mature landscape style in Germany. Other important garden designers of this period were Maximilian Friedrich Weyhe (1775–1846), active in the Rhineland, Wilhelm Hentze (1793–1874) in Hessen, and Eduard PETZOLD, who worked in Muskau and other places.

The first park donated for the use of the public, the ENGLISCHER GARTEN in Munich, was created by Friedrich Ludwig von Sckell with the help of Count Rumford in 1789. The first public park, Volksgarten Kloster Berge (People's Garden, Berge monastery), initiated by a city council was designed by Peter Joseph Lenné in Magdeburg (Saxony-Anhalt) in 1824. More municipal parks followed in the second half of the 19th century. The Bürgerpark at Bremen (1866 onwards) by Wilhelm Benque (1814–95) resulted from the initiative of a group of interested citizens. Other parks came into existence as improvement schemes for redundant fortifications—in Hamburg, Bremen, and Frankfurt. Newly established municipal parks departments paid attention to the emerging middle-class interest in displaying its status in public places and were also motivated by social concerns, e.g. as places of recreation for the working class. Such ideas are reflected in the design of such parks in Berlin as Humboldthain, Friedrichshain, and Treptower, which were planned by Gustav MEYER (1816–77), who was from 1870 the first municipal garden director of Berlin. Meyer was also the author of *Lehrbuch der schönen Gartenkunst* (Manual of Beautiful Garden Art) (1859/60), which for many decades was the essential textbook for garden architects at the *Gärtnerlehranstalt*. In 1871 the German Empire was founded as a federal state after the war against France. The statutes of the Verein Deutscher Gartenkünstler (Association of German Garden Artists), founded in 1887, explicitly promoted designs such as those by Lenné and Meyer as a model for a distinctive German garden style. Carl Hampel (1849–1930), who simplified Meyer's models, successfully published books such as *Die deutsche Gartenkunst* (German Garden Art) (1902) and promoted a primitive version of the late landscape style known as Lenné–Meyersche Schule.

Garden culture before and during the First World War

At the turn of the 19th century garden design attracted much criticism. A growing interest in historical gardens led some garden designers to evoke the styles which antedated the period before the landscape garden, while others evoked the flavour of country gardens with geometrical arrangements of flowers and vegetables. Famous artists like Joseph Maria Olbrich, Max Läuger, and architects such as Hermann MUTHESIUS and Paul Schultze-Naumburg demanded a return to architectonic garden design. Muthesius, influenced by the English ARTS AND CRAFTS movement, on his return to Germany in 1903 advocated a closer relationship between house and garden. Schultze-Naumburg wrote in 1902 an influential book about the relationship between gardens and houses. His design advice was often sought, for example at Cecilienhof in Potsdam (1912–17). In the course of the next two decades Willy LANGE's ideas about garden design became influential. Contrary to the architectonic design of gardens and landscapes he proposed a biological aesthetic which he derived from the arrangement of plants in botanical gardens according to their geographical origin in order to create a kind of national garden based upon the imitation of regional plant formations (as may be seen at Lunenburg Heath). Different stylistic tendencies, as well as an interest in the related arts, helped to diminish the influence of the one-sided late landscape garden concept. Visits by German garden artists to England (1909) and France (1912) helped to broaden the perception of possibilities in garden design. Unfamiliar aspects of garden making, such as town planning, garden preservation, and a social orientation in landscape architecture, including allotment gardens and people's parks, became important immediately before the First World War. The garden architect Leberecht MIGGE's book *Die Gartenkultur des 20. Jahrhunderts* (Garden Culture of the 20th Century) (1913) introduced social concerns to landscape architecture. The garden director of Lübeck, Harry Maasz (1880–1946), and the Berlin garden architect Ludwig Lesser (1869–1957) had similar interests. Work on lavish gardens almost ceased during the First World War. However, the design of cemeteries, the layout of garden cities, as well as settlements for war veterans occupied contemporary professional interests.

Garden culture during the Weimar Republic

The Treaty of Versailles in 1919 resulted in the loss of about 20% of the German territory and imposed high reparations. Forced to deal with this, the newly constituted Weimar Republic (1918–33) had to face a series of economic and political crises. However, the promise of democracy created ideas which were reflected in a number of design issues in garden architecture. Directors of municipal park administrations such as Otto Linne (1869–1937) in Hamburg, Fritz Encke (1861–1931) in Cologne, Max Bromme (1878–1974) in Frankfurt, Hermann Kube (1866–1944) in Hanover, and Erwin BARTH in Berlin implemented an innovative open space policy. This included the design of public parks with a wide range of facilities for various activities (often with special provision for children) and the layout of KLEINGÄRTEN (allotments). The functionalist style of large housing estates often provided small gardens for tenants. The Hufeisensiedlung (Horse Shoe Settlement) in Berlin-Britz, and Onkel-Toms-Hütte (Uncle Tom's Cabin) in Berlin-Zehlendorf, and the Römerstadt (Roman City) in Frankfurt, are examples of this social concern from about 1925 onwards. The democratic atmosphere of the Weimar Republic also spurred discussions about art. Landscape architects such as Hans Friedrich Pohlenz (b. 1901), Otto VALENTIEN, and Georg Béla PNIOWER introduced into garden design avant-garde ideas from De Stijl, from German expressionism, and the Bauhaus. A professional hope almost a century old was fulfilled when the first chair of landscape architecture was established in 1929 at the Landwirtschaftliche Hochschule (Agricultural College) in Berlin. The chair was given to Erwin Barth, the garden director of Berlin.

Landscape architecture and National Socialism

The promising professional impetus stimulated during the Weimar Republic was almost totally abandoned with the beginning of National Socialism in 1933. Professional organizations such as the Bund Deutscher Gartenarchitekten (BDGA—League of German Garden Architects), and the Verband Deutscher Gartenarchitekten (VDG—Union of German Garden Architects) were disbanded. The National Socialist Reichskammer der Bildenden Künste (Reich Chamber of Fine Arts) forced all Aryan German landscape architects into membership as a prerequisite for further design commissions. Those considered non-Aryan, such as Georg Béla Pniower, Ludwig Lesser, and many others, for racial and political reasons, could not become members. Garden architects such as Gustav Allinger (1891–1974), Alwin Seifert (1890–1972), and Heinrich Friedrich WIEPKING-JÜRGENSMANN supported National Socialist 'blood and soil' ideology. After Barth committed suicide Wiepking-Jürgensmann succeeded him in 1934 as professor of landscape architecture at the Agricultural College in Berlin. In full accord with National Socialist thinking he advocated to his students regional themes in landscape design according to characteristics of supposed German tribes. With the National Socialist invasion of Poland in 1939 he anticipated much work for his students associated with the Germanization in the east. He collaborated with Konrad Meyer (1901–73), professor at the Institute for Agriculture and Agricultural Politics, to implement the Generalplan Ost (1942) which provided for the expulsion and extermination of millions of Slavs, Jews, and other people from the occupied territories in the east to make way for German settlers.

An important field in this period was the landscape planning of motorways, an idea which had first been conceived during the Weimar Republic. The architect Alwin Seifert engaged in this together with a team of colleagues who called themselves Landschaftsanwälte (Lawyers for Landscapes) from 1934. With Gustav Allinger, who had designed some large garden shows during the 1920s and the 1930s, Seifert was among the most successful garden architects of this era. Landscape design had turned into a highly political profession—its representatives often took on an active role in the propagation of National Socialist ideas.

Post-Second World War garden architecture

In the Second World War Germany's major cities, including their parks and other open spaces, were badly damaged. The establishment of two German states in 1949, the Federal Republic of Germany (BRD), and the German Democratic Republic (DDR), led to different developments in the two states. While the BRD became integrated politically and economically within Western Europe and North America, the DDR became dependent on the Soviet Union.

With the establishment of the first 'antifascist state on German soil' in the DDR, former supporters of National Socialism lost their influence. In 1946 Georg Béla Pniower, who had been forbidden to work under National Socialism, received the chair of garden architecture and landscape design at the University of Berlin (which became Humboldt University in 1949) which Wiepking-Jürgensmann had vacated when the Russian troups reached Berlin in 1945. In the BRD the two major chairs were occupied by former supporters of National Socialism. In 1952 the Technical University of Berlin gave a newly created chair for landscape architecture to Gustav Allinger. The other chair in landscape architecture at Hanover University was given to Wiepking-Jürgensmann in 1949.

Curved paths, softened lines of lawns, perennials, shrubs, and trees as in the late 1930s continued as a late landscape style for several decades after the Second World War. An example of this is the so-called Englischer Garten as part of the TIERGARTEN created by garden architect Willy Alverdes (1896–1980) from 1951 to 1952. Also in the DDR the old-fashioned heath garden motif received considerable attention, for example at the Treptower Park in Berlin in 1961 from a design by Pniower. Compared with the development in architecture, sculpture, and painting, landscape architecture lacked genuine innovation. Avant-gardist garden designs exhibited at the international garden show in Hamburg in 1963 seemed to signal a change, but they were mostly seen as formalistic. At the beginning of the 1970s the anti-modernistic concept of a bio-, eco-, or nature garden became a major design issue in Germany. A completely new approach which emerged from the students' revolt was the establishment of a professorship in planning-related sociology at the University of Hanover in 1974. In the DDR the influence of the Soviet Union made itself felt in what became called the *Kulturpark* with its origins in the public park of the 1920s. An important example is the implementation of a *Kulturpark* in the historical park of BABELSBERG by the garden architect Walter Funcke (1907–87) from 1953 to 1957. Another artistic orientation in landscape architecture took place after the return of high-ranking officials and politicians from an excursion to Moscow in 1950. The Deutsche Bauakademie developed a programme for a national architecture which was implemented, for example, from 1952 in the construction of Stalin-Allee (now, once again, Frankfurter Allee) in Berlin. It included wide open spaces of historicist design by Reinhold Lingner (1902–68) along the characteristically symmetrical axis of high-rise buildings. The 'first socialist city in the country', Stalinstadt, later renamed Eisenhüttenstadt, was planned and built from 1951 to the early 1970s. The open space design by Lingner and others was poor. As design vanished from the open spaces within large housing estates in both East and West Germany urban open space design became contemptuously known as *Abstandsgrün* (spacing green)—green spaces between buildings with scarcely any attempt at design.

In the late 1970s in both German states a renewed interest in garden history provided the means for the reconstruction of castle gardens, municipal parks, city squares, and other open spaces. This tendency also influenced the layout of new spaces in the historical setting after the reunification of Germany in 1989–90. The city of Berlin created a large number of parks and other open spaces following the principle of the so-called 'critical reconstruction' of the city combined with an interest in new design solutions from the mid 1990s. Examples are the Mauerpark (to replace part of the former Berlin wall) by Gustav Lange (1996), the monument to the destroyed synagogue by Zvi Hecker (1997), as well as the garden courtyards in the Federal Ministry of Finance by Regina Poly (2000).

The profession of the gardener—history and types of jobs

Due to the enormous importance of gardens for the nutrition of the population, the position of gardeners in Germany was already regulated in medieval times by law. But this was true only for market gardeners who were integrated into the medieval guild system of the big cities. Besides professional gardeners there existed a large number of private gardeners who were the main readership for the *Hausbücher* (husbandry books) from the 16th century onwards. This kind of literature refers to the obligations of large households to be self-sufficient, with instructions on beekeeping, hunting, fishing, as well as horticultural techniques. Some *Hausbücher* included instructions for ornamental gardens. Already in the 16th century specialized garden designers existed at some German courts. Some were capable of constructing complicated waterworks such as Salomon de CAUS, who was responsible for the layout of the Hortus Palatinus. Qualified architects and military engineers such as Balthasar Neumann (1687–1753) were often employed to do such work. In addition, German courts employed gardeners from France, Italy, or the Netherlands. Professional court gardeners had been employed for several generations (for example Sckell and Effner who worked for the Bavarian court, and Fintelmann and Sello who worked for the kings of Prussia). They were highly qualified in such subjects as fruit growing and the cultivation of ornamental plants. Ideally the court gardener knew different languages and had a solid knowledge not only of plants and botany, but also of mathematics and land surveying. However, there were many badly qualified gardeners. This was one of the reasons in the 19th century for the establishment of colleges specializing in the training of gardeners.

The training of gardeners and notable institutions

Although Hirschfeld had suggested academic training for gardeners in 1779 it needed the foundation of the Königliche Gärtnerlehranstalt in Berlin and Potsdam in 1823 by Lenné and others to start such a programme. Here, as well as in the other programmes that followed during the 19th century, gardening was taught in its main branches as fruit growing, plant cultivation, ornamental gardening, and garden design in practice and theory. Other important colleges were founded much later in Proskau (1868), Geisenheim (1872), Köstritz (1887), Weihenstephan (1892), and Pillnitz near Dresden (1922). The second half of the 20th century saw the additional establishment of landscape architecture programmes at several polytechnic schools, such as Osnabrück (1950), Nürtingen (1969), Oranienburg (1897, 1948), Bernburg (1948), Erfurt (1946), Neubrandenburg (1996). At university level landscape architecture was offered in Hanover (1946), Berlin (1946, east; 1952, west), Essen (1966), at Höxter-Paderborn (1978), and at Kassel (1978).

Garden conservation

A major precondition for ideas about the conservation of a garden is the acceptance of its historical value. Already in 1892 the Verein Deutscher Gartenkünstler demanded that excellent gardens from the Renaissance and rococo periods as well as landscaped parks should be preserved in their original form. The scattered proposals for garden conservation before the First World War became important only after the war, when the gardens of the former rulers became public property. Proposals for the conservation and maintenance of these gardens as well as a collection of historical documents and the establishment of a register of valuable gardens were made. Although these regulations were generally accepted, success was limited. Only in some cases were artistically free reconstructions made, for example at the garden of BRÜHL with the reconstruction of the old parterre (1728) in 1935. The old formal garden at HERRENHAUSEN was reconstructed in 1936 according to its original layout of 1714. After the Second World War an institutionalized, research-based, conservation movement in both German states began. Hermann Schüttauf (1890–1967) became a central figure in the early conservation activities in the DDR and he was followed by others, such as Harri Günther (b. 1928) at Potsdam. The appointment of garden architect Hugo Namslauer (1922–99) for the care of historical gardens within the Institut für Denkmalpflege (National Institute for the Preservation of Historic Buildings and Monuments) in 1970 was the most important step for the institutionalization of garden conservation in the DDR. The development in West Germany was much slower. Although from the 1960s onwards a small group of garden historians was very active (such as Gerda Gollwitzer, Dieter Hennebo, Ursula Gräfin zu Dohna), institutional garden conservation only came in 1978 when the federal state of Berlin installed a highly successful department for this purpose with Klaus von Krosigk as its head. Garden conservation today plays an important role in the work of the administrations of castles and gardens. Of special significance for the academic development in this field are departments at the University of Hanover, the Fachhochschule Weihenstephan, the Fachhochschule Erfurt, the Fachhochschule Neubrandenburg, and the Technical University of Dresden.

Garden shows
Garden shows had already appeared in Germany during the second half of the 19th century. They informed professionals and the general public about contemporary trends in landscape and garden architecture as well as about horticultural techniques and plants. In some cases they were highly important for the development of garden design. For example at the Internationale Kunst- und große Gartenbauausstellung (International Exhibition of Art and Gardening) at Düsseldorf in 1904, the JAPANESE GARDEN significantly encouraged a fashion for Japanese gardens. The Jahrhundertausstellung (Centennial Exhibition) in Breslau from 1913 showed English ideas such as crazy paving and drystone walls which became important for German garden design. Many garden shows exhibited specialist collections of exotics. Cacti, for example, were shown in several exhibitions in the 1920s, initiating a fashion for these plants. However, the garden exhibitions in the 1930s, such as the Reichsgartenschau in Dresden in 1936, were problematic because they propagated National Socialist ideology. After the Second World War garden shows again became very popular in both German states. After unification in 1990 they also addressed town planning matters, such as at the Bundesgartenschau in Potsdam in 2001.

Nurseries
Although some private nurseries already existed in the 17th century, they were created on a bigger scale only after the Thirty Years War. Their main purpose was to supply the gardens of the aristocracy. The nursery for the castle garden of Hanover-Herrenhausen, for example, was founded in 1665. *Vom Garten-Baw* (Treatise about Gardening), published in this period by the Berlin physician and royal gardener Johann Sigismund Elßholtz (b. 1623), deals especially with the creation of nurseries. The nursery that was founded in the 1760s at the castle Solitude near Stuttgart by Duke Karl Eugen von Württemberg (1728–93) contained an exceptional number of trees and shrubs (about 224,000). Its head was Johann Caspar Schiller (father of the poet), who also wrote a treatise on tree nurseries, *Die Baumzucht im Großen* (1785). The introduction of the landscape garden which needed a large number of different trees and shrubs significantly encouraged the establishment of nurseries in Germany. The gardener John (Johann) BUSCH who established a nursery in London in 1753, sending trees and seeds to Germany, played an exceptional role in the trade between English nurseries and the then Anglophile German courts. Important writers in this field were Friedrich August Ludwig von Burgsdorff (1747–1802) with his treatise *Anleitung zur sicheren Erziehung und zweckmäßigen Anpflanzung der einheimischen und fremden Holzarten* (1787) and W. A. Borchmeyer with *Deutschlands Baumzucht* (1823) which describes 898 different species of trees and shrubs. A large number of private nurseries were founded, especially in northern Germany, from the end of the 18th century onwards. The Flottbecker Baumschule, founded jointly by Baron Caspar von Voght (1752–1839) and James Booth in 1795, specialized in North American trees. The garden artist Carl Ferdinand Bosse (1755–93) who had seen rhododendrons in England in 1782 first introduced these plants to Germany at the court of Rastede near Oldenburg. In Saxony the Seidel family cultivated camellias and rhododendrons near Dresden from 1813. The Späth nursery in Berlin, which was to become the biggest nursery on the continent before the First World War, was established in 1720. Nurseries in northern Germany deliver more than half of the whole plant production in Germany.

Garden historiography
Garden historiography has had a significant tradition in Germany for about 40 years. Between 1962 and 1965 Dieter Hennebo's and Alfred Hoffmann's *Geschichte der deutschen Gartenkunst* (History of German Garden Art) appeared as the pioneering German study in this field. Hennebo also worked as editor of the series *Geschichte des Stadtgrüns* (History of Urban Greenery) from 1979. In the 1980s and 1990s research into garden history became a very rich field. The Wernerscher Verlag in Worms began publishing the Grüne Reihe (Green series) of monographs. The manual *Grüne Biographien* (Green Biographies) by Gert Gröning and Joachim Wolschke-Bulmahn appeared in 1997. With its 2,700 biographies of garden architects in Germany it offered the first exhaustive survey and set the standard for biographical studies in this field. The publication and registration of archives and private collections of plans for parks and gardens reflected a strong interest in historical sources. Reprints of historical books on landscape and garden architecture by the Werner Verlag, by Alfons Uhl, and by the late Roger Gorenflo as well as the database **www.garden-cult** (2003) by Uwe Schneider and Gert Gröning support this. The ideological implications of landscape architecture have been addressed especially by Gert Gröning and Joachim Wolschke-Buhlmann with a focus on the 20th century. Garden conservation became another important field. In 1985, Dieter Hennebo, its Nestor, edited *Gartendenkmalpflege* (Garden Conservation) which gathered together methodological contributions. In addition a large number of garden guides and local garden histories serves an increasing public interest in garden history. Further fields of study are the history of plant introduction, glasshouses, and orangeries, and the history of cultural landscapes. More recently, garden history has been enriched by social and art-related topics, such as gardens and sexuality, gardens and memorials, gardens and literature, gardens and movies.

Documentation of garden history/garden societies
The most important location for the documentation of garden history is the Verein Bücherei des Deutschen Gartenbaues (Association of the German Horticulture Library) in Berlin, founded in 1936. The library of the Berlin Botanical Garden, the Deutsches Kleingärtnermuseum (German Museum for Allotment Gardeners) in Leipzig, and the Deutsches Gartenbaumuseum in Erfurt, founded in 1995, also hold collections dedicated to garden history. A museum of garden history was founded at Schloss FANTAISIE in 2000, and another at Schloss BENRATH in 2001.

Garden societies with an interest in garden history are the Pückler-Gesellschaft in Berlin, founded in 1979, and the Deutsche Gesellschaft für Gartenkunst und Landschaftskultur (German Association for Garden Art and Landscape Culture), founded in 1887, with its Arbeitskreis Historische Gärten (Study Group for Historical Gardens). Important journals are the biannual *Die Gartenkunst*, founded in 1989, the monthly journal *Garten + Landschaft* with more than 50 years of publishing, primarily serving the interests of freelance landscape architects. The journal *Stadt und Grün* (City and Greenery) was founded in 1951 and places a special emphasis on municipal parks administration. Since 1998 the *Grüner Anzeiger* (Green Advertiser) bimonthly gives information about exhibitions, lectures, and other public activities related to garden culture and its history. The journal *Zandera*, founded in

1986, provides information about the activities of the Verein Bücherei des Deutschen Gartenbaues, and pays special attention to the history of the introduction of new plants to Germany.   GG/US

Gernyeszeg (Gornești and Teleki Park) ⊛ near Tirgu Mureș, Romania. The house and park of Gernyeszeg were built by the Teleki family, on the site of a medieval castle with kitchen gardens, surrounded by a moat filled with water. The baroque house in its present form (with a huge cupola in the middle) was erected in 1772–82 for Count László Teleki, probably to the designs of András Mayerhoffer. The garden started to be laid out between the building and the moat in 1782, during the ownership of József I Teleki. The earliest known garden scheme, dating from *c.*1792, features ornamental parterres. However, József I Teleki, probably inspired by ROUSSEAU, with whom he was personally acquainted, wished to lay out a landscape garden at that time. In the early decades of the 19th century, his son József II Teleki, who had travelled in England as well, brought the landscape garden to completion. For this purpose, the moat at certain points was widened to form pools, and filled up at others. The garden's most significant edifice is József II Teleki's monument erected by his widow after his death in 1817 in the middle of the park. A design dating from 1831 features, in addition, a GLORIETTE and an obelisk. A fine collection of deciduous trees were enriched with conifers from the 1850s. The garden's last significant phase of improvement took place at the beginning of the 20th century when Domokos Teleki aquired some 18th-century statuary for the park. Seven mythological statues may originally have stood in the garden of Starhemberg Palace in Vienna before being transported to a private garden in Buda in the 19th century. Also among these newly acquired statues is a group of four gnomes, originally part of a series. The house was expropriated by the state after 1945 and has been functioning as a sanatorium ever since. Its park still exists, though it is badly in need of conservation.   GA

JÒZSEF BIRÒ, *A gernyeszegi Teleki-kastély* (Teleki House at Gernyeszeg) (1938).

ANNA ECSEDY, *Huszadik századi szerzemények a magyarországi kertek barokk szoboranyagában: Schmidt Miksa kertdekorációs tevékenysége a 'gernyeszegi sorozat' kapcsán* (20th Century Collecting of 18th Century Statuary in Hungarian Gardens: The Work of Max Schmidt through the 'Series of Gernyeszeg') (2003).

ANNA ECSEDY, 'Wandernde Statuen: Vorstudien zur Geschichte der Gartenplastik in Ungarn und Österreich im 18. Jahrhundert und in der Zeit des Historismus', *Acta Historiae Artium* (in preparation 2005).

Getty Center ⊛
Los Angeles, California, USA, was founded in 1992 as the headquarters of the Getty Museum and its related research offices on a site of 32 hectares/80 acres, and consitutes two widely divergent approaches to landscape order. Perched on a mountain site commanding views of downtown Los Angeles and the Pacific Ocean, the group of six structures forms an acropolis of culture that is approached by a small automated tram. The buildings are placed on platforms faced with travertine marble within a grid of native coast oak trees. The buildings front onto paved courts with simple fountains and groups of camphor trees, Italian stone pines, and native sycamores. Outside the south-east corner of the museum complex a circular prow is planted with cacti, forming an effective foreground to the view of downtown. The two main building groups frame a shallow valley within which lies the Central Garden designed by the artist Robert Irwin, who was commissioned to create a 'work of art'. A stream paved with carefully selected cobbles descends the slope beneath a large grove of London plane trees to a large terrace above a circular garden. The stream was engineered to create a sequence of sounds which are experienced from a path, contained by low vertical cor-ten steel sheets, zigzagging down the slope. The stream crosses the terrace, on which are high trees created out of cages of reinforcing rods with bougainvillea planted inside, to plunge over a CHADAR into a large circular pool with a raised island maze of azaleas. The pool is surrounded by three terraces of gardens derived from a variety of styles and planted with a great diversity of plants accentuating varied lights, colours, and reflections.   DCS

Getty Museum ⊛
Malibu, California, USA, opened in 1974 on a site close to the Pacific Ocean, and consitutes a controversial reproduction of a luxurious *villa suburbana*. This reconstruction of the Villa dei Papyri, near POMPEII, sits in a small valley commanding views of the Pacific Ocean. The villa is built over a large parking garage which forms the main approach. The main space is a long peristyle garden defined on three sides by Doric colonnades paved in terracotta. The panels of the outer walls are frescoed with panels framed with *trompe l'œil* columns and swagged garlands. The long pool in the centre is flanked by geometric beds enclosed with low clipped Japanese box hedges and planted with myrtle, roses, oleanders, and clipped laurel standards. Since the original villa lies beneath 19.5 m/65 ft of solidified ash the planting is speculative and is based on exacavations at Pompeian houses. The inner garden in the two-

storey villa has similar planting. On the cross-axis is an outer garden with a mosaic-encrusted *aedicula* NYMPHAEUM which replicates that in the House of the Large Fountain at Pompeii. The long herb garden is planted with scarlet anemones, poets' narcissus, campanula, violas, red and white tulips, plums, peaches, cherry apples, and pomegranates. Despite the strident criticism of the architecture this is a successful evocation of the sumptuousness of a fashionable wealthy villa.   DCS

Geuze, Adriaan
(b. 1960), Dutch landscape gardener specializing in large-scale public spaces who, in 1987, founded the group West 8 Landscape Architects. For the Interpolis Garden (Tilburg) he laid out a series of rectilinear but irregular raised canals juxtaposed with similarly shaped paths, and lawns animated by specimen trees and slabs of slate are arranged to form a naturalistic flow. Usually severely functionalist in style, Geuze displayed a surrealistic tendency for a design at CHAUMONT-SUR-LOIRE in 2000 with a bed filled with bones among which were two bright orange pumpkins. His characteristic work may be seen at Schiphol Airport (Amsterdam), Schouwburgplein (Rotterdam), and at Teleport Park (Amsterdam).   PT

Ge Yuan ⊛
Yangzhou (formerly Yangchow), Jiangsu province, China, was a private garden located in the city. It was owned by Huang Yingtai, a Qing-dynasty salt tycoon and once a governor of the salt trade in the Huai river region. Its name can be interpreted as 'Individual Garden' but a duplication of the character for 'ge' makes the character for bamboo, a major feature of the garden. It was built (according to Liu Fenggao in his *On 'Ge Yuan'*) at the end of the 18th century on the site of an older garden, Shouzhi Yuan, and it is said that its original artificial hill was designed and executed under the direction of Shi Tao, but no reliable information has yet been found to prove this. This hill, as it is today, is the best-known feature of the Ge Yuan. A rare example of its type among Chinese gardens, it uses various kinds of rock to distinguish different areas of the garden and to symbolize the four seasons. Thus, an idea of the Mountain Forest in Spring is suggested near the entrance moon-gate, where needle-like inverted stalactite rocks known as stone bamboo shoots have been planted among living bamboo groves to make a juxtaposition between real and false.

In the west, summer is symbolized by an artificial hill of Taihu stones (the rock most prized for artificial 'mountains') overshadowed by the dense foliage of pine trees. Crossed by a zigzag bridge, the neighbouring pool runs on underneath a rocky overhang which then widens into a shadowy room lit by water-reflected light. This cave, quiet and deep, remains pleasantly cool in Yangzhou's heavy summers, and the grey rock shapes, wet with summer rain or dappled with light and shade, seem almost alive.

In the east, a labyrinthine hill of yellow rocks rises sharply to steep peaks. Narrow rocky passageways wind up and through it, sometimes by steep steps or across deep chasms, to tiny courtyards and a central cave room. An aged cypress grows from a crevice and on the crest—an ideal place for ascending the heights in autumn—a gazebo overlooks the mountainous miniature landscape all around and the scenery of the slim West Lake beyond it. When this hill turns rosy at sunset it is thought to look exactly like a painting of autumn mountains. The fourth and last of the hills completes the theme of the seasons. Laid out along the wall of a courtyard facing a large hall in one corner of the garden, it uses white-capped rocks to suggest snowy peaks in winter. The Ge Yuan's artificial hill of the four seasons is Yangzhou's most unusual contribution to China's gardening tradition. G-ZW/MK

Ge Yuliang, a native of Changzhou, China, living at some time around the late 18th century, was one of the best-known Chinese garden designers of artificial rockery hills. His skill was in bonding rocks together by interlocking their natural edges like hooks. It is said the longer his rockworks stand, the more stable they become. Many gardens in the lower Changjiang (south of the Yangtze river), such as the artificial hill of HUAN XIU VILLA, are said to have been his work. D-HL/MK

Giambologna (Jean Boulogne) (1529–1608), Flemish sculptor in Italy; his name refers to the port of Boulogne, not the Italian city of Bologna. In 1550 Jean travelled to Florence, where he entered the service of the Medici, eventually becoming court sculptor. One of his first Medici commissions was a bronze statue of Venus (from a model by Niccolò TRIBOLO) for the MEDICI villa at Castello; it now stands in Villa PETRAIA. In the early 1560s Giambologna modelled and cast two *Fishing Boys* (now in the Bargello) for a fountain in the garden of Casino Mediceo in Florence. In the same period he made the exuberant figures for Tommaso Laureti's Fountain of Neptune (1566), which still stands in the Piazza Nettuno in Bologna; the statues include sirens, boys with dolphins, and a massive figure of Neptune. In Florence he designed the Ocean Fountain (1576) to stand in front of the Pitti Palace, but the

fountain was first moved to the amphitheatre of the BOBOLI GARDENS behind the palace and in 1636 moved again to its present location in the Isolotto; the marble statue of Neptune is in the Bargello, and has been replaced by a copy. Giambologna's most unusual garden statue is the colossal figure of Apennine (1570–80), who arises from a pond at PRATOLINO, pressing the head of a monster out of whose mouth the water flows. GC

Giardini Giusti. See GIUSTI, GIARDINI.

giardino segreto.

The *giardino segreto*, literally 'secret garden', was an important ingredient of Italian Renaissance gardens. It was a small, enclosed garden planted with herbs and ornamentals close to the villa with a more private atmosphere than that of the greater garden. Claudia Lazzaro in *The Renaissance Garden in Italy* (1990) quotes the garden historian A. Rinaldi who stated that the characteristic 16th-century villa garden had three ingredients—the *prato* (a lawn or meadow), the *selvatico* (a grove, the same as a BOSCO), and the *giardino segreto*. Examples may still be seen in surviving Renaissance gardens. Georgina Masson, in *Italian Gardens* (1961), wrote evocatively of the main garden terrace at the Villa MEDICI (Fiesole): 'It is only on the prolongation of this terrace, in the little *giardino segreto* behind the house, that the Renaissance world lives still in the green shade of this garden room with its simple box parterres and gently trickling fountain'. The Palazzo PICCOLOMINI preserves a *giardino segreto* of a rare kind. It is immediately adjacent to the palazzo, only glimpsed from the ground floor, but overlooked by the triple-height loggia which forms the façade of the palazzo on this side. From within the garden are exquisite framed views of the landscape of the Val d'Orcia. The principle of the *giardino segreto* may still be seen in modern gardens. Jacques WIRTZ often designs a small, hidden flower garden with a pattern of box-edged beds shielded from the chief layout by impassive hedges of yew. PT

Gibberd Garden ⊕

Harlow, Essex, England, was made from 1956 when the architect Sir Frederick Gibberd (1908–84) came here to work on the design and building of Harlow New Town. Despite its proximity to the town his 6.4-hectare/16-acre garden lies in a serenely unspoilt rural setting. Although a modernist architect his garden is a most eclectic mixture, looking more to the past than to the present. The remains of a Corinthian colonnade loom in a clearing in woodland, a thoroughly 18th-century evocation of the charms of the classical past. Many pieces

of 20th-century sculpture decorate a pool and terrace close to the house and vistas lead outwards to enclosures where more sculptures are seen. A concrete MIRADOR rises above hedges, a walk of pollarded hazels is underplanted with shimmering silver dead nettle (*Lamium*), a 20th-century version of a mount is crowned with a castle of wood and concrete. This is a garden of compartments but it manages to be unlike any other. It is populated by graceful explosions of inventiveness which at their best are dazzlingly successful—such as the sprawling limbs of a venerable quince above a magnificently rotund terracotta urn. After uncertainty about its future the garden is now owned by the Gibberd Garden Trust. PT

Gibraltar ⊕

Wilmington, Delaware, USA, named for its high, rocky site, is a restored early 20th-century garden that was formerly the estate of Hugh Rodney and Isabella du Pont Sharp. Landscape architect Marian Cruger Coffin (1876–1957) designed a series of garden rooms on the 2.4-hectare/6-acre property and, between 1917 and 1923, supervised construction of an Italianate formal garden. A magnificent marble staircase connects the mansion with three terraces. The uppermost allows the visitor a splendid overview of the garden. The Evergreen Terrace boasts a collection of sculpture, set against conifers and broadleaf evergreens. The Pool Terrace features a rectilinear reflecting pool and *Wisteria*, and the Bald Cypress (*Taxodium distichum*) Allée leads to a garden pavilion and fountain. Throughout the garden, Coffin created niches for some of the antique sculpture and garden ornaments that the Sharps collected. Other ornaments she placed as the focal points of grand vistas. Each of the 33 carved limestone and seven lead ornaments is an integral part of the garden. When, after the Sharps' deaths, the mansion and garden fell into disrepair, Preservation Delaware, Inc. lobbied the Delaware Open Space Council for the unprecedented funding of an urban property. Their successful efforts led to the preservation of an elegant, peaceful urban oasis. Inside Gibraltar's ivy-covered walls, the visitor has the sensation of entering a time warp, a secret garden that is protected from the pulsing life of the city around it. In 1998, Gibraltar was listed on the US National Register of Historic Places. CO

Gilpin, Revd William (1724–1804), schoolmaster at Cheam School in Surrey. Gilpin devoted many of the school holidays to travelling in Britain. He recorded what he saw in a series of books which pay particular attention to picturesque scenery.

The first of these, *Observations on the River Wye, and Several Parts of South Wales*, illustrated with his own sketches, was published in 1782. This, and subsequent volumes, were very successful and fostered an interest in the idea of the picturesque which had a profound influence on garden taste. Gilpin himself rarely commented on gardens although when he did it was to great effect. His *Dialogue upon the Gardens of . . . Stow* (1748) is both a valuable early account of the garden and a clever dialogue between formality and informality. Of The LEASOWES he was critical of Shenstone's formality—'he might have thrown down more of his hedges' and most relished those parts where Shenstone's hand was least visible—'(he) has succeeded the best in his rock-scenery, because he has done the least'. Gilpin's *Remarks on Forest Scenery and Other Views* (1791), elegantly illustrated with aquatints, went through several editions and was much admired by Horace WALPOLE—'his Essay on forest trees considered in a picturesque light . . . is perfectly new, truly ingenious, full of good sense in an agreeable style'. In *Three Essays: On Picturesque Beauty; On Picturesque Travel; and On Sketching Landscape* (1792) he explains that '*roughness* forms the most essential point of difference between the *beautiful* and the *picturesque*'.   PT

Gilpin, William Sawrey

(1762–1843), English garden designer, nephew of Revd William GILPIN. He is an intermediate figure, stylistically lying between the picturesque landscapes of his uncle and the full-blown Victorian rediscovery of formality. His work can be seen in the great flower parterre he laid out *c.*1831 for Audley End in Essex, which has been recently reinstated. Based on an 18th-century plan its sharp edges are blurred by lavish plantings of flowering shrubs, herbaceous perennials, and bedding plants. At SCOTNEY CASTLE in the 1830s he advised Edward Hussey on the siting of his new house, with its picturesque valley views of the old castle which, probably under Gilpin's influence, was partly demolished to become even more picturesque. He was the author of *Practical Hints on Landscape Gardening* (1832).   PT

Ginkakuji ⊛

Kyoto city, Japan, is a temple of the Sōkokuji branch of the Rinzai sect of Zen Buddhism located in eastern Kyoto city just at the base of Mount Daimonji. Ginkakuji, the popular name of the temple, means the Temple of the Silver Pavilion, but the proper name is Jishōji. The land was originally the site of a temple called Jodōji but was taken over by the military lord Ashikaga Yoshimasa (1436–90) in 1482 and used as his private villa, Higashiyama-dono (The

Villa of the Eastern Hills). Until Yoshimasa's death, the villa was the site of a cultural salon through which developed what has come to be known as Higashiyama Culture, including the arts of Noh theatre, flower arrangement, tea ceremony, *renga* poetry, and landscape gardening. Yoshimasa based his design for the villa on that of SAIHŌJI temple, of which he was enamoured and which he often visited, and also on that of KINKAKUJI, which had been built by his grandfather Ashikaga Yoshimitsu (1358–1408). Yoshimasa is known to have duplicated Saihōji for his mother at her residence, Takakura-gosho, because the actual temple was closed to females. The various halls of Higashiyama-dono were conceptual replicas (though not necessarily literal replicas) of buildings at Saihōji. The garden, as well, had a similar design, specifically, a long, narrow approach, an upper and a lower portion, and a similar development of a central pond divided by isles.

After Yoshimasa's death, the villa was made into a temple and named Jishōji, the Temple of Shining Compassion, after Yoshimasa's posthumous Buddhist name, Jishōin-dono. Most of the original buildings were destroyed by fire in the mid 16th century and the temple became derelict. In 1615, the Konoe family obtained the property and had Toyomori, Lord of Miyagi-tanba, do a large-scale restoration of the garden. The size of the pond and certain bridges were reworked at that time, and the large mounds of white sand, which are the focus of the present garden, were added: one tall, conical, and 'mountain-like', and the other low, flat, and 'water-like'. What remains today of the original estate are the Silver pavilion (which was never actually covered in silver); Tōgudō, a classic *shoin*-style (architectural style associated with samurai dwellings) structure; and some rockwork such as the Sengetsusen waterfall. The Ginkakuji-style fence (a low fence made of half-split bamboo) and the Ginkakuji-style water basin (a cube-shaped, geometrically decorated granite basin) have their origins at this temple.   MPK

giochi d'acqua.

The Italian term means 'water games' or 'water tricks' although they are often referred to as 'water jokes', but the essence of the idea is playfulness rather than humour. These were found in Italian Renaissance gardens and were constantly commented on by foreign visitors unfamiliar with such things in their own countries. Some *giochi d'acqua* involved the wetting of visitors by concealed water jets. At PRATOLINO a grotto had water-powered automata that played music and emitted sudden explosions of water which soaked

visitors. But the inventive and decorative use of water as a lively ornament was integral to the Renaissance garden idea. The water chain at the Villa LANTE, for example, is a cascade with serpentine edging running down the centre of a flight of steps, making a sparkling chain of light flowing down the stone. At the Villa MEDICI, Castello, MONTAIGNE, on his travels of 1580–1, saw 'a bronze statue of a hoary very old man, sitting down with arms folded, from whose beard, forehead and skin water flowed without cease, emerging drop by drop from every part, representing sweat and tears'. An attractive modern echo of the *giochi d'acqua* may be seen in the vertical water jets emerging from paving in such modern public spaces as the Parc André Citroën in Paris (see PARIS PARKS AND GARDENS) and Somerset House in London. The spirit is also evoked in Jacques Wirtz's great cascade of 2001 at Alnwick Castle (Northumberland) with its soaring randomly fired water jets.   PT

CLAUDIA LAZZARO, *The Italian Renaissance Garden* (1990).

Girard, Dominique

(*c.*1680–1738), French water engineer and garden designer, student of LE NÔTRE, first employed as *garçon fontainier* (fountain boy) at VERSAILLES. In 1714 Louis XIV placed him at the disposal of Elector Maximilian Emanuel of Bavaria, then in exile at Saint-Cloud, who in 1715 on returning to Munich took Girard with him as royal master of fountains and inspector of pleasure gardens and waterworks. He oversaw royal gardens in NYMPHENBURG, SCHLEIßHEIM, Lustheim, and Fürstenried. His major work was the famous water features and two great canals in Nymphenburg gardens. The pleasure gardens were developed by court master of works J. Effner, garden director after Girard's death. Girard also prepared plans for Schleissheim gardens, with variants derived from examples by A.-J. DEZALLIER D'ARGENVILLE. From 1717 Girard was commissioned by Prince Eugene of Savoy for the water features of BELVEDERE park in Vienna. In 1728 he devised garden plans in Brühl and Falkenlust for Joseph Clemens of Cologne.   MR

Girardin, Louis-René, Marquis de

(1735–1808), French army officer, landowner, garden maker, and garden theorist whose garden at ERMENONVILLE was one of the most celebrated of its time. A passionate admirer of Jean-Jacques ROUSSEAU, he brought up his own children in accordance with Rousseau's ideas set down in *Émile* (which argued against the existence of original sin). Rousseau came to live at Ermenonville in 1778 just before his death. Girardin recorded his own ideas about garden making in *De la composition des paysages* (1777) in which he firmly rejects symmetry ('born of idleness and vanity') and emphasizes the difficulties of laying out a naturalistic landscape. Painting and poetry, he argues, have as their goal to represent the most beautiful effects of nature. In both cases the art depends on arranging, embellishing, and selecting. The 'picturesque effect', by which he meant an effect of the sort to inspire artists, depended on exactly the same principles. It was in the spirit of painting or poetry that one should design landscapes, not as an architect or gardener. When you have abandoned 'la triste clôture de vos murailles' (the dismal enclosure of your walls) you will see opening out in all its majesty 'la voûte azurée des cieux' (the blue vault of the heavens). There was also a political dimension to Girardin's philosophy. He thought that a taste for picturesque landscapes to please the eye would lead to philosophical landscapes to please the soul—'for the sweetest and most touching spectacle is that of ease and universal contentment'. So Girardin saw the picturesque garden as the landscape equivalent of a just and natural social order.   PT

Giulia, Villa ⊛

Rome, Italy. Built for Pope Julius III 1550–5 outside the Porta del Popolo, originally in dense woodland, the villa and garden were designed by all the best known architects and decorators of the day. Giorgio Vasari (1511–74), Jacopo Barozzi da VIGNOLA, Bartolomeo AMMANATI, and Michelangelo (1475–1564) all played a part. Its design and perfect proportions with a series of interlocking spaces, clearly derived from Bramante's Cortile del Belvedere (see VATICAN GARDENS) constructed in the early years of the century, were to influence the development of future Renaissance gardens. Da Vignola was probably responsible for the curving loggia in the courtyard from which steps descend to a sunken NYMPHAEUM, fountain, and grotto, decorated with herms above a patterned marble paving. The first courtyard, in the shape of a 'U', was decorated by statues in niches with a portico leading to the loggia and nymphaeum. Originally a vegetable garden and vineyards were carved out of the wooded slopes but today a few box hedges, bay laurels, roses, and oleanders are all that remains of planting although the sunken nymphaeum is still preserved in its 16th-century form.   PHo

Giusti, Giardini ⊛

Verona, Italy. Although their detail has been considerably altered over the centuries the Giardini Giusti, set on a high hill above the river Adige, still retain the main 16th-century elements which define a Renaissance garden:

a geometric layout of box, fountains, grottoes, mythological statues, and a MAZE. Made for the Giusti family in the 1570s it is one of the oldest gardens in northern Italy. Although united by numerous spires of cypresses it is divided into three sections. The highest point provides a BELVEDERE and terraces reached through a mysterious wooded section containing a mythological stone mask and a GROTTO. Below is a parterre, once geometrically Italian but later set with French-style scrolls of box, possibly in 1786 when the original labyrinth (recently again restored) was redesigned by Luigi Trezza (1752–1823). The garden has been much visited by travellers, among them John EVELYN, President de Brosses, and Goethe, the last inspired by the 'huge cypresses which spire into the air like owls'. The American architect Charles PLATT, who deplored its poor state in the 1890s, would be reassured by its present immaculate condition.   PHo

Giverny (Fondation Claude-Monet) ⊛

Giverny, Eure, France. The artist Claude Monet came to live at Giverny in 1883 and made a garden—'I am good for nothing except painting and gardening,' he wrote. After his death, in 1926, the garden decayed but was splendidly brought back to life in the 1980s by Gerald van der Kemp, since when it has become a tourist phenomenon, one of the most visited gardens in France. The garden falls into two quite different parts. In front of the pink and green house is what Monet called the Clos Norman, a rectilinear pattern of beds and gravel paths whose hard lines are hidden in an explosive profusion of planting with thickets of herbaceous plantings above which rise standard roses, ornamental trees, and arches festooned with roses and sweet peas giving off their sweet scents. A tunnel under a railway line leads to the water garden where a long pool is dappled with water lilies. A bridge of Japanese inspiration, draped with wisteria, spans an inlet to the pool—providing one of the most photographed views in modern garden history. Paths among trees snake about the pool which composes itself from time to time into Monet paintings. The garden became famous in Monet's lifetime—*Le Figaro* published an article on it in 1901—but it was not universally admired. A dissenter was the English artist Sir Gerald Kelly who visited Monet and found the garden unexciting: 'It was nice and large and covered with rambling crimson roses which, you know, you get practically speaking in any suburban garden all over England. And there was a little piece of water where there were some common or garden water lilies' (Derek Hudson, *For Love of Painting: The Life of Sir Gerald Kelly*, 1975).   PT

Glasnevin.

See NATIONAL BOTANIC GARDENS, GLASNEVIN.

glasshouse.

The need to protect certain plants from a climate harsher than their native one was understood quite early in garden history. It was also realized that it was possible to bring on precocious growth in hardy plants by protecting them early in the season. The ancient Romans understood this and, unable to make panes of flat glass, used mica to glaze small houses. An example of such a house was found in the excavations of POMPEII. In the Renaissance a lemon house was used to protect citrus plants in the winter but these were really ORANGERIES. There was much circulation of tender plants in the 16th century. In the 1560s Sir William Cecil took delivery of oranges, lemons, myrtles, and pomegranates for the garden of his house in the Strand in London. There were means of protecting tender plants with an opaque roof which would help to ward off frost, but there was nothing resembling a glasshouse. The glasshouse proper, with a fully glazed roof, had to wait until a technique existed for making appropriate glass. By the beginning of the 18th century small panes of glass were easily, if expensively, made, and one of the earliest buildings to incorporate the true idea of the glasshouse was made for the Duke of Chandos at Cannons in Hertfordshire after 1717. Designed by Alessandro Galilei (1691–1737), it was crowned with a cupola glazed on its south side so as to receive the sun from dawn to dusk. A pioneer glasshouse, by an unknown designer and manufacturer, was made at Chiselhampton in Oxfordshire in about 1800. Built against a wall, it has five fully glazed walls and a steeply sloping glazed roof with an ingenious ventilation opening at the aperture. Its framework is of fine cast iron, permitting glazing bars much narrower than is possible with wood and thus allowing more light into the glasshouse. Furthermore, the panes running up and down overlap so there are no horizontal glazing bars. The problem with this technique is that water tended to gather at the overlap which, if it froze, could crack the glass. Furthermore, the overlap tended to become dirty. An ingenious solution was found to the problem by shaping the lower edge of each pane into a curve, like fish scales, which caused water to flow off the surface more rapidly. Furthermore, with glasshouses that had wooden glazing bars, this technique helped prevent the wood from rotting, for water ran down the centre of the panes instead of along the glazing bars. The new techniques were soon exploited by architects to make buildings that not only worked well but looked beautiful. At

Bicton Park in Devon is a superb early 19th-century glasshouse of futuristic design. Built against a wall and with cast-iron glazing bars and fish-scale panes, it is in the form of three billowing lobes of graceful shape. Designed as a palm house, the central lobe rises much higher than those on each side, allowing big trees—a date palm (*Phoenix dactylifera*) is grown there today.

The 19th century was the most fertile period of glasshouse design. The Palm House at Kew was built between 1844 and 1848, designed by Richard Turner and Decimus Burton (1800–81), and was one of the most admired garden buildings of its time; being open to the public, it had great influence on popular taste. The brilliant figure of Sir Joseph PAXTON was behind some of of the century's most dazzling achievements in glasshouses. His Great Conservatory for CHATSWORTH, completed in 1841, was designed in collaboration with Decimus Burton. It was in its day the largest glasshouse in England, 84 m/277 ft long, 37 m/123 ft wide, and 18 m/61 ft high, and cost £33,099 (over £1.2 million in today's money). Constructed with Paxton's ingenious ridge and furrow system of glazing, with the glass angled to permit maximum light, it was designed in a remarkably streamlined and elegant form. A noble carriage drive ran down its centre, wide enough for two carriages. The interior was skilfully landscaped, with outcrops of rocks, a pool, and large trees giving a naturalistic appearance. Charles Darwin saw it in 1845 and was 'transported with delight . . . more wonderfully like tropical nature than I could have conceived possible'. It was planted with an immense range of tender exotics, some of them very large mature specimens brought in for the purpose. A *Zamia*, a species of cycad, weighed 12 tons and was brought all the way from Surrey. The glasshouse was heated with eight underground boilers whose fuel was provided by an underground tramline which in winter brought 300 tons of coal and coke—more than was required to heat the house. The smoke from the boilers was piped away in an underground flue 242 m/795 ft long emerging in a high chimney on top of a hill so that the environs of the glasshouse were free from pollution. The Great Conservatory fell victim to the economies made in countless gardens after the First World War. The cost of heating it, and the wages of the ten gardeners required to manage it, made it impossible to maintain. It was blown up in 1920, needing several charges before the superbly built structure yielded. Paxton's glasshouse designs survive other English gardens, a notable example being the pair of lean-to ridge and furrow glasshouses at SOMERLEYTON HALL in Suffolk which date from the mid 19th century.

In England the tax on glass was abolished in 1845. In 1847 James Hartley patented the sheet glass process by which large panes of glass could be produced cheaply in quantity. Glasshouses became much cheaper and were regarded as an essential adornment of even modest gardens. They were used as the permanent home of some plants but also for raising the tender bedding plants which became so fashionable in Victorian gardens. Articles in garden journals promoted glasshouse gardening, and many books on the subject appeared in the 19th century ranging from Charles M'Intosh's *The Greenhouse, Hot House and Stove* (1838) to the influential James Shirley Hibberd's *The Amateur's Greenhouse and Conservatory* (1875).

The 20th century was not an exciting period for glasshouses but the 21st century started with an entirely novel concept. The future of the glasshouse lies probably with such structures as the biomes of the EDEN PROJECT designed by Nicholas Grimshaw & Partners and completed in 2001. These great geodesic domes, of which the largest is 240 m/800 ft long, 55 m/180 ft high, and 110 m/360 ft wide, are made of an external skeleton of steel hexagons which serve as frames for cushions of layers of EFTE (ethyltetrafluoroethylene) which are filled with dry air, providing very efficient insulation. This transparent foil is less than 1% of the weight of an equal area of glass. The future looks like being a glasshouse that does without glass.
PT

The DUCHESS OF DEVONSHIRE, *The Garden at Chatsworth* (1999).
MAY WOODS and ARETE WARREN, *Glass Houses* (1988).

Glemme, Erik,

(1905–59), Swedish designer, chief architect at the design office of the Stockholm parks department (1936–56) for most of the period under the direction of Holger BLOM. Glemme was a multi-talented designer who had the ability to work with a wide range of features within the landscape, from street furniture to the urban green structure. Glemme designed some of the most distinguished Swedish examples of modernistic parks, among them Mälaren Lakeshore Promenade (1941–3), the Tegner Grove (1941), and the Vasa Park (1947), all in Stockholm. These parks took the local landscape as a point of departure for their design, an early form of the contextualism which was later to be called the Stockholm School of Park Design.   TA

Glenveagh Castle ⊛

Churchhill, Letterkenny, County Donegal, Ireland, is at the heart of Glenveagh National Park, one of the wildest and most beautiful parts of the north-west of Ireland. The garden occupies a lakeside area of 11 hectares/28 acres in the park which covers an area of 16,548 hectares/39,881 acres. The castle was built in the 1870s to the designs of John Townsend Trench for John Adair. In 1937 it was bought by Henry McIlhenny, an American with Irish antecedents. The castellated and picturesque castle overlooks the lake, with the garden behind it and spreading along the banks. McIlhenny had the advice of James Russell in the planting of the garden, who recommended shrubs and trees suitable for the acid soil and the mild and very wet climate. Here are azaleas, eucryphias, excellent species rhododendrons like *R. cinnabarinum* and *R. sinogrande*, the tender and lovely Himalayan *Michelia doltsopa*, and much else that is rare and distinguished. Griselinia hedges conceal a garden of Italianate formality and the walled former kitchen garden behind the castle has been enriched with lively borders, statuary, and urns and a splendid castellated orangery.   PT

gloriette,

a small ornamental pavilion. The French word is derived from *gloire* meaning something glorious. A gloriette is often placed in a position of prominence where paths meet. Because of this, the word came to mean the point where paths meet (the Spanish word *glorieta* has both the primary meaning and the meaning of a traffic roundabout).   PT

Glorup ⊛

Funen, Denmark. Around 1760 romantic ornamental buildings in Denmark were often introduced into baroque gardens, with an informal layout being added only later. The gardens at Glorup were created in a transitional period and represent several styles. In the 1740s the older four-winged building complex was rebuilt, the moat filled in, and a broad parterre laid out in front of the south wing. Between 1762 and 1775 the manor was rebuilt in the baroque and then the classical style, and N.-H. Jardin (1720–99) created two very elongated rectangular spaces between three parallel avenues of lime trees. The parterre was made narrower, and a 220 m/720 ft long basin was dug, with a round islet and fountain. The basin was flanked by urns in Louis XVI style. The remotest part of the garden became a romantic garden with a spiral maze, hermit's hut, and rotunda. The rotunda was later moved to the south-eastern corner and reconstructed in 1868. Throughout the 1860s, the landscape gardener H. A. FLINDT changed and extended the gardens. A special feature was two brick towers holding a suspension bridge over a ravine. The poet Hans Christian Andersen (1805–75) wrote several fairy tales at Glorup, and was at the towers' inauguration. Today they are a ruin.   AL

Gnoll Estate ⊛
Neath, Glamorgan, Wales, bought in the late 17th century by Sir Humphry Mackworth, a copper smelter who was drawn to the place by the presence of a prolific water supply. He came to regard the water as a thing of beauty as well as an essential prerequisite for his industrial activities. Formal gardens were laid out here in the 1720s to the design of Thomas Greening (1684-1767), who made a long formal cascade which has been restored in recent years. In the 18th century the wooded valley above the cascade was ornamented with planned walks, a MOSS HOUSE, and an arcaded battlemented LOGGIA. At the head of the valley an astonishing naturalistic cascade was created in the 1740s, with an overall fall of 55 m/180 ft. It descends in a sequence of falls at the densely wooded curved head of the valley. Its date makes it one of the oldest naturalistic cascades in Britain. The Mackworth family house was destroyed by fire in 1957 and its grounds acquired by the local authority which has restored the surviving garden features and opened it as a public park. Despite its popularity it retains its secretive and Arcadian atmosphere.   PT

Godinton House ⊛
Ashford, Kent, England, is one of the best surviving works by the architect and garden designer Sir Reginald BLOMFIELD. The house dates from the early 17th century but was built on a much older site and is set in a magnificent medieval DEER PARK with fine old parkland trees. In 1898 Blomfield designed new gardens for G. Ashley-Dod. Yew hedges to the south and east of the house have been clipped into sweeping gables mimicking those of the house. Pan's Garden is also of strongly architectural character—a mazelike arrangement of giant shapes of box clipped into stumpy pyramids clusters about a statue of Pan rising high on a plinth. Lawns sweep across to the west where a figure of Ceres is flanked by a pair of weeping silver pears (*Pyrus salicifolia* 'Pendula'). Beyond the pears are a pair of flowering cherries (*Prunus × subhirtella* 'Taihaku') which stand at the head of a pair of mixed borders whose airy planting allows views of the parkland beyond them. Closer to the house is the Italian Garden, a concealed GIARDINO SEGRETO behind a colonnade veiled in wisteria and statuary. A lily pool with an Italian cypress (*Cupressus sempervirens*) at each corner stands at the centre surrounded by a lawn and raised beds on each side filled with eryngiums, lavender, *Perovskia atriplicifolia*, and *Pittosporum tobira*. The garden is 5 hectares/12 acres in area but repeatedly takes advantage of long parkland views. Blomfield's design responds to both the house's architecture and its surrounding landscape with exceptional success. The garden has been finely restored in recent years and is one of the outstanding examples of its period.   PT

Golden Gate Park ⊛
San Francisco, California, USA, was established in 1872 on a site of 410 hectares/1,013 acres, and is one of the finest city parks in the country. The long rectangular park has two distinct sections. The western section adjoining the Pacific Ocean is buffeted by fierce winds and salt-laden air, while the more sheltered eastern section is entered through the long, narrow Panhandle boulevard. It is the most remarkable 19th-century landscape improvement, since two-thirds of it comprised shifting sand dunes. The designer, William Hammond Hall, a surveyor and field engineer for the US Army Corps of Engineers, devised a successful reclamation programme that was a form of accelerated plant succession. Using fast-growing evergreen trees, he created a forested park with meadows similar to Olmsted's parks in the eastern states within five years. The lawn near the Sharon Quarters, one of the earliest children's playgrounds in the country, typifies his skill as a landscape designer. Several other notable Victorian features survive, including the decorative Arizona Garden, a popular form of gardening using desert plants, not necessarily from Arizona. The large and elaborate Conservatory (1878) is one of the finest in the country, and the sandstone Richardsonian Romanesque style McLaren Lodge (1895) stands near the main entrance. Hall was succeeded as superintendent by the Scottish horticulturist John McLaren (1847-1943), whom he had trained. McLaren continually claimed complete authorship of the park, when his true contribution was to extend Hall's design, by greatly increasing the range of broad-leafed evergreen plants from Asia, Europe, and Australasia. McLaren attempted to recreate natural scenes and was responsible for developing the Chain of Lakes, Stowe Lake, a naturalistic reservoir, and the polo field. The Music Concourse is a large formal arena with pleached London plane trees and an Italian Renaissance colonnade (1899) that is flanked by the California Academy of Sciences and the M. H. De Young Memorial Museum. The Japanese Tea Garden was created by Makoto Hagiwara (1854-1925) as a commercial tea garden with plants brought from Japan. The oldest features are the Main Gate, and the Moon Bridge. In 1915 the Pagoda, Temple Gate, and South Gate were installed. Irrigation was a major problem from the inception of the park and the continued drilling to tap ground water culminated in 1905 with the erection of two windmills close to the ocean. The Strybing Arboretum was initiated in 1937 on a site of 24 hectares/55 acres. The present layout dates from 1966 with South African, eastern Australian, New Zealand, and California areas, and collections of dwarf conifers, succulents, and fragrant plants arranged around a large oval lawn with a focal fountain.   DCS

Golistan Palace ⊛
Tehran, Iran. Reconstructed by Karim Khan Zand in the 18th century from Shah Tahmasp's original 16th-century citadel, and extended by Fath Ali Shah (*c*.1797-1834) in 1806, the Golistan became the 19th-century centre of the royal Qajar court. A large complex, it was often enlivened with carpeted tents set among lawns sprinkled with tulips and narcissi, anemones, and poppies. Robert Ker Porter attended one of Fath Ali Shah's receptions where the Shah appeared in a blaze of dazzling jewels, a lofty tiara of three elevations on his head. Divided originally into a public reception area and private royal dwelling it contained several water features and a Rose Garden—the word 'Golistan' actually means a rose garden—only destroyed during the Pahlavi period (1925-79). It was considerably altered after 1875 by Naser-ud-din Shah who inaugurated a museum and built a twin-towered building which overlooked a large basin. Today it is approached by the Dari-e Sadat or Gate of Happiness, a rectangular canal, flanked by plane trees, framing a view to the Divan Khaneh (public reception hall) where the marble throne is displayed. The garden needs restoration.   PHo

Gołuchów ⊛
between Poznań and Kalisz, Poland, is a landscape garden of the arboretum kind. The first manor house at Gołuchów was erected by Rafał Leszczyński before 1560. In 1600-19 Wacław Leszczyński remodelled it into a splendid four-wing Renaissance palace with a LOGGIA. On the southern side of the palace there existed an Italianate garden divided into four parts. The residence, falling into ruin, was rebuilt in 1875-85 by Izabella Działyńska, wife of Jan Działyński the owner of KÓRNIK. She decided to create 'mon eldorado . . . mon paradis terrestre' here. The palace was erected in French Renaissance (François I) style, mainly after designs by Maurice Ouradou, with the use of the surviving original fragments. In 1876-89 a landscape park designed by Adam Kubaszewski (1848-1927) was laid out round the palace, covering an area of 220 hectares/543 acres. It is an elongated rectangle in plan, stretching along the valley of the small river Ciemna which was

dammed to form a series of irregular pools. As in Kórnik, the Działyńskis brought here a large number of exotic trees and other plants, mainly Australian and Japanese conifers. The outer part of the park is a forest in character, whereas the inner one is composed of trees gathered in picturesque groups.   WB

Gongwangfu ⊛

Beijing, China. Once the mansion of the Qianlong Emperor's favourite, Heshen (1750-99), who was responsible for the small gate in the Jesuit baroque style fashionable in the late 18th century, it was later inhabited by Prince Gong (1833-98). The mansion, elaborately ornamented, consisted of three lines of courtyards which were joined at the back by a 160-m/525-ft long two-storeyed building of 40 bays. Lying behind this, the garden was composed as a 'mountain-water' landscape, with tree-covered hills, mounds, and rockeries set among winding brooks. The eastern part of the garden was enclosed by short walls and shaded by green bamboos. North of this a sheltered stage stood in front of a hall, planned in the shape of a bat, in which the audience was seated during performances, while to the west were various different scenes, including Elm Pass, Green Shade Mount, and the Mid-lake Pavilion. The monumental and luxurious style of this mansion and the freedom and elegance of its garden support the popular belief that they were the models for the Rong Mansion and Daguan Yuan described in the classic novel *Hong lou meng* (A Dream of Red Mansions).
C-ZC/MK

goose foot. See PATTE D'OIE.

Gordon, James

(c.1708-1780), Scottish gardener and nurseryman who came south to work for Dr James Sherard (1666-1738) in his garden at Eltham in Kent and for Lord Petre (1713-42) at Thorndon Hall, Essex. Later he opened his own nursery at Mile End, transferring to the city of London and a seed shop at 25 Fenchurch Street. Gordon became skilled in raising plants from American seed given him by Peter COLLINSON and collected by John BARTRAM and was renowned for getting the difficult *Kalmia* to germinate. For twenty years he patiently trialled a tree which was eventually named in his honour, *Gordonia lasianthus*, the loblolly bay. He also grew rhododendrons and azaleas collected from the USA, and from China he coaxed the newly collected (1754) gardenia and camellia plants to grow, as well as the extraordinary *Ginkgo biloba*. Gordon corresponded with LINNAEUS and was one of the 18th century's leading nurserymen.   MC-C

Gothenburg Botanic Garden ⊛

Gothenburg, Sweden, was founded, designed, and constructed in 1915-23 (inaugurated in 1923), on a site chosen by Professor Rutger Sernander (1866-1944) belonging to the farm Stora Änggården, south of Slottsskogen in Gothenburg. The first director (1919-48) was Sernander's disciple, the legendary university reader Carl Skottsberg (1880-1963), who planned and organized the garden and later participated in several plant hunting expeditions (Easter Island, South America). With an area of 175 hectares/432 acres containing about 12,000 species, it is owned by the city of Gothenburg and is Sweden's greatest botanic garden and one of the finest in Europe; 155 hectares/382 acres consist of a nature reserve, Änggårdsbergen, a typical cultural landscape of western Sweden with heather moors, a Naturparken (nature park), and Vitsippsdalen (the valley of wildwood windflowers (*Anemone nemorosa*)). The rock garden (Klippträdgården), planted in around 1920 with about 5,000 species arranged geographically, is one of the most notable features of the garden. Other notable parts are the Bambulunden (Bamboo Grove), and the Rhododendrondalen and Japandalen (Rhododendron and Japanese Valleys) dating from the 1950s. The 15-hectare/37-acre arboretum was planted in 1953 with about 6,000 specimens, planted in 500 groups representing the continents of North America, Asia and Europe. Besides the thematic gardens Gothenburg has botanical order beds (see BOTANIC GARDEN), demonstration gardens of roses and bulbs, and a kitchen garden. Greenhouses built in 1983 contain about 4,500 tender species. During the 1990s the most attractive compositions of annuals have won great admiration. The garden receives about 400,000 visitors every year.   KL

Gothenburg Parks ⊛

Gothenburg, Sweden. Gothenburg acquired its current town privileges in 1621, but its origins go back to the Middle Ages. Dutch fortification engineers made the first town plan, a walled city with an angled moat and acute bastions. Beginning in 1807 the wall was removed and, beyond it, the parks were built— Trädgårdsföreningen and Kungsparken together with an avenue, Nya allén. Trädgårdsföreningen was founded in 1842 on former meadowland—it is one of Sweden's oldest surviving public parks and the first to be listed. Several plans were drawn up and rejected, until a German-inspired landscape style, emphasizing garden plants and public attractions, was chosen. Around 1900 the park was completed with various buildings of which

the oldest and best preserved is Direktörsvillan (1847). There are also a restaurant (1887, burnt 1995, rebuilt 1998) and a music pavilion. The palm house (1878), together with the rose collection (with 3,800 cultivars, laid out in the 1980s), are the park's greatest individual attractions. Connected to the Trädgårdsföreningen is Slottsskogen (The Castle Wood) of about 140 hectares/346 acres, inaugurated as a public city park in 1876. It had its origin in the oak woods of Älvsborg's 15th-century royal demesne. After the foundation of Gothenburg, King Gustav II Adolf gave the woods as a public amenity, but because of vandalism the public was excluded in 1719. Slottsskogen went through many changes, becoming by 1874 a park of very diverse character and ingredients. From the beginning of the 20th century Björngårdsvillan, originally a bear house, became the park's greatest attraction—it now houses a collection of endangered tropical plants. Later attractions include a seal pond, a theatre, a museum of natural history and an observatory, and a children's zoo. Slottsskogsvallen (a sports ground) was laid out by the architect Lars Israel Wahlman (1870-1952) in 1923.   KL

Granja de Ildefonso, La ⊛

near Segovia, Madrid, Spain. The estate at La Granja, in the foothills of the Sierra Guadarrama, goes back to the 14th century when it was owned by Henry III of Castile who used it as a country retreat. Its present fame dates from its ownership by Philip V, the first Bourbon King of Spain, who came here in 1720. The new house was started to the designs of Theodore Ardemans and continued by Felipe Juvara after whose death Giovanni-Battista Sachetti took over. It was not, however, completed until the reign of Philip V's son Charles III, who came to the throne in 1759, but its essential character was established by that time. Philip V was a grandson of Louis XIV of France and as a child had lived at VERSAILLES. The garden at La Granja is certainly in the tradition of that at Versailles in so far as the limitations of the rise and fall of the irregular site would allow. The variations in level, however, gave La Granja an advantage that Versailles lacked. A pool in the highest part of the garden (1,325 m/4,347 ft higher than the palace) provides the water pressure to feed the spectacular fountains which are such a notable feature of La Granja.

The making of the garden here was an epic in itself. The rocky, infertile soil was immensely hard to work but terraces were built and huge quantities of earth were imported. The laying out of the grounds was initially in the charge of René Carlier, who had worked on the garden at the ESCORIAL; he died in 1722 and was succeeded by Esteban Boutelou II. A very large team of mainly French sculptors worked, initially under the direction of Carlier, on statuary for the garden, directly inspired by the example of Versailles and in some cases using designs by LE BRUN. Carlier was responsible for the large double parterre below the palace's façade and for the great cascade which continues its axis dramatically up the slope beyond. A parallel axis is formed by a series of pools linked by cascades, the Carrera de Caballos, which ascends the slope each with its vertical water jet soaring into the sky—the ends of the Carrera are marked by set-piece fountain pools with statues of Andromeda and Neptune. South of the palace, set in its own parterre, is the Fuente de la Fama (Fountain of Fame) whose jet rises 47 m/154 ft. The whole area of the gardens is 146 hectares/360 acres. The pattern of axes, ornamental eyecatchers, countless pools, and fountains is blurred by billowing trees and distant views of the mountainous scenery.

In the end La Granja has little in common with Versailles. It was never a centre of government—it was more a rural pleasure house. The pink and white stone of the palace, its cheerfully decorative architecture, and the exuberant eruptions of the fountains are light-hearted compared with the gravitas of Versailles. Lastly, the wild mountain setting of La Granja, constantly revealed, is a different world.   PT

grasses.
The grass families (Gramineae and Poaceae) contain over 10,000 species of both annual and perennial grasses as well as the bamboos. They are found in almost every habitat and display endless variations on an essentially simple architecture. Many such as wheat, rye, barley, maize, millet, and rice provide the staple diets of mankind, while others provide sugars and the starches for alcohol.

Gardeners use the term loosely to embrace not only the true grasses but also sedges, rushes, restios, and cat-tails. The true grasses (Poaceae or Gramineae) have cylindrical, usually hollow, stems and flat leaves produced at the base of the plant and at the nodes (joints) along the stems, while the sedges (Cyperaceae) have solid, three-sided stems and mostly basal leaves that are strongly V-shaped in section, the flowers appearing just short of the tip of the unjointed flowering stem. The rushes (Juncaceae) have round but solid and unjointed stems, all the leaves being basal and the flowers carried in a flat-head cyme two-thirds of the way up the stem. The cat-tails (Typhaceae) have basal leaves in two ranks springing from aggressively spreading rhizomes, and bear flowers at the tops of straight, solid unjointed stems, the female flowers looking like dark brown cigars surrounding the stem just below the male flowers, which are smaller and fleeting. The bamboos differ from other grasses mainly in their greater stature, in their usually woody stems, in that their stems branch, and in their leaves having stalks.

Grasses have been slow to be appreciated as ornamentals. For a long time their main use in gardens was for lawns and paths, and as green ground cover under orchards. In Victorian times a few such as pampas grass (*Cortaderia*), eulalia grass (*Miscanthus*), and fountain grass (*Pennisetum*) were displayed in isolation on broad sweeps of lawn, more as curiosities than beauties, and a limited number of bamboos, mainly invasive *Sasa* species, were an essential ingredient of the Victorian shrubbery. The present interest springs largely from the naturalistic movement, and since more plants on earth are grasses than plants of any other sort any imitation of nature must include an abundance of grasses. William ROBINSON in *The Wild Garden* (1870) advocates planting both natives and exotics in rough grasses and leaving them to grow, while in America in the first quarter of the last century Jens JENSEN pioneered the 'Prairie Style' of gardening (see NATURALISTIC PLANTING), making landscapes in the mid-west using only the indigenous prairie flora. In Germany Karl FOERSTER, whose nursery was offering over 100 grasses in the 1940s, advocated a style of planting based on naturally occurring plant associations. His book *Eintritt der Graeser und Ferne in den Garten* (Introducing Ferns and Grasses into the Garden), (1957) though never translated into English, had a profound influence on a whole generation of nurserymen and designers who took his ideas across Europe and to the Americas, most notably the nurserymen Richard Simon, whose Bluemount Nursery was the first in America to offer a collection of ornamental grasses, and Kurt Bluemel, whose eponymous Maryland nursery has been responsible for introducing many new grass species and varieties. His influence can also be seen in the work of landscape architects such as Oehme and VAN SWEDEN in America, whose stylized prairie gardens are composed of about 50% grasses relying on a basic palette of genuine prairie plants enlivened with exotic introductions, and Piet OUDOLF in Holland, whose naturalistic gardens, which contain about 20% grasses, seek to evoke wild landscapes, as well as on Roberto BURLE MARX in South America.

The true grasses are valued in gardens for the ability of their flower and seed-heads to capture the light of the sky and bring it down into the garden, as well as for the sense of movement they bring and for the length of time through which they remain ornamental. Many are also grown for their coloured or variegated foliage. In recent years the variety of grasses available has been greatly increased by careful selection through trials of the indigenous grasses of the United States, through work carried out at Longwood Gardens at Kennet Square in Pennsylvania, by breeding, particularly of Miscanthus by Ernst Pagels in Germany, and by the introduction to the West, mainly by staff of the US National Arboretum in Washington, DC, of grasses long cultivated in the East.

The pampas grasses, *Stipa gigantea*, and feather reed grass and many eulalia grasses are most often used as isolated specimens, either to draw the eye in the landscape or in a border, or as markers to create rhythm in borders or, more formally, in pairs each side of steps or an arch, though they can of course be massed. Other grasses such as Panicum, Molinia, and Pennisetum, as well as many Stipa, are more often grouped in threes or fives, or massed, and indeed most grasses are at their most effective in bold drifts, even in small gardens where it may be better to create drifts of five or ten of one kind of grass than to use five or ten different kinds. The flowers of grasses are best seen against a dark background with the sun shining through them from beyond or beside them. This is also true of many grasses with coloured or variegated leaves, particularly those with white or cream striped leaves such as *Miscanthus sinensis* 'Variegatus', *Phalaris arundinacea* 'Picta', and *Glyceria maxima* 'Variegata'. Grasses with gold-or yellow-striped leaves such as *Hakonechloa macra* 'Aureola' and *Alopecurus pratensis* 'Aureomarginata' look best with the light falling on them. The sedges (carex), especially variegated ones such as *Carex oshimensis* 'Evergold', *C.* 'Ice Dance', and *C. pendula* 'Moonraker', and woodrushes (Luzula) are particularly useful in more shaded parts of the garden, while the rushes and the cat-tails require moist soils and look best growing at the water's edge or even in shallow water, the linearity of their vertical stems in counterpoint to the horizontality of the water.   RG

RICK DARKE, *The Color Encyclopedia of Ornamental Grasses* (1999).
ROGER GROUNDS, *The Plantfinder's Guide to Ornamental Grasses* (1998).
MICHAEL KING and PIET OUDOLF, *Prachtig Gras* (1996). Translated as *Gardening with Grasses* (1998).

gravel garden.
Using gravel as a garden mulch to retain moisture in pots or beds is an old technique. Much more recent is the use of gravel on a much larger scale as the background for a whole garden. The pioneer in this style of gardening

was the English gardener and nurserywoman Beth CHATTO. On a visit to New Zealand in 1989, walking in the southern Alps, she was inspired by the beauty of a partly dry river bed with diverse wild plants. In her very dry garden in Essex she started to make a gravel garden of 0.3 hectare/0.75 acre on very poor soil in which the whole area was mulched in gravel and no artificial irrigation would be permitted. Apart from retaining moisture in the soil it also made a good-looking background to the planting, which is of a naturalistic style much of which resembles the river bed Beth Chatto saw in New Zealand. Apart from moisture loss through evaporation on the surface of soil the plants themselves, through transpiration through the foliage, are a major cause of moisture loss. Plants from dry climates have leaves which are designed to retain as much moisture as possible and it is these that Beth Chatto used. The motive for this kind of garden is partly ecological, to conserve water, and partly aesthetic. By making such a garden you are creating an important part of an ecology appropriate to a particular range of plants. The gravel also provides a perfect germination medium, so that self-sown plants will add to the naturalistic atmosphere.   PT

BETH CHATTO, *The Gravel Garden* (2000).

Gray, Christopher

(1693/4–1764), English nurseryman whose business in Fulham, London, using part of Mark CATESBY's garden, specialized in North American plants, having acquired in 1713 some of Bishop COMPTON's American collection. Philip MILLER regarded him as one of the ten leading nurserymen in London. In 1730 Gray joined in the publication by the Society of Gardeners of the *Catalogus Plantarum Officinalium* and in 1755 he published his own *Catalogue of Trees, Shrubs, Plants and Flowers*. Gray's interest in American plants continued. Miller inspected his custard apple (*Annona reticulata*) and the newly arrived (1734) *Magnolia grandiflora*, reputedly the first specimen grown in England. In 1763 Gray published Catesby's *Hortus Britanno-Americanus*, which included the author's own engraving of the tree, drawn in the garden of Admiral Sir Charles Wager, a keen gardener. Following the death of Gray the nursery continued for nearly a century, closing in 1810.   MC-C

Great Dixter ⊛

Northiam, East Sussex, England, has a timbered late 15th-century house which was much added to in 1910 under the supervision of Sir Edwin LUTYENS. Lutyens's client was Nathaniel Lloyd, a retired printer who had developed a passion for architecture. Nathaniel's wife Daisy was a knowledgeable plantswoman and gardener and together, with advice from Lutyens, they made a garden of ARTS AND CRAFTS style in keeping with the vernacular tradition of the house. Their son Christopher LLOYD also became a gardener and, starting with the fine framework of yew hedges, topiary, and enclosures, greatly added to the garden, in particular enriching the planting. One of his chief interests was the Long Border, 60 m/200 ft × 4.5 m/15 ft, in which he practised a style of mixed planting of shrubs, herbaceous perennials, and annuals which, in the late 20th century, had a strong influence on garden style. Meadow planting of a naturalistic kind, initiated at Great Dixter by Daisy Lloyd, was much extended. An enclosed formal rose garden laid out by Lutyens was dug up and replanted with a flamboyant 'subtropical' scheme of bananas, cannas, dahlias, and ginger plants (*Hedychium flavescens*). Great Dixter, of all the English gardens open to the public in the late 20th and early 21st centuries, has most inspired a generation of gardeners. Among the lessons they have learnt have been the importance of knowing your plants and of forming your own judgement of their relative merits.   PT

CHRISTOPHER LLOYD, *The Year at Great Dixter* (1987).

Greece, ancient.

The gardens and parks of the ancient Greek world in the Classical (5th–4th century BC) and Hellenistic (3rd–1st century BC) periods are known from archaeological exploration, from epigraphic, documentary, and literary sources, and from depictions in art. The available evidence suggests that the ancient Greek garden (κῆπος) typically lay outside the city, either in the suburban areas near the circuit walls or further away in rural areas. Within the walls of the city, houses were closely huddled together, and the density of the urban landscape was relieved only by scattered sanctuary groves or gardens of varying but modest size, and by the main public square or agora that was often shaded by the planting of trees. There was rarely any excess space available for a garden on the property of the houses of city dwellers. The plots for these houses were modest, and the small central courtyard of the house was generally paved, leaving only potted plants in this area as a possibility.

Market gardens and farms outside the city supplied the urban inhabitants with food. The gardens in these locations were kept alive with a plentiful source of water from the rivers and streams in the vicinity. Literary sources refer to gardens in the countryside, and property lists preserved in inscriptions record the location of gardens in suburban and rural locations near a source of water. Supplying urban areas with water was a problem in ancient Greece, and it was not until the Roman period that private homes were connected to city water pipes allowing the maintenance of a garden within the house.

Utilitarian gardens were mixed gardens planted with fruit trees and vegetable beds. The produce of these gardens named in written sources include figs, mulberries, nuts, herbs, melons, and vegetables such as leeks, lettuce, cabbages, asparagus, and onions. Gardens on farms were accompanied by fields of grain, vineyards, and olive groves, the staple crops of ancient Greek farming. Utilitarian gardens, usually fruit orchards, were also owned by cult organizations, and they were frequently rented out for profit. Roses and other flowering plants were grown commercially on farms for use in garlands and wreaths at religious festivals and weddings, but there were also merchants and dealers in wildflowers who collected these from the mountains and fields for these purposes. Flowers and vegetation were of special significance in the cult of Aphrodite, the goddess of fertility, and it is in Athens and in Paphos on Cyprus that she had a sanctuary called 'in the gardens'.

Groves of olive, pine, cypress, oak, and laurel trees commonly surrounded ancient Greek temples. Throughout the Greek world, sacred gardens and groves were revered as places belonging to and inhabited by the gods. Some of these groves were natural and of great antiquity, others were intentionally planted from time to time. Small sacred groves adorned public squares in many cities. A grove surrounding the temple of Hephaistos in Athens from the 3rd century BC to the 1st century AD is known through archaeological excavations. Here on the edge of the agora in the centre of the city, American archaeologists uncovered rows of planting pits containing ceramic pots for trees or bushes on three sides of the temple. Outside Athens in the districts of Academy, Lykeion, and Kynosarges were ancient sacred groves and cult sites. From the 4th century BC public gymnasia and private schools of philosophy operated as educational institutions in close proximity to these groves on the river banks. The gymnasia included athletic grounds, baths, and rooms for literary instruction in this environment. The plane, elm, poplar, and olive trees shading the gymnasium in the Academy district were praised in the ancient sources. The philosophers Plato, Aristotle, and Epicurus, among others, established their schools in these suburban areas, and all of them possessed a garden. Of all the philosophers, Epicurus was the most closely associated with a garden, his school commonly being referred to as 'The Garden'.

Cemeteries were occasionally planted with trees, but tomb gardens are best known in the Hellenistic period when sources refer to gardens associated with tombs. Those outside Alexandria in the fertile Nile delta were established and rented out as utilitarian gardens for fruit and vegetables. The profit from these gardens supported cultic activities associated with the tomb and funerary festivals in honour of the dead.

The Greek monarchs who ruled after the death of Alexander in 323 BC built palatial residences in their capitals at Alexandria, Pergamon, Pella, and Antioch, but the only palace at which gardens are attested is that in Alexandria. Groves were planted in the grounds of the palace itself, and in the palace district as a whole were many public and religious buildings, as well as tombs, that were surrounded by plantings of trees.

Professional gardeners existed in Classical Greece, but since most landowners at that time worked their own farms and estates, there appears to have been little demand for them. In the Hellenistic period, however, and particularly in Egypt under the Ptolemaic kings, Greek gardeners were regularly employed on royal plantations and vineyards. Detailed papyrus documents have survived that illuminate the organization, personnel, and produce of these estates. Books specifically dealing with gardening also seem to have been written at the earliest in the Hellenistic period, although treatises on botany and handbooks on farming had appeared since at least the 4th century BC. These contained, among other things, tips on how to plant crops, how deep to dig planting pits for trees, and how to irrigate and fertilize plants. Theophrastus, in his 4th-century treatise *On Plants*, for example, discussed methods of inducing flowers to bloom throughout the year.

Neither in the excavated remains, nor in the ancient written sources is it evident that nature in the form of a garden was considered a qualitative improvement of living conditions within the ancient Greek city, but on the borders of and beyond it, where gardens and groves prospered naturally due to favourable conditions, gardens were cultivated and appreciated.   MC

Green Animals ⊛

Portsmouth, Rhode Island, USA, like many American gardens open to the public, grew from a private country estate. From 1872 to 1972, members of the Brayton family resided here and indulged their sculptural garden fantasies. The topiary collection was created by gardener Joseph Carreiro and continued by his son-in-law George Mendonca. It is the oldest and most

northern TOPIARY garden in the United States. Miss Alice Braydon, the last family member to reside here, adopted the name 'Green Animals' when the animal count reached 21 pieces. Another 60 topiary geometric forms complete the sculptural collection. Topiaries and the hedges are from box, yew, and privet. The gardens are laid out in grids of squares and rectangles defined by gravel paths and low evergreen hedges. Each of these serves as a sort of plinth for a major topiary, and is filled in with richly coloured annual bedding. Some perennials, including grasses, are also used to good effect for the framed beds. Arbours, lily pools, fruit trees, and other garden features serve to display a wide variety of plant forms and colours, but it is the animals that truly delight visitors. Animals stand at attention, or cavort and gambol in the gardens. Giraffe, teddy bear, elephant, lion, and camel join the more expected swan and peacock in this leafy menagerie. The gardens surround a modest white house, overlooking Narragansett Bay, across from the summer palaces of Newport. Green Animals is owned by the Preservation Society of Newport, which also manages some of those palaces.   PC

Greencombe ⊛

Porlock, Somerset, England, has an unusual site on a wooded north-facing slope overlooking the sea with a notably benign microclimate. With high rainfall and acid soil the circumstances are perfect for the cultivation of camellias and rhododendrons in which the garden is very rich. The garden was started in 1946 by Horace Stroud but has been brought to its present state of perfection by Joan Loraine who bought the estate in 1966. Her skills as a plantswoman and practical gardener are allied to her sensitive understanding of the character of the place. Close to the house the ground is sculpted into lawns and sweeping terraces which are lavishly planted. The old woodland to the west is the setting for the finest part of the garden. Long mossy walks follow the contours and give views of the flowering shrubs and ornamental trees (in particular acers) which grow among the oaks, holly, and coppiced sweet chestnuts which have been grown here since time immemorial. Here, too, are beautifully grown erythroniums, of which a National Collection (46 species and cultivars) is held. These are the perfect conditions also for a very large National Collection of polystichum ferns of no less than 124 species and cultivars. Of more recondite interest, but skilfully woven into the landscape, are the National Collections of gaultherias (52 species and cultivars) and vacciniums (51 species and cultivars). At Greencombe the plant interest

and beauty of landscape are inextricably intertwined.   PT

Greene, Isabelle

(b. 1934), American landscape architect practising in Santa Barbara, California. She devised a new kind of garden, making use of native plants and inspired by the natural landscape. Historically the finest gardens in Santa Barbara, in particular those in Montecito, were inspired by European models. Isabelle Greene, with her interest in sustainability, uses a wide range of drylands plants including many of those native to southern California and to those countries with similar climates. In a garden such as the VALENTINE GARDEN in Montecito she deployed a rough stone dry creek bed scattered with agaves, anigozanthus, and yuccas as the setting for an austerely beautiful modern house. With the firm she founded, Isabelle Greene & Associates, she has produced a large body of work, ranging from gardens of modest size to extensive land planning in which a concern for the environment and a great knowledge of plants are the essential ingredients.   PT

greenhouse. See GLASSHOUSE.

Grew, Nehemiah

(1641–1712), physician and microscopist born into a dissenting family, and a pioneer of plant classification. He studied at Pembroke Hall, Cambridge, then at Leiden University practising medicine. Grew studied the structure of plants and carried out exhaustive experiments. In 1672 he published *The Anatomy of Vegetables Begun* which was particularly concerned with the study of seed structure. This was followed in 1673 by *An Idea of Phytological History Propounded* which related to the roots of plants. In Grew's most influential and controversial book, *The Anatomy of Plants* (1682), he correctly postulated that the male organs of a plant were the stamens which produced the pollen, or 'farina' as he called it, to fertilize the female organ (the pistil). This was a highly controversial view and prompted fierce discussion and disagreement and was totally disbelieved by de TOURNEFORT, who considered pollen existed for 'merely excrementitious' purposes.   MC-C

Grimsthorpe Castle ⊛

near Bourne, Lincolnshire, England, was built in the 13th century but transformed in the 16th century by the Willoughby de Eresby family (who still own it) with changes in the 17th century and, most particularly, in the early 18th century when it was partly rebuilt by Sir John VANBRUGH. An engraving by Jan KIP in *Britannia*

Illustrata (1707) shows the garden laid out in the 1680s by George LONDON with a pattern of enclosures corresponding closely to the garden today. Drawings by William Stukeley of 1736 show a star-shaped pattern of rides through the woods south of the castle, each ending in a bastion on the wood's perimeter. This is thought to have been designed by Stephen SWITZER afer 1720. Capability BROWN was consulted in 1772 and made plans but nothing is known of the result. Today the old bowling green east of the house is a rose parterre and to its south is a formal kitchen garden and orchard. The site of London's parterre below the south front is simplified but it retains noble urns of the period and a new topiary garden has been laid out south of it. A pair of modern herbaceous borders runs between yew hedges along an escarpment from which are magnificent views of the park. There are 1,200 hectares/3,000 acres here and the atmosphere of park and garden preserves much from the past. PT

Groen, Jan van der

(c.1635–1672), Dutch gardener best known as the author of a popular late 17th-century gardening manual. In 1659 he succeeded his late father-in-law as gardener to Prince William III for whom he worked at his various estates. Initially he was at Paleis Noordeinde (The Hague), from 1665 till 1670 he worked at HONSELAARSDIJK and possibly at Huis ten Bosch (The Hague), while from 1671 till his death in 1672 he was at Huis ter Nieuwburch (Rijswijk). His manual *Den Nederlandtsen hovenier* (1669) (The Dutch Gardener) is largely concerned with the cultivation of plants. The introductory section includes general horticultural information. A final section provides a series of engravings of garden features, based largely on early 17th-century foreign works with some inspired by features in the princely gardens. This book remained in print in various editions until 1721 and was translated into French and German.
JW

JAN VAN DER GROEN, *Den Nederlandtsen hovenier*, new edition ed. Carla S. Oldenburger-Ebbers and D. Onno Wijnands (1988).

Großsedlitz ⊛

Dresden, Germany, covering 18 hectares/44 acres, is in the care of the Saxonian State Palaces, Castles, and Gardens authority. The origins of today's gardens can be traced to plans drawn up under Elector Frederich August I (1670–1733) between 1723 and 1732, integrating existing parts of the garden design by architects Matthäus Daniel Pöppelmann (1662–1736) and Johann Christoph Knöffel (1686–1752) executed under August Christoph, Duke of Wackerbarth (1662–1734), between 1719 and 1723. Wackerbarth took account of the natural contours of the site by laying out two gardens, to be linked with an

Johannes Kip's engraving of the garden at **Grimsthorpe Castle** published in *Britannia Illustrata* (1707).

Güell, Park ✤

Barcelona, Spain, is a public park designed by Antoni GAUDÍ. It has its origins with Gaudí's patron the industrialist Don Eusebi Güell I Bacigalupi. Güell had studied the English GARDEN CITIES and resolved to create something similar in Barcelona. He found a mountainous site north-west of the city centre and from 1900 work began under Gaudí's supervision. The venture was a failure and only three of the projected 60 houses were completed. After the Second World War the site was acquired by the city of Barcelona and it became a public park. The south-westerly entrance is unlike that of any public park in the world and immediately proclaims Gaudí's individuality. The boundary wall is decorated with repeated medallions, worked in a mosaic of broken china, with the words Park and Güell. The entrance is guarded by two rustic stone pavilions, as though made of gingerbread, and crowned with undulating roofs covered, again, in coloured ceramic pieces and erupting in curious towers. A double flight of steps inlaid with white ceramic rises past a brilliantly coloured dragon spouting water into a trough. At the head of the stairs is the monumental Hall of a Hundred Columns which supports on its roof a huge esplanade with, snaking across one side, a curving bench inlaid with mosaic. Further up the hill paths wind among naturalistic groves of trees—palms, umbrella pines (*Pinus pinea*), holm oaks (*Quercus ilex*), and thickets of scented *Pittosporum tobira*. Terraces in this part of the park are supported by arcades of tufa with occasional stalactites and columns sometimes breaking out into figures. Gaudí's artistry restrains his decorative exuberance from tumbling over into kitsch and Park Güell is both immensely popular and much admired.   PT

Guevrekian, Gabriel

(1900-70), modernist architect and garden designer born in Turkey, educated in Austria, who practised in France and Iran. His garden designs are sharply geometric with much use of brilliant colours, triangular forms, and plants treated as part of the colour scheme. Only three gardens designed by him are known. His Jardin d'Eau et de Lumière (Garden of Water and Light) for the Exposition des Arts Décoratifs et Industriels Modernes (Paris, 1925) had zigzag planting, a coloured globe, stepped pools, triangular shapes, and clinical water spouts. It was admired by Charles de Noailles, who asked him to design a garden for the Villa NOAILLES, his house at Hyères on the French riviera. The result, a cubist garden laid out in 1928, is one of the few really well-known modernist gardens. Triangular, like the sharp prow of a ship, it had orange trees in square beds, brilliantly coloured mosaics, a slender pool, and blocks of planting in geometrically shaped beds. It was reinstated, somewhat sketchily, in modern times. At the Villa Heim (Neuilly, Paris) in 1927 Guevrekian designed both house and elaborate terraced garden for the couturier Jacques Heim.   PT

DOROTHÉE IMBERT, *The Modernist Garden in France* (1993).

Guilfoyle, William Robert

(1840-1912), landscape gardener and botanist, celebrated for his remarkable remodelling of Melbourne's ROYAL BOTANIC GARDENS during his long directorship 1873-1909. The Guilfoyle family migrated to Australia from England in 1853—father Michael was a nurseryman who trained under Sir Joseph PAXTON. In the following twenty years, Guilfoyle worked in the family's Sydney nurseries, collected plant specimens in eastern Australia, explored the South Sea islands, including Fiji, and helped grow sugar and tobacco on the family property in northern New South Wales. Through his travels, Guilfoyle came to appreciate the form and structure of tropical and subtropical trees; these became a major inspiration in his reworking of the Melbourne Gardens where he planted stands of his favoured trees, particularly the long-lived date palm, *Phoenix canariensis*. Other hallmarks of his style include the use of architectural plants, such as yuccas, agaves, and cordylines; the wide openness of sweeping lawns; and a love of curving lines in landscape work. In addition to his public work—in Melbourne and in Victorian country towns, such as Colac and Camperdown—Guilfoyle designed many private gardens, including MAWALLOK, Mooleric, and Turkeith, all in western Victoria, following the same strong approach to design.   CMR

Gulbenkian, Calouste, Parque do Museu ✤

Lisbon, Portugal. The Gulbenkian Museum, a magnificent collection of art and antiquities, was opened to the public in 1969. The buildings for the museum, library, and auditoria were designed by a large team of architects and the grounds were landscaped by Gonçalo Ribeiro Telles and António Viana Barreto. The low-lying rectilinear buildings are contrasted with a gently undulating landscape with something of the English landscape park about it. Open spaces of lawn, glades of trees and shrubs, well-placed sculptures, and a large expanse of naturalistic water create an admirable free-flowing foil to the severe modernist buildings. Good use is made of ornamental grasses, as landscape ornament rather than as ingredients in borders, and passages of naturalistic planting (yellow flag irises, *Iris pseudacorus*, on the edge of a stony creek, for example) add an informal note. The park is an admirable setting for the museum and it has become a popular public amenity for the citizens of Lisbon.   PT

Gunnebo ✤

Mölndal, Sweden, was built 1784-96 as a summer residence for a merchant, John Hall. Gothenburg's city architect Carl Wilhelm Carlberg (1746-1814) drew up plans for the house and gardens that are considered to be one of Sweden's best examples of neoclassical architecture and landscaping. Carlberg's garden plan consists mainly of a north-south axis aligned on the house. On the entrance side, in the north, a series of terraces is flanked with cone-shaped hornbeams and tender plants in pots with, to the south, a lime BOSQUET and a pond. An orangery, now a ruin, was built to the south and kitchen gardens with a conservatory to the east of the main building. During the 1800s a landscape garden was laid out west of the house. Walter BAUER proposed restorations for the gardens when the municipality bought the estate in 1949. Only some of these proposals have been realized but large parts of the garden were restored and reconstructed 1996-9 including the kitchen gardens and conservatory.   AJ

Gustafson, Kathryn

(b. 1951), American landscape designer, who studied fashion in New York before landscape design at the École Nationale Supérieure du Paysage de Versailles. She completed her first major land movement piece, Morbras (1986), in Roissy-en-Brie. Inspired by what she calls a 'visceral rather than linear' approach, Gustafson's sculpted, stylish spaces reflect her commitment to a site's historical, geological, and cultural elements. At Terrason, Les Jardins de L'Imaginaire (1995) appeals both as reinterpretation of ancient and modern garden history and features, and also as a sensual, contemporary place. Contoured land, sleek structures, and restrained plantings dominate her works, evidenced by the Shell and Esso gardens (1992) in Rueil-Malmaison: in the latter, straight lines, right angles, and flat stones merge with rolling lawn, flowing water, and draping willows, elegantly fusing the corporate property with the public esplanade it abuts. Additional designs include a curving bridge in Costa Mesa, California (2000); New York's lunar-eclipse-inspired Arthur Ross Terrace (2000); and the Diana, Princess of Wales Memorial fountain (2004) in Hyde Park, London.   LCJ

Gwinn ✿

Cleveland, Ohio, USA, on the shores of Lake Erie, is one of the finest preserved examples of early 20th-century American country house architecture and landscape. Charles PLATT, artist, architect, and landscape architect, and Warren Manning (1860–1938), a leading plantsman of his time, were asked in 1907 by William Mather, a Cleveland industrialist, to collaborate on the design of a new house and surrounding garden. Charles Platt was a formalist who was greatly influenced by Italian architecture and gardens; Warren Manning, a disciple of Frederick OLMSTED, on the other hand, advocated informality in the landscape. The tension they brought to their collaboration resulted in a superior design for Gwinn, Platt creating the formal structural framework, Manning softening the effect with lush plantings. Primarily because of the designers' sensitivity to the dramatic site and their use of local materials and native plants, Gwinn was considered an original American work. Platt's classical Italianate design of the house and terraces, set at the water's edge, embraces the vast lake as if it were the sea. An eye for detail and fine workmanship is apparent in the many ARTS AND CRAFTS details indoors and out. Manning relied heavily on native plants for the landscape, planting the entrance drive with a double row of vase-shaped American elms, with an understorey of *Viburnum dentatum*, the local witherod. Dogwood (*Cornus florida*), fringe tree (*Chionanthus virginicus*), silverbell (*Halesia carolina*), and redbud (*Cercis canadensis*) bordered the large formal garden to the side of the house.

Charles Platt called on Ellen Shipman, considered one of the great flower garden makers of the time, to come to Gwinn in 1914 to make planting plans for the formal flower garden. She returned after the Depression and the Second World War to restore the plantings. These have been simplified today, but the formal garden and tea house retain their charm. The third generation of the Mather family now owns and maintains Gwinn, opening it to the public. Among the memorable features of the garden is sculptor Paul Manship's magnificent 2-m/6-ft vase carved in the classical manner depicting Great Plains Indians on a hunt.   PD

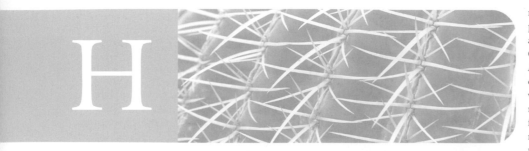

H

Haar, Kasteel de ⊛

Haarzuilens, Utrecht, the Netherlands, a medieval castle, destroyed in 1482, rebuilt in 1554, a ruin once again by the end of the 19th century. It then became the subject of the most spectacular restoration project of a castle in the Netherlands at this time. In 1892 the architect P. J. H Cuypers was commissioned by Étienne Baron van Zuylen van Nijevelt and his wife Helene Caroline Betsy (née Rothschild), to restore the castle, much inspired by the creative restorations of Viollet le Duc in France. He also made some preliminary proposals for the grounds, which were developed further by the landscape architect Hendrik COPIJN from 1894 onwards. The design covered a much larger area than the former gardens. It involved the removal of the village of Haarzuilens over a distance of 2 km/1 mile in order to create two instant parks for which some 7,000 mature trees had to be moved. The formal gardens surrounding and relating to the building lie alongside the north and south parks which are typical 19th-century continental landscape parks with large curvaceous walks crossing extensive vistas. The gardens represented the ancient history of the family, evoking Roman associations and the connection with the ancient Colonna (= column = Zuylen) family, by inclusion of a hippodrome and features included in Francesco Colonna's HYPNEROTOMACHIA POLIPHILI, such as the columned rose arbour. Much of this survives, although the layout has now been simplified and parts have become overgrown. An extensive restoration scheme of castle and gardens commenced in 2000, under the auspices of a trust in which the Zuylen family is represented.
JW

H. H. J. TROMP, *Kasteel De Haar/Castle De Haar* (n.d.).

Hacienda de la Concepción.

See CONCEPCIÒN, HACIENDA DE LA.

Hadrian's Villa (Villa Adriana) ⊛

Tivoli, Italy. One of the great monuments of antiquity, the 2nd-century villa and garden complex was constructed over twenty years by the Emperor Hadrian after he became emperor in AD 117. Situated on the plain at the foot of the Tivoli hill, the vast area contained water features, working on hydraulic systems which connected canals, pools, fountains, and reservoirs. The Emperor drew much of his inspiration straight from Ptolemaic Egypt, where eastern influence from Persia and the Hellenic empire had established a taste for the opulent gardens developed by Sasanian kings. The Canopus, recalling the long pool connecting Alexandria with Canopus on the delta of the Nile, was shaped like a hippodrome and surrounded by a colonnade while the Marine Theatre on a small island was surrounded by a circular portico of Ionic columns. Other features came from Greece and included baths, libraries, an odeum, a theatre, and dwelling houses for guests, courtiers, and soldiers, each surrounded by gardens with fountains and basins. The villa has been frequently excavated and often pillaged, especially so by Pirro LIGORIO between 1550 and 1560 while he was working on the Villa d'ESTE for Cardinal Ippolito d'Este. More recently systematic archaeology has revealed the main features. Today pines and cypresses provide some shade and wild flowers are scattered through the meadows and ruins.   PHo

Hafod ⊛

Cardiganshire, Wales, was one of the best-known landscape gardens of the late 18th century. Thomas Johnes of Croft Castle in Herefordshire inherited the estate and from 1786 began to animate the wild countryside of the valley of the river Ystwyth adopting as his principle 'that by *beautifying* it I have neither *shorn* nor tormented it'. Johnes was a cousin of Richard Payne KNIGHT whose notions of a picturesque untamed landscape strongly attracted him. He fully recognized the natural beauties of the river which he adorned with rustic bridges, built a cavern over a waterfall, and clothed the rocky banks with huge

numbers of trees. Planned walks and viewing points were laid out to concentrate the view and display sublime landscape compositions. George Cumberland in his *An Attempt to Describe Hafod* (1796) conveys the experience of visiting the cavern: 'As we creep along the winding and slippery path, a dark hollow in the rock attracts our notice on the right; the din of falling water reverberates through the cave, and makes us hesitate about committing ourselves to its damp and gloomy recesses. . . . on turning suddenly to the left, a rude aperture admits the light, and a sparkling sheet of water, in front of the aperture, urges its perpendicular fall from the rock above, into a deep hollow below the cave.' Johnes died in 1816 and the estate subsequently changed hands more than once. By the end of the Second World War the gardens had started to decline. In 1994 the Hafod Trust was set up to restore them and in 1998 received a Heritage Lottery Fund award of £330,000.   PT

Haga ⊛

Uppland, Sweden, has royal pleasure grounds containing miscellaneous buildings, pavilions, and gazebos forming one of the best-preserved parks in Sweden in the style of the English landscape school. The park originates from a purchase in 1771 of a farm intended as a summer retreat for King Gustav III. The landscape architect commissioned by the King, Fredrik Magnus PIPER, was well trained for the task, having spent eight years abroad making field studies at places such as STOURHEAD and STOWE. Piper began his work at Haga upon his return to Sweden in 1781. Haga is truly a Swedish interpretation of an English park, where Piper skilfully used the natural features such as the lake of Brunnsviken and the hilly terrain, thus avoiding costly construction work. However an estimated 26,000 trees and shrubs were planted during the work on the park. Among the buildings, Piper was commissioned to design only one, the Turkish Pavilion. Olof Tempelman (1745–1816) designed the King's Pavilion, beautifully located by a lake inlet, and also the great summer palace. This latter project was abruptly interrupted in 1792 when the King was assassinated, after only the foundation had been built. The French artist L. J. Desprez (1777–1863) designed several of the other buildings in the park, among them the so-called Copper Tents, of which there were several, inspired by an idea from the tent camp of a Roman army. These tents stand on top of a sloping lawn, which is the main feature of the park, and face the water of Brunnsviken. In its scale and well-tempered proportions, Haga is considered one of the most outstanding parks in its style and of international significance. Added to this is the central historical and cultural importance that the park has, as the favourite residence of King Gustav III, who in Sweden is known for having founded many cultural institutions.   TA

ha-ha.

In English gardening a ha-ha is often described as a sunken fence. It is a walled ditch which allows uninterrupted views over ground in which animals graze to which they are restricted by the ha-ha. The earliest known use of a ha-ha in England is at LEVENS HALL where the Frenchman Guillaume Beaumont worked in the late 17th century. It is described in a letter that remains at the house, dated April 1695, as 'the Ditch behind the Garden' and is still in place. In England, from William KENT onwards, the ha-ha became a vital part of the landscape garden, allowing views of the park without permitting grazing animals to escape. The term, however, is French in origin and had originally a slightly different meaning, being another term for CLAIRE VOIE. It became the practice in France to have an opening in a wall, a *claire voie*, with a ditch beyond it known as a *saut de loup* (wolf jump). The earliest known *saut de loup* was designed in the 1640s by François MANSART for the Château de Maisons. By the end of the 18th century ha-ha had the same meaning in both France and England.   PT

Hakusasonsō

Kyoto, Japan, the Villa of the White Sands, was the estate of Taisho-period (1912–26) painter Hashimoto Kansetsu (1883–1945). Kansetsu built his estate on what were formerly rice fields near the famous temple GINKAKUJI, in eastern Kyoto. Starting with flat, terraced land, all of the landforms and waterways that exist now are creations of his devising. The name of the residence refers to the fine, white-granite sand that is carried in the streams of that area (and is used extensively at Ginkakuji). The main residence and studio were completed in 1916, and he spent the next 30 years continually working on the design of the garden, eventually extending the pond to the south and adding there two tea houses and an arbour. In all, the property now covers about 1 hectare/2.5 acres. His interest as a collector can be seen in the great number of high-quality stone garden ornaments (stone lanterns and stupas), unusual plants (such as lacebark pine, *Pinus bungeana*), and various prized garden stones to be found in the garden. Kansetsu travelled to China often and the name of his studio at Hakusasonsō, Sonkorō, was also the name of his studio in Shanghai. Hakusasonsō is an excellent example, of relatively recent completion, of an artistic person creating his own private garden.
MPK

Hall Barn

Beaconsfield, Buckinghamshire, England, is a late 17th-century house built for the poet and statesman Edmund Waller. The garden is chiefly the work of his grandson Edmund Waller III, in the 1720s and 1730s. Edmund Waller III was much influenced by his stepfather John AISLABIE of STUDLEY ROYAL who lived at Hall Barn 1711–20. Much of the garden survives with a canal, buildings by Colen CAMPBELL, a grove with serpentine walks, a grotto, avenues, and a park. With an area of 200 hectares/494 acres this is one of the most complete layouts of its period.   PT

Halprin, Lawrence

(b. 1916), American landscape architect and environmental planner, who joined a kibbutz at the age of 17 before going on to study plant science and landscape design at Cornell, the University of Wisconsin, and ultimately with Bauhaus innovators at Harvard. He settled in San Francisco in 1945, apprenticing with Thomas CHURCH and contributing to the design of El NOVILLERO at Sonoma before starting his own practice in 1949. Throughout the north-west, Halprin's passions for urban life and the environment quickly found an outlet in his garden, shopping centre, transport system, and plaza designs. Fine urban reclamation achievements include the rejuvenation of historic buildings in San Francisco's Ghirardelli Square (1965) and Lovejoy Fountain Plaza in Portland, Oregon (1966), a vigorous and clearly man-made waterfall that evokes what Halprin might call an 'experiential equivalent' of nature. Along the more rural Sonoma coast, his talent for balancing the needs of both environment and community is evident at the Sea Ranch (1965), a place where houses, trails, and people blend with the meadows, forest, and beaches that surround them. A lifelong advocate of the collaborative design process and user needs, Halprin has publicized his beliefs through lively lectures, workshops, and writings like *Cities* (1963), *RSVP Cycles* (1970), and *Notebooks 1959–1971* (1972). Characteristically, his linear, 3-hectare/7.5-acre memorial to Franklin Delano Roosevelt in Washington, DC (1997), encourages the motion and participation of its visitors. His many awards include the American Society of Landscape Architects' Design Medal, the 2002 National Medal of Arts, and the American Institute of Architects' Gold Medal for Distinguished Achievement.   LCJ

Hamburger Stadtpark

Hamburg-Winterhude, Germany. In the last decades of the 19th century the city of Hamburg expanded very rapidly. Parks and green spaces of a new type were required. Alfred Lichtwark (1852–1914), director of the Hamburg Museum of Art, asked himself in 1897 whether Hamburg 'will remain a liveable city if a large park were not created'. For many years intensive public discussions about the 'correct' style followed throughout Germany. The new *Volkspark*, which was required to provide for recreation, sports activities, and the enjoyment of art, was designed in a functional and architectural style. In 1910 Fritz Schumacher (1869–1947), director of building and planning, and Fritz Sperber, head of the engineering department, developed the design, and in 1914, the park of more than 149 hectares/368 acres was opened to the public. Otto Linne (1869–1937), Hamburg's first director of the green spaces department, completed the park in 1928, adding several formal gardens, trees, and shrubberies. The Stadtpark today represents the great architectural and artistic vision of its time. Although some of Schumacher's buildings were destroyed during the Second World War some of his vernacular brick buildings can still be seen. The most important landscape feature is the great axis (more than 1,700 m/5,570 ft long) from the Saarlandstraße to the water tower by Oscar Menzel (1912—today it houses a Planetarium). With the Stadtpark the transformation of 19th-century public gardens to a modern *Volkspark* was completed and international standards for park design were set. Today, the park still has more than 200,000 visitors on sunny weekends.   HG

Ham House

Richmond, London, England, was built in 1610 and remodelled from 1672 by the Countess of Dysart who had married the Earl of Lauderdale. A new garden was also made which is shown in a painting of c.1675 by Henry Danckerts. It is seen from a formal wilderness ornamented with statues on plinths, potted plants, and seats. Beyond it is a rectilinear pattern of lawns and a raised terrace below the south front of the house. John EVELYN saw it in 1678 and thought it 'inferior to few of the best villas of Italy', admiring 'the parterres, flower gardens, orangeries, groves, avenues, courts, statues, perspectives, fountains, aviaries'. Nothing of this, except an orangery, survived when the NATIONAL TRUST was given the estate in 1948. In 1981 they embarked on the creation of appropriate new gardens, modelling them on Danckerts's painting and a 1671 plan attributed to John Slezer. The wilderness is once again in place, with platts of turf and raised terrace. To one side of the house is a great parterre with a pattern of santolina and lavender surrounded by a hornbeam tunnel. In an area of 7 hectares/18 acres Ham House and garden, with its riverside position, gives a vivid notion of the way of life of a great family of its time.   PT

Hamilton, Hon. Charles

(1704–86), Anglo-Irish garden designer and Member of Parliament (in both England and Ireland) who was the youngest son of the 6th Earl of Abercorn. Born in Dublin, he was educated at Westminster and Christ Church, Oxford, going on the grand tour and studying in France. In 1738 he bought land at PAINSHILL where he made a remarkable garden that consumed whatever slender resources he had— his most lucrative post seems to have been as receiver general of taxes for the island of Minorca. In 1773 he was forced to abandon Painshill and went to live in Bath. In the west country he advised on a cascade at BOWOOD and on the landscape at STOURHEAD. He also possibly gave advice to his great-nephew William BECKFORD at FONTHILL.   PT

Hamilton Palace ⊛

Lanarkshire, Scotland, was one of the greatest houses in Scotland. The Hamiltons had lived here since the Middle Ages and their 16th-century house was rebuilt for the 3rd Duke of Hamilton in the late 17th century with advice from Sir Christopher Wren (1632–1723) and Sir William BRUCE whose designs were executed by James Smith (c.1645–1731). Great formal gardens were laid out for the new palace by Alexander Edward (1651–1708), with parterres in the French style, and a little later by William ADAM. In 1732 Adam designed Chatelherault, a spectacular eyecatcher at the end of an avenue 1.6 km/1 mile long linking it to the north façade of the palace. Chatelherault, a banqueting hall, kennels, and MENAGERIE of exotic creatures, had elegant formal gardens of its own. The palace, its foundations weakened by coal mining, was demolished in 1927. The remains of the pleasure grounds and park, however, survive and are now a public park surrounded by suburban development. Chatelherault has been finely restored, with an elegant box parterre. The ruins of the medieval Cadzow Castle still stand on the edge of a rocky ravine and remarkable 15th-century oaks survive in parkland.   PT

Hammarby (Linnés Hammarby) ⊛

Uppland, Sweden, was a farm in the countryside near Uppsala bought by Carl LINNAEUS (Linné) in 1758. Here he gardened and farmed and also gave private lectures. After Linnaeus's death in 1778 his widow Sara Lisa lived there until her death in 1806. Hammarby was bought in 1879 by the government and is today managed by Uppsala University. It is considered to be one of Sweden's best-conserved 18th-century

small farms in terms of architectural style, furnishings, and as a cultural monument. The ground comprises a main building (1762), two wings, and the museum (1769) where Linnaeus kept his collections. Linnaeus's main old garden has become a grove with over 40 naturalized species such as the Turk's cap lily (*Lilium martagon*) and alpine barrenwort (*Epimedium alpinum*). The chief flower beds have been reconstructed and the Hortus Sibiricus, once filled with species received from Empress Catherine II of Russia, still remains. In addition there is 'Upplandsträdgården', a 'Linnaeus-style' garden (1886), and an orchard of mid-Sweden varieties including 'Linnés äpple'.   KL

MARIETTE MANKTELOW, 'Linnés Hammarby—ett blommande kulturarv', *Svensk Botanisk Tidskrift* (2002).

Hammerbacher, Herta

(1900–85), German landscape architect, member of the Society for Experimental and Applied Ecology, founding member of the Karl Foerster Foundation for Applied Vegetation Science. After an apprenticeship in Potsdam-Sanssouci from 1917 to 1919 and training at the Teaching and Research Institute for Horticulture in Berlin-Dahlem from 1924 to 1926 she began working as a landscape architect in the garden planning department of the firm Ludwig Späth, Berlin. From 1928 until 1948 she collaborated with Karl FOERSTER and Hermann MATTERN, her husband from 1928 until 1935. In 1950 she became the first woman professor of landscape architecture at a German university, becoming emeritus professor at the Technical University Berlin in 1969. She designed numerous private gardens, parks, cemeteries, school playgrounds, and open space surrounding hospitals, industry, and in residential communities. Her work was influenced by the progress in ecology and plant sociology in the early 20th century, and the nature garden as propagated by Willy LANGE. She designed gardens as outdoor rooms mediating between the architecture and surrounding countryside. Her modelled undulating lawns won her the nickname of 'Mulden-Herta' ('Herta-Hollows'). After the Second World War she promoted city planning with integrated landscape plans, and based on topography. Her own designs culminated in the visionary cityscape for Ratingen-West (1966). Besides publishing her work in short articles she produced an overview of the development and design characteristics of Berlin private gardens from the late 19th century until the early 1970s ('Die Hausgärten', *Berlin und seine Bauten*, Vol. C: No. 4 (1975).   SD

JEONG-HI RI, 'Visionärin der Neuen Stadt', *Stadt und Grün*, Vol. 52: No. 3 (2003).

JOACHIM WOLSCHKE-BULMAHN and GERT GRÖNING, 'Der 100. Geburtstag von Herta Hammerbacher', *Stadt und Grün*, Vol. 50: No. 1 (2001).

Hampton Court Palace ⊛

Richmond upon Thames, Surrey, England, was started by Thomas Wolsey in 1514 and built on a grandiose scale in the Gothic style with about 810 hectares/2,000 acres of land surrounding it. In 1525 Wolsey gave the estate to Henry VIII who enlarged the palace and greatly added to the gardens. The Privy Orchard was ornamented with several sundials made by the royal horologist Nicholas Kratzer and by the most distinctive ornaments of early Tudor gardens— carvings of heraldic beasts mounted on poles. In the 1530s three new gardens were made running down to the river Thames south of the palace—the Mount Garden, Pond Garden, and Privy Garden. These are seen in a remarkable, very detailed drawing by Anthonis van Wyngaerde of c.1555 and show rectilinear layouts, many upright ornaments (presumably the beasts), a banqueting house, and a terrace walk running down to the banks of the river. The Mount Garden was planted with apple trees and the mount itself was surmounted by a glazed arbour crowned with a leaden cupola. The Privy Garden, which lay below the windows of the King's apartments, was described by a German visitor, Thomas Platter, in 1599. He described knots whose patterns were marked by red brick dust or sand and topiary in 'all manner of shapes, men and women, half men and half horse, sirens, serving-maids with baskets, French lilies and delicate crenellations all round made from dry twigs bound together'. Roy Strong believes it likely that these features dated from Henry VIII's time. In Henry's time it is plain that the garden was regarded as a magnificent royal status symbol, even grander than any garden made by Henry's great French rival François I.

In the 17th century there were many changes in the garden. Charles II, having acquired a taste for French gardens in exile, had made a great PATTE D'OIE east of the palace, possibly designed by André MOLLET and in place by 1662. The central avenue of the *patte d'oie* encloses a canal, the Long Water. After 1688, in the reign of William III, even greater changes were made. In 1689 John EVELYN described a 'spacious garden with fountaines was beginning in the parke at the head of the canal'. This was the Great Fountain Garden, a semicircular garden below the east façade of Wren's new building with PARTERRES *de broderie* and fountains, probably laid out by Daniel MAROT, seen in Leonard Knyff's painting of 1702 which still hangs at the palace. At about the same time George LONDON and Henry WISE designed a formal wilderness to the north of the palace and a great avenue linking it to Bushy Park which then formed part of the Hampton Court estate. Only a small part of the wilderness survives, a fragment of a yew maze, the earliest known hedge maze to survive in England. Another development associated with Wren's extension to the palace was the Privy Garden running from the south façade to the banks of the river. The Privy Garden was probably designed by Daniel Marot and is seen in an engraving by Sutton Nicholls of c.1696. It was originally in the form of *gazon coupé*, sweeping shapes cut out of turf. An early 18th-century plan shows much more elaborate parterres here, the work of Henry Wise who had already completed one of the parterres by 1701. At about this time magnificent screens of wrought iron by Jean Tijou, originally made for the Great Fountain Garden and costing £2,160 (about £172,000 in today's money), were erected at the river end of the Privy Garden.

In the 18th century there were no great additions to the garden. Capability BROWN was appointed royal gardener in 1764 and came to live at Wilderness House in the grounds of Hampton Court Palace. He did not introduce any informal landscaping scheme here but could not bring himself to have the topiary clipped. When Thomas JEFFERSON visited Hampton Court in 1786 his journal noted laconically, 'Old fashioned. Clipt yews grown wild.' Brown is credited with planting in 1768 the surviving and still productive black Hamburgh dessert grape (now correctly *Vitis vinifera* 'Schiava Grossa') in the glasshouse south of the palace. George II (d. 1760) was the last monarch to live at Hampton Court Palace. In 1838 Queen Victoria opened the grounds as a public park which they have remained ever since. Later, in the 20th century, Ernest Law studied the history of the gardens and inspired the replanting of the gardens south of the old palace, dating from Henry VIII's time, with cheerful but unhistorical bedding schemes. In the 20th century the Privy Garden, most of whose statuary had been removed by George IV, became a lugubrious and labyrinthine shrubbery in which the original yew topiary grew unchecked. Bedding schemes of municipal splendour were laid out in the Great Fountain Garden where the old yews, under the influence of Ernest Law, were clipped into their present dumpy conical shapes. In recent times incomparably the most important development has been the thoroughly researched restoration of the Privy Garden inspired by the pioneer restoration of Het LOO. In 1993 the site was cleared and excavations laid bare the original pattern of the garden. Ring counting of the old yews showed them to be the

original trees. Yews and holly were propagated, so that the ancient clones could be preserved. No list survived of the original ornamental planting but contemporary lists (including two lists of 1701 showing plants ordered for the garden) gave a clear idea of the historical repertory. These plants were disposed in accord with what is known about planting systems of the first years of the 18th century. Much research was done into precisely the right clone for dwarf box (*Buxus sempervirens* 'Suffruticosa') of which 30,000 plants were propagated to edge the parterres. Statues were copied from surviving originals and Tijou's wrought-iron screens were superbly restored. Queen Mary's Bower, a tunnel of wych elm (*Ulmus glabra*) running along the western side of the Privy Garden of which original plants survived to the 1970s when they were killed by elm disease, has been reinstated using hornbeam (*Carpinus betulus*). The result is a restoration faithful to both the history and character of the place. It is to be hoped that other parts of this great garden will be brought back to life with similarly inspired restoration.   PT

MAVIS BATEY AND JAN WOUDSTRA, *The Story of the Privy Garden at Hampton Court* (1995).
ROY STRONG, *The Renaissance Garden in England* (1979).

Hanbury Gardens (La Mortola) ⊛

Ventimiglia, Italy. The 45-hectare/112.5-acre garden, bought by the Hanbury family in 1867, lies on a steep clifflike slope down to the sea, the Ligurian Riviera, on the border with France, with the planting taking advantage of the protected south-facing site which allows a wide range of tender plants. La Mortola (named for the thickets of wild myrtle on the rocky shore) has a superb collection, including cycads and succulents on the highest and sunniest part of the garden, built up by the Hanbury family over more than a century. Fortunately the garden is also beautiful, with steps, pergolas, pathways, pools, and belvederes integrating the design into a united whole as the prolific planting sweeps down to the Mediterranean. Sir Thomas Hanbury and his botanist brother Daniel were determined to grow all exotics that could flourish in the favoured site. Among many others, these included tender eucalyptus from Australia, Mexican cypress (*Cupressus guadalupensis*), acacias, melaleucas, and metrosideros. There are important collections of genera such as *Salvia*, *Rosa*, *Agave*, *Aloe*, and palms besides historic citrus fruits. The long pergola is clothed with red passion flowers, bignonias, and the scented *Jasminum polyanthum*. A part of the garden has always been retained for native plants. Since 1960 the gardens have belonged to the

University of Genoa and are in the process of restoration.   PHo

PIA MEDA, *Guida agli orti e giardini botanici* (1996).

Hanging Gardens of Babylon.

See BABYLON, THE HANGING GARDENS OF.

Hangzhou ⊛

Zhejiang province, China, situated at the southern end of the Grand Canal, near the mouth of the Qiantang, is famous for its silks and handicrafts and for the beauty of its West Lake, Xi hu, the place that, more than any other, epitomizes the Chinese ideal of 'hills and waters'. It covers some 500 hectares/1,235 acres and is surrounded by an amphitheatre of gentle hills. Since flooding was always a danger to the city, willow-planted dykes named after two famous poets, Bai Juyi and Su Dongpo, who both became governors of the province, divide the lake into three unequal parts.

After 1126 imperial survivors of the Northern Song made Hangzhou their capital and built palaces and gardens round the lake. During the Qing period, the Kangxi and Qianlong emperors paid lengthy visits to Hangzhou, and this encouraged the building of villas by the lake. A few of these villas survive today (one recently opened to the public) and a fine ARBORETUM, parks planted with peach trees along the water's edge, and the two larger islands in the lake are open to the public. Of these, the Xiaoyingzhou island, composed of a clover-leafed causeway surrounding four reflecting pools, is one of the most seductive places in China. Just off the northern shore of this island, three small hollow stupa lamps rise above the lake surface: on warm nights they used to be lit, so that their three lights mingled with the reflected moon and the shadows of the willow branches.   MK

Hansen, Sven

(1910–89), Danish landscape architect and IFLA (International Federation of Landscape Architects) founding member. He worked 1936–45 with G. N. BRANDT and developed MARIEBJERG CEMETERY for many years, 1936–65. At the same time he designed other cemeteries, such as Hillerød Cemetery and Skansebakke (1956) and Glostrup Cemetery (1960); green spaces for housing developments; and educational institutions such the Danish Contractors' Association School in Ebeltoft (1967). At Copenhagen County Hospital in Glostrup (1950–8) he shaped the terrain like a great rampart and surrounded a clearing with forest-like planting near the nine-storey building. Special gardens include a large mirror pool, also found at several of Hansen's other projects, for example at ÅRHUS CONCERT

HALL PARK and at the Broadcasting Centre in Århus (1971). When the School of Architecture in Århus was founded in 1965 he began teaching and developed the department of landscape architecture, becoming professor 1976–80.   AL

Hardouin-Mansart, Jules

(1645–1798), French architect who practised in a refined baroque style. He rose to particular prominence at VERSAILLES, being appointed *premier architecte du roi* to Louis XIV in 1686. The great-nephew of François MANSART, with whom he served his apprenticeship, he formed an early association with André LE NÔTRE. Mansart worked with Le Nôtre at SAINT-GERMAIN-EN-LAYE (1669–73), DAMPIERRE (1682–4), CHANTILLY (1683 onwards), SCEAUX (1685), and Saint-Cloud (1688–9). At MARLY from 1778 he designed both the chateau and its ranges of pavilions. The accounts suggest that Mansart alone was responsible for the layout of the gardens. Elsewhere, in particular at Versailles, it is not always possible to assign responsibility for garden features to Mansart or to Le Nôtre. Among his notable surviving garden buildings are the orangery and the Grand Trianon at Versailles and the orangery at Sceaux. Not a garden building, but a work of great garden importance, was the aqueduct of Marly (1681–5), designed with Robert de Cotte (his brother-in-law), which also survives. Mansart's skill in designing space may also still be seen in Paris in the place Vendôme where, from 1677, he was one of the speculative developers of the site as well as its chief architect.   PT

Harewood House ⊛

near Leeds, West Yorkshire, England, was built in the mid 18th century, designed by John Carr of York (1723–1807) for Edwin Lascelles in whose family it remains. Capability BROWN came to advise on the landscape in 1758 and draw up a 'general plan for the Ground'. Brown had an uneasy relationship with Lascelles and it was not until the 1770s that his plan for a lake in a vital position below the south side of the house was put into place. Much later, between 1844 and 1851, on this side of the house a dashing Italianate terrace was laid out by Sir Charles BARRY when Barry was also working on the house. A parterre, possibly designed by W. A. NESFIELD, ornaments the terrace. It is decorated with elaborate fountains, 18th-century urns, scrollwork of box, topiary of yew, and gravels of contrasting colours. In a scalloped central pool is a late 20th-century bronze of Orpheus by Astrid Zydower. Spring and summer bedding schemes fill the box-edged beds. The balustraded terrace commands fine views over the wooded Gawthorpe valley where Brown

dammed the stream to form a long serpentine lake. The contrast between the Victorian exuberance of the terrace and the Arcadian restraint of Brown's landscape is memorable. In the 1760s both Richard WOODS and Thomas WHITE worked on the 'northern pleasure grounds' but nothing is known of the outcome.   PT

Hårleman, Carl

(1700–53), considered to be the most influential architect and garden architect of his time in Sweden. He was the son of the royal gardener Johan HÅRLEMAN and was taught in Paris 1721–6 by André LE NÔTRE's great-nephew Claude DESGOTS. He also travelled to Italy where he stayed until 1727, when Nicodemus TESSIN the younger asked him to come back to Sweden and assist him at the Royal Palace. Hårleman succeeded Tessin as superintendent of the royal buildings. He worked in a holistic way with both main building and garden. His garden plans could often be seen to differ somewhat in shape and features from what was known as the French formal garden. Often they were simplified and included features of the landscape garden even before this style was accepted and commonly used. In a plan for Svartsjö in Uppland, for example, Hårleman transformed the parterre towards the lake into a grass lawn. Among his works, a few following on from the work of Jean de la VALLÉE, are Stockholm Royal Palace, Karlberg in Stockholm, ULRIKSDAL and Ekolsund in Uppland, and Övedskloster in Skåne. Few of his projects remain today, among which are the BOSQUETS at Ulriksdal.   AJ

TORBJÖRN ANDERSSON, TOVE JONSTOIJ, and KJELL LUNDQUIST (eds.), *Svensk trädgårdskonst under fyrahundra år* (2000).

Hårleman, Johan

(1662–1707), one of the most widely talented gardeners of Sweden's baroque period combining the role of gardener, garden designer, and courtier. For 25 years he was involved with all the royal garden projects and most of the larger private landscape designs in the country. He often worked with Nicodemus TESSIN the younger and it is sometimes difficult to separate their work. Hårleman was born into the gardening profession of Stockholm, in his youth working as gardener with his father, Christian Horleman, at KUNGSTRÄDGÅRDEN, DROTTNINGHOLM, Strömsholm, and ULRIKSDAL. After his grand tour in Europe (1680–85) he was appointed inspector of all Sweden's royal gardens (1688). On his second journey (1699–1700) to France and Holland, he met André LE NÔTRE in whose later style Hårleman worked. Noor Manor in Uppland is a full-scale

miniature example of the style, both in detail and in overall design. Parterres and *plate-bandes* (see BORDER), from 1690 at Drottningholm, Ekolsund, Stora Wäsby, Leufsta, and Östanå, are characteristic of Hårleman's work. So is the feeling for plants, hardy and tender, and their skilful cultivation. In 1703 he claimed his collection at Ulriksdal was 'next to Versailles the best in Europe'. In 1708, the first century plant (*Agave americana*) ever to flower in Sweden (at Noor), with 4,863 flowers on a single stem, was presumably the result of Hårleman's care and skills. He was the father of Carl HÅRLEMAN.   KL

Harlow Carr ⊛

Harrogate, North Yorkshire, England, was founded 1950 as the display gardens of the Northern Horticultural Society and in 2001 it was taken over by the ROYAL HORTICULTURAL SOCIETY. With 28 hectares/68 acres this is a valuable resource for gardeners showing a wide range of the kinds of plants which will thrive in acid soil in a wet and rather cold climate. The valley site is diverse, with an especially attractive area of ancient woodland, with old beech and oaks, where flowering shrubs such as   ▶

Colour plates

The Arthur Ross Terrace at the American Museum of Natural History, New York, designed by **Kathryn Gustafson**, Jennifer Guthrie, and Shannon Nichol

Sculpture by Simon Thomas in the garden at **Lismore Castle**, Ireland

The gardens of the great basin at **Chicago Botanic Garden** designed by James van Sweden

The gardens at **Monticello**, Virginia, USA, with the kitchen garden in the lower right-hand corner

camellias, magnolias, and rhododendrons are cultivated. A stream garden has an excellent collection of Himalayan meconopsis and primulas. An arboretum, a wildflower meadow, and a limestone rock garden are also to be seen. A most unusual National Collection is that of over 100 cultivars of rhubarb (*Rheum* spp.), a traditional market garden crop in this part of Yorkshire.   PT

Hartweg, Theodor

(1812–71), German plant collector who worked at the Jardin des Plantes in Paris (see PARIS PARKS AND GARDENS) before moving to England in his early twenties, being employed by the (Royal) Horticultural Society at their gardens in Chiswick. In 1836 he was dispatched by the society to the Americas to collect plants, where he travelled widely for the next seven years, in Mexico, Guatemala, Ecuador, and Jamaica, returning to England in 1843 before setting off again two years later to revisit Mexico. Due to unrest caused by the Mexican–American War Hartweg moved to California where he remained, plant hunting, for three years. In 1854 he visited Madeira before becoming inspector of gardens for the Duke of Baden in the Rhineland. His introductions include *Fuchsia fulgens* (1830) from Mexico, and the Monterey cypress *Cupressus macrocarpa* (1838) and *Ceanothus cuneatus* var. *rigidus* (1847), both from California.   MC-C

Hasht Behesht ⊛

Isfahan, Iran. The Pavilion of Hasht Behesht, or Eight Paradises, constructed around 1670, with high balconies and elaborate decorations, was conceived as part of the CHAHAR BAGH AVENUE, an extension of the Garden of Nightingales. Of an open, airy construction allowing views through central arches to the front canal, with vertical water spouts, and the pine tree grove at the back, projecting corners confirm its 'octagonal' theme. Planned as a base for open-air receptions, the garden revolved around the water tank with a RILL (now dry) completely encircling the building. The trees were cut down during the Afghan invasion of 1722 but elms and plane trees have been replanted to provide shady alleys.   PHo

Hatfield House ⊛

Hertfordshire, England, was built between 1607 and 1612 for Robert Cecil, chief minister to both Elizabeth I and James I. There was already a notable royal house here, Hatfield Palace, where Elizabeth I was born and of which part remains. Robert Cecil embarked on a garden as the new house was being built, with the help of Mountain Jennings, John TRADESCANT the elder, and Salomon de CAUS. De Caus laid out a water garden which is the only part of the original garden which is known about in detail, with a diamond-shaped lake with an island and banqueting house. A French visitor, Samuel Sorbière, saw it in 1663—'We Dined in a Hall that looked into a Greenplot with Two Fountains in it, and having Espaliers on the sides . . . you have a Prospect of the great Water Parterre.' No trace of the Jacobean garden at Hatfield survives. Walled courts and terraces survived until the early 18th century but by the end of the century they were gone and the grounds were landscaped up to the walls of the house. The Cecil family still owns the estate and from 1972 the Marchioness of Salisbury, a very knowledgeable gardener and garden historian, reinstated gardens of formal character. These are not historicist reconstructions, rather an evocation of the period in modern terms, including planting of Tradescant's period. With a very wide range of excellent plants, the 12-hectare/30-acre garden is cultivated organically throughout and is bursting with vigour.   PT

Hatley Park Estate ⊛

Victoria, British Columbia, Canada. The site has known many uses, from its days as a Coastal Salish Indian burial site, to the elegant estate of Premier and then Lieutenant-Governor James Dunsmuir (1851–1920), to a training school for military officers in the 1940s, to its present incarnation as part of the Royal Roads University campus. In 1999, the Friends of Hatley Park Society and Royal Roads University established the Hatley Park Museum, which encompasses the preservation of the estate grounds and gardens. Today the 263-hectare/650-acre property is a National Historic Site. The Scottish-style castle, designed by prominent Victoria architect Samuel Maclure (1860–1929), was built with local materials such as Satuma Island stone. The grounds were designed by the Boston landscape firm Brett, Hall & Co. with a formal Italian garden (boxwood hedges enclose seasonal plantings and at one end there is an endangered Mexican flannelbush, *Fremontodendron mexicanum*); and a rose garden with a formal geometric design which was retained in a 1987 renovation. There is a rare section of old growth forest. The exquisite Japanese garden was designed by Japanese landscape architect Noda with all elements of a contemplative garden including sinuous paths, bridges, and subtle buildings. Wildlife, including deer and peacocks, are frequently seen wandering about. The sweeping lawn with view of the sea and Washington State's Olympic Mountains to the south is an extraordinary setting for the annual Victoria Flower and Garden Show in July.   MH

Haussmann, Baron Georges-Eugène

(1809–91), French adminstrator who under the Emperor Napoleon III transformed the face of Paris. This work was carried out from 1853 when Haussmann was appointed *préfet* of the Département de la Seine and continued until his retirement in 1869. The largely medieval street pattern, and much of the ancient detail, was succeeded by a bold pattern of avenues and boulevards, with housing of suitably imposing character designed for the administrative classes. All this was supplied with an elaborate infrastructure of water supply and drainage. The new street pattern, apart from its aesthetic qualities and convenience, also had a strategic purpose, to allow the easy movement of troops if there was need for them. Haussmann's *Mémoires* (1893) give lavish credit to the initiative of the Emperor—'The creation of promenades, parks, gardens and squares, specifically planned for public use, is virtually without precedent before the second part of this century. Always preoccupied with that which contributes both to the health and well-being of the urban population, the Emperor Napoleon III provided the inspiration, recognised by all, for this valuable enterprise of which the results are visible and much admired by foreigners.' There is a character of ruthlessness about the creation of Haussmann's Paris which involved the forced redistribution of households, compulsory purchases, and the destruction of countless historic buildings, among them virtually all the 17th-century and many earlier houses on the Île de la Cité; 350,000 people were moved from their homes and Haussmann felt able to make a joke of his skills as a 'demolition artist'. Without such ruthlessness the harmonious pattern of streets, the creation of public parks and square gardens, and street planting would have been, if not impossible, very much more difficult. Under the supervision of ALPHAND, BARILLET-DESCHAMPS, and the architect Gabriel Davioud (1824–81), Paris was given a fine repertory of green spaces which remain one of the most attractive aspects of its atmosphere (see PARIS PARKS AND GARDENS).   PT

COLIN JONES, *Paris: Biography of a City* (2004).
PIERRE PINON and JEAN DES CARS, *Paris Haussmann* (1998).

Hautefort, Château de ⊛

Hautefort, Dordogne, France, a spectacular ornament in its landscape, rising high on its outcrop and visible for many miles about. The estate is an ancient one, going back at least to the 12th century when it was owned by the de

Born family of which the troubadour Bertrand de Born (mentioned by Dante in the *Divine Comedy*) was a member. The present chateau, with its domes and towers, dates chiefly from the 16th and 17th centuries. Nothing is known of early gardens here and the present gardens are 20th century, based on 19th-century records and put into place after 1929 when the estate was bought by Baron Henri de Bastard. The entrance courtyard is ornamented with a shady tunnel of clipped western red cedar (*Thuja plicata*) furnished with 'windows' and 'doors'. The *jardins à la française* are laid out on terraces above the chateau's ramparts, chiefly to the south. A parterre of *Santolina chamaecyparissus* includes a cipher of the letters H and S, the initials of the Baron and Baronne de Bastard. Other parterres have topiary shapes of box rising above sweeping beds edged with box and filled with bedding schemes. Pleached against the chateau walls is a series of finely trained and wired plants of *Magnolia grandiflora*, their glistening foliage shimmering against the stone and the tropical scents of their flowers suffusing the garden in summer. The whole area of the garden is 2.5 hectares/6 acres and it provides a lively and decorative, if unhistorical, setting for the splendours of the chateau.   PT

Hawksmoor, Nicholas

(*c.*1661–1736), an enigmatic but very attractive English architect born in Nottinghamshire. He is probably best known for the six churches he built from 1711 in the city of London to replace those lost in the great fire of 1666. With Sir Christopher Wren he worked on the ORANGERY at Kensington Palace (1704–5), and John VANBRUGH was also involved. He worked as Vanbrugh's assistant on the building of CASTLE HOWARD and BLENHEIM PALACE. At Blenheim he designed the Triumphal Gateway (*c.*1722) which forms the entrance to the park from Woodstock village. At Castle Howard he designed for the 3rd Earl of Carlisle a spectacular MAUSOLEUM (1729–36), a PYRAMID (1728), and, in the 1730s, a Temple of Venus which has not survived.   PT

Hawkstone Park ⊕

near Shrewsbury, Shropshire, England, was owned by the Hill family from the 13th century. From the 1740s two generations of Hills, Sir Rowland and Sir Richard, laid out a rare picturesque landscape park of unique character. The site lent itself particularly well to the kind of wild landscape they wanted to create for it is ornamented with dramatic outcrops of cliffs of red sandstone which was the scene of the greatest activity in the latter part of the 18th century. From the start it was seen as a public attraction and a *Description* of Hawkstone was

published as early as 1766. In the 1780s they had the help of William EMES who made a serpentine lake. A remarkable many-chambered grotto built in a rocky outcrop was started in 1765, with winding passages and the occasional glimmer of light. A description of 1787 records that it was 'curiously ornamented with spar petrifactions, stained and painted glass and other suitable appendages'. The Hill family went bankrupt and the estate changed hands. Since 1993 much of the original park has been finely restored and is once again open to the public. Only a few of the original ornamental buildings survive, among them a Gothic gazebo and the Monument, an immensely tall column (with an internal spiral staircase) surmounted by a giant statue of the Tudor Sir Rowland Hill, the first Protestant Lord Mayor of London.
PT

Heale House ⊕

near Salisbury, Wiltshire, England, is a 17th-century house, with sympathetic early 20th-century additions, in a beautiful site on the banks of the river Avon. In 1901 a JAPANESE GARDEN was made on the banks of the river, with a tea house built over a tributary stream, snow lanterns, Japanese maples, and a red-painted bridge—a startling but charming sight among the willows. In 1906 Harold PETO laid out new formal gardens close to the house. Shallow terraces raise from a scalloped pool west of the house culminating in a paved terrace flanked by borders. Peto recommended herbaceous borders here but today they are mixed borders planned by Lady Anne Rasch, who lived here until 1998. Peto also laid out a paved terrace to take advantage of river views. Close to the Japanese garden is an exceptional ornamental KITCHEN GARDEN, dating from the 18th century but given its present appearance by Lady Anne. Walled on three sides in cob the fourth side is closed by a pergola swathed with roses and grapevines. The garden is divided in four, with magnificent domes of yew about a pool at the centre. Tunnels of apples or pears line the paths and lavish borders run along the walls. This is still a working kitchen garden and fruit and vegetables flourish in well-tended beds arranged in the traditional four-part fashion.   PT

Hédervár ⊕

Szigetköz, Győr-Moson-Sopron county, Hungary. This landscape garden on Szigetköz, an island in the Danube, was created by the art collector Count Mihály Viczay around 1793, designed and supervised by Bernhard PETRI. Petri transformed the former baroque garden, but made use of the two pavilions standing symmetrically in front of the house, a

valuable centaur statue, and the medieval church that served as the family burial place. He embellished the garden with new statues rich in Freemasonic symbolism, and with water channelled from the Danube. He placed great emphasis on grouping trees and shrubs and on varying the character of the place. This park, melting into its surroundings as it did, was one of the first in Hungary to follow not an irregular or transitional style but the traditions of the classical Arcadian landscape garden.   GA

⊃ page 213

hedge.

The hedge is one of the most ancient and perennially valuable of garden features. It was known in classical times—PLINY THE YOUNGER's Laurentian garden is described in his letters, 'All around the drive runs a hedge of box, or rosemary to fill any gaps.' Hedges as field boundaries in the English countryside are often of remarkable antiquity. The Romans and Anglo-Saxons planted them, and many surviving examples are over 1,000 years old. The earliest literature on hedges in English is concerned with field boundaries. John Fitzherbert's *Boke of Husbandry* (1523) explains how to make a hedge—'Gette thy quickesettes in the woode-countreye, and let theym be of whytethorne and crabtree . . . holye and hasell be goode.' All these—hawthorn (*Crataegus monogyna*), crab apple (*Malus sylvestris*), holly (*Ilex aquifolium*), and hazel (*Corylus avellana*)—are English natives and still form the ingredients of countless hedges. Sixteenth-century knots and 17th-century parterres elaborated the language of hedging and the PALISSADES of French BOSQUETS in the 17th century are really a precursor of the modern hedge. When John EVELYN recommended yew for hedges in his *Sylva* (1664) he wrote that he 'may . . . without vanity be said to have been the first who brought it into fashion'. He says that it is 'preferable for beauty' and adds that it forms a 'stiff defence'. Hedges within gardens, however, have become truly common only since the 19th century. J. C. LOUDON's *Encyclopaedia of Gardening* (1822) discusses the subject only briefly and deals chiefly with boundary hedges.

As the boundary of a country garden, using appropriate plants, the hedge is an especially sympathetic way of managing the transition between garden and countryside. Within the garden, hedges are the living bones, and the best of all ways of dividing the space in an attractive fashion. As protection from the wind they are better than walls because they absorb much of the impact. YEW (*Taxus baccata*) remains the most distinguished evergreen hedge plant for the formal garden. Its rich, deep colour makes a marvellous background to more colourful planting. Today almost all yew plants are propagated vegetatively so the colour within a hedge is absolutely uniform. In the past, yew was propagated by seed and old yew hedges often show striking colour variation, a sort of patina which adds to their air of antiquity. BOX (*Buxus sempervirens*, or its small-leafed form *B.s.* 'Suffruticosa') is outstanding for smaller hedges. There are many cultivars of *B. sempervirens*, with foliage varying in size and shape, from quite narrow and elegantly pointed to almost circular. Leaf colour varies, too, the best being dark and glistening green. Those with glaucous or variegated foliage are not attractive for hedges. Holly, with its shining foliage, has its charms but many gardeners fear its fallen leaves. The only virtue of × *Cupressocyparis leylandii* as a hedge plant is that it is cheap and quick growing. It is not easily defended on grounds of beauty or distinction.

Among deciduous hedge plants the hornbeam (*Carpinus betulus*) is exceptionally attractive. The leaves, finely toothed and with emphatic veins, turn a lovely buttery yellow before falling. Beech (*Fagus sylvatica*) has similar charms, but with a warm russet autumn colour; but some think it has a rather suburban air. Hawthorn and field maple (*Acer campestre*) if sharply clipped can make excellent hedges but their character makes them more suitable for the less formal parts of the garden—they are ideal for boundary hedging.   PT

heempark.

The term *heem* literally denotes 'environment, home, yard', but in the context of parks it implies the recognition that plants derive from, and the manner of planting should be inspired by, their native country, region, or local area. The idea was conceived by landscape architect Chris Broerse (1902–95) director of parks in Amstelveen, the Netherlands, and the historian H. J. Scharp, in 1946, and the prototype was the Jac P. THIJSSE PARK, Amstelveen. The *heempark* philosophy acknowledges the inspiration of the schoolteacher THIJSSE, who had promoted gardens in which natural plant communities were recreated for educational purposes. These aimed to encourage nature conservation and he proposed them for all towns. The *heemparks* differed in their planting strategy in that the emphasis was to provide an aesthetically pleasing picture with native plants so that in most instances it represented an ideal of what might be achieved in nature, but was frequently better. The municipal authority of Amstelveen (where the parks department was successively headed by Broerse, Koos Landwehr (1911–96), and Hein Koningen (b. 1940)) led the movement for this kind of planting and served as an inspiration for similar green spaces in municipalities, such as Delft, Leeuwarden, Leiden, Schiedam, Venlo, Vlaardingen, and Zaandam, with professional organizations providing the know-how. The 1974 publication *Wildeplantentuinen* (Native Plant Gardens) by Landwehr and Cees Sipkes (1895–1989) encouraged private gardeners, while naturalistic gardens have also become the main focus of community gardening. In the process of popularization *heemparks* have evolved to become layouts that primarily use native trees, shrubs, and herbs, and the concept now incorporates a range of wild, naturalistic, and ecological gardens.   JW

Heian Jingū ✿

Kyoto, Japan, was built in 1895 as part of the celebration for the 1100th anniversary of the founding of the Heian capital (present-day Kyoto). It enshrines the spirit of Emperor Kammu, the founder of the Heian capital. The buildings represent, in two-thirds scale, the central Court of State (Chōdōin) of the Heian capital, a rectangular courtyard of white sand surrounded by brilliant vermilion and green buildings indicative of the classical Tang-dynasty court architecture that was used for the Heian-period (794–1185) bureaucracy. The gardens lie behind the buildings, to the west, north, and east.

Only the two gardens to the north were completed at the time of the festival. The names

The park at **Hédervár** shown in an engraving of a watercolour (*c.*1800).

of the ponds in those gardens, Blue Dragon Pond and White Tiger Pond, hark back to the geomantic design of the Heian period (see JAPAN; SAKUTEIKI) but in fact the garden was not designed according to the rules of geomancy and is not representative of Heian-period design in any other way. Rather, it was designed as a beautiful stroll garden in a style typical for its period. The two ponds were connected with a stream in 1897, and work continued until 1916 on a large pond garden to the east of the main courtyard and a smaller stream garden to the west. The designer of all of these gardens was the well-known gardener Ogawa Jihei (1860–1933), commonly known by his artisan name, Ueji.

Some of the salient features of the four gardens are: weeping cherries grown over broad bamboo trellises (west garden) and winding streams; irises in beds along the pond shore (north-west garden); a stepping stone path through water made by setting old bridge piers into the pond bed (north-east garden); and a long, roofed bridge with benches that acts as an arbour over water (east garden).   MPK

Heijōkyō Kyūseki Garden ⊛

Nara city, Japan, is a Nara-period (710–84) garden that was discovered through archaeological work in 1975 and restored over the next ten years. There is no historical name for the garden; Kyūseki simply means 'Palace Remains'. The garden is historically important because, along with the TŌIN GARDEN, it is one of only two restored Nara-period gardens. It is thought the garden may have been used as an imperial entertainment facility even though it lies outside the palace grounds within the precincts of the ancient city.

The garden centres on a 55-m/190-ft long meandering stream that varies in width from 2 to 7 m/7 to 22 ft. The stream is quite shallow and slow moving—somewhat like a long, undulating pond —and the stream bed has been neatly lined with rounded, hand-sized stones that are exposed above the waterline where the stream bows, forming curved 'pebble beaches' (*suhama*). Where the stream bends sharply to form peninsulas, rock arrangements were built in the rocky shore style (*ara-iso*). Wooden conduits made from hollowed-out cypress (*Chamaecyparis obtusa*) trunks controlled the flow of water into and out of the stream and at two places within the stream, wooden boxes were embedded in the stream bed to hold ornamental water plants, as has been determined from pollen samples taken from the soil within the boxes. Likewise, pollen, leaf, and bark remains have pointed to the use of Japanese black pine (*Pinus thunbergii*) and plum (*Prunus mume*) that have been replanted in the

garden in theoretical positioning. In addition to the stream, one of the garden buildings and many of the sturdy wooden walls that existed along the property edge have been reconstructed.   MPK

Hein, János

(Johann Friedrich) (1866–1935), German-born Hungarian landscape gardener. A native of Hamburg-Altona, after completing his studies in around 1890 he was drawn to Hungary by its great construction boom. He was soon to found an independent garden design and construction company, and became one of the most eminent in his field. By the First World War he had designed and constructed some 250 parks and gardens in Hungary, the majority of them using trees from his own nurseries. His style was typified by a grand, spatially elegant historicism that mixed naturalistic with geometric elements, but by the start of the 20th century his work began to display art nouveau motifs. He worked in almost every genre of landscape architecture known to the period: the modernization of old parks (e.g. the Károlyi Park at Fehérvárcsurgó; the estate of Count Majláth at Perbenyik (today Pribeník, Slovakia), where he constructed a baroque PATTE D'OIE motif in front of the mansion), gardens for new country houses (e.g. the Orosdy Park at Pilisszántó; the Deutsch Park at Vecsés, the estate of Baron Rothschild at Cséhtelek), villa gardens (principally in Budapest), public parks (e.g. Szombathely, Zombor; he also made a submission to the international competition to design the Stadtpark in Hamburg), the design of spas and their gardens (e.g. Pöstyén (today Piešťany, Slovakia)). He is associated with the gardens of institutions and factories, but he was also known as a specialist in grottoes decorated with mock stalactites. He was one of the first landscape gardeners in Hungary to work on the planning of suburbs. His plans won him the gold medal at the Paris World Exhibition in 1900. He abandoned landscape architecture after the First World War, the only exception to this being the design of Governor Miklós Horthy's Kenderes estate in 1926.   GA

Heligan ⊛

near St Austell, Cornwall, England, is an old estate of the Tremayne family who came here in the 16th century. There was a fine walled garden here in the 17th century which, in the early 18th century, had an elaborate formal garden. The grounds were later landscaped and in the early 19th century John Hearle Tremayne started the collection of rare exotics for which the garden became famous. Close to the coast, and with a protecting ravine, the microclimate here is benign. In 1825 Tremayne received seed of

Bentham's cornel (*Cornus capitata*), discovered as recently as 1821 by Nathaniel WALLICH in Nepal. Throughout the 19th century newly introduced plants came here, including those raised from seed collected by J. D. HOOKER on his Himalayan expedition of 1847–50. The tradition continued into the 20th century—the magnificent *Rhododendron sinogrande*, collected by George FORREST in 1912, first flowered at Heligan, in 1919. The fortunes of the garden declined in the 20th century and by the early 1990s the garden was in a state of advanced neglect. In 1991 restoration was begun, led by Tim Smit, who transformed the garden into an exceptionally attractive tourist attraction under the alluring name of The Lost Gardens of Heligan. With many remarkable old exotics, a dramatic site, excellent working kitchen gardens, and fascinating garden buildings (including a working pinery) it remains an excellent garden. As a phenomenon of marketing and mass tourism it is also of great interest.   PT

Hellbrunn ⊛

Salzburg, Austria. The patron of Hellbrunn, Markus Sittikus of Hohenems (1574–1619), was Archbishop of Salzburg from 1612 to 1619. He was a humanist who had lived in Italy and was well acquainted with Italian gardens, and he commissioned the Italian architect Santino Solari (1576–1646) to erect Hellbrunn's villa and gardens. The ground floor of the villa contains five grottoes, decorated with stucco, tufa, shells, and mirrors. The Neptune GROTTO has a figure of Neptune in a niche and north of it are two grotto rooms: the first decorated with frescoes, coloured stucco, and shells; the second, the Ruin Grotto, with its broken lintels and cracks all over the walls and the ceiling, creates the terrifying impression that the house might collapse at any moment. South of the Neptune Grotto are the Grotto of Mirrors and the Birdsong Grotto. The Altems Fountain opposite the Neptune Grotto is the focal point of the main axis. To one side of the villa the Roman Theatre is an EXEDRA flanked by two small pavilions. Beside a pool near the Roman Theatre the Orpheus Grotto, a cube-shaped pavilion, has a fountain and a statue of Orpheus playing his lyre. Through the BOSQUET to the left of the Altems Fountain runs a path, the Fürstenweg, accompanied on both sides by an irregular sequence of statues, fountains, and grottoes with waterworks. The Crown Grotto is decorated with statues of Apollo and Marsyas and a metal crown that can be lifted up by a water jet. A water-powered marionette theatre, showing the life of an 18th-century town, was added between 1748 and 1752 by Lorenz Rosenegger. The Stone Theatre a little further south was originally a quarry used for the construction of the villa. About 1617 it was transformed into an open-air theatre with an artificial stone stage that was probably used for pastoral plays.   BH/GH

Helmingham Hall ⊕

near Stowmarket, Suffolk, England, is a rare early Tudor house, started in 1480, which survives intact. It was built for the Tollemache family, who still live here, and is set in memorable old parkland, probably established in the early 17th century, in which fallow and red deer still graze. In the park to the west of the house is an old mound surmounted with an 18th-century obelisk. The house is moated, as is the old walled kitchen garden to which it is connected by a bridge. The brick walls were built in 1745 replacing a wooden PALISSADE of great antiquity. Fruit and vegetables are still grown here but the garden has been turned largely to ornamental purposes. It retains its old four-part division with its long central walk lined with boisterous herbaceous borders and the paths of its cross-axis with tunnels festooned with sweet peas, climbing beans, and ornamental gourds. At the entrance to the kitchen garden is a box parterre and beds of hybrid musk roses. On the far side of the house a new garden has been laid out since 1982 by Lady Tollemache, a professional garden designer. The compartments of a box knot garden are filled with herbs and a quadripartite arrangement of enclosures of hyssop or lavender is lavishly planted with old shrub roses underplanted with campanulas, geraniums, and violas. This modern planting successfully evokes the decorative atmosphere of a Tudor garden. Helmingham Hall is one of the outstanding surviving houses of its period and its present owners have given it a garden thoroughly in keeping with its sprightly and decorative spirit.   PT

Henry, Augustine

(1857–1930), Irish plant collector and dendrologist from County Derry who received his medical degree from Edinburgh, joining the Imperial Chinese Customs Service in 1881 and remaining in China for twenty years. Here he explored in the provinces of Hubei, Sichuan, Yunnan, and the islands of Hai-nan and Taiwan, sending back to Britain 158,000 herbarium specimens representing over 6,000 species (some 20% of the known Chinese flora). It was he who directed the young Ernest WILSON to where he might find the tree *Davidia involucrata*. On his return to Europe in 1900 he and Henry Elwes (1846–1922) wrote the classic seven-volume monograph *The Trees of Great Britain and Ireland* and in 1913 Henry became the

first professor of forestry at University College, Dublin. Amongst the many trees and plants bearing his name are *Acer henryi*, *Lilium henryi*, and *Cypripedium henryi*, also a Chinese deer, *Kemas henryanus*.   MC-C

herbaceous border. See BORDER.

herbaceous perennials.

The Englishness of English gardens is strongly identified with herbaceous perennials. These non-woody, usually hardy plants die down in winter (sometimes leaving a basal clump or rosette of evergreen leaves) and grow again in spring each year. Familiar perennial wildflowers include buttercups, ox-eye daisies, cranesbill, ragged robin, scabious, knapweed, and campion.

Range of plants

Our temperate climate also allows us to grow an astonishing range of perennials from other parts of the world. We use them not only in herbaceous and mixed borders but also under trees and shrubs, as ground cover in sun and shade, for cut flowers, and, most recently, with grasses as components of 'prairie planting'. Herbaceous perennials provide flowers from January, when hellebores and the sweet-scented *Iris unguicularis* bloom, to November or even December when, in mild seasons, *Schizostylis coccinea* and *Nerine bowdenii* linger on. Although perennials are grown above all for their colourful flowers, they also provide, more than any other class of plant, spectacularly varied and beautiful foliage. The majesty and *gravitas* of acanthus leaves inspired their use as an architectural motif in classical Greece, carved in stone or marble. Similar sculptural qualities can be enjoyed in the leaves of cardoons (*Cynara cardunculus*), *Crambe cordifolia*, and the waterside giant *Gunnera manicata*. In contrast, the fine threads of fennel leaves (*Foeniculum vulgare*) create a soft, hazy effect, specially in its bronze form, and the leaves of *Dicentra formosa*, *Myrrhis odorata*, and *Thalictrum delavayi* are lacy and delicate. Many evergreen perennials make excellent ground cover, such as *Bergenia*, *Campanula persicifolia*, *Dianthus*, and *Phlomis russeliana*. Others thrive in adverse conditions. *Anthemis*, *Aubrieta*, *Helianthemum*, and some sedums are suitable for hot, dry situations with very little soil, whereas *Epimedium*, *Euphorbia robbiae*, *Lamium maculatum*, and *Tiarella cordifolia* make effective cover in shade.

History

In the early history of garden making there were relatively few perennials to choose from. Prized for the beauty, and sometimes also the scent, of their flowers, they were spaced out so that each

individual plant could be enjoyed, in turf or in rectangular flower beds. Medieval paintings, manuscripts, and tapestries show borage, carnations and pinks, columbines, cowslips, rose campion, daisies, flag irises, hollyhocks, lily of the valley, peonies, periwinkles, sweet rocket, violets, and violas. The layout and content of gardens remained virtually unchanged until, during the reigns of Queen Elizabeth and her Stuart successors, travel and exploration brought new plants to Britain. At the same time, gardening advice and plant descriptions became available in book form for the first time. Herbaceous plants introduced in the 17th century included *Heuchera americana*, *Monarda fistulosa*, *Smilacina racemosa*, and *Yucca gloriosa* from North America, *Aster amellus*, *Campanula persicifolia*, *Delphinium elatum* (parent of the flamboyant garden hybrids), *Eryngium alpinum*, *Hemerocallis lilioasphodelus*, *Lavatera olbia*, *Lychnis coronaria*, and *Veronica teucrium* from Europe, and *Anchusa azurea* from the Caucasus.

From the mid 18th to the 19th century introductions came thick and fast. In 1730 Robert Furber, a London nurseryman, listed 285 bulbs and herbaceous plants. By 1778 William Malcolm could offer 1,100. Garden owners longed to grow them all, and a new style of gardening developed to accommodate them. Formal gardens of clipped evergreens gave way to flower gardens, a fashion embraced by an emerging, prosperous middle class with gardens of more modest size than those of established landowners. Flower beds might be laid out symmetrically in simplified parterres, disposed informally along serpentine walks, or included in walled gardens with fruit and vegetables. They were planted with a mixture of shrubs, bulbs, and perennials. Beds planted exclusively with herbaceous perennials became fashionable during the 19th century. The first known herbaceous BORDERS were planted before 1846 at ARLEY HALL and were still flourishing in 1889 when George Elgood painted a watercolour showing them in their summer glory. They still flourish today, full of colour from June to September, backed by a high brick wall on one side and a yew hedge on the other. Towards the end of the 19th century, Victorian gardeners were seduced by the brilliant flowers and lush foliage of tender plants from South America, South Africa, and other warmer regions. The technology for raising plants and overwintering them under glass was perfected, and bedding became all the rage, pushing perennials out of fashion. But William Morris and other members of the ARTS AND CRAFTS MOVEMENT castigated the garishness of bedding schemes, and William ROBINSON, in his influential weekly journal *The Garden* and his book *The English Flower*

Garden (1883), extolled the simplicity of cottage garden flowers. He recommended borders of informally arranged perennials and in *The Wild Garden* suggested using perennials that would thrive without special care in shrubberies and other wilder parts of the garden. Robinson's friend and colleague Gertrude JEKYLL also promoted unpretentious perennials, designing borders with carefully planned colour schemes, moving from cool to warm colours and back again. She also planned borders using variations on a single colour.

Plant societies

The success of the Hardy Plant Society, formed some 40 years ago, confirms the enduring popularity of perennials. It has 12,000 enthusiastic members. Some herbaceous perennials are held in such high esteem that they have their own society. The National Viola and Pansy Society was formed in 1911, the British Iris Society in 1922, and the Delphinium Society in 1928. Changes in taste led, in the second half of the 20th century, to the breeding of numerous new forms of *Hosta* and *Hemerocallis* species, and they too have had their own society since 1981. Surprisingly, the Peony Society was not formed until 2001, although peonies have never been out of fashion, in spite of their short flowering season.

Using herbaceous perennials

Successful herbaceous borders need more space than is available in most gardens today. It is difficult to achieve the desirable combination of harmonies and contrasts in a border less than 3 m/10 ft deep. Nevertheless, Robinson's and Jekyll's ideas are still relevant. They are perpetuated in immensely influential gardens like SISSINGHURST and HIDCOTE, where a classic, timeless English garden style is demonstrated, applicable to gardens of any size. It consists of luxuriant informal planting within a formal layout near the house, grading to 'wilderness' at the boundaries. Herbaceous perennials are essential components of the style. They are especially valuable in providing strong vertical emphasis among shrub roses and other plants with rounded or indeterminate shapes. The upright, spirelike flower stems of lupins, delphiniums, and penstemons, and the sword-shaped leaves of *Crocosmia*, *Hemerocallis*, irises, and *Sisyrinchium*, contribute structure and contrast in such groups. There are perennials for all soil types and climatic conditions, and the correct choice for the site gives each garden its special character. Many suitable plants for free-draining soil in areas of low rainfall have grey leaves and pale flowers, their soft colouring giving a very different effect from the lush exuberance of clay-tolerant *Hemerocallis*, *Hosta*, and *Rodgersia*. There are a few perennials that

should come with a warning. They increase so rapidly and are so tenacious they should be regarded as weeds. *Saponaria officinalis* (soapwort or bouncing Bet) will bounce through a border, smothering more delicate plants as she goes. The pink-flowered Japanese *Anemone tomentosa* is an aggressive colonizer only to be planted where aggressive colonization is desirable, in the wilder parts of large gardens. On a smaller scale, *Ajuga reptans* 'Catlin's Giant', *Alchemilla mollis*, and *Viola labradorica*, although wonderful ground cover, are difficult to control.

Cultivation

Perennials are not labour saving. They need feeding at least every few years, and annual mulching to suppress weeds and conserve moisture. Regular dead-heading is advisable for appearance and to prolong the flowering season, unless a winter display of seed-heads is wanted. The flowering season of some plants including phlox can be delayed by cutting the stems down to 15 cm/6 in when they have reached 45 cm/18 in: if some shoots on each plant are cut and others left to flower at their natural time, the flowering season is prolonged. Spent flower stems should be cut down and decaying leaves removed in autumn or spring. Herbaceous borders can be strimmed and the debris raked off and composted, but in mixed borders where shrubs or roses might be damaged by a strimmer, each plant must be dealt with separately. Although peonies can be left alone for decades, with their health undiminished, most perennials need dividing and replanting at regular intervals to maintain a good performance, every three years in the case of irises. Some, like *Alcea rosea* (hollyhock), and *Hesperis matronalis* (sweet rocket), deteriorate so rapidly they are best treated as biennials. Some perennials need support: wide mesh netting can be stretched horizontally over the entire border, or twiggy hazel or birch branches stuck in the ground around each plant. Metal or plastic supports are also available. Supports should be put in place in spring soon after the new stems emerge. Later, the flower stems of delphiniums need support, with one cane to each stem. The time and effort required to grow herbaceous perennials successfully is more than repaid by the results.

JF-W

herbarium.

A herbarium is a systematic collection of dried plants, or the building that contains it. It has been a vital part of botanical studies since the Linnaean revolution of the 18th century. All great botanic gardens possess a herbarium and gardens of the size and age of the ROYAL BOTANIC

GARDENS, KEW have gigantic collections—Kew has several millions of items in its herbarium. The Jardin des Plantes at MONTPELLIER has over 4,000,000 items in its herbarium and the MISSOURI BOTANICAL GARDEN has 5,300,000. The largest herbarium in the western hemisphere is that of the NEW YORK BOTANICAL GARDEN which contains almost 7,000,000 items. One of the most important aspects of the herbarium is to verify the identity of a plant. A herbarium specimen, with its accompanying data of provenance, will serve to authenticate a plant. In the case of a specimen which was the first to be collected it may also serve to establish the priority of a name (see PLANT NOMENCLATURE).

PT

herb garden.

The first herb gardens would have been made for largely utilitarian purposes, to cultivate plants of medicinal, culinary, or practical (dyeing, for example) purposes. All these were a vital part of the domestic economy of the Middle Ages. It was the monastic communities which brought the craft of cultivating such gardens to its peak. The 12th-century Abbaye Royale de FONTEVRAUD on the Loire in France has a reconstructed *hortulus*, or kitchen garden, which has areas devoted to medicinal and useful herbs. It includes many of plants listed in Charlemagne's *Capitulare de Villis* of *c*. AD 800 which lists the plants considered especially worth growing in his empire. There is, as John Harvey has shown in his *Mediaeval Gardens* (1981), much difficulty in identifying exactly which plants were meant in the list, but they include such herbs of medicinal value as artemisia, coriander, fennel, fenugreek, lovage, rue, rosemary, and sage. The ST GALL plan of the ideal monastery (*c*.816–20) shows a garden of medicinal herbs next to the physician's house. From the 16th century lay gardens were devoted to medicinal herbs, in the form of physic, or apothecary's gardens. In modern times the herb garden, very broadly interpreted, has become a common feature. Vita SACKVILLE-WEST was a pioneer in this, making herb gardens at her first house, Long Barn (from 1915), and later at SISSINGHURST CASTLE (from 1930). She was no cook and in both cases the gardens are at a very considerable distance from the kitchen, so they were considered chiefly as ornaments. Eleanor Sinclair Rohde's *A Garden of Herbs* (1920) was influential in the 20th-century rediscovery of herb gardening.   PT

KAY N. SANECKI, *History of the English Herb Garden* (1992).

herbicides

are phytotoxic substances often referred to as weedkillers that are used to remove unwanted vegetation. They include both inorganic and organic chemicals and may be used selectively and for total vegetation control. Non-selective inorganic substances include salts such as sodium chlorate. Common salt, sodium chloride, may be the earliest example of a total non-selective herbicide following its application to soil after the sacking of Carthage in 146 BC. Ferrous sulphate is still widely used to control mosses in lawns either alone or in combination with dichlorophen. Earliest examples of organic substances as herbicides date back to the 1st century BC using olive processing waste (amorca). Until the mid 20th century selective weed control was achieved from a combination of inorganic and organic chemicals. The era of modern weed control began with the discovery of selective herbicides during the 1940s with the introduction of 2,4-D, MCPA, and related growth regulator type products that selectively removed broad-leaved species from monocotyledonous crops including grass.

Herbicides may be classified depending on their time of application, type of activity, and mode of action. In agricultural and horticultural situations they may be applied pre-planting, pre-emergence, and post-emergence of the crop, although in the garden they are most likely to be used in unplanted areas or lawns. Activity is described as residual, contact, or systemic. Residual herbicides are generally soil applied where they provide extended weed control over a number of months. Examples are provided by dichlobenil, applied as a granular formulation to provide slow release activity around ornamental shrubs and trees. Diuron is also a residual herbicide for use on hard surfaces such as paths and patios. Formerly, simazine was widely used to prevent weed seedling emergence, following root uptake. It still retains a role for weed suppression in non-cultivated areas such as paths and drives. Contact non-selective herbicides include diquat and paraquat for total vegetation control on paths and prior to planting. Treated plants show symptoms of desiccation, restricted to the area of foliar contact, and hence not suited for control of perennials, albeit paraquat shows limited translocated activity. Glyphosate is a non-selective translocated herbicide suitable for total vegetation control. Systemic selective herbicides include MCPA, mecoprop-P, dicamba, and dichlorprop, all of which have growth regulator type activity. However, EU Directive EU91/414 requiring further environmental registration of products introduced prior to 1993 has resulted in the loss of products containing dichlorprop. Nonetheless, it may be replaced by dichlorprop-

P. Such chemicals are used for selective removal of broad-leaved weeds from lawns and turf. Other selective systemic herbicides for use in lawns include fluroxypyr and clopyralid. Mixtures of 2,4-D, mecoprop-P, and dicamba are particularly suitable for control of woody weeds. Selective removal of grasses from flower beds may be achieved using graminicides, the first discovery of which was alloxydim-sodium, albeit no longer registered for use.

Selectivity may also be achieved by directional placement such as at the base of ornamental trees whilst avoiding direct contact. Often herbicides are applied in combination to include both foliar contact/systemic and residual activity. Thus, chemicals with foliar activity remove existing vegetation while those with residual activity prevent further weed growth. Herbicides may also be classified on the basis of their chemical structure and mode of action. Although many chemical groups have been shown to have herbicidal activity, relatively few modes of action have been exploited. Thus herbicides registered for use in the garden include the bipyridyls diquat and paraquat which interfere with photosynthesis by disruption of Photosystem I, resulting in the production of superoxides and peroxides causing desiccation, whereas the s-triazines including simazine and the phenylures such as diuron interfere with electron flow in Photosystem II. Symptoms are expressed as chlorosis and necrosis. Growth regulator type herbicides represented by dicamba, fluroxypyr, and clopyralid elicit symptoms of physiological mayhem as a result of epinasty or contorted growth. Other herbicides permitted for use in the garden include aminotriazole, an inhibitor of carotenoid (pigment) bio-synthesis resulting in symptoms of albinism, while glufosinate ammonium causes toxic accumulation of ammonia as a result of enzyme inhibition. Similarly, glyphosate interferes with protein synthesis through enzyme inhibition thus preventing cell division, whereas dichlobenil inhibits cell wall formation through inhibition of cellulose synthesis. Other modes of action include inhibition of lipid synthesis and of essential amino acids. Microbial and natural plant substances may also provide the basis of herbicidal products as demonstrated by the development of glufosinate ammonium, itself an analogue of phosphinothricin produced naturally by the bacterium *Streptomyces hygroscopicus*. Future herbicide developments are likely to involve natural products.   RJF-W

Herculaneum.

See POMPEII AND HERCULANEUM.

Hergest Croft Gardens ⊛

Kington, Herefordshire, England, are an especially distinguished example of a particular type of English garden—the plant collection built up by a family of devoted and knowledgeable plantsmen. William Hartland Banks started a garden here in 1896 on a site distinguished for its beauty but with no particular advantages of climate. Plants were acquired from VEITCH's nursery at a time when outstanding new introductions were being made. Two subsequent generations of the family have added to the garden which, in an area of 20 hectares/50 acres, now has an exceptional collection of trees and shrubs. There are touches of formality close to the house but it is the woodland gardens, especially in the exquisite hilly Park Wood, where excellent trees form the background to flowering shrubs, that the true distinction of the garden is seen. Still owned by the Banks family, it attractively conveys the excitement of gardening.   PT

Herkenrode ⊛

Haacht-Wespelaar, Vlaams Brabant, Belgium, contains a fine and well-catalogued dendrological collection of over 5,000 trees and 2,300 varieties of shrubs in around 10 hectares/25 acres of garden and woodland. Guillaume de Spoelberch purchased Herkenrode in 1923 and later added the neighbouring estate of Wespelaar. Philippe de Spoelberch has lived there since 1970, greatly enlarging the collection in the woodland gardens and in the arboretum of Wespelaar. Near the house are attractive gardens including mixed borders of trees, shrubs, and perennials underplanted with ground cover, lawns, and a pond, part designed by Jacques WIRTZ in 1979. The woodland garden has a large rhododendron collection (800 varieties) planted among species of stewartia and styrax. In the arboretum there are many rarities including exceptional collections of birch, planted among hybrid rhododendrons carefully arranged so that colours harmonize, oaks, beeches, magnolias, and maples which thrive in the acid soil.   BA

Hermelin, Sven

(1900–84), doyen of Swedish landscape architecture. He participated in many organizations in Scandinavia, was vice-president of IFLA (International Federation of Landscape Architects), and wrote numerous articles in the Scandinavian professional press. His landscape education included practical work in Danish nurseries and the parks department, Stockholm, followed by study in Germany, before he started his own practice in 1926. Hässelby Castle was probably his most outstanding historical project and, like that of all Scandinavian landscape architects, his work included churchyards and CEMETERIES, but he was most widely recognized for his work in nature conservation. Sven Hermelin was a pioneer, in that he refused to separate ecology from aesthetics, regardless of the situation. He was convinced that it is the responsibility of the landscape architect to unite science and art in practical work.   PRJ

hermitage.
The remote dwelling place of a holy man living in solitude was a curious notion for ornamental garden buildings. The earliest known garden hermitage was in France at the Château de GAILLON, in a secluded part of the garden called Le Lydieu. The hermitage is first mentioned in 1508 and is shown in Androuet DU CERCEAU's engraving made after 1550. It is an elegant little building, like a miniature chateau, with, behind it, a rocky MOUNT. No hermitages seem to appear subsequently in French gardens until the 18th century. Antoine-Nicolas Dezallier d'Argenville in his *Voyage pittoresque des environs de Paris* (1762) describes a BOSQUET, called an *ermitage*, which was decorated with paintings of notable hermits. At ERMENONVILLE the Marquis de GIRARDIN had a hermitage of *c*.1775 which is illustrated in Georges-Louis LE ROUGE's *Détails de nouveaux jardins à la mode* (1775–89). In British 18th-century picturesque gardens hermitages became a commonplace, and they took many forms. At Badminton House (Gloucestershire) in the mid 18th century Thomas WRIGHT designed one in the form of a rustic ROOT HOUSE which survives (just) to this day. A thatched root house, called a hermitage, ornamented the garden of Marino (Dublin, Ireland) *c*.1760—no trace of it remains but William Chambers's magnificent house does. Some hermitages were in the form of grottoes such as the very early one, made before 1721, at Carshalton House (London) which overlooks a lake. The view was plainly important to many hermitages. At Belle Isle (County Fermanagh, Northern Ireland) the 18th-century thatched hermitage was placed on the banks of a lake. The HERMITAGE in Scotland, a rather plain stone building, also 18th century, was placed on the edge of a spectacular natural cascade of which it was explicitly planned to display views. William Wrighte's pattern book *Grotesque Architecture or Rural Amusements . . . which may be Executed with Flints, Irregular Stones, Rude Branches and Roots of Trees* (1767) has engravings of hermitages. One, the Augustine Hermitage, was a hermitage de luxe. It has a central pedimented temple-like building, with columns in the form of palm trees, and was linked by a covered passage to a circular library on one side and a circular bathhouse on the

other. For the true hermitage effect it was necessary to have a resident hermit. Barbara Jones's *Follies & Grottoes* (1974 edn.) explains how difficult it was to recruit them. The hermit at PAINSHILL in the 18th century was allowed to walk in the grounds and was provided with a hassock, hourglass, and Bible. He found the solitude insupportable and after three weeks was sacked when he made a visit to a nearby pub. It seems that the tradition of hermits still retains a spark of life. In the *London Review of Books* (22 August 2002) an advertiser sought a 'resident hermit' for Great Haywood Cliffs, formerly part of the Shugborough estate in Staffordshire. A 'wilderness and stipend' would be provided for a suitable candidate.   PT

Hermitage, The ⊕
near Dunkeld, Perthshire, Scotland, the atmospheric remains of a picturesque garden made in the late 18th century by the 2nd Duke of Atholl for his estate of Dunkeld House. The Hermitage (originally called Ossian's Hall) dates from 1785, a pavilion overlooking the river Braan which here tumbles over a spectacular cascade. When Dorothy and William Wordsworth visited it in 1805 this view was suddenly revealed and the room 'was almost dizzy with waterfalls that tumbled in all directions—the great cascade which was opposite to the window that faced us, being reflected in innumerable mirrors upon the ceiling and against the walls.' The mirrors have long gone but the cascade and pavilion remain, as does a rustic grotto in the woods, Ossian's Cave. The woods contain exceptional specimens of Douglas fir (*Pseudotsuga menziesii*)—David DOUGLAS, who introduced it in 1826, came from Perthshire.   PT

Herning Art Museum ⊕
Herning, Denmark. The collaboration between the textile manufacturer Aage Damgaard and C. Th. SØRENSEN began in 1956 in the grounds of the Angli IV shirt factory, creating the Geometric Gardens in a reduced form, after a proposal originally made for the Vitus Bering Park in Horsens. When the factory moved further out in the 1960s, C. Th. Sørensen influenced the design of the entire area. He drew up the first draft for the round factory, today the Herning Art Museum, where a narrow passage leads to the inner court, consisting of a bowl-shaped lawn bordered by Carl-Henning Pedersen's (b. 1913) ceramic 220-m/720-ft long mural on the long wall. C. Th. Sørensen also designed the round sculpture park. Surrounded by a dense planting of oak, the sculpture park lies in a circular clearing 180 m/ 590 ft in diameter, and the sunken green centre was intended as grazing land. Along the edge

of the forest is a raised belt 15 m/50 ft wide where radial hawthorn hedges create separate enclosures to display sculptures. In 1983 the Geometric Gardens, called the Musical Gardens by Sørensen, were established in their original size. A series of nine enclosures, hedged in hornbeam, of varied geometric shapes (a circle, an oval, and six polygons) were disposed on a green surface in an oval clearing. The development of the Birk quarter and the location of future buildings follows a plan by Sven-Ingvar ANDERSSON.   AL

Herning City Hall Square ⊕
Herning, Denmark, was completely altered by Jeppe Aagaard ANDERSEN in 1996. The large trapezoid square, sloping from the church towards the pedestrian mall, was given striped paving of two types of granite ashlars, one pink, one grey. The cross-profile is concave, and the central axis is marked by narrow strips of granite. The main entrance to the city hall is indicated by a diagonal, dark red square in the paving, and the area occupied by an open-air café is paved with blackish-blue tile. At the top, a gravelled area with a QUINCUNX of horse chestnuts forms the end of the square, joined by four pools whose fountains spray water in varying patterns. The square also has a small parterre of flowers edged with steel, steel trees with creepers, varied lighting, and polished granite plinths that serve as benches. All the materials are of high quality and were used with great feeling for texture.   AL

Heronswood ⊕
Kingston, Washington State, USA, was developed from 1987 by Daniel J. Hinkley (b. 1953) and his partner Robert L. Jones (b. 1949). The garden and nursery, encompassing 3 hectares/7.5 acres, are filled with exemplary combinations of choice plants. Hinkley's intrepid travels, wit, and passionate collecting are reflected in the Heronswood Nursery catalogue, which combines travelogue, poetic plant portraits, and personal reflections. The woodland garden, filled with species rhododendrons, hydrangeas, and myriad bulbs and perennials, comprises half the property. Sunny spaces include a stylish kitchen garden; a long arbour smothered with vines; a blue and gold mixed border; and meticulously clipped hornbeam (*Carpinus*) arches.   BBA

Heronswood ⊕
Victoria, Australia, enjoys a spectacular site on the Mornington Peninsula, close to the southern coast of Australia and about an hour's drive from Melbourne. The Gothic Revival stone house, with its picturesque roof structure, was designed in 1871 by Edward La

Trobe Bateman (1816–97) and he is also credited with the landscape plans for the garden. Many of the fine specimen trees date from this 19th-century period, including Moreton Bay figs (*Ficus macrophylla*), cypress, oaks, and an *Araucaria cookii*. In the garden, they frame the views of Port Phillip Bay in a manner strongly reminiscent of French Riviera landscapes. Since 1982 Heronswood has been the home of Digger's Seeds, a company founded in 1978 by Clive and Penny Blazey as a mail-order garden club for enthusiastic Australian gardeners, specializing in offering hard-to-find plants. The Blazeys have been instrumental in reviving interest in both cottage gardening and heirloom vegetables, reintroducing many old cultivars both to Australian home gardeners and to commercial production. While Heronswood is primarily a perennial garden with a series of garden rooms featuring cottage flowers, vegetables, and perennials for a dry climate, many areas feature annual flowers and vegetables that thrive in Australia's hot summers. Clive Blazey's publications, *The Australian Vegetable Garden* (1999) and *The Australian Flower Garden* (2001), record his 30-year experiences using the Heronswood garden as a trial ground and as a showcase for Australian gardeners.   CMR

Herrenchiemsee Palace Park ⊗

Priem am Chiemsee, Upper Bavaria, Germany. Ludwig II of Bavaria (1845–1886) had great admiration for the Bourbon King Louis XIV whose palace and the gardens in VERSAILLES were a model setting for a retreat from the everyday world. In 1868 Ludwig embarked on a re-creation of Versailles, first in the mountains at Linderhof, and then, when this site proved too small, from 1873 onwards on an island in the Chiemsee in Upper Bavaria. The gardens were designed in 1875 by court garden director Carl von Effner (1831–84). They were considerably smaller and less complex than Versailles: only the central garden axis with the Parterre d'Eau, the Parterre de Latone, the Apollo Fountain, and the Grand Canal were reproduced at Herrenchiemsee. A further aspect of the Versailles programme was created in reverse: the axes that extend for kilometres into the surrounding countryside ended in Herrenchiemsee after only a few metres in high hedge walls. It was Ludwig's express wish that neither the lake nor the rural surroundings could be seen from the palace. After extensive levelling and reshaping of the site, it was not until 1882—four years after the foundation stone of the palace was laid—that detailed work on the gardens could begin. When the King died prematurely in June 1886, only a third of the planned 81 hectares/200 acres of gardens

had been completed. In the last two decades important garden areas such as the Latona Parterre, the Fama and Fortuna Fountains, and the Grand Canal have been restored, and the Palace Park of Herrenchiemsee is now as it was in Ludwig II's lifetime.   MSt

Herrenhausen ⊗

Hanover, Lower Saxony, Germany, was the summer residence of the dukes and later electors of Hanover as early as 1666; the first small garden also dates from this time. The celebrated baroque garden, the Großer Garten, was the creation of the wife of Ernst August, Sophie, who was a daughter of Friedrich V of the Palatinate. Her childhood in the Netherlands is reflected in the style of the Großer Garten; her gardener, Martin Charbonnier, was sent to the Netherlands to study garden design. Sophie started planning the garden in 1680, and extended it in 1692 to its present size of 50 hectares/124 acres. It is rectangular in shape and is enclosed by a canal in the Dutch style.

The layout is extremely regular, with a middle axis dividing the whole area. Thirty-two pieces of sculpture adorn the large parterre, in the middle of which stands a round *bassin* (formal pool). The parterre is bounded at the sides by high hedges, beyond which lie two large garden rooms: a hedge THEATRE on the left and a MAZE on the right. Immediately to the south of the parterre are four ponds and below them a number of small enclosed gardens of various styles. The other half of the Großer Garten consists of a star-shaped BOSQUET; in the middle stands the main fountain with a jet which reached a height of 350 m/1,148 ft (today it reaches 82 m/269 ft). *Bassins* with fountains stand at the intersections of the paths in the hedged lateral *bosquets*. Wide avenues lead around the whole garden and terminate at two pavilions at the southern corners.

The hedge THEATRE is an important feature of Herrenhausen. The stage, decorated with gilt-lead figures from the Netherlands, is in the shape of a trapezium (16 m/52 ft wide at the front, 8.5 m/28 ft at the back); beech hedges form the wings. A small orchestra pit lies in front of the stage, while the auditorium is constructed in the form of an amphitheatre. Sandstone statues once stood around the sides of the auditorium. The theatre is again used for performances in the summer.

Sophie's son became George I of England in 1714 and the court was moved to London. This meant that the English landscape style was not imposed on the garden which could therefore be restored in its original form.

The Schloss was destroyed in the Second World War and this gap in the total conception

of the garden detracts from the effectiveness of the parterre. Only the orangery survived; tubs of plants have been placed in front of the building.   UD

Herterton House Garden ⊗

Hartington, Northumberland, England, is a rare intermingling of the traditional and the unexpected. Frank and Marjorie Lawley, both artists, have made a garden radically unlike any other English garden, underpinned with ideas borrowed from early 20th-century painting. The Lawleys leased the ruinous 18th-century Herterton House from the NATIONAL TRUST in 1975, rebuilt it and its fine stone garden walls, and embarked on their garden, which is strongly formal, with a firm structural pattern of paths, hedges, and walls. The Flower Garden is divided into a geometric pattern of paths and beds disposed in a modular system (based on a unit of 1 m/3.5 ft) inspired by the grid paintings of Piet Mondrian. The planting is chiefly of herbaceous perennials with repeated use of geometric topiary shapes of box. In high summer the profuse planting of flowers masks the grid but the underlying harmony remains. Further harmony comes from subtle deployment of colour. The chief beds modulate from cool pinks, whites, and yellow close to the house, to intense blues and oranges at the centre and fiery reds and purples in the distance. Further enclosures are equally fastidious—a Fancy Garden with a tall stone gazebo and parterre-like beds, a Physic Garden with a totem of clipped silver pear, herbs, and roses, and the Formal Garden at the front of the house of serene topiary of box and yew underplanted with many different cultivars of dicentra. There is an extraordinary atmosphere to the garden, with all the harmony and intricacy of the Italian Renaissance clothed in a profusion of cottage garden planting.   PT

Hestercombe ⊗

near Taunton, Somerset, England, has two gardens, one of the 18th century and one of the early 20th century. In the 18th century the estate belonged to Coplestone Warre BAMPFYLDE who inherited it in 1750. Bampfylde was a gentleman landscaper and friend of Sir Charles Kemeys Tynte of Halswell (Somerset) and Henry Hoare II of STOURHEAD, both of whom made notable landscape gardens of their day. At Hestercombe Bampfylde had the advantage of a fine wooded valley which his father John Bampfylde had already beautified with an obelisk and ornamental tower. By the time Arthur Young visited Hestercombe in 1771 he admired a waterfall and a ROOT HOUSE. At the foot of the valley Bampfylde laid out a pear-shaped lake, fed by a stream flowing from the cascade, and built on one side of the valley a curious rusticated mausoleum crowned with an obelisk. The garden was well known in the 18th century (William SHENSTONE was an admirer) but swiftly faded from view. By the 20th century it was choked with undergrowth but not entirely forgotten. Intrepid garden historians made their way into the undergrowth to discover what remained and from 1995 a full-scale restoration was launched and the charms of the landscape were fully revealed. Although of approximately the same area as Stourhead, 18.5 hectares/46 acres, it has no buildings of real distinction and much less variety of scenery.

The second garden at Hestercombe is a masterpiece by Edwin LUTYENS and Gertrude JEKYLL laid out from 1903 for the Hon. E. W. B. Portman. This garden, of 1.5 hectares/3.7 acres, lies on the far side of the house from the 18th-century garden, where beautiful views are revealed of the Vale of Taunton. Lutyens disliked the clumsy late Victorian house (which replaced Bampfylde's elegant Queen Anne house) and designed his garden so that views are turned away from the house towards the rural landscape. At its heart is the Great Plat, a SUNKEN GARDEN flanked by terrace walks on three sides and with a pergola walk, swathed in roses, on the fourth side giving the best views. The flanking terrace walks each have a rill edged with irises which runs from a hemispherical lily pool let into a supporting terrace wall at one end to a water tank at the other. Gertrude Jekyll garlanded the drystone walls with cistus, *Erigeron karvinskianus*, and snow-in-the-summer (*Cerastium tomentosum*). A circular garden, the Rotunda, links two awkward axes to connect the Great Plat with the Dutch Garden. In the Rotunda a circular pool is enclosed in high stone walls garlanded with winter-sweet (*Chimonanthus praecox*) and roses. The Dutch Garden is a paved parterre with a characteristic Jekyllian planting of roses, lavender, and *Yucca gloriosa* and edgings of soft grey *Stachys byzantina*. Beyond the Dutch Garden is a magnificent ORANGERY, designed by Lutyens in his full Sir Christopher Wren style. The shifting levels, cunningly deployed vistas, varied enclosures, and beautiful details of stonework throughout the garden are masterly. Jekyll's planting is so much in keeping that the garden seems the work of a single person. From 1973 the Somerset County Council carried out a pioneer feat of restoration of this garden at a time when Lutyens and Jekyll while not exactly forgotten were woefully neglected.   PT

Het Loo. See LOO, HET.

Heveningham Hall,
Heveningham, Suffolk, England, is a magnificent house designed for Sir Gerald Vanneck by Sir Robert Taylor c.1778 with interiors by James Wyatt. An 18th-century landscape park has a fine lake and Brownian atmosphere but, although Capability BROWN worked here from 1781, he made no major changes to the park. He did design a new walled kitchen garden with a CRINKLE-CRANKLE WALL. In 1995 Kim Wilkie and Associates laid out behind the house an elegant fanned pattern of grass terraces embraced by a curved walk of pleached holm oak (*Quercus ilex*).   PT

Hever Castle ✹
near Edenbridge, Kent, England, dates from the 14th century and was bought in 1903 by William Waldorf Astor (later 1st Viscount Astor). Astor impeccably restored the moated castle to which he added lavish guest accommodation in the form of a 'medieval village'. Astor, when American ambassador in Rome, had built up a remarkable collection of classical antiquities, and he proposed to have a garden which would display these to advantage. The garden was designed by the architect Frank Pearson, who had restored the castle, and the nurserymen Joseph Cheal & Son. The Italian Garden is a walled enclosure with, on one long side, the Pompeian Wall which is divided into a series of compartments to display statues, architectural fragments, and ornaments—many of them of high quality. Each of the compartments is, in addition, planted with an elaborate spring and summer bedding scheme. The wall on the opposite side of the garden, facing north, has a long walk covered with a pergola shrouded in clematis, vines, and wisteria. The shady wall behind it is planted with camellias, and mossy niches are planted with ferns, hostas, and persicarias. A gate leads through to an enclosed rose garden. The walled garden is closed by a grand classical loggia designed by Frank Pearson beyond which is a terrace and pool with marble nymphs carved by W. S. Frith in 1908. The terrace overlooks a serene lake made for the garden. Close to the castle are a yew maze and Anne Boleyn's Garden with giant chess pieces clipped in golden yew. Today Hever Castle is run as a tourist attraction but the garden is very finely kept and has exceptional character.
PT

Hex, Kasteel ✹
Limburg, Belgium, the summer residence of Charles-François de Velbruck, Prince Bishop of Liège, who laid out formal gardens, a CHINESE GARDEN, and an English landscape park in 1770. The intricate parterres of the formal French garden were removed in 1915 but the symmetrical axial design remains. A simple area of grass, lightly embellished with flattened domes of clipped box, beds of perennial flowers, and urns—the whole enclosed by tall hornbeam hedges—leads from the front of the chateau to an attractive pair of gate lodges. The Chinese garden, enclosed by undulating yew hedges, has an 18th-century statue of a Buddha in polychrome wood sitting cross-legged beneath a small pavilion accompanied by bonsai trees and *Rosa yakushimanense*. The landscape park at Hex was one of the first in Belgium and has hardly been altered. There is a grotto, a column, a hermit's house, and an avenue of plane trees (1930), although recent storms have caused some losses among the trees. Hex has been known for roses since the 18th century. Three different china roses were brought back from the east for the Prince Bishop by the East India Company. These still grow in the Jardin du Prince, immediately outside what was the Prince's bedroom. Throughout the garden there are now 500 different old and species roses, collected by the late Comtesse Michel d'Ursel who came to the chateau in 1959. In 1990 Jacques WIRTZ redesigned three terraces which overlook the parkland. Parterres of gravel and grass are ornamented with original urns, buttressed with clipped box, and framed by old shrub roses and a group of domed hollies whose shapes are repeated in box. The 1-hectare/2.5-acre vegetable garden is overlooked by a long balustraded walk. Old climbing roses festoon the 18th-century cast-iron balustrade, and espaliered pears and other fruit trees grow against the retaining wall. Mulberries planted during the time of the Prince Bishop still fruit abundantly. The vegetable cellar, a rare survival, is used for storing and forcing vegetables for winter. Plant festivals are held at Hex in June (roses) and September (vegetables) each year.   BA

He Yuan ✹
Jiangsu province, China, also known as Jixiao Shanzhuang or the Retirement Manor, was named after He Zhidao, a local official who built it at the turn of the 19th century. It is the last known Qing-dynasty garden to have been made in the Yangzhou region, and is now blocked off from a large house, to which it was once attached.

It is composed of two sections separated by a double-storeyed *lang* (see CHINA) walkway. In the western part, a two-storeyed *lou* (see CHINA) of seven bays, called Butterfly Hall from its shape in plan, faces the central pond with other buildings and *lang* surrounding it. A square *ting* (see CHINA), or open pavilion, which was used sometimes as a stage, stands in the middle of this pond so that the masters and their guests might enjoy performances while sitting casually in groups along the galleries around it. Climbing the steps of the rockery south-west of the pond, one reaches the first floor of another hall which overlooks the whole view. The focal point in the eastern section is a square hall open on all of its four sides with a smaller hall and *ting* beside it.

The double *lang* between the two sections greatly increases the illusion of size in the garden by allowing views of its rocks, trees, buildings, and lake from above and all round. It also separates the very different atmospheres of both sections—the western more dynamic and vivid, the eastern more peaceful and secluded. Such a use of the *lang* is rare in Chinese garden planning.   D-HL/MK

Hezar Jarib,

Isfahan, Iran. In the early years of the 17th century Shah Abbas created a beautiful garden south of the city across the Zayandeh river, lying alongside the extended CHAHAR BAGH AVENUE on the road to Shiraz. On a natural slope, it had twelve terraces, at the very top of which stood the palace of Jahan-Nama, with a view back towards the city. Cascades, and 500 fountains worked by gravity, enlivened the scene. Today the garden has vanished under new building.   PHo

Hidcote Manor ✿

near Chipping Camden, Gloucestershire, England, has been one of the most influential English gardens of its time. The 17th-century house on a cold and windy hill was bought in 1907 by an American, Gertrude Winthrop, whose son Major Lawrence JOHNSTON started to make a garden after the First World War. The garden is broadly in the tradition of ARTS AND CRAFTS gardens with a firmly patterned layout of walks, hedges, and compartments. Johnston had a strong architectural sensibility which he expressed both in the layout and in the plants which formed the structure and the ornament of Hidcote. However, little is known today of the exact repertory of plants Johnston deployed beyond the fact that he was a very knowledgeable plantsman. Since 1948 when Johnston went to live permanently in France (see MADONE, SERRE DE LA) the garden has belonged to the NATIONAL TRUST, and the planting seen today in all likelihood owes more to it than to Johnston. Johnston's brilliantly conceived layout, however, remains in place and it is a great tribute to its strength and purpose that it retains its charms despite the uncertainty of the detailed planting. In 2004 some of Johnston's notes and diaries from the 1920s came to light and may help to put in place a more accurate Johnstonian planting.

The garden, quite unrelated to the house, is disposed on two chief axes. An east–west axis starts with a walled flower garden which leads into a grass circle. Beyond it are a pair of borders planted largely with red-flowered plants at the end of which, at the head of steps, is a pair of elegant pavilions. One gives an exhilarating view southwards along a very long grass walk hedged in hornbeam. The axis continues westwards through a hornbeam PALISSADE *à l'italienne* which is aligned on wrought-iron gates which reveal a view of the countryside beyond. The second axis runs south from the circle through a series of yew-hedged enclosures—a parterre of fuchsias, a giant circular pool, and a second circle of grass. Several other enclosures lead off the main axes, some of them of informal character. The Stream Garden has winding walks and waterside plantings of hostas, irises, lysichiton, Himalayan primulas, with a background of rhododendrons. WESTONBIRT, named after the great arboretum, is a miniature woodland garden with fine maples. Smaller patches—the Camellia Corner, the Hydrangea Corner—have collections of particular groups of plants. The mood is occasionally cottagey/ whimsical—the White Garden starts off, perhaps, with notions of being a yew parterre garnished with white tulips and roses but TOPIARY hummocks and birds introduce a more whimsical note. Such is the variety of atmosphere and planting that the garden seems even larger than its 4 hectares/10 acres. Vita SACKVILLE-WEST, who was strongly influenced by Hidcote, thought of it as 'a cottage garden on the most glorified scale'. In recent years the National Trust has been fund-raising to finance a restoration of the garden. Ordinary day-to-day maintenance may be thought of as a permanent process of restoration; but it can also be a permanent process of loss of focus. It will be fascinating to discover what surprises emerge from the new initiative.   PT

Highfield ✿

Tasmania, Australia, built 1832-5 as the residence for the Van Diemen's Land Company's first manager, Edward Curr, is an important site in Australian garden history, although little remains of the original garden today. Documents in VDL Company records describe Highfield, near the village of Stanley, in 1828 as situated 'where Nature has done everything in variegating this place with hill and dale and making it the most picturesque and best adapted soil for habitation on the North Coast of this island'. An oil painting, *c*.1835, shows the house set in a picturesque landscape with cows grazing in the foreground but with the bizarre addition of kangaroos and emus in the middle ground. However, five years later, a watercolour of Highfield, held in Hobart's Allport collection, shows a markedly different scene. Highfield's Regency villa and its garden in great detail has been transformed in GARDENESQUE style with winding, irregular paths and beds containing small flowering plants and stiff little conifers. The two paintings of Highfield are remarkable as evidence of a clear transition in garden fashion in a remote colonial outpost. Highfield's layout with its pattern of paths and coloured foliage is also in marked contrast to the Arcadian landscapes created around the grander houses, such as Panshanger, built in this colonial period. The VDL occupancy of Highfield ended in 1856; subsequent private owners made only minor alterations to the house, which remains remarkably intact. Significant garden restoration, using the 1840s watercolours as a guide, is being undertaken.   CMR

Highgrove,

near Tetbury, Gloucestershire, England, is the country house of Charles, Prince of Wales. Here, from 1980, he made a new garden as the setting for the late Georgian house. He had the advice of various notable gardeners, among them Rosemary VEREY, Sir Roy STRONG, Miriam Rothschild, and the Marchioness of Salisbury. The resulting very eclectic garden represents a conspectus of English gardening taste of its time. The Prince's interest in ecology is represented in a wildflower meadow, and a fine formal kitchen garden is cultivated organically—as is the whole garden as well as the estate's agricultural land. There are passages of formality—a walk of golden yew topiary underplanted with carpets of thyme—and salutes to earlier garden taste such as a stumpery (see ROOTERY) with ferns and hellebores. The garden is rich in ornamental buildings, among them a charming tree house, a pair of green-oak temples (with pediments filled with driftwood), and a Wall of Gifts made of stones presented to the Prince. The importance of the garden derives less from its intrinsic merits than from the influential example of the heir to the throne taking such an emphatic interest in gardening.   PT

Hildebrandt, Johann Lukas von

(1668-1745), Austrian architect born in Italy who trained in Rome and practised largely in Vienna. One of the outstanding figures of the Austrian baroque, among his best-known works is the BELVEDERE palace (1700-23) in Vienna where he also had strong influence on the garden design. Two other estates on which he worked that have notable gardens are MIRABELL in Salzburg in the 1720s and SCHLOSSHOF (1725-32) in Lower Austria.   PT

Hill, Thomas

(1529-*c*.1572), English author of gardening and

scientific books. His first book was *A Most Briefe and Pleasaunte Treatyse, Teachyng how to Dresse, Sowe, and Set a Garden* (*c.*1558), which went through several editions and its title changed to *The Proffitable Arte of Gardening* in 1568. *The Gardeners Labyrinth* (1577), published under the pseudonym of Didymus Mountaine, appeared posthumously, the text having been completed by Henry Dethick. The book is attractively illustrated, showing garden designs and scenes of practical garden work. Hill, like many another gardening writer, was a gatherer of other people's knowledge, but he did it most engagingly.   PT

Hilliers,

an English firm of nurserymen and plant breeders. Aged 24 and Veitch trained (see VEITCH FAMILY), Edwin Hillier (1840–1929) purchased a small nursery and florist business in Winchester and later, in 1874, began developing the West Hill Nursery. It was inherited by his sons, Edwin Lawrence (1865–1944), who was responsible for developing the collection of trees and shrubs, and Arthur Richard (1877–1963), who acted as the firm's administrative head. This period laid the foundation of the nursery's worldwide reputation, by cultivating, in particular, the new woody plants arriving from the various plant collectors in China, the Himalayas, and Japan. Despite the sale of the Shroner Wood Nursery in 1913, the business continued expanding under the guidance of (Sir) Harold Hillier (1905–85), grandson of the founder. His knowledge of temperate zone trees and shrubs made him a world authority and in 1957 and 1962 respectively his expertise was acknowledged by the ROYAL HORTICULTURAL SOCIETY when he was awarded the Victoria Medal of Honour, and the Veitch Memorial Medal. In 1953 Harold Hillier moved his home to Jermyns House, near Romsey, Hampshire, where there was a small garden, shrubbery, and some very mature beeches planted originally in 1844. Over the next twenty years he developed the grounds into the 73 hectares/180 acres of the Hillier Garden and Arboretum which now contains one of the most diverse collection of hardy woody plants in the world. In 1977 Sir Harold donated the site to public ownership, and Hampshire County Council continues to develop the gardens and arboretum for the public, including ten National Plant Collections.   MC-C

Hills and Dales.

See FERRELL GARDENS AT HILLS AND DALES.

Hirschfeld, Christian Cay Lorenz

(1742–92), the best-known theoretician and writer on garden art and landscape gardening in 18th-century Germany. The son of a parson, he was born at Kirchnüchel, became a Latin scholar of the Franckesche Stiftung in Halle, and studied theology at the university there. From 1770 he was professor of philosophy and aesthetics at the Christian-Albrechts-University at Kiel, where he was the founder and director of the Königlich Dänische Fruchtbaumschule (Royal Danish School for fruit trees). He was tutor to Peter Friedrich Ludwig von Oldenburg (later Großherzog von Oldenburg) who laid out three important landscape gardens at Rastede (1777–80, Niedersachsen), Eutin (1785–1802, Ostholstein), and Oldenburg (from 1803, Niedersachsen). His five-volume *Theorie der Gartenkunst* (1779–85), published simultaneously in German and French, became the bible of German landscape gardening. It was translated into English for the first time in an abridged version as *Theory of Garden Art* (2001). His influence also reached France, Hungary, Italy, the Netherlands, Russia, and the Scandinavian countries. Hirschfeld's intellectual roots lay in enlightened rationalism; he praised the nature of landscapes in poetic language and described numerous gardens of his time. His *Theorie* is the most extensive 18th-century compendium of its subject and was influenced by English romanticism intermingled with German idealism. He believed in the power of the natural world to foster everyone's moral forces. This universal right to enjoy the experience of gardens and landscapes gives the creation of public parks special importance. Hirschfeld ranks not only as the founder and discoverer of the German landscape garden but also as the father of popular gardening.   MMM

Historic Bartram's Garden ⊕

on the Schuylkill river in Philadelphia, Pennsylvania, USA, is recognized today as the oldest surviving BOTANIC GARDEN in North America. It was originally the pre-revolutionary home, garden, and nursery of Quaker plant hunter John BARTRAM who, according to LINNAEUS, was 'the greatest natural botanist in the world'. Between 1736 and 1766, Bartram travelled north to Lake Ontario, south to Florida, and west to the Ohio river in search of plants and natural history specimens for his own garden and for collectors at home and abroad: for example, George Washington at MOUNT VERNON and Peter COLLINSON in London. Among the plants he found on these journeys were numerous trees—pines, oaks, maples; the first large-leafed rhododendron, *Rhododendron maximum*, and flowers including liliums (*Lilium philadelphicum* and *L. superbum*), gentians, asters, and solidago. Bartram and his son William are credited with identifying and introducing

---

Garden design from **Thomas Hill's** *The Gardeners Labyrinth* (1577).

more than 200 North American plants into cultivation. Bartram's Philadelphia garden, in his 1785 sketch sent to Peter Collinson, shows a fenced 'common' flower garden, a 'new' flower garden, intended for plants from England, and a small shed, his 'Seed House'. Trees and shrubs were grouped in a 80–120-hectare/200–300-acre arboretum. They possibly included *Franklinia alatamaha*, which was last seen in the wild in 1803. A specimen, descended from those propagated and saved from extinction by the Bartrams, can be found in the garden today. Other significant trees still growing are a yellowwood, *Cladrastis kentuckea*, and a *Ginkgo biloba*, the last of three original ginkgos introduced to the USA in 1785, and a Bartram oak, *Quercus* × *heterophylla*. Bartram discovered a species of this rare but naturally occurring hybrid of the red and willow oaks growing on his own property. John Bartram's spirit lives on in the enchanting 18-hectare/45-acre site, which includes the furnished Bartram House, botanical garden, meadow, parkland, and wetland.   CMR

Hoare, Henry, and family.
The Hoare family began as goldsmiths in London. In 1672 Richard Hoare founded a bank in Cheapside, London, 'at the sign of the Golden Bottle'. The bank, C. Hoare & Co., still survives and is still solely owned by the Hoare family. Richard's son Henry Hoare (1677–1725) bought the Stourton estate in Wiltshire in 1717 and demolished the ancient manor of the Stourton family (which had lived here for hundreds of years) and created the Stourhead estate. He commissioned a noble new Palladian house from Colen CAMPBELL which was built between 1721 and 1724. Henry's son Henry Hoare II (1705–85) (known as Henry the Magnificent) from 1741 created the garden at STOURHEAD. He formed the lake and commissioned most of the buildings which today ornament the landscape. In 1783 the estate was passed to Henry II's grandson Sir Richard Colt Hoare (1758–1838). He maintained the garden, added a few buildings, and removed some of which he did not approve. He began the tradition of planting exotic trees and shrubs at Stourhead which, later in the 19th and 20th centuries, radically altered the appearance of the landscape. By the late 19th century the estate was practically derelict when Sir Henry Hoare (whose father had been a cousin of Sir Richard Colt Hoare) inherited *the estate* in 1894. Henry Hoare restored the garden and the agricultural estate. His only son Harry was killed in the First World War and in 1946 he gave it, with 810 hectares/2,000 acres of woodland, to the NATIONAL TRUST.   PT

Hobhouse, Penelope
(b. 1929), Anglo-Irish author, garden designer, garden historian, and plantswoman of wide-ranging skills and much influence on late 20th-century gardening. She has designed many gardens in Britain and other countries, especially in the USA—some of these may be seen in her book *Penelope Hobhouse's Garden Designs* (1997). She combines a reverence for Italian Renaissance principles with great knowledge of plants and an acute sense of history. Among her British gardens accessible to the public are the formal garden at Walmer Castle (Kent) commissioned in 1995 to celebrate the 95th birthday of Queen Elizabeth, the Queen Mother, and the Summer Garden designed at the Royal Horticultural Society's garden at WISLEY. Among her many books are *Plants in Garden History* (1992), *The Story of Gardening* (2002), and *Gardens of Persia* (2003). She was awarded the Victoria Medal of Honour in 1996.   PT

Hodkovce
(in Hungarian Hotkóc), Csáky Gardens, near Košice, Slovakia, one of the most characteristic examples of the early landscape garden in Slovakia (formerly in Hungary), with a large number of ornamental buildings and monuments. In around 1800 Count Emánuel Csáky had a garden built which made use of pattern books—like Grohmann's *Ideenmagazin*—to combine the former terraced structures of the baroque garden with the characteristic features of an irregular layout. A contemporary illustration (1802) shows that the relatively small grounds were home to a number of buildings—among them ancient and medieval mock ruins, statuary, an amphitheatre, and a Chinese pavilion. Despite its size, thanks to an 1806 work by Ferenc Kazinczy—the most universal Hungarian writer of the period—Hodkovce became the model garden of its day for Hungarian garden historical literature. The formerly elaborate garden preserves its original structure and some of its monuments to this day.   GA

Hofwijck ⊛
Voorburg, Zuid-Holland, the Netherlands, situated on land along the river Vliet was bought in 1639 by Constantijn HUYGENS with the intention of distancing himself from court life. A house, designed by Jacob van CAMPEN and Pieter Post (1608–69), was conceived inspired by classical Roman examples. The estate poem *Vitaulium Hofwyck* which Huygens published in 1653 exemplifies this, with its structure being based on Virgil's *Georgics*, celebrating country life, and the proportions of the garden relating to the (his) body, very much in the way proposed

by Vitruvius (fl. 46–30 BC) and ALBERTI. The moated, well-wooded symmetrical garden contained an orchard near the house and a mound in the centre of the layout. The last Huygens sold the property in 1750. In 1914 the Vereniging Hofwijck saved the building from demolition when a new railway was built through the grounds. The property was restored in 1925–8, and so was the remaining part of the garden, supervised by the landscape architect Dirk Tersteeg (1876–1942). The gardens were restored again in 1988, intending to evoke the garden of the Huygens period, with an attempt to make the lost part of the garden visible in the design of a new railway station.   JW

WILLEMIEN B. DE VRIES, 'The country estate immortalized: Constantijn Huygens' Hofwijck', in J. D. Hunt, *The Dutch Garden in the Seventeenth Century* (1990).

Hőgyész ⊛
Tolna county, Hungary. The construction of the landscape garden at Hőgyész is associated with Count Antal Apponyi, one of the most erudite Hungarian aristocrats of his time. From 1785 until his death in 1817, Apponyi gradually turned the grounds—built in the first third of the 18th century by the Mercy family with a modest baroque garden—first into an irregular transitional design with straight avenues and serpentine paths, then into an increasingly purist and large-scale landscape park. He had a range of elaborate designs prepared during this time. The designers were Georg Karl Zillack, Ambros Leihn, Johann Matthias Gacksch, Johann Hypman, and Fr. Le Febour—the last of these is probably the same as F. Le Febvre d'Archenbault, who created the parks of LAXENBURG and LAEKEN, which bears witness to the changes in taste during the lifetime of this one owner. The focal point of the gardens was a bridge arching over a stream, from where vistas branched out in a star shape, each with a building at its end, one of them leading to the palace itself. At the end of the 19th century geometric parterres were created around the palace. After the Second World War the 14-hectare/34-acre grounds were divided up, partly used for housing, and most of the garden's buildings were destroyed. The round Temple of Venus still survives, however, as the park's main ornament.   GA

Höhenpark Killesberg ⊛
Stuttgart, Germany, was begun in 1938 with an area of about 50 hectares/124 acres laid out to the designs of the Potsdam garden architect Hermann MATTERN in collaboration with the architect Gerhard Graubner from Berlin on the site of a former quarry for the Reichsgartenschau 1939 (the German Reich's

garden show). The permanent features of the garden show integrated allotments, a public swimming pool, playgrounds, an orchard, a vineyard, and several park features exhibiting a huge number of perennials within naturalistic as well as formally designed settings. The rugged stone formations of the former quarry became the most impressive element of the whole layout, for which, according to the competition of 1935, only indigenous plants were allowed. In addition to the rock formations of the quarry, Mattern created other naturalistic features like a waterfall, an artificial brook, as well as large meadows and a kind of vale which emphasized the scenic character of the undulating ground and made room for the display of various types of perennials. Having been partly destroyed during the Second World War, the park was reconstructed by Hermann Mattern for the first Bundesgartenschau (see SHOWS AND FESTIVALS) which was held in 1950. Mattern also integrated some of the existing buildings and enriched the park with new paths and roads which followed the natural contours of the ground, a cable railway, and light garden-architectural structures such as trellises. After other garden shows in 1961 and 1977, the area was finally used for the IGA 93 (Internationale Gartenbauausstellung—International Garden Show) in 1993, which was designed from a general layout by the Stuttgart garden architect Hans LUZ. This show presented a collection of individual national gardens and installations by modern artists. The entrance area displays a memorial stone which commemorates the deportation of Jews from Württemberg to the concentration camps.   US

Honselaarsdijk,

Honselersdijk, Zuid-Holland, the Netherlands, is best known as the country retreat of Stadtholder Frederik Hendrik, Prince of Orange-Nassau (1584-1647). It is situated on the site of the medieval Naaldwijck Castle and gardens, which he acquired in 1612. One of the first undertakings was the planting of a monumental approach avenue, c.1615, the first of such avenues in Western Europe. The initial garden within a double moated site was divided into compartments. In a continual process of enlargement and renewal it led the latest trends with contributions by fashionable designers, including André MOLLET, employed 1633-5 to implement some of the first PARTERRES de broderie in the Netherlands. The estate also performed an important political function—it was taken to symbolize a new Rome. This reinforced the age-old establishment and power of the Dutch Republic as a new Batavian stronghold, the emblematic 'Hortus Batavus' with the House of Orange as its protector. Little

happened to the estate after Frederik Hendrik's death until it became the property of William III in 1672 and after his death in 1702 when it was owned by Friedrich I of Prussia—each altered parts of the garden. However after Friedrich Wilhelm inherited the estate in 1713, it fell into general neglect, with buildings being demolished and the gardens becoming overgrown. There was a brief revival when the estate was returned to the House of Orange in 1754, until it was finally sold off and built over with greenhouses. Only one of the lower courts and the general structure of the layout survive.
JW

VANESSA BEZEMER SELLERS, *Courtly Gardens in Holland 1600–1650: The House of Orange and the Hortus Batavus* (2001).

Hooker, Sir Joseph Dalton

(1817-1911), English botanist and naturalist, born in Suffolk, son of William Jackson Hooker (1785-1865), botanist, plant collector, artist, and administrator, who for 21 years was professor of botany at Glasgow University, before being offered the directorship of the ROYAL BOTANIC GARDENS, KEW. Joseph took after his father in almost all particulars; after studying medicine at Glasgow, he was appointed surgeon-botanist on board HMS *Erebus* in 1839. Joseph departed for a four-year exploration of the Antarctic, Falkland Islands, Tierra del Fuego, and the Antipodes, publishing the results in *Botany of Antarctic Voyage* (1844-60). His most notable expedition took place 1848-51 when he travelled and botanized in Sikkim and Nepal, when he introduced some 43 new species of rhododendron, which resulted in *Rhododendrons of Sikkim-himalaya, Himalayan Journals* (2 vols., 1854), and *Illustrations of Himalayan Plants* (1855). Hooker thereafter always maintained an interest in the area. In 1855 he became assistant director to his father, and on the death of Sir William ten years later took over as director of Kew, a post he held for twenty years. Although administrative tasks took much of his time, he continued his botanical researches, publishing with George Bentham (1800-84) *Genera Plantarum* (3 vols., 1862-83) and completing *Flora of British India* (7 vols., 1872-97). Hooker maintained an interesting correspondence with Charles Darwin on the origin of species and his global view of economic botany continued the work begun by his father, gaining him many honours and awards.   MC-C

Horticultural Centre of the Pacific ⊛

Victoria, British Columbia, Canada, the creation of Victoria citizens who wanted a horticultural training centre with gardens demonstrating plants of the Pacific Rim. Begun in 1979, the non-profit Horticulture

Centre of the Pacific has a garden staff heavily supplemented by volunteers. Today it encompasses 3.25 hectares /8 acres of teaching and demonstrations garden set amidst a 50-hectare/123.5-acre woodland setting of old growth Douglas firs (*Pseudotsuga menziesii*) complete with walking trails next to Viaduct Flats Lake. There are more than 10,000 varieties of plants on display. Its speciality gardens include a perennial mixed Hardy Plant Border, the Takata Japanese Garden and Zen Garden, a Native Plant Garden, and the recently added Drought Tolerant Garden. The Doris Page Winter Garden features 500 kinds of plants perfect for a winter garden of Victoria's moderate Mediterranean climate, including a dazzling hellebore display (*Helleborus niger, H. orientalis, H. argutifolius,* and *H. foetidus*) as well as such fragrant shrubs as witch hazels (*Hamamelis mollis*), *Daphne odora* 'Rubra', *Gaultheria mucronata,* and *Corylus avellana* 'Contorta'. Ornamental grasses contrast with colourful dogwood (*Cornus stolonifera*) and willow (*Salix* spp.) stems. Masses of delicate snowdrops (*Galanthus nivalis*) and winter aconites (*Eranthis hyemalis*) give way to *Anemone* species and *Cyclamen* species in February and March. The three amazing Hardy Plant Borders are each run by a team of professionals with amateur designer-gardeners and are among the best-designed public gardens in Canada.   MH

hortillonages ⊛

Amiens, Somme, France. A large area, originally over 300 hectares/740 acres, of market gardens made in reclaimed marshy ground on the banks of a network of inlets, canals (called *rieux* in these parts) and pools by the Somme river in the centre of the city of Amiens. The origins of these gardens are very ancient, certainly dating back to the Middle Ages and probably even earlier. Today only 25 hectares/62 acres of the gardens are still cultivated and these are mostly pleasure gardens with only a handful used as market gardens. Even these, occupying valuable inner city land, are threatened and there is an active Association pour la Protection et la Sauvegarde du Site et de l'Environnement des Hortillonages. They present a charming sight, with a handsome background of substantial poplars and willows, decorative arched bridges over the canals, and the toing and froing of the *bateaux à cornet,* the flat-bottomed boats designed to take large quantities of vegetables. The *hortillonages* may be visited by boat or by exploring the towpaths.   PT

JOY LARKCOM, 'The floating gardens of Amiens', *The Garden* (Sept. 1996).

Hortus Botanicus.

See LEIDEN BOTANICAL GARDEN.

Hortus Bulborum ⊛

Limmen, Noord-Holland, the Netherlands, a garden of historic bulb varieties that finds its origin in the collection of historically important tulip cultivars started in the 1920s by the schoolteacher P. Boschman gathered from the bulb growing areas of Noord-Holland. In 1928 a collection of bulbs from Dr W. E. de Mol from Amsterdam was added to this and it was then planted up as a scientific collection. When in 1934 the Neversie, the Dutch Society for the encouragement of scientific improvement of cultivated plants, was founded, it took over responsibility for the collection. Funded by the Dutch bulb growing industry it now serves as a gene pool for cultivation of new varieties and the collection has been extended to include daffodils, fritillarias, and various other bulbous species. As one of the very few repositories of the old varieties it is an invaluable resource for historic planting schemes, and several restoration schemes throughout the Western world have made invaluable use of it.   JW

hortus conclusus,

literally an enclosed garden, a secret garden within a garden. There is a literary/religious symbolism dating back to the Song of Songs which associated the Virgin Mary with the term: 'enclosed' represented her intact virginity, and the fruition of the garden represented the flowers of virtue. This garden was often contrasted with the lost Eden. When the medieval cult of the Virgin was at its height, Mary was identified frequently with the rose, and 'Mary gardens' would contain flowers each with its own meaning. In practice the enclosed garden was often a rose garden with fountains, walks, and arbours, surrounded by a hedge or wall, sometimes with turfed seats, a lawn, and paths. The term 'herber' was sometimes used synonymously. Some enclosed gardens were ecclesiastical, some secular, and their purpose was for delectation and entertainment.   MWRS

Hortus Palatinus,

Heidelberg, Germany. The Hortus Palatinus mannerist garden of Heidelberg Castle owes its creation to love. Following the marriage of Elector Friedrich V of the Rhineland-Palatinate and Elizabeth Stuart, daughter to the English King James I, in 1613, Friedrich commissioned Elizabeth's former drawing master, the French architect and engineer Salomon de CAUS, to create a new garden around the castle. In 1620, de Caus, who had travelled extensively through Italy and thus had a great knowledge of Italian garden design, published a detailed description of the garden containing 30 plates. Thus we are well informed about its layout as well as details of a structural and architectural nature. The garden was created between 1614 and 1619, replacing an existing garden near the castle. De Caus mastered the difficult topographic situation of the steep hill by laying out five superimposed narrow terraces; high retaining walls had to be built up from the river Neckar valley to support the lowest terrace. The terraces are organized in a large 'L' shape with the east terrace being at right angles to the rest of the garden, thus affording a splendid view over the river valley. The terraces were divided by hedges and pergolas. Embellished with typical Renaissance elements such as gazebos, a maze,

The **Hortus Palatinus** displayed in an engraving (1645) by Matthaeus Merian.

ornamental ponds and lakes, statuary, and tubs of plants, the Hortus Palatinus was a perfect example of a mannerist garden where no axes dominated the view. Visitors were invited to admire and experience different attractions in the garden, especially the overwhelming, innumerable waterworks and grottoes, most of which were musical—a unique phenomenon in German garden design of the time. The many grottoes, fountains, and statues spitting out water prove de Caus's elaborate skill in engineering and hydraulics, while reflecting his great knowledge of Italian garden design. Several architectural features indicate a pronounced political and panegyrical meaning, culminating in the statue of Friedrich V that dominated the highest point of the garden and stood directly above that of Neptune, the ruler over the element of water. Friedrich V became King of Bohemia in 1619 and left Heidelberg. Soon after he was forced to leave Bohemia for exile in the Netherlands and as a consequence the garden was never finished. Later damage during the Thirty Years War (1618–48) and several devastations destroyed the garden, but the terraces as well as a number of grottoes remain to the present day.   AK

SALOMON DE CAUS, *Hortus Palatinus a Friderico, Rege Boemiae, Electore Palatino Heidelbergae Exstructus* (1620). Reprint of French edn. (1981).
REINHARD ZIMMERMANN, *Hortus Palatinus: Die Entwürfe zum Heidelberger Schlossgarten von Salomon de Caus* (1986).

hospital grounds.

Various British therapeutic institutions occupied designed, ornamental estates. Of the few hospitals in the 17th century, Bethlem (London, 1674–6) was the first with substantial designed grounds. It was a charitable lunatic asylum overlooking Moorfields (the first public park see LONDON PARKS AND GARDENS), its magnificent building and forecourt flanked by two exercise yards, or airing courts. Two military hospitals followed shortly after, Chelsea (1682) and Greenwich (1694), each with lavish formal gardens for patients. A few large hospitals set in landscaped grounds appeared in the 18th century, including naval ones at Haslar (Hampshire, 1746–61) and Devonport (Devon, 1758–62), both using formal axial designs about which both buildings and landscapes were centred. At The Retreat (York, 1792–6), a Quaker asylum, designed grounds beyond the airing courts were provided for the first time for the lunatic patients. This idea was expanded greatly at Brislington House (Bristol, 1804–6), to resemble a landscape park with the asylum building and airing courts at the core next to the building. Most 19th-century hospitals followed a similar pattern when they required extensive rural grounds, taking the

country house estate model, with the flexibility of the informal landscape park and pleasure grounds, modified for their particular therapeutic needs.

County lunatic asylums spread across Britain by 1914, with at least 130 large asylums scattered across England alone. All were huge institutions set in extensive grounds, some more than 100 hectares/220 acres, the most notable including Crichton Royal (Dumfries, 1839), Colney Hatch (London, 1849–51, grounds by William Broderick Thomas (1811–c.98)), and the Royal Holloway Sanatorium (Surrey, 1874–8, grounds by John Gibson). Formal groups of airing courts surrounded the asylum building, enclosed by fences, walls, or HA-HAS to stop the patients escaping. Informal pleasure grounds accommodated supervised exercise, with recreation ground and parkland, and a kitchen garden and farm for male patients to work in as part of their treatment, sometimes with a cemetery, united by a network of drives guarded by lodges. Views out, over the estate and rural setting beyond, were considered essential for the patients. Epileptic and mental deficiency colonies developed from the asylum from the 1890s, with extensive designed grounds moving away from the landscape park towards the garden city model in the early 20th century. Groups of patient villas replaced the single asylum building, set in informal pleasure grounds instead of formal airing courts, within park and farmland, generally reusing country house estates. Asylums were built throughout Europe, North America, and the British Empire, the grounds laid out in similar fashion.

Other types of hospital developed requiring extensive grounds. Chest hospitals (which became tuberculosis sanatoria) needed clear air for their patients' treatment, with extensive grounds for measured exercise circuits, such as the Royal National Hospital for Diseases of the Chest (Isle of Wight, 1868, now Ventnor Botanic Garden). Gertrude JEKYLL produced designs for a similar landscape at the King Edward VII Sanatorium (Midhurst, Sussex, 1905–8). To combat infectious diseases such as smallpox, large isolation hospitals were built in remote areas with a *cordon sanitaire* provided by their extensive grounds. Joyce Green (Kent, 1903, grounds by Messrs H. E. Milner) overlooked the remote Thames marshes, with extensive lawns and gardens between the ward blocks, its own tramway, and detached cemetery.   SR

hothouse plants.

The use of artificial heat has enabled gardeners to make some attempt at growing plants indoors under glass in temperate regions since the 18th century, with a high point reached in

the 19th century. The beginning of the 20th century saw a variety of influences result in the steady decline of the hothouse: notably rising energy prices and a greater and more tempting range of hardy plants. During the 19th century the range of species grown reflected two main factors: the ability of the heating technology to provide a given temperature and the contemporary status of plant hunting. Fashion has also played a far more important role in the history of indoor plants than it has with hardy plants, as they are so totally dependent upon human intervention for survival. Nineteenth-century hothouse plant growing was characterized by a succession of infatuations with particular plant groups, with Britain very much leading the way. A great many of the species grown under glass in the 19th century are today no longer in cultivation outside their home countries, and many of the hybrids raised and cultivars selected have been lost. One of many examples is the heather-like genus *Epacris*, a range of hybrids being very popular in the latter half of the 19th century which today has been almost entirely lost, and does not appear to be cultivated much even in its native Australia.

Eighteenth-century orangeries housed citrus fruits and a number of Mediterranean evergreens. The latter half of the 18th century and the early 19th century were also the high point of pineapple growing in Britain. Pineapples can be successfully fruited in low glasshouses using very primitive heating methods, such the use of the heat from decaying manure or tan bark, a process which can be seen today in the reconstructed kitchen garden at HELIGAN. The use of flue-based heating systems during the latter years of the 18th century and the first two decades of the 19th and the botanical exploration of the South African Cape and Australia coincided to stimulate the first of several indoor plant enthusiasms amongst wealthy European gardeners. Needing only frost-free conditions and appreciating the dry heat of the flues, plants from the Mediterranean climate zones of these regions were ideal for early glasshouses.

With the development of heating using hot water flowing through cast-iron pipes during the second decade of the nineteenth century, gardeners at last had a reliable, safe, and efficient method. At last tropical temperatures could be achieved, and the repeal of the glass tax in 1845 added a further stimulus. With vast numbers of new plant species arriving from South America and tropical Asia, hothouse gardening could really take off, making the last half of the 19th century a true golden age of glasshouse gardening. Speaking very broadly, hothouse gardening was divided into 'cool', ▶

where minimum winter night temperatures of around 10 °C/50 °F were aimed at, and 'stove' with a minimum of 15 °C/60 °F. As well as growing plants under glass all year round, hothouses were used to start off warm climate species for summer cultivation outside, the so-called 'half-hardy annuals', and to provide winter protection for leafy exotics which were planted outside temporarily as centrepieces for colourful annuals—particularly palms and bananas (*Musa* spp.).

Of the waves of exotica which poured into the glasshouses of north-west Europe, and the east coast of the USA, ORCHIDS became the most sought after, with collectors ransacking the rainforests of the world for new rarities with which to tempt the palettes and wallets of hothouse owners. Orchids were frequently cultivated in their own orchid house, often divided into cool and stove sections, and also an 'intermediate' one, particularly useful for South American montane forest genera, such as cattleya and odontoglossum.

Nineteenth-century glasshouses were essentially functional growing spaces for plants, with those in flower being taken into the house for brief periods or into a special display

house. By the end of the century, however, conservatories were also extremely popular, heated glass structures attached to the main body of the house, with soil-filled beds for growing shrubs and particularly climbers such as jasminum and passiflora species, directly in the ground. Staging allowed for the temporary display of plants from the working glasshouses, and also for hardy perennials and bulbs which were 'forced', i.e. encouraged to make early growth in a hothouse so that they could be enjoyed a month or two earlier than they could be in the garden.

With the arrival of large numbers of colourful flowering shrubs such as magnolias and rhododendrons from temperate zone Asia in the late 19th century, hothouse gardening began to lose its appeal. The First World War then struck a blow from which hothouse gardening has never recovered. Today, a limited number of enthusiasts grow warm climate plants under glass, mostly in Germany, although keen orchid growers can be found in most cooler climates. With cheap and easy foreign travel and a wider range of exotic-looking but hardy species being introduced for garden cultivation, the appeal of hothouse gardening has been considerably reduced. Despite there now being a range of technologies for efficient indoor climate control, it is only botanical gardens which really exploit them to the full.   NK

Hotkóc. See HODKOVCE.

Huanxiu Villa (Huanxiu shanzhuang) ⊛ Jiangsu province, China, lies in Suzhou, on a site which in the 10th century had belonged to a prince of the Qian family. After innumerable changes of ownership, it came in the mid 19th century to a family named Wang who renamed it Huanxiu, meaning literally 'a mountain retreat surrounded by elegance'. Most of the site is now occupied by the Suzhou Embroidery Institute but the whole point of the garden lies in the huge artificial hill (*jiashan*) of Taihu rocks (the rock most highly prized for artificial 'mountains') that takes up nearly half of the site. Said to have been designed by one of the most famous of all rock artists, the Qing-dynasty Ge Yu-liang, it has long been ranked among the best of all such works in China. The main part lies on the eastern side of the garden, where its steep cliffs and peaks are said to imitate exactly in form and structure, and in the grains and veining of the rock, those of a natural rocky hill. Moreover, the 'mountain' is built around and above interior grottoes and chambers which add a sense of strangeness and adventure to the domestic beauties of the garden. The whole is regarded as an unusually

skilful and rare example of what can be done to reproduce the dramatic effects of a mountainscape in a limited space.   G-ZW/MK

Huaqinggong ⊛
Shaanxi province, China, lies 20 km/12 miles east of the city of Xi'an. The site of this garden below pleasant hills has long been famous for its hot spring. Early in the time of the Emperor Qin Shi Huang (who first united China in 221 BC), there was already a short-stay royal villa here which the Tang-dynasty Emperors later developed into an elaborate palace complex. Xuan Zhong (712–55), a cultivated as well as powerful ruler, spent each winter there with his favourite concubine, Yang (Guifei), whose legendary beauty is supposed to have so bemused him that he lost interest in affairs of state. The whole hillside was included in his garden palace, which was lavishly endowed with building complexes, bathing pools, pavilions, and hidden retreats. Above all, however, it was famous for the effects of its huge bluish-green fir and jade green pines in the evening twilight. Eventually there was a revolt against the Emperor and the palace was greatly damaged. What today is still called the Huaqing Spring, which includes a bathing pool said to be that of Lady Yang, is in fact only a very small part of what was then the palace. Its buildings, rebuilt and first opened to the public in 1956, nevertheless still preserve names like the 'Hall of Dancing Frost', and the 'Crab Apple Flower Bathing Pool' given them in Tang times. Rebuilding of Tang-style halls continues.
  G-ZW/MK

Huis Bingerden. See BINGERDEN, HUIS.

Humayun's Tomb ⊛
Delhi, India. Built between 1560 and 1573, this 12-hectare/30-acre garden, with a 360-m/1,080-ft quadrangle on one side, is a *parterre* in which the Persian motif of the CHAHAR BAGH (quadrant) is repeated in 36 smaller *chahar baghs*. The four central ones are occupied by the MAUSOLEUM rising on a high base. This is the first example of a tomb garden in India. The layout is composed of narrow water channels that intersect at right angles and are fed by wells outside the garden proper. The causeways are raised and pipes of clay irrigate the lower, square lawns. The axes are underlined by four monumental entrances and by the perfect symmetry of the mausoleum itself, crowned by a dome resting on a drum. All the original vegetation has been replaced and the fruit trees that once filled the quadrants have disappeared.   AP
  S. CROWE and S. HAYWOOD, *The Gardens of Mughul India* (1972).

Colour plates

The 18th-century Visconti Bridge in the gardens at **Pavlovsk**, St Petersburg, Russia

Fountain cascade and nymphs in the Italian garden at **Hever Castle**, England

Serene minimalism in **Fernando Caruncho's** designs for the water garden at S'Agaro and the cypress avenue at Mas Floris, both in Spain

Detail of the early 18th-century shell gallery at **Rosendael**, the Netherlands

E. B. Moynihan (ed.), *Paradise as a Garden in Persia and Mughal India* (1979).

C. M. Villiers Stuart, *Gardens of the Great Mughals* (1913).

Humboldt, Alexander von

(1769–1859), German scientist, explorer, and traveller. Enthralled by the natural world, Humboldt studied at Göttingen University, becoming a mining official but longing to travel. In 1798 the opportunity arose when he met the botanist Aimé Bonpland (1773–1858) in Paris where they had been invited by Louis de Bougainville (1729–1811) to join a proposed round-the-world voyage of exploration. Although that did not materialize, the two young men in 1799 set out on a five-year journey encompassing most of tropical America, including exploring the river Orinoco and the Casiquiare Canal and climbing Mount Chimborazo (6,267 m/20,681 ft) in Ecuador. Humboldt recorded all he encountered, and travelled back to Europe in 1804 via the United States, meeting and becoming friends with President Thomas JEFFERSON. The expedition returned with some 60,000 specimens and they were fêted in France. Their observations and conclusions on plant distribution were encompassed in *Essai sur la géographie des plantes* (1805), a precursor of the ideas of Charles Darwin (1809–82). This was the first of 30 volumes entitled *Voyage de Humboldt et Bonpland 1799–1804* (1805–34). Humboldt's unique contribution to 'provide an accurate scientific picture of the physical structure of the universe' is contained in *Cosmos* (1845–59), the five-volume tour de force which he worked on for the rest of his life. His visionary concept of seeing 'nature as a whole and man as part of that whole' places him at the forefront of the modern environmental world.   MC-C

Hungary.

The first gardens in the Carpathian basin are likely to have been those of the villas built in the Pannonia province of the Roman Empire, but at present we have only scarce data about them. After the arrival of the Magyars in the 9th century, and the adoption of Christianity in 1000, monasteries began to be built in the 11th century which would have small gardens, but the information we have on them is sketchy. The first unambiguous mention of a garden in Hungary is from the mid 15th century—the recreational garden of János Vitéz, Archbishop of Esztergom, which, with its shaded bowers and terraced hanging garden, already displayed characteristics of the Renaissance style. Vitéz was stepfather of King Matthias (Corvinus) Hunyadi (reigned 1456–90), who commissioned the reconstruction of Buda Castle and the

Royal Palace at Visegrád, largely under the inspiration of his second wife, Beatrix of Aragon.

For the reconstruction and for the creation of gardens and wells King Matthias invited such well-known Italian masters as Chimenti Leonardo di Camicia and Giovanni Dalmata, thus introducing the direct influence of Italian architecture and horticulture of the 15th century in Hungary. This early blossoming of the Renaissance was interrupted by the Turkish occupation, which was to last for a century and a half (1541–1686), and only continued to survive in the region to the fringes of the country not threatened by the Turks, drawing on outside resources. The characteristics of this style can be seen throughout the 17th century, and even into the 18th, especially in Transylvania. These late Renaissance Hungarian walled gardens, small in size, were usually divided into equal rectangular compartments. They were not decorated with many statues or other built elements, and tended to include fruit trees and vegetables as well as flowers and other ornamental plants. The Turkish influence was not only a negative one, however: they brought a number of crops, especially fruits, to Hungary, and thereby to Europe. At the invitation of Boldizsár Batthyány, the famous botanist Carolus CLUSIUS made a prolonged stay in Hungary, and created Batthyány's garden in Némétújvár (today Güssing, Austria). He was the first to record a number of ornamental plants (*Hemerocallis lilioasphodelus*, for example), and it was from here that it became known worldwide. The flowers that provided the main decoration for the gardens of the 16th and 17th centuries, however, came to the Carpathian basin from Western Europe. The most noteworthy garden of the Hungarian late Renaissance is that of Archbishop György Lippay, built in Pozsony (today Bratislava, Slovakia) in the middle of the 17th century, which, with its fountains, statues, bowers, labyrinths, grottoes, mound, and greenhouse full of exotic plants, displayed a profound Italian influence. THE ARCHBISHOP'S GARDEN was the subject of the first systematic series of garden illustrations, and the first garden treatise in Hungarian, *Posoni kert* (1664), was written by János Lippay, the Archbishop's brother. The widely known illustrations of the gardens of the Esterházy family also date from the end of the 17th century.

18th and 19th centuries

It was only in the decades following the expulsion of the Turks, in the first third of the 18th century, that Hungary saw the construction of its first real baroque palaces and their gardens. The style persisted until the

first decade of the 19th century, when baroque gardens were still found existing alongside the increasingly dominant landscape gardens. Palaces would often face their gardens with a *cour d'honneur* (see ATTRE, CHÂTEAU D'), and fences would divide them from their ornamental gardens, which usually had simple rectangular path systems and also included areas of crops. The fashion for PARTERRES *de broderie* continued until the 1760s and 1770s. The use of water tended to be modest, rarely appearing except in the form of wells and fountains (although cascades were found at Eszterháza—see FERTŐD), and the canals or larger-scale pools common in Western Europe were very rare. There are only a handful of eminent masters from the period (e.g. Anton Zinner, Louis Gervais, Franz Rosenstingl, Nicolaus Jacoby), who for the most part came to Hungary from Vienna or through Viennese connections. Since the task of design fell to the estate's master builder or surveyors, as in the case of KESZTHELY, many important gardens made use of pattern books—above all the treatise by A.-J. DEZALLIER D'ARGENVILLE. The construction of the most distinguished baroque gardens was associated with Hungarian aristocrats who also maintained palaces in Vienna (Esterházy dukes—Kismarton (today EISENSTADT, Austria), Eszterháza (today FERTŐD); Esterházy counts—Cseklész (today Bernolákovo, Slovakia); Széchenyi family—NAGYCENK; Batthyány family—Körmend; Magyarbél (today Vel'ky Biel, Slovakia); Grassalkovich family—Gödöllő, Ivánka (today Ivanka pri Dunaji, Slovakia); Festetics family—KESZTHELY; Pálffy family—Királyfa (today Král'ová pri Senci), Jeszenák family—Majorháza (today Tomašov, Slovakia), etc.) or with the major constructions of the Catholic Church (Jászó (today JASOV, Slovakia), Majk). The members of the ruling Habsburg family, meanwhile, built a substantial garden at Féltorony (today Halbturn, Austria) and at the Royal Castle of BUDA. Of the baroque gardens in Hungary, however, it was the park complex at Eszterháza (today Fertőd) that was the most prominent, in terms of both size and artistic design. In Transylvania—which was a Principality at that time—BONTIDA was the most eminent Baroque garden.

The earliest mentions of landscape gardens date back to the 1760s, but these represent at most a single detail of a garden, with an irregular layout. From the 1770s to the end of the century we know of more plans and completed gardens characterized by this transitional style of densely planted gardens with geometric layouts but with irregular path systems, bizarre, exotic buildings, and dense, winding paths (e.g. HODKOVCE, CSÁKVÁR,

HŐGYÉSZ, Keszthely—the botanic gardens of the Georgikon). From the 1780s onwards sentimental elements (mock ruins, monuments, and shrines) became increasingly fashionable, and were a staple characteristic of the whole Biedermeier period until 1848. After 1800 it was increasingly the grand, serene (so-called 'classical') landscape garden in the spirit of BROWN and REPTON that was popular (e.g. Kismarton (today Eisenstadt, Austria), DÉG, MARTONVÁSÁR), for the most part laid out by designers from abroad (Heinrich NEBBIEN, Bernhard PETRI, Charles MOREAU, and the Tost brothers). It was Nebbien who created the VÁROSLIGET (City Park) in Pest (today Budapest), a competition for the design of which was advertised in 1813, Europe's first large-scale park to be established by a city's residents. The creation of large landscape parks and introduction of new farming methods often went hand in hand, and improvement of model agricultural estates also resulted in the embellishment of landscapes (Dég, Nebbien's work at Martonvásár and at Alsókorompa (today Dolná krupá, Slovakia)).

It was also essentially in the first half of the 19th century that the cultivation of ornamental plants became widespread in Hungary, primarily in gardens associated with the large manorial estates (e.g. at ALCSÚT). The ornamental trees typical of the period were the plane (*Platanus* × *acerifolia*), the horse chestnut (*Aesculus hippocastanum*), the copper beech (*Fagus sylvatica* Atropurpurea Group), the Japanese acacia (*Sophora japonica*), the white acacia (*Robinia pseudoacacia*), the black walnut (*Juglans nigra*), and the weeping species and varieties (willow—*Salix babylonica*; birch—*Betula pendula*; Japanese acacia—*Sophora japonica* 'Pendula'). A favourite speciality was *Ginkgo biloba*, the first specimen of which was planted at Acsád in 1802. But it was the indigenous species—oaks, limes ashes, and elms—that formed the basis of the tree repertory of most gardens. It was around 1850 that the first generation of Hungarian landscape gardeners (e.g. Ármin PECZ, Vilmos JÁMBOR) emerged. Its exponents still worked as head gardeners on estates, and thus the careers of some (like Jámbor) were dominated by grand parks constructed for the aristocracy. Increasingly, however, they were playing a role (especially in Pecz's case) in the design of great gardens for industrial magnates and rich members of the bourgeoisie, as well as of public gardens and city parks. New genres of gardens grew up as a result of urbanization—factory gardens, public gardens, domestic gardens, institutional gardens, front gardens, and so forth. The number of gardens grew by leaps and bounds, too, leading to the establishment of private and public gardening companies.

A generation of entrepreneurial landscape gardeners and architects emerged, who, in addition to laying out plans, would bring the necessary plants and other materials from their own nurseries and workshops (Ármin PECZ Sr. and Jr., János HEIN, Gyula Bogyay). The garden construction boom also encouraged many professionals to move to Hungary from abroad, particularly from Germany, the Czech lands, and Moravia. In addition to the work of so many outstanding experts, the rapid advancement of horticulture was also helped by the appearance of national and local associations, and the development of professional training.

20th century

The trend in landscape gardens continued to thrive, but the proportion of exotic plants increased substantially, leading to the creation of arboretum-like landscape gardens (e.g. Nádasdladány, Füzérradvány, Szarvas, Szombathely-Kám). It was in the last third of the 19th century that geometrically shaped pleasure grounds and carpet beds became fashionable in Hungary (e.g. János Hein, Keresztély ILSEMANN). Historicism was the defining force in the direction taken by garden construction right until the beginning of the 1900s (e.g. Nagymágocs, Fehérvárcsurgó, Hatvan, Eszterháza (today Fertőd), Tiszadob, Perbenyik, and Zabola, the work of Achille DUCHÊNE). The breakthrough into art nouveau took place around 1910, primarily in the form of efforts to follow the clear geometric style represented by German and Austrian architects (like the Otto Wagner school). The full evolution of this style was interrupted by the First World War, after which Hungary lost more than two-thirds of its original territory (the Western territories were annexed to Austria, the Northern regions to Czechoslovakia, the Eastern territories—including Transylvania—to Romania, and the southern counties to Yugoslavia).

The inter-war period saw the slightly conservative, baroque-like geometric garden come to the fore again (e.g. Béla Rerrich's parks). The gardens in Hatvan, in Szeleste, and the one in Oroszvár (today RUSOVCE, Slovakia, designed by Gertrude JEKYLL), unusually displayed the influence of Edwardian garden design from England. From the end of the 1920s, but especially in the 1930s and 1940s, it was a modernist functionalist style that became widespread (e.g. László Solty, Imre Ormos, Kálmán Jonke). It was principally the German influence that was present throughout this process of development, just as it had been in the preceding two centuries.

The garden style of the 1950s was defined by the geometric, symmetrical, grandiose doctrine of 'Socialist Realism' dictated by the Stalinist Soviet Union. From the 1960s to the 1980s, however, it was the less regulated 'Socialist Functionalism' movement, serving the needs of the masses, that became dominant, with green areas for prefabricated housing estates, public gardens, and parks. In the construction of domestic gardens it was mostly the modern tradition that survived, though in this period significant commissions of this kind were infrequent. With the collapse of the socialist system in the 1990s, postmodern, high tech, and neo-historicism have emerged as forms of denial and rejection of the styles and ideologies of the preceding decades. The palette is furthered enriched by various organic approaches. Protection and restoration of historic gardens in Hungary first emerged in institutional form in the 1960s, under the aegis of the National Inspectorate for Historic Monuments, at the behest of Károly Örsi. However, many parks and gardens fell into disrepair or were divided up in the socialist period, and a number of palace gardens, public parks, and gardens of villas are still awaiting official protection and supervision, while some important parks have been restored according to the practices of the time (e.g. NAGYCENK, Seregélyes). Today a number of parks of value (especially country house gardens) enjoy protection as heritage sites and/or areas of natural beauty, and in the last few years art historians have joined landscape architects in devoting themselves to research into the history of gardens. Interest in this new, interdisciplinary field continues to grow.   GA

Huntington Library and Botanical Gardens ✿

San Marino, California, USA, was founded in 1925 as a botanic garden on a site of 82.8 hectares/204.5 acres, and now constitutes one of the country's most outstanding collections of desert and subtropical plants, and roses. From 1903 until 1925 it was the estate of Henry Huntington, and was developed by William Hertrich (1878–1966), an expert German horticulturist. Maturity was achieved through the pioneering transplantation of large trees in boxes, including many species of palm, California live oaks (*Quercus agrifolia*), and specimen trees such as *Araucaria bidwillii*, and *Cedrus deodara*. The garden developed without a master plan, one garden project succeeding another, and typified the prevailing passion for lush tropicality and specialized gardens. The palm garden was developed as an ornamental and experimental collection of palms from the semi-tropical regions of Australia, Asia, Africa, and America, and includes pinnate- and palmate-leafed species. By 1925 the Desert Garden had grown to 6 hectares/15 acres and is now the largest collection of cacti, succulent species, and fibrous desert plants in the world outside a natural desert. Unlike the early naturalistic gardens the North Vista and the Rose Garden are formal spaces. The long axial North Vista, oriented toward the mountains and a large terminal Renaissance fountain, is flanked by *Livistona decipiens* alternating with 17th-century Italian marble statues. It bisects a large grove of *Quercus robur* and *Q. englemani* sheltering extensive collections of azaleas and camellias. The Japanese Garden, created in 1912 in a canyon west of the Rose Garden, used all the plants and structures of a commercial tea garden. A prominent feature is a moon bridge, originally painted vermilion, built by a Japanese craftsman, and the lanterns and miniature pagodas came from Japan. In the 1960s numerous new gardens were created, including the Herb Garden, Shakespeare Garden, Zen Garden and bonsai court, Jungle Garden, and Australian Garden. The camellia collection was expanded, and additions were made to the collections of roses, magnolias, rhododendrons, and azaleas.   DCS

Huygens, Constantijn

(1596–1687), Dutch diplomat, author, and arts patron. Highly educated and cultivated, he served as a diplomat in Venice and London, and from 1625 acted as secretary and later councillor to three generations of princes of Orange. He was one of the main proponents of Dutch classicism, designing both his town house in The Hague (1634) and country seat HOFWIJCK (1639–42) with leading architects Jacob van CAMPEN and Pieter Post. The gardens of Hofwijck were designed according to classical proportions based on the Vitruvian human figure, and in true Virgilian tradition he celebrated them in an extensive court poem entitled *Vitaulium: Hofwijck* (1653).   JW

Hyde Hall ⊛

near Chelmsford, Essex, England, is a farmhouse where the Robinson family made a garden from 1955 which since 1993 has belonged to the ROYAL HORTICULTURAL SOCIETY. Few sites are less propitious for gardening—the top of a windy hill in the driest county in England. The Robinsons showed what was possible, building up a remarkable collection of plants. The RHS has developed it into a valuable show garden. Here is an excellent collection of roses, a miniature woodland garden, fine ornamental trees, and well-judged borders. The RHS has recently added a superb dry garden laid out among gravel and rocks of special interest to Essex gardeners and to anyone else who believes that global warming is here to stay.   PT

Hydro Park ⊛

Oslo, Norway, was laid out in 1961 next to the fourteen-storey administration building of the Norwegian Hydro Company, designed by the architect Erling Viksjø (1910–71). Landscape architects were Egil Gabrielsen (1932–98) and Morten Grindaker (b. 1925) in collaboration with the sculptor Odd Tandberg (b. 1924). The layout of the 0.5-hectare/1.3-acre triangular park incorporated some existing trees, e.g. a magnificent copper beech, famous in Oslo. On the sloping lawn a modern sunken garden was laid out in an asymmetrical rectangular design, defined at its upper side by a long retaining wall in rubbed-down concrete like the building, cut through by two flights of stairs. Benches are fitted on the wall. The space is covered in square quartzite flagstones and is overlapped by a rectangular pond with one tall jet of water. Four broad paths with the same type of flagstones, making them part of the space, lead across the lawn to the nearby streets. Two concrete 2-m/6-ft free-standing walls, covered in polished stone mosaics by Odd Tandberg, stand at a right

Illustration from the front jacket of *Hypnerotomachia Poliphili*.

FRANCESCO COLONNA

HYPNEROTOMACHIA POLIPHILI

The Strife of Love in a Dream

THE ENTIRE TEXT TRANSLATED
FOR THE FIRST TIME INTO ENGLISH
WITH AN INTRODUCTION
BY
JOSCELYN GODWIN

angle to the retaining wall, forming a shelter against traffic noise.   ME

MALENE HAUXNER, *Med himlen som loft* (2002).

Hypnerotomachia Poliphili

is a book written in about 1467 and published in 1499, printed in Venice by Aldus Manutius. The title means 'Poliphilo's battle of love in a dream' and describes the love of Poliphilo for Polia and their voyage to the garden island of Cytherea. The hero's emblematic name has two meanings—lover of many things, as well as lover of Polia. The book is full of lavish descriptions of architecture, ceremonies, jewellery, music, fabrics, and much else that is beautiful or curious. Poliphilo also has a particular love of antiquities. The book was illustrated with 174 woodcuts rich in the detail of architecture, garden buildings, and ornaments. There is much exact information of plants used in gardens and detailed designs of parterres. The author was probably a monk, Francesco Colonna (*c.*1433-1527), whose name appears as an acrostic derived from the initial letters of the chapter headings. The language in which it is written is an amalgam of classical Latin and Italian. Although a partial translation into English was published in 1592, the first complete translation into English did not appear until 1999. The translator was Joscelyn Godwin and the style of publication, in particular the typeface and layout, faithfully reflect the atmosphere of the original edition. For English readers it revealed the true nature of this curious but remarkably influential book. The first complete translation into French (*Le Songe de Poliphile*) was published in 1883. A scholarly new edition in the original language, edited and with a commentary by Giovanni Pozzi and Lucia A. Ciapponi, was published in 1968.   PT

I

IBM Headquarters ⊛

Kista, Uppland, Sweden, is an office building with landscape designed for the computer firm IBM in 1972–6. The red brick building is designed by Carl Nyren and Bengt Lindroos and the landscape design is by the landscape architects Söderblom & Palm. IBM is significant from a landscape point of view because of the extreme adaptation to the existing landscape and the ambition to preserve natural assets, an attitude characteristic of the political and environmental trends that characterized Western society in the 1970s. The grounds consist of a spruce forest with thin layers of soil. In the construction work, the typical *Calluna* vegetation was preserved, rolled up like a fitted carpet, and then rolled back again after the multi-storey building had been built from construction roads restricted in width to 2 m/7 ft. The traditional corporate image clichés such as the reflecting pool and rows of identical trees are interpreted in a way more in keeping with the *Zeitgeist*: in front of the building is an alder marsh serving as water feature, and the gravel-covered parking lots are carefully tucked in between the existing spruce trees. Practically no new plantings were done in the project and no storm drains were installed, which was radical at this time.   TA

icehouse.

As a building to store ice gathered in winter or brought from colder climates, the icehouse goes back, in England, to the 16th century. In France in the 17th century the *glacière* was a common, and often ornamental, garden building. By 1688 Louis XIV had thirteen icehouses in and around VERSAILLES. Charles II of England during his exile admired them and had one built in Upper St James's Park, London (now Green Park) in 1660. In British 18th-century gardens they were a common feature, sometimes worked into the scene of a landscape park. More often than not they were almost entirely underground, marked above ground by a grassy mound (as at Hanbury Hall, Worcestershire). At Gosford (East Lothian),

however, the icehouse has a rusticated façade, a grotto, and stone seats at ground level.   PT

ICOMOS.

See INTERNATIONAL COUNCIL ON MONUMENTS AND SITES.

Iford Manor ⊛

near Bradford-on-Avon, Wiltshire, England, is an Elizabethan house rebuilt in the 18th century and bought in 1899 by the garden designer Harold PETO. Peto seized upon the existing 18th-century terracing to make a garden of Italianate style which he embellished with his collection of sculpture, garden ornaments, and architectural fragments. A flight of stone steps links the terraces, with piers and urns or statues flanking the entrance to each level. The terraces vary in atmosphere—with lawns, gravel walks, pools, the occasional substantial tree (an old yew and a beautiful *Cercidiphyllum japonicum*), and ornaments. The uppermost terrace with a stately walk of Italian cypresses (*Cupressus sempervirens*) has at its eastern end a pretty 18th-century pavilion and at the western a loggia of pink Verona marble and glistening mounds of clipped *Phillyrea latifolia* and large Tuscan terracotta pots filled with clipped box. In the centre of the terrace an opening is marked by a group of flowering cherries and a pair of giant Ali Baba jars. The axial walk initiated by the terrace steps continues into the wooded slopes above. To one side is a shady JAPANESE GARDEN and pavilion. The walk continues to the summit of the hill which is marked by a stone column with the inscription 'To Edward VII the peacemaker Harold Peto dedicated this column in the midst of the great war in 1916'. Peto spent the rest of his life at Iford which remains his most complete and attractive garden.   PT

Ilm Park ⊛

Weimar, Germany. Weimar's best-known park evolved over the years by incorporating 17th-century gardens (Welscher Garten and Sterngarten) in the Ilm valley. After Duke Carl

August had given the manor to him as a present, Goethe started to alter the layout of his estate in 1776. The construction of a memorial to Christel von Laßberg, who had committed suicide in 1778, marks the beginning of a series of changes in the Ilm valley that, inspired by visits to Wörlitz (see DESSAU-WÖRLITZ GARTENREICH), Goethe and Carl August initiated. With regard to stately festivities, new paths and gathering places interspersed with monuments, ornaments, and buildings were added without, however, following any greater garden concept. Among these additions were a hermitage today called the Borkenhäuschen (Bark House) in 1778, Dessauer Stein (Dessau Stone) in 1782, and a sham RUIN in 1784.

Between 1786 and 1798 some older gardens were incorporated into the park and numerous smaller buildings and sculptures were added, such as the Sphinxgrotte (Sphinx Grotto) in 1786, the Schlangenstein (Snake Stone) in 1787, three pillars in 1788 (which collapsed in 1823), the Römisches Haus (Roman Villa, with Goethe's active involvement) 1791–8, and an orangery converted into the Tempelherrenhaus (Templar Hall) 1818–20—destroyed to a large extent in 1945. In addition an ideal landscape connecting to the encircling park grounds was created. By the time of Carl August's death in 1828 the garden design was more or less complete.

The ducal gardeners Eduard PETZOLD, Julius Hartwig, and Otto Ludwig Sckell (1861–1948) subsequently wanted to preserve the park, which has, by and large, remained unchanged to this day, as a testimony to the different eras of gardening art. Trying to preserve the original state, however, proved difficult in so far as the failure to replace the tree population in the 19th century led to an considerable thinning of trees. Beginning in 1969 the historic garden site underwent extensive monument preservation work, which culminated in 1999 with the restoration of the surroundings of the Römisches Haus, the Pompejanischen Bank (Pompeian Bench), and the Liszt memorial.
   USc

Ilnacullin ⊛

Glengarriff, County Cork, Ireland, has a remarkably beautiful position on Garinish Island in Bantry Bay with views back across the water to the pointed peaks of the Caha Mountains. The island was bought in 1910 by a Belfast East India merchant, John Annan Bryce, who commissioned Harold PETO to design a garden. Swept by wind, almost nothing grew on the rocky island which had only occasional patches of peat. Huge quanties of humus-rich soil had to be imported and any substantial planting place had to be blasted out of the rock.

Between 1911 and 1914 over 100 men worked on making the garden. There is no sign of such dramas today—the lavishly planted island, with its serene buildings, presents a scene of idylllic harmony. Peto designed a pair of Italianate buildings with fine views back to the mainland. The Casita overlooks a rectangular pool at the far end of which steps rise to an open pavilion with a balustraded viewing terrace from which to admire the mountain scenery across the water. Further along the coast Peto made a flight of stone steps leading up a slope at the top of which he designed a colonnaded rotunda with an eastern Mediterranean feel. A walled garden, originally intended as a kitchen garden, is now given over to ornamental planting, with boisterous mixed borders and climbing plants garlanding the walls. The climate is mild here and many rare and tender plants flourish. There is an exceptional collection of rhododendrons, especially species.   PT

Ilsemann, Keresztély (Christian)
(1850–1912), German-born Hungarian landscape gardener, son of a well-to-do Kiel horticultural family. In the 1870s, like so many of his contemporaries, he came to Hungary, where he worked in the gardens of various landowners, before teaching gardening at the Agricultural Academy in Mosonmagyaróvár. In 1892 he was invited to be head of gardens of Budapest (from 1896 he was director of parks), where it fell to him to plan all the public gardens and promenades in the rapidly developing capital. Hence his name became associated with the VÁROSLIGET (City Park), the similarly significant Népliget (People's Park), Döbrentei Square, Szabadság Square, Köztársaság Square, and with turning several open areas into parks. His work saw Budapest's public parks and gardens reach the highest European standards. He also designed private gardens (e.g. Dunaörs, Hatvan). Depending on the size and function of the area in question, his designs combined naturalistic and geometric elements in the spirit of historicism. His carpet beds—which emphasized the form of the flowers—earned him international recognition, as in Götze's work *Album für Teppichgärtnerei*, and Austrian and German professional journals. He himself edited periodicals, and published his own articles on the widest variety of horticultural subjects.   GA

GÁBOR ALFÖLDY, 'A Hatvany-család kastélyparkja Hatvanban' (The Park of the Hatvany Family in Hatvan), in László Horváth (ed.), *Hatvanyak emlékezete* (2003).
JÒZSEF SISA, 'Keresztély Ilsemann in Budapest', *Stadt und Grün* (1997).

Imperiale, Villa ✲
Pesaro, Italy. The spectacular Renaissance summer palace on the slopes of Mount Bartolo was built by Alessandro Sforza between 1469 and 1472 and later enlarged for Francesco Maria della Rovere by the architect Girolamo Genga (1476–c.1551), an associate of Raphael at both the Villa Farnesina Chigi and Villa MADAMA in Rome. In 1530 Genga was commissioned by Eleonora Gonzaga to turn the fortress-like *castello* into an elegant villa. He built a new main block, joining the two buildings with a complicated system of covered grottoes, porticoes, and shell-encrusted rooms, topped by symmetrical pavilions. On the fourth side of the courtyard, known as the *sala coperta*, which lies in shadow between the buildings, the main garden is terraced to slope upwards at the back. Over centuries it has been devoted to the cultivation of bitter oranges and lemon hybrids (known as *bizzarie*). Although suffering from neglect through the centuries the villa and its garden are now in the capable hands of Count Gugliemo Castelbarco Albani.   PHo

India
Peninsular India and its northern hinterland offer as varied a topography as any in the world. From west to east it stretches from the arid scrublands of Rajasthan to the heights of Assam and some of the wettest places on earth; and from south to north from the coastal rainforests below the thermal equator, over the dry Deccan tablelands to the great river systems of the Ganges and Indus and beyond to the Karakorams and some of the highest peaks in the world. For all this diversity the biggest hindrance to its cultural expression in gardens is a lack of water. Conservation of water for food production has always been a matter of life and death and is expressed only incidentally for aesthetic purposes in the gardens of the very wealthy and the very important. Within the villages there are no gardens and no parks. The children play in the streets, the house compounds are largely unplanted, and what time there is after working in the fields is given to cultivating useful plants. Several villages may share a *mali* or gardener but his function is to provide the flowers needed for temple offerings, festivals, and weddings.

Against this struggle to subsist, the gardens of the great assume a special and symbolic importance. They reflect a hierarchical, highly ordered society centred on the *chakravatin* ruler, or King of Kings; distinctive from at least the end of the 2nd millennium BC during the long period of cultural assimilation between the light-skinned Aryan pastoralists migrating down from the Iranian plateau, and the dark-skinned indigenous Dravidian peoples who were predominantly farmers.

Of these great Indian gardens, the first known, dating from the 4th and 3rd centuries BC, was that of the Mauryan King Chandragupta, at Patalipotra near modern Patna. A near contemporary account by Aelian refers to fish-filled tanks of remarkable beauty, tame peacocks and pheasants, cultivated plants and shaded groves, parterres planted with trees apparently trained or pleached, and buildings rivalling in splendour the Medean and Persian palaces of Ecbatana and Susa.

Therefore, even at this early period, the Indian garden seems to have owed at least something to Aryan skills of irrigation and water display; and planting had begun to combine aromatic shrubs and bright short-lived annuals of the arid north-west with the gaudy and teeming life of the rainforest.

Buddhist gardens
Central to Buddhism is the idea of a garden as a place of retreat and meditation—typically planted with mango, ashoka, and jaman trees, and furnished with great water tanks. The most celebrated of these retreats, at Gaya, Sarnath, Sanchi, and Nalanda, survive today not as gardens but as archaeological sites. The garden tradition to which they gave birth is stronger in Sri Lanka, Burma, CHINA, and JAPAN. In India the best traces survive in the square garden enclosures of the many excavated *viharas* or monasteries, each one cardinally oriented and containing the stone platforms and sometimes the railed enclosures of shrines, with tree temples dedicated to the *bodhi*.   JBy

Mughal gardens
This refers to the royal gardens created during the Mughal dynasty, which reigned in India from 1526 to 1857, even if in fact after the first half of the 18th century all the initiatives were transferred to the peripheral courts of the vassals. The Mughal garden is indebted to the autochthonous traditions and preceding Islamic dynasties especially for its different attitude regarding water. The India of the monsoon in fact does not suffer from a lack of water, as much as from the concentration of rains in a brief period of the year. The problem is that of conservation by means of huge artificial basins or the capturing of water in wells.

Furthermore, it was the task of the first Emperor BĀBUR (1508–30) to transfer to the plain a landscape technique that had had good results on the slopes of Afghanistan, solving the water problem through a series of slightly declining levels. The BAGH-I WAFA (Garden of Fidelity) in Dholpur, cut out like a platform into the ridge of red arenaria, into which follow levels with lotus-shaped tubs, joined by a water canal, is the first example of the brilliant integration of a Mughal project with Hindu techniques. The best-preserved garden is rather that around the tomb of HUMAYUN at Delhi, with its rigorous pattern of 32 parterres fed by a hierarchical network of small canals.

Most original was the decision to place the garden along the banks of a river, more often as a sequence to form a river front like the one at Agra, or, reviving a medieval Rajput tradition, on the banks of an artificial lake as at Fathpur Sikri or Ajmer, taking advantage in both cases of the effect of the cooling of the air by the water and the double access from both land and water. At Agra, Bābur's decision to place his own garden palace, the present RAM BAGH, on the left bank of the Yamuna river over time was followed by dignitaries and successors and finally comprised a green settlement called Kabul, of which remain the Zagara Bagh, the Chini ka Roza, the Wazir Khan ka Bagh, the garden tomb of I'TIMA-UD-DAULA, the CHAHAR BAGH and the Mehtab Khan ka Bagh. The waterfront garden would be one of the preferred models. Introduced to the palace on the bastions of the forts of Agra, Lahore, and Delhi, the different royal pavilions alternating with enclosures form a line of stone gardens. In addition, in the RED FORT of Delhi the water that runs in a marble canal (*nahr behesht*) through the pavilions becomes the connecting thread of the plan. The royal Mughal garden in its typical form is a sequence of defined spaces, designed with two intersecting 90-degree axes following a plan called CHAHAR BAGH. This refers to the layout of a military camp and is articulated in a series of four spaces: vestibule, Diwan-i Amm or place of public audiences, Diwan-i Khass (private audience hall), and harem, to which the plan of the palaces and especially that of the gardens are related.

The Persian influence (see IRAN) is present in the formal oasis garden, where moving water is shown symbolically as the spring of life, giving idealized form to the irrigation projects, and the shade-bearing plantings with their high trunks which emphasize the geometric layout of the plan. The Hindu and especially Jainist influence is present in the symbolic role played by the nodal elements of the composition regarding still water, like the pavilion set in water. Examples are the throne (*chabutra*) on the water in the NISHAT BAGH of the Dal Lake and in the SHALAMAR BAGH of Lahore, the water platform of the courtyard of the Kwabgah of Fathpur Sikri, and finally the Zafar Mahal immersed in the tank of the Red Fort in Delhi.

From the time of AKBAR (1556–1605) there remain the ruins of the gardens of Fathpur Sikri, and the small water garden in the fortress of Hari Parbat at Srinagar. The fortress was connected to an underlying palace garden,

NASIM BAGH, along the lake of which there remain few traces. JAHĀNGĪR (1605–27) and his court left instead an indelible sign: we remember the Wah Bagh near Taxila, which grew up on a camp ground, but the garden is under restoration and the main pavilion is unrecognizable; the gardens of Kashmir like VERNAG, built starting from a spring that empties into an octagonal pool with arches; ACHABAL, structured by a canal that imitates the course of a river from its source to its mouth; Jarogha Bagh on Manasbal Lake and the Nishat Bagh laid out on twelve terraces on Dal Lake; and then the Khusrau Bagh of Allahabad and the I'tima-ud-Daula of Agra, where the mausoleum–garden relationship is carried to a more intimate scale. Finally, we remember the Dilkusha Bagh of Shahdara near Lahore, where Jahāngīr is buried.

Shāh Jahān (1628–58) continued the work of his father in Kashmir with the CHASMA SHAHI and the Peri Mahal. In the plain are worthy of note the Shalamar of Delhi, no longer extant, and the SHALAMAR BAGH of Lahore. Its name is in any case connected to the mausoleum garden of the TAJ MAHAL at Agra. The three palaces at Agra, Lahore, and Delhi contain gardens that, although the vegetal element is limited, are the highest expression of the poetic of the pleasure and contemplation garden. To the time of AURANGZĪB (1658–1707) belong the complex of Pinjaur near Simla and the garden of the mausoleum of Rabi a Daurani at Aurangbad which are not distant from the officially approved schemes.

The plantings followed a scheme according to which cypresses in the form of obelisks, poplars, and plane trees were lined up to reinforce the axes of the main routes, then the willows, whose interwoven branches formed green, leafy canopies. A totally original form was the covering of the cypresses with climbing flowers. In the plain, the palm was added, along with the mango and the tamarind with their shading function. In the quadrants of the parterre laid out in geometric order are fruit trees, vegetables, aromatic plants, and flowers, all kept separate. Especially in Kashmir there grew every fruit tree, the most appreciated being apricot, pear (*nashpat*), guava (*amrud*), grape, and pomegranate; others that were imported became naturalized as the apple of Samarkand and the cherry (*sha-alu*) of Kabul. Miniatures, hard stone inlays, and literary descriptions of the time allows us to compile a list of flowers: in the plains: carnation, cockscomb, heliotrope, hyacinth, jasmine, larkspur, lotus, marigolds, narcissus, oleanders, tuberoses, violet, zinnia; in Kashmir: carnation, delphinium, hollyhock, jasmine, lilac, lotus, narcissus, saffron, stocks, and wallflower.   AP

Indian botanic gardens

While the botanic gardens of India arose as a result of European colonization, they took, in the subcontinent, a particular form. Among local influences were India's rich plantlife (some 16,000 species) and the traditional indigenous knowledge encountered, especially of the medicinal and economic properties of plants; in some cases existing pre-colonial gardens were developed for new functions and thus had an influence on their design. Leaving aside some 'proto-botanic' and physic gardens, notably those of the aptly named Portuguese Garcia da Orta, who cultivated plants as part of his medicinal studies in Goa and Bombay in the 16th century, and Hendrik van Rheede who had gardens at Cochin at the end of the 17th century, the great period of establishment was from the late 18th to the late 19th centuries, initially by the East India Company (EIC). This arose as a result of two major factors: as part of the process of economic/imperialistic expansion, and in the pursuit of scientific knowledge for its own sake, in the wake of the European Enlightenment. These factors, driven by figures such as Sir Joseph BANKS and Sir William Hooker in England, cannot be separated and there has been much debate over their relative importance, and the use of 'science' as an instrument of imperialist control. Such difficulties in defining aims and agendas are also encountered in defining a 'botanic garden', especially as their roles and administration changed, even before Independence, making a concise summary somewhat fraught. In India it is certainly impossible to separate a group of strictly 'botanical' gardens from the 'horticultural' ones run by the agri-horticultural societies established in the three presidencies in the 1820s and 1830s. Though their functions may have changed, botanic gardens in the widest sense still form an important subset of Indian public gardens.

That from the start the running of these establishments was entrusted to men with a scientific training, the company's surgeons (who had studied botany as part of their medical courses notably at Scottish universities), led to a diversity of motivation, and potential conflicts of interest with their employers. The company's agenda was to a large extent (though not quite entirely exclusively) commercial—investigating indigenous plants for potential exploitation, and introducing exotic species to be grown either as cash crops, or as sources of food, medicine, dyestuffs, etc. The surgeons, while supporting the aims of their paymasters, often had additional motives ranging from the philanthropic (such as investigating local and imported crops that might withstand droughts and alleviate famine), to taxonomic investigation of the Indian flora (not merely its economic species), using gardens to raise trees for reafforestation schemes, and as a base for wider scientific investigations such as the climatic effects of deforestation. The introduction of exotics for horticulture and agriculture ran parallel with the agri-horticultural gardens whose prime role was acclimatization and distribution, but these societies were also supported indirectly by government and many of the surgeons participated in these as well as in their botanic gardens.

The sites of the earliest botanic gardens were coastal, around Madras and Calcutta, in extreme tropical climates, but an obsession with introducing temperate fruit and vegetables led to the establishment of gardens in more temperate and montane regions. The gardens were established on more or less virgin sites, or sometimes based on earlier gardens. Layouts tended to be functional with paths enclosing beds capable of growing large crops of economic species, though most incorporated decorative elements since they were also expected to perform an aesthetic/recreational role, especially those in hill stations or associated with governor's residences. At Calcutta, Saharanpur and Ootacamund taxonomic plantings (initially Linnaean, later Candollean; see CALCUTTA BOTANIC GARDEN) were used for certain sections. Later in the 19th century (as their economic role declined) garden layouts tended to the GARDENESQUE.

It is only possible to give the briefest history of the major gardens here, arranged under the three administrative units of British India.

The Madras presidency

Edward Bulkeley, a surgeon and pioneer in the exploration of the flora of south India, had a garden near Fort St George in Madras around 1700 and William Roxburgh followed in this tradition, starting his Indian career in Madras to become the 'father of Indian botany'. Roxburgh established government-funded experimental gardens at Samulcottah in the Godavery delta in the 1770s, experimenting with economic plants such as indigo, pepper, and drought-resistant crops such as breadfruit. Slightly earlier a group of Moravian missionaries including J. G. König, a disciple of Linnaeus, had established a garden at Tranquebar, a Danish coastal settlement south of Madras, as part of their taxonomic study of the Indian flora. In the 1790s the EIC established the Nopalry in Madras, a garden devoted to the cactus *Opuntia* as a host for the cochineal insect, the brainchild of James Anderson, who also had his own private botanic

garden in Madras. The Nopalry was reused again briefly in the 1820s, but around 1800 Madras horticultural/botanical activities had moved inland to the higher and cooler Deccan plateau, to the Lal Bagh in Bangalore, a 16-hectare/40-acre garden founded in 1760 by Hyder Ali, Raja of Mysore. This garden, under various administrations, was developed throughout the 19th century (notably in 1856 under Hugh Cleghorn), eventually reaching its present size of about 40 hectares/100 acres. Still a fine garden, it retains the skeleton of its original Mughal-style rectilinear layout, has a fine collection of trees, and a large, unglazed, cast-iron conservatory, opened in 1899, used for flower shows and receptions. Like most botanic gardens in India it is really a public park, the plants are largely unlabelled, though some horticultural research activities are still undertaken there. In 1835 an Agri-Horticultural Society was founded in Madras and an fine garden established, which survives as an attractive oasis selling seeds and plants and as a backdrop for shooting Tamil movies. The Government Garden at Ootacamund ('Ooty') in the Nilgiri Hills was established on a steep, virgin site at around 2,280 m/7,500 ft, by W. G. McIvor in 1847, and from 1861 played a major role in the introduction of cinchona to India, and, rather more ecologically disastrously, the introduction of Australian eucalypts and acacias. Ooty had various outstations including Sim's Park at Coonoor, and is still one of the most attractive gardens in India, beautifully maintained, though devoid of plant labels and with little botanical interest beyond its magnificent trees.

Bengal and north India

After early experiments in Madras, the real focus of botanic garden activity shifted to the north; but CALCUTTA and SAHARANPUR, the pre-eminent establishments, dating from 1786 and 1819 respectively, will be described separately. Also in Calcutta, however, was an interesting 2-hectare/5-acre private garden at Serampore established in 1800 by the botanical missionary and linguist the Revd William Carey, and carried on after his death in 1834 by Joachim Voigt. The Agri-Horticultural Society of India was founded in Calcutta in 1820 and started a garden which moved several times (including a period within the Botanic Garden) before settling on a 10-hectare/25-acre site at Alipore in 1872. This society continues to thrive and its garden is beautifully maintained; research activities are undertaken in its Birla Laboratories, and a programme of spectacular flower shows is presented throughout the year, patronized by the well-heeled garden lovers of Calcutta. The Calcutta Botanic Garden had two

outstations in the eastern Himalaya—an establishment at Mungpoo near Darjeeling devoted to cinchona started in 1862, and the Lloyd Botanic Garden at Darjeeling. The latter was founded in 1878 on a steeply sloping site of 16 hectares/40 acres. It had an attached herbarium and library and under George Cave played a significant role in exploration of the flora of Sikkim. It still exists as a pleasant park, though it has been the victim of political disturbances and is little visited. Far in the interior is Lucknow (the capital of Oudh), where a garden called the Bodhi-Daroga-Ka-Bagh, adjacent to an early 19th-century royal garden called the Sikander Bagh, was taken over by the local Agri-Horticultural Society in the 1830s. This was developed in the 1950s as the National Botanic Garden; though the garden itself is really a park, its laboratories are a major centre of research into medicinal plants and horticulture. In the grounds of the Forest Research Institute at Dehra Dun, in the foothills of the Himalayas at about 610 m/2,000 ft, is an outstanding arboretum (incorporating a botanic garden), which has been developed since the 1920s; occupying over 400 hectares/1,000 acres, it contains a magnificent collection of trees from all over the world.

The Bombay presidency

Bombay was the last player in the Indian botanic garden game with the establishment of a 19-hectare/48-acre botanic garden around the Governor's summer bungalow at Dapuri near Poona in 1828, at the instigation of Sir John Malcolm. This was based on a British garden and orchard and survived until 1865, when it was moved by Nicholas Dalzell to a site near the relocated Government House at Ganeshkind. Under Alexander Gibson in the late 1830s the garden established several outstations around Junnar to the north of Poona, which were largely used for growing economic plants, but at the largest of these, Hewra, Gibson's interests as a pioneering forest conservator resulted in the formation of an arboretum. In the city of Bombay the Agri-Horticultural Society of Western India was formed in 1830 and had a garden at Sewree; this closed and in 1861 the society ran the Victoria Gardens at Byculla in Bombay until 1873, when the society fell into temporary abeyance. The society seems to have been relaunched, but to have transferred its base to more temperate Poona, and by the 1890s was undertaking major botanical activities at the Empress Gardens, This garden is still extant, and well maintained as an attractive park.

Most of these gardens still exist, often well maintained and performing a much appreciated amenity function, though really shadows of their former selves—their libraries and herbaria moribund or dispersed, and the number of species grown reduced by attrition (with replanting from a limited repertoire of pantropical species coupled with an oddly anachronistic desire to grow British favourites such as hybrid tea roses). Many fulfil a limited aspect of their original function as horticultural research stations. However, the modern concept of a botanic garden as a place to grow accurately named and labelled species of known wild origin, as centres of taxonomic research, conservation, and education, has generally not been adopted—through lack of funds and a narrowness of roles assigned to government-funded establishments and in the case of Calcutta, the headquarters of the Botanical Survey of India (BSI), trade union difficulties. Accurate identification and labelling is almost unheard of, and the most interesting plants are always, simply from their longevity, the trees—with virtually no herbs or shrubs of botanical interest.

Rather than a renaissance of the old establishments, and out of a sense of frustration, this is leading to the establishment of a new generation of botanic gardens fulfilling modern ideals. The BSI has started other gardens away from the problems of Calcutta such as one specializing in orchids at an unlikely site at Yercaud in the Shevaroy Hills in Tamil Nadu and more recently has embarked on a completely new National Botanic Garden at NOIDA, a development area on the eastern outskirts of Delhi. This 80-hectare/200-acre garden, started in 1997, but still in its planning stages, is to have education and conservation as a major part of its remit. Despite the horticultural research undertaken in many of the gardens mentioned, it is somewhat ironic that for the establishment of the Tropical Botanic Garden and Research Institute at Palode in 1984 advice was still sought from Kew. This fine 120-hectare/300-acre garden, in a remote part of Kerala, near Trivandrum, undertakes conservation and education activities, as well as taxonomic research, and is funded mainly by the state of Kerala. Mention must also be made of the visionary Botanical Sanctuary at Gurukala in Wyanad (also in Kerala), which on a small site, with limited funds, and no guarantee of long-term survival, undertakes highly effective work in the fields of conservation (of Western Ghat plants, especially balsams, ferns, and orchids) and education, being visited by thousands of school and college students every year.   HNo

R. DESMOND, *The European Discovery of the Indian Flora* (1992).

D. P. McCRACKEN, *Gardens of Empire: Botanical Institutions of the Victorian British Empire* (1997).

G. S. RANDHAWA, K. L. CHADA, and D. SINGH, *The Famous Gardens of India* (1978).

Innisfree ⊛

Millbrook, New York, USA, was home to painter Walter Beck and his wife Marion. Beck had studied at the Royal Academy of Fine Arts, in Munich, and returned to New York to teach at the Pratt Institute. When he married Marion Stone, they moved to her family property in Millbrook, and named it after the Yeats lyric: 'I will arise and go now, and go to Innisfree.' A substantial Queen Anne-style house was built in 1929, but the landscape followed different inspirations. Both Mr and Mrs Beck were intrigued by Chinese landscapes, viewed in museum scrolls. Images of 8th-century Chinese poet Wang Wei's famous villa and gardens resonated as a model for the aesthetic development of the Innisfree landscape. Focused around a 40-hectare/100-acre lake, more than 300 hectares/741 acres of rolling hills, woodlands, and outcrops were to be united into this vision, using the 'cup garden' concept to frame and connect distinct features and views within the larger landscape. Grading, stone moving, clearing, pruning, and changing of watercourses was done on a large scale, created a stroll garden of linked 'moments' of exquisite composition. Their passion was shared by a young landscape architect, Lester Collins, who continued the work and the vision after the death of the Becks, in 1960. Refinements to this stroll garden continued, under the mantle of the Innisfree Foundation, until Collins's death in 1993. The house was razed in 1982, favouring the visual balance of the landscape, an enduring vision.   PC

Innsbruck Hofgarten ⊛

Tyrol, Austria, is today the principal green space in the Tyrolean capital. It is divided into Großer (greater) Hofgarten, Kleiner (lesser) Hofgarten, Hofgarten-Gärtnerei (nursery), and Pflanzengarten (plant garden). The Hofgarten of the Renaissance period took shape simultaneously with AMBRAS from 1564 during the reign of Archduke Ferdinand II as an adjunct to the Ruhelust Palace where the monarch lived with his consort Katharina Gonzaga. The complex comprised six pleasure gardens, which gradually disappeared from the 17th century onwards but in their heyday contained houses for ball games, hothouses, pleasure pavilions, a lion house, a pheasant garden, pergolas, ponds, fountains, terracotta figures, and walks in the style of Vredeman de VRIES (all modelled on the royal gardens in Prague). From 1763 under Empress Maria Theresa the garden was remodelled in the rococo style, with geometric axes, a large rondel,

and PARTERRES *de broderie*. In 1805, under the Bavarian occupation, F. L. SCKELL was commissioned to modernize the grounds, and from 1839 there were further alterations in an English landscape style, while preserving baroque remnants such as pathways and a pavilion. Construction of the Rennwegstraße road in 1842 both divided the gardens and reduced their extent. Numerous exotic and rare trees, however, survive. The landscape character of the Hofgarten is romantically enhanced by the Nordwand high Alpine peak.   GH

Insel Mainau. See MAINAU, INSEL.

International Council on Monuments and Sites

(ICOMOS), founded in 1965 as a non-governmental organization for the conservation of historic sites (including designed landscapes) and monuments throughout the world. It established over 100 national committees one of whose chief purposes is to advise UNESCO of sites to be designated WORLD HERITAGE SITES and of any site in danger. A general assembly is held every three years which helps to disseminate conservation advice and information and seeks to establish and maintain international standards for the preservation, restoration, and management of the cultural environment. Sometimes it may help in the funding of conservation initiatives as it did, for example, to help complete the CADW/ICOMOS Register of Landscapes, Parks and Gardens of Special Historic Interest in Wales. It gives advice internationally and is active in the training of conservation specialists.   PT

Inverewe ⊛

Poolewe, Ross-shire, Scotland, is a garden created by a remarkably persevering man in a part of Scotland where no one had made such a garden before. Osgood Mackenzie came here in 1862 as a young man, knowing nothing about gardening. Jutting out into a windswept sea loch, this is a rocky promontory where nothing larger than a feeble willow 1 m/3 ft high grew when Mackenzie arrived. It is on the same latitude as Labrador and St Petersburg but the North Atlantic Drift warms the waters and there is an average rainfall of 150 cm/60 in. In such circumstances all sorts of tender acid-loving plants will flourish if only protected from the gales and from the salt. Mackenzie spent the first fifteen years of his gardening life establishing windbreaks. He started with evergreens, in particular Scots pines (*Pinus sylvestris*) and Austrian black pines (*Pinus nigra* var. *nigra*), gradually adding a wider range and introducing deciduous trees in clearings protected by the conifers. Once these were established he could get down to the serious business of cultivating the tender exotics which interested him. Mackenzie died in 1922 and his daughter, Mairi Sawyer, took over the running of the garden which she left to the National Trust for Scotland on her death in 1953.

The Inverewe promontory today presents an extraordinary scene—it is shrouded in dense planting whereas the coast on each side as far as you can see looks wholly barren. The 25 hectares/62 acres of the garden are of jungle-like complexity, with winding paths threading their way through plantings of exotics. There is little design here, beyond a convenient pattern of paths from which to admire the plants. The garden is especially rich in southern hemisphere plants—celmisias and olearias from New Zealand, acacias and eucalypts from Australia, the pretty *Asteranthera ovata* from Chile. There is an outstanding collection of rhododendrons including many of the tender *Maddenia* group and the National Collection of *R.* subsection *barbatum*. The garden also holds National Collections of two New Zealand genera, *Brachyglottis* (thirteen species and cultivars) and *Olearia* (46 species and cultivars). Close to the entrance is a marvellous kitchen garden, with decorative interludes, close to the sea and protected by a high curving wall.

PT

Iran,

today covering an area of 1,648,000 sq. km/ 636,000 sq. miles, is one of the highest lands in the world, at its heart a great saucer-shaped plateau 1,200–1,500 m/4,000–5,000 ft above sea level. The plateau is surrounded to the north and west by high mountain peaks, the Alborz to the north and the Zagros running almost parallel to the Iraq border and then on to the north-west. To the east lies desert extending beyond the frontiers. Except for narrow coastal strips only 30% of the country is inhabitable. The annual rainfall on the plateau, the centre of Iranian civilization, is very low, 5–25 cm/2–10 in, almost all rain falling between November and April, and in winter it is exposed to icy air masses from Central Asia and Siberia. The upland plain, a landscape in tones of brown and buff depending on changing light and shadows, combines desert and steppe conditions, any cultivation depending on the limited winter rains and availability of water from the melting snow from the mountains, brought by underground conduits (because water in open channels would evaporate) known as *qanats*, sometimes as far as 30 km/18 miles. The *Dasht-e Lut* southern desert has no precipitation while the Great Salt Desert (*Dasht-e Kavir*) further north covering 55,000 sq. km/21,000 sq.

miles is barren because of its salinity. The high-rainfall humid forest-clad north-facing slopes of the Alborz which sweep down to the Caspian littoral 30 m/100 ft below sea level have an entirely different climatic and ecological diversity. While on the plateau plane trees, elms, ash, and willow only flourish where there is sufficient water, with poplars in the north and date palms in the south, in the Caspian (or Hyrcanian) forest, the habitat contains 50 or 60 broad-leafed indigenous deciduous trees or shrubs, depending on altitude. Many of these are familiar in Western gardens—various oaks, hornbeam, wing nut, parrotia, oriental plane, and zelkova besides fruit trees and pomegranates on the lower levels. The warm subtropical climate permits extensive rice growing in the west near Rasht with lower foothills dedicated to tea, tobacco, and fruit, including citrus. In the 19th century the Caspian region exported cotton to the Western industrialized nations. Under Reza Shah, in an attempt to make Iran self-sufficient, tea plantations were established with government support.

Plants

More than 10,000 species of flora have been recorded and collected in Iran. But, over the millennia, human activity—collecting wood for burning, building, and charcoal—reduced forest areas on the south- and east-facing mountain slope, and persistent grazing has led to the disappearance of perennial grasses and their replacement by non-palatable plants and spiny shrubs. Although today on the plateau areas of semi-natural vegetation are in the process of deliberate regeneration with schemes to introduce drought- and salt-tolerant plants (halophytes) and to increase salt tolerance of wheat and barley, other regions are still in the process of destruction.

Many of the mainly spring-flowering indigenous bulbous plants from the high mountains and foothills including anemones, eremurus, fritillaries, iris, ixiolirons, muscari, and tulips, which retreat into dormancy after flowering, are not easily grown in gardens on the plateau, although almost certainly wildflowers were encouraged under the orchard trees in early gardens, growing amongst alfalfa and/or clover. Instead the bulbous plants have been translated into Western gardens or are, at the least, ancestors of 'cultivated' plants. As early as the 10th century plants from the Iranian uplands were carried to the eastern Mediterranean and from thence through North Africa to Spain. In the 16th century European plant collectors in the Levant found that gardens in the Ottoman Empire already contained 'improved' varieties of bulbs, tubers,

corms, and rhizomes, many originally brought from Persia.

The range of trees, shrubs, roses, and flowers actually planted in Iranian gardens has always been limited, with a predominance of native fruit trees which give sustenance and longed-for shade. Almonds, figs, wild plums, pears, pomegranates, and walnuts predominate, with apricots and peaches and white mulberries (to feed the silkworm) from China, the same trees which are grown in groves in the numerous orchards, surrounded by baked mud walls, which, established in a natural oasis or originally watered by *qanats*, are still a welcome feature in the desert landscape. Groves of pistachio trees are today grown commercially on the east-facing foothills of the Zagros. Other trees, watered by *jubs* (open canals), provide shade on town streets: elm (*Ulmus minor*), willows, ash, and large shrubs such as Russian olive. Trees and flowers have always had symbolic meanings for the desert dweller, as is evident from the low-relief carving of cypress, palm trees, and lotus (a motif imported from Egypt) on the staircase walls at Persepolis constructed under Darius I (521–485 BC). This tradition continued under Islam. The cypress represented immortality or eternity, the plane tree defined the presence of life-giving water. In Garden Carpets and Persian miniatures the cypress is portrayed entwined by a flowering almond—symbol of spring and rejuvenation—while oriental plane trees are shown around water basins. Although the traditional Iranian garden had comparatively few plants, irises, narcissus, roses, and tulips are often portrayed in miniatures painted from the late 14th century. One of the few summer-flowering native annuals is *Amaranthus caudatus* (love-lies-bleeding). Today summer gardens are augmented by plants from the New World, such as sunflowers, marvels of Peru, tobacco plants, and salvias that follow scented stocks and pansies performing in spring. Weeping white mulberries were popular ornamental features in 19th-century gardens.

Early history

In Iran at least 4,000 years ago nomadic tribes became settled agriculturists in the desert oases, watered by natural springs and enclosed by walls to keep out marauders and drifting sand. Although, over the next millennia, the topography, climate, and consequent lack of water determined how gardens could develop in Iran, their history begins in lands beyond the boundaries of the modern state. Gardens in the Mesopotamian deltas of the Euphrates and Tigris rivers (now part of Iraq), the area of the 'fertile crescent' where wheat and barley were first tamed by man, and in the western foothills of the Zagros mountains (today the Iranian province of Khuzestan), are mentioned in cuneiform writings from 2000 BC, their recording in myths and literature often confirmed by 19th-century archaeological discoveries. The earliest gardens were shaped by delta conditions, canals drawing water from the great rivers dictating a geometric system of irrigation, while other pleasure parks were made in the cool foothills where water was more freely available.

The qanat system

On the Iran plateau farming and gardening were dependent on natural oases until the 7th century BC, when a pattern of underground conduits was developed to bring melting snow water from the base of the mountains. Known as qanats, these were invented by the ancient Medes and Persians, immigrants from the Russian steppes; they made village life and the development of gardens possible even in the desert. A main shaft would be sunk at the base of the mountains followed by further shafts at regular intervals, until reaching a village settlement. The flow of water along a very slight natural gradient was adapted by water availability. Water was distributed within a highly formalized system based on ownership of land and maintenance of the qanat. The wealthy took the best of the water supply—in some cases allowing the creation of ornamental as well as productive gardens—while the poor, further down the contour of the land, got the least, by then a muddy trickle. Communities were locked together in a virtually enclosed hierarchical system. The linear and rectilinear pattern of irrigation ditches (jubs) drawing water from a qanat established the geometry of streets in a village just as it regulated the running water in ornamental courtyards, the stone-lined water rills which established a garden pattern. Although many of the qanats, highly dangerous to build and maintain, were destroyed during the 13th-century Mongol conquests, they continued to be a vital part of the plateau economy until very recently and many are still functioning. Many of Iran's most important historic gardens have their own qanat-supplied water: the BAGH-E FIN at Kashan, the Shazadeh at Mahan, the BAGH-E DOULATABAD in Yasd. The British legation in Tehran for years had its own qanat bringing water straight from the Alborz Mountains above the city. Attempts at land reform during the 20th century and the introduction of central planning in agriculture led to a lack of communal responsibility in villages. The better-off introduced well and diesel pumps to provide their own irrigation water, often threatening the continued viability of existing qanats, as well as causing permanent damage to aquifers.

The Achaemenid and Sasanian gardens

Although Elamites established their own civilization in the province of Khuzestan, bordering Mesopotamia, c.4,000 BC, and their culture was to influence the future development of Persian arts, its destruction by the Assyrians in 650 BC ensures there are no records of gardens, even in their capital of Susa. The earliest known Iranian garden was made by Cyrus the Great (reigned 558-530 BC), the first Achaemenid Emperor of ancient Persia. Its foundations still exist today. At PASARGADAE the ancient gravity-fed water rills and basins (originally fed by an aqueduct), once overlooked by shade-giving pavilions, trace out a basic geometric pattern, establishing the elements of what was later known as the CHAHAR BAGH or 'fourfold' garden, developed under Islam over 1,000 years later. The enclosed gardens of the Achaemenid dynasty (558-323 BC), where fruit trees were grown in ordered rows, were known as *pairidaeza* in Persian (*pairi* meaning 'around' and *daeza* meaning a 'wall'), later translated by Xenophon into Greek as *paradeisos*, the word used for the Garden of Eden in Greek versions of the Bible. Cyrus also restored the ancient city of the Elamites at Susa, destroyed by the Assyrians in 650 BC, leaving Darius I (521-485 BC) and Artaxerxes (465-425 BC) to construct further palaces and gardens. The desert gardens, hunting parks, and orchards of the Achaemenid, Parthian (223 BC-AD 226), and Sasanian (AD 224-642) dynasties demonstrated royal power and prestige, making use of the qanat system to allow more elaborate water features. A hundred years after Cyrus the Great, his namesake Cyrus the Younger, satrap of Sardis in Lydia 423-404 BC, laid out orchards in a park, its beauty and its ordered rows described by Lysander to Xenophon, who, in his *Oeconomics* in 399 BC, mentioned how the satrap grew and transplanted saplings with his own hands. Both the Achaemenians and the Sasanians, whose empires encompassed an area far larger than Iran, borrowed skills from other cultures, using craftsmen for carving stone reliefs and adapting decorations such as the lotus motif from Egypt for their palaces and garden buildings. In Roman Italy generals returning from service against the Sasanian armies built luxurious parks and gardens in emulation of Persian schemes. Plants such as peaches and apricots travelled west along the Silk Road from China, while Iran exported pistachios to Aleppo, sesame to Egypt, and rice to Mesopotamia, and lucerne (alfalfa) travelled to Greece as fodder for the horses of Darius I as well as east to China. Attar of roses, from red roses grown on the plain near Firuzabad, was also exported to China. In 62 BC the general Lucullus introduced peaches, apricots, and cherries into his garden in Rome, the first to be grown in Italy.

The ruins of Sasanian gardens can still be seen at Firuzabad south of Shiraz, at Taq-e Bostan near Kermanshah, and at Taq-e Kisra at Ctesiphon outside Baghdad, where massive barrel-vaulted halls known as *aywans* (invented by the Parthians) once overlooked wide pools and orchards.

In 642 the conquering Arabs found the famous 'Spring of Khrosrau' carpet at Ctesiphon lying on a marble pavement in the vast hall. Woven in heavy silk, its design represented a garden pattern with golden threads to represent earth, shimmering crystal for water, and pearls for paths. Lost to posterity (the Arabs cut it up to distribute to the troops), it was the first of the so-called Garden Carpets made in the following centuries which illustrate the basic layout of a fourfold garden. The earliest carpet to survive was woven in Persia in the 17th century (Jaipur Museum).

Elements of the Islamic garden

The descriptions of the gardens of paradise found in the Qur'ān are clearly based on the existing pattern of desert gardens, but the basic pattern is now reinterpreted by Islam and given a spiritual dimension. The earthly garden became for the Muslim a symbol or foretaste of heaven to come, the paradise to be enjoyed by the faithful in the next life as revealed to Muhammad in the Qur'ān. As the Islamic empire expanded, its territories eastward mainly included desert countries, such as Persia (modern Iran) in which this basic garden formula had developed. The Garden of Eden mentioned briefly in Genesis is described much more vividly in verses of the Qur'ān, with more than 100 references to the paradise garden. Imbued by the Muslim with a sacred meaning, the water rills of the ancient Persian garden came to represent the four rivers of life of the Qur'ānic Revelations, dividing a garden into quadrants where fruit trees and flowers grew in beds, sunk below the level of the water and walkways, irrigated by periodic flooding. In paradise, reveals the Qur'ān, 'of every fruit there shall be two kinds . . . green pastures, therein fountains of running water, fruits and palm trees, and pomegranates'. Fruit trees were to provide shade and sustenance, water would cool the air and incidentally purify the soul, and flowers would give scent and colour. The desert dweller's love of nature came to be reflected in decoration of buildings and gateways of mosques and gardens, with floral motifs and geometric patterns derived from twining branches of vines, linking the new faith with the idea of abundance and fertility. By the first millennium these gardens were called *chahar bagh* (from *chahar* meaning 'four' and *bagh* meaning 'garden'). Enclosed by a high wall, and shaped as a rectangle which could be expanded to encompass extensions of the 'fourfold' scheme, the garden, entered by a massive gateway, contained pavilions built as mausoleums or as shady sites for contemplation. At first functional, water channels soon became part of decoration with more sophisticated water features developing over the centuries, to emphasize reflective surfaces and to cool the air rippling over carved screens. With plane trees, cypresses, fruit trees, and flowers, often with symbolic meanings, the original Persian or Iranian garden, with individual cultural and topographical interpretations, has remained the basic model for Islamic gardens in Iran, North Africa, Spain, Central Asia, and India.

Under Islam

By the 8th century Persia and Mesopotamia (a part of the Sasanian Empire) were ruled by the Abbasid caliphs in Baghdad, with the sophisticated Persians, often newly converted to Islam, becoming administrators, introducing the Arabs to their ancient traditions of garden making both in Persia and in the river deltas. The caliphate, although in decline, lasted until the 11th century, but in Iran itself and further east various regional dynasties assumed power over the intervening centuries. Although gardens had developed a sacred interpretation, rulers continued to make hedonistic pleasure parks, encouraging poets to eulogize their reigns with garden imagery. In the 10th century the Buyids from the Caspian provinces revived Sasanian palace architecture with 'Aud ad-Douleh making his capital at Shiraz in south-west Iran calling himself *Malek al Muluk* (King of Kings) and laying out orchards and groves around his palace, with water flowing through the rooms and arcades. In Ghazni in eastern Afghanistan, its territories extending to Khorasan in Persia, the gardens of Sultan Mahmud (998–1030) were celebrated by the poet Farrukhi. Trees, flowers, and birds figure largely, with images of spring and joy giving rise to thoughts of love. The Seljuks (1037–1220), who were responsible for many of the great monuments of Iran, bringing a more three-dimensional approach to architecture, also contributed to gardening: the third Seljuk ruler, Malek Shah (1072–92), built four gardens in Isfahan, each about 1 hectare/2.5 acres in extent. A contemporary poet mentions gardens fragrant with narcissus, myrtle, and saffron, with shaded seats and cooling breezes. One, the

Bagh-e Fallasan, had a high pavilion overlooking streams and vineyards, another, the Bagh-e Karan, planted with fruit trees and rows of cypresses and pines overlooking the river, still existed in the 14th century, its praises sung by the famous Shirazi poet Hāfiz (c.1324–1389).

The Mongol invasion

Although the civilized world cultivated by Islam for seven centuries was ravaged in the 13th century by the Mongol hordes of Genghis Khan destroying ancient *qanats*, breaking down canal banks, and filling in wells, the Mongols, converting to Islam, soon established an Iranian dynasty, with gardens reflecting a nomadic way of life. In 1302 near Tabriz, Ghazan Khan (1295–1304) laid out his garden with tented pavilions set in orchards and meadows becoming the centre of court life. By 1369 Timūr (1335–1405), known in the west as Tamerlane, a prince from Central Asia, seized power in Samarkand across the Oxus river, expanding his territories to include Iran, some of India, and part of Russia, destroying many of the old trade routes. Although a brutal conqueror, he was also a great builder, gathering artisans and craftsmen from his conquests to Samarkand to create palaces and gardens on a vast scale, well described by the Spanish ambassador from Castile who visited Timūr in his last years in 1404. The gardens while retaining their basic 'fourfold' format had acquired a more public ambience. They had become the settings for receptions with sumptuous silken tents and awnings raised on clover-rich lawns watered by streams, a style which was to influence how gardens developed in Safavid Persia and in the Mughal Empire in India. At least eleven gardens were made around the city to inspire poets and miniature painters. His son Shah Rokh (1408–47) established a school of miniature painting at Herat during the 15th century in which gardens were portrayed in delicate brushwork, often illustrating the great epic poems of Persia, Firdausi's 11th-century *Shahnameh* and Nezami's 12th-century *Khamsa*, with scenes set in beautiful gardens. Although stylized, the paintings of walled gardens and countryside amply record contemporary garden fashions, confirmed by poetry suffused with garden imagery.

Safavid gardens

Many of the most interesting gardens which remain in Iran date to the Safavid period (1500–1736). Those constructed in Isfahan in the 17th century were developed from the 'tented' Timurid gardens and reflect an integration between 'inside' and 'outside' and with pavilion reception rooms opening into the garden at

ground level. Shah Abbas I (1587–1629) had moved his capital from Qasvin to Isfahan in 1598, where he set about planning a new garden city alongside the old, using water from a series of canals diverted from the river Zayande. His own palace, the ALI QAPU, behind which were extensive gardens cooled by fountains, looked out over a vast new town square, the *maidan,* or the *naqsh-e jahanan* (Mirror of the World). The main CHAHAR BAGH AVENUE, stretching from north to south across the river, was flanked by gardens of his courtiers. The vast HEZAR JARIB, south of the river, no longer exists and Sa'adatabad on the north bank vanished under buildings. The CHEHEL SOTUN and HASHT BEHESHT were built by his descendants later in the 17th century. Shah Abbas, besides building caravanserai all over the country, also constructed at least six gardens on the Caspian shores in the province of Mazanderan, where with ample water he could use the gradient of the north-facing slopes to have more elaborate cascades and fountains. On a vast scale the architecture, a series of interconnected pavilions and gardens, although set in a lush green landscape, still reflected the 'desert' principles with a central water feature, rills, and sunken flower beds. The gardens at Farahabad have totally vanished but at Ashraf, modern Behshahr, the reconstructed town garden retains elements of Shah Abbas's original layout. One of the most beautiful gardens in Iran, the BAGH-E FIN near Kashan, probably dates to the early Safavid period, but was considerably augmented by Shah Abbas, and later restored by the Qajars. Fortunately 17th-century travellers to Persia such as the Italian Pietro della Valle, the Englishman Sir Thomas Herbert, and the Anglo-French jeweller Sir John Chardin have left vivid contemporary accounts of the Safavid gardens.

The city of Shiraz in the south-west, with a milder winter climate than Isfahan allowing citrus and date palms to flourish, has always been associated with gardens, with images of roses and nightingales evoked by poetry and miniature paintings. Many of the gardens made by merchants in the 19th century had earlier origins, although they had been damaged by earthquakes and floods during the 17th and 18th centuries. The BAGH-E TAKHT with seven terraces was first constructed in the 11th century but has now virtually disappeared below hotel foundations. The BAGH-E DELGOSHA or Garden of Heart's Ease, originally Safavid or even earlier, is much reduced in size with a 19th-century pavilion. The BAGH-E ERAM, with a distinguished 19th-century pavilion and a traditional Persian garden, is now the botanical garden of the university. The NARANJESTAN garden was part of the town house of the

Qavam ul-Mulk, hereditary head of the Khamseh tribal federation. Built in 1870, the central water features are flanked by palm trees and orange groves. Modern gardens with attractive trees and annuals in terracotta pots surround the mausoleums of the two famous Shirazi poets, Sa'dī (c.1207–1291) and Hāfiz (c.1324–1389).

Later gardens
In spite of political turbulence during much of the 18th century some gardens are of considerable merit, although the BAGH-E DOULATABAD in Yazd, surrounding a pavilion and tall wind tower, needs restoration (which began in 2000). The BAGH-E GOLSHAN in the remote desert town of Tabas retains its shape and beauty in spite of the town's destruction by an earthquake in 1978. At only 610 m/2,000 ft with a mild climate for date palms and citrus, this traditionally styled garden with gushing water channels and wide tanks has the most interesting plants well maintained by enthusiastic gardeners. The SHAH-GOLI at Tabriz in the north may have been constructed earlier than the 18th century but much of its present appearance dates to the Qajar era. At Mahan near Kirman the BAGH-E SHAHZADEH, although only constructed in the 1880s in a typical large *chahar bagh* pattern, conveys the true spirit of the desert garden, a walled enclosure where water brought by *qanat* from the mountains feeds central cascades and fountains, and provides irrigation for the flourishing orchards.

Tehran became the capital of the country under the Qajar dynasty in the 1780s. The cultivated ruler Fath Ali Shah (reigned 1797–1834) initiated building and restoration work completing the GOLISTAN PALACE and gardens in 1806, to become the centre of court life. Although grand and ostentatious in the 19th century with carpeted tents and flowers in the meadow, today the glory has wholly departed. Another palace and garden, the Negarestan, built by Fath Ali Shah in 1810 with a pool and garden set within an octagonal pavilion, has disappeared as has the QASR-E QAJAR outside the city walls, the latter rivalling in splendour all other contemporary gardens. Many of the 18th- and 19th-century gardens of Tehran were built by rulers and nobles on the cool slopes of the Alborz above the city, as summer retreats. Fath Ali Shah built a hunting lodge near his birthplace near Damghan. Chesmeh-e Ali lies among the southern foothills where spring water irrigates a green valley lined with groves of poplars and willows, wild plums, and pear trees. Today white-stemmed poplars, willows, ash, and ancient plane trees are the only garden plants, lining a wide pool in which the romantic

windowless hunting lodge sits on an island. The last Qajar palace of any importance was built a few miles east of Tehran by the spendthrift Muzaffar od-Din Shah after 1896 but this extravaganza, the Qasr-e Farahabad, a glaring white palace modelled on the Trocadero in Paris, with terraces and cascades descending to a vast lake, has now vanished.

The National Botanic Garden of Iran (now the Research Institute of Forest and Rangelands) was established in the 1970s near the village of Karaj 20 km/13 miles west of Tehran at the instigation of the department of conservation and, in particular, an environmentalist, Eskander Firouz, with considerable input from his English sister-in-law Ana Ala, who oversaw a wild bulb collection and the making of a library. Edward Hyams helped prepare a master plan based on the classic Persian garden. Radiating walks defined separate geographical regions of Iran and were planted accordingly: the Caspian, the Zagros, the Alborz, and desert regions. A rock garden was laid out by the English nurseryman and alpine specialist Will Ingwersen.

Landscape architecture in the 20th century
In spite of the cultural heritage of Iran, home to some of the earliest recorded gardens in Western civilization, modern landscape architecture is a relatively new field in post-revolutionary Iran. Following the First World War and the growth of cities as people moved off the land, developing parks were largely modelled on European lines with the principles of the ancient *chahar bagh* forgotten. Park-e Shahr, Park-e Mellat, Park-e Sar, and Park-e Laleh were developed in the capital Tehran. On the other hand the Jamshid-e yeh, a garden on the northern slopes of the city, was conceived by the architect Ghollamreza Hazrat in 1975 on more traditional lines, with cascades and pools descending the contours. More recently, after the eight-year war with Iraq, this garden is being extended to incorporate cultural centres representing regions where tribal peoples, such as the *Bakhtiari* and *Qasghai* from the Zagros, are indigenous. A geometric scheme based on rills and pools for Park-e Haft-o-do Shahid (72 Martyrs Park), north of the sacred city of Qom, devised in the 1980s, is still largely unrealized. The Bagh-e Ghadir in Isfahan, a few kilometres east of the Chahar Bagh Avenue, was designed from 1987 by Hossein Zainnadin of Bavand Associates, with the landscape architect Farhad Abozzia, as a conscious reinterpretation of a traditional *chahar bagh*, with an emphasis on facilities for the public, local office workers, and children, including picnic areas. Water, circulating by gravity, runs through shallow blue-coloured channels. Most of the large

projects are completed by architects who are in charge of outdoor design and oversee installations. An exception is Farhad Abo-Zia with his business firm Baft Shahr, who has been awarded a UNESCO award for a project completed in Mashad. Another firm, Manzar Pira, with Dr Ghazal Rouhani (trained in the United States), has recently completed a project of 23 hectares/58 acres around the Tangooyeh Dam in Sirjon in Kirman.

Historic gardens
As a result of the lack of experts in the field, few restoration projects of historic gardens exist, except on a local level. The Ministry of Cultural Heritage deals primarily with buildings. Under the municipality of Tabriz an ambitious plan for restoration and enlargement of the Qajar garden Shah-Goli, was conceived under the direction of Farhad Arhmadi, with 70 hectares/173 acres extra incorporated to provide many new facilities. Although 19th-century merchants' houses in Kashan and Tabriz, constructed on traditional lines each with a central courtyard containing a pool, have recently been admirably restored, little attempt has been made to implement any authentic planting schemes. In general 'restoration' of historic gardens has involved reinstating and repairing the essential water features and ancillary buildings. Too often intrusive modern lamp standards and planting of purple-foliaged shrubs, bright flowers, and modern roses mar effects. An exception is the garden of the Abbasi Hotel in Isfahan, originally a caravanserai, which retains the basic attributes of the spiritual fourfold garden with graceful trees and flowers surrounding a long canal.

In the last four years landscape architecture has been introduced as a university course, attached to departments of horticulture in four different campuses, but the shortage of trained teachers means that students are taught by architects and horticulturists with little knowledge of garden design. Garden magazines are all published with government support: *Green Space* by the municipality of Tehran, *Sabzineh* by the municipality of Sistan, *Payam Sabz* by the Landscape Organization, and a newsletter published by a Horticultural Society. There are also several agricultural magazines that specialize in the environment.   PHo

Irchel Park ⊗
University of Zurich, Canton of Zurich, Switzerland. Between 1979 and 1986, Atelier Stern & Partner and Eduard Neuenschwander (b. 1924) created one of the largest new urban parks in Switzerland, covering an area of around 32 hectares/79 acres, according to the current, ecologically influenced principles of

the quasi-natural landscape park. From 1973 a new campus for part of the University of Zurich was built in the grounds of a former school of agriculture, not far from the city centre on a prominent ridge between Zurich and Waidberg. In the emerging spirit of environmental awareness and the ecological movement, the park was conceived in the landscape style as an idyllic natural space, extending into the city like a green wedge. Large earth mounds, made from the spoil from university buildings, protect the park from traffic noise in adjacent roads, bring variety to the topography and create diverse landscape spaces that appear natural but were artificially produced. Two reinstated streams and the large lake, whose uncontrived appearance is the result of considerable technical efforts, create a natural-seeming water system. A wide, grassed bridge links the separate parking areas, letting visitors forget that they are crossing an important traffic artery. In contrast to the high-tech university buildings the park feels like a natural oasis, an artificial Arcadia in the middle of the city, shaped by natural materials and unconstrained plants. The diverse sculptures in the park and the buildings are worthy of note. The idea of a 'natural' idyllic park that imitated the forms of an intact natural landscape but was essentially highly artificial provoked repeated and fierce controversy in professional circles. The grounds, so 'un-Swiss' in their sweeping, generous dimensions, are on the other hand held in great affection by Zurich's citizens and students and offer a remarkable example of ecological design in the 1970s and 1980s.
UW

Ireland. See BRITISH ISLES.

Isola Bella ⊛
Stresa, Italy. The vast baroque palace and gardens built for Count Carlo Borromeo on a barren rock were begun in 1632, and work continued until 1671 under his sons Count Vitaliani and his brother Ghiberti. The palace itself was never completed. Seen from the lake Isola Bella seems to float on its surface like a great galleon, its prow the theatrical ten-terraced garden, rising some 30 m/100 ft above the lake, with statues on the marble balustrades, a dramatic silhouette only softened today by three centuries of planting. Dal Re's engraving of 1726 shows the ambitious project before any planting had matured to disguise the 'bones' of the design. The print also shows the 'bows' of the fabulous 'craft', a feature which was never constructed. Although Dal Re's print also reveals a series of elaborate PARTERRES of French-style *broderie* with little relief of BOSCO, it seems from the accounts of

contemporary travellers that much more planting had been done. The English Bishop Burnet visited the island in 1684 and Président de Brosses in 1739, both describing the garden as one of the loveliest spots on earth, filled with exotic trees and fruit espaliered against the walls of the terraces.

An architectural masterpiece, Isola Bella, its palace and garden skilfully integrated at an angle disguised by a small entrance courtyard and tall trees, is also of interest to the botanist. The high rainfall, hot summers, and winter temperatures modified by the expanse of water provide exceptionally favourable conditions for exotic trees and shrubs from many parts of the world. By the 21st century any severity of design is disguised by masses of foliage and blossom. Magnolias, camellias, jasmine, pomegranates, and citrus frame the fantastic theatre where statues of gods, putti, and a prancing unicorn reign in baroque splendour. Angelo Crivelli drew up the first plans for the fabulous pleasure palace and garden but died before the work was far advanced; other architects, artists, and sculptors, including Francesco Castelli (1599–1667) and Carlo Fontana (d. 1587) from Rome, continued with the project.   PHo

Isola Madre ⊛
Stresa, Italy. In his *Description of All Italy* written in 1568 Leandro Alberti speaks of an 16th-century building on an island in the middle of Lake Maggiore. Lancilotto Boromeo, 'a Milanese gentleman, has built a sumptuous palace and ornamented it with an agreeable garden'. The original garden, around the unfinished Renaissance villa with formal terracing providing shelter for citrus, was greatly extended by Prince Gilberto during the early 19th century. He swept away the regimented orchards to introduce a romantic informal atmosphere, enhanced by lush planting in the favourable climate. From 1850 Count Vitaliani established a serious botanical collection, growing palm trees on the terraces and experimenting with new introductions. Today crape myrtles, hibiscus, leptospernums, acacias, and the rare *Nolinia longifolia* from the deserts of Central America greet the visitor as he arrives by boat. In the woodland native trees—aromatic cypress, bay laurel, and pine—mix with exotics such as the camphor tree (*Cinnamomum camphora*), pepper trees (*Schinus molle*), and a rare specimen Kashmir cypress (*Cupressus cashmeriana*), and white peacocks stroll among the glades.   PHo

Isuien ⊛
Nara, Japan, was developed in two distinct phases, one in the early Edo period (1600–1868)

and the other in the Meiji period (1868–1912). The clear waters of the Yoshiki-gawa river, which runs near the Great Buddha Hall of Tōdaiji Temple, were well suited to the production of a bleached white cloth called *nara sarashi*. A merchant of such cloth built a villa for himself along the river in the 1670s or 1680s that took in the view of three mountains: Kasuga-yama, Wakakusa-yama, and Mikasa-yama. When a Chinese Zen Buddhist priest named Mokuan (Chinese: Muan) visited the villa, he named the main building Sanshūtei, the Arbor of Three Excellences. This thatch-roofed building now sits at the western end of the garden. The pond of this first garden remains but not any other stylistic attributes from the early Edo period.

Around 1879, another *sarashi* merchant, Seki Tōjirō (b. 1864), obtained the property, built a villa for himself just east of the older garden, and joined it to the older garden. He created a pond in the shape of the Chinese character for water, and a building called Suishintei, the Arbor of the Water Spirit. The view of the mountains is now best seen from this newer garden and the technique of incorporating the distant scene as part of the garden—BORROWED LANDSCAPE—is one of the salient features of this garden. The name of the garden, Isuien, the Garden Born of Water, was given by Viscount Sugi Chōu (1835–1920) and may have been drawn from a poem by Tang-dynasty (618–907) poet Du Fu, but may as well simply refer to the clear waters that fed the garden and supported the merchants who built it.   MPK

Italy,
separated from the rest of Europe by the magnificent mountain barrier of the Alps to the north, is a peninsula jutting deeply into the Mediterranean. A less elevated chain of mountains, the Apennines, extends as a spine all the way down the peninsula leaving the country (301,000 sq. km/116,000 sq. miles) only 21% of plain, with 40% hilly and 39% of mountains with ranges higher than 702 m/2,300 ft. The plains, however, constitute only one-quarter of the land under cultivation; agriculture in the hills has been made possible by modifying the natural landscape and resources through extensive terracing and irrigation, factors which have influenced the development of garden layouts over the centuries. The most extensive plain is that of the Po valley, its lower fertile reaches providing land for intensive agriculture. Around Naples near Vesuvius, Campania has been famed since Roman times for its crops and roses grown in volcanic soil, and in Sicily the central plateau was the granary of the Roman Empire, while the Catanian Plain is today a centre for citrus fruit

and with a drier climate has encouraged gardens with succulents and cacti.

Geographically lying in the temperate zone, the Italian climate varies between its northern extremities and the Mediterranean south and coastal districts. For plants and garden making, rainfall, latitude, and microclimates are all important, with coastal areas on the west warmer and wetter than on the Adriatic Sea. With almost no frost the Ligurian Riviera, the Tyrrhenian Sea, the Bay of Naples, and the coast of Sicily are especially favoured for growing semi-tropical vegetation, although the low rainfall (68 cm/27 in) at Ventimiglia on the French border, the site of the famous plant collection at the HANBURY GARDENS is a limiting factor. For comparison, further south La Spezia has 112 cm/45 in, the inland city of Florence on the Arno has 75 cm/30 in, while Naples has 77 cm/31 in and Palermo 57 cm/23 in. The southern island, Sicily, is subject to the hot humid sirocco, a wind from Africa and the Middle East. In the north a hot dry wind, the foehn, blows from Switzerland and Austria, while in the east the bora brings cold dry winds and strong gusts.

The natural vegetation of the country divides into three distinct zones, the Alps, the Po valley, and the Mediterranean-Apennine area, reflecting the diversity of physical environment. On the lower foothills of the Alps vines and olive trees are fruitful, while slightly higher beech and sweet chestnut are ubiquitous, gradually changing with higher altitude to larch and Norway spruce. In high altitudes stunted shrubs, including junipers, give way to pastures, with grasses, sedges, and wildflowers such as gentians, dryad, and saxifrage, then mosses and lichens on the snow line, of more interest to the Alpine gardener than of influence in gardens. In the 1st century BC the poet VIRGIL, besides celebrating country life and agriculture, gives a list of the native trees and crops of his Mantuan homeland on the northern plain, including orchard trees and field crops. In the Alpine foothills the lakes in the valleys, Maggiore, Como, and Garda, surrounded by olive groves and citrus orchards, provide mild winters and a higher rainfall, factors exploited by Prince Gilberto Borromeo on ISOLA MADRE in the 19th century and by the Scot Neil McEacharn at Pallanzo (Villa TARANTO) from the 1930s. In the Apennines winters vary in severity according to altitude, with native evergreens predominating in the lower hills. The *macchia* thickets, in areas where man has thinned out original woodland for building, fuel, and grazing, consist of brambles, broom, bay laurel, and mastic plants (*Pistacia lentiscus* and *P. terebinthus*). In limestone areas the destruction of woodland and subsequent loss of soil results in a *garrigue*, where aromatic herbs such as rosemary, thyme, sage, and lavender flourish. In the foothills, in the river valleys, and in the plains, native evergreens provide the foundation planting in historic gardens: holm oaks, cypress, arbutus, pines (three different sorts—the Aleppo pine (*Pinus halepensis*), the umbrella pine (*Pinus pinea*) with edible seeds, and the maritime pine (*Pinus pinaster*), often planted as seaside windbreaks), bay laurel (*Laurus nobilis*), myrtle, laurustinus (*Viburnum tinus*), and oleander. Carob and cork oak grow in coastal regions.

The Roman garden

Italy's garden heritage is an inescapable presence in the development of garden styles throughout the West. The history of Italian gardens and gardening evolved from the varied topographical conditions, the Mediterranean-type climate with hot dry summers and cool wet winters, as well as from successive civilizations which drew in their turn on earlier cultures. Although many of the villas and gardens of the Roman Empire crumbled to ruin with their empire, their legacy inspired the great architects of Renaissance Italy to establish a grammar of architectural design which still dominates European and American gardening styles. Archaeological scrutiny of Roman ruins, combined with new mathematical understanding of perspective, allowed Renaissance builders to discover the secrets of classical proportion. Less directly, classical literature—the letters of PLINY THE YOUNGER describing his country villas, the poems of Horace, Virgil's *Georgics* idealizing country life where working the earth could be 'a happy compulsion that makes labour sweet' (from *The Eclogues*) and Ovid's tales of metamorphoses—established a link between man and nature which had a special appeal to the 15th- and 16th-century Italian humanist and would be exploited in full in the naturalism of the 18th-century English landscape movement.

The Romans, as evidenced by archaeological remains and contemporary frescoes, established strong architectural principles to garden layout, with axial and symmetrical lines matching those of the building, with an interplay between 'inside' and 'out', using precepts set out by Vitruvius in *Ten Books of Architecture* (before AD 27). The commonest feature in a domestic villa was the peristyle garden. A one-storey building included an inner courtyard and pool, surrounded by a covered colonnaded walkway, decorated by flower beds, pots, statues, and occasionally frescoes, as discovered in the excavation of POMPEII AND HERACULANEUM, depicting a wider *trompe l'œil* landscape. Although destroyed by the eruption of Vesuvius in AD 79, the civilization of these towns and those in the surrounding Campania, a history of 400 years, was preserved by a covering of *lapilli* to be revealed by archaeologists, to allow authentic restorations of public places, private gardens, and planting. The medieval cloisters found in monasteries from medieval times are derived from the Roman peristyle gardens.

The confined Pompeian gardens bore little resemblance to the grander concepts of the wealthy Romans who drew inspiration both from Greece and from the luxurious walled parks discovered on their eastern campaigns. From Greece came porticoes, shady tree-lined walks, springs or groves dedicated to a god or goddess, temples, and NYMPHAEUMS. The statues in Roman gardens were often late Greek in origin or copies of the great Greek sculptors. The Greek writer Xenophon (*c.*435–354 BC) described the gardens of the Persian Empire in some detail including the ordered orchards arranged in QUINCUNX, the central water features, and hunting parks. From the 2nd century BC generals could see for themselves the opulent *paradeisoi* of the Persian kings (see IRAN), and returned to create similar gardens in Rome or in other outposts of the empire, bringing with them new fruit trees such as peaches and apricots. The Emperor Hadrian drew his inspiration directly from Hellenic (Ptolemaic) Egypt for his vast villa and garden at Tivoli, laid out in the 1st century AD, with buildings, baths, theatres, pools, and libraries contained within a complex of gardens, concepts travelling originally to Egypt from Persia and Mesopotamia. HADRIAN'S VILLA had water features such as the Canopus, shaped like a hippodrome and surrounded by a colonnade, and the Marine Theatre, located on a small island, its surrounding water sheltered by a circular portico, to inspire garden design in later ages, while in the 16th century Pirro LIGORIO was able to plunder the villa for statues and sculptures for the nearby Villa d'ESTE.

Pliny the younger, nephew to PLINY THE ELDER, author of the *Natural History,* in letters written in the 1st century AD describes his villas in Latium (modern Ostia) and in the hills of Tuscany, giving details of garden layout and planting, including topiary, and spelling out his gardener's name. Besides detailing porticoes, vine-covered pergolas, courtyards, pools, cascades and watercourses, rooms oriented with the sun, and plants, Pliny, particularly in Tuscany, emphasizes the importance of surrounding landscape 'not as real land but as an exquisite painting' (from *Pliny's Letter to Domitius Apollinaris*). Pliny's recommendations were to influence the 16th-century architect Andrea PALLADIO, confirming Renaissance humanist ideals and belief in a partnership between man and nature, a prelude to the later landscape movement. The Roman interest in countryside was depicted in frescoes, often a temple or grotto set in wild hills or in a grove of trees, showing a reverence for the gods as well as for nature and its unknown forces. Nero's Golden House in Rome, disapproved of by contemporaries for its size and opulence, although containing formal elements also incorporated true landscape features, vineyards, woodland, pastures, lakes, and even ploughed fields. Within 50 years of Nero's death (AD 68) it had disappeared (although modern archaeologists are working on part of the site).

Although Romans exploited ideas from other cultures it is obvious from their manuals of agriculture written by Cato (c.160 BC), Varro (c.40 BC), COLUMELLA (c. AD 60), and Palladius (4th century AD), all of which contained sections on gardening, that they were innovators in agricultural techniques, particularly in management of water. These books, copied by hand in monasteries through centuries, remained the principal source for garden practice throughout the Middle Ages, only to be superseded by *Liber Ruralium Commodorum* (1305), many of the ideas of the author, the Bolognese Pietro de' CRESCENZI, culled from Columella's earlier 1st-century treatise.

The Middle Ages
As the Roman Empire collapsed Islam, at first in Baghdad and then Córdoba, became the centre of learning for the known civilized world, bringing Arab taste and scholarship to Sicily and southern Italy by the 9th century. The Arabs built pleasure palaces in Sicily based on Persian paradise gardens. Although conquered by the Normans in 1091, and the gardens destroyed, Arabic traditions remained, with the Norman Christians modelling their new palaces and gardens around the city of Palermo on eastern lines. Although nothing remains of these hedonistic hunting parks dotted with pavilions, except for that of the Ziza in Palermo, it seems that the grandson of Roger the Great, the Hohenstaufen Emperor Friedrich II (1194–1250), built hunting boxes and gardens throughout southern and central Italy, with enclosed pool gardens, vine trellises, meadows with fish ponds, and menageries for exotic animals and birds, a blend of exotic orientalism culled from both Sicily and the Roman country villa. Between 1277 and 1279 under Pope Nicholas III a *Viridarium Novum* was established inside the Vatican grounds where plants for medical use were grown. At Salerno around 1317 the famous school of medicine attached to the university (the oldest in Italy) was responsible

for a public garden instigated by the doctor and 'botanist' Matteo Silvatico, where medicinal plants were also grown for study. Undoubtedly the southern Arab-influenced gardens became a source for Pietro de' Crescenzi's *Liber Ruralium Commodorum*, a treatise which was to remain an unchallenged agricultural and garden authority until the 16th century. Except for a few early frescoes (notably those in the Campo Santo in Pisa of the *Garden of Eden* and the *Triumph of Death*) and miniatures of medieval manuscripts we know little of secular gardens of medieval origin in Italy, although the 13th-century Villa RUFOLO at Ravello, with a distinct Moorish style and an open-air loggia with splendid views over the Gulf of Salerno, still exists today.

The Renaissance
The Italian Renaissance garden by reinterpreting the classical traditions of the ancient world established a new formula for garden design. Giovanni Boccaccio (1313–75), with the poet Francis Petrarch (1304–74), early humanists with a passionate interest in classical literature and with a love of nature, heralded the Renaissance. The elder, Petrarch, astonished his contemporaries by ascending Mont Ventoux in Provence just to see the view; anticipating by 100 years the Piccolomini Pope Pius II who extolled the beauties of the countryside in his *Commentaries*. Petrarch also made gardens wherever he lived, often following Virgilian precepts set out in the *Georgics*. In his *Visione Amorosa*, completed in 1345, Boccaccio paints a picture of Neapolitan life and the gardens of Naples filled with sculptures, possibly a legacy of Friedrich II, little streams, flowers, and grassy plots, a prelude to his better-known *The Decameron*, which vividly portrays *villeggiatura* (the custom of withdrawing to a country residence). His descriptions may have been based on the medieval garden of the Villa Palmieri in Florence. Seeking refuge from the plague, characters danced, sang, told stories, and dined by a central fountain amidst flower beds containing scented roses, jasmine, and citrus fruits. Another major influence was Leon Battista ALBERTI, who wrote *De Re Aedificatoria* in 1452 drawing heavily on the Latin authors and restating ancient Roman principles of villa and garden design, reviving the integrated intimacy between villa and garden established in classical times, largely absent when during the troubled medieval period fortification of villas was necessary. Alberti recommended hillside sites both for the views and for health. Many of his instructions were lifted almost verbatim from earlier sources, such as Pliny the younger's letters and the Roman manuals. The

Florentine Villa QUARACCHI (1459) was built on Alberti's precepts by Giovanni Rucellai on a simple axial plan with a pergola leading into a GIARDINO SEGRETO from the main entrance and an avenue stretching down to the Arno, combining medieval and classical features. At Pienza Pope Pius II had Rosselino build the Palazzo PICCOLOMINI (1462) with its small hanging garden, laid out with four rectangular beds, with four paths forming a cross, and framed views over the wild Val d'Orcia, a perfect early example of Renaissance symmetry and balance. The influential HYPNEROTOMACHIA POLIPHILI, written by Francesco Colonna and published in 1499 (although available from 1467), was illustrated with lively woodcuts of pergolas, fountains, porticoes, and flower beds. Within an allegorical romance the erotic dream of the narrator Poliphilo gives specific details of garden design as well as plant detail, showing parterre patterns later adapted as forerunners of elaborate knots. The description of the Island of Cytherea combining stone, water, topiary, and flowering plants is especially evocative of gardening possibilities. Its descriptions and woodcuts were to influence both Italian and French garden design in the next two centuries.

Other important 15th-century writers include Filarete (c.1400–c.1469) and Francesco di Giorgio (1489–1501/2) at the end of the century, both imbued with classical learning and recommending unified garden schemes and grand axial compositions. Although the lunettes portraying Medici gardens by Giusto UTENS are dated 1499, paintings of the earlier villas such as Cafaggiolo and Il Trebbio, both conceived in 1451 and built by the architect Michelozzo, reveal their early appearance. Basically still fortresses rather than country villas, their gardens although reflecting an axial formality have no relationship with the building. All this changed within a few years, with the Villa MEDICI in Fiesole, also built by Michelozzo (1458–61) on a steep hillside, with projecting garden terraces aligned with the villa and magnificent views over the valley of the Arno.

The Renaissance architects did not rely only on classical literature. They had innumerable Roman ruins to study and measure, establishing the ancient principles with gardens visualized as a series of 'rooms' aligned with the main entrance of the villa. Donato BRAMANTE designed the Belvedere Court (see VATICAN GARDENS) in 1503 for Pope Julius II, a layout combining these precepts with a new three-dimensional approach which was to influence the next 200 years of garden development. Other Roman villas, such the Villa MADAMA by Raphael (1516 but never completed) and the

Villa GIULIA by AMMANATI, VIGNOLA, Vasari, and Michelangelo from 1550, both with a series of interlocking spaces, reflect Bramante's influence. Two other villas near Rome remain essentially as originally planned, the Villa d'Este built for Cardinal Ippolito d'Este by Pirro Ligorio from 1550 and the Villa LANTE built for Cardinal Gambara by Jacopo Vignola from 1566, both built on steep slopes with an orchestration of terraces, steps, and water features. At Este lavish fountains dominate an allegorical theme dedicated to Hercules (an indicator of power) and Hippolytus (symbol of chastity). At Lante the adjoining park, through which visitors originally approached, had a 'wild' nature artfully balancing with the architectural features in the formal garden.

In Tuscany gardens, particularly those of the MEDICI FAMILY in the middle of the 16th century, reflected the outer landscape, a countryside of terraced olive groves and vineyards, from which their pre-banking wealth was derived. There was none of the drama of the Roman designers. At Villa MEDICI Castello outside Florence the garden was designed by Niccolò TRIBOLO from 1537, for the Grand Duke Cosimo I. Fountains and statues expressed an allegory of Medici rule in the city, reflecting victory over tyranny and eternal spring. Laid out on shallow terraces the simple garden contained a collection of citrus augmented by a garden for rare plants and newly introduced species, an animal grotto, and a labyrinth of cypress surrounding a statue by GIAMBOLOGNA. The famous BOBOLI GARDENS were laid out from 1549 behind the newly acquired Pitti Palace in a natural amphitheatre (once a stone quarry) by Tribolo (after his death by other architects) for Cosimo and his wife Eleonora di Toledo. Aligned on the palace, sloping paths and planting areas reflected an acceptance of existing landforms, rather than the sophisticated terraces, ramps, and stairways of Roman design. In the next century the green amphitheatre was transformed into a series of concentric stone steps and the garden much enlarged to take a baroque form with long vistas.

The most influential of the Medici villas in Florence was PRATOLINO, created by Bernardo Buontalenti for Francesco I from 1569. Known as 'the garden of miracles', for its large park, grottoes, organs worked by hydraulics, fountains, and water jokes, it was renowned throughout Europe for its sophistication and many of its features were imitated. The Pergola of Water at Pratolino was wide enough, according to John EVELYN, for a man to ride on horseback beneath. It was drawn by Giovanni Guerra in 1604. Water games—GIOCHI D'AQUA— were a feature of late Renaissance gardens, designed to soak the unsuspecting spectator.

The baroque garden in Italy

By the second half of the 16th century axial gardens had developed into a form of mannerist art in which intricate iconographical and allegorical features, besides complicated hydraulic and mechanical devices, were employed to project garden architecture into realms of fancy. Art's infinite capacity to outdo natural things, while still seeming to imitate them, became a rule. Later baroque gardens developed an even more theatrical approach. Laid out on steep slopes, they included dramatic terraces and water cascades deliberately distorting simple proportions and perspective and visually extending the garden into the countryside, the latter idea particularly captivating the French and adapted in Italy when the terrain was appropriate. Depending on climate and topography the baroque style developed in Italy in different ways in different regions, but by the middle of the 17th century garden creativity was strongly influenced by France, instead of depending on Italian Renaissance principles.

The Villa BORGHESE gardens, just outside the Porta Pinciana in Rome, begun in 1608, were virtually complete by the 1630s. Losing all sense of intimacy, its gardens and those of the Villa DORIA PAMPHILI on the Janiculum (1644) were large parks laid out with long formal avenues each terminating in a statue, in which the public were welcome, only the intimate walled flower gardens around the Casino Nobile remaining private. A group of villas at Frascati south-east of Rome on the fringe of the Alban Hills personify the baroque era. Built on steep slopes with commanding views to the Roman Campagna, the villas were backed by natural oak and chestnut forests. A flat area was carved out of the hillside for each villa and a semicircular retaining wall forming a NYMPHAEUM at its back, with niches for statues and for fabulous water displays and cascades. Water appeared to descend naturally from a rustic fountain above but in reality had to be conveyed there by pipeline. Typical was the Villa ALDOBRANDINI, begun in 1598. Other baroque gardens varied in style with geography and climate. They included Villa GARZONI and the Villa REALE (Marlia) near Lucca, CETINALE near Siena with a long formal axis, and CICOGNA MOZZONI near Varese in Piedmont with a fine water staircase. On ISOLA BELLA in Lake Maggiore gardens were designed over a period from 1630 to 1670 for Count Carlo Borromeo. Designed in a series of terraces with a magnificent theatre, its site, surrounded by snow-capped Alps, is incomparably dramatic.

Plants and planting

Although Pope Nicholas III (1277-80), the first pope to live in the Vatican, had a garden for growing herbs and vegetables, it was the physician of Nicholas IV (1288-92), Simone da Genova, who added a 'garden of simples' for medicinal use, a small vineyard, and a *boschetto* (see BOSCO). This first 'botanical' garden was established 300 years before, in the Renaissance age, new plants from the Orient and from the New World stimulated serious scientific study of plants for their own sake rather than for their medicinal use. Italy can also claim the first modern BOTANIC GARDENS to be established in Europe. PISA and PADUA were founded in 1545, within a few months of each other, soon to be followed by the Botanic Garden of Florence (1550). Both were conceived as gardens of medicinal herbs for the university medical students, but, receiving the flood of new plants both from the eastern Mediterranean and from the New World, rapidly attracted scientific botanists who started herbarium collections and began to study plants scientifically. The Italian Pierandrea Mattioli (1501-77), botanist and physician, who spent twenty years in the service of the Archduke Ferdinand and the Emperor Maximilian in Prague, published his *Commentarii in Sex Libros Pedacii Dioscoridis* in 1544. Although without pictures, it was to become the standard work on medical botany for European physicians. By the 1550s it was illustrated with fine woodcuts. In 1565 an edition printed in Venice and translated into Italian, French, German, and even Czech, included woodcuts and descriptions of many plants newly arrived from the Levant, including horse chestnut, lilac, grape hyacinths, sea holly, auricula, and four different pine species. In Rome the *Horti Farnesiani* were laid out by Vignola at the instigation of the Farnese Pope Paul III in the middle of the 16th century. The terraces descended to the Forum from the Palatine Hill. Little remains today except for aviaries, but the rich collection of plants was catalogued by Pietro Castelli in 1625 to give an indication of the contemporary knowledge of plant species and cultivars, many of which had been collected and grown by wealthy amateurs such as Francesco Caetani, Duke of Sermoneta, whose garden at Cisterna south of Rome became famous for rarities from 1625. Caetani and other collectors benefited by the interchange of botanical knowledge and plants between Italy and northern Europe. From the 1560s a small but intensely active world of scholarship developed as the flood of plants, mostly bulbs, corms, or tubers, arriving from the eastern end of the Mediterranean increased in volume.

Renaissance garden literature and art

In Italy various 16th-century writers such as

Girolamo Fiorenzuola (1552) recommended plants for hedges and fruit while Agostino del Riccio's treatise *Del giardino di un re* (1597) suggested the planting of citrus fruits, including fourteen sorts of lemons as well as the citron, *Citrus medica*, to be followed by Vincenzo Leonardi's famous watercolours of lemons collected in the Paper Museum of Cassiano dal Pozzo early in the 17th century. Descriptions of a variety of plants and their use in gardens are found in G. B. Ferrari's *De Florum Culturum* (1633). The Italian influence spread throughout northern Europe through published designs. Sebastiano Serlio's plans for geometric flower beds appeared in the fourth volume of *Tutte l'opere d'architettura e prospettiva* (1569, although these were available in 1537). The Flemish Hans Vredeman de VRIES showed designs for Italian-type parterres, pergolas, and tunnels in his *Hortorum Viridariorumque Elegantes et Multiplicis Formae* (1583) and Porro's engraving of the circular Padua Botanic Garden was published in 1591. Painters such as Claude Lorraine (1600–82) and Nicolas Poussin (1594–1665), although incorporating Roman ruins in their landscapes of the Italian countryside to influence the developing 18th-century English landscape style, did not paint existing Italian gardens. The Flemish painter Giusto Utens, who portrayed fourteen of the Medici gardens in and around Florence in lunettes for the Villa Artimino towards the end of the 16th century, is a useful source for detailed planting. The lunettes are now in the topographical museum in Florence.

Many engravings show gardens as they were soon after their creation. Giovanni Battista Falda's *Li giardini di Roma* (1683) is an invaluable guide to the gardens of Rome, while G. Zocchi's 18th-century engravings cover most of Tuscany. Marcantonio dal Re's book of prints of the gardens of Lombardy was published in the 18th century. Italian Renaissance gardens were also exceptionally well documented by contemporary travellers such as the French essayist Michel de MONTAIGNE in the 1580s, John Evelyn in the 1640s, and Président de Brosses from Dijon in the 18th century, whose descriptions have added to our knowledge of the gardens when just finished or even sometimes when in decline. In his *Lives of the Artists* (1550 and 1568) Giorgio Vasari (1511–74) describes gardens made by architects such as Michelozzo Michelozzi (Cafaggiolo, and the MEDICI Villas at Careggi, Fiesole, and Castello).

The French influence
Although through almost two centuries the French (and the rest of Europe) absorbed the principles of garden design from Renaissance Italy, by the mid-17th century France took the lead in establishing the baroque form, most readily adaptable to its flatter forested landscape. Thereafter, with Italian city states in relative decline and France a unified nation and centre for the arts with designers such as LE NÔTRE in control, Italian garden design acquired a French finish, although the vast linear gardens with avenues marching to infinity were hardly suitable for much of the Italian countryside. Four such gardens were outstanding: Crivelli Sormani-Verri in Lombardy with a famous cypress alley stretching for 1 km/0.6 mile (now almost disappeared), Juvarra's radiating avenues planted at STUPINIGI outside Turin, the Villa PISANI at Strà on the Brenta Canal laid out in the 1730s, and Vanvitelli's gardens at the Palazzo REALE in Caserta built for the Spanish King Charles III from 1762 to 1779 to rival those of Versailles, although never completed.

The 19th and 20th centuries
By the end of the 18th century, with the Atlantic taking the place of Mediterranean trade, Italy was in serious economic decline. Many of the 18th-century travellers on the grand tour saw gardens in which hedges had grown too high, stonework was crumbling, and parterres were flowerless. Many of the most elegant trend-setting earlier gardens were converted into a *giardino inglese*, including Pratolino, in 1822, often lifeless imitations of the great landscape compositions first conceived in England. A neoclassical architect, Giuseppe Japelli (1783–1852), was responsible for many minor English-type gardens in the Veneto and Friuli. A 19th-century landscape park, Parco CELLE near Pistoia, with some romantic buildings, lakes, and temples, has proved a successful setting for a sculpture museum since 1964.

Towards the end of the 19th century foreigners, attracted by the climate and planting possibilities, established new gardens combining Italian formal design with an extravagant use of plants from many corners of the world. The most important were the HANBURY GARDENS on the Italian Riviera at Ventimiglia from 1867 onwards and TARANTO established on Lake Maggiore from the 1930s. In Sicily the Whitaker family took advantage of the benign climate to make collections of tender plants in various gardens in Palermo, including MALFITANO. At the same time there was a revival of interest in the Renaissance garden, instigated by English and American writers such Charles PLATT, Edith Wharton, Charles Latham, Sir George SITWELL, and Inigo Triggs towards the turn of the century, followed by Shepherd and Jellicoe's *Italian Gardens of the Renaissance* in 1925. Other foreigners bought old villas and established or restored Renaissance-type gardens such as La PIETRA and GAMBERAIA from the early 1900s. Cecil PINSENT, an English designer, composed new gardens on classical Italian lines for Bernard Berenson at I TATTI, and built the villa and garden at Le BALZE, and the La FOCE garden in southern Tuscany, besides helping restore old gardens. As the countryside became depopulated, with changes in farming methods, wealthy industrialists were able to convert old villas and farmhouses.

Georgina Masson's *Italian Gardens* (1961) remains the most important and serious introduction to Italian garden history, although other scholars such as John Dixon Hunt and Claudia Lazzaro have added immeasurably to our knowledge of Renaissance gardens. After 1950 English designers such as Russell PAGE created private gardens for the Agnelli family near Turin and for Sir William Walton at La MORTELLA. Geoffrey JELLICOE worked from 1984 at Modena on city development. Pietro PORCINAI and Maria PARPAGLIOLO SHEPHARD brought a modern approach to garden design as did the architect Carlo Scarpa (1906–78) in his Garden of Rest (1970) for the industrialist Brion at San Vite di Atavole. Interesting gardens were restored and created by Tommaso Buzzi: La Scarzuola at Montegiove near Terni (1956) being the most famous. Modern landscape architects include Paolo Pejrone, president of the Association of Landscape Architects, who has undertaken projects for the Agnelli family. There are many young landscape architects: Massimo Semola working in the north of Italy, Ermanno Casasco from Sicily who works in Milan and has done a project at the Thermal Park Negombo in Ischia, Giulio Crespi and Patrizia Pozzi also from Milan, to name but a few.

By the middle of the 20th century many of Italy's greatest gardens were under threat from neglect. Others such as Pratolino had long been transformed into English-style parks, the 'garden of miracles' lost for ever. The garden of the 16th-century Palazzo Principe Doria in Genoa, once covering a hillside above the bay, was divided in two by a motorway. The 17th-century Villa Venaria Reale in Turin was derelict. But during the last 50 years there has been a renewed interest in historic gardens and there have been a number of fine restorations, with many privately owned gardens being opened to the public on a fee-paying basis. The Villa Gamberaia, still in private hands after its partial redesign in the early 1900s, has been restored since 1945 and well maintained. Pinsent's Villa Le Balze has been restored by Georgetown University. La Pietra is currently under restoration by New York University. Other individual owners have made some fine restorations. The unique 17th-century Villa BARBARIGO PIZZONI ARDEMANI at Valzanzibio and the 17th-century Villa Cetinale near Siena now belonging to the British Lord Lambton have had a remarkable awakening, restored over 30 years with skill and taste. Private owners have organized themselves into an organization, Grandi Giardini Italiani, to promote visits to their gardens. They also promote an annual design competition for designers, the Premio Martini. The garden of the Villa Della Porta BOZZOLO near Lake Maggiore has been restored by the Fondo per l'Ambiente Italiano (FAI), a private non-profit-making organization that can acquire, by donation, inheritance, or even purchase, properties of historic, artistic, or environmental value to ensure their future conservation. The Villa d'Este at Tivoli was restored during the 1980s. Three Medici gardens in Florence, the villas Castello and Petraia, and the Boboli, have been restored (including the famous grottoes at Castello and Boboli (still under reconstruction)). In Rome the 17th-century Medici garden, owned by the French Academy, is in the process of restoration by Giorgio Galletti, and the *giardini segreti* at Villa BORGHESE were renovated with a historically-based design by Ada Segre. She also planned the restoration of the 16th–17th-century south garden of the Doria Pamphili Palace at Genoa. A few new gardens have been

recently created by foreigners in Renaissance style. The Villa Massei near Lucca, a 16th-century hunting lodge, has an immaculate layout with modern planting. Quite different is the philosopher's garden in pine and oak woods south of Siena, the Ragnaia of San Giovanni. Made by the American painter Craig Sheppard, it is a modern version of the Sacro Bosco at Bomarzo, with a series of inscriptions and quotations from the classics.

During the last 50 years Italian nurseries, with admirable climatic advantages, have developed to supply the rest of Europe and the Mediterranean countries, particularly with evergreen trees and shrubs from large wholesale nurseries near Pistoia in Tuscany and at Chiusi and Tor San Lorenzo south of Rome. Many, such as Barni Roses, Innocenti for irises, Tintori for citrus in pots, have been in business for many years, while new retail nurseries have sprung up to provide perennials and herbs, tropical plants, interesting vegetables, cacti, and water plants. Nurseries such as the Archeologia Arborea Foundation in Città di Castello in Umbria preserve old varieties of fruit, and Susigarden at Aiello (Udine) specializes in old cultivars of perennials and annuals. There are a number of garden shows where plants are displayed by nurseries, including one at Masino near Turin, the Orticola at Milan, the Landriana Fair south of

Rome, and, in autumn, Le Corti near Florence and the Murabilia in Lucca.   PHo

I'tima-ud-Daula ⊛

Agra, India. A tomb garden on the Yamuna river front not far from RAM BAGH. It is a pure CHAHAR BAGH with the mausoleum in the centre resting on a low base. The composition is absolutely symmetrical, as indicated by the four entrance gates from which the causeways branch off, the four pools, one on each side of the tomb, and the four corner towers. The garden may be reached by land via a tree-filled enclosure, once used for horticulture, and on the opposite side by water, where a landing on the river is marked by a pavilion with a false door. There are hardly any trees. The grass parterres enhance the tomb architecture, which, unlike that of HUMAYUN, is on a more intimate scale. The tomb, in the form of a casket, belongs to the Prime Minister of Jahāngīr, father of Nūr Jahān, and is a jewel of bichromatic inlaid stone, in which the motifs of the vine, flowers, and plants (including the famous cypress with climbing flowers) predominate.   AP

S. CROWE and S. HAYWOOD, *The Gardens of Mughul India* (1972).

E. B. MOYNIHAN, *Paradise as a Garden in Persia and Mughal India* (1979).

C. M. VILLIERS STUART. *Gardens of the Great Mughals* (1913).

Jacobsen, Arne

(1902–71), Danish architect and industrial designer known as a leading figure in Nordic functionalism. Besides his architecture, starting with the design of many single houses, he usually created green spaces for his buildings. In 1953 he designed terraced houses, Søholmhusene at Klampenborg near Copenhagen, a model for housing design. Living in one of the end houses he created a highly individual garden. Clipped larch hedges were used to divide the garden into compartments and serve as a backdrop for a varied selection of plants. His concern for integrating the landscape with the building is expressed in the many courtyards at Munkegaard Elementary School (1948–57) in Vangede, Copenhagen. At Danmarks Nationalbank (1965–78) he designed a wide and deep courtyard with concrete columns overgrown with climbing plants, like a temple ruin. Much of his later work was abroad, including St Catherine's College, Oxford (1964) (see OXFORD UNIVERSITY COLLEGE GARDENS), which is remarkable for the unity of landscape and architecture. AL

Jahāngīr

(1569–1627), 4th Mughal Emperor (1605–27), first accompanied his father to Kashmir, and developed a lifetime's attachment to the country. He married, late in life, the Persian Nūr Jahān, and together they became the leading figures in designing the gardens of Kashmir. They created the superb royal gardens there of ACHABAL, SHALAMAR, and VERNAG, which became their summer homes. They visited the country regularly, and the Emperor put in hand the improvement of the roads to Kashmir, building rest houses along the way, some of them with gardens. His courtiers followed his example, and a count in his time recorded 700 gardens along the shores of Lake Dal, producing a considerable income from flowers. All this has vanished, leaving only Shalamar and NISHAT BAGH, the creation of Asaf Khān, together with the later Chasma Shahi.

Jahāngīr travelled widely also in the rest of his empire, for travel was a way of life with the Mughals, and court business was conducted along the way. Great pains were therefore taken over the comfort and luxury of their temporary homes along the route. While in India, the Emperor's time was divided chiefly between Agra, Ajmer, and Lahore, and it is clear from his records that BĀBUR's gardens in Agra were well maintained in his day. Many distinguished minor works are also attributed to him. His wife Nūr Jahān also created great gardens—the Tomb of I'TIMA-UD-DAULA at Agra and the Shahdara at Lahore.

Jahāngīr wrote his own memoirs, the *Tuzuk-i-Jahāngīri* (trans. A. Rogers, ed. H. Beveridge, 1968), which recall those of Bābur in his delight in trees and flowers, and his understanding of nature as a whole. The memoirs give, too, a detailed picture of the times, and of the creation and development of the gardens. The Mughal school of painting, already developed by Akbar through the Persian painters introduced by HUMAYUN, reached its zenith under Jahāngīr, and included superb illustrations of birds, plants, and flowers. SMH

Jakobsen, Preben

(b. 1934), Danish landscape architect. After an early reaction against plants instigated by his family's involvement in the nursery business, Jakobsen began to study horticulture. He worked in a number of well-known nurseries in Denmark, France, and Britain before becoming a student at the ROYAL BOTANIC GARDENS, KEW, where he became interested in landscape design. After returning to Denmark for military service he studied landscape architecture at the Danish Royal Academy of Fine Arts, where he came into contact with teachers who had worked with or been influenced by Alvar AALTO, Le Corbusier, and Frank Lloyd Wright; and particularly with the Danish landscape architect Carl Theodor SØRENSEN. He returned to England to work for the architects Eric Lyons and Ivor Cunningham on the Span housing estates in which he was able to develop his design ideas. In 1969 he left to set up his own practice with his wife Margaret. He has acquired a reputation as a designer of outstanding ability working with equal facility in the manipulation of hard architectural elements and in the use of plants. His contribution to *Design with Plants*, edited by Brian Clouston (1977), is outstanding for his clear analysis of the subject of planting design, on which he has lectured in many institutions. Although the range of his work is wide and varied, his strong belief that landscape architecture is an art form is best expressed in the smaller scales of urban and garden design.

At Hounslow Civic Centre (1977) he divided the site into a series of 'garden' areas of great intricacy and impeccable quality. In a private garden at Stanmore (1977) all items—fences, pergolas, paving, lighting, and plants—are designed and selected with the care and attention to detail which is a characteristic of his approach to design. MLL

Jámbor, Vilmos

(1825–1901), Hungarian landscape gardener. Together with Ármin PECZ Sr., he was the first professional exponent of landscape gardening to be of Hungarian origin. He was born in Somogyhárságy, where his father was gardener to the Pálffy estate. He spent his student years in Pozsony (today Bratislava, Slovakia) and at the Brunswick estate at Alsókorompa (today Dolná Krupá, Slovakia), then in gardens in Vienna, before continuing his studies in Germany, France, and England. He returned to Vienna and became a successful independent landscape architect, before coming back to work in Hungary, first on the Pálffy estate, then, until 1867, on the estate of Count Esterházy at Pápa. It was then that he entered the court of Archduke Joseph Habsburg as head gardener, working on the reconstruction of the parks of ALCSÚT, then MARGITSZIGET, until 1873, before going into retirement in 1876. To celebrate this, and at the Archduke's recommendation, he was awarded a title and an estate at Recsk, where he planted his own garden and tree nursery. He is associated with the design and construction, or remodelling, of the parks of the mansions of Parádfürdő and Parádsasvár, and later those at VÁCRÁTÓT, Tápiógyörgye, Tóalmás, and Nagykároly (today Carei, Romania). His work is typified by a strong, visual animation of the land, the construction of mounds and cliff valleys, and the emphatic use of exotic species. GA

James river plantation gardens,

Virginia, USA. The majestic colonial mansions of tidewater Virginia—Westover, Sherwood Forest, Berkeley, Evelynton, and Shirley—still stand at discreet distances from each other along the James river, handsome legacies of the tastes and accomplishments of Virginia's prominent families. In colonial times the river was the chief highway of commerce and social activity, therefore these houses faced the water, presiding with grace and dignity over the traffic of generations. Stately terraces of mown grass elevated houses above the river, further enhancing their commanding positions as the centre of plantation life. Towering trees created a living green framework against brick and timber, and lined inland driveways. The cultivated garden was usually walled, often off to one side, and complete with decorative iron gates. Westover is considered one of the finest examples of these estates, reflecting the formal garden tradition of contemporary French and Dutch style and arguably influenced by the ornamental gardens at nearby WILLIAMSBURG. Although no garden detail is shown in early drawings of Westover, a plan of 1701 shows three avenues radiating out from the house; in 1705, William Byrd II began improving the property with a collection of American plants, encouraged and influenced by a visit from English plant collector and author Mark CATESBY. Byrd corresponded with and obtained plants from English botanist Peter Collinson and Sir Hans SLOANE. By 1738 John BARTRAM described Westover as having 'new gates, gravel walks, hedges and cedars finely twined and a little green house with two or three orange trees with fruit on them'. Westover's formal gardens were re-established in 1900, with the elaborate tomb of William Byrd I as the centrepiece. Shady tulip poplars (*Liriodendron tulipifera*), more than 150 years old, frame the buildings, and boxwood hedges still enclose the lawns. At Sherwood Forest, the original 17th-century tobacco barn, garden house, milk house, and many other outbuildings comprise one of the few complete and extant plantation yards in America, while at Shirley, a number of superb brick outbuildings, built in 1723, form a Queen Anne forecourt unique in colonial America. They include a large two-storey kitchen, laundry, barns, stable, smokehouse, and dovecote. They are evidence, together with their enclosed flower and kitchen gardens, of the settlers' need for domesticated order and a safe haven in the wilderness around them. These gracious manor houses and their grounds along the James river remain even today in a rural oasis of tidal waters, thick woods, and richly cultivated farmland. Although all privately owned, they are, however, open for visitors to experience and enjoy.   CMR

James Thompson Garden.
See THOMPSON, JAMES, GARDEN.

Jane Platt Garden.
See PLATT, JANE, GARDEN.

Japan

is an archipelago consisting of four large islands and many smaller ones that stretch in a north-east-south-west arc off the east coast of China. There are several factors regarding Japan's geography and geology that have affected its gardening culture, the first of which is its elongated, north-south disposition. The entire landmass of Japan is only a little bigger than Germany, or a little smaller than the state of California, but the extremes of latitude of the central isles are great, spanning from approximately 46 degrees in the north to 31 degrees in the south. This compares roughly to the span between Montréal, Canada, and Jacksonville, Florida, USA, or that between Milan, Italy, and the southern end of Tunisia in northern Africa. This north–south orientation results in a wide variety of ecological zones that would most likely not be found if the country covered the same territory on an east–west axis.

Another important geographic factor is Japan's location in the Pacific Ocean, within the Japan Current, or Kuroshio (Japanese; Black Current), that flows northward from the Philippine Sea and surrounds the archipelago. That warm ocean current, and warm air associated with it, ameliorate Japan's climate, making it far more temperate than it would otherwise be. The current also increases the regularity and quantity of precipitation on the islands which ranges between 50 cm/20 in and 4 m/160 in per annum but averages 1–2 m/40–80 in. All of the above factors have led to the development of a diverse flora that is adapted to the various ecological zones that exist on the islands and that is succoured by the plentiful supply of water.

Plants

The diversity of Japan's flora is attested by the large number of horticultural plants now used around the world with the species names *japonica* and *japonicus*. Japanese plants have greatly influenced gardens in other parts of the world. Japanese gardens, in contrast, have been primarily created with native species. A few notable exceptions to this are plums (*Prunus mume* Siebold & Zuccarini, *Prunus salicina*, *Prunus armeniaca* var. *ansu* Maximowicz) and some bamboos (*Phyllostachys nigra*, *Phyllostachys aurea* Rivière & C. Rivière, *Sinobambusa tootsik*) which were native to China, and weeping willow (*Salix babylonica*) which was introduced via Korea. All of these have been used in gardens since ancient times. More recent introductions from North America and Europe that have become especially popular include the

flowering dogwood (*Cornus florida*) and many varieties of lawn grasses that stay green through the winter months unlike the native Japanese grass (*Zoysia japonica*).

The varieties of plants most typically used in gardens are called *niwaki* (garden plants) as opposed to *zōki* (miscellaneous plants). Most traditional garden designers use the relatively limited palette of *niwaki* to create the structure of a garden and it can be correctly said that the collection and display of a wide variety of diverse plant materials is not the focus of Japanese gardening. Although there is a recent movement by some garden designers purposefully to use *zōki* in their designs to create a more 'natural' feeling, most traditional garden designers still rely primarily on the rarefied *niwaki* palette. The plants used most commonly in Japanese gardens today include: Japanese black pine (*Pinus thunbergii*), Japanese red pine (*Pinus densiflora*), Japanese cedar (*Cryptomeria japonica*), camellias including sasanqua (*Camellia sasanqua*) and many other flowering varieties (*Camellia japonica* cvs.), Japanese evergreen oaks (*Quercus glauca*, *Quercus myrsinifolia*), gardenia (*Gardenia jasminoides*), sweet osmanthus (*Osmanthus fragrans*), Japanese maple (*Acer palmatum*), plum (*Prunus mume* and others), Yoshino flowering cherry (*Prunus × yedoensis* 'Yedoensis'), Japanese aucuba (*Aucuba japonica*), Japanese andromeda (*Pieris japonica*), winter daphne (*Daphne odora*), Japanese enkianthus (*Enkianthus perulatus*), and Satsuki azalea (*Rhododendron indicum*).

The geology of the Japanese archipelago also has played a key role in the development of the gardens. Japan lies on the eastern edge of the Eurasian tectonic plate just where it meets the Pacific and Philippine plates. The volcanic activity and crustal uplift resulting from the latter two plates being constantly forced under the Eurasian plate has created the islands themselves and given Japan the steep mountains and narrow river valleys that are characteristic of its landscape.

These geological and geographical features deeply influenced how Japanese gardens developed. In a broad sense, they formed the underpinnings of all aspects of Japanese culture—social, technological, and spiritual—that formed the larger cultural context within which gardens were developed, but in a more specific sense, images of nature as it exists in Japan became the palette that garden designers worked with so that mountains and narrow valleys, quick streams and waterfalls, islands rising from the sea, and windswept rocky shorelines became the standard motifs found in the gardens. Likewise, the changing seasons became a focal point of Japanese culture—for instance, the favoured motif of poetry—and as gardens developed, they were specifically designed to take advantage of that fluid aspect of nature as found in Japan.

The ancient religion of Japan, now known as Shinto or the Way of the Gods, is fundamentally a 'nature religion'. The gods, *kami*, are believed to inhabit higher planes (such as the tops of mountains) but can be drawn into the world of man through exceptional natural objects such as ponds (*kami ike*), boulders (*iwakura*), and trees (*shinboku*). The belief that seemingly ordinary aspects of the natural world are sacred became a fundamental aspect of Japanese culture that would later be revealed in garden design. In addition, although ancient Japanese sacred spaces were not highly designed or manipulated, certain specific aspects of those spaces—their simplicity and the importance given to ponds, stones, and irregularly shaped, ancient trees—can also be seen in the design of the gardens of later eras.

Early beginnings—4th to 8th century AD

During the Kofun period (300–552), several clans in the Yamato region (present-day Nara prefecture) vied for superiority and formed the foundation for what would later become the imperial and aristocratic lineages. The period is named for the large burial mounds of clan leaders, which give evidence of the ability of the peoples of that time to restructure the landscape—the largest *kofun* rivalling the pyramids of Egypt in size. There are written records from the early to mid 5th century that mention boating parties and Winding Stream Festivals (*kyokusui no en*), implying that the Japanese elite were aware of Sino-Korean garden culture. The earliest archaeological evidence of sites that were clearly manipulated into garden-like spaces comes from this period; for instance, a stone-lined artificial river discovered at Jō no Koshi in Mie prefecture. There is debate over whether this archaeological finding, which resembles the rivers in gardens of later periods, is actually the remains of a garden, or whether it represents a religious site or simply a functional waterway.

The following Asuka period (552–710) was marked by the active importation of Sino-Korean culture by the dominant Japanese clans in an attempt to organize their developing social structure. The first capital city of Japan, Fujiwara-kyō, was built in what is now Nara prefecture, and to accomplish that task, information, goods, and skilled craftsmen were sought from the kingdoms of Korea, in particular Paekché. That culture included writing, religion (Buddhism), textile and metal technology, architecture, and the art of gardening. A record for the year 612 in the *Nihon shoki* (Chronicles of Ancient Japan) mentions a

craftsman from Paekché, called Michiko no Takumi in Japanese, who built an image of the sacred Buddhist mountain, Shumisen (Sanskrit: Sumeru), in the garden of Empress Suiko.

At that point in time, it was primarily the foreign artisans and scholars who had the knowledge and skills required to develop gardens, and the remains of gardens from this period have strong similarities to those that have been unearthed from similar periods in Korean history, such as the pond garden at Anapji, in Kyongju. Various sites in the Asuka district of Nara prefecture have been excavated in Japan since the 1950s including some small pebble-lined streams, several carved stones which were either used as water features in gardens or for rituals involving flowing water or *sake* (rice wine), and a large pond garden.

In the following Nara period (710–84), a new capital was established called Heijō-kyō (present-day Nara city). Aristocratic families became formally established and, accordingly, the palaces and entertainment villas they built became more elaborate and well developed. The people for whom those gardens were built, having become more accustomed to the techniques and aesthetics of garden design, were able to design their own gardens, rather than rely on foreign artisans or scholars for that service. From what can be discerned from excavations of gardens from this period, they express a softer design sense than those of the previous era. The shorelines of the ponds, for instance, are not reinforced with rigid stone walls (as in the ponds of Asuka and Anapji) but have gently shaped, pebbled beaches. Two such examples, both of which have been recently reconstructed, are the TŌIN and Heijōkyō Kyūseki gardens.

The golden age of aristocratic gardens—8th to 12th century AD

The Heian period (794–1185), named after the great capital city Heian-kyō (present-day Kyoto), represents the apotheosis, and then disintegration, of the aristocratic class as governors of society (from 784 to 794 there was a brief, ill-fated capital situated at Nagaoka). The gardens of this time became highly developed, were requisite elements of any aristocratic residence, and were often the locus for formal gatherings—anything from performances of court dance to raucous cockfights. We know about the gardens through extensive archaeological work, historical scroll paintings, and numerous records in the daily journals of courtiers that reveal the gardens through casual comments. One record that specifically addresses garden

building is the SAKUTEIKI (Records of Garden Making).

The shape of the Heian capital was a simple rectangle, as were the individual properties assigned to aristocrats, each ranging from 0.3 to 1.4 hectares/0.7–3.4 acres in size. In a typical residence, wooden halls attached to each other by roofed corridors were situated in the central and northern portions of the property. To the south of those lay a flat, sand-covered court used for formal gatherings, and further to the south was a garden. The gardens usually had a pond as a central feature, as well as streams, hillocks, and a variety of plantings. Unlike the gardens from the medieval period onward, which are known for their rarefied palette, gardens in the Heian period included a variety of flora, such as wildflowers, grasses, and vines.

Gardens were also built outside the confines of the capital city, some in the surrounding areas where aristocrats had country villas and others in outlying provinces at the residences of the lords who acted as governors. Gardens were also built at Buddhist temples, especially those that enshrined Amida *nyorai* (Buddha of Infinite Light, Amitabha). Amida was believed to preside over a western paradise (*saihō jōdō*) and to evoke this image, gardens were built with an Amida hall situated on the west side of a pond. These gardens are now called Pure Land gardens (*jōdō teien*), extant or reconstructed examples of which include BYŌDŌIN, JŌRURI-JI, and MŌTSUJI.

The people for whom gardens were built were, at times, also the designers of the gardens. More likely, other members of the aristocratic society helped them in their work, perhaps those of somewhat lower rank, who had an affinity for such things. In addition, there was a group of Buddhist priests who began to design and build gardens, not as a profession (for no such profession would exist for centuries to come) but as part of their religious work and their position in society. A euphemism for gardening in the Heian period was 'setting stones' and the priests who did that sort of service were known as 'stone setting priests' (*ishi tate sō*).

Warrior elite and Zen Buddhism—12th to 16th century

The Kamakura period (1185–1333) begins with the foundation of a military government in the northern city of Kamakura (near Tokyo) and represents the completion of a long shift away from aristocratic rule to the rule of the warrior class (*bushi*). It was also the age when the Zen sect of Buddhism, due to the active patronage of the warrior elite, became a strong cultural force in Japan. Zen Buddhism focuses on meditation as the means toward its goal of enlightenment, unlike other sects of Buddhism that focus on prayers to higher deities. The teachings of Zen Buddhism were being introduced from China (then in the Southern Sung (1127–1279) and Yuan (1271–1368) periods) by émigré Chinese priests as well as Japanese priests who travelled to China, studied, and returned. Along with Buddhist teachings, the general culture of the Chinese people of those eras was also introduced to Japan, including ink landscape painting, the art of tray landscapes, and formalized drinking of tea, all of which would eventually have an influence on garden design. These changes, however, were not immediate and the gardens that exhibit their influence do not appear until the following Muromachi period (1333–1568). Kamakura-period aristocrats still made gardens in the manner of the Heian period, and the newly established warrior elite, in an attempt to emulate the aristocrats, made their residences in a similar style. Another example of the continuation of earlier cultural forms is Pure Land gardens (*jōdō teien*) in temples, such as the one built at SHŌMYŌJI at the end of the Kamakura period.

The Muromachi period begins when the military government in Kamakura moves its seat of power to the Muromachi district in Kyoto (formerly called Heian-kyō). Muromachi-period society was marked by a hitherto unseen mixing of social classes and it was the vitality of that mixing that gave rise to many of the arts of the period, including Noh theatre, *renga* poetry, flower arrangement (*ikebana*), tea ceremony (*chanoyu*), and dry landscape gardens (KARESANSUI). The classes mixing in Kyoto included military lords, aristocrats, Zen Buddhist priests, and wealthy merchants. To generalize the contributions of the various groups, the military lords were often the patrons and set the rigorous tone of the age; the aristocrats, being the bastions of traditional culture, injected a sense of refinement; the Zen Buddhist priests were the primary connection to China and its religious and literati culture; the merchants, who were just beginning to develop standing as a social class, often financed voyages to China and shared in the collecting and display of Chinese and Japanese artwork. The gardens of those four groups, however, developed somewhat separately.

The gardens of the aristocrats continued, for the most part, to be developed in the tradition of the previous eras. A gardening text reputed to have been written in this era, *Sansui narabi ni yakeizu* (Illustrations of Mountain, Water, and Field Landscapes), exemplifies this remaining interest in traditional gardening techniques. The treatise covers themes such as geomantic principles and gives comments on the use of stones, ponds, and plants.

The military lords, in their residences in the city of Kyoto as well as, to some degree, at their residences in their home provinces, built gardens that included many of the features of the older gardens—such as central ponds and waterfalls—but began to limit the palette of materials used, especially of plants, to create gardens of greater control. The development of metal tools meant that pruning could be done with greater efficiency and accuracy, prompting an increase in the degree to which gardeners controlled garden flora. The rockwork in those gardens—along the shores of ponds, in waterfalls, and in free-standing groupings—was given particular attention and became one of the salient features indicative of gardens of that age. Extant examples of this sort of rockwork can be found at KINKAKUJI and GINKAKUJI, both estates of shoguns (chief military lords) within Kyoto, as well as in the garden remains at the provincial estates of lords ASAKURA in Fukui prefecture and KITABATAKE in Mie prefecture.

Zen Buddhist priests developed a novel form of garden during this period that has become a hallmark of Japanese design simplicity, namely the *karesansui* or dry landscape garden. The beginnings of this development can be found in the late Kamakura and early Muromachi periods in the application of symbolic Buddhist imagery and names to rockwork at gardens such as SAIHŌJI and TENRYŪJI, and it culminates in the refined, painterly expressions found in the strictly confined courtyard *karesansui* such as that at DAISENIN.

The Buddhist mountain Shumisen continued to be used as a garden motif as did Mount Hōrai (Chinese: Penglai), a theme drawn from Chinese legend of a mountain-island populated by Immortals, cranes, and tortoises. These images were included in gardens as a symbolic request for the longevity of those associated with the garden.

The names connected with garden design during the Kamakura and Muromachi periods include the owners of the various gardens, whether aristocrat or warrior elite, as well as the aforementioned 'stone setting priests', and also include a new class of gardener—the 'river bank people' (*kawaramono*). Due to pestilence and periodic flooding, the banks of the rivers were considered the least desirable places to live; those who lived there were considered social outcasts and forced to do lowly work such as slaughtering and earthwork. Doing the latter also gave these social outcasts skills required in garden making and, over time, some among them developed reputations as skilled gardeners, eventually to the extent where they were invited to build gardens for the shogun and emperor. These men had the appellation 'garden' (*senzui*) added to their class title and became known as *senzui kawaramono*.

Tea and stroll gardens—16th to 19th century
The Momoyama period (1568–1600) was only 32 years long but is noted for the particular quality of the arts at the time often referred to as 'Japanese baroque' because of their overt, stylized aesthetic. Control over the nation was being consolidated by a succession of military lords through a series of civil wars and, in light of the scale of the brazen push for complete dominance, the fact that this overt, lavish aesthetic appeared at this time is understandable. With regard to garden design, this aesthetic was revealed in the use of certain exotic plants, such as sago palm (*Cycas revoluta*) and the use of unusual flat-topped or blue-coloured stones in great numbers as seen at SANBŌIN and the NISHIHONGANJI Taimensho Garden. To some degree this taste continued into the following Edo period (1600–1868) as exemplified in the garden at NIJŌJŌ.

At the same time that opulence was being played out in full, a counter-movement was also under way, focused on the appreciation of subtlety, meagreness, and rustic simplicity; a movement championed by those artists who were developing the tea ceremony (*chanoyu*). The formal service of powdered green tea (mixed with hot water and whisked to a froth in a ceramic bowl) had originally been developed in Chinese temples of the Zen sect and was introduced to Japan during the Kamakura period. By the end of the Muromachi period, the service of this tea had become associated with tea-tasting contests (*tōcha*); large gatherings where contestants attempted to discern tea types and the host provided a display of collected artwork and plenty of food and alcohol. Taking a hint from the intimate gatherings of linked-verse (*renga*) poets, and the aesthetic of meagreness they pursued, which they called 'chill' (*hie*), the early tea ceremony masters developed a new, subdued form of tea gathering called 'rustic tea' (*wabi cha*).

Whereas the tea competitions had taken place in formal halls built expressly for large gatherings (*kaisho*), the setting for the rustic tea was a small, thatch-roofed hut (*sōan*). Everything about the rustic tea gathering was subdued—the architecture, the utensils used, the artwork displayed—and in order to prepare for the gathering, physically as well as inwardly, an entry garden was created. The garden, called a *roji*, which has the various meanings of 'alleyway', 'dewy ground', and 'sacred ground', simulated the sensory qualities of a journey out of town to a hermit's hut in the mountains but did so in the narrow space between outer gate and tea house. Plantings were primarily broadleaf evergreens or conifers; flowers were shunned, as were ornamental rocks. A water basin was provided for the purpose of cleansing one's hands and mouth, and a small waiting bench was situated midway through the garden to allow guests to sit and commune with the garden while they waited to be called forward by their host. The tea gardens would develop in formality and size over the next centuries but still maintain the same basic intent.

The most famous, historical tea gardens are still in the possession of the families descended from the original tea masters, for instance Konnichian (of the Urasenke family), Fushinan (of the Omotesenke family), and Kankyūan (of the Mushanokoji senke family), all descendants of Sen no Rikyū (1522–91). Some, however, are open to the public, for instance Joan, Aichi prefecture; Kōtōin, Kyoto city; Nishida Residence, Ishikawa prefecture; and Shōkadō, Kyoto prefecture.

In the Edo period two forms of garden developed that are particularly noteworthy: the stroll garden and the *tsubo* garden. The former is associated with the provincial lords (*daimyō*) and the latter with the townsfolk (*chōnin*) of Japan's great cities. The Edo period was a time of relative peace throughout the country that was maintained through strict control over the provinces by the central military government in Edo (present-day Tokyo). In order to bolster this hierarchical structure, classicist thought (which forwarded traditional Japanese culture) and Confucianist thought (which promulgated an ordered, hierarchical society) were promoted by the government. With regard to gardens, the state of relative peace meant that gardens could be fine tuned, and enlarged, by successive generations, setting the foundation for the expansive stroll gardens we find in that period. The cultural focus on tradition also informed the gardens to some degree as designers began to include images in the garden that were drawn from classic Japanese or Chinese texts.

Provincial lords were often owners of several stroll gardens: one built at their residences in their home provinces and also one each at the residences they were required to keep in Edo (often three or more). The gardens of minor lords were not extensive and may have comprised no more than a well-developed tea garden, so not all *daimyō* gardens were stroll gardens. The gardens of the more powerful lords, however, were large and featured a central pond that was circumambulated by a path that took the stroller through a series of carefully developed scenes that were laid out along the path. The themes of the scenes was varied, including famous landscapes of Japan and

China, images from classical poetry, images related to Confucian thought, and amusing scenes such as fake country villages complete with gift stores and wine shops. The central pond, and large areas of lawn, created an expansive atmosphere not found in earlier Japanese gardens. Some of the most famous, extant examples (which were turned into prefectural parks in the late 19th century) are KENROKUEN, KOISHIKAWA KŌRAKUEN, KŌRAKUEN, RIKUGIEN, RITSURIN PARK, and SUIZENJI.

The townsfolk, too, were building gardens during the Edo period, especially the wealthy merchants (*shōnin*). Their residences in dense urban centres were typically designed with a shop along the street (*omoteya*), a residence behind the shop, and storehouses further back on the lot. In the tightly confined spaces between the three architectural units, viewing gardens were developed based on the aesthetics and design motifs of tea gardens. These gardens are known as *tsubo* (courtyard) gardens or *senzai* (plantings), both of which are terms used by Heian-period aristocrats, revealing the townsfolk's desire for cultural acquisition.

The aristocrats, too, continued to build gardens. The finances of that class, however, were strictly controlled by the government so it was only the upper echelon (retired emperors and imperial princes) that could build gardens of any size. KATSURA DETACHED PALACE, SENTŌ GOSHO, and SHŪGAKUIN Detached Palace are all excellent examples. The garden at ENTSŪJI temple may also be considered in this category if the theory that it was created when the building was an imperial villa (before it was a temple) is accepted. In addition, many other temples and residences had gardens built during the Edo period that do not fit the category of stroll or *tsubo* garden. These include the borrowed scenery (SHAKKEI) garden at Jikōin, the *karesansui* gardens at Konchiin, and the KATSURA residence in Yamaguchi prefecture.

The designers of gardens in the Edo period include the owners of gardens, whether provincial lord, aristocrat, or merchant, but no longer include the *senzui kawaramono* of medieval times. Instead we find a new kind of designer, the professional gardener (*uekiya*). By the mid to late Edo period, the profession of gardening had developed to the point where it resembled that of modern times: raising, hybridizing, and selling plants; dealing in garden stones and garden ornaments; building and designing gardens. Horticultural varieties of certain plants became a great interest among the general populace of urban centres, often displayed in the form of potted plants (*hachi no ki*) including camellia, chrysanthemum (*Dendrathema grandiflora*), morning glory

(*Ipomoea nil*), and iris (*Iris ensata*). With the development of woodblock printing and papermaking techniques, gardening manuals became popular as did guides to famous gardens. *Tsukiyama teizōden* and *Tsukiyama sansuiden* (both translate as Instructions on Making Hills and Gardens) are the two well-known examples of the former and *Miyako rinsen meisho zue* (Illustrations of Famous Gardens around the Capital) an example of the latter.

Modern times—19th century to the present day
The Meiji period (1868–1912) ushered in a new age. Emperor Meiji was installed as head of state, the system of military lords was abolished, and, in a wave of ultra-conservative Shinto thought, Buddhist temples were suppressed or destroyed; the gardens they held, of course, were also lost. In 1852 the US Admiral Matthew Perry in command of the East India Squadron was given the task of opening up isolationist Japan. Perry forced Japan to open its ports to trade and Western culture and technologies became the new focus of Japanese society. The old expression Wakan Kansai (Japanese Spirit, Chinese Genius) was replaced by Wakan Yōsai (Japanese Spirit, Western Genius), in other words, keeping Japanese culture but importing Western technology. Residential architecture and gardens reflected this dichotomy in their design with, for instance, a Western-style hall attached to, but not integral with, a Japanese-style residence, or a lawn area for Western garden parties tucked behind a larger Japanese garden. The FURUKAWA residence in Tokyo exemplifies this separation with its rose garden on the hilltop and Japanese pond garden down below.

Other gardens built during the Meiji period more successfully blended the new with the old, such as the gardens at the HEIAN Shrine and at MURINAN, which reveal a light, open quality that seems at once modern and yet is clearly still within the tradition of Japanese gardens. Still other Meiji-period gardens, such as ISUIEN, were designed completely within the Japanese tradition and do not reflect the massive changes in society that were happening at that time.

Another Western concept which was imported during the Meiji period was that of public parks, which were developed, initially, by converting four types of existing lands into designated areas for public access: temples and shrines (Ueno Park, Tokyo; Maruyama Park, Kyoto), castles (Himeji, Hyōgo prefecture; Matsuyama, Matsuyama prefecture), *daimyō* stroll gardens (Kenrokuen, RIKUGIEN), and, finally, traditional scenic areas that were not previously delineated but, as public property, were given formal structure (Matsushima,

Miyagi prefecture; Amanohashidate, Kyoto prefecture).

The dismantling of the military class and suppression of Buddhism in the Meiji period meant that provincial lords and Buddhist priests were no longer among those designing or requesting new gardens. The garden makers of this era were the newly ascendant aristocracy and wealthy industrialists. Although newly founded universities trained architects and engineers, landscape architecture did not develop at that time as a separate profession and gardeners continued to work in a traditional manner, training by apprenticeship.

The following Taishō period (1912–26) was a brief period that developed its own romantic design style, Western in its foundation but fully tempered by Japanese taste. The vast collector's paradise SANKEIEN, and the lovely artist's residence HAKUSASONSŌ, were products of this period.

The greatest changes, with regard to gardens, in the Shōwa (1926–89) and Heisei (1989–   ) periods happened after the Second World War. To some degree, the traditional manner of garden building and of training gardeners through apprenticeship still continues through to today, but the numbers of people involved in that work as professionals, or requesting traditional gardens as clients, has greatly reduced. In recent years (the 1990s) English-style gardening has undergone a boom in Japan and the English word *gardening* has become part of the Japanese language. It refers, however, not to Japanese gardens but to Western-style gardens or horticulture, especially the do-it-yourself aspect of gardening that was not a part of social-elite culture in the past but is an element of popular gardening culture now. Large, warehouse-like garden centres, which are now appearing all over the country, support that culture by marketing do-it-yourself gardening products.

Although there are many excellent large-scale wholesale nurseries in Japan that produce uniformly sized, catalogued plants, as do their counterparts in America or Europe, the stockyard of traditional Japanese gardeners is utterly different. The plants, which are each individual in shape and size, are not laid out in rows but fitted together as space allows. Neither are they priced, tagged, or catalogued; the whole resembling an antique shop more than a supermarket. Each gardener comes in, selects what he needs, and arranges the details of the purchase with the proprietor, perhaps over a cup of tea and a cigarette.

Some gardens have been designed in recent years that are neither traditional works nor copies of Western styles. These have primarily been the work of artists or other individuals who were not trained as gardeners, including sculptors Isamu NOGUCHI (Dōmon Ken Museum, Sakata), Asakura Fumio (Asakura Sculpture Museum, Tokyo), and Nagare Masayuki (Canadian Embassy rooftop, Tokyo), Buddhist priest Fukaya Kōki (Keio Plaza Hotel in Tokyo), and architect Hasegawa Itsuko (Shonandai Culture Centre, Shonandai), all of whom have created novel forms of gardens, often heavily influenced by the *karesansui* style. Two modern designers who were also garden researchers are Nakane Kinsaku and Shigemori Mirei, and some exemplary designers of recent years are Ogata Kenzō (Showa Kinen Park, Tokyo), Araki Yoshikuni (Mitsui Insurance Co. Headquarters, Tokyo), and Nakajima Ken (Japanese garden at the Montréal Botanic Garden).

Education has also changed; Japanese universities now offer training in horticulture and landscape architecture but the graduates of those courses are not likely to be engaged in Japanese garden design, least of all design of gardens in the traditional manner, which is still done primarily by traditional gardeners trained under a system of apprenticeship. Research on Japanese gardens, which for all intents and purposes did not exist before the Meiji era, has developed to a very high degree, and there are at least three academic societies and many research centres focused on historical research, garden archaeology, and garden restoration.

MPK

Japanese garden.

The word japonaiserie, the Japanese counterpart of CHINOISERIE, is first recorded in English use in 1896, the heyday of Western interest in Japan. In S. R. Crockett's *Cleg Kelly* an alcove is described as 'cobwebbed with the latest artistic Japonaiseries of the period'. With the end of the Edo dynasty in 1868 Japan gradually became accessible to the West and an intense interest in Japanese culture was aroused. Japanese art was fashionable in the 19th century, especially among the French impressionist painters, who were particularly interested in Japanese graphic art, especially woodcuts. Monet collected Japanese prints, and they may still be seen at his house at GIVERNY, and in his garden he made an arched bridge of Japanese style. The idea of the Japanese garden exerted a powerful influence on the horticultural imagination in the latter part of the 19th century and in the early years of the 20th century. The world of Japan was largely closed to the West with rare contacts such as those with Portugal in the 16th century and with the Netherlands in the 17th century. There are no Japanese gardens in Portugal although the Portuguese were probably the first in Europe to cultivate *Camellia japonica*, of which ancient specimens may still be seen in Portuguese gardens. Nor were Japanese gardens especially fashionable in the Netherlands and only one example may be seen today, at CLINGENDAEL. The Baroness van Brienen visited Japan in 1895 and collected garden ornaments, statuary, and snow lanterns, much of it of very high quality, with which to embellish a Japanese garden at Clingendael. She also brought from Japan a tea house, a red-painted bridge, and a collection of rocks. The garden survives today and its exceptional interest is an extraordinary moss garden in which 50 species are disposed in sweeping patterns of subtly varying colour and texture. It is impeccably cared for—the delicate hand weeding was in recent times done by patients from a nearby psychiatric hospital who found the atmosphere of the garden therapeutic.

In England in the early years of the 20th century there was a craze for Japanese gardens. Several firms in London met the demand. By the 1920s the firm of Pulham & Son (see PULHAM, JAMES) constructed Japanese gardens, Liberty's of Regent Street sold model miniatures of them, and J. Suzuki, a professor of Soami School, set up in Oxford Street as a designer of Japanese gardens. Smart country house gardens laid out Japanese gardens often in quintessentially English settings. At Batsford (Gloucestershire) A. B. Freeman-Mitford, who had been a diplomat in Japan, published *The Bamboo Garden* (1896) and laid out a Japanese garden rich in bamboos with a Japanese rest house, a figure of Buddha, and a Foo Dog (the sacred oriental temple dog). Another English diplomat who had been posted to Japan, the Hon. Louis Greville, in 1901 had a Japanese garden on the banks of the river Avon at his estate of HEALE HOUSE in Wiltshire. Among the bulrushes and ferns a tea house was built over a stream which was spanned by a graceful orange-red bridge. In France a curious Japanese garden was made after 1905 at the Villa Ephrussi de ROTHSCHILD with a ceramic garden house. An exceptionally good example was that made on the edge of Paris for for the banker Albert Kahn between 1895 and 1910—it survives today in slightly dishevelled state. In Eastern Europe Japanese gardens were made in Romania at KOLOZSVÁR after 1919 and in Bulgaria in KING BORIS'S GARDEN after 1934. The JAPANESE GARDEN at Wrocław in Poland is a fine example. A rare example in Scandinavia is a bizarre hybrid, the Swedish/Japanese garden designed by Sven-Ingvar ANDERSSON at Ronneby Brunspark in 1987.

In North America by the late 1890s there was a great fashion for Japanese gardens. In California Henry Huntington (in what is now

the HUNTINGTON LIBRARY AND BOTANICAL GARDENS) in 1912 made an early example which survives. Others may be seen in Washington State at the CHASE GARDEN and in Colorado at the DENVER BOTANIC GARDENS. At LOTUSLAND in Santa Barbara, California, a late example may be seen dating from after the Second World War. In Canada the Nitobe Memorial Garden in the University of BRITISH COLUMBIA Botanic Garden in Vancouver is considered to be among the finest examples outside Japan. Also in Canada is a Japanese garden of exceptional beauty at Les QUATRE VENTS where, with superb buildings made by a Japanese craftsman for the site, it is integrated into the magnificent natural setting of a wooded (and finely planted) ravine.
PT

Japanese Garden ✿

Wrocław, Silesia, Poland, located in the centre of Szczytnicki Park, once a part of the Garden Exhibition (1913) containing reconstructed European historical gardens and contemporary layouts designed by gardeners and landscape architects. These were partly removed after the exhibition. Founded by Count Friedrich Maximilian von Hochberg, a oriental art collector and connoisseur, German ambassador in Japan, the garden was laid out by the Count, his gardener Josef Anlauf (1870–1944), and a Japanese designer, Minkichi Arai. It was modelled on the Japanese garden in Hochberg's Iłowa estate (Lubuskie Voivodeship province), 1905. The original composition imitated woodlands surrounding a heated pool with a cascade. The garden was renovated between 1994 and 1997 by Ikuya Nishikawa and Yoshiki Takamara. But it was damaged during the 1997 flood and reconstructed 1997–9. The current composition combines a stroll garden (see JAPAN) with the Japanese tea garden (see JAPAN). The main elements are a pond with an island, two cascades (female and male), a bridge, a view pavilion, and a tea pavilion. A water garden and a stone garden complete the composition. IB

jardin anglais.

The English garden, also referred to as a *jardin à l'anglaise*, has been an object of much interest, and occasional derision, to the French (see AESTHETICS OF THE GARDEN). It is the 18th-century landscape garden which they found to be especially attractive. This informal, irregular kind of garden, so radically different from the *jardin à la française* with its sublime symmetry, deeply intrigued the French. A garden such as ERMENONVILLE is as close as any garden in France gets to the essence of the English landscape style. French gardeners were reluctant to believe that the English were capable of devising anything so original as

the landscape garden and came up with the idea that it was, at least in part, a Chinese invention. Thus was born the term *jardin anglo-chinois* which is still widely used among French garden historians to denote the 18th-century English landscape garden. English lawns have long been regarded with fascination, and often admiration, in France (see LAWN). The BOULINGRIN, a Gallicization of bowling green, was well established in France by the early 18th century. In the *parterre à l'anglaise* the French and English garden traditions seem to achieve a state of happy concord. This was a parterre whose pattern was formed by shapes of trimmed turf. A BOSQUET *à l'anglaise* was a *bosquet* which was turfed and overlooked by a bench. The picturesque tradition of gardening in France, which reached its apotheosis in the late 18th century with gardens such as the Folie SAINT-JAMES and MAUPERTHUIS, undoubtedly owed much to the English relish for sometimes exotic garden buildings. At first a distinctly aristocratic taste in the 19th century, it had a renaissance among the bourgeoisie. At the same time a supposedly English-style park became common in France, consisting of an open space planted with groves and groups of often exotic trees. Much later, at the end of the 19th century, there was a slight interest in Gertrude JEKYLL who worked on only one garden in France, at Le Bois des MOUTIERS. In Italy the *giardino inglese* of romantic informality, such as that at the Palazzo CORSINI, is found in gardens from the 19th century.   PT

jardin anglo-chinois.

See JARDIN ANGLAIS.

Jardin Atlantique.

See PARIS PARKS AND GARDENS.

Jardin des Plantes, Montpellier ✿

Hérault, France, the first botanic garden in France and among the earliest in Europe, founded in 1593 at the instigation of Henri IV to grow herbal plants for the Faculté de Médecine. Its first director was Pierre Richer de Belleval, a botanist who founded the HERBARIUM (which today has 4,000,000 specimens, the second largest in France) with a collection of plants native to the Languedoc. Among later directors were Pierre Magnol (1638–1715), after whom Linnaeus named the genus *Magnolia*, and Pierre Broussonet (1761–1807) whose name was given to the paper mulberry, *Broussonetia papyrifera*. At the heart of a very large wine-growing area, Montpellier was particularly involved with viticulture. It was Professor Planchon of Montpellier who first identified *Phylloxera vastatrix*, which decimated French vineyards in the 1860s. The garden was influential in the

distribution of grapevines to the New World, in particular to South Africa, Australia, and the Americas. James Busby, the father of Australian wine-growing, assembled 300 varieties of grapevines at Montpellier, part of the consignment of 570 varieties he took to Australia in 1833. The garden today has a collection of around 3,000 hardy plants and 2,000 tender species housed in tropical and temperate glasshouses. It has suffered from underfunding and neglect in recent years and was closed to the public in 2001 but by 2004 was partly accessible once again. The grounds, with an area of 4 hectares/10 acres, are attractive with a distinguished orangery (1804, by Claude Matthieu Delargadette) and a statue celebrating François Rabelais, an unexpected alumnus of the medical school in 1530.   PT

Jardin des Plantes, Paris.

See PARIS PARKS AND GARDENS.

Jardin Dumaine.

See DUMAINE, JARDIN.

Jardins de Métis.

See MÉTIS, LES JARDINS DE.

Jasov Monastery Garden (Hungarian: Jászó) ✿

near Košice, south-eastern Slovakia, is the only garden surviving structurally more or less intact from the baroque period in present-day Slovakia. The complex of the Premonstratensian monastery was built between 1745 and 1765 to the plans of Viennese architect Franz Anton Pilgram who was also the designer of the garden. The 200-m/ 640-ft long axis of the rectangular garden terminates in a great orangery the trees from which were originally placed in the parterre which lies before it. In the late 19th century new patterns were created within the quadrangular compartments and exotic trees were planted. The now overgrown yew cones, box hedges, and deciduous ALLÉES create a unique atmosphere in this small 1.6-hectare/4-acre garden. GA

GEYZA STEINHÜBEL, *Slovenské parky a záhrady* (Slovakian Parks and Gardens) (1990).

Jefferson, Thomas

(1743–1826), American statesman who became the third President of the USA. He was also a remarkably cultivated man, designing his own house at MONTICELLO and also some of the buildings of the University of Virginia at Charlottesville. Throughout his adult life he was keenly devoted to gardening, from both a practical horticultural as well as an aesthetic point of view. He kept a garden notebook from the age of 23 until two years before his death in which he listed plants, commented on the rotation of crops, noted the weather and the best way of clipping hedges, and recorded his first crop of peas which became an annual obsession. The vegetable garden at Monticello (overlooked by an elegant pavilion from which he could survey his estate) was a special focus of his gardening interest. On his travels to England in 1786 he was guided by Thomas WHATELEY's *Observations on Modern Gardening* (1770)—noting that 'While his descriptions, in point of style, are models of perfect elegance and classical correctness, they are as remarkable for their exactness.' Jefferson's own notes, laconic and pithy, on such English gardens as CHISWICK, CLAREMONT, HAMPTON COURT, PAINSHILL, STOWE, and WOBURN ABBEY give precious information of them at that time.   PT

EDWIN MORRIS BETTS (ed.), *Thomas Jefferson's Garden Book 1766–1824* (1944).

Jekyll, Gertrude

(1843–1932), English author, artist, nurserywoman, plantswoman, and garden designer—one of the most variously influential gardening figures of her age. E. V. Lucas wrote of her that she 'changed the face of England more than any, save the Creator himself and, perhaps, Capability BROWN'. Born in London, she spent most of her life in Surrey, latterly in a house designed for her by Edwin LUTYENS at MUNSTEAD WOOD. She designed some of the best gardens of the early 20th century, often in partnership with Lutyens. Trained as an artist, her astute sense of colour played an important role in her garden design, especially her deployment of complementary colours and her use of single colour harmonies (although she firmly recommended that a white garden, for example, would always be improved with the inclusion of another colour). She devised a method of planting in 'drifts'—closely planted diagonal swathes of herbaceous perennials to avoid gaps as one variety stopped flowering. She collaborated with William ROBINSON in his magazine publishing (*The Garden* and *Gardening Illustrated*) and was an admirer of wild and woodland gardening—a chapter of one of her books is entitled 'When to let well alone' and she wrote: 'no artificial planting could ever equal that of Nature.' Other aspects of her garden style have remained influential—the planting of walls, use of plants to enhance architectural features, the use of English natives, and her use of particular groups of plants (e.g. shrub roses). Her style of gardening is generally labour intensive and none of her gardens has survived as she left them, though some have been resurrected (such as

HESTERCOMBE) and some brilliantly reconstructed (such as The MANOR HOUSE, Upton Grey). She designed around 400 gardens in all, the vast majority in south-east England. Over 70 of her gardens were designed in collaboration with Lutyens but she worked with many other architects, among them Sir Herbert Baker (1862–1946), Oliver Hill (1887–1968), Sir Robert LORIMER, Robert Weir Schultz (1860–1951), and C. F. A. Voysey (1857–1941). She was 36 when she started designing, so in her 52-year career she averaged eight gardens a year, in addition to her writing, and the running of her own garden and nursery (which supplied many of her gardens in the later part of her career). Mrs Amy Barnes-Brand once asked her how she managed it all—'By not going to Tea Parties', she replied. She was a skilled practical gardener—when she received her Victoria Medal of Honour (the first woman ever to do so) Dean Reynolds Hole described her as 'The Queen of Spades'. After her death her reputation decayed but her influence did not—Russell PAGE in his *Education of a Gardener* (1962) wrote that he could think of few English gardens that 'did not bear the mark of her teaching'. Christopher Hussey regarded her as 'the greatest artist in horticulture and garden-planting that England has produced'. Her gardening books, all worth reading, are as follows: *Wood & Garden* (1899), *Home & Garden* (1900), *Lilies for English Gardens* (1901), *Wall & Water Gardens* (1901), *Roses for English Gardens* (1902), *Some English Gardens* (1904), *Colour in the Flower Garden* (1908), *Children & Gardens* (1908), *Gardens for Small Country Houses* (with Lawrence Weaver) (1912), *Annuals & Biennials* (1916), *Garden Ornament* (1918), *A Gardener's Testament* (1937). See also BORDER.   PT

JANE BROWN, *Gardens of a Golden Afternoon* (1982). SALLY FESTING, *Gertrude Jekyll* (1991).

Jellicoe, Sir Geoffrey

(1900–96), English landscape architect, garden designer, and author. Widely cultivated, and with very eclectic tastes, he was the leading figure of his profession in England for much of the 20th century. It is relatively easy to describe the influences which formed his work but hard to define the qualities of the landscapes he designed. He trained as an architect at the Architectural Association school and became particularly interested in Italian Renaissance gardens—the subject of his first book, *Italian Gardens of the Renaissance* (1925), written in collaboration with J. C. Shepherd. His early designs are refined but unsurprising exercises in formal layouts with a strong axis, distinctly Renaissance in character. Examples may be seen in his first commission, at Ditchley Park (Oxfordshire, 1933), and, on a much

more intimate scale, at SANDRINGHAM HOUSE (Norfolk, 1947). The John F. Kennedy Memorial at Runnymede (Surrey), laid out in 1964, shows Jellicoe in thrall to the past. The fact that Magna Carta, the guarantee of English liberties, was sealed here in 1215 must have been profoundly attractive to him. The subtle glade, with its simple memorial to Kennedy, is very moving. At SHUTE HOUSE one has the impression he found a setting, also with ancient undertones, much to his taste. From 1968 he fashioned a beguiling mixture of Renaissance panache, Mughal discipline, and sacred groves. At SUTTON PLACE, despite the splendours of an early Tudor house, the flat landscape is scarcely lovable. From 1980 Jellicoe laid out a series of enclosures of dramatically varying character—but the whole scheme was never put into place. Nor was his final work, the Moody Historical Gardens at Galveston, Texas. The book of his that probably gives the best picture of his ideas is *The Landscape of Man* (1975), written with his wife Susan.   PT

Jenischpark ✿

Hamburg-Altona, Germany. Towards the end of the 18th century, Caspar Voght created a FERME ORNÉE with meadows, belt walks, trees, and shrubberies in Klein-Flottbek/Teufelsbrück. Poets and artists were frequent guests at his home. The large park, divided into four parts, was bought in 1828 by Martin Johann von Jenisch who built a new white manor house, designed by F. G. Forsmann (1795–1878) and K. F. SCHINKEL. Agriculture was abandoned and the area transformed into a landscape park. In 1939 the Jenischpark, one of the original four parts, was sold to the city of Altona, having been open to the public for some years. The manor (Jenischhaus) is today part of the Altonaer Museum. The nearby Barlach-Haus is a modern museum devoted to the artist Ernst Barlach (1870–1938) and its white walls complement the Jenischhaus. Small bridges and a timber pavilion were built in 1994 in a historic style. Magnificent 300-year-old oaks (*Quercus robur*) and other trees, wide meadows, and shrubberies encourage wildlife. A stream, the Kleine Flottbek, flows towards the river Elbe, adding to the romantic scenery. Today the Jenischpark, with 42 hectares/104 acres, is the largest and best-kept park in the western suburbs of Hamburg. It evokes the great days when the rich traders of Hamburg built their houses and parks along the Elbchaussee.   HG

Jensen, Jens

(1860–1951), American landscape architect. He was born in Denmark but emigrated to the United States in 1884, and settled in Chicago in 1886, where he began professional activity as a gardener. By 1900 he had risen to be superintendent of Humboldt Park. Sacked for political reasons, he developed a private practice, and returned to be appointed landscape architect and superintendent for the West Park system in 1906. In 1920 he again severed his connections for political reasons, to concentrate on private commissions.

His work is known for its compositions of indigenous plant material. This style, advertised as the 'Prairie Style' (see NATURALISTIC PLANTING), was well suited to public parks (such as Columbus Park, Chicago, and the parks of Racine, Wisconsin) and corresponds to the development of the 'Prairie School' of architects (such as Frank Lloyd Wright) in the mid-west at that time. Most of Jensen's work was on estates, and few examples have survived. His work for an estate in Kentucky was illustrated in *American Landscape Architecture* (1924).

Although Jensen had a devoted following in the mid-west, he was largely ignored by the profession. He closed his Chicago office in 1935, and retired to his summer home in Ellison Bay, Wisconsin. In 1939 he published a volume of his writings, *Siftings*.   WLD

ROBERT E. GRESE, *Jens Jensen: Maker of Natural Parks and Gardens* (1992).

Jianzhanggong,

Xi'an, Shaanxi province, China, was an imperial palace built in 104–101 BC during the reign of Han Wudi, to the west of the ancient capital of Chang'an (north-west of today's Xi'an) in Shaanxi province. Though now only the ruins remain, according to records the palace enclosure was *c*.15 km/9 miles in circumference, included many halls, terraces, and towers, and was known as a palace possessed of 'thousands upon thousands' of doors.

Jianzhanggong faced another imperial palace inside the capital and was linked to it by 'flying corridors' above the city wall. The front hall of Jianzhanggong, higher than that of its twin palace, had a *feng que*, or gateway with watchtowers, ornamented with bronze phoenixes on its roof ridge. On the Terrace of Divinities, the statue of an Immortal held up a wide dish to collect the dew of immortality, while lying north of the palace the Taiyi, or Pool of Heavenly Water, contained three islets bearing the names of those mythic islands in the Eastern Sea thought to be the homes of Immortals—Penglai, Fangzhang, and Yingzhou. The garden, which was celebrated in a series of great prose-poems, contained rivers and mounds, collections of pedigree birds and beasts, and many rare flowers and trees.

C-ZC/MK

Jichang Yuan ⊕

Wuxi, Jiangsu province, China. Though the original was destroyed in 1860, the fine reconstruction of this masterpiece of Ming garden design is said to have followed its original plan with accuracy. Also known as the Garden of Ecstasy, it was built in the early 16th century at the foot of Hui Shan, a hill to the west of Wuxi. The site was already well known as a Buddhist monastery under the Yuan, and the country villa of a Minister of Revenue in the early Ming period.

Though it covers only about 0.4 hectare/1 acre, the garden has 'borrowed views' (JIE JING) of the hills around it and the Dragon Light pagoda nearby, to extend its views. A great artificial mountain of earth and yellow rock credited to the rockwork artist Zhang Yue, a nephew of Zhang Lian, takes up all of the north-west part of the garden, but is so skilfully made that it seems to be part of Hui hill beyond the trees planted on its crest. From it the musical sounds of the Stream of the Octave, fed by the Hui Shan spring, bubble down a rocky gully leading to the long and narrow pool, which takes up the eastern side of the garden. This pool also manipulates the available space to create an illusion of depth and distance: its rocky edges curl out of sight into small coves, and a tiny peninsula, jutting out on the west bank at the Beach of a Crane's Stride, draws the eye to the opposite shore where a swoop-eaved open pavilion with balustrades leans out over the water. Though this is in fact very near the garden's eastern boundary, a whitewashed wall and roofed *lang* (see CHINA) corridor cut the remaining space down to a sliver, its trees and rocks only half visible and enticing behind and above open *louchuang* (see CHINA) windows. At the far end of the pond the Bridge of Seven Stars cuts diagonally across the water and the small space beyond it is again divided by pavilions, trees, and open corridors so that the nearby boundary wall no longer seems a barrier.

Though small, the garden's many subdivisions allow it to contain very different effects. On his inspection tour of the south, the Qianlong Emperor was so taken with its simplicity and peace that, within the Imperial Garden of Clear Ripples (now the YIHE YUAN or Summer Palace), near Beijing, he had the XIEQU YUAN built in its imitation.   G-ZW/MK

Ji Cheng

(b. 1582), native of Wujiang in Jiangsu province, China, was a prominent Ming-dynasty landscape and rock artist. He was also known as Ji Wufou and by the pseudonym Pi Daoren, meaning Taoist Pi or the Negative Taoist. Like many other famous Chinese gardeners, he was also an artist and writer, and the many gardens

he made south of the Changjiang (formerly Yangtze river) such as the Shadow Garden, Ying Yuan, in Yangzhou, and Wu or Awakening Garden in Yizheng, Jiangsu province, owed much to ideas derived from poetry and painting. None of his known gardens has survived, but his greatest contribution to landscape architecture was the *Yuan ye*, a treatise on garden planning which is the classic work in Chinese on the subject.

C-ZC/MK

jie jing

means 'borrowed views'. In China, as in Japan (see SHAKKEI), buildings, trees, or natural scenes outside either a garden or a courtyard within a garden are adopted whenever possible into the composition and become part of the view. It is a technique often used in small city gardens to give an illusion of greater space. See also BORROWED LANDSCAPE.   X-WL/MK

Jikōin Temple ⊕

Nara prefecture, Japan, the Retreat of Compassionate Light, is a temple of the Daitokuji branch of the Rinzai sect of Zen Buddhism, founded by Katagiri Sekishū (1605–73) in 1663 in memory of his deceased father, Sadataka. Sekishū was born into a samurai (military ruling class) family and became lord of Iwami province (at present in Shimane prefecture) at the age of 23. At 29, he became magistrate of construction for Chionin, the head temple of the Jōdoshū sect of Buddhism, in Kyoto, and through that position came to understand the arts of architectural and garden design. He was socially adept, and among his acquaintances was the tea master and garden designer Kobori Enshū (1579–1647) who influenced his sense of design. In 1661, Katagiri wrote his seminal treatise on tea culture, *Wabi no Bun*, and two years later was made tea master to the shogun (chief military lord). He developed his own style of tea ceremony and, throughout the Edo period (1600–1868), Katagiri-style tea was popular among the ruling military class.

The architecture of Jikōin is more akin to *sukiya*-style tea architecture than customary *shoin*-style temple architecture (style associated with samurai dwellings). The garden near the main hall is very simple; it has no stone arrangements or ornamental lanterns, just a flat expanse of sand beyond which is a view over a broad valley to distant mountains, many of which are part of the historic Eight Scenic Landscapes (*hakkei*) of the Yamato area. This technique of capturing a distant view as part of a garden is known as SHAKKEI, or borrowed scenery. Alongside the hall is a small hillock covered with tightly clipped evergreen shrubs (mainly azaleas such as *Rhododendron indicum*) the form of which mimics the distant mountain range.   MPK

Jing Shan

or Hill of Scenic Beauty, Beijing, China, is an imperial garden lying just outside the back gate of the Forbidden City. It is also known as Mei Shan or Coal Hill. The hill itself is 43 m/141 ft high, and was the highest point in the capital until the new buildings of the 1950s. Before the 12th century, however, it did not exist. Earth and sludge dug out to make the Taiyi or Pool of Heavenly Water first created a mound here during the Jin dynasty (1115–1234); then, when the moat which encircles the Forbidden City was being dredged at the beginning of the 15th century, this became again a convenient dumping ground. Later pines, cypresses, flowers, and lawns were laid out below the hill, a paddock was opened for raising deer and cranes (symbols of longevity), and the whole place became an imperial garden. During the Ming dynasty, a hall named Guande, or the Observance of Virtue, was built behind the hill to the north, with a courtyard round it where the nobles practised archery. The last Emperor of the Ming hanged himself from a pagoda tree (said to have survived until the early years of this century) on the northern slope of the hill. In 1749, the fourteenth year of the Qianlong Emperor's reign, mass construction began to the north of the hill on an architectural complex including the Shouhuangdian, or Hall of the Ageing Sovereign, and Liulifang, or Glaze-Work Lane, which formed an organic system of their own and were used by the imperial family as private altars. The following year saw the building, on top of the hill, of five pavilions roofed over with glazed and coloured tiles. The biggest of these is Wanchunting, the Pavilion of Everlasting Spring. A square structure with double eaves, it not only makes a dramatic silhouette on the horizon at the end of many vistas in the imperial palace, but from it there are panoramic views across the whole capital, with the Imperial City itself spread out below, the Three Seas, BEIHAI, ZHONGHAI, and Nanhai almost underfoot, and the outlines of the Western Hills rising beyond the suburbs in the distance.   G-ZW/MK

Jingu Yuan,

China, was a private garden north-east of the city of Luoyang (Henan province) in the Western Jin dynasty (265–316) and took its name from the nearby Jingu Jian or Golden Valley Stream. It belonged to Shi Chong (249–300), a man of such extravagant wealth that he once put up brocaded silken screens extending for 10 Chinese li (*c*.5.7 km/3 miles) for a garden party.

Though he described his estate as a simple country retreat, its 'many thousands' of cypresses, numerous buildings, and a private orchestra helped it to become a classic symbol of luxurious living. In addition, its name carries the allure of association with one of the Four Great Beauties of Chinese history: during the tyranny of King Sima Lun, Shi Chong was falsely arrested after refusing to give up his concubine Lu Zhu (the Green Pearl) who then jumped to her death from a tower in the garden.   D-HL/MK

J. Irwin Miller Garden.

See MILLER, J. IRWIN, GARDEN.

Joensuu Estate Park,

near Salo, Halikko, Finland. The park at Joensuu was designed *c*.1810 in the landscape style by Count Armfelt. The estate remained in the possession of the Armfelt family until *c*.1910 when parts of the 1810 design that had never been executed were put into place and some new elements characteristic of the time were added. During the last decades maintenance of the gardens has concentrated on the surroundings of the main building, and the English-style landscape park has slowly become overgrown. Now a new period has begun in Joensuu. On the initiative of the current owner, the park and the gardens have been restored to their old splendour, assisted by a restoration plan that emphasizes the history of the park.   ITL

Johan Maurits.

See NASSAU-SIEGEN, JOHAN MAURITS VAN.

Johanna-Park ⊛

Leipzig, Germany, situated south-east of the city centre with a site of 11 hectares/27 acres. It connects the heart of the town, which is surrounded by the PROMENADENRING, with other parks and the floodplain forest to the south-west of the city. The Johanna-Park is an important monument of horticultural art. Its development goes back to a charitable trust founded by the banker Wilhelm Theodor Seyfferth, who initiated the park in memory of his short-lived daughter Johanna. Seyfferth asked Peter Joseph LENNÉ to design the park; he used themes taken from one of his other works, the Marly-Garden at Potsdam. The city gardener Carl Otto Wittenberg (1834–1918) was responsible for realizing the project but he did not execute the sightlines which were characteristic of Lenné. Sitting places, however, with ornamental plantings on banks were characteristic of Lenné's design and Wittenberg arranged belts of trees to form an undulating boundary with specimen trees nearby. After

finishing the park in 1863 Seyfferth opened it to the public. In his will he decreed that the park must not be developed, Lenné's design must not be changed, and the name Johanna must be retained. In 1896 a monument to the founder was created by Melchior zur Strassen (1832–96) and Hugo Licht (1841–1923). In the 1990s the park was carefully restored to preserve its horticultural heritage.   HN

Johnston, Lawrence

(1871–1958), garden owner and designer. He was born in Paris to American parents, educated at Trinity College, Cambridge, and took British nationality. He fought in both the Boer War and the First World War, rising to the rank of major. Living at HIDCOTE MANOR from 1907 he made one of the best, and most influential, English gardens of the 20th century. He also had a hand in designing the garden of his neighbours Mr and Mrs J. B. Muir at KIFTSGATE COURT. From 1924 he also made a garden on the French Riviera at Serre de la MADONE at Menton. In both his gardens he displayed a very strong sense of design and skilful plantsmanship, especially in view of the radically different climates of the two gardens. Johnston, alas, never wrote about his gardens and remains an enigmatic figure, very little having been written about him in his lifetime.
    PT

Jones, Inigo

(1573–1652), English architect of Welsh origins. He travelled to Italy, and entered the service of Queen Anne of Denmark for whom he designed his first court masque. Between 1605 and 1640 he staged over 50 masques and other entertainments, often in collaboration with Ben Jonson. The importance of these masques in garden history is that they, in the words of Roy STRONG, 'propagated a garden style which looked far more directly to Italy and also to new currents in French garden making under the aegis of the Mollet dynasty. Classical statuary and architecture appear along with the parterre of clipped box, soaring Italianate cypresses, elegant fountains and cavernous grottoes.' At Arundel House he designed a court to display the Arundel Marbles and advised Isaac de CAUS on the garden at WILTON HOUSE. As an architect he is best known for introducing the ideas of Andrea PALLADIO to England.   PT

ROY STRONG, *The Renaissance Garden in England* (1979).

Jordan, Dr, Park ⊛

Cracow, Poland, is the first town park in the world to be laid out specifically for children. In 1888 Dr Henryk Jordan (1842–1907), physician and Cracow councillor, secured the creation of a park on the site of the National Industrial-Agricultural Exhibition for Galicia (part of Poland at that time under Austrian rule). It was laid out in the following year according to a design by Bolesław Malecki, a municipal gardener. Since 1891 it has been the property of the city of Cracow. After the Second World War its area was extended to its present size of over 21 hectares/52 acres. The park is laid out on a triangular plan in the so-called mixed style, combining a geometrical composition (the straight main avenue with a hippodrome, terminating in a circus) with a landscape arrangement. In addition to the existing trees a number of new species were planted, such as hornbeams, alders, thujas, horse chestnuts, and oaks. The exhibition pavilions were converted into sports facilities and some playing fields marked out separately for boys, girls, and small children. Dr Jordan's guiding principle was to combine sports with the patriotic education of the young. The latter idea was to be served by a gallery of sculptured busts of great Poles set up round the circus and by military exercises for boys. Today the park no longer functions as a sports centre for the young (the wooden pavilions and playing fields have ceased to exist), but is one of the ordinary town parks. However, the idea of the gallery of great Poles is continued by the addition of new busts (now along the main avenue).   WB

Jōruri-ji ⌾

Kyoto prefecture, Japan, is a temple of the Shingon Risshū sect of Buddhism. The general disposition of the garden, which covers roughly 1.5 hectares/4 acres, remains from the mid Heian period (794–1185) and is an example of what is known as a Pure Land garden (see JAPAN). The temple developed over more than a century, beginning with the construction of the main hall in 1047 and continuing until 1178, when a three-storey pagoda was moved from Heian (present-day Kyoto). After that, there are records of fires, and repairs to the pond, but the primary form of the garden had been created.

At the centre of the garden is a pond within which is an elongated central island. The island is laid out with its tip on the axis with the centre of the main hall, a positioning that is in accordance with the rules prescribed in the Heian-period gardening treatise SAKUTEIKI. To the west of the pond is a hall in which are enshrined nine sculptures of Amida *nyorai* (Buddha of Infinite Light; Sanskrit: Amitabha). The sculptures were enshrined in 1107 but probably came to their present location in the west in 1157. To the east of the pond, enshrined in the three-storey pagoda, is the original deity of the temple, Yakushi *nyorai* (the Healing Buddha; Sanskrit: Bhaisajya-guru). To the north of the pond is enshrined an image of Dainichi *nyorai* (the Universal Buddha; Sanskrit: Mahavairocana).

This enshrinement of deities in specific directions around the pond creates a Buddhist cosmology in the landscape. Amida, believed to preside over a Western Pure Land (Saihō Jōdo) is placed in the west; Yakushi, believed to preside over the World of Pure Lapis Lazuli (Jōruri Sekai, traditionally ascribed to the east), is represented in the east; and Dainichi, the Buddha which oversees all others, is represented in the north looking southward over the whole.   MPK

J. Paul Getty Museum.

See GETTY, MUSEUM.

K

Kaempfer, Engelbert

(1651–1716), German physician and botanist. After studying medicine in Cracow (Poland) and Königsberg (Russian Kaliningrad) he accompanied a Swedish diplomat travelling through Russia and Persia (Iran). Kaempfer explored in the latter for several years. In 1688 he went to India and the following year to Java, becoming the Dutch East India company's chief surgeon at Nagasaki, Japan. Despite severe restrictions on travel, he was able to make two journeys to the Emperor at Edo (Tokyo). He observed the natural and cultivated flora, collecting where possible, and published his results in *Amoenitates Exoticae* (1712). Kaempfer was the first to record the species aucuba, hydrangea, skimmia, 30 different types of camellia, and *Lilium tigrinum*.   MC-C

Kaivopuisto (Brunnsparken) Park ⊛

Helsinki, Finland, was established in 1834 as a sea bathing and mineral springwater company for affluent Russian tourists and local elite. A spa park was laid out on the seashore as a rustic adaptation of German models. The lime-lined main walk, connecting the principal entrance to the park, and the water cure building, still exist from the period, but the sea baths were destroyed in 1944. During the Crimean War artillery batteries were built in the park, and after the war the Russians stopped coming, and the land was let for residential villas. The dwindling park, however, remained a popular place of recreation, maintaining an aristocratic although decayed air. In 1886, the city of Helsinki restored the park. The built-up area was set aside and the rest converted into a public park with a site of 20 hectares/50 acres, redesigned in 1889–90 by the new city head gardener, Svante Olsson (1856–1941). The restoration, generally following the late 19th-century German landscape garden style, was completed by 1912. As in the 'hill parks' of Stockholm (see STOCKHOLM PARK SYSTEM), bare cliffs were turned into undulating green parkland accentuated by lookouts, natural rocky outcrops, rare trees, or carpet bedding.

The composition was tied together with gently curving drives or paths and carefully framed vistas onto the Baltic. Further additions were made by the city head gardener Bengt Schalin (1889–1982) in 1946 and, in the 1990s, by the landscape architect Gretel Hemgård (b. 1948), in connection with a restoration plan.   MHay

Kalmthout Arboretum ⊛

Kalmthout, Antwerp, Belgium, was originally a nursery, started by Charles van Geert in 1856. Many of the mature trees date from that time but the site has only developed as an important arboretum since it was purchased by Georges and Robert de Belder in 1952. They were soon joined by Robert's wife Jelena de Belder-Kovacic, a trained horticulturalist and inspired plantswoman. The 12-hectare/29-acre arboretum has evolved over the years. The result is a series of informal island beds, remarkable for their subtle groupings of trees, shrubs, and perennial plants, amid beckoning grass walks. The individual beds are often designed around one of the huge, original trees. In the spring, flowering cherries are followed swiftly by rhododendrons, azaleas, and magnolias. High summer sees the flowering of roses and herbaceous plants and in late summer there are beds of fuchsias and hydrangeas. In autumn the garden is a vivid mixture of conifers, berrying shrubs, and changing leaf colour. In winter there are special open days to see the witch hazel (*Hamamelis*) in flower—several notable cultivars have their origin here: *Hamamelis* × *intermedia* 'Diane', *H.* × *intermedia* 'Jelena', and *H.* × *intermedia* 'Pallida'. There are two ponds, and a country house surrounded by old rhododendron hybrids and reached by an avenue of large conifers, planted in the days of the original nursery. In 1978 a foundation was created to safeguard the future of the arboretum and in 1986 it was bought by the province of Antwerp.   BA

Karaca Arboretum ⊛

near Yalova, Turkey. In 1980 Hayrettin Karaca retired from his clothing manufacturing business and established a private arboretum on his apple orchard along the south coast of the Sea of Marmara. The site covers covers 13.5 hectares/33 acres and is on heavy clay. This venture was completely financed by Mr Karaca. Originally planted with deciduous plants and conifers collected from all over Turkey, the collection has now been extended to include plants from all over the world. This successful venture now distributes woody plants to various sites throughout Turkey, which assists the running of the arboretum. The arboretum collection currently holds 7,000 species and at present there are plans to extend the collection on another site nearby.   LJD

karesansui

is the proper term for those Japanese gardens made primarily of stone and raked sand that are often referred to as Zen gardens or meditation gardens. Neither of the latter two expressions exists in Japanese and, although the gardens are at times found in Zen Buddhist temples, they were not built to be the focus of seated meditation (*zazen*). The word *karesansui* (also pronounced *karasenzui*, *kosensui*, and otherwise) literally means 'dry, mountain, water' or 'dry landscape' since *sansui* (mountain-water) was an appellation for the landscape. *Karesansui* refers to a garden that depicts a landscape scene without the use of water, though water is often represented with sand raked into wave patterns.

The word *karesansui* first appears in the 11th-century gardening manual SAKUTEIKI: 'There is also a way to create gardens without ponds or streams. This is called the Dry Garden (*karesansui*) Style.' In this case, the word refers to a section of a garden that is 'dry' and has rockwork. Through the ensuing Kamakura (1185–1333) and Muromachi (1333–1568) periods, *karesansui* developed from loose rock arrangements built within the context of larger gardens, to very precise arrangements built in small courtyards associated with the main halls of Zen temples and the military-class elite. The influence of Chinese ink landscape paintings (*sansuiga*) and tray landscapes (*bonzan*, *bonseki*) on the design of these gardens is unmistakable.   MPK

Karlsaue Staatspark ⊛

Kassel, Hesse, Germany. A 16th-century Renaissance garden created for Landgrave Wilhelm IV von Hesse-Kassel (1532–92) was succeeded in the 18th century by a 150-hectare/370-acre French-style baroque garden for a new house, the Orangerieschloss palace, built for Landgrave Karl (1644–1737). A fan-shaped ALLÉE and canal system provides the framework   ▶

of the grounds. In front of the orangery lies the great parterre that had already been reworked as a BOULINGRIN lawn at the end of the 18th century. To the south the Siebenbergen island marks the end of the park. In the late 18th century the work of Daniel August Schwarzkopf (1738–1817) for Landgrave Wilhelm IX (1793–1874) brought about the first reshaping as a landscape park. Further alterations by director of the royal gardens Wilhelm Hentze (1793–1874) under Landgrave Wilhelm II led in the mid 19th century to a layout that permitted a sweeping landscape park while retaining the dominant geometrical structures within the framing canals and *allées*. The Siebenbergen island is particularly striking for its botanical variety. Destruction during the Second World War, followed by the 1955 federal garden show designed by Hermann MATTERN and another in 1981, brought about massive changes. Recent work has restored most of the 19th-century layout.   BM

Karlsruhe ✿

Baden-Württemberg, Germany. The baroque Schlossgarten at Karlsruhe is among the most original of this period in Germany as it is

designed in the shape of a star. At the centre stands the high hunting tower built in the Hardtwald by Margrave Carl Wilhelm of Baden-Durlach; 32 avenues radiate from this central point. It was in keeping with the spirit of absolutism of the time that, when the town was founded in 1715, the plans for both town and Schloss should be based on this same strict geometrical star design. A circle runs round the tower at a distance of 440 m/1,443 ft and forms the boundary of the garden. The segment of the circle between the two wings of the Schloss contained a pleasure garden with a parterre and a BOSQUET, while the main area around the tower was left as a hunting park.

This woodland park was rearranged for the Bundesgartenschau (see SHOWS AND FESTIVALS) of 1967 to a design by Professor W. Rossow, who also directed the work. He had the difficult task of on the one hand creating a permanent leisure park for the population of Karlsruhe, while on the other accommodating the Gartenschau with its different aims and requirements. It comprised a large number of individual gardens, mainly of plants, and also had various attractions, such as the miniature railway which ran through the park, and architectural works, such as the pools constructed from pre-cast concrete: all things which cannot easily be brought into harmony with a historic garden around the Schloss. The garden at Karlsruhe represents an attempt to integrate modern garden design, architecture, and the visual arts.
    UD

Kasteel Amerongen.
See AMERONGEN, KASTEEL.

Kasteel de Haar.
See HAAR, KASTEEL DE.

Kasteel Twickel.
See TWICKEL, KASTEEL.

Kasteel van Leeuwergem.
See LEEUWERGEM, KASTEEL VAN.

Kasteel Weldam.
See WELDAM, KASTEEL.

Katsura Detached Palace ✿
Kyoto, Japan, or Katsura Rikyū in Japanese, is located on the banks of the Katsura river in the west of Kyoto city. It is an excellent example of an Edo-period (1600–1868) aristocratic villa garden (see SENTŌ GOSHO and SHUGAKUIN). Prince Toshihito (1579–1629), brother of Emperor Goyōzei (1571–1617), commenced work on the garden around 1620. Adopted as heir by the childless shogun (chief military lord) Toyotomi Hideyoshi (1537–98), Toshihito was

later disowned when the shogun's wife bore a son. In compensation, he was granted new titles and a new name, becoming the founder of the Hachijō no Miya family. Toshihito's studies of Chinese and Japanese classics, and interest in arts such as tea ceremony, provided the inspiration for many of the landscape images that were recreated in abstract form within the garden. In its early days, the garden was referred to with self-effacing names such as the Simple Teahouse in the Melon Fields (Uribatake no Karoki Chaya) and only became designated as a Detached Palace (Rikyū) in 1886, five years after the property was taken over by the Imperial Household Agency.

After Toshihito's death the garden fell into disrepair until around 1642 when his son Toshitada (1619–62) married the daughter of the lord of Kaga province and the garden was refurbished. Though descendants carried out some work in later years, the garden we see today, which covers about 5.6 hectares/14 acres, is primarily the work of the first two generations of Hachijō princes.

The garden centres on a complexly shaped pond with many inlets between hillocks that provide a constantly changing sequence of views to someone circumambulating the pond. The refinement of details makes this garden renowned among professionals and laymen alike, including the architecture of the various tea houses and residences, the subtly abstracted landscape scenery, the understated garden ornaments (such as stone lanterns), and the brilliantly designed pathway.   MPK

Katsura Residence Garden ✿
Yamaguchi prefecture, Japan, not to be confused with KATSURA DETACHED PALACE, is a 90-sq. m/295-sq. ft courtyard garden built by Katsura Unpei Tadaharu (1664–1747) in 1712. Tadaharu was a vassal of the Mōri clan of Hagi. When the lord he served, Mōri Narikatsu (1673–1707), moved to Hōfu province (now Yamaguchi prefecture) to participate in the development of the lower reaches of the Sabagawa river, Tadaharu moved with him. It is believed that this garden was created as part of a ceremony intended to ensure the success of the project. Unlike other dry landscape gardens (see KARESANSUI), the rock placement here is overtly sculptural, with unusually shaped stones placed on pedestal stones rather than buried directly in the soil. Annually, on the 23rd day of the 11th month of the old calendar (24 December in 2005), a lunar blessing ceremony is held in the garden. A rice cake to represent the sun is placed centrally in the garden and surrounded by twelve rice cakes that symbolize the moon. When the moon aligns with the centre of an L-shaped stone, a

sacred light is offered to the moon. The stone is known as the Rabbit Stone because Japanese traditionally perceive the image of a rabbit in the moon, like the Western 'man in the moon'. The distant view beyond the garden wall is of Tenjinyama Mountain, the site of the local Tenmangu Shrine, which enshrines Sugawara no Michizane, deity of sagacity.   MPK

Kazanlak,

Bulgaria, is the main town in the beautiful Valley of Roses at the foot of the Balkan Mountains. Dating back to antiquity, the town gained importance in the late 17th century due to the essential oils industry, based on the cultivation of *Rosa damascena*. The rose was brought from Persia in the Middle Ages and found better climatic and soil conditions than in its place of origin. It is said that around 1590, a Turkish judge had a large, splendid garden of fragrant roses in the Kazanlak area and was ordered by Sultan Murat III to extend their growth and supply the palace. Gradually, vast areas of land were used to produce rose bushes and oil for the Ottoman and Russian empires. In 1820 the first Bulgarian-owned distillery was established and the fame of the superior quality of Bulgarian rose oil spread across Europe. Thus, for more than 300 years, every May through to June the fields have been magically transformed into a sea of beauty with a glorious scent and colour as far as the eye can see. The dominating pink swathes of *Rosa damascena* have been diversified with lavender, mint, and clary. Kazanlak holds the Festival of Roses annually in early June with magnificent street processions and performances of beauty and craft. The delightful decoration of private gardens, as well as all phases of oil extraction, can all be seen in the Museum of Roses, which opened in 1969.   ASG

Kellie Castle ⊛

near Pittenweem, East Fife, Scotland, was built in the 15th century and much altered in the 16th and 17th centuries. It was rescued from dereliction by Professor James Lorimer whose son Robert LORIMER in 1880, at the age of 16, laid out a garden in the old walled enclosure below the castle walls. Divided by paths into four spaces, with herbaceous borders, often edged in box, lining the paths and rose arbours rising above them, Lorimer sought to evoke the spirit of 17th-century Scottish gardens. Beds of fruit and vegetables lie below the walls and espaliered pears run along behind borders. Gallica roses are underplanted with lavender and noble drifts of ghostly *Galtonia candicans*. It may be unhistorical but it is devastatingly charming.   PT

Kemp, Edward

(1817–91), English gardener and garden designer who was apprenticed at CHATSWORTH to Joseph PAXTON, and served as his foreman of works on BIRKENHEAD PARK (1843–7). On its completion, he became its superintendent for over 40 years, while pursuing a career as a garden designer. In 1850 he published *How to Lay out a Small Garden*; by its third edition (1864) it had dropped the word 'small' and become a widely influential manual on the design of country estates. Among his major commissions were Hesketh Park, Southport, and Stanley Park, Liverpool, in which he continued Paxton's later trend towards increasing formality of design and the use of viewing terraces within the park.   BE

Kendall, Donald M., Sculpture Gardens ⊛

Purchase, New York, USA, on the grounds of the Pepsi Corporation, the last great project of English landscape architect Russell PAGE. In 1981, Page was commissioned by Donald M. Kendall, the chairman and chief executive of PepsiCo, to create a park around his collection of 20th-century sculptures. Four hectares/10 acres of the 58-hectare/144-acre site had originally been landscaped by Edward Durrell Stone Jr. to extend from the complex of contemporary corporate buildings designed by Stone's father. Russell Page's primary task was to achieve a vibrant spatial relationship between the land and the vast works of art. First he created a path of tawny gravel to weave around and past the sculptures by Henry Moore, Alexander Calder, Louise Nelvelson, Isamu NOGUCHI, Max Ernst, Arnaldo Palmidoro, and Barbara Hepworth. Page called it his 'golden pathway'. The path made exploring the garden an adventure and successfully linked together the disparate artworks. Then he planted trees—hundreds in the first year alone: 'I use the trees as sculptures and the sculptures as flowers, and then I take it from there. It's a cross-current thing,' he said. Smaller gardens were made within the larger landscape, a grass garden, a pool garden, and a perennial border. After Page died in 1985, landscape architect François Goffinet became his successor. He strives to keep Page's design in balance, and at the same time continues to develop areas along the edges of the park with the idea of enhancing the garden. Among Goffinet's achievements are a woodland garden (the West Wood Garden), and a Japanese iris garden, planted along a stream, which is stunning in flower in late June.   PD

Kennedy, John F., Arboretum ⊛

New Ross, County Wexford, Ireland, one of the finest collections of woody plants in Ireland.

The old estate was bought after 1963 and opened as an arboretum in 1968. It was an especially appropriate site, for Kennedy's Irish ancestors came from Dunganstown 5 km/3 miles away. The site is also very beautiful—252 hectares/622 acres of rolling land in a high and hilly position rising at its peak, the hill of Slievecoilta, to 271 m/889 ft. The arboretum is ingeniously laid out in two major parts. A grid of forest plots—echoing the grid pattern of a US city—groups plants according to their place of origin—Asia, Australasia, Europe, and North America. The chief part is arranged more naturalistically with a winding path linking its various parts. Here the plants are grouped by genera regardless of country of origin. These sometimes follow the path—the cherry walk, birch walk, oaks walk—or are arranged in naturalistic groups. In all there are over 4,500 taxa of woody plants from temperate climates. The arboretum has a research programme but in addition to that it is a beautiful landscape, and as a reference collection of trees and shrubs it is of great value to the gardener. Many of the groups of shrubs—buddleias, escallonias, magnolias, rhododendrons (over 500 here), and spiraeas—are of particular interest to gardeners.   PT

Kenrokuen ⊛

Kanazawa city, Japan, a public park since 1874, was originally the estate garden of the Maeda family, lords of Kaga province (now the southern part of Ishikawa prefecture). The garden began as a simple lotus pond outside the castle moat during the administration of the second lord, Maeda Toshinaga (1563–1614), and was developed by succeeding generations. It is possible that Kobori Enshū, who was tea adviser to the Maeda family, and the well-known gardener Kentei, who is known to have visited Kenrokuen from 1630 to 1632, were involved in the early design and implementation. The form we see today, however, was influenced in particular by the work of the twelfth lord, Narinaga (1782–1824), and thirteenth lord, Nariyasu (1811–84), in the late 18th and early 19th centuries. As such, it is one of the most recently created provincial stroll gardens, having come into its present form just decades before it was made a public park.

Kenrokuen is known as one of Japan's Big Three Parks, along with Okayama KŌRAKUEN and Mito Kairakuen, and is famous for the unusual garden ornaments it holds: the Harp-Stand Lantern (Kotoji-dōrō) which is now the symbol of Kenrokuen, the Flying Geese Bridge (Gankō-bashi), and others. The name was suggested by Mastudaira Sadanobu (1758–1829), lord of Ōshū (a province that existed at the northern end of Honshū island) and well-known poet-painter. He in turn drew it from Sung-dynasty poet Li Gefei's *Luoyang mingyuan ji* (Record of the Celebrated Gardens of Luoyang, written in 1095) in which are mentioned 'six attributes' (*kenroku*) for gardens: expanse (*kōdai*), reserve (*yusui*), human effort (*jinriki*), patina (*sōko*), a water source (*suigen*), a grand view (*chōbō*).   MPK

Kent, William

(*c*.1685–1748), English architect, garden designer, and artist, pioneer of the early period of the 18th-century informal landscape style. Kent went to Rome in 1709 to study to become an artist, returning in 1719. Little of his work survives, except for drawings for landscapes designed by him, and these are certainly not of high quality. He was a protégé of the 3rd Earl of BURLINGTON, whose garden at CHISWICK HOUSE Kent helped to design, and intimate of Alexander POPE for whose translation of *The Odyssey* he did engravings and for whose garden at Twickenham he designed ornaments. He was famous because, in the words of Horace WALPOLE, 'He leaped the fence, and saw that all nature was a garden.' Among the gardens where his work survives are Badminton (Gloucestershire), CLAREMONT, Euston Hall (Norfolk), Holkham (Norfolk), ROUSHAM, and

STOWE. Rousham is Kent's most complete surviving garden. Among the best surviving garden buildings by him are the Temple of British Worthies (Stowe, *c*.1735), an octagonal domed temple at SHOTOVER PARK (Oxfordshire, *c*.1730), and the exquisite Worcester Lodge (Badminton House, *c*.1740). Of the famous garden made for Henry Pelham at Esher Place (Surrey), hailed by Walpole as 'Kentissimo', only tantalizing fragments of architecture survive at Esher Green. This was the garden referred to in James Thomson's poem *The Seasons* (1726–30)—'Esher's peaceful grove, | Where Kent and Nature vie for Pelham's love.'

PT

JOHN DIXON HUNT, *William Kent: Landscape Garden Designer* (1987).

Kerdalo ⊛

Trédarzec, Côtes d'Armor, France, is a rare type of garden to be found in France, an amateur plantsman's garden of a kind more commonly associated with England. It was the creation of the late Prince Peter Wolkonsky who came here in 1965 attracted by a handsome granite manor house and its valley setting close to the sea in northern Brittany. The mild climate, acid soil, and relatively high rainfall encouraged him to plant flowering shrubs, especially rhododendrons, but he ranged widely in his

tastes in plants. Essentially informal in character, the garden has passages of formality close to the house which overlooks terraced gardens with decorative architectural detail. To one side a slender canal runs between ramparts of rhododendrons and is centred on a CHINOISERIE kiosk. The valley of a stream flowing through the garden is the setting for wilder planting—the spires of self-sown *Echium pininana* rise among groves of *Trachycarpus fortunei* and *Chamaerops humilis*. The banks of the valley are lavishly planted with trees and shrubs—cherries, dogwoods, *Gevuina avellana*, magnolias, maples, and many rhododendrons. A bridge across the stream incorporates a grotto/pavilion with mermaid sirens formed of shells and glass fragments. Beautiful plants, a very attractive site, and the idiosyncratic charm of Prince Wolkonsky (very potent in his life and still to be felt today) are the distinguishing ingredients of Kerdalo.   PT

Keszthely ⊛

Zala county, Hungary. Kristóf Festetics acquired the Keszthely estate in 1739, and had

Bird's-eye view of the park at **Keszthely** (1885) from Charles Schilberszky's *Monographie de la horticulture en Hongrie* (1900).

the palace built directly facing the street, with a baroque ornamental garden behind the rear *cour d'honneur* (see ATTRE, CHÂTEAU D'), and behind that an enormous orchard, all according to plans by Christoph Hofstädter, the estate's master builder. A number of different plans for these gardens have survived, all from the second half of the 18th century. The construction of the landscape garden, involving the removal of the baroque pleasure garden and the orchard turned into parkland, occurred in a number of stages in the course of the first half of the 19th century. This took place under the ownership first of György Festetics, founder of the Georgikon, Europe's first agricultural academy, and later, and more significantly, under that of his son László. The Georgikon's botanic garden, which neighboured the estate and whose *théâtre de verdure* (see THEATRE) was home to significant literary readings (the Helikon Festivals), and later opera performances, was annexed to the Count's park after the academy was dissolved in 1849. The 1880s saw a further large-scale renovation of the palace and its grounds, the latter in 1885 on the basis of plans by the English landscape gardener Henry Ernest MILNER. Milner demolished houses and redirected the town's traffic to create a semicircular park in front of the palace, while constructing an imposing formal parterre behind it. He opened up long vistas in the grounds, and built mounds and a small lake with a waterfall. These gardens, redesigned and extended to an area of around 40 hectares/100 acres—Milner's first independent garden work—became one of Hungary's outstanding parks. After 1945 a museum was established in the palace, while the 18-hectare/44-acre section of the park that remained was renovated in the 1970s and 1980s. The larger part of the grounds to the back became a military base, however, and in front of it a busy road divides the park in two, which has led to the complete degradation of the area. The park still awaits reunification and conservation.
GA

GÁBOR ALFÖLDY, 'A brief history of Festetics Park at Keszthely', in Gábor Alföldy (ed.), *Principal Gardens of Hungary* (2001).
HENRY ERNEST MILNER, *The Art and Practice of Landscape Gardening* (1890).

Keukenhof, De ⚘

Lisse, Zuid-Holland, the Netherlands, the archetypal and probably best-known Dutch bulb display garden. It has its origins in the Middle Ages as the kitchen garden (= *keukenhof*) of Castle Teylingen. In 1641 Adriaen Maartensz Block built a new house, Keukenhof, and formal gardens with profits made from trade with the East Indies. Successive generations

carried out improvements until part of the property, on which the bulb show is now held, was sold off. The new owner, Baron Du Tour van Zandvliet, redesigned his part in landscape style. The main part of the estate was altered in the landscape style by the end of the 18th century. In 1854 J. D. Zocher and L. P. ZOCHER made improvements for both Keukenhof and Zandvliet, as the smaller part had become known. The latter part contained the main pond, now the focal point for the exhibition area. In 1949 the Keukenhof Foundation acquired this property with the aim of creating a display garden for the Dutch bulb industry, asking the landscape architect W. van der Lee to prepare designs. Initially the framework was provided by the woody planting from the historic layout and served as a setting for temporary exhibitions. This is now being revised occasionally, while the arrangement and exhibition of bulbs is redesigned on an annual basis. The organization employs its own landscape architect for the purpose. There is also an extensive range of greenhouses, which serve as display units.
JW

Kew Gardens.

See ROYAL BOTANIC GARDEN, KEW.

Kiftsgate Court ⚘

Chipping Camden, Gloucestershire, England, has a garden of a very English kind. Its creator, Heather Muir, was a plantswoman of strong and independent views who, from 1920 onwards, made a garden of great character. She was an immediate neighbour of Lawrence JOHNSTON at HIDCOTE MANOR with whom she became friendly. Kiftsgate and Hidcote might broadly be described as belonging to the Gloucestershire tradition of ARTS AND CRAFTS gardens but they each have their own identity. Heather Muir was one of those gardeners who rediscovered the beauty of old shrub and species roses. A *Rosa sericea* seedling 'Heather Muir' is named after her and the great rambler *R. filipes* 'Kiftsgate' was discovered by her (the original plant survives at Kiftsgate). The garden falls into two parts—a cluster of formal areas about the house and an area of much wilder character where the ground falls away down a precipitous slope with immense views of the Vale of Evesham. In a rose garden hidden behind yew hedges a path is lined with *Rosa gallica* 'Versicolor' behind which are beds of shrub roses. A square garden enclosed by an 'L' shape of the house has a four-part arrangement of beds filled with mixed plantings in which purple dominates. Paths lead down the side of the steep well-wooded valley where abutilons, cistus, hebes, phlomis, and teucrium thrive in the sharply drained position. At the foot of the

slope is a lawn, pool, and temple from which fine views of the landscape are revealed. Heather Muir's taste in plants dominates the garden but her granddaughter who now owns the garden has put her stamp on it: a former tennis court was converted in 2000 into a modernist pool with stepping stones, an island, and a dazzling fountain.
PT

Kiley, Daniel Urban

(1912–2004), American landscape architect. He received his professional education in landscape architecture at Harvard University's Graduate School of Design where he joined Rose, ECKBO, and CHURCH in effecting the transition from the Beaux-Arts system to a modern approach to design. His early work was dominated by a preoccupation with form rather than function in the solution of design problems, but was later tempered by the belief that form is achieved as a by-product of the several functional solutions to a problem. His great strength lay in his ability to make a rapid assessment of the functional relationships of buildings on a large site in order to establish a clear spatial hierarchy and appropriate scale. 'Landscape', he said, 'is not mere adornment but an integral part of the disposition of space, plane, line and structure with which it is associated.' The geometry and layout of his schemes were frequently reminiscent of the formal qualities of 17th-century French gardens (which he much admired) and reflected his opinion that the man-made landscape should be an obvious contrast to the world of nature. Although much of his work is on a large scale associated with public and commercial buildings, it includes a number of gardens; notably the roof and terrace gardens for the Oakland Museum and an indoor garden for the Ford Foundation in New York city.
MLL

DAN KILEY and JANE AMIDON, *Dan Kiley: The Complete Works of America's Master Landscape Architect* (2003).

Killerton ⚘

near Exeter, Devon, England, was an old estate of the Acland family. In the late 18th century Sir Thomas Acland started to enrich the planting with help of John Veitch (see VEITCH FAMILY) who had started a nursery at Budlake quite close to Killerton. Veitch was the founder of the great dynasty of nurserymen who later set up business in Exeter and London. For well over 100 years the Aclands bought plants from Veitch who were in that time one of the finest nurseries in Europe. The house is set in lawns which give way to handsome parkland. Trees and shrubs are planted on the lawns, sometimes as lonely, magnificent specimens and sometimes in groups. Here are beautiful old magnolias and rhododendrons (mostly species) among superb old trees. The trees include fine specimens of *Quercus* × *hispanica* 'Lucombeana', *Saxegothaea conspicua*, *Sciadopitys verticillata*, and *Zelkova serrata*. The borders above the terrace close to the house were designed by William ROBINSON in about 1900. Robinson's original planting of roses was replaced by a mixed planting of herbaceous perennials and small shrubs in 1957 by the NATIONAL TRUST which has owned the estate since 1944.   PT

Killesberg.

See HÖHENPARK KILLESBERG.

Killruddery

Bray, County Wicklow, Republic of Ireland, dates from the early 17th century when it was acquired by Sir William Brabazon (later 1st Earl of Meath) whose descendants still live here. One of the most remarkable survivals of its period in Ireland, the garden was started in the late 17th century and completed early in the 18th century, designed by a Frenchman named Bonet about whom nothing, apart from the evidence of this garden, is known. South of the house (a picturesque neo-Elizabethan extravaganza by Sir Richard Morrison) two long parallel canals point away to a great lime avenue which extends the vista far into the distance. West of the canals is a mazelike pattern of triangular spaces enclosed in hedges of beech, hornbeam, or lime, separated by walks which are embellished with statues as eyecatchers. This part of the garden, known as the Angles, has something of the character of a French baroque BOSQUET. In woodland to the east of the canals are rides with occasional ornamental interludes—a statue of a stricken warrior rising from a sea of wild garlic (*Allium ursinum*) and a statue of Venus. In J. N. Brewer's *The Beauties of Ireland* (1825) the author notes 'the long avenues of stately elms, the close-cut yew hedges, and regular terraces of this little St Cloud'. A magnificent domed glasshouse of *c.*1850 overlooks a Victorian parterre and pretty dairy.   PT

King Boris's Garden

Sofia, Bulgaria, considered the finest example of garden design in the country, was conceived in 1882 at the city's edge. Due to the post-war urban expansion, however, it is now the capital's large green heart, with an area of 90 hectares/220 acres. Over four distinctive periods of development the park acquired its rich appearance and diverse vegetation. The spatial concept is based on a modular system, mainly borrowing from Austrian and German baroque patterns with clear continuity in each

designer's contribution. In the 1880s, the Swiss landscape architect Daniel Neff (1843-1900) prepared the park's first plan, featuring the 'Fish Pond', and organized a large nursery to supply the necessary plants. After planting rows of false acacias (*Robinia pseudoacacia*), making flower beds, and growing extensive oak and hawthorn hedges, he established a large mixed woodland of native species: oak, beech, sycamore, birch, pine, and spruce. In 1906, Josef Fray (1873-1953) from Alsace extended the territory and elaborated its original concept, laying out several structural ALLÉES and adding sculptural elements like the limestone Bigor Fountain. His passion for flowers was expressed in spectacular flower beds and a rosarium. From 1934, under the Bulgarian garden specialist Georgi Duhtev (1885-1955), the rosarium was enriched with 1,400 new varieties and the park acquired a Japanese garden and several fountains. By 1942, with a large lake at its entrance, the park served diverse social functions, accommodating a summertime swimming complex, an observatory, an open-air library, two stadiums, tennis courts, and a cycling track. After 1945, the imposing obelisk of the National Resistance was erected and several children's playgrounds were established.   ASG

Kingdon Ward, Frank.

See WARD, FRANK KINGDON.

Kinkakuji

Kyoto city, Japan, the Temple of the Golden Pavilion, properly named Rokuonji, is a temple of the Sōkokuji branch of the Rinzai sect of Buddhism located in north-western Kyoto city just near Kinugasa Mountain. The property was first developed in 1224 by Fujiwara Kintsune (also Saionji Kintsune, 1171-1244) as his residence, Kitayamadai. A diary entry from 1225 mentions a pond like lapis lazuli and a large waterfall, but the details of the garden at that time are not clear. His descendants lived there until 1397 when military lord Ashikaga Yoshimitsu (1358-1408) took possession of the land. In 1394 Yoshimitsu had retired from the official position of shogun (chief military lord) and taken priestly vows but in fact was running the government from retirement. At the same time, he focused on the construction of the lavish estate he called Kitayamadono, Villa of the Northern Mountains. Yoshimitsu established trade relations with Ming-dynasty China, which brought him great wealth and introduced Chinese art and culture to his court and to the ruling society in general. The architecture and gardens at Kinkakuji reflect this influence.

Prominent among the many buildings on the estate was a three-storey, lakeside Buddha hall (*shariden*). The first floor was built in the style of aristocratic residences (*shinden*), the second floor in the style of samurai residences (*shoin*), and the third floor in a style associated with Zen Buddhist architecture (*karayō*), a mixture that aptly describes the blend of cultures that informed the design of the estate in general. The surfaces of the second and third floors were gilded, thus the name Kinkaku, or Gold Pavilion. The pond contained many small islands planted with pines which represented Taoist and Buddhist themes: tortoises, cranes, Mount Hōrai, and Mount Shumisen (see JAPAN). The rockwork of the islands' shores and of the Dragon's Gate waterfall (see TENRYŪJI), north of the pavilion, is indicative of Muromachi-period (1333-1568) gardens.

Upon Yoshimitsu's death, the estate was turned into a temple and named Rokuonji, Temple of the Deer Park, after his posthumous Buddhist name Rokuonin-dono. Yoshimitsu's son Yoshimochi dismantled many of the buildings and the temple fell into disrepair until the early 17th century, at which time the Tokugawa military lords lent their patronage which lasted through the Edo period (1600-1868). Hōrin Shōshō, head priest in the mid-17th century, conducted repairs on the garden, including fixing the stones of Dragon's Gate waterfall and planting pine trees. An aficionado of tea culture, Shōshō also commissioned tea master Kanamori Sōwa (1584-1656) to build a tea house, Sekkatei, which remains to this day. The temple opened to the public in 1894. The only structure remaining from Yoshimitsu's time, the Golden Pavilion itself, was burnt intentionally by an acolyte priest in 1950 and rebuilt five years later. Finally, in 1988, it was repaired and gilded once again, creating one of the most famous landmarks in Japan.   MPK

Kinross House

Kinross, Kinross-shire, Scotland, was built for his own use to the designs of Sir William BRUCE, the most distinguished Scottish architect of his day. House and garden, also designed by Bruce, were completed by 1693 and Bruce's original plans in the Scottish Record Office show that they were conceived as a whole. The estate is on the edge of the town of Kinross whose High Street originally formed the approach drive to the house. The garden is enclosed in stone walls with the house standing at its centre. A central axis not only unites house and garden but also fixes both firmly in the landscape, for it takes as an eyecatcher the ruined castle standing on an island in Loch Leven beyond the garden's boundaries. This view is revealed through a gate set in the garden wall surmounted by a carved urn filled with fish—all freshwater species and all originally found in Loch Leven. Two other openings in the garden walls were also part of the planned landscape: one ('kirk wynd') led originally to the church and the other revealed a fine grove of trees. The garden walls are built of stone and finely ornamented with piers and finials forming a distinguished background to the excellent late 20th-century mixed borders that run along below them. Close to the house is a hidden walled garden overlooked by a pavilion with the characteristic ogee-shaped roof which Bruce often designed. This is a modern rose garden with a lead statue of Atlas at the centre and a 17th-century multi-faceted SUNDIAL. This is one of the very few gardens of its date in Britain whose original layout, and almost all of its architectural detail, survives intact.   PT

kiosk

is derived from the Turkish word *kiûsk* which meant a light, usually open, garden pavilion sometimes of an ephemeral kind. In England and France (*kiosque*) the word was used to denote this from the early 17th century. Such buildings were common in the Ottoman Empire and were sometimes lavishly decorated. Lady Mary Wortley Montagu (1689-1762) on her travels saw one 'adorned with a profusion of marble, gilding and the most exquisite painting of fruit and flowers'. Some kiosks survive at TOPKAPI. In England the word often carries exotic connotations, not necessarily Turkish. At STOWE, for example, is a 'Chinese Kiosk'.   PT

Kip, Johannes. See KNYFF, LEONARD.

Kirby Hall ⊛

Corby, Northamptonshire, England, is the ghostly and beautiful remains of a magnificent Elizabethan house. It was bought in 1575 by Sir Christopher Hatton, Lord Chancellor to Queen Elizabeth. He and his descendants made the house even grander and in the late 17th century, in the time of another Christopher Hatton, embellished it with a Great Garden. It was possibly designed by George LONDON who is known to have come here in 1693. In all probability it was finely planted, for Christopher Hatton's brother Charles was a notable plantsman of the day. By the 18th century the estate had started to collapse. Only parts, but magificent parts, survive, and under the ownership of English Heritage they were given a new garden in 1994—a parterre of shaped lawns, gravel walks, and topiary copied from a George London design (for Longleat in Wiltshire).   PT

Kirstenbosch National Botanic Garden ⊛

is situated on the Cape peninsula 13 km/8 miles from the centre of Cape Town on the landward slope of Table Mountain, which makes a magnificent backdrop for the garden. The 528-hectare/1,300-acre garden has 36 hectares/89 acres that are cultivated. The remainder is diverse fynbos flora (the distinctive vegetation of the Cape) as well as an area of natural forest. Kirstenbosch is the flagship of the National Botanical Institute network of botanic gardens, and like all gardens in this group aims at displaying the indigenous flora of South Africa. Being situated in the south-western Cape, naturally its focus is on the local fynbos flora. Specialized gardens at Kirstenbosch include a fragrance garden, a medical garden, the peninsula garden, a protea garden, a restio garden, and a water-wise garden. Curiosities include The Dell, the oldest part of the garden, where a brick-lined pond fed by a mountain stream, 'Colonel Bird's bath', is overhung with tree ferns, and 'van Riebeeck's hedge'. This line of indigenous bitter almond trees (*Brabejum stellatifolium*) was planted in 1660 to mark the eastern boundary of the Dutch enclave at the Cape of Good Hope. The botanic garden was established in 1913, thanks mainly to the efforts of Sir Lionel Phillips, Harold Pearson, and Neville Pillans, on an old estate that dated back to the 1650s and which subsequently was owned by Cecil John Rhodes, who had left the farm to the state. The founding director, the eminent botanist Professor Harold Pearson, died in 1916 and his grave—with Wren's epitaph, 'If ye seek his monument, look around'—is to be found in the protea garden. He was succeeded in 1919 by fellow English botanist Robert Harold Compton, who remained director for the next 34 years. From 1954 to 1983 the position was held by Brian Rycroft, the first South African director. These pioneering days were not easy: money was short, the labour force small, and in the early days transport from Cape Town for the general public infrequent. It is fortunate that the early directors realized that the natural setting of the Kirstenbosch garden should not be dramatically altered. As Professor Compton said, 'The idea of "landscaping" Kirstenbosch was always rendered futile by the grandeur and diversity of its setting.' Kirstenbosch is one of South Africa's major tourist attractions and one of the world's great botanic gardens. It is Africa's most famous and most prestigious garden, a fact frequently recognized by the award of gold medals for its annual exhibits at the Chelsea Flower Show in England. It has the large Botanical Society Conservatory, the Kirstenbosch Research Centre, the famous Compton Herbarium, a Visitors' Centre complex, an open-air amphitheatre for the ever-popular concerts as well as a much-frequented tea garden and a restaurant. Kirstenbosch is also the home of the Botanical Society of Southern Africa, which publishes the popular magazine *Veld and Flora*.   DPMcC

Kitabatake Villa Garden ⊛

Mie prefecture, Japan, is noted for its rockwork, which exemplifies the gardens of provincial lords during the Muromachi period (1333-1568), as do Shūrinji Temple in Shiga prefecture and the ASAKURA VILLA Garden in Fukui prefecture. The present size of the garden, just under 3,000 sq. m/10,000 sq. ff, is perhaps only a third of the original. Of note in the remaining garden is the excellent selection of sculptural river rocks, the aesthetic strength expressed through their careful placement, and the rock-setting skill revealed by the fact that the rocks have not shifted over the centuries. The garden is thought to have been made under the direction of military lord Hosokawa Takakuni (1484-1531) around 1529 while he resided at the villa on the occasion of his daughter's wedding to Kitabatake Harutomo (1503-1563). Takakuni was an aristocrat and warrior who enjoyed both the cultural and military arts. The pond in the garden is said to have allowed for the aristocratic pastime of the Winding Stream Festival (*kyokusui no en*; see JAPAN) while at the same time the rockwork is praised for its rugged strength.   MPK

kitchen garden,

the most utilitarian department of the garden, and also the most ancient. The cultivation of an orchard-cum-vegetable garden in close proximity to the household or community to which it belongs is considered by the archaeologist Helen Leach to be the earliest form of gardening. She cites evidence for kitchen gardens in the Near East dating from 3,500-3,000 BC, and these may well have evolved some two or three millennia before that ('The origins of kitchen gardening in the ancient Near East', *Garden History*, Vol. 10: No. 1 (1982)). The usefulness—not to say the necessity—of a kitchen garden thereafter ensured its presence in virtually all domestic gardens, barring the smallest town gardens, until recent times.

Size and extent

The prestige of the household was reflected in the kitchen garden which served it. At the lowest end of the scale, the whole of a humble cottager's small garden might be devoted to the cultivation of vegetables, with a few fruit trees and currant bushes and perhaps a beehive (see BEEKEEPING AND GARDENS), hen coop, and rabbit hutch. The supply of fruit and vegetables would be strictly seasonal, and limited to those which thrive without artificial heat or protection from the elements, such as cabbages, leeks, onions, root vegetables, peas, and beans. Ornament would be provided, if at all, by an edging of flowers (often planted to deter insects or disease), or by small decorative flower borders. The kitchen garden of a wealthier middle-class household would occupy a relatively large space in relation to the rest of the garden. An area of 2.5 hectares/1 acre was considered enough to supply garden produce for twelve people—a moderately large family with several children and indoor servants—and would require one man and a boy to work it. It was usually enclosed by high walls to protect the garden from thieves and the weather, provide warmth and support for trained fruit trees, support lean-to glasshouses, storerooms, and work sheds, and screen the activities of the gardeners from those enjoying the recreational parts of the garden. Depending on the depth of the owner's pocket and the skill of his gardeners, the cook could expect a succession of temperate fruits, cut flowers, and vegetables all year round. At the highest end of the scale, the kitchen gardens of the aristocracy could run to many acres. These would be situated on or even beyond the boundaries of the pleasure grounds, and were often enclosed and subdivided by a series of walls. In England the royal kitchen gardens at WINDSOR CASTLE occupied 12.5 hectares/31 acres and the kitchen gardens of the Duke of Portland at Welbeck Abbey covered 9.3 hectares/23 acres. Both gardens had extensive hothouses, from which came year-round supplies of figs, grapes, peaches, nectarines, melons, pineapples, and strawberries, as well as exotic ornamental plants. In their heyday at the end of the 19th and the beginning of the 20th century, Windsor's kitchen gardens and glasshouses employed 150 gardeners; at Welbeck, where the family fortunes rested literally on coal, the glasshouse boilers consumed 60 to 70 tons per month.

Layout and design of the walled garden

Regardless of size, the layout of all walled gardens is similar; all have the same basic requirements. They are usually rectangular in plan, with the longest walls running east–west to take advantage of the sun, and with the glasshouses for the most tender fruits and plants ranged against these south-facing walls. An outer 'slip', bounded by more walls, hedges, or fences, provides further compartments for work sheds and the storage of composts, manure, and fuel, and space for the cultivation of the coarser sorts of vegetables, an orchard or nursery, and a frameyard for forcing. The open ground within the inner walls, preferably lying

on a gently sloping southern incline, is divided into 'quarters' by axial paths running north–south and east–west, and borders below the walls are bounded by a peripheral path. A central dipping pond or well traditionally provides water; alternatively, the site may be watered from a nearby reservoir or stream, or even by a stream flowing through the garden (as at Ston Easton, in Somerset). The four-square, quartered layout derives from the layout dictated by the earliest form of irrigation, when field crops and gardens were watered by a system of channels between the beds, the channels acting as paths when not conducting water. High walls provide a sheltered microclimate but, to give further protection, a shelter belt of forest trees is often also planted on the 'weather side'. If the kitchen garden is situated at a distance from the house (as was the fashion from the later half of the 18th century), a decorative walk or drive will bring visitors from the mansion to the garden. The produce, however, may be taken to the kitchens by a circuitous, hidden back route which may also allow fresh and rotted manure to be brought to the garden from the stables or home farm. Accommodation for a watchful head gardener, with bothies for the garden boys, would be nearby.

History

The horticultural skills of successional sowing, grafting, taking cuttings, hybridizing, selecting, improving, forcing, watering, and manuring were all practised in the earliest kitchen gardens in order to ensure a fresher, more succulent, and constant supply of the fruits and vegetables that were hitherto foraged for in the wild. The Greek and Roman husbandries of COLUMELLA, PLINY, and Varro give details of the bed-and-channel form of irrigation, the sowing, saving, and selection of seed, the preservation of crops, the use of manures, formation of composts, and recipes for pesticides. These instructions were handed down in monastic treatises, and followed by gardeners, well into Renaissance times. The Moorish Arabs perfected the use of the hot bed (a flat-topped mound of fresh, fermenting horse manure, capped by loam and used for raising tender or early seedlings) in the 10th and 11th centuries in southern Spain. This technique, first mentioned in about 961 in the 'Cordovan Calendar' (*Le Calendrier de Cordoue*, ed. C. Marinescu, J. M. Millàs-Vallicrosa, and H. Monés, 1961), does not appear to have reached the rest of Europe until the 14th century, when it was mentioned under 'melons' by Pietro de' CRESCENZI (*Liber Ruralium Commodorum*, c.1304). Its first use in a British garden occurs in the 16th century (Thomas HILL, *Gardeners Labyrinth*, 1577).

Renaissance gardens were used as much for beauty as utility, as places for flowers, walks, arbours, and ornament, as for culinary plants, and the walls were low. But significant changes in both horticultural techniques and layout arrived in Britain at the end of the 17th century, introduced by the Dutch King William III and his English Queen, Mary, who both loved gardens. Gardeners in the Netherlands had perfected the arts of growing fruit by dwarfing, pruning, grafting, and training, and had succeeded in growing pineapples by using tan bark instead of horse manure in their hot beds. To accommodate the new style of fruit tree growing, kitchen garden paths were lined with dwarf trees and espaliers, while lofty walls were built for taller, fan-trained trees. When dwarf trees went out of fashion at the end of the 18th century, tall armatures supported fruit trees trained as goblets or pyramids, while cross-paths were lined with herbaceous plants or covered with tunnels of trained fruit trees. Hot beds, heated walls, and primitive glasshouses began to be used extensively only in the 18th century. Hitherto, gardeners had relied on dark, insulated sheds heated by charcoal to provide winter shelter for the tender and previously unknown plants that were beginning to be brought into Europe by 16th- and 17th-century voyagers. Throughout the 18th century the heating, ventilation, and design of the GLASSHOUSE was improved, largely due to the desire to grow pineapples. In the 19th century, technological innovations in iron- and glass-making, as well as in heating, made hothouses for all kinds of fruit much more widely available. By now the walled kitchen garden was the hub of the whole garden. Besides supplying the kitchens, all the ornamental plants for the house and for the pleasure gardens would be raised here, and here the under gardeners learned their craft. In the back sheds behind the glasshouses was the head gardener's office, the mess room for the under gardeners, potting sheds, boilers, and often a mushroom house.

The future of kitchen gardens is encouraging. Their neglect began in the 1950s, but in the early years of the 21st century some are being brought back to life. The kitchen gardens at West Dean (Sussex), Audley End (Essex), and HELIGAN have been restored to Edwardian productiveness, and are now open to the fee-paying public; others are being developed by local communities to provide fresh organic produce for local consumption; others are used as therapeutic gardening centres for the physically and mentally disabled (see DISABLED PEOPLE, GARDENS FOR). Their potential as living repositories of horticultural technology, or for other practical purposes, is now well recognized.   SC

SUSAN CAMPBELL, *A History of Kitchen Gardening* (2005).

Kleingärten.

Small gardens, called *Kleingärten* in Austria, Switzerland, and Germany, ALLOTMENT gardens in the United Kingdom, *ogródek działkowy* in Poland, *rodinná zahrádka* in the Czech Republic, *kiskertek* in Hungary, *volkstuin* in the Netherlands and in Belgium, *jardins ouvriers* and *jardins familiaux* in France and Belgium, *kolonihave* in Denmark, *kolonihage* in Norway, *kolonitraedgard* in Sweden, *siirtolapuutarhat* in Finland, *shimin-noen* in Japan, community gardens—historically 'Victory Gardens'—in the USA and Canada. These, and many more names in other countries around the world, are a specific expression of the human interest in the growth of plants both for food and for aesthetic reasons. These gardens are part of the civilization in many societies and with ongoing worldwide urbanization they gain in meaning as a special kind of urban garden culture. *Kleingärten* have often been associated with the rural and the proletarian backgrounds of people who migrate to cities. True as this may be in many instances, they are cultivated by the middle classes as well. Most of these are urbanites whose families have settled in cities for several generations and like to practise gardening in small gardens which in almost all cases are grouped together in associations. The number of gardens assembled in specific locations in the inner city as well as on the periphery may range from a very few to several hundred. Even if there are a number of *Kleingärten* in rural areas most of them are located in cities. Different from home gardens, *Kleingärten*, allotment gardens, and community gardens are not attached to the urban home or apartment. There is always some distance to be covered between the home and the site where the little gardens stretch. Usually the gardens are rented on a contract basis for one or more years. Few are privately owned. Contrary to the temporary status of many of the early versions of these gardens, those with a longer history tend to turn permanent. In Germany there are about 1,000,000 *Kleingärten*, the earliest of which date back to the early 19th century, some of them still on the very first location where they were established. Most of them are organized in the Bundesverband der Gartenfreunde, the federal union of garden friends, which unites some 15,000 associations of allotment holders. In the United Kingdom many of the some 500,000 allotment gardens are organized in the National Society of Allotment and Leisure Gardeners (NSALG). In Berlin, Germany, for example, close to 900 associations have formed for the some 80,000

Kleingärten this city hosts. In order to reduce speculation in the land on which *Kleingärten* are operated and in order to avoid arbitrary cancellation of contracts, the allotment holders have organized themselves at local, provincial, and state levels and send their representatives to the respective diets, boards, commissions, and councils who decide on these matters. *Kleingärten* can be found on land which belongs to cities, states, churches, railways, industrial and commercial corporations, and private landowners. In a few countries, such as Germany and Austria, there are special laws which among many other issues rule land provision and inclusion in land use planning processes for these little gardens. Their size varies from several square metres to almost 1,000 sq. m/3,600 sq. ft. The average *Kleingärten* in Germany, the United Kingdom, and other European countries, measures about 300 to 400 sq. m/984 to 1,312 sq. ft. Most community gardens in the USA and Japan are much smaller than *Kleingärten* and allotment gardens. Their size may range from a few square metres to about 100 sq. m/328 sq. ft. In the USA the community gardens are organized in the American Community Gardening Association. A toolshed, an arbour, or a little hut can be found in most of these small gardens. Also a community house and a community playground are often part of the land for *Kleingärten* and for community gardens. In Germany a number of these small gardens are called *Schrebergärten*. This refers to a special branch of *Kleingärten* which for family kinship reasons are associated with the name of a surgeon who historically served as a name patron for early *Kleingärten* in Leipzig, Germany, but who had no particular involvement with *Kleingärten* (see SCHREBERANLAGE).   GG

Klein-Glienicke ⊛

Berlin, Germany. Situated between Berlin and Potsdam at a narrowing of the Havel river, Glienicke marks a central location within the cultural landscape of Potsdam. Peter Joseph LENNÉ undertook the work on State Chancellor Hardenberg's pleasure grounds in the years 1816–17 as his first project in Potsdam. Even in this early work, the high quality of Lenné's ground modelling is apparent. Under Prince Carl of Prussia, the next owner of Glienicke, a fruitful cooperation developed between the architect Karl Friedrich SCHINKEL, who was responsible for the conversion and expansion of the buildings, and Lenné. During this time the former billiards house, situated on the banks of the Havel, was converted to a CASINO and the mansion was enlarged to become a residence. The *casino* was visually extended by pergolas

and, by framing views, connected to the Havel river landscape. Glienicke offers a classical sequence from the courtyard of the residence, which is designed as a flower garden, to the intensively designed pleasure grounds and on to the larger spaces of the park and landscape. Under Prince Carl, whose visit to Italy from 1822 to 1823 had a decisive influence on the design of Glienicke, the park grew to over 100 hectares/247 acres. In 1837, the architect Ludwig Persius (1803–1845) built the steam engine house, with the help of which the park as well as the pleasure grounds could be watered. Numerous waterworks were integrated in the flower garden and the pleasure grounds. The park offers romantic settings with artificial waterfalls, picturesque bridges, artificial rock formations, and ornamental boulders. After Prince Carl's death in 1883, the park grounds were neglected. Further disturbance occurred in 1938 when parts of the pleasure ground were covered by excavation material from a street expansion. Careful restoration work, beginning in 1978, has restored the former quality of Glienicke.   APa

KLAUS VON KROSIGK and HEINZ WIEGAND, *Glienicke* (1992).

Knight, Richard Payne

(1750–1824), English author and garden theorist. Inheriting the estate of Downton Castle in Shropshire in 1770 he rebuilt the castle in extravagantly picturesque Gothic style. He also embellished the banks of the river Teme which flowed through the estate with rustic bridges, grottoes, viewpoints, and planned walks. In a 'didactic poem', *The Landscape* (1794), he criticized the landscape style of Capability BROWN, that 'genius of the bare and bald' with his 'sheets of vapid lawn'. Knight loved the picturesque style and wrote, no doubt thinking of his own estate: 'Bless'd is he, who, 'midst his tufted trees, | Some ruin'd castle's lofty towers sees; | Imbosom'd high upon the mountain's brow, | Or nodding o'er the stream that glides below.' In his *Analytical Inquiry into the Principles of Taste* (1805) he emphasized the power of the picturesque to stimulate the imagination.   PT

Knightshayes Court ⊛

near Tiverton, Devon, England, was built for Sir John Heathcoat Amory to the designs of William Burges (1827–81) from 1867. Where the house faces south over parkland Edward KEMP, shortly after the house was built, designed terracing with a flight of steps leading down to a pool, lawns, gravel and paved walks, and ornaments of urns and yew topiary. At the upper level, close to the house, he laid out a bowling green enclosed in monumental yew hedges. In the 1950s Sir John and Lady

Heathcoat Amory made changes to the garden. A circular lily pool was made at the centre of the bowling green, new borders planted along the top terrace, and to the east, in existing woodland, they laid out a woodland garden of exceptional quality. Against a background of beeches, larches, oak, and Scots pines they introduced ornamental trees and shrubs. Here are acers, Japanese flowering cherries, dogwoods (*Cornus* spp.), with camellias, hydrangeas, magnolias, rhododendrons, and viburnums planted in glades. Lavish underplantings of exotic bulbous plants— cyclamen, erythroniums, fritillaries, narcissi, and scillas—intermingle with the native bluebells (*Hyacinthoides non-scripta*), wild garlic (*Allium ursinum*), and wood anemones (*Anemone nemorosa*). A fine form of the American *Erythronium revolutum* discovered here, 'Knightshayes Pink', has become naturalized. The exotic planting in the woodland is introduced into the largely native woodland with a deft hand and plants are the only ornament. More subtle, and less ostentatious, than many of the Cornish woodland gardens, it is a masterpiece of its kind. The estate has belonged to the NATIONAL TRUST since 1973. PT

knot garden.

The knot garden, a pattern of intertwined hedges or other low planting, dates from the Renaissance and is a precursor of the PARTERRE—indeed it is impossible to say at what stage the knot became the parterre. It seems likely that the idea of the knot garden had its origins in Renaissance Italy. The earliest detailed descriptions are found in Francesco Colonna's HYPNEROTOMACHIA POLIPHILI (1499). Colonna describes knot gardens in words and illustrations, showing several designs. One has an elaborate pattern of intertwined hedges breaking out into repeated circles and with a rosette at the centre. Colonna describes the hedging woven 'alternately above and below each other' and mentions the plants used— marjoram, thyme, germander, 'amethystine violets', primulas, cyclamen, wormwood, and hyssop. He illustrates another knot, planted with simples (that is, herbs), with a linear pattern of octagons overlapping with squares interconnected by their corners. Here 'the lines of the pattern were made with bands of white marble fixed in the ground, and four and a half inches wide on their surface and bordered on either side with simples'. Many different plants were used—achillea, wild thyme, groundsel (!), and tarragon—and 'Every free square was covered with flowering cyclamen, and their bands were of myrtle'. A further design shows an eagle with an inscription—'the herbs . . . were always green and of uniform height. . . .

Tiny pipes in orderly arrangements irrigated it with a spray of fine droplets.' Designs of this sort made their way to France in the reign of François I (1494-1547) and in the course of the 16th century were frequently found in great gardens of the time. Many are illustrated in Androuet DU CERCEAU's *Les Plus Excellents Bastiments de France* (1576-9). At the Château de DAMPIERRE, for example, a moated garden is illustrated with no less than 24 square knot gardens with no pattern repeated.

In England the knot garden dates from early Tudor times. Grose's *Antiquarian Repertory* (1808) quotes a description of the garden of Henry VII's Richmond Palace as it was in 1501 when Prince Arthur married Catherine of Aragon, 'under the King's window, Queen's, and other estates, with royal knots alleyed and herbed; many marvellous beasts, as lions, dragons, and such other divers kinds, properly fashioned and carved in the ground, right well sanded'. Thomas HILL's *A Most Briefe and Pleasaunte Treatyse* (c.1558) has a frontispiece depicting a modest garden with a knot enclosed in a trellis-work fence and he included many patterns in *The Gardeners Labyrinth* (1577). Hill does not describe knots but mentions in a caption 'Tyme, or Isop' as appropriate plants. College gardens at Oxford (see OXFORD UNIVERSITY COLLEGE GARDENS) had knot gardens by the end of the 16th century. By the early 17th century knots were still being made and were popular but probably no longer fashionable. Books such as Olivier de Serres's *Le Théâtre d'agriculture et mesnage des champs* (1600) and William Lawson's *The Countrie Housewifes Garden* (1617) both illustrate them. No original knot garden survives but good modern re-creations may be seen at HATFIELD HOUSE, at Moseley Old Hall (Staffordshire), and at the Musée Carnavalet in Paris. See also HERB GARDEN. PT

Knyff, Leonard

(1650-1721), Dutch artist from Haarlem who, from 1676, painted houses and their gardens in England. His paintings, engraved by Johannes Kip and published in collections such as *Britannia Illustrata* (1707), are both very ornamental and richly informative about an especially important period of garden making in England. Knyff's magnificent view of Hampton Court (c.1704), exhibited at Hampton Court, is one of the relatively few oil paintings by him to survive. PT

ROY STRONG, *The Artist and the Garden* (2000).

Koishikawa Kōrakuen

Tokyo, Japan (not to be confused with KŌRAKUEN in Okayama), about 7 hectares/17 acres at present, is a classic example of the large

stroll gardens built during the Edo period (1600-1868) by provincial lords (*daimyō*; see JAPAN). The paths that lead around the large, central pond traverse a number of garden 'scenes' ranging in imagery from famous landscapes (*meishō*) of Japan and China to Confucian symbols.

The garden was begun in 1629, when Tokugawa Yorifusa (1603-61), first lord of Mito province, received a deed of land from the shogun (chief military lord) Tokugawa Iemitsu (1604-51), to be used for his residence near Edo castle. The initial garden design was done, at least in part, by one Tokudaiji Sahei, whose name is connected with gardening though little is known of his personal history. Also, Iemitsu is recorded to have visited and personally overseen the reconstruction of the ponds.

The next phase in the development of the garden happened during the time of the second Mito lord, Tokugawa Mitsukuni (1628-1700), who is known for his interest in Chinese culture, especially Confucianist theories. He hosted Zhu Zhiyu (Japanese: Shu Shunshui, 1600-82), a Confucian scholar who fled to Japan from the collapsing Ming dynasty in 1659. Shunshui named the garden Kōraku after a maxim in the Northern Sung-dynasty text *Yueyanglou ji*, 'A true Lord takes his pleasure (*raku*) after (*kō*) the nation (or emperor).' Mitsukuni's general interest in China, along with Shunshui's influence in the late 1660s, resulted in an abundance of Chinese images being built into the garden. Some of the scenes included are: the West Lake Causeway (Seikō no tsutsumi) and Little Mount Lushan (Shōrozan) which are images of China; the Pavilion of Gaining Virtue (Tokujindō) which enshrined an image of the Zhou-dynasty Boya and Shuji brothers, a Confucian image; the Ōi river, Tōgetsukyō bridge, and Tsūtenkyō bridge, all of which are scenes from the ancient capital of Kyoto. During and after the Meiji period (1868-1912), the Ministry of the Army used much of the property, and what is left today is only the central core of the old garden. MPK

Kokei no Niwa.

See NISHIHONGANJI.

Kolozsvár.

See CLUJ BOTANIC GARDEN.

Komarov Botanical Institute ⊛

St Petersburg, Russia, named after the botanist V. L. Komarov (d. 1945), has its origins in the Apothecary's Garden, established on an island (later known as Apothecary's Island) in the delta of the river Neva in 1714, when it was concerned with the collection and cultivation of herbs for pharmaceutical purposes. The range of plants soon grew wider, embracing those with economic and aesthetic potential, with introductions from Western Europe and as far away as Siberia and China. In 1736 1,275 species were recorded. Following the death in 1822 of Count Razumovsky, the owner of the famous private botanical garden at Gorenky near Moscow, his botanical library, part of his herbarium, and a number of his plants were acquired by the St Petersburg garden, while F. E. L. Fisher, a distinguished botanist who had been in charge at Gorenky, became director (1823–50) in St Petersburg. Another director, E. L. Regel (1855–66 and 1875–92), was both a distinguished botanist and a leading authority on ornamental gardening and landscape design. Under his direction many exotic plants from all parts of the world became available to Russian gardens. and it was on his initiative that the Russian Horticultural Society was founded. By 1917 there were about 5,000 species in the open ground and many more in the 28 glasshouses. Enormous damage was suffered by the garden and particularly by the glasshouses during the Second World War, but a good recovery was made in the decades which followed.   PH

Konchiin ⊗

Kyoto city, Japan, is a sub-temple of Nanzenji, a large temple of the Rinzai sect of Zen Buddhism. The garden of note is a dry landscape garden (KARESANSUI) in the southern court of the main hall (*hōjō*), approximately 3,800 sq. m/12,464 sq. ft in size. The garden is noteworthy because of its striking design but also because of the clear documentation regarding its construction found in the diary of the head priest, Ishin Sūden (1569–1633), and other sources. From this we know that Kobori Enshū (1579–1647), the Minister of Construction, was clearly involved with the garden's design, and Murase Sasuke and Kentei, two well-known gardeners, guided the construction. The entries describe the busy lives of Sūden and Enshū, the difficulties they had beginning and completing the work on schedule, and Sūden's great satisfaction at hearing of the garden's completion in 1632 (though he died before actually seeing it).

The forward portion of the garden area (northern, close to the main hall) is a flat expanse of fine white gravel raked in the pattern of waves. In the rear, in front of a steep slope covered with large, tightly clipped shrubs, are two hillocks with stone arrangements representing a crane and a tortoise isle, images relating to Mount Hōrai (see JAPAN) and longevity. The crane and tortoise were considered appropriate images to create a solemn and respectful atmosphere for the main

hall. The evergreen (*Juniperus chinensis*) that grows on the tortoise isle (the eastern of the two) is most likely original. In between the two isles lies a large flat stone called the *reiseki* or Stone of Obeisance. The mausoleum of the founder lies on a bluff overlooking the garden and it is thought that visitors to the temple would have crossed the garden from a gate on the east side and paid their respects to the founder from the *reiseki*, before entering the main hall.   MPK

Kōrakuen ⊗

Okayama prefecture, Japan, a public park since 1884, was originally the estate garden of the Ikeda family, lords of Okayama province. Covering about 11.5 hectares/28 acres, the garden lies on the curve of the Asahi river just across the river from Okayama castle, which is prominently visible, and purposefully incorporated as a scenic view, from the garden. The garden was initiated by Ikeda Tsunamasa (1638–1714) in 1686 with work continuing until around 1700. Construction was overseen by Tsuda Nagatada (1640–1707), the Minister of Construction for the province, who had also rebuilt the province's finances through clever agricultural and irrigation projects. Originally, the garden was known by names such as Saenba (the Vegetable Fields), Chaya yashiki (the Tea house Villa), and Kōen (the Park Behind [the castle]), with the comparatively recent name, Kōrakuen (see KOISHIKAWA KŌRAKUEN for the meaning), dating from 1871.

Some portions of the garden stem from the mid to late 18th century, such as the central, azalea-covered hillock, Yuishinzan, and the large areas of lawn that replaced the cultivated fields that used to exist within the garden area. Agricultural imagery still features prominently in the garden, however, for instance the carefully pruned rows of tea shrubs (*Camellia sinensis*) and plum orchards on the west side of the site. There is, as well, a small square rice paddy, divided into nine equal sections, which was built in the mid 19th century as a 1 : 100 scale model of a Zhou-dynasty agricultural land division scheme that had been experimented with in the province. Kōrakuen underwent extensive renovation through the 20th century and the gardens and architecture are now in excellent repair. As with most Edo-period stroll gardens (see JAPAN), the design of Kōrakuen centres on a large, shallow pond, which, combined with the extensive areas of lawn, gives the garden a feeling of openness and breadth not found in other forms of Japanese gardens.   MPK

Kórnik Arboretum ⊗

near Poznań, Poland. The Kórnik castle, built in

the 15th century by Lake Kórnickie and surrounded by a wide moat, was remodelled *c.*1570 and renovated in the second half of the 18th century by Teofila Potulicka. She also created the first known baroque garden. Tytus Działyński (1796–1861) decided to arrange a library in the castle that—in view of the lack of national institutions (the Polish state did not exist then)—would function as a national cultural institution. In 1839–42 the castle assumed the neo-Gothic form of a fortress surrounded by a moat (partly designed by Karl Friedrich SCHINKEL). From 1842 Działyński replaced the formal garden by a landscape park. He also begun to introduce exotic trees and flowers. In his time magnolias and tulip trees (*Liriodendron tulipifera*) among other species were planted. This interest was continued by his son Jan Działyński (1829–80), who consciously converted the Kórnik park into botanical gardens, so that in addition to the subject of history studied in the library, botany became a subject of research at Kórnik. In addition the orchards were cultivated and much care was taken with the development of fruit farming, and agricultural exhibitions were organized. In the early 20th century the arboretum comprised 216 species of trees and shrubs and until up to the Second World War the number of trees in the park significantly increased until *c.*4,000 species of trees and shrubs were grown in an area of *c.*40 hectares/99 acres. In 1949 Kórnik was taken over by the Polish Academy of Sciences, which arranged a library and museum in the castle and now maintains the park.   WB

Kozłówka ⊗

near Lubin, Poland. The garden was created in the first half of the 18th century together with a baroque palace of the *entre cour et jardin* (between courtyard and garden) type designed by Jakub Fontana in 1742. On the axis of the palace there was a *salon de verdure* (see CABINET) with parterres, bordered by double rows of trees, while the lateral axis in a southerly direction was formed by twelve rectangular BOSQUETS. After Kozłówka passed into the hands of the Zamoyski family (1799), the garden underwent a transformation through the removal of the *bosquets* and the conversion of the whole into an irregular composition. In 1897–1911 the palace was rebuilt, transformed into a grand neo-baroque residence. Franciszek Szanior (1853–1945) imparted a neo-baroque character to the garden in the immediate vicinity of the palace. The access ALLÉES in front of the *cour d'honneur* (see ATTRE, CHÂTEAU D') assumed the form of a PATTE D'OIE, ornamental parterres were restored, and the principal garden axis was extended beyond the pleasure grounds. This neo-baroque garden was surrounded by a landscape park. The 1920s saw the introduction of a spacious bowling green in the *cour d'honneur*. After 1945 a museum was established in the palace, and in the course of the last twenty years the garden has been restored, thereby regaining its character from before the Second World War.   WB

Krelage Nursery,

Haarlem, Noord-Holland, the Netherlands, dominated the bulb trade during most of the 19th century. Arriving as an apprentice in the Netherlands in 1804 the Hanover-born Ernst Heinrich Krelage (1786–1855) founded his own nursery in Haarlem in 1811. This area had been the centre of the Dutch bulb industry since the 17th century. Over the years he expanded the nursery by acquiring others, including that of Voorhelm and Schneevoogt, which had dominated the bulb trade during the 18th century. It was however Krelage's son Jacob Heinrich (1824–1901) who made the firm world famous through efficient marketing, which he also brought to bear on the Dutch Bulb Growers' Society that he founded in 1860, which flourished as a result. By starting this society he provided the foundation for the success of the Dutch bulb trade during the late 19th and the 20th century. Today he is perhaps best known for the launch of the Darwin tulips in 1886, which he named after Charles Darwin (with the latter's son's permission). They had however derived from a collection of bulbs he had bought at the sale of the collection from the nursery of Jules Lenglart in Lille the previous year. His business acumen was fully established when he seized the opportunity to provide the 1889 Exposition Universelle in Paris with large-scale bedding schemes consisting wholly of this tulip. In 1921, the final year of the firm's existence, it launched a new race which from 1923 has been distinguished as Mendel tulips.   JW

Krieger, Johan Cornelius

(1683–1755), Danish architect and gardener. One of the greatest garden architects in Denmark, he had an unusual career from the 1720s as both royal garden inspector and chief national building master. When a series of Scandinavian wars was concluded in 1720, King Frederik IV started several large-scale projects, three of which were undertaken at the same time: FREDENSBORG PALACE, FREDERIKSBORG CASTLE, and Frydenlund Manor. Krieger's great skill in shaping the terrain can be seen not only at Frederiksborg, but also in the cascades of FREDERIKSBERG GARDENS, at CLAUSHOLM, and at Ledreborg. At the same time, Krieger altered

the gardens at Rosenborg Palace, and planned the gardens at Hirschholm Palace and the King's Gardens in Odense. Influenced by André LE NÔTRE, but not slavishly copying him, Krieger created both level, classic baroque gardens and Italian-inspired terraced gardens. After the Copenhagen fire of 1728 he recommended a model for gentry terraced houses with uniform street façades in brick.
                                                        AL

Kröller Müller Museum, Beeldentuin ✤

Hoenderloo, Gelderland, the Netherlands, is located on De Veluwe, an area of sandy heathland acquired by Anton George Kröller between 1909 and 1917. He regarded his estate, De Hoge Veluwe, mainly as a hunting ground, displacing farmers and fencing an enormous area, to restore the natural landscape. Helene Kröller-Müller conceived the idea of building a museum in the centre of this area as a symbol of the unity of decorative arts, architecture, and nature. The recession halted any further developments and the estate was donated to the government on the condition that it would complete the plan and create a National Park to protect the whole area. While the museum was finished in 1938 to designs by Henri van de Velde, the sculpture garden was only established after the Second World War. In 1955 A. M. Hammacher, director of the museum, commissioned designs from the landscape architect J. T. P. BIJHOUWER, with a second phase by him in 1965. Situated within uniquely wooded sand dunes, the first part immediately behind the museum consists of a layout with well-maintained lawns with winding paths, and a small pond, with stands of trees. Thus a number of open-air rooms were created, for displaying the sculptures. The second part has larger rooms, of a more naturalistic appearance, with fewer walks. Work displayed here is of the best international modern sculptors. A further extension took place in 1988. During 1995 West 8 (see GEUZE, ADRIAAN) landscape architects reviewed the 21 hectares/52 acres of the layout and proposed to diversify the predominantly native vegetation with ornamental planting, which is being implemented over a number of years.   JW

GILES WATERFIELD, 'Art in a woodland setting: the Kröller Müller Museum, Holland', *Country Life*, Vol. 170: No. 4383 (1981).

Kultaranta (Gullranda) Garden ✤

Naantali, Finland, is currently the summer residence of the Finnish presidents. The industrial magnate Alfred Kordelin (1868–1917) originally established Villa Gullranda and its garden in 1909–17 on a site of 56 hectares/165

acres. The National Romantic villa with its lookout tower was designed by the architect Lars Sonck (1870–1956) in 1913, together with a BANDSTAND. The granite buildings were characteristically located on a forested hilltop by the sea. The garden proper consisted of two parts, an informal forest garden terraced on the hill and a formal garden on sheltered even ground next to the hill (there also was a roof garden, now disappeared). These were designed from 1914 on by the city of Helsinki head gardener Svante Olsson (1856–1941) and his son, garden architect Paul OLSSON, and were carried out by 1920.

The composition of the formal garden or 'Medaillon' reflects the German *Architecturgarten* style adopted by Paul Olsson from his training in Köstritz. It is surrounded by a dark *Picea abies* hedge and the plan is rigorously disposed about the main axis, which is not directly linked with the villa building. A rosary, ornamental fountains, a colonnade PERGOLA, labyrinthine walks, and colour gardens follow each other in the course of the axis, accentuated by the cypress-like *Populus tremula* 'Erecta' and articulated by cross-axes. Kultaranta presents an extraordinary synthesis between the richly detailed rectilinear garden, the harsh coastal climate, and the irregular terrain.

The central parts of the garden have been remarkably well maintained in their original form. In the 1960s, a modernist element—the 'Chain'—was added by landscape architect Professor Maj-Lis ROSENBRÖIJER. The garden today also houses a collection of sculpture.
                                                        MHay

Kungsträdgården ✤

Stockholm, Sweden, is together with Humlegården (from 1619 onwards), the oldest surviving garden of the capital, although it has undergone several substantial remodellings. Today it serves as the public's living room, intensely used with weekly entertainment and cultural events, with about 3 million visitors a year. Kungsträdgården has its origin in a cluster of small medieval KITCHEN GARDENS and orchards close to the church of St Jacob and from 1430 there was a royal garden. King Gustav Vasa's gardener, the Dutchman Hans Friese (from 1545), may have worked in the grounds as well as his successor, the Frenchman Jean Allard, during the late 16th century. At that time the garden was both enlarged and improved, and given its still extant strict rectangular shape. Between 1620 and 1645 the grounds were developed lavishly as an enclosed pleasure garden. A detailed inventory of 1648, when gardener Hendrich Locher handed over the garden to André MOLLET, shows a formal garden with a great summer house (which also served as an orangery), box parterres, a labyrinth, rare fruit trees, and a kitchen garden. A later inventory, of 1661, shows Mollet's influence—larger beds, PARTERRES *en broderie*, a GIARDINO SECRETO—a unity. In 1666 gardener Christian Horleman (1633–87) was called in from the Netherlands. His work was continued by his son Johan HÅRLEMAN who in 1688 was appointed comptroller for all royal gardens in Sweden. They transformed Kungsträdgården into a LE NÔTRE-style baroque garden with a central axis, avenues, BOSQUETS, *parterres en broderie*, and a central fountain. In 1796 Fredrik Magnus PIPER redesigned Kungsträdgården with inspiration both from Italy and England, with a central oval lawn, viewpoints, avenues, and several shrubberies. In addition he redesigned the ORANGERY as a Temple of Flora. King Gustav III opened Kungsträdgården to the public in the 1780s.

At the beginning of the 19th century all greenery between the avenues was removed and replaced with sand, functioning as a military exercise area. Greenery was replanted in the middle of the 19th century. Kungsträdgården got its character of a modern city park for everyday use when it was remodelled by the city of Stockholm in the 1950s. The theatre, pavilions, tea house and a new fountain date from that time. In 1971 Kungsträdgården became a worldwide scene for the 'Elm Battle' in which environmental activists occupied the elms (*Ulmus glabra*) and prevented the felling of one to allow the building of a new subway station, as a general protest against the frenzy of demolition in Stockholm. Today Kungsträdgården functions as both a square and a park. A new axial rebuilding took place during the 1990s, something of a pastiche; adding a sunken pool, a public ice rink, and cherry groves.   KL

Kuskovo ⊛

near Moscow, Russia. The palace and the formal gardens (31 hectares/77 acres) have survived of the country estate of the Sheremetevs, 10 km/6 miles from Moscow. Though the gardens were begun in the 1720s, they date from the middle of the 18th century in their present form, while the palace was rebuilt in the 1770s. The gardens were planned by the architect Fyodor Argunov (1732–68), a serf, who also designed some of the buildings in the garden. The large central parterre is embellished with marble statues. Beyond the parterre Argunov's impressive orangery faces the palace along the central axis. A network of paths leads from the parterre to form *étoiles* (star-shaped patterns) in the flanking BOSQUETS. The trees bordering the paths frequently frame garden pavilions or views of the palace. Argunov's Dutch House (1749), the earliest of the garden buildings, once had a small garden planted with typical Dutch flowers. RASTRELLI's influence is evident in the Grotto (by Argunov) and the HERMITAGE, at the meeting place of eight paths, which was also designed by serf architects. There used to be an elaborate green THEATRE and a menagerie with a collection of birds and animals. On the other side of the palace, concealed from the garden, is an artificial lake, and beyond it a canal continued the central axis and was aligned with the village church of Veshnyaki.

Kuskovo was designed as a great parade garden and was frequently the setting for receptions, theatrical performances, concerts, fêtes, and FIREWORK displays. There has been considerable restoration.   PH

Kwekerij Piet Oudolf.

See OUDOLF, KWEKERIJ PIET.

Laberinto de Horta, El ✿

Barcelona, Spain. The slopes north-west of Barcelona were by the late 18th century a fashionable place for the estates of the gentry. Joan Antonio Desvalls i d'Ardena, Marqués de Llupiá, came here in 1791 and built an eclectic house—a mixture of Muslim, Roman, and Gothic—designed by Domenico Bagutti. In his large garden, of 9 hectares/22 acres, he introduced various features of which the best known is a MAZE. Fashioned of beautifully clipped Italian cypress (*Cupressus sempervirens*) it has as its goal a statue of Eros framed in arcades of cypress at the centre. The sloping site is laced with winding or straight paths shaded by many excellent trees, for the most part evergreen—among them umbrella pines (*Pinus pinea*), deodars (*Cedrus deodara*), and cotton palms (*Washingtonia filifera*). In the upper reaches of the garden a Palladian *tempietto* overlooks a large balustraded pool which serves as an irrigation cistern. Ornaments everywhere enrich the garden—nymphs stand or recline in rustic grottoes, urns and busts line a grand staircase, a Tuscan temple has a figure of Diana, and a hermitage stands in the shade. The estate remained in private hands until recent times, but it was acquired by the city of Barcelona and opened to the public in 1971.   PT

labyrinth.

See MAZE.

Ladew Topiary Gardens ✿

Monkton, Maryland, USA, were designed and developed by Harvey S. Ladew, a bon vivant and avid fox-hunter. After serving in the First World War, he spent twenty winters fox-hunting in England. In 1929, the sport drew Ladew to rural Maryland where he purchased the 81-hectare/200-acre Pleasant Valley Farm, adjacent to a Hunt Club. After completing renovations and additions to the house, with a superb collection of English furniture, he turned his attention to the grounds. Years abroad had exposed him to English and Italian gardens. Drawing upon these traditions, he designed a 9-hectare/22-acre garden with two long axes crossing at an oval swimming pool. Along the axes are fifteen garden rooms, each dedicated to a single theme and discreetly apart from the others. These include a White Garden, a Garden of Eden, and a Temple of Venus. The highpoint is the Topiary Sculpture Garden with its unicorn and seahorses of hemlock (*Tsuga canadensis*) and yew (*Taxus* spp.). Ladew had once seen a topiary hunting scene on a hedge in England and recreated it in his garden. Today, a fox, followed by hounds, can be seen bounding across a lawn and over a hedge. Ladew Topiary Gardens was opened to the public five years before Ladew's death in 1971. The Garden Club of America has called it 'the most outstanding topiary garden in America'. In 1999, a 2.4-km/1.5-mile nature walk was added. It leads through the woodland, fields, and, via a boardwalk, over a marsh.   CO

Laeken ✿

(Domaine Royal de Laeken and Serres Royales), Avenue du Parc Royal, Brussels, Belgium. The estate of Laeken was started by the Austrian governors-general in 1781 and is today the main residence of the Belgian royal family. It was the first complete example in Belgium of the English landscape style—paths wind between copses and temples, grottoes, an artificial waterfall, large ponds, and a canal are set in an undulating landscape. Some of the Domaine Royal can be seen when the Royal Glasshouses open to the public each year in the spring. These are attached to the Orangery designed by G. J. Henry around 1817–18. Leopold II, who had travelled widely in North Africa, India, and China and seen tropical flora growing in the wild, added first the large circular domed Winter Garden, designed by Alphonse Balat (1818–1905) after 1874. This magnificent iron and glass curvilinear structure, 57 m/187 ft in diameter and supported by Doric columns, contains many mature palms. It was planted originally by John Wills, an English landscape gardener. This was the beginning of the expansion of the glasshouses to their present area of 1.4 hectares/3.5 acres. Separate greenhouses containing palms, tropical ferns, azaleas, hibiscus, medinillas, and hydrangeas are linked by a series of glass corridors lined with pelargoniums, fuchsias, and curtains of *Abutilon megapotamicum*. The public Parc de Laeken, of 26 hectares/64 acres, contains a monument to Leopold I. The Japanese Tower and the Chinese Pavilion, bought by Leopold II at the 1900 Paris Exhibition, can be seen nearby.   BA

Lake Dal,

Kashmir. In the Srinagar valley, where the Jhelum river expands into Lake Wular and Lake Dal, a propitious climate and a sheltered location favoured the permanent settlement of a farming community. Lake Dal is a shallow, reclaimed marshland and is intensely cultivated both along its shores and on its floating islands, rafts built of woven vegetable fibres. In the Mughal period the aesthetic value of the lake gardens began to take precedence, beginning with Akbar (1556–1605), and in the 18th century the pleasure gardens and vegetable gardens were said to number over 700. Queen Victoria's red mantle (mid 19th century), conserved at the Victoria and Albert Museum in London, faithfully reproduces the local topography, with Lake Dal, Jhelum river and its canals, the city of Srinagar, and the gardens, including the names of the most famous ones, NISHAT BAGH, SHALAMAR BAGH, CHASMA SHAHI, and NASIM BAGH. The land conformation, shut in by the mountains and the lake, and the numerous springs have influenced building methods and the shape of the lake gardens, in which the considerable quantity of water needed to be regimented. The flat and static pools of the dry plains of India were replaced by lively waterfalls, fountains, and canals, while the slopes were modelled in a series of terraces. Not only was Lake Dal the focal point of this watery world, it also represented its route network, since the gardens were only accessible from the lake for the grandees of the Mughal Empire, who would exchange courtesy visits while out boating.

AP

A. PETRUCCIOLI, 'Gardens and religious topography in Kashmir', in *Mughal Pomp and Ceremonies, Environmental Design*, Vols. 1–2 (1991).

Lancaster, Roy

(b. 1937), English plantsman and botanist. A schoolboy fascination with the local flora led Lancaster to his first job in Bolton parks department to which he returned after two years' National Service in Malaya, having collected over 1,000 plant specimens. A student at Cambridge University Botanic Garden, he joined HILLIER's Nursery in 1962 as horticultural botanist, playing a major role in producing

Hillier's Manual of Trees and Shrubs (1971). Becoming curator of the Hillier Arboretum, he participated in the plant collecting expedition to east Nepal, resulting in his book *Plantsman in Nepal* (1995). From 1980 to 1986 he participated in six China expeditions, described in *Travels in China a Plantsman's Paradise* (1989). A most distinguished plantsman and outstanding communicator, Lancaster is the recipient of many honours, including the Royal Horticultural Society Veitch Memorial Medal, the Victoria Medal of Honour, and in 2002 the Garden Writers' Guild Lifetime Achievement Award.   MC-C

land art

is a form of art whose most distinctive characteristic is a relationship with landscape. It emerged in the 1960s and has developed a large body of works which, while certainly not gardens, share with garden design a desire to create, manipulate, or embellish a landscape. Although the term is a modern one the practice has ancient antecedents. One of the great inspirations of land art has been the enigmatic ancient markings or monuments on the earth's surfaces whose original purpose remains unknown. The monumental circle of standing stones at Stonehenge in Wiltshire (England) is thought to date from *c.*3500 BC and possesses extraordinary presence in the landscape. It is only one example, although a particularly large one, of numerous mysterious stone ornaments which are found along the western fringes of Europe presumably of Celtic origin. Even if the purpose of Stonehenge was utilitarian or ceremonial its makers must surely have been aware of its purely visual qualities. In Peru the Nazca Lines in the desert south of Lima are patterns of lines etched in the land, abstract rectilinear patterns, or depictions of birds, insects, and animals. Some of the lines are many miles along and the patterns reveal themselves only when seen from the air. The earliest patterns date from around 200 BC but were recognized as such in modern times only in the 1930s when a plane first flew over them. A more recent form of early land art is the 18th-century turf terraces found in Britain in such landscape gardens as CASTLE KENNEDY in Scotland and CLAREMONT in England. The late 20th-century work of Charles Jencks (b. 1939) and Maggie Keswick (1941–95) at PORTRACK, with voluptuously curving turf terraces embracing sweeps of water, is in the same tradition.

There has never been a land art 'movement' in any kind of organized way, rather a gradually emerging number of artists whose activities have certain similarities. One of the first of them was the American Robert Smithson (1938–73), primarily a sculptor but who worked in several different media. One of his most beautiful works is the stone *Spiral Jetty* (1970) shaped like the head of a bishop's crozier but of immense size, 450 m/1,500 ft long, jutting out into the waters of the Great Salt Lake in Utah. As the water rises and falls the jetty is submerged or displayed, sometimes with a fringe of algae. Smithson was inspired by the remarkable pre-Columbian earthworks of the Great Serpent Mound in Ohio and, indeed, *Spiral Jetty* has all the inscrutable presence of the archaeological remains of some enigmatic ancient culture. James Turrell (b. 1943) has been involved in an epic work-in-progress of land art since 1972, still incomplete in recent times. This is the Roden Crater, an extinct volcano in Arizona, which Turrell has been transforming into a celestial observatory. Michael Heizer (b. 1944) also works on an immense scale. As a painter he made shaped canvases with voids sculpted in the centre. In the Mojave desert from 1968 he created *North, East, South, West* by excavating pits in the sand similar in shape to the holes in his canvases. He now lives in a remote part of the Nevada desert where he has been exploring ways of fashioning the landscape—motorbike trails across the sand, patterns of dyes scattered across the surface, and immense trenches dug into the ground at random intervals and covering huge distances. Since 1971 he has been at work on *City*, a pattern of giant concrete upright shapes rising from the sand.

These North American practitioners of land art work on the grand scale, no doubt in response to the grandeur of the landscape and the ferocity of the climate. In England land art takes a very different form, usually more intimate and often with an elegiac quality. Richard Long (b. 1945) from 1967 made walking an art, at first striking out in a straight line across a grass field—the work being visible only as the ephemeral traces of his passage. Long's book *A Walk across England* (1997) is a series of photographs and occasional brief captions describing a 382-mile walk from coast to coast. Other land artists, in particular Andy Goldsworthy (b. 1956), make structures out of material, such as fallen wood, leaves, snow, or ice, that will swiftly decay or be dispersed. The only way of making a permanent record of such events and objects is by written description, drawings or photography. A graphic, and permanent, record is the artist's (and the dealer's) only way of making money out of something whose essence is transitory. Andy Goldsworthy photographs his work and often exhibits it with related texts. The images he creates are extraordinarily beautiful and many are shown in his book *Andy Goldsworthy* (1990).

PT

Landhaus Cramer,

Berlin, Germany, Berlin-Dahlem, was built in 1912–13 for the grain merchant Hans Cramer according to designs of the German architect Hermann MUTHESIUS. The garden, also designed by Muthesius, was executed by the garden firm of Jacob Ochs from Hamburg. The geometric-architectonic garden in a space of about 0.4 hectare/1 acre is subdivided into several functionalized areas related to specific parts of the house. In front of the southern part of the house is an elevated, spacious terrace, partly planted with roses. It is divided from the garden by a massive stone pergola. Below follows a lawn tennis court and subsequently a lawn used for children's games which is surrounded by a double row of linden trees. Adjacent to the children's room which lies beside the living room on the terrace was planned a small playground. The servants' wing on the northern part of the property had a vegetable garden (now parking places), being divided from the southern garden by a short alley of lime trees which leads to the entrance of the house. The whole site is separated from the streets by a hedge of *Thuja* plants. The garden design, influenced by ARTS AND CRAFTS prototypes, follows the idea of 'the garden as an amplification of the house' which Muthesius got to know during his studies of English country houses and gardens 1896–1903. The whole design is a typical example of his endeavours to reform villa architecture as well as contemporary German garden design. Since 1988 the estate has been used by Stanford University.   US

HERMANN MUTHESIUS, *Dekorative Kunst*, Vol. 27 (1918–19).

Landriana, Villa La ✿

Anzio, Italy. Only started since 1956, this modern garden, created on derelict farmland near the sea (not far from where PLINY THE YOUNGER had his Latium villa), is the work of the late Marchesa Lavinia Taverna. The garden combines Italian geometry and control and ebullient planting of roses, shrubs, and perennials to give a distinctly English look. After the first ten years of acclimatizing plants the Marchesa invited Russell PAGE to create a more serious structure to the garden. He introduced a series of axial paths which linked various areas as well as creating a formal Orange Garden with fruit trees clipped to spherical heads interplanted with the low-growing 'balls' of evergreen *Myrsine africanus*. In an olive garden the trees make patterns of dappled shade over beds filled with mauve and pale yellow flowers. The Viale Bianca descends steeply to the valley with steps made from tufa stone, white tulips, and narcissus followed by the delicate *Gaura lindheimeri* and white roses. *Salvia leucantha* gives a touch of blue and continues to produce its flowers throughout the winter. The Marchesa made her own selection of viburnums and magnolias. There is a field of *Rosa* × *odorata* 'Mutabilis' (syn. *R. chinensis* 'Mutabilis') and arum lilies and irises grow by a lake.   PHo

landscape architecture.

The term 'landscape architecture' was used intermittently throughout the 19th century, but it was only in the 20th that it developed the implications of a distinct discipline. J. C. LOUDON had used the term in the title of his volume of Humphry REPTON's collected works, *The Landscape Gardening and Landscape Architecture of the Late Humphry Repton* (1840), probably because a significant portion of Repton's writings dealt with the theme of architectural styles in the landscape. As a professional label, however, English practitioners in the 19th century followed Repton in using the terms 'landscape gardening' and 'landscape gardener'. In America, the title of 'landscape architect' was adopted by F. L. OLMSTED and Calvert Vaux in their plans for Central Park, New York, in the 1850s (see NEW YORK PARKS AND GARDENS). Thereafter, it gradually became a professional label, and in 1899 the American Society of Landscape Architects (ASLA) was founded.

In Britain, the development of the ARTS AND CRAFTS style of gardening at the end of the century, with its emphasis on the architectural framework of the garden, and on matching the style of the garden to the style of the house, shifted the emphasis away from the planning of the broader landscape park. A proponent of architectural gardening such as Reginald BLOMFIELD used 'landscape gardening' as a pejorative term for the promotion of horticulture over architecture. Between the 1890s and the 1920s the terms 'garden architecture' and 'landscape architecture' gradually replaced 'landscape gardening' as a label for formal garden design. Patrick Geddes appears to have been the first designer to advertise himself (in 1907) as a 'landscape architect', but it was Thomas MAWSON who popularized the term. In 1909, he took up the first university post as a lecturer in landscape architecture, in the Liverpool department of civic design, and three years later changed his title from 'garden architect' to 'landscape architect'.

In 1928 the ROYAL HORTICULTURAL SOCIETY (RHS) convened an international conference on garden design, and some of the younger designers thus assembled proposed the creation of a professional institute. Mawson was invited to become the first president, and the British Association of Garden Architects was founded in 1929, to change its name to the Institute of Landscape Architects (ILA) the following year. In 1934, the institute began to publish a journal, *Landscape and Garden*, edited by Richard Sudell. This was succeeded by the smaller *Wartime Journal of the Institute of Landscape Architects*, which dropped the 'Wartime' in 1946, and continued until 1971, when it was retitled *Landscape Design*.

Among the early members of the institute were established figures like Edward White and Barry Parker, associated with the design of private gardens and municipal parks. Richard Sudell, the first of the younger generation to become prominent, shared their emphasis on the domestic garden. E. Prentice Mawson, son of Thomas, summed up their goals in a 1934 statement: 'The function of the Landscape Architect is that of guide and counsellor in all matters relating to the preservation of beauty, the creating of added amenities, whether they be parkways, parks, recreational areas or cemeteries, so that they will minister . . . to the practical needs of the community.' But among the founders were people like Brenda COLVIN, Sylvia CROWE, and Geoffrey JELLICOE, who were soon to take the institute in a different direction.

During the second quarter of the twentieth century, the meaning of the term 'landscape architecture' began to change, as the attention of the newly organized professionals shifted from the architectural garden towards environmental planning on a larger scale. The GARDEN CITY movement and the parallel development of garden suburbs had already led architects like Unwin and Parker into the planning of gardens, while Mawson was consulted on the planning of Port Sunlight and in 1908 published a massive book on *Civic Art*. After the First World War, Mawson was active in encouraging the planning of new villages to provide housing for demobilized soldiers, and eventually became president of the Town Planning Institute. The generation that came of age in the 1920s thus had before them the twin ideals of social amelioration and of landscaping on a wide scale instead of concentrating on the private garden. A similar development took place in America, with the vogue of the 'City Beautiful' movement around the turn of the century; its proponents, like Mawson, favoured a Beaux-Arts approach to urban design.

During the 1930s, town planning expanded into the design of road systems. The planting of roundabouts and arterial roads was becoming an issue, and resulted in the formation of the Roads Beautifying Association (RBA) in 1928 under the direction of Wilfred Fox; but Fox's approach was seen by the younger members of the ILA as too horticultural (the RBA was wound up in the 1950s). Peter Youngman, writing in *Landscape and Garden* in 1939, saw in the emerging road system the beginning of logical planning for the countryside, and looked forward to 'the new environment of which it is a forerunner'. This statement indicated the direction which the ILA would take after the Second World War.

During the war, the ILA made proposals for the planning of post-war reconstruction, and supported the County of London Plan drawn up by Holford. As a result, when the New Towns project was initiated in the late 1940s, prominent members of the ILA were involved in the planning of all the sites: Sylvia CROWE at Harlow New Town, Brenda COLVIN at East Kilbride, Geoffrey JELLICOE at Hemel Hempstead, Frank Clark at Stevenage, Peter Youngman at Cumbernauld. The Beaux-Arts approach taken by the institute's senior founders had now been abandoned for ideas based on modernism, the revival of the English landscape garden, a new interest in the picturesque, and the accommodation of the automobile. The Festival of Britain, in the planning of which Peter Youngman, Frank Clark, Peter Shepheard, and Maria PARPAGLIOLO SHEPHARD were involved, provided an opportunity to propagandize for the importance of the new ideas in urban landscape.

The ILA also extended its influence into the agricultural and industrial landscape. In 1943 the institute set up a Forestry Committee, which issued a report on the planning of afforestation the next year; Crowe and Colvin became particularly involved with forestry schemes, and in 1963 Crowe was appointed the first landscape consultant to the Forestry Commission. She also became involved with the planning and planting of motorways in the 1950s, and published *The Landscape of Roads* in 1960. Post-war legislation on industrial development in the countryside increasingly included amenity clauses that required the involvement of landscape architects; S. Colwyn Foulkes was the first landscape architect to be employed on an industrial scheme by virtue of an Act of Parliament (the Dolgellau reservoir project in the early 1950s). Crowe and Jellicoe were to become involved in the landscaping of nuclear power stations in the 1960s.

At the beginning of the 20th century, landscape architecture had been distinguished from landscape gardening by its concentration on the architectural garden. By the 1960s, it had reversed its meaning, absorbing all the areas that had once been allocated to landscape gardening, while the Arts and Crafts architectural garden was being eclipsed. Most of the institute's members continued to design private gardens as part of their practice, but their main enthusiasms lay elsewhere. The sort of project that lay closest to the formal remit of landscape architecture was the design of university campuses—most famously Frank Clark's work at the University of York. Garden design as such was sometimes dismissed as a relic of individualism when the emphasis ought to fall on the communal. Sylvia Crowe in particular (*Garden Design*, 1958 and later editions) attempted to maintain links between landscape design and horticulture; but ideas on garden design were in flux, because of the perceived need to adapt it to the demands of modernism. Christopher TUNNARD's *Gardens in the Modern Landscape* (1938) was looked to as pointing the correct way, but as Peter Youngman later said, 'there was nothing else in this country to learn from. One had to look abroad.'

International relations among landscape architects were by that time long established. In America, the founding of the ASLA in 1899 had had three purposes: to establish landscape architecture as a recognized profession in America, to develop educational studies in landscape architecture, and to provide a voice of authority in the 'new profession'. Just as the British institute was to be dominated initially by Mawson and the garden city architects, so the American institute was dominated by the influence of Olmsted. Olmsted had long since retired from practice when the ASLA was formed, but his sons and his former associate Warren Manning were founder members, as were Calvert Vaux's son Downing Vaux, and Samuel Parsons, an associate of Vaux's firm, who was much involved with Central Park. Thereafter, Britain and America exhibited parallel stylistic developments, from Mawson and the City Beautiful designers at the beginning of the century, to an interest in modernism, and a parallel expansion of interests, through campus planning (e.g. Beatrix FARRAND at Princeton), to countryside planning through institutional involvement in the Tennessee Valley Authority and the National Parks Service. In 1948 the International Federation of Landscape Architects (IFLA) was founded, with Geoffrey Jellicoe as its first president.

Professional organization required the establishment of qualifications and training programmes. Liverpool, which had organized the first degree course in architecture in 1894, followed with the first course in landscape architecture in 1909, with Mawson as the lecturer. Reading University followed during the 1930s, but it was not until the post-war years that such courses multiplied, with Durham, Edinburgh, Sheffield, and London setting up courses, generally within departments of town planning. Brian Hackett, Frank Clark, and Peter Youngman were the most important of the early instructors. The first full-time honours degree course in London was set up at the Hammersmith School of Arts and Crafts, by Michael Lancaster. During the war, the ILA proposed collaborating with the RHS, which already ran a wide range of examinations, but in 1946 set up its own external examinations and standards for entry into the profession. It was not until 1969 that A. E. Weddle's *Techniques of Landscape Architecture* was published under the ILA's auspices, and served as an effective textbook of practice. Similarly, in America, the ASLA set up a Committee on Education in 1918, which then modulated into the National Conference of Instructors in Landscape Architecture, and in 1970 was renamed the Council of Educators in Landscape Architecture.

In the 1960s, the ecological movement began to have a significant impact on landscape architecture. Brian Hackett and Brenda Colvin had already encouraged ecological assessment in landscape planning, but Colvin, for example, could treat naturalized exotics like rhododendrons as part of the site ecology, while a later generation took up ideas of ecological restoration and the removal of invasive aliens. The new concerns were first manifested in America, where work on national parks had made environmental protection a major concern; in 1965 Ian McHarg reorganized the University of Pennsylvania's programme to include regional planning and environmental science in the landscape architecture syllabus. The concepts of biodiversity, ecosystems, and renewable resources became part of the American vocabulary of landscape architecture long before they became common in Britain. At the Green Towns and Cities Conference in 1984, American landscape designers criticized some of the major British firms for being too accommodating of environmental damage caused by industry, instead of using their status to campaign for social change. A new emphasis on ecological restoration and habitat creation had begun in the 1970s, and became increasingly popular.

At the end of the 20th century, British landscape architecture found that many of the once prestigious and highly publicized programmes of the mid century had fallen from favour. Coniferous forests and motorway planting, power station landscaping, and early industrial reclamation schemes were criticized on ecological grounds, and the planning of the New Towns increasingly questioned. Even some of the attempts at ecological restoration were incurring criticism for falsifying the history of the sites, as debates over the nature of ancient woodland were aired in the press. Meanwhile, the concern with the preservation from destruction of historic gardens (most notably in the work of the GARDEN HISTORY SOCIETY in dealing with threats to landscape gardens from motorway development) led some major firms into historical assessment and conservation, and so once again back into questions of garden design.   BE

Lange, Willy

(1864–1941), German garden designer. He started his career in 1903 as teacher and head of the department for plant production (Pflanzenbau) at the Royal Horticultural College, which had been moved from Potsdam to Berlin-Dahlem in the same year. He withdrew from this office in 1915 for health reasons. In 1907 the first of his several books on garden design appeared, the last of which was published in 1927. From 1906 until before the First World War Lange served as a consultant to a land agency and designed a number of gardens for houses of wealthy clients designed by the architect Otto Stahn on lots along the southern shore of the Kleiner Wannsee in Berlin. Although quite a few landscape architects of the Weimar Republic seem to have shared Lange's teachings he professionally became an outsider. However, Lange felt personally rewarded when the National Socialists came to power in 1933. Then the racist and nationalist ideas for garden design Lange had already developed much earlier became mainstream. In 1934 Lange was made honorary professor at the agricultural college in Berlin, and on the occasion of his 75th birthday the National Socialist Führer, Adolf Hitler, conferred on him the Adolf-Hitler-Medal.   GG

Langkilde, Eywin

(1919–97), Danish landscape architect. An early success was his own small terraced house garden (1949) where he used granite setts to make an abstract pattern in grass, and combined this with exotic foliaged plants such as *Rhus typhina* and *Arundinaria nitida*. Many drawings by the landscape architect Troels Erstad (1911–49) show a marked Islamic influence, and when Langkilde took over his practice he continued to work with ornamental patterns, but in the form of modern and abstract figures, such as he used in a small exhibition garden (1955) in the Royal Danish Horticultural Society's garden. The widely acclaimed courtyard garden for Baltica Insurance in Copenhagen (1958) is a tour ▶

de force in abstract cubism; the interlocking elements of paving, pools, walls, and planted beds show superb craftsmanship. The gardens at the housing complex Frederiksgården (1959) have ornamental patterns and demonstrate great knowledge of planting design. Langkilde wrote several books, among them *Nye Danske haver* (Modern Danish Gardens) (1956) and *Danske blomsterløgparker* (Danish Bulb Parks) (1960). AL

Langley, Batty

(1696–1751), English architect, garden designer, and author influential in popularizing the Gothic style in architecture, especially in garden buildings. His best-known architectural book, *Ancient Architecture Restored and Improved by a Great Variety of Grand and Usefull Designs, Entirely New in the Gothick Mode for the Ornamenting of Buildings and Gardens* (1741–2), was a recipe book of Gothic detail which builders could seize upon as a source. The Gothic Octagon (1750) at BRAMHAM PARK is typical of the buildings produced under Langley's influence. His *New Principles of Gardening: or, the Laying out and Planting Parterres, Groves, Wildernesses, Labyrinths, Avenues, Parks,*

&c. after a more Grand and Rural Manner, than has been Done before (1727) was influential in the transition between the severely formal and the landscape style. In it he attacks 'that abominable Mathematical Regularity and Stiffness' and emphasizes the 'Pleasure of Imagination', anticipating the taste for the picturesque. One of his 'Directions' was 'That such Walks, whose Views cannot be extended, terminate in Woods, Forests, mishapen Rocks, strange Precipices, Mountains, old Ruins, grand Buildings, &c.' He recommends statues of appropriate classical deities and warns against the dangers of putting '*Neptune* on a Terrace-Walk, Mount, &c. or *Pan*, the God of Sheep, in a large basin'. PT

Lante, Villa ✤

Bagnaio, Lazio, Italy This is one of the most important Renaissance gardens in Italy, designed by the architect Jacopo Barozzi da VIGNOLA and an engineer, Tommaso Ghinucci (d. 1587), for Cardinal Gianfrancesco Gambara in the 1560s. Although twin *casini* (see CASINO) are placed symmetrically on either side of the main axis as part of the overall garden plan, the main focus is on the superb garden architecture and water features rather than on a domestic villa. The garden, originally approached through the adjoining park to reach the Grotto of the Deluge and the tufa-built reservoir (the source of the garden's water) shaded by plane trees, is on five descending levels. Its central component is a rippling cascade or *catena d'acqua*, shaped like an elongated crayfish (symbol for Cardinal Gambara), which is fed by the Fountain of the Dolphins decorated with eagles, harpies, and monstrous heads which sits in the midst of a pool below the grotto. The water chain drops into the shell-shaped basin of the Fountain of the River Gods, to provide water for a table with a trough of water for cooling wine, as described by PLINY THE YOUNGER in the 1st century AD. Another fountain lies below on the fourth terrace, while water emerges on the final level as four balustraded tanks surrounding another fountain which MONTAIGNE in 1581 described as 'a high pyramid which spouts water in a great many different ways' (*Voyages en Italie*, 1581). The Fountain of the Moors as it is called today is comprised of four naked men holding up the arms of Cardinal Peretti Montalto who owned the property after 1590, altering this fountain to celebrate his name. In each of the water tanks a small ship, carved in stone, recalls the *naumachia*, performances of marine battles noted in the literature of classical Rome. The water features were completed by Carlo Moderno (1556–1629) in 1612.

Although water is of such importance, the twin *casini*, and simple planting play a considerable part in enhancing this important garden. The original Italian-style flower parterres surrounding the lower water panels were replaced by the fashionable box-patterned shapes in the 17th century. Today the entrance is through a gate straight into the lower garden instead of the ascent to the topmost grotto through the BOSCO to the side, so the whole complex is viewed in the reverse order to what was originally intended. Even today some of the original fountains are preserved in the wood, which was quite a formal affair with rides and vistas. The Fountain of Pegasus, its winged horse carved by GIAMBOLOGNA, is in a pool at the bottom of the site. A faded fresco in the west casino c.1578 and a print of 1569 show how little the main elements of the Villa Lante have been altered in the last five centuries. PHo ⊃ page 276

Lanting ✤

near Shaoxing, Zhejiang province, China, situated 13 km/8 miles south-west of the city, is famous as the garden where, on the third of the third lunar month AD 353, the great calligraphist Wang Xizhi composed his *Preface to the Anthology on Orchid Pavilion*. Since then, great changes have obscured the exact place which provided his poetic inspiration, but the Pavilion of the Winding Brook and Floating Cups, standing since the 16th century on the north bank of the stream, is said to be where Wang and his friends floated their wine bowls while they recited the poems and prose which were later collected in the *Anthology*. Each had to compose a poem by the time the floating cup passed in front of him—a literary game copied by countless gentlemen poets in the following centuries. Fittingly, this pavilion stands on the garden's main axis, with the entrance and the Temple of the God of Literature or Wen Chang Ge in front of it and, at its back, a Pavilion for the Royal Stone Tablets recording visits of the Kangxi and Qianlong emperors. A triangular gazebo has been built to hold another stone tablet engraved with calligraphy of two words only, 'Geese Pond', supposedly in Wang Xizhi's own hand. The Ink Pond, enclosed by *lang* (see CHINA) and with the Pavilion of Talent in Ink in its centre, suggests a type of mid-lake pavilion surrounded by *lang* along the water's edge which was developed in the Song dynasty, and is rare today in Chinese gardens. C-ZC/MK

Larchill Arcadian Garden ✤

Larchill, County Kildare, Republic of Ireland. The house at Larchill dates from the late 18th century but the landscape garden, of 18th-

Colour plates

The **Taj Mahal**, India

The Pebble Garden at **Dumbarton Oaks**, Georgetown, DC, USA

The mid 18th-century summer palace at **Sanssouci**, Germany, overlooks a vineyard with parabolic terraces

The late 19th-century box parterre and exotic conifers in the arboretum of **Volcji Potok**, Slovenia

century flavour, seems to date from a later period. The landscape here is ornamented with curious buildings which stylistically seem more early 19th than 18th century. In a field to the south of the house is a lake with a triangular island on which is a castellated fortress-like building with gun ports named Gibraltar. On the edge of the lake is a Gothic boathouse, and a second lake has a temple—a circle of columns—which was formerly connected to the mainland by a CHINOISERIE bridge and a causeway. At the centre of the lake there used to stand a fine 18th-century stone figure of Bacchus which is now in the ornamental walled garden at Larchill. One of the oddest buildings, in a corner of the field, is the Foxes' Earth, a stone temple with massive columns standing on a grassy mound which has two tunnels to allow a fox to escape from the hounds. The present owners have restored the garden and added a farmyard in the spirit of the FERME ORNÉE in which rare breeds of pigs, chickens, and geese are housed in picturesque Gothic buildings. In the walled garden is a

charming three-storey Gothic tower with stained-glass windows whose interior is decorated with shells.   PT

La Reggia. See REALE, PALAZZO.

Larnach Castle ⊕

Dunedin, New Zealand. The story of Margaret Barker's restoration of the garden is one of determination against all odds. She battled on almost alone while simultaneously restoring the castle. Her family bought the dilapidated property with its 14 hectares/35 acres of garden and grounds in 1967—the roof of the castle leaked, it was practically stripped of furnishings, and the garden had all but vanished. William Larnach, financier and Minister of the Crown, had commenced building the castle and garden for his first wife in 1871. Two hundred workmen toiled on the project, and craftsmen from Europe worked on the decoration of the interior for a further

eleven years. The site high on the Otago Peninsula has panoramic views of the harbour far below but it was exposed to every wind that blew. Larnach planted a shelter belt of *Cupressus macrocarpa* on all sides and some specimen trees still stand.

Margaret Barker has boldly removed some of this shelter in exchange for the view, creating a spectacular vista through a laburnum tunnel and down to the harbour at one point, and a totally new planting concept—a 'South Seas' garden, in another. Although there are many exotics throughout, it is the 'difficult' New Zealand endemics and plants from the outer islands—Chatham, Stewart, and the Snares—that bestow a special character. Separate colonies of the blue and the white *Myosotidium hortensii*, *Brachyglottis repanda* var. *fragrans*, *Olearia semidentata*, *O. chathamica*, and the great

Giacomo Lauro's engraving of the **Villa Lante** from *Antiquae Urbis Splendor* (1612–28).

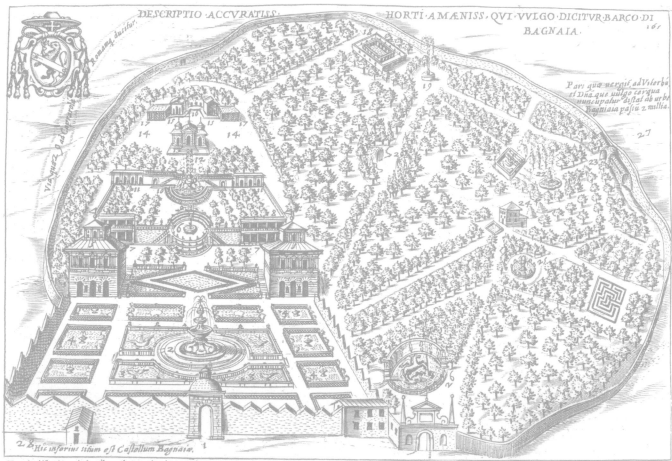

tree daisy, *O. lyalli*, are well suited, as are astelias, celmisias, and aciphylla. *Leucogenes grandiceps*—the South Island 'edelweiss'—grows alongside *Geranium traversii* in the rock garden behind which a venerable *Fuchsia excorticata* displays its flaking bark. An avenue of the coveted mountain 'palm' (*Cordyline indivisa*), so difficult in cultivation, heralds the 'rainforest' garden home to dracophyllum, richia, berberidopsis, *Rhododendron falconeri*, and bustling colonies of *Lobelia tupa*. In the 'South Seas' garden there are plantings of *Eucalyptus ficifolia* and numerous representatives of the seventeen-strong metrosideros genus. *Araucaria columnaris* from New Caledonia is here too along with palms from Lord Howe Island, coastal Queensland, and the Kermadecs, all reflecting Margaret Barker's botanical journeys.   GC

Laskett, The,

Much Birch, Herefordshire, England, the garden of Sir Roy STRONG who came to live here with his wife Dr Julia Trevelyan Oman in 1973. On a flat site they made a garden of vistas, hidden enclosures, knot gardens, temples, and eyecatchers lavishly laced with ornaments. What makes the garden truly original is the autobiographical theme that underlies it. Episodes in the garden commemorate, sometimes wittily, events in the lives of the owners—a temple celebrates Sir Roy's directorship of the Victoria and Albert Museum, the Ashton Arbour salutes Sir Frederick Ashton for whom Julia Trevelyan Oman designed ballets, and so on. The planting is less expressive than the pattern of hedges and the choreography of the ornaments. However, there are beautiful collections of quinces and of crab apples (*Malus* spp. and cvs.) and a thriving kitchen garden.   PT

ROY STRONG, *The Laskett* (2003).

Lassus, Bernard

(b. 1929), French garden designer who trained as an artist (with Fernand Léger) and at the ecole Nationale Supérieure des Beaux-Arts where he subsequently taught. He began to design gardens and his Jardin d'Antérieur (1975) won the competition for the new town of Isle d'Abeau but was never executed. In 1982 he shared first prize in the competition for the Parc de la Villette (Paris) but here against his plan was not executed. His first major scheme, won by competition in 1982, was the Jardin des RETOURS for the 17th-century Corderie Royale at Rochefort. In 1992 he won the competition for a motorway rest area at Nîmes-Caissargues (Exit 25 on the A9). His work emphasizes the power of imagination and the importance of a historical dimension and is in general a highly intellectual approach to landscape design. In

1996 he won the Grand Prix du Paysage in France.   PT

BERNARD LASSUS, *The Landscape Approach* (1998).

lawn.

In its modern sense of an area of close-mown turf the lawn dates from the early 18th century. The French equivalent, *pelouse*, derived from the word *poilu*, meaning 'hairy', originally meant, in the 17th century, an area covered in uniformly low plants; it came to be identical to the English lawn in the 18th century, often in the form *pelouse de gazon* (lawn of turf). In the 18th century in England, at the height of the fashion for landscape parks, lawn is used to refer to parkland grass grazed by cattle, deer, or sheep. The lawn came to be one of the most treasured features of gardens in England where the wet maritime climate was particularly favourable for its cultivation. LOUDON's *Encyclopaedia of Gardening* (1822) has a paragraph on 'The superiority of British turf'. This superiority is recognized elsewhere, too. The *Robert-Collins Dictionnaire Français–Anglais Anglais–Français* (1980) translates *gazon anglais* as 'well kept or smooth lawn'. In the 20th century the lawn was an almost universal feature of British gardens. Lawnmowers (see TOOLS AND TECHNOLOGY) pushed by hand whose wheels turned the blades gave way to self-propelled petrol or electric mowers. Ingenious mowers floating on a cushion of air were invented to cope with awkward slopes. Ride-on petrol-driven lawn tractors became fashionable for very large lawns where in the 19th century mowers were drawn by horses shod in soft shoes like padded bedroom slippers to protect the fine surface. Gardeners in modern times have been encouraged to worry about their lawns and to embark on dictatorial seasonal regimes of feeding, weeding, scarifying, and aerating their lawns in addition to the regular mowing and trimming of edges (widely recognized as the easiest way of imparting a possibly delusive well-kept air to a garden). Garden journalists used to fret about the urgency of the various tasks to be performed to arrive at the perfect lawn. Selective, 'broad-leafed' weedkillers were developed so that nothing but grass should be found in the lawn. To the dismay of lawn purists many gardeners actually enjoyed some of the 'weeds' in their lawns, in particular daisies (*Bellis perennis*) and speedwell (*Veronica filiformis*). In the late 20th century anxiety about the use of chemicals in the garden, and about the consumption of carbon-fuels in lawnmowers, began to reduce the popularity of lawns. A slow growing cultivar of lawn grass was introduced as a means of reducing the amount of mowing but this seems not to have been popular. GRAVEL GARDENS, having the additional

ecological advantage of requiring no watering, were thought of as a possible substitute.   PT

Laxenburg

Niederösterreich, Austria. The hunting ground of Laxenburg was Habsburg property from the 14th century. A new era began with the imperial couple Maria Theresa and Franz Stephan I who in 1755 decided to erect a more comfortable new garden palace near the old castle, designed by Nicolo Pacassi with a geometric garden by Jean Beaulieu. In 1782 Joseph II ordered the transformation and extension of Laxenburg into a naturalistic JARDIN ANGLAIS. This work was planned by Isidore Ganneval in 1782-5. The geometrical network of ALLÉES was retained, with, between them, irregularly shaped meadows and clumps of trees. The final and most important changes took place in the early years of the Emperor Franz II (I), who reigned from 1792 to 1835, and his vivacious wife Neapolitan wife Maria Theresa II (1772-1807). The construction of the Rittergau (District of Chivalry) in a landscape with an artificial lake and several islands is the greatest achievement of Austrian garden architecture around 1800. The designer of this picturesque extension was Johann Michael Riedl, chief surveyor of the buildings and gardens of Laxenburg from 1798 to 1849. The Gothic Bridge (finished in 1808) and the Grotto (finished in 1821) were built but a proposed Habsburg castle was abandoned. Various neo-Gothic structures—the Franzensburg castle, the Tilt-Yard, the Gothic Bridge, Knight's Column, and Knight's Tomb—were constructed between 1798 and 1810 in cooperation with the architect and sculptor Franz Jäger the elder. Between 1820 and 1849 the lake was extended to the east, where a neo-Gothic pavilion was finished on Mariannen Island in 1840.   GH

Łazienki

Warsaw, Poland, was a suburban residence of the last King of Poland, Stanislas Augustus Poniatowski (1764-1795). In the second half of the 17th century Stanisław Herakliusz Lubomirski built below the Ujazdów Castle, in the middle of what had been a zoo, a baroque Łazienka (bathhouse) on an island. Stanislas Augustus Poniatowski transformed the former zoo grounds, turning them into a formal garden. His chief seat was arranged in the old Bath House, which was remodelled by Dominik Merlini (1730-97) into a Palladian villa (the Palace on the Island), mainly in 1784-8. The palace stands between two reservoirs and to the north is a regular canal closed by a bridge on the Agricola road (with a monument to John III Sobieski in the centre) and to the south are two irregular pools separated by a cascade.

On the island in the pool closer to the palace is the antique-style Theatre on the Water (Jan Christian Kamsetzer, 1792). After 1784 Jan Christian Schuch (1752–1813), a royal gardener, began to introduce into Łazienki elements of an irregular composition without, however, destroying the regular arrangement of the whole layout. In the 19th century Łazienki was a residence of the Russian Tsar, becoming a public park in the latter part of the century. It was then that the park was extended southwards. After 1815 the part of the garden around the Belvedere Palace was excluded from Łazienki, and in 1818 botanic gardens were created near the Ujazdów Castle.   WB

leadwork.

Garden ornaments made of lead have the chief advantages of cheapness—once a mould has been made large numbers of identical copies can be produced inexpensively—and imperviousness to the weather. William SHENSTONE in *Unconnected Thoughts on Gardening* (published posthumously 1764) thought they were perfectly suitable as 'part of a scene or a landskip' but would not survive scrutiny indoors. The first use dates from the 17th century. They were used in LE NÔTRE's Versailles (sometimes enclosed in gold leaf to conceal their humble material) but were soon abandoned in favour of bronze which not only produced a distinguished patina but which was capable of being moulded with much finer details. In England in the late 17th and early 18th centuries lead figures and urns were produced in very large numbers by the van NOST family and John CHEERE. Leadwork was sometimes painted to resemble marble or fine stone. At first leadwork was used to ornament formal gardens in the Le Nôtre style but it also appeared frequently in 18th-century landscape parks. In the late 20th century in England there was a renaissance of leadwork, casting statues, urns, and CISTERNS in the old style.   PT
  JOHN DAVIS, *Antique Garden Ornament* (1991).

Leasowes, The ⊛

Halesowen, West Midlands, England, the creation of William SHENSTONE from around 1743. He inherited the farming estate in 1735 and was dependent on its slender income both for living and for the making of his garden. His letters often refer to financial difficulties. At The Leasowes he was able to put into practice in a modest way some of the ideas about the landscape whose purpose he considered to be to please 'the imagination by scenes of grandeur, beauty and variety'. Robert Dodsley's *Description of the Leasowes* (1764) gives a vivid account of the kind of garden it was. Dodsley describes a wooded and well-watered valley in which 'the

hand of art is no way visible either in the shape of ground, the disposition of trees, or (which are here so numerous and striking) the romantic fall of cascades'. A ROOT HOUSE was inscribed with a long poem (starting 'Here in cool grot, and mossy cell, | We rural fays and faeries dwell'). A 'ruinated wall' had some lines of Virgil, and simple benches—'two stumps with a transverse board'—serve more to draw attention to a scene of beauty than to provide a resting place. A figure of Faun pipes under oaks and a rustic Temple of Pan ornaments the scene. In his lifetime Shenstone's garden was very well known and much visited but after his death in 1763 it declined swiftly. When Thomas JEFFERSON saw it in 1786 he found the cascades beautiful and 'the walk through the wood is umbrageous and pleasing' but noted that 'Many of the inscriptions are lost'. Many of Shenstone's ornaments were ephemeral; he could afford nothing more enduring. The house at The Leasowes is now a golf club, a golf course occupies part of the grounds, and the remainder, which has been partly restored, gives only the vaguest impression of Shenstone's Arcadia. In 2004 it was announced that the Heritage Lottery Fund had granted a £1.3 million award for its restoration.   PT
  CHRISTOPHER GALLAGHER, 'The Leasowes: a history of the landscape', *Garden History*, Vol. 24: No. 2 (1996).

Le Bouteux family,

a family of French gardeners with particular connection with royal gardens in the 17th century. Jean Le Bouteux (d. 1636) was a master gardener in Paris. His son Michel Le Bouteux (c.1600–50) was gardener to the Duc de Vendôme. He laid out a garden of rare plants for Gilles Renard, captain of the King's guard, in the Tuileries garden (see PARIS PARKS AND GARDENS). His son Michel II Le Bouteux (b. c.1623; d. between 1696 and 1716) worked at the Trianon for Louis XIV where he was *fleuriste ordinaire du roi* (King's florist in ordinary). He was married to a great-niece of André LE NÔTRE. He was a gardener at the Tuileries, at the Château de Maintenon, and at FONTAINEBLEAU with special responsibility for orangeries. His son Michel III Le Bouteux (c.1648–c.1694) under the patronage of Le Nôtre shared responsibility as *contrôleur général des bâtiments du roi* (comptroller of the King's buildings) and was also a specialist in flowering plants. Le Nôtre also secured for him, jointly with Claude DESGOTS, the post of *dessinateur des plans et jardins du roi* (draughtsman of the King's plans and gardens). Late in his career he published a collection of designs *Plans et dessins nouveaux de jardinage*. In the 1680s he also engraved and published a long illustrated list of Parisian

gardens designed by Le Nôtre. It is, however, far from certain that Le Nôtre designed them all.
    PT

Le Brun, Charles

(1619–90), French artist who early in his life met André LE NÔTRE in the studio of Simon Vouet where they were both pupils. Le Brun worked on several gardens with Le Nôtre, among them SCEAUX, VAUX-LE-VICOMTE, and VERSAILLES, where he had overall charge of the garden sculptures. In this role he determined the iconography and often made preparatory drawings from which the sculptors, of which there was a team of up to 50, would work. He became *premier peintre du roi* to Louis XIV and a member of the committee, the Conseil des Bâtiments, which oversaw royal building works.
    PT

Lee, James

(1715–95), Scottish gardener and nurseryman born in Selkirk who came to England to work as a gardener, first at Syon House, Middlesex, and later with the 3rd Duke of Argyll (1682–1761) on his Whitton estate in Twickenham. By 1745 Lee was a partner in the Vineyard Nursery at Hammersmith (present-day Olympia) with Lewis Kennedy, whose identity is not clear; he may be the father of Lewis Kennedy (c.1721–1782) and the grandfather of John (1759–1842), both of whom later became partners. Lee brought out the book *Introduction to Botany* (1760) which although mostly a translation of Linnaeus' *Philosophia Botanica* (1751) proved immensely popular. Peter COLLINSON referred to him as 'the ingenious Mr. Lee of Hammersmith'. The nursery specialized in growing exotics, particularly those received from the Antipodean expedition of James Cook (1728–79) in 1771, and the South African introductions of James Niven (c.1774–1827). In 1788 Lee is credited with being the first to raise the Australian *Banksia serrata* (saw banksia) and was instrumental in propagating the Chilean *Fuchsia magellanica* which he purchased from a seaman in Wapping. Following Lee's death his son James Lee (1754–1824) and John Kennedy continued the nursery, numbering among their clientele the Empress Joséphine (1763–1814) who in 1803 purchased plants to the sum of £2,600 and the Marquess of Blandford, who in the following year reportedly spent £15,000. By 1822 John LOUDON reported that the Nursery was 'unquestionably the first nursery in Britain or rather the World'.   MC-C

Leeuwergem, Kasteel van ⊛

Leeuwergem, Oost Vlaanderen, Belgium, a moated chateau in the French style c.1745 on a much older site; the formal garden layout probably dates from the same time. The approach is along a magnificent avenue of the same date, with a faithfully restored orangery to one side. On the other side a large *miroir d'eau* (see ANNEVOIE, CHÂTEAU D') reflects both the south façade of the chateau and the avenues of limes that edge the water. At the end of the *miroir* is the Bassin des Sphinxes, with two imposing female sphinxes, and a further canal, cut straight through the woodland and bordered by beech trees and stone plinths dating from the period of Louis XIV. The most outstanding feature of the garden is the unique *théâtre de verdure* (see THEATRE). Everything in this open-air theatre is of turf and hornbeam—it is still used for performances and the acoustics are said to be very fine.   BA

Leiden Botanical Garden (Hortus Botanicus) ✤

Leiden, Zuid-Holland, the Netherlands, is the earliest surviving botanic garden in northern Europe; it dates back to 1585 when a former monastery was incorporated in the university (founded in 1575). The old kitchen garden was used for medical research and teaching, leading to the creation of the Hortus Botanicus in 1593-4. Supervised by Carolus CLUSIUS, the layout was the responsibility of Dirck O. Cluyt (or Clutius) and emphasized the study of plants for their own sake, rather than for medicinal purposes only. The arrangement consisted of a series of rectangular order beds (see BOTANIC GARDEN) within a system of cross-paths. Internationally well-known directors of the garden include Paul Hermann (d. 1695) and Herman Boerhaave (d. 1738). They encouraged the garden to be extended; first in 1686 (designed by Jacob ROMAN) and in 1736 a doubling of the area (with the new beds arranged according to the Linnaean or natural system by Adriaen van Royen). A large new ORANGERY designed by Daniel MAROT followed in 1740-4. In 1818 the garden was further extended along the former defence works. In 1936 L. G. M. Baas Becking created a scaled-down version of the original layout on a smaller site in a different location, naming it the Hortus Clusianus. A year later saw a substantial redesign of the layout of the garden. The late 1980s and 1990s saw renewed activity, with a Memorial Garden dedicated to Philipp von SIEBOLD, who introduced many plants from Japan. Makoto Nakamura and Wybe Kuitert designed the garden. The entrance area to the botanic garden, which is the site of the original Hortus, was redesigned by M. T. D. Buys and van der Vliet with a garden inspired by the 1739 plan. A large winter garden on one side of it designed by Hubert-Jan Henket complements the arrangement of an area that still contains the *Laburnum alpinum* planted in 1601.   JW
> ERIK DE JONG, *Nature and Art: Dutch Garden and Landscape Architecture, 1650–1740* (2000).

Lenné, Peter Joseph

(1789-1866), one of the most influential German landscape gardeners of the 19th century. Born in Bonn, Germany, as son of the electoral head gardener by the same name, he was apprenticed under Clemens Weyhe at BRÜHL. While travelling through southern Germany, Italy, Austria, France, and England, he worked with Gabriel Thouin in Paris, whose formal style strongly influenced the young German disciple. In 1814 he became garden engineer at LAXENBURG near Vienna, where he helped to design the park.

In 1816 he was employed as journeyman by the royal garden director at the Prussian court in Potsdam. Immediately he produced several extensive designs for SANSSOUCI and the NEUER GARTEN, which were, however, not executed.

His first fully autonomous responsibility was the designing of the pleasure ground at KLEIN-GLIENICKE (1816). In 1824 he was appointed a member of the Potsdam garden superintendence to which he was elected as garden director in 1828. In the meantime he had extended the park of Sanssouci by adding the Charlottenhof in 1826 and the Hopfenkrug in 1827. But Lenné had a strong vision that included all different aspects of gardening; thus his influence on Prussian gardening was not limited to his position as garden director: Already back in 1822 he had set up a highly influential Association for the Encouragment of Gardening (Verein zur Beförderung des Gartenbaus) and in 1824 he had suggested establishing the Royal State Nursery (Landesbaumschule) that supplied a vast assortment of plants, especially trees and shrubs, to Prussia and several other countries. Further efforts were focused on the founding of the Royal Gardeners' Education Centre (Gärtnerlehranstalt) in Potsdam (1824), of which Lenné became the first director, and which was the first school for gardeners worldwide. Backed by these three important institutions, Lenné had an enormous influence on gardening in the German-speaking world.

During his 50 years in Prussia virtually every one of the numerous royal gardens was redesigned by him. Probably his most famous plan is the 'Improvement Plan for the Isle of Potsdam' from 1833, in which he suggested a designed landscape on a vast scale, stretching approximately 18 km/11 miles from Peacock Island (PFAUENINSEL) in the north to Caputh in the south. He united the various palaces and parks into a unique park landscape by incorporating the river Havel and its banks as well as the neighbouring rolling woody hills. The whole designed landscape was designated as a World Heritage Site by UNESCO in 1990. A similar, but less sophisticated plan was made for the Reichenbach estate (now Poland) in 1820. During his whole career he provided numerous plans for new gardens and parks all over Germany, including Mecklenburg, Anhalt, and Bavaria, as well as for rearranging them. Many of his plans survive at the Neues Palais in the Potsdam archives.

In addition to his manifold work with parks and gardens, Lenné also became involved in town planning, especially in Berlin. He also drew plans for people's parks (*Volksparke*) at Magdeburg (1824), Frankfurt am Oder (1835), and Dresden (1859). However, he did not leave a 'garden theory' or a theoretical work on gardening, as did his rival Prince PÜCKLER. Two rather extensive essays on his works in Magdeburg and Reichenbach were published in the *Verhandlungen des Vereins zur Beförderung des Gartenbaus* though. As a teacher Lenné had many pupils, who established the so-called Lenné-Mayer School of Garden Design which influenced garden design in Germany until around 1900. Lenné can surely be considered to be the best-known German landscape architect.   AKl

Le Nôtre, André, and family.

André Le Nôtre (1613-1700), the greatest and most influential of French garden designers, was born into a notable horticultural dynasty. His father Jean Le Nôtre (c.1575-1655) was a gardener at the Tuileries (see PARIS PARKS AND GARDENS) and was appointed designer of the King's gardens to Louis XIII in 1619. His grandfather Pierre Le Nôtre (c.1540-before 1603), a gardener and fruit merchant, was charged with the upkeep and planting of six parterres at the Tuileries gardens in 1572. His sister Françoise (1615-72) married Simon Bouchard (d. 1638) who was master of the gardens at the Palais-Royal (Paris) and looked after the orange trees at the Tuileries. Bouchard's aunt was married to Michel II LE BOUTEUX (1623-before 1713) who also came from a gardening dynasty who worked at Versailles, the Tuileries, and Fontainebleau. Le Nôtre's other sister Élisabeth (1616-before 1640) married Pierre Desgots, a gardener whose father Jean had been a gardener at the Tuileries and whose grandson was Claude DESGOTS. André Le Nôtre's godfather, after whom he was named, was André Bérard de Maisoncelles, *contrôleur général des jardins* (surveyor general of gardens) to Henri IV and Louis XIII, and his godmother was Claude de Martigny, wife of Claude I Mollet (see MOLLET, ANDRÉ, AND FAMILY). Thus he was connected to a formidable network of gardeners all of whom had worked for the royal estates. He studied painting in the studio of Simon Vouet (*premier peintre du roi* to Louis XIV) and acquired great skill as a draughtsman. As a young man he met the architect François MANSART who made many valuable introductions for him. In 1635, at the age of 22, he was appointed 'premier jardinier to Monsieur, frère du Roi', that is, Louis XIII's younger brother Gaston d'Orléans who lived at the Palais du Luxembourg (see PARIS PARKS AND GARDENS), and only eight years later he was put in charge of all the royal gardens. In 1653 he was given even wider responsibilities when he was appointed *contrôleur des bâtiments royaux* (surveyor of royal buildings).

Le Nôtre was a man of astonishing energy, combining the management of the royal gardens, entailing both maintenance and new works, as well as design work for private clients. The court records show how demanding was the maintenance. In 1672, for example, the records spell out the works required for the newly planted parterres in front of the Tuileries Palace—the cleaning and raking of the great terrace, the great central ALLÉE and subsidiary *allées*, including the half-moon PALISSADES planted with firs, yew, and cypress, the cross *allée* of box, the *allée* of elms, the eight squares of PARTERRES *en broderie* which will be clipped, cleaned and kept up, as well as the *plate-bandes* (see BORDER), cross-*allées*, and the edges of pools, mulching the evergreen shrubs of the parterres and garnishing them in season with such flowers as there may be. Perelle's 1680 engraving of the Tuileries gardens shows a formidably elaborate layout. André Le Nôtre's first design dates from 1645 when he laid out an elaborate four-part parterre for the Jardin de la Reine at FONTAINEBLEAU. Other parterres are certainly attributable to him but it should be emphasized that, although his name may certainly be associated with certain gardens, the precise contribution he made to them is, so far, impossible to determine. At Vaux-le-Vicomte and Versailles he was part of a team associated with the whole development of the site. The fact that no garden he worked on has survived intact—all are either reconstructions or sites that have been radically altered over the years— makes it even harder to identify the essence of his work. His first private commission, which made him famous, was at VAUX-LE-VICOMTE from 1656 to 1661. Immediately subsequently he was involved with the new gardens at VERSAILLES and in 1662 he started work on the huge and problematic new gardens at CHANTILLY. New gardens were laid out at SAINT-GERMAIN-EN-LAYE from 1663 and at Saint-Cloud from 1665. In 1673 he designed an especially

complex layout at SCEAUX, requiring the shifting of immense quantities of earth, and at Maintenon (Eure-et-Loire) in 1676 he redesigned the old garden for Madame de Maintenon. Many other gardens are attributed to Le Nôtre, sometimes fancifully, and in the absence of documentation such attributions have little value. The following have been ascribed to him: Ancy-le-Franc (Yonne), Chateauneuf-sur-Loire (Loiret), Jardin Bossuet (Seine-et-Marne), Château de CASTRIES (Hérault), Château de la Caucherie (Pas-de-Calais), Château de la Chaise (Rhône). At Castres (Tarn) a *parterre de broderie* in the Bishop's Palace (designed by Hardouin-Mansart) has been convincingly attributed to Le Nôtre.

No complete garden by Le Nôtre survives and his major landscapes—such as Chantilly, Vaux-le-Vicomte, and Versailles—are either reconstructions or gardens whose detail scarcely corresponds to their original appearance. Thus, although it is possible to have a fairly clear idea of the character of a Le Nôtre layout, nowhere can one experience the lavish intricacy of planting and ornamentation which is shown in 17th-century engravings and paintings. Le Nôtre rarely worked on a virgin site and sometimes, as at Chantilly, the site made it very hard to impose the harmony he sought, but he nonetheless solved the problem with great ingenuity. At Vaux-le-Vicomte an immense central axis is disposed on land that dips and rises, allowing Le Nôtre to conceal a very long cross-canal. The parterres are elaborate close to the chateau, becoming simpler the further away they are. The axis appears to terminate between groves of trees on the horizon, now marked by a giant statue of Hercules, but it continues beyond the summit, sweeping on through woodland as if without end. At Versailles the Grand Canal which forms the chief axis also appears to be limitless. At Sceaux the site made such vistas impossible and at great labour he contrived two vistas meeting within the garden.

Le Nôtre was by all accounts an attractive figure, admired at court (not least by Louis XIV himself), and confident in his abilities but without ambitions beyond his status. An anonymous biography of 1730 describes his reaction to the King who in 1681 wanted him to take arms. Le Nôtre replied that 'he had his own, which were three slugs crowned by a lettuce heart. Sire, he added, how could I forget my spade? How precious it is to me. Is it not to it that I owe the kindnesses with which the king honours me?' He is buried in Paris at the church of Saint-Roch, in the rue Saint-Honoré quite close to the Tuileries where he was born and lived, and is commemorated by a magnificent

posthumous bust of him carved in 1707 by Antoine Coysevox, Louis XIV's court sculptor who did much work at Versailles.   PT

Le Rayol. See RAYOL, LE DOMAINE DU.

Le Rouge, Georges-Louis

(*fl.* 1740–80), French engraver and cartographer with the royal appointment of *ingénieur géographe du roi* to Louis XV. He made engravings of many of the most notable 18th-century French gardens, with a few Chinese, English, and German subjects, and published them in a series of 21 parts (*cahiers*) between 1775 and 1789 under the title *Détails de nouveaux jardins à la mode*. Of very high quality, these are especially valuable for the gardens for which little other evidence exists. *Cahier* 13 (1785), for example, has 26 plates illustrating the DÉSERT DE RETZ which are a key source for our knowledge of that garden. The *cahiers* vary in value and some of the engravings are either borrowed from other books (including English pattern books of the time) or are Le Rouge's own inventions in which imagination has triumphed over actuality. As corroborative evidence they are invaluable and as evidence of the taste of the time they are delightful.   PT

Le Vau, Louis II

(1612–70), French architect particularly associated with VAUX-LE-VICOMTE and VERSAILLES who also worked for Louis XIV at the palaces of the Tuileries and the Louvre. At both Vaux-le-Vicomte and Versailles he worked in partnership with André LE NÔTRE and Charles LE BRUN. At Versailles, apart from his work on the chateau itself he designed three exceptional buildings none of which survives. A great MENAGERIE (1662–4), an exotic octagonal miniature chateau for animals with two fine pavilions, fell into decay in the 18th century. His ORANGERY (1663), part of the terracing which transformed the site of Versailles, was redesigned by Hardouin-Mansart in 1685. The posthumous Trianon de Porcelaine, completed just after his death in 1670, was replaced in 1687 by Hardouin-Mansart's Grand Trianon.   PT

Levens Hall ⊛

Kendal, Cumbria, England, dates from the 13th century but the present house is largely 16th century. A garden was made here from 1694 for James Grahme who had the help of a Frenchman, Guillaume Beaumont, about whom almost nothing is known apart from the evidence of his work at Levens. A portrait of him painted in around 1700 survives at the house inscribed 'Monsieur Beaumont Gardener to King James II and Col. Jas. Grahme. He laid out the gardens at Hampton Court Palace and at

Levens.' There is no other evidence known of Beaumont working at Hampton Court. In 1695 Beaumont built the first HA-HA known in England—'The Ditch behind the Garden' is mentioned in surviving estate correspondence and may be dated to April of that year. Also at the house is a plan of the garden of around 1730 showing the results of Beaumont's work. It shows a layout roughly corresponding to what may be seen today, in particular a long axial walk of beech hedges with a spacious roundel at its centre. The most striking, indeed unique, feature of the garden today is an astonishing collection of yew TOPIARY, much of it lopsided and deformed with age. These are contained in box-edged beds and some of them may date back to the late 17th century but most are of the 19th century (including golden forms of yew unknown before that time) and later. Underplanted with spring and summer bedding schemes they present one of the most enchanting sights of any English garden. The garden, still privately owned, is maintained to exemplary standards.   PT

Lewis, Meriwether

(1774–1809), American explorer who was secretary to Thomas JEFFERSON, third President of the United States, when in 1803 the Louisiana Purchase was negotiated with France. The land gained stretched from the Mississippi to what is now Wyoming and Montana and increased by 150% the amount of new unexplored territory held by America. Lewis received grandiose instructions from Jefferson to lead a military expedition to survey the land and detail the whole of the natural environment. Accompanying Lewis was his friend William Clark (1770–1838) when they departed from St Louis during spring 1804. Using the river systems of the Missouri and Columbia rivers they reached the Pacific in November 1805. The presidential instructions were fully carried out and they returned having amassed many plant specimens; including species of the genera named for them *Lewisia* and *Clarkia*, as well as *Philadelphus lewisii* and *Mahonia aquifolium*.   MC-C

Lexington Cemetery ⊛

Lexington, Kentucky, USA, was founded in 1849 to meet the needs of a cholera outbreak a few years earlier. The initial 16-hectare/40-acre purchase of Boswell Woods soon expanded and followed the 'garden cemetery' design of MOUNT AUBURN (1831) in Boston, Massachusetts. The current 69-hectare/170-acre arboretum-like setting includes historic monuments to local legends like the statesman Henry Clay (1777–1852), John Hunt Morgan (1825–64) 'The Thunderbolt of the Confederacy', and William

'King' Solomon (1775–1854), the town drunk who became a local hero during the cholera plague of 1833. Equally noteworthy—among the living—are impressive specimen trees including American basswood (*Tilia Americana*), cucumber magnolia (*Magnolia acuminata*), blue ash (*Fraxinus quadrangulata*), and the nearby Kentucky coffee tree (*Gymnocladus dioicus*) that has become curiously twisted and misshapen. Dozens of burr oaks (*Quercus macrocarpa*) line the roadways. No less spectacular in the early spring are the unfurling leaves of buckeyes (*Aesculus pavia*) followed by the flowering of weeping cherries (*Prunus subhirtella*), redbuds (*Cercis canadensis*), and magnificent dogwoods (*Cornus florida*).   AB

l'Haÿ-les-Roses, Roseraie de.

See ROSERAIE DE L'HAŸ-LES-ROSES.

Liberato, San ⊛

(Chiesa Romanica, e Giardini Botanici), Bracciano, Lazio, Italy. In 1964 the noted art historian Conte Sanminiatelli invited Russell PAGE to make an appropriate garden around a Romanesque church, with views over Lake Bracciano and the Rocco Romana beyond. Page chose to implement a simple scheme of small rectangular beds in medieval style, where he grew grey-leaved shrubs, rosemary and sage, and roses spilling out on the pathway under olive trees. Later he and the Count laid out an ARBORETUM in an adjacent meadow with exotic trees and shrubs: pines, tulip trees, black walnut, scarlet oak, and magnolias from North America and acers from Japan.   PHo

Lichtenwalde Castle Gardens ⊛

near Chemnitz, Germany. This notable formal garden, whose designer is unknown, was constructed between 1730 and 1737. The undulating terrain of a rocky ridge was skilfully used to create a composition full of captivating contrast. Representative of the spirit of the rococo, the park consists of relatively small, inward-looking spaces which are axially related to each other. At various points, views into the valley of the river Zschopau and of the distant mountains of the Erzgebirge testify to the integration of the larger environment into the design, a feature not uncommon in baroque landscape art. In contrast, there is little correspondence between the park design and the architecture of the castle, built between 1722 and 1726 and which today houses several museums. With only a balcony mediating between the building and the surrounding terrain (about 10 hectares/25 acres in size), an ALLÉE provides the backbone for garden spaces that vary in elevation and contain numerous fountains. Since the 1950s, in what is now a

public park, efforts have been made to preserve what survived and reconstruct missing features, a project that gained momentum in the mid 1990s. As a result of extensive restoration, visitors can now enjoy a formal garden which illustrates a number of late baroque and rococo ideas about form and space.   PFi

BARBARA BECHTER, *Schloss und Park Lichtenwalde* (2000).

HUGO KOCH, *Sächsische Gartenkunst* (repr. 1999).

Ligne, Charles-Joseph, Prince de

(1735–1814), Belgian landowner, courtier, writer, and garden theorist whose family had lived at BELŒIL since the Middle Ages. His father, Prince Claude-Lamoral II de Ligne, made the great formal garden at Belœil to which, after he inherited in 1766, Charles-Joseph de Ligne added ingredients of a picturesque kind. His book *Coup d'œil sur Belœil et sur une grande partie des jardins de l'Europe* (A Glance at Belœil and at Many Gardens in Europe) (1781) describes his own and other gardens and is laced with aphorisms and digressions on all sorts of subjects apart from gardening. He was an interesting representative example of the cultivated gentleman-amateur of gardens. His book has continued to be reprinted but it is unlikely to have been of any profound influence on the appearance of gardens.   PT

PHILIP MANSEL, *Prince of Europe: The Life of Charles Joseph de Ligne* (2003).

Ligorio, Pirro

(*c.*1513–1583), Italian architect, painter, and antiquary. In 1558 he was appointed papal architect, in which capacity he designed the Villa Pia (1560), the CASINO of Pope Pius IV in the VATICAN; this charming *casino* was the first in Italy to have its own GIARDINO SEGRETO. Ligorio subsequently entered the service of Cardinal Ippolito II d'Este, for whom he designed the gardens of the Villa d'ESTE in Tivoli (1560–75), at once the most magnificent and most influential of all Italian gardens.   GC

Limahuli Garden and Preserve ⊛

Ha'ena, Kauai, Hawaii, USA, was given to the National Tropical Botanical Garden in 1976 by Mrs Juliet Rice Wichman with a subsequent gift in 1994 by her grandson Chipper Wichman and his wife Hau'oli. The site, located in the lush tropical rainforest of the island of Kauai, encompasses about 405 hectares/1,000 acres. Of this area, 15 hectares/37 acres are occupied by the garden and visitors' centre, while the remaining 390 hectares/963 acres are the Limahuli Preserve. It was Mrs Wichman's vision to protect the endangered species of native Hawaiian plants in the area. In 1997, the American Horticulture Society named Limahuli Garden and Preserve as the best

natural botanical garden in the United States. The area is a living museum not only of botanic specimens but of the cultural heritage and stewardship practices of the first Hawaiians who settled the area between AD 200 and 300. The agricultural terraces built more than 1,000 years ago for the cultivation of taro (*Colocasia esculenta*) have been restored and replanted. The hillside, with its magnificent view of the Pacific Ocean, has also been replanted with native species, many of which are endemic to Limahuli valley, including *Pritchardia limahuliensis,* an extremely rare palm, and *Cyanea kuhihewa,* a native lobelia that has been reduced to a single individual growing in the Limahuli Preserve. Polynesian-introduced species growing in the garden include food plants such as breadfruit (*Artocarpus altisis*), medicinal plants such as kava (*Piper methysticum*), and plants such as paper mulberry (*Broussonetia papyrifera*), used to make tapa cloth, and ti (*Cordyline fruticosa*), important in rituals. The preserve above the garden is a steep, forested valley divided by the pristine Limahuli stream and its 243-m/800-ft waterfall. The area above the waterfall is accessible only by helicopter, and is a refuge for endangered native plants and birds.
LTC

Linderhof Palace Park ⊛

near Garmisch-Partenkirchen, Upper Bavaria, Germany. The little palace and the gardens were developed between 1868 and 1880 around a hunting lodge in the Bavarian Alps. Here King Ludwig II of Bavaria (1845–86) sought seclusion and distraction in decorative palace rooms and gardens arranged like scenes from the theatre. He originally wanted to build a copy of VERSAILLES, but this proved too large for the site. Ludwig II then constructed a garden out of elements from other well-known complexes which he disposed around his palace rather like stage sets to shut out the ordinary countryside beyond: terrace gardens modelled on the Italian Renaissance Villa GARZONI on the south side of the palace; two BOSQUET gardens, one on the west and one on the east side, based on the hermitage of Louis XIV, MARLY; and a cascade in front of the bedroom on the north side based on the one in the La GRANJA gardens in Spain. Allegorical stone figures and fountain sculptures with the same themes as the Versailles sculpture programme evoked the residence of the Sun King. Court garden director Carl von Effner (1831–84), a landscape gardener comprehensively trained in all types of garden design, satisfied the King's requirements to the full with his particular talent for decorative arrangements. As a proponent of the mixed style, which he had learned from the Potsdam School, Effner

added a landscape component to the formal elements of the Linderhof gardens. Winding paths linked the palace and gardens with a park of around 58 hectares/143 acres, where groups of trees alternated with spacious meadows in imitation of the ideal landscapes of English parks. With its variety of style elements, the Linderhof Palace Park is one of the finest existing examples of the mixed style of garden.
MSt

Linderud Mansion ⊛

Oslo, Norway, is one of the large estates that were swallowed up by urban expansion from the 1950s. Today's 4.2-hectare/10.4-acre property includes the main building, now a museum, the entrance area to the north with a long lime avenue, and the gardens to the south, overlooking the eastern parts of the Oslo valley. The house and gardens, restored in the 1950s, date from the 1730s and 1750s with 19th-century additions. The house overlooks a symmetrical terraced garden, but has no direct access to it. From the house four terraces descend to a rectangular lawn below with a 70-m/230-ft rectangular pond at the bottom. The garden was enclosed on two sides by hazel tunnels on broad ramps (of which only one remains) and on the third by a 180-m/590-ft avenue of clipped lime trees, originally extended to the west into a BOSQUET where in 1788 a famous garden party was given for Crown Prince Frederick. Enclosed by vegetation on all three sides with no long vistas, the formal terraced garden may be seen as a hybrid of the Renaissance and the baroque. West of this garden are an orchard and a kitchen garden, and on a level above is a former parterre garden, today a lawn with a few flower beds.   ME

Lindley, John

(1799–1865), the son of a Norwich nurseryman, who worked for the Horticultural Society of London (later ROYAL HORTICULTURAL SOCIETY) for over 40 years as administrator, botanist, shows organizer, editor, and head of examinations. In addition he was, from 1827, professor of botany at University College London; from 1835 to 1853, professor of botany at the CHELSEA PHYSIC GARDEN; and from 1841, the founder editor of the weekly gardening newspaper the *Gardeners' Chronicle*. For over twenty years he used its leader columns to attack the growing fashion for formal and historically revivalist gardens, to campaign for the abolition of taxes on glass, to advocate planting by complementary colours, and to promote an Anglicized nomenclature for plants (among his coinages were 'conifers' and 'orchids' to replace 'coniferae' and 'orchises'). In 1838 he compiled a report on the condition

of the royal gardens at Kew, which led to the establishment of the ROYAL BOTANIC GARDENS. He developed a private garden at Bedford House, Acton, near the Horticultural Society's garden; after his death this garden was turned into the Bedford Park Garden Suburb, whose roads were planned with dogleg bends to retain as many of his trees as possible on site.
BE

Linnaeus, Carl

(1707–78), Swedish professor of botany. Linnaeus was the first person consistently to adopt the system of binomial (two-word) nomenclature for plants and animals and he thus initiated the modern concept of species classification. He was born on 23 May 1707 at Rashult, Smaland, in southern Sweden, the son of a Lutheran clergyman. The surname Linnaeus had originally been chosen by his grandfather to record both the former family ownership of the Linnegard estate, whose name was derived from the Smaland dialect word *linn* for the linden or lime tree, and to remember the great tree which grew there. When he was ennobled Linnaeus took the name Carl von Linné by which he is always known in his native country. It was from his father Nils Ingemarsson Linnaeus (1674–1733), an enthusiastic horticulturist and botanist, that Carl learned his love of natural history and the importance of the correct naming of plants. In 1727, aged 20, Linnaeus entered the University of Lund as a medical student, concentrating on botany, geology, and zoology, but in the following year he moved to the University of Uppsala where he assisted the dean, Olof Celsius (1670–1756), with his two-volume work on biblical plants *Hierobotanicon* (1745 and 1747). Subsequently, following the writing of a paper on the sexuality of plants, Linnaeus was appointed assistant to Professor Olof Rudbeck (1660–1740). A student friend, Petrus Artedi, shared his interest in natural history and the two young men conceived the awesome idea of classifying and naming all minerals, plants, and animals according to a system of their own devising. For several years they worked on the idea while Linnaeus botanized and explored Lapland, travelling over 4,827 km/3,000 miles. In 1736 Artedi drowned, leaving Linnaeus to shoulder the full responsibility of their grand concept. The same year he moved to Holland to the University of Harderwijk in order to obtain a master's degree and to have some of his work published; he also became physician to George Clifford (1685–1760), the Anglo-Dutch banker, who had a magnificent garden filled with plants from around the world. Linnaeus was entranced—there was nothing comparable in Sweden—and he wrote a detailed catalogue of the garden's plants, which was sumptuously illustrated by Georg Dionysius Ehret (1708–70) and entitled *Hortus Cliffortianus* (1738). In July 1736 Linnaeus travelled to London with a letter of introduction to Sir Hans SLOANE. In England he also met Philip MILLER as well as Johann Jakob Dillenius (1684–1747), the first occupant of the chair of botany at Oxford (see OXFORD BOTANIC GARDEN). In general during his stay, the 30-year-old Linnaeus with his modern idea of reclassifying all plants—and the natural world—was received with reluctance, but gradually over the following years not only Britain but the whole of Europe came to realize that the binomial system of nomenclature was a reliable and yet simple method of classification.

Linnaeus remained in Holland until in 1741 when he returned to Sweden, being appointed professor of medicine and botany at his alma mater of UPPSALA, a position he held for the next 36 years. As well as teaching, his duties included the supervision of the university's Botanic Garden, which flourished under his guidance. Linnaeus' lectures and practical botanical forays became renowned and inspired many of his students to pursue a career in medicine or botany, with 23 of them becoming professors in their chosen subject. He named many of the new plant introductions after both colleagues and students. Writing occupied much of Linnaeus' time, with the most important botanical work being *Philosophia Botanica* (1751) a complete exposition of his binomial system; there were also *Systema Naturae* (1735), *Genera Plantarum* (1737), and *Species Plantarum* (1753 with a second edition 1762–3). In this, his last work, he classified some 6,000 plant species known to him according to the sexual system and the number of stamens and stigmas present, which he had devised and which was variously described by some of his contemporaries as 'his lewd method' and 'such loathsome harlotry'. The Linnaean system of nomenclature became universally accepted, but the system of sexual classification has long been outgrown, with different and wider classifications coming into use.

Linnaeus' influence was felt particularly strongly in Britain, and following his death in 1778, his widow sold his library of 2,500 books, his manuscripts, correspondence, and vast collections including 20,000 herbarium sheets, over 3,000 insects, 1,500 shells, and mineral specimens, to Sir James Edward Smith (1759–1828) for 1,000 guineas. Sir James was encouraged to make this important purchase for Britain and in 1789 was instrumental in founding, and becoming the first president of, the Linnean Society of London where the whole collection is now housed.   MC-C

Linyou,

Shaanxi province, China, is one of the earliest imperial parks recorded in Chinese history. It was made in the middle of the 11th century BC during the reign of Wen Wang, a wise and benevolent ruler of the semi-mythical Zhou dynasty. Located in or just near the capital Fengjing, south-west of the present city of Xi'an, it was what today would be called a preservation area with a perimeter of some 35 km/21 miles. Wild deer and crane roamed freely in this enclosure, which was used for breeding, herding, and hunting by the King and was open also to the common people for hunting, fishing, and wood gathering. It contained a high terrace, the Lintai, and a large pool, Linzhao (from which perhaps the terrace had been dug), where fish were bred. Since *lin* means mana and suggests a concentration of benevolent spiritual power, both terrace and pool probably had some magical significance; the philosopher Mencius praised the park as a contribution to the welfare of the empire.   G-ZW/MK

Lipik Spa Garden ⊛

Požega-Slavonia county, Croatia, was founded at the end of the 19th century with a site of 10 hectares/25 acres. It is the most precious late romantic spa garden of Croatia. It was started in 1860 and work continued, to the plans of an unknown garden designer, until the beginning of the 20th century. The spa garden, with a hotel and health centre, is in the centre of the town of Lipik and forms its main square garden. It falls into two parts, a neo-baroque garden with a geometric ground plan in front of the Kursalon and hotel and a later romantic garden with laid out in the style of a landscape park. The latter is furnished with pavilions, a gazebo, sitting places, pergolas, and arched promenades. Woodland of native oak (*Quercus robur*) forms a background to varied plantings of trees, shrubs, and flowers. The garden was severely damaged during a war 1991–2 and renovation is in progress. Lipik Spa Garden was the only spa garden of the Habsburg monarchy to be awarded a prize at an international exhibition of flowers and garden pleasure grounds that was held in Budapest in 1910. According to a newspaper (*Obzor*, No. 135, 19 May 1910) Lipik was honoured with a large gold medal because of the quality of its plants, the design of its swimming pool, and its luxuriant exotic vegetation.   MOŠ/BBOŠ

MLADEN OBAD ŠĆITAROCI, 'Hrvatska parkovna arhitektura', *Encyclopedia moderna*, Vol. 13: No. 2 (38) (1992).

— 'Il giardino di Lipik—rinnovamento del giardino tra i metodi le possibilità', Atti del convegno '*La trasmissione delle idée dell'architettura*' (1988).

Liselund ⊛

Møn, Denmark. Liselund is situated in dramatic terrain near Møns Klint, an ideal landscape for a romantic garden. The gardens were designed between 1783 and 1803 by the owner Antoine Bosc de la Calmette (1752–1803), assisted by the architect Andreas Kirkerup (1749–1810), who also designed the small manor house. An irregular clearing in the forest was transformed into a landscape garden with rolling lawns and paths winding between specimen trees, and water was dammed to form a series of lakes with islands and monuments. Buildings such as the Swiss Chalet, the Norwegian House, and a Chinese tea pavilion served as the garden's ornaments and fixed points, and have been preserved. They were placed at the edge of the clearings, to give the best views of the landscape. There is a fall of 52 m/170 ft from the clearing to the sea—a ravine can be crossed via a bridge to reach the shore.

AL

Lismore Castle ⊛

Lismore, County Waterford, Republic of Ireland, dates back to the 12th century but the present castle is largely of the 17th-century reworked in the 19th century. The estate has belonged to the Cavendish family (dukes of Devonshire) since 1753. The most remarkable survival here is the 17th-century terraced Upper Garden. This, the earliest garden of its kind surviving in Ireland, was in its day a KITCHEN GARDEN. It was built when the 1st Earl of Cork lived here who noted in his diary in 1626 payments 'for compassing my orchard and garden at Lismore with a wall two and a half feet thick and fourteen feet high of lyme and stone and two turrets at each corner'. Walls and corner pavilions survive but the garden is now planted largely with ornamental plants. However, the essentially four-part layout of the old kitchen garden remains and there is a fine orchard of apples and quinces. The south-facing wall running along the topmost terrace gives protection to such tender exotics as *Acacia dealbata*, *Drimys winteri*, *Luma apiculata*, and *Melianthus major*. The Lower Garden, below the castle walls, is laid out with lawns and fine flowering trees and shrubs, among them camellias, magnolias, and an avenue of *Eucryphia* × *intermedia* 'Rostrevor'. An ancient yew walk is ornamented with a sculpture by Antony Gormley, one of several well-placed modern sculptures in both parts of the garden.

PT

Little Sparta ⊛

Dunsyre, Lanarkshire, Scotland, was made by Ian Hamilton FINLAY and his wife Sue from 1966. The stone croft—originally known as

Stonypath—is in the wild and austerely beautiful countryside of the Pentland Hills south of Edinburgh. Finlay's work as a poet, artist, and embellisher of the landscape comes together most completely at Little Sparta. The garden is rich in inscriptions but these are quite different from those common in 18th-century landscape gardens such as The LEASOWES. Finlay's inscriptions are sometimes witty (BRING BACK THE BIRCH on a tombstone-like slab alongside a silver birch), sometimes poetically enigmatic (See POUSSIN Hear LORRAIN in a marshy part of the garden), and sometimes dramatic and thought provoking. A quotation from the French revolutionary Louis de Saint Just, THE PRESENT ORDER IS THE DISORDER OF THE FUTURE, is carved word by word on a series of stone slabs lying in grass near a pool with grand views over the landscape—the effect is unsettling rather than Arcadian. A bird table is in the form of an aircraft carrier mounted on a column—a collision of nature and war. The planting—cottagey, floriferous, shady, and uncontrived—lulls the visitor into a false sense of security, unprepared for sometimes worrying messages. There is much to admire and enjoy, and much to think about at Little Sparta. It powerfully creates its own world and makes most other late 20th-century British gardens seem both insipid and insubstantial.   PT

JESSIE SHEELER, *Little Sparta* (2003).

Liu Yuan ⊛

Suzhou, Jiangsu province, China, in the north-western suburbs of Suzhou, was the only garden in the district to survive the Taiping rebellion (1851–64). When first built between 1522 and 1566 by Xu Shitai, a retired official of the Ming dynasty, it was called the East Garden or Dong Yuan. However, in 1798 the property was bought by a provincial official, Liu Shu and despite his new title for it, Hanbi Shanzhuang, it was thereafter always popularly known by his family name. In 1876, when the garden was enlarged by the Lius, they cleverly kept the sound 'Liu' but changed the character to mean Lingering Garden. Its four sections cover about 2 hectares/5 acres, but are so complexly planned that the whole seems much bigger. From the entrance courtyard a narrow whitewashed passage, some 50 m/160 ft long, twists and turns past various tiny open spaces and leads eventually to a corridor with views, through open *louchuang* (see CHINA) windows, of the main pool. Bordered to the north and west by rockeries and to the south and east by varied grey-tiled buildings, this is the heart of the garden. Around it many of the garden's 700 m/ 2,296 ft of covered *lang* (see CHINA) corridors rise and fall following the terrain while, to the east, groups of halls, courtyards, open corridors, and

garden rooms lead through and around each other to make a varied and complex architectural labyrinth. South of this, a more open section brings the visitor round to the double Hall of Mandarin Ducks (see *ting* in CHINA) overlooking a small pond and the 6.5-m/ 21-ft high Cloud-Capped Peak, a water-worn Taihu stone (the rock most highly prized for artificial 'mountains') said to have been originally chosen for the Song-dynasty imperial garden GENYUE. To the west of this, the last part of the garden wraps around the central section, its earthy hills (*jiashan*) capped by an open pavilion with views across the garden's internal walls to the central pond and its surrounding trees. An enclosure within the garden here houses a large and remarkable collection of miniature landscapes and bonsai (penjing). Liu Yuan has been designated a key place of national historic and cultural importance.

G-ZW/MK

Li Yu

(1611–79), alias Li Liweng and Zhe Fan, was a native of Lanqi, Zhejang province, China. This author, playwright, and theorist of drama was also an amateur master of garden art. His designs included BANMU YUAN and the Mustard Seed Garden in Beijing, while his immensely popular *Random Notes in a Leisurely Mood*, a book on various aspects of culture and the art of living, is considered one of the most important works on garden design in China. Published in 1671 during the reign of Kangxi, it contains fourteen chapters of which VIII to XI are devoted to house furnishing and garden planning. Chapters VIII and IX discuss the positioning of windows to 'borrow' near or distant landmarks (JIE JING), and the arranging of hills and rocks both to accord with local conditions and to express a cultivated man's delight in the antique and his appreciation of landscape painting.   D-HL/MK

Ljubljana Riverside ⊛

Ljubljana, Slovenia. The river Ljubljanica encircles the castle hill in the centre of the old city of Ljubljana. Here, along the banks of the river and its tributary Gradascica, the architect Joze PLEČNIK designed several new features of modern character between 1930 and 1942. The Trnovski pristan links the river with the southern suburb through a gentle graded slope, which softens the effect of the concrete water channel. Together with a lyrical avenue of weeping willows this design gives much atmosphere to the river scene. Plečnik used a similar gradation of the bank along the Gradascica, intended for suburban washerwomen. Here, in front of the Trnovo church, he designed a broad bridge, forming

a square, featuring two side footbridges for pedestrians, and ornamented with birches and pyramidal ornaments. The idea of a bridge as an urban square was repeated in the case of Shoemakers' Bridge (Cevljarski Most) down the river, with its lamps, reminiscent of a classical colonnade. Plečnik's Three Bridges (Tromostovje) to the north are the spatial centre of Ljubljana. They link two important city squares and accentuate the passage to the oldest part of the city with two groups of Lombardy poplars as a river portal in the visual axis to the castle. Plečnik expanded the original stone bridge 1831–2 with two additional footbridges, viewing balconies, and staircases connecting the lower river terrace, arranged with Venetian balustrades, accentuated with rhythmical aligment of lamps and globes.   AK

ANDREJ HRAUSKY, JANEZ KOZELJ, and DAMJAN PRELOVSEK, *Plecnik's Ljubljana: Architectural Guide* (1996).

DAMJAN PRELOVSEK, *Arhitekt Joze Plecnik, 1872–1957* (catalogue to the exhibition in Ljubljana) (1986).

Lloyd, Christopher

(b. 1921), English author and gardener, owner of GREAT DIXTER. Through his voluminous writings—in books, magazines, and newspapers—Christopher Lloyd's own garden has become one of the best known, and admired, in the country. He is, above all, a very experienced practical gardener and a profoundly knowledgeable plantsman. He has one of the liveliest pens in the business and his weekly column in *Country Life* has appeared without interruption since 1963. His gardening credo is set down most appetizingly in his best book, *The Well-Tempered Garden* (1970). He has great contempt for 'low-maintenance' gardening—'Effort is only troublesome when you are bored'—and he wrote 'for gardeners who have not been dragged into this pursuit but are here because they love it'. Among his other especially successful books on plants are *Foliage Plants* (1973) and the excellent *Clematis* (1977). Throughout his writing career his own garden has been his central subject—in *The Year at Great Dixter* (1987) he gives a good general view of it. Apart from passing on precious knowledge of plants and how they behave, his greatest influences have been to encourage gardeners to study plants, to pay less attention to fleeting fashion, and to have the courage of their own convictions—rather than any great influence on garden design.   PT

L'Obel, Matthias de

(1538–1616), Flemish botanist who studied medicine under the eminent zoologist Guillaume Rondelet (1507–66) at Montpellier and as an exceptional student inherited

Rondelet's botanical manuscripts. L'Obel was almost the first to observe plants *in situ* with an instructor, and studying primarily medicinal flora he began a taxonomy of the 'natural classification of plants'. He moved from Montpellier to England where his book *Adversaria Nova* (1571) was published and where he met John PARKINSON and the TRADESCANT family. In Antwerp L'Obel published a supporting book *Observationes* (1576). For seven years he was physician to William the Silent but later returned to England as director of the Hackney botanic garden of Lord Edward Zouche (c.1556–1625), himself a botanist, to whom L'Obel dedicated the 1605 edition of *Adversaria*. At the age of 78 he became royal botanist to James I. The species lobelia was named in his honour. MC-C

Lockwood de Forest Garden,

Santa Barbara, California, USA, was completed in 1927 on a site of 0.2 hectare/0.5 acre, and constitutes an early compactly planned modern California garden with distinct zones for entry, service, social, and recreational uses. Lockwood de Forest Jr. (1896–1949) designed his own house at the centre of the garden with a series of roomlike spaces. The small single-storey Mediterranean-style courtyard house is approached via a circular motor court defined by high clipped hedges of blackwood acacia (*Acacia melanoxylon*) contrasting with a bold New Zealand flax and a pink dombeya on the pergola leading to the front door. The east, north, and south sides of the house overlook a series of compactly designed gardens. On the east side a path bisects a series of small richly planted areas defined by clipped myrtle balls, terminating in a larger area with a collection of lavenders. On the north side the square lawn is planted with kikuyu grass (*Pennisetum clandestinum*), which is never watered, defined by low seat-high walls of the local Calabassas stone. The view north toward La Cumbre Peak in the Santa Ynez mountains is an apparently unbroken vista framed by the flanking trees and a gently rising bed. This rock garden is planted around existing rocks with South African bulbs, cotoneasters, junipers, and *Rosmarinus officinalis* 'Lockwood de Forest'. The careful choice of plants represents a deliberate artistic attempt to capture the spirit of this dry landscape and is an early example of sensitive drought-tolerant design. DCS

Loddiges, Joachim Conrad

(c.1738–1826), German nurseryman in London. Born into a gardening family in Hanover, on qualifying Loddiges moved to the Low Countries and then to England in 1761 where he was gardener to Sir John Silvester in Hackney.

Ten years later Loddiges took over the nursery business of his fellow Hanoverian Johann (or John) BUSCH. Over the years Loddiges Nursery became one of the most prestigious in Britain, and throughout Europe and the empire. Until 1814 it was known as Paradise Fields, and thereafter as Hackney Botanic Nursery Garden. Its facilities included a Grand Palm House, an arboretum, and a rosarium. The nursery maintained contact with a number of plant collectors and is responsible for introducing about 150 new plants. It continued to flourish under the Loddiges family until 1854 when due to the expiry of the lease it ceased trading.

MC-C

DAVID SOLMAN, *Loddiges of Hackney* (1995).

Logan Botanic Garden ✿

Port Logan, Stanraer, Wigtownshire, Scotland, is part of the group of gardens belonging to the ROYAL BOTANIC GARDEN, EDINBURGH. It formed part of the garden made in the 19th century by the McDouall family which had lived here since the 13th century and was acquired by the Royal Botanic Garden Edinburgh in 1969. The site, on a narrow isthmus jutting into the Irish Sea, has an exceptional microclimate, warmed by the Gulf Stream Drift, with plenty of sun and a moderate annual rainfall of around 100 cm/40 in. The garden is well protected from fierce salt-laden winds by shelter belts. Southern hemisphere plants flourish here and the garden is rich in such plants as the Chatham Island forget-me-not (*Myosotidium hortensia*), *Lapageria rosea*, olearias, *Polylepis australis* (with extraordinary peeling bark), and much else. Such formal planting as there is is found in the old walled garden where an avenue of *Cordyline australis* underplanted with brilliant tender plants marches down one side of a large pool. A raised terrace, and the high wall behind it, provides a site for especially tender plants such as *Caprobrotus edulis*, *Cedronella canariensis*, and *Mutisia ilicifolia*. Outside the walled garden specimen trees and shrubs are planted in lawns, and woodland gardens are rich in rhododendrons, in particular the tender Maddenia species. In all around 2,500 taxa are represented here in an area of 12 hectares/30 acres—not a huge collection, but many of them are rarely seen cultivated out of doors in mainland Britain. PT

loggia.

An open arcaded building, often attached to a house to provide a sheltered room leading into the garden. In hot countries it gives welcome shade, in cold and wet countries protection from wind and rain. A common feature of Italian Renaissance gardens, an outstanding early example is that still to be seen in the

garden of the Palazzo PICCOLOMINI (after 1485) in Pienza. Here the cloister-like loggia is three storeyed and provides the only view, and access, to a hidden garden (see GIARDINO SEGRETO). In some Renaissance gardens the loggia was built into the retaining wall of a terrace with a cool, shady *sala terrena* within. The principle was adopted in Britain in gardens such as the 17th-century terraces at POWIS CASTLE and the terraces of the same date at CLIVEDEN, both of which were probably designed by William Winde (d. 1722). The earliest known loggia in England may still be seen at Horton Court in Gloucestershire, built by 1521 for William Knight, a courtier to Henry VIII. In 19th-century English historicizing gardens the loggia made a fashionable reappearance—outstanding examples were those designed around 1840 by Sir Charles BARRY for the Italianate garden at Trentham (Staffordshire). ARTS AND CRAFTS gardens made much of the loggia. Harold PETO designed one for his own garden at IFORD MANOR and at Wayford Manor (Somerset) after 1902 built a new loggia at the end of a Jacobean terrace. PT

Lomonosov. See ORANIENBAUM.

London, George

(c. 1640–1713), English garden designer and the most important figure in the explosion of new gardens which were made in the period of William and Mary and early in the 18th century. His partnership with Henry WISE formed one of the greatest garden design practices in the history of gardening in Britain. Joseph Addison, by no means naturally disposed to their style of gardening, called them 'our heroick Poets'. He worked under John Rose, the royal gardener at St James's Palace, and in 1675 for Henry COMPTON, Bishop of London, at Fulham Palace. He was co-founder, in 1681, of Brompton Park Nursery which also undertook garden design and construction. By 1689 London was royal gardener to William and Mary and sole partner in the firm with Henry Wise. Working in partnership, or individually, they designed formal gardens in the tradition of LE NÔTRE for some of the grandest estates in the country. Among those designed by London were GRIMSTHORPE CASTLE (c.1690), Dyrham Park (Gloucestershire, c.1692), Hampton Court (Herefordshire, c.1693), Hodsock Priory (Nottinghamshire, 1692/3), CASSIOBURY PARK (1697), Chicheley (Buckinghamshire, 1699 onwards), Lumley (County Durham, 1701), Rokeby (County Durham, 1701), Burley-on-the-Hill (Leicestershire, 1701), NEWBY HALL (1701), Canons (Middlesex, after 1706), and Wanstead (Essex, 1706 onwards). None of these survives even partially, although in some cases subsequent designs have followed alignments established by London. The best evidence for their appearance is in the engravings in KNYFF and Kip's *Britannia Illustrata* (1707) which include several London gardens. See also LONDON PARKS AND GARDENS.　PT

London parks and gardens.

From its Roman and Saxon foundations on the banks of the Thames, London gradually expanded. By the late 14th century (as shown by a poll tax return) it had a population of around 20,000 and by the early 16th century this had reached some 35,000. (However, the population of Roman Londinium in the 3rd century AD is estimated (the first census was only taken in 1801) at 45,000.)

In the early Middle Ages London was confined to the square mile that is today the City of London. We know nothing in detail about the gardens attached to houses at this time; only that they existed. The history of London's gardens really starts with the rise in importance of Westminster, to the west of the city. A Benedictine monastery and abbey had been founded there in the 8th century, and in the 11th century, when Edward the Confessor came to the throne in 1042, he established Westminster Palace as his primary royal residence. It is known that by the late 13th century the abbey had an orchard and herb garden and paths strewn with sand, and under Edward III (who came to the throne in 1327) a royal privy garden was established at the palace.

The Strand, linking the city to Westminster, became a major thoroughfare from the 12th century onwards, and from the 13th century many notable town houses (or 'inns' as they were sometimes called) were built for bishops along its southern side, overlooking the river. By the end of the 13th century the Bishop of Ely's Ely Place, on the western edge of the city, had a garden of 2.4 hectares/6 acres; in the late 14th century the garden was given a new hedge, requiring four cartloads of thorns; and in a map of c.1558, attributed to Ralph Agas, it is seen divided into four, with a series of striplike beds. Essex House (where Essex Street stands today, immediately west of the Temple) was originally a property of the Knights Templar but in the 14th century was used by the bishops of Exeter as their London palace, and in the 16th century it belonged to Robert Dudley, Earl of Leicester; his stepson Robert Devereux, Earl of Essex, inherited it in 1588. Hollar's map of c.1660 shows it with elaborate gardens running down to the river—a pattern of knots disposed about a central axis. To the west of Essex House was Arundel House, originally the medieval residence of the bishops of Bath and Wells, with a garden on the river. In the early 17th century it

belonged to Thomas Howard, Earl of Arundel, whose great sculpture collection, the Arundel Marbles, was displayed in a courtyard between the house and the river in a setting created 1613–20 by Inigo JONES. Roy Strong in his *The Artist and the Garden* (2000) describes this as 'the first Italianate garden filled with classical statuary ever to be laid out in this country . . . one of the crucial images in the history of gardening in Britain'. By the mid 17th century the garden also had an elegant four-part knot garden. Nearby, to the west, was Somerset House, first built for Lord Protector Somerset in the mid 16th century on the site of the demolished medieval house of the bishops of Chester and Worcester. In the early 17th century James I's Queen, Anne of Denmark, made a great Renaissance garden here, probably designed by Salomon de CAUS; its centrepiece was a grotto fountain, Mount Parnassus, and west of this was a four-part formal garden overlooked by terrace walks. A German visitor, Neumayr, accompanying the Duke of Saxony, saw the garden in 1613 and found it 'very well laid out, and divided into diverse beautiful plats of curious shapes'. Immediately adjacent to Somerset House was Savoy Palace, built in the 13th century for Peter, Count of Savoy; it was sacked in the Peasants' Revolt (1381) and succeeded by a hospital built in the early 16th century. Hollar's map of London (1646) shows the hospital's courtyard filled with formal gardens. The Savoy Chapel is all that remains today. The most magnificent of the former palaces of the princes of the Church was created from the Archbishop of York's house, York Place, in what is today Whitehall. In 1539 Henry VIII took it over from Thomas Wolsey and turned it into the largest palace in Europe. A garden of matching splendour was made (the Great Garden), of which details can be glimpsed in the background to the portrait of Henry VIII and his family by an unknown artist (c.1545) in the Royal Collection. Some idea of its layout can be gained from the map of c.1558, attributed to Ralph Agas, which shows a quadripartite design with a pattern of narrow beds and an elaborate tiered fountain at the centre. The garden was described by a visitor, Leopold von Wedel, in 1584: 'there are thirty-four high columns, carved with various fine paintings; also different animals carved in wood, with their horns gilt, are set on top of the columns . . . In the middle of the garden is a nice fountain with a remarkable sundial, showing the time in thirty different ways.' Nothing, apart from Inigo Jones's much later Banqueting House (1619–22), now remains of the palace, which was destroyed by fire in 1698.

In later Tudor, and Stuart, times the population of London grew with great rapidity, expanding well beyond the city walls into the

surrounding liberties. By the early 17th century it had reached 225,000, of whom 75,000 lived within the city walls. A map of c.1550 shows the great concentration of houses within the city, many with private gardens, but the same map also shows the development of Moorfields, north of the city walls at Moorgate. Here is 16th-century ribbon development, with houses fronting the road (modern Bishopsgate) on each side, backed with gardens, some of them very elaborate, with hedged fields beyond. By the early 17th century Moorfields was regarded as a place of retreat: there was laid out 'a garden . . . and a pleasurable place of sweet ayres for Cittizens to walk in' (on the site of modern Finsbury Pavement). A little later, inspired by the example of Moorfields, a proposal was put forward that Lincoln's Inn Fields should also be laid out with walks as a public amenity, but the land was sold for development and by 1658 building had begun. However, the Society of Lincoln's Inn raised objections and as a result it was agreed that a large part of the fields should 'for ever and hereafter be open and unbuilt'. Laid out with diagonal walks by 1682, it remains public open space to this day.

The royal parks

The most important ingredient of the London landscape, and its greatest public amenity, is the extraordinary sequence of royal parks which embellish central London and its fringes and which remain royal property to this day. The oldest, *St James's Park*, takes its name from St James's Hospital for lepers, founded in the 11th century. From 1531 Henry VIII drained the marshy land to form a deer park and built St James's Palace (which largely survives). In the 17th century the park was open to the public and early in the century James I had a MENAGERIE here, which was admired by John EVELYN in 1665, especially for the pelicans—'a fowle between a Storke and a Swan; a melancholy waterfowl' (there are still pelicans in the park). After the Restoration (1660), Charles II, filled with enthusiasm for the gardens he had seen during his French exile, had the park redesigned, probably by André MOLLET, to create a new vista westwards from Whitehall. A PATTE D'OIE of avenues radiated out from a semicircle of trees and a great canal ran between the trees of the central avenue. To the north, the Mall was laid out with a quadruple avenue (planted today with London planes (*Platanus* × *hispanica*)), and to the north of that were very elaborate parterres on the site of what is now Carlton House Terrace. Between 1828 and 1829 the park was landscaped by John NASH, who turned the canal into an informal lake with eyecatchers at each end—Buckingham Palace and Horse Guards—and introduced informal plantings of trees. With an area of 36 hectares/89 acres it remains today a popular green space in one of the busiest parts of London.

Hyde Park was a Saxon estate which was acquired after 1066 by Geoffrey de Mandeville who bequeathed it to the Benedictines at Westminster. At the dissolution of the monasteries it was acquired by Henry VIII, who from 1536 made it into a royal hunting forest. In the early 17th century, still used for hunting, it was opened occasionally to the public by James I and became fashionable. From 1637, under Charles I, it became the first of the royal parks to open permanently to the public, but was sold during the Commonwealth, in 1652, and only returned to royal ownership at the Restoration in 1660. In 1730 the Serpentine lake was made and there was much tree planting. The Serpentine was possibly laid out with advice from William KENT; the charming Queen's Temple on its western bank may also have been designed by him. The ensemble, even today, vividly evokes the spirit of early 18th-century landscaping. Hyde Park still has an outstanding collection of trees, some of which, such as the sweet chestnuts (*Castanea sativa*) to the east of the Serpentine, survive from 18th-century plantings. Deer were still hunted in the park as late as 1768.

On the western edge of Hyde Park, *Kensington Palace* was built for William III from 1689. A great garden of ornate parterres laid out south of the palace is usually attributed to George LONDON and Henry WISE but may show the influence of Daniel MAROT. By the time of John Rocque's map of *c*.1756 this garden had gone and elaborate gardens had been laid out, 1726–33, to the east and north of the palace by Charles BRIDGEMAN, with the help of Henry Wise, for George II's Queen Caroline. This layout, with its axial pattern of avenues, a giant pool, serpentine walks in wildernesses, and immense parterres, survives remarkably intact, though shorn of its detail, with the pool (now the Round Pond) remaining and later tree plantings exactly following the old alignments. Also surviving is the beautiful ORANGERY to the north of the palace, built for Queen Anne in 1704 and probably designed by Nicholas HAWKSMOOR and John VANBRUGH. An attractive piece of Victorian neo-formality is the Italian Water Gardens of 1861, close to Lancaster Gate on the northern edge of the park, and an Italianate pumping house by Robert Banks (1813–72) and Charles Barry (1824–1900) overlooks a water parterre with four pools and fountains. In the 20th century there was much replanting of trees throughout the park, and one of the avenues, running south from G. F. Watts's bronze *Physical Energy* (1907),

was slightly bent in order to make Sir George Gilbert Scott's (1811–78) Albert Memorial (1863–72) into a spectacular eyecatcher. The overall area of Hyde Park and Kensington Gardens is 237 hectares/585 acres. Had it not been for the fact that it was royal property it is unlikely that such precious real estate would have survived undeveloped.

Henry VIII's hunting forest ran from Hyde Park northwards to *Regent's Park*, then known as Marylebone Park, which remained a hunting park until 1646 when Charles I mortgaged it to help finance the Civil War. It was sold by Cromwell during the Commonwealth, returned to the crown at the Restoration, and let out as farmland until 1811. At this time John Nash was asked to advise on its development and, in particular, on a way to link it with the Prince Regent's (later George IV's) residence, Carlton House, overlooking St James's Park. The link was never completed—Regent Street forms part of it—nor were the plans to build detached villas in the park and a circus of terraced houses at its centre ever implemented. Nash, sometimes working with Decimus Burton (1800–81), did, however, design a series of terraced houses on the periphery of the park—in streets such as Park Crescent, Hanover Terrace, Cornwall Terrace, and Cambridge Terrace—and the park itself was initially set aside for the exclusive use of the residents of the new houses. In 1826 the Zoological Society established itself in the park, with zoological gardens following. From 1839 the Royal Botanic Society made a lake and an AMERICAN GARDEN, and introduced a collection of medicinal plants. From 1863 W. A. NESFIELD, working with his son Markham (*c*.1842–74), laid out a dazzling ornamental garden, Avenue Gardens, with a lime avenue, box-hedged walks, Italianate urns, topiary, and a feast of bedding schemes (all handsomely restored in 1994). In the 1930s Queen Mary's Garden replaced the Botanical Society's garden. Its centrepiece, lovingly maintained today, is an immense rose garden, now a rare period piece.

The largest of all the royal parks is *Richmond Park*, 1,012 hectares/2,500 acres, in south-west London. It was royal property, as the manor of Sheen, under Edward III in the 13th century. Henry VII built a new palace at Richmond after 1499, where a visitor in 1501 saw 'goodly gardeyns, lately rehersid'. Henry VIII hunted in the park here and his hunting stand, or mound, may still be seen. Under James I a new garden was made, 1610–12, on which Salomon de CAUS worked. In 1637 Charles I enclosed a new park—as distinct from the old park near the palace—(the wall was 13 km/8 miles long) but the palace was destroyed during the Commonwealth. Some ancient oaks may still be seen in the

park but the oldest substantial feature of the landscape is the mid 18th-century Queen's Ride, an avenue of sweet chestnuts (*Castanea sativa*) and English oaks (*Quercus robur*) close to the centre. A very large area, Isabella Plantation, was planted with trees from 1831, and since the 1950s turned into a remarkably beautiful woodland garden with acers, camellias, and rhododendrons. The park has been open to the public since the early 20th century. Although a substantial part of it is today given over to two golf courses and fields for football, polo, and rugby, a herd of deer recalls the park's origins as a hunting ground.

Bushy Park, also in south-west London and, with an area of 450 hectares/1,099 acres, the second largest of the London parks, was enclosed in the late 15th century and became part of Thomas Wolsey's HAMPTON COURT estate in 1514. After the estate passed to Henry VIII in 1529, Bushy Park became a royal deer park. A great avenue of limes (*Tilia × europaea*) (now called the Chestnut Avenue) was planted in 1622 to form the chief north–south axis of the park, and in the 1630s Charles I had an irrigation canal built to bring water to the park; it survives and is today handsomely embellished with streams and pools. Between 1689 and 1699 four rows of horse chestnuts (*Aesculus hippocastanum*) were added on each side, under the supervision of George London. The avenue and some of the original trees survive. In a pool at the southern end of the avenue is the Diana Fountain with, rather confusingly, a statue of Arethusa which originally stood in the early 17th-century garden at Somerset House. With its fine trees and mixture of wildness and formality, Bushy Park is one of the best, and least known, of the London parks.

Greenwich Park on its hilly site overlooking the Thames in south-east London was enclosed in the early 15th century by Humphrey, Duke of Gloucester, the brother of Henry V. His manor house was destroyed to build the Queen's House, to the designs of Inigo Jones from 1616. In the late 17th century André LE NÔTRE was asked to make a design for the park, for which a drawing dated 1662 survives, but it seems this was never executed. However, Sir William Boreham, keeper of the park, laid out a pattern of avenues at this time, of which traces survive, including some 17th-century sweet chestnuts (*Castanea sativa*). Later replantings of avenues have followed some of the original alignments. Charles II appointed an astronomer royal in 1675 and the Royal Observatory, designed by Sir Christopher Wren (1632–1723) and Robert Hooke (1635–1703), was completed in 1676. The view northwards from Observatory Hill of the Queen's House, the former Royal Naval Hospital, and the towers of Canary Wharf with the city beyond is a rare historical panorama. Greenwich, with an area of 73 hectares/183 acres, has been a public park since the 18th century and was in the 19th century a popular retreat for Londoners.

Public parks and pleasure gardens

As the population of London grew (reaching around 600,000 by 1700 and over 900,000 by 1800), public gardens began to be seen as a valuable amenity. PLEASURE GARDENS such as Vauxhall (founded c.1660) and Ranelagh (1742) were designed for public entertainment and were popular in the 18th century. From the early 19th century a very different kind of PUBLIC PARK, far larger and of much greater horticultural interest, made its appearance away from the centre. Victoria Park in Hackney, with an area of 87 hectares/215 acres, was laid out by James Pennethorne and opened to the public in 1845. Pennethorne also laid out Battersea Park, opened in 1858 and seen as an important part of the new residential development south of the river. Also dating from the 1850s was one of the greatest of all London public parks, Crystal Palace Park, laid out in Sydenham by Sir Joseph PAXTON. Many others followed and became popular amenities as well as sources of civic pride. By the late 20th century all had suffered from neglect, although in recent years some restoration has been done, in particular at Battersea Park.

Square gardens and communal gardens

There has never been a systematic programme of tree planting in London such as that associated with the avenues and boulevards of PARIS, laid out in the 19th century by Baron HAUSSMANN. However, London square gardens, for the most part privately owned, fulfil something of the same purpose. In the late 17th- and 18th-centuries development of London, expanding westwards from the city, communal gardens for the private use of residents were seen as an important ornament to the London squares. St James's Square, for example (developed from 1662), had a central garden laid out in 1727 by Charles Bridgeman; it was redesigned by John Nash 1817–18 and by John Brookes in 1974. In Grosvenor Square, built from 1725, Todd Longstaffe-Gowan in his *The London Town Garden* (2001) shows how the expensive central garden was seen as a vital attraction in this speculative development. Square gardens of this sort, in addition to the private individual gardens which the houses also had, were a universal feature of Georgian developments in such areas as Mayfair, Bloomsbury, and Islington. In Notting Hill some streets were planned so that the back gardens of the houses gave onto, and had access to, an enclosed communal garden (the west side

of the upper part of Lansdowne Road, developed in the 1860s, is a good example).

One of the most striking features of London is that houses with gardens, including those of public housing schemes, have continued to be built even after the Second World War. To this day far more Londoners live in houses with gardens than in the blocks of flats that in other countries, from the 19th century onwards, were seen as the solution to housing an increasing urban population. In London today, over 200 gardens, mostly privately owned, open to the public for charity every year under the National Gardens Scheme, giving a vivid idea of the importance of gardens to life in the capital.

The nursery trade

John Harvey's *Early Nurserymen* (1974) finds hints of nurserymen in London as early as the 13th century. By the 16th century the Banbury family appear to have been established in the trade in Westminster. Ralph Tuggie (d. 1632) also of Westminster was described by Harvey as 'the leading plantsman of his day. As a nurseryman . . . he reigned supreme.' As the population grew the nursery trade retreated to cheaper available land on the periphery, particularly east of the city. In the late 17th century Leonard Gurle's Whitechapel Nursery was a major supplier of fruit trees and of ornamental shrubs. By the end of the century there were several firms of seedsmen trading in London. The establishment in 1681 of the Brompton Park Nursery in west London, in which George London was a partner, was important not merely for London gardens but for gardens all over England which the nursery supplied. As Todd Longstaffe-Gowan shows in his *The London Town Garden* (2001) the 18th-century development of London stimulated the nursery trade immensely. Loddiges Nursery (see LODDIGES, JOACHIM CONRAD), founded in Hackney in 1771, was probably the finest nursery of its time and continued to supply London gardeners until 1854.   PT

Long Hill ⊛

Beverly, Massachusetts, USA, was the summer country home of Ellery Sedgewick (editor of *Atlantic Monthly*) and his wife Mabel Cabot Sedgewick, author of *The Garden Month by Month* (1907). The original 46-hectare/114-acre tract had a cover of woodlands, meadows, and wetlands, with views out over the surrounding countryside. Mr Sedgewick was inspired to salvage the magnificent interior details from the Isaac Ball Mansion, c.1802, of Charleston, South Carolina, and incorporate them into a new house at Long Hill, in 1921, through architect Philip Richardson. Mabel Cabot Sedgewick designed the original gardens with

an accomplished eye, combining indigenous and exotic trees and shrubs to create a strong framework for a rich collection of spring bulbs and borders of flowering shrubs. Mabel Sedgewick's death in 1937 brought this design chapter to an end, and the marriage of Mr Sedgewick to Marjorie Russell, in 1939, opened a new one at Long Hill. Marjorie's English origins carried collecting passion to the gardens. She added tree peonies, koelreuterias, oxydendrums, rhododendrons, stewartias, and Japanese maples to prolong the flowering and foliage seasons, added new gardens, and developed a close relationship with the ARNOLD ARBORETUM, in Boston, for new plant sources and cultural information. The core collection at Long Hill has been rebuilt to 400 species, with Mabel Sedgewick's meticulous cataloguing of her original collection. There are now eighteen noted landscape and garden elements, ranging from specimen beeches to a Chinese Pagoda. The property was given to the Tustees of Reservations, a conservation and preservation trust, in 1979.   PC

Longue Vue ⊛

New Orleans, Louisiana, USA. Edgar and Edith Stern's adaptation of a Greek Revival plantation house, built in 1939–42, was axially positioned to take advantage of existing garden rooms laid out in 1935 by Ellen Biddle Shipman (1869–1950). Within the 3.2-hectare/8-acre property's symmetrical framework, a cobblestoned courtyard opens to an entrance driveway canopied by live oaks (*Quercus virginiana*) that frame the western façade of the house designed by William (1897–1984) and Geoffrey (1905–85) Platt, replacing an earlier house. The main garden extends south from a portico terrace planted with boxwood (*Buxus microphylla* var. *japonica*) parterres edged by white 'Summer Snow' roses and accented with standard gardenias. A lush Bermuda grass (*Cynodon dactylon*) lawn, bordered by brick paths, perennial beds, and lattice-patterned walls (punctuated with fountains), extends to two canal-linked pools backed by a semicircular, colonnaded, wisteria-clad loggia. With twenty water jets arching dramatically over the rectangular pool, the so-called Spanish Court was inspired by the ALHAMBRA and reworked by William Platt. Turning abruptly west, a canalled passageway leads into to a brick-walled kitchen garden, an octagon of beds arranged around a sunken sugar kettle pool. Past fragrant plantings of sweet olive (*Osmanthus fragrans*), the path divides into three and then rambles through woodland gardens of camellias, wildflowers, and Louisiana irises to a brick *pigeonnier*. Maintained by a non-profit foundation, Longue Vue has been open to

the public since 1980 and offers ongoing educational programmes for children in its 0.2-hectare/0.5-acre interactive discovery garden.
HSS

Longwood Gardens ⊕

Kennett Square, Pennsylvania, USA, is the horticultural wonderland created by industrialist Pierre S. du Pont in the first half of the 20th century. Mr du Pont purchased the property from Quaker farmers in 1906 to save its collection of trees, and then transformed it into 425 hectares/1,050 acres of woodlands, meadows, gardens, conservatories, and his residence. Extensive travels exposed Mr du Pont to a broad array of cultural and horticultural influences. From a childhood visit to Philadelphia's 1876 Centennial Exposition, to the Exposition Universelle in Paris, the World Columbian Exposition in Chicago, the Crystal Palace and Kew Gardens in England, and villas and palaces across Europe, he catalogued impressions of gardens and their features. Many forays to exotic regions of South America, the Caribbean, Hawaii, and California fed his botanical curiosity, and formed the inspiration for the exotic plant collections that distinguish Longwood Gardens. His first garden effort was a 180-m/600-ft long Flower Garden Walk, in 1907, that featured old-fashioned cottage flowers and flowering shrubs. As his vision matured, new gardens reflected Italian and French influence. With the addition of an Open Air Theatre, in 1914, the use of the gardens for entertainment was an important facet of their design. The construction of the Conservatory—complete with pipe organ—set a new direction for the plant collections and their display. An appreciation for spectacle and a facility for engineering led to more elaborate garden features, in the form of a series of pools and fountains in the Fountain Garden, modelled after the Villa GAMBERAIA, facing the Conservatory. Illumination then made the fountains and their gardens a magical evening performance experience, and these pleasure gardens became the favoured venue for Mr du Pont's entertaining—to the delight of his guests. All developments at Longwood were directed for the ultimate enjoyment of the public, and Longwood Gardens was turned over to the Longwood Foundation for management in 1946.

Mr du Pont died in 1954, but the gardens continued to grow according to his visionary plan. A visitors' centre welcomes the public. The domestic greenhouses were converted to display houses, and a series of new greenhouses were added, including a Desert House and tropical collection, to make a total of 1.6 hectares/4 acres under glass. There are now twenty outdoor gardens on display, and the concept of indoor gardens under glass was developed—twenty in all—to complement the outdoor gardens. A bold design initiative of inviting prominent designers—such as Isabelle GREENE and Roberto BURLE MARX—to add new gardens to the collection brings a dynamic evolution to Longwood and promises modern additions to the collection of garden ideas. The mix of horticulture and display intensity here is unequalled in America. Longwood Gardens are also noted for scientific research, plant exploration, horticultural education programmes, and performing arts, all important components of the modern Longwood mission. The outstanding element continues to be pleasure gardens—for the pleasure of all guests, as Mr du Pont wished.
PC

Loo, Paleis Het ⊕

Apeldoorn, Gelderland, the Netherlands, one of the most influential garden revivals of its time after completion of the restoration of palace and formal gardens in 1984. When William III acquired the medieval castle of Het Loo at the edge of the Veluwe in 1684, he intended to build a new hunting lodge alongside it, which he envisaged according to the latest French models. While requesting designs from Paris, he settled for a design from Jacob ROMAN that was started the following year. What followed was a remarkable and protracted design process that saw Hans Willem BENTINCK and Romeyn de Hooghe in charge, with contributions from Claude DESGOTS and Daniel MAROT. The botanist Daniel Desmarets was responsible for horticultural aspects in the layout. There were two principal phases—the palace with its King's and Queen's Garden on either side and the main lower parterres to the north. The latter was extended in 1692 with the upper parterres, terminated by the colonnade that had formerly connected the two wings of the palace. The richly planted and decorated formal gardens were considered the most exuberant in the Netherlands, vying in many ways with Louis XIV's VERSAILLES, indeed exceeding it in some aspects, including the waterworks designed by van Cleeff. The gardens remained throughout the 18th century, but in 1773 Pieter W. Schonck produced alterations for areas near the house for Stadtholder Prince Willem V and in 1778 a variant of this proposal was executed. This was an early landscape-style arrangement of shrubberies with both classical and chinoiserie-inspired garden buildings. The layout otherwise respected the baroque framework and detailing. However when King Louis Napoleon selected Het Loo as one of his residences, this involved a more rigorous approach. The building was altered and stuccoed, and in 1808 a landscape plan for the small park by Alexander Dufour (1750–1835) was executed by Johan Philip Posth (1763–1832). At his return in 1814 after the French Period King Willem I found the gardens ruined. Yet he not only maintained the new layout but extended it, including the creation of two large lakes from a series of old fish ponds in 1818–24. The upper lake was made into a bathing pool in 1856, and the park continued to be modified during the 19th and 20th centuries. King Willem III (1817–90), who had a passion for trees, added an arboretum, planted exotic trees in the park, and also numerous clumps of rhododendrons. His widow Queen Regent Emma continued the passion for developing the park, with the 'Regent's park' on the site of the former home farm. A large maze was also planted, which remains today. Queen Wilhelmina (1880–1962) and Prince Consort Hendrik extended the layout with the 'Achter park' (the park beyond) which respected the features of the original landscape, while the 'Prins Hendrik park' designed in 1902 consisted of a woodland park with a formal layout respecting the lines of an old military camp. The PATTE D'OIE arrangement in front of the palace was completed in 1911 with the planting and replanting of double beech avenues on a location where there had been only two.

In the early 20th century the house was extended, but apart from the additional avenue the landscape remained largely unaltered. In 1957 the architect C. W. Royaards was asked to explore possibilities for restoration, proposing in 1965 to liberate the building from later additions and return it to the original form as it had been during the era of William III. The idea was to transfer the palace from a royal residence and to turn it into a national museum dedicated to the royal family. A lengthy debate followed as to the nature of the restoration, but was finally agreed for the palace in 1976 and for the gardens in 1978. The architect in charge J. B. Baron van Asbeck commissioned working parties for the research required, and based the restoration on a plan by Christiaan Pieter van Staden c.1714 after this had been verified with archaeology. A restoration of the park followed from the mid 1990s onwards.   JW

ERIK DE JONG, *Nature and Art: Dutch Garden and Landscape Architecture, 1650–1740* (2000).
EELCO ELZENGA, *Het Witte Loo: van Lodewijk Napoleon tot Wilhelmina 1806–1962* (1992).

Lorimer, Sir Robert

(1864–1929), Scottish architect and garden designer born in Edinburgh and educated at Edinburgh Academy and the University of Edinburgh. His work is characterized by a devotion to Scottish vernacular architecture, and to the gardens of the past, in particular those of the Italian Renaissance and the 17th century in Scotland. In a lecture in 1899 he described his ideal of the old Scottish garden: 'Great intersecting walks of shaven grass, on either side borders of brightest flowers backed by low espaliers hanging with shining apples.' He is sometimes referred to as 'the Scottish LUTYENS' and it is true that they have much in common, in particular a respect for local building materials and techniques, and a sense of humour. Like Lutyens he also designed furniture and the interior fittings of his houses and this delight in craftsmanship had a strong influence on his garden designs. Virtually all his architectural work, and all his gardens, were carried out in Scotland. His work as a garden designer may be admired at two country houses in East Fife open to the public: KELLIE CASTLE and Hill of Tarvit House (where he also designed the house). Gardens by him also survive at Balmanno Castle (Perthshire), Earlshall (East Fife), Gibliston (East Fife), and, possibly, Torosay Castle (Mull). They have much in common—a love of TOPIARY and finely crafted hedges, a delight in symmetry and axial vistas, a fastidious treatment of levels, and a lively use of garden ornaments.   PT

L'Orme, Philibert de

(c.1510–1570), French architect and theorist, the first Frenchman to synthesize the Italian Renaissance and native traditions in an individual style. Between 1533 and 1536 he studied Roman antiquities in Italy, where he met Cardinal Jean Du Bellay, who commissioned him to design a house at the Abbey of Saint-Maur.

In 1547 Henri II appointed L'Orme *architecte du roi*. His most important work during this period was for Diane de Poitiers at ANET, where he included gardens in a symmetrical design which by its scale imposed regularity on the old buildings. He wrote that an architect should show imagination when building on marshy ground, using the canals necessary to drain it to increase pleasure and profit, as he had done at Anet, where, despite a waterlogged site, he had made a garden as pleasant as could be seen anywhere. He also worked for Diane de Poitiers at CHENONCEAUX. At SAINT-GERMAIN-EN-LAYE he designed the Maison du Théâtre (later called the Château-Neuf), on steep ground overlooking the Seine. However, the death of Henri II in 1560 ended the project with only the upper terrace finished.

Catherine de Médicis employed L'Orme throughout his life, first at Montceaux-en-Brie, where he is recorded as having designed a garden pavilion, a grotto, and a building for the game of pall-mall; then at Saint-Maur, acquired after Jean Du Bellay's death. He was engaged on her palace of the Tuileries (see PARIS PARKS AND GARDENS) when he died.

L'Orme's treatises combine theory derived from Vitruvius, ALBERTI, and Sebastiano Serlio with practical knowledge from his own experience. *Nouvelles Inventions pour bien bastir et à petis frais* was published in 1561; *Le Premier Tome de l'architecture* in 1597. Besides the originality of his designs, he established the architect's responsibility for the laying out of grounds, and he pioneered the ornamental use of water in basins and canals.   KASW

Lotus Garden ⊛

Dholpur, Rajasthan, India. A garden made by BĀBUR which was forgotten for 400 years before it was identified by Elizabeth Moynihan and described in her book *Paradise as a Garden in Persia and Mughal India* (1979). Bābur came here in 1527, admired an outcrop of sandstone, had a pavilion made of it, and laid out a garden. He described the making of the pavilion, which was carved out of the stone, and the garden as we may read in Annette S. Beveridge's translation of his memoirs, *The Babur-Nama in English* (1969). Bābur described the levelling of the sandstone and the making of a water tank and a well. He had watercourses made and a hot bath. Elizabeth Moynihan found traces of these, of pools in the shape of various parts of the lotus (its buds or flowers), and a hexagonal pool. The hot bath remained in perfect state, but in use as a stable. She describes the garden as 'the first example of the brilliant assimilation of Mughal design with Indian skill and creativity in garden architecture'.   PT

Lotusland ⊛

Santa Barbara, California, USA, with an area of 15 hectares/37 acres was developed by Madame Ganna Walska between 1941 and 1984, and now constitutes one of the most exuberant collections of temperate and subtropical plants in the country. In the 1880s Kinton Stevens had developed a nursery here and several large specimens of palm and *Araucaria bidwillii* and a huge Monterey cypress remain. The Mediterranean-style house was built in the early 1920s and several associated formal features survive, including the original swimming pool, flanked by semicircular pools planted with lotus and *Victoria amazonica*, an olive ALLÉE, and a Spanish garden. Ganna Walska created several specialized collections in which literally hundreds of one plant species were used to create visual fantasies. These include the collection of golden ball and barrel cacti and eccentrically shaped euphorbias along the main drive, a large grove of *Dracaena draco*, and a bromeliad collection. The aloe garden contains small aloes and tree aloes, and a milky white pool with an eccentric fountain of abalone and giant tricadana clam shells. The remarkable blue garden is a grove of blue foliage trees, including cedars, palms, and spruces, underplanted with blue fescue grass and paths lined with lumps of blue coke waste. A small lake was transformed into a JAPANESE GARDEN. The Cycad Garden created in 1978–9 contains Australian, African, and Mexican cycads planted on low mounds so that their unusual structure can be studied more easily. Since Madame Walska's death several areas have been partially redesigned, including the new swimming pool and the Japanese garden.
                                        DCS

Loudon, Jane Webb

(1807–58), English author and garden journalist who married J. C. LOUDON in 1828. They met as the result of Loudon's review of her futuristic novel *The Mummy!* in the *Gardener's Magazine*. The book, whose first line is 'In the year 2126, England enjoyed peace and tranquility under the absolute dominion of a female sovereign', is a pioneer of science fiction. She became her husband's amanuensis, taught herself about gardening, and in 1840 started her own periodical the *Lady's Magazine of Gardening*. She was an outstanding popularizer of gardening knowledge for women and wrote a series of influential books for that readership. *The Ladies' Companion to the Flower Garden* (1841) went through four editions, and she wrote a series of books devoted to particular groups of plants starting with *The Ladies' Flower Garden of Ornamental Annuals* (1840). After her husband's death in 1843 she wrote many more books (diversifying into *Domestic Pets: Their Habits and Management*, 1851) and produced new editions of her husband's books. Jane Loudon was the first distinguished woman garden writer in what has become a great tradition.   PT

Loudon, John Claudius

(1783–1843), Scottish author and garden theorist of protean talents and energy born in Cambuslang, Lanarkshire. He came to London at the age of 20 and embarked on a career of gardening journalism and authorship. From 1803 onwards (*Observations on the Laying out of Public Squares*) he poured out a stream of books and articles of high quality and independent opinion. His *Encyclopaedia of Gardening* (1822) was a book of great influence which came out in many new editions, continuing after his death, the last edition appearing in 1878. It embraced the whole art and practice of gardening, and remains of great value—if you want to know how to cultivate cherries, and what are the best cultivars; what are the most interesting gardens in Russia or Denbighshire; the best designs of beehives; what are the important British books on gardening from 1502 onwards (with critical notes); and almost anything else whatsoever about gardening, the *Encyclopaedia* will tell you. He founded the *Gardener's Magazine* (1826) which catered to the burgeoning new middle-class interest in gardening. His *Arboretum et Fruticetum Britannicum* (1838) in eight volumes gathered together an immense range of information on trees and shrubs with 2,500 engravings. He designed BIRMINGHAM BOTANICAL GARDENS (1831) and DERBY ARBORETUM (1839–40), executed a planting plan of Brompton Cemetery (London, 1839), and made landscape designs for a few great country houses such as HAREWOOD HOUSE (1806) and Ditchley Park (Oxfordshire, 1810).

In garden aesthetics Loudon swithered between a devotion to the irregular landscape style and the formal garden. In the *Encyclopaedia* he struck what seems to be a happy balance—'to say that landscape gardening is an improvement on geometric gardening, is a similar misapplication of language, as to say that a lawn is an improvement of a cornfield, because it is substituted in its place. It is absurd, therefore, to despise the ancient style, because it has not the same beauties as the modern, to which it never aspired. It has beauties of a different kind, equally perfect in their kind as those of the modern style.' In the *Gardener's Magazine* in 1832 Loudon coined a new term—'it is necessary to understand that there is such a character of art as the gardenesque, as well as the picturesque'. The GARDENESQUE emphasized the garden's intrinsic rather than imitative powers. It adopted a style of planting in which trees and shrubs were planted as isolated specimens so that their intrinsic beauties may be displayed to the greatest advantage. In the Derby Arboretum trees planted by Loudon may still be seen—raised on mounds so that the upper part of their roots may be seen and the whole tree shown in a position of prominence. See also LOUDON, JANE WEBB.   PT

Louisenlund ⊕

Güby, Schleswig-Holstein, Germany. The garden of the Danish governor, the Landgrave Carl von Hessen (1744–1836), inspired by the ideas of Freemasonry and laid out between 1770 and 1804, lies on the banks of the Schlei, a fjord of the Baltic Sea. The name of the garden derives from his wife Louise, a sister of King Christian VII, and the Danish word *lund* which means forest. Like a FERME ORNÉE the estate includes woodland, grazing, hedges, gardens, brooks, and ponds. Formal avenues and naturalistic plantings intermingle the baroque and landscape styles in a distinctive way. The manor house, enlarged by Johann Hermann von Motz (1743–1829), was used as a summer house for the family. Close to the house are parterres, a cascade in the form of a water stair, and a natural waterfall with a grotto and pool. In the grounds are a hermitage with an Irrgarten (Labyrinth), a Norwegian chapel, an altar, a Felsenberg (Mount of Rocks), a column of marble and a wooden Freimaurerturm (Tower of Freemansonry). Of the cellar where Carl experimented on an *Athanor* (a special furnace) with the famous alchemist Earl of Saint-Germain (who died in 1784) only some stones from the walls remain. A sundial on a broken column stands today at the centre of a new parterre garden in front of the manor house. The sandstone Egyptian gateway of the main entrance of the Tower of Freemasonry was moved to the wall of the earlier stable block. The masonic garden of Carl von Hessen still presents many unsolved mysteries.   MMM

Louisiana Museum of Modern Art ⊕

Humlebæk, Denmark. The museum park has been developed since 1958 on the site of a 19th-century manor house with rolling terrain, fine views, and old full-crowned trees surviving from the 19th-century garden. The first museum building by architects Jørgen Bo (1909–99) and Vilhelm Wohlert (b. 1920) was built sensitively among the mature trees and created a precedent for how the museum and the park were to be united as a place with a sculpture garden with works of Jean Arp, Enzo Cucchi, Max Ernst, Henry Moore, Nobuo Sekine, and Richard Serra. The building opens onto special enclosures: kerbstones laid like stepping stones through a reflecting pool, a fern-filled ravine, and Henry Heerup's (1907–93) granite sculptures on a surface of green ivy. In recent years the Pond Garden has been developed by landscape architects Lea Nørgaard (b. 1952) and Vibeke Holscher (b. 1948) as an adventurous BOSQUET *sauvage*, accentuated by Alfio Bonanno's (b. 1947) woven birds' nests, bridge structure, and red cottages. Also George Trakas's *Self Passage*, a progression of stairs, paths, and bridges leading to the water, beautifully fits the site. The graphics wing was built underground and terrain around modelled like a steep slope, bordered by an undulating wall.   AL

Lowveld National Botanical Garden ⊕

Nelspruit, Mpumalanga province, South Africa, is part of the botanic garden network of the National Botanical Institute. Summers here are hot with high humidity and winters are pleasantly mild. The 159-hectare/393-acre garden, founded in 1970, has one of the most dramatic settings of any botanic garden in the world. The garden straddles the Nels and Crocodile rivers, the former cascading down a waterfall into the latter. The riverine area affords the visitor interesting riparian forest vegetation. Only some 25 hectares/62 acres of the garden have been landscaped and laid out taxonomically, making this garden more of a botanical bush arboretum than a conventional botanic garden. It lies between the great eastern escarpment and the true lowveld and is dominated by sour and mixed lowveld bushveld. But it also has examples of sand forest, rain and afromontane forest, and mopane bushveld. Some 65% of South Africa's indigenous trees can be seen here. It also has an interesting collection of cycads. As in the other NBI gardens, botanical research is carried on and there are a small library and herbarium.   DPMcC

Ludwigslust ⊕

Mecklenburg-Western Pomerania, Germany, is one of the most noteworthy parks in northern Germany since two garden styles intermingle in a most magnificent way: formal late baroque elements are enriched by classicist influences so that both French and English sections overlap. The park was designed during two major phases: the first followed the foundation of a new town, Ludwigslust, where Duke Friedrich of Mecklenburg transferred his small residence in 1764. The then court architect Johann Joachim Busch supervised the planning and construction of town, palace, and park. On either side of the new palace the garden had typical baroque elements—a Great Cascade, a lawn parterre, BOSQUETS, statuary, a well-worked-out system of canals, fountains and several waterworks, and garden buildings (e.g. a sham RUIN of 1788, a Swiss Cottage of 1789, and a pheasantry). The various scattered formal parts of the park were combined and brought together into a unified landscape after 1852, when the Prussian court gardener Peter Joseph LENNÉ developed a large-scale project where long vistas integrated the park into the surrounding landscape. Groups of trees encircled areas of meadowland, water basins were created, and winding paths gave access to the open grounds. Though some parts have grown into woodland, the once magnificent and lavish layout, bounded by a HA-HA, is still clearly recognizable today.   AK

Luisium.

See DESSAU-WÖRLITZ GARTENREICH.

M

Machchi Bhawan

(Fish Square), Agra Fort, India, was once one of the two major Mughal gardens of the fort at Agra. Named after its tanks of sacred fish, it was richly planted, and its fountains and channels repeated the pleasures of running water which Niccolao Manucci described. In the 18th century, however, it was pillaged by the Jats, who removed much of the marble work to the palace of Deeg at Bharatpur. Later, during the administration of Lord William Bentinck, the remaining marble and mosaic work was sold, and no trace of the garden now remains, other than its name. SMH

Macleay, Alexander

(1767–1848), Australian colonial politician who arrived in Sydney in 1826 to become New South Wales Colonial Secretary. Macleay, with interests in etymology, horticulture, landscape design, and botany and a foundation member of Sydney's Botanic Gardens, established two of the grandest gardens in the colony, one at his marine villa, ELIZABETH BAY HOUSE overlooking Sydney Harbour, and a country estate, BROWNLOW HILL, near Camden. Macleay developed Elizabeth Bay as a celebrated landscape garden retaining the native bush and planting exotics to enhance its botanical interest. Macleay's development of his garden reveals his informed taste and romantic enthusiasm. CMR

McMahon, Bernard

(c.1775–1816/18), Philadelphia nurseryman, born in Ireland. At 21 he emigrated to America and in Philadelphia founded a successful seed and nursery business, becoming one of the main distributors of native American flora into Europe. In 1806 he published *The American Gardener's Calendar* which for 50 years was the standard reference work in several fields of gardening, including, unusually, recommending the use of native flora. McMahon was entrusted by Thomas JEFFERSON with the cultivation of the seeds and plants from the LEWIS and Clark transcontinental

expedition. McMahon was the principal founder member of the Pennsylvania Horticultural Society in 1827. He is remembered botanically by the species *Mahonia*. MC-C

Madama, Villa ⊛

Rome, Italy. Built between 1516 and 1520 the villa and garden, although never completed, was designed by Raphael (1483–1520), Giulio Romano (1492–1546), and Antonio Sangallo the younger (1485–1546) for Giulio de' Medici (afterwards Pope Clement VII) on the eastern slopes of Monte Mario outside the walls of Rome in what was still unspoilt countryside. The house was planned as a series of open courts and loggias of some magnificence, integrating indoor and outdoor spaces but leaving little living accommodation. The LOGGIA to the east commanded a superb view over the Tiber valley, while that to the north was entrance to a GIARDINO SEGRETO and on the west to a great semicircular theatre excavated out of the hillside. At Raphael's death in 1520 less than half the building was completed and the project more or less abandoned after burning during the Sack of Rome in 1527. The garden, however, a series of terraces on the contours of the hill, was already used for entertainments, although it appeared to lack the strong axial alignments used by BRAMANTE for the Cortile de Belvedere (see VATICAN GARDENS) constructed twenty years earlier. The most notable survival at Madama is the Elephant Fountain by Giovanni da Udine (1487–1561), ornamented with swags of fruit and backed by handsome mosaics, originally placed over an antique sarcophagus, a copy of a subterranean Temple of Neptune discovered shortly before on the Palatine Hill, part of Nero's Golden House. Today only the elephant's head and a plain stone tank remain. Another fountain by da Udine is recorded in a woodland setting away from the formal terraces, a fine artifice with water falling over rustic stones with dripping stalactites. PHo

Madinat al-Zahra ⊛

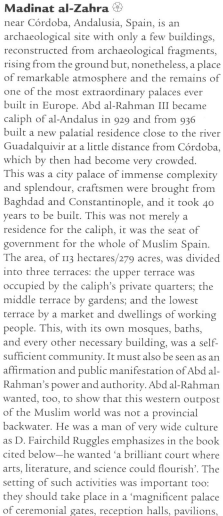

near Córdoba, Andalusia, Spain, is an archaeological site with only a few buildings, reconstructed from archaeological fragments, rising from the ground but, nonetheless, a place of remarkable atmosphere and the remains of one of the most extraordinary palaces ever built in Europe. Abd al-Rahman III became caliph of al-Andalus in 929 and from 936 built a new palatial residence close to the river Guadalquivir at a little distance from Córdoba, which by then had become very crowded. This was a city palace of immense complexity and splendour, craftsmen were brought from Baghdad and Constantinople, and it took 40 years to be built. This was not merely a residence for the caliph, it was the seat of government for the whole of Muslim Spain. The area, of 113 hectares/279 acres, was divided into three terraces: the upper terrace was occupied by the caliph's private quarters; the middle terrace by gardens; and the lowest terrace by a market and dwellings of working people. This, with its own mosques, baths, and every other necessary building, was a self-sufficient community. It must also be seen as an affirmation and public manifestation of Abd al-Rahman's power and authority. Abd al-Rahman wanted, too, to show that this western outpost of the Muslim world was not a provincial backwater. He was a man of very wide culture as D. Fairchild Ruggles emphasizes in the book cited below—he wanted 'a brilliant court where arts, literature, and science could flourish'. The setting of such activities was important too: they should take place in a 'magnificent palace of ceremonial gates, reception halls, pavilions, and gardens'.

A great aqueduct was built to bring water from the mountains. The garden terrace at Madinat al-Zahra, which included orchards, had rills and pools and much water was required for everyday needs. We know that there were pavilions, MIRADORS, and ornamental basins and that the gardens were laid out symmetrically, disposed on a cross-axial plan, and that individual courtyards were planted. Nothing is known of the detailed plantings within the gardens. Planned vistas within the garden complex were carefully calculated and vistas beyond the city walls were also regarded as important. There were small, enclosed gardens but from these much longer views were also valued. The caliph's palace overlooked gardens and it also contained a pool of mercury which would reflect the sun through an open door and fill the room with dazzling, liquid light.

Madinat al-Zahra lasted a very short time. Abd al-Rahman III died in 961, his successor al-Hakam II died in 976 leaving a 2-year-old heir.

Power was seized by Muhammad ibn Amir (later known as al-Mansur) who was succeeded by his son al-Muzaffar, but a state of civil war ensued. Groups of Berbers became increasingly powerful and they burnt and sacked Madinat al-Zahra in 1010. The caliphate formally disappeared in 1031 and Madinat al-Zahra was repeatedly plundered for building materials and for treasures so that this greatest of Islamic palaces receded into oblivion. Archaeological investigations of the site started in the early 20th century and have been continuing spasmodically ever since. By 2001 only about 10% of the site had been investigated. In its day the buildings here were among the most beautiful in the Muslim world—in all likelihood of greater beauty and sophistication than the very much later buildings which survive at the ALHAMBRA. The site today is beautiful and poignant. Some walls have been rebuilt, some interiors (with superb architectural detail) pieced together, footings of other buildings revealed. Italian cypresses, date palms, and strawberry trees (*Arbutus unedo*) rise among the ruins. It is hard to imagine that the 10th-century Muslims who made Madinat al-Zahra would have enjoyed anything as commonplace as the bougainvillea that may now be seen.   PT

D. FAIRCHILD RUGGLES, *Gardens, Landscape, and Vision in the Palaces of Islamic Spain* (2000).

Madone, Serre de la ⊛

Menton, Alpes-Maritimes, France, an Italianate farmhouse on the outskirts of Menton which was bought in 1924 by Lawrence JOHNSTON. Here he found a climate and site entirely different from those of his English garden, HIDCOTE MANOR. Olives and lemons were originally cultivated here, in terraced ground protected by hills to the north. The mild Riviera microclimate immensely extended the range of plants which Johnston could grow. On the terraced ground south of the house he had all kinds of tender plants—banksias, clivias, melaleucas, and tender mahonias (including the orange-flowered *Mahonia siamensis* from Thailand, introduced by Johnston). After Johnston's death in 1958 the estate changed hands many times, with little interest shown in the garden. It now belongs to the Conservatoire du Littoral, a French government agency dedicated to protecting coastal sites, which has embarked on its restoration. Some fine plants survive from Johnston's time, among them a huge *Afrocarpa falcata* (formerly *Podocarpus gracillimus*), a noble *Magnolia delavayi*, and several mature stone pines (*Pinus pineaster*). An enormous *Rosa* 'La Follette' scrambles through the trees. Much work remains to be done, on planting as well as the architectural

fabric of the garden (including glasshouses)—it is potentially one of the best gardens of the French Riviera.   PT

Madoo ⊛

Sagaponack, New York, USA, an idiosyncratic 0.8-hectare/2-acre garden on the south-eastern flats of Long Island, the quirky creation of artist Robert Dash (b. 1931). Supported by a charitable trust since 1994, the garden boasts more than 12,000 species of trees, shrubs, perennials, and bulbs, planted in a succession of playful compositions—the Templum Barbecuem, an arbour of granite stumps, and a hermit's hut, among several. Colourful architectural features abound: the mirrored shed, a gazebo painted flashy purples, a loo trimmed in lime green, the frozen red hoops seeming to roll off a bridge. The overall scene incorporates several weathered 18th-century farm outbuildings (reinvented as artists' studios and utility sheds), a pod of small ponds spanned by an oriental bridge, and decorative connecting paths of various materials including pebbles, brick, grass, and telephone pole sections. Since 1967 the garden has cheerfully if unpredictably devoured the once barren land, from the original buildings to the outer property limits, so that today it resembles a vivacious horticultural carnival. The mix of plant material is as eclectic as the garden's unorthodox features. Reliable natives like clethra, monarda, *Kalmia latifolia*, *Magnolia virginiana*, *Ilex glabra*, and ferns intermingle with exotics which include *Ginkgo biloba*, Irish junipers, tree peonies, and *Rosa rugosa* from Japan. The garden is strictly organic, enriched annually with numerous truckloads of manure and scores of mulching hay bales, as described in Dash's engaging *Notes from Madoo* (2000). Madoo is a year-round wildlife refuge for birds and is regularly open to the public.   HSS

Mainau, Insel ⊛

Bodensee (Lake Constance), Germany. The island, connected to the mainland by a bridge, covers an area of 44 hectares/109 acres and is situated in the north-western part of Lake Constance close to the city of Constance. From AD 724 it belonged to the monastery of Reichenau and was from 1272 to 1805 the property of the Deutscher Orden, an order of knight Crusaders founded in 1190 which was abolished in 1809 by Napoleon. The surviving baroque church and the castle with its terraced garden were started in the 1730s by Giovanni Gaspare Bagnato (d. 1757). In 1806 the island became part of the newly created archduchy of Baden. One of the several owners during this period was Prince Nikolaus Esterházy-Galantha, who carried out the first exotic

plantings, made possible by the mild local climate. The island was acquired as a private retreat by Großherzog Friedrich I of Baden in 1853. He laid out an Italian garden and extended the existing evergreens with the help of Ludwig Eberling (1823–98) who became court gardener in 1858. In 1866 they also created a collection of conifers. In 1928 the island was bequeathed to Queen Viktoria of Sweden, who in 1932 gave it to her grandchild, Count Lennart Bernadotte. He, together with his wife Sonja, restored and extended the gardens and developed the island into a famous garden. The formal rose garden with about 30,000 plants deserves special mention. Its original layout dates back to the time of Friedrich I. The island derives much of its character from huge subtropical plants including banana trees, eucalyptus, and palms as well as a long avenue of *Metsasequoia glyptostroboides*.   US

H. LIEDEL and HARALD SCHUKRAFT, *Gärten und Parks in Baden-Württemberg* (1993).
—— *140 Jahre Mainau-Arboretum* (1995).
—— *Rosen auf der Mainau* (1995).
J. RAFF and R. KELLER, *Pflanzenschätze der Mainau* (1979).

Maksimir Park ⊛

Zagreb, Croatia, was founded in 1787 and completed in 1847 as a public park. It was the first public park in the whole of south-eastern Europe, and is older than most public parks in other parts of the world. Maksimir was named after its founder, the Zagreb Bishop Maksimilian Vrhovac (1752–1827). Bishop Juraj (Georg) Haulik (1788–1869) actually realized Vrhovac's idea of a public park. The land set aside for the park was once covered by a forest of common oak (*Quercus robur*), sessile oak (*Quercus petraea*), and hornbeam (*Carpinus betulus*). The park and its surrounding woodland cover an area of 402 hectares/1,005 acres. In relation to the population of Zagreb, which in the first half of the 19th century was c.10,000, this is an exceptionally large space. Bishop Vrhovac began the layout in baroque style but it was never finished (and the only remaining part that still retains its baroque character is an entrance ALLÉE). Bishop Haulik transformed the site into a romantic landscape park. Thousands of oak trees were cut down, the ground was levelled, pits were dug out for lakes, meadows were opened out, paths were laid out, and bridges were built. Many of the architectural structures belong to the period of romantic neoclassicism, coinciding with the Biedermeier style, and have elements of historicism. The design of the garden was inspired by the park surrounding the Habsburg summer residence at LAXENBURG near Vienna. The layout was the work of several people:

Bishop Haulik, landscape architect Michael Sebastian Riedel (1763–1850), architect Franz Schücht, gardener Franjo Serafin Körbler (1812–66), and sculptors Josip (Joseph) Kässmann (1784–1856) and Antun Dominik Fernkorn (1813–78).   MOŠ/BBOŠ

MLADEN OBAD ŠĆITAROCI, 'Maksimir: a romantic episcopal park in Zagreb, Croatia', *Journal of Garden History*, Vol. 14: No. 2 (1994).

Malahide Demesne ⊛
Malahide, County Dublin, Republic of Ireland, was the ancient estate of the Talbot family who lived at Malahide Castle from the 12th century until the estate was sold to the local authority in 1973. The site is a handsome one, on the coast north of Dublin Bay, with old parkland and fine mature trees extending to an area of over 100 hectares/247 acres. There are areas of woodland garden here but the soil is alkaline so it is one of the few Irish gardens of Robinsonian character that is devoid of rhododendrons. The parkland setting, with the castellated medieval castle at its centre, is wonderfully romantic but gives no indication of the true garden interest here. The 7th Baron Talbot de Malahide, who inherited the estate in 1948, was one of the great gentleman plant connoisseurs of the 20th century. He was a tireless traveller and collector of plants, taking a special interest in the flora of Tasmania where his family had owned an estate since the 18th century. In the Talbot Botanic Garden at Malahide are many rarities, often tender and usually from the southern hemisphere. Here are the Chilean *Schinus latifolius*, the Tasmanian cedar *Athrotaxis cupressoides*, and many species of such Australasian genera as *Eucalyptus*, *Hebe*, *Olearia*, and *Pittosporum*. Since Lord Talbot's death in 1976 further appropriate new plants have been added to the collection which today contains over 5,000 taxa of woody plants.   PT

Malfitano, Villa ⊛
Palermo, Sicily, Italy. The neoclassical villa, built between 1886 and 1889 by Isaac Whitaker, a marsala marchant from England, is now open to the public. The Whitakers, already known for their collections of plants, grew a selection of rare exotic trees from all over the world, succulents and cacti which flourish in the frost-free Sicilian climate. The garden, laid out as a landscape park, has a formal section behind the house overlooked by an assortment of palm trees (*Phoenix dactylifera*, *P. canariensis*, *P. reclinata*, and *Washingtonia filifera*) with a rampant wisteria, a Banksian rose, and a *Rosa* 'Maréchal Niel' draped over the portico. The garden is noted for its vast Australian banyan tree (*Ficus macrophylla*) planted in the 1890s, rare nolinos, *Yucca elephantites*, and a dragon tree (*Dracaena draco*). Malfitano now belongs to the

Whitaker Foundation created by Delia, the last surviving family member, and although reduced in size to 4 hectares/10 acres instead of 7 hectares/17 acres it still retains an atmosphere of botanical excitement.   PHo

Malle, Château de ⊛
Preignac, Gironde, France, built in the early 17th century for Jacques de Malle, one of whose descendants, Jeanne de Malle, married Alexandre-Eutrope de Lur-Saluces, whose family still owns the estate. Excellent Sauternes is made here, and the greatest of all Sauternes is made at the Lur-Saluces's chief estate of Château Yquem. Early in the 18th century Alexandre-Eutrope laid out a garden behind the chateau with a series of parterres and, beyond them, a terraced walk with a parade of stone figures mounted on tall plinths. The garden was Anglicized in the 19th century and restored after the Second World War—the parterres have gone but the terrace and its statues remain, as well as a NYMPHAEUM in the form of a loggia with masks and statues of *commedia dell'arte* characters. At the other end of the terrace a balustraded viewing platform gives views of the vineyards. The ensemble of beautiful house, Italianate garden, and a setting of rolling vineyards is especially memorable.   PT

Malmaison, Château de ⊛
Rueil-Malmaison, Hauts-de-Seine, France, built in the early 17th century but much altered before it was bought in 1799 by Joséphine Bonaparte who, as the Empress Joséphine, lived here after her divorce in 1809 until her death in 1814. Here the Empress pursued her interest in botany and zoology, introducing all sorts of exotic animals—kangaroos, black swans, llamas, orang-utans—and an immense range of plants, with the advice of the botanist A.-J. G. Bonpland (1773–1858), many of them tender and some newly introduced. She had a *parc à l'anglaise* laid out by Louis-Martin Berthault, who also designed a Temple de l'Amour, with columns taken from various Parisian churches during the Revolution, which survives but in separate ownership. The great flower painter P. J. Redouté (1759–1841) worked as a botanical artist to the Empress and under her patronage produced his greatest book, *Les Liliacées* (8 vols., 1802–16), and also illustrated Bonpland's *Description des plantes cultivées à Malmaison et à Navarre* (the Empress's other estate) (1812–14). In 1805 the Empress had a great glasshouse built 50 m/164 ft long by 19 m/62 ft wide heated by twelve stoves—nothing survives of it. The chateau is today a museum of the First Empire and the gardens, with a rather perfunctory rose collection, reflect little of the splendours of Joséphine's time.   PT

Malmö parks ⊛
Malmö, Sweden, are partly a result of a transformation of the town's old defence system, military areas, and private estates into promenades and public parks. The cigar manufacturer Frans Suell donated the grounds to *Folkets Park*, which opened in 1893 as the first park in Sweden owned by the public. The layout was inspired by the TIVOLI amusement park in Copenhagen. King Oscar's park, *Kungsparken*, opened in 1872 and was designed by the Danish landscape architect Ove Høegh-Hansen (1832–1910) in 1869 with exotic specimen trees along winding paths planned for slow walking and conversation. Linked to Kungsparken, on the military area next to the city castle, Edvard Glæsel (1858–1915), also a Dane, designed *Slottsparken* in 1896 with open areas for activities surrounded by dense vegetation. In the middle a lake is encircled with paths, wider for carriages and narrower for walking. The 76-hectare/188-acre area of the Baltic exhibition 1914 was transformed into *Pildammsparken*, one of Sweden's best examples of new classicism in the 1920s. Remaining from the exhibition are Margaretapaviljongen (the royal pavilion) and Princess Margareta's flower borders. Of Erik Erstad-Jørgensen's (1871–1945) design of 1915 there remains a lake surrounded by willows and winding paths. The city engineer Erik Bülow-Hübe (1879–1963) made a new plan in 1926, on monumental lines, carried out by the city gardener Birger Myllenberg (1883–1974). Straight paths, edged with high clipped beech trees, radiate from a broad grass circle and thereby connect the park to the city.   AJ

Malonya.
See MLYŇANY ARBORETUM.

Manin, Villa ⊛
Codroipo, Veneto, Italy. The curving white *barchesse* (wings) of the 18th-century villa, like a great bird spreading its wings over the flat plain in Friuli, were clearly inspired by Bernini's colonnade at St Peter's. Making a semicircle the wings terminate with twin *columbaie* (dovecotes) overlooking formal fish ponds. Built by Domenico Rossi (1657–1737) in the early 18th century for Ludovico Manin, the last Doge of Venice, it was considerably altered and embellished during the 19th century. In 1863 the northern part of the garden was transformed into a romantic landscape, leaving only relics of formality with strange mounds, representing Etna and Parnassus, once accompanied by allegorical statues by Giuseppe Toretto. Napoleon signed the Treaty of Campodoglio at Manin in 1797 and commented that the villa was too rich and sumptuous to be a private palace.   PHo

manor gardens ✤

north Croatia. These were built from the 17th century until the beginning of the 20th century. Comparable with similar smaller gardens in other Central European countries about 100 examples are still preserved. Of baroque gardens (such as Valpovo and Gornja Bistra) only fragments remain, partly because very few baroque gardens were laid out and in the 19th century many were redesigned. Most of them are now landscape parks, which became fashionable in the 19th century (the most important are Našice, Valpovo, and Trenkovo in Slavonia and Stubički Golubovec and Veliki Bukovec in Croatian Zagorje). Romantic, picturesque gardens date from the second half of the 19th century (for example, Trakošćan (1861) and OPEKA ARBORETUM). At the beginning of the 20th century historicizing gardens were made, among them Donji Miholjac and Oroslavje.

During the 20th century much of the contents of the gardens was lost—sculptures, orangeries, pavilions, fences, and bridges were destroyed or stolen. Many trees are found in these gardens, both native and exotic. Typical native trees are yew (*Taxus baccata*), lime (*Tilia platyphyllos*), hornbeam (*Carpinus betulus*), oak (both *Quercus petraea* and *Q. robur*), maple (*Acer campestre*), ash (*Fraxinus excelsior* and *F. ornus*), sycamore (*Acer platanoides*), beech (*Fagus sylvatica*), and spruce (*Picea abies*). Exotic trees include Caucasian fir (*Abies nordmanniana*), Weymouth pine (*Pinus strobus*), Douglas fir (*Pseudotsuga menziesii*), maidenhair tree (*Ginkgo biloba*), oriental plane (*Platanus orientalis*), horse chestnut (*Aesculus hippocastanum*), *Catalpa bignonioides*, tulip tree (*Liriodendron tulipifera*), Caucasian wing nut (*Pterocarya fraxinifolia*), *Sophora japonica*, and *Paulownia tomentosa*.

MOŠ/BBOŠ

MLADEN OBAD ŠĆITAROCI and BOJANA BOJANIĆ OBAD ŠĆITAROCI, *Dvorci i perivoji u Slavoniji* (1998); trans. as *Manors and Gardens in Croatia—Slavonia* (2001).

Manor House, The (Upton Grey) ✤

near Basingstoke, Hampshire, England, an ARTS AND CRAFTS house designed, on the basis of a Tudor house, by Ernest Newton (1856–1922) for Charles Holme, the founder of the very influential journal *The Studio*. The house was bought in a neglected state in 1984 by Rosamund and John Wallinger, who discovered that the garden had been designed by Gertrude JEKYLL. Mrs Wallinger also found that the original plans survived in the Reef Point Gardens Collection in the University of California in Berkeley. Despite Miss Jekyll's fame no garden by her survives in its original state and very few have been restored with

fidelity. Mrs Wallinger acquired copies of the garden plans and discovered as much as she could about Miss Jekyll. With help from the Hampshire Gardens Trust and others she embarked on a restoration. It is probably the most meticulously revived Jekyll garden in the country and the best kept. The garden was laid out in 1908 and covers an area of 2 hectares/5 acres with chalk soil. At the back of the house is a formal terraced garden with pergola, a rose lawn flanked with raised borders, a bowling lawn, and tennis lawn. The front of the house overlooks a wild garden with a pond, thickets of wild roses (such as *R. virginiana* and *R. glauca*), winding walks through long grass, and trees. The garden gives the most vivid idea of the repertory of plants used by Miss Jekyll and the manner in which she used them. In the formal garden, for example, the retaining drystone walls are planted with her characteristic plants—alyssum, aubrieta, cerastium, miniature phlox, sedums, and many others. Apart from giving a clear account of Miss Jekyll's style of gardening it is also an exceptionally attractive place. PT

ROSAMUND WALLINGER, *Gertrude Jekyll's Lost Garden* (2000).

Mansart, François

(1598–1666), French architect practising in a refined Renaissance style who was influential in the early period of the baroque garden. At BALLEROY (1626–36) he united house and garden about a single axis and also related it to the landscape outside the garden. At Maisons (1642–51) he first used the *saut de loup* (wolf jump), an early form of HA-HA, and conceived the chateau, outhouses, and gardens as a single unit—the chateau and much of its layout survives. Other estates where Mansart conceived chateau and garden as a unity do not survive—Berny (1623–4), Fresnes (c.1644–50), Petit Bourg (late 1640s–1660s), and Gesvres (1650s and 1660s). He designed several houses in Paris, as often as not disposing the house *entre cour et jardin* (between courtyard and garden), the classic arrangement for Parisian *hôtels*. Surviving examples are the Hôtel Guénégaud, the Hôtel de la Vrillière, and the Hôtel Carnavalet. He met the young André LE NÔTRE (they both worked for Gaston d'Orléans), on whom he had much influence. PT

Marfino ✤

40 km/25 miles north of Moscow, Russia, is notable for its impressive buildings by a lake in a romantic landscape park. The castle-like palace (architect M. D. Bykovsky, 1800–85), replacing the 18th-century palace seriously damaged during Napoleon's invasion, stands on an eminence overlooking the lake and is

approached by a monumental, colonnaded, pseudo-Gothic brick bridge. Balustraded terraces descend from the palace to a landing stage, flanked by a pair of winged griffins and with a spectacular fountain nearby. Two 18th-century estate churches add to the scene. The park has a music pavilion and a two-tiered domed rotunda with a statue of Apollo Belvedere. In the 18th century the palace was surrounded by a series of pools linked by a canal, and there were conservatories near the palace and two theatres and a MENAGERIE in the park. PH

Margam Park ✤

Port Talbot, Glamorgan, Wales, is an ancient place. There was an Iron Age hillfort here, an early Christian settlement was established in the 9th century, and a Cistercian abbey founded in the 12th century whose remains still ornament the landscape. The estate was owned by the Mansel family (later Mansel Talbot) from the dissolution of the monasteries. The original 'faire and sumptious house' of the 16th century was succeeded by the present 1830 Tudor Gothic mansion by Thomas Hopper (1776–1856). The most notable feature of the garden is an extraordinary ORANGERY designed by Anthony Keck (1726–97) and built in around 1787: 100 m/327 ft long, it is built of beautiful pale sandstone, with rusticated surrounds to its windows and a parapet bristling with urns. It was built to house a remarkable early 18th-century collection of citrus plants which even in 1727 included '10 Larg Chaney [China] Oranges, som 8 som 10 som 12 feet Diameter'. Also in the garden, but brought here in 1835, is a fine 17th-century banqueting house—the Temple of the Four Seasons. PT

Margitsziget (Margaret Island) ✤

Budapest, Hungary. The first gardens on this narrow 96-hectare/236-acre Danube island lying between Buda and Pest date back to the 13th century, and were the setting for the monasteries built here. The development of the island as a park was only begun at the end of the 18th century, when it came into the hands of the Habsburg dynasty. From 1808, during the ownership of Palatine Joseph, a garden enthusiast, it was under the direction of head gardener Károly Tost that the island properly became a landscape garden. The natural vegetation on the river bank was left intact, as was the existing agricultural land, pastures, and vineyards. The ruins of the medieval monasteries that had stood at various points on the island were used to build a dairy and a pleasure house, while other ruins added to the garden's atmosphere. Plane and other decorative trees were planted, but in contrast to the Palatine's BUDA ROYAL CASTLE GARDENS, most of the planting was made up of native Hungarian species. The park was renovated at the end of the 1860s at the request of Archduke Joseph (son of the Palatine), following the designs of landscape gardener Vilmos JÁMBOR, and under the direction of György Magyar. Exotic flora were also planted, and on discovering an artesian well that was a source of thermal waters, baths, a hotel, a restaurant, and a waterfall were also built, all designed by Miklós Ybl. The park was popular from the outset with Budapest residents and visitors alike, and in 1909 Archduke Joseph sold it to the city of Budapest. It was then that the water tower was erected (1909–11), followed in the 1930s by the rose garden and a number of sports buildings. The island continues to be one of Budapest's most popular public parks.   GA

María Luisa, Parque ⊛
Seville, Spain, a public park laid out in the grounds of the San Telmo estate in 1929 to the designs of J. C. N. FORESTIER. The land was given to the city by María Luisa, Duchess of Montpensier, in 1893. Best known for his

work in Paris, Forestier also travelled widely in Spain, designing several private gardens and immersing himself in the flavour of the Islamic gardens of the south. At María Luisa he had been invited to design a site for the Hispano-American Exposition which was due to take place in 1914. His plan, dated 1911, shows an elaborate rectilinear grid system with patterns of bold axes embracing a network of smaller spaces and curved or winding paths. The exposition did not take place until 1929 when María Luisa, which was adjacent to the exposition site, was opened as a public park. Water was an essential theme of the park, ranging from the central, irregular duck pond to countless pools, fountains, and canals. Many of the pools are raised and their external walls surfaced with AZULEJOS. Forestier, a learned plantsman, laid out a rose garden and a garden of water lilies and deployed many excellent and varied trees—among them *Ailanthus altissima*, the Australian bunya bunya (*Araucaria bidwillii*), maples, planes, and tulip trees (*Liriodendron tulipifera*). Flowering shrubs are used profusely—abutilons, magnolias, myrtles, and oleanders. With its many sitting places, areas

of intimacy or of long views, cascading or still water, and abundance of plant interest the Parque María Luisa is a model park. Forestier's inventive use of water, and of *azulejos*, makes attractive reference to Seville's Islamic past.
                                        PT

Maribor City Park ⊛
Maribor, Slovenia, is in the north-east of Slovenia on the river Drava close to the Austrian border. The park of 25 hectares/62 acres is located at the northern edge of the old city with views of the characteristic silhouettes of wine-growing hills of Piramida, Mestni vrh, and Kalvarija. The area was connected with the city in the early 19th century by an alley along the stream that supplied water to the moat around the city walls. The eastern part of the park, with a lake, was created by gardener Franz Marauscheg from Graz (1830–1902) in 1872–83, while the western part was designed by lawyer Julius Feldbacher

---

Medieval ruins in the park at **Margitsziget** shown in a lithograph by Eduard Weixelgärtner *c.*1860.

between 1889 and 1896. The park was expanded to include the Kalvarija hill with its church, and woodland was planted there at the turn of the 19th century. The main promenade leads to the landscape climax of the park—The Three Ponds with walks and a boathouse. The layout was influenced by 19th-century historicism with additional romantic elements. Among the surviving original features are a cast-iron BANDSTAND, small footbridges across the stream, a rose hill, picturesque groups of shrubs, circular flower beds with carpet bedding, ponds with fountains, park sculptures, an aquarium, and a terrarium. The rich collection of trees is disposed like an ARBORETUM, flanking meandering paths and lawns. The park gives an impression of spaciousness combined with the intimacy created by richly articulated park motifs.   AK

Mariebjerg Cemetery

Kgs. Lyngby, Denmark. From 1926 to 1936 the planning of this large cemetery (25 hectares/62 acres) became a major commission for G. N. BRANDT. The plan is completely regular, with nearly 50 rectangular enclosures surrounded by hedges of yew. Clearly defined avenues create structure. There are two rectangles of avenues, a smaller one with hornbeam placed within a larger one with rows of Scots pine, and both rectangles are intersected by two broad axes. The individual spaces were developed over a span of many years, some by Brandt, others by Sven HANSEN in the 1960s. The spaces have a highly diverse character, with distinctive rules. There is an area for children with simple stones embedded in the grass, spaces with a very forest-like look, and a more pantheistic area in a grass-covered irregular valley, where uncarved fieldstones mark the sites of urn burials. A very fine complex, this is an excellent Danish parallel to forest cemeteries in Stockholm and Hamburg.   AL

Mariemont Park

Morlanwelz, Hainaut, Belgium. Mariemont has had a dramatic history. In the middle of the 16th century Mary of Hungary, sister of Charles V, chose the site for a hunting lodge and laid out extensive terraced gardens in the Italian style. After her death the estate was half abandoned until the arrival in 1598 of Archduke Albert of Austria and his Spanish wife Isabella. The gardens then showed a Spanish influence (1620 painting by Denijs van Alsloot (1570-1626)). Isabella died in 1633 and again the domain was abandoned and in 1668 it was appropriated by Louis XIV. In 1756 Charles of Lorraine rebuilt the castle and transformed the gardens in the French classical style—neither

gardens nor castle survived the French Revolution. In 1830 an industrialist, Nicolas Warocqué, bought part of the estate and he and designer C. A. Petersen laid out the present romantic landscape park and important ARBORETUM. Warocqué had a castle built and the family lived there until 1917 when the property was left to the Belgian state. The castle became a museum but was destroyed by fire in 1960—a modern building replaces it. The grounds today are a mixture of open lawns and woodland traversed by paths bordered with shrubs. In the glades are groups of rhododendrons or clumps of bamboo. Trees, many dating from the 19th century, are grown as specimens in the grass. A monumental *Acer pseudoplatanus* 'Atropurpureum', a fine *Phellodendron amurense*, and a *Populus lasiocarpa* are striking. There are good collections of ash, walnuts, oaks, birches, limes, and acers as well as a hundred different conifers including imposing groups of *Sequoiadendron giganteum*. Among the trees are statues and fountains, a wrought-iron gate and screen, and the ruins of Charles of Lorraine's chateau. There is also a striking circular modern rose garden.   BA

Marimurtra Botanic Garden

Blanes, Gerona, Spain, was founded by Karl Faust (1874-1954), who started buying land here in 1924. The site, on the cliffs of the Costa Brava, is very beautiful and here Faust built up a collection of plants particularly suitable for the microclimate. Here are many drylands plants, collections of medicinal plants, scented plants, and poisonous plants. Of special interest is a collection of Catalan ferns. The finely laid out garden now occupies an area of 5 hectares/12 acres and displays c.4,000 species. A domed temple dedicated to Linnaeus takes advantage of the magnificent Mediterranean views.   PT

Maritime Park (Bourgas)

Bourgas, Bulgaria, emerged with the first city master plan of 1881 and covered 1.25 hectares/3 acres on high land by the steep Black Sea coast. In 1910 a large-scale extension to 8.8 hectares/22 acres, designed and supervised by landscape architect Georgy Duhtev (1885-1955), brought a solid structure with ornamental vegetation to the park. Many exotic plants and trees of various shape, colour, and scent were acquired and by the 1930s the park earned its reputation of a 'perfume garden'. After the Second World War, it was further enlarged and partly lost its identity along with loss in species diversity due to dry and windy climate. Since the early 1980s however, Maritime Park Bourgas has hosted twice a year the oldest flower exhibition in Bulgaria, Flora. Thus the harmonious spatial

layout and scenic views out to the sea are beautifully complemented by numerous blossoming flower beds.   ASG

Maritime Park (Varna)

Varna, Bulgaria, was established for recreation in 1862 by the then Turkish city governor on agricultural plots along the Black Sea coast. The initial modest size and amateur layout underwent significant transformations to accommodate diverse social and cultural functions in an ever-increasing area, currently 120 hectares/300 acres. In the early 1890s, the design and its realization were commissioned from the Czech landscape architect Anton Novak (1889-1945), who gave the park its baroque appearance. The 'central' and 'coastal' promenades parallel to the beach and several alleys, connecting the city with the sea, form the park's skeleton. Diverse vegetation arranged in picturesque groups and specimen trees combines native and exotic species: lime trees, beeches, maples, cedars, silk trees (*Albizia julibrissin*), and magnolias. The finely designed ornamental landscape is enriched with various facilities for entertainment—a casino, an open-air theatre, an aquarium, a zoo, a lake, and fountains. The patriots' walk, with busts of famous Bulgarians, and the pantheon honour the national past. Particularly since the 1950s, the Maritime Park has reflected Varna's standing as the country's main port and seaside resort, hosting at times industrial fairs and music festivals.   ASG

Marlia, Villa. See REALE, VILLA.

Marly, Château de

Marly-le-Roi, Yvelines, France. In 1678, according to SAINT-SIMON, Louis XIV 'lassé du beau et de la foule se persuada qu'il voulait quelquefois du petit et de la solitude' (fatigued with finery and crowds convinced himself that he sometimes wanted minor pleasures and solitude). Between Saint-German-en-Laye and Versailles he had built a new chateau and gardens in the wooded, swampy valley of Marly—after Versailles this was the most extravagant building project of his reign. The architect was Jules HARDOUIN-MANSART who, in consultation with André LE NÔTRE and Michel LE BOUTEUX III, also laid out the grounds. The design was elegant and original—the chateau standing at the head of a great sunken pool with fountains which was flanked on each side by two-storey pavilions to provide lodging for guests. It was habitable by 1686 and every part of the estate completed by 1698. J. B. Martin's painting of the complete estate shows a garden of restrained splendour with the pool as the prelude to a great water garden ending with the huge *abreuvoir*, a horse trough combined with an equine plunge pool. A gigantic pump, the *machine de Marly*, brought water via an aqueduct from the Seine. The terraced slopes between the central pool and the pavilions were lined with chaste ALLÉES but later on, however, the garden took on much greater complexity and vast numbers of elaborate BOSQUETS, BERCEAUX, and PARTERRES were laid out. Staggering numbers of plants were deployed—14,000,000 bulbs in four years. The garden continued expanding until Louis XIV's death in 1715 and Louis XV continued to use the chateau, but it was sold in 1792, became ruinous, and was demolished in 1816. All that remains is the *grande pièce d'eau*, the curiously atmospheric lie of the land, gently undulating greensward edged with woodland, a 17th-century iron gate, the rather battered *abreuvoir*, and modern copies of Coysevox's splendid prancing horses, *les chevaux de Marly*.

PT

GÉRARD MABILLE and LOUIS BENECH, *Vue des jardins de Marly* (1998).

Marnock, Robert

(1800–89). Beginning his career as head gardener at Bretton Hall, Yorkshire, in 1833 Marnock won a competition to design the Sheffield Botanic Gardens, of which he then became curator. In 1840 he won the competition to design the Royal Botanic Society's gardens in Regent's Park, and similarly became curator there in 1841. From 1836 to 1842 he edited the *Floricultural Magazine*, and the *United Gardeners' and Land Stewards' Journal* from 1845 to 1847. After his retirement in 1869, he returned to garden design. Among his later commissions were Weston Park, Sheffield; Alexandra Park, Hastings; Rousdon, Devon; and WARWICK CASTLE. By that time he had collected a group of acolytes, one of whom, William ROBINSON, who worked under him at Regent's Park, founded a magazine, *The Garden*, in 1871, which lauded Marnock as the greatest landscape gardener of the day, and as the saviour of English gardening from the formality of the High Victorian years. In his last years Marnock helped Robinson in the design of his garden at Gravetye Manor, Sussex. Parts of the Royal Botanic Society's gardens survive in the Inner Circle of Regent's Park, including Marnock's lake and rockwork.   BE

Marot, Daniel

(1661–1752), French Huguenot artist who trained under Jean Bérain in Paris before emigrating after the Revocation of the Edict of Nantes in 1685 to the Netherlands, where he became designer to William III. With an ebullient baroque flourish Marot adapted the Louis XIV style of garden ornamentation to the Dutch classical canal garden, resulting in a Franco-Dutch style. His designs of garden ornaments, many motifs of which echo those of his interiors, were disseminated by his engravings (*Œuvres de Sieur Daniel Marot*, 1703 and 1712; repr. P. Jessen, *Das Ornamentwerk des Daniel Marot*, 1892), which illustrate elaborate and exuberant PARTERRES, intricate BOSQUETS and labyrinths which prefigure the rococo, fountains, statues inspired by those of LE BRUN, urns, seats, pavilions, TREILLAGE arbours, and BERCEAUX.

Marot collaborated with Jacob ROMAN on the ornamentation of Het LOO, ZEIST, and De VOORST. At ROSENDAEL he designed a pavilion and ornate shell gallery and at TWICKEL parterres and bosquets. That Marot did not excel as a landscape designer is shown by two disjointed and heterogeneous rococo plans of *c.*1730 of Huis ten Bosch and Meer en Berg, in which he introduced garden theatres inspired by the Galli di Bibiena. His influence is reflected in Belgium and Germany, and at HAMPTON COURT where he designed the parterres of the Great Fountain Garden and possibly the Privy Garden and the Wilderness.   FH

Martinsson, Gunnar

(b. 1924), Swedish landscape architect who trained in nurseries in Sweden and Denmark prior to attending the School of Agriculture and Horticulture in Stockholm; he gained experience in landscape architectural practices in Switzerland, Germany, and Italy before returning to Sweden to work with Sven HERMELIN. In 1956 he started his own practice and later taught at the College of Art in Stockholm. Since 1965 he has been professor of landscape architecture at Karlsruhe University, West Germany. Martinsson has his own unique style of drawing, well illustrated in his *En bok om trädgårdar* (A Book about Gardens) (1959) and *Mitt hem och min trädgård* (My Home and my Garden) (1963). He has won numerous competitions, some of which designs have been carried out, and he has also designed the landscape site plans for the universities of Bremen and Karlsruhe, and urban developments in Stockholm and Ludwigshafen, for which he was awarded the BDLA (German Landscape Institute) prize in 1981. In addition, he has also received the State Prize for Town Planning and Architecture, Rheinland Pfalz, in 1982 and the Friedrich Ludwig von Sckell Honour from the Bavarian Academy of Fine Arts in 1983.   PRJ

Martires, Carmen de los ⊛

Granada, Andalusia, Spain. The site, on the southern slopes of the ALHAMBRA hill where a Carmelite convent was built in 1573, is very handsome. In the mid 19th century a distinguished neoclassical house was built and gardens laid out which are a beguiling mixture of the picturesque and the neoclassical. In the 1970s the estate was acquired by a property company with plans to build a hotel. Many ancient trees, and parts of the garden, were

---

The **Château de Marly** in an engraving by Matthias Diesel in *Erlustierende Augenweide in Vorstellung hortlicher Gärten und Lustgebäude* (*c.*1717).

destroyed and such was the public outcry that the city of Granada stepped in and bought the estate. The house and gardens have now been restored and are open to the public. Alongside the house a colonnade of Muslim character leads through to a narrow canal and grotto. In the centre of a spacious box-hedged parterre a large circular pool has a figure of Neptune with *Zantedeschia aethiopica* rising in the water about his feet. Other statues and urns stand in the shade of date palms, and in the compartments of the parterre are peonies, roses, and orange trees. From the parterre are giant views of Granada. Beyond the house another, three-tiered fountain is hidden among trees with, to one side of it, a romantic lake. An arched bridge crosses to a wooded island with a grotto, and black swans swim in the water. On the island and to one side of the lake are fine trees, some of which date from 19th-century plantings, among them *Cupressus lusitanica*, *Magnolia grandiflora*, and *Arbutus menziesii*.   PT

Martonvásár ⊛

Fejér county, Hungary. The estate's reputation is primarily a result of Beethoven's repeated visits here at the invitation of one of the Brunswick countesses, the composer's 'eternal admirer', and of Antal Brunswick Jr. It was in 1777 that the Brunswick family obtained the estate of Martonvásár, which was a muddy, woodless wilderness at the time. Garden making began at the time of the younger Antal Brunswick, at the end of the 18th century, following preliminary tree planting and drainage work commissioned by his father. In 1809 the estate was inherited by Ferenc Brunswick, who set about reconstructing the park, following the designs of and under the leadership of Heinrich NEBBIEN, as part of a general programme of improvement and modernization for the estate as a whole. As a result of the large-scale shaping of the area, an English traveller was in 1814 able to describe the beautiful landscape garden he saw here. The large lake with its island and a neoclassical stone bridge remain central features of this landscape park, but in its original form it had many picturesque buildings and monuments. Teréz Brunswick erected a monument to her father, and planted the 'Linden Rondeau Republic', in which every tree bore the name of a family friend, and to mark a visit Beethoven become one of those thus remembered. In line with Nebbien's vision, the park merged with its improved surroundings, its area grew to more than 200 hectares/500 acres, later reduced when the railway was built. Today an agricultural research institute belonging to the Hungarian Academy of Sciences and a Beethoven memorial museum operate in the palace buildings, while every summer concerts are held on the island in the lake.   GA

Mason, Revd. William

(1725–97), English clergyman, poet, and garden designer whose very long didactic poem *The English Garden* (1772–81) celebrated the triumph of the landscape garden, achieving its apotheosis in the work of Capability BROWN. In his *An Heroic Epistle to Sir William Chambers* (1757) he ridiculed the taste for CHINOISERIE and formality in general. Although his poetry was successful in his lifetime, passing through several editions and *The English Garden* being translated into French (1788), few today would read Mason for the quality of his verse. Among garden historians he is remembered chiefly for the flower garden at NUNEHAM PARK which he helped to design. This, with its eclectic mixture of ornament, winding walks, flowery interludes, and jumbly character, is a laissez-faire style of gardening congenial to English taste and has its influence to this day.   PT

MARK LAIRD, *The Flowering of the Landscape Garden: English Pleasure Grounds 1720–1800* (1999).

Masson, Francis

(1741–1805), English plant collector who trained at Kew and in 1772 was chosen as the first professional plant collector by Sir Joseph BANKS. The destination was the Cape region of South Africa where for three years he travelled and botanized, accompanied on occasions by Carl THUNBERG. Masson returned to Britain bringing with him among many other plants *Amaryllis belladonna* and *Strelitzia reginae* (the bird of paradise plant). For five years Masson travelled through the Atlantic islands and Iberia, but in 1786 he returned to South Africa, spending a decade in the Cape and its interior. Four hundred new species are credited to him including Cape heaths, *Pelargonium*, *Kniphofia* (red-hot poker), *Mesembryanthemum*, *Agapanthus*, *Lobelia*, *Protea*, and the glorious *Zantedeschia aethiopica* (arum lily). Unable to settle in England, Masson was invited to plant hunt in North America, visiting New York and Montréal, where during the winter of 1805 he died.   MC-C

Mata Nacional de Buçaco.

See BUÇACO, MATA NACIONAL DE.

Mateus, Casa (Solar de Mateus) ⊛

Vila Real, Portugal. The house, dating from the first half of the 18th century, is marvellously decorative. Of stone and stucco, it has a dashing double entrance, external staircase, decorative window cases, and a roofline that erupts with ornamental pinnacles and statues. The mood of sprightly ornament is one that is continued in the garden. The garden's layout, although by no means all of the planting detail, must date from the same period as the house. At the front is a calm, square pool with, overshadowing one corner, a grand deodar (*Cedrus deodara*). Behind the house is an elaborate and close-packed parterre of dwarf box (*Buxus sempervirens* 'Suffruticosa'), the corner of each compartment marked by a clipped mound. Trees and substantial shrubs decorate the compartments—a pair of bulging mounds of *Chamaecyparis obtusa*, treelike camellias, and a pair of old *Lagerstroemia indica*. Beyond a grove of camellias is a cavernous tunnel of *Cedrus lusitanica* which leads down to a magnificent pergola supported on fine granite obelisks and covered in grapevines. Beyond it are a kitchen garden, vineyards (a famous and once fashionable rosé wine is made here), and open countryside. A long terrace walk leads to other parterres. A PARTERRE *de broderie* has slender arabesques of box against pale gravel. Another has triangles, lozenges, and circles of box with a *Lagerstroemia indica* in the centre of each circle underplanted with arum lilies (*Zantedeschia aethiopica*), forget-me-nots, and tulips. A long walk of box hedges with arches overhead leads past an orchard and a rose garden. All this is very finely kept.   PT

Mattern, Hermann

(1902–71), one of the most influential figures in post-war German landscape architecture, both as a designer and as a teacher. Following a horticultural apprenticeship, he studied landscape design at the horticultural college in Berlin, and after working briefly for the city of Magdeburg and with Leberecht MIGGE, he went in 1927 to head the design section of Karl FOERSTER's nursery near Potsdam. Here, together with Herta HAMMERBACHER and under the influence of Foerster's enthusiasm for rich herbaceous planting, he developed a very sensitive style of garden design which soon moved away from the formality and geometry of the prevalent architectural garden to become particularly characterized by the use of subtle ground modelling to define spaces.

This collaboration continued in various forms until the Second World War, and Mattern was successful in several larger competitions, including a house and garden exhibition in Munich in 1934, and the 1939 Gartenschau (see SHOWS AND FESTIVALS) in Stuttgart in which the Killesberg Park (see HÖHENPARK KILLESBERG) was created out of a disused quarry. This was reconstructed by Mattern as the first post-war Gartenschau in 1950, and he followed it with the reconstruction of the Aue-Park in Kassel for the 1955 Bundesgartenschau. He was also involved in the initial planning of Bonn as a new capital city. His interests in the wider landscape and in design beyond the confines of landscape architecture is illustrated by his involvement in the resettlement of farmsteads as part of an agricultural resettlement programme, to which his contribution included the design of the agricultural buildings and farmhouses.

After the war Mattern was closely associated with the founding of the Werkakademie in Kassel, where he taught landscape design as a subject on equal terms with art and architecture. In 1961 he became professor of garden and landscape design at Berlin University.　RSt

Mauperthuis, Château de,

Mauperthuis, Seine-et-Marne, France, the estate of the Montesquiou-Fézensac family where c.1763 Claude-Nicholas Ledoux (1736–1806) designed a new chateau on the banks of the river Aubetin. Here, between 1775 and 1780, Alexandre-Théodore Brongniart (1739–1813), possibly taking over from Ledoux, laid out an extraordinary sequence of FABRIQUES. These supposedly corresponded to the stages of initiation of a Freemason—the Marquis de Montesquiou-Fézensac, Ledoux, and Brongniart were all masons. The entrance started in a grotto connected by an underground passage to a huge pyramid, built to resemble a semi-ruin, with the initiate emerging from the gloom into the dazzling light of wisdom. Here, on the banks of the river spanned by an ornamental bridge, was a column and the tomb of Admiral Coligny, a notable Protestant whose death was supposed to have sparked off the St Bartholomew's Day massacre of 1572. There was also a Renaissance-style Pavillon de Clèves, a picturesque cottage, a Gothic tower and a Chinese pagoda on stilts. Today only fragments survive, among them the remains of the grotto and pyramid, and the estate has been dismembered. In its day this was one of the most celebrated gardens in France, painted by Hubert ROBERT and Claude-Louis Châtelet, and illustrated in Cahier 12 of LE ROUGE's *Détails de nouveaux jardins à la mode*.　PT

mausoleum.

The word is derived from Mausolus, a Persian satrap (provincial ruler) who governed Caria from c.376 BC until his death in 353. He planned a great tomb before his death which was ordered to be built by his widow Artemisia. One of the wonders of the ancient world, it was described by Lucian—'Nothing is equal to it either in size or in beauty . . . the perfect model of all tombs.' It was built in Asia Minor at Halicarnassus (modern Bodrum, on the Aegean in south-west Turkey) but was

gradually weakened by earthquakes and looted for stone by Crusaders in the 13th century. Its last remains, including statues of Mausolus and Artemisia, are in the British Museum. The word mausoleum came to mean any imposing tomb. The Roman Emperor Hadrian also planned a mausoleum for himself, and for his successors, which was completed in AD 139. In 271, however, it was incorporated into the Emperor Aurelian's defensive buildings for Rome and became the Castel Sant'Angelo. In 18th-century England, when classical culture and the grand tour were an essential part of education, the mausoleum became a feature of the landscape. HAWKSMOOR's mausoleum built from 1729 for the 3rd Earl of Carlisle at CASTLE HOWARD was inspired partly by the tomb of Cecilia Metella on the Appian Way near Rome. Standing in an isolated position on ground sloping down to the New River, and visible from all directions, the noble and gigantic building (it is 30 m/100 ft high) has a dramatic presence in the landscape. At BOWOOD Robert ADAM designed a mausoleum, completed in 1764, set in woodland and planned so as to be visible from the house that lies at some distance from it. One of the finest mausoleums was designed at Cobham Hall (Kent) in 1783 by James Wyatt (1746–1813) for the 3rd Earl of Darnley. It stands in woodland almost one mile from the house of which it has views. With columns and arches it is surmounted by a pyramid, just as the first mausoleum at Halicarnassus was. Derelict in recent times, it is now restored. At Wentworth Woodhouse (West Yorkshire) in 1785 John Carr of York (1723–1807) designed a three-storey mausoleum, crowned with a columned cupola—'not to entertain the eye, but to instruct the mind'. One of the most extraordinary, and poignant, mausoleums, and one of the few in Scotland, is that built in 1850 for HAMILTON PALACE to the designs of David Bryce (1803–76): 36 m/120 ft high, it is in the form of a square base with blind arches surmounted by a drum crowned with a dome. Originally standing at the head of the Grand Avenue (of which a few 18th-century trees survive), it is now isolated by the ring roads and industrial development of Hamilton town. The mausoleum, with its classical antecedents making it so suitable for the 18th-century landscape park, is an especially English feature, but not uniquely so. After all, the TAJ MAHAL was built as a mausoleum although here the landscape was designed to suit it rather than its being added to an existing landscape.　PT　➲ page 303

Mawallok,

Victoria, Australia, was laid out by William GUILFOYLE in 1909, the year of his retirement

from the Melbourne Botanic Gardens. The 2.8-hectare/7-acre garden design is one of his last private works and perhaps his grandest. As in many 19th-century properties on the plains of western Victoria, the homestead and garden at Mawallok is surrounded by thickly planted belts of trees, especially conifers, creating an environment protected from the wind. Within this framework, Guilfoyle's plan was designed to complement the newly built homestead, a picturesque composition of gables, sweeping roofs, and cream roughcast walls. He used the drama of sentinel-like palms on sweeping lawns to frame the northern vista in a formal landscape design with the house as a centrepiece. However, in the 1930s the palms were removed and the garden was modified, further extending the view across the extensive lawn, HA-HA, golf course, and spring-fed lake to distant Mount Cole. In recent years, sympathetic garden renovation has returned paths and garden beds to their position on Guilfoyle's original plan. Sinuous walks now weave through the perimeter shrubberies and beneath mature deciduous trees, including horse chestnut, copper beech, planes, limes, and oaks. With the restoration, Mawallok is an elegant reflection of the style of the 18th-century English landscape movement, albeit in an Australian context.　CMR

Mawson, Thomas

(1861–1933), English garden designer and landscape architect practising in a largely ARTS AND CRAFTS style. In 1884 Mawson founded, with his two brothers, the firm of Lakeland Nurseries in Cumberland which gradually expanded into garden design, at first in the north-west of England but increasingly in the south. Of his surviving work the best example is probably DYFFRYN. Most of Mawson's work was in an architectural style but he was capable of designing romantic, informal gardens such as the large rock and shrub garden made in 1893–8 for MOUNT STUART. The weakness of Mawson's work is a lack of refinement and a tendency towards a ponderous monumentalism. The Hill in London, for W. H. Lever (later Lord Leverhulme), one of his most assiduous clients, is an example. Here Mawson designed a giant pergola of great complexity overwhelming the finer detail of the garden. Mawson's *The Art and Craft of Garden Making* (1900), illustrated with his own garden designs, was an influential text in the garden taste of its period, running through five editions.　PT

Mayer, Johann Prokop

(1735–1804), born in Smečno (Bohemia). After studies in Prague he began an apprenticeship of three years as a pleasure gardener in the palace garden in Smečno. After 1755 he worked as a travelling journeyman in different manorial gardens throughout Europe—in Germany, Austria, France, the Netherlands, and England. During these years of travel he acquired excellent horticultural skills and knowledge of the art of gardening. In 1768 the Prince Bishop of Würzburg, Adam Friedrich von Seinsheim, appointed him as court gardener at the magnificent Würzburg Residenz. Mayer drew some beautiful plans for the rearrangement of the court gardens. These showed his characteristic richly intricate rococo style. The redesign was based on these plans but the work stopped after a few years when the Prince Bishop died in 1779. His successor did not have any interest in continuing this costly project and Mayer had to modify and simplify the design. Between 1776 and 1801 Mayer published his *Pomona Franconica* in three volumes in which he describes in French and German all the fruit trees cultivated in the WÜRZBURG court gardens. It contains also more than 250 very fine hand-coloured copperplate engravings showing the described fruits. When Mayer died in 1804, his celebrity was mainly founded on this famous work, proving him to be one of the outstanding pomologists in Germany in the 18th century.   JA

maze.

The maze is sometimes distinguished from the labyrinth by asserting that the labyrinth always has a central goal which makes the tortuous journey worthwhile whereas the maze is simply an infuriating network of deceptions and dead ends. This is not a distinction reflected in usage and nor do we propose to make it here. It is not known when the maze first appeared but the idea is one of great antiquity. In the Western tradition the greatest influence is the Greek myth of the Cretan labyrinth at Knossos made by Daedalus, with the Minotaur lurking at its heart. The great Egyptian maze, dating from around 1800 BC, known from the 5th-century AD description of Herodotus, was excavated by Flinders Petrie in 1882, but not enough of it survived to give a clear idea of its pattern. Some early writers thought it was the forerunner of the Cretan maze. Mazelike patterns are found in many parts of the world—among the Aborigines of Australia, the Hopi Indians of Arizona, in India, Sri Lanka, and Indonesia. An English maze, carved into stone at Tintagel in Cornwall, although discovered as recently as 1942, is said to date (on very little authority) from between 1800 and 1400 BC. Mazes featured in gardens in the Roman Empire—an excellent one laid out in mosaic, surviving from the 3rd century AD, may be seen in Portugal in the

Roman city of CONIMBRIGA. In Christian symbolism the maze was taken to signify the tortuous wanderings of the soul in search of perfection. Mazes were laid out in the floor of the early 13th-century cathedral of Chartres and of other French Gothic churches such as Amiens, Bayeux, and Saint-Quentin, all of which survive. A small 15th-century example may be seen in the English church of St Mary Redcliffe, Bristol. Mazes appeared in gardens in the Middle Ages—at Hesdin in northern France by 1311 and at the Hôtel de Tournelles in Paris in 1431. They were found in later French gardens such as Catherine de Médicis's Tuileries Palace (see PARIS PARKS AND GARDENS) made between 1564 and 1572 and in the Petit Parc at VERSAILLES by 1677. An attractive late 20th-century example, designed by Bernard LASSUS, may be seen in the JARDIN DES RETOURS. In Italy several patterns are shown in a book by Giovanni Fontana of *c*.1420 and mazes were found in several Renaissance gardens such as the Villa d'ESTE by 1573 and the Villa Medici (Rome) *c*.1576 (see MEDICI FAMILY). In Britain the earliest garden maze seems to have been the yew maze

The **mausoleum** of Augustus in Rome with its 16th-century garden in an engraving by A. Sadeler after Dupérac (1606).

Vestigii del Mausoleo d'Augusto qual fu un bellissimo sepolcro che lui edificio, dove vuole che si sepellissero i suoi descendenti e un che dove la morte sepeli, lo chiema Mausoleo però detto come figlia il Epulcro che fu edificato a Mausolo Re di Caria da Artemisia sua moglie, del quale non si vede altro che un muro di mattoni di forma circulare con dentro certe volte et uscite a quelle e un obelisco di granito rotto in più pezzi per terra et un altro ne è sotto terra quali servivano per ornamento al detto sepolcro oggidì sopra questo edificio ne è un bellissimo giardino che serve alla casa di ng™ Soderini.

laid out for HAMPTON COURT PALACE in 1690. The 19th century was a particularly rich period for British mazes of which an oustanding example is W. A. NESFIELD's surviving design of the 1840s for SOMERLEYTON HALL (Suffolk). In the late 20th century there was a renaissance of maze making in British gardens led by Adrian Fisher. Examples of his work in gardens open to the public may be seen at Floors Castle (Roxburghshire), Greys Court (Berkshire), Kentwell Hall (Suffolk), and Leeds Castle (Kent). More or less contemporary with this renaissance has been the appearance of crop circles which have sometimes presented themselves in appropriately labyrinthine form. PT

HERMANN KERN, *Labyrinthe: Erscheinungsformen und Deutungen* (1982). Translated as *Through the Labyrinth* (2000).
W. H. MATTHEWS, *Mazes & Labyrinths: Their History and Development* (1922).

meadow garden.
In miniatures and tapestries depicting medieval gardens turf scattered with flowers, often of clearly identifiable species, is a common and most attractive image. In modern times meadow gardens have aroused interest partly for reasons of conservation. Ancient meadowland, rich in wildflowers, and a vital part of the ecology, has been all but destroyed in many parts of Europe. The occasional surviving patches of it are marvellously beautiful. William ROBINSON, when writing about growing plants in grass in his *The Wild Garden* (1870), was concerned chiefly with aesthetics. Budding's patent lawnmower, introduced in the 1830s, and many similar machines, introduced a craze for close-mown lawns. Robinson thought that meadow grass, mowed only in late summer when seed had been scattered, was a far more beautiful sight. Meadow gardening in the Robinson style has been practised in gardens such as GREAT DIXTER since between the wars. In the late 20th century, with growing awareness of the depletion of habitats, it was seen as ecologically as well as aesthetically valuable. It is a style of gardening very difficult to do well. In rich soil more delicate flowering species will tend to be overwhelmed by invasive grasses. In Britain much of the finest old meadowland, richest in native flowering plants, is on thin, poor soil. However, when successfully established it is relatively easy to maintain. PT

PENELOPE HOBHOUSE, *Natural Planting* (1997).

Medici, Villa (Careggi) ⊛
Florence, Tuscany, Italy, the meeting place of the Platonic Academy, under the leadership of the celebrated Neoplatonist Marsilio Ficino (1443-99). In 1462, the villa's owner, Cosimo de'

Medici, invited the philosopher as follows: 'Yesterday I came to the villa of Careggi, not to cultivate my fields but my soul. Come to us, Marsilio, as soon as possible. Bring with you our Plato's book *De Summo Bono*.' The land and the old manor with court, loggia, and tower were acquired by the MEDICI family in 1417. Cosimo de' Medici asked Michelozzo Michelozzi (1396-1472) to transform the fortress-like manor into a villa, adding on the west side a double loggia, which defines a small private garden. This was an imitation of a Roman villa garden, with bay, box, cypress, myrtle, and also various scented flowers, and flower beds. The house is now the property of the Hospital of S. Maria Nuova in the suburbs of Florence, with little of the garden remaining. PG

Medici, Villa (Castello) ⊛
Florence, Italy. The gardens, transformed from orchards from 1537 by Cosimo I, soon after his election as Grand Duke of Tuscany, were amongst the most important made by the Medici family during the 16th century. They were designed by Niccolò TRIBOLO, inspired by Benedetto Varchi (1502-65), who devised an allegorical programme of statues and fountains to glorify Medici rule, the city of Florence, and the Tuscan state, reflecting victory over tyranny and eternal rejuvenation. Laid out on a simple slope with shallow terraces, framed by pleached alleys, the garden contained a collection of citrus, and was augmented by a garden for rare plants and newly introduced species, an animal GROTTO, and a labyrinth of cypress surrounding the famous Venus statue by GIAMBOLOGNA, today replaced by *Ercole e Anteo*. Unlike contemporary 16th-century gardens around Rome, Castello retained its country feel, carved out of original orchards and farmland. Apart from the iconography the most innovatory feature was the Grotto degli Animali started by

Tribolo in 1550, its walls decorated with shells and three-dimensional sculptured animals saved from the flood. Marble basins are carved with garlands of shells and fishes. Tribolo, whose work was carried on by Georgio Vasari (1511-74) after his death in 1550, devised complicated hydraulic projects in order to supply all the fountains. MONTAIGNE describes the famous tree house in which hidden fountains and copper tubes filled with water emitted strange musical noises, a foretaste of the more sophisticated hydraulics installed at PRATOLINO later in the century. Double stairways lead to an upper garden terrace where in a dark wood of holm oak a pond contains a bronze statue of Apennine (or possibly *Inverno*) modelled by Bartolomeo AMMANATI in 1564. The lunette in the Topographical Museum in Florence, painted by Giusto UTENS before 1599, shows the villa as described by Georgio Vasari and by Montaigne in the 1580s and later in the next century by John EVELYN and other travellers. Pierre Belon (1518-63), the French plant explorer, visited between 1546 and 1549 and recorded the plants. PHo

Medici, Villa (Fiesole) ⊛
Italy. Built by Michelozzo Michelozzi (1396-1472) between 1458 and 1461 for Giovanni de' Medici, the villa, thrusting out over the valley on the steep Fiesole hillside, was a considerable engineering feat of great expense, its terraces providing incomparable views as well as allowing the cultivation of tender plants and citrus. It is one of the earliest Renaissance villas,

A design for a **maze** from *The Theory and Practice of Gardening* (1712), the English edition of A.-J. Dezallier d'Argenville's *La Théorie et la pratique du jardinage* (1709).

at the time a landmark, a transition from the fortress-like dwellings of the earlier Medici. Extensive alterations over the centuries have almost obliterated its 15th-century character. Inherited by Lorenzo the Magnificent the villa became a centre for philosophical discussions between early humanists such as the poet Politian, Pica della Mirandola, and Marsalio Ficino.   PHo

Medici family,

the ruling family of Florence from 1434 and of Tuscany from 1569 to 1737. Members of the family became prominent bankers, statesmen, churchmen (including two popes), and soldiers; their patronage included palaces and villas around Florence, and in the case of the two Medici women who married into the French royal family, palaces and chateaux in France. The family had some fourteen villas near Florence, including Cafaggiolo, CAREGGI, CASTELLO, FIESOLE, and Poggio a Caiana (See opposite). Within Florence, their most important garden was the BOBOLI GARDENS, behind the Pitti Palace. There was also a Villa Medici in Rome (now the Académie de France), of which both the layout and statues of the sixteenth-century garden have been preserved. In France, Catherine de Médicis commissioned the palace and gardens of the Tuileries (see PARIS PARKS AND GARDENS) and Marie de Médicis initiated the palace and gardens of the Luxembourg (see PARIS PARKS AND GARDENS); both gardens have marked Italian features, and the latter is particularly indebted to the Boboli Gardens.   GC

medieval gardens.

Gardens made in Europe between the collapse of the Roman Empire and 1500 (to take a slightly arbitrary date) are generally poorly documented. The beautiful illustrations which make modern books on medieval gardens seem so attractive are for the most part Flemish miniatures of the 15th century, almost none of which are known gardens and thus their accuracy cannot be corroborated from other sources. One rare exception to this is the early 15th-century painting in the *Très Riches Heures du Duc de Berry* showing the Château de Dourdan. Here is a lake below the chateau walls, formal alignments of trees, and a separate walled garden with a tunnel ARBOUR, overlooked by an elaborate lodge at some distance from the chateau. Although the identity of gardens shown in illustrations is usually unknown the features shown, appearing repeatedly in different pictures, must certainly correspond to the style of gardens of their period. Arbours, TOPIARY, raised beds, tiered fountains, turf seats, grass spangled with flowers, and trellis fences with climbing roses

are the usual ingredients of gardens that are generally enclosed and quite small. The gardens invariably show human activity—reading, playing music, feasting, and flirting. Some tantalizing images show most unusual gardens. The hunting book of Gaston Phoebus, for example, dating from the second half of the 14th century, shows what appears to be a formal woodland garden, with plants edging a cruciform pattern of paths in which there are netted traps to catch hares which are being chased up the paths by huntsmen armed with spears. Gardens depicted are generally of the formal type but one late 15th-century engraving, from the *Hausbuch* of the *Hausbuchmeister*, shows a garden of quite different type. Here is a scene of a bucolic picnic in a fenced enclosure with a tiered fountain on the banks of winding stream overlooked by picturesque rocks. Delight in plants, and their expert cultivation, is plainly displayed in many illustrations. A 15th-century miniature illustrating the *Roman de la Rose* shows a Flemish town garden in the spring. A herb garden enclosed in brick walls has a pattern of square beds separated by paths. Gardeners are shown at work—holding a basket for weeds, training a plant against a wall, and discussing with the owner. A well, or dipping pool, is seen in one corner.

Although there are very few surviving contemporary theoretical writings on medieval gardens the illustrations show something that remains for many people the chief delight of gardens—a love of plants and the pleasures of cultivating them. It is also worth saying that in later garden literature, in 18th-century England for example, writings on garden aesthetics seem to turn their back on this fundamental delight. Part of the encyclopedia compiled by Bartholomew de Glanville and completed *c.*1240 is devoted to plants. John Harvey described this book as 'one of the most widely used encyclopaedias in the whole Middle Ages'. In it he defines a herber (*virgultum, viridarium,* or *viretum*) as 'a green place and merry with green trees and herbs'. The herber was the pleasure garden as distinct from the kitchen garden. The Dominican monk Albertus Magnus, from the German duchy of Swabia, in his *De Vegetabilibus et Plantis* (*c.*1260) borrowed material from Bartholomew, especially that dealing with herbers. Some of this material found its way into Pietro de' CRESCENZI's *Liber Ruralium Commodorum* (*c.*1304-9), which was one of the most influential gardening manuals of the Middle Ages.

The finest gardens made in the medieval period in Europe were almost certainly the Islamic gardens of Andalusia in the south of SPAIN from the 10th century until the 14th

century. The surviving layouts, such as the ALHAMBRA, date from the later period but at a site like MADINAT AL-ZAHRA, dating from the 10th century, enough remains to give a good idea of the splendour of the place. Elsewhere in Europe we have only occasional glimpses of great medieval gardens from documentary sources. In England, at Woodstock in Oxfordshire (close to the site of the later BLENHEIM PALACE), Henry I *c.*1100 enclosed a park and had a collection of exotic wild animals. Later in the 12th century Henry II created a maze at Woodstock where he is supposed to have made love to his mistress, Rosamund Clifford. Here, too, was Everswell, also known as Rosamund's Well (which still exists), a remarkable water garden. At WINDSOR CASTLE early gardens, chiefly for vegetables and herbs, were made within the castle walls— 'the King's herbary' is referred to in the late 12th century. In the same century ornamental gardens were established and in 1246 'unum pulcrum virgultum' (a beautiful herber) was ordered to be laid out. At Hesdin in the north of France, close to modern Arras, Robert d'Artois at the end of the 13th century made a great park of 940 hectares/2,322 acres enclosed in a wall 13 km/8 miles long. The troubador poet Guillaume de Machaut (1310-77) described the garden, which he saw in the 1330s, in his poem *Le Remède de la fortune.* 'I had never seen, nor will ever see anything so beautiful, noble and agreeable', he wrote, and also commented on the 'works of art, machines, canals, games and strange things'. The 'machines' are thought to be very early automata of which Robert d'Artois may possibly have seen examples in Sicily where they had been introduced by Islamic craftsmen.

In Europe generally the most important influence on gardening in the Middle Ages was that of the monasteries. In terms of horticultural techniques, and the cultivation of herbs, fruit, and vegetables, the monks were profoundly influential. The 9th-century plan of the monastery of ST GALL shows the wide range of medicinal plants, vegetables, and fruit and nut trees to be grown in an ideal monastery. Parts of monastic gardens were also thought of as places of spiritual nourishment. The Benedictine order, with its emphasis on hospitality, was especially known for its horticultural skills.   PT

JOHN HARVEY, *Mediaeval Gardens* (1981).
DIETER HENNEBO, *Gärten des Mittelalters* (1987).

Melbourne,

Australia, settled in 1835 and named after Queen Victoria's Prime Minister, was developed on a simple ground plan of 4-hectare/10-acre squares with exceptionally wide major streets, 33 m/99 ft across, set beside a broad bend of the river Yarra. This imposed pattern of geometric development, initially for land speculation, has left Melbourne with a precious legacy of spacious city streets and grand boulevards, the latter forming majestic approach avenues to the inner city. These avenues are undeniably enhanced by extensive plantings of mature exotic deciduous trees, chiefly elms (*Ulmus* spp.) and planes (*Platanus* spp.).

Clustered around the city's precincts is an expansive network of parks and gardens, established in the mid 19th century. They range from the 180-hectare/445-acre Royal Park (1851–4), where the major planting focus is on indigenous species, to the historic Flagstaff Gardens (1840) and the King's Domain complete with floral clock, south of the river. The most recent addition is Birrarung Mar (2000), a riverside park which features spectacular use of Australian plants. The world heritage-listed Carlton Gardens, embracing the Royal Exhibition Building of 1880, are the major example of 19th-century classicism in an Australian public garden, particularly evident in the imposing fountain, while the Fitzroy Gardens' elm avenue is the most famous of all Melbourne's tree-lined paths. However, the city's central garden ornament remains the picturesque ROYAL BOTANIC GARDENS extending down to the Yarra's banks. All of these numerous parks evoke Melbourne's garden city image, inspiring affection in the public imagination, typified by the much-loved walking track, colloquially known as 'the Tan', encircling the Royal Botanic Gardens and paralleling the placid river.

In Melbourne's 19th-century suburban development, John Claudius LOUDON's *The Suburban Gardener and Villa Companion* (1838) was enormously influential. His recommendations of a geometric style for the front gardens of Italianate mansions, villas, and cast-iron decorated terrace houses echoed the central city's orderly planning. Loudon's precepts are still evident in Melbourne's spreading suburbia where formerly dry, rural paddocks are now landscaped with bright-green instant lawns and pop-up sprinklers. Meanwhile, in the tree-lined streets of long-established suburbs—South Yarra, Toorak, and Kew—contemporary landscape designers continue to incorporate the artifice of Loudon's gardenesque in box (*Buxus* spp.) and privet (*Ligustrum* spp.), while others abhor this style and are working with a more natural design approach using Australian plants, mindful of limited water resources.

In both the city's public and domestic gardens, an eclectic mix of plants from all regions of the world can be discovered thriving in the temperate climate. Trees from the Australian rainforests, temperate shrubs, desert cacti, and even alpine wildflowers flourish alongside rhododendrons and roses, camellias, and cannas.

The overall picture of 'marvellous Melbourne', G. A. Sala's description in 1880, is of leafy spaces; a Victorian capital city dressed at every corner in varying shades of green with a heritage of magnificent exotic trees, their changing canopies reflecting the city's colours and seasons. CMR

Melbourne Botanic Gardens.
See ROYAL BOTANIC GARDENS, MELBOURNE.

Melbourne Hall ⊛
Melbourne, Derbyshire, England, is an early 18th-century house, on earlier foundations, built for a courtier, Thomas Coke, who served both Queen Anne and George I. In 1704 Coke had commissioned a new garden from George LONDON and Henry WISE, asking them to lay out the grounds 'to suit with Versailles'. The garden, although formal, has no resemblance to Versailles but it is a fascinating, and delightful, example of what became of French ideas in English hands. It was not in its day a famous garden—there seems to be no description of it before the late 19th century. What makes it famous today is that it is one of the very few gardens of its date to survive with its original design, and much of its detail, intact. East of the house, where gently terraced gardens already existed, PARTERRES were put into place—the terraces survive today but the parterres do not. A yew arbour south of the terraces was made, which is today a magnificent sight. At the foot of the terraces a stream was dammed to form the Great Basin, overlooked by a superb wrought-iron arbour made by Robert Bakewell in 1706. On undulating land to the south an elaborate BOSQUET was made with pools and fountains and a pattern of walks hedged in lime. Beautiful lead urns and statues by John van NOST, made for the garden, also survive. PT

Melzi, Giardini di Villa ⊛
Bellagio, Italy. Built between 1801 and 1810 on the shores of Lake Como, the elegant neoclassical villa, the summer residence of Francesco Melzi d'Eril, Vice-President of the Italian Republic in the days of Napoleon I, is surrounded by gardens of some botanical interest adorned with classical statues. Pollarded plane trees and flower beds near the villa establish some formality but it is the landscape garden developed and planted during the 19th century which is of interest to the plantsman. The tender *Pinus montezumae*, giant redwoods, pines, tulip trees, and camphor trees grow to a vast size in the favoured climate with its mild winters, hot summers, and high rainfall. PHo

Memorial University of Newfoundland Botanical Garden ⊛
St John's, Newfoundland, Canada, is a unique display of Newfoundland's native plants as well as exotics amenable to the local climate. It has an extensive trail system which wends its way through a 45-hectare/110-acre coniferous forest, across fens, through barrens, and mature boreal forest. Open to the public since 1977, and a non-profit corporation since 1994, the garden is a resource centre in basic and applied botanical research. Perennials beds are jammed with plants surprising even to sophisticated gardeners. The Medicinal Garden consists of nine formal beds laid out anatomically with each bed devoted to plants used to treat specific body parts. The Shade Garden celebrates the indigenous Boreal Forest; under the conifers, over 250 plants and 30 varieties of hostas thrive, while the blue poppy (*Meconopsis betonicifolia*) and Jack-in-the-pulpit (*Arisaema triphyllum*) thrive along with such plants as *Philadelphus* 'Starbright', *Ranunculus aconitifolius*, *Sanguinaria canadensis*, and *Rhododendron* 'Madison ▶

Colour plates

The Blue Steps framed by white paper birch (*Betula papyrifera*) in Fletcher Steele's **Naumkeag**, Massachusetts, USA

The orientalist water garden designed by Michael White for the Bali Hyatt Hotel, **Bali**, Indonesia

Woodland formality and abundant planting in the garden of **De Wiersse**, the Netherlands

Massed flower plantings and magnificent natural scenery in the **Kirstenbosch National Botanic Garden**, South Africa

Snow'. The Cottage Garden is an informal riot of colour and the Heritage Garden, started in 1978, preserves plant collections from old Newfoundland gardens with old-fashioned common names such as boy's love and grandmother's bluebells. A Quiggly fence, the traditional Newfoundland windbreak fashioned from vertically woven saplings, provides shelter. Peat, an important feature of this environment, provides a bed built in 1976 from locally cut peat, featuring *Rhododendron canadense*, *Andromeda polifolia*, and *Ledum groenlandicum* as well as exotic plants. New Found Plants Inc. was formed in 2000 to bring rare ornamentals and the breeding and selection of new plants into the trade.   MH

menagerie.

Collections of exotic and curious animals have a long history in gardens, at first in parks and later in sometimes elaborately designed buildings. In AD 802 the Emperor Charlemagne at Aachen received an elephant as a present from the Caliph Harun al-Rashid. At Woodstock Palace *c.*1110 Henry I enclosed a park and, according to Teresa McLean in *Medieval English Gardens* (1981), stocked it 'with lions, lynxes, leopards, camels and a porcupine sent from Montpellier'. A painting of *c.*1400 illustrating the *Roman de la Rose* shows exotic animals in a walled enclosed park. In French Renaissance gardens menageries were occasionally built—an outstanding example was the one at SAINT-GERMAIN-EN-LAYE designed by Philibert de L'ORME in 1548 and in the 1560s Catherine de Médicis had one at the palace of FONTAINEBLEAU.

In French baroque gardens menageries were often built. The most spectacular was that at VERSAILLES, which does not survive but is vividly depicted in a 17th-century engraving by Adam PERELLE. Designed by Louis LE VAU in around 1663 its centrepiece was a miniature domed chateau from which railed and walled enclosures radiated, overlooked by a raised walk giving views of the creatures below. There were also buildings in which different animals and birds were accommodated. It formed an eyecatcher at the southern end of the cross-canal off the Grand Canal. Visitors were usually taken to it by ornamental boats rowed on the canal and accompanied by music. Antoine-Nicolas Dezallier d'Argenville in his *Voyage pittoresque des environs de Paris* (1762) describes an elaborate menagerie at the Château de CHANTILLY: 'Several pavilions serving to house various rare animals from foreign countries, such as the royal bird, two eagles, white hinds, an Angolan or Syrian ram, a wolfhound, etc. Each courtyard of the pavilions has a rockwork fountain with animals painted in their natural colours.'

In 18th-century English landscape gardens the menagerie sometimes served as a landscape ornament. The Menagerie at Horton Hall (Northamptonshire) designed by Thomas WRIGHT in the late 1750s was planned as a banqueting house but immediately adjacent to it, in a moated enclosure, was a collection of exotic creatures. Capability Brown made designs in 1762–8 for a 'great water menagerie' for Lower Gatton Park (Surrey). At Osterley Park (London) a menagerie was built, possibly to the designs of Sir William CHAMBERS, which Horace WALPOLE described in 1773 as 'full of birds that come from a thousand islands'. Menageries in public parks, and zoos open to the public, took over from privately owned menageries in the 19th century. One of the earliest English public parks, Victoria Park (London), had a menagerie when it opened to the public in 1845.   PT

Menkemaborg, De ✿

Uithuizen, Groningen, the Netherlands, a 14th-century country house that was extensively refurbished *c.*1700, but which has changed little subsequently. The gardens lie within a double moated site and were designed *c.*1705 by the

The **Ménagerie** at Versailles in a 17th-century engraving by Adam Perelle.

architect Allert Meijer (1654–1722) for the Alberda van Menkema family. Afterwards there were but few alterations of structural significance, although the design was made more intricate and included a series of 18th-century lattice-work structures. The last member of the Alberda van Menkema family to inhabit the property died in 1902, after which the family donated it to a museum, opening in 1927. The restoration of the gardens by Hendrik COPIJN and Son in 1921 used the early 18th-century plan as a basis, but modified this freely in places, with an emphasis on a collection of modern roses. In 1981 the Copijn firm continued this approach incorporating later 18th-century features.   JW

Mercogliano, Pacello da

(d. 1534), Neapolitan priest and garden designer brought to France in 1495 by King Charles VIII. The gardens with which he is associated, at Amboise, Blois, and GAILLON, were all laid out in rectangles and squares, and all provided with pavilions in the Italian style. The garden at Amboise was constructed on a terrace within the castle precincts. At Blois, the garden was built on three terraces, of which the middle (like Amboise) was laid out as ten rectangular compartments. The garden at Gaillon was laid out on a level terrace, and planting was organized in 24 squares and two rectangles. Pacello is the first gardener known to have grown citrus trees in tubs with a view to moving them into sheltered storage during the winter months.   GC

Méréville, Château de ⊛

Méréville, Essonne, France. The estate was bought in 1784 by Jean-Joseph, Marquis de Laborde, banker to Louis XVI, and the grounds were laid out at first by François-Joseph BÉLANGER who in 1786 was succeeded by Hubert ROBERT. A picturesque landscape garden, rich in FABRIQUES, was created taking every advantage of the river Juine which flows through the grounds. Robert's paintings of the park at Méréville, splendid as they are, are deceptive for it is not always certain what was merely a project and what was executed. Bélanger refashioned the river, making it wind across the landscape, created cascades, and diverted its waters to feed a great lake. Mahogany bridges, some of which survive, crossed the river and gave access to the *fabriques*. CHATEAUBRIAND fell in love with Nathalie de Laborde and was a visitor in the garden's great days—he described it as being 'crée par le sourire d'une muse' (created by a muse's smile). As all this was being made the Revolution was about to erupt. The Marquis de Laborde was guillotined in 1794 and the estate decayed in the 19th century. A few of

the grottoes, cottages, and ruins survive today in ruinous state. The best-known *fabriques*, all designed by Robert, were rescued in 1896–7 and are now to be seen in the Parc de Jeurre nearby. Here, in fine condition, are the Rostral Column (on an island at Méréville), the Temple of Filial Piety (which stood on a rocky outcrop above the river), the façade of an ornamental dairy, and a monument to Captain Cook.   PT

Mesopotamia, ancient.

Two different types of garden are attested. A northern type, known from the inscriptions of Assyrian kings and some 8th–7th-century relief sculpture, imitates a natural landscape, intended for royal sport and recreation. A southern type, Sumerian and Babylonian, laid out in a formal, geometric manner, was often associated with temples and supplied produce for the cult. In addition to these two types, Bronze Age palaces in Syria had trees planted in their internal courtyards. They may have included vines and fruit trees; grafting was practised for vines on the Middle Euphrates by c.1800 BC. In the earliest texts there is no distinction between the word for an orchard and a garden. In the mythical days of Gilgamesh, King of Uruk in the early 3rd millennium BC, civic pride boasted a city of which one-third consisted of gardens or orchards. At Ur the excavator thought bushes or trees might have been planted on the stages of the ziggurat, but this is now refuted.

Second millennium BC

By the 2nd millennium BC there is more evidence. Kings might have a royal garden in which festivals and banquets took place, and the huge internal courtyards of palaces were planted with trees and perhaps also flowers. At Mari on the Middle Euphrates a courtyard in the 19th-century palace had palm trees and an ornamental pool, and perhaps also pet female kids. At Ugarit on the north Syrian coast in the 15th century one internal courtyard of the palace contained a large stone pond; and another courtyard had flower or vegetable beds laid out with walkways, and a pavilion with a well and a large trough. A fable of this time relates how a king planted a date palm and a tamarisk in the courtyard of his palace, and held a banquet in the shade of the tamarisk; and ration lists show that a gardener was regularly attached to the staff of the palace. In Babylonia some temples had gardens providing fresh fruit and vegetables to the deities. Gardens there were also used for making love, and for swearing oaths before judges.

First millennium BC

By the 1st millennium BC there is evidence for large public parks in Assyria. Tiglath-Pileser I

(1114–1076) formed herds of deer, gazelle, and ibex, and he imported foreign trees including cedar, box, Kanish oak, and rare fruit trees. He may also have tried to keep in his parks a crocodile and an ape which he received from Phoenicia. For the garden of Ashurnasirpal II (883–850) at Nimrud, ancient Kalhu, mountain water from the upper Zab river was diverted to the city through a rock-cut channel, and the orchards which it watered included vines, cedar, cypress, juniper, almond, date, ebony, olive, oak, tamarisk, terebinth, ash, Kanish oak, pomegranate, fir, pear, quince, fig, and apples, as well as other unidentified species. Many of them had been collected abroad on campaign as young plants or seeds; the failure rate is unknown. Like his predecessor he bred herds of wild animals which were probably enclosed in a zoological park: wild bulls, lions, ostriches, and apes. Presumably flowering plants also featured, for on the stone relief sculptures of Sargon II (721–705) and Sennacherib (704–681), kings of Assyria, courtiers, and protective deities had a flower called *illuru* which had a red flower and red berry.

Sargon laid out parks around his new capital Khorsabad, north-east of Nineveh, and they are depicted on his narrative sculptures with many different trees and with a small pavilion with Doric columns serving as a boathouse beside a lake. Sennacherib built his palaces at Nineveh, and constructed the Hanging Gardens of 'BABYLON' beside his south-west Palace, imitating the fragrant landcape of the Amanus mountains. In his various parks and gardens he planted imported trees and plants including cotton bushes, mountain vines, and olives. He tried in one place to recreate the marsh environment of southern Babylonia which had captivated his interest on campaign; he made a swamp and filled it with cane brakes and wild boar, and relates with satisfaction how herons came to nest there. His son Esarhaddon planted a great garden with fruit and resinous trees in imitation of a garden landscape; his grandson hunted lions in parks around Nineveh and celebrated victory by feasting with his queen to music in a garden planted with trees and vines. One Assyrian temple garden is known for this period from Ashur on the Tigris. Excavations of the Temple of the New Year Festival outside the city walls revealed the regular layout of garden plants in a rectangular, enclosed space which extended all around outside it. One of Esarhaddon's inscriptions tells of a temple garden in Babylon with fruit trees, channels of water, and burgeoning vegetable beds.

Many real-estate records of this period mention gardens in northern Mesopotamia on the estates of wealthy men. Vines are very common, fruit trees quite frequent; pools, ponds, wells, and vegetable plots, a gardener's house, and the Euphrates poplar are also found.

From Babylon comes a clay tablet naming plants in the garden of King Merodach-Baladan II (721–710, 703). The text was a literary set piece, copied by scribes of later time. The plans are listed in sections, possibly corresponding to the beds in which they were planted. Vegetables and herbs are there but no fruit trees. Many of the 67 plant names are Aramaic, and many cannot be identified with certainty. However, all are edible, and some occur in contracts for supplying temple offerings. There are leeks, various onions, and garlic; various salad vegetables including lettuce, radish, purslane, and rocket; spices including cardamom, caraway, coriander, cumin, and fenugreek; herbs including mint, dill, thyme, oregano, and fennel; other edible plants include the snake-gourd, some kind of cucumber or gherkin, the mung bean, and lucerne, possibly imported from north-east Turkey in the 9th–8th century. Since herbal remedies were important in Babylonian medicine, many of the plants would have been valued for their curative or protective properties, in particular rue, colocynth, and sagapenum. Nebuchadness II mentions in his inscriptions that he grew fruit and vegetables as offerings for Marduk god of Babylon, but he had to import wine and raisins, for vines do not flourish in southern Mesopotamia. Temple garden contracts show that dates, figs, and pomegranates were cultivated on plots of land that flanked the processional road up to the temple, and each plot provided offerings for one month of the year. Gardens within the temple precinct included cypress and juniper trees. There is no evidence for public parks in southern Mesopotamia, nor for lion hunts and falconry.   SD

Métis, Les Jardins de (The Reford Gardens) ✿

Grand-Métis, Québec, Canada. The gardens are located at the mouth of the Métis river along the St Lawrence's south shore. In 1926, when Elsie Reford (1872–1967) inherited Villa Reford, she transformed the property into an enduring ornamental garden spanning 8 hectares/20 acres. Over the next 33 years, she imported plants from England, and had seeds sent from collectors and garden societies around the world. She developed a collection of over 3,000 species and varieties of plants, both native and exotic. Sixty species of lilies earned her international respect, and she is believed to be the first gardener to successfully cultivate *Rhododendron* species in such an unforgiving climate. By the time it was sold to the Québec government, the garden had expanded to 16 hectares/40 acres and opened to the public in

1962. The Blue Poppy Glade contains a rare gathering of more than 10,000 *Meconopsis betonicifolia*. Other features include the Long Walk (an amazing perennial border in the style of Gertrude JEKYLL); the Azalea Walk and a wildflower meadow; the Entrance Garden featuring a native forest filled with woodland plants, added in the 1960s; and the Moss Garden, a contemporary work of art by artist Francine Larivée 1990. It was privatized in 1965 and became host to the International Garden Festival in 2000. It now has landscape architects and architects vying to produce the most stunning installation of the year which stays *in situ* for five months.   MH

Meyer, Gustav

(1816–77), German garden designer, from 1840 royal gardens director and influential teacher at Potsdam's college of gardening within the Prussian gardens administration and from 1859 to 1870 royal court gardener. Under LENNÉ's overall direction, he was active in many projects at SANSSOUCI (including Marlygarten, Pfingstberg, and Ruinenberg), and at Feldafing and Bad Homburg. Over 100 garden and park plans include Friedrichshain (1845), Treptower Park (1864), and Humboldthain (1866) in Berlin, Wrisbergholzen near Hildesheim (1864), Bremer Bürgerpark (1866), the Prussian Garden at the Paris world exhibition (1867, executed by Niepraschk), Glacies (1858), and the 1873 world exposition grounds in Vienna. From 1870 Meyer was Berlin's first director of gardens, mainly responsible for (along with villa gardens, avenues, and squares) municipal parks: Humboldthain, Kleiner Tiergarten, Köllnischer, and Treptower Park. He published the influential *Lehrbuch der schönen Gartenkunst* (1860), including a comprehensive history of the garden arts and technical instructions. His park designs are of mixed style, integrating formality and functionally varied structures, a style referred to as the 'Lenné-Meyeresque school'.   MR

Michael, J. G.

(1738–1800), German architect and landscape architect who settled in the Netherlands. Michael was one of the proponents of what is often referred to as 'the early landscape style', the Batty LANGLEY type of wilderness designs with winding but geometric walks, within the formal framework of the garden. He was the first of a series of German landscape architects who worked and settled in the Netherlands, and lived at Beeckestijn near Velsen when he was referred to as a 'boschgardenier' (a woodland or wilderness gardener) and later at Rozenstein nearby, where he ran his own nursery. He designed various properties near

Haarlem, but also several pleasure grounds in Gelderland, including Kasteel Biljoen, Kasteel Doorwerth, and Kasteel Staverden. He employed, and his daughter later married, the garden architect J. D. ZOCHER Sr.   JW

Michaux, André

(1746–1803), French plant collector and explorer who was taught horticulture by his father at Versailles. In the 1770s Michaux explored western Asia and Persia (Iran) for two years, returning to France in 1785 with a collection of plants which he donated to the royal gardens. With his breadth of vision and erudition Michaux was ideally suited to be sent to the United States to forward French interests in their colony of Louisiana. Accompanied by his son François-André Michaux (1770–1855), he was instructed to make a horticultural collection, particularly of trees suitable for masts which would flourish in France. Within a month Michaux dispatched several boxes of seeds and trees, establishing holding gardens near New York and later at Charleston, South Carolina; and then for eleven years he traversed the continent from Florida to the Canadian tundra, frequently alone, meeting the Indians, and learning the Cherokee language. Probably knowing more about the geography and physical aspect of America than anyone else in 1793 Michaux planned, with the support of the Philadelphia Philosophical Society, to undertake a cross-continental journey to the Pacific; this did not materialize, and instead he explored in North Carolina. Although Michaux eventually shipped 60,000 plants to the government nursery at RAMBOUILLET, near Paris, little material survived and funding for the American enterprise ceased with the French Revolution. With his son he wrote *The History of North American Oaks* (1801); a second book followed shortly before his death, *Flora Boreali Americana*, which described some 40 new genera and 1,700 plants, the most complete work of its time on American flora, both books being illustrated by Pierre-Joseph Redouté (1759–1840). The genus *Michauxia* was named in his honour.   MC-C

Middachten ✿

De Steeg, Gelderland, the Netherlands, originally a medieval castle, was rebuilt twice during the 17th century. It achieved its present form when rebuilt between 1694 and 1697 for Godard van Reede, later 1st Earl of Athlone. The architects were Steven Vennecool and Jacob ROMAN, who may also have designed the formal gardens. Large parts of the moated gardens were dedicated to the cultivation of fruit trees, and two large mazes flanked a central parterre. This arrangement was not altered substantially until the early 19th century when winding walks and shrubberies changed the character of the garden. During the late 19th and early 20th centuries there were a number of changes. Eduard PETZOLD produced a partly executed plan in 1878, whereas Hugo POORTMAN redesigned and altered the area of the formal gardens, creating in 1901 a modern but asymmetrical formal garden with croquet lawn, bowling green, parterre and a rose garden. One side of this design was altered as early as 1908 by R. E. André, and Poortman himself removed the maze for a second rose garden in 1926. With wartime shortage of labour Jan BIJHOUWER, Mien RUYS, and J. H. R. van Koolwijk produced a plan for simplification in 1942. They required the removal of the parterre and of most of the hedges. During the 1970s the gardens were renovated by Heidemij, while during the 1980s a group of specialists aimed to return some of the early 20th-century glory to the gardens. JW

Middleton Place ⊛

Charleston, South Carolina, USA, is among the oldest (if not the most senior) landscaped estates in America, a gracious 18th-century southern plantation (then some 20,000 hectares/50,000 acres) amassed by Henry Middleton (1717–84) in 1741. Hewn from the swampy wilderness, 26 hectares/65 acres of magnificently restored gardens blaze with spring colour today amid the bones of rice and indigo fields that thrived for 120 years before the Civil War (1861–5). Through marriage, Middleton inherited a Jacobean-style, four-storey brick house set high above a bend in the Ashley river. The couple added two Georgian brick houses in 1755, one a library and conservatory, the other, gentlemen's quarters. Three succeeding generations of Middletons. Arthur (1742–87), Henry (1770–1846), and Williams (1809–83), shaped the land, agriculturally and ornamentally. The younger Henry invited André MICHAUX to Middleton in 1786 and with him came perhaps the earliest camellias to be planted in America. But it was Williams who introduced the azalea (*Rhododendron indicum*) which remains the hallmark of Middleton Place today. Sherman's army slashed and burned in 1865; a year later an earthquake tumbled shells of charred bricks, leaving only the noble gentlemen's quarters standing. The property lay in ruins until the mid-20th century when Middleton descendants began the exhausting work of renovation. The plantings, however—live oaks hung with Spanish moss, southern magnolias (*Magnolia grandiflora*), *Camellia japonica*, tulip poplars (*Liriodendron tulipifera*), bald cypress (*Taxodium distichum*), crape myrtles (*Lagerstroemia*

anagyroides), and sweet olives (*Osmanthus fragrans*)—had, in fact, revelled in neglect.

The original garden design was rooted in a colonial interpretation of LE NÔTRE. The plan is geometric, a main axis descending from a height where house and flanking buildings once perched, bumping down six terraces of lawn (which took 100 slaves nine years to shape), across two excavated butterfly-shaped lakes, to a broad reach of the river. The gardens lie within the bounds of a perfect triangle to the west of the central ALLÉE. The plan is as prettily precise on paper as the gardens are intricate and fun in leaf, with walkways connecting fussy parterres, bowling green, sundial room, green galleries sectioned off by clipped hedges, and quiet pools. One simply must see around the next corner—the rewards are spectacular. There is a 1,000-year-old live oak with a moss-bedecked reach of 44 m/145 ft, a lovely marble wood nymph drying her feet, a path strewn with dropped camellia petals, or an old but nimble alligator sunning himself at the river's edge.

In the 1930s, 35,000 azaleas were planted on a hillside climbing from the rice mill pond to the south of the main garden axis. The pale to deep pink blossoms swim together in waves, their reflection broken in the pond below by the wake of a pair of black swans. Each generation of the Middleton family has made its contribution to this remarkable property; the current being the establishment of a non-profit foundation that has opened the gardens, house, and stableyards to the public as a National Historic Landmark. HSS

Migge, Leberecht

(1881–1935), German landscape architect, from 1904 artistic director of the landscape gardeners Ochs-Hamburg (gardens for private houses in Hellerau-Dresden garden city, Hohenhof garden in Hagen with H. v. d. Velde, Wegmann garden in Rhede with H. MUTHESIUS). He opposed 'mixed garden art' and the idea of W. LANGE's 'nature garden'. He travelled to England in 1910 and in 1911 designed the *Volkspark* (see PUBLIC PARKS) in Oldenburg with architectural forms and a wide range of facilities. Migge was among the advocates of the reform movement in Germany, and the author of around 120 articles, among them critiques (1908) of designs for the HAMBURG STADTPARK and those of M. Läuger in Hamburg and Baden-Baden. In 1913 he published *Deutsche Gartenkultur* and had an office in Hamburg working on *Volksparks*: Rüstringer Stadtpark in Wilhelmshaven (with H. Maasz and M. Wagner), Uelzen, and Mariannenpark in Leipzig. After 1945 he designed cemeteries and allotment garden colonies and took an interest in self-sufficiency and urban settlement

issues. In 1920 he moved to Worpswede artists' community and was involved with the 1923-9 publication of *Die Siedlungswirtschaft* magazine. In 1926 he founded an office in Berlin for urban planning, collaborating with such architects as H. Poelzig, B. Taut, and E. May. MR

Mignarde, Château de la ⊛

near Aix-en-Provence, Bouches-du-Rhône, France. The 18th-century chateau is an elegant country house which, in the 1760s, was garnished with a curious and unusual garden. On the terrace in front of the house lions spout water into a pool and a rectangular pool is decorated with dolphins. At its far end Venus sits on a sea monster's tail and a white marble Hercules struggles with the Nemean lion. Below the terrace an open area of grass is framed by groves of plane trees, and statues on plinths gaze at each other or towards an oval pool at the end of the garden beyond which the land falls away sharply. This is a modest but gentlemanly garden of its time, with an agreeably Arcadian charm. PT

Miguel, Puente de San ⊛

near Torrelavega, Santander, Spain, the ancient estate of the Botín family with gardens of varied and unusual interest. Excellent old trees are largely of 19th-century plantings of the conifers fashionable at that time. An exceptional *Magnolia grandiflora*, however, must date from the 18th century. In the 1950s the artist and garden designer Javier de Winthuysen (1874–1956; of a Flemish family settled in Seville in the 17th century) laid out charming and subtle formal gardens. A pattern of narrow, hedged rose beds extends about a square fountain pool. An arcade of roses runs along one side and a stone table and chairs is enclosed in hedges. A later garden, added in the 1980s, has a circular pool and rose garden and a naturalistic lake and cascade with a circular pavilion. PT

CARMEN AÑÓN FELIÚ, MONICA LUENGO AÑÓN, and ANA LUENGO AÑÓN, *Jardines artísticos de España* (1995).

Mikler Dionizy (Denis MacClair)

(1762–1853), Irish garden designer. After studying natural sciences in Dublin and horticulture in London he arrived in Poland c.1790 and apart from brief intervals lived there for the rest of his life. He laid out numerous gardens: for example, at Dluga stret in Warsaw, behind the palace of Chancellor Chreptowicz, and, above all, in the Wołyń and Podole regions—Beresteczko, the Palestyna park in Dubno, Gródek, Iwańczyce, Kodeń, Laszki, Mizocz, Podłużne, Poryck, Szpanów, the botanic garden in Krzemieniec (1809), and many others. Mikler Dionizy was also involved in establishing the parks of PUŁAWY (1797) and ARKADIA. He found growing in the wilderness on the banks of the river Slucza *Rhododendron luteum* which he planted in many of his parks and sent to the United Kingdom, though not for the first time.   LM/PG

Miller, E. C., Botanic Garden ⊛

Seattle, Washington State, USA. It was founded by Elizabeth Carey Miller as a small botanic garden in 1994 on a 2-hectare/5-acre site in a private gated community and now constitutes one of the country's finest collection of unusual plants. Elizabeth and Pendleton Miller purchased the property in 1948 and the house was completed in 1949. Mrs Miller became a discriminating collector of rare plants which she arranged with great artistry, emphasizing plant form and texture. Since 1996 the original collection has been augmented with plants designed to extend the garden's range of colours and textures. The garden is arranged on the sloping site as a series of zones determined by existing vegetation, prospects, and microclimate. The gently sloping area above the house is the least changed area. Second growth Douglas Firs are underplanted with a collection of species rhododendrons, native ferns, and other ground cover plants. Immediately above the house is a gully treated as a rockery with Japanese maples and dwarf conifers. Below the west side of the house a narrow lawn commands framed views across Puget Sound toward the snow-capped Olympic Mountains. This space is dominated by a large *Parrotia persica* and several large maples. The open dry slope below was originally planted with a large collection of ceanothus, which are now being re-established. A masonry-clad stair, built in 2001, provides access across a steep slope from the central parking area to a collection of *Nothofagus*, and a small bog garden.   DCS

Miller, J. Irwin, Garden ⊛

Columbus, Indiana, USA. Compared to estates of other 20th-century American industrialists, the Irwin home and gardens are tiny, occupying about 0.4 hectare/1 acre, in the heart of downtown Columbus. The size allows for an immediate, intimate appreciation of the gardens, designed in 1910 by Henry A. Phillips; at the same time he outfitted the 1864 house with a new façade adorned with four, whimsical, carved stone heads that depict the seasons. Family members drew on their travels, especially to Italy, for the design of the gardens. The first steps down from the house, past the busts of four Greek philosophers that sit in open pergolas, to a centre fountain adorned by a sculpture of a child riding on a dolphin, then

back up the stepped waterfall to the 'garden house', whose only purpose is another view of the landscape. A special feature in the centre garden is a replica of a bronze Japanese elephant from the 1904 World's Fair. Purchased for the garden, the original elephant deteriorated after 25 years and a replacement was made by a local foundry. Across from the elephant is a medieval Italian well-head and, nearby, a Florentine crane in the evergreen courtyard. Heavy plantings of spring and summer annuals complement seasonal bulbs, perennials, shrubs, and trees. A charming nook is the formal herb garden, planted with a wide selection of salvias and scented pelargoniums. The bench by the knot garden is the perfect place for a quiet respite in a shady retreat.   JEMS

Miller, Philip

(1691–1771), curator of CHELSEA PHYSIC GARDEN. Miller worked in his father's market garden before becoming a florist in Pimlico. He came to the attention of Sir Hans SLOANE on whose advice the Apothecaries' Society appointed him curator of what is now the CHELSEA PHYSIC GARDEN, which post he held until his death. The garden under his direction attained an international reputation assisted by his various publications, pre-eminent amongst them being *The Gardeners Dictionary* (1731). The book went into eight updated editions to 1768, with the seventh edition of 1756 including the new nomenclature details of LINNAEUS; it was translated into several European languages. Miller received propagation material from around the world and his practical and experimental work earned him an unparalleled horticultural reputation. He distributed much of the fruits of his labour throughout Europe and America. Miller remained at the Physic Garden until he was nearly 80, finally retiring on 6 February 1771.   MC-C

HAZEL LE ROUGETEL, *The Chelsea Gardener* (1990).

Miller, Sanderson

(1716–80), English architect, rococo garden theorist, and builder of ruins. At Honington Hall (Warwickshire) in the 1740s Miller advised Joseph Townsend on the laying out of the grounds in the rococo manner, and built a grotto and several garden buildings none of which survives. At Hagley Hall (Worcestershire) he designed a new Gothic house for Sir George Lyttelton (later 1st Lord Lyttleton) and a ruined castle in the park. Horace WALPOLE came here in 1753 and admired it extravagantly—'the enchanting scenes of the park . . . such lawns, such wood, rills, cascades, and a thickness of verdure . . . a ruined castle by Miller . . . has the true rust of the Barons' Wars'. A ruined castle he designed for WIMPOLE HALL in 1751 was not built

until Capability BROWN landscaped the park in 1768–72 and put it into place as an eyecatcher. In the grounds of Enville Hall (Staffordshire), laid out as a FERME ORNÉE in the mid 18th century, possibly by William SHENSTONE, Miller designed a Gothic greenhouse in 1750. Wroxton Abbey (Oxfordshire) was probably his most elaborate garden design. Virtually nothing of the buildings survives, and what remains is dishevelled but not without charm.   PT

Milner, Edward (1819–84), and his son Henry Ernest

(1845–1906). Edward Milner was apprenticed to Joseph PAXTON at CHATSWORTH; after studying in Paris, he became Paxton's foreman at Prince's Park, Liverpool, and Crystal Palace Park (1852–54). After collaborating with Paxton on People's Park, Halifax (1856), he launched an independent career. Among his commissions were Miller and Avenham Parks, Preston, Lancashire; the Lincoln Arboretum; the Buxton Pavilion Grounds; the first stage of the development of BODNANT; and overseas commissions such as Knutenborg Park in Denmark. In 1881 he became the principal of the Crystal Palace School of Gardening.

Henry Milner entered his father's practice in the 1870s. Among his important commissions after his father's death were the enlargement of the Princes Street Gardens, Edinburgh; Friar Park, Henley, for Sir Frank Crisp; and overseas commissions such as Gisselfeld in Denmark and works on the Swedish royal gardens. In 1890 he published *The Art and Practice of Landscape Gardening*, most of the examples in which were taken from Edward Milner's work. In 1897 he was one of the original recipients of the Victoria Medal of Honour. His practice was taken over by his son-in-law Edward White, and the firm survived into the late 20th century as Milner White and Partners.   BE

Milner Gardens and Woodland ⊛

Qualicum Beach, British Columbia, Canada, is a seamless collaboration of garden and woodland, initially designed by Veronica Milner (1909–98) and her husband, business tycoon Horatio 'Ray' Milner (1889–1975). She renovated her first husband's estate, Glin Castle, Ireland, and in 1954 Mrs Milner transformed the grounds of her second husband's summer retreat into a wild garden à la William ROBINSON. She donated the property to Malaspina University College in 1996 and continued to live in the house until her death. The house was designed in 1931 by A. N. (Alex) Fraser in a style reminiscent of a Ceylonese tea plantation. The garden contains a very wide range of plants with a stand of 500 varieties of rhododendrons designed to give colour for months. The most significant aspect of the estate is the woodland. Paths wind through the astounding Douglas firs (*Pseudotsuga menziesii*), grand fir (*Abies grandis*), and western red cedar (*Thuja plicata*). Since this is one of Vancouver Island's increasingly rare old growth forests, conservancy as well as discovering how these intricate ecosystems function have become major goals. Of the 28-hectare/70-acre estate, 4 hectares/10 acres are garden, the rest is forest. The garden includes gorgeous specimens of stewartia (*Stewartia pseudocamellia*), a dove tree (*Davidia involucrata*), cultivars of beech (*Fagus sylvatica*), birch (*Betula pendula*), golden chain tree (*Laburnum* × *watererii* 'Vossii'), katsura (*Cercidiphyllum japonicum*), dawn redwood (*Metasequoia glyptostrodoides*), and Spanish chestnut (*Castanea sativa*).   MH

Mindelunden in Ryvangen ⊕

Hellerup, Denmark, was laid out 1946-50 by Aksel Andersen (1903-52) and architect Kaj Gottlob (1887-1976) on a site Germans used for executions during the Second World War. The entrance is a 10-m/30-ft high gateway, which adjoins a low memorial hall and a wall with plaques for 151 fallen resistance fighters whose graves are unknown. The square ground is bordered on three sides by a stone embankment, and on the fourth by the wall. The gateway effect of the entrance continues in a long avenue. A clearing in the forest covered with ivy holds the graves of 31 resistance fighters whose bodies were returned to Denmark after the war. The forest contains tombstones irregularly arranged in a circular area. On a large lawn with scattered hawthorn lies the central, rectangular burial section of natural stone, raised two steps above the ground. A broad yew planting forms the background for the large monument, *Mother with her Murdered Son*, by the sculptor Axel Poulsen (1887-1972), and uniform rows of heather for 196 resistance fighters executed by the Germans. Today the execution site in the southern corner is marked by three wooden posts and a memorial plaque with verses by the priest and poet Kaj Munk (1898-1944).   AL

Minneapolis regional park system ⊕

Minneapolis and St Paul, Minnesota, USA, consists of 2,590 hectares/6,400 acres of land and bodies of water, and now constitutes one of the finest unbroken natural open space systems in the country. It was conceived by the landscape architect Horace William Shaler Cleveland (1814-1900) in 1872 as a system of parkways and parks that would bring identity to the region by emphasizing and celebrating its distinctive geography. Cleveland believed

in the necessity of encountering nature on a daily basis. His design displays a remarkable intuitive understanding of regional hydrology and ecology. Parks of varying dimensions were developed around the numerous lakes reflecting their differing catchment areas. Connected by parkways this system of the 'Grand Rounds' provides an unbroken experience of moving through natural landscapes unembellished by non-native plants. Cleveland designed broad parkways along both banks of the Mississippi river. The crowning feature of the system is Minnehaha Falls, combining both powerful visual imagery and a deeply felt cultural resonance with Longfellow's famous poem *Song of Hiawatha*. Cleveland's system was extended in the early years of the 20th century. Later additions include the Sculpture Garden of the private Walker Art Museum. The original formal garden of hedged outdoor rooms was extended in 1980 and contains larger pieces of sculpture, the most notable being Claes Oldenburg's *Spoon and Cherry*. This garden is linked to Loring Park, the oldest city park, by a suspension bridge over an eight-lane freeway created by Siah Amajani which uses perspectival illusion and poetry to direct the eye toward the park.   DCS

HORACE WILLIAM SHALER CLEVELAND, *Landscape Architecture as Applied to the Wants of the West with an Essay on Forest Planting on the Great Plains* (1873).

Mirabell ⊕

Salzburg, Austria. The first garden on this site was created by Prince Archbishop Wolf Dietrich for his consort Salome Alt in 1606. The name Mirabell is from Archbishop Marcus Sitticus, who between 1612 and 1619 chose Hellbrunn as his favourite place. Between 1620 and 1646 the Mirabell garden on the banks of the river Salzach was enclosed in fortifications, and from 1687 Archbishop J. E. von Thun-Hohenstein had the garden modernized by architects Johann Bernhard Fischer von Erlach (1656-1723) and Matthias Diesel; the centre of the parterre facing the Hohen-Salzburg castle with its octagonal *bassin* (formal pool) and the four larger-than-life groups depicting the *Rape of the Sabine Women* by Ottavio Mosto survives from this period. Between 1721 and 1727 architect Johann Lukas von HILDEBRANDT remodelled the palace, having already altered the Sala Terrena in 1710. Royal inspector of gardens Franz Anton Danreiter (from whom we have the important German translation of A.-J. DEZALLIER D'ARGENVILLE's *La Théorie et la pratique du jardinage* (1709)) altered the great parterre in rococo style. He worked for Prince Archbishop F. A. Graf von Harrach, an important patron of the arts. In 1811 under the Bavarian occupation

landscape gardener F. L. von SCKELL drew up plans for remodelling the Mirabell gardens in the landscape style which, however, were not executed. Since 1975 the parterre sections with their monotonous flower beds have created a very poor impression. The orangery and orangery parterre were reinstated in 1980, and since the late 1990s the city council has been reconstructing the baroque beds by the central fountain *bassin*.   GH

mirador.

From the Spanish *mirar*, meaning to look at, the word originally meant a balcony or bay window but has assumed the meaning, especially in the garden context, of a building that commands a view. The *mirador* has a similar meaning to BELVEDERE or GAZEBO. The Mirador de Lindaraja overlooking the lower garden of the ALHAMBRA is a quintessential example.   PT

Missouri Botanical Garden ⊕

St Louis, Missouri, USA, the oldest continually operating botanical garden in America, was a flat prairie when Englishman Henry Shaw (1800-89) discovered it in 1819. Forty years later, he transformed it into a public garden, beginning with the 4-hectare/10-acre rectangular plot north of his Italianate-style villa, Tower Grove (1849). Shaw's garden plans were inspired by CHATSWORTH, the Crystal Palace, and the ROYAL BOTANIC GARDENS AT KEW; his mission—to provide not only displays, but also research and education—was influenced by botanists Asa Gray, Sir William Hooker, and George Engelmann. Initially, a central axis linked parterres arranged around a statue of the goddess Juno (1885) to the Linnean House (1882), an elegant brick building which currently houses camellias. To the east, the Museum (1859) housed the library and HERBARIUM (which today holds 5.3 million specimens). Notable features on the site's now 32 hectares/79 acres include the Climatron® (1960), a domed CONSERVATORY with more than 1,400 tropical species, and Seiwa-en (1977), 5.6 hectares/14 acres of lawns, gravel, lake paths, and islands landscaped in a style that was popular among 18th-century Japanese landowners. Among the garden's smaller, but no less authentic, displays are a Chinese garden with mosaic-decorated paths and a pavilion, a naturalistic German garden, English woodland abloom in spring with dogwoods and trilliums, a Victorian garden with geometric beds, and two rose gardens boasting nearly 3,000 plants combined. The home gardening centre has fine examples of city, fragrance, and bird gardens. Plant collections include orchids (more than 8,500 plants) and Victoria water lilies.   LCJ

mixed border. See BORDER.

Mlyňany Arboretum ⊛
(Hungarian: Malonya), near Nitra, Slovakia.
The botanist aristocrat Count István Ambrózy-
Migazzi inherited the Malonya estate in Upper
Hungary from his wife's family in 1892 and
extended it by purchasing the neighbouring
forest of oak and hornbeam. The construction
of the house was finished two years later, and
the Count with his Bohemian head gardener,
Josef Mišák, started to develop the park of
32 hectares/79 acres around the house. A
systematic collection of exotic woody plants
from different foreign nurseries lasted for two
decades, and resulted in a unique ensemble in
the Carpathian Basin. Microclimates for plants
of different habitats were skilfully achieved
with the use of the natural umbrella of the
existing forest. These protective trees were
gradually replaced by coniferous species.
During the First World War (at the end of
which this part of Hungary became part of
Czechoslovakia), the Count left the estate
entrusting it to Mišák's care, and moved to
Tana in western Hungary where he created
another arboretum in Kám-Jeli with a similarly
rich collections of rhododendrons.

After the nationalization of the estate, the
territory of the park was extended to 46
hectares/114 acres and new plantings were
made, with experiments in the acclimatization
of East Asian species. The great variety of
rhododendrons and azaleas gives a special
character to the site which is, with almost 2,000
taxa of woody plants, the richest and best-
known plant collection in Slovakia.   GA
  IVO TÁBOR and RADEK PAVLAČKA, *Arboretum
Mlyňany* (1992).

Moerheim Nursery, Royal.
See ROYAL MOERHEIM NURSERIES.

Mogilany ⊛
near Cracow, Poland. The wooden manor house
at Mogilany was built between 1560 and 1568
by Wawrzyniec Spytek Jordan, a humanist
educated in Italy. The residence was provided
with a garden most probably designed by
Bartolomeo Ridolfi. A special terrace, opening
southwards onto a vast panorama of the
Beskids and the Tatra Mountains, was the
site of an ornamental quadripartite garden
and adjacent orchards. After the founder's
death the garden fell into decline and in the
18th century Michał Stefan Jordan tried to save
the estate. It was perhaps in his lifetime that
hornbeam hedges, BOSQUETS, and a balustrade
with baroque sculptures of putti were added,
closing the garden on the south side. Probably
before 1800 a new stone house was erected. A

later extension, accompanied by the addition of
a new garden on the north side, took place in
the early 20th century. In 1945 the estate was
nationalized; since 1968 the house and garden
have been the property of the Polish Academy
of Sciences, which has its Conference Centre
here. Today the Mogilany garden consists of
the northern landscape and the southern
geometric layout. The latter part is composed of
four quarters with a circular bed in the middle,
enclosed by hornbeams hedges, and of two
bosquets on the west side.   WB

Mollet, André, and family.
André Mollet (d. 1665) was a French garden
designer and author, a member of a remarkable
family of gardeners. André became *jardinier
du roi* at the Tuileries (see PARIS PARKS AND
GARDENS) and the Louvre. Early in his career
he came to England where, in around 1630, he
worked at St James's Palace and in 1642 made
new gardens at Wimbledon House for Charles
I's wife Henrietta Maria. Between 1633 and 1635
he was in the Low Countries where he designed
gardens at Buren and HONSELAARSDIJK for
Prince Frederik Hendrik of Orange. From
1648 until 1653 he worked in Sweden as royal
gardener to Queen Christina. Here he wrote his
influential book *Le Jardin de plaisir* (1651) which
was dedicated to the Queen. The book contains
designs for PARTERRES *en broderie*, BOSQUETS,
compartiments de gazon (shaped lawns), and
other garden features. It is also full of practical
horticultural knowledge—its first chapter
discusses in detail different types of soil and
emphasizes the importance of compost.
Subsequent chapters deal with nurseries, fruit
trees, grafting, kitchen gardens, flower gardens,
and trees before he broaches the subject of
parterres. He emphasizes the importance of
progressively less ornate elements extending
from the chateau—the *parterres de broderie*,
leading to *parterres de gazons* and then to
bosquets. In 1661 he was once again in London
where he laid out new gardens for Charles II
at St James's Palace and became keeper of St
James's Park gardens (see LONDON PARKS AND
GARDENS).

André's father Claude I (*c*.1560–*c*.1649) was
the royal gardener in charge of FONTAINEBLEAU,
SAINT-GERMAIN-EN-LAYE, Montceau-en-Brie, and
the Tuileries. His father, Jacques I, was gardener
to the Duc d'Aumale at ANET where Claude met
the royal architect Étienne Dupérac (1535–1604),
under whose influence he evolved the first
parterre de broderie, laid out at Anet after 1582.
Claude was the author of the posthumously
published *Théâtre des plans et jardinages* (1652)
which is a valuable account of gardening at the
moment when Renaissance ideas were giving
way to early baroque. In it he also describes

his encounter with Dupérac. André's brothers
Pierre (d. before 1656), Claude II (d. 1664),
Jacques (d. 1622), and Noel were all gardeners
in the royal service. Claude II was especially
important, becoming in 1632 *jardinier ordinaire et
dessinateur des plans, parcs et jardins des maisons
royales* (gardener in ordinary and draughtsman
of plans, parks and gardens of the royal houses).
In this role he laid out new gardens at
VERSAILLES for Louis XIII in 1639.   PT
  DOMINIQUE GARRIGUES, *Jardins et jardiniers de
Versailles au grand siècle* (2001).

monastic gardens. See MEDIEVAL GARDENS.

Monet, Musée Claude. See GIVERNY.

Monforte ⊛
Valencia, Spain. The house was built in the mid
19th century for Juan Bautista Romero in what
was then countryside outside Valencia. Today
it is engulfed by urban expansion but the 0.8-
hectare/2-acre garden, enclosed in walls,
preserves a thoroughly rural character, even
more precious as it is now in the heart of the
city. This is a garden of lively formality spiced
with romantic ingredients. Great arcades of
clipped cypress divide the space, hedges of box
or myrtle frame parterres, and orange trees
repeatedly rise at the centre of beds. A rose
garden has a large bay tree in a central circular
bed from which a parterre of segmental rose
beds radiates with, in one corner, a large coral
tree (*Erythrina crista-galli*). A MOUNT is climbed
by a helical path and crowned with thickets of
ivy intertwined with *Plumbago auriculata*. Fine
statuary ornaments the scene—a series of white
marble nymphs rises from a box parterre and
Neptune sprawls on the rocaille island of a
pool. A small and intricate courtyard garden
lies below the neoclassical villa. Scrolls of
clipped myrtle surround a fountain pool,
tritons rise from a goldfish pool, and putti
play on the surrounding balustrade. Away
from this decorative feast the view of banal
skyscrapers rises above the garden walls. Since
1971 Monforte has belonged to the city of
Valencia and is finely cared for.   PT

Mon Repos ⊛
near Vyborg, Russia, is situated on the Island
of Linnasaari in the Gulf of Finland and is
approached from Viborg by a bridge. The
property was acquired in 1784 by the governor
of Karelia, Prince Friedrich of Württemberg
(1754–1816), who was the brother of the Grand
Duchess, later Empress, Maria Fedorovna.
When Friedrich left Russia in 1787 it was bought
by Ludwig von Nicolay (1737–1820), a poet and
academic from Strasbourg, who was tutor to
the Grand Duke Paul and later secretary to

Maria Fedorovna and president of the Russian Academy of Sciences. It was he who made Mon Repos one of the great parks of Europe.

In an idyllic northern setting of rugged granite rocks, surmounted by trees and surrounded by sea, long walks led past a succession of picturesque views. Elegiac monuments served as reminders of life's transience and induced moods of pensive melancholy, which were then fashionable. Maria Fedorovna presented a memorial for another Strasbourg poet, Franz Hermann Lafermière, who had been a fellow student and friend of von Nicolay. During her brother's time at Mon Repos she had given a Chinese viewing pavilion, the interior of which she had personally decorated. An OBELISK was erected by Ludwig's son Paul in memory of his two brothers-in-law who had died fighting Napoleon. Ludwig von Nicolay and other members of his family were buried on the small, closely neighbouring island of Ludwigstein, where there is a structure in the style of a medieval castle by the English architect C. H. Tatham (1772–1842).

Mon Repos came through the 1939–45 war largely unscathed, but from 1945, after it had been ceded to the Soviet Union, it was used as a military rest home, and the park buildings suffered wanton destruction. In 1954 it became a so-called Park of Culture and Rest, which led to further damage. Some restoration was undertaken in the 1990s.   PH

Monserrate, Parque de ✣

near Sintra, Portugal. The house was built in 1789 by an Englishman, Gerard De Visme, in the Gothic style in a beautiful elevated position overlooking old woodland. In 1795 it was rented by William BECKFORD who was especially fond of it and its setting—'here I remain spellbound', he wrote to a friend. Beckford built a Gothic pavilion, a rustic cascade and a bizarre outhouse of gargantuan rockwork (which survives). Of Beckford's planting nothing is known and the garden's distinction dates from the time of Sir Francis Cook, who bought the estate in 1856. He remodelled the house, with Renaissance and Manueline features giving it the bizarre appearance it has today. Cook also introduced an immense number of plants— exotic ferns, conifers, eucalyptus, and much else. *The Gardener's Chronicle* described the garden in an article in 1929 expressing the opinion that 'it is a great achievement and vies with only one other garden of the same kind that I know—La Mortola' (see HANBURY GARDENS). By the end of the 20th century the estate was derelict and it now belongs to the state. The house was under restoration in 2004 and there were rumours of a restoration of the

landscape. At that time it presented a desolate appearance but the beauty of the landscape was still visible, as were many remarkable plants, some of which are now grown to great size. A huge *Metrosideros excelsa* was flaunting its aerial roots, a *Rhododendron falconeri* was in full flower, tree ferns and agaves flourished cheek by jowl, and a giant magnolia spread its limbs among the ruins of a Gothic chapel. In 2004 the Sintra Tourist Office, somewhat worryingly, listed it as a 'Theme and Amusement park'.   PT

Montacute House ✣

near Yeovil, Somerset, England, was built in the late 16th century for a lawyer, Sir Edward Phelips, who was also an MP and became chancellor to the household of Henry, Prince of Wales. Phelips made a garden shortly after the house was built and by 1630 Gerard was able to describe 'large and spacious Courtes, gardens, orchards, a parke'. There had been a park at Montacute in the 12th century but Phelips's park must have been a new one enclosing, as it did, common land—ridge and furrow patterns are still visible. The essential layout of Phelips's garden survives today—one of the very few English gardens of its period to do so. The East Court, originally the entrance court, is enclosed in balustraded walls decorated with obelisks and openwork stone 'Turrets of Ornament' as a 1667 description calls them. In each outer corner are 'faire Turretts with lodging Chambers'. All this, made of the beautiful golden Ham Stone quarried nearby, survives in fine condition. It is now laid out with lawns and with mixed borders lining the walls. Originally put into place in the late 19th century they were replanned by Phyllis Reiss of TINTINHULL HOUSE in the 1950s. The north garden has lawns and a raised walk planted with rows of thorn trees (*Crataegus* × *lavallei*) and, at the lower level, rows of clipped Irish yews (*Taxus baccata* 'Fastigiata'). At the centre is a balustraded, scalloped pool and fountain of the 1890s. On one side is a fine border of shrub roses. The Cedar Lawn, a former bowling green, has a magnificent *Cupressus arizonica* var. *arizonica*—the largest specimen in England of this unusual tree.   PT

Montaigne, Michel Eyquem de

(1533–92), French writer, philosopher, statesman, and diarist. In 1579 he travelled to Italy and recorded lively and observant accounts of the Medici gardens as well as the Villa LANTE and the Villa d'ESTE (Tivoli) in their heyday. His greatest work was his essays on which he was still working when he died, full of clear-eyed wisdom and candour on topics ranging very widely, among them sadness, smells, coaches, conscience, thumbs, and books.

He was one of the most attractive great men of the Renaissance.   PT

Monte Palace ✣

near Funchal, Madeira, Portugal. Monte is an attractive area in the wooded hills above Funchal with splendid views. Monte Palace was an old estate, the Quinta do Prazer, which in the 18th century had belonged to the British consul Charles Murray, and in 1904 was converted into a grand hotel, and a garden was laid out with a lake and exotic planting. After the Depression and the Second World War the fortunes of the hotel declined and for some years it was empty. In 1987 it was bought by a local businessman, José Berardo, who restored the house and garden, opening it to the public from 1991. The garden, disposed on sloping wooded ground, is rich in both plants and ornamental interludes. The collection of cycads is remarkable, with over 700 specimens of some 60 species. They find a perfect climate here and are finely displayed in the naturalistic setting of the steep slopes. The soil here is acid and there is a collection of ericaceous plants. Orchids are grown, in particular species of *Cymbidium* and *Paphiopedilum*—some of these require protection from frost. Among all these exotics the indigenous flora of Madeira is well represented—with splendid shrubby milk thistles (*Sonchus* spp.), the purple-flowered germander *Teucrium betonicum*, and the rare endemic orchid *Goodyera macrophylla*. Among the ornaments in the garden of special interest are the many examples of AZULEJOS, for the most part pictorial tableaux, ranging in date from the 16th to the 20th century. The garden is well watered, with ornamental pools, and gardens of Japanese inspiration seem entirely at ease here. Statuary appears throughout the garden, some of it of fine quality; particularly attractive are the fragments of Portuguese architecture of different periods.   PT

Monte Palace: A Tropical Garden (1999).

Monticello ✣

Charlottesville, Virginia, USA, is the home and estate created by Thomas JEFFERSON, author of the Declaration of Independence and third President of the United States. Jefferson levelled a small mountaintop on inherited land in 1768 for its prospect and adjacency to what he called the surrounding 'workhouse of nature'. He was a Renaissance man in the New World, and his talents as architect, land planner, farmer, inventor, scientist, ornamental horticulturist, and author—literate in seven languages—all came to bear in the creation of Monticello. The house was begun in 1770, designed by Jefferson in the Roman neoclassical style. He was elected to the Continental

Congress in 1775 and began his political career. Posted to Europe in 1784, as a Commissioner and then Minister to France, he undertook considerable remodelling and enlargement of the house in 1796. Jefferson's interest in botany, agriculture, and ornamental horticulture were well established from his youth. His education at William and Mary College in WILLIAMSBURG exposed him to the most sophisticated town planning and gardens of the day. Benjamin Smith Barton honoured Jefferson's botanical curiosity and his political contributions by the naming of a new genus and species *Jeffersonia binata* (*Jeffersonia diphylla* L.), the twinleaf, after him in 1792. During the course of his diplomatic career, he often exchanged plants with friends and garden enthusiasts abroad. He received new plants from the famous expedition of LEWIS and Clark, which he initiated, and also purchased many plants for trials at Monticello. The gardens consist of a Winding Walk Flower Border around the West Lawn, the Oval Flower Beds (twenty in all), a 300-m/1,000-ft long Vegetable Garden terrace, Fruit Gardens (including orchards, vineyards, and a 'fruitery'), and The Grove—an ornamental forest. There was painstaking recording of experimentation with varieties of flowers, fruits, vegetables, and ornamental trees—more than 160 tree species. Jefferson wrote to a friend, in 1811, 'No occupation is so delightful to me as the culture of the earth, and no culture comparable to that of the garden . . . But though an old man, I am but a young gardener.'

Monticello was a working plantation, with five satellite farms, totalling more than 10,000 hectares/24,729 acres, and was home to the Jefferson family and a large contingent of free workers and African-American slaves who laboured in the fields and gardens. It was sold after Jefferson died there, in 1826, and fell into neglect, and the gardens disappeared. Purchase of the property for a public memorial in 1923 led to the research and restoration of Monticello. Extensive garden archaeological studies undertaken in the last quarter of the century informed meticulous restorations of the gardens. Research programmes on historic plants and gardens and multi-level education programmes are now centred at Monticello. The impression is of a more modern place, due to Jefferson's well-tempered landscape philosophy and vision, and with its rich mix of Old World and New World in horticulture and design, Monticello stands apart as a unique and influential early American landscape.   PC

Montjuich ⊗

Barcelona, Spain, is a hill south-west of the centre of Barcelona. There had been great expansion on this side of the city in the late 19th century and the need was felt for public green space. Work had started towards the end of the 19th century but little had been achieved. The turning point came with the involvement of J. C. N. FORESTIER who, from 1917, collaborated with the architects Nicolau Maria Rubió I Tudurí (1891–1981) and Josep Puig I Cadafalch (1867–1956). It was the intention to develop the site both as a public park and as a site for international exhibitions. Forestier planted many trees and designed a sequence of gardens which have been added to subsequently. Each had its own name—Parc Laribal, Miramar, Amargós, and others. Advantage was taken of the sloping site and Forestier was adept in deploying eclectic detail—a modernist pergola at Amargós, neo-Renaissance terraces at Miramar, and brilliant use of water ranging from spectacular fountains to Islamic-style rills. There were the scents of a rose garden, of citrus plants, and of hedges of *Pittosporum tobira*. The whole area covered by the gardens is 200 hectares/494 acres. Time has taken its toll on some of the detail of the gardens but the value of the site's essential conception has kept its currency. This huge space is a very popular public park that also from time to time lends itself to other activities. From 1936 to 1975 Montjuich was the site of Grand Prix motor racing. In 1992 the Olympic Games took place in Barcelona and the stadium for them was built at Montjuich.   PT

Montréal Botanic Garden ⊗

Montréal, Québec, Canada, a multicultural garden, is among the largest of its kind in the world. In 1931, Brother Marie-Victorin (1885–1944) founded the garden; his ambition was to create a site that combined conservation with research activities, and the botanical education of visitors. Together with botanist, horticulturalist, and landscape architect Henry Teuscher (1891–1924) who became MBG's first garden director, Brother Marie-Victorin made an impassioned appeal to Montréal's citizens to give their city a gift for her 300th anniversary and, slowly, the Montréal Botanic Gardens took shape. Over the years, many gardens and pavilions have been added to the 75-hectare/185-acre site. The long winding walks through various gardens settle into a gentle landscape. There are more than 22,000 species and cultivars of plants housed within ten exhibition greenhouses and 30 thematic gardens. The latter include a fern exhibition, the exciting Garden of Innovations where new plant varieties and the latest landscaping trends are showcased; the Perennial Garden (the oldest exhibition garden); a new First Nations Garden highlighting their integral relationship with the plant world; a traditional Monastery Garden of the Middle Ages, featuring medicinal and aromatic plants; the City Gardens, designed by various landscaping experts to inspire with new concepts and themes; and the Corner of Quebec, a pocket of maple-hickory forest typical of the region. Two of the most dazzling exhibitions are the CHINESE GARDEN designed by Le Weizhogm of Shanghai and the JAPANESE GARDEN designed by Ken Nakajima in the traditional manner with a pavilion designed by Hisato Hiraoka in 1989.   MH

Moratalla, Palacio de la,

Moratalla, near Córdoba, Andalusia, Spain. The estate is an ancient one—Roman mosaics were found here and the Muslims built an outlook tower on the banks of the river Guadalquivir nearby. In the 19th century the house was remodelled and in the early 19th century the gardens were laid out by J. C. N. FORESTIER. Noble wrought-iron gates provided the original entrance to the estate but today what had been the drive is an ornamental ALLÉE. A narrow rill of Islamic character runs down the centre and the allée is flanked by myrtle hedges with statues and Irish yews with thickets of shrubs behind—*Elaeagnus angustifolia*, oleanders, philadelphus, and others punctuated by Italian cypresses. A myrtle parterre is decorated with statues of the four seasons. Shading the façade of the house is a double oval of lofty plane trees (*Platanus × hispanica*) at the centre of which is a circular pool with a picturesque fountain supported by putti. The pool is edged with arum lilies (*Zantedeschia aethiopica*) and radiating from it are box-edged segments of a parterre whose compartments are filled with waves of blue and white agapanthus and bergenias. Urns, statuary, and topiary add further ornament to the parterre. The house and garden are today finely cared for by the Duke of Segorbe who bought the estate in 1988.   PT

Moreau, Charles-Jean-Alexandre

(1760–1810), French architect, painter, and landscape gardener. As a student of F. Trouard at the Academy of Architecture in Paris from 1782 to 1785 he became an exponent of revolutionary architecture. He first completed designs for an 'English garden' while still at the academy. From 1785 to 1790 he studied and worked in Rome, then on his return to Paris became a student of painter Jacques-Louis David (1748–1825) at the Academy of Painting. Between 1798 and 1803 he worked as an architect in France, and in 1803 was invited by Prince Miklós Esterházy II to Kismarton—today EISENSTADT, Austria—to design the complete reconstruction of the residence. Only part

of the neo-classical renovation work was completed, but the landscape garden, including the Leopoldina Tempel, the Steam Engine House (housing the first steam engine on the continent, which circulated the water flowing through the park) and the hilltop GLORIETTE, still stands today, a composition which, without question, was one of Hungary's most significant picturesque landscape gardens. Also associated with Moreau are the landscape garden at Pottendorf (Austria) with a spectacular rotunda, the conversion of the medieval castle in the centre of the TATA estate of another member of the Esterházy family, Count Ferenc Esterházy, into a mock ruin romantic garden house, and the neoclassical reconstruction of Count János Esterházy's palace at CSÁKVÁR. He was responsible for the design of the house and its outstanding park at Somlóvár (today Doba) for Count Károly Erdődy at the beginning of the 1820s.
GA

STEFAN KALAMÁR, 'Daten zu Leben und Werk der Pariser Architekten Charles Moreau zwischen 1760 und 1803', *Zeitschrift für Kunst und Denkmalpflege*, No. 4 (2001).
FRANZ PROST (ed.), *Der Natur und Kunst gewidmet: Der Esterházysche Landschaftsgarten in Eisenstadt* (2001).

Moritzburg ⊛

Saxony, Germany, is named after Duke Moritz of Saxony (1521-53), who had a hunting lodge built here between 1542 and 1546, not far from Dresden on an outcrop of rock in the midst of the Friedewald, an area of woodland, lakes, and marshes. The original Renaissance building was altered and extended several times, acquiring its baroque form between 1723 and 1733 in the reign of King Augustus the Strong (1670-1733). Schloss Moritzburg has been the symbolic and formal centre of this hunting, fishing, forestry, and farming region since the 16th century. The woodland was already criss-crossed with ALLÉES and forest rides in the 16th and 17th centuries. The early 18th century saw a complex reshaping of the landscape whose effects are visible to this day. The plans may be mainly ascribed to the King himself, to Marcus Conrad Dietze (1658-1704), and to Matthäus Daniel Pöppelmann (1662-1736), with a chain of large lakes and radial axes segmenting the woodland areas serving both the needs of the hunt and the aesthetic concept. The palace itself, a palatial hunting lodge, lies on a symmetrical artificial island in the lake. To the north of it, the modest horseshoe-shaped pleasure garden begun in 1726 to plans by Pöppelmann was probably completed around 1740 by Georg Gottlob Meister. It was reconstructed in the latter half of the 20th century. The pleasure grounds and

island together cover around 4 hectares/10 acres. In 1728 the first pheasantry in Moritzburg was laid out as the termination of the east–west axis through the palace; 2 km/1.2 miles away, on the direct sightline from the palace dining hall, the CHINOISERIE Fasanenschlösschen (Little Pheasant Palace) built on the site between 1769 and 1776 was the centrepiece of a hermetic 'far-off land'. In the grounds created under the Saxonian Elector Friedrich August III (1750-1827) and probably strongly influenced by the Italian Duke Camillo Marcolini (1739-1814) one could undertake a 'world tour in miniature'. The area, in the charge of the Saxonian State Palaces, Castles and Gardens Authority, is to be revived, and parts of it have already been restored.   RP

Moro, Campo del ⊛

Madrid, Spain. Campo del Moro means literally the Moor's field or countryside. This was the site of a Muslim fortress which remained in place until the early 18th century. Here, close to the river Manzares west of the old city of Madrid, Philip V (reigned 1700-46) built a palace to the designs of J. B. Sachetti which remains a royal palace today. The palace grounds had initially been used for hunting in the reign of Philip IV and there was no garden here until 1840 when, to the west of the palace, a park was laid out and a great fountain of tritons was moved here from ARANJUEZ. It stands today as the chief ornament of an axial vista aligned with the palace. The whole site here is 20 hectares/49 acres which is crossed with avenues with informal plantings of groves and groups of trees some of which go back to the original plantings.   PT

Morris Arboretum ⊛

Philadelphia, Pennsylvania, USA, began as a private estate. 'Compton', as it was known, was the summer home of siblings John and Lydia Morris. Through wide travels and broad interests in art, horticulture, and gardens, the Morrises developed a series of eclectic gardens containing collections of plants and sculpture. The ARBORETUM covers 175 hectares/433 acres, containing living collections of more than 2,500 taxa from North America, Asia, Africa, and Europe. The original residence no longer exists, but a fernery, visitors' centre, and other structures punctuate the landscape. Collections of note include magnolias, maples, native azaleas, roses, hollies, conifers, and members of the witch hazel family. Many of the Asian plants here are from the expeditions of E. H. WILSON, of the ARNOLD ARBORETUM, and collecting expeditions continue under the sponsorship of the arboretum. A number of record or champion trees—the largest on record—are

found here. There are two dozen theme gardens or garden features listed for the visitor, from a Rose Garden, to a Japanese Hill and Water Garden, to a Log Cabin, all laid out along a serpentine route through the arboretum. The Morrises planned a future of laboratories and a school of botany and horticulture at Compton, and the estate was given to the University of Pennsylvania in 1932 as an educational and research centre. Today, a Center for Urban Forestry and the Flora of Pennsylvania Program provide valuable research and resources for the region, and the Morris Arboretum is a prime teaching resource for local universities.   PC

Mortella, La ⊛

Ischia, Campania, Italy. In the hot southern climate much of the exotic planting at La Mortella is dependent on the elaborate system of fountains and sprays which keep the air humid. Laid out in part by Russell PAGE for the composer Sir William and Lady (Susana) Walton in the late 1950s (before the house was completed), the main garden lies in a deep south-facing gully, with thick planting of semi-tropicals allowing a very naturalistic and almost jungle-like appearance while a strong axial and cross-axial structure holds the design together. Page imposed a grid system of Islamic-type water rills linking pools and fountains and framed views to the distant peak of Mount Ipomeo, an extinct volcano. Large volcanic boulders were rearranged to make pool and rock gardens. Trees were initially planted around the perimeter to give shade and protection. Inspired by Russell Page, Lady Walton became a talented and very knowledgeable plantswoman, the garden reflecting her choice of exotics. Camphor trees, chorisias from her native Argentine, tree ferns, *Metrosideros excelsa* (the New Zealand Christmas tree), and tulip trees are underplanted with alocasias, ginger, arisaemas, zantedeschias and brugmansias, hostas, and self-seeding *Geranium maderense*. Below the house in full sun a collection of palms contains a specimen blue-fan palm, *Brahea armata*, from California. Over the years Lady Walton, who makes the garden a setting for performances of her husband's music, has greatly extended its extent in the higher cliff above the valley, choosing appropriate plants for each site. On the exposed cliff grey-leaved Mediterranean-type aromatics cling to the rocks, while in woodland beyond she has constructed shaded rock pools for ferns and bamboos.   PHo

Mortola, La. See HANBURY GARDENS.

Morton Arboretum ⊛

Lisle, Illinois, USA, with an area of 570 hectares/

1,425 acres, was founded in 1922 by Joy Morton, and now constitutes one of the country's outstanding collection of woody plants. Thornhill Farm was Morton's country estate, which was redesigned by Ossian Simonds (1855–1932) as an arboretum around the Morton home. Simonds's naturalistic plan emphasized the subtle and gently undulating terrain and the existing stands of oak, hickory, and maples, which were augmented with extensive new plantings of trees and by the creation of Lake Marmo, close to some splendid specimen oaks. The new collections were set out in the areas best suited to their needs. Waste areas surviving from the earlier history of farming were developed to demonstrate improved forestry techniques. The arboretum site is bisected by a public road. Its larger part lies east of the road and includes the floodplain of the east branch of the DuPage river. The Visitor Center is located at the head of Meadow Lake, and this area is designed to provide expansive pastoral landscape views. Much of the newer planting groups here comprise mixed families. There are a number of special collections such as the hedge and coloured foliage collection. Almost half of the east section lies higher and contains a climax forest of oak, hickory, and maple. Recognizing the widespread phenomenon of the disappearance of mid-western prairies, in 1963 a former area of pasture was developed with mesic prairie plants.   DCS

mosaïculture

is a French word for ornamental bedding, especially CARPET BEDDING. French and Belgian gardeners began to follow the English fashion for patterned flower beds in the late 1860s, about the time that carpet bedding was being introduced there; while in England flower bedding and carpet bedding were regarded as separate genres and kept distinct, on the Continent they were grouped together into a unified style. The word *mosaïculture* was coined by J. Chrétien, superintendent of the Parc de la TÊTE D'OR in Lyon. The patterns used started with simple circles and ovals; after the creation of beds in the shapes of a butterfly and a flower vase at the Exposition Universelle of 1878, emblematic and zoomorphic shapes became popular instead. By the end of the century, historically revivalist patterns made their appearance, and some proponents of *mosaïculture* justified their bedding schemes by claiming that they were a revival of the spirit of the age of Louis XIV. These claims were dismissed in the early 20th century as the demand for period accuracy in garden reconstruction increased. However, it continued to form a major part of municipal park decoration. In England, William ROBINSON

attempted to popularize the word *mosaïculture* as a term for beds of dwarf succulents, to distinguish them from conventional carpet bedding, but the word was not adopted outside his own circle.   BE

Moscow Botanic Garden

Russia, is pleasantly situated in north Moscow in the Ostankinsky Forest Park and covers 360 hectares/890 acres. It was established in 1945, replacing the much smaller 18th-century botanic garden in the centre of the city. It made rapid progress under its first director, N. V. Tsitsin, who remained in that post for thirty-six years. The gently undulating terrain, crossed by the valleys of rivers Yauza, Likhoborka, and Kamenka, provides varied soil conditions to facilitate the cultivation of a wide range of plants. In the former Soviet Union there were 59 botanical gardens from which plants could be obtained for the new Moscow garden. Of particular interest is the area devoted to the display of the flora of the Soviet Union, with each of the main regions represented by its plants in appropriate landscaped settings. The arboretum (75 hectares/185 acres) features a large collection of those trees and shrubs from all parts of the world which have been able to adapt to the harsh Moscow winters, while 50 hectares/124 acres of natural oak woodland (*Quercus robur*) has been preserved. Among ornamental plants, tulips, narcissi, hyacinths, lilies, peonies, gladioli, irises, and phlox are each represented by some hundreds of varieties, while the rose collection exceeds 2,000 species and varieties. A wide range of tropical and subtropical plants are grown under glass.
PH

Mosigkau.

See DESSAU-WÖRLITZ GARTENREICH.

moss house.

Of all the picturesque and melancholy buildings that ornamented the 18th-century English landscape garden the moss house was the most ephemeral. It was usually made of rustic wood, in a shady place, and moss was encouraged to grow on it. In the 18th-century woodland at the GNOLL ESTATE in Wales the moss house was an important building and part of the garden to this day is called Moss House Wood. No extant example of a moss house is known.   PT

Mōtsuji

Iwate prefecture, Japan, is a temple of the Tendai sect of Buddhism, founded in 850 by the priest Ennin, but the garden, which remains today only in its general form, dates from the early 12th century when the temple was rebuilt

by the Fujiwara family who were governors of the region. The first two generations, Fujiwara no Kiyohira (1056–1128) and his son Fujiwara no Motohira (d. *c*.1157), are associated with the design of the temple and garden. At the time Mōtsuji was built, it lay on the very northern frontier of the Japanese nation, which made its original gilded splendour all the more unusual. The temple buildings were destroyed by fire in 1226 and nothing but their foundation stones remains today. Although the garden, too, is just a remnant, it is important historically because it represents an example of late Heian-period (794–1185) Pure Land garden design (see JAPAN). Originally, a large southern gate opened onto a broad pond over which bridges were built, first to a central island, then on to an Amida Buddha hall on the far shore. The pond and island remain, as do some areas of rockwork that are representative of Heian-period aristocratic gardens, including a Rocky Shore (*ara-iso*), Pebble Beach (*suhama*), and Winding Stream (*kyokusui*).   MPK

Mottisfont Abbey

near Romsey, Hampshire, England, was an Augustinian foundation dating from the 13th century. A new house was built in the 1740s incorporating some of the monastic buildings. Although there are some fine old trees here, including one of the largest London planes (*Platanus* × *hispanica*) in the country, most of the garden interest dates from the 20th century. Sir Geoffrey JELLICOE designed a deft formal garden after 1934—turf terracing, an octagon of clipped yew and a walk of pleached limes underplanted in spring with blue chionodoxa. In 1938 Norah Lindsay designed a box knot garden, whose pattern is copied from an 18th-century fanlight, planted with spring and summer bedding schemes. In 1952 the estate was given to the NATIONAL TRUST and twenty years later Graham Stuart THOMAS, then gardens adviser to the National Trust, installed his rare collection of shrub roses in the walled former kitchen garden. Today, this forms the National Collection of pre-1900 shrub roses, with over 300 species and cultivars. It was ingeniously laid out by Thomas, retaining the quadripartite division from its kitchen garden days and a few old fruit trees up which some of the roses are prettily trained. Beds are edged in box, Irish yews give strong structure and everywhere there is skilful underplanting of the roses. A collection of more recent cultivars was added in an extension a few years later.   PT

mount.

An artificial hill of regular shape usually resembling a steamed pudding turned out on a plate. Its chief purpose seems to have been to provide an elevated view of the garden, or anything else of note, below. Mounts (*montagnette* or *montagnole*) were found in Italian Renaissance gardens from the mid 15th century. Giovanni Rucellai had one in his garden at QUARACCHI, planted naturalistically with evergreens such as arbutus, box, and juniper. A mount in the garden of the Villa Medici in Rome (see MEDICI FAMILY), in place by the end of the 16th century, had a helical walk lined with cypresses leading to the summit. The mount was found, too, in English Renaissance gardens of which the most spectacular was at HAMPTON COURT, made in 1533-4 with paths hedged in hawthorn and lined with statues of the king's beasts leading to the summit crowned with the elaborate Great Arbour with its onion-shaped lead dome. OXFORD UNIVERSITY COLLEGE GARDENS sometimes had mounts. An engraving of 1675 shows the garden of Wadham College with an unplanted pudding-shaped mount standing at the centre of a formal garden. It had an ornate staircase, with a viewing platform and a statue of Atlas at the top—it lasted until the mid 18th century. The mount at New College survives, in a rather blurred state. Celia Fiennes saw it before 1691 and described 'Myrtle Oringe and Lemons and Lorrestone [laurustinus] growing in pots . . . and a great mount in the middle which is ascended by degrees . . . and on top is a Summer House'. At ZORGVLIET in the Netherlands a remarkable mount, Parnassus, was made in the 1650s with zigzag paths, conical trees, and surmounted by a tree. In the Jardin des Plantes in Paris (see PARIS PARKS AND GARDENS) a mount, the Grande Butte, was built in the early 17th century, with a spiral path leading to a belvedere—it still survives, shrouded in trees. By the end of the 17th century mounts seem to have fallen out of fashion.   PT

Mount Auburn Cemetery ⊛

Cambridge and Watertown, Massachusetts, USA, America's first pastoral CEMETERY, was established in 1831 by the Massachusetts Horticultural Society and is today a private, non-profit corporation. Conceived of and designed by amateur botanist Henry A. S. Dearborn (1783-1851) and Jacob Bigelow (1787-1879), a Harvard physician, Mount Auburn's naturalistically planted original 29 hectares/72 acres, handsomely adorned as it was with classical monuments, was a novel concept at that time, a large-scale, rural commemorative garden open to the public. The now 71-hectare/175-acre property's maze of roads winds around elaborate cast-iron fence lots (belonging to distinguished New England families), crests ridges ablaze in autumn gold, ginkgos (*Ginkgo*

biloba), fiery reds, threadleaf Japanese maples (*Acer palmatum* 'Dissectum'), and sourwoods (*Oxydendrum arboreum*), and carves out surprisingly quiet and inviting spaces. An intimate vernal pool lined with Norway spruce and Japanese stewartia (*Stewartia pseudocamellia*) hosts the endangered yellow-spotted salamander in spring and rare migrating birds throughout the year. More encompassing vistas from the 18-m/62-ft Washington tower take in the Boston skyline and a spectacular collection of 640 varieties of trees, including many pre-dating the cemetery and others the largest of their species in New England. In 1860, England's Edward VII planted a European beech (*Fagus sylvatica*) that now shades an elegant stone sphinx and Victorian-inspired garden fronting a Gothic-inspired granite chapel. Commemorating the founder of Christian Science Mary Baker Eddy, a white marble Corinthian-columned temple is mirrored in a lake edged in majestic bald cypresses and dawn redwoods. Mount Auburn continues to implement new ideas as a memorial landscape, like multiple-burial sites.   LJ

Mount Congreve ⊛

Kilmeaden, County Waterford, Republic of Ireland, is one of the most remarkable gardens made in the 20th century. In the tradition of the 19th-century plantsman's woodland gardens Ambrose Congreve created an outstanding plant collection taking advantage of the acid soil, mild climate, and relatively high rainfall. The Congreves have lived here since the 18th century but Ambrose Congreve, inspired by visits to Lionel de Rothschild's Exbury (Hampshire) between the wars, laid out a startling new garden. In 73 hectares/180 acres of attractively sloping ground on the banks of the river Suir Congreve accumulated plants and disposed them according to firmly held notions. He despised spotty planting and thought that plants, of whatever size, always looked better planted in masses. The minimum number was six, even of large plants like magnolias, and was frequently far greater. A walk 1 km/0.6 mile long, for example, is lined on one side by 100 trees of *Magnolia campbellii* and on the other by 100 *Magnolia sargentiana* var. *robusta*. Paths run along the slopes above the river, with clearings and paths leading off. It is flowering shrubs—camellias, magnolias, and rhododendrons—that are the central theme here but there is an enormous collection of trees and rich plantings of herbaceous perennials. There is only the very occasional use of ornament—a pillared temple, a Chinese pavilion—and the chief focus is overwhelmingly on plants. With a very large garden staff, as

many as 35 in recent years, the garden is impeccably maintained.   PT

Mount Cuba Center, Inc.

Greenville, Delaware, USA, the home of Lammot du Pont Copeland and his wife Pamela from 1937 until her death in 2001. They sited their Georgian house (Victorin and Samuel Homsey, architects) atop one of Delaware's highest hills with magnificent views across steep hills and deep valleys of the Eastern American Piedmont, to the Delaware river and the Coastal Plain below. Thomas W. Sears was engaged to lay out the drive and formal gardens which were almost completed as the Second World War broke out. Terraces for outdoor living and floral displays surround two sides of the house, with walkways leading through formal plantings, to the large cutting garden and out into the larger landscape. After the war, and on the advice of Henry F. du Pont of WINTERTHUR, Marian Coffin (1880-1957) was commissioned to complete the formal gardens. The Round Garden, a small, formal flower garden, with a dipping pool in the form of a Maltese cross, was designed for seasonal displays of tulips, delphiniums, lilies, roses, and a variety of annuals and chrysanthemums. Mount Cuba is most celebrated for its naturalistic plantings of native wildflowers, ferns, shrubs, and trees begun in the early 1950s, fulfilling a love of native plants Pamela Copeland had since childhood. In young tulip tree (*Liriodendron tulipifera*) woodland, grown up on an eroded cornfield abandoned in the late 1920s, a series of ponds was created, connected by sounding rills, and accessed on paths surrounded by foliar tapestries and, in spring, a wealth of wildflowers, trilliums, wood poppies, foamflower, Virginia bluebells, and deciduous azaleas.   RWL

Mount Edgcumbe ⊛

Torpoint, Cornwall, England, with its extraordinary coastal position, was acquired in the early 16th century by the Edgcumbe family, who enclosed a DEER PARK here in 1539. By the 17th century there was a formal landscape garden which was depicted in a Thomas Badeslade engraving of 1737. A broad double avenue descended the slope leading down towards the sea and on each side patterns of rides are cut into woodland. This garden was seen by Celia Fiennes in 1698—'a hill all bedeck'd with woods which are divided into severall rowes of trees in walkes'. In the 18th century a pattern of walks, the Zigzags, was laid out above the cliffs and ornamental buildings put up—a picturesque ruin, a Gothic seat, and an Ionic rotunda (Milton's Seat)—with a planned walk,

the Earl's Drive, to link the beauties of the landscape. In the late 18th century formal gardens were added—the Italian Garden with a double staircase, statuary, an orangery, and citrus plants in pots; the French Garden with a box parterre (now used for bedding schemes); and the English Garden with a pedimented garden building overlooking a flower garden. A late 20th-century development was the National Collection of camellias which is now held here, with ten species and 500 cultivars which flourish in a protected valley. There are 350 hectares/865 acres of designed landscape at Mount Edgcumbe. It is the contrasting wild beauty of the clifftop walks, and their ornamental buildings, with the unexpected formal gardens that makes it so memorable.
PT

Mount Stewart ⊛

Newtownards, County Down, Northern Ireland, was built in the early 19th century for the 1st Marquess of Londonderry to replace an 18th-century house. All that survives from the 18th-century garden is a superb garden building, the Temple of the Winds, designed by James 'Athenian' Stuart (1713–88) and built in the 1780s. At some distance from the house, it stands on a wooded hill overlooking the waters of Strangford Lough. At the time of the 3rd Marquess it was suggested that the temple be converted into a mausoleum after the suicide of his son Lord Castlereagh. He rejected the idea: 'I have no Taste for Turning a Temple built for Mirth and Jollity into a Sepulchre—The place is solely appropriate for a Junketing Retreat in the Grounds.' A lake was laid out in the 1840s, with plantings of trees and shrubs about its banks. On dry banks leading to the family burial ground, called Tir Nan Og, are southern hemisphere plants relishing the mild climate—banksias, callistemons, hakeas, and leptospermums. Formal gardens behind the house and to one side of it were laid out from 1921. The sunken garden, with a giant pergola, has an ARTS AND CRAFTS flavour but the Shamrock Garden, with jokey topiary and bedding plants, is of thoroughly independent style. The Italian Garden behind the house is in the form of a great parterre, with a central pool. Beds are edged in unusual hedging plants, golden thuja and purple berberis, and colour schemes within them are sometimes explosive. Curious animals, made of concrete, decorate the garden. The 32 hectares/ 78 acres of the garden present a varied scene—Arcadian lakeside views, many excellent and sometimes rare plants, and decorative exuberance. Since 1955 it has belonged to the NATIONAL TRUST. PT

Mount Stuart ⊛

near Rothesay, Isle of Bute, Scotland, is the estate of the Stuart family (later earls and marquesses of Bute) who have lived in these parts since the 14th century. The present house is a spectacular Gothic palace, built to the designs of Rowand Anderson (1834–1921) in the late 19th century to replace an 18th-century house destroyed by fire. In the 18th century this was the estate of the 3rd Earl of Bute, George II's adviser at KEW, who laid out a garden here from 1739. Noble traces of his garden survive—magnificent lime avenues and a triumphant stone column—but the great parterre in front of the house has not survived. Planned walks along the water's edge seem to date from the same time and there are the remains of an 18th-century GROTTO. In the late 19th century Thomas MAWSON laid out a picturesque rock and shrub garden. The climate here in the Firth of Clyde, warmed by the North Atlantic Drift, is mild, and many tender plants such as embothriums, *Hoheria sexstylosa*, and the rare *Pittosporum dallii* flourish here. PT

Mount Usher ⊛

Ashford, County Wicklow, Republic of Ireland, is an admirable example of a type of garden important in the Irish garden tradition—the Robinsonian garden taking every advantage of a rare site. The river Vartry flows through the gently undulating grounds at Mount Usher and this is the central feature in the garden that the Walpole family made after they came here in 1868. William ROBINSON himself visited Mount Usher in 1883 and described it as 'a charming example of gardens that might be made in river valleys'. This was a great age for Irish plant collections and the Walpoles had the advantage of contacts with Sir Frederick Moore at the NATIONAL BOTANIC GARDEN and the plant collector Augustine HENRY. The Walpoles built a series of weirs in the river which today are one of the great beauties of the place. Much ornamental planting, especially of flowering shrubs, decorates the banks of the river and the placid pools below the weirs act as mirrors reflecting the beauties of the flowers and foliage. The climate is mild here, rainfall fairly high and the soil acid. Today, in 8 hectares/20 acres, there are over 3,000 species grown here. Rhododendrons loom large but there are excellent collections of trees—among them acers, eucalyptus, nothofagus, and rowans. Many of the trees and shrubs are propagated from wild-gathered seed. Many of the plants, especially those from the southern hemisphere, are rarely seen in European gardens—*Agathis australis*, *Bowkeria citrina*, and *Telopea truncata*. Still privately owned, this is one of the best and most attractive of Irish gardens. PT

Mount Vernon ⊛

Virginia, USA, was the home for more than 45 years of the first President of the United States, George Washington (1732–99). The estate was originally granted to Washington's great-grandfather in 1674 and was inherited by Washington in 1761. The present-day house, built by Washington around an earlier small farmhouse, sits on a bluff above the Potomac river and the prospect was described by traveller William Loughton Smith in 1791 thus: 'the view extends up and down the river a considerable distance . . . embracing the magnificence of the river with the vessels sailing about; the verdant fields, woods, and parks.' Another visitor, Samuel Vaughan, four years earlier, had drawn a plan of the house and grounds that reinforces this description and emphasizes Washington's own comments in 1793 that 'no estate in America is more pleasantly situated than this'. Washington designed his garden at Mount Vernon himself, landscaping an entire 200 hectares/500 acres at the centre of his 3,200-hectare/8,000-acre estate. Garden historians have praised Washington's attention to detail, in both the architecture and landscape, including the placement of buildings—from the approach in serpentine curves to the HA-HA; from the selection of native American trees for the shrubberies to the 'necessaries' and even the poignancy of a 'botanick' garden full of exotic plants sent from east and west. His embellishments reveal his understanding of Batty LANGLEY's *New Principles of Gardening* (1728)—Washington had his own copy—in which Langley recommended a softening of the earlier fashion for rigid formal schemes. This can be seen in the groves and woods planted to frame the view across the river. However, the Vaughan plan reveals the essential regularity of Washington's designs with only a hint of naturalism in the winding paths through the shrubberies. Benjamin Latrobe's description of the garden in 1796 is the faithfully restored garden we see today. 'The ground on the west front of the house is laid out in a level lawn bounded on each side with a wide but extremely formal serpentine walk . . . on the side of this is a plain kitchen garden, on the other a neat flower garden laid out in squares and boxed with great precision . . . I saw here a parterre, clipped and trimmed with infinite care into the form of a richly flourished Fleur de Lis.' The formality and precision of the gardens at Mount Vernon echo the traditional pattern of colonial gardening seen in other plantation gardens in the Chesapeake Bay area and along the James river to the south. Mount Vernon is one of the best-documented properties in the United States. The 1787 Vaughan plan and the bird's-eye view engraved in 1859, a year after the far-sighted purchase of the property by the Mount Vernon Ladies' Association, have provided pictorial documentation for accurate restoration. Washington's own planting records have been invaluable in the restoration to its 1799 appearance, the last year of Washington's life, and defining Mount Vernon as an 18th-century gentleman's country seat.

CMR

Moutiers, Le Bois des ⊛

Varnegeville-sur-Mer, Seine-Maritime, France. The house was built in 1898–1900 to the designs of Edwin LUTYENS for a Protestant banker, Guillaume Mallet, and Gertrude JEKYLL designed the garden. The site, of 12 hectares/30 acres, is a very beautiful one, with the ground sloping away east of the house towards the sea of the Channel which is just glimpsed from the house and which Monet loved to paint on his visits here. West of the house Lutyens devised a series of enclosures, of beautifully detailed stone, brick, tile patterns, and stucco, and yew hedges. A pattern of square box-edged beds decorates the entrance courtyard which is enclosed in yew on two sides. Here the planting is white, with massed 'Iceberg' roses, *Dicentra spectabilis* 'Alba', hydrangeas, lupins, and in spring drifts of 'White Triumphator' tulips. Immediately below the west gable of the house, and aligned on it, a long walk laid with basket-weave bricks runs between mixed borders with a planting scheme dominated by silver, grey, and purple. Substantial buttresses of yew on each side divided the borders and create intimate enclosures, and structure within the borders is given by shrubs—silver-leafed *Elaeagnus commutata*, sombre purple-leafed *Berberis thunbergii* f. *atropurpurea*, and rhododendrons and roses. These are underplanted with cranesbills, hostas, irises, Jacob's ladder (*Polemonium caeruleum*), lilies, and *Thalictrum aquilegiifolium*. An opening leads to a bold pergola of oak beams on brick columns veiled with clematis, roses, and *Vitis coignetiae*. Behind the house is a garden of wholly different character made by the Mallet family in the early 20th century. The attractively undulating site, with paths winding among trees, is a dazzling woodland garden with magnificent displays of camellias, enkianthus, eucryphias, pieris, and rhododendrons.   PT

Muckross ⊛

Killarney, County Kerry, Republic of Ireland, has a site of rare beauty among the mountains and lakes of the 10,000-hectare/25,000-acre Killarney National Park. The Herbert family came here in the 16th century and in the 18th century cleared the land by the lake and made a feature of the picturesque ruins of a 15th-

century Franciscan friary. In the high rainfall and mild climate trees grow superbly well here: 19th-century plantings of conifers, such as Monterey pines (*Pinus radiata*), have grown to vast and characterful size. Such native trees as the Durmast oak (*Quercus petraea*) are as fine as you will see anywhere. The arboretum is a good tree collection enlivened with many flowering shrubs, especially camellias and rhododendrons. Muckross is now a much used public park but the interests of plant lovers are well catered for.   PT

Munstead Wood,

near Godalming, Surrey, England, was the garden of Gertrude JEKYLL where she put into practice the gardening ideas she made famous and experimented with a wide range of plants. The house was built for her to the designs of Edwin LUTYENS and completed in 1897. The site was a triangle of ground of 6 hectares/15 acres with lime-free soil which she described in *Gardens for Small Country Houses* (with Lawrence Weaver, 1912) as 'the poorest possible soil, sloping a little down towards the north'. In one corner of the triangle, close to the house, she made formal gardens, including a nursery (which supplied many of her garden commissions) and a kitchen garden. But the bulk of the site, to the east and south of the house, was a wild woodland garden laced with paths two of which formed long, broad straight walks. Woodland gardening was one of Gertrude Jekyll's special loves which she described so well in her *Wood and Garden* (1899), many of whose illustrations are photographs of the garden at Munstead. For Gertrude Jekyll Munstead was not merely a garden but a whole way of life. It was also a place of pilgrimage for many who became notable gardeners themselves, among them Beatrix FARRAND, Mien RUYS, and Russell PAGE. After Gertrude Jekyll's death the Munstead estate was dismembered but the house and 4 hectares/10 acres of land remain, and the present owner has carried out much restoration.   PT

JUDITH B. TANKARD and MARTIN A. WOOD, *Gertrude Jekyll at Munstead Wood* (1996).

Murinan ⊛

Kyoto city, Japan, the villa of Yamagata Aritomo (1838–1922), army general and Prime Minister of Japan after the Meiji Restoration (1868), lies just outside Nanzenji temple in the east of Kyoto city. Yamagata obtained the property in 1894 and but was immediately called away as commander of the Japanese army in Manchuria. The work on the villas was left to Kuhara Shōzaburō, an entrepreneur from his home village, to oversee. Upon Yamagata's return, Kuhara introduced him to the gardener

Ogawa Jihei (1860–1933, also known as Ueji), whom Yamagata directed in the design of the garden. Yamagata, being deeply involved in the modernization of Japan (which in many ways meant Westernization), purposefully disregarded the stylistic trends of the previous Edo period (1600–1868)—such as overt pruning of tree forms and ornate rockwork—and searched for a new, 'bright' expression. The freely growing trees (originally *Abies firma*) that surround the property, the open lawn that fills the foreground, and the focus on a central, flowing stream rather than a pond, were all means to this end.

Yamagata's move to this site, away from his previous Nijō residence, stemmed in part from a desire to make use of the plentiful water made available to the Nanzenji area through the Biwako canal project and, in part, from an attraction to the view the site commanded of the eastern mountains. Yamagata framed that view with trees, incorporating the mountains into the garden through the technique of 'borrowed scenery' (see SHAKKEI).   MPK

Murndal,

Victoria, Australia, has been developed by six generations of the Winter Cooke family. Near Hamilton, in the rich Wannon river valley, Murndal was first settled by Samuel Pratt Winter, of Anglo-Irish descent, in 1837. The area immediately around the substantial homestead has no significant garden. However, the 1,850-hectare/4,532-acre estate is a cultivated parkland strongly reminiscent of the 18th-century English landscape style. Extensive groups and avenues of trees—many of them elms and oaks—are arranged in prominent positions or follow the contours of the land in hills and valleys; Murndal boasts a Coronation Avenue, and many single specimen trees have been planted throughout the property to commemorate significant events in England and Australia. A series of five artificial lakes, each flowing into the other, are surrounded by more elms, willows, holm oaks, pines, and monkey-puzzle trees. Somewhat surprisingly, these lakes are out of sight of the house. Unlike the English model, Samuel Pratt Winter did not embellish his domain with allegorical temples, and the agile deer likely to appear in an English landscape of the period have been replaced in the Australian context by the solidity of Hereford cattle. Murndal's designed landscape is thought to be the largest of its type in Australia and is unknown elsewhere in Victoria.   CMR

Museumpark ⊛

Rotterdam, Zuid-Holland, the Netherlands, is a museum quarter first proposed by the city of Rotterdam in 1985. The site was a neglected villa garden in a polder adjoining the 1932 Museum Boymans van Beuningen. The former gardens were proposed as a public park with the Netherlands Architectural Institute at one end, the old Villa Dijkzigt as the proposed natural history museum, and the newly proposed Kunsthal for modern art on the other. The commission for the Kunsthal was given to OMA, the office of Rem Koolhaas (b. 1944), who was then also asked to design the park. Koolhaas had made a name for himself in 1982 with his entry for the Parc de la Villette competition, where he had challenged the concept of the public park. In 1988–9 he employed the French landscape architect Yves Brunier (1962–91) to help him with the design. They divided the site into four different character blocks, a grove, a tarmacked events area, a flower garden, and a paved area surrounding the Kunsthal. The events area with stage has been detailed in the manner of a motorway, thereby challenging the concept of the park as an escape from the urban rat race. This concept is strengthened with a large curved bridge which passes the flower garden as if a flyover. This flower or 'romantic' garden retained many of the existing trees while introducing a bolder river provocatively in the shape of a spermatozoid. Shrubs, perennials, and annuals were produced in strong patterns below the trees, but in practice the shady location has inhibited this concept from flourishing.   JW

Museumplein ⊛

Amsterdam, Noord-Holland, the Netherlands, was created on a much-disputed site in the centre of Amsterdam about which discussions had already started even prior to the building of the adjoining Rijksmuseum in 1875. Various proposals were made and the area was last redesigned after the Second World War with a wide central avenue, dubbed 'the shortest

motorway in the Netherlands', of which the sides were used for car parking. In 1990 the decision was taken to eliminate the car from this area and recreate a people space suitable for large events. The Scandinavian landscape architect Sven-Ingvar ANDERSSON was given the task of designing a new square. In a lengthy process, which was completed in 1999, the central avenue of trees was removed in order to create a large, open multifunctional space, and underground garages were provided for cars. A small section of the central avenue is remembered in the small basin, around which there are cafés and sports facilities, with this area becoming the hub of the park. The large central area, which feels a bit like an underappreciated part of the city, as the Rijks, Stedelijk, and Van Gogh Museums have all turned their backs on it, is left open, the only feature being a lighting strip which cuts through it. Unfortunately the enormous popularity of this space for informal sports activities and as a shortcut was not foreseen and the design has had to be adapted with a cycle path associated with the lighting strip, while the large central space has to be regularly closed off in order to give it time to recover from heavy usage.   JW

ALLE HOSPER, 'Sven-Ingvar Andersson in Amsterdam', in Steen Højer, Annemarie Lund, and Susanne Møldrup (eds.), *Festskrift Tilegnet Sven-Ingvar Andersson September 1994* (1994).

Muthesius, Hermann

(1861–1927), German architect, architectural historian, theorist, critic, and garden designer. Muthesius played a decisive role for fundamental changes in German architecture, industrial design, and aesthetic education after the turn of the 20th century. He was also a key figure for the adoption of English garden design principles (the functional and formal relationship between house and garden; geometric-architectonic garden design

principles) as well as for the introduction of certain ARTS AND CRAFTS elements in German garden design. Educated as an architect, he first worked with a German architectural firm in Tokyo (1887–91); on his return to Germany he joined the Ministry of Public Works, a position in which he showed his strong ability as a writer on architectural issues. On 1 October 1896 he was sent to England as technical attaché at the German Embassy in London (1896–1903). In England he especially dealt with the history and design principles of the traditional English country house. In this respect he also occupied himself with garden design. His intensive studies in this field resulted in the publication of the three-volume book *Das englische Haus* (1904–5). The ideas about the layout of country house gardens in this book had been taken from a small range of English contemporary writers (Reginald BLOMFIELD, Thomas H. MAWSON, Gertrude JEKYLL) as well as from historical writings. Muthesius also had studied contemporary English country houses and was acquainted with leading architects of the Arts and Crafts movement. Immediately after his return to Germany in 1903 he initiated a polemical debate against landscape gardening. Though he had been criticized for his sometimes aggressive position, his ideas were discussed in German garden design circles and led to the highly influential trip of German garden architects to England in 1909. Muthesius designed many country houses and gardens throughout the German Reich from 1904 to 1927 (about 70 in all), but his importance lay in his writings (he published about 50 books and 500 articles).

US

UWE SCHNEIDER, *Hermann Muthesius und die Reformdiskussion in der Gartenarchitektur des frühen 20. Jahrhunderts* (2000).
—— 'Hermann Muthesius and the introduction of the English Arts and Crafts garden to Germany', *Garden History*, Vol. 28: No. 1 (2000).

N

Nærum allotment gardens ⊛

Nærum, Denmark, are considered one of C. Th. SØRENSEN's most important creations. In 1948 40 oval allotment gardens, each measuring *c*.25 × 15 m/80 × 50 ft, were laid out on a rolling lawn, a common green, in a fluid progression. The gardens are mostly placed so that the oval lies across the curves of the slope. This use of the rolling terrain, combined with the sweeps and curves of the hedges, accentuates the dynamic impression. The individual garden plots are enclosed compartments surrounded by hedges; their cottages may be situated in different ways, but comply with the overall plan. The hedges were originally intended to be both clipped and unclipped, using such species as hornbeam, hawthorn, privet, and roses, but today there are mostly privet and hawthorn, clipped in different heights and forms. The design of the individual garden plots was left up to each owner, but a guide from C. Th. Sørensen shows various models. The allotment gardens are situated close to a large public housing scheme, Nærumvænge, with flats and terraced houses, characterized by its homogeneous look and red hipped roofs. C. Th. Sørensen landscaped the green spaces here also.   AL

Nagycenk ⊛

Győr-Moson-Sopron county, Hungary. At the same time that a baroque palace was built, around 1750, General Count Antal Széchenyi commissioned a decorative but modestly sized baroque garden for which a number of alternative designs have survived by Louis Gervais, Kaspar Kollmann, and Andreas Kneidinger. The composition of the park included a 2.5-km/1.5-mile lime tree avenue along the palace's axis, with a hermitage at its end. In the last third of the 18th century Ferenc, the son of Antal Széchenyi, and founder of the Hungarian National Museum and Library, turned it into a picturesque landscape garden, which included small lakes, mock ruins, watermill, grottoes, and a HERMITAGE. In 1820 the estate was inherited by his son, István Széchenyi, a crucial figure in Hungarian

history. István was a believer in reform in every sphere. Inspired by his visits to England, he created a pleasure ground near the palace, and constructed a cast-iron greenhouse. It is probably at his bidding that most of the buildings belonging to the picturesque garden were pulled down. Following István Széchenyi's death in 1860, his son Béla redesigned the park according to plans made by the Austrian landscape gardener and architect Lothar Abel, enriching the gardens with fine trees, especially conifers. The palace and park, having fallen into complete disrepair, were renovated as a museum and hotel. According to designer Károly Örsi, this provided the only opportunity in Hungary—where during the 19th century all baroque gardens were completely remodelled as landscape parks—to conjure up an 18th-century baroque ornamental garden. The work on the park was completed in 1981.   GA

Nai Lert Park Hotel,

Bangkok, Thailand. Opened some twenty years ago as the Hilton Hotel, this is now managed by Raffles International. The building underwent a complete renovation in 2004 and the garden (the largest of any Bangkok hotel) was extensively replanted by Thanpuying Lursak Sampatisiri, owner of the property, and William Warren, who were also responsible for the original selection. The property consists of two ponds, the smaller planted with hybrid water lilies and a larger one planted with *Victoria amazonica* (formerly *V. regia*), as well as an artificial waterfall. Pathways lead through lawns planted with such flowering trees as *Plumeria*, flamboyant (*Caesalpinia pulcherrima*—both the usual red and a rarer yellow variety), buttercup tree (*Cochlospermum religiosum*), *Jacaranda*, *Brownea*, *Saraca*, and *Angsana*, as well as local fruit trees such as guava, breadfruit, and pomelo. Many of the trees and coconut palms had grown to such heights over the years that there was insufficient sunlight for lower flowering plants like *Ixora*, *Alpinia*, *Gardenia*, *Heliconia*, and jasmine. Accordingly, a number of these were removed during the renovation,

opening up views of the garden from the glass-walled hotel lobby. Plants with colourful foliage, among them *Codiaeum*, *Cordyline*, and *Graptophyllum*, were also added for accents.   WLW

Nanjing

(formerly Nanking), China, is situated on a curve of the Changjiang (formerly Yangtze river), with the Purple Gold Mountains (the tiger crouching) to the east. This capital of Jiangsu province has several times in its long history also been capital of the empire and a major cultural centre. The first three Ming emperors are buried in the Purple Gold Mountains, which are also famous for their monasteries set among cliffs and wooded hills. Just beyond the northern city walls is the Xuanwu lake park, covering today about 400 hectares/988 acres, which 'borrows' views of the distant hills (JIE JING) and has several large islands linked by bridges. Outside the western wall is the pleasant Mochou—meaning light-hearted—Lake garden which commemorates a Liang dynasty heroine. Originally laid out under the Song dynasty, it was restored in the 1950s with bamboo groves, crab apple orchards, and pavilions around the lake. Within the city is the Zhan Yuan, an intricate Ming-dynasty garden, now overlooked by buildings but with a fine rockery imaginatively restored and enlarged in the 1950s. Once known as one of the three furnaces of China because of its unbearable summer heat, Nanjing has become much cooler with the planting of 24 million trees under the People's Republic.   MK

Naranjestan (Bagh-e Qavam) ⊛

Shiraz, Iran. Begun in 1870, the garden and reception hall visible today are part of the public area, the *biruni*, where the merchant Qavam received visitors. The hall or *talar*, reflecting 19th-century Qajar taste, is elaborately decorated with mirror mosaic and coloured glass, the latter of Russian origin. The stone-edged garden beds, filled with roses, perennials, and annuals, form an intricate pattern around the central water feature, the whole framed dramatically by tall date palms, casting dappled shade over a scented orange orchard. The reception room is decorated with glittering mirrors on walls and ceilings and coloured glass in the windows.   PHo

Naranjos, Patio de los ⊛

Córdoba, Andalusia, Spain. The courtyard of orange trees immediately adjacent to the Mezquita (mosque) of Córdoba was probably laid out in the late 8th century making it one of the oldest continuously gardened sites in Europe. It is a symmetrical pattern of   ▶

regular rows of trees each planted in a circular bed let into paving stones. The beds are linked by narrow irrigation rills fed from a cistern and two fountains ornament the patio. It occupies a rectangular space precisely the width of the Mezquita. Until the early 16th century, when a Christian cathedral was built inside it, it was open on the side of the Patio de los Naranjos whose water also served to allow worshippers to wash before entering the mosque.   PT

Narváez, Jardines de ⊛

near Antequera, Andalusia, Spain. In the 19th century the estate was owned by the Duke of Valencia and it was in his time that the garden was made. The ingredients are formal but the atmosphere picturesque. A serpentine box hedge curves across the ground and a mossy path runs through a tall tunnel of box. A parterre-like garden has curved irregularly shaped beds. An octagonal moated fountain is surrounded by blue and whire irises and box hedging and a cool *glorieta*, or summer house, is fashioned of clipped box in which one can sit on stone benches. Waves of scented violet (*Viola odorata*) lap at the feet of fruit trees—apples, mulberries, persimmons, and pomegranates.

Colour plates

The **Valentine Garden** designed by Isabelle Greene in California, USA

Innovative **public parks** in Paris: trees reflected in the stainless steel Géode in the Parc de la Villette and the computer-controlled fountains in the Parc André Citroën

The Mussenden Temple at **Downhill Castle**, Ireland

An estate from the heyday of the French Riviera, **Villa Ephrussi de Rothschild**, France

Walls and garden furniture inlaid with china fragments at the **Maison Picassiette**, France

Substantial trees shelter the garden to the north—date palms, *Magnolia grandiflora*, and umbrella pines (*Pinus pinea*). This is a country garden of unpretentious charm with touches of more sophisticated formality.   PT

Nash, John

(1752–1835), English architect and landscape designer especially associated with the picturesque landscape. From 1796 he was in partnership with Humphry REPTON but they parted company in acrimony in around 1800. From 1811 he laid out Regent's Park (see LONDON PARKS AND GARDENS) and the elaborate urban development associated with it. In 1813 he was appointed surveyor-general of the works, resulting in much work for the royal family, including rebuilding Buckingham Palace. Between 1815 and 1822 he designed the ROYAL PAVILION and its grounds for the Prince of Wales. His reworking of the 17th-century landscape at St James's Park (London), between 1828 and 1829, including the transformation of a 17th-century canal into a picturesque lake, is masterly. At BLAISE HAMLET in around 1810 Nash designed picturesque thatched estate cottages set in a miniature village setting. On a more extravagant scale in 1813 he designed Royal Lodge in Windsor Great Park, a cottage *orné* (see AVELEDA, QUINTA DE) which became a large and expensive house. Nash also laid out the grounds in collaboration with William AITON.   PT

Nasim Bagh,

Lake Dal, near Srinagar, Kashmir. This corresponds with the Emperor JAHĀNGĪR'S description of a lakeside palace belonging to his father AKBAR who visited Kashmir in 1586. He found it already fallen into disrepair, and he describes in his journals how, out of respect for his father's memory, he gave instructions for its repair and decoration. Only a few fragments of masonry now remain near the water's edge. The site was planted out in the reign of Shāh Jahān with an immense grid of plane trees, and this, when viewed from the lake, forms a powerful feature in the landscape.   SMH

Nassau-Siegen, Johan Maurits van

(1604–79), Dutch politician, arts patron, and gardener. After a successful military career Johan Maurits acted as governor of the West India Company administering the Dutch colonies in Brazil between 1637 and 1644. During his period there Maurits built four houses in Recife in north-east Brazil, the most important two being the Palace of the Two Towers, or Vrijburg Palace, completed in 1642 and Boa Vista completed in 1643. These palaces had extensive gardens. In 1644 he returned

to The Hague where the Mauritshuis and its garden had been finished for him in his absence by Jacob van CAMPEN and Pieter Post. Becoming the Elector's stadtholder at CLEVES in 1647, he continued his building and gardening activities in and around Cleves creating an extensive network of parks and gardens. He retired to Bergendal after being dismissed from the service of the Dutch States General in 1676.
                                                              JW

WILHELM DIEDENHOFEN, ' "Belvedere", or the principle of seeing and looking in the gardens of Johan Maurits van Nassau-Siegen at Cleves', in J. D. Hunt, *The Dutch Garden in the Seventeenth Century* (1990).

MARIA ANGELICA DA SILVA and MELISSA MOTA ALCIDES, 'Collecting and framing the wilderness: the garden of Johan Maurits (1604–79) in north-east Brazil', *Garden History*, Vol. 30: No. 2 (2002).

National Botanic Garden of Wales ⊛

Middleton Hall, Llanarthne, Carmarthenshire, Wales, funded partly by National Lottery funding and opened to the public in 2000. The site is a very beautiful one, 237 hectares/586 acres, in the undulating rural landscape of Carmarthenshire. The Middleton family came to live here in the 17th century and in 1789 sold the estate to Sir William Paxton who had the park landscaped by Samuel Lapidge (1740–1806) and had the curious notion of founding a spa here—which was not then, and is not now, one of the more populous parts of Wales. For this purpose he dammed streams and formed lakes but the spa was never made. Work on making the National Botanic Garden started in 1996. Norman Foster & Partners designed the Great Glasshouse which is substantially underground (providing excellent insulation) and covered by a podlike glass roof—all that is seen above ground—which ingeniously echoes the landforms here. The interior, with terraced beds filled with plants from Mediterranean climates, was landscaped by Kathryn GUSTAFSON. From the entrance paths leading uphill are decorated with herbaceous borders and with a collection of Welsh rocks arranged in order of antiquity. The lakes, drained between the wars, are being restored to provide habitats for flora and fauna. Sustainability and organic principles are recognized and heating for administrative buildings is provided by a stove fed with recycled timber or woodland thinnings. By the end of 2003 there were problems about the continuing funding of the garden.   PT

National Botanic Gardens, Glasnevin ⊛

Dublin, Ireland. The garden was founded at the end of the 18th century at the instigation of Dr Walter Wade who, in 1790, petitioned the Irish

Parliament to found 'a public botanical garden, in this city, or its environs'. In 1795 the Dublin Society bought land at Glasnevin, then on the edge of the city but today part of it, and a year later Wade was appointed the society's professor of botany. The first map of the garden, drawn by Thomas Sherrard in 1800, shows the garden layout much as it is today, without the magnificent glasshouses that later adorned it. From 1838, under the direction of David Moore, the garden entered one of its most flourishing phases. Moore was particularly interested in cycads and orchids of which he built up large collections. It was he, from 1843, who had the great Curvilinear Range of glasshouses built, initially by William Clancy, with later additions by Richard and William TURNER. A beautiful palm house was built in 1883–4 replacing an earlier one damaged by a gale. David Moore's son Frederick (later Sir Frederick) replaced him as director in 1879 and continued his father's work. He was also a great influence on gardening in Ireland, distributing plants widely among keen gardeners. The site, 19 hectares/48 acres in area, is attractive, gently undulating, with the banks of the river Tolka forming its north-west boundary. The gardens today, with cheerful bedding schemes as well as a plant collection of around 20,000 taxa, are a very popular public amenity, exactly fulfilling the role for which they were planned. There is a fine arboretum, a rose garden, alpine house, rock garden, and many tender plants under glass.　PT

National Council for the Conservation of Plants and Gardens

(NCCPG), set up in 1978. Christopher Brickell, then the director of the Royal Horticultural Society Gardens WISLEY, persuaded the RHS Council to host a conference titled 'The Practical Role of Gardens in the Conservation of Rare and Threatened Plants'. The concern was the uncertain future of the unique range of plants that survives in cultivation in the United Kingdom and the value of the biological and cultural resource this represents. The conference had delegates from over 100 organizations and as a result the NCCPG was formed with the following mission: 'To conserve, document, promote and make available Britain's great biodiversity of garden plants for the benefit of horticulture, education and science.'

Financed by membership subscriptions and the fund-raising efforts of regional area groups who run lectures and plant fairs, the NCCPG's main conservation endeavour is the National Plant Collection® scheme. There are 650 collections around the country most of which are based around a taxonomically related group of plants, mainly at the genus level. Examples include *Phlox paniculata* cultivars and *Musa* species. By organizing the scheme systematically the areas being conserved can be identified and collections can be actively recruited to fill the gaps. Plant groups covered include trees, shrubs, herbaceous perennials, orchids, cacti, ferns and glasshouse plants. The NCCPG harnesses the energy of enthusiastic collectors, whatever sector of horticulture they may come from. Private collections may be held on allotments or in large country estates. Collection holders include botanic gardens, historic gardens, commercial nurseries, schools, and even a zoo. All collections can be visited and are listed on the website www.nccpg.com and in the annual *NCCPG National Plant Collections® Directory*. All collection holders meet set standards of documentation, reserve plants, establishment, representative coverage, and cultivation set down by NCCPG. There are mechanisms to test applicants against these standards and to monitor the existing collections. To do this the National Office coordinates a network of volunteers who visit the collections. These volunteers also work with the National Office to support collection holders with short-term problems and relocation of collections. The NCCPG also trains applicants for collection status. For example they may not know about the record keeping or labelling necessary if a collection is to be a useful research resource as well as having a long-term future. The expertise of the collection holder is as important as the plants themselves, and many research and document their plants' history, cultivation, and nomenclature. NCCPG has a responsibility to try and capture this information, by publishing the *Plant Heritage Journal* and booklets written by collection holders. It is also developing plant recording software called *Demeter®* to help them keep electronic records of their plants.

To quote Colin Chapman, a *Syringa* collection holder: 'A National Collection is an awesome responsibility. Plants could come to you, which are virtually unique. You must know how to reproduce them and you must record them even if they are in the last throes of their existence. You are not just the holder of a collection of plants; you are also the holder of the physical history of your genus. And do remember "history" is defined as the "recorded" evidence of existence.'　RJ

National Trust.

The leading conservation organization of houses, gardens, and the landscape for England and Wales was founded in 1895 at a time when conservation was much in the air. Also founded at the end of the 19th century were the Society for the Protection of Ancient Buildings (1877), the National Footpaths Preservation Society (1884), and the Royal Society for the Protection of Birds (1889). The founders of the National Trust were Canon Hardwicke Rawnsley, Sir Robert Hunter, and Miss Octavia Hill, whose aims initially were to preserve the countryside (in particular Canon Rawnsley's beloved Lake District), to provide green space for urban dwellers, and to protect common land. Later on it broadened its scope, especially as regards buildings and their gardens.

From slow beginnings it has become a very large and influential organization. By 2004 it had over 3,000,000 members, and owned 248,000 hectares/612,000 acres of land, 600 miles of coastline, and more than 200 buildings and gardens. An independent charity, the National Trust receives no money from the state. Apart from the value of pooling resources, and large economies of scale, it has the advantage over private ownership of paying no capital transfer tax. It will usually take on a house or garden only if it is accompanied by sufficient estate to make it self-supporting, but in exceptional circumstances it may buy an estate, raising the money by public appeal. This was done, for example, in 2002, to secure the remarkable Victorian estate of Tyntesfield in north Somerset which was bought for £24,000,000. In some very rare cases it will acquire a garden of outstanding interest whose original house has been destroyed (as at WESTBURY COURT).

Some of the most notable gardens in England and Wales are owned by the National Trust, among them POWIS CASTLE, SISSINGHURST CASTLE, STOURHEAD, and STOWE. For the most part the policy on garden conservation is an exceedingly conservative one, with the existing fabric maintained. Any additions must be historically justifiable (such as the Victorian parterre reinstated at Charlecote Park in Warwickshire). New gardens of contemporary design had never been commissioned until 2003 when it was announced that a new garden (designed by Arne Maynard) was to be laid out for the late 17th-century house of Dyrham Park in Gloucestershire.

Criticisms of the National Trust often refer to an institutional flavour, distasteful to some, which pervades the properties in its care. Certainly greater individuality is possible in estates which are privately owned and have no need to please committees and the very large number of paid-up members upon whom the National Trust depends. Some of the best gardens owned by the National Trust have benefited from the continuing influence of the original owners, such as the Rothschilds at Ascott Park and WADDESDON MANOR or the Aberconways at BODNANT. The occasional powerfully independent head gardener, too, can introduce a sometimes welcome note of individuality. On balance, however, any niggles are very minor compared to the immense achievements of the National Trust.   PT

naturalistic planting
can be defined as a planting style that is inspired by the aesthetics of wild plant communities and that aims to match closely the ecological requirements of plants with the conditions that prevail at the planting site. It covers a wide range of different approaches, from the planting style used in WILD GARDENS to a more heavily managed and self-consciously aesthetic style, notably the planting that has become associated with German garden shows and parks, sometimes known as *Lebensbereich* (habitat) style, and is particularly associated with Richard Hansen (1912–2001). Whether the work of practitioners such as OEHME, VAN SWEDEN, or the Netherlands-based Piet Oudolf is truly naturalistic is a matter of opinion.

History and philosophy
In seeking its inspiration from nature, naturalistic planting makes a clear statement about the relationship between humanity and the natural world, so it is not surprising that it has occasionally developed a definite political charge, and attracted lively debate and controversy. William ROBINSON made a forceful case for wild gardens but was only one of several practitioners in the late 19th and early 20th centuries; others include the Austro-Hungarian Ernst Graf Silva Tarouca and the German Willy LANGE. The latter was associated with the nationalistic and mystical range of ideas around the concept of the 'Nordic' in the early 20th century, which also inspired Jens JENSEN. Both strongly favoured the use of regionally native plants, and were openly racist in their political views and contempt for the 'architectural' garden styles of southern European origin. In the USA the landscape architect Warren H. Manning (1860–1938) promoted naturalistic planting as part of an attempt to develop a distinctively American garden style. Unlike Jensen, he did not see non-natives as being inherently unsuitable, as for him the garden was a 'cosmopolitan' place. Another early North American proponent was Wilhelm Miller (1869–1938), author of *The Prairie Spirit in Landscape Gardening*, which developed the idea of gardens that celebrated regional distinctiveness and echoed the dominant features of the landscape. The specifically naturalistic influences of Robinson, JEKYLL, Tarouca, and others is today very

difficult to judge, as the very nature of the style is that it leaves very few and subtle traces in gardens, so there are real problems in identifying any remaining naturalistic elements.

Whether or not naturalistic planting should involve only regionally native plants or whether it should use species from anywhere with a similar habitat has always been a central debate, which has been to some extent resolved by a separation between naturalistic planting which aims to restore a functioning local ecology, as in the Dutch HEEMPARKS, in MEADOW GARDENS and in the increasingly widespread prairie movement in the mid-west of the USA and Canada, and a more horticultural and intentionally aesthetic style. The latter owes much to Gertrude Jekyll, who took over the editorship of *The Garden* magazine from William Robinson in 1899 and continued to promote natural-style gardens, especially the WOODLAND GARDEN, which has been the most distinctive British contribution to naturalistic planting, and one that is very definitely in the 'cosmopolitan' camp.

Amongst those working with a cosmopolitan approach, Beth CHATTO has from the 1950s onwards been enormously influential in promoting a close linking of plant selection with habitat and an informal quasi-naturalistic style, to a large extent building on the ecological research of her husband Andrew Chatto. In Germany, nurseryman and writer Karl FOERSTER has been enormously influential, largely through his promotion of perennials, ferns, and grasses rather than with naturalistic planting *per se*. Foerster was a pacifist, and post-war naturalistic planting in Germany can to some extent be seen as part of a wider left-environmentalist and counter-cultural movement.

Native plant gardening
The use of native plants in naturalistic planting schemes is widespread, although there is a huge range of practice between those who eschew any plants not native to the region and those who combine them with non-natives. For open environments, meadow-based schemes tend to dominate in Europe, and prairie in the USA, both based on a matrix of grasses, with non-grass perennial wildflowers as a minority element. Both are characteristically sown from seed mixtures supplied by specialist companies. Prairie seed mixtures can, to some extent, be manipulated for visual effects, for differerent heights of growth, flowering seasons, and colour schemes. In the UK, work by James Hitchmough and Nigel Dunnett at the landscape department of the University of Sheffield has shown that seed-sown meadow

mixtures comprising both native and non-native species are feasible, offering a greater visual appeal for urban public space schemes than purely native-based planting combinations. In woodland and wetland environments, the use of seed mixtures is not so feasible, for a variety of reasons including the lower seed production of many suitable species, and naturalistic planting schemes tend to be smaller scale. The use of dry meadow-inspired planting schemes has a particular, and rapidly growing application, in extensive green roof technology, where low drought-tolerant vegetation such as wildflower meadow is used to cover flat roofs. Pioneered in Germany, extensive green roofs are essentially functional rather than aesthetic, offering a variety of public and private environmental benefits, such as reduction in run-off from precipitation and building insulation. Whilst most native plant gardening is carried out in North America and north-west Europe, interest is growing elsewhere. Mediterranean and arid climates particular offer considerable scope, as a challenging climates tend strongly to favour the use of plant material known to survive. The work of Steve Martino in Arizona (USA) is particularly notable for his use of desert natives, and for his use of selected clones of natives for aesthetic reasons—a practice that tends to be frowned upon by many in the field, as it can reduce genetic diversity. Isabelle GREENE in southern California is also noted for using a large proportion of native plants in sustainable gardens and landscapes.

Naturalistic planting schemes using non-native plants
Individual practitioners have created a number of gardens with naturalistic schemes over the years, often with little reference to any wider or previous body of work. The only systematic work has been done in Germany, where Richard Hansen's work at the SICHTUNGSGARTEN (SHOW GARDEN) in Weihenstephan in Bavaria has resulted in a considerable body of knowledge on plant compatibility and longevity. The majority of landscape and garden designers have however only tended to apply very simplified versions of his planting schemes in their work. However, a number of practitioners have created elaborate and highly successful habitat-based planting schemes in the garden shows that are a regular feature of German horticultural life, notably in the GRUGA-PARK and the WESTPARK. The Hermannshof garden in Weinheim (Baden-Württemberg), developed originally by Urs Walser, who was director from 1983 to 1998, is also a good example of the Hansen-inspired style, with a strong emphasis on aesthetics and, more recently, on the

development of a prairie style planting for European conditions. In Britain, the most extensive example is to be seen at PORTMEIRION, where a very wide range of species, mostly woody, has been used in mixed native woodland, with the intention that species should be seen as they would be in the wild. The use of southern hemisphere species such as cordyline and richea is particularly dramatic. Fairhaven garden (Norfolk) is an example of a wetland habitat garden, where there is extensive self-sowing of primulas and other non-native species in semi-natural woodland. Lady Farm (Somerset) is a good example of a style inspired indirectly by the German parks using a combination of perennials and grasses.

Practicalities
Naturalistic planting requires particular skills in both design and management. Unlike conventional planting schemes, plant development is expected to be dynamic, i.e. species populations will ebb and flow over the years. The role of subtle and skilled management is thus crucial, in order to limit the growth of stronger-growing species and thus maintain the high level of diversity which is needed to maintain visual and wildlife interest. The control of weeds is also vital. Whilst well-designed naturalistic plantings are very robust and can continue to function well with little maintenance, natural succession processes (such as the germination of aggressive grasses and woody species) will inevitably result in degradation if there is no intervention. Maintenance needs to be only infrequent, but it does need to be skilled, with staff needing a relatively high level of plant knowledge.

High-fertility soils which favour the growth of aggressive weeds present more of a problem for naturalistic planting schemes than drought-prone or low-fertility ones. In the latter, there is less opportunity for unwanted species to become established, and the stressful conditions tend to ensure that the species used grow more sparsely and thus compete with each other less and so maintain a higher level of diversity. It is no coincidence that the most spectacular and successful naturalistic plantings are often reckoned to be the steppe areas in the Westpark and other German parks, where a combination of a continental climate and difficult growing conditions ensure a high level of floristic diversity.   NK

Naumkeag ⊛
Stockbridge, Massachusetts, USA, on 20 hectares/49 acres set in the picturesque Berkshire hills, was originally a summer home built in the 1890s by architect Stanford White

(1853–1906). It is celebrated today for its remarkable garden, designed over a period of 30 years, starting in 1926, by landscape architect Fletcher STEELE in collaboration with Mabel Choate, the daughter of Naumkeag's original owner. Steele, schooled in the Beaux-Arts tradition, was nevertheless open to new ideas, and his work is considered transitional between the classical designs of the early 20th century and the avant-garde modernists creating gardens in mid-century. Naumkeag, with its bold sense of theatre and fun, and Fletcher's imaginative use of curves and colour, is the captivating result of this play between traditional and abstract design. A terraced garden room just outside the shingled house, with a view to Bear Mountain, is airily enclosed with tall, carved and painted oak posts, made from piers salvaged from Boston Harbor, which resemble Venetian gondola piers. Between the posts swags of ship rope support clematis. On the ground swirls are repeated in the patterned stonework and a curved pool filled with black glass and an inch of water. On a south-facing slope, Steele cut narrow, snaking ribbons of gravel in the lawn, an expression of land art echoing the curves of the mountain in the view. The Blue Steps are Steele's last project at Naumkeag and his signature work. In a grove of white paper birch (*Betula papyrifera*) on a steep hillside, Steele designed a double stone stairway supported by four arches painted blue. White-painted pipe railings sweep up the staircase on each side, seeming to contain the birches. The result is graceful fantasy, an innovative, light-hearted stage set.   PD

NCCPG.
See NATIONAL COUNCIL FOR THE CONSERVATION OF PLANTS AND GARDENS.

Nebbien, Christian Heinrich
(1778–1841), German landscape gardener, estate improver, architect, economic adviser, and multifaceted philanthropist. Born in Lübeck, after lengthy travels in Russia, England, Italy, and Holland, he fled before the Napoleonic wars to Hungary, where he joined the service of the Brunswick family in Alsókorompa (today Dolná Krupá, Slovakia), at MARTONVÁSÁR, and in Soborsin (today SĂVÂRŞIN, Romania) as landscape gardener, and to develop the estates both economically and aesthetically. According to some sources, he also worked for other Hungarian aristocratic families: for the Andrássy family in Betlér (today BETLIAR, Slovakia), the Prónay family in Tóalmás (in 1812), for the Koháry family in Hontszentantal (today St Antol, Slovakia), Felsőbalog (today Velky Blh, Slovakia). Before 1818, he designed gardens in Lower Hungary (today Yugoslavia):

in Elemér (today Elemir), Bégaszentgyörgy (Želište), and in Écska (today Ečka). After 1821 he left Hungary and worked in Koźmin, near Breslau (today Wrocław, Poland), at the Krzyżanowicz estate, then, from 1808 to 1834, in eastern Prussia and Bavaria. One of his most important works was the VÁROSLIGET (City Park) in Budapest. The influence of the style of BROWN and REPTON can be felt in the parks he designed. His view was that the objectives of agricultural reform, the improvement of parks and estates, bore moral significance, and thereby transcended mere aesthetic and practical considerations. He was also notable for his theoretical work, which bears witness to a thorough knowledge of international landscape gardening literature. Moreover, his foresighted convictions proved to be pioneering in a number of ways.   GA
Géza Galavics, *Magyarországi angolkertek* (Landscape Gardens in Hungary) (1999). Heinrich Nebbien, *Ungarns Folks-Garten der Koeniglichen Frey Stadt Pesth* (1816), ed. Dorothee Nehring (1981).

Nei Yuan,
Shanghai, China, literally the Inner Garden, was built in 1709 on some 700 sq. m/2,289 sq. ft to the east of the City Temple complex in the old city of Shanghai. Today it has become part of YU YUAN which lies to its west, so it was also called Dong Yuan or East Garden. It is a tiny, intensely planned enclosure, its main Hall of Sunny Bright Snow or Qingxuetang facing and embraced by rockery hillocks on three sides. These are piled up above hollows and a rocky tunnel with pavilions and secret paths built among them. A Dragon Wall, identical to those in Yu Yuan, winds across these rocks ending in a realistically modelled head. Below it, water flows out through an opening and runs into the tiny Nine Dragon Pond surrounded by *meirenkao* (see CHINA). A fine brick carving of an Immortal in paradise animates one tiny enclosure, while on the west hillock a small tower once 'borrowed' (JIE JING) a distant view (blocked now by structures built this century) of the busy Huangpu river.   G-ZW/MK

Nesfield, William Andrews
(1794–1881), a respected painter before he began designing gardens. His first garden to become known was his own villa at Fortis Green in north London, which was publicized in J. C. LOUDON's *Gardener's Magazine*; here and elsewhere he worked with his brother-in-law Anthony Salvin, and also worked extensively with William Burn and Edward Blore. In 1843 he was commissioned to lay out the ROYAL BOTANIC GARDENS, KEW, where his works included the broad walk, the parterre, PATTE-D'OIE, and lake around the Palm House, and the PAGODA, Syon,

and cedar vistas. Among his country house commissions were parterres for CASTLE HOWARD; Eaton Hall, Cheshire; Combe Abbey, Warwickshire; and Holkham Hall, Norfolk. He became identified in the public eye with the revival of the box-and-gravel parterre in the manner of Louis XIV; he assembled a scrapbook of parterre designs from period literature which he drew on in his commissions. In 1859 he was commissioned to design the ROYAL HORTICULTURAL SOCIETY's garden in Kensington, and issued a press statement on the merits of parterres composed entirely of patterns in coloured gravels, which he termed 'winter gardens'. The RHS garden was greeted with immense enthusiasm when it was opened in 1861, but a decade later his gravel parterres were falling from fashion, and by the time of his death his style was condemned. In his later years, including his alterations to the royal parks in the 1860s, he was assisted by his sons Markham (c.1842–1874), a gifted landscape designer who died young, and William Eden (1835–88), who became a pioneer of the Queen Anne revival in architecture.   BE

Nes Mansion and Ironworks ⊛

Tvedestrand, Aust-Agder, Norway, is a large private estate with an 18th-century main building and a romantic park of 2 hectares/5 acres from the early 1800s. The mansion is situated on the bank of a river which from 1665 to 1959 powered the large Nes ironworks which is today a museum. The open agricultural landscape west of the mansion has been transformed into a golf course. The romantic park named Lunden (The Grove) was laid out around a small artificial lake, created by altering the course of the river and fed by a stone-lined canal. The park was restored in the 1990s with serpentine gravel walks and shrubberies replanted with species rescued from the formerly overgrown park under the guidance of the Agder Nature Museum & Botanical Garden in Kristiansand, Vest-Agder. The lake was dredged and cleared of excessive water vegetation, the white tea house by the lakeside was repaired, and a cast-iron bridge reinstalled. Future restoration projects may include the ruined grotto and the former aviary on a small island in the lake. Restoration architects: SMS Landskap MNLA.   ME

AASE HØRSDAL, 'Den romantiske parken ved Nes Verk', *Lustgården* (2001).

Netherlands, the

With its north–south extent of about 300 km/ 180 miles and width of 200 km/120 miles the kingdom of the Netherlands is one of the smaller countries in Europe. Yet despite its limited size there is a great variety in landscapes. The hilliest part with the highest point of 321 m/1,053 ft—the Vaalserberg—lies in the very south. In the lower parts peat and moor districts once covered extensive areas, but they have virtually all been drained, as well as lakes, and land has also been reclaimed from the sea. The resulting polders provide a lowest point of almost 7 m/23 ft below sea level (in a polder north of Rotterdam). About half the country lies below sea level. With its total size of 41,526 sq. km/24,915 sq. miles and a population of just over 16.2 million the Netherlands is one of the most densely populated countries in the European Union, with 468 inhabitants per square kilometre. In slightly over one century the nation has moved from a predominantly agricultural (and horticultural) base to a nation of city dwellers, with 89% of the population now living in cities.

Climate

The Dutch climate is moderated by the proximity of the Gulf Stream which ensures cool winters and mild summers with an average annual temperature of about 16 °C/63 °F during the summer and 3 °C/37 °F during the winter near the coast. Inland average temperatures are slightly higher during the summer and slightly lower during the winter by 1 °C/28 °F. The lowest recorded temperature is –27.8 °C/–20 °F and the highest 38.6 °C/101 °F. The average numbers of days above 25 °C/77 °F varies from five on the islands to the north to 25 in the south of the country. Snow occurs regularly during the winter. Precipitation is spread fairly evenly throughout the year and throughout the country, with an average of about 780 mm/30 in.

Flora

Due to a diverse landscape the Dutch flora is reasonably varied with a total of 1,881 native plant species. With its position at the north-eastern edge of the continent, there is a remarkable range of plants that includes Central European species, as well as southern influences and relics of northern vegetation types. The Dutch flora is recorded in the 'Heukels', the most scientific of the floras which has traditionally been the responsibility of the Rijksherbarium in Leiden and since 1999 has been available on CD-ROM as *Heukels' Interactieve Flora van Nederland.*

A brief history of gardening

The earliest evidence of gardening activity is of Roman gardens in the south of the country, as for example town gardens in Venlo. There is however little information about the gardening activities during the Dark Ages that followed. In the medieval era monasteries had a considerable input in land reclamation, but while this can still be appreciated today, there is little surviving evidence of the gardens created during the medieval period, as much was lost during the Reformation. Traditionally monasteries have been associated with the cultivation of herbs for medicinal purposes, and evidence of this survives in a treatise such as the herbal by Prior Matthias Paulli of the Augustine monastery in Maastricht, *Een niev tractaet . . .* (1636). Most of the surviving monasteries and gardens are in the Catholic area south of the Rhine.

The oldest surviving evidence of courtly gardens is that of the counts of Holland at Het Binnenhof, The Hague. They created a large garden consisting of a series of enclosed spaces and a great fish pond (c.1350), which survives today. The gardens of the dukes of Gelder at ROSENDAEL incorporated a renowned MENAGERIE with exotic animals, but visual evidence of this is lacking. A more profound record is provided of 16th-century late Renaissance/mannerist gardens in the imaginary schemes of Jan Vredeman de VRIES that show compartmented gardens with hedged mazes and flower beds, which would have been particularly suited for plant collections of Dutch 'florists'. This style of gardens was superseded with the emergence of the Dutch Republic after liberation from the Spanish in the early 17th century. The aspirations of the new state became those of the ancient Roman republic, with Virgilian court poetry and Vitruvian and Albertian classical symmetry and balance in architecture and garden design, which has become known as Dutch classicism. Prince Frederik Hendrik's HONSELAARSDIJK was one of the earliest examples that positioned the palace within a large rectangular moated plot and displayed a formal tree-lined approach, and in 1625 was the first example with a grand central avenue in modern history. Honselaarsdijk retained its leading position in garden design by being one of the first to introduce the PARTERRE de broderie, designed 1633–5 by André MOLLET, who also designed those at Buren. With increasing wealth through trade the developing bourgeoisie laid out their country seats along canals, rivers, and in new polders, such as De Beemster. In design they followed the princely examples. The next development in garden design takes place after William III became stadtholder, when after the 1680s ornamentation increasingly followed French examples, exemplified by the work of the Huguenot Daniel MAROT, who was initially employed by William III in 1685–6 to decorate Paleis Het LOO.

The following period of the 18th century is sometimes referred to as the Dutch Régence, which can be seen as a gradual step towards a more informal style. Winding walks appear within the formal framework of gardens, and one of the first gardens that shows an asymmetrical plan within a geometric layout is that of Duin en Berg, Santpoort (*c.*1730). The remainder of the century saw a more general application of informal designs within a formal framework that are often referred to as the 'early English landscape style', but were in fact a typical Dutch (and German) interpretation of various foreign influences, from France, England, and Germany. Many estates contrasted French and English BOSQUETS, with the latter being an interpretation of the shrubbery-type wildernesses with graduated plantings, known from the translation of Philip Miller's *Gardeners Dictionary.* J. G. MICHAEL, originating from Germany, was one of the proponents of this style, and so was Philip Willem Schonck (1735–1823), who prepared designs for courtly gardens, such as Het Loo, Noordeinde, Oranjewoud, Soestdijk, and Dieren.

The principles of the landscape style, as stereotyped in the designs by Capability BROWN and Humphry REPTON, developed gradually with the designs of Michael and his son-in-law Johann David ZOCHER Sr., with Biljoen (Velp) being an early example. While Gijsbert van Laar's (1767–1829) *Magazijn van Tuin-sieraden* (1802–9) became the standard pattern book for ornamentation of picturesque gardens, the market for garden design during the 19th century was largely cornered by the ZOCHER FAMILY, particularly J. D. Zocher Jr. Examples of his work include TWICKEL, Delden, Groeneveld (Baarn), Slot ZEIST, and De Schaffelaer (Barneveld). Other landscape architects at the end of the 19th century who made a significant contribution to Dutch garden design include Hendrik COPIJN and Leonard SPRINGER, who continued largely in the landscape style, although he also adopted features of the mixed style, promoted by one of the most significant French designers of the time, Édouard ANDRÉ.

The early 20th century saw a number of tendencies, from nature-style gardens to ARTS AND CRAFTS style gardens, or mixtures thereof as in the work of J. P. Fokker (1889–1963). Gertrude JEKYLL's writings became the main source of inspiration in this, with the Arts and Crafts-style gardens being referred to in the Netherlands as the 'cottage style'. Other promoters of this style include Dirk Tersteeg (1876–1942) and John Bergmans (1892–1980). It can also be noted in the early work of Mien RUYS. Modernism and the Bauhaus became significant sources of influence in development from the 1930s onwards, with Cor van Eesteren being a central figure in developing the

modernist concept of the open city in Amsterdam, with the AMSTERDAM BOS being the largest city park developed in the 20th century. Landscape architects Jan BIJHOUWER, Mien Ruys, and Wim BOER were all part of the CIAM (the International Congress of Modern Architecture) and all explored new approaches, especially immediately after the Second World War. Many of the designs of this period incorporated ecological design principles that were popularized by Jac. P. THIJSSE, with one of the best-known parks of the time named after him at Amstelveen.

A small revolution took place in the person of Louis Le Roy from the late 1960s onwards. An artist and teacher, who called himself an 'ecotect', he reacted against the burgeoning consumer society, promoting recycling and art as part of a process of community participation. Ecological principles became the flavour of the 1970s and early 1980s, culminating in Project Stork (1987) and the Ecological Framework for the Netherlands (1990). The changing emphasis meant an end to the principles of the modern movement, and when landscape architecture and garden design re-emerged in the 1980s there were new names of practices which have determined the face of international landscape architecture since. The practice Bakker en Bleeker produced a significant output, but it is the West 8 practice (see GEUZE, ADRIAAN) that has featured worldwide through its avant-garde approaches. While this has worked well in public works, the general public has been more conservative, which can be seen in the continuing popularity of box-edged gardens which have been revived since the late 1970s.

Allotments or people's gardens
During the Middle Ages there was a tradition for renting out cabbage plots of land outside the city defences for the benefit of the poor. In 17th-century Rotterdam there were so-called *laanorganisaties*, or avenue organizations, which acquired land along the avenues leading from the city in order to rent out plots to individuals. As from 1818 the Maatschappij van Welddadigheid, a welfare society, commenced with allotting land in so-called colonies in the north-east of the country in order to combat poverty, letting plots with accommodation to the unemployed. After 1838 labourers' gardens were a feature in the north and were the actual forerunner of allotments. Occasional schemes with rented plots occurred elsewhere at the end of the 19th century, but in 1909 a Comité voor Volkstuinen (Committee for People's Gardens), in Amsterdam, was founded with as its aim the promotion of allotments, as they were considered an antidote to unemployment, alcoholism, and tuberculosis. The years 1917

and 1919 saw the foundation of the first unions of allotment holders. These allotments proved their use particularly during the world wars in providing much-needed food, but as from 1920 there was consent for building huts and growing ornamental plants, which changed the character substantially. This development was seen particularly in the urbanized west of the country, and in Groningen. In 2000 there were 2,308 allotment complexes covering a total of 4,000 hectares/9,880 acres; and in 1995 there were some 34,000 allotments with a hut which may be used as seasonal accommodation (see also ALLOTMENT; KLEINGÄRTEN).

Cemeteries
Following health concerns about the traditional style of burial inside churches, or in overfull cemeteries, the first new burial grounds were created outside towns in a series of model cemeteries, with one in Scheveningen, named Ter Navolging, to 'serve as a model'. In 1825 a royal decree prohibited burial within town centres and in churches as from 1829. This resulted in a wave of new cemeteries completed that year, all in landscape style with informal shrubberies; Jan David Zocher Jr. designed one in Soestbergen near Utrecht and one in Zutphen; Lucas Pieters ROODBAARD (1782–1851) designed the general cemetery in Leeuwarden. While in the Catholic south most cemeteries were laid out on a grid pattern, the landscape-style tradition continued elsewhere. The Westerveld cemetery (Driehuis; 1888), by Louis Paul Zocher, was laid out at the edge of the dunes, of which full use was made in the layout. In 1913 it incorporated the first crematorium in the Netherlands. In 1925 it was also the location of a remarkable columbarium by the architect W. M. Dudok (1884–1974). After the Second World War there was a considerable number of well-designed cemeteries, particularly in the newly made Noordoostpolder, with Mien Ruys designing one in Nagele. An influential example was the woodland cemetery designed by Wim BOER in Doorn (1954) that created burial rooms within an existing woodland structure. The creation of cemeteries outside, or at the edge of, towns was being questioned by designers in the late 1960s, which led to the idea of making cemeteries part of everyday life. This was most successfully done by the cemetery designed by Chris Zalm (b. 1943) at Almere Haven, a new town in 1975. The proposed position was immediately outside the town centre and the cemetery was designed as part of an open space network, in which it was fully integrated.

Public gardens
While there have been well-established traditions of opening private gardens to a select public, the proclamation of the Batavian

Republic in 1795 meant that former princely properties, such as Valkenberg, Breda, went into state ownership and were—for this short period—open to the general public. Other opportunities for outdoor recreation were provided by the Haarlemmer Hout (Haarlem, before 1349), Alkmaarder Hout (Alkmaar, 1607), Haagse Bos (The Hague, 1600), Maliebaan (Utrecht, 1636), and De Plantage (Amsterdam, 1682), while other towns had their 'star' wood, a wilderness plantation in a double cross pattern that provided opportunities for promenading. When it was shown in the early 19th century that city defences had become redundant there was a gradual move to convert these into city parks, commencing with Leeuwarden, Haarlem, and Utrecht in a tradition in which other towns followed, with late examples until the early 20th century. In the process the ramparts were laid out in the prevalent landscape style (designed by Lucas Pieters Roodbaard, J. D. Zocher Jr., Hendrik Copijn, and Leonard Springer), with the building of villas on the periphery to pay for the works.

While Rotterdam adapted a country seat to become its first public park, Maaspark (1857, J. D. Zocher Jr.), a number of citizens of Amsterdam raised funds for a walking and riding park that was realized as VONDELPARK (1867, J. D. Zocher Jr. with subsequent additions by L. P. Zocher). Additional municipal parks were proposed as part of the General Development Plan for Amsterdam (1867), but it was some time before these were established as Sarphatipark (1881) Westerpark (1886, both by J. G. van Niftrik (1833–1910)), and Oosterpark (1891, Leonard Springer). By this stage there was already a tradition of park design in other parts of the country, with people's parks being provided by rich industrialists and bankers, for example Volkspark (Enschede; 1872, Dirk Wattez), Volkspark (Rijssen; 1914, Springer), and Philips–de Jonghpark (Eindhoven; 1920, D. F. Tersteeg). These parks were all in the landscape style and were fairly prescriptive with respect to their usage. This altered gradually after c.1920, with the emphasis on multifunctional recreational use, with Zuiderpark (The Hague; 1908, H. P. Berlage; 1920, P. Westbroek) being one of the best-known examples. The next development was led by Cor van Eesteren with the General Development Plan for Amsterdam (1934), who for the first time used and developed normative green space allocation from Martin Wagner's *Städtische Freiflächenpolitik* (1915)—using the recreational needs of the population as a starting point, this established the requirement for local parks, neighbourhood parks, and also for a city park. This provided the rationale for an approach that made green space an integrated part of any new development, rather than a separate afterthought. It also provided the reasoning behind the establishment of such parks as AMSTERDAM BOS.

As a result of the Amsterdam approach to green space, which was mirrored with that in Rotterdam, the post-war emphasis on park design was on how to integrate parks seamlessly as part of the living environment. Wim Boer's competition entry for the Gijsbrecht van Aemstelpark (Amsterdam-Buitenveldert; 1959) is exemplary of this. A rational Mondrian-like plan linked new rectilinear neighbourhoods and provided a green heart that was to serve various neighbourhood and district uses. While one might argue that the greenness of such modernist examples represents some rural ideal, the latest development in park design takes its cues from the urban environment, which is most clearly expressed by the MUSEUMPARK, ROTTERDAM, inspired by motorway architecture. The work of the landscape practice West 8 has continued this trend, with designs such as Schouwburgplein (Rotterdam, 1990), and is leading it internationally. This seems far removed from the emphasis in the latest community parks, which is driven by a concern for the loss of nature; as a result they have been designed in a naturalistic manner.

Plant collections

From the 16th century there has been a tradition of plant collections in the Netherlands, and during the 17th century there were literary hundreds of private collections. Additionally there were university gardens in LEIDEN (founded 1587), Franeker (1589), Utrecht (1639), Groningen (1642), and Harderwijk (1649), and other educational gardens at Breda (1646), Amsterdam (1682), and Haarlem (1696), the last serving mainly for medicinal purposes. The tradition of educational gardens was revived with the resurgence in horticultural education at the end of the 19th century, with well-known gardens in Frederiksoord (1884, A. C. Ide (1857–1925)) and Wageningen (de Dreijen; 1896, Leonard Springer) and Belmonte (1953, Jan Bijhouwer); and the Hortus Botanicus Vrije Universiteit Amsterdam (1967, C. P. Broerse (1902–95)). Private collectors have continued to play an active role; the most important arboreta in the Netherlands were initiated by industrialists and shipping merchants, including Poortbulten (De Lutte; 1912, Leonard Springer), Von Gimborn Arboretum (Doorn; 1924, Gerard Bleeker (1882–1956)), Pinetum Blijdenstein (1929, H. Copijn and son), and TROMPENBURG ARBORETUM (Rotterdam; by its owners; 1920s, Griettie Smith-van Stolk and later her son James van Hoey Smith).

Other important plant collections include herbs at Kruidhof (Buitenpost, 1930) and the herb garden in the open-air museum in Arnhem (1927). The most important collection of historic bulbs is HORTUS BULBORUM (Limmen, 1928), while one of the latest fruit collections is Fruithof (Frederiksoord, 1998). An important contribution is formed by the decentralized national plant collections, whereby individuals take responsibility for a particular genus.

Ecological gardens/heem gardens

The earliest nature-like gardens in the Netherlands were commenced as a response against artificiality in garden design at the end of the 19th century. By the early 20th century there were attempts to recreate plantings of specific geographic settings in order to achieve a more naturalistic appearance. At the same time Jac. P. Thijsse promoted educational (or 'instructive') gardens that were to contain the plants of the locality in order to create awareness for conservation. One of the first of these gardens was THIJSSE HOF (Bloemendaal, 1925), and other such gardens were to follow elsewhere, including Heimanshof (Vierhouten, 1935) and Zuiderpark (The Hague, 1933–5). The best-known examples were the so-called HEEMPARKS where plantings are inspired by native plant communities, first conceived in Amstelveen, with the Jac. P. Thijssepark (1939) being the most famous example. Louis Le Roy challenged gardens laid out by specialists and from the 1960s advocated community projects in order to achieve his wild gardens. Since then naturalistic gardens have become the focus of community-led projects, and have since 1991 been promoted by the Oase Foundation, which publishes an attractive guide to more than 100 of them.

Nurseries and horticulture

From the late Middle Ages horticulture has played a significant role in the west of the Netherlands, where rapid urbanization was encouraged by trade. The towns and cities ensured a continuous demand for agricultural produce. As land was not managed by large landowners as in other countries, but instead was occupied by small-scale family-run units, this led to a greater intensity of cultivation and variety that was also able to respond quickly to developing market forces. Thus growing garden plants was one way of diversifying and achieving higher profits. By the second half of the 16th century the many branches of horticulture flourished and the Netherlands became a main producer with more trees, shrubs, and plants grown in the Netherlands than in Germany, England, France, and Spain. It also became the main exporter of avenue and fruit trees and bulbs.

The fashion for plant collecting in country houses, and the many plants introduced to the Netherlands from warmer climates, led to the development of heated greenhouses (now generally referred to as orangeries), stoves, and hothouses. The advances made in horticulture were eagerly adapted by the trade, and there was a rich culture in floristry, bulbs, and cultivation of exotic plants that had an international reputation. Dutch manuals on plant cultivation were translated into other languages, so for example Jan Commelin, *Nederlantze Hesperides* (1676), and Henri van Oosten, *De nieuwe Nederlandsche bloemhof, ofte sorghvuldige hovenier* (1700), were translated into English and Jan van der Groen, *Den Nederlandtsen Hovenier* (1669), and Pieter de la Court van der Voort, *Byzondere aenmerkingen over het aenleggen van pragtige en gemeene landhuizen, lusthoven, plantagien en aenklevende cieraeden . . .* (1737), were translated into both French and German. Dutch gardeners could be found in important gardens in other countries during the 17th and 18th centuries.

Horticulture lost its leading position during the French period (1795–1815). Yet despite some improvement over the following years, by the time of the 1865 International Congress of Botany and Horticulture, held in Amsterdam, Dutch horticulture was found to be lagging behind its European counterparts. One of the main reasons for this was the lack of provision for horticultural education, which, once addressed, saw remarkable improvement. Also, from the early 20th century a framework for the development of the industry was put in place that included national and regional organizations for quality control, cooperatives in order to buy and sell more cheaply, and with an emphasis on export. It also included the setting up of an efficient large-scale network of supply and processing. This vision was moreover shared between the government and the trade, and the process was assisted by education, research, and publicity.

By 1950 17% of employment in the Netherlands was in agriculture and horticulture, assuring 14.4% of the national income. While this had diminished by 1996 to 4% of employment and 3% of national income, the Netherlands is today the third largest exporter of agricultural produce, and horticulture is by far the most important agricultural sector. It remains the largest producer and exporter of ornamental plants, the amount of trade representing 70% of the total of EU trade in ornamental plants, while for bulbs this is 90%. Today there are some 4,000 nurseries growing over 20,000 different species and varieties on a total area of some 12,500 hectares/30,875 acres. A characteristic feature of the Dutch nursery trade is the various centres, with Boskoop, specializing largely in ornamental shrubs and conifers, being the best known. Zundert is the centre for forestry plants and hedge material, whereas Lottum is well known for roses and rose stocks. There are three centres for standard trees: Haaren, Oudenbosch, and Opheusden. Fruit trees are largely cultivated in the provinces of Flevoland, Limburg, Noord Brabant, and Zeeland. Bulbs are grown along the coast between Haarlem and The Hague.

Plant collecting

The continuous demand for new plants by private collectors led to a remarkable record of plant introduction that in turn generated skills and facilities on which the nursery trade was eventually founded. A herbal such as that by Rembert DODOENS, *Crüÿdeboeck* (1554), indicates the range of exotic herbs available at the time. This was hugely extended afterwards with the advancement of trade and particularly with the establishment of the Dutch East India Company (1602) and the Dutch West India Company (1621). These companies were granted a monopoly to trade with the various corners of the world and ensured a continuous flow of exotic plants coming into the country. The enticement of discovery also drew foreign botanists to the Netherlands, and to work for the companies. Carolus CLUSIUS, who arrived at the recently established Hortus in Leiden in 1592, brought with him horse chestnut, plane, cherry laurel, potato, and the tulip which he had been given by Ambassador Busbeq in Vienna. He later hugely extended the collections with the aid of the Dutch East India Company, but became famous for developing new varieties of tulip that led to a craze in cultivation with inflated prices that reached its pinnacle in 1637 when the market collapsed (see TULIPS).

The introductions from the East and West Indies meant plants arriving from North America whilst there was a Dutch colony there, and from South America where from 1630 the Dutch administered the colonies from Mauritsstad (now Recife), Brazil, and where from 1640 Johan Maurits van NASSAU-SIEGEN was in charge. He was actively involved in collecting plants that made their way to the Netherlands. The East India Company with their headquarters in Batavia, Java (now Jakarta, Indonesia), provided not only plants from that region, but also from Japan, where Protestant Dutch merchants only could trade from Deshima, an artificial island off the coast of Nagasaki. En route back from the Far East to the Netherlands a trade post was established at the Cape of Good Hope in 1652, with Jan van Riebeek as first commander of this Dutch colony till 1662. Various individuals have been credited with the new plant introductions; those who ordered the collecting, or who first planted them up, or who described them. Riebeek has been credited with a range of Cape plants, including: agapanthus, *Erica* species, gladiolus, helichrysum, mesembryanthemum, oxalis, pelargonium, silene, and zantedeschia. Back in the Netherlands there were a whole host of collectors, with the Leiden botanist Paul Hermann (1646–1695) taking a central position, as well as the Amsterdam-based Jan (1629–92) and Caspar Commelin (1667–1731), the latter being credited with the introduction of the sweet pea (*Lathyrus odoratus*). Engelbert KAEMPFER, a German physician with the Dutch East India Company, is credited with introducing *Ginkgo biloba*. During the early 18th century one of the main private collections was that of George Clifford (1685–1760), mayor of Amsterdam and director of the Dutch East India Company. At his garden De Hartekamp he employed Linnaeus, who developed his ideas about plant species here in his *Hortus Cliffortianus* (1737/8), and described a range of new plants including the banana (*Musa* × *paradisiaca*). The Swedish physician Carl Peter THUNBERG (1743–1828) named more than 250 new plant and animal species whilst employed by the Dutch East India Company. Important introduction of Japanese plants followed, due to the physician Philipp Franz von SIEBOLD (1796–1866), who afterwards settled near Leiden. Here he extended his range with Chinese and Korean species which were initially cultivated by Rodbard & Co., and then Siebold & Co. The total range of 367 new introductions included many now popular garden plants, including: epimedium, *Dicentra spectabilis*, various *Hosta* species, *Hemerocallis* species, *Iris kaempfer*, and *Primula japonica*. One of the main results of the exotic introductions since the 17th century was the development of greenhouses (orangeries) and hot stoves, in the technology of which the Netherlands continues to lead. The many introductions of temperate plants found their way into so-called English woods, which were a feature of the larger late 18th-century gardens, inspired by translations of Philip Miller's *Gardeners Dictionary*.

Besides the range of exotic species, the Dutch nursery trade has been renowned for its horticultural improvement and creation of new cultivars. Of late they have been the main promoters of the Plant Variety Rights Act in order to protect what is in most cases many years of investment in creating better varieties. These cover the full range of garden plants. As from the 19th century the occurrence of bigger plants and better colours has provided an interesting dilemma for garden designers. Whereas 'good taste' dictated that informal landscape-style gardens remained the norm, the continuous flow of improved varieties meant that they were crammed into gardens, having to be maintained with judicious pruning, providing gardens with an artificial appearance. This treatment generated a response in the late 19th century, such as by Geertruida Carelsen (Pseudonym of A. G. de Leeuw, 1843–1938), the granddaughter of J. D. Zocher, and last of a well-known family of garden designers. She called for respect for plant material in garden art (*Eerbied voor het levend materiaal in de tuinkunst*, 1902), for use of less artificial plants in a more naturalistic manner. While this has remained an undercurrent during the 20th century with native plant gardens taking an important position in garden design, the majority of gardeners are of course only too happy to try the newest and latest varieties.

Garden conservation

The main interest in garden conservation in the Netherlands has been from museum curators looking to interpret the past, while alluding to the Golden Age, with the other main group being nobility looking to affirm their historical lineage. One of the early re-creation projects was that of the Museum Het Broekerhuis, Amsterdam (1881), where Leonard Springer provided a new layout in the 'Old Dutch' style, in contrast to the then predominantly landscape style of the time. The museum was built to house a collection of 17th-century Dutch art and was similarly in a period style. Édouard André was asked to design gardens at Kasteel Weldam and Kasteel Twickel in 1885 and 1886 respectively, which were both historicizing layouts carried out for him by Hugo POORTMAN (1858–1953). The latter also altered the gardens at Middachten in 1901 as a free interpretation of their 17th-century appearance. A more remarkable example was Kasteel Sypesteyn (Loosdrecht), which was restored in 1902–7 by C. H. C. A. van Sypesteyn (1857–1937) as a monument and museum to his family. Despite his interest in garden history—he wrote one of the earliest historical reviews of Dutch garden design—the garden did not set out to provide an accurate representation of the 17th-century original.

Other examples of restored and recreated gardens include: MENKEMABORG, Uithuizen (1921), HOFWIJCK (1928), vernacular gardens at the Nederlandse Openluchtmuseum (Open-Air Museum) near Arnhem, the Clusius Garden, HORTUS BOTANICUS (1932), Prinsenhof (Groningen, 1938), Museum Willet-Holthuysen (Amsterdam, 1972), and gardens at the Zuiderzeemuseum (Enkhuizen, 1983). The majority of the conservation projects were free interpretations of the past, rather than an accurate record of it, which changed with the restoration of Paleis Het Loo, when this was being turned from a royal residence into a state museum in 1984, under the supervision of Jan van Asbeck. This set new standards with respect to research and reconstruction work.

As from the early 1980s the state has, through its Ministry of Agriculture, been responsible for grant aiding restoration work in gardens, initially via a scheme assisting specific projects combating neglect, with dredging expanses of water, rebuilding walls, and restoring pavements. After 1993 this was supplemented with a separate scheme specifically directed towards aiding repair work of architectural features and garden ornaments by Rijksdienst voor de Monumentenzorg, the state's monument advisory service. This scheme pre-empted the listing of private country estates of national importance dating from before 1850, which was completed in 1999 with 434 country estates being included under the Monument Act. As a result of the restricted official remit, a private organization, Nederlandse Tuinenstichting (the Dutch Gardens Foundation), was created to support gardens created after 1850. A private foundation, it was founded in 1980 and is dependent on donations from over 5,000 members. It carries out an active conservation role by initiating surveys of parks and gardens, and recommending to the state those that are suitable for conservation as monuments. It also provides advice to managers, owners, and the state on repair and restoration plans. Additionally it engages large numbers of people in the process by organizing an annual 'gardens open today' scheme amongst its membership.

There have been some enlightened public–private partnerships that have analysed and provided a solution to one of the most pressing problems confronting private estate owners, that of maintenance. The Stichting tot Behoud van Particuliere Historische Buitenplaatsen (Foundation for the Conservation of Private Historic Estates) was established in 1973 by a small group of private owners of country estates as a joint venture with the Ministry of Culture, Recreation, and Social Work. The organization serves as an intermediary between the two parties and aims to encourage the conservation of privately owned country estates. It has encouraged the government to create a climate in which conditions for conservation are created, with tax allowances, grants for the restoration and maintenance of buildings, but also support in the maintenance of parks and gardens. This has been available to estates of historic value since 1982. Under this scheme the government bears the costs of producing a comprehensive historic study and a ten-year management plan. Once the management goals have been established the owners can make bids to a central pool of qualified gardeners employed by the foundation, who will carry out conservation-guided maintenance work for a nominal charge. This innovative solution has inspired others, both in the Netherlands and abroad, to find similar partnerships.

Documentation of garden history

The main collection of landscape and garden design in the Netherlands and of landscape architects is the collection TUiN, held in the Department of Special Collections of Wageningen University and Research Library. It commenced with the collection of Leonard Springer, and now includes the material of some 26 further landscape architects. This material is in the process of being accessed and catalogues are being made available online as they are completed (**http://library.wur.nl/speccol/tuin.html**). The TUiN collection also includes a database with descriptions of gardens which originate from the four-volume *Gids voor de Nederlandse tuin- en landschapsarchitectuur* (1995–2000) by Carla Oldenburger, Anne Mieke Backer, and Erik Blok. Additionally there is an exquisite library with an international collection of historic gardening treatises, a collection of nursery catalogues from 1830 onwards, as well as a collection of historic maps and aerial photographs.

Garden Societies

The largest horticultural society in the Netherlands with 72,000 members is the Koninklijke Maatschappij voor Tuinbouw en Plantkunde, founded as the Nederlandse Maatschappij voor Tuinbouw en Plantkunde in 1872. Its forerunner, the Koninklijke Nederlandse Maatschappij tot Aanmoediging van de Tuinbouw, was founded in 1842, and was mainly concerned with organizing horticultural exhibitions, like its successor. This changed by the end of the 19th century, when it became primarily a professional organization engaged in the debate surrounding horticultural education and in vocational guidance. In 1908 it was one of the initiators of Nederlandse Tuinbouwraad, which represents the horticultural trade in government. After 1960 it shifted from a professional organization to one primarily dealing with amateur gardening. It publishes *Groei en bloei*, which is the main horticultural magazine in the Netherlands.

Garden shows

There has been a long tradition of horticultural shows in the Netherlands, but these were primarily held in temporary venues. While these continue in various locations throughout the country, since the Second World War more have found homes in permanent sites. Thus since 1949 the bulb trade provides an annual exhibition at the KEUKENHOF that uses a well-established 19th-century landscape park as its setting. Once every ten years the Nederlandse Tuinbouwraad organizes Floriade, an international exhibition that promotes horticultural achievement in association with innovative ideas in landscape architecture. The first Floriade was held in 1960 in Rotterdam; Amsterdam followed in 1972 and 1982; in 1992 it was held in Zoetermeer, and in 2002 in Haarlemmermeer. In each of these cases a park was created, which has been left as a public amenity. These garden shows, as well as the indoor flower festivals and the so-called 'corsos' of flower- and fruit-ornamented wagons, have kept horticulture in a prominent position, both nationally and internationally. The nursery trade has been successful in promoting itself, particularly through insistence on quality, continuing research, and from the public's point of view through its efficient marketing by effective sales techniques, making pioneering use of the Internet, with a supply and demand registration system during the early 1980s to a provision that covers a wide range of needs, from **groeninfo.com** to **plantscope**, which provides free use of digital images of plants, as well as free advice through Plant Publicity Holland (**http://pph.wis-interaxion.nl/Page/ml2/sp328/index.html**). This has not necessarily been the case with garden design and making, which has tended to become a commercial venture appealing to popular taste, such as Tuinen van Appeltern, the largest of a series of 'garden ideas parks'. Yet the popularity of gardens and gardening can be measured in the increased demand for produce and products, as well as the media, the television programmes, and the many available publications. There is a generous provision of periodicals catering for the ordinary public through to the connoisseur, ranging from *Bloemen en planten*, *Groei en bloei*, *Onze eigen tuin*, to *De tuin exclusief*. Professional journals include *Tuin en landschap* intended for landscape contractors and gardeners, *Groen* for landscape management, and *Blauwe kamer* for urban design and landscape.

Horticultural education

After the 1865 International Congress of Botany and Horticulture in Amsterdam showed that Dutch horticulture was trailing behind Germany, France, and Belgium, the main reason identified for this was the lack of education in which future generations of horticulturalists might learn theory and practice and the latest techniques. This stimulated the establishment of such courses, initially mainly due to private initiatives; one of the best-known courses at the time was the Tuinbouwschool Linnaeus at Frankendael, Amsterdam (1867), while a trade school commenced in Boskoop in the same year. The other well-known and longest surviving school was the Gerard Adriaan van Swieten Tuinbouwschool, Frederiksoord (1884), with an emphasis on practical training. Other courses included those in Maastricht and Sempercrescens in Naarden (1890s). A garden design course started in Rotterdam (1892), which was afterwards transferred to the Academy of Arts. The debate on horticultural education remained an important issue and by 1896 the state confirmed its interest by establishing a Rijkstuinbouwschool or state horticultural college in Wageningen, and various Tuinbouwwinterscholen intended to provide theoretical knowledge during the winter; others were established at Aalsmeer (1899), Naaldwijk (1897), and in Boskoop (1898).

More than 80,000 students are currently following agricultural courses in the Netherlands. This includes *c*.30,000 students following vocational education from the age of 13; 25,000 students following vocational education after secondary school (equivalent to British GCSE levels), 8,000 students who study the topic after their equivalent of A levels, and 4,000 students at Wageningen University and Research Centre. A characteristic of the Dutch educational system in horticulture remains its close links with practice, which is directed by a board in which the government is represented together with employers and employees from the various agricultural sectors. While this system has served the profitable aspects of agriculture well, this is may be less true for amenity horticulture where the 1990s saw the restructuring of educational establishments into a smaller number, closing many well-known schools, such as Boskoop, Utrecht, Frederiksoord, and Huis te Lande, and incorporating them either in regional agricultural education centres or a national specialized centre. Higher education for landscape design and management is now at Hogeschool Larenstein, shortly to become a university. Besides formal schooling there is a range of opportunities for evening and day release courses, which may be taken by working professionals. There is a separate landscape architecture course at the faculty of architecture at Delft University of Technology.

A special mention is reserved for the Academie voor de Bouwkunst in Amsterdam where practising professionals in architecture, landscape architecture, and planning can follow a joint course, which is likely to be one of the important reasons for recent advances in the progressive nature of contemporary Dutch landscape design. Recent additions to the field of education are a Clusius chair in garden history at Leiden (2003) and a course on management of historic parks and gardens at Hogeschool Utrecht (2004).   JW

Neuer Garten ⊗

Brandenburg, Potsdam, Germany, is a 122-hectare/301-acre park which encloses the Heiliger See on three sides and extends northwards to the banks of the river Havel (at the Jungfernsee). After his accession in 1786 Friedrich Wilhelm II bought up a large number of small gardens and vineyards to provide land for his park, whose plans were executed by J. August EYSERBECK. Considerable alterations were made in the first half of the 19th century by LENNÉ. In the middle of the western shore of the lake stands the Marmorpalais (1787–92, by Gontard and Langhans). An avenue of pyramid oaks leads straight to the park entrance, which is framed by gatehouses in the Dutch style but with slightly curved roofs in the Chinese manner. Along the length of the avenue is the Holländisches Etablissement (1789–90), a number of gabled houses intended to suggest a Dutch village.

Between the avenue and the southern shore of the lake are winding ALLÉES and small groups of trees, with a neo-Gothic library (1793–4) on the shore, which corresponded to a Moorish temple (demolished 1869) on the northern shore. Directly next to the Schloss on the shore is a kitchen, in the form of a sunken temple (1789), and an obelisk (1793–4). Facing the avenue is the decorative façade of the Orangery (1791–2) with antique motifs depicting the sphinx and Egyptian gods. A flower garden (1879–80) lies in front of the plant hall. On the garden side of the Marmorpalais is a formal flower parterre (1846, by Lenné). A narrow park extends to the north with many diagonal vistas. A commemorative urn stands in a dense plantation of trees; in the meadows are a pyramid (1791–2) and a Chinese parasol. In the northern part of the park are appreciably larger garden rooms and a hermitage with urns and a grotto. Schloss Cecilienhof was built in this part of the park in 1913–17. Thirteen hectares/32 acres of the park edging the river Havel were occupied and destroyed 1961–90 by the Berlin Wall. They are now restored.

Adjoining the Neuer Garten is the Pfingstberg on which stand the Temple of

Pomona (1800, by SCHINKEL) and a copy of the picturesque Belvedere Torso, and which offers long views of town and landscape. The plans by Persius, Stüler, and Hesse from sketches by Friedrich Wilhelm IV were only partially executed in 1849–52. Lenné designed the surrounding park, connecting it with the Neuer Garten. HGÜ/MS

Neuhardenberg ⊛

Brandenburg, Potsdam, Germany. The landscape park of Neuhardenberg, on the banks of the river Oder, is one of the most beautiful designed landscapes in Brandenburg. The park opens into the landscape to the south of the castle. In the beginning of the 18th century Count Albrecht-Friedrich of Brandenburg/Sonnenburg created a formal garden with a castle and moat. The pleasure grounds contained an ORANGERY and were bordered with water (as shown in a map of 1722). The remains of an tree-lined avenue are still recognizable to the present day. In 1763 Obrist-Leutnant Joachim Bernhard of Prittwitz senior settled at Quilitz (which is the former name of Neuhardenberg). The basic design can be traced back to these times and follow his artistic ambitions to create a landscape park. This layout was fundamentally extended and refined by his son Friedrich Wilhelm of Prittwitz. The most significant redesign of the landscape park was between 1818 and 1822 in the time of the Prussian State Chancellor, Karl-August von Hardenberg. It is at this time that Quilitz was renamed as Neuhardenberg. The young and ambitious architect Karl Friedrich SCHINKEL was commissioned in collaboration with the landscape architect Peter Joseph LENNÉ (as shown in a map of 1822) to redesign the entire estate (castle and grounds) as a prominent modern example of local cultural landscapes. Lenné united the architectural arrangement of Schinkel with a landscape of picturesque spatial sequences and clumps of trees, sweeping meadows and watercourses, interwoven with the framing backdrop of forests, agricultural farmland, and forest-like groves. In multiple use the park remained neglected up to the turn of the 1990s. Since 2001 the original views along the axes between the castle and church, Friedrich memorial and park, can be experienced once again. The newly designed courtyards and gardens within areas of fully renovated buildings are united with the revitalized landscape park in a garden-artistic ensemble, as if it had always been that way. A country refuge in Brandenburg with cultural charm reawakens to a new life. AS

Neuwerkgarten ⊛

Schleswig, Schleswig-Holstein, Germany, was the third, largest (12 hectares/30 acres), and most ambitious garden of Castle Gottorf, the main residence of the dukes of Schleswig-Holstein-Gottorf (1544–1713). The castle stands on an island at the centre of a lake. In 1637 Duke Friedrich created a terraced garden in the Italian manner on the south-facing slopes of the Schlei, a fjord of the Baltic ocean. Under the direction of the botanist and gardener Johannes Clodius (1584–1660) a water staircase was built on the castle's axis. West of it lies a great pool with a monumental sculpture of Hercules slaying the Lernean hydra and, to the south, a semicircular walled flower garden. The Friedrichsburg, a pavilion overlooking the garden, accommodated the famous Gottorfer Globus, an astronomical globe in which twelve persons could observe a painting of the starry sky. In the time of Christian Albrecht (1641–94) six further terraces were added linked by water stairs. At the highest level in the 17th century was an orangery which contained a wide range of exotic plants. All the plants that once grew in the gardens were described in a codex, containing 1,180 botanical illustrations of plants (see Helga de Cuveland, *Der Gottorfer Codex von Hans Simon Holtzbecker*, 1989). At the end of the Great Northern War (1713) the duchy of Schleswig was incorporated in the Danish kingdom. The ally of Denmark, Tsar Peter the Great, received the famous Gottorfer Globus as a spoil of war and with its removal began the garden's decline. Today Castle Gottorf is the seat of the State Museum of Schleswig-Holstein. MMM

Newby Hall ⊛

near Ripon, North Yorkshire, England, was built in the 1690s and added to by Robert ADAM in 1767. Celia Fiennes visited Newby in 1697 and described the garden in detail, and it was illustrated by KIP in *Britannia Illustrata* (1707). The garden then had a PATTE D'OIE of avenues leading to an entrance forecourt with topiary. On each side of the house formal groves of trees surround rectilinear arrangements of beds or lawns. The latter are described by Celia Fiennes: 'fine gravel walks between grass plots 4 Square with 5 brass Statues great and small in each Square, and full of borders of flowers.' The Brompton Nursery supplied plants to Newby 1690–2 and the head gardener, Peter Aram, had worked with George LONDON who designed the garden at Newby. Of this garden only something of the pattern, and a few lime trees from the avenues, survive. South of the house today, where the 'grass plots' were, is the strong axis of a broad grass walk descending a gentle slope to the banks of the river Ure. These deep borders, chiefly of herbaceous perennials, are backed by yew hedges. A cross-axis, just below the house, is a walk edged with Irish yews and Venetian statues. This was reputedly designed by the architect William Burges (1827–81) who designed a church (consecrated in 1876) in the grounds at Newby. Paths lead off on either side to formal enclosures filled with flowers, and excellent trees and shrubs rise up behind the formal plantings. The National Collection of dogwoods (*Cornus* spp.) is held here and everywhere are excellent, sometimes surprisingly tender, plants. This is a tribute to the skills of the Compton family who own it. PT ⊃ page 334

New Delhi ⊛

India. At the Delhi Durbar of 1911 it was announced that the seat of government of British India was to be transferred from Calcutta to Delhi. Edwin LUTYENS and Herbert Baker (1862–1946) designed the complex of buildings, now known as New Delhi, in a style that incorporated both Western and Indian features. The Rajpath—the 3-km/1.8-mile ceremonial approach flanked by reflecting canals and lines of ashoka trees—and the garden to the west of the viceroy's house, laid out in 1917, were inspired by the geometry of the traditional Mughal garden. Spectacular fountains fashioned in overlapping tiers of sandstone discs, gazebos, pergolas, flights of steps, and topiaried trees combine to give a sculptural quality to a garden that is dominated by water. The garden, which is raised above the level of the surrounding plains, is contained within two massive retaining walls on each of which stretches a long narrow terrace. In the planting of the garden, which was largely carried out during 1928–9, Lutyens was assisted by William Robert Mustoe (1878–1942), formerly a Kew gardener who came to India in 1905 to become superintendent of the Lawrence Gardens in Lahore. The geometry of the Mughal garden was softened with English flower borders and lawns. RD

Newton, Peter, Garden ⊛

St Helens, California, USA, a 2-hectare/5-acre series of eleven gardens cascading down a mountain in the Napa valley. Its English designer, Peter Newton, feels that an English garden in California provides the best of both worlds, and has carefully selected plants that flourish and retain their appeal in this sun-soaked climate. Vineyards are all around. Garden making on a mountain requires bold, imaginative terracing to create usable space. Here, the separation of terraces provides opportunity for contrast between succeeding garden enclosures. A simple entry leads to a parterre lined with weeping trees. There is a formal rose garden limited to those with white and yellow flowers, a strikingly unusual water garden, a croquet lawn and herbaceous border, a quartet of rose arbours, a wild garden with spectacular viewpoint, and more. The approach to the garden is lined for 300 yards with trimmed standards of *Wisteria sinensis* 'Cook's Purple', preparing the visitor for the generosity and originality of the planting to follow. Nearer the house the driveway branches and is lined with a handsome variant of golden desert ash (*Fraxinus excelsior* 'Aurea'); a large bank of the vigorous, white-flowered rose 'Gourmet Popcorn' marks the terminus. Immediately in front of the house the English manner is set aside, and a large Zen courtyard is laid out with an expanse of raked granite chips, carefully placed rocks, and well-chosen *Acer palmatum*. This is the work of Su Hua Newton, Peter's wife, who believes that the temple garden concepts of her native land accord with the Chinese house, which she also designed.   WGW

Newydd, Plas ⊛

Llanfairpwll, Anglesey, Wales, built by James Wyatt (1746–1813), on the basis of an older house, for the 1st Earl of Uxbridge in around 1795. The setting, overlooking the Menai Straits with grand views of Snowdonia, is magnificent. In 1798 Humphry REPTON was consulted—he planned a new drive and recommended much tree planting, in particular to shield the house from the road. To his layout of lawns and trees has been added much planting of shrubs, in particular rhododendrons, seen to particular advantage in the part of the garden called West Indies, to the south of the house. In the 1930s a garden of quite different character was made to the north of the house overlooking the water. Here a pavilion overlooks enclosed terraces with skilful planting, some of it in the brilliant colours so fashionable in the late 20th century. The estate was given to the NATIONAL TRUST in 1976.   PT

New York Botanical Garden ⊛

The Bronx, New York, USA, established in the late 19th century, is set on a beautifully preserved 101-hectare/250-acre parcel of land in the middle of urban New York. A National Historic Landmark, the garden is distinguished by its diverse and comprehensive array of plant collections and display gardens, as well as its international renown as an important scientific research centre and teaching institution.

America's pre-eminent Victorian glasshouse (1902), the Enid A. Haupt Conservatory, offers an ecotour of the world, including lowland and upland rainforests, deserts of the Americas and Africa, carnivorous plants, aquatic plants, subtropicals, and temperate and tropical pools. Two galleries within the glasshouse are devoted to seasonal exhibitions for the public. The 15-hectare/37-acre Conifer Arboretum, planted in the early 20th century, has magnificent specimens of pines, firs, and spruces from around the world. Major collections of oaks, maples, legumes, magnolias, cherries, and crab apples are among the mature trees that grace the property. The garden also boasts an extraordinary 20-hectare/50-acre tract of the original, uncut forest of beech, tulip tree, and oak that once covered New York City.

Forty-eight gardens and collections celebrate good design with a large variety of specimen plants. The 1-hectare/2.5-acre rock garden is well known for its colourful display of thousands of alpine plants. The Jane Watson Irwin Perennial Garden is a handsome example of mixed borders including herbaceous plants, ornamental grasses, and shrubs, many with plumes of red foliage. The Ornamental Conifer Collection, first planted in the 1930s and newly redesigned, contains the cultivated forms of

---

Johannes Kip's engraving of **Newby Hall** in *Britannia Illustrata* (1707).

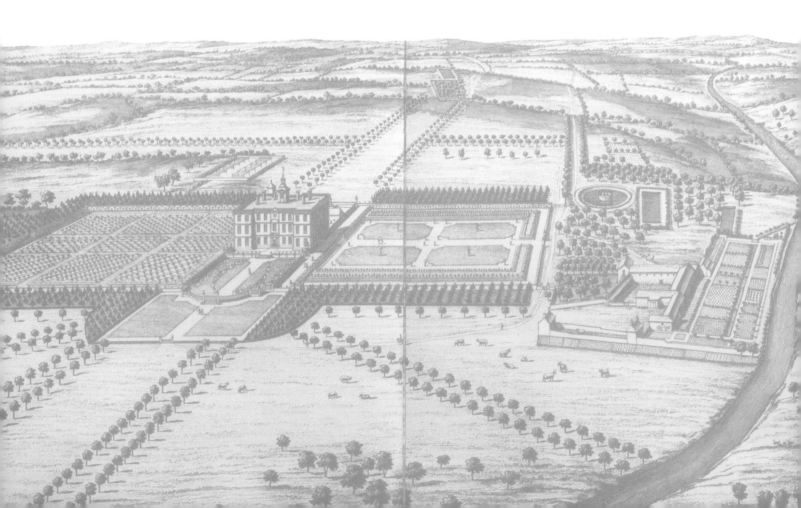

a number of rare evergreens. Other features include an enclosed garden of herbs, redesigned by Penelope HOBHOUSE, the Peggy Rockefeller Rose Garden, a native plant garden, and collections of peonies, iris, day lilies, daffodils, and chrysanthemums.

The garden's extensive science programmes and collections document and preserve plant biodiversity. A new facility, the Pfizer Plant Laboratories, to be completed in 2005, will expand the latest technology capabilities for studies on molecular systematics and plant genomics. The International Plant Science Center, opened in 2002, includes the largest HERBARIUM in the western hemisphere with nearly 7 million plant specimens. The LuEsther T. Mertz Library, considered one of the world's great plant science libraries, holds ongoing exhibitions of botanical prints and rare horticultural books for the public.

The garden's education programmes embrace all ages. A pace-setting programme for Ph.D. candidates helps address the shortage of scientists handling the need for more biodiversity data. More than 800 classes are offered yearly to adults who participate in the Continuing Education programme in gardening and plant studies. Children from toddlers to teenagers are offered classes and activities in the Everett Children's Adventure Garden.   PD

New York City parks and gardens.

New York's first public spaces reflected the functional needs of a 17th-century colonial outpost. In 1625, Dutch merchants established Fort Amsterdam at the foot of what became Broadway with an open market and parade ground in front of the main gate. Part of this space later became Bowling Green, often hailed as the city's first park. On the seaward side, the Battery assured a field of fire into the harbour for the settlement's cannon. A common (now City Hall Park) lay at the colony's northern limits. British conquest caused New Amsterdam to be rechristened New York in 1664. By the 1730s, the former trading outpost had grown into an important commercial centre with a population approaching 10,000. A Common Council of elected aldermen, which had jurisdiction over all common and unallocated land on Manhattan Island, began taking control of public spaces. Fenced and planted with trees and grass, Bowling Green began to resemble a contemporary London square. Because the Battery had become a popular waterfront promenade, a law prohibited building on the site. However, the aldermen directed construction of an almshouse on the site of City Hall Park, the first of numerous public buildings that

would eventually cover much of the old common.

Despite rapid expansion in the following decades, government did little to secure public open spaces. The council acquired land for a potter's field (later Washington Square) in the 1790s, but in general, ad hoc plans for street openings and drainage improvements determined the outlines of urban growth. The Commissioners' Plan of 1811 reserved 190 hectares/470 acres of open space, mainly for utilitarian purposes—parade grounds, markets, and small residential squares. But as the city grew, these areas were further reduced. Union Place had extended from 10th to 17th Streets where Broadway met the Bowery, but it became the much smaller Union Square when improved and opened in 1832. The original 22.25-hectare/55-acre 'market' between First Avenue and the East river became 4-hectare/10-acre Tompkins Square in 1833. When Madison Square opened in 1847 at 23rd Street, it covered only 2.5 hectares/6 acres of a 44-square block 'parade' that had been proposed between 23rd and 34th Streets.

By the mid 19th century, when the city's population had surpassed 500,000, development reached north to 42nd Street. While a number of small parks and residential squares had been set aside, including Stuyvesant Square and the private Gramercy Park, none was larger than 4 hectares/10 acres, and in total amounted to only 25.5 hectares/63 acres. For New Yorkers who saw their city as the London of North America, the example of London's royal parks was compelling. By the 1840s, a number of influential citizens advocated the creation of a large park in northern Manhattan. William Cullen Bryant (1794–1878), the lawyer and poet, and landscape gardener Andrew Jackson DOWNING (1815–52) pressed for a park of several hundred acres to preserve significant open space within the metropolis. In 1850, both mayoral candidates endorsed the idea, and in 1853 the 'central' site in the middle of Manhattan Island was chosen. The State of New York passed enabling legislation, and acquisition of parcels of land within the proposed park's defined boundaries began. The state legislature created a Board of Commissioners for Central Park in 1857 and hired Frederick Law OLMSTED to supervise clearing operations. Following a design competition, the board selected as the winning entry the plan titled 'Greensward', which Olmsted submitted in partnership with the English architect Calvert Vaux (1824–95). Olmsted and, later, Vaux supervised the construction and management of the park over the next several years. Central Park immediately captured the hearts and imaginations of New

Yorkers when the lake was opened for ice skating during the winter of 1858. Other American municipalities observed the popular success—and its effects on adjacent land values and development—and acted to build their own municipal parks. In Brooklyn, Olmsted and Vaux designed Prospect Park (1865) and, three years later, proposed connecting 'parkways' to extend park planning into a comprehensive framework for urban growth. By the 1890s, many American municipalities had developed park and parkway systems based on the precedents of New York and Brooklyn.

In 1870, a new department of public parks, which oversaw the redevelopment of many city squares and small parks, replaced the Board of Commissioners. Typically, these were designed in the GARDENESQUE style and, later, according to the principals of neoclassical design derived from the École des Beaux-Arts in Paris. Other large parks in Manhattan, including Morningside and Riverside Parks, were built in the 1870s. In 1888, the annexation of adjacent areas of Westchester County added almost 1,416 hectares/3,500 acres of parks and connecting parkways to the northern suburban area known as the Bronx. Despite such acquisitions, park planners had begun to emphasize the need for small parks in the congested tenement wards of Lower Manhattan. In 1887, the state legislature passed the Small Parks Act allowing the city to condemn tenement blocks and replace them with playgrounds. In 1897, the mayor appointed a Small Parks Advisory Committee, with social reformer Jacob A. Riis (1849–1914) as secretary, to recommend a system of small parks in response to an analysis of local crime and disease statistics in overcrowded areas. Over the next ten years, Mulberry Bend (site of the Five Points slum, now Columbus Park), Seward, Hamilton, Jefferson, and other small parks appeared in tenement districts of the Lower East Side, Hell's Kitchen, and Harlem. Equipped with outdoor gymnasia and staffed by 'play supervisors', they indicated the new emphasis on organized recreation programmes, rather than on horticulture and the maintenance of landscape scenery.

In 1898, Brooklyn, Queens, and Staten Island incorporated with Manhattan and the Bronx to create the five boroughs of Greater New York. A restructured department of parks administered parks and recreation programmes in each borough through separate borough commissioners. While state, county, and national park development flourished in the United States as networks of rail lines and then automobile highways were built, in New York (and many other cities) municipal budgets for parks shrank, and their maintenance and popularity declined. But the situation in New

York changed dramatically in 1934, when Mayor Fiorello LaGuardia (1882–1947) appointed Robert Moses (1888–1981), the state park commissioner for Long Island, as commissioner of a newly unified department of parks. Moses consolidated the agency into a centralized citywide administration, and, during the 1930s, thanks to Franklin D. Roosevelt's (1882–1945) New Deal programmes, he spent millions of federal dollars acquiring and developing city parks and automobile parkways. Throughout the five boroughs, Moses oversaw the construction of hundreds of playgrounds, zoos, golf courses, swimming pools, and beach parks, including Orchard Beach, Jacob Riis Park, and a redeveloped Coney Island. He built river crossings and a parkway system connecting with regional parkways in Westchester and Long Island, thereby creating the first metropolitan arterial highway system in the world. Through acquisitions, transfers, and landfills, Moses more than doubled the acreage of New York's park system, while also augmenting its administration and workforce.

During the post-war period, federal investment in municipal park development effectively ended. Subsequent commissioners found it difficult to maintain, much less expand, the system of the Moses era. In the 1970s, New York's fiscal crisis imposed severe budget cuts on municipal agencies, worsening an already difficult situation. By the end of the decade, the condition of Central Park had become a national scandal. In 1978, Mayor Edward I. Koch appointed Gordon J. Davis as park commissioner and, a year later, Elizabeth Barlow as the first Central Park administrator. In 1980, Davis and Barlow enlisted a group of private citizens as the first trustees of the Central Park Conservancy, the public–private partnership they founded to make the park clean, safe, and beautiful once more. The conservancy, in partnership with the department of parks, oversaw the restoration of the park's 340 hectares/840 acres and, in 1997, entered into a contract with the city to assume the management of the park on a day-to-day basis. The conservancy became the model for public–private partnerships for other parks in New York and elsewhere. Citizens of Brooklyn formed the Prospect Park Alliance to support their major park, the landscape masterpiece of Olmsted and Vaux. The Battery Conservancy, incorporated in 1994, has spearheaded the renovation of that historic area according to a management and restoration plan by Saratoga Associates, creating a rebuilt Promenade and linear planting beds by Piet Oudolf (b. 1945). The Riverside Park Fund has gardens donated and maintained by neighbourhood volunteers

and a group from the New York Committee of the Garden Club of America. Friends of Brooklyn Bridge Park spurred the initiative to convert decommissioned piers at the foot of Fulton Street and adjacent industrial frontage beneath the Brooklyn Bridge into a waterfront park. Friends of Hudson River Park advocate the completion of a new 223-hectare/550-acre pier-and-waterfront park, a joint city and state project extending from 59th Street to Battery Park City's chain of parks. By 2004, two segments were completed, one designed by the landscape architectural firm of Sasaki & Associates, another by that of Abel Bainson Butz.

When the World Trade Center's foundations were laid in the 1980s, Battery Park City was built on landfill from the excavated materials. At the same time, the Battery Park City Authority sponsored a 1.2-mile long waterfront promenade with adjacent parkland featuring gardens and commissioned works of art. With richly planted perennial beds and shade trees, the Hudson River Esplanade (1983) runs from North Cove to South Cove where environmental artist Mary Miss (b. 1944) collaborated with landscape architect Susan Childs and architect Stanton Eckstut (b. 1942) to create a landscape that evokes the original shoreline with its tumble of boulders, wooden pilings, and maritime vegetation. Rockefeller Park at the northern end is a sports park with playing fields and ball courts set within sculptural berms designed by the Boston landscape architectural firm Carr, Lynch, Hack, and Sandel. It also contains beds of ornamental grasses by OEHME, VAN SWEDEN (1992).

Gardens
Although the garden history of New York city dates from colonial times, the bouweries of the Dutch West India Company were really farms with livestock, not embowered gardens. Maps depict a garden attached to the company director's house, but the first significant gardens were created for 18th-century mansions built by the colonial British, wealthy Dutch-descended landowners, post-American Revolution merchants, and other affluent members of New York society. The Morris-Jumel Mansion (1765) in Upper Manhattan and the Bartow-Pell Mansion (1842) in the Bronx have revivalist gardens that echo original ones. Private pleasure gardens were also an important, if more ephemeral, part of life by the mid 18th-century. Modelled on London's famous pleasure grounds (see LONDON PARKS AND GARDENS), New York's relatively modest Ranelagh and Vauxhall gardens were located between Broadway and the Hudson river, north of the common.

In 1801, Dr David Hosack (1769–1835) established New York's first botanic garden, the Elgin Botanic Garden, on the site of the present-day Rockefeller Center. It served as a teaching garden for medical students of Columbia University, then located there, as well as a showcase for newly introduced ornamental species. Philanthropic citizens formed the NEW YORK BOTANICAL GARDEN (1891) and the BROOKLYN BOTANIC GARDEN (1910). In the borough of Queens, a group of residents established the Queens Botanical Garden Society (1947), the progenitor of the 16-hectare/39-acre Queens Botanical Garden. The Staten Island Botanical Garden (1977) lies within the Snug Harbor Cultural Center and boasts a Chinese Scholar's Garden (1999) built by 40 craftsmen from the southern Chinese city of Suzhou.

Several gardens are found within New York City parks. Designed as two garden rooms flanking a central grass parterre, the 2.5-hectare/6-acre Conservatory Garden in Central Park (1936) was reclaimed through private philanthropy. The New York Committee of the Garden Club of America spearheaded its recovery (late 1970s), and garden designer and Central Park Conservancy trustee Lynden Miller (b. 1938) subsequently turned it into a horticultural cynosure (early 1980s). Miller serves as the garden's director and is also the designer of several other gardens within New York City parks, including two 90-m/300-ft long herbaceous borders framing the central lawn in Bryant Park. Also within Central Park, the Shakespeare Garden (originally called the Garden of the Heart), a post-Olmsted addition dating from 1913, covers a hillside below the Belvedere. Its restoration began in the 1970s when a group of volunteers revived the existing beds. In the 1980s, with support from the Samuel and May Rudin Foundation, the Central Park Conservancy hired landscape architects Bruce Kelly and David Varnell to redesign it as a perennial garden incorporating many plants mentioned in Shakespeare's plays. The Heather Garden in Fort Tryon Park (1920s), commissioned by John D. Rockefeller Jr. (1874–1960), and designed by Frederick Law Olmsted Jr. (1890–1957), also suffered a period of neglect before the park department developed a plan (1983) to replant its terraces overlooking the Hudson river, a project advanced by private fund-raising and the landscaping skills of gardener Tim Steinhoff. WAVE HILL (1843), an 11-hectare/28-acre former estate in the Bronx, was deeded to the city in 1960 and is managed as a public garden by a private board of trustees. Between 1967 and 2001, gardener Marco Polo Stufano enriched the gardens with impressive horticultural artistry. In the Wild Garden a variety of evergreens anchor seasonal plants that spill down the hillside in an apparently unstudied and naturalistic manner.

New York also has several museum gardens. The Museum of Modern Art's sculpture garden, designed by Philip Johnson (b. 1906) in 1953, was restored in 2005. A gift of John D. Rockefeller Jr. to the city along with Fort Tryon Park, the CLOISTERS, which houses the medieval collection of the Metropolitan Museum, includes three gardens dating from 1938: the Cuxa Cloister Garth Garden, the Bonnefont Cloister Herb Garden, and the Trie Cloister Garden. The Frick Museum Garden (1973), designed by Russell PAGE, complements that museum's neoclassical architecture. Its vine-covered trellises, boxwood-bordered planting beds, green lawn, and limestone-edged reflecting pool can be viewed through a handsome iron fence on East 70th Street as well as from inside the museum. Further uptown at 90th Street and Fifth Avenue, the long-neglected garden of the mansion built by Andrew Carnegie (1835–1919) in 1901, now the Cooper-Hewitt National Design Museum, was revived in 1992 with new plantings installed by garden designers Lynden Miller and Mary Riley Smith (b. 1941). In 1985, in the industrial neighbourhood of Long Island City, Queens, modernist sculptor and garden designer Isamu NOGUCHI (1904–88) opened the Garden Museum that bears his name. Here art and nature are thoroughly integrated in a disciplined space where Noguchi's works in stone and water are displayed in granite-outlined gravel beds set off by carefully placed trees, shrubs, and ground cover.

Several New York churches are built on parcels of land large enough to accommodate gardens. The Biblical Garden at the cathedral of St John the Divine contains plants mentioned in the Bible. The Hope Rosary displays a large collection of English roses, and Pulpit Lawn hosts a small population of peacocks. Protected by high brick walls, the garden at the church of St Luke's in the Fields on Hudson Street offers a sheltered location where several southerly species—fig, pomegranate, crape myrtle (*Lagerstroemia*), and camellia—flourish along with an aged central crab apple tree.

Elsewhere in the city, there are notable privately operated public gardens. The sloping Channel Gardens (so named because they occupy the space between the British Empire Building and the Maison Française) were built with the rest of Rockefeller Center in 1934. They provide the foreground axis for a sunken plaza that becomes a skating rink in winter. Sculptor Paul Manship's (1886–1966) gilded figure of Prometheus soars at the axial terminus above the far end of the plaza. Under the direction of

garden manager Dave Murbach, raised beds are planted according to seasonal themes. Always popular, the Channel Gardens draw the most visitors during the year-end holidays when a 27-m/90-ft illuminated Christmas tree soars above the ice skating rink at the terminus of the central axis. Designed by the firm of Robert Lewis Zion in 1967, Samuel Paley Plaza on East 53rd Street (site of the former Stork Club) is a small urban oasis in which a 12-m/40-ft wide, 6-m/20-ft high waterfall provides a dramatic backdrop and effective sound buffer. Ivy-covered walls and granite paving blocks with honey locust trees planted in a modified QUINCUNX pattern complete the architecture of this pleasant outdoor room. Movable chairs allow visitors to relax and enjoy a snack. Nearby, on East 51st Street, Greenacre Park, designed in 1971 by Hideo Sasaki and Associates, also features a copious waterfall that blocks noise and accommodates four distinct areas on three garden levels.

Dotting the city landscape with welcome greenness are numerous community gardens. Liz Christy, founder of the Green Guerillas, initiated the movement to reclaim vacant lots as gardens. The memorial garden located at Bowery and Houston Streets bearing her name contains more than 1,000 plant species and a rose-covered pergola. Since 1978, under a programme called Operation Green Thumb, the city has leased vacant lots to community gardeners for one dollar a year. Their popularity has sometimes set sponsors at odds with municipal agencies wanting to designate city-owned properties for resale and redevelopment as housing. However, more than 100 community gardens have achieved permanent status, thanks to the Trust for Public Land and the New York Restoration Project. Some are used to grow vegetables; some have 'casitas', homey Puerto-Rican-style structures that serve as neighbourhood gathering places; others express the artistic intentions of their creators, often displaying great design originality in garden ornaments fashioned from recycled materials. The Jefferson Market Garden (1974) and the Sheridan Square Viewing Garden (1982), both created by Greenwich Village garden designer Pamela Berdan, are filled with striking combinations of perennials.

Healing gardens constitute another category of New York city garden culture. The Glass Garden at the Howard A. Rusk Institute of Rehabilitation Medicine at 34th Street and First Avenue provides patients with contact with plants year round. Wheelchair-accessible paths meander through a perennial garden and an urban woodland filled with specimen trees donated by the Brooklyn Botanic Garden. Bellevue Hospital's Comfort Garden (2001),

designed by Patricia McCobb of McCobb & Associates, offers a welcoming entrance to New York's oldest medical institution.

Less visible than these gardens, which are mostly accessible to the public, are the city's many private gardens. These town house and penthouse gardens, as well as the many gardens attached to single-family residences in the Bronx, Queens, and Staten Island, all make New York far greener than its image as a city of steel and glass leads one to believe. ECa/EBR

New Zealand

stretches 1,600 km/974 miles in the South Pacific Ocean. It enjoys a temperate climate with mean temperatures ranging from 7 °C/ 45 °F to 17 °C/65 °F. No garden is far from the ocean. Topography varies from coastal plains to high mountains in both islands. The far north and some coastal areas are virtually frost free, allowing an enviable range of plants to be grown. In other regions and in the south of the two main islands, cold winters are normal but snow seldom lies more than two days at a time. With good fertile acid soils, gardening is the preferred leisure activity for many of the 3.6 million inhabitants.

Flora

The native flora is almost totally unfamiliar to the first-time visitor. About 2,100 species of flowering plants, 80% of which are endemic, colonize a series of island habitats isolated from others over aeons of time. Further, about 80 million years ago, the land separated from the ancient continent of Gondwanaland—thus many plants are related to those in other lands in the southern hemisphere and around the Pacific Ocean. Some of the most notable plants are the mega herbs from outlying and subantarctic islands. *Myosotidium hortensia* and *Astelia chathamica* from the Chatham Islands are coveted worldwide. Unfortunately the magnificent *Pleurophyllum speciosum* with corrugated leaves up to 50 cm/20 in in size and pinkish mauve rayed flowers on 1-m/40-in stems, from New Zealand's subantarctic islands further south, defies cultivation. *Xeronema callistemon* from the Poor Knights, a northerly outlying group, is another exciting plant bearing brushlike fiery red flowers on 1-m/40-in stems. Phormium is ubiquitous in the gardening world. The two species have been much hybridized and there are now many outstanding cultivars. Among the woody plants many have unusual characteristics; some pass through a distinct juvenile stage before reaching adulthood—the lancewood (*Pseudopanax crassifolius* and *P. ferox*) is a typical example. *Clianthus puniceus* (there are three colour forms) has always been desirable—it is critically endangered in the wild. Three trees stand out for their beauty and interest: the iconic cabbage tree (*Cordyline australis*), so called because the hearts of the unfurled leaves were a staple food for the Maori (kouka) and eaten also as a green food supplement (cabbage) by the early settlers; the rimu (*Dacrydium cupressinum*), highly prized for its timber and as a slow growing weeping specimen tree; and the kowhai (*Sophora*), of which seven species are now recognized, spectacular when covered in their yellow pea flowers. Of the ten species of tree fern, *Cyathea dealbata*, the silver fern is the best known, famous for its symbolism but not widely grown in gardens.

History

There is a presumption that gardening began with the arrival of the European settlers in 1840. Archaeologists, however, have shown that the Maori, New Zealand's indigenous people, raised crops long before that. The date these Polynesian settlers arrived is uncertain—some historians suggest as early as AD 700 but others consider 1200 more likely. Whatever the date the Maori brought a collection of fruit and vegetables—sweet potato (*Ipomoea batatas*—kumara), taro (*Colocasia esculenta*), yam (*Diosorea* spp.), gourds (*Lagenaria siceraria*), ti (*Cordyline terminalis*), and the paper mulberry (*Broussonetia papyrifera*). They were successful in cultivating these crops with little more than a primitive digging stick with which to work the soil. Archaeological surveys reveal that stone boundaries were raised to provide shelter and to clear the ground and that occasionally the soil was modified by the addition of sand or shell to improve drainage. Cultivating food crops from the Pacific was a necessity of life for at least six centuries before the missionaries arrived from the cooler climate of Great Britain. By 1821 the early missionaries were cultivating gardens in the English manner, food crops and soon ornamental plants—sweet-brier (*Rosa rubiginosa*) is thought to be the first of these. English settlers from 1840 onwards brought with them other woody plants (often planted singly in grass), and flower seeds and bulbs frequently displayed in circular beds—the cottage style was evolving. Until around a century ago, horticulture was in many ways a fusion between these two ancient gardening traditions. Palms, notably *Trachycarpus fortunei*, still persist in derelict gardens as evidence of the Victorian fashions of the early 20th century, but are now highly fashionable once more.

Alfred Buxton (1872–1950, Christchurch) was a noted designer and builder of gardens in the early years of the 20th century. Buxton worked mainly for rural clients and specialized in pergolas, rockeries, rustic constructions, and other ornamentation. In one of his gardens, Panikau (Gisborne), created in 1919–20, the pergola constructed from locally quarried stone remains in perfect condition as does the garden itself. Many other of his gardens survive in part. Buxton's time was one of the most influential and affluent periods in the development of New Zealand gardens. Much later Ted Smythe (b. 1937, Auckland) designed modernistic gardens where water and stones play against a hard landscape—his use of plants is minimal.

There were many small nurserymen and seedsmen in the first two decades of settlement but there is a dearth of records. There was a nursery in Dunedin in 1853, but again, no name. These were trained gardeners from England who put their skills to use in the new colony. From the 1880s nurserymen began to influence garden style—Buxton, Nairns, and Hale were prominent at that time. In the 20th century two nurseries stood out for the scope of their catalogues and their influence on gardens—R. E. Harrison of Palmerston North and Duncan and Davies of New Plymouth.

Additional gardens

In New Plymouth picturesque *Pukekura Park* is famous for the view of Mount Taranaki afforded down a man-made lake fringed with tree ferns, and for an underground fernery. Begun in 1876, the first trees planted were an oak, a puriri (*Vitex lucens*), a Norfolk Island pine (*Araucaria heterophylla*), and *Pinus insignis*. There has been a policy of planting native species ever since.

A private garden in the same city was a major influence in its time. *Tupare* (New Plymouth) began on a steep, weed-infested hillside in 1932 constructed by Russell Matthews, later Sir (1896–1987), over many years on a scale seldom seen. In its heyday, the garden attracted thousands of visitors in spring when the many flowering shrubs, especially rhododendrons, were in bloom. Tupare was considered a premier landscape garden of its time where trees and shrubs made up the majority of plantings, for annuals, though still used in public parks, especially in gardens and around factories in the city of Christchurch, and perennials were viewed as labour intensive. Tupare along with *Hollards* (Kaponga), a great plantsman's garden, is now owned by the Taranaki Regional Council.

The coastal *Jury* garden (Tikorangi, Waitara) contains an astonishing collection of plants from diverse countries and climates. Felix Jury (1911–97), a third-generation New Zealander, plantsman, and hybridizer, began his garden in 1944 and, although sheep farming was his livelihood, he soon made his mark in horticulture. He imported plants, mainly from England, and began to hybridize over a long period of time an extensive range, hoping for hybrids better suited to his climate. He had significant success with a number of genera but his magnolia hybrids are the most widely acclaimed—*Magnolia* 'Iolanthe' and *M.* 'Vulcan' are just two of these. In 1958 Jury introduced the first vireya rhododendrons from New Guinea including the original *R. macgregoriae*, and began hybridizing this and other species with great success. Mark Jury follows in his father's footsteps.

On the other side of the North Island in a much drier climate, *Eastwoodhill* has possibly the most comprehensive collection of woody plants south of the equator. Douglas Cook (1884–1967) was one of the most knowledgeable plantsmen of his time and imported truckloads of plants to establish his park and garden. Cook was also critically involved in the establishment of PUKEITI Rhododendron Trust (New Plymouth). Eastwoodhill Arboretum is now administered by a trust set up when Cook died. Nearby is *Hack Falls Arboretum* (Tiniroto), containing over 2,500 taxa, including 200 species of oak, 70 of which are Mexican, many collected in the wild.

Cashell (Ohoka, Christchurch) is an outstanding new garden commenced on a bare site in 1993 and designed by John Trengrove (b. 1925) and Pauline Trengrove (b. 1931) along architectural lines marked by hornbeam and immaculate *Cupressus macrocarpa* hedges. Garden rooms each side of the Palladian-style house are planted in yellow and green on one side and purple and red on the other. A further border is furnished in the grand manner with indigenous plants.

The *Trevor Griffith Rose Garden* (Timaru) was established in 2001 to display and preserve the Griffith collection of old roses. It was designed along formal lines by Sir Miles Warren of Christchurch and contains a number of elegant structures. Further south near Dunedin, *Glenfalloch* (Otago Peninsula) dates back to 1872 when many of the old deciduous trees were planted. For a few decades from 1920, the garden became famous for rhododendrons and daffodils which flourished in the woodland areas.   GSC

Neyelov, Vasily Ivanovich

(1722–82), Russian architect who worked for Catherine the Great in the park at TSARSKOE SELO (Pushkin) with John BUSCH and Charles CAMERON. In 1771 he was sent to England by Catherine to study English gardens and stayed for six months. His Palladian Bridge at Tsarskoe Selo was based on the bridge at WILTON, while his buildings there in the

Chinese style were influenced by the publications on Chinese architecture by Sir William CHAMBERS and William and John Halfpenny. The Admiralty and the Hermitage Kitchen, both in the neo-Gothic style, are also by V. I. Neyelov. Of his sons, Ilya Vasilevich (1745–92) assisted his father and Charles Cameron with the Chinese Village and designed the Upper and Lower Baths and the Chinese Theatre. Pyotr, who had accompanied his father to England in 1771, became architect at Tsarskoe Selo in 1794. He designed the Evening Hall.

PH

Nijōjō Castle 🏵

Kyoto city, Japan, covers nearly 30 hectares/74 acres within the confines of its outer moat, but the garden of note is a pond garden covering only approximately 0.45 hectare/1.25 acres in between the inner and outer moat that was built to be seen from formal meeting halls situated next to it. The castle was constructed as the Kyoto residence for Tokugawa Ieyasu (1542–1616), the first shogun (chief military lord) of the Edo period (1600–1868), who normally resided in Edo (present-day Tokyo). Work on the castle—including the outer moat, meeting halls, and residence—was completed by 1603 and it is presumed that the garden, in its original form, was completed by that time, too. The garden was reworked to some degree in 1636 when a large hall (no longer extant) was built on the south side of the garden to accommodate a visit by Emperor Gomizunoo. The form of the present garden stems from that period.

The garden was intended as a grandiose backdrop for meetings between the shogun and important visitors. The stone arrangements along the shoreline of the pond were set in a powerful, overtly expressive style as a display of strength, and images of immortality—such as the Isle of the Immortals (Hōrai), and Tortoise and Crane Isles—were used as the principal motifs in the garden.   MPK

Nikitsky Botanic Garden 🏵

Yalta, Ukraine, was established by government decree in 1811. The first director, Carl Steven (1812–26), chose the site, a steeply wooded slope leading down to the sea, near the village of Nikita. There was almost no soil on the rocky surface and vast quantities of black earth were transported from the Ukraine. Steven was succeeded by Nikolai Hartvis (1826–60) and, as a result of their efforts, a large collection was built up from many parts of the world; considerable contributions were made to the study of the local flora, viticulture, and fruit culture; and a wide range of ornamental trees, shrubs, and herbaceous plants was made

available for the great gardens, among them Alupka, Livadia, and Massandra, which were being developed along the coastal strip by the Black Sea. The site covers 272 hectares/672 acres (almost 1,000 hectares/2,471 acres with satellites). The garden is not laid out along the usual systematic lines of botanical gardens but with the object of creating exceptional visual effects. Box-edged paths lead past remarkable ornamental planting, with intermittent sea and mountain views to enhance the experience. Among the trees are some large cypresses, cedars, pines, and sequoias planted by Carl Steven. Even older trees include a 500-year-old olive tree and a pistachio tree thought to be 1,000 years old. Roses are represented by almost 2,000 species and varieties. The Nikitsky Botanic Garden has become both a leading research establishment and a major tourist attraction.   PH

Ninfa, Giardini di 🏵

near Latina, Lazio, Italy. The flower-covered ruins of the ancient town of Ninfa make one of the most romantic gardens in Italy. Medieval Ninfa, already recorded by PLINY THE YOUNGER in the 1st century AD for its natural springs, and containing a cathedral and seven churches, was sacked in 1382 when the owners, the Caetani family, opposed the Pope. Deserted for the hills above, the village remained empty until the early 20th century when the Caetani reclaimed the land, canalized the river, stabilized the ruins, and converted the medieval town hall into a dwelling. In 1920 it was Gelasio Caetani who instigated the draining of the unhealthy marshes, infested by malaria-carrying mosquitoes. With his English mother Duke Gelasio began to plant among the ruins, planting cypresses along the old streets to create semi-formal axes. At first they used native trees only but soon discovered the possibility of acclimatizing exotics from the rest of the world. Abundant water from the hills above was stored in a vast reservoir. Duke Gelasio's brother, married to an American, Marguerite Chapin, enriched the garden further, while their daughter Lelia Howard, an artist, continued to add new specimens until her death in 1971.

Even when deserted Ninfa had been famous for its wildflowers, but today there are meadows, and a rock garden, in which native and foreign plants jostle together. Paths are lined with native rosemary, a broad stream is flanked by *Zantedeschia aethiopica*, and each ancient wall provides a home for a climbing rose or tender twining plants. Tender trees and shrubs such as *Drimys winteri* from Chile, the rare *Cladastris sinensis*, New Zealand Hoherias, and *Pinus montezumae* from Mexico have grown large. Today the garden belongs to the Caetani

Foundation and the region around has become a nature reserve. The only threat remains the possibility of industrial development which could take Ninfa's water supply.   PHo

Nishat Bagh 🏵

Kashmir. Situated on the eastern shores of Lake Dal, the garden, whose name means Garden of Gladness, is attributed to Asaf Khān, Grand Vizier to Jahāngīr (1605–27). The design recalls that of SHALAMAR Garden, though it is on a more monumental scale, originally in order to give a better view of the lake and surrounding mountains. The garden is laid out along twelve lawn terraces, corresponding to the twelve signs of the zodiac; these are planted with *Celosia* and descend towards the lake. There is just one canal, punctuated by thrones (*chabutras*) and slides, that flows through the uppermost pavilion into the lake. The whole is crowned by a double row of chenars (*Platanus orientalis*), which thicken near the top to form a wood in the women's garden (*zenana*). Two fine octagonal three-storey gazebos at either end of the *zenana*'s retaining wall give a panoramic view of the lake and the rice paddies on the opposite slope.   AP

S. CROWE and S. HAYWOOD, *The Gardens of Mughul India* (1972).

Nishihonganji 🏵

Kyoto city, Japan, is the head temple of the Honganji branch of the Jōdoshinshū sect of Buddhism. The garden of note, designed as a dry landscape garden (see KARESANSUI), is found in a 760-sq-m/2,492-sq-ft courtyard to the east of the Taimensho (Audience Hall), thus the formal name, Nishihonganji Taimensho garden. The garden stems from the beginning of the 17th century, built originally in the first decade along with the Audience Hall, and adjusted to some degree during the reconstruction of neighbouring halls in the second and third decades of that century.

The familiar name of the garden is Kokei no Niwa, the Tiger Glen Garden. The name makes reference to a story of the Chinese Buddhist priest Huiyuan (334–416) who lived in a secluded temple on Lushan mountain. The Tiger Glen, which Huiyuan swore never to cross, divided his temple (sacred space) from the outside world (secular space). An apocryphal story about Huiyuan describes him as forgetting his vow and crossing the Tiger Glen while enjoying the company of two dear friends—one Taoist, the other Confucist—symbolizing the unity of the three creeds: Buddhism, Taoism, and Confucianism. The garden at Nishihonganji evokes this story primarily in the rear section through a dry waterfall made of large bluish stones (the Glen) and a view of the massive roof of an adjacent temple hall (Huiyuan's mountain). The forward part of the garden evokes the image of a sea through the use of raked white sand and contains standard symbols of longevity and felicity: Tortoise and Crane Isles, and Hōrai (Chinese: Penglai) stone arrangements. These motifs created the proper backdrop for audiences held between important individuals in the Audience Hall. The dramatic arrangements of large bluish stones, and the use of groupings of non-native plants such as sago palms (*Cycas revoluta*), lend the garden an exotic atmosphere.   MPK

Niven, Ninian

(1799–1879), the principal garden designer of the Victorian age in Ireland. Born at Kelvin Grove, Glasgow, at the age of 14 he was apprenticed in the gardens of Bothwell Castle, then studied painting and drawing in Glasgow, after which he returned to Bothwell as head gardener. He soon came to Ireland as head gardener at the official residence of the Chief Secretary for Ireland in PHOENIX PARK, Dublin. In 1834 Niven was appointed curator of the Royal Dublin Society's Botanic Garden at Glasnevin (see NATIONAL BOTANIC GARDENS, GLASNEVIN). In 1838 he published *The Visitor's Companion to the Botanic Gardens*, but in the following year resigned his position to become a professional landscape gardener and nurseryman.

After the collapse of one of his earliest projects, the establishment of a national arboretum in Phoenix Park, he went on a tour of French gardens, on his return from which he resolved to practise an intermediate style in which the natural English and formal French styles would be 'judiciously blended'. His subsequent designs for gardens around the great houses of the Victorian nobility included those at Baronscourt, County Tyrone, for the Duke of Abercorn, at Kilkenny Castle for the Marquis of Ormonde, and at Santry Court and Templeogue House, both in County Dublin, for Sir Compton Domville, Bt., but he also designed for industrial magnates such as Mr Roe, the distiller, at Nutley Park, Dublin, and Mr Reeves, the miller, at Athgarvan, County Kildare, and for hotels like the Royal Marine Hotel at Kingstown. A major part of his work consisted of laying out parks for public use such as the People's Park in Phoenix Park, Monkstown Public Park, and the park for the Dublin International Exhibition of 1863.

He was also gardener to the court of the lord lieutenants of Ireland, laying out the grounds of the Viceregal Lodge, the Chief Secretary's Lodge, and the Under-Secretary's Lodge. He was obliged to widen the gravel sweep in front of his nursery at Glasnevin to accommodate the carriages of the Lord Lieutenant and his entourage when they came to buy plants, and he conducted the ceremonial plantings of trees at the Viceregal Lodge during the visits to Ireland of the British royal family. In his latter years he published various religious tracts and a volume of verse. He died in 1879 at Garden Farm, Glasnevin, Dublin, where he had lived and conducted his nursery and a horticultural school since 1838.   PB

Noailles, Villa ⊛

Hyères, Var, France. In 1924 Charles de Noailles commissioned Robert Mallet-Stevens to design a modernist villa in a fine position in the Riviera town of Hyères with views of the Mediterranean. In 1928 Gabriel GUEVREKIAN designed a modernist garden to suit the house—a triangular enclosure jutting out like the prow of a ship. With a glittering statue by Jacques Lipchitz (*La Joie de vivre*) it had a rectilinear pattern of coloured glazed tiles, pools, and small beds for ground cover plants, orange trees, and tulips. It has been restored in recent times, but very half-heartedly, conveying little of the brilliance and dash of the original design. A quite different garden is spread out among the old terraced olive groves below the house with thickets of *Heliotropium arborescens*, *Melianthus major*, and *Beschorneria yuccoides*.   PT
DOROTHÉE IMBERT, *The Modernist Garden in France* (1993).

Noguchi, Isamu

(1904–88), Japanese designer. He was born of Japanese and American parents in the United States but travelled to Japan at the age of 2. Subsequently he travelled widely, expressing an envy for 'those who belong'. In Japan he went to a Jesuit school, and later, at the age of 20, went to Paris to work as a stonecutter for the sculptor Brancusi, and subsequently began to work as a sculptor. But his interests soon expanded to include design for the theatre and environmental design including memorials, bridges, play parks, and gardens, including a Japanese garden for the UNESCO building in Paris and a number of small courtyards and roof gardens for the Beinecke Rare Book and Manuscript Library, Yale University (1963), the Chase Manhattan Bank (1964), and the IBM Headquarters (1964), in New York, using symbolic sculptural forms to great effect, often with the minimum number of plants.   MLL

Nong Nooch Garden ⊛

Pattaya, Thailand. First opened in the mid 1990s as an attraction for tourists visiting the popular beach resort of Pattaya, on the Gulf of Thailand, this has developed into one of the most impressive collections of tropical plants in the country. The owner has gathered them from many places, including South-East Asia, Australia, Hawaii, South America, and the West Indies, and, at one time or another, has brought in foreign experts to advise on their cultivation. The beautifully maintained garden covers a very large site near the sea and is divided into a number of sections, each devoted mainly to a certain species. Particularly outstanding are the palm and heliconia collections. Among the palms are *Kerridoxa elegans*, native to southern Thailand, on which the leaves have black petioles and are silver on the undersurface; the large silver-leafed *Bismarkia nobilis*; several species of *Johannesteijsmannia*; and the rare double coconut (*Lodoicea*), found only in the Seychelles Islands. The heliconias, mostly from South America, include almost every known species and cultivar, over 100 in all. In other landscaped areas are various flowering trees and shrubs, gingers, cycads, and cacti, while a fernhouse displays numerous more delicate plants.   WLW

Nonsuch Palace,

Surrey, England, was a hunting lodge in Hampton Court Chase built for Henry VIII in 1538–46 at the centre of a great park. In 1579 it was inherited by John, Lord Lumley, who created a new garden inspired by what he had seen on a visit to Italy in 1566. A visitor, Baron Waldstein, saw it in 1600 and considered it 'the finest in the whole of England'. Roy Strong in his *Renaissance Garden in England* (1979) described it as 'the first large-scale symbolic garden in the Italian Mannerist style to have been attempted in England'. The garden celebrated Lumley's own ancestry and was also an allegory in honour of Queen Elizabeth. A walled garden had knot gardens in which a German visitor, Henzer, saw 'many columns and pyramids of marble . . . fountains that spout water'. A fountain had a statue of Diana and a pelican—both of which had iconographic associations with Elizabeth. Informal gardens, with groves of trees, were decorated with statues and ornamental buildings like a Renaissance BOSCO—one of the groves was dedicated to Diana. Nothing remains of the palace or garden today.   PT
MARTIN BIDDLE, 'The gardens of Nonsuch', *Garden History*, Vol. 27: No. 1 (1999).

Nørgård, Edith (1919–89) and Ole

(1925–78), Danish landscape architects, who worked with the surroundings of buildings and forming the landscape. The Nørgårds created not only some of the most exquisite Danish landscape architecture in the 1960s in gardens but also greater landscapes such as those for motorways, the reclamation of the gravel pit

Hedeland (1978–96), the campuses around universities at the TECHNICAL UNIVERSITY OF DENMARK and Amager University, the landscapes of STORE VEJLEÅ VALLEY with Kongsholm Park, Vallensbæk Moat, and Herstedvester Lake. Perfectionism and simplicity are dominating features, but lavishly planted gardens can be found as well, for example at Louisiana's SCULPTURE GARDEN.   AL

Norway

constitutes the west coast of the Scandinavian Peninsula towards the North Atlantic with 1,750 km/1,090 miles between its southern and northern points, its long and deep fjords and valleys, and its range of mountains from the north to the south. The climate is influenced by both westerly winds and the temperate Gulf Stream, which creates a maritime climate west of the mountain range and a continental climate to the east. Average yearly rainfall varies from c.2,000 mm/80 in around Bergen on the west coast to c.400 mm/16 in on the Finnmark plain. Temperatures in Finnmark vary from an average in winter of –15 °C/3 °F to in summer 14 °C/57 °F, the equivalent in Bergen being 1 °C and 15 °C. The climate is favourable for plant life even above the Arctic Circle at 66 ° 33′ N, but the mountainous landscape with only 3% arable land represents great challenges for horticulture.

The history of gardens in Norway is influenced by the fact that the country was part of a union with Denmark for nearly 300 years (1536–1814) and with Sweden for almost 100 years (1814–1905), during which periods the royal court was situated in Copenhagen and Stockholm respectively. In spite of prosperous times for the important Norwegian timber trade during the 18th century only few major architectural or horticultural works were created before 1814, when the capital Christiania (later Oslo) saw a range of new building projects. Norwegian gardens in general are small compared to the grand gardens of continental Europe.

There is little archaeological evidence of gardening in Norway before the 11th century. Recent research has shown that small, fenced-in vegetable gardens within the boundaries of the medieval towns became common at that time. *Angelica archangelica* was grown both as a vegetable and for medicinal purposes, and was exported within Europe. At the UNESCO World Heritage Site Bryggen in Bergen there still remains part of the garden area behind the wooden houses. Other types of secular medieval gardens, like castle and manor gardens of kings and the aristocracy, no longer survive. The monastic orders that arrived from the 12th

century had considerable influence on Norwegian gardening. Orchards were laid out both within the monasteries and at their farms. On the North Sea coast fruit production is still an important part of modern horticulture. Out of the c.25 monasteries only Utstein near Stavanger is still standing, but its gardens are very much changed. The other monasteries were destroyed before or during the Protestant Reformation in 1537, and no monastery garden in its original layout can be seen in Norway today.

Extensive trade, in particular with the Netherlands, Germany, and Denmark, brought new impulses to Norwegian gardening during the Renaissance. The commercial capital Bergen was the gateway for cultural influences from continental Europe. The well-to-do would employ experienced gardeners from abroad. The Flemish head gardener to the first Lutheran bishop in Bergen after 1537 created a magnificent garden that became a model for the new style in gardening from the 17th century onwards: an enclosed formal garden, divided into compartments by paths, preferably laid out with white shell gravel. Until after 1945 this type of garden would exist as an archetype in rural areas and fishing ports, in spite of all later changes in style. The best-preserved Renaissance garden in the country is found at ROSENDAL BARONY south of Bergen (1660s). The restored garden at the small rococo DAMSGÅRD MANSION in Bergen is of the same type, although a century younger, like the LURØY GARDEN just south of the Arctic Circle. An example of the larger gardens near the capital can be seen at LINDERUD MANSION, laid out c.1740 as a terraced garden—the delay in relation to the Italian Renaissance is about 300 years. Baroque influences in the 18th century never had a great impact on Norwegian gardening. A few officers of the crown and wealthy farmers and merchants built large mansions with elaborate formal gardens and long axes lined with avenues. Some of these avenues still exist, in particular in the Trøndelag and Østfold regions.

The landscape style was introduced around 1780 at BOGSTAD MANSION near Oslo, not much later than the rest of Europe. While many formal gardens in England were completely reshaped in the new style, in Norway it was easier to use the nearby naturally picturesque landscape, leaving the old garden unaltered. The vegetation would be a mixture of indigenous and newly introduced species, as in the well-restored landscape park at NES MANSION AND IRONWORKS. During the 19th century an artificial and exotic landscape style flourished, in particular in the villa gardens that grew up in the outskirts of the expanding

industrial cities. The garden at the villa BREIDABLIKK is a typical example. Many of the 19th-century public parks still remain intact, such as the Nygårdsparken in Bergen and the royal palace park Slottsparken in Oslo.

The new formalism of the first decades of the 20th century can be seen at BJERKEBÆK where hardy perennials, shrubs, and trees are abundant. The best-known public park from this period is the VIGELAND PARK in Oslo, created by the sculptor Gustav Vigeland. The campus park at the Agricultural University of NORWAY represents the transition from the formal to the functionalistic style in gardening. The modern garden was further developed after 1945 by a growing number of landscape architects. One of the best examples is the HYDRO PARK at the main administration building of Norsk Hydro, Oslo. Norwegian gardens today vary in style from minimalist to naturalistic to eclectic, and there is a growing interest in historic gardens and gardening with heritage plants.   ME

MAGNE BRUUN, 'Historic gardens in Norway', *Monuments & Sites, ICOMOS Bulletin*, No. 7 (1987).
KARSTEN JØRGENSEN, 'Nature and garden art in Norway', *Journal of Garden History*, Vol. 17 (1997).
CARL W. SCHNITLER, *Norske Haver i gammel og ny tid* (1916).

Norway, Agricultural University of ⊛

Ås, Akershus, Norway, founded in 1859 and the faculty of horticulture in 1887. The 55-hectare/135-acre campus park was laid out in a Victorian landscape style until 1925–35, when it was changed into the formal (neoclassical) style of the period designed by Olav Leif Moen (1887–1951), who became the first professor of garden design in Norway in 1921. Moen's plan of 1924 created a unity between the 19th-century building complex and the new buildings of 1901 and 1924 by the architect Ole Sverre (1865–1952). The central feature in the park is the rectangular Great Lawn, shaped like a BOULINGRIN with a rectangular pond and monumental flights of stairs in the main axis and a PATTE D'OIE vista towards the surrounding moraine landscape. Outside the central area elements from the older park were incorporated, such as the romantic Swan Pond. The park contains the university arboretum, started in the 1880s and developed from the 1930s to contain 1,400 species and subspecies of woody plants, including a collection of 300 roses and a perennial garden. Outside the park is the North Forest arboretum with around 50 species of woody plants, mostly evergreen.   ME

Nost, John (Jan) van

(*fl.* 1677–1710), sculptor of Flemish origin who set up in business making lead statuary around 1677 in London. He had two workshops, in the Haymarket and in Hyde Park Road, where, with several assistants, he produced fine-quality figures, usually of classical inspiration. Surviving examples of his work may be seen in the gardens at Cholmondeley Castle (Cheshire), MELBOURNE HALL, and ROUSHAM. On his death his cousin, also John van Nost, took over his business followed by his son, a third John, and it continued until 1729.   PT

JOHN DAVIS, *Antique Garden Ornament* (1991).

Novillero, El,

Sonoma, California, USA, created in 1937 on a site of 2 hectares/5 acres, and one of the finest modernist gardens in the country. The garden, designed by Thomas D. CHURCH, sits on an eminence in the middle of a large cattle ranch. A long drive, following a former cattle trail, winds through picturesque outcrops of rock and groves of *Quercus agrifolia*, the native California live oak, and debouches into the motor court. This space is dominated by a large screen of carefully pruned back-lit oaks forming an abstract living sculpture. The garden comprising a narrow lawn around the house and the larger and higher area around the swimming pool is separated from the expansive ranch land by a juniper hedge. The levelled low hill above the house is both an abstract space for swimmers and memorable art. Meticulously pruned existing oak trees frame the outward views and provide a visual counterpoint to the abstract ground plane of scored concrete and redwood decking and the contrasting volumes of a glazed pavilion and a blank-walled dressing room/guest house structure. This composition is experienced like a cubist composition, the overlapping planes appearing to lead the eye simultaneously out to the sweeping forms of the ox-bow bends in the river below and inward to the free-form sculpture by Adeline Kent. Planting is limited to abstract panels of grass, beds of zoysia grass, and bold clumps of *Strelitzia regina*.   DCS

Nuneham Park,

Nuneham Courtenay, Oxfordshire, England, became famous in the 18th century when the 1st Earl of Harcourt destroyed the village to clear the ground for his landscaping activities in the 1760s in this beautiful site on the river Thames. By no means the only example of such destruction, this case became notorious because of the publicity given to it in Oliver Goldsmith's poem *The Deserted Village* (1770) with its mournful line 'The country blooms—a garden and a grave'. The ancient church was rebuilt by James 'Athenian' Stuart (1713-88) to give it the air of a classical temple, a suitable ornament for the new landscape. The Earl opened up distant views of Oxford's spires

and domes. The 2nd Earl, an admirer of Jean-Jacques ROUSSEAU, in 1777 commissioned a garden designed by William MASON and modelled on Julie's garden in Rousseau's *La Nouvelle Héloïse*—a walled flower garden, a rare feature in the 18th century. Capability BROWN landscaped the park to the south of the house from 1778. In the 1830s W. S. GILPIN added a picturesque PINETUM. Today this forms part of the Harcourt Arboretum, since 1962 a department of the University of OXFORD BOTANIC GARDEN.   PT

nursery.

The nursery as a place in which plants are propagated and young plants cared for until large enough to be planted out in garden or woodland, or as a business selling garden plants, is of the greatest importance to horticulture. The propagation and dissemination of plants is at the heart of a vigorous garden culture. For J. C. LOUDON the nursery gardener, or nurseryman, was 'the highest species of tradesman-gardener' (*Encyclopaedia of Gardening*, 1822). The raising of plants and their early care must be as old as gardening itself. In England, as John Harvey showed in his *Early Nurserymen* (1974), it was the monasteries, distributing plants and seeds, that acted as de facto nurseries in the latter period of the Middle Ages, between the 11th century and the beginning of the 16th century. There is also evidence of private gardens of the Middle Ages having nurseries and these, too, would have been informal sources of plants in their locality. Most of the early trade in plants and seeds was to do with food plants or trees rather than with ornamental flowering plants.

Exploration and the introduction of exotics immensely stimulated the nursery trade, and the great number of new gardens made by the aristocracy and gentry after the Restoration of 1660 saw the trade taking on something like its modern character. George Rickets established a nursery at Hoxton (London) which was flourishing in the 1670s. He did not supply only gardens of the London area. A bill of 1689 for plants supplied for the new garden at LEVENS HALL in the north-west of England included '22 Peaches & Nectarines, 400 Gooseburys & Currants, 45 Spruce Firrs' and many ornamentals (including '200 Good Tulipps mixt'). Rickets's list of 1688 is the earliest surviving English nurseryman's catalogue—in it he described himself as 'the great Collector and Improver of the beauties of a Garden'. He sold tender plants (such as oranges and lemons), flowering trees (including shrubs), hardy evergreens (including such fashionable plants as *Phillyrea angustifolia*), and herbaceous perennials. In addition he lists a wide range of

fruit trees. Some of the plants he lists had been introduced very recently, among them the cedar of Lebanon (*Cedrus libani*) which was introduced c.1650. Seedsmen in this period (such as Edward Fuller of Strand Bridge, London) seem to have specialized in vegetables. The Brompton Park Nursery was founded in London in 1681 (on the site of what is today the Victoria and Albert Museum) by George LONDON with three partners (William Looker, Moses Cook, and John Field) joined in 1687 by Henry WISE. All had valuable connections in the gardening world and in 1702, on the succession of Queen Anne, Henry Wise became royal gardener, an appointment that was renewed in 1714 on the accession of George I. London and Wise became the sole partners in Brompton Park Nursery which, through their connections and garden design business, supplied many of the royal gardens and aristocratic estates—a position of power unique in the history of English gardens. The 18th century saw an extraordinary increase in the nursery trade in Britain and the establishment of the first commercial nursery in North America, the PRINCE NURSERY. Robert Prince founded the business, at Flushing on Long Island, as early as 1737. The nursery became very important both for the dissemination of North American plants to Europe as well as for the introduction of new plants. It continued in business until 1864, latterly under the name The Linnaean Gardens, and a second nursery was opened north of Broadway. At the beginning of the century the most notable firm in England was the Brompton Park Nursery but throughout the century the numbers increased, slowly at first but gathering pace from the middle of the century.

The VEITCH family of nurserymen, in business from 1808 to 1914, were profoundly influential on gardening, not least for their patronage of great plant collectors such as William Lobb (1809-64), William Purdom (1880-91), and, most magnificently, E. H. WILSON. In France Maurice de Vilmorin, a member of the French dynasty of plantsmen, seed merchants, and nurserymen as influential as the Veitches, in the second half of the 19th century patronized such plant collectors as Armand DAVID (1826-1900), Jean Marie DELAVAY (1838-95), and Paul Guillaume Farges (1844-1912), all of whom collected in China. In Scotland in the 20th century one of the most remarkable nurseries, still very much in business, is Glendoick (Perthshire). Here, four generations of the Cox family, some of whom have also been plant collectors in China, have built up a rare collection of rhododendrons and other ericaceous plants. In the 20th century after the Second World War the growth of garden centres and the radical change of large firms like HILLIERS, which in its great days stocked virtually every woody plant hardy in the British Isles, caused a profound change in the nursery trade. The garden centres concentrate on the heart of the market and indeed a very large part of their business is not in plants at all but in 'garden sundries', which includes furniture, barbecues, plastic pools, and so forth. Garden centres of this sort dominate the market for garden plants throughout Europe and North America. Virtually all plants sold by garden centres are bought in, with no propagation done on the premises. This means that many garden centres sell only those plants easy to propagate en masse. In England the growth of these garden supermarkets has stimulated a new generation of small specialist nurseries, sometimes short-lived but often selling discerningly chosen plants hard to propagate and therefore hard to find elsewhere. This is especially true of cultivars of herbaceous perennials (such as hellebores) which are slow to propagate by division but may not be in sufficient demand to justify the expense of micropropagation. The 2003/4 edition of the *RHS Plant Finder* lists more than 65,000 plants, species and cultivars, commercially available in well over 700 nurseries in the British Isles.   PT

Nuttall, Thomas

(1786–1859). Born in Yorkshire, Nuttall was a self-taught botanist fascinated with the United States to which he travelled in 1808, and where, apart from a brief interlude caused by the British–American War in 1812, his whole working life was to be spent. On Nuttall's arrival in Philadelphia he was engaged as a plant collector for the university and for eleven years he explored the eastern United States, Arkansas Territory, and the upper reaches of the Missouri river. His knowledge of the flora was contained in *Genera of North American Plants* (1818). Between 1822 and 1833 Nuttall was curator of Harvard Botanic Garden, Boston, retiring to Britain in 1842 having between 1836 and 1841 updated François-André Michaux's *North American Sylva* (1810–13). Nuttall was responsible for several plant introductions including *Ribes odoratum* and the Californian farewell-to-spring, *Clarkia amoena*.   MC-C

nymphaeum.

In classical Greece the nymphaeum was a temple dedicated to nymphs which were spirits associated with natural settings. Dryads, or hamadryads, were associated with trees (sometimes specifically oaks or ash trees); naiads were nymphs of water and potamaiads specifically of rivers. An especially noted nymphaeum was the Corcyrian cave on Mount Parnassus mentioned in Aeschylus' (d. *c*.456 BC) *Eumenides*—'the Nymphs, who dwell where is the Corcyrian caverned rock, delight of birds and haunt of powers divine'. The cave survives and the poet George Seferis described his visit to it in *Delphi* (1965) where he was still able to see 'the half-obliterated inscription to Pan and the Nymphs'. The Romans used the term nymphaeum to denote fountains dedicated to nymphs. A 3rd-century nymphaeum of this sort, the Castell dell'Acqua Marcia, survives in Rome. The idea of the nymphaeum was rediscovered in the Renaissance and became a notable feature of Italian gardens and, later on, of gardens in France. In Italy surviving examples may be seen at BOMARZO (*c*.1550), the Fontana Papacqua at Soriano nel Cimino (Lazio, *c*.1561), and the Villa GIULIA (1550–5). In France a magnificent nymphaeum, with a direct Italian connection, was made for the Château de Wideville (Yvelines) in 1635 designed by Tommaso FRANCINI. Finely restored in recent years it has a sumptuous interior of patterned shellwork and a figure of a nymph standing in a niche above a pool. At the Château de RAMBOUILLET the Queen's Dairy (1785) contains a nymphaeum in the form of a grotto in which a nymph perches on a rock with the goat Amaltheia, restrained on a leash, drinking from the pool below. Here the nymph is associated specifically with Zeus who shortly after his birth was taken to Crete where, in a cave at Lyktos, he was fed by the goat Amaltheia. So the nymph here has the pastoral role of goatherd, appropriate to a dairy. The Queen's Dairy was built for the Queen, Marie-Antoinette, for whom the fantasy pastoral life of the Hameau at VERSAILLES was also created, in 1783–5. Perhaps the most astonishing surviving nymphaeum in France is that which was built for the Château de Chatou (Yvelines) in 1779–80 to the designs of Jacques-Germain Soufflot. The chateau, which no longer survives, was built on the banks of the Seine. The nymphaeum, with rusticated Doric columns, has a vast open vault, like a giant shell, facing the river. In England, despite a fondness for grottoes, the nymphaeum as such is not found in gardens.

The closest is the mid 18th-century grotto at STOURHEAD with its 'nymph of the grot' reclining above a pool.   PT

BERND H. DAMS and ANDREW ZEGA, *Pleasure Pavilions and Follies: In the Gardens of the Ancien Régime* (1995).

NAOMI MILLER, *Heavenly Caves: Reflections on the Garden Grotto* (1982).

Nymphenburg Palace ⊛

Munich, Germany, with its approximately 180-hectare/445-acre park, is located in the west part of the city. Once the summer residence of the Bavarian rulers the palace was begun in 1664 by order of Elector Ferdinand Maria and his consort Henriette Adelaide, who called it the 'borgo delle ninfe' (village of nymphs). In 1671 a small garden in the manneristic style was laid out, which did not survive the subsequent enlargement of the complex. From 1701 to 1704 Elector Max Emanuel commissioned the French garden designer Charles Carbonet to design a new, much larger garden that was to be supplied with water by means of an artificial canal. Between 1714 and 1726, finally, the Bavarian architect Joseph Effner and the French garden designer Dominique GIRARD created Nymphenburg's famous baroque park. The extensive grounds also acquired a hermitage (Magdalenklause, 1725–8) and several pavilions or miniature palaces with separate gardens (Pagodenburg, 1716–19; Badenburg, 1718–21; Amalienburg, 1734–9). In 1765–92 twelve figures of gods and goddesses and huge marble vases were erected close to the palace in the Large Parterre. From 1804 to 1823 the baroque complex was transformed by Friedrich Ludwig von SCKELL into a classical landscape park. Elements of the formal garden were retained: the central canal with the cascade and the adjoining avenues and the basic structure of the parterre together with its sculptures. The diagonal axes with their avenues however were replaced by Sckell with a variety of scenic settings with artificial hills and lakes, and HA-HAS which gave a glimpse of the surrounding countryside. The main architectural features in the spacious landscape park are the 18th-century pavilions and the Monopteros (see TEMPLE) designed by Leo von Klenze in 1865. Between 1807 and 1820 three greenhouses were also built near the palace from designs by Sckell for the extensive plant collection of the first Bavarian King Max I Joseph.   RH

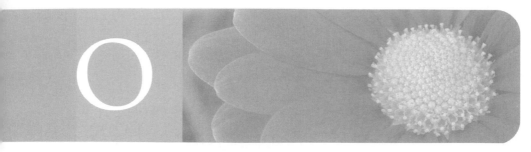

O

Oatlands Park,

near Weybridge, Surrey, England, was a medieval palace rebuilt by Henry VIII from 1538. After 1730, when it was inherited by the 9th Earl of Lincoln, an immensely elaborate late 17th-century formal garden was gently landscaped by William KENT, Joseph Spence (1699–1768), and, possibly, Philip SOUTHCOTE. Terraces overlooked a long narrow lake and the landscape was embellished by a grotto by the Lanes of Tisbury, a menagerie and temples by Kent, and a gateway by Inigo JONES from the old Oatlands Palace. The last, and Kent's temples, were broken up to make a rockery and the grotto was destroyed in 1948. The lake and one temple survive.   PT

obelisk.

The obelisk, a tall tapering square-section shaft of stone, first appeared in Egypt, around 1500 BC made of polished granite, usually from Aswan, and embellished with gold. From Roman imperial times obelisks were much valued in the West and many were removed from their original sites—there are more ancient Egyptian obelisks scattered throughout the world than remain in Egypt today. In 16th-century Rome Pope Sixtus V built a new system of roads with obelisks marking the junction of major thoroughfares. These served both as ornaments and as reference points to help pilgrims make their way about the city, and many remain in place. In St Peter's Square he erected an Egyptian obelisk (dedicated to the True Cross, of which a fragment was attached to its apex) brought to Rome in imperial times. The most ancient, dating from the 15th century BC, and the tallest in the world (42 m/140 ft), is that in the Piazza di San Giovanni in Laterano. That at the centre of the Piazza del Popolo, dating from the 13th century BC, was brought to Rome by the Emperor Augustus.

The obelisk shape became a common decorative feature of Italian Renaissance gardens seen, for example, in the first terrace of the Villa LANTE. Under the influence of Italy the obelisk made its way into English gardens remarkably early on. After 1579 at NONSUCH PALACE Lord Lumley erected a marble obelisk decorated with the Lumley arms. It never went entirely out of fashion as a motif in British gardens. It may still be seen at the late 16th-century MONTACUTE and, in the form of a sundial, dated 1630, at DRUMMOND CASTLE. In the 18th century it came into its own as a valuable distant eyecatcher in the landscape park. It may still be seen at CASTLE HOWARD (1714), at STOURHEAD (1746–7), and at BRAMHAM PARK (c.1768). It is found in Ireland, too, in the 18th century, most memorably at CARTON in the bizarre form of Conolly's Folly (1739). In the 19th century it was found in historicizing formal gardens and in the ARTS AND CRAFTS gardens of the end of the century, of which ATHELHAMPTON is the outstanding example. In France stone obelisks were rarely found in gardens (although there was one at MARLY). As a decorative shape however, in the form of topiary or trellis-work, it was common in French gardens from the 17th century onwards. In the 19th century two notable ancient Egyptian obelisks made their way into gardens. In England the Philae Obelisk, dating from 100 BC, was brought by William Bankes to Kingston Lacy (Dorset) and erected in 1839 in a particularly fine garden setting in company with other Egyptian antiquities. In the USA Cleopatra's Needle, dating from the 15th century BC, was moved to Central Park (see NEW YORK CITY PARKS AND GARDENS) in 1881.   PT   ⊃ page 345

Oca, Pazo de ✵

San Esteban de Oca, near Santiago de Compostela, Galicia, Spain. The word *pazo* means a manor house or manorial estate. The word also embodies *paz*, the Spanish for peace, and the Pazo de Oca, with its secretive air, has a memorably peaceful air. The estate goes back at least to the Middle Ages and in the 12th century there was a fortified house here. By the early 18th century it was in the possession of the Gayoso family who rebuilt the house and made the garden that exists today. In the entrance courtyard the house is linked by an arcade to a pretty baroque chapel with two bell towers. A circular pool is surrounded by a deep box hedge whose top is clipped at regular intervals into monumental hemispheres. Beyond it a very large maze of box hedges is overlooked by a loggia. From the entrance courtyard a door opens into a mysteriously shady garden of sandy paths and large box-edged beds with mature trees and shrubs—*Magnolia grandiflora*, a huge old *Cryptomeria japonica* divided into several branches, venerable yews underplanted with camellias, hydrangeas, and rhododendrons. Corners of the enclosures are often marked by stone columns with ceramic urns painted in blue with exotic scenes. To one side is an open stone washhouse with huge troughs of stone through which water rushes. Water is the chief ingredient of the garden and sounds of rushing water are never far away. Two great rectangular pools, one slightly lower than the other, are linked by water rushing through a spout. The pools are separated by a wide stone bridge with a fine pergola swathed with grapevines supported on stone pillars. Each of the pools has a stone island, shaped like a boat and seeming to float in the water. At the prow of each boat is a stone fisherman. The parapets of the enclosing walls of the pools are decorated on one side with stone shapes, spheres alternating with pyramids, and on the other side with old box trees underplanted with hydrangeas whose flowers hang down towards the water. At the head of the upper pool an old mill house stands on a balustraded terrace—stone tables and benches are furred with moss. To one side of all this is a canal and a long ALLÉE of lime trees beyond which is an orchard hedged in box. Pazo de Oca is a garden of exceptional character, unlike any other in Spain but in its inventive use of water showing kinship with the gardens of Islam.   PT

Ocampo, Villa,

San Isidro, Buenos Aires province, Argentina. Originally the garden here had an area of 15 hectares/37 acres but today only 1.12 hectares/2.8 acres remains. The garden was originally the characteristic setting for a prosperous country house of the late 19th century. In the middle of the 20th century it was changed into a garden of romantic beauty by the writer Lady Victoria Ocampo (1890–1979) who was an outstanding cultural figure in South America. She came from a family of gardeners and redesigned the garden herself. She used such indigenous species as *Chorisia speciosa* and the jelly palm, *Butia yatay*, together with foreign species especially from Asia and Australia, and created a layout with a magical ambience.

She was particularly interested in the changing colours of plants, their texture and movement, their fragrance, and their desirability to birds, whose sounds and brilliant colours were one of the garden's ingredients. The garden also had an unusual dimension, as the meeting place of many of the notable cultural figures of Victoria Ocampo's day who would walk among the plants and sit in the shade of ancient trees. Among them were Rabindranath Tagore, Albert Camus, Jorge Luis Borges, André Malraux, Igor Stravinsky, and many more. Victoria Ocampo donated this landmark to UNESCO but unfortunately it was disregarded: the house and the garden are abandoned, although Thays Landscapers designed a restoration project. The restoration began in 2004, first by Thays Landscapers and then under the supervision of Sonia Berjman and Ana María Ricciardi.

SLB

Odense University.

See SOUTHERN UNIVERSITY DENMARK IN ODENSE.

Oechsberg Horticultural College ⊗

(Cantonal School of Gardening), Oeschberg, Koppigen, Canton of Berne, Switzerland, was built in 1920 and provided with a garden by Albert Baumann (1891–1976) that is one of the few remaining examples of the architectural garden style of the period. The school was founded at the initiative of the Swiss fruit and vegetable gardeners' association to give young gardeners a sound professional education; traditionally they had been apprenticed to companies and acquired further theoretical and practical expertise for themselves. Garden architect Albert Baumann was responsible, along with his teaching duties, for the design of the 9-hectare/22-acre grounds. Among Baumann's principle mentors were two German garden designers—Paul Schultze-Naumburg (1869–1949), whose 1902 book *Gärten* argued for garden design as an architectural task, and Leberecht MIGGE. It is thus hardly surprising that the kitchen garden and display garden at Oeschberg reflects a strongly architectural approach. An avenue of limes leads from the main road to the school building on its elevated site, facing south with geometrical garden terraces behind stone retaining walls. The layout of the garden in the vicinity of the house is closely related to the plan of the house, emphasized by the southern parterre, the lake, and the summer floral garden. At some distance the productive parts of the garden are arranged on the same strict lines. A park area, adjacent to the east, is laid out in landscape garden style with extensive lawns and an interesting collection of trees. The two park areas, used for theoretical and practical teaching, are linked with a circuit walk. One notable feature is the extensive plant collection with over 5,000 species.   UW

Oehme, van Sweden, & Associates,

garden design partnership founded in 1975 by James van Sweden, an American architect, landscape architect, and urban designer, best known for his public and residential landscapes, and Wolfgang Oehme. They are credited with establishing the 'New American Garden', a style of planting perennials and grasses in massed groupings, which takes its inspiration from the native American biome of the Great Plains. Described by van Sweden as a metaphor for the American meadow, it provides a year-round display of foliage and flower interest in an unstructured plan. Plants are selected for their ability to form self-sustaining communities, lessening weeding, watering, and other aspects of long-term maintenance. Built elements of the landscape receive equal attention and the emphasis on simplicity and honesty of materials and forms is evident in the balance between hard and soft landscape features. Water, too, is present in some form in most designs. Van Sweden holds a bachelor's degree in architecture from the

An **obelisk** at the centre of a firework display at Versailles in 1674.

University of Michigan, and studied landscape architecture and urban design at the University of Delft. Among his most notable projects are the Gardens of the Great Basin at the Chicago Botanic Garden and the Second World War Memorial on the National Mall in Washington, DC, the city in which many of his residential projects may be found. He is the author of *Architecture in the Garden* (2003), *Gardening with Nature* (1997), and *Gardening with Water* (1995), and with Wolfgang Oehme, co-authored *Bold Romantic Gardens: The New World Landscapes of Oehme & van Sweden*.   EC

Oerliker Park ✿

Zurich, Canton of Zurich, Switzerland, is a 2-hectare/5-acre park laid out in 1999 and 2000 by Swiss landscape architects Zulauf Seippel Schweingruber on a contaminated industrial site in the Oerlikon district of Zurich, which opened up new directions in process-oriented open space design. The park, designed for a competition in 1996, is the largest of four new neighbourhood parks created as an integral part of an urban construction project on disused industrial land. One serious problem for the designers was that contaminated soil could not be removed but had to be sealed under a layer of asphalt, over which the park was laid out as if on a tray. Furthermore, when construction commenced it was unclear how quickly the surrounding residential and commercial areas would be built, and there were no buildings to provide a frame for the park. Because of these imponderables the team of landscape architect, architects, and artists devised a simple, flexible project idea: trees planted in a grid formation with a maximum spacing of 8 m/28 ft to create a dense spatial volume, cared for on forestry principles, as a 'green hall' to accommodate a variety of uses. A regularly shaped central clearing, emphasized with a red pavilion on a wooden platform with a fountain, was designed as a link between the two sections of the park separated by a road. A blue lookout tower has already become the landmark and symbol of the park, giving views over buildings and treetops. Stylistic godparents of the design were the enchanting views of Lindenhof in Zurich, Petersplatz in Basle, and the Jardin du Luxembourg in Paris. It was clear from the outset that such impressive green space could not, despite considerable technical measures and expense, be installed within a short period and be ready to use. Indeed, this would have contradicted the intentions of the landscape architects, who were concerned with emphasizing natural processes; the park is not finished, but should grow over the years, develop, and mature along with local residents.   UW

Ohinetahi ✿

Bank's Peninsula, Christchurch, New Zealand, is a garden where plants, design, and style combine to make a place of quality. Sir Miles Warren (b. 1929), the owner, is a distinguished architect who with his sister Pauline and her architect husband John Trengrove conceived the garden over a number of years after taking over a derelict house, the remains of an orchard, and some old trees planted in the 1860s by T. H. Potts, New Zealand's first botanist. The trio adopted a style influenced by gardens they had seen abroad, HIDCOTE MANOR in particular. Of medium size, 1.2 hectares/3 acres, Ohinetahi has a dramatic setting on the edge of the Lyttleton Harbour overlooked by the jagged peaks of the Port Hills. It contains many of the elements of Hidcote being designed along strict architectural lines with cross-axes planted in an informal style. Approached by broad herbaceous borders in strong pinks and blues, a timbered gazebo echoes the ornamentation on the house. When his sister and brother-in-law left to begin their own garden in 1993, Sir Miles changed the white garden colour scheme to red, and built a tall stone tower for the view it provides and to give the garden a vertical accent. Sir Miles has ornamented the garden with sculptures by prominent New Zealand sculptors including Paul Dibble, Graham Bennett, and Neil Dawson. The Dibble is displayed besides an immaculately clipped hedge of *Cupressus macrocarpa* and the Dawson against the open sky.   GSC

Ohlsdorfer Friedhof ✿

Hamburg-Ohlsdorf, Germany. The first municipal cemetery in Hamburg was planned as a large central cemetery north of the town. The landscape architect Johann Wilhem Cordes (1840–1917) began his work in 1877 in traditional design with belt walks, trees, and shrubberies. In the 1920s, Otto Linne (1869–1937), Hamburg's first director of the green spaces department, doubled the surface area and designed the new part in a modern, functional style with water channels, reservoirs, avenues, and formal hedges. With about 400 hectares/988 acres the cemetery today is one of the largest in the world. Visitors admire its distinctive atmosphere with the old trees and hundreds of rhododendrons contrasting with the later part. Memorials of many celebrated men can be seen, among them Fritz Schumacher, Alfred Lichtwark, Gustav Gründgens, and Ida Ehre. The open-air Museum of Tombs, the Jewish Cemetery, and the Cemetery for Celebrated Women are also of particular interest.   HG

Old Company Garden, The ✿

Cape Town, South Africa. The garden lies in the heart of the city, adjacent to St George's cathedral and the parliament buildings. It was the initial *raison d'être* for white settlement in South Africa. It was here on the slopes of Table Mountain, running down to Table Bay, that the Dutch East India Company established a garden to supply fresh fruit and vegetables to their ships sailing between Europe and the East. Several generations later the garden had taken on more of a parklike appearance and it was not long before 'the wild plants of Africa' were being grown. For part of the 18th century a MENAGERIE was located in the grounds. The garden had very mixed fortunes until 1848 when it was re-established as Cape Town Botanic Gardens. The most eminent curator was Paul MacOwen (1830–1909). In 1892 control of the garden was moved from the commission which had run it for the municipality and soon the garden was little more than a public park. Today the Old Company Garden is a favourite city park especially for office workers at lunchtime. The once 17 hectares/42 acres is now reduced to about 5 hectares/12 acres. There is a pleasant avenue of oaks running up the side of the garden which is much frequented by grey squirrels. In the centre of the garden is a statue of Cecil John Rhodes. He is pointing and the inscription reads, 'Your hinterland is there'.   DPMcC

Old Vicarage, The ✿

East Ruston, Norfolk, England, one of the most outstanding new gardens made in England since the Second World War. The ARTS AND CRAFTS vicarage was bought in 1973 by Alan Gray and Graham Robeson—at first a weekend house, it became their permanent abode in 1986. A weekend garden expanded into a full-time garden and by 2003, when it occupied 5 hectares/12 acres, Gray and Robeson showed no signs of ceasing its expansion. The site, as flat as only Norfolk knows how to do, is close to the sea, which has a pronounced effect on the microclimate and also exposes the garden to fierce, cold east winds. Windbreaks have been established, which, with skilful gardening, permit the cultivation of unexpectedly tender plants. The space has been divided with strong axes and long walks which sometimes borrow a distant church spire as an eyecatcher. Ornamental garden buildings, walls, and terracing south of the house have been built. Much box, holm oak (*Quercus ilex*), and yew hedging has been put into place. A drylands garden (inspired by Arizona) has agaves, aloes, dasylirions, and Californian poppies (*Eschscholzia californica*). The exotic garden spills over with the bold foliage of bananas and cannas and is jewelled with brilliant salvias. There are borders, a meadow garden, a Mediterranean garden, and walks of topiary, lines of apple trees or *Robinia pseudoacacia*. The planting is lavish and exuberant but it is always disciplined by strong formal structure.   PT

Old Westbury Gardens ⊛
Old Westbury, New York, the Long Island estate of John Phipps (1874–1958), a steel magnate, and Margarita Grace Phipps (1876–1957), a member of England's Grace shipping-line family, encompasses 65 hectares/160 acres of sweeping lawns, formal gardens, woodland walks, lakes, ponds, grand tree-lined ALLÉES, and wilderness. Built in 1904–6 on a rise, the rosy-bricked Charles II-style mansion and 28 hectares/68 acres of landscaped grounds were designed by London-based George A. Crawley, a designer influenced by the Edwardian sensibilities of his time. The ivy-clad north façade of the house with its limestone-pillared entrance is edged in a yew hedge and faces a rectangular gravel courtyard approached from parallel driveways that fan east and west past an avenue of magnificent beech trees. Much of the planting on the estate was already mature when transplanted in the early 1900s, so today there are mature specimen trees and shrubs that pre-date the garden by decades. The imposing south terrace, brick with stone balustrades punctuated with flower-filled urns, focuses afar on a long linden tree *allée*. Twin stairways descend to the great lawn, bordered by a hedge to set it peacefully apart from gardens out of view on either side. Shaded by a massive American beech (*Fagus grandifolia*), the west terrace overlooks a boxwood garden that encircles a lily pond and a reflecting pool backed by a Grecian colonnade. A lilac walk leads to the brick-walled, sunken Italian garden, 0.8 hectare/2 acres of geometric beds of ever-changing annuals and perennials, planted in English-cottage exuberance (irises, dahlias, daisies, hollyhocks, climbing roses) in waves of seasonal colour. An elegantly colonnaded pergola clad in wisteria and crowned by a latticed and domed summer house, forming a decorative exclamation mark at the south end of the grandest garden within the garden, abuts a serene lily pond banked by Japanese iris. From the Italian garden event follows event, a series of pleasure gardens unfolding along the master path. A hemlock tree (*Tsuga canadensis*) tunnel opens onto a box-bordered traditional rose garden. Overhung by a rustic, locust-post pergola, the now mossy brick passage lined with primroses emerges in a stand of dogwood and hawthorn trees that shelters, surprisingly, a charming thatched playhouse cottage. It could belong to Hansel and Gretel. The stucco and wood-beamed cottage, smothered in flowers and surrounded by a picket fence dotted with bright blue morning glories, was built as a birthday present for the Phippses' 10-year-old daughter. While Peggie gave tea parties for her dolls, her brothers played in three adjacent (and austere) log cabins. The common sandbox, however, is canopied with roses. The tacit invitation from here is to wander eastward, crossing the south lawn that rolls away from the house, into woodland where arched bridges cross streams and trails, glancing by statuary and a temple, and weave around a lake. Old Westbury Gardens opened to the public as a non-profit institution in 1959, a gift from the Phipps family to preserve an extraordinary American country estate in Long Island of the early 20th century.   HS

Olmsted, Frederick Law
(1822–1903), landscape architect and principal founder of the profession of landscape architecture in the United States. Prior to creating the plan for New York's Central Park in 1858 in collaboration with the English architect and landscape architect Calvert Vaux (1824–95), Olmsted had many years of indirect preparation for his profession. His father's love of natural scenery strongly influenced him, and while very young he read the writings of Uvedale PRICE, William SHENSTONE, William GILPIN, and other British landscape theorists whose works influenced his later approach to design. An eye infection in 1837 prevented him from entering college and he spent the next three decades pursuing a varied, informal education and engaging in several professions as a farmer, travel writer, publisher, and administrator. During three trips abroad in those years he became familiar with the parks of Paris and London, and was especially influenced by BIRKENHEAD PARK near Liverpool. In 1865 he entered a nine-year partnership with Calvert Vaux, the first stage of a 30-year career in landscape architecture. Their principal contribution was in the design of public recreation grounds, making distinctive innovations in the planning of parks, parkways, and park systems.

Olmsted developed the concept of the urban park as a place devoted primarily to the experience of scenery that provided a restorative antidote to the stress of city life. The key was immersion in landscape that acted on the viewer through a powerful and 'unconscious' process. All elements of the design, including architecture and engineering, were subordinated to this purpose. Decorative display of plants or objects used for their individual beauty or referential significance were to be avoided. Instead, he sought to produce a feeling of extended space in some areas through gracefully graded meadows with indefinite boundaries, while elsewhere he introduced richness and profusion combined with delicacy, intricacy, and variety of textures in plantings intended for close viewing. The concepts of the pastoral and the picturesque that he had learned from British writers provided the basis for the experience of landscape he sought to produce.

The circulation systems of Olmsted's parks were crucial design elements, since he planned them so as not to intrude on the visual experience while at the same time providing gentle grades and curves that reduced exertion and the need for conscious decisions about the route to take. They provided all-season and all-weather access to the scenery while protecting it from damage through overuse. As illustrated by Central Park (see NEW YORK CITY PARKS AND GARDENS), separation of ways was also a hallmark of Olmsted's parks—separation of city traffic from the park by sunken transverse roads, and separation of potentially conflicting internal traffic through separate ways for pedestrians, equestrians, and carriages.

In his choice of plant materials, Olmsted based his plans on vegetation native to the region. Wishing to have the richest possible palette from which to draw, he supplemented those plants with non-natives that could thrive in the particular microclimate. Much as he valued landscape effects based on the scenery of the British isles, he sought to develop regional styles for the drier climate of the United States. For the semi-arid climate of California and the western mountain states he devised a landscape style based on the Mediterranean (most fully realized in the campus of Stanford University, Palo Alto, California).

When designing the grounds of private residences, Olmsted emphasized creation of 'attractive open-air apartments' where domestic activities could be pursued outside the house. He planned these spaces either to provide extensive greensward for active use or to evoke a sense of richness, variety, and mystery by means of dense planting of shrubbery. He preferred subtle mixing of tints of green and chose plants for complexity of texture of leaves and delicacy of bloom. This was true whether he was planning the grounds of a country estate or a city row-house. He restricted flower gardening to walled enclosures so as not to intrude on broader landscape effects, and there is no record that he ever designed a flower garden. His most notable plan for a walled garden was at BILTMORE Estate in North Carolina, where he proposed to create a 1.6-hectare/4-acre KITCHEN GARDEN with special emphasis on cultivation of fruit on arbours and walls.

Olmsted and his partners produced designs for some 500 landscape commissions between 1857 and his retirement in 1895, of which more than 150 involved laying out the grounds of private estates.   CEB

Olsson, Paul

(1890–1973), garden architect, son of Svante Olsson (first head gardener of the city of Helsinki). He studied in Köstritz, Germany, and later, after training in Stockholm, Germany, and England, worked as assistant head gardener at the city of Helsinki. In 1920, he started his own practice in Helsinki and a nursery in Björkgården, Kauniainen. He designed public parks and other green spaces, private villa and estate gardens, suburban gardens, courtyards, farmyards, public building and factory surroundings, and cemeteries in many parts of Finland. His archive comprises about 2,000 designs. His starting point was a strict *Architekturgarten* style, skilfully using axes to link buildings and various formal garden elements with surrounding landscape. Later, in the 1930s, he moved over to functionalism, and then to international modernism. Among his notable works are Eiranpuisto and Municipal Winter Garden parks, Helsinki; Villa KULTARANTA; and Hahkiala estate garden, Hauho. He employed many second-generation landscape architects, including Maj-Lis ROSENBRÖIJER, Erik Sommerschield, and Onni Savonlahti, and was a prolific writer.

MHay

PAUL OLSSON, *Trädgårdskonst i Finland* (1946).

Opeka Arboretum

Varaždin county, Croatia, was founded as a manor house garden in the 19th century. The house was built by the family of the counts Drašković at the end of the 18th century and was rebuilt, designed by an unknown architect, for the family of the counts Bombelles at the end of the 19th century. Marko Bombelles (1830–1906), the proprietor of Opeka, laid out the garden, which was enlarged and altered on more than one occasion in the late 19th and early 20th centuries and by 1947 was known as an ARBORETUM. Together with park woodland it is spread out over an area of more than 52 hectares/130 acres. It is characterized by a romantic landscape style. The woodland, on rising ground, is planted with sessile oak (*Quercus petraea*), hornbeam (*Carpinus betulus*), and such exotic conifers as Douglas firs (*Pseudotsuga menziesii*), Canada hemlock (*Tsuga canadensis*), and Weymouth pine (*Pinus strobus*). The arboretum in the valley below cultivates 182 different exotic species (about 14,000 specimens) from the Far East, North America, and Europe.   MOŠ/BBOŠ

MLADEN OBAD ŠĆITAROCI, *Dvorci i perivoji Hrvatskoga Zagorja* (1991, 1993). Translated as *Castles, Manors and Gardens of Croatian Zagorje* (1992; 3rd ed. 1996).

Opinogóra

near Ciechanów, Poland. The village belonged to the Krasiński family as early as the 16th century. In 1828–43 a neo-Gothic Little Castle was erected for Zygmunt Krasiński (1812–59), one of the foremost Polish Romantic poets. It was then that the creation of a landscape park was commenced. The garden was given its final form in 1895 by the well-known landscape architect Walerian Kronenberg (1859–1934). The landscape park, covering an area of 21 hectares/52 acres, extends over three hills between which there is a large lake with an irregular shoreline. About 1,000 trees grow about it, including maples, oaks, ashes, and horse chestnuts. Two oaks (Zygmunt and Eliza) and two ashes (Szwoleżer I and Szwoleżer II) are ancient natural features of historic importance. Nineteenth-century stone ornaments and a monument to Zygmunt Krasiński are additional attractions of the park. The Little Castle now houses the Museum of Romanticism.   WB

orangery,

a building in which to protect orange trees or a garden dedicated to their cultivation. The orange, in the form of the bitter orange (*Citrus aurantium*) from South-East Asia, came to Europe with the Islamic occupation from the 8th century AD. The surviving Patio de los NARANJOS (patio of orange trees) in Córdoba (Spain) was laid out in the late 8th century and is possibly the oldest continuously gardened site in Europe. The sweet orange (*Citrus sinensis*) coming from China is a much later introduction but was certainly known by the 16th century. Orange trees are first mentioned in any French garden at the Château de Blois (Loir-et-Cher) where the gardens were made for Louis XII by the Neapolitan Pacello de MERCOGLIANO between 1499 and 1510. They were visited in 1517 by the Cardinal d'Aragon who described 'many lemon and orange trees in wooden tubs. In the winter they are kept in a big wooden shelter which protects them from snow and malicious winds.' Oranges were supplied to François I's new garden at FONTAINEBLEAU in 1538 but it is not known how they were displayed, but in 1645–7 a new orangery was designed by Jacques Le Mercier and later on, after 1682, a gardener, Michel LE BOUTEUX, had specific reponsibility for the care of the orange trees. In Germany an orangery was designed by Salomon de CAUS for the HORTUS PALATINUS at Heidelberg and the design published in his *Les*

Raisons des forces mouvantes (1624). In England oranges seem to have been grown for the first time at Beddington (Surrey) by Francis Carew, who inherited the estate in 1539 and brought orange trees from Italy. They were still cultivated in the 17th century and John EVELYN saw them in 1658—'the first Orange gardens in England . . . planted in the ground, and secur'd in winter with a wooden tabernacle and stoves'. The word orangery is French in origin (*orangerie*) and in England until the 19th century it meant merely a place were oranges were grown. In France, where orangeries were much used, the word also combines the two meanings, an orange garden overlooked by a building in which to give winter protection. One of the earliest examples of this arrangement (no longer surviving) was designed for the Château d'ANET by Philibert de L'ORME and built between 1547 and 1552. Standing outside the walled pleasure gardens it formed an entity of its own, with south-facing windows opening onto a raised terrace ending in ramps to allow the easy movement of the potted plants between the orangery and the walled enclosure below where they would spend the summer months. It is illustrated in Androuet DU CERCEAU's *Plus Excellents Bastiments de France* (1576–9). Such orange gardens were sometimes laid out in an ornamental way, with the pots of citrus plants forming part of an elaborate parterre. Antoine-Nicholas Dezallier d'Argenville in his *Voyage pittoresque des environs de Paris* (1762) describes such an arrangement at the Château de Villeneuve-l'Étang with 'compartments of cut turf with two pools displaying fine orange trees disposed in two diagonal *allées*'. This was exactly the arrangement, in its heyday, of the great *orangerie* at VERSAILLES. Israël Sylvestre's engraving of it *c*.1690 shows six parterres of *gazon coupé* (cut turf) with a central circular pool, the whole overlooked by the south-facing winter quarters, built like a vaulted cavern in the supporting wall of a terrace. The parterres have long since gone but the Versailles orangery still houses citrus plants (including some said to date from the 17th century) to which have been added many large palm trees. The interior of the winter room, with its great vaulted space, is an astonishing sight.

The arrangement of an orangery overlooking its own space in which to display citrus plants out of doors, forming its own decorative interlude, is found in many European gardens from the 17th century onwards, continuing well into the 19th century. In England the earliest example of this seems to have been at Bretby Hall (Derbyshire) where the Earl of Chesterfield made a great garden in the 1670s, seen in a KIP engraving in *Britannia Illustrata* (1707). Seven bays wide and pedimented, it faced south over a walled garden with a central pool—nothing survives of this house and garden. There are, however, many surviving examples in British gardens. A modest three-bay orangery at HAM HOUSE was built by 1677, overlooking the kitchen garden and today used to house a restaurant. At Kensington Palace (London) is one of the most splendid orangeries, built in refined baroque style, probably a collaboration between Nicholas HAWKSMOOR and Christopher Wren, it was completed in 1704. The interior, also now used as a cafeteria, is outstanding and among its ornaments are two 17th-century garden urns, by C. G. Cibber (1630–1700) and Edward Pierce (d. 1695), originally from HAMPTON COURT. Increasingly orangeries became indistinguishable from CONSERVATORIES, housing any plant that required winter protection. At Hanbury Hall (Worcestershire) there is a noble nine-bay orangery built of brick and stone decorated with a pediment and urns along the parapet. Its date, and designer, are unknown but it must be a little later than the house which was completed in 1701. Now finely cared for by the NATIONAL TRUST, with citrus plants in *caisses de Versailles* (see CONTAINER), it has an unusual feature—an entrance behind it, on its north side, leads to a mushroom house built into the back of the orangery. The most astonishing orangery in Britain is at MARGAM PARK. Dating from 1787, designed by Anthony Keck (1726–97), and built in beautiful pale honey-coloured stone, it has 29 bays and is 97 m/327 ft in width. In the later period it is impossible to distinguish an orangery from a conservatory—both were glasshouses for cultivating tender ornamentals. One of the last great orangeries dedicated to orange trees to be built in Europe was that in the Tuileries gardens in PARIS, built in 1853 to the designs of Firmin Bourgeois and Ludovico Visconti and since 1927 a museum (Musée de l'Orangerie).   PT

MAY WOODS and ARETE WARREN, *Glass Houses* (1988).

Oranienbaum (Germany).
See DESSAU-WÖRLITZ GARTENREICH.

Oranienbaum ⊛
(Lomonosov), Russia, 41 km/26 miles from St Petersburg on the Gulf of Finland, is the site of the palace and park of Prince Alexander Menshikov, associate of Peter the Great. Begun by D. M. Fontana in 1710 and then continued by J. G. Schädel from 1713 until 1727, Oranienbaum was one of the most magnificent residences of the early 18th century. Like PETERHOF, the palace was built on a terrace facing the sea and was connected by stairways and terraces to the Lower Park, which was formally laid out with straight walks, parterres, fountains, and statues. There was a small harbour by the entrance to the park, linked to the sea by a canal, which was a projection of the central axis of the park.

In 1743 Oranienbaum became the summer residence of Grand Duke Peter Fedorovich (later Peter III), for whom Rinaldi (1709–94) designed the palace-fortress complex, Peterstadt (1756–61), by the river Karost. The same architect also designed the Chinese Palace (1762–8), so-called because of its interiors, in a formal setting for Catherine II. Most of the formal areas of the park were landscaped in the 19th century.

Rinaldi's elegant blue and white Katalnaya Gorka (Coasting Hill) Pavilion is still a striking focal point in the Upper Park. It was once a viewing stand, a place of rest and refreshment, and gave access to the starting platform of the remarkable coasting hill which was built between 1762 and 1769. Sliding hills, *montagnes russes,* are a traditional Russian amusement and the forerunner of the modern roller-coaster. Rinaldi's coasting hill, which was 532 m/1,745 ft long, was not just a simple single descent, as was usually the case, but a series of descents, the first three of which were followed by ascents, switchback fashion. 'It is thus used: a small carriage containing one person, being placed in the centre groove upon the highest point, goes with great rapidity down one hill; the velocity which it acquires carries it up a second; and it continues to move in a similar manner until it arrives at the bottom of the area, where it rolls for a considerable way' (William Coxe, *Travels into Poland, Russia, Sweden and Denmark*, 1784). This structure was surrounded by a colonnade with a flat roof as a promenade, protected by balustrades which were embellished with vases and statues. There was a slightly earlier sliding hill at TSARSKOE SELO. The Chinese Palace, the Palace of Peter III, and the Coasting Hill Pavilion have been restored.   PH

orchard.
An orchard is an enclosure devoted to the cultivation of fruit trees, in England the apple, pear, plum, and cherry. Domestic or commercial, its history is that of fruit, the long evolution of its varieties, husbandry, and consumption. But orchards have never been merely utilitarian: fruit trees were ornaments of the pleasure ground, valued as much for their exquisite blossom, glowing fruits, and gentle shade as their harvest. It was princely demand for luxury and rarity that drove the development of fruit cultivation from its origins in the ancient world—our very orchard fruits come, in the main, from species native to areas stretching from southern Europe to the Caucasus, Iran, Central Asia, and China. By the first millennium BC fruit cultivation had become an essential part of civilized life. Homer's King Alcinous owned 'a large orchard of four acres, where trees hang their greenery on high, the pear and the pomegranate, the apple with its glossy burden, the sweet fig and the luxuriant olive'. The Persian King Darius I, who in the 6th century BC ruled an empire stretching from the Mediterranean to the Indus, fostered fruit cultivation by establishing in all his provinces a *pairidaeza*, a 'walled space' planted with trees. From *pairidaeza* through the Greek *paradeisos* comes our word and vision of paradise—an enclosure filled with fruit trees watered by pools and canals, a pattern that still survives in Iranian gardens and an image of beauty combined with utility that has never left orchards and fruit trees.

The early history of the orchard in England
The tradition came to England with the Romans, who grew such a range of varieties that, according to Horace, Italy became one vast orchard. How much survived the fall of the western empire is impossible to say, but new stocks came with the Normans and later royal and monastic networks. Orchards were both profitable and pleasurable. The 100 pear trees planted for Henry III in 1264 at Everswell, the cloistered pleasance of orchards and pools near the palace of Woodstock, must have been remarkable in the spring sheeted in white blossom. They were, no doubt, also remunerative, like the orchard of pearmain apples at Runham in Norfolk that paid the rent in 1290 to the royal exchequer and the orchards of Battle Abbey in Sussex, which also provided meditative walks for the monks (John Harvey, *Mediaeval Gardens*, 1981).

Most of the fruits of the medieval orchard, such as the well-known costard apple and warden pear, were destined for the kitchens and press, too sharp and hard to be eaten fresh with pleasure. Quality, however, began to improve from Tudor times as the renewed continental interest in fruit crossed the Channel. In 1534 new varieties of apples, including the first 'pippins', pears, and cherries collected from the Low Countries by Henry VIII's entrepreneurial fruiterer Richard Harris were introduced to Kent. Soon new orchards to supply the metropolis transformed the county into the 'Garden of England' where William Lambard revelled in apples and cherries 'of the most delicious and exquisite kinds' in his perambulation of Kent in 1570. England was also to benefit from cheaper supplies of sugar, fruit's perfect partner, its sweetener and preservative, which was beginning to arrive from colonies in the West Indies. The stage was set for the emergence of the increasingly elaborate Fruit Banquet, a glittering array of fresh fruit and fruit sweetmeats which formed the finale to the feast and was often taken outside in a banqueting house in the garden among the fruit trees.

Fruit was a prominent feature of the new pleasure gardens, such as those of Wimbledon Manor, bought by Charles I for his wife Queen Henrietta Maria in 1639. Nearly 100 cherry trees were set around fountains and statues in the Great Garden in front of the manor, where several banqueting houses were conveniently placed. In its upper section many more fruit trees were planted—'divers kinds of apples, pears, pleasant and profitable'—and elsewhere walls sheltered muscat vines and figs. The adjoining 4-hectare/10-acre walled orchard of fruit trees was divided into sections by avenues of lime trees and with borders of currants and strawberries (A. Amherst, *Gardening in England*, 1895).

Orchards have always varied considerably in size and content, but they were and still are usually bounded by a hedge, fence, or wall, which might have been set behind a ditch for further security. This boundary not only protects the precious trees and fruits from damage or theft by intruders and animals, but also from wind; even very large modern orchards are subdivided by windbreaks. The sheltered microclimate helps ripen the fruit, prevents it being blown off, and most importantly encourages the activity of bees and other pollinating insects, which ensures a good set of fruit; bee hives are an essential part of a fruitful orchard. The trees are set in rows for ease of cultivation. They may be grown in grass, or the ground kept free of any herbage, or cultivated, and at least three broad categories of orchards existed by the 17th century.

Types of orchard

Farmers' orchards were of tall, standard trees, with grass beneath grazed by sheep or cows. Long established in Kent, orchards were increasing all over the country by the end of the century as farmers diversified into fruit with the decline in the prosperity of mainstream agriculture. This created the regional pattern that endured up to the late 19th century, in which Kent with access to nearby London grew fresh fruit, such as apples and cherries, while the west country and west midlands, with less market opportunities, concentrated on cider orchards. Market gardeners' orchards were usually smaller than those of the farmer and more diverse and intensive. Tree fruits formed an upper storey of top fruit grown in cultivated ground, in which an undercrop of fruit bushes,

vegetables, or flowers was planted. Every city had its market gardens with the largest in the Thames valley supplying London. Intensive orchards also developed in the Vale of Evesham in Worcestershire with an expanding market in Birmingham. The domestic orchard, which supplied the mansion, vicarage, or farmhouse with all its fruit requirements, was closer in size and content to that of the market gardener. Many probably resembled the plan advised by the Revd William Lawson in 1617. Surrounded by a sturdy, yet fruitful hedge of hawthorn interplanted with damson, bullace, plums, and filberts, it was planted with apples, pears, and quince trees set 18 m/60 ft apart to allow for considerable size at maturity. There were borders of fruit bushes and strawberries and from the broad walks and camomile seats owners could enjoy violets, primroses, honeysuckle, and roses, as well as fruit (William Lawson, *New Orchard and Garden with The Country Housewifes Garden*, 1617).

Developments in fruit cultivation

The Age of Enlightenment brought a more scientific approach to fruit cultivation. The aim became quality rather than mere quantity, a direction that was facilitated by the new dwarfing rootstocks for apples and pears, enabling them to be grown as smaller trees, which could be carefully pruned and were easier to pick and protect against frost, predators, and pests. These were taken up in country house gardens where, throughout the century, fruit increased in range and prominence and its cultivation became split between the orchard and the walled fruit garden, a separation that was already becoming apparent at Wimbledon Manor. The fruit garden was considered second in importance and beauty only to the flower garden, according to John Rea in his *Flora Ceres and Pomona* (1665). It was the domain of the choicest and most tender fruits—the best pears and apples, the superior gage plums, peaches, apricots, figs, and vines—while most of the apples, baking pears, and stewing plums were consigned to the orchard. Trees were also trained or palisaded into two-dimensional forms, such as fans, espaliers, and palmettes, which further improved their quality. Trained fruits, thus receiving maximum sunshine, developed good colour, built up sugars and flavours, especially if grown against a wall, and produced perfect specimens for the increasingly demanding requirements of the dining table and banquet. Grown in the open these forms could edge paths and create avenues of delight throughout the pleasure grounds. 'A perpetual tapestry, covered in spring with flowers, in summer and autumn with fruit and foliage, beautiful even in winter

with bare branches laced together in cunning artifice,' wrote Antoine Le Gendre, the French pioneer of fruit training, whose instructions were translated into English as *The Manner of Ordering Fruit Trees* (1655). By the end of the century, not only were orchards very much in evidence following agriculture's investment in fruit, but this enthusiasm, especially for apples, was also apparent in the 'many very good gardens' which boasted an 'abundance of fruit of all sorts' (*The Illustrated Journeys of Celia Fiennes c.1682–c.1712*, ed. C. Morris, 1988).

The walled fruit gardens evolved into the great fruit and vegetable gardens of the 18th century, where extensive espaliers of trained trees were said to be prominent features and their owners' pride and joy. Here experiments were under way in growing fruit under glass in preparation for the revolution in fruit cultivation that occurred during the 19th century. With improvements in glass manufacture and the development of hot water boilers to heat the houses, all the tender fruits now came under glass in peach and fig houses and vineries. Pineapples and citrus fruits even became standard crops in some establishments. The Victorian fruit and vegetable garden was not only an enclosure of traditional temperate fruits, but also orchards of Mediterranean and tropical fruits and flowers redolent with imperial splendour. The stimulus was the Victorian dessert, the triumphant climax to the formal dinner party and a telling statement of the host's wealth and refinement. Fruit sweetmeats of the past were cast in the shade by the magnificence of home-grown fresh fruit (Joan Morgan and Alison Richards, *A Paradise out of a Common Field*, 1990).

Among the hardy fruits there was an immense increase in diversity and quality, especially in pears, and the 19th century also saw the development of the modern, large-fruiting strawberry. The trial grounds for all this new material were the country house where gardeners were constantly searching for quality and novelty to satisfy the demands of the dessert. Very many varieties of each fruit were needed so as to provide the greatest selection and longest possible season. This could be best met from the trees of the walled fruit and vegetable garden, grown on improved and more dwarfing rootstocks and in the most intensive trained system, that of cordons, which from about the 1860s became the fashionable way to grow a large collection of apples or pears. For estate owners who lived in less clement parts of the country the orchard house provided the means to achieve this perfection. The orchard house was a large, airy glasshouse designed, said its inventor, nurseryman Thomas Rivers, to create the climate of Nice without its biting winds. In this protected environment, apples, pears, and other fruits were grown in large pots which, with skill and a little luck, enabled the finest varieties to ripen and achieve exhibition quality, even in chilly Scotland or amidst the rains of Wales.

Orchards of large standard trees, free of any dwarfing trends, were still a feature of these 19th-century supply centres. Their heavy crops were mostly destined for the kitchens and were primarily of cooking apples, routine pears, and plums for puddings, jams, and preserves. Depending upon the locality, there might also be blocks of cherries and nuts outside the walled garden. Meanwhile, commercial orchards had risen to the top of the political and economic agenda in response, on the one hand, to almost overwhelming competition from imported American and continental fruit and, on the other, to the severe decline in mainstream agriculture by the 1880s. Orchards were modernized, new ones planted, and farmers all over the country invested in fruit growing. In traditional regions, like Kent, many farms now turned over completely to fruit and planted intensively. Apple orchards around Maidstone, for example, were sheltered by damson hedges and also grew gooseberries; the fruit bushes would be removed when the trees attained full size. Cherry orchards, grazed by Romney Marsh sheep, predominated around Sittingbourne and Faversham, where pears were also grown. In the west midlands, plums were the speciality of the Vale of Evesham. New plantations in Herefordshire were often of fresh fruit rather than cider orchards, as the railways brought previously isolated areas into swift and easy contact with the cities. Gloucestershire and adjoining counties remained the place for perry pear trees and in the west country orchards were planted mainly for cider. New orchards developed in East Anglia, particularly Cambridgeshire and Essex. Areas in which orchards are almost forgotten now were supplying markets—for example, around Kendal and Nottingham, and in Lancashire, Cheshire, and Cornwall in the Tamar valley, where they grew early cherries with narcissi in between the rows. Thames valley orchards stretched out to Uxbridge and beyond as the growth of London pushed the market gardeners westwards. By the end of the century every county had seen an expansion of its orchards and the modern fruit industry was established (Joan Morgan and Alison Richards, *The New Book of Apples*, 2002).

The heyday and decline of orchards

By the 1890s, not only the professionals, but also the general public were caught up in the Fruit Campaign to save the English orchard and especially the English apple from predicted extinction by the Yankee imports. In these competitive, rapidly changing times, not only did the English apple achieve the status of a fine wine, discussed and debated with as much intensity as the claret at connoisseurs' dining tables, but apples and orchards also came to symbolize a gentler, more appealing age, when garden design was deemed to be free of the foreign excesses of Italianate terracing and French parterres of the High Victorian period. Designers turned to 16th- and 17th-century England for their ideas and an era when fruit trees were ornaments of the pleasure garden. William Lawson's inspirational claims and plans of 1617 became the model for the artistic orchard promoted by the ARTS AND CRAFTS movement. 'What can your eye desire to see your eares to heare, your mouth to taste, or your nose to smell, that is not to be had in an orchard?' he asked. Accordingly large apple trees, garlanded with climbing roses, were grown in grass in which snowdrops, narcissi, and crocuses were naturalized and perhaps a brood of nightingales was also present 'to clense your trees of caterpillars, and all noysome worms and flies'. The tree's blossom and its habit were now of interest, and gardeners and nurserymen's catalogues guided their readers as to a variety's suitability for enlivening a shrubbery or forming a spreading lawn tree. At a more formal level, fruit trees trained as arches, tunnels, and espaliers were planted in gardens all over Britain— Tyninghame in East Lothian, for example, boasted an apple tunnel 45 m/150 ft long.

Since those glorious times and especially during recent decades, orchards have declined everywhere. Thames valley market gardens, enveloped by urban expansion, finally disappeared under Heathrow Airport, farmhouse orchards have shrunk or vanished altogether, and modern gardens have little space for an orchard. Orchard varieties have been reduced as horticulture moved away from the diverse needs of the private garden to the profitable few of the commercial man. Today's commercial orchard is tended as meticulously as a Victorian fruit garden, but its appearance has dramatically changed since the 19th century. Tall standards have been replaced by dwarfed, closely spaced trees, a trend that has spread to cider orchards. Even cherry trees are low growing enough to net and protect. Instead of lasting for 50 years or more orchards are renewed every fifteen or twenty years. The loss of these traditional fruit tree landscapes, which were a feature of Kent, the west midlands, and the west country, has brought orchards into the conservation arena. Over the last decade or so there has been a call for the return of old-fashioned, tall, standard trees grown in grass, while old and regional fruit varieties are being rediscovered and promoted as we seek to conserve our fruit heritage. As a consequence, the range of orchard varieties readily available has greatly increased; interest in local specialities almost reduced to a memory, such as the mazzard cherries of north Devon and the damsons of Westmorland, has burgeoned; the spread of farmers' markets has brought new outlets for local fruits; stewardship schemes and grants are available for the restoration of orchards and creation of community orchards; and Apple Day, 21 October, founded by the environmental charity Common Ground, has become a focus for orchard celebrations. Public awareness of the riches of our orchards has been awakened, but this has done little to halt the erosion of British commercial fruit growing, where large trees and old varieties have no place in an international industry. The orchard could once again be a shady paradise, but its bounty is fast disappearing.   JMo

orchids

are found wherever there is not permanent ice and snow, permanent desert, or water. They grow terrestrially (in the ground, or even completely underground), epiphytically (on trees), lithophytically (on rocks), bryophytically (on mosses), can be monopodial (with a single growing point) or sympodial (with a rhizome), saprophytic but never parasitic, and (at least in the seedling stages) dependent on a symbiotic relationship with various root mycorrhiza for germination and sugar synthesis. They may be leafless, synthesizing carbohydrates from chlorophyll in aerial roots, tiny (a few millimetres high) or gigantic (the record weighing in at over 2 tons). There are some 800 genera, 30,000 species, 130,000 recorded artificial hybrids, and an estimated 400,000 unregistered artificial hybrids. The species and the genera interbreed vigorously, usually producing fertile offspring; intergeneric hybrids containing up to ten different genera are recorded. All have flowers with three sepals (although in some genera there may be fusion of two or more sepals) and three petals and have left–right symmetry. All have their pollen in clumps called pollinia, often on the end of narrow stipes ending with a sticky plate, the viscidium. The pollinia and the stigma are found at the end of a central column, an extension of the ovary formed from the fusion of its three stamens and three pistils, at the centre of the flower. They are, when not self-pollinating, pollinated by an endless list of insects, hummingbirds, bees, butterflies, and moths, with which they have an intense symbiotic relationship—usually of benefit to both insect and flower. Even outside the pollination process, so well described by Charles Darwin, orchids have symbiotic relationships with spiders, ants, and even snakes—providing a mutual benefit to each other. The seeds are wind borne, and among the smallest in the plant kingdom, with 80,000 seeds in a single capsule of an *Orchis* and as much as 3 million in the seedpod of a *Cymbidium*. They can colonize huge areas and are suspected of rapid evolution by hybridization and mutation—an argument supported by the continuous appearance and discovery of new species in certain genera, but not all. In 1970 there were 200 known species of *Masdevallia*, a showy small-flowered South American orchid, but more than 600 have been found since then.

The British Isles has some 60 species, Ecuador more than 3,000—wet, mountainous areas in the tropics being the areas of greatest diversity. Their cultivation is first recorded from China in 800 BC and Confucius sang the praises of *Cymbidium*. The word *Orchis*—from which 'orchid'—was first used by Theophrastus between 370 and 285 BC and refers to the tubers of plants in the genus *Orchis* that resemble testes, for which *Orchis* is the Greek word. Under the Doctrine of Signatures these tubers had medicinal powers related to sexual function and fertility, but despite the clear lack of such activity they are still collected in Eastern Europe to make a protein-rich drink called 'salep'. In the New World, the *Badianus* manuscript, an Aztec herbal of 1552, illustrates *Vanilla*, an orchid still used today for the aromatic oils produced by its seed-pods. In Africa orchids have many herbal aficionados, the strangest being the belief that the tiger orchid, *Ansellia africana*, can—if fastened to the roof of a house—ward off lightning.

Neofinetia falcata has been prized in cultivation in Japan since the 17th century and specimens with uniquely coloured foliage still command huge prices—$US 50,000 being requested for the cultivar 'Brown Bear' in this century. The transatlantic orchid trade began nearly 400 years ago, for PARKINSON records an American *Cypripedium* (slipper orchid) in 1640. Cultivation of tropical orchids in Europe began with the introduction of *Brassavola nodosa* to the garden of Casper Fagel in the Netherlands, from Curaçao in 1698. The introductions were few and far between initially, with two orchids from China being introduced by Dr John Fothergill in 1778. Sir Joseph BANKS and Daniel Solander collected orchids in Australia in 1780 and various naval captains, such as Captain Bligh, were bringing back a few plants to Kew or to friends as the century ended. John LINDLEY in 1818, working for William Cattley, described

some of the exotic orchids being introduced, and the interest in tropical orchids for cultivation increased. At the Horticultural Society he sent out plant collectors and described the introductions—and by the 1830s, led by the Duke of Devonshire, there was a great upsurge of enthusiasm for collecting, naming, and growing new orchids throughout the British Isles and into Europe. John Lindley, H. G. Reichenbach, and other botanists made their reputations on the back of their descriptions of the flood of new orchid introductions, collected by the plantsmen sent out by rich amateurs and professional nurserymen to find new species to satisfy the increasing demand. The orchid nurseries of James VEITCH, Jean Linden, Frederick Sander, and others importing, breeding, and growing them became major industries that continued into the 20th century. In 1946 the export of orchids from the UK was its third largest export in cash value.

The artificial breeding of orchids in Europe was first recorded on April Fool's Day, 1 April 1856 with the announcement of the production of *Calanthe dominyi*—a hybrid raised in the Veitch nursery at the suggestion of Dr Harris, a local doctor. At the present time orchid breeding and the production of mericlones (from *in vitro* multiplication of meristemmatic tissue) has become a major international industry, with over a thousand million orchid pot plants being produced in the Netherlands each year. Huge greenhouses covering many acres are filled by seedlings raised in sterile flasks containing agar, sugar, and minerals. Here they are watered by machines, potted on by machines, and monitored by computers—a single acre producing up to 2 million flowering-size orchids each year. Millions of *Phalaenopsis* hybrids flood into an insatiable market from the Netherlands and Taiwan, to be sold as window-sill plants for the world. *Vanda* and its relatives are produced in Thailand, and the cut-flower industry using *Cymbidium* is a flourishing business from Europe to South Africa.

Botanists continue to study orchids, following in the footsteps of Linnaeus, but are now armed with the tools of genetic analysis, phylogenetics, enabling accurate and impartial classification of difficult groups and the merging of those which are indistinguishable. It is, however, their colour and form, their heady fragrances and long flowering times, with their association with all that is exotic, that maintains their perpetual fascination in orchid growers and non-orchid growers alike.

Excellent collections of orchids are to be seen in many specialist gardens. Among the best in the United States are the American Orchid

Society Visitors Center and Botanical Garden (Delray Beach, Florida) with a 1,220-sq.-m/ 4,000-sq.-ft display greenhouse complete with waterfall and a 1.4-hectare/3.5-acre garden with hardy orchids growing on trees or in flower beds. BROOKLYN BOTANIC GARDEN (New York; 1,005 taxa) has an extensive collection of orchids, grown by curator David Horak. Denver Botanical Garden (Denver, Colorado; 963 taxa) has a dramatic, huge artificial tree (made of cork bark) housing many of the orchids displayed in a multi-level conservatory. Golden Gate Park Conservatory (San Francisco, California; 2,400 taxa) displays an extensive collection of cool-growing orchids in a conservatory which has just completed a major renovation. Marie Selby Botanical Gardens (Sarasota, Florida; 1,470 taxa) is a lovely display greenhouse with orchids and other tropical plants, some also grown outdoors in a tranquil waterfront garden. NEW YORK BOTANICAL GARDEN (New York) has a spectacular conservatory, one of the wonders of the glasshouse world, with magnificent orchids grown by curator Marc Hachadourian.

In Britain there are notable collections at the Eric Young Orchid Foundation (Jersey, Channel Islands) which is solely dedicated to raising superb orchids for exhibition—the display house has among the finest hybrids and species in the world. The ROYAL BOTANIC GARDENS, EDINBURGH, ROYAL BOTANIC GARDENS, KEW, and Royal Horticultural Society Garden, WISLEY, all have good collections.   HFO/JBW

Orczy Gardens,

Budapest, Hungary. It was outside the then boundary of Pest that Baron László Orczy turned bleak wasteland into the landscape garden that would soon become the Hungarian capital's most often visited public park. The construction of the gardens began in 1794, to the designs of Bernhard PETRI, who succeeded, with great difficulty, in establishing a splendid park in this poor soil, together with a lake, hills, a vineyard, a GROTTO, and a mock RUIN. This is where one of Hungary's largest greenhouses was built from 1817 to 1820, which in 1867 was later to fall victim to a fire. In 1829 the park was purchased for the construction of the Ludovika Military Academy, though it remained visitable until the end of the 19th century. Between 1848 and 1867 Ármin PECZ Sr. was the head gardener. The area of the park has since contracted considerably, but work on its conservation has partially begun.   GA   ⊃ page 353

organic gardening

is easier to practise than it is to describe succinctly. The word organic itself has several dictionary definitions, including 'of living origin' or 'relating to organic chemistry', which do not pertain to gardening. A common definition of organic gardening is that it 'avoids the use of industrially manufactured chemical fertilisers and pesticides'. This is less than helpful, negative, and not entirely truthful. Organic gardening is a very proactive system of growing, it is not a question of 'not doing'. Organic gardeners work with nature, harnessing and enhancing natural systems of soil fertility and pest and disease management. Organic gardening aims for long-term sustainability, minimizing adverse impact on the local and wider environment. Other names for this type of gardening include biological, green, and ecological, but organic is probably the term most widely used.

The history
Organic gardening, as a distinct concept, came into being in the early 20th century. This was when the development and use of artificial fertilizers and chemical pesticides in commercial growing was really beginning to take off. A minority of concerned individuals saw the new growing methods as breaking the vital relationship between the health of soil, plants, animals, and man. Determined to maintain their more natural, holistic systems of growing, they were the spearhead of what is now known as the 'organic movement'. Lawrence D. Hills D.Sc. (1911–90) was one of these visionaries, and he can well be called the father of organic gardening in the UK. Due to illness, he received little in the way of formal education, but he was knowledgeable, imaginative, and widely read. He was also a professional horticulturalist, particularly expert in alpines. Hills's concerns about the direction that agriculture, and gardening, was taking led him to start the Henry Doubleday Research Association (HDRA). This was basically a club for experimenting organic gardeners. HDRA was formally established as a registered charity in 1954. Hills was a journalist and prolific writer, with several organic gardening books to his name. In recognition of his life's work, he was awarded an honorary D.Sc. by Coventry University in 1990. Henry Doubleday, after whom the association was named, was a 19th-century Quaker naturalist whose work Hills admired.

Now known as 'HDRA—the organic organization', the association is run by scientists Alan and Jackie Gear, who have taken it through a period of sustained growth, to become the largest organic membership organization in Europe. The Prince of Wales is its patron. HDRA is the UK's leading organization for organic gardeners, providing advice, information, and support for its 30,000 amateur and professional gardening members. Its organic display gardens in the Midlands (Ryton Organic Gardens) and Kent (Yalding Organic Gardens) are open to the public. HDRA members also open their gardens under the Organic Gardening Weekends scheme. HDRA is also a prime player in the research and development of commercial organic horticulture.

Organics today
In the mid 20th century, organic gardening was often seen as the province of hippies and 'back to the land'-ers. Organic methods were used primarily for food growing, and not always very successfully at that. Now things have changed. Organic methods are recognized as a valid, and

---

The park at **Orczy** in a lithograph by Rudolf Alt (1845).

354   **organic gardening**

successful, way of managing the whole garden—ornamentals and lawns as well as fruit and vegetables. Organic gardening is popular across the population as a whole, from domestic gardeners and allotment holders to managers of large estates. The Victorian KITCHEN GARDEN at the English Heritage property Audley End in Essex is run organically, in conjunction with HDRA. The NATIONAL TRUST now manages some of its properties organically, as do the Prince of Wales, Lady Salisbury (at HATFIELD HOUSE), the Duke of Westminster, and other owners of large gardens. Interest in organic methods, from the general public, commercial food producers, and amenity landscape managers alike, continues to grow. This is fuelled by an increasing awareness that organic gardening methods are effective, and by food health scares, pesticide worries, and concerns for public health and the environment.

Organic standards

Across Europe, and in other countries, there is a legally binding definition of the word 'organic' when used in relation to food for sale. In the UK, this definition comes as a lengthy and comprehensive organic growing manual—known as the 'organic standards'. The content will vary to some extent in different countries. There are also internationally recognized standards. Organic standards are fluid in that they are revised and updated as knowledge grows. Although there is no legal definition of organic gardening, some sort of guidelines are needed for gardeners. HDRA has produced a gardening version of the official food production standards, the *Guidelines for Organic Gardeners*. HDRA is also compiling standards for organic landscaping.

The market for organic gardening products has expanded with the increasing interest in growing this way—but unfortunately there is currently no *legal* definition of the word organic when used in this context. A fertilizer, soil improver, or pesticide labelled as organic may not necessarily be suitable for use in an organic garden. Manure from intensive farming systems, for example, can legally be labelled as organic, but it would not be acceptable in an organic garden. Some products, however, do carry an accredited organic logo.

Modern organic gardening uses many valuable techniques from the past, as well as the most recent developments from scientific research, as long as they meet the organic ethos. Pest- and disease-resistant cultivars, for example, can prove invaluable, but those produced by genetic engineering are regarded as an unacceptable step too far. It is interesting that modern research, into the use of compost, or growing flowers to attract predators for

example, is validating traditional organic techniques.

A summary of the basic principles of organic gardening follows:

Soil management. Where possible, grow plants to suit existing conditions. Maintain and improve soil structure and fertility as appropriate, using bulky organic materials such as garden compost and leafmould. Soil improvers brought in to the garden should not be from intensive production systems. They should be composted for six months before use. Organic fertilizers—slow release materials of animal, plant, or mineral origin—are available to provide additional fertility if required. Requiring breakdown by micro-organisms before nutrients are available to plants, these are seen as more appropriate for soil and plant health than soluble artificial fertilizers that provide an almost instant supply of a limited range of plant foods.

Pest and disease management. A prime aim is to capitalize on the natural pest/predator interactions, both in the soil and above ground, to provide a basic level of pest and disease control. Predators are encouraged by the avoidance of harmful pesticides, and by the enhancement of habitats. Biological control agents can be purchased for introduction into the garden and greenhouse. Research has shown that plants grown on soil improved with composted organic wastes are less attractive to pests. The natural systems are backed up by sound horticultural practice to encourage healthy plant growth. Physical barriers and traps are used to keep pests and diseases at bay. A very limited range of naturally based pesticides are 'permitted', as it is recognized that at times other methods are not enough. It is hoped that in time these will be superseded by treatment more appropriate to organic ideals. Traditional home-made sprays are of course illegal.

Weed control. Weed control is achieved, primarily, by mechanical means and mulching. Thermal weed control (both flame and infrared) is increasingly being used on hard surfaces. Traditionally there are no 'organic' herbicides, though some standards are beginning to include them.

Plant raising. Organic growing media for plant raising and container growing are made from bulky organic materials and organic fertilizers. In the UK, for environmental reasons, they do not contain peat. The development of growing media that are both organic and peat free has not been easy, particularly with regard to supply of nutrients. Research continues, with

particular emphasis on using recycled waste, such as composted green waste. Organically grown seed has only been available in reasonable quantities since the late 20th/early 21st century. The range, and quantity, on offer increases annually. It is primarily vegetable seed that is available as this is required for organic commercial growers. Otherwise, organic gardeners use 'conventional' seed that has not been treated with pesticides post-harvest. Organically grown plants of fruit, herbs, and some ornamentals can be found, though they are not as yet widely available.

Wider issues. Wider environmental and ethical issues, such as fair trade, and the distance products travel, have begun to impact on organic growing. All are part of the striving for sustainability. Locally sourced materials are always the preferred choice. Wood should come from sustainably managed forests, such as those accredited by the Forest Stewardship Council (FSC). Products not ethically produced will become unacceptable. As standards are developed for organic landscaping, guidelines will also be needed for the whole gamut of hard landscaping materials.   PP   ▶

Colour plates

Pavlovsk palace, St Petersburg, Russia, seen through wintry silver birches

Venus surveys a terrace border at **Powis Castle**, Wales

The gardens of the great basin at Chicago Botanic Garden designed by **James van Sweden**

Grotto of the Sleeping Venus at the **Villa d'Este** (**Tivoli**), Italy

ornaments.

Movable decorative objects have long been an important feature of gardens. The fragmentary but richly atmospheric remains of HADRIAN'S VILLA, dating from the 2nd century AD, with statuary playing a vital role in the layout of the gardens, is an early reminder of how valuable garden ornaments may be. The modern history of the use of ornaments in gardens begins, like much else in garden hstory, with the Italian Renaissance. Donato BRAMANTE's Belvedere Court in the VATICAN GARDENS was a brilliant design to create a garden which both linked the papal palace with the lofty belvedere, created harmony in an awkward site, and arranged space in which to display Pope Julius II's collection of antique statuary. Built in the early years of the 16th century, it was complete by 1523 when the Venetian ambassador to the Vatican described what he saw: 'a very beautiful garden . . . In the centre . . . are two enormous men of marble, one is the Tiber, the other the Nile, very ancient figures, and two fountains issue from them'. The river god became an enduring image in gardens. It is found in many Italian Renaissance gardens of the 16th century (such as the Villa LANTE and the Palazzo FARNESE (Caprarola)); in 18th-century England it is found in a grotto at STOURHEAD and a little later, in 1784, it is moulded in Coade stone and sold at 100 guineas a piece—an example may be seen today in the entrance courtyard at HAM HOUSE.

In England in 1613-14 Inigo JONES designed a garden court at Arundel House (London) to display the collection of classical statuary acquired by the Earl of Arundel—the first English garden designed for the purpose. Throughout Europe classical forms of statues dominated taste in garden ornaments. Some were priceless originals, others were skilful copies, and even more were original statues in the classical style. French gardens of the baroque style used statuary in great quantities. At VERSAILLES, with its programme of Apollonian imagery and other symbolic references, a vast number of statues and urns, in bronze or marble, were woven into the fabric of the garden. It contains one of the most remarkable collections of garden ornaments in the world. Other 17th-century baroque gardens such as Het LOO, HERRENHAUSEN, and NYMPHENBURG also made lavish use of ornaments.

John Worlidge (*fl.* late 17th century) wrote of ornaments: 'In all places where there is a Summer and a Winter, and where your Gardens of pleasure are sometimes clothed with their verdant garments, and bespangled with variety of Flowers, and at other times wholly dismantled of all these; here to recompence the loss of past pleasures, and to buoy up their hopes of another Spring, many have placed in their Gardens, Statues, and Figures of several Animals, and a great variety of other curious pieces of Workmanship, that their walks might be pleasant at any time in those places of never dying pleasures' (*Systema Horti-culturae: or, The Art of Gardening,* 1677). When Worlidge was writing the demand in England for garden statuary stimulated an outpouring of works verging on mass production. The intense demand continued until around 1750, by which time formal gardens of French inspiration had given away in fashionable taste to the landscape park. From 1677 the Flemish artist John van NOST, succeeded by his cousin John, produced quantities of high-quality lead figures of animals, gods, and putti. Their workshop was taken over by John CHEERE who produced, according to an anonymous author, 'numberless figures in stone, lead or plaster . . . spruce squires, haymakers with rakes in their hands, shepherds and shepherdesss, bagpipers and pipers and fiddlers, Dutch skippers and English sailors enough to supply a first-rate man-of-war'. Another great producer of lead ornaments was Andries Carpentiere (or Andrew Carpenter) from the 1670s to 1737. In the second half of the 18th century Eleanor Coade (1733-1821) invented Coade stone, a ceramic which was capable of being finely moulded. She set up her business in 1769 in Lambeth (London), going into partnership with John Sealy in 1799, producing architectural detailing (swags, masks, gatepiers, keystones, funerary monuments, and so forth) and garden ornaments, in both classical and Gothic styles. Her catalogue in her heyday listed 778 items. Virtually every British architect of consequence used Coade stone in the latter part of the 18th and early 19th centuries—among them Robert ADAM, Sir Charles BARRY, Sir William CHAMBERS, Henry Holland (1745-1806), John NASH, Sir John Soane (1753-1837), and Sir James Wyatt (1746-1813). Much of her work was exported to the colonies, Russia, and North and South America. Many Coade stone ornaments are still to be seen in English gardens—a fine urn at KILLERTON, a pair of crouching lions at Audley End (Essex), busts of Nelson and Raleigh in Bicton Park (Devon), and a caryatid at ANGLESEY ABBEY.

European gardens from Roman times onwards were sometimes embellished with works of art by some of the greatest artists of their time. The tradition continued throughout the 20th century with notable sculptures by artists such as Jacques Maillol (1861-1944), Auguste Rodin (1840-1914), Eduardo Chillida (1924-2002), Henry Moore (1898-1986), Richard Serra (b. 1939), and Barbara Hepworth (1903-75) exerting their powerful influence on the atmosphere of many landscapes. The marvellous work of Andy Goldsworthy (b. 1956) (see LAND ART), ephemeral as it often is, has an altogether special affinity with its settings. In the past the purpose of most garden statuary was to make some connection with another world. Andy Goldsworthy's art, however, has a different purpose, to assert the individuality of the landscape.   PT

JOHN DAVIS, *Antique Garden Ornament* (1991).

Oroszvár. See RUSOVCE.

Orotava, Jardín de Aclimatación de la ⊛

Tenerife, Canary Islands, Spain. The garden was founded in 1788 with the express purpose of receiving tender plants from Spain's colonies overseas and studying their performance in a different environment. The climate here is remarkably benign, with an average annual temperature of 19.5 °C/66 °F and an average temperature of the coldest month of 16 °C/61 °F. In an area of 6 hectares/15 acres there is an outstanding collection of tropical and subtropical plants. Of particular interest is the collection of plants endemic to the Canary Islands. Most of the collections are grown in the open but there are also glasshouses and shade houses (with collections of aroids and bromeliads). Because of the long history of the garden many of the plants displayed are exceptional mature specimens, some of them early introductions of trees which have grown to great size. Apart from displaying the plant collections the garden also has a programme of botanical research chiefly concerned with conservation and education. Seed is distributed from a very wide range of families. The garden is managed by the ICIA, the Canary Islands agrarian council, with a particular interest in plants of agricultural potential, but it also takes an interest in new ornamental species. The garden also has a small subsidiary, the Hijuela, a formal garden in the town of Orotava which is notable for a good example of the dragon tree *Dracaena draco* subsp. *draco*, an endemic plant of the Canary Islands.   PT

Orsan, Prieuré Notre Dame d' ⊛

Maisonnais, Cher, France. In the valley of the river Orsan in the rural landscape of Berry two architects, Sonia Lesot and Patrice Taravella, seized upon the setting of medieval priory buildings to create an original garden of medieval inspiration. They came here in 1991, restored the surviving priory buildings, and embarked on their garden which was opened to the public in 1995. A square pool is surrounded by cloisters of hornbeam threaded with clematis and roses. A pattern of square raised beds, edged in sweet chestnut wattle, is planted with medicinal herbs. Two cross-shaped beds are planted with corn or with broad beans. A garden of pink and white roses and madonna lilies celebrates the Virgin and a hornbeam maze is enclosed in ramparts of different varieties of plums. Wood-framed BERCEAUX are garlanded with roses or grapevines. Much fruit is grown, an orchard occupies the site of the monks' graveyard, and a vineyard cultivates the great white grape of the Loire, Chenin Blanc. There is no attempt at historical purism—modern plant cultivars are used with abandon. The garden is full of uncontrived charm—this is essentially a modern garden inspired by ideas from the Middle Ages.   PT

Orsini, Villa. See BOMARZO.

Osborne House ⊗
East Cowes, Isle of Wight, England, was started in 1845 as a holiday home for Queen Victoria and her husband Prince Albert. The house was designed by Thomas Cubitt (1788–1855) with much collaboration with Prince Albert. The Prince was also involved in the detail of the gardens whose designer was his artistic adviser, Professor Ludwig Gruner of Dresden. This was very much a place for family holidays, not for official receptions. North of the house, from which there are fine views across the Solent to the mainland, terraced gardens were laid out. These, recently superbly restored by English Heritage, present a feast of ornament from the early Victorian period. A tiered fountain pool stands at the centre of a parterre of curved turf shapes set in gravel decorated with topiary stags fashioned of clipped *Lonicera nitida* which rise from plantings of *Felicia amelloides*, *Festuca glauca*, and scarlet pelargoniums. Nearby, the balustraded upper terrace has a great central vase filled with annual plantings and supported on sphinxes. It is surrounded by L-shaped beds edged in stone and filled with bedding schemes, the whole lavishly decorated with TOPIARY. The lower terrace is overlooked by a three-arched loggia where Queen Victoria liked to sit and read or write—her journal describes the scents of jasmine, orange blossom, and roses. It looks out onto a sunken circular pool with a figure of Andromeda surrounded by sea monsters. Shapes of turf, with beds of annuals, are let into the gravel and a great pergola runs across the east side of the terrace. At some distance from the house is a Swiss cottage which had its own garden, now restored, where the royal children were encouraged to grow vegetables which Prince Albert undertook to buy from them at the market rate. Their miniature garden tools

and wheelbarrows, bearing the children's initials, may be seen in a thatched summer house. The original walled kitchen garden has been excellently restored by English Heritage, preserving the original setting (in particular the fine old gardeners' bothies) with a lively new layout and excellent ornamental planting by the garden designer Rupert Golby. Osborne House is one of the most attractive gardens associated with the royal family and an exceptional example of early Victorian garden taste.   PT

Osuna, El Capricho de la Alameda de ⊗
Barajas, Madrid, Spain. In the late 18th century this was the Arcadian garden of the Duchess of Osuna enlivened by all manner of ornamental buildings. *Capricho* means caprice and *alameda* means avenue, which conveys the essential notions of whim and formality that informed the garden. The Duchess was a cultivated woman, a great reader and patron of the arts—Goya was commissioned to execute paintings for her. In laying out the garden of El Capricho she must have been influenced by what she knew of the English landscape garden and, possibly, by the picturesque gardens of late 18th-century France. With advice from Spanish and French gardeners she devised a landscape of a kind then unique in Spain. After the Duchess's death the estate passed first to her nephew and then to her grandson, the last Duke of Osuna, who squandered his fortune, and the estate was sold and divided. In recent times what remained of El Capricho has been overtaken with suburban development—the Barajas airport is nearby and so is the A10 motorway. Since 1977 El Capricho has belonged to the city of Madrid, which has carried out much restoration and made it a public park. Part of the garden has the character of a landscape park with lakes and a serpentine river. Here are such picturesque buildings as a rustic 'old man's house' and a hermitage. A formal garden close to the palace has a parterre and a restored EXEDRA—a monument to the Duchess, today shorn of the statue of her and the canopy that protected it and several other sculptures. A woodland garden has grottoes and winding walks among dense plantings of trees.   PT

Oudolf, Kwekerij Piet ⊗
Hummelo, Gelderland, the Netherlands, is one of the most renowned nurseries of the end of the 20th century. It was started in 1982 by Piet (b. 1944) and Anja Oudolf (b. 1948), who have made an important contribution to the popularization of ornamental GRASSES, and to the introduction of a large range of new and

forgotten plants and their varieties. In this he is part of a group of traditional nurserymen, including Coen Jansen, Romke van de Kaa, Rob Leopold, and Hans Kramer. The nursery was extremely successful because of their new introductions, but particularly due to the efficient marketing by means of Piet's garden designs, which have given him an international reputation. The emphasis in his designs is the retention of a year-round display. There is particular interest in a wide range of grasses and other plants that retain their structure after flowering, such as monardas and eupatoriums. Their private garden, which is adjacent to the nursery in front of an old farm De Koesterd, is both experimental and for plant displays to attract customers. Tiered wave-shaped yew hedges form the background structure to the luxuriant planting that has a naturalistic character and thus contrasts with the architectural framework.   JW

Ou Yuan ⊗
Suzhou, Jiangsu province, China. *Ou*, meaning couple, is the name of a garden (*yuan*) situated to the east and west of an old city residence in the north-east district of the town. Lu Jin, a district magistrate in the early Qing dynasty, built the eastern part first, calling it She Yuan, and the garden acquired its present form only when the property came into the hands of Shen Bingcheng, a government official in the 19th century.

The western side was divided by a studio building into two courtyards: the one in front with an unusual rockery, the one behind accentuated by a two-storeyed study with finely carved balustrading. The eastern garden, occupying about 0.25 hectare/0.6 acre, is now much the larger. Inside its entrance, a small courtyard leads into an open space bounded by a meandering white wall with several ornamental *louchuang* (see CHINA) windows cut into it and a fine moon gate framing the garden beyond. From here the main hall, two storeyed and double eaved, is hidden by a high artificial mountain of yellow rock (*huangshi*), which falls steeply on its eastern flank to a narrow splash of reflecting water. Winding steps are cut along this cliff to give visitors the sensation of walking by a 'profound Valley', Suigu, which is its name. Then, the pond runs southwards down the garden to a summer house with many pivoting, lattice-worked windows. A path which follows the water here was paved in the 1960s with a chequerboard of black and white stones: while the path runs straight, the checks slant off to the right, pulling the eye towards a succession of decorative windows in the gallery that runs along the enclosing wall. Along the eastern boundary, a double-storeyed *lou* (see

CHINA) rising above the walls allowed at one time views of the canal and city outside the garden. This is a garden well worth studying for its delicate manipulation of space and light and its many peaceful and hidden corners.
G-ZW/MK

Oxford Botanic Garden ✿

Oxford, England, was, in 1621, the first botanic garden founded in Britain. As part of the University of Oxford its purpose was to provide plants for students of botany and biology. Enclosed in noble stone walls it has three grand gateways, built, and possibly designed, by Nicholas Stone (1587-1647). Today the garden has an area of 1.8 hectares/4.5 acres, having substantially spilled over from its original enclosure to colonize the banks of the river Cherwell which flows alongside. The area within the old walls retains a layout close to its 17th-century appearance with much space devoted to botanical order beds (see BOTANIC GARDEN). The economic beds display plants used for dyeing, food, and medicine, and those that give useful fibre and oils. Excellent old trees survive, among them a yew planted by the first director (Jacob Bobart, 1569-1679) and a beautiful *Sorbus domestica* f. *pomifera* planted in 1790. There is much to interest the gardener, with a National Collection of euphorbias (well over 100 species and over 30 cultivars), borders of irises, variegated plants, ferns, and many tender ornamentals on the south-facing wall. Beyond the walls are several glasshouses with collections of succulents, orchids, tender lilies, alpines, and ferns. Here too is a rock garden and boisterous herbaceous border along the south-facing wall and a pool with fine plantings and walks on its margins. With over 8,000 species of hardy and tender plants, retaining its original beautiful architectural setting, and with a lively educational and public programme, it is a botanic garden of exceptional merit. Since 1963 the garden has been the owner of the Harcourt Arboretum, originally part of NUNEHAM PARK at Nuneham Courtenay.   PT

Oxford University college gardens ✿

Oxford, England. The two ancient English universities of Oxford and CAMBRIDGE have a remarkable range of historic and often very beautiful college buildings among which gardens have been made from very early times. In Scotland some of the old universities, in particular St Andrews and Edinburgh, have exceptional buildings, but none of the Scottish universities is collegiate and none has notable gardens. With very few exceptions (of which the University of Exeter (Devon) is a rare and distinguished one) none of the

more recent British universities has paid much attention to gardening or landscaping.

The most striking difference between Oxford and Cambridge is that Cambridge has a most rare group of colleges, whose gardens flow into each other, running along the banks of the river Cam, whereas Oxford colleges are scattered and nowhere, although they may adjoin each other, do they form an ensemble. All Oxford colleges have a garden of some sort, if only a lawn in a quadrangle, but some possess memorable landscapes or an interesting horticultural past, and sometimes both. Those described below give a notion of the range and character of them.

Christ Church, although by no means among the older colleges (founded in 1525 as Cardinal College and refounded in 1546 as Christ Church), has strikingly grand scenery. Its chief quadrangle, Tom Quad—the largest quadrangle in Oxford—is scarcely a garden but it is a noble piece of landscaping. It has a sunken lawn, divided into four by paths, with at its centre a large circular lily pool decorated with a copy of Mercury by GIAMBOLOGNA placed here in 1928 and mounted on a pedestal designed by Sir Edwin LUTYENS. Christ Church has the exceptional setting of Christ Church Meadow south-east of the college which had planned walks by the 17th century—the college records show a payment in 1624 'for setting plants in ye walks'. Broad Walk, laid out in 1668, by 1670 had an avenue of elms which succumbed to the elm disease and were felled in 1975. They were replaced with alternate oriental planes (*Platanus orientalis*) and London planes (*Platanus* × *hispanica*).

Magdalen College (founded in 1458) like Christ Church benefits from a magnificent extent of land. The college grounds run along the river Cherwell where walks were known by the 16th century. Loggan's plan of the college in *Oxonia Illustrata* (1675) marks them as 'Magdalen College Water Walkes'. Joseph Addison (1672-1719), the writer, politician, and garden philosopher, was a student and Fellow of Magdalen and especially loved the 'water walkes' which, he thought, reflected the 'beautiful wildness of nature'. In the 19th century the walks were renamed Addison's Walk. The path is shaded by trees and at a certain point the great tower of the 15th-century college chapel is seen across a meadow—a favourite view of Addison's, scarcely changed from his time even to the extent of the stone bench on which he used to sit to take in the view. The meadow here is notable for having a marvellous wild community of snake's head fritillaries (*Fritillaria meleagris*). Early in the year the college deer herd, established in 1705, graze

here but before the fritillaries emerge are moved to another meadow, in front of the New Building (1733). Here, in front of the stately classical façade of the New Building, they create the impression of an ancient deer park of some country estate. There are other pleasures at Magdalen, including a good mixed border and a wonderful London plane planted to celebrate the Treaty of Amiens in 1801.

Trinity College (founded in 1555) is finely kept and notable for the traces still visible of the great formal garden known chiefly from an engraving in *Oxonia Depicta* (1732). About a central axis leading from the college buildings to grand wrought-iron gates six rectangular lawns are outlined with topiary and two of them have a mount crowned with a column. To one side are four rows of clipped trees with, beyond, an intricate wilderness clipped into a mazelike pattern. The axis survives and so do the gates on their piers capped with urns, placed here in 1713. Most remarkably, some ancient yews, deformed with age, remain on the site of the clipped trees.

New College (founded 1379) had a notable formal garden seen in an engraving in *Oxonia Depicta* (1732). Within the college walls terraced walks with regular rows of trees overlook a quadripartite garden with intricately patterned beds which are overlooked by a great mount in the form of a pyramid surmounted by a pavilion. Celia Fiennes saw it before 1691 and admired 'Myrtle Orinter and Lemons and Loorestine [laurustinus (*Viburnum tinus*)] growing in potts . . . a great mount in the middle which is ascended by degrees . . . and on the top is a Summer House'. All that remains today is the mount, its shape blurred by overgrowth.

St Catherine's College (founded in 1962) is a rarity—a new college and its landscape designed by the same man. The Danish architect Arne JACOBSEN designed it down to the last detail (including the college silver). The site is close to the river and Jacobsen made a watery connection by creating a canal running along the entrance façade with a Barbara Hepworth bronze overlooking it. The plan of college buildings is perfectly symmetrical but the designed landscape for the college buildings is very varied. Here is a mixture of intricately designed intimate spaces, with plenty of sitting places, and sudden long vistas or open spaces dominated by one or two fine specimen trees. Today parts of the garden are slightly dishevelled but it, and the college buildings, remain an exhilarating piece of lively modernism in a world largely given over to the past.   PT

MAVIS BATEY, *Oxford Gardens* (1982).

P

Pacello da Mercogliano.
See MERCOGLIANO, PACELLO DA.

Packwood House ✿
Lapworth, Warwickshire, England, is a 16th-century house which by the mid 18th century had a handsome garden walled in brick with a summer house. At some time, possibly in the early 18th century, a MOUNT was made beyond the garden walls to the south on the axis of a gateway in the garden walls and the garden door of the house. Long known as the Sermon on the Mount it is crowned with a single yew with, clustering about it on the slopes, further yews representing the twelve apostles and the four evangelists. More shapes of yew, clipped into rounded cones, are gathered below, with some of them forming an axial walk to the garden gate. This latter group probably dates from the 19th century. Christian symbolism is very unusual in English gardens and it is surprising that there is no early reference to the Sermon on the Mount. A drawing of the garden dating from the mid 18th century survives but there is, puzzlingly, no trace of the mount. The earliest known description of it is in Reginald BLOMFIELD's and F. Inigo THOMAS's *The Formal Garden in England* (1892). Blomfield was told that it represented the Sermon on the Mount by the gardener who was clipping the yews when he visited. The old garden walls today enclose pretty flower gardens, largely the work of the NATIONAL TRUST which has owned the estate since 1941.   PT

Padua Botanic Garden ✿
Padua, Veneto, Italy. Of the greatest historical and botanical interest the *giardino botanico* was founded in 1545, its establishment ratified by a decree of the Venetian Republic. It was the first botanic garden in Europe (except for PISA founded a few months earlier), and designed as an apothecary's teaching garden for medical students at the university in order that living plants could be studied. Inspired by Daniele Barbaro, the Venetian scholar, its foundation was approved by Francesco Buonafede, doctor

and naturalist, holder of the chair of *Lectura Simplicium,* and the plans were realized by the architect Andrea Moroni di Bergamo. The first curator was Luigi Squalerno (Anguillara) from 1546 to 1561. The famous circular walled garden, imagined as the world of four continents, containing order beds (see BOTANIC GARDEN) laid out in geometric patterns, was constructed in 1551, and is still in existence. The *Horio dei semplici* of Padua published by G. Porro (1591) lists all the 1,168 plants in the garden, with details of their sites. Goethe visited in 1768 and studied a specimen fan palm (*Chamaerops humilis*), originally introduced to Padua by Prospero Alpini, the author of *De Plantis Aegypti*, in 1581. The palm inspired Goethe's search for the primeval plant from which all others are descended, thus prompting early ideas about evolution. It can still be seen in the garden today. Several exotic introductions were first grown at the botanic garden, including potato, lilac, and sunflowers. A chaste tree (*Vitex agnus-castus*), introduced in 1550 and now 20 m/60 ft high, still flourishes, as does an oriental plane planted in 1680. Other trees such as a *Ginkgo biloba* and a *Magnolia grandiflora* date to the 18th century. Today there are sections devoted to flowers of local regions, including the *macchia* (Mediterranean scrub).   PHo

Page, Russell
(1906–85), English garden designer and author who started his career in collaboration with Geoffrey JELLICOE from 1935 to 1939. His work was classical in inspiration, strongly influenced by Renaissance Italy and 17th-century France, but he was also a learned plantsman—as he accurately said, 'I know more about plants than most designers, and more about design than most plantsmen.' He worked in Britain, France, Belgium, Italy, Spain, and the USA. Most of his gardens were designed for private clients but his work may be seen by the public at Longleat (Wiltshire), PORT LYMPNE (Kent), Leeds Castle (Kent), La MORTELLA (Italy), the Frick Collection (New York), and, one of his last works, the Donald M. KENDALL SCULPTURE GARDENS at the

PepsiCo Headquarters in New York State. The gardens he designed in Battersea Park (London) for the Festival of Britain in 1951 were partly reinstated in 2003. He combined the skills of a designer with the practical gifts of a skilful horticulturist—certainly in his early days he often carried out his planting schemes himself—and frequently returned to the gardens he had designed to see how they were evolving. His book *The Education of a Gardener* (1962) remains one of the finest and most approachable books on the principles of garden design with many acute opinions of famous gardens. Acknowledged or not, he has been one of the most influential 20th-century garden designers.   PT

RUSSELL PAGE, *The Education of a Gardener* (1962).
MARINA SCHINZ and GABRIELLE VAN ZUYLEN, *The Gardens of Russell Page* (1991).

pagoda
first appears in English at the beginning of the 17th century and is derived from an Indian word meaning a holy place or sacred building. As a garden building it comes into prominence in the 18th century when it appears in gardens as a CHINOISERIE tower-like building becoming increasingly slender as it rises. William CHAMBERS's design for his Chinese pagoda (1761) in KEW GARDENS, inspired by a brief visit to Canton, was the most influential example and remains one of the most beautiful. The Pagode de CHANTELOUP (1775–8) was modelled on it and many other CHINOISERIE buildings subsequently. The term is sometimes loosely extended in France to signify any pavilion of Chinese inspiration such as the grotto/pagoda built for the Château de RAMBOUILLET *c.*1780 (which does not survive) and the pavilion at CASSAN of a slightly later date (which triumphantly does survive). Gabriel Thouin's *Plans raisonnés de toutes les espèces de jardin* (1819) gives many examples of chinoiserie designs for pagodas and, a bizarre hybrid, a *pagode turque* (Turkish pagoda). One of the last outstanding pagodas to be built is Robert Abraham's magnificent surviving building (1827) at ALTON TOWERS.   PT

Pagode de Chanteloup
see CHANTELOUP, PAGODE DE.

Paine, James
(1717–89), English architect born in Hampshire who designed notable garden buildings. Among those surviving are: a temple at BRAMHAM PARK (1760) a mausoleum at Gibside (County Durham, 1760–6), a Temple of Diana and a Roman bridge at Weston Park (Staffordshire, *c.*1765–70), and a bridge in the park at Chillington Hall (Staffordshire, *c.*1770).

At Hardwick Park (County Durham) between 1754 and 1757 Paine designed a Gothic gatehouse, a park bridge, Temple of Minerva, Gothic summer house, and bathhouse—which survive only partially. Of his designs for houses Humphry REPTON wrote (in the *Red Book* for Panshanger, Hertfordshire), comparing him unfavourably as an architect with Capability BROWN, '[he] never built a house that was comfortable without great alteration'. This is not an opinion universally held. Paine's Wardour Castle (1770–76) in Wiltshire is an exceptionally beautiful house and Paine may also have designed the temple in the grounds here.   PT

PETER LEACH, *James Paine* (1988).

Painshill ✿

Cobham, Surrey, England, is a landscape garden created between 1738 and 1773 by the Hon. Charles HAMILTON who improverished himself in the process. Somewhat surprisingly the garden was well maintained until after the Second World War when pressure on building land in this increasingly populous area provoked the sale of some of the grounds for building. In 1980 a large part of the original site—64 hectares/158 acres—was bought by the local authority and the Painshill Park Trust was established to carry out a restoration. This has been one of the best organized and most valuable of all English garden restorations. The garden is historically important, with features covering a wide span of time reflecting the evolution of 18th-century landscaping ideas. The site, a valley with the river Mole dammed to form a long serpentine lake, now has much of its original ingredients restored. A castellated Gothic tower rises high on a wooded knoll, a delightful Turkish tent commands views of the lake, a ruined abbey (built as such) stands by the water's edge, and a Gothic temple surveys the scene. An island on the lake, connected by a CHINOISERIE bridge, has a superb GROTTO by Joseph Lane of Tisbury (1717–84), lavishly decorated with stalactites and glittering with crystals, through which rowing boats can pass. An amphitheatre of tiered evergreens is embellished with a copy of the statue of the *Rape of the Sabine Woman* by GIAMBOLOGNA. Hamilton's vineyard has been replanted with Chardonnay, Pinot Noir, and Seyval Blanc (the last an anachronism, it is a 20th-century cultivar). In 1998 Painshill was awarded a Europa Nostra medal for 'the exemplary restoration from the state of extreme dereliction of a most important 18th-century landscape park and its extraordinary buildings'.   PT

Painswick Rococo Garden ✿

near Stroud, Gloucestershire, England, was a forgotten garden until 1982 when two garden and architectural historians, Timothy Mowl and Roger White, investigated the site and discovered traces of the original garden beneath dense undergrowth. Surviving in the house was a painting by Thomas Robins (1716–70) of *c.*1748 showing the house and a garden of highly ornamental character rising up on apparently very steep ground. The garden at Painswick was visited in 1757 by Bishop Pococke who saw 'a very pretty garden . . . on an hanging ground from the house in a vale, and on a rising ground on the other side and at the end; all are cut into walks through wood and adorn'd with water and buildings, and in one part is the kitchen garden' (J. J. Cartwright (ed.), *The Travels through England of Dr Richard Pococke*, 1888–9). Pococke's description accords with Robins's painting but by 1982 the 'hanging ground', at a little distance from the house, was choked with saplings. Mowl and White demonstrated that features of the garden shown in Robins's painting survived and this, and more evidence, was laid bare by later archaeological excavation. Whether Robins's painting was a design for the garden, or an account of what he saw, is not known. Armed with the new-found evidence the owner of the estate embarked on a restoration which is now complete. The wooded valley is overlooked by decorative buildings—the Gothic Red House (so called because of the colour of its stucco) and the airy Eagle House on the edge of the valley. A filigree EXEDRA overlooks a diamond-shaped formal kitchen garden. In the eastern part of the garden, below fine old beeches (*Fagus sylvatica*) and close to a Gothic seat, is an astonishing spread of the snowdrop *Galanthus* 'Atkinsii', a cultivar named after James Atkins, a 19th-century snowdrop grower who lived at Painswick. There are traces of formality in the garden, the alignments of paths and eyecatchers, and passages of near symmetry, but the effect is informal, intimate, and decorative. Other paintings by Robins survive—of Marybone House (Gloucestershire), Woodside House (Berkshire), and Honington Hall (Warwickshire)—but only at Painswick may we see, laid out before our eyes, the type of garden that delighted him.   PT

Palacio de las Dueñas. See DUEÑAS, PALACIO DE LAS.

Palacio de Viana. See VIANA, PALACIO DE.

Palagonia, Villa ✿

Bagheria, Sicily, Italy. During the 18th century the nobility of Palermo had their country estates in Bagheria, a seaside village a few miles to the east of the city. The baroque Palagonia, known as the 'Villa of the Monsters', was built in 1715 for Prince Francesco Ferdinando Palagonia Gravina, and is today, with no land attached, famous only for its grotesque statues in local tufa stone which line the encircling walls. Representing mythological figures, dwarfs, warriors, musicians, hunchbacks, and dragons, these are arranged on the wall between the two gateways. Goethe visited here in 1787 and already found the 'paving . . . overgrown with grass and the courtyard . . . like a dilapidated graveyard' (*Travels in Italy*). He considered the villa 'bad taste and folly of an eccentric mind'. The villa itself, with a concave façade and dramatic double staircase, is still striking, with the ceiling of the ballroom decorated with 'angled' mirrors to distort the viewer horribly.   PHo

Palais de la Berbie. See BERBIE, PALAIS DE LA.

Palais Idéal du Facteur Cheval. See CHEVAL, PALAIS IDÉAL DU FACTEUR.

Palais-Royal. See PARIS PARKS AND GARDENS.

Palermo, Orto Botanico di ✿

Palermo, Sicily, Italy. One of the most interesting botanic gardens in Italy, and unique in Europe for its tropical plants, the Palermo garden is distinguished by significant collections of Cactaceae, Agavaceae, Liliaceae, Euphorbiaceae, Amaryllidaceae, and Moraceae. It was first opened in 1779 near the Porta Carini but by 1786, needing more space, it was moved to the present locality adjoining the Villa Giulia. The French architect Leon Dufourny built the neoclassical buildings still in use today: a gymnasium, library, herbarium, and warm and hot greenhouses. The garden was organized into four large rectangles, each quarter separated by an avenues of trees; that nearest the buildings is bisected by cross *viales* (avenues) of palms—*Washingtonia robusta*, *Phoenix dactylifera*, *P. canariensis*, sabal, and chamaerops. Another avenue is today composed of bombac, the false kapok (*Chorisia insignis*), underplanted with clivias and variegated tradescantias. Established at a time of intense interest in post-Linnaean botany and under the patronage of the Bourbon King Ferdinando III, the new garden inaugurated a programme of research for both agricultural and industrial improvement. The director Giuseppe Tineo (1795–1812) introduced trees such as *Parkinsonia aculeata*, *Broussonetia papyrifera* (paper mulberry), and *Eyrthrina viarum*, and various aloes for growing in the city. Other plant species such as citrus were a particular study, proving especially suitable for growing on a commercial scale in Sicily. Tineo was

responsible for introducing the mandarin (*Citrus deliciosa*) in 1810 which, by overproduction within 30 years, caused a crisis in citrus cultivation. The garden's prime role is in studying useful plants, notably cotton, sugar cane, soya, sorghum, *Bohemeria nivea* which produces a natural fibre, besides plants of agricultural interest such as varieties of banana and *Opuntia*. Today notable trees in the garden include a vast Moreton Bay fig (*Ficus microphylla*) introduced in the middle of the 19th century and an Indian banyan (*Ficus benghalensis*). A section devoted to Mediterranean flora includes many spring-flowering euphorbias, *Phlomis* species, and bulbs such as *Urginea maritima*. There is still an emphasis on scientific research, in particular the use of plants in medicine and agriculture.
PHo

Palheiro, Quinta do ⊛

near Funchal, Madeira, Portugal. The English connection with the island of Madeira, in particular because of the wine trade, is a long-established one. Some of the English families resident here made gardens of distinctive atmosphere, in which unfamiliar exotics are used in an English way. The Blandy family, long connected with Madeira wine, bought the old estate of Palheiro in 1885. It had formerly been a hunting lodge belonging to the Conde de Carvalhal who planted many trees here, in particular oriental planes (*Platanus orientalis*). The long curving entrance drive is memorable—in summer vast numbers of blue and white agapanthus flower with, behind them, an avenue of camellias, themselves a dazzling sight in winter. The long border is a distinctive example of an English-style mixed border using an unfamiliar repertory of plants. Descending slightly, the path between the borders is surfaced in swirling patterns of finely laid pebbles. Such plants as *Strelitzia regina*, *Pittosporum tobira*, and *Anigozanthus bicolor* consort with such English border familiars as dahlias, day lilies, and phlox. Climbers overarching the path show a similar mixture—roses are here but so also are *Aristolochia gigantea* (from Panama) and *Clerodendrum ugandense* (from tropical Africa). A parterre of curious topiary snails and box hedges has a central pool and is planted with pale sempervivums. A delightful chapel, both Palladian and baroque, with fine interior plasterwork dates from the time of the Conde de Carvalhal. A canal is edged with orange tritonias and the Lady's Garden has curving

beds edged in box and filled with exotics. All about are notable trees, several of them (such as a huge *Metrosideros obtusa* with billowing foliage) exceptional specimens. The garden's atmosphere is unusual; despite the unfamiliar plants it has an unassuming English informality and at any moment the visitor may expect to see wicker chairs and a table laden with tea and scones.   PT

palissade.

A French word (the English is usually spelled palisade) for one of the essential ingredients of the 17th-century French garden. It means a regular planting of trees whose surface is clipped to form a wall and whose size is restricted by clipping the top growth. It is, in fact, a hedge, but with greater pretensions, and was used to line ALLÉES, BOSQUETS, or

Designs for **palissades** from Dezallier d'Argenville's *La Théorie et la pratique du jardinage* (1709).

terraces. A.-J. DEZALLIER D'ARGENVILLE's *La Théorie et la pratique du jardinage* (1709) illustrates different types of *palissade*. The *palissade à l'Italienne* leaves the lower part of the stems of the plants exposed so that it appears to be raised on stilts (an excellent 20th-century example is to be seen at HIDCOTE MANOR, planted with hornbeam (*Carpinus betulus*)). The *palissade de Chantilly* had regular clipped arched 'windows' and was capped with lollipop finials. At MARLY the *bosquets*, of which there were countless different designs, were often edged with *palissades* in which, at regular intervals, a tree was allowed to rise bare stemmed above the top of the hedge and left with a mophead. The *palissade* was, thus, seen as a decorative ingredient in the garden but it could also be used for more mundane purposes. Louis Liger's *La Nouvelle Maison rustique ou économie de tous les biens de campagne* (1700) explains that it may be used to 'give shade, to cover walls, outhouses, compost heaps and other unsightly places'.

PT

Palissy, Bernard

(*c*.1510–1590), French potter, garden theorist, virtuoso, scientist, fantasist, and author. His book *Recepte véritable, par laquelle tous les hommes de la France pourront apprendre à muliplier et augmenter leurs thrésors* (True Recipe by which Every Man in France may Learn to Multiply and Augment his Riches) (1563) contains a section entitled 'Le Dessein du jardin délectable' in which he sets out the principles of the perfectly delectable garden. It should be close to a river, be rectangular in shape, divided into four, and enclosed by walls or terraces. Water, a stream or a fountain, was essential to the garden. He emphasizes the importance of being able to look down upon a geometric garden in the making of which it was essential to have a knowledge of geometry. In all this he prefigures many of the principles which ruled garden design in France, and elsewhere, in the 16th and 17th centuries. He was a devotee of grottoes and designed one for Catherine de Médicis at the Tuileries garden (see PARIS PARKS AND GARDENS). In his taste for exotic garden ornament he shows a more mannerist tendency, with a fondness for musical weathervanes and automata, naturalistically painted statues of animals and people, and intricate arbours woven of living trees of exactly the sort seen in the HYPNEROTOMACHIA POLIPHILI. No garden designed by him survives but his pottery does. It swarms with naturalistically rendered creatures, fruit, flowers, and vegetables, in brilliantly coloured high relief.   PT

Palladio, Andrea

(Andrea di Pietrodella Gondola) (1508–80), Italian architect born in Padua who was brought up in Vicenza, where he spent much of his working life, and all of whose work was executed in the Veneto. He designed churches, palaces, and villas and was also absorbed in the study of the design of bridges. His *I quattro libri dell'architettura* (1570) describes many of his own projects and also reveals his deep knowledge of the architecture of antiquity. Unlike many of the earlier books on architecture Palladio's deals more with practicalities than with theory. Although he plainly took much interest in the sites of his buildings, and their exact position in relation to the topography, he was not himself involved in landscape design. His chief interest strictly from the garden point of view comes from his profound influence in England in the 18th century among those who were also influential makers of gardens. His influence was also strongly felt in Ireland and in America where Thomas Jefferson's MONTICELLO has a pronounced Palladian flavour. In England he influenced the architects Colen CAMPBELL, Inigo JONES, and William KENT all of whom designed garden buildings or gardens. Palladio's Villa Rotonda inspired Lord Burlington's CHISWICK HOUSE and Colen Campbell's Mereworth Castle (1723). Palladio's magnificent rejected design for the Rialto bridge in Venice gave birth to a family of delightful smaller versions, each of which was a notable 18th-century garden ornament: the Palladian bridges at STOWE, WILTON, PRIOR PARK, and TSARSKOE SELO (see BRIDGE).   PT

BRUCE BOUCHER, *Andrea Palladio* (1998).

Palmengarten ⊛

Frankfurt am Main, Hesse, Germany. The creation of the Palmengarten is closely linked with Schloss Biebrich near Wiesbaden, which Herzog Adolf von Nassau was forced to relinquish on his deposition in 1866. The Bockenheim garden designer and nurseryman Heinrich Siesmeyer was employed to assist the Duke with the sale of the palace's world-famous plant houses, erected by court master gardener Thelemann in 1847, together with the plant collection with its famous camellias and palms, and saw an opportunity of acquiring them for the city of Frankfurt. On 6 May 1868 the Palmengartengesellschaft company was founded to acquire the Biebrich winter gardens, and within a year a public appeal had amassed sufficient capital to purchase 6.5 hectares/16 acres of land beside the Bockenheimer Landstraße. Siesmeyer took on the planning of the gardens and became their first director. Between 1869 and 1874 the grounds were laid out and the Biebrich plant houses re-erected. Some 7.5 hectares/19 acres of adjoining land were purchased in 1883, the new grounds being designed by Siesmeyer's successor August Siebert. In 1896 the gardens were extended again by 22 hectares/54 acres from the grounds of Baron von Rothschild's Villa Leonhardsbrunnen, used for nurseries and greenhouses.

The centrepiece of the garden today is the 1871 Palmenhaus, modelled on the *jardin central* at the 1867 Paris Exposition by Frankfurt architect Fritz Kayser as a single-span cast-iron and glass construction with a flower gallery on three sides. From their inception the Palmengartengesellschaft saw the gardens as having a dual function, as a botanical show garden and as an attractive social and recreational amenity for Frankfurt's middle classes. Siesmeyer planned the landscape garden with a belt walk and winding paths, a boating lake with a waterfall, rocky grotto, tower, and playgrounds. In addition there were such sports facilities as sixteen lawn tennis courts, a cycle racetrack, and a skating rink. In 1891 the assembly rooms burnt down and were rebuilt immediately in neo-Renaissance style, and most of the old plant houses from Biebrich were replaced in 1906, when wings to accommodate tropical and subtropical species were added to the 61-m/200-ft high central hall. The grounds and their built features reflect late 19th-century German middle-class tastes and ideals and are typical of the historicist period. During the 1920s Depression they declined in importance and fell into disrepair; social upheavals after the First World War further affected the role and use of such amenities, and elements such as the Swiss Cottage (Schweizerhäuschen) were removed and the number of tennis courts reduced. Reshaping and simplifying the grounds in the 1930s progressively lent it the character of a people's park (*Volkspark*), and the assembly rooms were also rebuilt in the Neue Sachlichkeit style, by Ernst May. However, the most radical alterations were made in the post-war era and have continued until recently. The tennis courts have gone and the entire eastern grounds have been reshaped to harmonize with the new Tropicarium Nord and Süd plant houses.

Today the Palmengarten offers a mixture of overlapping styles and periods. The pre-1920s historicist park can still be seen in the Palmenhaus and in the south-eastern and western areas, while the north-eastern areas have been reworked. With its 29 hectares/72 acres of grounds and 1 hectare/2.5 acres of glasshouses—comprehensively restored between 1979 and 1990—the Palmengarten is an immensely popular garden. The Palmenhaus displays subtropical flora, while the Tropicarium has eight biotopes from various tropical zones. There are splendid collections of palms, orchids, bromeliads, cacti and other succulents, carnivorous plants, azaleas, camellias, and fuchsias.   BM

Panshanger,

Tasmania, Australia, an elegant house in the Greek Revival style, was built by Englishman Joseph Archer, between 1831 and 1834. Early lithographs of Panshanger show the house sited on a commanding point above the Lake river, framed by clumps of trees with the aptly named mountain range the Great Western Tiers in the background. These depictions, c.1835, relate directly to the 18th-century Claudean ideal of romanticized poetic landscapes, especially in the relationship of the house to the natural topography. Today the general effect at Panshanger is more one of enclosure than openness. The long entrance avenue and surrounding parkland are heavily wooded. Mature trees—conifers, oaks, and elms—and thick and expansive shrubberies protect the house, screening the view to the river. The grassy void at the front of the house, however, has been retained. Finely worked 19th-century iron gates open to a charming and protected flower garden, resplendent with roses, created within the projecting wings of the house. Especially notable at Panshanger is the unique pigeon tower, a crenellated cylindrical building, positioned to be seen from the house terrace as an eyecatcher in the classic 18th-century manner. A water tower, also castellated, stands nearer the house, a silent tribute to Joseph Archer's engineering skills in the pumping and distribution of water from the river to house and garden. Panshanger is one of three important houses and gardens developed by the Archer family near Longford, in the Tasmanian midlands. Joseph's brother Thomas was responsible for Woolmers and a third brother, William, owned Brickendon.   CMR

paradeisos.

Great estates with large enclosures filled with wild animals were first introduced to the Western world by the Greek writer Xenophon (c.430–354 BC), who described the parks of the kings and nobles of Persia (Iran) that he had seen in his travels. He uses the Greek word of Persian origin, *paradeisos*, to describe these royal gardens, which were vast enclosures that included fruit and ornamental trees, flowers, birds, and mammals.

The hunting ground was an essential part of the oriental *paradeisos*. Xenophon, in his description of the education of Cyrus, describes the animals that the young prince was taught to hunt: bears, boars, lions, leopards, deer, gazelles, wild sheep, and wild asses. When Alexander the Great (356–323 BC) conquered the Persians, he took possession of their *paradeisoi*. His successors also acquired such parks, and when the Romans conquered the Hellenistic world they, in turn, acquired a taste for them.

Varro (116–27 BC), in describing the large hunting preserves found on the great estates in Italy, gives a vivid description of the wild animals on the estate of Quintus Hortensius, near Laurentum. Gardens at POMPEII and Herculaneum were frequently decorated with large animal paintings, suggesting that even the city dweller could create the illusion that he owned a *paradeisos*.   WFJ

Paris parks and gardens.

Paris is an ancient place but most of our knowledge of gardens is relatively recent. There was a neolithic settlement here in the 5th millennium BC—on the site of the modern quai de Bercy to the east of the city's epicentre—but Paris may be said to have started when the Celtic tribe of the Parisii established itself in the 2nd century BC on what is today the Île de la Cité which by the 3rd century AD was fortified to repel the barbarians. The Île de la Cité has remained the historic heart of Paris from which the city expanded outwards. For the Romans Paris, which they called Lutetia, was not as important as several other cities in Gaul. Autun, Lyon, Narbonne, Nîmes, and Rheims under Roman occupation had populations between 20,000 and 30,000 whereas Lutetia had only around 6,000. We know of no Roman gardens

Paris parks and gardens: the Tuileries gardens in Adam Perelle's late 17th-century engraving.

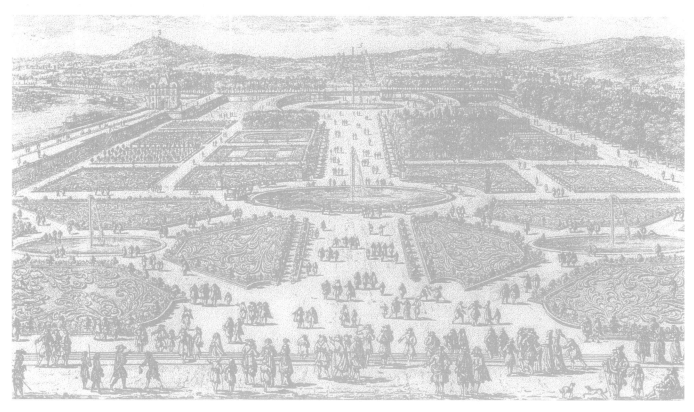

here but the Romans opened up the left-bank expansion of Paris when they built a forum and a great arena to the north-west of what is today the Jardin des Plantes—celebrated in the present square des Arènes in the 5th arrondissement. Three public baths were also built on the left bank of which the largest, built in the 2nd century, partly survives at the Hôtel de Cluny on the boulevard Saint-Michel. After the collapse of the Roman Empire the Merovingian Frankish King Clovis made Paris his base in 508 and thus established the royal presence which was to be vital to its history. Clovis's son Childebert I was a Christian and founded the church of Saint-Vincent-Sainte-Croix which formed the basis of the later Abbey of Saint-Germain-des-Prés. With the rise of the Carolingian dynasty in the 8th century, with its emphasis on the eastern parts of France, and beyond, Paris lost its importance. In the 9th century, after many destructive raids by Vikings, the city defences were reinforced and in 885-6 a Viking siege was resisted under the leadership of Eudes, the Comte de Paris. The great-nephew of Eudes was Hugues Capet, the first of the Capetian kings, who became King of France in 987 and established himself in a palace on the Île de la Cité. This, the Palais at the west end of the island, had been a Gallo-Roman fortress which the Merovingian kings had taken over. It remained the royal palace until the reign of the Valois King Charles V who came to the throne in 1364, after which it remained the seat of the exchequer and of justice. The building became, and remains, the Palais de Justice of which, today, the oldest part dates from the 13th century.

By the early 14th century Paris was one of the greatest of European cities, with a population of around 200,000, at the heart of a kingdom with a population of 20,000,000. King Charles V moved from the Palais to the Hôtel Saint-Pol which no longer exists but was in the Marais to the north-east of the Île de la Cité. The King laid out large pleasure grounds, an area of 8 hectares/20 acres in the care of his gardener Philippart Persant. It had, according to John Harvey (*Mediaeval Gardens*, 1981), 'trellised pavilions, a labyrinth, tunnel arbours, plantations of cherry trees and many kinds of ornamental plants of which rose, rosemary, lavender, wallflower, marjoram and sage are recorded'. The earliest known depiction of any Paris garden is seen in a miniature from the *Très Riches Heures du Duc de Berry* (1413-16). It shows the Palais on the Île de la Cité from the south and precious glimpses of a tunnel arbour entwined with flowering plants are visible rising above the crenellated walls. On the banks of the river haymaking is in progress (it is the month of June) and a row of pollarded willows runs along the river bank.

Very early churches and monastic communities were established in and around Paris and several of these had gardens, but detailed knowledge of them comes only from the later periods of their history. To the north of the city, and just beyond its modern boundary, the church of Saint-Denis (since 1963 the cathedral of Saint-Denis), named after the 3rd-century Roman martyr and first Bishop of Paris, had its origins as a basilica erected over the tomb of St Denis. Later still it became an abbey church, with superb 12th-century architecture and stained glass. It is the burial place of the kings of France from the 7th century to the end of the 18th century. An engraving in *Monasticon Gallicanum* (1690) shows an elaborate garden in the cloisters—four rhomboidal PARTERRES *de broderie* about a central circular pool. The abbey of Saint-Germain-des-Prés (originally called Saint-Vincent-Sainte-Croix) was founded in the 6th century by Bishop Germain. It expanded greatly and at the beginning of the 17th century was adopted as the mother church of the Benedictines of Saint-Maur. Magnificent gardens were laid out and are seen in an engraving by P. Saury *c.*1723. A physic garden spread out to the east of the infirmary and the abbot's garden had triangular parterres and a BOSQUET with irregular spaces among the trees. A quadripartite arrangement of parterres filled the central space of the cloisters and, to the west of the infirmary, the Great Garden (Grand Jardin) had a central fountain pool, *parterres de broderie*, and other parterres with rectilinear arrangements of beds. The Abbaye du Val-de-Grâce (later a military hospital), founded in 1621 with a church designed by François MANSART, had an extensive garden by the time Jean Marot published his engraving of it in the late 17th century. Behind the domed chapel is seen an extensive pattern of ALLÉES lined with trees and to one side a four-part walled garden each of whose quarters is divided into four parterres. In 1606 Henri IV started to build a hospital to cope with the plague, the Hôpital Saint-Louis, outside the city walls to the north-east—it still survives, close to the 19th-century Buttes-Chaumont. Claude Chastillon's engraving of it published in *Topographie française* (early 17th century) shows that it was garnished with fine gardens—four courtyards are seen with parterres and topiary and there are several alignments of trees. Princes of the Church also had great houses with gardens. The town house of the bishops of Sens, the Hôtel de Sens, was established in the 14th century. By the late 17th century when it was engraved by Roger de Gaignières it was ornamented by a great *parterre de broderie*—with the house *entre cour et jardin*

(between courtyard and garden) as is the classical arrangement of great Parisian houses.

As far as modern Paris is concerned the two most important influences on the parks and gardens of Paris were the various royal houses and the 19th-century replanning of the city by HAUSSMANN. These, with their fascinating history, determine not only the garden character of the city today, but much of its essential atmosphere. There are no really large parks in the centre of Paris—easily the largest, the Bois de Boulogne and the Bois de Vincennes, each over 900 hectares/2,220 acres, are just outside the city boundary. But the city is immensely rich in small parks, far too numerous to describe here. It is also exceptionally enterprising in the creation of large-scale new parks—the Parc André Citroën and the Parc de la Villette are described below but the 14-hectare/35-acre Parc de Bercy, laid out from 1994 along the Seine in the 12th arrondissment, is also a fine addition to the city landscape.

Tuileries
The site just west of the city walls, which had been a tile (*tuile* means 'tile') factory since the 13th century, was bought in the early 16th century by François I. His daughter-in-law Catherine de Médicis, the widow of Henri II, started to build a palace here in 1564 to the designs of Philibert de L'ORME. A drawing of 1570 by Jacques Androuet DU CERCEAU shows the walled gardens which were built below the palace's western façade along the Seine. Here was a rectilinear pattern of over 40 beds, some laid out as parterres, one as a maze (planted with willows), and there were many fruit trees—cherries, pears, and plums. From 1572 Pierre Le Nôtre, grandfather of André LE NÔTRE, was in charge of some of the parterres. The palace was added to in the 17th century and in 1664 André Le Nôtre redesigned the garden. Israel Silvestre's drawing made shortly after the garden's completion shows a bold central axis and the gardens immediately to the west of the palace opening with triumphant *parterres de broderie* and three circular pools with fountains. The tree-lined central axis continues to an octagonal pool further east. In this design Le Nôtre laid the foundations to one of the most spectacular of all urban set pieces. Today the axial vista which starts at the Tuileries is continued by the avenue des Champs-Élysées and the Arc de Triomphe and beyond it by the avenue de la Grande Armée and the avenue Charles de Gaulle culminating in the Grande Arche de la Défense (1989) beyond the western boundary of the city. In the 1990s, as part of President Mitterrand's Grands Projets, the Tuileries gardens were reinvigorated. A new

garden was designed by Jacques WIRTZ for the Arc du Carrousel which marks the eastern end of the great vista, with radiating yew hedges and BOSQUETS of pleached lime—a powerful and elegant design. The planting in the beds to the west was enlivened, to the designs of Pascal Cribier and Louis Benech, with much freer use of herbaceous perennials and shrubs. The pattern of Le Nôtre's garden, with two of his pools, remains in place.

Luxembourg Gardens

The palace and gardens were created at the instigation of Marie de Médicis, the second wife of Henri IV, who in 1610 on the death of her husband became Queen Regent during the minority of Louis XIII. Wanting a residence of her own, she commissioned a palace then well outside the city walls to the south of Paris. In 1615 the palace was started to the designs of Salomon de Brosse (1571–1626). The gardens were already under way in 1612 and in 1613 the great aqueduct of Arcueil was built to bring water from Rungis 11.5 km/7 miles away. The Italian specialist in water features, Alessandro FRANCINI, designed a grotto in 1612 which survives in a different position (and heavily reworked in the 19th century) on the eastern boundary of the garden to the north of its original site. Jacques BOYCEAU DE LA BARAUDERIE probably laid out the garden whose plan is seen in an anonymous drawing of 1627. South of the palace an octagonal pool stands at the centre of four square beds beyond which the ground rises and is sculpted into semicircular terraces. Israel Silvestre's engraving of about the same date shows elaborate *parterres de broderie*. The estate remained in the royal family until, after the Revolution, in 1791, it became national property and became the Senate, which it still remains. The gardens became a public park which still retains much of its original layout but, apart from the grotto, almost none of its detail. The most interesting planting today, which is otherwise strongly municipal in flavour, is the remarkable collection of tender plants—lemons, oleanders, oranges, and pomegranates—some of great age—which are displayed in huge *caisses de Versailles* (see CONTAINER).

Jardin des Plantes

It was founded in 1626 as the Jardin Royal des Plantes Médicinales under the patronage of Louis XIII. The King's physician Guy de La Brosse urged him to found the garden, arguing that 'plants are to medicine as stone, mortar and timber are to architecture', and explained to him how the garden might be established and laid out. Scalberge's painting of 1636 shows an axial plan with a rectilinear pattern of beds and to one side, beyond an *allée*, a less formal

garden with a mount and helical walk. John EVELYN saw the garden in 1644 and described 'all varieties of ground for planting and culture of medical simples. It is well chosen, having in it hills, meadows, wood and upland, natural and artificial, and is richly stor'd with exotic plants.' As early as 1640 the garden was opened to the public, the first in Paris to do so, and a seller of lemonade was licensed to ply his trade in the shade of the trees. Throughout the 17th century the garden was dedicated to the cultivation of medicinal plants and to teaching students of medicine and pharmacology. In 1718 it changed its name to the Jardin Royal des Plantes and assumed a much wider role in the study of botany. The great natural scientist Georges-Louis Leclerc de Buffon became director of the garden in 1739, remaining until 1788. He was joined, as curator of the garden, in 1774 by Jean de Lamarck whose work on the mutability of species anticipated Darwin. After the Revolution, in 1793, the garden lost its royal appellation and greatly widened its scope, becoming the Jardins des Plantes of the new Muséum National d'Histoire Naturelle dedicated to the study of natural history generally. Thus a zoo was introduced, with animals brought from the royal MENAGERIE at VERSAILLES. Today the layout of the garden corresponds generally to its 17th-century appearance. The formal garden, about the axis of the Allée Centrale, has gaudy bedding schemes sternly overlooked by statues of Buffon and Lamarck, but the *Robinia pseudoacacia* planted in 1636 and a *Sophora japonica* planted in 1740 remain. To the north the less formal garden has winding walks, an aviary, a menagerie, and a fine alpine garden. The mount survives, recreated as the Labyrinthe under Buffon, and there are several noble trees planted in the 18th century.

Palais-Royal

Originally the Palais-Cardinal, it was built in the 1630s for Cardinal Richelieu but became the Palais-Royal when Anne of Austria, Queen Regent of France during Louis XIV's minority 1643–51, came to live here in 1643. The garden, in Richelieu's time the largest in Paris except for the royal gardens at the Tuileries and the Palais du Luxembourg, was laid out by Pierre Le Nôtre (the grandfather of André Le Nôtre) with a flower parterre and a *parterre de broderie* to the designs of Jacques Boyceau de La Barauderie, with elm bosquets and hedges added in 1634. However, it was radically redesigned by André Le Nôtre for the Duc d'Orléans in 1673. La Boissière's engraving of 1679 shows an axial layout centred on the palace with a circular and octagonal pool and lavish *parterres de broderie*. The Palais-Royal today owes its appearance

to the early 19th century when it was largely rebuilt. A sketch of a *jardin à la française* is in place, with lime *allées* running down each side and the great circular pool, but lawns in the centre are framed with late 20th-century mixed borders. In 1986 the entrance courtyard was filled with regular rows of striped stubby truncated columns by Daniel Buren—they delight children but garden lovers are more uncertain.

Château de Bagatelle

In 1775 the estate, now in the north-western part of the Bois de Boulogne, was bought by the Comte d'Artois, the brother of Louis XVI. He replaced a simple earlier building with a beautiful new small chateau designed by François-Joseph BÉLANGER and built in 1777. It was set in a formal garden *à la française* (whose layout survives) but, to the south, Thomas BLAIKIE laid out an English-style picturesque park with lakes, a winding stream, and a pattern of serpentine paths completed in 1786. Today only traces of this remain and nothing is to be seen of numerous FABRIQUES—Chinese, Dutch, Egyptian, Indian, and Swiss—which were scattered in the landscape. In 1835 the estate was bought by Lord Seymour (later Marquess of Hertford) who left the estate to his illegitimate son Sir Richard Wallace, who in turn left it to his secretary Sir Henry Murray Scott, who sold the estate to the city of Paris in 1905. J. C. N. FORESTIER laid out a magnificent romantic rose garden which survives today and is very well looked after. With 24 hectares/60 acres, its delightful chateau (though rather clumsily altered in the 19th century), and richly varied grounds, it is an outstanding garden. C. C. L. Hirschfeld in his *Theorie der Gartenkunst* (1779–85) admired the 'Peaceful voluptuousness of this hidden retreat'.

Parc Monceau

In the 18th century the site, now in the heart of the 8th arrondissement, was in the country. It was bought by the Duc de Chartres who commissioned a picturesque garden from Louis Carrogis, known as CARMONTELLE, an artist who became *ordonnateur des plaisirs* to the Duke. This, known as La Folie de Chartres, was his most famous work. He started work in 1773, disposing numbers of exotic *fabriques*—a windmill, sham ruins, columns, a Turkish tent, a pyramid, and much else. Carmontelle wrote a booklet, *Le Jardin de Monceau* (1779), explaining his ideas. He believed that one should 'change the scenes in a garden like the stage sets at the Opéra'. In 1783 Thomas Blaikie was asked to take charge of Monceau which he found 'a confused Landskipe . . . the walks Serpenting and turning without reason'. In the 1860s, during Haussmann's replanning of Paris, part of it became the Parc Monceau, and today it is a popular public park in a fashionable residential district, with only the faintest traces of Carmontelle's work surviving.

Père-Lachaise

Properly known as the Cimetière de l'Est, the CEMETERY of Père-Lachaise was designed *c.*1810 by Alexandre-Théodore Brongniart (1739–1813). By 1804 the city of Paris had forbidden any further burials within the city. A country estate belonging to the Jesuits, named after a priest, François de La Chaise, was acquired for a new cemetery then outside the city walls. Brongniart's original plan, a picturesque landscape garden decorated with *fabriques*, was only partly executed. The sloping southern part, closest to the boulevard Ménilmontant, has a central axis off which winding paths wander among the monuments with many trees and shrubs. The northern part is disposed in a much less sympathetic grid pattern. Many notable people are buried here, often with outstanding and appropriate memorial stones. Among them are Frédéric Chopin (1849, romantically shaded by a weeping willow), Alfred de Musset (1857), Oscar Wilde (1909, a sphinx with pouting lips by Sir Jacob Epstein), and Marcel Proust (1922, a sleek horizontal slab of gleaming black marble).

Bois de Boulogne

Although just beyond the western city boundary the Bois de Boulogne, which belongs to the city of Paris, must certainly be considered a Paris park. The site, today with an area of 845 hectares/2,087 acres, has its origins as part of a royal hunting ground called Rouvray (*chêne rouvre* is the French for *Quercus robur*, the common oak). An abbey was founded here in the 13th century by Ste Isabelle, the sister of St Louis, who gave it the name Longchamp—the name given today to a famous racecourse. François I built a palace here, the Château de Madrid (so named because it was inspired by a Spanish country house), which is illustrated in Androuet DU CERCEAU's *Les Plus Excellents Bastiments de France* (1576–79). A spectacular building, its façade was clad in intricate majolica architectural ornaments by Girolamo Della Robbia—it was destroyed during the Revolution. In the 1550s Henri II enclosed the park in a wall and in the 17th century, when the park was still used for hunting, Louis XIV laid out a star-shaped pattern of rides. The perimeter of the park became a fashionable place for new houses in the 18th century—Bagatelle and the Folie SAINT JAMES date from this period. In 1852 Napoleon III gave the Bois de Boulogne to the city of Paris to be used as a public park. It was laid out by Louis-Sulpice Varé (1802–83) and J. C. A. ALPHAND. The park

was girdled with boulevards, and a pattern of paths, sometimes straight and sometimes serpentining, divided the interior space. Several lakes were floated of which the largest, the lower lake, had two islands, one of which had a famous restaurant, the Chalet des Îles, which survives. Unlike other Hausmannian parks the Bois de Boulogne was at some distance from the more populous parts of Paris so attractions were needed to draw the public. Restaurants and cafeterias were established, the Longchamp racecourse built, and, to the north of the park, a great zoo, the Jardin d'Acclimatation, was laid out. The municipal architect Gabriel Davioud (1824–81), who worked on many Parisian parks, designed several garden buildings, of which the Emperor's Kiosk at the southern end of the lower lake is a pretty survival rising among the trees. Pleasure gardens, the Pré-Catelan, were laid out with a smart restaurant, a puppet theatre, and an open-air theatre. In 1953 it was decided to transform the theatre, by then neglected, into a Shakespeare garden in which every plant mentioned in the plays is cultivated. Throughout the park many different trees have been cultivated—native oaks and beeches but also countless exotics. Proust was moved by the character of the Bois de Boulogne and in *Le Côté de Guermantes* gave a memorable description of the narrator's autumnal walk with Albertine 'while the wind, like a conscientious gardener, shook the trees, causing fruit to fall and sweeping up the dead leaves'.

Parc des Buttes-Chaumont

The park was laid out between 1865 and 1867 by Jean C. A. Alphand. The 25-hectare/62-acre site is dramatically hilly—a rocky promontory soars to 50 m/164 ft and is crowned with a copy of the Temple of the Sibyl at Tivoli and a great cascade plummets into the lake below. Engravings of the newly made park give it the atmosphere of an 18th-century picturesque landscape park. Now that the planting is fully mature, dense with groves of trees enlivened by sudden hidden glades, it has a secretive and mysterious air—one of the most attractive of Paris parks. It was much loved by the surrealists—Louis Aragon wondered if it was the preserve of 'seuls rêveurs en quête de mystère' (solitary dreamers in search of mystery) (*Le Paysan de Paris*, 1926). In the 19th arrondissement close to the north-eastern boundary of the city, this is not a park much frequented by tourists—it retains a quintessentially Parisian character.

Champ-de-Mars

The martial connotations of the Champ-de-Mars come from the École Militaire (designed by Ange-Jacques Gabriel (1698–1782) in 1751 (but subsequently much altered) which stands nobly at its southern end. The *champ* (field), which

ran all the way north to the river Seine, was let out by the École Militaire to market gardeners until, in 1881, it was sold to the city of Paris. It was laid out as a public park, from 1881, by J. Bouvard, J.-C. Formigé, and J. C. N. Forestier who designed an open central space flanked by informal groves of trees, shrubberies, pools, and flower beds. Its northern end is marked by the world's supreme eyecatcher, the Eiffel Tower, built in 1889. To celebrate the millennium Le Mur de la Paix (The Wall of Peace) designed by Clara Halter was put in place in 2000 at the southern end of the park where it abuts with the esplanade of the École Militaire. An open pavilion walled in glass is engraved with the word peace in 32 languages as are the pale grey free-standing stone columns that flank it, sixteen on each side.

Parc de la Villette

The former cattle market and abattoir in the north-east of Paris was, from 1983, transformed into a park with several public buildings for different purposes. The site is a large one, with an area of 55 hectares/136 acres, and among the buildings are a museum of science and industry, a museum of music, a cinema with a hemispherical screen (the Géode), a multipurpose auditorium, and much else. The landscaping was designed by the architect Bernard Tschumi (b. 1944) and consists of a series of episodes involving several different designers linked by a serpentine walk. Scattered hither and yon are curious skeletal buildings painted bright red. Designed by Tschumi these are said to evoke the 'follies' of an 18th-century landscape park. The setting is very strongly architectural and the planted episodes, which provide occasional hidden retreats, have only a modest, sometimes perfunctory, presence in the landscape. The surface is busy with different materials—concrete, cobbles, stainless steel, or pebbles. Some of the plantings are attractive—thickets of *Salix elaeagnos* subsp. *angustifolia* below a parade of maples, a grove of *Catalpa bignonioides*, a *bosquet* with vertical mirrors, and a deep canyon of bamboos. But the most memorable features of the landscape are certainly the buildings. The Géode, designed by Adrien Fainsilber (b. 1932), is a sphere clad in stainless steel, 36 m/118 ft in diameter, which rises above a huge placid pool.

Parc André Citroën

This park occupies the site of the former Citroën armaments and car factory, with an area of 13.8 hectares/34 acres, which now has residential and office buildings about a central open space. The site was landscaped by Gilles CLÉMENT and Alain Provost (b. 1938) who won the competition for its design in 1985. Clément's colour-themed planting and wild garden, the garden's calmly expansive great central lawn crisply framed in a surrounding canal, subtle plantings of groups of trees, and explosive computer-controlled fountains resulted in a very popular public garden which gives a new urban development on a former industrial site a true sense of place and character.

Paris has an exceptional range of public parks and the sometimes ponderous lines of Haussmann's new avenues and boulevards are everywhere enlivened by trees. Of all cities Paris has shown that it has the political will and determination to devote precious land to green amenities. It will even make them on the roof of an office block. The Jardin Atlantique is a 3.5-hectare/8.6-acre public amenity on the roof of an office block immediately adjacent to the Gare Montparnasse (which serves the Atlantic coast of France, hence the garden's name). Here in 1994 the landscape architects Brun, Pena et Schnitzler designed lawns, *bosquets*, a children's playground, a meteorological centre disguised as a sculpture (surrounded by GIOCHI D'ACQUA), tennis courts, a pergola, and much else. The whole is garnished with bold plantings of grasses and willows with magnificent individual trees—black walnut (*Juglans nigra*), nettle tree (*Celtis australis*), and Hungarian oak (*Quercus frainetto*). There is no phrase in English for *tour de force*.   PT

MARTINE CONSTANS (ed.), *Jardiner à Paris au temps des rois* (2004).
DOMINIQUE JARRASSÉ, *L'Art des jardins parisiens* (2002).

Parkinson, John

(1567–1650), English apothecary and plantsman. Although probably from Nottinghamshire Parkinson lived, and created his famous garden, in Long Acre, London. Appointed apothecary to both James I and later Charles I, Parkinson helped found the Society of Apothecaries in 1617, and was its warden. However he soon resigned to devote time to his garden, and to writing *Paradisi in Sole Paradisus Terrestris* (1629) which emphasized both the pleasure and detail of flowers, mostly described from his own garden. The book was dedicated to Queen Henrietta Maria, and Charles I was so impressed that he created Parkinson *botanicus regius primarius*—the King's first botanist. Parkinson knew both the TRADESCANTS, and Matthias de L'OBEL, from whom on his death in 1616 he inherited his botanical manuscripts. In 1649 Parkinson published *Theatrum Botanicum*, a larger work in which he describes some 4,000 mainly herbal plants. It has been described as the first great gardening book.   MC-C

Park Wilhelma. See WILHELMA GARDENS.

Parmentier, André

(1780–1830). A Belgian, Parmentier was influenced by his horticulturist brother Joseph to become a nurseryman, and when he emigrated to the United States in 1824 Parmentier immediately established a nursery and vineyard overlooking Brooklyn Harbour, New York. He introduced to America the landscape style of garden, and became its foremost exponent, travelling from the far south of the United States to Canada fulfilling commissions. In Toronto he remodelled the grounds of King's College and Moss Park, as usual laying out the grounds himself and stocking them from his own nursery. His most famous garden, where much of his planting remains intact, is Hyde Park, the Vanderbilt residence overlooking the Hudson river in New York, where in 1828 he received a commission to redesign the estate. In 1828 the flourishing business employed 30 agents, and his influence long affected the gardens of the United States.   MC-C

Parpagliolo Shephard, Maria Teresa

(1903–74), Italian landscape and garden designer, member of the British Institute of Landscape Architects, the Associazione Italiana degli Architetti del Giardino e del Paesaggio, the Società Italiana 'Amici dei Fiori', and the Società di Orticultura di Lombardia. As one of the few women pioneers of European landscape design she played a central role in revitalizing and developing garden culture and landscape design in Italy, working in her home country and in Britain from the late 1920s until her death on small- and large-scale private and public projects. She complemented her autodidactic studies by training in Percy CANE's office in 1931–2, travelling throughout Europe, attending the first international conferences of European landscape architects, and contributing to the foundation of IFLA in 1948. Characteristic of her design work is the blending of design motifs from different garden cultures and movements, e.g. the naturalistic garden and ARTS AND CRAFTS movement. Her early works reveal a preference for Italy's garden tradition as a source of inspiration, strengthened during her work as head of the planning department for parks and gardens at the International World Exhibition (E'42) in 1940–2 under fascist dictatorship. In contrast to the early architectural garden designs the biomorphic forms used in the Regatta Restaurant Garden at the Festival of Britain in 1951, where she acted as deputy landscape consultant collaborating with Frank Clark, show her reception of the

modern movement in landscape architecture and her openness to experiment. Other work includes the winning design for the French War Cemetery in Rome (1944), open space and landscape planning for residential developments and garden suburbs outside Rome (1950–1960s), prestigious projects at the Roman Hilton (1963) and RAI headquarters (1966), and the restoration project for the 16th-century Mughal garden Bagh-i Bäbur in Kabul in 1970–2 (*Kabul: The Bagh-I Babur. A Project and a Research into the Possibilities of a Complete Reconstruction*, 1972). Teaching activities at the Roman professional school for the training of gardeners in 1932–7, a book on trees and botany for the Girl Guides (*Conoscere le piante*, 1946), numerous articles in *Landscape and Garden*, *Journal of the Institute of Landscape Architects*, *Domus*, and *Il giardino fiorito*, and her initiatives together with Pietro PORCINAI for the foundation of a school for landscape architecture in the 1960s document her commitment to develop a stronger public awareness of garden cultural, landscape, and environmental affairs in Italy.   SD

SONJA DÜMPELMANN, *Maria Teresa Parpagliolo Shephard (1903–1974): Ein Beitrag zur Entwicklung der Gartenkultur in Italien im 20. Jahrhundert* (2004).

Parque 3 de Febrero ⊛

Buenos Aires, Argentina, is a public park with an area of 90 hectares/222 acres. The first public park in Argentina, it was inaugurated in 1875, built over the ruins of a Versaillesque private park whose original name was Palermo, by which it is sometimes still known. The design was influenced by European and American landscapers such as Jean Charles Adolphe ALPHAND and Frederick Law OLMSTED. The Argentine President, Domingo Sarmiento (1811–88), thought of it as a combination of New York's Central Park and the Bois de Boulogne in Paris. It was designed and built by a group of European professionals, among them Jordan Wysocki (Polish, 1839–83), Ernest Oldendorff (Prussian), Fernand Mauduit (French), Jules Dormal (Belgian 1846–1924), Adolph Methfessel (Swiss 1836–1909), and Carlos Burmel (Swiss). The present layout, which intermingles the influence of the French formal style and a more romantic and informal English style, is by Charles THAYS and his Argentine disciple Benito Carrasco (1877–1958). Among outstanding planting surviving from the original layout is a *Magnolia grandiflora* and a magnificent entrance avenue of the indigenous queen palm (*Arecastrum romanzoffianum* syn. *Syagrus romanzoffianus*). The park contains an open-air collection of sculpture and monuments by 19th- and 20th-century European and Argentine artists, ornamental buildings, lakes

with islands, bridges, fountains, a botanical garden, and a zoo. It is a favourite place of recreation for an immense number of people. Due to poor maintenance, and parts of the park being turned over to commercial enterprises, in 1993 members of the public formed an organization to restore and protect the park.
SLB

parterre.

The word, meaning literally 'on the ground', whose first use in France is recorded in 1546, came to mean a garden bed with a regular pattern. It is essentially a later, and much more elaborate, development of the English KNOT GARDEN and first made its appearance in 16th-century France, becoming in the 17th century, with increasing elaboration, an essential ingredient of the *jardin à la française*. Claude MOLLET (*c*.1560–*c*.1649) was a central figure in the development of the parterre. At the Tuileries gardens (see PARIS PARKS AND GARDENS) towards the end of the 16th century he laid out a parterre which included the arms of France and of Navarre traced in low clipped plants set off by a background of coloured earth. At the HORTUS

PALATINUS in Heidelberg Salomon de CAUS designed a quadripartite garden with a different pattern of parterre in each quarter. Hedges of clipped box, lavender, or rosemary traced the interlacing pattern, and the compartments were filled with hyssop and mint clipped lower than the hedges. The *parterre de broderie* (embroidered parterre), with a pattern of swirling arabesques, first appeared at the Château d'ANET in the late 16th century and began to replace the earlier style of interlacing hedges. The *parterre d'eau* (water parterre) was a 17th-century development in which patterns of water, often on a very grand scale, were the chief ingredient. A fine surviving example by André LE NÔTRE may be seen at CHANTILLY (1671–2). Two books were particularly influential on the design of *parterres de broderie*. Jacques BOYCEAU DE LA BARAUDERIE's *Traité du jardinage selon les raisons de la nature et de l'art* (1638) illustrated parterres in several of the royal gardens—the Louvre, LUXEMBOURG, SAINT-GERMAIN-EN-LAYE, Tuileries, and VERSAILLES—and gave much detail of their planning and planting. André MOLLET's *Le Jardin de plaisir* (1651) gives many illustrations of plans for *parterres de broderie* and very detailed

information on recommended sizes and planting. Design number 8, for example, has a central octagonal fountain pool, four parterres with patterns of fleur-de-lis and crowns, each edged in *plates-bandes* (see BORDER) six *pieds* wide planted with clipped evergreens evenly spaced and underplanted with smaller plants such as anemones, ranunculus, and tulips. *Parterres à l'anglaise* (English-style parterres) were much simpler, and much cheaper both to put into place and to maintain. They were lawns in which simple curved patterns may be cut into turf (*gazon coupé*), the whole usually edged with *plates-bandes* planted with flowers. In England knots were followed by parterres, often very much in the French style, by the end of the 17th century in gardens designed by George LONDON. A London design for a cut turf *parterre à l'anglaise* originally made for Longleat (Wiltshire) has been laid out at KIRBY HALL.

Designs for **parterres** from *The Theory and Practice of Gardening* (1712), the English edition of A.-J. Dezallier d'Argenville's *La Théorie et la pratique du jardinage* (1709).

A Parterre after ye English manner.

A Parterre of Cutwork for Flowers.

A Parterre of Orange Trees.

Parterres fell out of fashion in England as the landscape garden swept all before it in the 18th century. However, in the 19th century they made a return in the gardens of such designers as Sir Charles BARRY and W. A. NESFIELD, often using the newly fashionable bedding plants within the compartments. Outstanding examples of this style of parterre may be seen in Scotland in the 16th-century walled garden at PITMEDDEN, based on 17th-century designs, but only put into place from 1955. PT

Pasargadae ⊛

province of Fars, Iran. The ruins of Cyrus the Great's palace at Pasargadae, built by the Achaemenid Emperor after 548 BC in the great plain of Marvdasht east of the Zagros in south-west Iran, and preserved in the desert, are those of the earliest Iranian garden. Its geometric arrangement of limestone rills and square pools, revealed by archaeologists, gives a glimpse of what was to become the traditional Persian fourfold or CHAHAR BAGH pattern, later adopted in Islamic garden architecture. Except for a few glimmering white columns, little remains of the palace and pavilions from which the garden would have been viewed. The watercourses were fed originally by a now vanished aqueduct. Almost certainly the inner royal garden, measuring 230 × 200 m/766 × 666 ft, will have been planted with productive orchard trees, sheltered by dark cypresses and/or poplars. PHo

paths.

The garden path is not a subject that has much commanded the attention of garden historians yet it is an ingredient of gardens that greatly contributes to their atmosphere. It is both practical, keeping feet dry and providing an alternative route preventing damage to, say, frozen or waterlogged lawns, and at the same time it is a powerfully expressive aspect of garden design. The reason that it is often overlooked is that successful paths are often the least obtrusive. Russell PAGE in his *Education of a Gardener* (1962) laid down the rules. He was emphatic that the path should have a purpose, it must go somewhere—aimless paths make aimless gardens. He also believed that a path should take the most direct route to its goal or, if deviating from it, do so only for a very good reason, such as a tree or building blocking its way. This is not a new idea, for William Lawson in his *A New Orchard and Garden* (1618) wrote that 'universallie walks are straight'. The front garden of a cottage typically has a path leading directly from the entrance gate to the front door, a route that usually divides the garden into two equal spaces. This is what J. C. LOUDON

believed, too, articulating the matter very firmly in his *Encyclopaedia of Gardening* (1822): 'The principle of *a sufficient reason* should never be lost sight of in laying out walks . . . that is, no deviation from a straight line should ever appear, for which a reason is not given in the position of the ground, trees, or other accompanying objects'. This is, on the whole, the prevailing European approach to paths, but in China different notions apply. The gardening manual *Yuan ye* (1634) recommends that 'the paths meander like playing cats'. A curved path, too, suggesting no great urgency, will encourage a visitor to walk at a more leisurely pace and consider the views. A path curving away towards some unknown destination is a tantalizing sight. In informal and woodland gardens the curving path will often seem more natural. William GILPIN in his *Remarks on Forest Scenery* (1791) wrote, 'Let it wind: but let it not take any deviation which is not well accounted for.' In Gertrude JEKYLL's own garden at MUNSTEAD WOOD the woodland garden, occupying most of its space, has two straight paths dividing the space and meeting at an angle. All other paths wind off these central walks, ambling through glades and among thickets of planting. In Chinese and Japanese gardens the path is, in effect, a means of orchestrating the experience of being in a garden—what is revealed in what order. The path itself may often be an object of contemplation. Marc P. Keane in his *Japanese Garden Design* (1996) points out that the use of uneven stepping stones in a path forces the visitor to look down and focus on the path's materials.

The path is usually one of many ingredients that divide the space of a garden but it can sometimes rise above the humble role and assume major importance. The TERRACE WALK is a kind of garden path elevated to the high status of a major garden feature. The 18th-century terrace at RIEVAULX is a broad grass walk following the natural curve of the ground. From it a series of views are revealed, through openings cut into the woodland, of the ruins of Rievaulx Abbey below and its exquisite setting in the rural landscape. Each view is different and each adds to the cumulative impact of the scene below. The family that made the Rievaulx terrace, the Duncombes, also made another terrace at DUNCOMBE PARK which has a similar purpose. Here the views of the ruins of Helmsley Castle, and of the river Rye flowing past it in the valley below, are vaguely glimpsed through the trees' branches and foliage. In Renaissance gardens terraced walks were made to provide views of elaborate parterres laid out below. The more naturalistic grass paths in these 18th-century Yorkshire gardens

were made for a similar purpose, but to relish a very different kind of view.

The materials chosen for surfacing a path are important to the character of the garden and are often all of a piece with the larger visual environment. In old gardens of the Low Countries paths are often made of the narrow Flemish bricks used for buildings. The same bricks were used to pave courtyards and are seen in Flemish paintings of the 17th century by artists such as Pieter de Hooch. They are integral to the atmosphere of such places. In England, in those parts of the country such as East Anglia where there is little stone and bricks are the almost universal building material, bricks are found surfacing old garden paths, often laid in beautiful herringbone patterns,. In English ARTS AND CRAFTS gardens the materials and patterns of paths were carefully considered. At Barrington Court (Somerset), for example, the architect J. E. Forbes was brought in to restore the Tudor house in the 1920s. He also laid out superb paths surfaced in handmade bricks in patterns of herringbone or basket weave of marvellous virtuosity which perfectly suit the character of the old house and of the garden on which Gertrude Jekyll worked. Gravel paths add the dimension of sound, crunching under foot, to the garden's atmosphere. The more refined hoggin—fine gravel mixed with clay and pounded down—makes a distinguished path. In seaside places beach pebbles are often used to surface paths, sometimes laid in patterns taking advantage of different colours. Mown grass remains among the most attractive of materials for paths. A close-mown path across a meadow of flowers and long grass is one of the most beautiful forms of path. In modern times, with transport making everything universally available, the local use of vernacular materials has become much less common. The mass production of paving slabs and of paviours, the same designs available in every garden centre or building supplier, has eroded regional differences. PT

patio.

In Spanish the word means a courtyard but in modern English it has come to mean a terrace for sitting, sometimes planted, sometimes with a 'water feature', and often equipped with a barbecue. The patios of the Islamic gardens of southern Spain, however, of the sort seen in the ALHAMBRA, are a distinctive form of enclosure in which exquisite architectural detail, shade, and the soothing sound and glitter of water are prime ingredients. That form of patio is, thus, very much influenced by the climate. There was sometimes planting within the patio but paving and water occupied most of the space. The Islamic patio is invariably connected with the rooms of the building that encloses it and very often the relationship of the spaces is emphasized by water rills which link inside and outside. In the intense midday heat the inner rooms would provide shade but light would be reflected into the rooms from the patio. The serenity and inwardness of the patio has an atmosphere quite different from that, say, of Italian Renaissance gardens in which views out of the garden were a central ingredient. The Renaissance garden may be serene but it does not turn its back on the world outside. The essence of the atmosphere of the Islamic patio was caught by James Dickey, in *The Islamic Garden* (ed. E. B. MacDougall and R. Ettinghausen, 1976) when he referred to its 'emphasis on the intimate and the within'. Although the most complete surviving examples of Islamic patios may be found in Andalusia the form is found throughout the Islamic world. It has also been adopted in countries sharing a similar climate.   PT

patte d'oie.

Literally a goose's foot in French, the term came to mean a multiple (usually three- or five-part) arrangement of avenues or walks radiating from a single point. Its first use dates from 1624 and it became a common feature of French and English gardens in the latter part of the 17th century. It was characteristically found radiating from the entrance front of a house with the central avenue forming the entrance drive. The arrangement was susceptible to many variations. At Badminton House (Gloucestershire) in the late 17th century, for example, the *patte d'oie* was only part of a sunburst of avenues exploding from the house on all four sides.   PT

pavilion.

Derived from the Latin *papilionem*, a butterfly, the word had the meaning of a tent, whose flapping or furled material might resemble a butterfly's wings. In garden terminology it has an imprecise meaning that can easily blend with GAZEBO, BELVEDERE, BANDSTAND, KIOSK, TEMPLE, and CASINO. Like these it is a free-standing ornamental building usually woven into the design of a garden to occupy a place of importance, often to form an eyecatcher or a decorative incident. Such buildings were common in Italian, French, and English Renaissance gardens, and in French gardens of the 17th and 18th centuries they assumed greater prominence. At MARLY a whole series of pavilions was built to house Louis XIV's guests, in two rows of six buildings. At their head was the *pavillon du roi*—a two-storey eleven-bay palace. In the garden of the Petit Trianon at VERSAILLES in the 18th century the Pavillon Français, an exquisite building of 1749–50 designed by Jacques-Ange Gabriel, was built as the centrepiece, at the meeting place of two ALLÉES. Lavishly decorated, it is built like a miniature one-storey chateau. In 18th-century English gardens pavilions often had more than ornamental purposes. The island Music Pavilion at WEST WYCOMBE PARK dating from *c.*1778 was built for concerts and theatrical performances. At Audley End (Essex) Robert ADAM's Teahouse Bridge Pavilion of 1782 was simultaneously an eyecatcher, a tea house, and a bridge spanning a river.   PT

Pavilion Gardens ⊛

Charlottesville, Virginia, USA, designed by Thomas JEFFERSON, are part of his campus plan for the University of Virginia. It included a central rotunda, moving out from which two rows of pavilions flank a central lawn. Behind the pavilion living quarters for students and professors are the gardens, numbered I to X. Some still retain the 'necessaries', privies of brick construction, now used as sheds. Though the serpentine walls that divide gardens I to VI were completed by 1824, no record exists of

---

The Chinese **pavilion** at the Désert de Retz from Georges Le Rouge's *Détails de nouveaux jardins à la mode* (1775–89).

La Maison Chinoise vûe du côté du Couchant

Jefferson's actual garden plans. It is thought that his ideal was an academic village in which the professors living in the pavilions would maintain their gardens for both scholarly contemplation and utilitarian purposes. This came to pass, resulting in the greatly differing characters of the various gardens. Garden IV, the Boxwood Garden, was meticulously cultivated by Professor Schele de Vere from 1845 to 1897. Garden VI contains the Merton Spire, constructed for Oxford's Merton College Chapel in 1451 and given to the university in honour of Jefferson's ideals. It also includes a grove of native shrubs and trees, including sweet bay (*Magnolia virginiana*), rhododendrons, and mountain laurel (*Kalmia latifolia*). Garden VII, one of the smaller gardens, is used for functions by the Faculty Club. Its lawn serves for large gatherings and the secluded niches, fitted with benches, allow for more intimate conversation. In 1948, the Garden Club of Virginia hired landscape architect Alden Hopkins to restore the West Gardens and, later, Donald H. Parker the East Gardens.   CO

Pavlovsk ⊛

near St Petersburg, Russia, is the site of Paul I's palace and extensive landscape park (600 hectares/1,482 acres) on the banks of the Slavyanka, 25 km/16 miles from St Petersburg and 3 km/2 miles from TSARSKOE SELO. Charles CAMERON designed the palace for Paul and Maria Fedorovna when Paul was Grand Duke, but it was considerably altered by Vincenzo Brenna (1740–1819) and others. Cameron also laid out the private gardens nearby; began to design the 'natural' landscape along the wooded slopes of the river; and designed a number of fine buildings in the park. His Temple of Friendship, a large domed rotunda with Doric columns, is an important focal point and was the forerunner of many similar temples in Russia. The role of the park as a sanctuary was underlined by the Apollo Colonnade with its statue of Apollo (one of three in the park), the protector of valleys and groves and patron of the arts. Among Cameron's other classical buildings are the Aviary and the Temple of the Three Graces. Less prominently situated rustic buildings—a rustic dairy, a hermit's cell, and a charcoal burner's hut—reflected the sentimental tastes of the Grand Duchess and the changing fashions of Western Europe, where the exotic had yielded ground to the pseudo-vernacular.

When Paul succeeded to the throne in 1796 and Pavlovsk became briefly an imperial residence, Brenna made alterations to the park to give it a more ceremonial character. The Old Sylvia is his most important addition. In a central clearing, from which twelve paths

radiate, stands a statue of Apollo surrounded by Mercury, Venus, Flora, and the nine Muses on the circumference of the clearing in the spaces between the radiating paths. Andrei Voronikhin (1759–1814) designed the open-air theatre, the Visconti Bridge, and the Rose Pavilion; while Carlo Rossi (1775–1849) contributed pretty summer houses and arbours and some distinguished ironwork, including the Iron Bridge.

The last major landscape designer was Pietro Gonzaga (1751–1831), and he, like Cameron, sought to improve nature, but, while Cameron perhaps had English models in mind, Gonzaga, particularly in the area called the White Birches (273 hectares/675 acres), looked to the meadow and forest landscapes of northern Russia for inspiration. His training as a stage desiger is reflected in the way he placed trees in the landscape, using clumps of trees as receding side screens to create a remarkable feeling of depth. His laying out of the former parade ground of Paul I, nearer to the palace, has a different character, with water playing an important role and reflecting the trees which he grouped so effectively. Combining different kinds of trees for their form, colour, and for the mood each conveyed to him—some gay, some proud, some mournful—he sought to vary his effects by the way he concentrated them. The Empress Maria Fedorovna was devoted to Pavlovsk, and it was she who controlled its development, deciding on what buildings should appear and where, and issuing instructions for the architects. She was a talented artist, a knowledgeable and enthusiastic plantswoman, and an experienced practical gardener, whose children were taught to garden. At her request plants were sent to Pavlovsk from many parts of the world including two large consignments from Kew.
PH

Paxton, Sir Joseph

(1803–65), English gardener, architect, and garden designer. In 1826 he was appointed head gardener at CHATSWORTH. An entry in his diary describing his arrival at Chatsworth is characteristic: 'I left London by the Comet coach for Chesterfield, arrived at Chatsworth at half past four o'clock in the morning of the ninth of May, 1826. As no person was to be seen at that early hour, I got over the greenhouse gate by the old covered way, explored the pleasure grounds, and looked round the outside of the house. I then went down to the kitchen-gardens, scaled the outside wall, and saw the whole of the place, set the men to work there at six o'clock; then returned to Chatsworth and got Thomas Weldon to play me the water-works, and afterwards went to

breakfast with poor dear Mrs Gregory and her niece: the latter fell in love with me, and I with her [they married the following year], and thus completed my first morning's work at Chatsworth before nine o'clock.' Paxton transformed the garden at Chatsworth, becoming manager of the whole estate, and also worked on the Cavendishes' Irish estate at LISMORE. At Chatsworth he laid out an ARBORETUM, a ROCK GARDEN, and a PINETUM, designed several glasshouses (including the Great Conservatory, in its day the largest glasshouse in Britain), built a new terrace, and managed one of the great gardens of its day. He designed great houses and laid out their grounds for the Rothschilds at Mentmore (Buckinghamshire) and at FERRIÈRES. He also rebuilt three Chatsworth estate villages. Paxton invested successfully in the railways, became a Member of Parliament, was knighted, and, for the Great Exhibition of 1851, designed the astonishing Crystal Palace and its park. He was also a pioneer in public park design, laying out the Pavilion Gardens (Buxton), BIRKENHEAD PARK, Prince's Park (Halifax), and others. Paxton wrote several books, articles, and pamphlets. He was the epitome of the energetic, immensely gifted Victorian man of parts, achieving a huge amount in a relatively short life.   PT

Pazo de Oca.

See OCA, PAZO DE.

Peckerwood Garden Conservation Foundation ⊛

Hempstead, Texas, USA. Formerly known as Peckerwood Gardens, the 2.8-hectare/7-acre landscape is the creation of artist and designer John Fairey. Started in 1971 as his private garden, the garden later developed into a hugely varied botanical collection featuring plants native to the Piney Woods and tropical east Texas coast and the mountains of the Sierra Madre in north central Mexico, at approximately 900 m/3,000 ft. Fairey credits his introduction to native Texas plants and the botanical treasure chest of mountainous north Mexico to the fabled Texas plantsman Lynn Lowrey. Fairey's mission, expressed through the collection and the creation of the Conservation Foundation, is to introduce a wide range of native and 'counterpart' plants (i.e. adapted exotics) into the difficult subtropical and tropical climate zones of the south. This was facilitated by his partnership (begun in 1983) with plantsman Carl Schoenfeld and his nursery, YuccaDo. Allied to the plant collection is Fairey's exceptional collection of Mexican folk art. Contemporary sculpture by several celebrated American artists is on display in the garden. Peckerwood's conservation   ▶

subtext is that the plant and folk art collections provide a bridge across the cultural gap between Mexico and United States. The foundation's stated mission is to encourage a mutual understanding and respect between these neighbour nations for their common heritage, shared ecology, and cultural experiences, and generally to foster a greater appreciation of and desire to conserve the natural environment. Peckerwood also serves conservation with a wide-ranging seed distribution programme.   EC

Pecz, Ármin, Sr. (1820–96), and **Ármin, Jr.** (1855–1927), Hungarian landscape gardeners. Born in Pest (today Budapest), after his schooling Ármin Pecz Sr. worked as an assistant gardener first in the FÜVÉSZKERT (botanical garden) in Pest, then, under the direction of Antal Tost, chief gardener to the Palatine, at the Royal Buda Castle Gardens. Afterwards he made a study tour of Vienna, the Bohemian lands, and Germany, before working for a year at SANSSOUCI. It was here that he studied landscape design in the school run by Peter Joseph LENNÉ, and this can be felt in his distinctly landscape style, which bears almost

no signs of geometric elements. After returning to Hungary he became head gardener at the ORCZY GARDENS in Pest. He continued to deal with garden design and construction, setting up a company in 1856, under the aegis of which he created a tree nursery, which went on to become the largest in Hungary, as well as designing more than 240 gardens across the country, many of which he constructed himself. They include Budapest Zoo, the gardens of the National Museum, the first designs for the Népliget (People's Park), a number of institutional, public, and private parks in Budapest and across the country, as well as the grounds of the palaces at Tura, Acsa, and Gyöngyös. In his time he was a major figure in Hungarian horticulture, and was one of the first important landscape gardeners to be of Hungarian extraction. His designs were honoured at the World Exhibitions in London in 1871 and Vienna in 1873. In 1882 he handed over control of the company to his son, Ármin Pecz Jr. The latter is associated with the design and construction of more than 500 parks and gardens, in every horticultural genre, including parts of the BUDA ROYAL CASTLE GARDENS, the modernization of the Városliget on the occasion of the National Exhibition of 1855, the Kazinczy Memorial Park at Széphalom, and the public gardens in Győr. He was relatively conservative in style, rarely making use of geometric elements, and it was only around 1910 that he began to follow art nouveau traditions. Like his father, he played a key role in the development of Hungarian landscape gardening and Hungarian horticulture in general.   GA

Pedregal de San Angel,
Mexico City, Mexico. A private luxury housing development in the southern part of the city designed and directed by Luis BARRAGÁN, one of the greatest landscape architects in Mexico. It was built between 1945 and 1953, covering an area of 504 hectares/1,245 acres. The original landscape is the result of the eruption of the Xitle volcano in the 1st century BC, leaving behind an arid but extremely attractive field of lava beds. Barragán made use of this view and designed gardens filled with luxuriant greenery to contrast with the existing stone formations, and even penetrating into the interiors. For Barragán the gardens were an integral part of the living spaces, using great windows to show the splendid contrast of the green garden with the arid and irregular ground formed by lava rocks that give way to plants disposed naturalistically. Among these are such native plants as *Erythrina coralloides*, *Buddleja cordata*, *Senecio* species, exotics such as *Jacaranda* species and *Schinus molle*, and foliage plants such as

Philodendron species, *Monstera* species, trailing plants such as ivy (*Hedera helix*), and grasses amidst the volcanic rock. Within the gardens, plants are lavishly disposed among the lava crags, and water flows from fountains in the arid rocky landscape. Barragán's great influences in landscaping were the ALHAMBRA, his travels on the Mediterranean coast, and the work of Ferdinand Bac (1859–1952), who inspired his landscapes as places for meditation and contemplation, but always remaining Mexican, strongly influenced by the haciendas.
SAO/LTT

Pedro II, Dom, Parque ⊗
São Paulo, São Paulo state, Brazil, is an example of the vicissitudes of an open space in South America's largest metropolis. The region, of great beauty at the time of the city's foundation, was known as the Várzea do Carmo, an area prone to flooding by the river Tamanduateí, and consequently considered a health risk and an obstacle to progress in the expanding city. The first effort at urbanization was a landfill used to create an island—Ilha dos Amores—in 1872, a short-lived attempt at making a public garden. Based on a proposal in 1911 by the French urban planner Joseph-Antoine Bouvard (1840–1920) to turn the Várzea do Carmo into a large urban park, the landscape designer E. F. Cochet developed a project that was implemented between the years 1918 and 1922 on an area estimated at 45 hectares/111 acres. However, in 1938 Mayor Prestes Maia's road plan for the city—*Plano de Avenidas*—and the subsequent urban plans giving priority to traffic meant that the Parque Dom Pedro II was gradually sacrificed, with areas lost to new roads and overpasses, so that by 1970 the park was completely disfigured. In 1993 the city hall offices were relocated to the old Palácio das Indústrias (Palace of Industry) (inaugurated in 1924) as part of a strategy to recuperate the whole area of the Parque D. Pedro II. In 1994, as part of the celebrations commemorating the 450th anniversary of the city's founding, a partial restoration of the park was planned, following a project by landscape designer Fernando Chacel (b. 1931).
HS

ROSA GRENA KLIASS, *Parques urbanos de São Paulo* (1993).

Peleş Castle ⊗
Sinaia, Romania. One of the favourite summer residences of the Romanian royal family, Sinaia was created by Prince (later King) Carl of Hohenzollern-Sigmaringen between 1873 and 1883 following the designs of Viennese architect Wilhelm Doderer and Johannes Schultz on a wooded slope of the Carpathian

Mountains. The palace is a mixture of different styles. Seven Italianate terraces decorated with balustrades, PARTERRES, LOGGIAS, FOUNTAINS, CASCADES, sculpures, vases, and elegant stairs create a grand surrounding to the palace. The most spectacular feature in this area is the Neptune Fountain, which, together with the other statues, is the work of Italian sculptor Romanelli. The park, cut out of the surrounding forest, consists of massive coniferous woodlands and scattered trees. A unique three-room tree house, the so-called 'Le Nid', was designed by English ARTS AND CRAFTS architect W. H. Baillie Scott (1865–1945) in 1897-8. Built high up in a group of pines, it could only be reached by rope ladder. The heyday of the gardens was in the 1910s–1920s under the direction of the English Queen Mary, granddaughter of Queen Victoria and wife of King Ferdinand I. She lightened the rather heavy structure with iron pergolas and created a series of flower gardens. The park was partly redesigned by German architect F. von Rebhuhn at the beginning of the 20th century. Now the palace serves as a museum and luxury hotel, and the grounds around are open to the public.   GA

Pena Palace ✿

Sintra, Portugal. The wild, and wildly picturesque, scenery of Sintra, with rocky outcrops erupting from high wooded hills, was immensely attractive to foreigners by the 18th century. The English poet Robert Southey in 1796 thought it was 'too good for the Portuguese'. Foreigners came here to build houses, often seeking in the theatricality of the architecture they commissioned an echo of the drama of the landscape. Of all the extraordinary houses that were built Pena Palace remains the most remarkable. There had been a monastery here, high on a peak of the Serra de Sintra, since the 16th century. It was severely damaged in the 1755 Lisbon earthquake and only a handful of monks remained. It was acquired by the King Consort, Dom Fernando II (Prince Ferdinand of Saxe-Coburg and Gotha), who had married, as her second husband, Queen Maria II of Portugal (reigned 1834–53). From the 1830s, with the help of Wilhelm Ludwig, Graf von Eschwege (b. 1777), he created the Pena Palace. Dom Fernando was a collector and a highly cultivated man and Eschwege, a military engineer by training, was an intimate of Goethe and of HUMBOLDT. The palace was a collaboration between Dom Fernando and Eschwege. The resulting building is a gallimaufry of styles—Gothic, neo-Manueline (referring to the reign of Manuel I in the early 16th century), and Islamic.

When the palace was started its surroundings were devoid of planting. Dom Fernando created a huge park, with an area of c.200 hectares/494 acres, which today clothes the land below the castle in luxuriant vegetation. He sought a landscape of romantic profusion and planted camellias, cork oaks (*Quercus suber*), cryptomerias, cypresses, figs, rhododendrons, tree ferns, and walnuts. Lakes, streams, cascades, and pools were created and rocky outcrops valued. In the centre of one lake an island has a castellated tower, like the remains of a medieval keep. A Temple of Columns, a domed building whose roof is supported by stumpy columns with elaborate ponderous capitals, was built as an eyecatcher but is now lost in vegetation. Various pavilions dotted the park—a domed hexagon was faced in pink and blue tiles, a banqueting house (the Casa do Regalo) was a cottage *orné* (see AVELEDA, QUINTA DE). The composer Richard Strauss thought that 'This park is the most wonderful thing I have seen in the world, this is the veritable garden of Klingsor and, above it, is the castle of the Holy Grail.' House and landscape today constitute one of the most extreme and memorable expressions of the romantic impulse.   PT

Penicuik House,

Penicuik, Midlothian, Scotland, was the family seat of Sir John CLERK who inherited the estate in 1722. He planted 300,000 trees (many arranged in avenues), made a remarkable GROTTO bearing the inscription *Tenebrosa occultaque cave* (beware of dark and hidden things), built several landscape ornaments, and planted many ornamental shrubs amd trees. While not exactly a FERME ORNÉE, the productive aspects of the estate—livestock, fish ponds, timber—were regarded by Clerk as part of the beauties of the scene. An early proponent of the landscape park, he thought ''Tis a beauty to see things natural'.   PT

Penshurst Place ✿

near Tonbridge, Kent, England, dates from the 14th century and was acquired in the 16th century by the Sidney family (later viscounts De L'Isle) who still own it. This continuity of ownership has allowed the preservation of garden features of different periods. A medieval deer park has English oaks (*Quercus robur*) that probably date from that time and an avenue of limes (*Tilia × europaea*) that was planted to celebrate the accession of William III in 1688. The most remarkable feature of the landscape is the 4-hectare/10-acre enclosed garden whose walls are built of fine 16th-century bricks. A KIP engraving of c.1700 shows this garden laid out with the same cruciform pattern and

disposition of compartments that it has today, making it one of the oldest surviving layouts in the country. The garden was restored in the mid 19th century when an Italianate garden was laid out by George Devey (1820–86). A circular central pool is surrounded by shaped lawns with box topiary and beds of pink bedding roses. On two sides yew hedges are clipped into regular humps. To one side a pair of mixed borders by Lanning ROPER leads into the chief part of the garden. John Codrington (1899–1992) designed an enclosure of magnolias, a great parterre is laid out in the form of a union jack with lavender and red and white roses forming the colours, and a charming semi-formal orchard in a meadow has different cultivars of a local speciality, Kentish cobnuts (*Corylus avellana*), and many fruit trees.   PT

peonies.

In China peonies have been cultivated as garden plants certainly since the 4th century AD and probably for much longer. In China and Japan, they were revered by courtiers, poets, and philosophers for their beauty, as status symbols, and as emblems of prosperity and friendship. Today they are China's national flower and in Luoyang and Heze annual festivals are held to celebrate their brief flowering season in late spring and early summer.

'Tree' peonies or moutans are not trees, but shrubs with gaunt stems carrying huge single, semi-double, or double flowers, in white, yellow, and shades ranging from pink and crimson to deep red-purple, almost black, some scented. Their average height is 1.2 m/4 ft, but some varieties reach 3 m/10 ft. A wide range of garden forms (Ouyang Xiu (1007–72), poet, scholar, and statesman, described 90) was bred first in China, then in Japan, from the native Chinese *Paeonia suffruticosa*. They came to the attention of European gardeners in 1656 when a representative of the Dutch East India Company reported seeing, in Peking (Beijing), flowers twice the size of roses, and without thorns. By the 19th century collectors such as John Reeves and Robert FORTUNE were sending specimens of Chinese garden varieties to the Horticultural Society in London.

P. lactiflora, the parent of the majority of herbaceous peonies, also originated in China and is grown as a crop for its roots which, like those of the moutan, have long been an important commodity in traditional Chinese medicine. Other species, such as the single yellow *P. mlokosewitschii* from the Caucasus, the Himalayan *P. emodi*, and the Greek *P. peregrina*, are highly prized garden plants. Europe has its own native peony, *P. officinalis*. Its crimson, pink, or white double flowers have been familiar cottage garden plants since the 16th century. But a new phase in the development of garden-worthy peonies took place from the early 1800s. In France, Empress Joséphine grew both herbaceous and tree peonies at MALMAISON, and many peonies introduced by French breeders are still grown today, such as Modeste Guérin's 'Duchesse d'Orléans' (1846) and 'Alexandre Dumas' (1862), and Auguste Miellez's enduring classics 'Festiva Maxima' (1851) and 'Madame Calot' (1856). In the early 1900s Victor Lemoine and his son Émile introduced the herbaceous 'Sarah Bernhardt' and 'Solange', and a new strain of tree peonies with single or double flowers of yellow and orange-apricot colouring: P. × lemoinei. Pivoines Rivière, a nursery founded in 1849 by another dedicated peony family, is still thriving today.

The pattern was echoed in England, where James Kelway began breeding peonies in the 1860s. In both France and England, the style of peony flowers, with their elaborate, heavy blooms on slender stems, was in tune with the fashion of the time, and they became immensely popular. When the Kelways' peony fields at Langport in Somerset were in full bloom, special arrangements were made for trains carrying sightseers to stop at a temporary railway station called Peony Halt. Kelway's (which still thrives) exported peonies to the USA, Canada, and New Zealand. In these countries the cultivation of existing varieties and the breeding of new ones increased throughout the 20th century, wherever the climate was suitable. Herbaceous peonies are very hardy, and will grow outdoors in northern Canada and Finland. In fact they need a spell of cold weather during their dormancy in order to thrive. Oliver Brand, a USA peony pioneer in the 1870s, combined the production of peonies and apple trees in his Minnesota nursery, and his son Archie continued to build the business in the 1920s. Four generations of the Wild family of Missouri produced thousands of cut flowers as well as peony plants. Like Kelway's, their nursery was a huge tourist attraction every May. Professor A. P. Saunders, Don Hollingsworth, and Allan Rogers, author of Peonies (1995), were all notable hybridizers.

In the 1960s Tochi Itoh of Japan made peony history by crossing a tree peony with a herbaceous P. lactiflora. The resulting hybrids, of compact habit with yellow flowers, were brought to the USA by Louis Smirnov of New York, and have been further developed by, among others, Roger Anderson of Wisconsin.

In China there are nine recognized peony flower shapes, but the ROYAL HORTICULTURAL SOCIETY recognizes four: single, semi-double, double, and Japanese (also called imperial or anemone form), with a central tuft of narrow petals surrounded by larger ones. Flowering mostly during the gap between spring and summer, and lasting well as cut flowers, peonies became indispensable components of herbaceous and mixed borders throughout the 20th century and are still much loved and collected today.   JF-W

JANE FEARNLEY-WHITTINGSTALL, Peonies (1999).

Père-Lachaise.
See PARIS PARKS AND GARDENS.

Perelle family,
a family of French artists whose drawings, paintings, and engravings of French 17th-century gardens are a valuable record of their appearance. Gabriel Perelle (1595–1677) had two sons, Nicolas Perelle (b. 1631) and Adam Perelle (1640–95). They all practised in similar style and their work is often difficult to attribute individually; engravings are often signed simply 'Fait par Perelle'. Gardens which they depicted include Berny, Clagny, Le Raincy, Palais-Royal (Paris), RUEIL, RICHELIEU, Saint-Cloud, SAINT-GERMAIN-EN-LAYE, and the Tuileries. Several of these gardens were shown in many different views, adding immensely to our knowledge, in particular, of those gardens which no longer exist, such as Rueil. In other cases they give a precious record of parts of gardens, such as the Grotto of Thetis at VERSAILLES, which have been destroyed.   PT

KENNETH WOODBRIDGE, Princely Gardens (1986).

⊃ page 374

pergola.
The word is Italian (the form pergolato is also found) meaning a framework tunnel on which are trained climbing plants. The essential idea, of plants trained overhead, was found in ancient Roman gardens and in all likelihood in gardens of an earlier date. It has been seen in Italian gardens over a long period. Boccaccio's Decameron (1358) describes 'wide walks covered with vines trained in arches'. An exceptional later Italian pergola, dating from the mid 18th century, may be seen at the convent of Santa Chiara in Naples where the supporting octagonal columns are covered in polychrome tiles. In England it was a favourite device of ARTS AND CRAFTS garden designers. LUTYENS designed a characteristically ingenious example for HESTERCOMBE which forms a garden boundary and presents views both into the garden and outwards over particularly beautiful countryside. In gardens it is a valuable feature in many different ways. It is a strong structural device giving form to the pattern of a garden. It is an admirable way of introducing variety into a long and possibly monotonous path. In hot countries it provides a shady, and possibly sweetly scented, walk. Narrow beds running along the pergola, planted with shade-loving plants, are very decorative. In gardens with limited wall space it allows the cultivation of more climbing plants. From the practical point of view it requires skilful maintenance. In an exposed space in cooler countries the more tender climbers may suffer being exposed to the elements.   PT

PAUL EDWARDS and KATHERINE SWIFT, Pergolas, Arbours and Arches (2001).

pest control.
Before the 1940s, pest control options in the garden were pretty limited, mainly to problem-specific solutions. Examples were sticky bands round the trunks of apple trees to trap the flightless winter moth females emerging from the soil, and discs around the stems of brassica plants to prevent cabbage root flies from laying eggs on the soil there. General techniques were labour intensive and/or of limited efficacy—such as pinching out the tops of broad beans against blackfly, hand picking of caterpillars, squashing of eggs and aphids, and varying the position of vegetables each season. Some gardeners planted rows of plants (garlic, marigolds) thought to be repellent to pests in the vegetable plot. There were few chemical pesticides, mainly arsenicals and plant toxins used by African tribesmen for hunting game and fishing (such as pyrethrum from a chrysanthemum-like flower and derris). The toxicity of tobacco was exploited as 'nicotine chips'—ignited for fumigation or diluted in water, and tar oils were sprayed in the orchard in late winter to suffocate insect eggs.

All this was changed in the late 1940s by the appearance among garden products of DDT, a chemical first synthesized as an academic exercise in 1874. DDT (an organochlorine or OC) was the first commercialized synthetic organic insecticide. Gardeners soon also had BHC available as a soil insecticide. These two chemicals were all that a gardener needed. They killed most pests, were cheap, usually needed just one application, and were remarkably safe for humans to use. However, the commercial success of DDT in farming was also its downfall. The long persistence of most OCs (it can take 150 years for the dieldrin levels in soil to reduce to 25%) led to their progressive withdrawal from sale in many countries.

By the late 1960s two other major groups of insecticides, the organophosphates (OPs) and carbamates, had become available to gardeners. The carbamates were still fairly long-lasting residual pesticides which—like DDT—had to be contacted by the insect, but the first OPs were

short-lived and more benign to natural enemies and environmentally. Many were much more toxic to humans than the OCs. Their particular strength was the variety of modes of action in addition to residual activity. There was fumigant action, enabling the compound to reach inside rolled leaves (e.g. malathion), systemic activity (absorbed by the plant and translocated into the sap to kill sucking insects, e.g. metasystox), translaminar activity (penetration from the upper to the lower leaf surface—many OPs). Later longer-lasting OPs in granular formulation became available to control soil pests such as cabbage root fly. Malathion and fenitrothion became two very commonly used broad spectrum garden insecticides. The main carbamate available to

gardeners was carbaryl for caterpillars and ants, but later came pirimicarb—a specific aphicide very safe to nearly all other forms of life. In the 1980s a number of synthetic insecticides based on the pyrethrum molecule (e.g. permethrin, resmethrin) became another group of broad spectrum garden insecticides, in spite of their solely residual mode of action and their high toxicity to beneficial insects.

Largely as EU policy, most of the above chemicals have recently been withdrawn from garden use—indeed it is now illegal to use, or even possess, many of them. This restriction has been based on the common action of most of them in preventing the recycling of the enzyme cholinesterase in the nervous system of animals including man. Thus all 'anti-cholinesterase'

A treillage portico designed by André Le Nôtre in an engraving by the **Perelle family** of c.1700.

compounds have been removed from sale to gardeners, although many of them (particularly the almost totally selective pirimicarb) pose negligible risk once diluted. Very few insecticides are now available. A few pyrethroids (especially bifenthrin) are still marketed and a fairly recent chemical against soil pests—imidacloprid—has appeared on the shelves.

The early cultural and physical controls as well as more recently discovered non-insecticidal methods (such as beer traps for slugs and sticky traps in glasshouses) are in use again. Also gardeners are using biological

control agents; these include ones which feed on insects, spider mites, and slugs, and a bacterial disease of caterpillars which can be applied as a spray. All these can be very effective, but differ from insecticides in that they have a limited 'shelf-life', act more slowly, are better at preventing pest populations getting excessive than at wiping out large populations, and are very dependent on favourable environmental conditions. It is therefore absolutely essential that they are applied strictly in accordance with the suppliers' instructions; this means that familiarity with the instructions should precede placing an order!   HFvE

Peterhof ⊗

near St Petersburg, Russia. Peter the Great's Versailles-inspired summer palace and park (120 hectares/297 acres) on the Gulf of Finland lies 30 km/19 miles from St Petersburg. Peter chose the site and probably conceived the overall plan. J. F. Braunstein was the first architect but Le Blond took charge from his arrival in Russia in 1716 until his death in 1719, and much of the layout dates from that time. His successor was Niccolo Michetti (d. 1759), who designed some of the fountains, CASCADES, and summer houses and added pavilions to the palace. Later Bartolomeo Francesco Rastrelli (1700–71) considerably extended the palace for Elizabeth (1709-62, Empress from 1741) and designed buldings and fountains in the park. Alterations and additions to the park continued well into the 19th century. The remarkable water system, feeding the many fountains from a source 22 km/14 m away, was the work of hydraulic engineer Vasily Tuvolkov.

The palace is imposingly situated on a natural terrace 15 m/49 ft high, and the cascades below the sea-facing north façade are among the most impressive in the world. The water tumbles down the marble steps of the double cascade into the basin with its spectacular Samson Fountain. Samson has prised apart the jaws of the lion and a jet of water gushes 20 m/66 ft into the air. This fountain, and indeed all Peterhof, celebrates Russia's recovery of its Baltic lands from the Swedes. Numerous gilded fountains and statues of ancient gods and other mythological figures grace the basin and the cascade, acclaiming Samson's prowess. The water then flows along the canal, flanked by fountains, to the sea, Russia's vitally important new access to Europe. It is to the presence of the sea, as background, as foreground, and symbolically, that Peterhof owes much of its special character.

On both sides of the canal the lower park is formally laid out with ALLÉES, BOSQUETS, a great variety of fountains including some good trick fountains, two cascades, and three small palaces—Monplaisir, the Hermitage, and Marly. Monplaisir, Peter's first residence here, was the work of Braunstein, Le Blond, and Michetti, but Peter determined its position by the sea's edge and the style, which is that of a modest Dutch house. He also made sketches for the garden, which was laid out with box hedges, trellised galleries, gilded statues, and fountains. The Hermitage, by Braunstein, is also by the sea and is surounded by a moat. The Marly Palace, again by Braunstein, is an elegant small country mansion set in a mirror parterre of fish ponds.

The upper park, on the south side of the main palace, was originally designed by Braunstein and Le Blond and laid out by gardeners Harnigfelt and Borisov between 1714 and 1724. In the 1750s it was widened to reflect Rastrelli's extensions to the palace. The large formal parterre, between the palace and the entrance gates, with *allées,* grass plots, basins, fountains, and statues, is bounded on each side by covered galleries and lines of clipped trees.   PH

Peto, Harold

(1854–1933), English architect and garden designer in the ARTS AND CRAFTS tradition inspired by Italian Renaissance architecture and gardens. He formed a fashionable architectural partnership with Ernest George which ended in 1895. His garden philosophy may be summed up in this quotation from his own *The Boke of Iford* (published posthumously): 'old buildings or fragments of masonry carry one's mind back to the past in the way that a garden of flowers only cannot do. Gardens that are too stony are equally unsatisfactory; it is the combination of the two in just proportion which is the most satisfying.' He in any case disapproved of the English taste in planting 'running riot in masses of colour irrespective of form'. He designed gardens or garden features at Bridge House (Surrey, 1906), BUSCOT PARK, Easton Lodge (Essex, 1902), Hartham Park (Wiltshire, c.1903), HEALE HOUSE, High Wall (Oxfordshire, c.1912), IFORD MANOR (his own house, 1899 onwards), ILNACULLIN, Wayford Manor (Somerset, 1902), and West Dean House (West Sussex, 1910). He also practised in the south of France on the Côte d'Azur from 1893 to 1910 where he designed gardens at Villa Bella

Vista, Villa Les Cèdres, Château Isola Bella, Villa Maryland, Villa Rosemary, and Villa Sylvia. Easton Lodge was one of his grandest gardens but little remains of it today. The best places in which to admire his work, all open to the public, are Buscot Park, Iford Manor, and Ilnacullin.   PT

HAROLD PETO, *The Boke of Iford* (1994).

Petraia, Villa ⊛

Florence, Tuscany, Italy. An older fortress was remodelled in 1537 by Duke Cosimo I. After 1587, under Ferdinando I, the second son of Cosimo, the garden was completed by Raffaello Pagni who laid out three terraces, the Terrace of the Little Statue, the middle terrace or GIARDINO SEGRETO with geometric parterres, and the lower terrace which became a formal *frutetto* (orchard). The circular tunnel arbours framing the fruit trees were fitted into the rectangle on the last terrace as shown in the UTENS lunette in the Topographical Museum in Florence. In 1872 Villa Petraia was occupied by King Vittorio Emmanuele II of Savoy and the upper garden completely transformed with 19th-century bedding-out schemes. A recent restoration has attempted to recapture some of the 16th-century atmosphere with collections of suitable plants on the lower terraces while exploiting the bedding schemes on the top level. The famous statue of *Venus Wringing out her Hair* by GIAMBOLOGNA which first stood at nearby Villa MEDICI (Castello) is now protected from weather in the vestibule at Petraia.   PHo

Petri, Bernhard

(1767–1853), German landscape gardener. His father Johann Ludwig Petri created the famous circular parterre at SCHWETZINGEN. He pursued his studies in his home town of Zweibrücken as a student of Ludwig SCKELL, before being sent by the Prince Elector of Pfalz on an agricultural and horticultural study tour of England. He also travelled across France, Holland, and Germany, and on his return worked in the Prince Elector's gardens. After the outbreak of the French Revolution he fled to Vienna, where he was to design gardens for a number of aristocrats, also submitting plans to Emperor Leopold II for a 'National Garden' to be built in Brigettenau, with temples erected in memory of Austria's leading personalities. In around 1793 Palatine Leopold Alexander Habsburg invited him to Hungary, where he was again to take on aristocratic commissions: the Zichy Park in Vedrőd (today Voderady, Slovakia), the Viczay Park at HÉDERVÁR, and the Sándor Park in Ráró. In Pest (today Budapest) he designed and built the ORCZY GARDENS. He wrote a detailed report on these works in his volumes for the *Taschenbuch für Gartenfreunde* in Leipzig. From

Hungary he went to the estate of Johann, Prince of Liechtenstein, in Eisgrub (today Lednice, Czech Republic), where in addition to creating the system of lakes in the park, he also worked on the introduction of new methods of agricultural production. He achieved such success with the latter that the rest of his life was largely dedicated to agricultural questions, like the breeding of merino sheep and the introduction of modern fodder crops. He worked the estate he had bought at Theresienfeld, near Vienna, and devoted most of his professional life to writing about these topics.   GA

Petworth House ⊛

West Sussex, England, is an estate that goes back at least to the early 12th century when it was owned by the Percy family (later dukes of Northumberland). In the late 18th century it passed by marriage to the Wyndham family (earls of Egremont). The present house was built from 1688, and shortly after George LONDON came to replace the 16th-century pleasure grounds to the north of the house with a layout of formal groves and walks. There was a bowling green, a banqueting house, a black marble fountain, and 'flower pottes upon peeres goeing up the ramparts'. Capability BROWN worked here from 1751 to 1763, creating new pleasure grounds on the original Elizabethan site. Brown planted a wide range of ornamentals here as his account of 1753-7 with the nurseryman John Williamson shows, listing 'spireas, Persian jasmins, Virginian sheemachs, tamarisks, bird and double cherries, American maples, sea buckthorns, trumpet flowers, roses, candleberry trees, broom, sweet briars, laburnums, lilacs and acacias'. Brown also laid out a great park of 276 hectares/682 acres which was not only one of his masterpieces but also one of the finest surviving examples of his work. West of the house he created a serpentine lake with islands. Beyond the lake the chief part of the park spreads out on rising land, with groups of English oaks (*Quercus robur*), beech (*Fagus sylvatica*), and sweet chestnut (*Castanea sativa*). Loudon saw the park at Petworth and described it in his *Encyclopaedia of Gardening* (1822). He does not mention Brown but notes that the park was 'well stocked with every variety of British oxen, and also those of the Calmucks and of Astracan; there is also a breed from the East Indies; the Scottish bison, and the shawl goat of Thibet'. The estate has belonged to the NATIONAL TRUST since 1947.   PT

Petzold, Eduard

(1815–91), German landscape designer (full name: Carl Eduard Adolf Petzold), apprenticed 1831-4 to Prince PÜCKLER-MUSKAU, after journeyman years and travels in Europe. From 1844 to 1852 he was Weimar court gardener, working on the reinstatement of Goethe's ILM PARK, on TIEFURT, and independent commissions. Subsequently he became royal gardens inspector to Prince Frederik of the Netherlands in Muskau Park, which he completed in the Pückler spirit, extending it by over half again to around 600 hectares/1,500 acres and, with Kirchner, creating the Arboretum Muscaviense. Until 1881 he was director-in-chief of MUSKAU Park and active on committees for international exhibitions (e.g. Vienna 1873, Amsterdam 1877, Berlin 1885). Petzold is, with G. MEYER, among the most important late 19th-century German garden artists. He designed, replanted, renewed, and supervised around 170 mainly privately owned gardens and parks in Europe including De Paauw, Heinrichau, Zypendaal, Salaberg, Finckenstein, Rhederoord, Josephstal, Sandrowo, and TWICKEL. He sought a sense of space, taking nature and painting as his models, and was deeply devoted to the landscape style. As a notable dendrologist he ran his own nurseries and disposed woodland more densely and subtly than e.g. Pückler. He often laid out the pleasure grounds extensively around the house. His paths were few but broadly spaced. Petzold often treated grounds in the spirit of the FERME ORNÉE. He published around 30 works including *Landschaftsgärtnerei* (1867), which adopted the principles of Humphry REPTON. He addressed issues of woodland aesthetics and park cemeteries, opened up the fundamentals of colour and perspective for landscape gardening, and was the first German garden artist to formulate principles of park maintenance.   MR

Pfaueninsel ⊕

Berlin-Zehlendorf, Germany, is an island covering 67 hectares/165 ares. It lies in the river Havel 4 km/2.5 miles east of the NEUER GARTEN. Friedrich Wilhelm II's enthusiasm for the South Sea islands was the reason for the use of the island as a retreat. Four hundred old oak trees already growing there were integrated consciously into the new design. To this day they give the island an atmosphere of romantic wilderness. The summer castle was erected in 1794–5 using the half-timber technique for a building of two storeys, integrating the elements of a ruin. A FERME ORNÉE with a neo-Gothic building which was used as a kind of dairy farm came into being on the eastern end of the island. The peacocks from which the island gets its name have been there since 1795 (at present there are 45 birds). Peter Joseph LENNÉ was commissioned to design the island together with the estate gardener, F. Fintelmann, from 1816 onwards.

He created long perspectives which focused on objects of particular interest such as ornamental buildings and statuary. He established a MENAGERIE at the centre of the island which was given to the Berlin Zoo in 1842. This menagerie was designed after a building at the Jardin des Plantes in Paris (see PARIS PARKS AND GARDENS). The first Prussian rose garden was created on the island in 1821. The palm house (which does not survive), built in 1839–41 to a design by K. F. SCHINKEL and decorated in the 'Indian' style, encouraged a fashion for hothouse plants. Pfaueninsel can be reached by a small ferry.   MS

Phoenix Park ⊕

Dublin, Ireland, is one of the largest PUBLIC PARKS in Europe with an area of around 728 hectares/1,800 acres running along the banks of the river Liffey for 5 km/3 miles. After the Anglo-Norman Conquest the estate belonged to the Knights of St John of Kilmainham Priory but after the dissolution of the monasteries it passed to the crown and became a royal deer park. From 1740 the viceroy, Lord Chesterfield, laid out new grounds, planting clumps of trees and avenues in an informal style. He also had built a fluted column crowned with a phoenix. In 1747 it was opened to the public and was then the largest city park in the world. J. C. LOUDON described it in his *Encyclopaedia of Gardening* (1822): 'a public promenade and royal park . . . beautifully diversified with woodland, champaign and rising grounds tastefully adorned with extensive sheets of water, and plentifully stocked with deer.'   PT

photography and gardens.

A garden makes a desirable subject for a picture. Painters have incorporated gardens into their work since the 15th century. When photography emerged in the early 19th century, a garden was one of the first subjects to be illustrated in the new medium. William Henry Fox Talbot (1800–77) did numerous studies of his garden at Lacock Abbey (Wiltshire), as well as portraits of the plants that he grew there. The stark factual statement of the early photographs makes a striking contrast with the more idealistic and romantic depictions of gardens in paintings of the late 19th century. The Pre-Raphaelites, for instance, looked back nostalgically to an earlier period. Their imagined gardens, often with a Tudor formality, were embowered with honeysuckle and rambling roses, the understorey embroidered with a tracery of old-fashioned pinks and dog roses. Later in the century, Helen Allingham was to romanticize the peasant garden in her watercolours of humble cottages, their gardens aglow with delphiniums and hollyhocks that reached from

the ground to the eaves of the billowing thatch. But from the outset, photography became the medium of record. It is through photography, and not painting, that we are made aware of the scale and grandeur of the opulent 19th-century parterres of the stately homes in their golden age. True, the garden was not always the central subject of such photographs. More often the garden formed the background to a studied casual grouping of grandees and their guests; the purpose of the photograph being to demonstrate their wealth and status. At an early stage, then, garden photography was used to serve the rich.

To reach a wider market, photography had to wait for mass printing technologies to catch up. That moment can be traced, in England at least, to 1883 when the *Gardeners' Chronicle* magazine introduced half-tone reproductions of photographs. Previously photographs could only be reproduced by line engravings, the same technique as was used for paintings. By the time that the influential magazine *Country Life* was launched in 1897, half-tone reproduction of photographs was the norm. The photographs of gardens published in *Country Life* at the turn of the 20th century are reproduced in black and white, of a murkiness that is off-putting to the modern eye. The original glass plates and prints, however, were of impeccable quality. Their subject matter was mainly the architectural context of the garden and its structures. Details of flowers and borders did not reproduce well in black and white and were hardly attempted. The names of the individual photographers were not always acknowledged, but among them were Arthur Gill, A. E. Henson, F. Sleigh, F. W. Wesley, and Charles Latham. It was Latham who provided most of the photographs for one of *Country Life*'s earliest ventures into book publishing, the three-volume *Gardens Old and New* of c.1901.

In France, the photographer Jean-Eugène-Auguste Atget (1857–1927) set out around 1890 to make a record of his beloved Paris. Supporting himself by the sale of postcards, often for use as reference by artists, Atget documented the parks of Paris, particularly Saint-Cloud and Parc de SCEAUX, with pictures of marvellously evocative atmosphere. Atget's Paris is devoid of people, but worn and decayed artefacts in his pictures imply a constant human presence.

In America, a land of wide open spaces and true wilderness, there has been a tradition of landscape and nature photography since pioneering days. Among the great names of 20th-century American landscape photography, Edward Steichen, Ansel Adams, and Edward Weston only rarely made forays into the garden for subject matter. Even then their subject of choice might have been a single plant or, in the case of Weston, sometimes a solitary pepper fruit suggestive of the human form.

It was in Europe that the gardening tradition was the deepest rooted. It was here that garden photography became increasingly more specialized to serve the need for images of gardens, both for publication and for private record. Making gardens is itself an art form and, at its simplest, garden photography is no more than a record of a work of art. As such, it is equivalent, say, to a photograph of a painting. Gertrude JEKYLL made photographs of her own plantings. In these, it is the garden that speaks to us and not especially the photographer's art. Actually it is remarkable that Miss Jekyll produced photographs of such competence at all. With her notoriously poor eyesight she had already been forced to abandon her chosen skills of painting, silversmithing, and embroidery but had been able to turn to the broader brush arts of gardening and garden making. She does not dwell upon her photography in her writings, even when, around 1910, she was responsible for a series of colour photographs of the borders of her garden at MUNSTEAD WOOD. Technically such photographs were highly advanced for their time. This would suggest that she could have employed a professional to undertake the photography under her direction, without feeling the need to acknowledge his or her contribution to the result.

The ROYAL HORTICULTURAL SOCIETY in London has long been a sponsor of photography as a medium of record, both for the displays of plants at flower shows and for gardens. In the 1940s, black and white photographs by Ernest Crowson, J. E. Downward, and Harry Smith were used to illustrate practical manuals of gardening. In turn, around 1950, these three passed down their expertise to the distinguished gardener Valerie Finnis (b. 1924), who became a dominating influence in garden photography for the next 25 years. Valerie Finnis's work was mainly in colour, and her pictures, taken originally as visual aids for lectures, eventually found their way into print when printing techniques became progressively more sophisticated, enabling colour to be used in the 1960s and 1970s. There are colour pictures by Edwin Smith in Edward Hyam's book *The English Garden* (published 1964), but it is Smith's black and white images, printed in rich, velvety photogravure, that have the most impact. There have never been more atmospheric and evocative images of English gardens, great and small. Edwin Smith was primarily an architectural photographer and his pictures of cathedrals, churches, and houses great and small give the impression of a golden age, with discreet signage and streets without yellow lines and parked cars. His gardens, too, suggest a time of innocence, before mass garden visiting and the accompanying health and safety laws compromised something of the rough-edged Eden-like innocence of the English garden.

Contemporary garden photography

From the 1980s the explosive growth of gardening as a pastime has been accompanied by an equally rapid expansion of the media supporting it. Books, magazines, and television programmes on gardening have multiplied. To supply the demand, at least 80 professionals have come to specialize in gardens and plants in Britain alone, with more in France, Germany, Japan, Australia, New Zealand, and the USA. Their convergence from other disciplines of photography accounts for differences in approach to the subject. Horticulturalists, like Valerie Finnis and more recently Tony Lord and John Fielding, produce some of the most informed pictures of plantings and associations of plants. Photographers who were originally landscapists, such as Clive Nichols and Clive Boursnell, respond especially to the effects of light and atmosphere of the whole garden. Several self-taught garden photographers have entered the profession from a background of painting. These include Marijke Heuff (in Holland), John Glover, and Andrew Lawson. Jerry Harpur's first experience in photography was industrial; Derek St Romaine's was in food; and Marianne Majerus' early work was in portraiture and architecture.

Certain key publications have marked the progression of garden photography through the decades. *Visions of Paradise* (1985), containing photographs of gardens around the world by Marina Schinz (USA), was a landmark, as was the launch of *Gardens Illustrated* in 1993. This magazine has been a strong influence in photographic style and has set a fashion for shallow focus, extreme close-ups, and a partial return to black and white. Tessa Traeger, renowned as a still-life and food photographer, published *A Gardener's Labyrinth* in 2003, a book about many of the dominant personalities in British horticulture, with outstanding photographs of their gardens.

Professional garden photographers often use more simple technical means than their amateur counterparts. Making a good garden picture involves judgement of light and weather conditions, and also an understanding of the special qualities of the garden itself. It is usually a matter, quite simply, of being in the right place at the right time. It is rarely dependent upon arcane photographic techniques. The future is probably digital, but the amateur garden lover has been quicker to embrace the digital revolution than the professional garden photographer and picture editor. At the moment, colour film remains the material of choice for the photographer who is intent upon capturing the elusive magic of a garden at peak condition in an ephemeral moment of transcendent light.   AWL

physic garden,
a garden set aside for the cultivation of medicinal plants or simples, as they were known by the 16th century. The use of plants for the treatment of physical and mental disorders is of immense antiquity and is found throughout the world. In 1960, for example, the archaeologist Ralph Solecki excavated a site at Shanidar in north-eastern Iraq and discovered the remains of a Neanderthal and a wreath. Pollen analysis showed that all the plants in the wreath were of medicinal value. China has a particularly long and sophisticated tradition of herbal medicine, still very much alive today. In ancient Egypt physicians drew on a pharmocopoeia which described 700 ingredients most of which were plants, some being exotics introduced from as far afield as India. Ancient Greeks and Romans were learned in herbal medicine and much of their ancient knowledge was set down in DIOSCORIDES' 1st-century *De Materia Medica*. With the collapse of the western Roman Empire much of this knowledge was lost, surviving only because of the interest of Christian monks. However, some early Christians believed that it was God who should cure, not herbs, and it was not until the Carolingian period that physic gardens began to be an important feature of the monastic community. The ST GALL plan, drawn up in the 9th century as a model of the perfect monastic estate, shows a physic garden immediately alongside the physician's house on one side and the infirmary on the other. Many gardens founded as physic gardens were attached to universities, in particular to the medical department. In the medical school at Salerno, established in the 12th century, the physician Mattheus Platearius compiled a herbal describing 273 plants of which 229 were medicinal. At Montpellier a school of medicine, founded by Arab physicians, was established by 1221, and it must certainly have had a physic garden; the JARDIN DES PLANTES, MONTPELLIER, not founded until 1593, had the specific role of providing herbs for the medical school. The two earliest botanic gardens in Europe, at PADUA and PISA, both founded in the middle of the 16th century, had a particular interest in medicinal plants. A physic garden had existed in Padua before the botanic garden and was seen by John

Evelyn in 1645–'I went to see the Garden of Simples, rarely furnish'd with plants.' Physic gardens soon came to be associated with the cultivation of exotics, or plants of particular botanic interest, and became (like the Oxford Physic Garden) botanic gardens. Some physic gardens, such as the CHELSEA PHYSIC GARDEN, have maintained their specifically medicinal function into modern times. The Chelsea Physic Garden was founded by the Society of Apothecaries in 1673, is still owned by that body, and still pursues research into herbal therapies. In Paris Louis XIII founded the royal physic garden (Jardin Royal des Plantes Médicinales) in 1626 and it later became the Jardin des Plantes (see PARIS PARKS AND GARDENS) and later still was subsumed under the Muséum National d'Histoire Naturelle. Although physic gardens as such are rarely found today the tradition of research into the medicinal properties of herbs is very much alive. A significant proportion of all prescribed drugs have some herbal content and much research has been done on the efficacy of traditional herbal treatments. The ancient use of snakeroot (*Rauvolfia serpentina*) in India to treat nervous disorders was proved in the late 1940s to have a scientific basis. It was found to reduce blood pressure, and since 1954 an extract from snakeroot, reserpine, has been used as a effective tranquillizer that has no unpleasant side effects. Despite such remarkable discoveries there remains much credulous quackery associated with the use of herbal treatments in 'alternative' medicine.   PT

CHRISTINE STOCKWELL, *Nature's Pharmacy* (1988).

Pia, Villa. See VATICAN GARDENS.

Picassiette, Maison ⊕
Chartres, Eure-et-Loir, France, the creation of a foundry worker and later street sweeper, Raymond Isidore (1900–64). From 1938 he formed the habit of collecting fragments of broken pottery and glass and using them to make mosaic tableaux to decorate the walls and outhouse of his garden in suburban Chartres. The name Picassiette is a play on the name Picasso and *assiette* (meaning plate). Much of Isidore's work has religious symbolism and he was particularly interested in the architecture of cathedrals—Notre Dame de Chartres looms large but also several other favourites. In the garden mosaics decorate statues of the Eiffel Tower and of the artist and his wife. There is no planting of any consequence but the mosaics are of exceptional beauty. Isidore showed real artistry in both his use of colour and the skill with which he built up his pictures—the effect is delightful. The Maison Picassiette was listed as a *Monument Historique* in 1983.   PT

Piccolomini, Palazzo ⊕
Pienza, Tuscany, Italy. The Piccolomini Palace and its hanging gardens, revealing stupendous views of the San Quirico valley and Monte Amiato to the south, was built 1459–62 by Bernardo Rossellino (1409–64) for the humanist Piccolomini Pope, Pius II. The magnificent three-tiered LOGGIA of the palace fronts onto the early Renaissance garden, arranged as four box-edged beds with three arches allowing vistas into the landscape. Rossellino followed ALBERTI's precepts outlined in his *De Re Aedificatoria* of 1452 in which he recommends a site for a villa overlooking the countryside. The palace and garden were restored between 1905 and 1933.   PHo

picturesque.
In everyday life today the word conjures up ideas of excessive prettiness—hollyhocks nodding at the door of a deeply thatched cottage swathed in swoony roses—but this meaning is a modern one. Samuel Johnson's *A Dictionary of the English Language* (1755) includes no definition of the word but he uses it when defining 'graphically'—'In a picturesque manner; with a good description or delineation.' In the 18th century the word had two other meanings—a scene or object that might inspire a painting or a scene that resembles a painting. It was this second meaning that Horace WALPOLE intended, after visiting the garden at STOURHEAD, describing it as 'one of the most picturesque scenes in the world'. What he meant was that views in the garden were composed like those seen in paintings. The pictures in mind were those of landscape artists like Claude whose work, often of mythological scenes set in the Roman Campagna, had been seen, admired, and often bought by those on the grand tour. The lake overlooked by a temple on rising wooded ground, seen in many such paintings, is certainly a scene that is familiar in gardens such as Stourhead. Such dramatically romantic scenery was already current in literature, some of it inspired by landscape. John Dyer's poem *Grongar Hill* (1726) describing the scenery of the river Towy in Wales could be a manifesto for picturesque gardening: 'Deep are his feet in Towy's flood, | His sides are cloth'd with waving wood' | And ancient towers crown his brow, | That cast an awful look below; | Whose ragged walls the ivy creeps.' Such ideas were influential in the early development of the English landscape garden which in its later phase underwent a radical change. The movement, many people believe, reached its apotheosis in the designs of Capability BROWN, who from the 1750s was the most fashionable landscaper in the country. Later in the 18th

century, when Brown had dominated garden taste, there was a feeling that his smooth landscapes, with their neat clumps of trees, placid water, and shaven turf, were too tame. They had lost touch with the wildness, drama, and irregularity of the paintings that had inspired landscapers and poets before Brown's time. William GILPIN in his *Essay on Prints* (1768) defined the picturesque as the 'kind of beauty that would look well in a picture'. In his essay 'On Picturesque Beauty' (1792) Gilpin distinguished between the picturesque and the beautiful—the latter was smooth and finely finished whereas the former was rough and wild. This distinction is followed by Uvedale PRICE in his *An Essay on the Picturesque* (1794) which criticized the 'high polish and flowing lines' of 'modern improvers'. Such an approach to landscape, Price maintained, omitted two of its most important qualities, variety and intricacy. The first, Price argued, was the 'great and universal source of pleasure . . . independent of beauty'. 'PICTURESQUENESS', Price argued, 'therefore appears to hold a station between beauty and sublimity.' The picturesque is to be distinguished from the beautiful by its roughness, sudden variations, and evidence of the passage of time, even of decay. Picturesqueness is to be distinguished from the sublime which tends towards great size whereas the former is independent of dimensions. The sublime is 'founded on principles of awe and terror' whereas the characteristics of the picturesque 'are intricacy and variety', making it 'equally adapted to the grandest and gayest scenery'. Uvedale Price's friend Richard Payne KNIGHT wrote *The Landscape: A Didactic Poem* (1794) savaging the work of Capability Brown 'whose innovating hand | First dealt thy curses o'er this fertile land'. Humphry REPTON was also a target for Knight's criticism—his Red Book for Tatton Park (1791) does nothing but show the owner's 'wealth in land, and poverty in mind'. Repton amusingly responded to this— 'Are we to banish all convenience from close-mown grass, or from gravel-walks, and bear the weeds, and briers and docks, and thistles, in compliment to the slovenly mountain nymphs?' Repton was perfectly aware of the charms of the 'romantic wildness of nature' but regarded something less wild as a more appropriate setting for the house. The modern understanding of the word picturesque is sometimes overlaid with notions of chocolate box excess, with definitely pejorative meaning. No garden would be recommended except jokingly for its picturesque qualities.   PT

EDWARD MALINS, *English Landscaping and Literature* (1966).

Piercefield ⊛

Chepstow, Gwent, Wales, is the richly atmospheric remains of an outstanding 18th-century landscape park. It belongs to a tradition of garden design inspired by the beauties of the natural landscape. Between 1752 and 1772 Valentine Morris, who inherited the estate from his father, embellished the dramatic scenery here where the river Wye flows through a precipitous wooded valley. A winding path, with viewpoints, was made along the river gorge and Morris arranged all sorts of interludes along the path—a grotto, a druid's temple, a Chinese seat, the giant's cave, the double view, and various viewing platforms with seats. The path occasionally passed through archways cut into the rock. Some of these survive as do the sublime valley views whose beauties they were planned to display. The landscape of this part of Wales was particularly admired by William GILPIN who published *Observations on the River Wye* in 1783. Piercefield became an essential visiting place on the late 18th-century PICTURESQUE itinerary. It was visited in 1787 by John Byng, Viscount Torrington, who admired 'the noble and romantic walks' but found them neglected since his last visit. In 1784 Morris had been forced to sell the estate to pay off his debts and it changed hands several times until being sold in 1923 to Chepstow Racecourse. The remains of the park, and beautiful walks along the river, may still be enjoyed—with, on race days, the distant sound of the cheering spectators.   PT

Pietra, Villa La,

Florence, Tuscany, Italy. Arthur Acton and his American wife bought the 15th-century villa (1462) at the beginning of the 20th century and proceeded to lay out the garden, earlier converted into a 19th-century landscape park, in a 'Renaissance' manner between 1908 and 1910. Acton briefly employed the French landscape architect Henri DUCHÊNE, but much of the transformation may have been his own work. The gardens were further restored by Diego Suarez in 1915. It is a bold Anglo-American interpretation of a 16th-century Italian garden with architectural features and plants used to define garden 'rooms' and axial walks. Features included triumphal arches, pergolas, and a green theatre (see THEATRE), where yew provided a backdrop and balls of box represented the footlights. A collection of marble statues, mainly from the Veneto, decorated steps and terminated vistas. During the lifetime of his son Sir Harold Acton, the many evergreen oaks, cypresses, and bay trees grew to obscure views in the garden and to hide the neighbouring houses and fields, thus distorting the original design. The most interesting part of the garden is the 17th-century *pomario* (walled garden), primarily for citrus fruit, encircled with *rocaille*-encrusted walls, where a baroque pool, vines, fruit trees, and clipped evergreens have been recently renovated. Today the whole garden is being restored by New York University to Arthur Acton's original concept.   PHo

Pilatos, Casa de ⊛

Seville, Andalusia, Spain, built in the 15th century for the Marqués de Tarifa. The chief patio is an airy cloistered space with a white marble fountain pool at the centre. The cloister walls are decorated with busts of Roman emperors. The entrance to the gardens leads through magnificent rooms decorated with AZULEJOS, and through a grille in the northern wall are tantalizing glimpses of the Jardín Grande. Here is a pattern of eight rectangular beds arranged about a central axis with a fountain pool decorated with *azulejos* at the centre. An iron pergola covered in a Banksian rose (*Rosa banksiae*) shades the central path. Beds are hedged with euonymus or privet and filled with lemon trees, pomegranates, roses, philadelphus, and the occasional large tree, such as *Erythrina crista-galli*. This shady garden is packed with plants and for much of the year rich in scents with the tinkling of water always in the background. Handsome loggias overlooking the garden were built in the 16th century to house the collection of antiquities formed by the 3rd Duque de Alcalá at that time, some of which had been collected by his father when viceroy of Naples. A smaller garden, the Jardín Chico, to the far side of the main patio, has a rectangular pool, gravel paths edged with narrow blue tiles, fig trees, and *Magnolia grandiflora*, and a climbing heliotrope on a high wall. The gardens seen today are a fragment of the original site and the planting is wholly modern. The atmosphere of the place, however, is delightful and gives a lively notion of the effect that a flowery enclosed Andalusian garden of the 15th century might have created.   PT

Pillnitz Palace and Park ⊛

Dresden, Saxony, Germany, covering 31 hectares/77 acres, lie to the east of Dresden directly on the river Elbe. The manor of Pillnitz was first mentioned in 1403, and a modest pleasure garden already existed in around 1600. In 1694 Elector Augustus the Strong (1670–1733) acquired the manor for his mistress, Duchess Anna von Cosel, who in 1712–13 commissioned the plantings of the geometrical enclosures hedged in hornbeam. Augustus repossessed Pillnitz in 1718, and created a wonderful project for the grounds in the baroque style, of which however only a part was ever completed. The Wasserpalais (Water Palace) with its flight of steps and two sphinxes on the river bank was erected in 1720 to plans by Matthäus Daniel Pöppelmann (1662–1736), followed in 1722–3 by the twin Bergpalais on the side towards the hills, with a baroque parterre between them. In 1723–5 the Große Schlossgarten was added, and the main axis laid out as a chestnut avenue, used from 1765 for the game of pall-mall. Furthermore an amusements garden was laid out, its ring game house converted to an orangery in 1774. After the accession of Elector Friedrich August III (1750–1827), Pillnitz became the summer residence of the Wettin court; the Englische Garten in *anglo-chinois* (see JARDIN ANGLAIS) style was laid out from 1778 onwards, where the Elector collected foreign, mainly North American trees. The architectural highlight is the Englische Pavillon (*c.*1781) in the form of a circular classical temple. Outside the park, in 1780 work began on enhancement of the Friedrichsgrund as a landscape garden of sensibility. The year 1785 saw the creation of the Holländische Garten, and a little later the Chinesischer Garten, in which the Chinesische Pavillon was erected in 1804. When the old palace burnt down in 1818 the Neues Palais was built on the same spot and its courtyard planted in 1866 with lilac trees. Under King Friedrich August II (1797–1854) the Pillnitz botanical collections expanded considerably. A palm house was erected in 1859 for exotic hothouse plants. In 1863 King Johann of Saxony (1801–73) commissioned Peter Joseph LENNÉ to redesign and improve the gardens, and accordingly the pleasure garden and the English garden were refashioned under the direction of master of the Royal Saxonian Gardens Gustav Friedrich Krause (1821–95). On the site of the former Spielgarten, in 1874 a conifer garden with over 200 varieties was laid out. Today the Saxonian State Palaces, Castles, and Gardens Authority is responsible for the care and retention of this culturally and historically significant ensemble.   JS

Pineapple, The ⊛

Dunmore, Stirlingshire, Scotland, built in 1761, in the form of a magnificently carved giant stone pineapple, as a banqueting house in a walled kitchen garden. The estate was dismembered and The Pineapple survived in a derelict state until 1974 when it was given to the National Trust for Scotland. It has now been finely restored and converted into a house let out for holidays by the Landmark Trust. Built into a south-facing wall, it was originally flanked by long ranges of glasshouses. Pineapples were cultivated in Scotland by

1732 and it is likely that they were grown here in the heated glasshouses.   PT

pinetum.

The idea of an arboretum specializing in coniferous trees dates from the first part of the 19th century at a time when exciting new introductions were being made in British gardens especially of trees from the Pacific coast of North America. By the time the word was first used, in 1842, the idea had already taken root. Among 19th-century conifer introductions from the Pacific coast were the Monterey pine (*Pinus radiata*, 1833), the Monterey cypress (*Cupressus macrocarpa*, c.1838), the coastal redwood (*Sequoia sempervirens*, 1843), and the Wellingtonia (*Sequoiadendron giganteum*, 1853). Notable conifers were introduced from other parts of the world in this period such as *Cunninghamia lanceolata* (1804, from China), the deodar (*Cedrus deodara*, 1831, from the Himalayas), and the Atlas cedar (*Cedrus atlantica*, 1840, from North Africa). A 2.4-hectare/6-acre pinetum was established by Joseph PAXTON at CHATSWORTH shortly after 1829. One of the best surviving examples is that at Scone Palace in Perthshire established by the 4th Earl of Mansfield. The plant collector David DOUGLAS was an apprentice at Scone, and a specimen of one of his discoveries, the Douglas fir (*Pseudotsuga menziesii*), propagated from his original seed in 1826, still grows in the garden. The pinetum at Scone was established by 1848 and now includes over 50 species of conifer, some of which go back to the original plantings. Scone became famous in its day and new introductions made their way quickly to the pinetum. The pinetum at BOWOOD dates from the same period. Exotic conifers were fashionable garden plants throughout much of Europe in the 19th century, but it seems only in Britain were gardens specifically devoted to them. See also CONIFERS.   PT

Pingquan Villa,

Henan province, China, was the country retreat of a celebrated Tang-dynasty Prime Minister, Li Deyu (787–850). The Plain Spring Villa was situated near the Huang He (Yellow river), somewhere south of the present city of Luoyang. A large estate (it was said to have been surrounded by a wall 20 km/12 miles long), its bamboo groves and streams were embellished with 'more than a hundred' halls and terraces, and pavilions of several storeys. Li's particular passion, however, was collecting both rare plants, brought back from various political postings, and unusual rocks: the garden is still famous in China today because of his elegant literary record of these collections, 'On Trees and Rockeries at Pingchuan Villa'.   C-ZC/MK

Pinsent, Cecil

(1884–1963), English architect who, on arriving in Italy in 1906, met Bernard and Mary Berenson who engaged him to take on the renovation of their property, Villa I TATTI. Mary Berenson introduced Pinsent to her protégé Geoffrey Scott, and encouraged them to become business partners, a condition that endured until 1918. Through the Berenson connection, Pinsent soon became the architect of choice for the Anglo-American expatriate community in Florence while Scott, author of *The Architecture of Humanism,* served as an occasional administrative assistant and interior design consultant. The partnership ended with the First World War, and Pinsent resumed his practice alone in 1918. Between 1921 and 1928, Pinsent executed eight major formal gardens, seven new buildings, 36 alterations and additions, six libraries, and numerous other decorative projects. He retired in 1938 with the onset of fascism, and never practised architecture again.

In his designs for villas and gardens (Villa I Tatti; Villa le BALZE; Villa MEDICI, Fiesole; La FOCE; Gli Scafari (Lerici) among others) Pinsent demonstrated his ability to interpret the historical record, and the aspirations of his clients to revive and restore their villas and gardens *all'italiana*. As his work matured and the expatriate community became more assimilated, Pinsent turned his abilities to creating simple buildings that—while referencing the vernacular and historical—were more forward looking, setting him at the crossroads of neoclassicism and modernism. Sir Geoffrey JELLICOE, who met Pinsent in Florence in 1923, regarded him as his 'first maestro on the placing of buildings in the landscape'.   EC

Pinya de Rosa Botanic Garden

Blanes, Catalonia, Spain, was started by Dr Fernando Riviere de Caralt who bought the land in 1945. It has a splendid coastal position on the edge of cliffs plummeting down to the Mediterranean. With the mild climate and sharp drainage it was the perfect place to cultivate the succulents that interested Riviere de Caralt. He built up an exceptional collection of agaves, aloes, opuntias, and yuccas which today numbers some 7,000 species, making it one of the largest collections in Europe. Many plants are now venerable specimens of great size and groups of them are a dramatic ingredient of the landscape.   PT

Piper, Fredrik Magnus

(1746–1824), Swedish architect, who introduced the English landscape style into Sweden. He studied painting and architecture at home and, between 1773 and 1780, in France, Germany,

Italy, and, most of the time, in England. He was much impressed by the English landscape garden and made a thorough study of the best parks of his time. After returning home he was commissioned by Gustav III to lay out parks in the English style at DROTTNINGHOLM and HAGA, and made several plans for other royal gardens. Among private parks laid out by him the one at Forsmark, north of Stockholm, is still well preserved. He made a great number of descriptions and drawings of famous gardens in Italy and England which are kept in the Royal Academy of Arts in Stockholm, of which he was made superintendent in 1803.   GA

Pisa, Giardino Botanico dell'Universita

Pisa, Tuscany, Italy. Founded in 1544 by Medici decree under Cosimo I, the botanical garden in Pisa had the naturalist Luca Ghini as its first director. He first introduced a HERBARIUM or 'dry garden' where plants could be collected for scientific study. During the century the garden was moved twice, in 1564 and again in 1595 under the Flemish botanist Joseph Goedenhuitze (known in Italy as Casabona) to its present position near the *duomo*. It was laid out in eight square compartments with geometric divisions for plant genera and species which were at first chosen for their curative qualities as required in Galenic medicine. Later the complex geometric patterns were altered to narrow rectilinear shapes more suitable for scientific study. At Pisa, as at other early BOTANIC GARDENS, many natural objects besides plants were also collected and displayed in the adjacent *galleria*: skins, stuffed animals, bones, minerals, together with the herbarium and paintings of plants. In the mid-18th century the museum was enlarged and in 1841 and 1900 the garden extended to allow space for an ARBORETUM. Six surviving compartments with central fountains show the original layout.
PHo

Pisani, Villa

Stra, Veneto, Italy. The villa, built originally in the 17th century for the Pisani family, was radically altered around 1720 by Girolamo Frigimelica (1653–1732) and later by Francesco Maria Preti (1701–74), work ending in 1735, the year that Alvise Pisani was appointed as Doge of Venice. The grandiose villa, decorated with baroque statues, fronts the Brenta Canal, the direct link with Venice, and the main French-style garden, with a labyrinth, a Temple of Minerva and a hexagonal archway where six rides meet, gives the illusion of a great park. The stables were a triumph of Frigimelica. In 1911 a new canal was built to join the main villa and the stables, mirroring the buildings in its still waters.   PHo

Pitmedden ⊛

near Ellon, Aberdeenshire, Scotland, is among the oldest gardens in Scotland whose exact date is known. On one of the entrance gates is the inscription 'Fundat 2 May 1675' together with the initials of its maker, Sir Alexander Seton, and of his wife Dame Margaret Lauder. The Great Garden retains its original stone walls enclosing a sunken space with a pair of dashing ogee-roofed pavilions in two corners and a double stone staircase leading down into the garden. In the 19th century the garden was in a state of decay after the house was destroyed by fire in 1818. It is probable that Seton knew Sir William BRUCE who might have advised on the garden but nothing whatever is known about the original planting. After 1951, when the estate was given to the National Trust for Scotland, an archaeological excavation showed evidence of an axial layout with, at its centre, a fountain of which fragments were discovered. It was decided to lay out a new garden in the spirit of a decorative Renaissance garden inspired by an engraving of 1647 showing the parterres of Holyroodhouse (Edinburgh). Dr James Richardson laid out a four-part pattern of parterres edged in clipped box separated by a central walk of yews clipped into pyramids. The planting within the parterres is of annual bedding schemes some of which represent the Seton arms and the saltire and thistle of Scotland. Unhistorical as this may be in detail, the effect is delightful and makes excellent use of the fine period setting.   PT

Pitmuies, House of ⊛

Guthrie, Forfarshire, Scotland, an 18th-century house whose grounds were landscaped in the late 18th century. Since 1945 the estate has been owned by the Ogilvie famaily who carried out much tree planting. Farquhar Ogilvie inherited it in 1966 and he and his wife Margaret gave the garden its particular modern distinction. The walled garden south of the house, retaining its 18th-century divisions, has outstanding borders. Some of these, including a collection of old cultivars of delphinium, date back to the first half of the 20th century but much has been added by Margaret Ogilvie. Two sets of colour-themed double herbaceous borders are backed by hedges of *Prunus cerasifera* 'Pissardi' whose purple-brown foliage, increasingly dark as the season passes, makes a fine background to flowers. One of the borders is aligned on the windows of the drawing room and echo its colour scheme of blue, cream, white, and yellow. A parallel pair of borders is rich in purple and pink with much silver-leafed foliage.

Both pairs of borders are separated by a narrow grass path so that the visitor passes through a chasm of flowers. A gateway leads out of the walled garden past a 17th-century dovecote Gothicized in the 19th century to a woodland garden with fine trees among which are an outstanding *Acer griseum*, a *Ginkgo biloba*, and a tulip tree (*Liriodendron tulipifera*) which is thought to be one of the largest and most northerly in Scotland.   PT

place, the spirit of.

The *genius loci*, the spirit of place, is often easy to experience and impossible to define. Alexander POPE in his poem *An Epistle to Lord Burlington* (1731) urges, 'In all, let *Nature* never be forgot. Consult the *Genius* of the *Place* in all.' The *genius loci* of a garden in the first instance, before the gardener has put hand to spade, is a matter of its given setting, in terms of topography, climate, soil, and historical associations. Once the garden is made its spirit depends on many things, for a garden has a greater range of ingredients than any other work of visual art. A garden is a multidimensional work—the usual three dimensions with the added dimension of time. Time changes the appearance of the garden—the time of day, the season, and the weather. Plants change all the time, grow at different speeds, decline, die, and are replaced hither and yon. The person who designs the garden and the person who tends it have only a limited control over its spirit. The buzzing of bees, the chatting of visitors, the distant siren of a fire engine, a sudden burst of rain, a screaming baby, a brilliantly coloured anorak against the subtle harmonies of the border—all are part of the spirit of the place and all are beyond the control of the garden artist. The garden is never the same twice and the way in which it is experienced varies at every visit. You scarcely ever follow exactly the same route twice, so the sequence of events, never mind the events themselves, will never be repeated. In French gardens you sometimes see a slightly dictatorial sign indicating the *sens de la visite* (visitor's route), and this was something very much in Louis XIV's mind when he wrote his *Manière de montrer les jardins de versailles* (six versions between 1689 and 1705) which tells the visitor precisely where to go and what to admire. The film director Jean-Luc Godard was once asked by a perplexed interviewer, 'Don't you think a film should have a beginning, middle, and end?' 'Oh yes, certainly,' he replied, 'but not necessarily in that order.' Many garden visitors reject dictatorial proposals and wander at will and who knows what is going on in their minds? They could still be recovering from a particularly disgusting lunch or an argument over breakfast with their husband. How can a

garden ensure that a visitor will be in the appropriate frame of mind to experience the spirit of the place?

Different cultures have very different views of what emotions might be elicited by the experience of visiting a garden. In *The Gardens of Japan* (1928) Jiro Harada describes a garden designed to evoke 'the solitude of the soul still lingering amid shadowy dreams of the past, yet bathing in the sweet unconsciousness of a mellow spiritual light, and yearning for the freedom that lay in the expanse beyond'. Such delicate notions of the spirit of the place make Western garden aesthetics seem horribly coarse. An exception to this is the character of Italian Renaissance gardens, more worldly than those of Japan, perhaps, but of marvellous and subtle distinction. Gertrude JEKYLL caught their spirit perfectly when she wrote of the 'princely grace that unites impressive dignity with the modesty that comes from refinement and due proportion; a charm only to be likened to the human charm of a perfect manner' ('The idea of a garden', *Edinburgh Review*, July 1896). The spirit of French 17th-century gardens is a matter of splendour rather than charm. These are gardens of ostentation, designed to dominate the landscape and to appear to be without end. Nothing cosy here, you have to be on your best behaviour and could scarcely relax in such a garden. The spirit of the English flower garden, however, is like an extension of the drawing room with its capacious, well-stuffed armchairs. Like the Italian gardens it has a charm, but the English charm is of a more rumpled kind. Only an English writer could have written a gardening book with a name like *A Gentle Plea for Chaos* (Mirabel Osler, 1989). The idea of the garden as 'the Greatest Refreshment to the Spirits of Man', as Francis BACON wrote in his essay 'Of gardens' (1625), is surely the most frequently sought quality of a garden, the most desirable spirit of a place. If you cannot be at ease in your own garden, where can you be? See also AESTHETICS OF THE GARDEN.   PT

Plantbessin ⊛

Castillon, Calvados, France, is a garden created since 1986 by Colette and Hubert Sainte-Beuve. The climate of Basse-Normandie, with a relatively high rainfall and hot summers, is particularly favourable for gardens. The Sainte-Beuves had, in 1974, already opened an excellent nursery, specializing in herbaceous perennials which were then not in France the fashionable garden plants which they have since become. The design and planting of their garden was strongly influenced by what they had seen of English gardens. The site is precisely square, 50 m × 50 m/170 ft × 170 ft, and presents a harmonious yet varied succession of planted episodes skilfully linked. Hedges of hornbeam (*Carpinus betulus*) form the backdrop to double herbaceous borders with carefully controlled colour schemes—red, yellow, and orange modulating to white and cream and ending in pink, purple, and red. Columns of Irish yews punctuate the lavish planting. The grass path between the borders leads to a simple space enclosed in yew hedges with an octagonal water lily pond and a pair of *Catalpa bignonioides* clipped into mounded shapes. This forms the linking passage to a hidden water garden concealed behind yew hedges. Here is a long canal edged with a narrow path and along its banks are plants with striking foliage—hostas, rodgersias, *Rheum palmatum*, *Gunnera manicata*, and such ornamental grasses as *Hakonechloa macra* 'Alboaurea'. An open area of flawless sweeping lawns is decorated with ornamental trees and shrubs—*Acer griseum*, *Betula utilis*, and *Viburnum plicatum*—and a great pergola is draped with *Wisteria floribunda* 'Alba' and *W. floribunda* 'Multijuga'. At the head of the pergola a gate opens into a formal garden of scented plants—flagged paths and a four-part arrangement of raised beds. As an example of skilful design and excellent planting Plantbessin is an exceptional garden of its time.

PT

plant collecting.

Where plants come from and when are fundamental to the development of both landscape and gardens and indeed the whole countryside. Plant introductions mirror historical events, and although collecting plants is usually deliberate it can be inadvertent, and seeds and nuts may also be scattered by animals and birds. Traders, Crusaders, travellers, explorers, missionaries, government officials, pirates, and soldiers all have played a part in introducing plants from one country to another, although it was only during the 19th century that the profession of plant collector was recognized.

The first deliberate transplantation must have been in the collecting of edible plants, but one of the earliest records of plants being taken to another country was *c*.1495 BC when the Egyptian Queen Hatshepsut and her nephew returned with horticultural trophies from Somalia and Syria respectively. In China *c*.180 BC records show that six cedars (*Cedrus deodara*) were collected from the Western Himalayas and transported to the mountain and temple of Tai Shan in Shandong province about 400 km/240 miles south-east of Beijing. The Taoist temple, the holiest in China, is still believed to have remnants of the original trees. In 153 BC during the Qin dynasty of the Chinese Empire and again some 800 years later in the reign of the

Emperor T'ai Tsung the choicest plants were required from each subjugated area to supply the royal gardens. Enlarging empires and occupying forces required familiar food (they still do) and the Romans in their expansion throughout Europe spread and planted the Mediterranean horticulture they knew. Following their arrival in Britain in AD 43 it is believed they were responsible for introducing about 600 plants during their 400-year sojourn. Their legacy includes *Castanea sativa* (the Spanish, or sweet, chestnut) as well as walnuts, asparagus, parsley, rue, sorrel, and coriander—all reminders of Britain's Roman past. Later during the exploration and discovery of South and North America, the Antipodes, Asia, and the Himalayas, many European plants, both economic and ornamental, were taken around the world to remind the travellers of their own home environment.

The arrival of a new plant in a country is rarely a random event; it is usually the result of a particular happening, and if the source and dates of a number of plant arrivals are analysed a pattern emerges which reflects events in that geographic area and at that specific time. Over the past 1,000 years eight amorphous groupings of plant introductions can be identified: the first is from AD 1000 to *c*.1560 when European plants dominate; the second period of 60 years (1560-1620) traces plants arriving from South and Central America, the Near East and Asia. The third phase highlights the father and son TRADESCANTS and focuses on plant arrivals from Virginia and Canada from 1620 to 1686; the fourth period from about 1680 lasts for about 100 years and encompasses two areas, the Cape of Good Hope and the eastern seaboard of North America; the fifth period 1772-1820 is dominated by the Australasian flora arriving; next comes an 80-year period (1820-1900) where two areas of the world are dominant, the western seaboard of North America and South America. Period 7 from 1900 to *c*.1930 is when the Chinese and Asian ericaceous plants come to the fore, and the eighth and last period brings us from 1930 to the present day, when plant collecting has gradually established itself in a different form, dominated by the developing idea of plant conservation.

In Europe, including Britain, the slow spread of Christianity with its concomitant monastic orders brought an international exchange and trade in plant material. Herbs, vegetables, and fruit were sent for the garden, as well as dried and ground material for medicinal use. However it is the isolation from the Continent, not Britain's proximity to it, which has made the country so horticulturally hedonistic, and above all it is the mercantile activity and colonizing which developed from the 16th

century onwards that has added such a global dimension to the gardens of Britain. Early on it was events such as the Norman invasion, the Crusades, pilgrimages to Jerusalem, Rome, or Santiago de Compostela, and trade which helped to swell the meagre native plant population. Later exploration and trade also helped, but it was two events in the 18th century which thrust Britain into the premier horticultural position: the first was the result of the Seven Years War (1756-63) when Britain briefly took over the mantle of the leading world power from France and brought in geographical terms vast new territories for exploration and trade; and the second event was the discovery of New Zealand and Australia by Captain Cook in 1771, thus bringing further new lands into the British orbit.

It is of course that very exploration of unknown and undeveloped lands which led in the first instance to returning travellers bringing home to Europe unrecognized botanical species. However it was quite different in the sophisticated Chinese and Japanese empires. China has both the oldest gardening heritage in the world and the richest flora, but their philosophy towards their gardens and to plants differed fundamentally from the Western mind. Symbolic and literary associations of a plant were crucial to its selection in an Eastern garden; the idea of including a rare or unusual plant for its own sake would have been in Chinese eyes quite unacceptable behaviour. Both countries were hostile to foreigners and placed restrictions of every sort in the way of communication. Several attempts from the 17th century onwards were made to bring China and Japan into the sphere of influence, and horticulturally one of the most successful was the overtures made by the French King Louis XIV (1638-1715) who, wanting to establish good diplomatic relations with China, arranged for some Jesuit missionaries to reside there. The order remained in China for some 250 years, during which, with little to do (evangelizing was mostly forbidden), these highly intelligent and learned men meticulously recorded the flora, and in some cases the fauna, of China. In 1792 and again in 1816 Britain sent high-powered diplomatic missions to the Chinese court but neither proved successful. Trading foreigners were confined to the 16 sq. km/6 sq. miles of Macao, the island across the Zhu estuary from Hong Kong, with occasional visits to Canton (Guangzhou) when the merchant fleet was in. This situation continued until about 1842 when, following the Treaty of Nanking (Nanjing), restrictions began to ease. In Japan the situation was worse; all foreigners including missionaries had been banished in 1639 and access was only eventually tolerated on a tiny artificial walled island in Nagasaki Harbour measuring about 236 paces by 82 paces, and then it was to the Dutch East India Company only. A yearly visit to the Emperor in Edo (Tokyo) with a carefully controlled journey was all the contact that was allowed. It was not until the 1860s that Japan also opened its doors to foreigners. By the end of the 19th century travel in both countries although still dangerous and difficult was usually allowed; the Western world, aware of what horticulturally they had to offer, were only too eager to begin introducing some of the marvellous botanical species that for so long had been a hidden world.

Despite all the difficulties and years of isolation a few Chinese and Japanese plants had managed to journey to Europe, mainly due to the good offices of the East India Company whose employees seem to have assiduously managed to collect and pack their specimens. At the beginning of the 18th century China's floral exports probably amounted to no more than about 50 plants, while Japan was represented in Western gardens with a mere ten. All that changed in the early part of the 20th century when plant collectors, alerted by the distinguished work of the earlier missionaries, arrived from Europe and America to seek samples of the native flora.

By now collecting the flora of one country and sending it to another country had become a global activity; it included not only plants being discovered for development by nurseries, to be bought by the gardening public, but also economic crops being taken from one country to another. Much of this was instigated by Sir Joseph BANKS, whose example was followed by Sir William Hooker and his son Sir Joseph HOOKER, successively directors of the ROYAL BOTANIC GARDENS, KEW. Britain's imperial power enabled it to transfer many useful plants from one part of the globe to the other. The policy resulted in enormous economic growth in some countries, as for example when the tea plant (*Camellia sinensis*) was introduced from China to India, thus starting the Indian tea industry. The same policy had earlier been used when breadfruit, *Artocarpus communis* (syn. *A. altilis*), was shipped, despite the famous mutiny of 1787, from Tahiti to the West Indies to help relieve the constant food shortage of the slaves working the sugar plantations (sugar was itself an earlier introduced plant (*Saccharum officinarum*), native of tropical Asia). Quinine, the extract from the bark of the South American tree *Cinchona succirubra* (syn. *C. pubescens* 'Succirubra'), and long known as a cure for the relief of malaria, was taken, amid some subterfuge, from Ecuador and Peru first to Kew, and then shipped onward for India.

Britain was here emulating what had been done earlier, when in the 15th century maize (*Zea mays*) was brought to Europe by the Spanish, and later introduced into Asia by the Portuguese, and there are examples of coffee, chocolate, fruit, herbs, and vegetables all being transported to other countries to help feed, clothe, or assist the local population, as well as for trade.

The professional services of plant hunters really began during the 18th century when Sir Joseph Banks and Kew employed Francis MASSON to travel to South Africa and in particular the Cape of Good Hope, collecting material specifically for Kew. Naval voyages of exploration and chart making were also used to help garner plants, exchanges of native horticultural material via newly set up botanic gardens were encouraged—usually via Kew—throughout the empire, and in the 19th century the (ROYAL) HORTICULTURAL SOCIETY sent David DOUGLAS to the western seaboard of North America to collect for the society. Astute nurseries were showing their commercial enterprise by sending employees abroad to gather specific flora to bring home to propagate and sell. The Indian subcontinent was a particularly fruitful source of collecting where both civilian collectors and members of the East India Company and then the Indian army spent much of their time botanizing, especially in the Himalayas, collecting or making herbarium specimens, many of which were later to be sent to British and European seats of learning. ORCHIDS and RHODODENDRONS were among the most favoured to be introduced—tropical orchids were much admired, but their continued delicacy and difficult requirements meant they eventually were too complicated to survive, whereas a large number of rhododendrons found conditions in northern Europe much to their liking.

By the early part of the 20th century plant collecting from, in particular, China, Japan, the Far East, and South America was attracting botanists from all over Europe and America, and new introductions began flooding into Europe. However by the middle of the century and following the two world wars a complete change of attitude had begun to prevail regarding the collection from the wild of such an enormous number of plants, and the idea of conservation, a word only coined 100 years previously, became a major influence. Such was the alarm that Kew helped compile a list of threatened flowering plants and gymnosperms throughout the world. Known as the Red Data Book it was published in 1970 and estimated that some 20,000 species were in danger. In 1973 the first meeting was held of the CONVENTION ON INTERNATIONAL TRADE IN ENDANGERED SPECIES OF WILD FAUNA AND FLORA (CITES).

The fundamental understanding of the fragility of the world's flowering plants—and ecology—brings to a close thousands of years of indiscriminate plant collecting. The taking of plant material from the wild is now a more disciplined and scientific affair, usually undertaken as a joint project with the host country, and under the aegis of a university or botanic garden. For gardeners, in most cases, the plants now grown are the result of an ad hoc policy of garnering from the global resource of wild plants. With fewer new arrivals, developing and hybridizing the available material already collected will be the way forward, as will be the propagation of the existing stock, all helping to conserve the world's biodiversity.   MC-C

Planting Fields Arboretum ⊛

Oyster Bay, New York, USA, was the estate of James Byrne, with a house designed by Grosvenor Atterbury (1869–1956) in 1906 and grounds and gardens by landscape architect James Greenleaf (1857–1933). In 1911, William R. Coe and his wife leased the 353-hectare/871-acre estate, and purchased it in 1913. Coe began the ambitious importation of trees and shrubs from England, Asia, and from American nurseries, and Guy Lowell (1870–1927) and A. R. Sargent (1882–1918) were engaged as landscape architects for the transformation. Greenhouses and a CAMELLIA HOUSE were added, and two monumental purple beeches from Mrs Coe's childhood home, in Fairhaven, Massachusetts, were transported on the deck of a ship in the winter of 1915. The house burnt in 1918, and Coe Hall was built on the old foundations—primarily to fit among existing plantings. The Olmsted Brothers firm carried on landscape improvements, planting to create the naturalistic look of an English park. English 18th-century iron gates were installed to create an impressive approach. After more than three decades of family, social, and economic change, Planting Fields was transferred to New York State in 1929, for a school of horticulture and agriculture. This endeavour failed and the present role as a public arboretum and historic site began in 1971. The outstanding plant collections (notably camellias, magnolias, rhododendrons, heathers, dwarf conifers, hollies, and dahlias) and signature gardens, such as the Italian Blue Pool Garden and the Garden Court, are striking relics of the great days of Oyster Bay's 'Gold Coast' landscapes.

PC

plant nomenclature.

The accurate naming of plants, in a language universally understood, is essential for their study. This was well recognized by the 16th-century plantsman William TURNER, who is often referred to as the founding father of botany in England. His book *The Names of Herbes* (1548) recognizes the impossibility of talking about plants unless there is some agreement about their names. He gives the names of herbs in 'Greke, Latin, Englishe, Duche [by which he meant German] & Frenche wyth the commune names that Herbaries and Apothecaries use'. Before the introduction of printing, oral traditions in countries in which plants were important had developed a bewildering, if delightful, vocabulary of plant names. In the British Isles the common names of native plants were memorably catalogued by Geoffrey Grigson in *The Englishman's Flora* (1955) in which he showed how even within a single county the name of a plant may vary. The wood anemone (*Anemone nemorosa*), for example, was known in Somerset as candlemas caps, chimney smocks, cuckoo-flower, granny's nightcap, granny thread the needle, lady's milkcans, milkmaids, silver bells, smell foxes, snakes and adders, and woolly heads. Printed books gradually encouraged a widely accepted if makeshift way of referring to plants, based on the writings of DIOSCORIDES and PLINY THE ELDER, but it was the Linnaean revolution in the 18th century, with its set of nomenclatural and taxonomic principles, that provided the foundations for the systematic, universally accepted way of naming plants. The essence of this is that a plant should be assigned to a genus and its species determined. The plant name is thus binomial—the generic name followed by the specific name. Thus, *Rosa glauca* is a species called *glauca* within a genus called *Rosa*.

Changes in plant names are the bane of gardeners and of nurserymen. New names for old favourites—such as the very ugly *Iris unguicularis* for the euphonious *Iris stylosa*, the beautiful winter-flowering Algerian iris—are often ignored. Occasionally, if one waits long enough, an old name may come back into favour. The decorative New Zealand endemic whose common name is the Marlborough daisy was known as *Pachystegia insignis* but this was changed to *Olearia insignis* (although the change seems, perceptively, to have been ignored in New Zealand). It has now reverted to *Pachystegia insignis*. William Stearn in *Stearn's Dictionary of Plant Names for Gardeners* (1996 edn.) traces the eight different names of the South American spring starflower allocated between 1830 and 1963 which assigned the plant to eight different genera. In the 2003–4 edition of the *RHS Plant Finder* it has reverted to the name *Ipheion uniflorum* which it was first given in 1834. The layman must wonder why names are ever changed. In some cases the change is made in accordance with the rule of priority by which the name given to the earliest known scientifically valid description of a plant is the name that must stand. This explains the occasionally odd spelling of plant names—*Acer pensylvanicum* is spelled thus because that was the spelling used when the plant was first named.

The principles by which plants are correctly named, a profoundly technical matter, are guided by the International Code of Botanical Nomenclature (whose 16th revision was published in 1999) and the International Code of Nomenclature of Cultivated Plants (whose 7th edition was published in 2004). The Royal Horticultural Society's Advisory Panel on Nomenclature and Taxonomy exists to advise on the thornier problems of the subjects. Gardeners and the nursery trade are understandably reluctant to adopt new names and, in any case, are often unaware of them. Confusions can easily occur. The lovely late summer-flowering *Cyclamen hederifolium* was previously known as *Cyclamen neapolitanum* but some garden writers have treated them as two distinct species and commented on their particular charms. For gardeners and nurserymen the most valuable source of current names of garden plants is the annually revised *RHS Plant Finder* which is available in book form or on the internet. The 2003–4 edition lists over 65,000 plants with sources for buying them.   PT

Planty ⊛

Cracow, Poland. In the early 19th century the medieval defences of Cracow were pulled down, the moats filled in, and the terrain was levelled off (the name 'Planty' derives from the word *plantować*, to level off). In 1820 the Senate of the Free City of Cracow passed a resolution to create a park on the site of the demolished fortifications. The design was made in 1821 by Feliks Radwański Sr. (1756–1826) whose plan, which provided for straight tree-lined avenues, was carried out in 1822–30. In the second half of the 19th century a number of public buildings were erected along a street marked out around the Planty (in imitation of Vienna's Ringstraße), but, unlike many European towns, Cracow retained the old park in its entirety. Between 1878 and 1914 the town gardener Bolesław Malecki converted the Planty into a landscape garden. While preserving the earlier chestnut-lined avenues as an element integrating the whole composition, he treated each park section—separated from its neighbour by radiating streets linking the old town with new districts—individually. Thus a sequence of garden enclosures was created with meadows and 'forest' parts, as well as an artificial lake with a fountain and a number of flower beds. Private individuals erected several monuments in honour of Polish poets, composers, and painters. The park, covering an area of 21 hectares/52 acres, has survived in the form given it in the first century of its existence. Neglected during the Second World War and in the post-war period, since 1985 it has been undergoing an extensive restoration.   WB

Plas Brondanw. See BRONDANW, PLAS.

Plas Newydd. See NEWYDD, PLAS.

Platt, Charles

(1861–1933), American landscape designer, architect, and organizing leader in his field. Born to a wealthy New York family, Platt initially trained as an artist, studying at the National Academy of Design and the Art Students League, and later at Paris's Académie Julian in the 1880s. Although his paintings and etchings received acclaim during this time, various visits to Italy provoked an interest in Italian architecture and garden design that ultimately dominated his career. Platt's return from Europe to the United States in 1887 coincided with the start of what would come to be known as the Country Place era, a time when many Americans possessing largely untaxed fortunes were eager to design homes in the European style, but unsure of how to do it. The solution, said Platt, was to adapt, rather than impose, the Italian style to American soil. A complete integration between house and garden, achieved via terraces, garden rooms, and plantings aligned along one sightline, was important, as was respect for the site's naturally present plants and functionality. Platt's ideas, along with sketches he published in *Harper's* magazine in 1893 and in his book *Italian Gardens* (1894), encouraged commissions, among them Faulkner Farm, Charles E. Sprague's estate in Brookline, Massachusetts (1897); and GWINN, an elegant collaboration with Warren Manning in Cleveland, Ohio (1912). Later, he turned to more public and institutional projects; a shift toward the Georgian aesthetic is reflected in his buildings and master plans for the University of Illinois, Urbana-Champaign, and Phillips Academy in Massachusetts.   LCJ

Platt, Jane, Garden ⊛

Portland, Oregon, USA, designed and planted by Jane Kerr Platt, daughter of Peter Kerr who developed ELK ROCK. The 1-hectare/2.5-acre garden, begun in 1941, reflects the passion of a plant collector with an artist's sensibility. 'I like to think of my garden as a painting—which I hope never to finish,' wrote Jane Platt (*The American Woman's Garden*, 1984). Over the years she showed thousands of gardeners and nurserymen through the garden with a mentor's enthusiasm, sending them home with plants, cuttings, and seeds. The ranch-style home designed by Pietro Belluschi (1899–1994) looks out on a spacious lawn ornamented by mature conifers that give the garden good bones, including *Sequoiadendron giganteum* 'Pendulum', *Sciadopitys verticillata*, and *Abies koreana*. At the entry an enormous *Cedrus atlantica* 'Glauca' makes a blue curtain. Trees chosen for winter bark (*Prunus serrula*, *Acer griseum*, and *Betula utilis* var. *jacquemontii*) and early flowering trees and shrubs (*Hamamelis, Corylopsis, Parrotiopsis, Edgeworthia*) light up winter borders. *Magnolia, Erythronium*, and *Trillium* illuminate spring, while *Acer, Hamamelis, Disanthus, Stewartia*, and *Parrotia* contribute fiery autumn colour. The rock garden began in 1978 when John Platt rented a crane and a flatbed truck and moved tons of layered basalt from an abandoned quarry near Mount Hood. Four round trips were a labour of love. Mrs Platt filled the ROCK GARDEN with unusual dwarf conifers, trees, shrubs, and alpines that shine against the black rock, a study of texture, form, and foliage colour.

BBA

pleasure garden.

The term pleasure garden has been used very loosely to denote any garden that gave pleasure. However, a specific use denotes a particular kind of garden open to the public in London from the late 17th century. The first pleasure garden in this specialist sense was that of New Spring Gardens, renamed Vauxhall Gardens in 1785, which were founded *c*.1660 on the south bank of the Thames close to the modern junction of Vauxhall Bridge and the Albert Embankment—no trace of them remains. The gardens quickly became popular. Samuel Pepys visited them in 1667 and recorded his impression in his diary: 'It is very cheap going thither, for a man may go to spend what he will, or nothing, all is one—but to hear the nightingales and other birds, and here fiddles and there a harp, and here a jews trump, and here laughing, and there fine people walking, is mighty divertising'. At first the layout of the gardens was quite simple with walks edged with trees, and the only building was the proprietor's house. Later many ornamental buildings were added and they are shown in detail in J. S. Muller's engraving of *c*.1751. This shows a grid of walks among trees with a series of grand archways ornamenting one of the walks. These walks were illuminated at night by hundreds of lanterns. At the centre of the garden is an elaborate three-storey building which had a bandstand on its first floor. There were musical

performances and in a rotunda at the entrance to the gardens was placed a bust of the composer Handel (by Roubiliac) which is now in the Victoria and Albert Museum. A series of arcaded 'Chinese' pavilions housed 'supper boxes' where visitors took their evening meal. The opening arrangements varied but by the 1730s they were opened daily except Sunday from May to September and an entrance fee of one shilling was charged. The gardens continued to open in the 19th century with further novelties (such as, in 1816, a lady tightrope walker, Madame Saqui, performing surrounded by exploding fireworks). After several changes of ownership the gardens closed in 1859.

The other great London pleasure garden was Ranelagh Gardens in Chelsea. They were named after Ranelagh House, built for Lord Ranelagh, east of the Royal Hospital. After his death the estate was bought in 1741 and opened as a public pleasure garden the following year. It was ornamented with a spectacular building, the Rotunda, designed by William Jones (d. 1757) who also laid out the grounds. The Rotunda had a galleried interior in which tea or coffee was consumed and concerts performed. Jones's design for the gardens survives in the British Library and shows tree-lined ALLÉES, an octagonal fountain pool edged with a curiously undulating hedge, a long canal, and what appear to be circular or oval pools. Various ornamental buildings and statues were later added. Ranelagh was fashionable but with a rather more sedate atmosphere than that of Vauxhall. The historian Edward Gibbon thought that Ranelagh was 'the most convenient place for courtship of every kind—the best market we have in England'. In New York (see NEW YORK CITY PARKS AND GARDENS) versions of London pleasure gardens were opened between Broadway and the Hudson river by the mid 18th century. In London versions of Vauxhall and Ranelagh on a smaller scale sprang up in different parts of the city and continued, with varying success, until the end of the 19th century.   PT

pleasure grounds.

The term, often used in the forms pleasure grounds or pleasure ground, has a slippery meaning although it was widely used in 18th-century writings. Edward Holdsworth in *Remarks and Dissertations on Virgil* (1768) wrote, 'The Romans seem . . . to have used the word Tempe, as the Greeks did Παράδεισοι [paradise] . . . for any very pleasing place; or pleasure-grounds, as our gardeners of late call them.' It may be taken to refer to that part of an estate that is planned to give pleasure as distinct from that which gives produce. A modern authority,

Mark Laird, in his book *The Flowering of the Landscape Garden* (1999), defines the pleasure ground as 'the ornamental area that was separated from livestock'. However, he goes on to refer to 'The tripartite division of the landscape garden—the park, the pleasure ground, and the flower garden'. The 18th-century English landscape park, with its grazing cattle, deer, or sheep and plantations of trees for timber, was planned for both pleasure and profit. The HA-HA was used in the 18th century precisely with the purpose of allowing views of the park with its livestock, and such BORROWED views were thought of as part of the charm of the pleasure grounds. It some cases the term is used to denote specifically that part of the grounds laid out as a garden close to the house reserved for the private use of the owner, friends, and family—rather like the privy garden of a royal domain in 16th-century England. It is this meaning that J. C. LOUDON gives in his *Encyclopaedia of Gardening* (1822)—'garden scenery devoted to show and recreation, generally placed near the house, and consisting of lawn, shrubbery, flower-gardens, walks, water, seats, &c.' Pleasure grounds are often taken to mean PUBLIC PARKS or PLEASURE GARDENS. The *Oxford English Dictionary* (2nd edn. 1997) includes the definition of a charming-sounding building called a helter-skelter lighthouse which, according to *OED*, was 'A tower-like structure used in fun fairs and pleasure-grounds, with an external spiral passage for sliding down on a mat'.   PT

Plečnik, Joze

(Josip, Josef) (1872–1957), Slovene architect, founder of the Ljubljana School of Architecture. His work was influenced by Otto Wagner's idea of modernizing the historical language of architecture, by the example of antiquity, and also by Bohemian culture and folk design. His interior designs were inspired by the Etruscans. His urban planning, landscape, and garden design respected the natural elements of the urban landscape, in particular its historic features, and expressed the modernistic influence, perfected with his own artistic style and symbolism. Among his best works are the Langer Villa and Zacherl House in Vienna, renovation of the Prague Castle, and the design of its gardens. In LJUBLJANA he designed the University Library, the Krizanke complex, the Riverside with the Three Bridges and markets, the port and bridge in Trnovo suburb, as well as Shoemakers' Bridge, Congress Square, Tivoli Promenade, and Zale Cemetery. He designed numerous sacred and cemetery buildings in Slovenia, in particular the church at Bogojina.

AK

ANDREJ HRAUSKY, JANEZ KOZELJ, and DAMJAN PRELOVSEK, *Plecnik's Ljubljana: Architectural Guide* (1996).

DAMJAN PRELOVSEK, *Arhitekt Joze Plecnik, 1872–1957*, catalogue to the exhibition in Ljubljana (1986).

Pliny the elder

(Gaius Plinius Secundus) (23/4–79), commander of the Roman fleet stationed at Misenum across the Bay of Naples from Pompeii, lost his life when he went to rescue friends endangered by the eruption of Vesuvius. In his *Naturalis Historia*, a vast encyclopedia in 37 books, he quotes extensively, but uncritically, from previous literature, and adds numerous observations of his own. His work contains much that is valuable that is not found elsewhere. Much of Book 19 deals with KITCHEN GARDENS, their history, the preparation of the soil, the making of paths for access and irrigation, the plants to be grown, their varieties, cultivation, and uses. In Book 21 Pliny says that he 'includes everything about flowers that will seem worthy of record'. Flowers, both cultivated and wild, are discussed, and their use in chaplets, ointments, perfume, and in connection with apiaries. The identification of the many plants mentioned is difficult in any pre-Linnaean treatise; in antiquity the same name was often given to very different plants, and the same plant was often given several names. A valuable index of plants, with probable or possible identifications, is included in volume vii of the Loeb Classical Library edition of the *Naturalis Historia*.   WFJ

Pliny the younger

(*c*.61–112), Roman statesman and the nephew and adopted son of PLINY THE ELDER, published nine books of literary letters in the last quarter of the 1st century AD, two of which (2. 17 and 5. 6) describe the gardens of two of his villas: the Laurentian Villa (at Laurentum) on the coastal plain near Rome, not far from what is now Castel Fusano; and the Tuscan Villa, *c*.70 km/42 miles north of Rome, in the upper valley of the Tiber, at Tifernum Tiberinum, today the Città di Castello.

Both these gardens are essentially 'open', making use of the vast perspectives of the surrounding countryside (hills, mountains, vineyards, and cultivated land around the Tuscan Villa, pasture and sea views for the Laurentian Villa). However, some elements are enclosed, such as the hippodrome at the Tuscan Villa and the little courtyard with a fountain and four plane trees, which resumes the old theme of the atrium, at the same place. The essence of their design consists in the interpenetration of nature and house. For every season, light and warmth linked to the corresponding vegetation (violets and evergreen shrubs in winter, plane trees and rose arbours in summer) make everyday life extremely agreeable. Even the baths are, as far as possible, open onto the garden: the cold bath at the Tuscan Villa, for example, makes a water feature to adorn the terrace, which is dominated by the triclinium; the water falls in a cascade into the *bassin* (formal pool) and animates a fountain of white marble. The diners in the triclinium see the water falling into the marble and hear the noise of the cascade.

This aim of intimately uniting house and garden leads to a marked articulation of the different parts of the house and to a multiplication of the façades, frequently provided with porticoes, open or closed (the crypto-porticus), and to the scattering in the landscape of little pavilions, such as the tower at the Laurentian Villa, which looks over the garden and the *gestatio* (an ALLÉE for walking in). The overall effect was similar to what we see in representations of villas in contemporary landscape painting.

Around this architectural core stretch the terraces: sometimes they are the site of *allées* bordered by a lawn (the *pratum*, as at the Tuscan Villa, parallel to the swimming bath), or by an acanthus plantation; or, as at the Laurentian Villa, by box and rosemary. Sometimes the terrace is called a *xystus*, on the model of those used by the athletes in Greek gymnasia.

At the Tuscan Villa, Pliny's favourite garden was his 'hippodrome'. The word is borrowed from Greek civic architecture but it also refers to a very widespread Roman feature (as, for example, at the Palatine, the palace of Domitian). Pliny writes: 'The hippodrome stands in an open space, and is surrounded by plane trees, which are clad in ivy . . . The ivy twines around the trunk and branches of each tree, and binds the trees to each other in festoons. Box is planted between the trees; laurel runs round the outside of the box, and mingles its shade with that of the plane trees. The right-hand *allée* along the hippodrome is interrupted at its extremity by a hemi-cycle . . . it is surrounded and covered by cypresses, which cast a shadow that becomes blacker and denser the further it goes. The ronds-points (circular spaces from which paths radiate) within are very brightly lit. Roses also grow there making this sunlit area a delightful contrast to the freshness of the shadows. After many curves, the *allée* becomes straight again, but branches into several parallel paths bordered by box borders. Here and there is a lawn, elsewhere, box, which is cut into a thousand shapes or even letters, which sometimes spell out the name of the owner, sometimes that of the designer. There are also little rows of boundary posts (*metulae*), which alternate with fruit-trees. Thus in the refined surroundings of the villa there suddenly arises before us an image of the countryside (*imitatio ruris*). The central space is adorned with two lines of small plane trees on either side. Behind these is acanthus, some pliant and vine-like, some cut into shapes, others into names. At the end, there is a curved seat of white marble, shadowed by vines, which are supported by four little columns of Carystian marble' (*Letters*, 5. 6. 32 ff.). The spectator taking his place here would be showered by jets of water.

It seems that Pliny's gardens had very few statues—not as an economy measure, but because the fashion was for natural elements, even when artificially formed. Apart from the lawns (probably of natural grass), the plants used were acanthus, box, rosemary, rose trees, sweet-smelling violets, ivy, perhaps periwinkle, vines, and above all cypress, plane trees, and laurel, as well as unspecified fruit trees. Water was plentiful, even at the Laurentian Villa, where it was drawn up from shallow wells. On the interior walls of this villa are paintings 'depicting birds perched upon leafy branches', and this is in a room where water flows and falls into a bowl 'with a most pleasing sound' (5. 6. 23).   PGr (trans. PG)

Pniower, Georg

(1896–1960), an outstanding garden architect in Germany from 1925 until his death in 1960. His importance is reflected in two positions he held before he became a freelance landscape architect in 1925. In 1922 he became head of the design department of the firm of Ludwig Späth (Berlin), then the largest tree nursery in Europe with an area of *c*.364 hectares/900 acres. In 1924 he switched to Hermann Rothe, the largest horticultural firm in Berlin. But in 1935 he was forbidden to continue to work as a garden architect by the National Socialist Reichs-chamber of plastic arts (Reichskammer der bildenden Künste) where every professional artist had to be accredited during National Socialism. Furthermore his outstanding 'Little Landscape', designed and built for the 1935 Berlin fair and exhibition, was destroyed. In spring 1938 he followed an invitation to work in England, mostly in Surrey and in London, and was received as a guest of the Royal Institute of British Architects. Due to pressure upon his family he was forced to return to Germany where he established a horticultural business and tried to continue to work as a landscape architect secretly. He was caught by the secret state police and had to work in a factory for textile fabrics as a compulsory worker from September 1944 until the end of the Second

World War. On 1 July 1946 Pniower received the chair and became director of the institute for garden art and landscape design at the faculty of agriculture at the University of Berlin. He initiated a number of research projects. Most remarkable was the research on 'exemplary landscapes' (*Beispiellandschaften*) which should follow a design which would prevent soil erosion and at the same time increase agricultural productivity by biological means.
GG

Poggio Reale, Villa,

Doliolum, Naples, Italy. Designed by the Florentine architect Giuliano da Maiano (1432–90) from instructions given by Lorenzo de' Medici, the villa was constructed after his death by Luca Fancelli with assistance from the eminent humanist and architect Fra Giocondo from Verona who was summoned to Naples. Both the Sienese architect Baldassare Peruzzi (1481–1536) and Sebastiano Serlio (1475–*c*.1554) wrote enthusiastically about Poggio Reale although their details were probably based on hearsay. A late 17th-century engraving by Bastiaen Stoopendael shows a reconstruction. The hillside site was laid out with terraces commanding views over the Bay of Naples; the upper terrace had canals meeting at the centre with a fountain, while the lower terrace was square with four compartments adjoining an open loggia, referred to by contemporaries as a 'grotto beside a pool, a place for entertainments'. Below stretched the park, aviaries for exotic birds, and groves of citrus.

Built as a 'pavilion of pleasure' or *hortus deliciarum* it was much admired by Charles VIII of France, who on his return to France in 1495, after his short-lived occupation of Naples, strove to emulate its main features, taking with him not only Fra Giocondo but also Dom Pacello (identified as Pacello da MERCOGLIANO) to implement his newly derived ideas. The latter was placed in charge of the gardens at Blois. Charles spent a night at the villa early in 1495 and returned there in March to recover from measles. The French King was totally seduced by the 'earthly Paradise' (from a letter of Charles VIII to the Cardinal de Bourbon). Nothing remains of the 15th-century villa.
PHo

Poland

Climate

Owing to Poland's geographical position in Central Europe, its weather is highly changeable, and the seasons differ considerably from one year to the next (cool and wet or dry and hot summers, mild or severe winters). The mean annual temperature ranges from 6 °C/ 32 °F to 8.8 °C/48 °F, the lowest (in mountain valleys) being *c*.–36 °C/–32 °F and the highest 40 °C/104 °F.

Flora. Poland lies in the Central European zone of deciduous and mixed forests, with the predominance of multi-species deciduous woods containing beech, hornbeam, and oak; meadows are usually the effect of clear felling. In the north-east are fragments of natural forest with hornbeam, lime, and oak. There are almost 2,500 native flowering plants with a large number (146) classified as rare and an almost identical number classified as vulnerable.

History of gardening

Garden layouts first appeared after the adoption of Christianity in 966. These were mainly monastic utilitarian gardens such as that at the Cistercian abbey at Mogiła (now Cracow) dating from the 14th century. Gardens were also composed within square cloister garths. Towards the end of the Middle Ages, between the 14th and 15th centuries, gardens began to be laid out at secular residences. Sources record a large garden in the mid 14th century for King Casimir the Great's summer residence at Łobzów near Cracow and also small castle gardens in which herbs and roses were grown. In the 16th century, with a predominant Italian influence in culture and architecture, there appeared Italian quadripartite gardens of symmetrical and rectilinear composition. Their presence was most conspicuous in Cracow and its environs. Quadripartite *hortuli* were created within the precincts of the Royal Castle on Wawel Hill in Cracow and also at suburban residences. The *villa suburbana* in Wola Justowska (today Cracow), originally surrounded by a large formal garden, and the layout at MOGILANY are characteristic examples. The Italian quadripartite garden became fashionable in Poland and survived as the principal kind of garden for smaller country residences of the gentry and at suburban burgher villas until the end of the 18th century, when Wacław Sierakowski recognized it as the most typical Polish type of garden (*Postać ogrodów*, 1798). The early 17th century witnessed growing Dutch influences, chiefly through the port of Gdańsk. This was manifested in the trimming of trees and bushes into decorative shapes and in the popularity of canals and moats. Terraced gardens, following Italian and French influences, were laid out in the course of the century by residences of the *palazzo in fortezza* (fortified palace) type (Krzyżtopór near Kielce and Podhorce, today in Ukraine). The influence of the school of LE NÔTRE was observable in the early 18th century. The French style was imitated both in the royal residences, such as the monumental Saxon Axis—partly completed—which linked the palace of King August II Wittelsbach with the Saxon Gardens in Warsaw (the garden opened to the public in 1720) and in those of the magnates such as Białystok (1711–30) and CHOROSZCZ.

Landscape gardens came into fashion in the second half of the 18th century. After 1770 a number of suburban residences with *jardins anglo-chinois* (see JARDIN ANGLAIS) appeared in the Warsaw area, designed by Szymon Bogumił ZUG—Powązki, Mokotów, Książęce, and Góra all date from the 1770s. Gardens were made with an intricate iconographic programme, with numerous park pavilions and varied landscape designed to evoke different emotions, such as ARKADIA and PUŁAWY where the first Polish museum was established. In the early 19th century the fashion changed and park pavilions began to be eliminated for the sake of 'improvement' in landscape (Natolin, 1806–15). Vast landscape parks were created throughout the century, often assuming the character of arboreta such as KÓRNIK and GOŁUCHÓW. In 1798 the first city park was laid out (Kalisz), and successive examples appeared in the landscape park style in the course of the following century. In place of the demolished fortifications the PLANTY park was laid out in Cracow. Also in the 19th century there developed a fashion for health resort parks—at Krynica (*c*.1810), Szczawnica (*c*.1830), Nałęczów (1822), and Ciechocinek (1825). The second half of the 19th century witnessed a return to formal gardens, especially in the neo-baroque style seen at such gardens as Posadowo and KOZŁÓWKA, which was to continue after the First World War. Between the wars private gardens were often laid out in geometric style and huge 'reform parks' with sports facilities were laid out (such as the People's Park in Łódź designed by S. Rogowicz between 1924 and 1939). After 1945 the Soviet idea of culture and recreation parks was popularized—the largest example, at Chorzów, was designed in 1955. Since the 1960s green space has been introduced into housing estates for utilitarian purposes and vast expanses have been shaped extensively in accordance with the principles of landscape architecture.

The first nurseries appeared in the 18th century, but efficient commerce in plants dates only from 1839 when Jan Bogumił Ulrich (1775–1844) founded his nursery in Warsaw. Gardening as a trade emerged in Poland very late and professional gardeners came from many Western European countries to supply the need—even in the 19th century gardeners of foreign descent still predominated. Gardening schools were established from the first half of the 19th century, at Ulrich in Warsaw, and a school attached to the Botanical Garden in

Lvov. Modern horticultural training was initiated by the Gardening College in Warsaw which lasted only briefly, from 1913 to 1922; it was also taught by the Main School of Farming (SGGW) in Warsaw. Today gardening is taught in the faculties of horticulture of agricultural universities such as Cracow and Poznań and SGGW in Warsaw. Landscape architecture was taught for the first time at SGGW in 1929 with Franciszek Krzywda-Polkowski (1881-1949) as the first professor. From 1945 it has also been studied in the faculty of architecture of the Cracow Technical University under Professors Gerard CIOŁEK and Janusz Bogdanowski (1929-2003). In addition the Cracow Technical University also teaches a course in the conservation of historic gardens. The conservation of gardens was initiated by Gerard Ciołek after the Second World War and great services in this field were also rendered by Longin Majdecki (1927-97), professor at SGGW, and Janusz Bogdanowski. An inventory of historic gardens was made, and work on their conservation initiated, by the National Centre for the Study and Documentation of Monuments which was set up in 2002. It absorbed the Centre for the Preservation of Historic Landscape (1994-2002) managed by Andrzej Michałowski, which had come into being as a result of the transformation of the Administration for the Protection and Conservation of Palace-Garden Ensembles, based at the National Museum in Warsaw from 1976. WB

Pombal, Palácio de Marquês de ⊕

Oeiras, near Lisbon, Portugal. This was the estate of the reforming statesman the Marquês de Pombal whose garden was laid out in the second half of the 18th century. The house, of the same period, has charming touches of CHINOISERIE—pagoda-like tiled roofs and window frames surrounded with AZULEJOS decorated in the Chinese manner. The entrance courtyard is inlaid with small stones with, at the centre, the figure of a compass traced in darker stone. Pots of cordyline and monumental statues of Pan and Hercules stand about the perimeter. Behind the house a terraced garden has a box parterre with TOPIARY, each compartment filled with dark red roses, and a central fountain pool. Statues of whippets stand to one side and the terrace wall is decorated with lively hunting scenes and cherubs rendered in pale green, faded yellow, and bistre *azulejos*. To one side a pair of huge bunya bunyas (*Araucaria bidwillii*) shade the terrace. A pair of statues flanks the landing of a grand double staircase with wrought-iron balustrade, and outer walls faced in pale blue *azulejos* leads down to the lower level. Here a

path leads southwards, over a bridge crossing a canal, towards a remarkable rustic GROTTO. A huge figure of Neptune reclines at the centre overlooking a a curved basin. On each side is a dolphin which originally spouted water into the basin. A curved apron is inlaid with a pattern of black and white pebbles and on each side pavilions with columns of ROCAILLE work are surmounted by giant busts of poets—Homer, Tasso, Virgil, and Camões. Concealed steps, finely inlaid with pebbles, lead up to the roofs of the pavilions (with fine views back to the house) and onwards to a large CISTERN which originally supplied water for the grotto.

West of this a path leads past an unexciting modern rose garden to a water parterre with geometric beds of annuals in a rectilinear pattern. A circular fountain pool stands at each corner and a grand central pool has as a centrepiece a rococo plinth where grotesque masks contain water spouts and the whole is crowned with figures of Ceres, Bacchus, Flora, and Prometheus. This seems to be a radical 20th-century reworking of an 18th-century feature retaining some of its original ornament. The whole is overlooked by a noble winery whose façade is decorated with busts of Roman emperors. On the western edge of the garden is its most beautiful feature, a formal fish pool overlooked by a Casa de Pesca (FISHING HOUSE). Its interior is exquisitely decorated with lavish rococo plasterwork, pictorial panels of *azulejos*, and murals with scenes of a fishy character. In the time of the Marquês de Pombal orchards of fields of lemon and orange trees extended along the banks of the canal. A building for housing silkworms survives north of the canal, and on rising land where vineyards once were cultivated is an ornamental dovecote—or *pombal* in Portuguese. The estate in the time of the Marquês, if not exactly a FERME ORNÉE, recognized the ornamental value of useful crops and the beauty of a productive landscape. In recent times this delightful and important place has been shamefully neglected, but in 2002 the estate was acquired by the municipality of Oeiras. Few gardens would be more worthy of a comprehensive restoration. PT

Pompeii and Herculaneum ⊕

near Naples, Campania, Italy. Increasingly professional excavations have revealed the details of the smaller Roman gardens in cities such as Pompeii and a few larger gardens attached to seaside villas at Herculaneum and others in the prosperous Campanian towns. Owing to its fertility, the rich plain of volcanic soils could bear four crops a year, and with its pleasant climate attracted many wealthy Romans. PLINY THE ELDER, author of *The Natural*

History, who lost his life in the eruption of Vesuvius in AD 79, called the Campania south of Naples 'the fairest of all regions, not only in Italy, but in the whole world'. After the eruption, the living and thriving cities were buried under a thick layer of tufa-like lapilli (about the size of peach stones), a layer up to 12-20 m/40-70 ft in places which preserved them intact for the archaeologists, an invaluable source for studying domestic architecture over a period of at least 400 years from the city's founding to its demise. Most of the gardens belonged to private houses but there were also orchards, market gardens, and nurseries. Walls frescoed in *trompe l'œil* country scenes, to make the garden seem larger, provide valuable data of flowers, birds, and animals known at the time. Views of wild mountains show an early appreciation of nature. Many gardens, such as the House of Veti (*c*.AD 60-70), were of the peristyle type with a central courtyard with a central pool surrounded by columns. Today the study of carbonized soil, soil contours, preserved stems and roots, pollen, seed, fruit, and bacteria can make it possible to identify the plants grown in beds and pots and against the walls. Nail holes in the walls indicate espaliered fruit. There were also religious shrines and statues of the Roman gods and goddesses. Garden development increased when the Emperor Augustus (d. AD 41) constructed an aqueduct which provided water for pools and fountains. In the House of the Wedding of Alexander a bubbling fountain sheltered white camomile and small-flowered chrysanthemums under a canopy of plane trees. In the House of the Marine Venus a fresco shows myrtle, ivy, oleander—which kept away mosquitoes—southernwood, and roses, with oriental planes, bay laurel, and arbutus in the background. The Villa dei Papyri at Herculaneum with a peristyle garden probably belonged to Lucius Calpurnius Piso at the time of the eruption. Its outlines have been reconstructed at the Paul GETTY MUSEUM at Malibu in California, with trimmed hedges of myrtles, box, and bay trees. At Oplontis near the sea a luxurious villa, possibly belonging to Nero's wife Poppaea, had thirteen separate gardens varying between informal and formal peristyle, one of the earliest compartmentalized gardens on record. Porticoes stretch out towards the sea and towards the mountains at the rear with views carrying the eye through the house. PHo

Poortman, Hugo A. C.

(1858-1953), Dutch garden designer. Following his horticultural training in Vilvoorde, Belgium, Poortman worked from 1880 for the office of landscape architect Édouard ANDRÉ in

Paris. The execution of André's commission for Kasteel WELDAM in 1886 was supervised by Poortman, who was persuaded in 1887 by W. C. P. O. Count van Aldenburg Bentinck to continue working there as a secretary and administrator and remained till 1915. Simultaneously he carried out private commissions, and after leaving Weldam continued his own practice until about 1928. The majority of his commissions concerned parks and gardens for large private estates, which were designed in the mixed style, intermingling historicist formal layouts and informal landscape style in the typical André manner. He often cooperated with garden architect Samuel Voorhoeve (1880–1948). He was an important public figure, chairing various committees, and was a co-founder of the Bond Nederlandse Tuinarchitecten (Society of Dutch Garden Architects), of which he was the first chairman from 1922 till 1928.　JW

BONICA ZIJLSTRA, *Nederlandse tuinarchitectuur 1850–1940: waard om beschermd te worden!* (1986).

Pope, Alexander

(1688–1744), English poet, gardener, and garden theorist whose maxim 'Consult the *Genius* of the *Place* in all' remains the single most useful principle of garden making and possibly the only rule which it is difficult to break successfully. Pope's own villa garden (see POPE'S GARDEN) on the Thames at Twickenham, 'Haunt of the Muses', where he went to live in 1719, was famous in his time and drew such distinguished guests as Voltaire and Frederick, Prince of Wales. The style of his garden hovered between such old-fashioned features as MOUNTS and formal groves and the new romantic idiom of winding walks, a temple, a GROTTO, and an OBELISK (in memory of his mother). Pope's garden writings were influential. In an essay in *The Guardian* (1713) he attacked topiary with splendid vigour—'ADAM and *Eve* in Yew; *Adam* a little shatter'd by the fall of the Tree of Knowledge in the Great Storm'. His *An Epistle to Lord Burlington* (1731) ridiculed the stiff formality of 'Timon's Villa' and emphasized the vital rule of consulting the Genius of the Place. He was an intimate of several contemporary gardeners whose ideas he influenced—among them Lord Bathurst (CIRENCESTER PARK), Lord Burlington (CHISWICK HOUSE), Robert Digby (Sherborne Castle, Dorset), Henrietta Howard (Marble Hill House, Richmond), and William KENT. Despite his famous recommendation that 'In all, let Nature never be forgot' his role as a possible pioneer of the informal landscape garden has in recent years been undermined.　PT

MAVIS BATEY, *Alexander Pope: The Poet and the Landscape* (1999).

Pope's garden,

Twickenham, London, England, was made by Alexander POPE from 1719 when he bought a Thameside house and turned it into a Palladian villa. All that survives of the garden is part of the grotto he built to ornament the passage passing under a road to link his house and garden. The garden he made was strongly formal in character with straight walks only occasionally breaking into serpentines. Horace WALPOLE admired 'the passing through the gloom from the grotto to the opening day . . . the dusky groves, the larger lawn, and the solemnity of the termination at the cypresses that lead up to his mother's grave'.　PT

Porcinai, Pietro

(1910–86), Italian artist, furniture designer, architect, and landscape architect, who began his career as a garden designer in 1937. His work was greatly influenced by the great Italian designers of the past, in his use of art to create a setting for life. Although he mastered the practical techniques of creating gardens in a Mediterranean climate, he was firmly convinced that 'science alone is nothing—we need poetry and science working together'. His belief was exemplified by his imaginative use of space and the placing of objects, sculptures, and items of furniture, each designed to stimulate the imagination. One of his outstanding achievements is the Villa Riva Saronno (1960), where he designed a mobile sculpture and a bright band of annual plants to link the new garden with the old.　DAB

Port Lympne ✥

near Hythe, Kent, England, was built *c.*1912 to the designs of Sir Herbert Baker for Sir Philip Sassoon. The position on a bluff overlooking Romney Marsh gave a fine site for a garden. The house overlooks a southern slope where Philp Tilden (1887–1956) laid out a series of terraces with at their head a pair of stone gazebos. These look out over a pair of remarkable art déco gardens: a chequerboard of squares of turf and of red and white bedding schemes; and strips of yellow or orange marigolds interspersed with electric blue lobelia. The terraces below have pools, a fig garden and a vineyard, and a delightful ARTS AND CRAFTS double staircase enclosing a finely made vaulted brick grotto/summer house. Within the house Tilden also designed a 'Moorish Patio'—a vision in pink and green. West of the house a lime walk leads to a grand statue of George II by J. M. Rysbrack (*c.*1693–1770) once in the garden at STOWE. In the 1970s the gardens were restored by Russell PAGE who added an avenue of *Magnolia grandiflora* and a pair of deep mixed borders on the west side of the terraced gardens.　PT

Portmeirion ✥

Penrhyndeudraeth, Gwynedd, Wales, is the creation of Sir Clough WILLIAMS-ELLIS 1925–72. In a beautiful coastal position, overlooking Tremadog Bay, Williams-Ellis built a charmingly heterogeneous village of architectural fragments and pastiche period buildings of baroque character. Williams-Ellis called it 'a home for fallen buildings'. He garnished the village with bold plantings of Chusan palms (*Trachycarpus fortunei*), slender Irish yews (*Taxus baccata* 'Fastigiata'), and brilliant splashes of bedding plants. Many of the houses have their own small front gardens. In 1941 Williams-Ellis bought the neighbouring land of the Gwyllt Woodlands where Henry Seymour Westmacott, from the mid 19th century, had planted excellent trees, many of which survive to provide a distinguished backdrop to the exotic flowering shrubs added by later owners. The microclimate is affected by the Gulf Stream Drift, permitting the cultivation of many tender plants, especially those of the southern hemisphere, including over 40 species of eucalyptus. With over 7,000 species and cultivars disposed in mature and varied woodland the atmosphere here is that of an outstanding woodland garden—a surprising adjunct to the decorative whimsy of the film-set village.　PT

Portrack House,

Holywood, Dumfriesshire, Scotland, is an 18th-century house in whose grounds, from 1990, Charles Jencks (b. 1939) and his wife Maggie Keswick (d. 1995) made a garden of rare originality which they called the Garden of Cosmic Speculation. As 18th-century landscapers took their inspiration from the ancient world and mythology so Jencks and Keswick sought theirs on the frontiers of scientific theory, especially of cosmology and of the origins and structure of the universe. Sweeping terraced banks of turf swirling among curved pools evoke fractal geometry. The new discipline of fractal geometry, dealing with irregular shapes, describes nature far more accurately than Euclidean geometry which deals with regular forms. The motif of the helical structure of DNA, the evolution of the universe symbolized in a cascade, the mysterious orderliness of biological growth are all woven into the pattern of the garden. The notion of order emerging from chaos, with which much modern science is absorbed, is also a way of describing a garden. At Portrack two apparently very different worlds, those of cutting-edge science and landscape design, intermingle to create a remarkable garden in which art and nature forge a new relationship. You do not need to be a scientist to appreciate it, just as a degree in classics is not required to love STOURHEAD.   PT

> CHARLES JENCKS, *The Garden of Cosmic Speculation* (2003).

Portugal.

The boundary with Spain is marked by ranges of mountains with many peaks of more than 1,200 m/4,000 ft. The highest mountain, in the Serra da Estrela in the central interior, is Malhão de Estrela (1,991 m/6,500 ft). The great bulk of the population lives between the mountains and the sea, in an area which has a generally benign maritime climate. Lisbon, on the Atlantic, has a most equable climate with a January temperature that very rarely goes below 8 °C/47 °F and a temperature in high summer which rarely exceeds 27 °C/82 °F. The annual rainfall is around 750 mm/30 in. The north is only a little cooler but it has a much higher rainfall of around 1,500 mm/60 in (very much higher in the northern mountains). Trees grow superbly here and the remarkable camellias (which the Portuguese were the first Europeans to cultivate, in the 16th century) grow to magnificent size. In the south, the Algarve, with a climate of a more Mediterranean character with even milder winters than the northern parts, the rainfall is as low as 350 mm/15 in a year. The Portuguese climate, thus, is one very favourable for gardening and, although a wide range of plants is seen, it could be far wider. The climate of the Portuguese islands in the Atlantic, the Azores archipelago and the Madeiran archipelago, is warm temperate with temperaratures rarely lower than 13 °C/55 °F and rarely higher than 23 °C/73 °F. Rainfall, however, has striking variations with an average annual rainfall on the north-west of Madeira of 3,000 mm/120 in and in the south of 530 mm/21 in. The annual rainfall in the Azores averages 850 mm/34 in.

The flora of Portugal has *c.*2,600 native flowering plants, with an additional *c.*500 of naturalized exotics some of which (such as eucalypts) have become dangerously invasive. The island of Madeira possesses the rare indigenous forest, the Laurasilva, in the mountains at a height of between 300 m/984 ft and 1,300 m/4,265 ft, on the northern part of the island. This, now a World Heritage Site, has a remarkable biodiversity. It derives its name from the many species of the laurel family that are found here such as *Apollonia barbujana* and *Persea indica*. The Botanic Garden of Madeira at Funchal specializes in plants from the Madeiran archipelago. Almost all the specimens in its herbarium, and many of those displayed in the garden, are native Madeiran species, several of them endemics.

History

The Romans, coming to Portugal in the second century BC, found the Portuguese exceptionally difficult to subjugate (as later did the Muslims who never succeeded in taking the whole country). In road building and irrigation the Romans made a deep impact. Great villas were built and, from the evidence of CONIMBRIGA, there were sophisticated gardens. The largest *domus* excavated here, Cantaber's house, is one of the largest known in the western Roman Empire. Here, as elsewhere, however, it is impossible to assess any long-term garden influence. It seems likely that some later estates were based on Roman foundations. The palace of Mitra (near Evora) has a great circular pool which in all likelihood dates from Roman times. The arrival of Muslims in the 8th century brought a new influence. The Muslims, who never conquered the north of Portugal, introduced AZULEJOS, a legacy still visible in gardens of many kinds and of almost all subsequent periods. There was also a great impact on agriculture and, significantly, Arabic had a particular influence on Portuguese plant names. Although the Romans had shown great skill in the use of water, as far as gardens were concerned it was the ingenuity of Muslim water engineers that had such an influence on the cisterns in gardens, and delight in pools and fountains, which is such a striking feature of Portuguese gardens to this day. Resistance to the Muslim invaders was protracted and eventually, in the 13th century, successful. Only traces of Muslim gardens survive today, such as those at the Palácio Nacional de SINTRA. However, the *azulejos* and pools are one of the most distinctive legacies of the Muslim period.

The Quinta da BACALHÔA, dating from the 15th century, shows the Muslim legacy in its exquisite water tank. It shows, too, a characteristic Portuguese eclecticism in the marvellous arcaded pavilion that overlooks it— built in the 16th century and decorated with *azulejos* with geometric patterns but showing a definite influence of the Italian Renaissance. The Parco dos Duques de BRAGANÇA also dates from the 16th century and displays both the Muslim influence in its decorative use of water as well as that of the Renaissance in its scalloped central pool and quadripartite parterre. The influence of the Renaissance is visible in the 16th-century Quinta das Torres (Azeitão) with its rusticated archways, loggias, and domed *tempietto* in a great pool. Such influences continued in the 17th century if only in the tendency to dispose the ingredients of the garden about a central axis. At the Quinta da Penha Verde (Sintra) in the mid 17th century we see the early use of pictorial tiles. A pavilion is entirely covered in *azulejos*, inside and out including benches. A fountain has a backdrop of a scene resembling the Garden of Eden with animals, some exotic, grazing on the banks of a stream. In the 16th century Portugal had contacts with Japan and it is thought, as a result, that the first specimens of *Camellia japonica* came to Europe in this period. At Vila Nova de Gaia two very ancient specimens are said to date from this time.

BOM JESUS DO MONTE, dating from the early 18th century, has something of an Italianate panache about it. Added to that is a Portuguese individuality—the use of a virtuoso staircase of great complexity, allied with skilful planting, to animate a precipitous slope leading from a pilgrim church. Elsewhere *azulejos* and water remained a major ingredient of 18th-century gardens. The 'hanging garden' at QUELUZ built over an enormous CISTERN, and the canal surfaced with *azulejos* in the same garden, convey the essence of Portuguese garden style as does the feast of *azulejos* to be seen at the Palácio FRONTEIRA. In the late 18th century the tradition of *azulejos* achieved its most lavish expression in the Quinta dos Azulejos (Lisbon) where walls, seats, archways, and much architectural detail is clad in largely yellow and blue tiles. The influence of French gardens of 17th-century character, seen in many 18th-century gardens (most notably at Queluz), was another widespread fashion, especially in the taste for parterres which is also seen in gardens of more modest size, such as the Casa MATEUS. The occasional GROTTO, for example at the Palácio de POMBAL, is an influence that may have come from Italy or England. Visitors to Portugal may be most forcefully struck by the charming heterogeneity of gardens. At Pombal we may see the inventive use of water, parterres, *azulejos*, a grotto, and even a hint of the FERME ORNÉE.

In the 19th century a picturesque tradition produced some memorable gardens. The Quinta da AVELEDA near Porto with its pools, romantic woodland, and rustic buildings is typical of that style. On an enormously grander scale a romantic garden that seems to connect with many of the European currents of culture of its time is the extraordinary PENA PALACE in the Sintra hills which took advantage of a rare natural setting to create a landscape of Wagnerian resonance. MONSERRATE, quite close to Pena, is a garden made by an Englishman in which exotic plantings of trees consort exceptionally well with a dramatic setting. On the island of Madeira an English family, the Blandys, also planted exotics, but here in the more domestic context of mixed borders against a background of trees. In Sintra, as the 19th century drew to its close, António

Monteiro built an extravagant castle in neo-Manueline style (that is, Gothic) and laid out a mysterious garden in the woods with pools, grottoes, and tunnels which, possibly, has undertones of masonic symbolism.

In the 20th century an exceptional public park was laid out in the centre of Lisbon—the Parque Eduardo VII, which was completed in the 1930s. With lavish bedding schemes, promenade walks, and shady ALLÉES it also includes zigzag rills of Muslim character. The ESTUFA FRIA, completed at the same time, is an inventive use for a quarry site which has been converted into a shaded house for tender plants, especially ferns. The Parque de SERRALVES is a rarity in Portugal and indeed in any country—a complete modernist garden by Jacques Gréber (1882–1962) for a truly remarkable art deco cultural centre designed in the 1930s. The grounds of the Parque do Museu Calouste GULBENKIAN, also in the centre of Lisbon, dating from the 1960s provide both a public park of romantic character as well as a suitable setting for a modernist building.

Botanic gardens and plant collecting
Although botanic gardens were late to develop here—the first two, at Ajuda and COIMBRA, both date from the 18th century—there is a notable tradition of plantsmanship in Portugal. The Mata de BUÇACO, with its magical woodland rich in fine trees, is as much a part of the Portuguese tradition as the decorative formal garden. Nor are the two traditions mutually exclusive—both Coimbra and Ajuda show the decorative charms of well-designed formality as well as displaying collections of plants. In the late 19th century an Englishman, William Tait, made a garden at the Quinta da Meio near Porto where he inherited some fine old trees, including venerable camellias. He, and his daughters Muriel and Dorothy, enriched the garden with a very wide range of plants. The tradition of plantsmanship is still alive, as may be seen at the MONTE PALACE on Madeira where since 1987 a successful businessman with a passion for plants, José Berardo, has built up an exceptional plant collection in a fine setting in the hills above Funchal.

In the 21st century there is little sign that hobby gardening is well developed although in the Portuguese countryside charming gardens of a simple kind are often visible. It is the historic gardens of their various periods that are the great horticultural glory of Portugal. These, open to all sorts of influences, are of great character. There are more remarkable and attractive gardens here relatively unknown to visitors than in any other European country.
PT

potager
is the French for KITCHEN GARDEN, or sometimes specifically the vegetable garden, although among English-speaking gardeners it is often taken to mean a kitchen garden of extreme and decorative formality such as the ornamental *potager* at VILLANDRY. The 17th-century Potager du Roi at VERSAILLES, with its original layout intact to this day, was designed to be practical and convenient—its beauty is a by-product of that. But its designer, Jean de La QUINTINIE, was well aware of the ornamental qualities of the *potager* and wrote in his *Instruction pour les jardins fruitiers et potagers* (1690): 'I am even so convinced of the innocent pleasure given by the sight of a handsome potager that in all large gardens I recommend building a pavilion, not merely to provide shelter in storms . . . but also for the pleasure derived from admiring in comfort land that is well used.' In England in the late 20th century the designer Rosemary VEREY made an ornamental kitchen garden for her garden at BARNSLEY HOUSE. Her *potager*, inspired by William Lawson's *A New Orchard and Garden* (1623) and by the Potager du Roi, was influential in British and North American garden taste.
PT

Potager du Roi. See VERSAILLES.

Potsdam, Neuer Garten.
See NEUER GARTEN.

Powerscourt ⊛
Enniskerry, County Wicklow, Republic of Ireland, was built between 1731 and 1740 for Richard Wingfield (later 1st Viscount Powerscourt) to the designs of Richard Castle (1695–1751). The house occupies a splendid site with wide views of the Wicklow Hills to the south-west. A terraced garden was laid out when the house was completed to take advantage of the views. John Rocque's map of 1760 shows this garden shortly after completion with the terraces descending to a large circular pool and the whole enclosed in a horseshoe of trees. It is possible that this design was made by Castle or another architect from his office. J. C. LOUDON's *Encyclopaedia of Gardening* (1822) describes Powerscourt as having 'a demesne of 600 acres tastefully planted'. From 1843 the terraced garden was refashioned by the architect Daniel Robertson (*fl.* early 19th century). Little is known of Robertson, but Lord Powerscourt's *Description and History of Powerscourt* (1903) says that 'He was given to drink, and always drew best when he was excited with sherry'. Robertson's work at Powerscourt introduced a note of Victorian exuberance in the terraces. Many statues were added to the terraces in this time and fine

walled gardens made to one side of the house above the terraces. Leading into the walled gardens are a pair of very beautiful wrought-iron gates made in 1770 for Bamberg cathedral in Bavaria. Gilded and painted black they form a *trompe l'œil* giving a sense of false perspective. After Robertson's time a splendid climax was added on the lowermost terrace which overlooks the lake made of Castle's formal pool. Professor Hagen of Berlin was commissioned in 1866 to make a pair of pegasi (the pegasus is the crest of the Wingfields) rearing up at each end of the terrace. In 1908, at the height of the craze for such things, a JAPANESE GARDEN was added in the woodland to one side of the lake. The entrance leads between mossy rocks which are the remains of a lakeside grotto made *c.*1740. A scarlet bridge spans a stream and stone snow lanterns stand on the edges of paths leading under flowering cherries, Japanese maples, and a group of *Trachycarpus fortunei*. Trees are a notable feature of Powerscourt. The entrance drive runs across parkland with magnificent beeches (*Fagus sylvatica*) planted in the 18th century by the 2nd Viscount Powerscourt. In the 19th century many conifers were introduced which have grown to great size in the benign microclimate and fairly high annual rainfall of 1 m/42 in. A walk of monkey-puzzles (*Araucaria araucana*) dates from the 1860s and running along one side of the formal terraces is a row of Wellingtonias (*Sequoiadendron giganteum*) of the same date. Well over 200 species and cultivars of trees and shrubs are found in the gardens, with many excellent specimens and several uncommon trees such as the crimson-flowered *Picea likiangensis*, the beautiful Japanese *Thujopsis dolabrata*, and an exceptionally large example of the slow-growing plum-fruited yew *Podocarpus andinus*. The central part of the house was gutted by fire in 1974 and its wonderful contents destroyed. The house has been restored, with some interiors replaced, and with its great garden is one of the most visited estates in Ireland. PT

Powis Castle ⊛
Welshpool, Powys, Wales, is an ancient princely estate going back at least to the 12th century. It was bought in the 16th century by the Herbert family whose descendant, the 4th Earl of Powis, left it to the NATIONAL TRUST in 1952. The present castle is a 17th-century remodelling of a largely 13th-century building. A rare feature of the garden at Powis is the sequence of south-facing terraces of distinctly Italianate character built below the castle walls in the 1660s probably to the designs of William Winde (d. 1722). Shortly after, by 1705, a great water parterre was laid out on the flat ground at the foot of the terraces. John Bridgeman saw it in 1705—'I din'd this

week at Powis Castle. The water works and fountains that are finished there are much beyond anything I saw.' A Buck print of 1742 shows topiary walks on the terraces with the water parterre of scalloped pools, statuary, and topiary. In around 1771 William EMES turned the water parterre into the Great Lawn with, beyond it, a wooded wilderness. When John Byng visited Powis in 1793 he found the terraces in a sorry state—'upon the terraces you cannot walk as the balustrades are fallen down'. Today the garden is well cared for by the National Trust which, under the direction of Graham Stuart THOMAS, laid out excellent mixed borders on the terraces. A series of lead statues dating from the early 18th century (possibly from the John van NOST workshop) decorates the terraces, and rising above the topmost terrace is a remarkable ancient yew hedge—possibly grown out of the topiary seen in the Buck print. The Wilderness has flowering shrubs among old oaks (*Quercus robur* and *Q. ilex*) and specimen trees. The view back from the Wilderness to the castle terraces is one of the most memorable of British garden scenes.
PT

Prasart Museum ⊛

Bangkok, Thailand. Prasart Vongsakul, the creator of this private museum in the Bangkok suburb of Hua Mark, is as keen a gardener as he is a collector of Thai, Chinese, and Khmer art. Among the structures on the property are a small Buddhist chapel, a classic Thai house, a colonial-style palace, and a Chinese temple. Around these examples of Thailand's religious and domestic architecture he has planted a remarkable garden, combining both traditional and contemporary concepts of landscape design. Tradition is reflected in a number of old gnarled trees, mostly *Plumeria*, selected as much for their form as for their flowers, and in plants that have been clipped and trained into assorted shapes, an ancient art known in Thai as *mai dat*. Elsewhere, pathways lead through jungle-like beds densely planted with assorted bamboos, heliconias, palms, gingers, and philodendrons, with accents of stronger colour provided by codiaeums and cordylines. The Buddhist chapel is reflected in a lily pond, edged with assorted water plants. WLW

Pratolino, Villa ⊛

Florence, Tuscany, Italy. Known as the 'garden of miracles' Pratolino, commissioned by Francesco I de' Medici from Bernardo Buontalenti (1536–1608) from 1569, was the greatest of the Medici gardens, its fountains, statues, grottoes, musical waterworks and GIOCHI D'ACQUA famous throughout Europe. Many of the Renaissance features were copied north of the Alps, only to be destroyed during the Thirty Years War which racked Europe between 1618 and 1648. The lunette of Pratolino in the topographical museum in Florence, painted by Giusto UTENS by 1599, shows the garden at its peak. Ten km/6 miles north of Florence the garden's sophistication marked the contrast with the surrounding wild countryside of woods and mountains, the site purposefully chosen by Francesco to show his mastery over nature, or at least the close relationship between nature and garden art. The painting reveals a mixture of formality and parklike scenery. A main axis below the villa is intersected by lateral avenues, some at right angles, others at diagonals. Irregularly placed pools meander down the slope between densely planted trees. There were labyrinths of bay laurel and meadows sprinkled with wildflowers, surprise fountains, and a 'pergola' of water jets. The hydraulics were described by Michel MONTAIGNE in the 1580s. Statues of Apollo, the Muses, and Pegasus were brought to animated life by a water organ inside the mount.

Pratolino was transformed into a landscape park in 1819 by the engineer Giuseppe Frichs and the villa destroyed in 1822. The enormous statue of Apennine by GIAMBOLOGNA created in 1879 and 11 m/35 ft high is all that remains, except for a web of rides through the woods and the *Fontane delle Maschere*. The courtesans' quarters have been turned into a villa for the Demidoff family. PHo

Price, Sir Uvedale

(1747–1829), English landowner, author, and theoretician of the PICTURESQUE. He put into practice his own ideas of the picturesque in his estate of Foxley (Herefordshire), where he laid out walks and rides 'diversified with different prospects'. He loved continuity in the landscape and admired 'the superior variety and richness of unimproved parks and forests'. A well-run and productive estate could also be beautiful—his woodland was managed with profit and beauty in view. Although the house at Foxley was long ago demolished, traces of his landscape survive. Price's *Essay on the Picturesque* (1794—in a third edition by 1810) was an influential book of its time. His view of the picturesque was less dramatic than that of his neighbour and close friend Richard Payne KNIGHT but they were united in their disapproval of the suave landscapes of Capability BROWN, which they saw as destroying the individuality of regions and landscapes. Humphry REPTON, who did much work in Herefordshire, was at first admired by Price but Repton believed that the *Essay on the Picturesque* was an attack on him. He replied to the attack in his published open *Letter to Uvedale Price* (1794) in which he argued that the 'health, cheerfulness and comfort of a country residence' was of greater importance than 'the wild but pleasing scenery of a painter's imagination'. Price immediately published a reply to Repton in 1794 to which Repton replied, and others also took sides in a long-simmering and inevitably inconclusive dispute.
PT

Prince Nurseries.

In 1735 the first American commercial nursery was established at Flushing by Robert Prince, later continued by his son William Prince (1725–1802); it concentrated and prospered on the sale of fruit and ornamental trees until the Revolutionary War (1775–83). Their catalogue of 1771 included many varieties of plum, pear, apple, and nectarine, and by 1774 the selection incorporated Portuguese grapevines and English and American strawberry plants. Prince introduced the Lombardy poplar (*Populus nigra* 'Italica') and was the first to propagate the native *Carya illinoensis*, the pecan nut. The nursery developed a plum called either Flushing or Prince's Gage, now *Prunus domestica* 'Imperial Gage'. Following the war the business became the leading exporter of American plants, and was visited by George Washington (1732–99), who purchased fruit trees. In 1793 the founder's grandson William Prince Jr. (1766–1842) worked with Thomas NUTTALL establishing a new nursery north of Broadway, named the Linnaean Botanic Garden. In Britain their reputation prompted the Earl of Liverpool to name a plant *Pelargonium* 'Princeanum' in their honour. William wrote several books including *Treatise on Horticulture* (1828), *A Treatise on the Vine* (1839), *A Pomological Manual* (1840), and *A Manual of Roses* (1846).
MC-C

Prior Park ⊛

Bath, Somerset, England, is a great Palladian mansion built between 1735 and 1748 to the designs of John Wood the elder (*c*.1705–1754) for Ralph Allen, the entrepreneur and quarry owner who supplied stone for the building of 18th-century Bath. The site, on the southern fringe of the city, lies at the head of a valley which slopes steeply to the north, giving magnificent views. When the house was being built a landscape park was laid out in the valley probably designed by Allen himself, and possibly with the help of his friend Alexander POPE. Pope certainly advised Allen's wife on the building of a GROTTO, writing to her in 1740 to express his pleasure that she had 'begun to imitate the Great Works of nature, rather than the Baubles most ladies affect'. An engraving by Anthony Walker of *c*.1754 shows the garden with a descending apron of turf centred on the house, with informal woodland and winding walks to one side and a formal pattern of walks on the other. Richard Pococke, writing before 1754, described 'a new Gothick building, higher up a statue of Moses with his hand striking the rock, and below it a beautiful cascade falls 20 feet' (*The Travels through England*, 1754). Shortly after this Allen's clerk of works, Richard Jones (b. 1703), designed a fine Palladian bridge in 1756, very similar to those at STOWE and at WILTON HOUSE, which stands on one side of the valley spanning the neck of a pool. Today the house is a school and the park, with the Palladian bridge intact, belongs to the NATIONAL TRUST. The whole area of Prior Park is 11 hectares/28 acres, of modest size as 18th-century landscape parks go, but it achieves a potent Arcadian atmosphere enriched by views over one of the greatest urban scenes in Europe. PT

GILLIAN CLARKE, *Prior Park: A Compleat Landscape* (1987).

Promenadenring ⊕

Leipzig, Germany. An outstanding monument of horticultural art, the park was established in the 1780s using the site of former fortifications. By *c.*1700 avenues had been planted about the city centre and in 1777 work began to fill in the moat between the northern and eastern city gates on the initiative of the mayor Carl Wilhelm Müller (1782–1801). It is also due to him that these areas were kept free of buildings. He was also responsible for the generous green belt around the city centre. In recognition of his services the citizenry of Leipzig in 1819 devoted to him the first monument in the Promenadenring. In 1857 the southern part of the moat was filled and the area was redesigned by Peter Joseph LENNÉ. In 1904–5 the area between the Hallisches Tor and the New City Hall was redesigned to the design of the garden director Carl Hampel (1849–1930). In 1910, because of the development of the Central Station, the adjoining part to the east was totally redesigned. A wide avenue for pedestrians, adjacent to a street and planted with exotic trees and shrubs, formed the edge of the park. It is thought that the Promenadenring was the first urban landscape park in Germany. Today it has an area of about 13 hectares/32 acres and from the 1990s the city of Leipzig has been gradually reconstructing it to honour its horticultural heritage. PF

propagation

—simply put, the production of new plants from old—must have been among the very first practical achievements of mankind to set him apart from the rest of the animal kingdom.

Almost certainly a start would have been made in the Stone Age by gathering seed of the wild ancestors of present-day cereals, like wheat, maize, and rice, and scattering it in a convenient position. Propagation by seed is the only practicable method for annual plants. It is also widely used for perennial species, and for their varieties that 'come true', that is to say where the offspring produced from seed is practically identical to the parent. Propagation by seed offers large advantages. Seeds are easy to store for long periods in cool, dry atmospheres. Plants raised from seed are usually cheap by comparison with ones raised from cuttings or by division, let alone by budding or grafting. Even when seed is harvested from parent plants that are diseased, the embryonic plant within the seedcoat is normally free of pathogens, including virus diseases. Propagation by seed is a near necessity in the breeding of new varieties of plants of all kinds. Its practical basis is the use of parent plants of different genetic characteristics, the one to provide pollen and the other to be the seed parent. Requirements for successful germination are usually simple, given an environment free from seed-eating pests and fungal pathogens of seedlings such as those causing damping-off disease. The essentials are then an adequate but not excessive temperature, and water and oxygen. Light is beneficial for the germination of seed of a very few common garden plants, such as celery, *Nicotiana*, and *Petunia*.

The commonest reason for propagating plants vegetatively, by division, cuttings, or grafting, is that if they are raised from seed the progeny will not be precisely identical to the parent. This is the case for almost all cultivated varieties of fruit, and for the great majority of garden varieties of trees, shrubs, herbaceous perennials, and flowering plants grown from bulbs, corms, and tubers. Other reasons for the use of vegetative propagation include the absence of fertile seed, for example in bananas. A significant penalty of all forms of vegetative propagation is that any diseases and pests afflicting the parent plant are very likely to be present in or on its progeny. Successful vegetative propagation requires the establishment and maintenance of high health standards in parent plants. Division will almost certainly have been the first type of vegetative propagation used by mankind, and remains particularly important for most hardy herbaceous perennials. Nevertheless it is the use of cuttings which has long been the most prevalent. Much the most commonly stem cuttings are used. Hardwood stem cuttings root readily for a limited range of deciduous shrubs, such as *Cornus*, *Forsythia*, and *Spiraea*, and for gooseberries and blackcurrant and redcurrant

bushes. Chrysanthemums, dahlias, fuchsias, bedding pelargoniums, and a very wide range of shrubs and other herbaceous plants are usually propagated by softwood cuttings. These comprise a short length of actively growing stem, with its growing point, and root swiftly in sufficiently warm conditions under which the loss of water through the foliage can be minimized. This may be achieved by covering with plastic film or by using a traditional propagating frame, or by artificial misting or fogging. There are several other types of cutting. Leaf bud cuttings, for example of *Clematis*, *Camellia*, and ivies, differ from softwood stem cuttings in being short sections of stem containing one or sometimes two leaf joints. Semi-hardwood cuttings are stem cuttings of conifers and evergreen shrubs, intermediate in nature between softwood and hardwood cuttings. They are normally taken in late summer. A limited range of plants can easily be propagated from root cuttings, usually taken in the dormant season. It includes herbaceous perennials such as *Anchusa*, *Echinops*, *Echinacea*, *Eryngium*, *Phlox*, and oriental poppy (*Papaver orientalis*), and shrubs such as *Rhus* and *Rubus* species. For a small number of genera, propagation by leaf cuttings is a practicable method. Examples are African violets (*Saintpaulia*), *Begonia rex*, and *Streptocarpus*. Layering differs from propagation by cuttings in that root formation from the stems takes place while they are still attached to the parent plant. The best-known example is the tip layering of blackberries, a minor refinement of what takes place in nature. The stems of many climbing plants also root readily when in contact with soil: *Hedera*, *Hydrangea petiolaris*, and *Wisteria* are examples. Layering is also used for some woody plants of which cuttings are difficult to root, for example *Daphne cneorum* and some rhododendrons.

Grafting is known to have been practised in China and Egypt by around 2,000 BC. It results in the union of a piece of stem from one plant, the scion, with the stem of another, the stock. In the resulting plant, the root system and the base is usually provided only by the stock, while from the scion grows all the upper parts of the plant. A close genetic relationship between stock and scion is essential. The best-known uses of grafting are in the propagation of grapevines, and of Japanese maples. Budding is an important variant of grafting in which the scion is a single bud with a very small piece of the surrounding bark and stem tissue. Its best-known applications are in the propagation of roses, and of apples, pears, plums, cherries, and their counterparts among ornamental trees, varieties of *Malus*, *Prunus*, and *Pyrus*. The principal reason for budding or grafting is that a root system of superior character is provided. For apples, pears, and cherries, this usually means one of lesser vigour, resulting in a smaller tree on which blossoming and fruiting occur at an earlier stage. In grapevines, grafting is carried out to provide a root system resistant to a very serious root pest, the vine louse (*Phylloxera*). For roses, propagation by budding rather than by cuttings is carried out to ensure greater vigour and the quicker production of fully grown bushes. In some cases budding or grafting is used because cuttings are difficult to root: this applies in the case of many varieties of the Japanese maples, *Acer japonicum* and *A. palmatum*.   JSu

public parks.

The park designed for the recreation of the public as it is understood today is essentially a 19th-century development, when, with the great increase of population, it was seen as an essential public amenity. However, it has ancient, if sometimes distant, antecedents and urban space accessible to the public had existed long before the 19th century. In ancient GREECE by the 5th century BC the agora, or assembly place, in cities would usually have water and a grove of trees. In ancient ROME there developed a tradition of great men creating public parks as an ostentatious public display. The pioneer of this fashion was Pompey the Great who in Rome in 55 BC had a grove of plane trees, theatre, basilica, and markets (see Maureen Carroll, *Earthly Paradises*, 2003). In Mexico CHAPULTEPEC, first laid out by the Aztecs, was opened to the public from 1530 by the Spanish conquistadors. In Spain the *alameda* (which originally meant a grove of poplars), a shady place to sit or saunter, has been an urban feature since time immemorial. A handsome example may be seen at Ronda (Andalusia) on the edge of an immense cliff with grand views. Royalty sometimes gave public access to their lands in cities. In Paris Marie de Médicis in 1638 opened the Cours-la-Reine, a promenade running along the river west of the Tuileries Palace. This was reserved for the use of the royal family but when they were not in residence the public had access to it. From 1640 the Jardin Royal des Plantes Médicinales (later the Jardin des Plantes; see PARIS PARKS AND GARDENS) was open to the public. A remarkable example of a large private garden which was opened to the public as soon as it was finished was the Parc de la COLOMBIÈRE laid out in the 1680s in Dijon which still survives. In England in the 17th century there were several different kinds of gardens to which the public had access. Moorfields, to the north of the city walls, and Lincoln's Inn both had public promenades. The Avenham Walk (Preston, Lancashire) was a

public promenade laid out in 1697 shaded by an avenue of limes on a spur of land overlooking the valley of the river Ribble. It still exists although today the view is thoroughly urban. In England the various royal estates (see LONDON PARKS AND GARDENS) admitted the public in certain circumstances. Under Charles II in the 1660s St James's Park, probably designed by André MOLLET, was opened to the public. Deer, goats, and sheep grazed the park and wildfowl (some of them exotic) flourished in pools. From *c*.1700 a regular Milk Fair was held at which dairy farmers exhibited different breeds of cow whose milk was sold.

All this, however, with its air of *noblesse oblige*, is far from the spirit of the municipal public park, open to all, and equipped with a wide range of amusements and amenities. One of the earliest examples of the desire to provide large areas of green space for the public is the remarkable PHOENIX PARK in Dublin. Formerly monastic land, later a royal deer park, it became in 1747 a city park with the gigantic area of 728 hectares/1,800 acres and it remains to this day one of the largest public parks in the world. Also in Dublin, but a little later than this, is the NATIONAL BOTANIC GARDENS, GLASNEVIN founded in 1795 as a scientific institution but soon becoming, in addition, a much-loved public park. The ENGLISCHER GARTEN in Munich has a strong claim to be the first public park of a truly modern kind. It was laid out from 1789 by F. L. von SCKELL and the American Benjamin Thompson (who was ennobled as Reichsgraf von Rumford). The latter described the purpose of the park as 'to benefit not just one class of society but the whole population'. Apart from this explicit populist intention the park was modern in the way it separated the traffic, with carefully planned footpaths, carriageways, and bridle paths. This was something that was uppermost in the mind of Sir Joseph PAXTON in England when in 1843 he was planning BIRKENHEAD PARK. Another similarity between the two parks, which became standard practice in 19th-century parks, was the intermingling of open space and more intimate areas with vistas and eyecatchers to animate the scene.

In Germany in the 18th century the writings of C. C. L. HIRSCHFELD, particularly in his *Theorie des Gartenkunst* (1779–85), inspired an interest in the idea of the public garden. Hirschfeld was strongly influenced by the naturalistic 18th-century English landscape park and his book, translated into many languages, did much to foster that tradition. Hirschfeld believed in the moral power of the natural world and of landscape—it was good for you—and he was a keen advocate of public parks. His notion of the *Volksgarten* was that it should be a public garden opened to all sections

of society. He also, however, believed that it should have a didactic role. It should remind citizens of the 'heroism of its patriots, and of its good fortune as a nation' and monuments and ornaments were not mere decorations of the landscape, for they should evoke this spirit of heroism. The first public park in Germany created by a municipality was Volksgarten Kloster Berge at Magdeburg (Saxony-Anhalt) designed by Peter Joseph LENNÉ in 1824. Between 1833 and 1840 Lenné also took the 17th-century baroque landscape at TIERGARTEN in Berlin and, retaining some of its old character, made it into a public garden with something of the character of a landscape park. More municipal parks followed in the second half of the 19th century. The Bürgerpark at Bremen (1866 onwards) by Wilhelm Benque (1814–95) resulted from the initiative of a group of interested citizens. Other parks came into existence as improvement schemes for redundant fortifications—in Hamburg, Bremen, and Frankfurt.

The restructuring of Paris under Haussmann (see PARIS PARKS AND GARDENS) from 1853 was the occasion of the introduction of public parks of the new style. The ancient Bois de Boulogne and the Bois de Vincennes, respectively just beyond the western and eastern limits of the city, were given a mixture of straight and winding carriage drives and separate pedestrian walks. Lakes were floated and gardens within gardens were laid out together with such amenities as cafés. Parisian parks were very inventive in both adapting historic sites, such as the Parc Monceau, as well as creating entirely new landscapes in what had been wasteland, such as J. C. A. ALPHAND's wonderfully romantic Parc des Buttes-Chaumont. At the end of the 19th century the Champs-de-Mars, partly designed by J. C. N. FORESTIER showed a new eclecticism in French parks—Arcadian groves of trees, pools, and flower beds were disposed about an axis of 17th-century strictness with the Eiffel Tower as an epic eyecatcher. Major and minor French cities were quick to follow the lead of Paris. In Lyon in 1856 the Parc de la TÊTE D'OR was laid out. This followed the new pattern of public parks but, in addition, provided an exceptional collection of plants, making it of outstanding interest to gardeners. This was designed by Denis BÜHLER who was also responsible, in 1865, for the Parc du THABOR in Rennes which adapted an old garden, formerly that of a convent, for use as a public park. In Bordeaux the 18th-century Jardin Public, finely integrated with the 18th-century town planning, was in the 19th century given by L.-B. Fischer the appearance of a modern park with a serpentine lake, new walks, and a botanic garden of great public interest. The Parc Borély in Marseille was designed *c*.1860 by the BÜHLER brothers who took an 18th-century estate and made it into a romantic public park with good trees, a lake, grotto, and cascade. The Jardin DUMAINE shows that excellent public parks were made in 19th-century France in quite small towns such as Luçon in the Vendée. The French tradition of laying out public gardens continued throughout the 20th century. The Jardin des Prés-Fichaux (Bourges) was laid out in the 1920s by Paul Marguerita (1886–1942) in a refreshing art deco style. The various new parks laid out in Paris (see PARIS PARKS AND GARDENS) in the latter part of the 20th century were a unique achievement in urban planning of its time. The Jardin Atlantique, 3.4 hectares/8 acres of public gardens on the roof of an office block, is a symbol of Parisian panache in these matters.

In the USA one of the first urban public spaces has its origins in New York (see NEW YORK CITY PARKS AND GARDENS) in Bowling Green which dates back to 1625. It stood at the foot of what later became Broadway and was, by the 1730s, fenced off and planted with grass and trees. The making of Central Park in the heart of Manhattan from 1857 was of great importance in the history of public parks in the USA. Frederick Law OLMSTED and Calvert Vaux followed the new pattern of separating routes but had the novel idea of sinking main thoroughfares below the surrounding level. They, too, were responsible for part of the revolutionary CHICAGO PARKS system with its chain of parks and parkways which took shape in 1869. Very shortly afterwards, in 1872, William Hammond Hall (1846–1934), laid out the GOLDEN GATE PARK in San Francisco where he conquered sand dunes and planted 155,000 trees, many of them indigenous Californian species like Monterey pines (*Pinus radiata*) and Monterey cypress (*Cupressus macrocarpa*). In the very early years of the 20th century the Olmsted brothers designed SEATTLE PARKS, a network of parks and parkways linking the city to the shores of Lake Washington.

In the Netherlands the first Dutch people's garden, the VONDELPARK, was opened in 1865 to the designs of the ZOCHERS. Largely laid out in landscape style it managed to combine something of the FERME ORNÉE (it had a dairy herd from which milk was sold to the public) and popular entertainment in the form of a bandstand. The AMSTERDAM BOS, designed in 1934, in what sounds like an act of political conviction, avoided the words 'garden' or 'park' which were thought to be tainted with bourgeois prejudice. This was to be a park for everyman (and, of course, woman) and it avoided references to the past by eschewing monuments. It was, however, well equipped

with sports and other recreational facilities. A little later, from 1940, there was developed the adjacent THIJSSE PARK, planted with native species, and designed to have a more contemplative air than the busy Bos. Such explicit attitudes to the mood of public space, with a strong social dimension, were a new development. For the MUSEUMPARK in Rotterdam Rem Koolhaas (b. 1944) and Yves Brunier (1962–91) in the late 1980s adopted a positively postmodern approach for the public landscaping of a large area linking several museums.

Spain at the turn of the 19th and 20th centuries produced some exceptionally good public parks. The PARK GÜELL in Barcelona, started in 1900, is the landscape masterpiece of the architect Antoni GAUDÍ whose eclecticism and unostentatious originality resulted in one of the most attractive of all public parks. From 1917, also in Barcelona, the MONTJUICH park was designed by J. C. N. FORESTIER, who devised a series of gardens and public spaces of great flexibility—so flexible that it was able to accommodate the stadium for the Olympic Games of 1992. Forestier showed himself the master of a different mood when he laid out, from 1929, the Parque MARÍA LUISA in Seville. Here he designed a park with a strong underlying rectilinear plan but softened by bold plantings of trees (with many exotics), and decorated it with brilliant AZULEJOS and sparkling water in the Muslim tradition.

Public parks were laid out in various South American countries in the 19th century. In Argentina the PARQUE 3 DE FEBRERO in Buenos Aires was laid out in the fashionable park style of its day and later revised by Charles THAYS, who had trained under Édouard ANDRÉ in Paris. The Parque del CERRO SANTA LUCIA in Santiago, Chile, on an ancient site with remains of 16th-century Spanish work, was laid out as a public park in 1872. It has pavilions, restaurants, and a museum set in a landscape of winding paths and grottoes contrasting with formal garden architecture. The Parque do FLAMENGO in Rio de Janeiro, Brazil, is a work by the great figure of Roberto BURLE MARX. In 1962 this seaside site was designed with lavish public amenities and a huge range of plants including many Brazilian natives.

The STOCKHOLM PARK SYSTEM in Sweden created from the 1930s is a remarkable instance of the design of public space being strongly influenced by high standards of social welfare. The design of this network of public parks took its cue not from garden aesthetics but from the wild, rocky, natural landscape outside the city. Amenities include public art and theatrical performances and, furthermore, staffed children's playgrounds are available

without charge. GOTHENBURG has public parks built outside the old city walls and at MALMÖ the town's former fortifications and other available space were transformed into public parks.

In England the public park was not always regarded primarily as an amenity for the common man. Royal Victoria Park in Bath was designed by the city architect Edward Davis and opened by Princess Victoria in 1830. It is overlooked by Royal Crescent, the finest 18th-century houses in the city, whose owners relished the view of the park laid out (at the expense of public funds) below their windows. In the 1880s a BANDSTAND was added which attracted a socially more diverse range of visitors. The public park was usually an urban phenomenon but the Crystal Palace Park laid out between 1852 and 1854 by Joseph PAXTON was at Sydenham, then well outside the southern limits of London overlooking the Kentish countryside. It took as its centrepiece Paxton's extraordinary Crystal Palace (in a slightly enlarged version). Paxton built a grand flight of steps leading up to the Crystal Palace decorated with statues and a great terrace was lavishly planted with bedding schemes. Further floral displays and spectacular fountains decorated the park and a boating lake was floated with, about its banks, monumental sculptures of prehistoric creatures. The erection of the Crystal Palace and the laying out of the park grounds cost over £1,350,000 (the equivalent of around £58,050,000 in 2004). Its opening, by Queen Victoria, was a great social event, and the park became immediately famous, attracting many thousands of visitors. This was perhaps the first example of a new phenomenon, the 'destination' park planned not in the first place as a public amenity but as an event. The palace was destroyed by fire in 1936 and the park survives now equipped with an athletics centre and other sporting facilities but, except for the prehistoric monsters, shorn of all the splendour that Paxton gave it. A public park with explicitly populist intentions was the People's Park designed by Joseph Paxton and Edward MILNER in Halifax. It was given to the city by a local industrial tycoon and philanthropist, Sir Francis Crossley. His statue in the park bears the inscription 'The rich and poor meet together—the Lord is maker of them all'. By the end of the 19th century every industrial city of any size in England had its own public park. In Scotland there is not the same tradition of municipal parks found in England. An outstanding public park in Glasgow, the Glasgow Botanic Gardens, had its origins as an early 18th-century physic garden belonging to the university. In 1839 it moved to its present site and was taken over by the

Glasgow Corporation, and it serves as a public amenity as well as an academic botanic garden. It has an outstanding 19th-century circular glasshouse, the Kibble Palace, designed in the 1860s probably by the architectural firm of Boucher & Cousland.

In the 19th century the public park was considered both an essential public amenity and, in well-run cities, a source of civic pride. In France, where the mayors of cities have power and parks are valued, the standard of maintenance is generally very high. In the USA in the late 20th century an instructive sequence of events overtook Central Park in Manhattan (see NEW YORK CITY PARKS AND GARDENS). By the 1970s it was in a state of dereliction, a haunt of criminals and a place which law-abiding citizens avoided. In 1978 the Central Park Conservancy, appalled by what the park had become, in association with the city of New York, launched a comprehensive restoration and undertook to supervise continuing maintenance. This collaboration not only restored a magnificent landscape but it also made the park safe for New Yorkers and a source of pride. Such a lesson has been slow to influence those in charge of public parks in England. Under the Conservative government in the 1980s local government was largely forced to abandon publicly financed public parks authorities and the maintenance of parks was to be put out to 'competitive tender', which usually meant that the cheapest bidder won. By the end of the millennium it was estimated in a report by the Policy Studies Institute (*Cultural Trends*, August 2001) that in the previous twenty years between 50 and 70% of bandstands, fountains, paddling pools, pets' corners, glasshouses, and other amenities had been lost. A rather smaller percentage, between 25 and 50%, of ornamental and amenity buildings (including lavatories and cafés) were out of action. £3.5 billion was required to restore public parks. By the end of the millennium the only major public parks to be in good condition were the royal parks of London which have never been funded by the municipality. Substantial funding for restoration has come from the Heritage Lottery Fund but this has been adequate for only a few parks, nor did it address the underlying problem of financing maintenance.   PT

Pückler-Muskau, Hermann, Prince of
(1785–1871), German landowner, gardener, and garden theorist who inherited from his father the principality of Muskau where, from 1816, he laid out a landscape park strongly influenced by the ideas of Humphry REPTON. Pückler-Muskau travelled in England between 1826 and 1829, visiting many notable gardens

of the day. His lively letters to his wife were published, anonymously, as *Briefes eines Verstorbenen* (Letters from a Dead Man) (1830). Translated into English as *The Tour of a German Prince* (1832) they were a great success, alleviating the Prince's financial straits and making him something of a celebrity in England where he was known affectionately as Pickling-Mustard. Repton's influence is visible, too, in Pückler-Muskau's book *Andeutungen über Landschaftsgärtnerei* (Hints on Landscape Gardening) (1834), which seems like a primer of Repton's later more picturesque and flowery style. The book, handsomely illustrated with Reptonian drawings, was influential on German garden taste. In 1846 Pückler-Muskau moved to another family estate, BRANITZ, where he laid out another landscape garden.   PT

Puente de San Miguel.
See MIGUEL, PUENTE DE SAN.

Pukeiti
New Plymouth, New Zealand, was begun in 1951 when a group of RHODODENDRON enthusiasts searched the country for an ideal site on which to grow their favourite genus. They eventually chose a 63-hectare/153-acre tract of land on the site of an ancient lava cone at a height of 490 m/1,601 ft called Pukeiti (meaning 'Little Hill' in Maori). Part of the nearby Mount Taranaki (Mount Egmont) volcanic range, Pukeiti was clothed in remnants of a great podocarp forest. A trust was formed to establish and maintain the fledgling garden which many people both in New Zealand and overseas joined as members, to promote the genus and to conserve the forest. Pukeiti Rhododendron Trust has remained owned and operated by its members ever since. Pukeiti eventually grew by gift to 364 hectares/900 acres. Goats and opossums had stripped the forest, and with 4 m/12 ft of rainfall annually, the founders faced enormous difficulties—Pukeiti must surely be one of the wettest gardens on earth. These difficulties were countered by the extraordinary enthusiasm of member volunteers who carved the garden from the forest. This enthusiasm remains unabated today.

Although many exotic trees, shrubs, and perennials are planted, Pukeiti has one of the largest collections of rhododendron species and hybrids in the southern hemisphere. These are planted informally along grassed walks through the forest where they associate well with the varied foliage of the indigenous trees and shrubs. Tree ferns proliferate, particularly the giant mamaku (*Cyathea medullaris*), as do damp-loving filmy ferns

as well as the world's largest moss, *Dawsonia superba*. Grandia, falconera, maddenia, and vireya rhododendrons are particularly successful in this temperate rainforest setting—the tender maddenias grow out of doors with ease. The most spectacular of the many large-leafed species is *R. protistum* var. *giganteum*, which at 12 m/40 ft in diameter carries annually up to 200 flower trusses the size of footballs. The extensive vireya collection is housed in linked open-sided structures where the large yellow trusses of *R. lowii* may be seen, grown from cuttings collected by member Keith Adams at 3,050 m/10,000 ft on Mount Kinabalu, Borneo, in 1980.   GSC

Puławy
near Lublin, Poland. The baroque palace was built and the formal garden was laid out between 1671 and 1678 on the high bank of the Vistula by Tylman of Gameren for Stanisław Herakliusz Lubomirski. The entire layout was transformed by Izabela Czartoryska (1746–1835). Around 1770 a 'wild promenade' appeared in the park and then a number of park buildings designed by Chrystian Piotr Aigner (1756–1841). The loss of Poland's independence (1795) was deeply embedded in the consciousness of Czartoryska. The Russian troops plundered and devastated Puławy. After 1796 James Savage transformed the Puławy garden, its geometric composition being replaced by an irregular arrangement. The park was gradually being transformed into an Arcadia in which Czartoryska decided to create a great national utopia. She was guided by the idea of rescuing Polish antiquities. In 1798–1801 Aigner built on the Vistula escarpment the first museum pavilion (the Sibyl's Temple). It housed the objects that had once belonged to Polish monarchs and their families which were to serve the purpose of consolidating the national identity of successive generations. Izabela's idea was expressed in the inscription above the entrance to the temple: THE PAST TO THE FUTURE. In the Gothic House (1809) the European collection was exhibited. Here Izabela assembled mementoes of great persons, e.g. Shakespeare's chair or a fragment of Petrarch's cupboard. Beside these romantic relics there were paintings, including Leonardo da Vinci's *Lady with an Ermine*, *Portrait of a Youth* by Raphael, and *Landscape with the Good Samaritan* by Rembrandt. After the fall of the November Uprising and the confiscation of Puławy by the Russians (1831), the collection was transported to Paris; today it is kept in Cracow.   WB

Pulham, James
(1788–c.1838), English craftsman and

entrepreneur, the founding father of a dynasty of makers of terracotta, stone, or artificial stone garden ornaments. Born in Suffolk, he was working for William Lockwood's cement works in Spitalfields (London) by *c.*1820, where he modelled a wide range of garden ornaments. The firm was taken over by Pulham whose son, also James Pulham (*c.*1820–1898), also worked for it. By *c.*1843 the younger James was established in Broxbourne (Hertfordshire) and began to make high-quality terracotta ornaments in large quantities and an artificial Portland stone, Pulham's Portland Stone Cement. In 1865 the younger James Pulham was joined by his son James Robert Pulham (b. 1845), and the firm was named Pulham & Son. They also undertook landscaping work, especially rock gardens and other features involving rockwork. Their invention, Pulhamite, an artificial stone made of industrial clinker mixed with cement textured to resemble natural stone, was greatly in demand, fuelling the fashion for ROCK GARDENS and FERNERIES. By the 1920s the firm had also made a speciality of

constructing JAPANESE GARDENS and it remained in business until 1945.   PT

Pure Land Garden. See JAPAN.

Pushkin. See TSARSKOE SELO.

pyramid.
The first pyramid was built in Egypt around 2,700 BC, with stepped sides, and the characteristic smooth-sided form first appeared towards 2,500 BC. They were objects of the greatest fascination to early travellers, in particular to Romans, who erected a MAUSOLEUM for Gaius Cestius in the form of a pyramid at the Porta San Paolo in Rome *c.*10 BC. The pyramid shape was found as an occasional motif in Italian Renaissance gardens, but in 18th-century European gardens it was used with special inventiveness. An ICEHOUSE in the form of a pyramid modelled on that of Gaius Cestius was built at the DÉSERT DE RETZ after 1774. At the Château de MAUPERTHUIS one of the best-known pyramids in a French garden was built between 1775 and 1780 to

serve as the entrance to a garden called the Elysium—fragments of it survive today. In English gardens the pyramid form was found from the early 18th century. Nicholas HAWKSMOOR designed a pyramid for CASTLE HOWARD in 1728. For one of the most beautiful of English garden buildings, Worcester Lodge at Badminton House (Gloucestershire), William KENT *c.*1740 flanked a banqueting house with lodges capped with pyramid roofs. James Wyatt's (1746–1813) superb mausoleum at Cobham Hall (Kent) designed for the 3rd Earl of Darnley (and never used) is crowned with a pyramid. At Blickling Hall (Norfolk) Joseph Bonomi (1739–1808) in 1796–7 designed a mausoleum for the 2nd Earl of Buckinghamshire explicitly modelled on the Cestius pyramid.   PT

A **pyramid** concealing an icehouse at the Désert de Retz from Georges Le Rouge's *Détails des nouveaux jardins à la mode* (1785).

Vue de la Glaciere.

Qasr-e Qajar (Castle of the Qajars), Tehran, Iran, was built by Fath Ali Shah (reigned 1797–1834), 4 km/2.4 miles outside the city walls. In the first part of the 19th century the castle and garden layout rivalled in splendour all other contemporary gardens. Built in the same tradition as BAGH-E TAKHT at Shiraz and the SHAH-GOLI in Tabriz, a series of terraces descending from the royal palace overlooked a large square lake on the flat plain below. Within 50 years its glory had departed as the shahs built summer residences in the cooler foothills of Mount Demavend.

PHo

Qianlong Garden ⊛

Ningshou Yuan, Beijing, China, built for the Qianlong Emperor in the 1780s, is one of three gardens that still exist within the walls of the imperial palace. Located near the north-east corner of the palace, the garden consists of five parts or courses arranged consecutively along a north–south axis, in form somewhat like a courtyard house with a garden or courtyard separating each of its halls. Each is 37 m/121 ft wide, and the whole series 60 m/197 ft long with a total area of around 0.6 hectare/1.5 acre. As, out of filial piety, Qianlong did not wish to rule longer than the 61 years of his grandfather Kangxi, he named most of the buildings to suggest the retirement he planned in the sixtieth year of his reign. Between the buildings the courtyards are laid out in the style of south-east China, freer and more lyrical in design than the other parts of the imperial palace. Pavilions, *lang* (see CHINA), rockeries, and artificial hillocks seem to be arranged spontaneously, but are in fact carefully placed in relation to each other to create a subtle balance of high and low, foreground and background, solid and void.

Besides its central hall, the most interesting pavilion in the first course is the Xishangting, commemorating an ancient ceremony for dispelling bad influences. Since the great calligraphist Wang Xizhi used the character *Xi* in his 'Preface for the Anthology on Orchid Pavilion', the floor here is engraved with the pattern of a running brook, an allusion to the 'wine-cup stream' where the original poems in the anthology were composed (see CHINA). The gardens of the third and fourth courses are almost entirely made up of rockeries and artificial hillocks built up over grottoes and with halls and pavilions scattered among them; but, in contrast, the second and fifth courses are simply planted with trees and flowers in paved ground. A famous well where Lady Zhen, royal concubine of the Guang Xu Emperor, was compelled to commit suicide in 1900 is on the east of the fifth course. The whole garden was restored and opened to the public in 1982. G-ZW/MK

Quaracchi, Villa,

Florence, Tuscany, Italy. The famous villa of Quaracchi, with its early Renaissance garden on the outskirts of Florence, is described in some detail in the diaries of the owner Giovanni Rucellai. Built from about 1459, the garden followed the precepts of Leon Battista ALBERTI as set out in his *De Re Aedificatoria* of 1452, in which he recommends an architectural approach to gardening, with a central axis and trees planted in symmetrical patterns. The garden also retained medieval features such as the evergreen arbours, and twining honeysuckle. At Quaracchi, the villa was surrounded by a moat and fish ponds, with an axial pathway stretching from the LOGGIA, through a barrel-shaped PERGOLA of trimmed holm oak and a small GIARDINO SEGRETO of sweet-smelling herbs in terracotta pots, to emerge as an avenue flanked by orchards, which extended 550 m/1,800 ft to the banks of the river Arno. Four openings in the pergola revealed lateral gardens which included topiary pieces, a rose garden, and an EXEDRA framed by clipped bay laurel. PHo

Quatre Vents, Les ⊛

Mont Murray, Québec, Canada, has the distinction of being Canada's largest private garden. It is open to the public during the month of July but demand requires reservations a year in advance (serious botanical groups are allowed in at other times by application). The garden is owned and designed by Francis H. CABOT, although his uncles, both architects, laid out the garden when the family obtained the 10-hectare/24.7-acre property in the late 1920s. One section—the White Garden—dates from 1928. In 1975, Cabot began to expand the garden into what is an amazing spectacle today. He created a series of garden rooms with walls formed by cedar hedges to enclose a rose garden, shade borders, a POTAGER, perennial ALLÉES, MEADOW GARDEN, and a TAPIS VERT all with borrowed views of a magnificent countryside. A whimsical sculpture comprised of a frog quartet plays Mozart's Flute and Horn Concerto once visitors trip a motion detector. Topiary includes cedar loaves of bread flanking the working outdoor oven. A gorgeous *pigeonnier* in the French style is reflected in all its elegant glory in a mirror-like pool. A stream meanders through the extensive woodland featuring many varieties of primula in its understorey; and for the *pièce de résistance*, a pair of Japanese pavilions is backed by a lake with nine waterfalls. The woodland filled with native plants leads to a 1936 swimming pool set against the stunning vista of the St Lawrence river. MH

FRANCIS H. CABOT, *A Greater Perfection* (2001).

Quedlinburg. See BRÜHLPARK.

Queluz, Palácio de ⊛

Queluz, near Lisbon, Portugal. Queluz had been a royal estate in the 17th century, reserved for the use of the monarch's younger sons. In the 18th century it was used by Dom Pedro (younger brother of King Jose I) who, by marrying his niece Maria who was heiress to the throne became, by an entirely unexpected route, King Pedro III in 1777. It was Pedro who, between 1747 and 1786, rebuilt the house, transforming it into a royal palace, and made gardens of a suitable splendour. The French architect Jean-Baptiste Robillion (d. 1782) worked on both the palace and on the gardens that were made immediately adjacent to the palace buildings. The Malta Garden, so called because Pedro III was Grand Master of the order of the Knights of St John of Malta, lies below the western façade of the throne and music rooms—a lively baroque building of great charm. Here is a parterre, slightly sunken with exquisite steps, elegantly scalloped at each end. A scalloped pool stands at the centre, decorated with statues, and box-edged paths and TOPIARY radiate outwards from it. At one time this was called the cherry laurel garden—in 1758 1,450 plants of cherry laurel (*Prunus laurocerasus*) were brought here from the Netherlands. To one side the much larger Pensile garden extends southwards from the Ambassadors' Room and Council Room of the palace. This is a remarkable feat of engineering for the garden is laid out above a water CISTERN which provides water for the lower garden. A mazelike pattern of box hedges has virtually no ornamental planting apart from pyramids and mounds of box, columns of Irish yew, and trees of *Magnolia grandiflora* which rise above the hedges. Magnificent fountain pools are decorated with stone or lead statues. The latter came largely from the London workshop of John CHEERE. Delightful blue and white garlanded pottery urns, made by the Fábrica do Rato, are the 18th-century originals, copies of which appear elsewhere in the gardens. To the south a broad central walk runs through woodland which is threaded with patterns of ALLÉES onamented with occasional statues on plinths. The walk ends with a gigantic vertical CASCADE made in the 1770s—a wall of craggy tufa over which water would tumble from a grotesque mask enclosed in scrollwork at the top. A semicircular pool is edged with richly carved acanthus leaves and shells. To one side of this a botanic garden was completed by 1776, with a CHINOISERIE pavilion, but nothing of it survives today. North-west of the palace is a rare and delightful garden feature—an ornamental boating canal. The walls of the canal are decorated with shaped plinths to support urns and with blue and yellow AZULEJOS which are also seen in the interior walls. The water in the canal was controlled by a sluice and on its waters the royal family and its guests sailed in ornamental pleasure boats. Queluz is one of the finest and most enjoyable estates in Portugal. The gardens in recent years have been fairly well looked after, but a little shaggy at the edges. In 2004, however, a comprehensive restoration of the garden was started, with several of the John Cheere statues being sent to London for restoration.   PT

quincunx,

an arrangement of five objects in a square or rectangle with one at the centre and one at each corner. The word first appears in this meaning in Thomas BROWNE's *The Garden of Cyrus* (1658), which has the subtitle 'The Quincunciall, Lozenge, or Net-work Plantations of the Ancients, Artificially, Naturally, Mystically Considered'. Browne describes how the Persian Prince Cyrus (424–421 BC) was 'Not only a Lord of Gardens, but a manuall planter therof: disposing his trees like his armies in regular ordination'. Browne says that according to Xenophon Cyrus planted in quincunxial patterns so that 'a regular angularity, and

through prospect, was left on every side'. This arrangement was common in formal plantings of trees in 17th-century gardens, for example in wildernesses. It remains a standard practice, especially in France where it is commonly used for commercial timber plantations to great decorative effect.   PT

Quinta da Bacalhôa.

See BACALHÔA, QUINTA DA.

Quinta de Aveleda.

See AVELEDA, QUINTA DE.

Quinta do Palheiro.

See PALHEIRO, QUINTA DO.

Quinta Presidencial

(Presidential Residence), Olivos, Buenos Aires province, Argentina, has a site of 37 hectares/91 acres. Also known as Quinta de Olivos, the house was built—and presumably the first garden too—in 1854 by Prilidiano Pueyrredón (1825–70). He was the best-known Argentinian painter, engineer, and landscaper of the time, trained in Paris. In those days, the Plata river was close by and the house stood on the brink of a cliff giving fine views which today are lost because of refilling and land occupation. The house and grounds used to be enclosed in iron railings allowing views from outside, but during the military dictatorship in the 1970s they were replaced by a high wall. In 1903 the park was redesigned probably by the German designer Hermann Böttrich (1871–1944) in a free-flowing romantic style evoking country life. In 1930 the garden was remodelled by Carlos Leon Thays II (1894–1962). The outstanding features were two new axes: one parallel to the façade, on the edge of the cliff, planted with London planes (*Platanus* × *hispanica*) which also serves as an entrance avenue leading to the *cour d'honneur* (see ATTRE, CHÂTEAU D'); the other visually connects the house with the river shore with a monumental succession of Australian bunya bunya trees (*Araucaria bidwillii*). A new area includes a formal garden, a huge mirror pool in front of the house, a remarkable avenue of *Tilia* 'Moltkei', and a rotunda of Italian cypresses (*Cupressus sempervirens* 'Stricta'). This remodelling transformed the old garden into a ceremonial environment suitable to its new role as Presidential Residence. Thays Landscapers have designed a restoration project.   SLB

Quintinie, Jean-Baptiste de La

(1626–88), French gardener who was in charge of the royal fruit and vegetable gardens under Louis XIV. After studying philosophy and

law and becoming a barrister Quintinie was so impressed by the JARDIN DES PLANTES, MONTPELLIER that he decided to make a career in gardening. He came to work at VERSAILLES in 1661 and was appointed *jardinier du roi* (king's gardener) in 1665, where he was in particular responsible for the *potager du roi* (king's kitchen garden). From 1670 until his death he was *directeur des jardins potagers royaux* (director of the royal kitchen gardens) and became *jardinier en chef* (head gardener) in 1675. He also worked for the Prince de Condé at CHANTILLY and Nicolas Fouquet at VAUX-LE-VICOMTE. His *Instructions pour les jardins fruitiers et potagers* (1690) was published in England under the title *The Compleat Gard'ner* (1693). Ostensibly translated by John EVELYN the work was almost certainly done by George LONDON. La Quintinie's book showed his deep knowledge of every aspect of kitchen gardening—and also his wisdom. He wrote, 'Il est donc vrai que dans le jardinage il y a des plaisirs, et des chagrins; il n'est pas moins vrai que les plaisirs sont pour les jardiniers intelligents et actifs, et que les chagrins arrive immanquablement à ceux qui sont paresseux ou mal habiles' ('It is therefore true that in gardening there are pleasures and disappointments; it is no less true that the pleasures come to gardeners who are intelligent and hard-working, and the disappointments to those who are lazy and clumsy').   PT

DOMINIQUE GARRIGUES, *Jardins et jardiniers de Versailles au grand siècle* (2001).

Qu Jiang,

near Xi'an, Shaanxi province, China, named after the river Qu which ran through it, covered an area of some 182 hectares/450 acres in a scenic site south-east of Chang'an in the Tang dynasty (*c*.5 km/3 miles south of what is now the city of Xi'an). Earlier, Emperor Wendi (581–600) of the Sui dynasty, delighted by the lotus which completely filled the river there, had frequented this place and called it the Lotus Garden. Later, during the Kaiyuan years (713–42) of the Tang dynasty, the river was dredged and the banks embellished with many buildings such as the Purple Cloud Tower and Coloured Cloud Pavilion. Three times a year on the festivals of Middle Harmony (first of the second lunar month), Double Three (third of the third month), and Double Nine (ninth of the ninth month), the emperors held imperial court banquets there. Then the inhabitants of Chang'an came out in crowds to temporary bazaars set up under coloured tents, silk shades, and screens, while gaily embellished boats floated on the river. The great Tang Emperor Xuanzong and his favourite concubine Yang Guifei (meaning Precious Concubine) often made excursions to this garden.   D-HL/MK

R

Raglan Castle ✿

Raglan, Gwent, Wales, was built in the 15th century and passed by marriage to the Somerset family (later earls of Worcester and dukes of Beaufort). The 3rd Earl inherited the estate in 1549 and made a new garden with terraces on two sides of the castle and a formal pool. It was described in verse in Thomas Churchyard's *The Worthines of Wales* (1587): 'The curious knots, wrought all with edged toole, | The stately Tower, that looks ore Pond and Poole: | the fountain trim, that runs both day and night | Doth yield in show a rare and noble sight.' Later in the 16th century the 4th Earl built a walk about the moat decorated with niches containing sculptures of Roman emperors and laid out a water PARTERRE at the head of the pool. Today the castle is a ruin but the niches and moat walk are still visible as are the earthworks of the parterre—the poignant remains of a great Welsh garden of the Renaissance.   PT

Ram Bagh ✿

Agra, India. The 1st Mughal Emperor BĀBUR's memoirs describe in detail the first garden he laid out by the river at Agra: the transformation of a flat site into a garden of great beauty. Various alternatives have been suggested as to its location, but the probability is that the site was that of the Ram Bagh, lying on a curve of the river Jumna. This, although much changed, is almost certainly the oldest surviving Mughal garden, and the details of design are in their simplest forms. A large well, an aqueduct, and water channels were first built, while the layout of the garden was the classic Mughal one of geometrical walks and terraces, which here are raised some 3 m/10 ft above the ground so as to bring them level with the blossom of the surrounding fruit trees; narrow irrigation channels run down the centre of the walks to water the trees planted at intervals. At the corners are *chabutras*, square stone daises, on which to rest and enjoy the view. Some fine pavilions overlooked the river, while provision was also made for dwelling houses and hot baths. The planting would originally have been one of fruit and flowers, but the site was later overgrown with forest trees. Also known as the Garden of Rest, it was probably here that Bābur was buried, before being taken to his final resting place at Kabul.   SMH

Rambouillet, Château de ✿

Rambouillet, Yvelines, France. The chateau goes back at least to the 14th century; damaged in the Hundred Years War it was restored in the mid 15th century and there were later changes. In 1699 the estate was bought by Fleuriau d'Armenonville, a courtier and financier, who laid out a garden of canals and pools which partly survives. This has traditionally been attributed to LE NÔTRE but there is no evidence and, given that Le Nôtre died in 1700, it is extremely unlikely. Between 1779 and 1780 a JARDIN ANGLAIS was laid out for the Duc de Penthièvre who had built various FABRIQUES of which the Chaumière is the most remarkable survival. The exterior is unexciting but the interior, of two rooms, is ravishingly beautiful. The first is a hall wonderfully decorated with shellwork disposed in niches, pilasters, vaulting, and a frieze. The second, the *garderobe*, is a panelled room exquisitely painted with swags, garlands, and ribbons with birds, butterflies, flowers, and fruit. In 1783 Louis XVI bought the estate and in 1789 had built for Marie-Antoinette the Laiterie de la Reine (Queen's DAIRY) to the designs of Jacques-Jean Thévenin, one of the finest and most remarkable garden buildings to survive from 18th-century France. The austerely classical exterior scarcely prepares the visitor for the splendour of the interior. The dairy proper is a great domed room with an inlaid marble floor and shelves bearing Sèvres porcelain vessels for milk, cream, and cheese. A second, vaulted, room has a pool and grotto with a statue of a nymph and the goat Almatheia. The influence of Hubert ROBERT has been suggested in connection with the Laiterie and he too may have designed the garden of rare trees and Roman sarcophagi that originally surrounded it.   PT

Rastrelli, Bartolomeo Francesco

(1700–71), Russian architect of Italian descent, born in Paris, the son of the Tuscan sculptor Bartolomeo Carlo Rastrelli. In 1716 Rastrelli moved to St Petersburg, where he worked as his father's assistant and, after his father's death in 1746, independently on a long series of palaces (and their gardens). His most important gardens are Letny Sad and PETERHOF. Letny Sad ('Summer Garden', 1704–12), in St Petersburg, was a Russian version of Versailles; the gardens have since been overlaid by a landscaped park. Peterhof, which was known from 1944 to 1994 as Petrodvorets, is a palace and garden 29 km/17 miles from St Petersburg. Rastrelli also contributed the grotto and the hermitage to the Yekaterinsky Palace (1749–56) at TSARSKOESELO ('the czars's village', now Pushkin) and, during a period in the early 1730s in Moscow, designed the gardens of the vast Summer Palace known as the Annenhof (destroyed 1746).   GC

Raxa ✿

near Palma, Mallorca, Spain, is a Mallorcan *son* (see ALFABIA) whose origins date from the Muslim occupation of the island which ended in 1229. The estate passed to the Despuig family of whom Cardinal Antonio Despuig y Dameto, on his return from a long sojourn in Rome, gave the garden its present form. On the axis of the north façade of the house a series of seven terraces descends the steeply sloping ground which Despuig linked with a grand staircase. Some of the antiquities he had collected in Italy were used to decorated the walls of the staircase—an EXEDRA with columns, fountain, and a figure of Apollo stands at its head. Water runs down each side in ducts, gushing out of masks, and paths lead to water CISTERNS one of which is overlooked by a MIRADOR facing over the water with views of the countryside beyond. Despuig had connections with the ROYAL BOTANIC GARDEN in Madrid from which he had plants but nothing is known of what species he introduced. Early photographs show great walls of Italian cypresses flanking the staircase but in more recent times there have been mixed plantings. The lower garden on the far side of the house is overlooked by a LOGGIA.
   PT

Rayol, Le Domaine du ✿

Le Rayol-Canadel, Var, France, the estate of a businessman, Alfred Courmes, who came here in retirement in 1910 and built a house to take advantage of a magnificent Mediterranean site. It looks down over densely wooded slopes which descend to a rocky bay. The site,

threatened with development, was acquired in 1989 by the Conservatoire du Littoral, which commissioned Gilles CLÉMENT to redesign the garden. It was decided to concentrate on plants from climates all over the world which are similar to that of the Mediterranean. Planting was as naturalistic as possible and disposed regionally—Australia, California, Canary Islands, and so forth. For the most part the plants are suitable for the climate here but there are exceptions—tree ferns (*Dicksonia antarctica*) need far more moisture than would be natural here and are artificially irrigated. However, here is a beguiling landscape covering an area of 20 hectares/50 acres with many fine plants grown in a marvellous setting. Some, such as a superb old *Eucalyptus globulus*, date back to the times of the Courmes family but most of the planting is relatively youthful. Here are many species of acacia, casuarina, eucalyptus, the coral tree (*Erythrina crista-galli*), dragon tree (*Dracaena draco*), and much else against a background of old pines (*Pinus halepensis* and *P. pinea*), cork oaks (*Quercus suber*), and strawberry trees (*Arbutus unedo*). The flora and fauna of the bay itself are also conserved and may be studied in organized snorkelling expeditions.
PT

Reale, Palazzo (Caserta) ✿

La Reggia, Naples, Campania, Italy. King Charles III, ruler of the kingdom of the Two Sicilies, in 1751 commissioned Luigi Vanvitelli (1700–73) to build a new town, a monumental palace, and gardens planned to rival VERSAILLES in splendour. Charles, the first Bourbon King, had succeeded to the throne in 1734, and determined to make Naples his new capital with a palace at Caserta in the hunting woods to the north. Vanvitelli's designs published as *Dichiarazione dei disegni del real Palazzo di Caserta* (1756) included parterres lying in front of the palace and a vast garden, divided into compartments placed around a series of central canals decorated with elaborate fountains. It was to stretch 3 km/2 miles north terminating with a 78-m/200-ft cascade and basin of Diana and Actaeon, with water tumbling over blocks of massive stones. The ambitious plans including a pool on a circular island, an orchard, and gazebos remained uncompleted at the architect's death in 1773, although the aqueduct, bringing water a distance of 48 km/ 30 miles, begun in 1753, was finished in 1762. Although early abandoned the original plans contained an avenue flanked by canals which was to continue to Naples south of the palace on the route of the ancient Appian Way. Charles had left for Spain in 1759 leaving the palace and garden to his 8-year-old son Ferdinand. Vanvitelli's son Carlo continued with the

project, excavating the canal and preparing embankments for the Fountain of Juno. Allegorical statues, triumphal arches, water cascades, and beds in *broderie* (see PARTERRE) patterns of flowers and pebbles, to be contained within woodland and regimented hornbeam hedges, had been too ambitious. Water was scarce and had to be brought 51 km/31 miles by aqueduct from Mount Taburno. The ENGLISH GARDEN adjoining the baroque park to the east was laid out for Queen Maria Carolina, wife of Ferdinand IV, Charles's son, and sister of Marie-Antoinette, during the late 1780s. The English ambassador to the Bourbon court, Sir William Hamilton, sought advice from Sir Joseph BANKS at KEW. John André Graefer was sent out from England to collaborate with Carlo Vanvitelli. Planned as more than a PLEASURE GARDEN, it contained experimental fruit trees and crops grown to encourage the development of agriculture in the region. By 1793 the garden was well established with open glades, meadows, and a dark cave—the Bagno di Venere—with a marble statue of Venus. It was visited by Sir William Hamilton, his wife Emma, and Lord Nelson. Paintings of the garden done in gouache by the contemporary German artist Jakob Philipp Hackert (1737–1807), many of which are in the palace, portray its romantic character. Graefer went on to lay out the gardens of Castello di Maniace in Sicily for Lord Nelson, although he was finally murdered by bandits at Caserta after his return in 1802. Today many rare magnolias, camphor trees, palms, and eucalyptus with tender nolinas and yuccas still survive.   PHo

Reale, Villa ✿

(Marlia), Lucca, Tuscany, Italy. The Villa Marlia is one of the most important and beautiful parks in Italy, with its baroque garden laid out in c.1651 by the Orsetti family and its landscape parkland dating to the early 19th century and the influence of Napoleon's sister Elisa Baciocchi, Princess of Lucca. Nestling at the base of the Pizzorne Hills just north of Lucca, the 17th-century gardens of the villa (originally called Villa Marilla) include high hedges of bay, ilex, and cypress hiding an elaborate balustraded pool lined with lemons in pots and presided over by statues of the rivers Arno and Serchio, under a NYMPHAEUM overlooked by a statue of *Leda and the Swan*. There is a green THEATRE of box and yew, with terracotta statues of Colombina, Pantalone, and Balanzone paying homage to the *commedia dell'arte*. In a hemisphere behind the main façade of the villa a water theatre is backed by dark hedges. Elisa Baciocchi, whilst enjoying performances by Paganini in the theatre, was determined to turn the Orsetti gardens into an English-style park,

employing the French naturalist designer Jean-Marie Morel (author of *Théorie des jardins*, 1776) who worked for the Empress Joséphine at MALMAISON. Although she extended the grounds by acquiring the 16th-century property of Vescovato belonging to the bishops of Lucca and buying up neighbours' property she was fortunately prevented from destroying the main baroque features by the arrival of British troops in 1814. The 16th-century Villa del Vescovi, decorated with grotesques with terracotta and pebble flooring, was restored at the end of the 19th century. The Princess was responsible for planting many exotic trees and camellias, which, in their maturity, grace the park today. Following the unification of Italy, Marlia became the property of Prince Charles, brother of the last King of the Two Sicilies, who lived there happily with his commoner English wife Penelope Smith. After the First World War Count Pecci-Blunt employed the French architect Jacques Gréber (1882–1962) to restore the park, woods, and lake, besides building a small-scale Islamic water garden.   PHo   ▶

Red Fort

Delhi, India, was a part of SHĀH JAHĀN's new city at Delhi, Shahjahanabad, but by no means all. A canal to provide water was built by 'Ali Mardān Khān along the main street, the Chandni Chauk, while outside the Fort lay richly planted gardens.

The Fort itself was surrounded on three sides by a moat, filled with fish, and within there lay a complex of houses, palaces, and gardens, all irrigated by running water. The principal buildings were sited overlooking the river, below which stretched a long level space that provided for all kinds of spectacle to be watched from above.

Two gardens were combined in one grand design: the Hayat Baksh, or Life-giving Garden, and the Mahtab Bagh, or Moonlight Garden. These were planted in contrasting colours: the Hayat Baksh glowing in red and purple, the Moonlight Garden in pale colours only. The Mahtab Bagh is lost, but the Hayat Baksh remains in part. It was designed as a water garden, with at its centre a great tank for bathing in which is set a red sandstone pavilion, the Zafar Mahal, added by Bahadur Shah in the 19th century. Details everywhere were lavish: delicate pavilions, illuminated waterfalls, gold and silver vases of flowers, and many hundreds of fountains. The palaces along the river front remain, carefully restored, together with a mosque, the Moti Masjid, added by AURANGZĪB. Much, however, has been lost: the entrance canal and moat have been filled in, the water everywhere is lacking, the flower gardens have been replaced by trees and grass, and much of the old inner city by official buildings.

Of all the Mughal gardens, the Red Fort would perhaps gain the most by some restoration of the water. SMH

Renaissance gardens.

The Renaissance garden was Italian in origin. It had two distinct phases, the first running through the Quattrocento and whose defining work was the great architect Leon Battista ALBERTI's *De Re Aedificatoria* (1451), the second signalled by the work of another major architect, Donato BRAMANTE, in his orchestration of the papal Villa Belvedere in 1503–4 (see VATICAN GARDENS). The garden in its Renaissance phase was over by *c.*1540 when one which can be categorized as mannerist was under way. The principles of the Renaissance garden revolution, however, were to take a century and more to cross Europe and reach its outer fringes like England and Scandinavia.

The Renaissance garden was a typical product of the principles of humanism, the earliest phases of which stressed the role of reason and order in relation to man in the workings of both the mind and of society. Central to that was the microcosm–macrocosm principle, of man as a direct reflection of a universe created by God according to mathematical principles. All Renaissance art expresses this aspiration, to recast the physical world in order to place man at harmony with his Maker. That was achieved first by subjecting the space around man to his optical perception. It was the Florentine architect Filippo Brunelleschi who invented linear perspective, placing man at the centre of a new visual perception by siting buildings according to the new optics. The medieval approach to the orchestration of space was variable, for instance in the incorporation of many viewpoints simultaneously. As a result medieval town planning was a jumble. Under the aegis of Brunelleschi that changed, and buildings together with town and villa planning worked from the principle of monocular perspective, that converging lines meant distance, that items became smaller as

Renaissance gardens: a fountain at Gaillon engraved (1576) by Jacques Androuet Du Cerceau.

they became closer to the vanishing point. This was an optical revolution teaching people to look in terms of vista, recession, and avenue. In this new scheme of things man no longer saw himself as just part of God's creation on which God looks down, but as himself the image of God reducing the physical world around him by his own perception through the application of geometry, itself a reflection of the structure of the cosmos. The first person to apply this to gardens was Alberti in his *De Re Aedificatoria* in his revival of the antique villa garden. None survived except in ruins, like HADRIAN'S VILLA which had to be recreated in the main from the letters of PLINY THE YOUNGER along with what could be gleaned from the 1st-century Roman architectural writer Vitruvius. Collectively these record a delight in views, the siting of the villa on a southern slope, the existence of topiary, fountains, pattern planting, naturalistic areas, grottoes, and seats and places for dining. Above all they record that the garden, like the house, was arranged as a series of geometrical shapes, circles, squares, and rectangles using pergolas, colonnades, and porticoes, all linking house and garden as a single unit. To the design revolution that such principles embodied must be added a changed social use. That we owe to Francis Petrarch (1304-74), who had also studied antique sources in which he discovered that the garden in the country was cast as a setting for cultural activity, philosophical and religious contemplation, as well as for pleasure. Petrarch himself had two gardens, one dedicated to Apollo and the Muses, and hence the arts, the other to Bacchus, god of wine, and therefore to pleasure.

The impact of all this on actual garden making was gradual, in the main reflected in reordering elements of the medieval garden in terms of the new imperatives. Michelozzo (1396-1472), for instance, reordered the garden at the Medici Villa Carreggi in the 1450s, by introducing a pergola to define separate gardens and thus link them to the house. The best extant garden which encapsulates these new impulses is that of the humanist Pope Aeneas Sylvius Piccolomini at Pienza, laid out in the 1480s. There palazzo and garden are locked into one geometric space, a rectangle quartered incorporating cross-axes and a central axis culminating in a vista to landscape (see PICCOLOMINI, PALAZZO).

The aspirations of the new gardening are summed up in one book, Francesco Colonna's HYPNEROTOMACHIA POLIPHILI (1499), later translated into French (1546) and English (1592). This includes a long description of a fantastic garden in which the old medieval elements are given a classical overlay. The illustrations,

like those for patterned flower beds, the earliest knots, exotic topiary, and that for a circular arcade, were to be hugely influential. Six years after the publication of that book, in 1502-4 the architect Donato Bramante ushered in a new phase by looking back not only to Pliny but to descriptions of the Roman Emperor Nero's *Domus Aurea* when responding to Pope Julius II's demand that the existing papal Villa Belvedere be linked to the Vatican. Bramante set out to recreate a Roman imperial villa garden by reshaping the terrain, excavating terraces and flights of steps facilitating a gradual descent from the villa to a vast courtyard for fêtes. Into that scheme he incorporated the papal collection of classical antiquities. Previously such items had adorned humanist gardens but now, for the first time, they were integrated into an architectural framework, statues being set into niches and ancient river gods deployed as sources for water.

The impact of these innovations can be followed in the plans for Pope Clement VII's Villa MADAMA (1516), in the Villa GIULIA (1553), and at the Palazzo FARNESE, Caprarola (1556). But, by 1540, the true Renaissance phase was over, although from it stem the fundamentals which still pertain to the formal style. These established the garden as the province of the architect, the subjection of the terrain to relandscaping in terms of humanist architectural principles, the central role of perspective in uniting house and garden in terms of axes, cross-axes, and vistas, the deployment of statuary, topiary, and trained elements like hedges, the importance of views and vistas, the concept that the garden was the setting for learned debate, dining, and festival.

To all of this we must add the mannerist phase, which assimilated all that its predecessors had achieved but superimposed onto such elements complex allegorical and symbolic programmes, in the main to the glorification of the owner, reflecting vividly the late 16th-century refeudalization of Italian society in a new age of the princes. The Medici led the way in a great series of gardens beginning with the Villa MEDICI, Castello (1537) and culminating in PRATOLINO (c.1569), both dynastic apotheoses. The other great gardens of this phase were the Villa LANTE (1573), the Villa Orsini, BOMARZO (1532-8), and the Villa d'ESTE, Tivoli (1560). During the mannerist phase the garden became far more complex and esoteric, responding fully to late Renaissance concerns with hieroglyphics and hermeticism, the purveyance of hidden mysteries by means of image and word. It also developed to the full its role as an arena for developments in the sciences, its deployment of water, for instance, in rills, fountains, jets, cascades, and the

animation of automata—a response to the Renaissance rediscovery of the mechanics of the 3rd-century BC School of Alexandria. The mannerist garden thus belongs firmly to an era when science and magic have not as yet parted company. The spread of all of this northwards was a piecemeal process, the adoption at first of certain features like a classical fountain as at GAILLON (1502-9). But it would be true to say that the most influential gardens by far were those of the mannerist phase whose aims coincided with those of a Europe moving towards its absolutist phase. Two great gardening families stand out as purveyors northwards of the new ideals, the de CAUS, who worked in France, the Low Countries, England, and Germany, and the MOLLET family, who worked in France, England, the Netherlands, and Denmark.

By far the most comprehensive introduction to the subject is Claudia Lazzaro, *The Italian Renaissance Garden* (1990). In addition see Terry Comito, *The Idea of the Garden in the Renaissance* (1979) and David R. Coffin, *The Villa in the Life of Renaissance Rome* (1979) and his *Gardens and Gardening in Papal Rome* (1991). Georgina Masson's *Italian Gardens* (1961), although now very dated, is still worth reading as a pioneer work.   RS

Renishaw Hall ✹

Renishaw, Sheffield, Derbyshire, England. The English love affair with Italy has taken many forms but nowhere with such memorable effect as in this Renaissance-style garden intrepidly laid out in industrial Derbyshire. The Sitwell family has lived in these parts since the 14th century. Sir George SITWELL, who inherited the estate in 1887, had made a scholarly study of Italian Renaissance gardens and, armed with this first-hand knowledge, laid out a new garden at Renishaw. On land that slopes gently away from the south façade of the house he designed a sequence of gentle terraces linked by stone steps centred on the axis of the house. Each terrace is enriched with yew topiary and hedges, and decorated with fine statuary and urns, most of which Sir George brought from Italy. In the centre of the final terrace is a large circular pool with a single, triumphant water jet. Cross-vistas lead into woodland on each side which is enlivened by ornaments and buildings like some shady Tuscan BOSCO. Sir George was not interested in flowers and believed that 'such flowers as might be permitted . . . should not call attention to themselves by hue or scent'. His successors have taken a different view and the yew hedges now form a fine background to outstanding mixed borders especially rich in shrub roses. Still owned by the Sitwell

family, Renishaw is one of the finest English gardens.   PT
SACHEVERELL SITWELL, OSBERT SITWELL, SIR GEORGE SITWELL, and RERESBY SITWELL, *Hortus Sitwellianus* (1984).

Rennsteiggarten ⊛

Oberhof, Germany, is a BOTANIC GARDEN of mountain flora laid out around Pfanntalskopf hill (at a height of 868 m/2,848 ft) in a former quarry between 1970 and 1975 by Professor Otto Schwarz in cooperation with the Institute for Special Botany of Friedrich Schiller University at Jena. The original layout was extended with a collection of native bog plants in 1980, of protected native species from 1985, and with a plant display garden of Thuringian medicinal herbs. Set on the ridge of the Thuringian forest, mountain plants develop their typical growth and flowers due to the favourable climatic conditions of low annual average temperature, high annual precipitation, and snow cover of up to 150 days. Covering an area of more than 7 hectares/17 acres, Rennsteiggarten grows about 4,000 mountain plant species from Europe, Asia, North and South America, New Zealand, and the Arctic region. The plants have been established in different sites according to their ecological needs and geographic distribution. Rennsteiggarten serves research, educational, and public relations purposes as well as leisure and recreation.   USc

Repton, Humphry

(1752–1818), English landscape designer and author. Repton, after William KENT and Capability BROWN, was the greatest English landscape designer of the 18th century and had virtues that neither of his predecessors possessed. He was a thoroughly professional and astonishingly prolific designer who was also anxious to explain the nature of his craft in his writings. He formed the habit of producing 'Red Books' (they were usually bound in red leather) which contained proposals for his clients' landscapes in the form of text and his own watercolour paintings ('better to elucidate my opinion than mere words'), often equipped with flaps of paper so that 'before' and 'after' views could be displayed. He produced over 400 Red Books of which fewer than 200 survive, giving a vivid idea of the way he went about his work. He was 36 when he took up garden designing, producing thereafter an average of well over one Red Book every month of his life. By no means all his proposals were accepted, and many were for relatively small areas, but the work of producing his submissions was enormous and time consuming.

For Repton the position of the house, its immediate surroundings, and distant prospects were paramount. The house should always appear as an integral part of its setting—its style of architecture must be appropriate to the character of the landscape, and architectural styles should never be mixed. The approach to the house was vital—the drive should curve smoothly away from the road, not turn at an abrupt right angle, which suggested that it was continuing 'to some object of greater importance'. Repton believed that the drive leading to the house should be full of incidents. At Bulstrode (Buckinghamshire), for example, the proposed new drive looped and swerved about the land taking in every feature of interest. A gentle shaping of the land was permitted but not radical transformations involving great earth moving. Above all he believed in a harmony of practicalities and aesthetic effect—'propriety and convenience are no less objects of good taste, than picturesque effect'. He was anxious to strike 'The happy medium between the wilderness of nature and the stiffness of art; in the same manner as the English constitution is the happy medium between the liberty of savages and the restraints of a despotic government'. He was also anxious that a client's landscape should reflect his social status and wealth. He would often propose that the entrance drive should take an indirect route to make the park appear larger. Later in his career he laid out parterres influenced by historic period styles and anticipated the parterre craze of the high Victorian era (an elaborate parterre is shown in the 1814 Red Book for Beaudesert, Staffordshire). His clients were often very different from those of Capability Brown, sometimes being rich industrialists. One of these, in 1810, was a Yorkshire mill owner, Benjamin Gott, whose house, Armley House near Leeds, had a magnificent view of the cloth mill. One of the first industrial buildings to be illuminated by gaslights it delighted Repton who made it the chief focus of his landscape—'A beautiful and interesting object it is.' Surviving gardens where his work may be seen include: ANTONY HOUSE, Attingham Park (Shropshire), BLAISE CASTLE, Bloomsbury Square (London), Cobham Hall (Kent), ENDSLEIGH HOUSE, Kenwood (London), SHERINGHAM HALL, Ston Easton (Somerset), Tatton Park (Cheshire), and WOBURN ABBEY. Another source of information about his work is the series of engravings produced from his watercolours for smaller commissions printed between 1790 and 1809 in the almanac called *Peacock's Polite Repository*. Repton's published writings include: *Sketches and Hints on Landscape Gardening* (1795), *Observations on the Theory and Practice of Landscape Gardening* (1803), *An Enquiry into the Changes of Taste in Landscape Gardening* (1806), *Fragments on the Theory and Practice of Landscape Gardening* (1816). After his death J. C. LOUDON organized the publication of Repton's complete works under the title *The Landscape Gardening and Landscape Architecture of the Late Humphry Repton* (1840).   PT
STEPHEN DANIELS, *Humphry Repton* (1999).

restoration of gardens.

See CONSERVATION OF GARDENS.

Retiro, El ⊛

Churriana, near Málaga, Andalusia, Spain. Brother Alonso de Santo Tomás, Bishop of Málaga, retired in 1692 to this old estate overlooking the valley of the river Guadalhorce. In the 18th century the estate belonged to the Conde de Villalcázar de Sirga who greatly added to the gardens, probably with the help of the architect José Martín de Aldehuela who, late in the century, worked on the house. The gardens fall into two parts—an upper garden following the escarpment and, at right angles to it, the water garden. In the upper garden, close to the house, is an arched entrance decorated with rocaille work leading to a covered walk. A very large fountain pool of baroque character stands at the centre of a four-part arrangement of beds. Intertwined sirens supported by dolphins and putti disport themselves on the edge of the basin. The surrounding beds are enclosed in box and planted with date palms and *Magnolia grandiflora* underplanted with orange clivias. A terraced walk gives views over the valley and further along the escarpment is the water garden, the great set piece of El Retiro. A giant staircase flanked by stepped water channels descends the slope. Two river gods flank a fountain, water gushes from their containers, and in the pool below them a piping figure sits on an island of rustic rockwork. Steps lead down on each side and everywhere there is rocaille work, statuary, and topiary shapes of clipped cypress. On each side are rows of tall nettle trees (*Celtis australis*). Above all this, linked by a long walk, are two pools to supply water for the cascades. The garden designer Russell PAGE came here before 1962 and sensed the garden must have Islamic origins. Exploring the less frequented parts he came across 'an octagonal fountain of the fourteenth century falling into pieces in a cabbage patch and a long canal-like reservoir which still feeds the later formal garden' (*Education of a Gardener*, 1962). In recent years the garden has been undergoing restoration. It is to be hoped that the secretive 'lost garden' atmosphere that this remarkable garden possessed in earlier times will not be restored into oblivion.   PT

Retours, Jardin des ⊛

Rochefort, Charente Maritime, France, a

garden designed by Bernard LASSUS as part of the restoration of the Corderie Royale, Louis XIV's great works for making ropes and sails for the French navy. Completed in 1670 the vast building is 374 m/1,227 ft long and built of fine golden stone. Running along the banks of the river Charente the 'garden of returns' seeks to evoke the world of sailors returning from their journeys laden with discoveries from the New World. A maze commemorates great naval battles and a path along the river passes plantings of native species—alder, ash, hazels, reeds, and willows. Nearby is the Conservatoire National du Bégonia with a collection of 1,300 species and cultivars of begonia. The genus was named after Michel Bégon, the 17th-century director of the Rochefort Arsenal who was also a botanist. His name was given to the genus by the priest plant collector Charles Plumier who brought begonias back from the Americas in the 17th century.   PT

Rheinsberg ⊕

Brandenburg, Potsdam, Germany. In 1734 the future Friedrich II of Prussia took over the territory of Rheinsberg and from 1734 to 1739 had the Schloss rebuilt by Kemmeter and Knobelsdorff; Knobelsdorff also drew up the plans for the 16-hectare/40-acre garden. The classical PARTERRE with two large flower baskets on the island on which the Schloss stands was restored in 1996. A short main axis with a long transverse axis leads from the wing of the Schloss to make the best use of the terrain. Work stopped in 1740, and in 1744 the property passed to Prince Heinrich (1726–1802), brother of Friedrich II of Prussia, who subsequently continued work on the park until his death by transforming parts of the garden in an early landscape style and adding such large areas as the Boberow-Kabeln, the Boberow Parl, and the Remus-island. Along the short main axis stretching from the south wing of the Schloss lies an orange parterre with the Sphinx Steps (by Glume) and at the end a columned portal with Flora and Pomona, to the east of which are a PYRAMID (the burial place of Prince Heinrich) and a hedge theatre—a Chinese pavilion (1765) no longer survives.

Along the long transverse axis, which extends between a gentle range of hills and the Grienerick Lake, lies an oval rond-point (circular space from which paths radiate) with the Salon, the central building of a former orangery, and woodlike BOSQUETS, originally enclosed by hedges. The ALLÉE terminates in the Egeria GROTTO. A second grotto of rustic stonework lies on the bank of the lake. Three wide terraces with an OBELISK (1791) lie on the banks of the lake opposite the Schloss. Rheinsberg is a rare example of a garden of transition in which elements of a rococo garden are in harmony with an early landscape garden.
HGÜ/MS

rhododendrons

were prized in Chinese gardens of the Tang dynasty (581–907) as relics of the native flora already being lost to deforestation and agriculture in the lowland landscape. Today, of some 1,025 known species of the genus, half are Chinese natives, and these have been collected in the past 150 years from the remote mountains of Sichuan and Yunnan.The genus was named by Linnaeus (*Species Plantarum*, 1753) from the Greek *rhodon* (rose) and *dendron* (tree): he knew the American rosebay or sweet mountain rose (*R. maximum*) and the Mediterranean *R. ponticum*, but he treated the alpine species, the alpenrose (*R. ferrugineum*) and *R. hirsutum* (introduced by John TRADESCANT THE ELDER), as a separate species, azaleas. Azaleas and rhododendrons were formally united taxonomically by George Don in 1834.

In the later part of the 18th century the American rhododendrons were sent to Britain by king's botanist John BARTRAM for customers of the Quaker merchant and gardener Peter COLLINSON. Seeds and young plants, the latter carefully packed in soil and damp moss, travelled well with Collinson's chosen sea captains, and rhododendrons were widely dispersed to British gardens as part of the fashion for American shrubs. Bartram's son William (1739–1823) was the first to report on the glories of the 'flame azaleas' (*R. calendulaceum*) in the mountains of Carolina (*Travels through the Carolinas, Georgia and Florida*, 1791, 1792) but American independence put a (temporary) stop to British collectors. President George Washington cultivated the Pinxterbloom (*R. periclymenoides*) which he brought in from the wild to his garden at MOUNT VERNON, and the famous 'azalea' gardens of the South (MIDDLETON PLACE, Magnolia Plantation (Charleston)) were started in this way.

The mauve *R. ponticum*, a Turkish native carried by Muslim gardeners to the Iberian peninsula, first flowered in London in 1760. It was soon popularized, and sold in large numbers by the LODDIGES nursery of Hackney. The first recorded hybrid was Turkish-American, *R. ponticum × periclymenoides*, and named 'Odoratum'; this was 'at Mr Thompson's Mile End Road (London) nursery at the turn of the 19th century' (Lionel de Rothschild, *The Rhododendron Story*, 1996). By that time the surgeon-botanists of the East India Company were collecting the Indian species. The common but magnificent Indian native, the blood-red *R. arboreum*, flowered at The Grange, Northington in Hampshire, in 1825 and the following year was hybridized with an American *R. catawbiense × ponticum*. The result was 'Altaclerense' (named for the place of its birth, Highclere Castle) which was propagated in thousands. The search for the rhododendron 'grail' of hardiness plus scent plus good colour was launched, and collectors were dispatched to east and west. Robert FORTUNE found the lilac-pink and scented 'cloud-brocade rhododendron' (*R. fortunei*) in Zhejiang province south of Shanghai and described many other species, but China was then closed to collectors because of the Taiping Rebellion (1850–64). Consequently J. D. HOOKER went to northern India and Sikkim in 1849–51, where he collected 43 of the magnificent Himalayan species which were successfully propagated and distributed from KEW. Hooker's Himalayan species and their hybrids inspired the creation of large woodland gardens especially on the peaty soils of southern England (Leonardslee, Exbury), in mist-drenched Cornish coves (CAERHAYS, Penjerrick, and TREBAH), and along the western shores of Britain (BODNANT, Muncaster Castle, BRODICK, and Lochinch) and at ROWALLANE and Kilmacurragh in Ireland. The owners formed themselves into the Rhododendron Society (founded 1916) and with the ROYAL BOTANIC GARDENS at Kew and EDINBURGH, they formulated knowledge of the culture of rhododendrons and financed the collecting expeditions of George FORREST and Frank Kingdon WARD. Forrest and Kingdon Ward found the rhododendron 'heartland' of the high valleys on the borders of Yunnan, Burma (Myanmar), and Tibet, and introduced many low-growing species suitable for smaller gardens. British, German, and Dutch nurseries developed a vast trade in species and garden hybrids, exporting to North America and Australasia during the first half of the 20th century, except for the war years. After 1945 rhododendrons reached a peak of popularity with the desire for low-maintenance gardens, and they became a worldwide favourite. The American Rhododendron Society encouraged hybridizing amongst its members, who favoured crosses between imported Waterer and Knap Hill hybrids and American native species: the resulting Dexter, Glenn Dale, and Lem hybrids have been most influential. Introductions of evergreen 'azaleas' from Japan and the collecting of the tropical and brightly coloured Vireyas, native to the islands of the South-East Asian archipelago (Malesia), have been the two notable innovations of the late 20th century. Vireyas are being developed for conservatory, patio, and small town gardens.

Enthusiastic rhododendron gardeners are now found in New Zealand, Australia, the

Pacific islands, the western and eastern coastal states of North America, as well as in Britain and Northern and Western Europe. Whilst there is an abundance of small and medium-sized hybrids to attract and challenge gardeners, there are also developments in the conservation of the world's species: in America the native species are playing an important role in the revival of the woodland garden. In Bhutan the habitats of 43 Himalayan species have been protected in National Parks, ranging from *R. arboreum* in low-level subtropical forest up to the dwarf shrubs of the alpine zone. The ROYAL BOTANIC GARDEN, EDINBURGH, and the Kunming (Yunnan) Institute of Botany are jointly re-establishing the Kunming Botanic Garden in China and the newly born Chinese Rhododendron Society celebrated its first show in 1987.   JBr

JANE BROWN, *Tales of the Rose Tree: Ravishing Rhododendrons and their Travels around the World* (2004).

Richelieu, Parc de ⊛

Richelieu, Indre-et-Loire, France, all that remains of one of the greatest French gardens ever made. This was the estate of Armand Jean Du Plessis, Duc de Richelieu (1585–1642), who became first minister to Louis XIII. At Richelieu he rebuilt the family chateau from 1631 to the designs of Jacques Le Mercier (1585–1654), who at the same time laid out a new town, designed as a regular grid of streets and axially linked to the garden of the chateau. PERELLE's engraving (before 1677) shows the entrance from the south, leading through courtyards, with parterres beyond, two of which are arranged in a semicircle with grottoes on each side. No trace of the chateau survives, but parts of outhouses, a pair of grottoes, and the grand west entrance remain. This last stands on the D749 (originally part of a PATTE D'OIE) south-east of the town—a pedimented archway is flanked by steeply roofed lodges with walls sweeping about in a semicircle. Alignments of paths in some places correspond to the garden's original layout. The estate now belongs to the University of Paris. Perfunctory planting of a municipal character fails to destroy the melancholy charm of the place. The town survives intact and its central Grande Rue leads, via a grand entrance archway, to an axial path west of the site of the chateau. Jean de La Fontaine, in his *Lettres à sa femme*, writing in 1633, called it 'the most beautiful village in the universe'.   PT

Rideau Hall Gardens ⊛

Ottawa, Ontario, Canada, were established in 1838 by Thomas MacKay (1792–1855), who bought 457 hectares/1,130 acres of land with views of the Ottawa river as his residence.

He converted over 32 hectares/80 acres into a garden based on the PICTURESQUE tradition of English gardening: captivating views, ponds (created), a sweeping driveway up to the house amidst parkland, as well as a Sugar Bush (a grove of maples) for rustic strolls. It was sold to the Canadian government in 1864 to become the official residence of the governor general. Architect F. P. Rubidge (1806–97) designed the new gardens based on Mackay's original 'zones' which are still in place today. It has become Canada's oldest historical picturesque garden. With a new steward every five years or so, it is a marvel that there has been such a continuous blending of formal gardens open to the public and a private home. Renovations began in 2001 resulting in stunning perennial beds, woodland borders near the Hall, a serious hosta bed, arboretum, and nuttery. The Lady Byng Rock Garden and Michener Rockery have been restored to new glory. The huge borders now feature a combination of trees, ornamental grasses, and a wide range of perennials. The focus of the garden renovations has been to use native plants (instead of mass tulips at the entrance there is a collections of trilliums), and to make the borders examples of what northern gardeners can do. All of these can be visited on specific days of the year.   MH

Rievaulx Terrace ⊛

Rievaulx, Helmsley, Yorkshire, England, was built in 1758 to take advantage of an exceptionally beautiful setting. Its builder was Thomas Duncombe of DUNCOMBE PARK, where he had already laid out a viewing TERRACE of similar kind. At Rievaulx he made a broad, curved grass walk with an ornamental building at each end, both probably designed by Sir Thomas Robinson (c.1702–1777)—a Tuscan TEMPLE and an Ionic temple. The latter, with a sumptuously decorated interior which may still be seen, now finely restored by the NATIONAL TRUST, was intended as a banqueting house. From the terrace are focused views, cut through woodland, revealing different aspects of the exquisite ruins of the Cistercian abbey below and its setting in the Rye valley. Few designed landscapes in Britain achieve so much with such simple means.   PT

Rigaud, Jacques

(c.1681–1754), French draughtsman and engraver. He was born at Versailles and seems to have lived in Provence until 1720, making topographical drawings and engravings. In 1730 he published *Recueil choisi des plus belles vues des palais, châteaux, et maisons royales de Paris et des environs*, which includes the Tuileries (see PARIS PARKS AND GARDENS), Luxembourg (see PARIS PARKS AND GARDENS), VERSAILLES,

MARLY, Meudon, SAINT-GERMAIN-EN-LAYE, FONTAINEBLEAU, Vincennes (see PARIS PARKS AND GARDENS), Choisy, Saint-Cloud, SCEAUX, Bellevue, La Muette, Madrid, CHANTILLY, Berny, Clagny, RAMBOUILLET, Chambord, Blois, ANET, Monceaux, and Saint-Maur. He visited England in c.1738–9 and made a series of drawings of STOWE and CHISWICK HOUSE.   KASW

Rikugien ⊛

Tokyo, Japan, now a public park, was originally built as the villa of Edo-period (1600–1868) lord Yanagisawa Yoshiyasu (1658–1714). Yoshiyasu was a close adviser to the 5th Tokugawa shogun (chief military lord) Tsunayoshi (1646–1709), and as such rose to be one of the most influential lords of his time. The scope of the garden, and the many specimen trees and stones in the garden that were received as gifts from provincial lords seeking favour, are reflective of his status.

The garden's history begins in 1695 when Tsunayoshi gave Yoshiyasu a large parcel of land on the outskirts of Edo (present-day Tokyo). Yoshiyasu worked for seven years building a garden that was based on the aesthetics and images found in traditional Japanese and Chinese poetry. The name Rikugien (which was originally pronounced Mukusaen) refers to the six forms of poetry described in the 10th-century Japanese poetry anthology *Kokinwakashū* and, before that, in the Chinese *Book of Odes* (*Shijing*, Spring and Autumn period, 770–476 BC). Although Rikugien never literally reflected the six poetic forms in its design, 88 images from specific poems of that oeuvre were distilled and recreated in the garden, each identified by a carved stone marker. Some of those 88 references are known and can still be seen in the garden today. Yoshiyasu's descendants did not use the garden actively and it fell into disrepair, was purchased by Iwasaki Yatarō (the founder of the Mitsubishi company) in 1888, and was donated to Tokyo city by Yatarō's son in 1938.   MPK

rill,

a narrow stream of flowing (or, occasionally, still) water. In Islamic gardens, such as those still seen in southern Spain, the rill was a common feature. An outstanding example is seen in the Patio de los Leones in the ALHAMBRA where four straight rills join a central fountain pool to the interiors of the rooms that overlook the patio. Islamic gardeners also used patterns of narrow rills to irrigate fruit and vegetable gardens. In Córdoba in the Patio de los NARANJOS (orange tree patio) these may still be seen linking small circular enclosures where the trees are planted. One of the most evocative rills is at ROUSHAM HOUSE, where a serpentine woodland rill neatly edged with stone winds enticingly among trees, glinting in the shade, to feed a pool below a grotto. The rill is found in many ARTS AND CRAFTS gardens. An exceptionally ingenious example designed by Edwin LUTYENS is found at HESTERCOMBE. On terrace walks on either side of the sunken garden a rill, breaking out from time to time into circular beds in which to plant water irises, links two pools. Here the rills are ornamental, provide an opportunity for planting, link features within the garden, and are themselves a strong part of its structure.   PT

Rio de Janeiro, Botanical Gardens of ✿

Rio de Janeiro state, Brazil. This refuge was created in 1808 by Prince Dom João (the future King D. João VI of Portugal), at the time of the Portuguese court's flight to Brazil upon Portugal's invasion by Napoleon. Based on the precepts of physiocracy, the first work to be carried out in the Botanical Gardens was focused on the identification and acclimatization of exotics, especially those from the East Indies. Knowledgeable men such as Manuel Arruda da Câmara (c.1752–c.1811) favoured the idea of establishing various botanical gardens, emphasizing their economic importance to agriculture in a country of such vast dimensions as Brazil. Despite this original motivation, the Botanical Gardens throughout the 19th century did not benefit from any scientific development that lived up to these founding principles, being in general disdained by naturalists but appreciated by visitors as a place of recreation. The Botanical Gardens function today as an institute for research and for public pleasure, featuring both recreational and cultural amenities in an area of 137 hectares/330 acres. Their exuberant vegetation, bringing together a collection of around 7,200 species, constitutes one of the most highly appreciated tourist attractions of Rio de Janeiro.   HS

Rippon Lea ✿

Victoria, Australia, survives almost intact as a superb example of a late 19th-century landscape around a suburban mansion. The 11-hectare/27-acre estate, built and developed between 1868 and 1903, was the creation of leading politician and businessman Sir Frederick Sargood. The garden, although reduced from its original size, still retains many important elements of the Sargood era, including the lake, mound and grotto, fernery, conservatory, serpentine carriageway, and sweeping lawns. The entrance drive, overhung with huge Moreton Bay figs (*Ficus macrophylla*), winds through shrubbery,

offering occasional glimpses of lawns, house, and tower and finally the entrance front. From the west front of the house, an expanse of lawn stretches to the thick perimeter planting of flowering shrubs, towering conifers, and spreading deciduous trees. On the far side of the garden is a large ornamental lake. The curving edges are fringed with willows and poplars; cast-iron bridges disguised as rustic woodwork link up the garden walk. Photographic records show a striking similarity between Rippon Lea's lake and bridge and Sargood's father's estate in Surrey. Rippon Lea's vast iron-framed fernery has been magnificently restored and includes more than 230 species of fern, including tree ferns, *Dicksonia antarctica*, some 10 m/35 ft high. Other recent restorations include the orchard replanted with an extensive collection of heritage cultivars and the enchanting archery house, just one of the outstanding collection of rustic garden buildings.   CMR

Ritsurin Park ✿

Takamatsu city, Kagawa prefecture, Japan, has been a public park since 1875 but originated as the private garden of Satō Dōeki around the year 1600. Dōeki, who was a retainer to the Ikoma family, then lords of Sanuki province (present-day Kagawa prefecture), built his residence by the eastern branch of the Kōtō River. Around 1630, in response to the great drought of 1624, Nishijima Hachibe, a retainer of the Tōdō family of Ise, was called to oversee riverwork in Sanuki part of which created a dry river bed near Dōeki's garden. The Ikoma family built their own villa, Ritsurinsō, on that new land and eventually incorporated Dōeki's gardens as part of their villa.

In 1642 the Ikoma family was exiled, and control over Sanuki province was assigned to the Matsudaira family. The first lord, Matsudaira Yorishige (1622–95), was a well-placed individual, being grandson to the reigning shogun (chief military lord) and son of Tokugawa Yorifusa (1603–61), lord of Mito province and builder of KOISHIKAWA KŌRAKUEN. Yorishige's descendants continued work on the gardens of Ritsurinsō for the next 100 years, in particular the fifth lord Yoriyasu, during whose reign many images of famous Chinese landscapes were designated throughout the garden. Also at that time, a herb garden was established that became the impetus for a local industry in medicinal plant remedies.

The name Ritsurin, Chestnut Grove, referred to the large numbers of chestnut trees which were planted on the estate to act as a food reserve in times of famine. Lord Yoritane cut all but three of those trees down in 1850 because they interfered with his duck hunting. Like all large-scale gardens of provincial lords in

the Edo period (1600–1868), the central feature is a large pond, surrounded by artificial hills, subsidiary ponds, arbours, and tea houses. The nearby low mountain, Shiunzan, is incorporated as part of the garden's scenery.
                                                    MPK

Rizzardi, Villa ✿

Negrar, Veneto, Italy. The garden of Villa Rizzardi on the shores of Lake Garda is distinguished by the famous green THEATRE, one of the best preserved in Italy, which was designed by Luigi Trezza (1752–1823) in 1796 with tiers of seats cut out in boxwood. Trezza had completed the rest of the garden for Conte Antonio Rizzardi between 1783 and 1791, incorporating many features of symmetry and proportion found in the classical Renaissance garden of earlier centuries. The garden lies on three levels with carefully aligned cross-alleys designed to catch vistas of the surrounding hills. Clipped alleys of hornbeam and *Ostrya carpinifolia* provide high green hedges to confuse a visitor and an avenue of cypresses and palm trees leads up the hill to a BELVEDERE.
                                                    PHo

Robert, Hubert

(1733–1808), French artist and garden designer. As an artist he had a particular interest in gardens and studied at the Académie Française in Rome between 1754 and 1765. He developed in this time a taste for romantic and richly atmospheric paintings of gardens in a state of decay such as those of the Villa MADAMA painted in 1760 and now in the Albertina Museum in Vienna and the Hermitage in St Petersburg. Paintings of the Villa Barberini (Rome), the Villa d'ESTE, the Palazzo FARNESE (Caprarola), the Villa ALDOBRANDINI, and many others give a vivid if occasionally romanticized idea of their 18th-century appearance. In France in 1778 he was appointed *dessinateur des jardins du roi*. He had already made dramatic paintings of the felling of the trees at VERSAILLES which took place between 1774 and 1776, and went on to paint many other views of Louis XVI's Versailles, in particular the newly completed Petit Trianon gardens. The exact nature of Robert's involvement in garden design is uncertain. It seems likely that, with the architect Richard Mique (1728–94), he helped to lay out the Petit Trianon gardens. His involvement with the royal estates of Compiègne and RAMBOUILLET, and with the Princess of Monaco's BETZ and J.-J. Laborde's MÉRÉVILLE also seems certain. Robert was imprisoned at the Revolution but was able to continue his career after his release.   PT

JEAN DE CAYEUX, *Hubert Robert et les jardins* (1987).

Robin, Jean

(1550–1629), French apothecary and gardener who established a reputation as an outstanding gardener at his Parisian home on the Île de la Cité and was appointed King's botanist to Henri III and subsequently to Henri IV and Louis XIII. Initially, the Louvre garden was his responsibility but in 1597 Robin created a garden for the faculty of medicine which ultimately became the Jardin des Plantes (see PARIS PARKS AND GARDENS). Robin received plants and seeds particularly from French North America and, being on friendly terms with John TRADESCANT, exchanged relevant plant material received from Virginia. It is not known whether *Robinia pseudoacacia*, the tree recording his name, was introduced by him or by John Tradescant, as each grew it but only the latter catalogued it. Robin was assisted by his son Vespasien Robin (1579–1662) who continued his work following his father's death. Robin's only book, *Histoire des plantes aromatiques*, was published posthumously.

MC-C

Robinson, William

(1838–1935), Irish gardener and author who spent most of his career in England in particular at Gravetye Manor (West Sussex), which he bought in 1884 and where he spent the rest of his life. He was the pugnacious enemy of excessively formal gardening (especially bedding schemes—'pastry-cook's gardening') and the proponent of WILD GARDENING. His book *The Wild Garden* (1870) stated his belief in the use 'of perfectly hardy exotic plants under conditions where they will thrive without further care'. Robinson was not the first to voice such thoughts; they gathered force throughout the 19th century until they became ingrained in British horticulture and have become fashionable again in the early 21st century in the guise of supposedly newfangled naturalistically planted communities of herbaceous perennials (see NATURALISTIC PLANTING).

Incensed by two books on formal gardens, *The Formal Garden in England* by Reginald BLOMFIELD and F. Inigo THOMAS and J. D. Sedding's *Garden-Craft Old and New*, Robinson published a majestic counter-blast in *Garden Design and Architects' Gardens* (1892) in which he attacked architects who involved themselves with gardens: 'not worth notice for their own sake, as they contribute nothing to our knowledge of the beautiful art of gardening or garden design . . . That such men should write on things of which they have thought little, is unhappily of frequent occurrence, but to find them openly avowing their ignorance of the art they presume to criticise is new.' It is wrong,

however, to think of Robinson as an enemy of formal gardening of every kind. His own formal flower garden at Gravetye Manor enchanted the novelist Henry James: 'Few things in England can show a greater wealth of bloom than the wide flowery terrace immediately beneath the grey gabled house, where tens of thousands of tea-roses . . . divide their province with the carnations and pansies . . . the medley of tall yuccas and saxifrage.' Robinson was also a publisher of genius, founding two magazines, *The Garden* in 1871 and *Gardening Illustrated* in 1879, which catered for the burgeoning middle-class market for horticultural information and employed many of the best garden writers of the day. One of the contributors to *The Garden* was Gertrude JEKYLL, who became a close associate. His most famous book was *The English Flower Garden* (1883), a great best-seller, appearing in repeated new editions throughout his life. It contains a directory of garden plants (constantly amended in new editions as he came across new plants) which remains very valuable. Although his originality has been questioned he was probably the most influential gardener of the late Victorian and early 20th-century periods and his influence may still be seen in many gardens.   PT

Roche-Areal ⊛

Sisseln, Canton of Aargau, Switzerland. The centre of an industrial district, it was designed by the Zurich garden designer Ernst Cramer (1898–1980) in the 1970s in contemporary style as a remarkable *Gesamtkunstwerk*. Cramer was commissioned to design the grounds of the new Roche AG chemical works in Sisseln. Cramer, who in all his works untiringly sought to unite visual arts, architecture, and garden architecture, devised a spatially exciting ensemble, unique of its kind in Switzerland, for the imposing forecourt of the new administration building. The central industrial road, Avenida Treadwell, leads to a grove of 79 clipped plane trees, planted to precise plans in eccentric circles, juxtaposed by Cramer as a garden-architectural green mass with the adjoining industrial and office buildings. A clearing in the grove is aligned with the main entrance to the building, like a green foyer, and dominated by an expressive sculpture entitled *Flamme*—14 m/45 ft high, a flickering structure of red-tinted concrete tongues, assembled from many identical prefabricated sections by Cramer and symbolizing the crucial chemical process of oxidation. The 'flame' rises above the tops of the plane trees and, together with the high industrial chimney and the distinctive water tower, forms the landmark of the industrial plant. Cramer's aim was to create a new landscape from green architecture and

'living concrete'—not derived from nature but emphasizing the shaping will of the human being and creating usable spaces. The ensemble of the precisely shaped green space and the sculpture anchored within it changes its appearance in the course of the day and through the seasons according to the weather and light conditions, and still today offers a new visual approach to an industrial landscape.

UW

Roche-Courbon, Château de la ⊛

Saint-Porchaire, Charente-Maritime, France. The chateau dates from the 15th century with 17th-century additions. A new garden was made in the 17th century but the estate became derelict after a bankruptcy sale in 1817. In the 20th century a new owner restored the chateau and commissioned the garden designer Ferdinand Duprat to reinstate a garden of 17th-century character which was laid out between 1925 and 1935. South of the chateau are rectilinear parterres planted with bedding schemes and decorated with topiary of box and yew. A balustraded viewing terrace overlooks a huge T-shaped pool with, on its far bank, a grotto and cascade flanked by giant steps.   PT

rock garden.

The use of rockwork in gardens may be thought of as either a picturesque form of ornament or as a means of providing the particular conditions required for cultivating certain plants, notably alpines. The rock garden proper, however, belongs to the latter category. The first rock garden was made in the CHELSEA PHYSIC GARDEN under the supervision of William Forsyth and completed in 1773, built of a mixture of stone from the Tower of London, Icelandic lava (brought to the garden by Sir Joseph BANKS), bricks, and flint. The heyday of the rock garden runs from the first half of the 19th century to the early years of the 20th century. From the 1840s James PULHAM (latterly Pulham & Son) made many rock gardens, sometimes intermingling natural stone with 'Pulhamite', an artificial stone made of clinker bound with cement and textured to ressemble stone. At Madresfield Court (Worcestershire) Pulham & Son made a rock garden for the Earl of Beauchamp which the *Gardeners' Chronicle* in 1903 described as 'one of Pulham's masterpieces . . . it is difficult to believe that man has had any hand in its arrangement and construction, so gradual and natural is the transition from prim lawns to what appears to be Nature in her bold and rugged beauty of form and arrangement'. One of the most remarkable rock gardens was that made at Lamport Hall (Northamptonshire) by Sir Charles Isham from 1847 until the 1890s. With a steeply sloping cliff of ironstone the garden was planted with dwarf conifers and decorated with garden gnomes bought by Sir Charles in Nuremberg which were disposed in nooks and crannies so that they seemed to be working the stone. The garden survives today, with replacement gnomes, but one of the originals survives at the house, believed to be the earliest garden gnome in England. William ROBINSON in *The Wild Garden* (1870) treated the subject of rock gardens with care—'rock-works, as generally made, are ugly, unnatural, and quite unfit for a plant to grow upon. The stones . . . are piled up, with no sufficient quantity of soil or any preparation made for the plants.' Robinson thought the rock garden should have more soil than rocks, 'to let the latter suggest itself rather expose its uncovered sides'. In the late 19th century the firm of Backhouse of York (see James BACKHOUSE) was one of the chief builders of rock gardens. At Friar Park (Oxfordshire) in 1896 they made a rock garden for Frank Crisp using 23,000 tons of stone and including a scaled-down Matterhorn. Although the garden was full of whimsy, with model chamois of china or tin and an Ice Grotto with stalactites of blue ice, Crisp was a learned plantsman and around 4,000 different alpine plants were cultivated in the rock garden. William Robinson thought that it was 'by far the best natural stone rock garden I have ever seen', particularly admiring the planting in large sweeps of a single species rather than the 'dotty, spotty planting [that] was so common'. The plant hunter Reginald FARRER was very influential in fostering a taste for rock gardening in its later period. His books *My Rock-Garden* (1909) and *The English Rock Garden* (1919) inspired many gardeners. Farrer thought that the only place for the rock garden was 'In the wild garden . . . out of sight of all formal and artificial surroundings'. He regarded the rock garden as a place to plant the alpines about which he was so knowledgeable. His books are chiefly concerned with descriptions of the merits of plants with information on how best to please them.

Although rock gardens in the early 21st century are no longer remotely fashionable, many survive from the great days. At the ROYAL BOTANIC GARDEN, EDINBURGH the 1-hectare/2.5-acre rock garden was originally made in 1870 by James McNab and rebuilt before the First World War to the designs of Sir Isaac Bayley Balfour. Since 1970 it has been given new soil and replanted. On a fine sloping site, with rocks occasionally jutting from the ground in naturalistic fashion, with a meandering stream and cascade, it provides a handsome setting for a bewildering range of plants coming from habitats ranging from the Mediterranean to the Arctic. Shrubs and conifers from montane habitats add much to the character of the place, among them a beautiful old Japanese temple juniper (*Juniperus rigida*). The scree garden, of granite chips, was made in the 1920s with the advice of the plant hunter George FORREST, who had worked for the botanic garden. It corresponded exactly to the terrain which Forrest had seen on his expeditions in the Himalayas. Reginald Farrer was scornful of the Edinburgh rock garden which he thought had been made according to the principle 'You take a hundred or a thousand cartloads of bald square-shaped boulders. You next drop them all about absolutely anyhow; and you then plant things amongst them. The chaotic hideousness of the result is something to be remembered with shudders ever after.' At the ROYAL HORTICULTURAL SOCIETY's Garden at WISLEY a rock garden was made of natural stone by James PULHAM & Son in 1911 to the designs of Edward White. On a slope running down to a pool, with paths zigzagging between outcrops of rocks and substantial plantings of shrubs and trees with underplantings of bulbs and herbaceous perennials, it is an excellent example of its period. A 0.8-hectare/2-acre rock garden made by Lionel de Rothschild at Exbury (Hampshire) was completed in 1930, fell into decay during the Second World War, but was beautifully restored in the 1970s. The rocks are treated as splendid ornaments, soaring dramatically among alpine rhododendrons, fastigiate conifers, and waves of heathers. The ideal rock garden, as natural as nature can make it, uses native outcrops of rocks to create a marvellous setting for planting. At ROWALLANE in County Down Hugh Armytage Moore used such a site to make a garden of rare charm. Set, as Robinson recommended, in the wild part of the garden, huge rocks of whinstone thrust out of the ground in sprawling shapes. They are planted with smaller flower shrubs such as azaleas and daphnes underplanted with celmisias, erythroniums, gentians, meconopsis, and Asiatic primulas.   PT

rococo gardens.

The idea of rococo has a curious history, with the word first appearing in the early 19th century to mean old fashioned. It derives from the French word *rocaille*, meaning rockwork, so perhaps originally it referred to the ancientness of rocks. The term gradually acquired all manner of meanings, none of them, despite the best efforts of art historians, exactly precise. The writer Edward Fitzgerald in his *Letters* (1889) uses rococo to mean outlandish—'Think of the rococity of a gentleman studying Seneca in the middle of February . . . in a remarkably damp cottage.' By this time rococo was a term used in the decorative and fine arts. Walter Pater (*Imaginary Portraits*, 1887) referred to the 'rococo seventeenth-century French imitation of the true Renaissance'. Peter and Linda Murray, however, in their *Penguin Dictionary of Arts and Artists* (1959), state firmly that it was an architectural style, with much use of wriggling curves, that appeared in France 'immediately after the death of Louis XIV' (1715). The term drifted into music—Albert Einstein refers to it as 'the last tremulous echo of the Baroque' (*Music of the Romantic Era*, 1947). The first use of the term in a garden context seems to date from the early 19th century when the Countess of Blessington (*Idler in France*, 1847) described the Jardins de la FONTAINE in Nîmes as offering 'a curious mixture of military and *rococo* taste', perhaps referring to the ancient Roman ruins there.

In more recent times rococo has been associated with a frivolous, light-hearted atmosphere, with carefree curlicues and possibly excessively abandoned ornamentation. In France such character is certainly found in garden buildings of the 18th century before the more sobre neoclassicism of Louis XVI (reigned 1774-93) of which the epitome is the Queen's Dairy at RAMBOUILLET. The idea of the rococo garden as a stylistic category appears for the first time in the writings of John Harris—*Gardens of Delight: The Rococo English Landscape of Thomas Robins the Elder* (1978) and *The Artist and the Country House* (1979). He rediscovered the paintings of Thomas Robins the elder (1716-70) which showed delightful gardens full of light-hearted ornament. His views of the gardens at Painswick House and Honington Hall (Warwickshire), and a few paintings of unidentified gardens, particularly reflect this character. The present owners of Painswick House, who restored the garden and open it to the public, refer to it as PAINSWICK ROCOCO GARDEN. However, it seems unlikely on the present evidence that there ever existed a substantial tradition of garden design of this kind. John Dixon Hunt in *The Picturesque Garden in Europe* (2003) concludes that rococo is not 'a particularly useful word for actual landscape architectural ensembles'.   PT

Rocque, John

(1704/5?-62), French surveyor who probably reached England in 1709 as a refugee, later serving as an apprentice and journeyman. In his first publication, a plan of Richmond (1734), he described himself as *dessinateur de jardins*. As usual with Rocque, the authenticity of details—extent of plantations, types of trees, garden developments as shown in revisions of plan—cannot be blindly accepted. Further garden plans, notably WREST PARK (1735), CLAREMONT

(1738), PAINSHILL (1744), and WILTON HOUSE (1746) followed. Usually the competent survey is more thought provoking than the marginal pictures, which tend to be unimaginative and may depict humans, animals, or boats out of proportion with the background. Rocque's town plans, including the often-reproduced 'London' (1746), show formal layouts predominating in suburban seats and details of agribusiness—cherry markets and nursery gardens. HB

Rogalin ❀

near Poznań, Poland. A spacious baroque palace of the *entre cour et jardin* (between courtyard and garden) type was completed between 1774 and 1776 for Kazimierz Raczyński. Alongside the palace a formal garden was created, which has essentially been preserved to this day. It consists of two enclosures. Adjacent to the palace is the so-called garden *salon*, originally surrounded by BOSQUETS of lime trees, with a central bed from which paths radiate outwards with hornbeam hedges on both sides. Behind the *salon*, on the axis of the layout, is a MOUNT called Parnassus with two oval CABINETS abutting onto it. Within this formal layout are several rococo sculptures representing mythological figures. After 1810 Edward Raczyński (1786–1845) enlarged the park and converted it into an informal landscape park. The *bosquets* were removed, the trimming of hornbeams was given up, and an irregular grove was planted round Parnassus. The entire park was considerably extended northwards, including the remains of an old Warta riverside forest with numerous specimens of old trees. Among these the best known are three oaks—each several hundred years old—bearing the names of Lech, Czech, and Rus (the legendary founding brothers of Poland, Bohemia, and Ruthenia). A classical chapel, the family mausoleum, was erected in 1824. Today the Rogalin complex is a branch of the National Museum in Poznań and the seat of the Raczyński Foundation.
  WB

Roman, Jacob

(1640–1716), Dutch architect. After being trained as a sculptor in his father's studio, he established himself as an architect. He is particularly known as a designer of country estates for courtiers in the circle of William III. Slot ZEIST established his basic pattern of a central axis upon a *corps de logis* (dwelling quarters) with wings, and to one side large symmetrical formal gardens that ended in an EXEDRA and were moated. His most important commissions include Paleis Het LOO, MIDDACHTEN, and De VOORST. In most cases he worked on the designs of house and garden with others, frequently with Daniel MAROT, who was responsible for the ornamentation. JW

Rome, ancient.

For Romans throughout the empire, both utilitarian and ornamental gardens were an integral part of their living areas in cities and in the countryside alike. Particularly important are the archaeological investigations in the Italian cities of POMPEII AND HERCULANEUM and at the farms around them that were buried, and therefore well preserved, by the volcanic eruption of Mount Vesuvius in AD 79. Beginning in the 1950s, the American archaeologist and historian Wilhelmina Jashemski pioneered the discipline of garden archaeology in these locations. In the decades since then, archaeology in other parts of Europe and the Mediterranean also has contributed significantly towards an understanding and appreciation of the role of gardens in the lives of other peoples once they came under Roman sway.

Domestic gardens

Early Roman houses in the 4th and 3rd centuries BC at sites such as Cosa on the west coast of Italy frequently had a small walled garden at the back that was used as a kitchen garden. This utilitarian *hortus* later diminished in importance when larger courtyards with columned walkways around them were adopted from Greek domestic architecture and added to the Roman house. Unlike the Greek use of the courtyard, however, the Romans transformed this area of the house into a garden that could either be laid out informally with fruit trees and vines or designed as a formal garden with ornamental plantings, statues, and fountains. The excavations at Pompeii and Herculaneum have shown that at least one garden was present in most houses, often at the very heart of the house. The constant supply of water to the house for drinking, cooking, washing, and irrigating the garden was assured by the building of aqueducts in Roman towns from the later 1st century BC. This also allowed the fanciful and abundant use of water in fountains and pools in the garden. The House of the Jets of Water at CONIMBRIGA, for example, had an ornamental courtyard garden designed as six masonry planter boxes in geometric shapes in the middle of a pool. Water spurted into the pool from 400 lead jets on the edges of the planter boxes and the surrounding basin wall.

Suburban and rural villas of wealthy Romans often were designed with courtyard gardens and leafy parks. PLINY THE YOUNGER's villas are described in his *Letters* in the late 1st century AD as pleasant havens with pools, colonnades, and rooms arranged around gardens planted with box hedges, vine pergolas, and fruit and plane trees. Physical remains of this type of luxury estate survive at Oplontis near Pompeii where archaeology has uncovered a large villa of the 1st century AD with more than a dozen formal and informal courtyard gardens as well as parks bordered by box hedges, oleanders, lemon trees, and plane trees. Fountains, pools, and statues made such gardens pleasant places to stroll. Pathways and the hedges flanking them mirrored and enhanced the architectural layout of such villas, and also shaped the open space by leading the visitor through it. Wealthy and educated Romans such as Cicero designed these gardens at their countryside villas to reflect the groves of the gymnasia and the gardens of the Greek philosophers in the suburbs of Athens, taking great delight in spending time in their villa gardens whilst discussing philosophy, literature, and art with their equally cultivated friends. The garden was a place of leisure and relaxation (*otium*), and a pleasant escape from the stresses of public life (*negotium*) in the city.

Imperial interest in vast parks, gardens, and villas in Rome is exemplified by the Emperor Nero who in AD 64 constructed a palace with its own lake in a landscaped park of fields, vineyards, pasture, and woodlands on the Esquiline and Palatine hills. The Emperor Domitian rebuilt and expanded the imperial palace on the Palatine hill at the end of the 1st century AD. This *Domus Flavia* included many ornamental gardens and pools, including a racecourse planted as a garden. The Graecophile Emperor Hadrian built a vast imperial villa (HADRIAN'S VILLA) at Tivoli near Rome in the early 2nd century AD that included parks and groves named 'Academy' and 'Lykeion' after the Athenian gymnasia.

Gardens cultivated for edible produce and associated with more modest houses are best known at Pompeii because of their excellent preservation and detailed archaeological exploration. Here in the south-eastern part of the city near the amphitheatre were several large gardens planted as vineyards, fruit orchards, and commercial flower gardens. These were not formal luxury gardens, but big plots of land reserved for market gardens, and the houses attached to them are quite plain and small. In one of the large vineyards, over 2,000 vines were planted and supported on wooden stakes.

Features associated with outdoor dining in domestic gardens are masonry dining couches (*triclinia*) and tables, but also portable and temporary furniture put in place when needed, as well as PERGOLAS, ARBOURS, and trellises surrounding the dining area. Visitors to the games and shows in the amphitheatre at Pompeii could dine alfresco and enjoy the products of the vineyard in the large market gardens, as is indicated by the presence of masonry dining couches for hire. These were shaded by trees and vines. Garden restaurants and taverns, like that of Euxinus at Pompeii, consisted of a snack bar on the street and a garden with vines and trees at the back. Although this dining establishment lacked *triclinia* in the garden, diners in the two small rooms adjacent to it were able to enjoy paintings of gardens on the walls and they also had a pleasant view from the rooms onto the garden outside. Outdoor dining probably was not limited to areas with a hot Mediterranean climate, although there is less surviving evidence in western and north-western Europe for dining al fresco. But even here, pavilions, pergolas, and other structures associated with gardens suggest that a popular activity in the Roman garden was dining and entertaining.

Sacred and sepulchral gardens
The adornment of temple precincts with groves and gardens was common practice in Roman Italy and the Roman provinces. Excavations at Gabii in Italy uncovered rows of square holes cut into the rock for the planting of trees and shrubs around the temple in the late 2nd century BC. In AD 75 the Emperor Vespasian celebrated his victory in Judaea, dedicating a temple with a courtyard called the Templum Pacis (Temple of Peace) in the forum in Rome. Recent excavations at the site suggest that the courtyard was laid out with water basins and sculpture, as well as beds of roses. At Pompeii, masonry dining couches were found in the courtyard of the Temple of Dionysos that were used during the festivities of the cult. These originally were surrounded and shaded by a vine arbour, and the rest of the temple precinct was also planted with rows of vines. Even in North Africa at Thuburbo Maius the precinct of a Roman temple was planted with trees or large shrubs.

The Roman appreciation of gardens extended to the provision of the tomb with orchards, vineyards, and flower gardens. Some of these gardens have been uncovered in archaeological investigations, others are known only by references to them in the inscribed epitaphs attached to the tombs. Often the flowers grown in these gardens, particularly roses, were brought to the tomb and strewn over the grave on the birthday of the deceased and during the festival of roses (*Rosaria*) in May and June every year.

Gardens in art
Gardens were a favourite theme in Roman wall painting, and they are some of the most stunning depictions in ancient art anywhere.

A garden with a profusion of plants and trees decorated the walls of the villa of the Empress Livia at Prima Porta in the early 1st century AD, now to be enjoyed in the Museo Nazionale in Rome. These, and garden paintings of the 1st century AD in Pompeian houses and dining rooms, depict a profusion of conifers, oak trees, quince and pomegranate trees, palms, laurels, oleanders, and plane trees, as well as flowering plants such as roses, chrysanthemums, daisies, poppies, lilies, and violets in luxurious gardens full of birds, fountains, and statues. Garden paintings such as these decorated the walls of entire rooms, transforming an indoor space into a virtual garden. In some Roman houses, garden paintings can be found on the walls in the colonnades surrounding the open courtyard. In this way, even a planted courtyard of very modest dimensions could be made to appear much larger. Also the walls of Roman tombs are occasionally painted with depictions of gardens full of trees and songbirds, in reference to a kind of eternal paradise in which the dead could enjoy the afterlife.

Plants and horticulture
From the middle of the 1st century BC, wealthy Roman aristocrats competed with each other in ostentatious display by constructing public buildings and establishing parks and gardens open to the public in Rome. In 55 BC Pompey the Great had a theatre, basilica, and markets built with an adjoining colonnaded square planted with avenues of plane trees. Pompey and other aristocratic Roman generals returning from their military campaigns in the eastern Mediterranean were interested in exotic trees and garden plants, and they brought back such specimens as the cherry, the peach, the apricot, and the pistachio for the public parks and their own villas, many of them located in or just outside Rome. Although these parks and villa gardens were called *horti*, they had little in common with the humble *hortus* of early Roman houses.

By the Roman period, the profession of gardener had become firmly established, and gardeners were in great demand on the luxury estates of Roman aristocrats and emperors. One of the specialist branches of the profession was the topiary specialist (*topiarius*). The *topiarius* created garden landscapes, making use of artistically arranged ivy and planting trees and bushes, such as box, laurel, cypress, and acanthus, that were planted in symmetrical patterns and clipped in various shapes. Roman written sources attribute this invention to a man named Gaius Matius in the late 1st century BC. Topiary specialists practised their art outside Italy as well. The personnel who designed and planted the garden with its

formal hedges at Fishbourne near Chichester in the 70s AD almost certainly were immigrant gardeners, probably from Italy, who brought not only imported plants with them but also the necessary expertise to design and lay out a formal garden in the Mediterranean style on British soil.

Roman writers on agriculture and gardening recommended a variety of fertilizers such as pigeon dung, straw, chaff, animal manure, human waste, shells, and seaweed. Although sometimes difficult to detect archaeologically in the soil, remains of molluscs, seaweed, charred plants, kitchen waste, and broken crockery are regularly found in Roman garden soil deposits. These writers also described methods for planting new trees such as lemons, pomegranates, quinces, rosemary, and oleanders by starting off shoots or planting seeds in clay planting pots with holes in the bottom. Once the plant had rooted, the pot could be set in a specially prepared trench or pit. Such planting pots have been found at many sites in Italy, North Africa, Portugal, France, and Britain. Plants could be raised in large numbers in plant nurseries or in existing orchards, and they could be brought in their pots to the gardens for which they were intended. The export of Mediterranean plants to the western and northern Roman provinces may have been facilitated by transporting them in such containers. Pliny the elder's remarks in his *Natural History* that the cherry tree native to the Black Sea area had got as far as Britain 120 years after it was introduced in the early 1st century BC to Italy may well reflect this practice. Remains of other plants such as box, holly, and the Portuguese laurel frequently recorded at sites in Europe represent Roman imports that were subsequently grown in the gardens of the more northerly provinces as ornamental trees and shrubs.   MC

Roodbaard, Lucas Pieters
(1782–1851), Dutch garden architect and portrait painter who worked in the north of the Netherlands. The son of a gardener, he initially followed his father's profession, but *c.*1814–23 exploited his skills as a portrait painter. He then moved from Groningen to Leeuwarden where he registered as an architect of country estates, commencing a successful career in designing not only gardens for the Frisian nobility, but also cemeteries and public gardens for several towns and cities. His landscape style layouts are particularly notable for their carefully contrived ground modelling with winding walks and organically shaped expanses of water with delicate bridges.   JW

R. L. P. MULDER-RADETZKY, *Tuinen van de Friese Adel* (1992).

rootery.

Also known as a stumpery, the rootery has its origins in the first part of the 19th century at the same time as the growing craze for ferns. It consisted of picturesque old tree roots or stumps, excavated and disposed in a group, usually in a shady place so that ferns could be grown in association and mosses would colonize the stumps. The effect, gloomy and romantic, was attractive to Victorian garden taste. Edward KEMP's *How to Lay out a Garden* (1850) recommends the use of roots as an alternative to stone, to make a rootery or stumpery instead of a rockery: 'In localities where stone is not easily procured or where it abounds so much that some other material may be preferable, the *rugged stumps* or *roots* of old trees.' Edward Kemp admired the use of roots at BIDDULPH GRANGE where the remains of an excellent stumpery may still be seen. It its heyday the stumps were piled high, overarching to form a tunnel with climbing plants like ivy and Virginia creeper encouraged to grow over it. Few rooteries survive but another, made at ARLEY HALL before 1875, may still be seen, a ferny dell with ancient tree stumps. Modern rooteries have been made at HIGHGROVE and in the arboretum at CASTLE HOWARD.   PT

root house.

In English 18th-century gardens ornamental garden buildings sometimes incorporated picturesque roots to add to an air of romantic antiquity. The term is often a synonym for HERMITAGE. William Wrighte's *Grotesque Architecture or Rural Amusements* (1767) includes designs for every kind of garden building which 'may be executed with Flints, Irregular Stones, Rude Branches and Roots of Trees'. Wrighte included an illustration of a 'Rural Bath', like an igloo bristling with root and branch work. One of the few surviving examples is the hermitage at Badminton (Gloucestershire) designed by Thomas WRIGHT and built in 1747. Wright believed that such buildings should 'be naturally supposed the only Production of the Age, before Building became a Science'. The Badminton hermitage is thatched and its structure a jumble of odd bits of wood, including roots, its doorway a curious rough Gothic arch of misshapen branches, and its interior encrusted with moss. Such buildings were ephemeral and, according to Eileen Harris ('Hunting for Hermits', *Country Life*, 26 May 1988), only one other survives in England, at Brocklesby Park (Lincolnshire). Many other root houses are known from 18th-century gardens. Eileen Harris mentions examples at Hagley Hall (Worcestershire), HAWKSTONE, The LEASOWES, PAINSHILL, and STOURHEAD. The Stourhead root house/grotto, built in 1770 and destroyed in 1814, was drawn by F. M. PIPER who described it as exceeding 'everything that art and taste combined with Nature have been able to contrive'. According to Henry Hoare, for whom it was built, it was 'lined inside and out with old Gouty nobbly Oakes'. Rootwork was used in garden houses in the 19th century and had a minor renaissance in English gardens of the late 20th century. Gervase Jackson-Stops incorporated it in a garden temple at the Horton Menagerie (Northamptonshire) and Julian Bannerman in a memorable grotto for Leeds Castle (Kent).   PT

Roper, Lanning

(1912–83), American garden designer and author who came to England when in Second World War service with the US navy. He practised in a relaxed English style with exuberant mixed borders and a refined sense of architecture, mostly in England but also in Ireland, France, and USA. Most of his work was for private, often quite small, gardens but among those open to the public it may be seen at Broughton Castle (Oxfordshire), Claverton Manor (Somerset), GLENVEAGH CASTLE, PENSHURST PLACE, SCOTNEY CASTLE, and WADDESDON MANOR. An excellent writer, he was garden

A **root house** from Thomas Wright's *Six Original Designs for Arbours* (1755).

correspondent of the *Sunday Times* 1951–75 and the author of several books, among them *Successful Town Gardening* (1957) and *The Gardens in the Royal Parks at Windsor* (1961).   PT

Rose, John

(1629–77), English gardener who worked for the Duchess of Somerset at Essex House (London) and in 1666 became André MOLLET's successor as keeper of the royal garden in St James's Park (see LONDON PARKS AND GARDENS). Rose is said subsequently to have been sent to VERSAILLES to meet André LE NÔTRE. Rose possibly helped to lay out Lord Capel's famous garden at CASSIOBURY. Stephen SWITZER in *Ichnographia Rustica* (1718) described Rose as being 'esteemed to be the best in his profession in those days'. Rose's name appears as author on the title page of the book *The English Vineyard Vindicated* (1666) which was, in fact, although based on Rose's material, actually composed by John EVELYN, who signs the preface under the pseudonym Philocepos. In a famous painting Rose is depicted on bended knee presenting a pineapple to Charles II.   PT

Rosemoor ✿

Great Torrington, Devon, England, was a distinguished private plantswoman's garden made by Lady Anne Palmer from 1959. In 1988 the estate was given to the ROYAL HORTICULTURAL SOCIETY which transformed it into a regional display garden. The RHS restored the old part of the garden and made a much larger new garden separated by a road and linked by an underground tunnel. The new garden has a large formal area of beds enclosed in yew hedges linked by a strong central axis flanked by deep mixed borders. There are collections of shrub roses, foliage plants, a winter garden, and a range of plants introduced by the great Devon nurserymen VEITCH & Son. In addition there are such thematic areas as a water garden, cottage garden, and vegetable garden. High standards of gardening are everywhere visible and Rosemoor gives gardeners a vivid idea of the range of plants that may be successfully grown in the south-west of England.   PT

Rosenbröijer, Maj-Lis

(1926–2003), Finnish landscape architect. She studied in Denmark during the 1950s where she acquired an artistic and architectural approach to garden design. Her works cover private gardens, churchyards, hospitals, official institutions, and office buildings. The characteristics of her design were simple forms with contrasting elements: wooden decks upon carpets of ground covering plants and pebbles; a few spiky plants or exotic plants against a background of evergreens, built horizontal structures contrasting with free-flowing landforms. In the 1970s she was confronted with the new movement of ecological planting but despite stylistic upheavals in the profession, she continued as a successful designer. Her last well-known work is the garden of the President's residence Mäntyniemi in Helsinki. With colourful garden plants against native forest vegetation, the garden is framed by rocks and views opened to the sea.   CR

MAJ-LIS ROSENBRÖIJER and ANNA-LIISA AHMAVAARA, *Pihoja ja puutarhoja* (1968).

Rosendael ✿

Rozendaal, Gelderland, the Netherlands, is a medieval castle that was owned in the late 17th century by Jan van Arnhem, one of William III's confidants, who embellished the gardens, which were famous for their waterworks. In 1721 Lubbert Adolf Torck inherited the estate, altering the house largely to its present form and developing the gardens. Daniel MAROT was commissioned to modernize the layout, and several features from this phase survive today; a shell gallery, a garden pavilion, a water cascade, and fountain jokes. In 1781 the architect Philip Willem Schonck provided the first changes in the landscape style, but it was more than 50 years later, between 1836 and 1838, that the landscape gardener J. D. ZOCHER Jr. proposed a complete reorganization of the park. This was done for A. L. Adolph Torck and created a generally more open valley with flowing lines and included a large ORANGERY, whilst maintaining the Marot features. When the ownership changed once more in 1854 to R. J. C. Baron van Pallandt certain areas were planted with exotic trees while the area in front of the orangery was redesigned by Dirk Wattez in 1875. A rose garden was added around 1904. The estate suffered during the war, losing the orangery, and further declined as a result of a lack of investment afterwards. In 1977 the estate was given to the Gelderland Trust, which restored the then neglected park and rebuilt the orangery. The castle was opened to the public in 1990.   JW

J. C. BIERENS DE HAAN, *Rosendael, groen hemeltjen op aerd: kasteel, tuinen en bewoners sedert 1579* (1994).
JOHN CORNFORTH, 'An extravagance of shells', *Country Life*, Vol. 164: No. 4233 (1978).

Rosendal Barony ✿

Kvinnherad, Hordaland, Norway. The mansion and Renaissance-style garden, one of the few remaining in northern Europe, were built in the 1660s. Rosendal became an entailed estate from 1745 to 1927 when it was donated to the University of Oslo, and is today a museum. The whitewashed stone building with its 10-hectare/25-acre park and gardens forms a striking contrast to the powerful surrounding scenery of snow-capped mountains and the Hardanger fjord. The west front of the building faces the rectangular garden, but without direct access to it. The 50 × 60-m/165 × 200-ft parterre contains nine of the original twelve compartments, edged with turf and filled with mainly modern roses. The old fruit trees that marked their corners are gone. A tall whitewashed stone wall that enclosed the garden disappeared before 1850 when the owner started laying out the landscape park towards the south-east. From a viewing point in the beech grove on the steep hillside the Hatteberg waterfall is seen as BORROWED LANDSCAPE within the park. The large kitchen garden north of the house was restored 1998–2003 in accordance with an 1893 map. Herbs, vegetables, and fruit from the garden are now used in the museum restaurant.   ME

Roseraie de l'Haÿ-les-Roses ✿

L'Haÿ-les-Roses, Val-de-Marne, France, also known as the Roseraie du Val-de-Marne, was created by Jules Gravereaux from 1890. Newly retired from the shop Bon Marché (which he helped to found), he commissioned Édouard ANDRÉ to design a pleasure garden devoted to a single genus of plants—the rose. Gravereaux formed a collection of 3,000 species and cultivars which he hunted down on his travels. He also built up a collection of the varieties which the Empress Joséphine had at MALMAISON. Today the garden has an area of 1.7 hectares/4 acres and its late 19th-century design and atmosphere have been impeccably preserved. Many of the roses are superbly trained on arbours, tunnels, and trellis-work. Paths are lined with hedges of box and there is the occasional ornamental building such as the rotunda Temple d'Amour. Roses are grouped thematically—species roses, Gallicas, tea roses, modern roses, roses known at Malmaison, and so on. In all there are 3,200 varieties, 120 of which date from before 1800. The breeding and cultivation of roses have long been crafts at which French gardeners have excelled. Here is a garden which displays these skills in the most attractive and informative way.   PT

roses.

The rose, perhaps more than any other flower, has an existence beyond the merely horticultural. It permeates literature, art, and religion, insinuates itself into opera and popular song, even serves the cause of social protest and revolutionary agitprop. It has been central to the cults of Isis, Venus, and the Virgin Mary, and to the related cult of courtly love. Arguably more poems have been written about the rose than any other flower. As a symbol it is magnificently complex, full of opposing tensions—the sweetness of the perfume and the ordure from which it springs; the allure of the flower and the sharpness of the thorns; the enduring nature of the plant and the evanescence of the individual bloom—making it especially apt for conveying notions of love. Sexual politics go right to the heart of our thinking about the rose. Freud saw in the shape of the flower a symbol of the female sexual organs. The profusion of the flowers has been seen as a symbol of fertility after the barrenness of winter; their colour an intimation of innocence or experience. It can suggest both bodily trial—the sweat of the prophet, the blood of the martyrs—and the reward of heavenly bliss which follows, whether sacred or profane: Sleeping Beauty's prince has to fight his way through briers to reach her. The flower's symmetry has been seen as suggestive of order in a disordered or chaotic world, of purpose and meaning; Jung saw it as a manifestation of the mandala, a symbol of the individual's attainment of oneness with the universe; Eliot and Yeats as a symbol of arcane knowledge, its petals folding in upon themselves around a secret heart. At its most literal, it stands simply for the best: the red rosette at the Pony Club gymkhana, the strikers' demand for bread and roses, the petals strewn before a triumphant Roman general.

Roses have been cultivated in gardens for thousands of years. They have been used in medicine, in cooking, for ritual purposes, for their oil, their perfume, their petals. Some of the earliest written records of roses are in the Chinese *Materia Medica* which date back several centuries before the birth of Christ. Homer (*Iliad* 23) speaks of the body of Hector being embalmed with rose oil. Herodotus described the scent of the roses in the garden of King Midas of Phrygia, in exile in Macedonia. The philosopher Epicurus had his own rose garden in Athens. The archaeologist Flinders Petrie retrieved a wreath of dried roses (identified as *R.* × *richardii*) from a 2nd-century AD tomb at Hawara, Lower Egypt. Images of roses recur on the frescoes of POMPEII; and in the palace of Knossos. At Paestum (modern Pesto, near Agropoli on the Bay of Salerno) roses were grown on an industrial scale to satisfy the Roman demand for rose petals. At Provins, in 13th-century France, *R. gallica* var. *officinalis* was the centre of a similar industry, producing dried rose petals for use in medicine and confectionery. By the 17th century, production was still measured in tons.

Distribution and early development
There are currently nearly 3,300 rose varieties commercially available in the UK, and more than 14,000 worldwide—though these are only a fraction of the total number of roses introduced over the centuries. All are derived from a handful of the 120 or so distinct wild species scattered throughout the northern hemisphere. Habitats range from the Arctic to the tropics, from the desert fringes of North Africa and New Mexico to the temperate regions of Europe, but by far the greatest number of species are found in Central Asia and China. The garden roses derived from the species and by hybridization amongst themselves are commonly divided into ten main groups: those derived from the European species (the Gallicas, Albas, Damasks, Centifolias, and Portlands); those derived from Far Eastern species (the Chinas and Teas); and the hybrids between the two (Noisettes, Bourbons, and Hybrid Perpetuals). Until the second half of the 20th century, such distinctions were based upon anecdotal evidence and morphological observation of characteristics such as hip and leaf shape. The pioneering work of C. C. Hurst ('Notes on the Origin and Evolution of our Garden Roses', *Royal Horticultural Society Journal* (1941), reprinted in Graham Stuart THOMAS, *The Graham Stuart Thomas Rose Book*, 1994) applied the science of genetics to the elucidation of the history of roses for the first time. Hurst established that *R. gallica* was the foundation species from which most of our garden roses evolved, and showed that *R. centifolia*, contrary to what had long been supposed, was not the 'hundred-petalled rose' referred to by PLINY THE ELDER and THEOPHRASTUS, but a complex hybrid of relatively late garden origin which reached its fully developed form in the hands of Dutch breeders in the early 18th century. Hurst and others also posited a hybrid origin for the Alba group of roses, a line of enquiry later pursued by French researchers at INRA Centre de Recherche, Antibes (N. Maia and P. Venard, *Cytotaxonomie du genre Rosa et origine des rosiers cultivés*, 1976)) who demonstrated that the Albas were European hybrids between *R. gallica* and various species of *R. canina* (the common dog rose) thus corroborating gardeners' own observations of the Albas' vigour and their ability to tolerate poor soil and low temperatures.

Perhaps the most interesting avenue of recent research has been the DNA analysis of the Damask group of roses, carried out at Hiroshima and in the USA, which demonstrated that the four oldest known Damasks ('York and Lancaster', 'Kazanlik', 'Quatre Saisons', and 'Quatre Saisons Blanc Mousseux') descend from a common ancestor, itself of hybrid origin, expressed as (*R. moschata* × *R. gallica*) × *R. fedtschenkoana* (Hikaru Iwata, Tsuneo Kato, and Susumu Ohno, 'Triparental Origin of Damask Roses', *Gene*, Vol. 259: Nos. 1–2 (2000)). The previously little-known *R. fedtschenkoana* is limited in the wild to parts of Central Asia and north-west China, and its rediscovery in this context revolutionized thinking about the geographical source and possible garden origin of the Damask rose, traditionally considered to have been a naturally occuring hybrid brought back from Damascus by returning crusaders in the early modern period. Also, the fact that *R. moschata* and *R. fedtschenkoana* are both capable of flowering for an extended period has had considerable impact upon our understanding of early modern repeat-flowering roses.

The coming of the China roses
The European family of species roses and the hybrids derived from them have important qualities of winter hardiness, floral complexity (including doubling), and disease resistance, but—with the notable exception of the 'Quatre Saisons' or Autumn Damask rose—had only one brief period of flowering each year. The whole course of rose-breeding history was revolutionized at the end of the 18th century by the introduction of continuous-flowering roses from the East. These roses had probably been trickling into Europe since the 1500s, but seem to have made no impact on rose breeding until the arrival of the so-called 'four stud Chinas' in the last decade of the 18th century and the first two decades of the 19th. The China roses were themselves hybrids (of the tea-scented *R. gigantea* and the wild China *R. chinensis*, possibly in combination with *R. multiflora*), and had been in cultivation in Chinese gardens for hundreds of years. When crossed with the European roses, they gave rise to the continuous or repeat-flowering Noisettes, Bourbons, and Hybrid Perpetuals, and ultimately to all our modern continuous-flowering roses: the Hybrid Teas, Hybrid Musks, Polyanthas, and Floribundas.

One rose alone among European garden roses had the capacity to flower more than once a year. This was the 'Quatre Saisons' or Autumn Damask rose (*R. damascena* var. *semperflorens*), a form of which was known to Jean de La QUINTINIE, gardener to Louis XIV, under the name 'Tous les Mois', and in 17th-century Italy as *la rosa d'ogni mese* (the monthly rose). Whether either of these is identical to Virgil's 'twice-blooming' roses of Paestum (*Georgics* 4. 119) has long been a matter for discussion, though there seems no reason to doubt the veracity of Virgil (normally an attentive and accurate recorder of agricultural and horticultural practice) on the existence of remontant roses in the ancient world—a point recently lent considerably more weight by the DNA analysis of early Damasks carried out by Iwata, Kato, and Ohno. The exact origin of the repeat-flowering Portland Rose, in cultivation in England by 1775 (*R.* 'Portlandica', from which the Portland roses descend), still remains unclear, but 'Quatre Saisons' would seem certain to be one of its parents, probably in combination with *R. gallica* var. *officinalis*.

Recent developments

After many years during which they were eclipsed by the popularity of the Hybrid Teas and Floribundas, the middle years of the twentieth century saw a return to favour of the old roses, pioneered by the gardener and writer Vita SACKVILLE-WEST and promoted by the rosarian Graham Stuart THOMAS, amongst others. Modern shrub roses, such as those bred by Wilhelm Kordes in Germany, and David Austin in England (the 'English Roses'), have vastly extended the number of good cultivars available to gardeners; and the development of prostrate or ground cover roses, miniatures, patio roses, and patio climbers have extended the ways in which roses can be used. More recent developments have included a trend towards roses with unusual colours (such as brown and 'blue'), roses with a central eye of a different colour (derived from hybridization with *Hulthemia persica*, a close relative of the rose), and roses with old rose characteristics bred especially for the cut flower trade.   AKS

Roseto, Villa II,

Florence, Tuscany, Italy. Designed by Pietro PORCINAI, Italy's most important 20th-century landscape architect, in the early 1960s, the garden reflects Renaissance ideas of balance and proportion with the garden irrevocably linked to the house. Porcinai moved the main entrance to the first floor and built the garden on the roof of the garage area, the original approach to the villa becoming a setting for parties with a pavement of pebbles in a circular pattern. An iron and stone spiral staircase leads to the garden level, dominated by a motif of circles, cut out in paving and clipped boxwood, with three circular pools. A main axis leads from the door of the villa to a fountain at the end of the hanging garden. Plane trees, planted at ground level, rise above the garden.   PHo

Rothschild, Villa Ephrussi de ⊛

Saint-Jean-Cap-Ferrat, Alpes-Maritimes, France, one of the rare opportunities to see a grand Riviera house and garden, dating from its great period, preserved much as it was when it was a private estate. Beatrice de Rothschild, who was brought up at the Château de FERRIÈRES, bought the land in 1905 and had built a pink and white Italianate villa, which she called a *palazzino*. The 7-hectare/17-acre site, on the crest of the Cap, has splendid views east and west and the garden makes the most of them. South of the house the rocky ground was levelled to take a formal garden. A terrace has

shaped lawns, yew topiary, bedding plants, and statuary, and at the lower level a shaped pool leads to a long canal ending in a colonnaded Temple d'Amour on raised ground which forms the axis of the formal garden. On either side are scalloped pools, shaped lawns, bedding plants, clipped citrus plants, agaves, and tall palms with seats in the shade. The perimeter of the garden is less formal, with winding walks among trees and shrubs, and delicious views. Formal episodes occur here, too, with a Spanish garden with a loggia and canal, a Japanese garden with a ceramic house, and an Italian garden with its sweeping double staircase. The house, with its exquisite interior and contents, is all of a piece with the sprightly decorativeness of the garden. It is a splendid place in which to admire the *goût Rothschild* in holiday mood.   PT

MIRIAM ROTHSCHILD, KATE GARTON, and LIONEL DE ROTHSCHILD, *The Rothschild Gardens* (1996).

rotunda.

The rotunda form, a circular, pillared, usually open building often capped with a dome, inspired many ornamental garden buildings particularly in 18th-century English landscape gardens and others inspired by them. In Charles

---

The **rotunda** at the Désert de Retz from Georges Le Rouge's *Détails de nouveaux jardins à la mode* (1785).

Temple au Dieu Pan.

BRIDGEMAN's design for STOWE, in place by 1720 but which does not survive, a rotunda mounted on an elevated grassy knoll stood at the meeting point of three axes, two long avenues and a great canal. The Ionic Temple on the terrace at DUNCOMBE PARK, possibly designed by Sir John VANBRUGH and built c.1730, is an early example. At VERSAILLES a rotunda, the Temple of Love, was built for Marie-Antoinette in 1777–8 to the designs by Richard Mique (1728–94). Standing on a picturesque island it contains a statue by Edmé Bouchardon of Cupid shaping his bow into the club of Hercules. The picturesque siting of the building may have been chosen by Hubert ROBERT and the building itself may have been inspired by Robert's drawings of the Temple of Vesta rotunda at Tivoli which certainly inspired the Temple of Philosophy (c.1775) at ERMENONVILLE. An unusually late rotunda, also based on the Temple of Vesta, is to be seen at GARENNE-LEMOT, built in 1822 on a rocky outcrop on the river Sèvre.   PT

Roundhay Park

Roundhay, Leeds, Yorkshire, England, is an intriguing example of what can happen to an old estate gradually engulfed by urban development. North-east of the city of Leeds, Roundhay had a deer park in 1341. Its later history shows industrial development with quarries and mine workings by 1803. The Nicholson family bought it and Thomas Nicholson built a house in 1826 and made two lakes. At the northern end of Waterloo Lake is a sham ruined castle, and a rustic HERMITAGE at the head of the Upper Lake—both these must date from early 19th-century landscaping. The estate was acquired by Leeds City Council in the 1870s, the house became a hotel, and the grounds were developed as a public park with the later addition of sports facilities which include two golf courses. A more recent development is Tropical World to the west of the house. Here are glasshouses with collections of plants, insects, birds, and butterflies—a Desert House, Australian House, and Amazon House—and a Monet Garden and Alhambra. Despite these varied activities, in an area of 290 hectares/700 acres, areas of old parkland, and mature trees, still survive.   PT

Rouse Hill

New South Wales, Australia, is one of Australia's most culturally important historic properties. It represents the most complete document of continuous family occupation of a country house in New South Wales and contains possibly the earliest surviving garden in Australia. Rouse Hill House, built of sandstone in Georgian style, was begun in 1813 by Englishman Richard Rouse (1774–1852) and his wife Elizabeth (1772–1849). It became the centre of a 486-hectare/1,200-acre estate to which the family eventually moved from Sydney in 1825.

At this time, the garden acquired its basic decorative elements. The squared form emerged with gravel paths laid and edged in the ordered vernacular forerunner to the GARDENESQUE, familiar to the Rouses from England and also used locally in the garden at Government House, Sydney. This design and physical details such as edging in a variety of materials, fencing, planting containers, and path placement are all still visible, witness to the garden's evolution and changing fashions in gardening practice. Surviving physical evidence in the gardens also includes outbuildings such as a fanciful Victorian summer house, gate remnants, fragments of arbours, trellis, and paving. The history of the plant stock, however, is more problematic because of the long period of almost continual replacement. Mature feature trees such as Moreton Bay figs (*Ficus macrophylla*), now flanking the front of the house, and stone pines (*Pinus pinea*) define the outlook over the main lawn to the mountains, their dark green outlines a vivid contrast to the house on its strategic site alongside the busy Windsor Road.   CMR

Rousham House

Steeple Aston, Oxfordshire, England, has one of the most remarkable and delightful gardens in England. It was made for General James Dormer, who had fought at the Battle of Blenheim, and desired a garden in which to enjoy a 'philosophic retirement' as Horace WALPOLE called it. It is in fact two gardens—a formal garden with informal yearnings laid out by Charles BRIDGEMAN from 1725 and a poetic Arcadian garden by William KENT made between 1737 and 1741. The surviving plan of the garden in the Bodleian Library attributed to Bridgeman shows a large rectangular open space north of the house pointing towards ground that slopes down sharply towards the river Cherwell. On the banks of the river is what appears to be a characteristically Bridgemanic amphitheatre facing the water. The banks of the river are shown to be straight and the river, quite narrow at this point, resembles a canal. In the north-western corner of the rectangle a long straight walk plunges into woodland which is animated with straight or serpentine walks and pools. This layout, and some of the details, Kent retained when he set to work. In the two outer corners of the rectangular space, now a lawn, Kent put an elegant pedimented alcove seat with, between them, a statue by Peter SCHEEMAKERS of a lion attacking a horse. From this point idyllic views over the Cherwell open

out, a peaceful prospect in relation to the ferocity of the statue. Bridgeman's THEATRE, slightly blurred, may still be seen on the slopes below and, near it, Kent's Praeneste, a stone sweep of arcading which, from within, frames views of the river and rural landscape. On a terrace above Praeneste is another Scheemakers statue, a figure of a dying gladiator. Walks lead into woodland where Bridgeman's pools were modified by Kent into Venus' Vale, with figures of Pan and a Faun (1701, by John van NOST) skulking in the shade of trees on either side. The goddess stands at the apex of a rustic cascade above an octagonal pool flanked by cupids riding on swans. A second cascade splashed below the octagon from which a winding rill serpents into the woods. Parallel to it is Bridgeman's Long Walk through the woods ending in a figure of Apollo. Nearby Kent's Temple of Echo faces out along the river where in the distance the medieval Heyford Bridge forms a lovely eyecatcher. It is these views of the landscape beyond the garden, often directed by the gaze of a statue, that are one of Rousham's marvels. The field to the south of the garden, often filled with grazing cattle, is overlooked on its western side by a Gothic seat designed by Kent. Rousham, still owned by a Dormer descendant, has no trace of the heritage industry—visitors have the impression of being in a private estate. There is no pressure, indeed no possibility, to buy postcards or cream teas. To wander in its finely cared-for 12 hectares/30 acres is one of the most marvellous pleasures that any garden can offer. Horace Walpole thought that Rousham was 'the most engaging of all Kent's works. It is Kentissimo.'   PT

Rousseau, Jean-Jacques

(1712–78), French author, amateur botanist, social philosopher, and influential protagonist of romanticism. He believed in innate virtue and consigned his five bastard children to orphanages. A passionate field botanist he wrote in his *Confessions* (1782–9), 'I know something about the work of nature but nothing about that of the gardener,' and in his *Rêveries du promeneur solitaire* (1782) he expressed his desire to write a book describing 'every grass of the meadows, every moss of the woods and every lichen that carpets the rocks'. In the latter book he also described the 'délicieuse ivresse' (delicious intoxication) with which he abandoned himself to the beauties of nature in which man might rediscover his prelapsarian innocence. In a novel, *La Nouvelle Héloïse* (1761), Rousseau described Julie's garden in which the visitor (her former lover) was struck by the cool shade, flowers scattered all about, the burbling of water, and the song of a thousand birds.

The flowers were all natives, fruit trees and ornamentals were jumbled together, and flowering hedges lined winding walks. He became a friend of the Marquis de GIRARDIN, whose ideas he influenced, and died at ERMENONVILLE. Rather than the pioneer of a style of romantic, naturalistic gardening Rousseau in his garden writings sounds more like an eloquent spokesman of the spirit of the times.   PT

Rousseau, Parc Jean-Jacques.
See ERMENONVILLE.

Rowallane Garden ⊕
Saintfield, County Down, Northern Ireland, combines great plant interest with a most beguiling atmosphere. The atmosphere is apparent as soon as you enter—the curving drive pierces woodland and is flanked from time to time by conical cairns of mossy stones. The house is Victorian but the garden is largely of the 20th century, for the most part the creation of Hugh Armytage Moore (d. 1954), whose style has been closely followed by the NATIONAL TRUST since they took over in 1955. The walled former kitchen garden, in two compartments, is filled with flowers. A National Collection of large flowered cultivars of penstemons is held here, prettily disposed in a parterre-like arrangement. Distinguished flowering shrubs are everywhere visible—*Hoheria lyallii*, several magnolias, noble tree peonies, and species rhododendrons—and many tender plants flourish in the warm microclimate, among them the deliciously scented *Rhododendron* 'Lady Alice Fitzwilliam'. There is much distinguished underplanting of astilbes, Himalayan meconopsis, primulas, and rodgersias. Beyond the walled garden, against a background of mature trees, are ramparts of rhododendrons lining a grassy walk to a rare ROCK GARDEN of natural outcrops of rock planted with small shrubs, such as azaleas, daphnes, olearias, and pieris with dazzling sheets of celmisias, meconopsis, and primulas.
PT

Royal Botanic Garden, Edinburgh ⊕
The Lothians, Scotland, was founded in 1670 as a garden of medicinal plants attached to Edinburgh University. The original site of the garden was at St Ann's Yard, close to the royal palace of Holyroodhouse, and it had other sites before settling at its present site in 1820. In this final move many mature trees were transported from the previous site using a huge cart designed by the curator William McNab. It was in the 19th century that the essential character of the garden was established. The layout, with its winding walks, lawns with groups of trees,

and pools, was fixed in this period. A fine late 18th-century house, Inverleith House, stands at the top of a hill close to the centre of the garden. The northern corner of the garden is dominated by glasshouses, the first of which, the octagonal Old Palm Stove (for tropical palms), was built in 1824. The adjacent New Palm House (for temperate palms), was built in 1856–8 to the designs of Robert Matheson—a handsome classical building with a double convex roof. New glasshouses were built in the 1960s to the designs of George Pearce and John Johnson. Together these glasshouses provide a wide range of climates and house an exceptional collection, some species of which (such as a West Indian thatch palm, *Sabal bermudana*) are over 200 years old. An outstanding ROCK GARDEN was built in 1870 and extended and altered in later years to cover an area of 1 hectare/2.5 acres with acid and alkaline habitats, areas of shade or sharp drainage, to house an exceptional collection of around 5,000 species from Alpine, Arctic, or Mediterranean climates. The naturally acid soil in the garden at large is favourable for the cultivation of ericaceous plants of which there are distinguished collections—RHODODENDRONS are a major interest. The largest part of the garden is the ARBORETUM with 2,000 trees disposed in a parklike setting. The Pringle Chinese Garden, laid out in 1993, reflects one of the garden's chief interests. Since the plant collecting work of George FORREST in the early 20th century Edinburgh has had a special connection with China. Here a sloping site has been designed to resemble a wild Chinese landscape planted with appropriate plants. The HERBARIUM with specimens going back to the 17th century, contains 2 million specimens with the largest collection of Chinese plants outside China. The site is large, 27 hectares/67 acres, and exceptionally attractive with its undulating terrain and its high, airy position with beautiful distant views—south towards Edinburgh Castle and north towards the Firth of Forth. The Royal Botanic Garden, Edinburgh, is part of a group of four botanic gardens in Scotland—Benmore (Argyll), Dawyck (Peeblesshire), and LOGAN (Wigtownshire), each with a different climate. Together they display around 40,000 taxa from a very wide range of habitats and thus constitute one of the greatest plant collections in the world.   PT

Royal Botanic Garden, Madrid ⊕
Spain. In 1755 King Fernando VI of Spain ordered the creation of a Royal Botanic Garden which he located beside the Manzanilla river in the old hothouse gardens of the royal palace. It contained more than 2,000 plants, most of them provided by the garden's first curator, Jose

Quer, who made numerous plant collecting trips and acquired many specimens from other European botanic gardens. By 1774, the garden had outgrown its site and King Charles III commissioned the architects Sabatini and Juan de Villanueva to design a new garden on a 10-hectare/25-acre site—a third of which it presently occupies—in the centre of Madrid, beside the Prado museum, which de Villanueva had also constructed. The new garden, created to promote plant finding expeditions (chiefly to the Americas) and teach botany, was opened in 1781.

Three main terraces were created, rising from the Paseo del Prado, and overlooked by a grand pavilion, El Pabellón Villanueva, in which tender plants were overwintered. The plants were arranged according to Linnaean principles of classification and this general design has remained largely intact, despite long periods of neglect and remodelling. The 1808 War of Independence took its toll on the garden and serious attempts to restore the site were not undertaken until 1857, by curator Mariano de la Paz Graells, who incorporated a zoo, (removed twelve years later to the gardens of the BUEN RETIRO palace close by) and a new greenhouse, which still bears his name. Between 1880 and 1890 the garden suffered significant losses. Two hectares/5 acres were given up to the construction of a new ministry building and the hurricane of 1886 uprooted nearly 600 valuable trees. The garden limped through the greater part of the 20th century, acquiring some status as a centre for mycological and micromycological studies, but the ravages of neglect and the Civil War led to its closure in 1974 so that a full restoration could be made. In 1981, on the 200th anniversary of its first opening ceremony, the gardens were reopened. Since then, they have flourished and there is now a school of practical horticulture alongside the research departments. A seed bank has been established and both the library and herbarium are active. In 2004 a new elevated garden, behind the Pabellón Villanueva, designed by Fernando CARUNCHO was opened, creating important new views over the terraces and greenhouses below.

In the world of botany, the garden still leads in the field of mycological studies and is a useful reference for plants endemic to the Iberian peninsula. Each of the three terraces is immaculately kept and the decorative planting and clear labelling has much to offer the casual visitor as well as the specialist. Fountains, pergolas hung with roses, vines, and wisteria, superb specimens of trees planted in the 18th century—survivors of the 1886 hurricane—and greenhouses offering both temporary exhibitions and permanent ▸

collections of tropical and desert plants offer extraordinary respite in the heart of the capital.
KF

Royal Botanical Gardens, Hamilton ⊗

Burlington, Ontario, Canada, granted their royal charter by King George V and opened to the public in 1932. Spread along Lake Ontario's Western Shore, they are organized into five garden areas: Rock Garden, Arboretum, Laking Garden (Dr Leslie Laking (b. 1916) was the director for 30 years), Rose Garden/Hendrie Park, and Mediterranean Garden (opened in 1986 to bloom brilliantly for plant-starved gardeners in winter); plus four nature sanctuaries, Cootes Paradise, Hendrie Valley, Rock Chapel, and Berry Tract, for a total land mass of 1,100 hectares/2,700 acres. Home to 8,000 taxa, detailed plant records, and interpretative displays are well maintained. It has the largest collection of lilacs in the world and operates an international registry. Only 127 hectares/297 acres are cultivated; the remainder grows naturally, albeit highly managed, including the 250 hectares/618 acres of coastal wetland, and 30 km/18 miles of beautifully

constructed nature trails which meander through some of southern Ontario's richest marshland, woodlands, meadows, up the Niagara Escarpment, and across agricultural land. RBG is part of many conservation projects, including the Cootes Paradise Sanctuary. Once a thriving freshwater coastal marsh habitat, it has been devastated by human intervention. In 1993, Project Paradise, the largest freshwater marsh restoration venture ever attempted in North America, was launched. Part of that project was to erect a carp barrier/two-way fish structure, the first of its kind to be seen on the Great Lakes.   MH

Royal Botanic Gardens, Kew ⊗

Richmond, London, England. The gardens are outstanding for the quality of the collection, the importance of the botanical research, and the beauty of the remarkable landscape to which several historical periods have contributed. The royal association of the site by the Thames goes back to the early 17th century when James I had a hunting lodge close to the river in what is today called the Old Deer Park, south of Kew. In the late 17th century when William III lived here this house was given a garden by George LONDON with an avenue running down to the river. In 1718 the Prince and Princess of Wales (later George II and Queen Caroline) had the house rebuilt by William KENT and it was renamed Richmond Lodge. By 1725 Charles BRIDGEMAN was laying out a new garden here to which, from 1729, William Kent added notable buildings—a pavilion, a dairy, a temple, hermitage, and Merlin's Cave. A little later further land was added to the north which included the Dutch House (now Kew Palace) and much of the area that is today Kew Green. In 1731, with George II on the throne, his son Frederick, Prince of Wales, leased the White House quite close to the Dutch House. The Prince of Wales added 'many curious & forain trees and exotics' to the garden and after his death in 1751 his widow, Princess Augusta, continued expanding the garden, most spectacularly from 1757 by commissioning a series of marvellous garden buildings from William CHAMBERS. The best known of these to survive is the magnificent Pagoda (1761) but the Ruined Arch (1759–60), the orangery (1757), and the Temple of Arethusa (1758) also remain as important ingredients of Kew's landscape.

From 1750 John Stuart, the 3rd Earl of Bute, a knowledgeable gardener and botanist, became Princess Augusta's garden adviser. He also became tutor to her son, the future George III, whom he later served as Prime Minister. In 1761 Bute, on the death of his uncle the 3rd Duke of Argyll who lived nearby at Twickenham,

acquired many of his precious exotics for Princess Augusta. Some of these, a *Ginkgo biloba*, a *Sophora japonica*, and a *Robinia pseudoacacia* survive, in varying states of fragility, at Kew today. In 1764 Capability BROWN was appointed master gardener at Hampton Court and George III asked him to refashion the landscape at Richmond Lodge. Bridgeman's garden and Kent's delightful buildings were swept away, to be replaced by parkland, a lake, and shorn grass up to the walls of the house.

By 1768 the first catalogue of plants grown at Kew, the *Hortus Kewensis*, listed 3,400 species. Princess Augusta died in 1772 and George III used her house as his rural retreat, living here with his family 'as the simplest country gentlefolk' as Fanny Burney wrote. Joseph BANKS succeeded Lord Bute, who had been a failure as Prime Minister, as the de facto adviser on Kew and, in effect, its first director. In 1773 he described himself modestly as having a 'kind of superintendence over [the] Royal Botanic Gardens'. Under the day-to-day management of William AITON, who became head gardener in 1784, and with the inspiration of Joseph Banks, Kew's plant collection took on a new sense of direction. By 1789 the first printed edition of *Hortus Kewensis* listed 5,600 species. In this year a Frenchman, D. de Courset, was able to write 'La collection de Kew est la plus belle qui existe.' The second printed edition of *Hortus Kewensis*, appearing in 1810–13, listed 11,000 species. Banks saw Kew as a world centre of information about plants, in particular about those which had economic importance, and emphasized the importance of links with colonial botanic gardens. In the early 19th century the boundary between Kew and Richmond Lodge was removed and a single estate was formed.

After 1820, when Banks died, there was a hiatus in the fortunes of the garden, so much so that the *Gardener's Gazette* in 1837 recorded that 'The state of the place is slovenly and discreditable, and that of the plants disgracefully dirty'. In 1841 the gardens became the property of the state and Sir William Hooker was appointed director. Under him, and his son Joseph (see HOOKER, SIR JOSEPH DALTON) who succeeded him as director, 1865–85, the garden flourished. In this period great glasshouses were built—the Palm House (1844–8) by Richard Turner and Decimus Burton and the Temperate House (1859, Decimus Burton). In the 1840s the landscape around the Palm House was designed by W. A. NESFIELD. The garden took on a role of economic importance with the distribution of tea and rubber plants. In the 20th century the garden flourished, taking on a newly important role in the conservation of plants. A striking new

glasshouse, the Princess of Wales Conservatory, with several different environments was built in 1987—close to the site of Princess Augusta's glasshouse. For a time from the late 20th century Kew had more paying visitors (around 900,000) than any other garden in the country—to be overtaken by the EDEN PROJECT in the year 2001–2. The historical landscape and its remarkable buildings are finely maintained and the garden remains a great centre of botanical research. It is also a delightful place to visit.   PT

RAY DESMOND, *Kew: The History of the Royal Botanic Gardens* (1995).

Royal Botanic Gardens, Melbourne ✦

Victoria, Australia, a much-loved city icon and a tribute to the vision of three men: Victoria's first lieutenant-governor Charles La Trobe, German botanist Ferdinand von Mueller (1825–96), and landscape designer William GUILFOYLE. It was La Trobe who chose the garden's site, a section of sloping natural bushland running down to the Yarra river, creating 'a public domain for the purpose of rearing and cultivating indigenous and exotic plants'. Ferdinand von Mueller was director 1857–73. He began a 'system garden' with beds arranged to show plants in their 'natural' order. Under his leadership the National Herbarium with its extensive collection of Australian and exotic species became recognized worldwide. But von Mueller's formal design and emphasis on science—his 1861 plan shows trees arranged in serried ranks—failed to appeal to the people of Melbourne. In 1873, von Mueller was replaced by Sydney nurseryman and landscape designer William Guilfoyle, who, using the existing La Trobe/von Mueller template, extensively remodelled the gardens. He moved at least 2,000 of von Mueller's trees, rearranging them in groups, and designed large ornamental beds; he introduced sweeping lawns and broad paths for promenading, inviting Melburnians to enjoy the gardens at their leisure. From the river's billabongs, he created a large ornamental lake to become the gardens' centrepiece. Guilfoyle also introduced much new plant material—including his beloved palms—from Queensland, New South Wales, and from international sources. Today the gardens' magnificent vistas are the legacy of Guilfoyle's search for the 'picturesque effect'. An expansive main entrance for the 21st century, Observatory Gate, has been built on the site of the historic Melbourne Observatory, embracing a wide range of visitor and interpretative facilities. The development of the RBG Cranbourne annexe, on remnant heath and bushland in Melbourne's south-east, continues, devoted

solely to the research, display, and conservation of Australian native plants on a 363-hectare/889-acre site. The gardens' emphasis has shifted from the 19th-century focus on acclimatization of introduced species to contemporary concerns relating to the conservation of the heritage landscape and the horticultural rarities within the bounds. They continue to be one of the great public gardens of the world, a living memorial to the pioneer vision of La Trobe, von Mueller, and Guilfoyle.   CMR

Royal Botanic Gardens, Peradeniya ✦

Sri Lanka. After seizure from the Dutch, the rich island of Ceylon (now Sri Lanka) became a crown colony in 1798 and so had a rather different history from that of adjacent India. Renowned from early times for its spices and economic plants, such as the dye plant gamboge (*Garcinia xanthochymus*), its flora formed the subject of several 18th-century publications, and the British proposed the establishment of a botanic garden on the island as early as 1809. William Kerr established two gardens between 1812 and 1814 and was succeeded as superintendent and chief gardener by Alexander Moon. After various false starts Moon established the garden at Peradeniya, near Kandy, in 1821, in a loop of the Mahaweli Ganga river, on the site of a royal palace; this was developed into the Royal Botanic Gardens, Peradeniya, and remains one of the most attractive of all tropical botanical gardens, covering 61 hectares/150 acres at 470 m/1,540 ft above sea level. The garden declined after Moon's death in 1825, but it gained a new lease of life with the appointment in 1844 of George Gardner, a Scottish surgeon who had already obtained great botanical expertise in South America. Gardner died prematurely in 1849, but his work on both the garden and studies of the Ceylon flora was continued by George Thwaites who was in charge until 1880 and who established outstations (notably at Hakgala in 1861) as part of a programme of growing economic plants such as cinchona, rubber, and tea. The scientific work of the garden continued under Henry Trimen (1880–96) and John Willis (1896–1911), resulting in important publications on the flora and the establishment in 1901 of a scientific journal (*Annals of the Royal Botanic Gardens, Peradeniya*). Extensive improvements in landscaping were carried out under Hugh Macmillan, the curator from 1895, and from this time date the avenues of araucarias and palms (royal, cabbage, and palmyra) that are still such a feature of the garden.   HNo

Royal Horticultural Society.

The Horticultural Society of London was

founded in 1804 by Sir Joseph BANKS and John Wedgwood; its object was 'to collect every information respecting the culture and treatment of all plants and trees, as well culinary as ornamental'. Its meetings provided a forum for discussions about the improvement of horticultural practice and for the exhibition of plants. In 1818 the society acquired a garden in Kensington, but relinquished this after it succeeded in leasing, four years later, 13 hectares/33 acres of the Duke of Devonshire's estate at Chiswick. Here it began holding a series of floral fêtes, the prototypes of the modern flower show. From the 1820s to the 1840s, the society sent out a distinguished series of collectors, such as David DOUGLAS and Robert FORTUNE, to introduce plants from abroad.

The 1850s were a time of financial crisis for the society, leading to the sale of its herbarium and library. In order to revive its fortunes, its then president, Prince Albert, arranged a new charter under the title of the Royal Horticultural Society in 1861, and secured for it the lease of a site for a new garden in Kensington, which remained its headquarters until 1888, when it became the site of the Imperial Institute and the current Science Museum.

In 1903, the garden of George Fergusson Wilson, a former RHS council member, at Wisley, Surrey, came onto the market; Sir Thomas Hanbury purchased it and presented it to the society as a new experimental garden. (The Chiswick garden was finally relinquished and subsequently built over; a street name, Horticultural Place, and some surviving trees, are all that today bear witness to the society's former garden.) For 80 years WISLEY remained the society's only garden. In 1987, however, it received a second garden: ROSEMOOR, near Great Torrington, Devon, the gift of Lady Anne Palmer—followed in 1993 by HYDE HALL, near Chelmsford, Essex, the gift of Mr and Mrs Dick Robinson. In 2001, the Northern Horticultural Society was amalgamated with the RHS, and its already established garden at HARLOW CARR, Harrogate, Yorkshire, became the fourth RHS garden.

The society's centenary year, 1904, saw the opening of its new offices and exhibition hall on Vincent Square. A further exhibition building, the New Hall, was opened in 1928 on an adjacent site on Greycoat Place. These halls serve as the venue for most of the society's flower shows. Its great spring show, after the move from Kensington in 1888, was staged at the Temple Garden; in 1913 this show was moved to the grounds of the Royal Hospital at Chelsea, where it has remained ever since, apart from gaps during the war years, and has become familiarly known as the Chelsea Flower Show. In 1993 it took over the management of the Hampton Court Flower Show, which had been begun in 1990 under the short-lived sponsorship of Network Southeast. Its third major show, at Tatton Park, Cheshire, was begun in 1999, and the society is involved as a partner in running other shows around the country.

The society began replacing its library almost immediately after the original library was sold in 1859. In 1866, it purchased the library of its former secretary John LINDLEY as a nucleus for a new collection; in 1868 this library was invested in the Lindley Library Trust as a safeguard against any future sale. Today the library holds some 50,000 books; 1,500 periodicals (350 of them current); 28,000 drawings; and the country's largest collection of horticultural trade catalogues, representing 3,200 firms, British and foreign.

The society's attempts to improve the scientific aspects of gardening have progressed from its researches into fertilizers in the 1840s, to its promotion of research into genetics at the turn of the century (Mendel's paper on heredity received its first English publication in the society's *Journal*), to its 20th-century work on plant pathology (including the hot-water treatment for daffodil eelworm). Its concern with the nomenclature of cultivated plants led to the first publication of a classified list of daffodil names in 1908; today the society is the International Registration Authority for more categories of plants than any other organization: clematis, conifers, dahlias, delphiniums, dianthus, lilies, narcissus, orchids, and rhododendrons. Since 1938, the society has issued a colour chart to aid in the standardization of plant descriptions. It has been making awards to plants since 1858, and administers a large number of committees, often joint committees with specialist plant societies, for this purpose.

The society's membership was initially confined largely to the nobility, aristocracy, and landed gentry, though from an early date practical gardeners were 'admitted to the privileges of fellowship' for a reduced fee. By the first surviving membership list (1818) there were 360 Fellows; the first female Fellows were admitted in 1830; figures fluctuated in the lower thousands for much of the 19th century, but rose steadily in the 20th, and reached 50,000 in the 1950s, 250,000 in the 1990s, and 330,000 at the beginning of the 21st century.

The society's first examinations for student gardeners were set in 1836, with Robert FORTUNE achieving distinction that year; a reading room and library for students were set up at Chiswick in 1846. Since that time the society has continually promoted professional standards

and education in gardening, from the setting of practical examinations in horticulture in 1865, through the establishment in 1893 of the RHS General Examination and in 1913 of the National Diploma in Horticulture, now succeeded by the Master of Horticulture (RHS). It has also set up the Institute of Horticulture as an organization for professional gardeners.

The amateur gardener has benefited from the society's lectures and demonstrations, and from the model gardens and the trials of plant varieties conducted at Wisley. The society has a long series of publications to its credit, ranging from its massive *Dictionary of Gardening* (completely revised 1992), through its periodicals—the *Transactions* (succeeded by the *Journal*, now called *The Garden*), the various yearbooks, *The New Plantsman*, and *The Orchid Review*—through its various registers and checklists of plant names, to practical handbooks such as *The Vegetable Garden Displayed*, first issued during the Second World War as an aid to home food production.

In 1948 a joint committee was set up with the NATIONAL TRUST to advise on the management of historic gardens in its care, which led to the trust's acquisition of important gardens for their own sake. In 1978, the society set up the NATIONAL COUNCIL FOR THE CONSERVATION OF PLANTS AND GARDENS, to aid in salvaging endangered parts of Britain's gardening heritage. From 2002, the RHS became responsible for the administration of the Britain in Bloom competition.   BE

BRENT ELLIOTT, *The Royal Horticultural Society: A History 1804–2004* (2004).

Royal Moerheim Nurseries ⊗

Dedemsvaart, Overijssel, the Netherlands, were founded in 1888 by Bonne Ruys (1865–1950) and were one of the most important perennial nurseries in the early 20th century. Ruys was encouraged by A. M. C. Jongkindt Coninck who had started a perennial nursery in his home town in 1872; inspired by English examples it was named Tottenham. Ruys was taught here as a youngster and founded Moerheim in 1888, expanding quickly from 2 hectares/5 acres to 35 hectares/86 acres in 1906 due to efficient marketing and comprehensive catalogues. The nursery was especially dedicated to export trade, and introduced many new varieties, including *Alstroemeria lutea* 'Moerheim's Orange', *Erigeron karvinskianus* 'Moerheimi', and *Helenium* 'Moerheim Beauty'. With declining export trade during the First World War the nursery expanded in garden design from 1916 onwards, producing designs without charge for the home market if plants

were supplied. This became an immediate success, and his daughters Ina and Mien later joined the firm. In 1925 Mien RUYS started an experimental garden on the nursery grounds which from 1982 has been named the Stichting Tuinen Mien Ruys. The nursery was closed in 1990, and the company reorganized into the Moerheim Group of Companies, which includes Moerheim New Plant and Moerheim Roses, which continue to trade from various locations. Mien Ruys's gardens survive, managed by a trust which opens them to the public and continues to add to the gardens. There is still a small nursery and plant shop.
                                                          JW

BONICA ZIJLSTRA, *Mien Ruys: een leven als tuinarchitecte* (1990).
TONY VENISON, 'A gallery of little garths', *Country Life*, Vol. 168: No. 4331 (21 Aug. 1980).

Royal Pavilion ⊗

Brighton, East Sussex, England, a building of irresistible splendour built for the Prince of Wales (later George IV), who had come to Brighton to live with his mistress, Mrs Fitzherbert. A farmhouse was remodelled by Henry Holland (1745–1896) and subsequently Humphry REPTON was asked to design the grounds and remodel the house. A Red Book was produced in 1806 outlining his proposals but the Prince rejected them and instead chose John NASH, Repton's former associate with whom he had parted acrimoniously. Nash, borrowing much from Repton, between 1815 and 1822 gave the house its present extravagant but charming orientalist appearance, a feast of minarets, pinnacles, domes, and towers. The atmosphere of the garden, too, was remarkably similar to that shown in the Red Book—an informal arrangement of lawns, specimen trees, walks, and flowering plants lining winding paths. In recent years this layout has been faithfully restored, even to the extent of leaving the grass of the lawns rather long to replicate the shaggy appearance they had before the days of mechanized lawnmowers. The Pavilion itself has also been restored and its magnificent interior, every bit as extravagant as its exterior, may be relished once again. The ensemble is a rare example of exotic Regency taste and it is slightly to be regretted that the garden is a public park with all the litter and scruffiness that is so often found in England.   PT

Royal Victoria Park ⊗

Bath, Somerset, England, was laid out in 1830 in a key position in the 18th-century new city of Bath. Financed by public subscription and designed by the Bath city architect Edward Davis (c.1802–1852), the park was opened by Princess Victoria in 1830. It was managed by a group of Bath citizens and financed privately until it was taken over by Bath City Council in 1921. With an area of 20 hectares/49 acres it runs on sloping ground below the magnificent Royal Crescent designed by John Wood the younger (1728–81) and built between 1767 and 1774. Beeches, horse chestnuts, and oaks are planted in grass and a rococo 19th-century bandstand ornaments the scene. A pair of exceptional urns made by Antonio Canova in 1805 as a present for the Empress Joséphine stand on either side. In the north-west corner of the park is Bath Botanical Gardens with outstanding trees and shrubs, good borders, and memorable plantings of spring bulbs in long grass.   PT

Rubenshuis ⊛

Antwerp, Belgium. Pieter-Paul Rubens acquired a house and land on the Wapper in Antwerp in 1610 two years after spending eight years in Italy. Rubens died in 1640 and in 1649 the house was rented by William Cavendish, Duke of Newcastle. It was sold by the Rubens estate in 1660. A long period of obscurity followed until the house was purchased by the city in 1937. City architect Emile van Averbeeke used engravings by Jacob Harrewijn of 1684 and 1692 as guides for the building restoration. These engravings also showed a French-inspired garden. It is not known exactly what Rubens's garden looked like but the garden there now has been reconstructed from Rubens's and his collaborators' painting *The Walk in the Garden* (Alte Pinakothek, Munich) in a Flemish–Italian Renaissance style closer to what is believed to be the original layout. Through the main gate lies an inner courtyard bounded by a magnificent baroque portico with, beyond it, a balustraded terrace leading to the garden with the Pavilion of Hercules, a small temple containing a statue of Hercules at the far end. It is divided into four parterres, each surrounded by yew hedges, entered by small gates beneath arbours. The parterres, variations of rectangular shapes punctuated by narrow conical yews, contain flowers common in Rubens's time and with varieties that resemble those of the 17th century. Oleanders, lemons, pomegranates, and figs in pots line the paths, and herms, painted satiny black like the gates and arbours, support a vine-clad pergola.   BA

Rueil, Château de,

Hauts-de-Seine, France, a 16th-century chateau which was bought by Jean de Moisset, who transformed both chateau and gardens between 1606 and 1620. The estate was bought in 1633 by the Duc de RICHELIEU, in whose ownership it achieved its greatest fame. John EVELYN visited it

in 1644 and was unimpressed by the house but thought that 'the gardens about it are so magnificent that I doubt whether Italy has any exceeding it for all rarities of pleasure'. After the revolution the estate was confiscated and later fell into ruins—nothing remains of it today. Kenneth Woodbridge, however, in his *Princely Gardens* (1986) notes that aerial photographs show how the modern street layout of Rueil-Malmaison reflects the garden's pattern of walks. Contemporary descriptions and illustrations are the only source of information about the garden. Israel Silvestre's engraving shows a giant cascade, probably the work of Tommaso FRANCINI, descending a long wooded slope—Evelyn noted its 'astonishing noyse and fury'. Water was a major ingredient in the garden—Evelyn saw a 'basilisc of copper, which . . . casts water neere 60 feet high and will of itself move round so swiftly, that one can hardly escape wetting'. The chateau faced north over a long *miroir d'eau* (see ANNEVOIE, CHÂTEAU D') with, at its far end, a rocaille grotto with an entrance like a gaping mouth. A large orangery was full of 'many exotic plants, pomegranates, lemon and orange trees' and nearby, painted on a wall, was a *trompe l'œil* view of Constantine's Arch.   PT

Rufolo, Villa ⊛

Ravello, Campania, Italy. Thirteenth-century in origin, the Villa Rufolo, with its buildings and garden, is one of the oldest surviving palaces in Italy. It was built for the Rufolo family, who incorporated Saracenic and Norman features in the layout of scattered towers, garden loggias, and terraced gardens overlooking the Gulf of Salerno. The rooms within the palace are richly ornamented with arabesques and twining vine leaves. The courtyard is lined with double loggias with pointed arches open to fresh breezes. In 1851 the villa was sold to a Scot, Frances Neville Reid, who employed Michele Ruggieri to restore the garden. Boccaccio is said to have discovered the garden in the 14th century and incorporated its setting into one of his stories in the *Decameron*. Richard Wagner based his description of the magic garden of Klingsor in *Parsifal* on the gardens at Rufolo visited in 1880. Today the lower terrace is planted with palms, cycads, and yuccas, accompanied by formal beds of bright annuals. Above, evergreen shrubs grow under tall, shade-giving umbrella pines beside dripping fountains and grottoes.   PHo

ruin.

To the poetic mind ruins must always have had their fascination, as they certainly did to Shakespeare, who wrote in Sonnet 73, possibly evoking the destruction of the monasteries, of

'bare ruin'd choirs, where late the sweet birds sang'. An early recognition of the visual power of ruins in the landscape is seen in John EVELYN's journals where, in 1675, he described a visit to Althorp House (Northamptonshire) from which were visible the ruins of Elizabethan Holdenby House. He admired the 'prospect to Holmby [Holdenby] House, which being demolished in the late Civil warre, shews like a Roman ruin shaded by the trees about it, one of the most pleasing sights that I ever saw'. Much later, in the heyday of the fashion for ruins, the ruined monuments of the classical world, especially those in Rome, fascinated grand tourists and they were seen as exceptional ornaments of the landscape. In the 18th century ruins, real or sham, came to be esteemed as ingredients in the designed landscape. The architect Sir John VANBRUGH was one of the first to admire their beauty and character. At BLENHEIM PALACE he tried, unsuccessfully, to persuade the Duchess of Marlborough to retain the ruinous medieval Woodstock Manor, but it was demolished in 1723. The romantically dishevelled views of Italian gardens painted by Hubert ROBERT in the 1760s defined a mood of the time and were thought of as an appropriate atmosphere for the landscape. French gardens in the picturesque tradition adopted the idea of creating new semi-ruinous buildings. The pyramid at MAUPERTHUIS, built in the 1760s, is of this kind but the most extraordinary garden building of its day is the ruined column (Colonne Détruite) at the DÉSERT DE RETZ dating from the late 1770s. The Temple of Philosophy at Ermenonville (after 1766), which was probably designed by Hubert Robert, seems ruinous but it was deliberately left unfinished as a symbol of the unending task of philosophy. In the 18th-century Jardins de la FONTAINE in Nîmes the Roman ruins were skilfully woven into a new layout. Existing ruins were immensely valued among 18th-century English landscapers. The gardens at RIEVAULX, DUNCOMBE, and STUDLEY ROYAL all capitalized on prospects of medieval ruins. This use of the BORROWED LANDSCAPE of ruins has a rare precursor in Scotland where, in the 1680s, Sir William BRUCE at KINROSS HOUSE showed an early relish for such things by borrowing the distant remains of Loch Leven Castle as the focal point for his garden design. Few modern garden designs make use of the poetry of ruins. Ian Hamilton FINLAY at LITTLE SPARTA comes closest, with inscribed architectural fragments animating the groves of his poetic landscape.
                                                    PT

Ruiz Lopez, Hipólito

(1754–1816), Spanish botanist and explorer. Studying pharmacy in Madrid, Ruiz developed botanical interests, and in 1777 was invited by the government to join an expedition to Spanish South America (now Chile and Peru) to collect plants, as well as minerals, 'antiquities', and 'natural curiosities'. Ruiz participated with fellow botanist José Antonio Pavón y Jimenez (1754–1840). Accompanying them was a French physician and botanist, Joseph Dombey (1742–94), as the initial plant hunting request had originated with the French government. The expedition lasted eleven years, although Dombey returned in 1785 with 73 boxes, the same year as fire destroyed much of what remained at the South American camp. Consignments were sent to Spain in 1778, but the 1779 vessel with the shipment aboard was seized by the British and disposed of in Lisbon. Exploration continued until 1788 when Ruiz and Pavon returned to Spain with their collections, including 102 live plants in 24 tubs. When Dombey returned there were disagreements over the division of the collections, Spain eventually retaining 37 of the 73 boxes. Dombey's boxes were badly stored, as was the later material brought back by the

two Spaniards, the authorities taking five years to find suitable accommodation. Ruiz and Pavon published what became *Flora Peruviana* (3 vols., 1792–1802). Special studies were made of cinchona, from the bark of which quinine is derived, and the value of *Araucaria araucana* for use in shipbuilding. Conifer seeds and specimens were sent to Aylmer Bourke Lambert (1761–1842), author of *Description of Genus Pinus* (1803). MC-C

Rusovce (Hungarian: Oroszvár) ✿ Bratislava, Slovakia. A significant landscape garden was created in place of an 18th-century baroque garden *c.*1800 beside a branch of the river Danube. In the 1840s, when garden enthusiast Count Emanuel Zichy-Ferraris had the house redesigned for his English wife as a 'Tudor castle', the alterations possibly extended to the garden as well. The owners of the estate in 1906 became Count Elemér Lónyay and his wife Stephanie, Princess of Belgium (widow of the assassinated Crown Prince Rudolph Habsburg), who modernized the residence. To redesign the grounds, they commissioned Anton UMLAUFT,

director of the Imperial Court Gardens, as well as Gertrude JEKYLL. It is quite likely that Jekyll was responsible for the informal herbaceous borders within the formal pleasure ground, ornamented with statues and vases, in front of the garden façade. This was her only work in Hungary. A well-equipped nursery, named 'Stephaneum' after the Princess, belonged to the park in the early 20th century. Oroszvár was annexed to Czechoslovakia in 1946. Before this, the glasshouse range and certain garden ornaments were taken to Eszterháza (see FERTŐD). The neglected garden is at the beginning of the process of conservation. GA

Ruspoli, Castello ✿ Vignanello, Lazio, Italy. Reputedly containing the oldest surviving 17th-century parterre in Italy, the gardens stretched out in a rectangle containing twelve equal compartments each retaining its original geometric pattern. The

---

Ruin: the Ruined Arch at Kew designed by William Chambers 1759–60.

boxwood which today delineates the flower beds—a different design in each compartment—may be a more recent introduction, with a mixture of sage, rosemary, and cotton lavender the most likely original planting. The garden which lies east of the castello, reached by a bridge over a sunken road, is attributed to Marcantonio Marescotti, who had married Ottavia, the daughter of Vicino Orsini, creator of the Sacro Bosco at BOMARZO, in the hunting park between wings of evergreen oak. It is likely that, after her husband's death in 1608, Ottavia elaborated the remarkable garden, adding her own distinctive mark by 'signing' her name in three of the parterres; in one her initials, another an eight-petalled flower derived from the Orsini coat of arms, and a third the initials of her beloved sons, Galeazzo and Sforza. The flower bed spaces were planned to contain some of the new bulbous plants being introduced from the east—tulips, iris, hyacinths, and fritillary. Sforza married a Ruspoli heiress from Siena, getting his wife's fortune on condition of adding Ruspoli to the family name. The intimate GIARDINO SEGRETO on a narrow terrace below the castle's walls already existed in Ottavia's time, but was remodelled at the beginning of the 20th century. A meticulous restoration programme for the whole garden has been completed, financed by the European Union and the Casa di Risparmio di Roma.

PHo

Russia

Climate

The territory is vast, stretching from the Baltic to the Pacific and from the Arctic to the Black Sea, with a corresponding range of climates. In most of European Russia winters are very cold and summers warm, but subtropical conditions are enjoyed by the Black Sea. In January the average temperature in Archangel is -16 °C/4 °F, while in Sochi the thermometer only rarely drops below 0 °C/32 °F. In summer Archangel's average of 15 °C/59 °F compares with Sochi's 23 °C/74 °F. For Moscow and St Petersburg the average January temperatures are -10 °C/14 °F and -9 °C/16 °F respectively, and the average July temperatures 18.5 °C/65 °F and 17.5 °C/63 °F. High evaporation during summer coupled with long freezing of the soil in winter has produced the black earth and consequent fertility of large tracts of European Russia. The flora varies little in this region but is much richer along the Black Sea coast.

Early gardens

It is not known precisely when the first gardens were made in Russia, but there were gardens in Suzdal and Vladimir in the 12th century and extensive gardens in Moscow by the end of the 15th century. An early 17th-century plan of Moscow published in Amsterdam suggests that there were many gardens, among them the Tsar's apothecary's garden, shown with an avenue of trees, and the large imperial garden, dating from 1495, by the river opposite the Kremlin, laid out with straight paths and rectangular divisions. There were hanging gardens in the Kremlin in the 17th century with pools fed by pumped water, summer houses, paths, and flower beds.

During the reign of Ivan IV (reigned 1533-84) numerous estates were established around Moscow, combining formally laid-out areas with groves, meadows, and ponds. Utility was an important element in early Russian gardens. A great deal of fruit and some cereals were grown; birch and cedar groves were planted; and there were fish ponds and beehives. There were many orchards on Ivan's estate at Kolomenskoye. On the estate of Tsar Aleksei Mikhailovich (reigned 1645-76) at Ismailovo there were elaborate gardens clearly influenced by western European Renaissance gardens, but a wide range of fruit and cereals was grown within their formal frameworks. Attempts were made to cultivate melons and grapes, and interesting experiments were undertaken into the acclimatization of plants.

Peter the Great

Considerable advances were made in the art of garden design during the early years of the 18th century, and, as with the remarkable progress made by Russia in so many fields, Peter the Great (reigned 1682-1725) was not only the driving force but also the source of many ideas. In England he is remembered for riotous behaviour in John Evelyn's garden at SAYES COURT, where he instructed his companions to push him repeatedly into a holly hedge; but he was deeply interested in the art of garden and park design, and his visits to Berlin, the Netherlands, and France were of great importance to the development of that art in Russia. He took back with him books on gardening and engravings of gardens, and he arranged for others to be purchased and sent to him in St Petersburg. He engaged, among others, the architects Trezzini (1670-1734), Braunstein (fl. early 18th century), and Le Blond (1679-1719) and the gardener Jan Roosen to create new gardens in Russia and to train Russians in their skills. Dutch gardens had a particular attraction for him, and their influence was evident in the first major garden in St Petersburg, the SUMMER GARDEN, and in the Monplaisir garden at PETERHOF. But the French formal garden was the major influence and Le Blond the most important of the designers he engaged, though plans in Peter's own hand show that he was much more than a mere patron and made a significant personal contribution to the shaping of the city's new gardens. He was directly concerned in arranging for the supply of plants from abroad and from other parts of Russia, in the import of sculpture from Italy, in the development of nurseries, and in the establishment of schools for gardeners and architects. Some Russian features were retained in the new gardens, particularly the planting of fruit bushes in formal areas and the use of native trees, including clipped fir trees and junipers. Among the great gardens made during Peter's reign were the Summer Garden, Peterhof, Prince Menshikov's garden on Vasilevsky Island, Strelna, ORANIENBAUM, Ekaterinhof, and Dubki, all in or near St Petersburg; Peterholm and Alexanderschantz near Riga; and EKATERINTAL (Kadriorg) near Tallinn.

During the reign of the Empress Elizabeth (reigned 1741-61) palaces became more magnificent and gardens more elaborate. It was for Elizabeth that RASTRELLI rebuilt the Catherine palace at TSARSKOE SELO and designed superb baroque pavilions for the remodelled gardens. The refashioning of Ropsha near St Petersburg, the palace garden in Kiev, and KUSKOVO and ARKHANGELSKOYE near Moscow date from this period.

The landscape park in Russia

The introduction of the landscape park to Russia was encouraged by the example of Catherine the Great (reigned 1762-96). 'I now love to distraction gardens in the English style', she wrote to Voltaire in 1772. Her enthusiasm was reflected in the famous Green Frog Service, with many views of English landscape parks, which she ordered from Wedgwood and Bentley. She sent architects to England to study English parks, and John BUSCH was persuaded to sell his Hackney nursery to Conrad LODDIGES and to work for her in Russia, where he played a major part in landscaping a large area at Tsarskoe Selo. The landscaping at PAVLOVSK was begun by Charles CAMERON and then continued by Vincenzo Brenna (1740-1819) and Pietro Gonzaga (1751-1831) over a period of 40 years to create Russia's greatest and one of the world's greatest landscape parks. Pavlovsk is particularly associated with the Empress Maria Fedorovna, wife of Paul I (reigned 1796-1801), the son of Catherine the Great. Paul's preferred park was GATCHINA, which John Busch helped to landscape. Catherine's favourite, Prince Potemkin (1739-91), shared the Empress's enthusiasm for the English style. William Gould from Lancashire planned the gardens of his TAURIDE PALACE in St Petersburg, which impressed J. C. LOUDON during his visit to Russia.

The landscape park soon enjoyed a wide following. The *ukaz* issued by Peter III (reigned 1761–2) releasing the nobility from service and the Charter to the Nobility of 1785 encouraged owners to settle on their estates and to develop industry and agriculture there. When they turned to gardening, the landscape style, emblematic of freedom, was a natural choice. Apart from their sentimental appeal landscape parks made better economic sense. The writings of A. T. Bolotov (1738–1833) provided a great deal of valuable advice not only on agricultural improvements and estate management but also on the Anglo-Russian style of gardening and landscape design, retaining some formality near the house, which he advocated. William Coxe, who travelled to Russia in 1772, found that 'the English taste can certainly display itself in this country to great advantage, where the parks are extensive, and the verdure, during the short summer, uncommonly beautiful. Most of the Russian nobles have gardeners of our nation and resign themselves implicitly to their direction' *(Travels into Poland, Russia, Sweden and Denmark*, 1784).

Elevated sites were favoured for country seats, usually with a wide grass slope descending to a river or lake. Meadows were often preferred to lawns and were mown only twice a year to encourage the growth of wildflowers. Garden temples were very popular, and Cameron's Temple of Friendship at Pavlovsk, a domed rotunda with Doric columns, was the inspiration of many similar structures, usually sentimentally named, in Russian parks. Temples, some of them based on English designs, were particularly abundant at Prince Kurakin's Nadezhdino in Saratov, where they celebrated Concord, Glory, Patience, Gratitude, Friendship, and Sincerity. The area near the house was often formal, as Bolotov had recommended, and straight avenues were frequently planted, usually of lime or birch. This formality, the choice of site, and the use of native trees all helped to give the Russian parks their own particular character. Among the best-known estates near Moscow are Sukhanovo, where the impressive mausoleum of the Volkonskys stood out among the buildings of the park; MARFINO with a formal garden and a landscape park; Seredniko, associated with the poet Lermontov; and Kuzminki, with its many garden buildings and striking cast-iron ornaments.

But the building of country seats, which had been checked by the French invasion of 1812, was subject to other pressures in the decades which followed. The capitalization of agriculture was subverting traditional land use, and the lifestyle of the owners of the estates was becoming increasingly insecure, since it was sustained by an indefensible social system which was to end with the abolition of serfdom in 1861. The maintenance of many parks was beyond the means of their owners, and the sound of the axe in the cherry orchard was to signal the end of a way of life. A few parks continued to be made for the very rich, and there were new gardens on a smaller scale, but there was no longer the universal commitment to an ideal which had inspired the making of the formal gardens of the 18th century and the landscape parks which followed.

Landscape design in the Soviet Union
The revolution in 1917 put an end to large private parks and gardens, and their place was taken by public works of landscape architecture. Much attention was paid to the provision of green open spaces in towns, while Parks of Culture and Rest, offering a wide range of facilities for physical recreation, entertainment, and relaxation in landscaped settings, became a feature of Soviet cities. The first of these parks to be completed was Gorky Park in Moscow. In 1933 work began on the Central Park of Culture and Rest in Leningrad, which was to embrace Yelagin, Krestovsky, and Kameny Islands. Unfortunately A.S. Nikolsky's plans for what promised to be a masterpiece of Soviet landscape architecture were not fully realized. The superimposition of a network of straight paths, a big wheel, and other apparatus on the 1820s landscape park encompassing Yelagin Island was most ill judged, but senstive restoration eventually followed, After the Second World War Krestovsky Island, on which Nikolsky's sports stadium stands, was rededicated as the Primorsky Victory Park, one of the numerous victory parks which continued a tradition, begun at Peterhof, of celebrating military success in park architecture. Another architectural consequence of the war is the very moving Piskaryovskoye Cemetry for the countless victims of the siege of Leningrad. Not the least of the achievements of the Soviet architects was the remarkable standard of restoration of the great historic parks after wartime devastation.

In the 1990s a scheme was under way to restore the old Moscow Botanic Garden and to develop a garden centre there supplying gardening equipment and traditional plants.

PH

Ruth Bancroft Garden.
See BANCROFT, RUTH, GARDEN.

Ruys, Mien
(1904–99), Dutch landscape architect. Ruys was one of the most prolific 20th-century landscape architects, completing well over 3,000 projects. Her father owned one of the largest herbaceous plant nurseries, the ROYAL MOERHEIM NURSERIES, where she commenced experimenting with planting arrangements. After landscape design education in Germany and England she headed the garden design department of the nursery, with designs showing ARTS AND CRAFTS influences. However, after becoming a member of CIAM, the International Congress of Modern Architecture, she developed modernist ideas, with designs that were functional and asymmetric. All her life she experimented with new materials, not only with plants but also hard landscape materials, which is best shown in her experimental gardens in Dedemsvaart, which survive today. Thus she developed concrete Grion tiles in the 1950s, initiated the use of railway sleepers in the 1960s, and developed recycled plastic materials for use in gardens in the 1980s. Besides being active as a garden designer, she also was a prolific author, starting a quarterly gardening magazine *Onze eigen tuin* (Our Own Garden) in 1955 with her publisher husband. Additionally she published a considerable number of books, of which the most influential include *Het vaste planten boek* (1950), reissued in 1973 as *Het nieuwe vaste planten boek* (The New Perennial Book) and *Van vensterbank tot landschap* (1981) (From Window Sill to Landscape), written with Rosette Zandvoort, which summarizes her theories and observations on landscape and garden design.   JW

Ryōanji ⊕
Kyoto city, Japan, is a temple of the Myōshinji branch of the Rinzai sect of Zen Buddhism located in the north-western corner of Kyoto city. The grounds are large but the garden of primary interest is a 250-sq.-m/820-sq.-ft dry landscape garden (see KARESANSUI) that lies to the south of the main hall. Enclosed against the main hall by a thick rammed-earth wall, the courtyard contains just fifteen stones set on a flat field of fine white gravel in groups of 5-2-3-2-3 going from east to west. This also can be interpreted as 7-5-3, a numerical pattern often employed in Japan. The austerity of the garden, which contains no plants (other than the moss that surrounds the rock groupings), makes it one of Japan's most striking garden designs.

Ryōanji was founded by Hosokawa Katsumoto (1430–73) in 1450 on the former site of Tokudaiji. The temple was burned during the Onin war (1477–8) and rebuilt by Katsumoto's son Masamoto (1466–1507) in 1488, and renewed in 1499, at which time the stone garden is traditionally said to have been built.

Historical records suggest, however, that the garden was rebuilt several times, the last being in 1797 when the main hall burnt down and was replaced with the hall of the sub-temple Seigenin.

The names of two men, Kotarō and Hikojirō, who are known to have been active gardeners at the end of the 15th century, are carved into the back of one of the stones. Additionally Katsumoto, Masamoto, the artist Sōami (d. 1525), and tea master Kanemori Sōwa (1584–1656) are all mentioned in texts as having built the garden. Ultimately, there is no conclusive proof as to who built the garden or when, but it is generally presumed that the garden stems originally from the late 16th or early 17th century, was reworked in later eras, and represents a highly abstracted landscape or oceanscape (see KARESANSUI) such as was popularly depicted in paintings and tray landscapes of the time.   MPK

Sabatini, Jardín de ⊕

Palacio Real, Madrid, Spain. The Sabatini garden was laid out in 1933–4 by the north façade of the Royal Palace on the site of the former royal stables. Its designer was Fernando García Mercadal (1896–1986) who was then architect to the parks and gardens department of Madrid. It is named after the Italian architect Francesco Sabatini (1722–97) who had worked for the royal family in Madrid, at the Pardo palace, and at ARANJUEZ. The Sabatini garden is a remarkable piece of modernism which consorts surprisingly well with the façade of the neoclassical palace. Mazelike parterres of clipped box have central fountain pools and columns of clipped cypress rise up from time to time. A square fountain pool is framed by *Abies pinsapo*, a tree native to southern Spain. To one side a canal is flanked by statues of Spanish kings on plinths. An equestrian statue of Charles III, for whom Sabatini worked, overlooks a pool.   PT

Sackville-West, Vita (Victoria)

(1892–1962), author and garden maker, the creator with her husband Harold Nicolson of the garden at SISSINGHURST CASTLE. She was a poet whose long poem *The Land* won the Hawthornden Prize in 1927, and an original novelist. In her gardening she was above all a plantswoman with a restlessly inquisitive and discerning mind and a romantic disposition—but she also possessed a highly developed visual sense and great skills as a practical gardener. These attributes, together with her poetic sense of place, allowed her to make of Sissinghurst, in collaboration with her husband, one of the most admired and influential English gardens of the 20th century. For gardeners her most precious writings are her weekly columns (or 'snippets' as she modestly called them) for the *Observer* which were gathered together in *In your Garden* (1951), *In your Garden Again* (1953), *More for your Garden* (1955), and *Even More for your Garden* (1958). All these, finely written and sparkling with life, remain well worth reading.
PT

JANE BROWN, *Vita's Other World: A Gardening Biography of V. Sackville-West* (1985).

Sacro Bosco.

See BOMARZO.

Saharanpur Botanic Garden ⊕

Uttar Pradesh, India. Saharanpur is in the foothills of the Siwalik Hills, at about 300 m/ 1,000 ft in the Doab plain between the rivers Ganges and Yamuna. The botanic garden was adapted from a 16-hectare/40-acre garden, the Farahat-baksh, which had been laid out in the mid 18th century by Intizam ud Dowlah. This was taken over by the East India Company, which appointed George Govan, a Scottish surgeon, as its first superintendent in 1819. Govan thought that the climate might allow the growth of temperate fruit and vegetables, and even tea, though he did not neglect a more scientific role, also establishing a Linnaean garden. This work was greatly expanded by John Forbes Royle, superintendent from 1823 to 1831, who was especially interested in medicinal plants, and who opened an outstation at the nearby hill station of Mussoorie, at an altitude of 2,133 m/7,000 ft. In a typical example of the longevity of traditions in India, both of these gardens are still known locally as the 'Company' Gardens. Royle maintained close links with the CALCUTTA BOTANIC GARDEN and borrowed its artists to draw the plants he was having collected as a basis for his great work *Illustrations of the Botany of the Himalayan Mountains*. Royle also had an early rock garden, shown on an 1831 plan of the garden. It fell to Hugh Falconer, better known as a palaeontologist, but also a keen botanist, and superintendent from 1831 to 1841, to effect Govan's suggestions about tea, setting up plantations in Kumaon and Garhwal after its discovery as a wild plant in Assam and the breaking of the Chinese monopoly. Falconer also distributed widely the seeds of numerous native Indian plants, as did his successor William Jameson (1841–75), notably vast quantities of the deodar (*Cedrus deodara*). J. F. Duthie, an academic botanist, had charge of the garden from 1875 to 1903, using it as a base for studies of the north Indian flora and enlarging the herbarium, which dated back to Royle's time, and was later (1908) donated to the Forest School at Dehra Dun. Despite the destruction of most of its trees by troops during the Second World War the garden still exists, reasonably well maintained, but unlabelled and little visited, run as a horticultural research establishment.   HNo

Saihōji ⊕

Kyoto city, Japan, is a temple of the Rinzai sect of Zen Buddhism located in the Arashiyama district of western Kyoto, lying just at the base of the heavily forested foothills found there. The temple is familiarly referred to as Kokedera, the Moss Temple, because of the carefully tended carpet of mosses that covers the entire garden. Of the ten or twenty varieties, polytrichum and leucobryum are the most common. The garden was, however, never intended to be a 'moss garden', but rather is simply the result of poor maintenance through the 18th and 19th centuries.

The temple was first founded by the priest Gyōki (668–749) in the mid-8th century, and then redeveloped in the 1190s by Nakahara no Morokazu as two temples, Saihōkyōin and Edoji. Saihō (westerly direction) refers to the Western Pure Land paradise of Amida Buddha and Edo (the antonym of Jōdo, Pure Land) to the mortal, impure world. In 1339, a descendent of Morokazu, Fujiwara no Chikahide, invited the eminent priest Musō Soseki (1275–1351, see TENRYŪJI) to become head priest and to convert the temple from the Pure Land sect to the Zen sect. Musō slightly changed the characters of the temple name thus creating Saihōji. The garden at Saihōji is divided into upper and lower sections, together covering roughly 1.7 hectares/4 acres. The upper area corresponds to the site of Edoji and the lower to the site of Saihōkyōin. It is most likely that much of the structure of both gardens stems from before Musō's time—in particular, the pond and islands of the lower are indicative of late Heian (784–1185) and Kamakura-period (1185–1333) gardens in their overall form and lack of riparian rockwork. The stone arrangement of the upper garden is an excellent example of the kind of early KARESANSUI described in the SAKUTEIKI.

What is interesting about Musō's relationship with the garden is how he related the gardens and the pavilions to Buddhism by giving them special names. In particular he drew from the writings of Sung-dynasty priest Dahui Zonggao (1089–1163), whose works were considered important to the Rinzai sect. In this way, he turned the garden into an allegorical

Buddhist dialogue. Saihōji was acclaimed for its beauty and many other later villas were modelled, at least in part, after it, including KINKAKUJI and GINKAKUJI. MPK

St Enda's

Rathfarnham, County Dublin, Ireland, was a bilingual boarding school for boys founded in 1910 by Patrick Pearse (1879–1916), the Irish nationalist, educationist, and writer. The house, originally called Hermitage, was built in the 18th century for Edward Hudson who, Pearse wrote, 'made himself a beautiful home . . . dotting his woods and fields with the picturesque bridges and arches and grottoes on which eighteenth century proprietors spent the money that their descendants would spend on motor-cars'. In the mid 19th century William Elliot Hudson built a series of Celtic Revival monuments—cairns, Odin's Cave, a Druidical HERMITAGE, and Emmet's Fort (named after the Irish patriot Robert Emmet). The garden was a vital part of the school's curriculum. Pupils cultivated the kitchen garden and performed plays in the picturesque grounds, and the demesne (of 20 hectares/50 acres) provided space for sports grounds. Today St Enda's is a public park with, in the view of the author cited below, much loss of its significance as a nationalist site of unique importance. PT

FINOLA O'KANE, 'Nurturing a revolution: Patrick Pearse's school garden at St Enda's', *Garden History*, Vol. 28: No. 1 (2000).

St Gall,

a Benedictine monastery in Switzerland where, in the 9th century, a plan was drawn up for the model monastic community, and the plan survives to this day. It included three gardens—a physic garden next to the physician's house, a kitchen garden, and a cemetery which was to be laid out as a decorative orchard. The physic garden was to be planted with ornamental (lilies, roses) as well as medicinal (fennel, mint, rue) plants. The kitchen garden was to grow a very wide range of plants—celery, garlic, leeks, lettuce, onions, parsley, parsnips, radishes, and much else. PT

Saint-Germain-en-Laye, Château de

Yvelines, France. For an exceptionally long period the chateau was the residence of kings—Louis VI (reigned 1108–37) was the first and Louis XIV (reigned 1643–1715) was the last. The courtier SAINT-SIMON thought Louis XIV was mad to leave Saint-German-en-Laye for 'Versailles, the saddest and most ungrateful of all places, without a view, without woods'. The site, high above the river Seine, remains beautiful, and an anonymous 17th-century engraving of the estate shows its beauties. The towered medieval Château Vieux stands at the top of the slope with the Renaissance Château Neuf designed by Philibert de L'ORME, with its many courtyards, spread out below. On the slopes running down to the river is the spectacular sequence of terraced gardens laid out by Claude MOLLET, supervised by Etienne Dupérac (1525–1604), with water features by Tommaso FRANCINI. Here were several grottoes, built into the retaining wall, decorated with rocaille work and enlivened with water-powered automata. One terrace was dominated by a parterre designed by Claude Mollet and another had canals. Between 1669 and 1673 the gardens were radically altered by André

An anonymous early 17th-century engraving of **Château de Saint-Germain-en-Laye**.

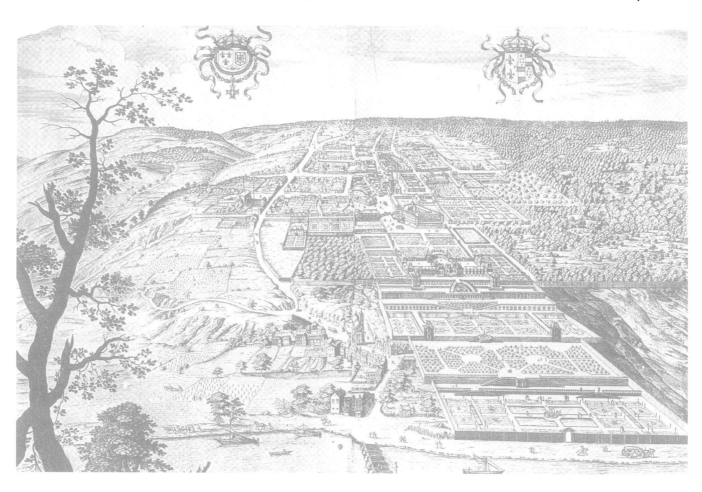

LE NÔTRE whose chief work was an immense terrace 30 m/98 ft wide and 2.5 km/1.5 miles long on the escarpment overlooking the Seine and the rooftops of Paris to the east. The Château Neuf was demolished between 1777 and 1782 and after the Revolution the Château Vieux became a prison and since 1862 has housed the Musée des Antiquités Nationales. The grounds today have the character of a public park and Le Nôtre's great terrace is intact.　PT

Saint-James, Folie,

Neuilly, near Paris, France, an extravagantly eclectic picturesque garden, busy with FABRIQUES of many kinds, designed by François-Joseph BÉLANGER for the Baron Saint-James between 1780 and 1785. The Scottish gardener and garden designer Thomas BLAIKIE, a friend of Bélanger, also worked on the garden which he called 'an example of extravagance more than of taste'. The Prince de LIGNE thought that it would be 'very beautiful if there were less of it, and if it were actually a garden'. A surviving drawing by Bélanger shows a gigantic rustic grotto/arch from the top of which a cascade pours down veiling a columned temple embedded in the rock. This was certainly built, for Blaikie described it in his memoirs—'an arch of prodigious large Stones . . . and a little temple in the midle in the Corinthian order and everything equally ridiculous as there is neither elevation nor mountain to form this huge pile of rocks'. The Baron enjoyed his garden only very briefly, becoming bankrupt in 1787, after which the estate swiftly declined and was dismembered. Today only part of the park survives, occupied by a school, and nothing of the *fabriques*.　PT

> BERND H. DAMS and ANDREW ZEGA, *Pleasure Pavilions and Follies in the Gardens of the Ancien Régime* (1995).

St Paul's Waldenbury ⊕

St Paul's Walden, Hertfordshire, England, has an early 18th-century house with a formal garden of the same period. Pleached lime walks lead to a PATTE D'OIE of three ALLÉES of beech hedges leading through woodland. Unlike a French garden of this kind the site is undulating and the *allées* swoop up and down in a thoroughly un-LE NÔTREAN fashion. An eyecatcher marks the end of each *allée*—statues of Diana and Hercules and, far outside the garden, the spire of St Paul's Walden parish church. Cross-axes lead to a lake overlooked by a pedimented temple by William CHAMBERS (brought here from Danson Park, Essex) and to a turf theatre. The garden was restored by Sir Geoffrey JELLICOE in the 1930s.　PT

St Petersburg Botanic Garden.

See KOMAROV BOTANICAL INSTITUTE.

Saint-Simon, Louis de Rouvroy, Duc de

(1675–1755), French soldier, courtier, and diarist whose *Mémoires*, completed in 1753 but not published in their entirety until 1856, are particularly remarkable for their account of court life at VERSAILLES under Louis XIV. Saint-Simon abandoned his military career in 1702 and became a courtier at Versailles. His opinions were influenced by his feeling that his merits were never truly recognized at court. The gardens at Versailles 'of which the magnificence astonishes, but of which the slightest experience contradicts, are of very bad taste. One only passes into an area of cool and shade after traversing a torrid open space . . . The violence which everywhere has been perpetrated against nature revolts and disgusts despite oneself. The abundance of water forced and gathered together from all over makes them green, dense and muddy; they breathe an unhealthy and palpable moisture, and a smell that is even more so.' Saint-Simon was perceptive about Louis XIV and gave devastating and often witty accounts of those who surrounded him. As a source of information about Versailles, apart from the sometimes dubious veracity of his evidence, he suffers from the fact that he only knew it in the last years of Louis XIV's reign and not in its heyday.　PT

Sakuteiki

(Records of Garden Making) was written in the mid 11th century in Japan, making it the world's oldest extant treatise on the design and construction of non-agricultural gardens. The authorship of the *Sakuteiki* is attributed to Tachibana no Toshitsuna (1028–94), a court noble well informed in the art of garden making, but this is only conjecture and the text may have been the combined work of several authors. The *Sakuteiki* describes Heian-period aristocratic residence gardens, in particular the courtyard area that lay to the south of the main hall of the main residence called the *nantei* or Southern Court. The information contained in the *Sakuteiki* falls into sections such as southern courts, ponds and islands, stones, gardening styles, islands, waterfalls, garden streams, trees, and wellsprings. The treatise offers technical information on garden making (i.e. how to set waterfall stones and seal them with clay); nature (i.e. how to respect natural dispositions and evoke those in the garden); the use of Chinese landscape physics (i.e. how to run water in a clockwise manner to fulfil certain geomantic requirements); Buddhism (i.e. how certain Buddhist deities were seen in garden features); and taboos (i.e. placing a tall stone in the north-east corner of the property or in the immediate proximity of a residence was taboo).　MPK

Sanbōin (Sanpōin) ⊕

Kyoto city, Japan, is the main temple of Daigo-ji, a Shingon Buddhist temple located in Yamashina, just east of central Kyoto. The garden, which includes a complexly shaped pond, isles connected by bridges, waterfalls, and many arrangements of stones, lies to the south of the main hall and covers about 0.55 hectare/1 acre. Although the temple was founded in 1115, and a garden existed there by the early 15th century, the garden as it is today stems from the time when military lord Toyotomi Hideyoshi (1537–98) took a personal interest in the temple in the last years of his life. In preparation for a grand flower viewing party that he held there in 1598, Hideyoshi ordered the reconstruction of the existing garden, adding waterfalls, islands, and bridges. The central isle held a *gomado*, a Buddhist hall for purification fire ceremonies. It is thought that this, and other garden elements, was designed to make the garden into a *mandala* (a symbolic representation of the Buddhist cosmos), as implied in the Buddhist name of the temple, the Mandala of Abiding Excellence (Yūryū mandara zan). The diary of the Chief Abbot, an excellent source of information on garden making at the time, records that Hideyoshi personally guided the initial layout of the garden and also notes the contributions, over the next quarter-century, of several magistrates and gardeners, the latter including Kentei, whose name appears in records of many contemporary gardens. Of particular note in the garden are the arrangements of stones, many of which were 'forcibly borrowed' from other lords' gardens through Hideyoshi's 'stone hunts' (*ishi-gari*). The most famous of these stones is the Fujito stone (a standing stone in the rear centre of the garden), the literary history of which begins with its mention in the 13th-century Tale of Heike.　MPK

Sandanski City Park ⊕

Sandanski, Bulgaria, is located in the southernmost corner of the country and enjoys warm a Mediterranean climate. Coupled with abundant healing thermal springs, the park is rightfully named Sveti Vrach (Medicine Man) and gives the city its spa resort character. The construction began in 1916 when pine, cedar, and Japanese pagoda trees (*Sophora japonica*) were planted, specifically selected to purify the air. After suffering severe damage by two river floods in the 1930s and 1950s, the park was finally shaped by landscape architects Boris Mitov (1927–2001) and Spiro Tatarev (1939–94) in the 1960s. The spatial concept of the 48 hectares/120 acres revolves around a central ALLÉE, which unites individual zones, such as the rock garden, the boating lake, and the grotto. Original architectural forms featuring a giant mushroom and a model of the adjacent Pirin Mountain complement the fountains, cascades, and pergolas, which along with the lively children's corner give the park a fairy-tale look. Plane trees form the planted backbone diversified by many Mediterranean and exotic species—ginkgo, magnolia, cypress, eucalyptus, pomegranate, and fig trees.   ASG

Sandemar ⊛

Södermanland, Sweden, is one of the country's best-preserved manors from the Carolingian era. *Corps-de-logis* (dwelling quarters) and wings (1693) were designed by Nicodemus TESSIN the elder and the garden probably by Johan HÅRLEMAN. The concept is traditionally baroque and very symmetrical, though minimalistic. The whole manor lines up about a main axis, starting in the north by a double avenue of limes ending with a bridge in Sandemar Bay far away in the Baltic Sea to the south. The buildings and garden are strung out like a pearl necklace on this axis. Five lines of limes on each side encompass the 1690s garden of six parterres, today dominated by trimmed hedges, spruce pyramids (*Picea abies*), and original dancing white wooden putti. The site is simple and exquisitely chosen.   KL

Sandringham House ⊛

Sandringham, Norfolk, England, has belonged to the royal family since it was bought by Albert Edward, Prince of Wales (later King Edward VII), in 1862. It is very much a country retreat and sporting estate rather than a place for royal receptions. The old house was replaced by a neo-Jacobean mansion and the gardens were laid out from the 1870s onward by William Broderick Thomas (1811–c.1898). Thomas created a landscape setting for the new house, taking advantage of some existing old trees and paying particular attention to water. He moved an existing lake and floated a new one in gently undulating ground south-west of the house. This, shrouded in trees, has a picturesque boathouse in the form of a grotto built of Pulhamite (see PULHAM, JAMES). To one side of it, rising on a craggy outcrop, is the Nest, an even more picturesque rustic belvedere, with a decorative panelled interior, built for Queen Alexandra in 1913. In 1947, below the north end of the house, a new garden was added to the design of Sir Geoffrey JELLICOE. To those familiar with his more radical later work

this comes as a surprise. A series of flowery enclosures is edged in finely detailed yew hedges and flanked with pleached lime avenues. In the 1960s Sir Eric Savill laid out a woodland walk and bog garden north-west of the house. The 24-hectare/60-acre site, with open lawns, a background of fine old trees, and varied pleasure gardens gives a vivid idea of the horticultural taste of the royal family over a long period.   PT

Sangerhausen Rosarium ⊛

near Lutherstadt Eisleben, Saxony-Anhalt, Germany, located in the foothills of the Harz Mountains, is counted one of the oldest and largest collections of roses worldwide. Today the collection covers about 500 species and 6,300 cultivars. From the beginning the approach of the rosarium has been twofold: to form a rose collection, and furthermore to study the science of rose breeding and of classification. Opened in 1903, in the care of the local amenity society, today it occupies *c.*12.5 hectares/31 acres of municipal ground which includes an arboretum with over 300 different kinds of trees. The area is divided into several departments. The oldest part was designed in 1899 by the landscape architect F. E. Doerr as a formal garden. H. Hoffmann, a resident of the town and member of the amenity society, gave his private collection of roses as a foundation. A further part was designed in 1902, one year before the great opening during a world rose congress, by P. Lambert from Trier. From 1910 onwards the garden was ornamented with several sculptures at the suggestion of Professor Gnau and a further extension of the grounds took place at the same time. As late as 1927, after constructing an alpine garden, the network of paths was finished. The post-Second World War changes, for example an open-air theatre, go back to the East German Public Park Programme. In more recent times, to improve the display, and to minimize rose replant problems, the rosarium expanded into new space which has been open to the public since 2003.   HM

Sankeien ⊛

Yokohama city, Japan, a 17.5-hectare/43-acre estate garden encompassing several hills and valleys, has been managed by a private foundation since 1953 but was originally the private villa of Meiji-period (1868–1912) entrepreneur Hara Tomitarō (1868–1939). Hara, who used the pseudonym Sankei, was the adopted son of wealthy silk merchant Hara Zenzaburō (1824–99). Sankei took over the business upon Zenzaburō's death and established himself at the family estate three years later in 1902. With the enormous wealth

that resulted from his business success, Sankei began sponsoring artists and collecting artwork, becoming one of the great patrons of his age. He also collected beautiful and historically important wooden buildings and stone garden ornaments, the artful placement of which became the key element in the design of his garden.

Among the many buildings, three in particular warrant mention. On top of a hill, seen beyond a large lotus pond from the entry to the garden, is a Muromachi-period (1333–1568) pagoda that has become the symbol of Sankeien. To the west of the lotus pond is an extensive villa hall, Rinshunkaku, which was built in 1649 for the lord of Kii province (present-day Wakayama prefecture) and moved to Sankeien in 1915. Further up one of the small valleys that feed into the garden is a tea house of unusual design, Chōshūkaku, originally from Nijō castle in Kyoto. The development of the walk through the stream valley by this tea house is particularly well done. Sankei was noted for his philanthropic work to support the local community, evidenced by his highly unusual decision in 1906 to open the grounds to the local citizens for their enjoyment while he was still alive.   MPK

Sanpōin. See SANBŌIN.

Sanspareil Rock Garden ⊛

Zwernitz Castle, Bavaria, Germany. The beech grove with its unusual rock formations near the medieval castle of Zwernitz came to the attention of Margrave Friedrich von Brandenburg-Bayreuth while he was on a hunting expedition. In 1744 he ordered the grove to be transformed into a garden. In 1746, when it was still under construction, a lady at the court is said to have exclaimed, 'Ah, c'est sans pareil!' (It has no equal!), and in the same year Margrave Friedrich had Zwernitz renamed Sanspareil. The garden consists of individual formal gardens inserted with very little alteration into the natural surroundings of a woodland setting dominated by rock formations. Small buildings with an exotic flavour such as the Belvedere with the 'Hanging Garden' were positioned on top of rocks, and rural huts were constructed to serve as retreats in the 'Sanspareil Hermitage'. The most unusual building in the grove, one of the few to have survived, was the ruined theatre, a mixture of grotto and RUIN. In addition to the many different types of building, Sanspareil also had a literary programme. Towards the end of the work on the garden, Margravine Wilhelmine named caves and rocks after events in the life of Telemachus, the son of Odysseus, who achieved enlightenment after a series of trials and adventures. In 1748 the rock garden was largely complete. When the Bayreuth margravate came to an end, the buildings, arcades, and small parterres became neglected, so that the garden eventually looked more like a landscape park. In 1942 Zwernitz Castle and the grove became the property of the Bavarian department for state-owned castles, gardens and lakes, which began restoring the garden in 1951. Boards have been placed in the rock garden with pictures to show visitors how Sanspareil would have looked in the time of Margrave Friedrich.   KG

Sanssouci ⊛

Brandenburg, Potsdam, Germany. Work on the 283-hectare/699-acre park went on almost continuously from 1715 to 1913, but it was extended chiefly between 1826 and 1860, and again between 1902 and 1908. In 1715 Friedrich I of Prussia laid out a kitchen garden, sarcastically called the Marlygarten, which was also used for recreation. In 1744 his son Friedrich II had a vineyard with six curving parabolic terraces planted 250 m/820 ft away and at right angles to the pleasure house belonging to the garden. Each terrace was divided by 28 glazed windows and 16 yew pyramids. Adjoining the vineyard stands the summer Schloss Sanssouci, built in 1745–7 to plans by Georg Wenzeslaus von Knobelsdorff (1699–1753). Vineyard and Schloss are situated on a hill and afford a splendid view of the countryside. The extensions to the garden took as their starting point the heights on which the buildings stand. In 1745 the terraces were extended to the south by a parterre comprising eight compartments to which a fountain and pond with a gilded Thetis group were added in 1748. Valuable statues by Pigalle and Adam animate the surroundings of the fountain. On the far side of the moat a short ALLÉE with the two famous sphinxes by Ebenhech (1755) leads through agricultural land to the gardeners' houses (1752).

East of the terraces there originally stood a hothouse (1747), which was replaced in 1755 by the picture gallery. A Dutch garden (1764–6) was laid out on the terraced beds, separated from the Oranier rond-point (a circular space from which paths radiate) with its fountain and hedged paths by a marble parapet with twelve sculptures of groups of children (1763–6). The Neptune Grotto (1751–7, by Knobelsdorff), with a small flower parterre and a rhomboid hedged area, forms another, separate garden room. Beyond it is the Obelisk Portal (1747, by Knobelsdorff) with a small flower parterre and, 120 m/394 ft away, the Obelisk (1748, also by Knobelsdorff). The various sections of the garden lie along the avenue which leads to the Neues Palais, 2 km/1.2 miles away. To the west

of Schloss Sanssouci are the Neue Kammern, which were built in 1747 as an Orangery on what was originally a fruit garden. They were rebuilt in 1771–4 as lodgings for guests. The remaining parts of the garden are divided into BOSQUETS; two *allées* with fountains run through them diagonally to the west, and in this part stands the Chinese tea house (1754–7, by Büring) with its own garden which later became the centre of several vistas. In the adjoining oak and beech plantations stood a marble colonnade (1751–63, by Knobelsdorff), which was demolished in 1797. At the end of the main avenue stands the Neues Palais (1763–9) by Büring, Manger, and Gontard. To the east of the large parterre with its statuary stand the Freundschaftstempel and the Antikentempel (both 1768, by Gontard).

Charlottenhof Park

In 1825 the future Friedrich Wilhelm IV was given a small estate adjoining Sanssouci by his father which he had redesigned as a landscape park from 1826 by LENNÉ; it was called Charlottenhof after the previous owners. In 1826–8 the old manor house was completely rebuilt to plans by Karl Friedrich SCHINKEL and connected directly to the park by a terrace enclosed by a pergola and exedra. To the east lie a regular rose garden (restored 1997) and a small waterworks (not preserved) by the so-called machine pond, formed by extending a moat on which building materials were transported to the Neues Palais. At the northern end of this pond stands the group of buildings known as the Roman Baths, built in the style of Italian villas: the Court Gardener's House (1829), the Tea Pavilion (1830) in the shape of a prostyle, the Hall of Arcades (1833, by Schinkel), and beyond, the Roman Baths (1834–6, by Persius), and the Servants' House (1832–3). Small, lavish flower gardens and fountains surround the buildings in front of which, facing the park, lay the Italian cultivation area with subtropical plants. To the west, by the Schloss Charlottenhof, lie the Poets' Grove, based on ancient models, with statues of famous poets and a cast-iron fountain; a large lawn with the Ildefonso group; and the vast open space of the hippodrome surrounded by trees (1836). Beyond the hippodrome lies a pheasantry (1841–4) with a group of Italianate buildings.

Lenné connected the Charlottenhof Park with the Frederican park round Sanssouci itself by means of an indirect route and three long axial vistas, so contrived that the eye is always directed inside the park, as there is no connection with the surrounding countryside. In 1827 a large area of land, known as the Hopfengarten, was purchased to the north of the Neues Palais, and Lenné redesigned this as

an elaborate landscape garden with statuary, a lake, and canals connected to the palace moat. The beauty of the garden prompted Friedrich Wilhelm IV to erect a bust of Lenné by C. D. Rauch.

After his accession in 1840 Friedrich Wilhelm IV extended the Sanssouci Park, particularly to the north. The hill Ruinenberg was laid out as a park including fields and connected by vistas with the ornamented farmland designed by Lenné. On a level with the Obelisk Lenné laid out a vineyard (1847) in the form of an Italian vineyard with a Vintner's House (1849, by Hesse and Stüler). Plans were made for a triumphal avenue to lead to the Schloss Sanssouci and on to the Orangery, but only the triumphal gate was built.

North-west of the Neue Kammern the Nordic and Sicilian Garden was created in 1857 with a large terrace and the Orangery (1,300 m/4,265 ft long, built in 1851–60), which in addition to the plant halls contains ceremonial rooms, including the Raphael Room, and living apartments. The regular terraces, in which Lenné introduced many Italian Renaissance elements into the garden, were not completed. The building plans were drawn up by Persius and Stüler from sketches by the King.

As the building which was to be the termination of the planned triumphal avenue was not connected to the Frederican park, Wilhelm II had the so-called Jubiläumsterrasse built in 1913 which H. Zeininger joined to the main avenue of the park by a 110-m/361 ft long parterre. To the west of the Orangery, G. Potente had laid out a 25-hectare/62-acre landscape garden in 1902–8 which formed the termination of the park on the north-west side at the Belvedere.

Extensive reconstruction work was carried out by Dr Gall and Georg Potente from 1922 to 1937; further work was undertaken from 1964 by H. Günther.   HGÜ/MS

Santa Barbara Botanic Garden ⊛

Santa Barbara, California, USA, was founded in 1939 on a site of 26 hectares/65 acres, and now constitutes one of the best collections of Californian native plants and centres of research and education. The site, close to the base of the Santa Ynez mountains, contains a variety of topographic settings, soils, and micro-climates together with substantial remains of the 1807 Santa Barbara mission aqueduct and dam. The first section developed around Founders Rock includes a group of large California live oaks (*Quercus agrifolia*) above a series of naturalistic pools and rock outcrops. The highly varied nature of the garden provides settings for the display of different native habitats, such as the Manzanita, Ceanothus, Desert, Arroyo, Woodland, and Santa Barbara Channel Island sections. The latter includes several rare species such as *Lynothamnus floribundus*. A grove of redwoods (*Sequoia sempervirens*), well south of their natural limit, was planted along the creek in 1930. Early planning was done by the first director assisted by Lockwood de Forest Jr. (1896–1949). Beatrix FARRAND and de Forest developed a new master plan between 1937 and 1942. Its principal features were the creation of a formal court serving the administration buildings and library, a new parking area and entrance stairs, and a large wildflower meadow with Cathedral Peak and La Cumbre Peak providing a dramatic backdrop. The original planting comprised blue-eyed daisies, lupins, penstemons, and California poppies. This was replaced in 1981 with low-maintenance plants such as bunch grasses, and native plants such as verbena, yarrow, salvias, monkey flowers (*Mimulus* species), and fremontias. More recently the entrance into the garden has been rearranged.   DCS

Santa Clotilde. See CLOTILDE, SANTA.

Santa Teresa Park ✿
Rocha department, Uruguay, is a National Park established in 1937 which now covers an area of 3,000 hectares/7,413 acres, with 2,000,000 trees and some land used for agricultural purposes. It lies between the Atlantic coast and the Rocha marsh and is part of the UNESCO-designated 'Bañados del Este' biosphere reserve. At its heart is Santa Teresa fortress built in the 18th century first by the Portuguese and latterly by the Spanish conquerors. Today it is managed by the Army Park Service. Horacio Arredondo, a local archaeologist and amateur botanist (1888–1967), devoted his life to transforming the ancient fortress and its surroundings in such a way that visitors believed it to be a natural park even though it is totally man made. This park was created in the 1930s to prevent the dunes from spreading and to make an appropriate setting for the ancient fortress. Arredondo designed a belt of planting surrounding the fortress in an informal style using plants from all over the world, with 250 species (64 indigenous and 186 exotic) producing extraordinary colour contrasts. Beyond this ring of planting he left the natural woodland of such trees as *Acacia cavenia*, queen palm (*Syagrus romanzoffianum*), parana pine (*Araucaria angustifolia*), and *Peltophorum dubium*. The park includes an area of cacti, nurseries, a rose garden with over 300 cultivars, and a museum. The whole is framed by the spectacular scenery of the seashore.
                                                            SLB

Sargent, Charles Sprague
(1841–1927), American dendrologist and plantsman born in Boston, Massachusetts. Sargent graduated from Harvard and then studied botany and horticulture. Aged 29 he became both director of Harvard Botanic Garden and in 1873 director of the newly created ARNOLD ARBORETUM, which under his tenure became a most prestigious collection. Sargent took part in the 1882 Northern Pacific Transcontinental Survey, and later travelled widely abroad collecting and introducing many trees, a number of which he also distributed to overseas horticultural bodies. In 1900 he began studying the American species of the genus *Crataegus*, describing 730 new species and introducing many into the arboretum. He was a prodigious author, publishing the fourteen-volume *Silva of North America* (1890–1902) among many other writings. He also edited E. H. WILSON's China records of the introductions made on behalf of the Arnold Arboretum in the three-volume *Plantae Wilsonianae* (1913–17).   MC-C

Săvârşin Park ✿
(Hungarian: Soborsin), Arad county, Romania. The landscape garden around the neo-classical house was created by Heinrich NEBBIEN for the Brunswick family in the early 19th century, and was partly redesigned by Hungarian landscape gardener Ferenc Óry in 1857. The estate changed ownership several times till the house and a large part of the grounds were bought by Michael I, King of Romania, in 1943. During the communist period it served as the dictator Nicolae Ceauşescu's residence.   GA

Narcis Dorin Ion, *Castele, palaste şi conace din România*, vol. i (2002).

Savill Garden ✿
Englefield Green, Surrey, England, in WINDSOR Great Park, was the creation of Eric Savill, the deputy surveyor of the park, from 1932. In 14 hectares/35 acres on a site of gently undulating acid soil enlivened by two pools and a stream, against a background of old beeches, oaks, and sweet chestnuts, Eric Savill laid out a subtle woodland garden of exceptional quality. The landscape has a naturalistic appearance intermingling long vistas and intimate glades. The trees and shrubs which form the chief part of the planting are often accompanied with underplantings of herbaceous perennials and bulbs. In moist areas, in particular on the banks of the stream and pools, are astilbes, many ferns, irises, *Lysichiton american* and *L. camtschatcensis*, and Himalayan primulas (especially *P. denticulata*). There are other planted features at the Savill Garden—among them a rose garden, a dry garden, and

herbaceous borders—all of which are good of their kind, but it is the outstanding shrubs and fine underplantings which make the Savill Garden of exceptional interest. The Savill Garden is immediately adjacent to the later Valley Garden, also within Windsor Great Park. Together they hold four National Collections of plants, all of great interest to gardeners: ferns (over 130 species and over 150 cultivars), mahonias (27 species and 51 cultivars), magnolias (30 species and 320 cultivars), and species rhododendrons (over 600 species). In each case these are among the finest collections of their genera in the country.   PT

Sayes Court,
Deptford, England, was, from 1652, the home of John EVELYN. Here he laid out a vast formal garden of 40 hectares/100 acres, rich in parterres and axial vistas, obviously inspired by what he had seen on his Italian and French travels. Evelyn's plan, surviving in the British Library, shows a double avenue aligned on the house with the gardens slightly awkwardly disposed on one side. Peter the Great stayed here for three months in 1698 during which time much damage was done to the garden— Evelyn subsequently referred to 'my now ruin'd gardens at Say's-court, (thanks to the Czar of Moscovy)'. Nothing survives of the Sayes Court estate today except its name, which has been given to a lugubrious public garden.   PT

Sceaux, Parc de ✿
Hauts-de-Seine, France, was the estate of Jean-Baptiste Colbert, Louis XIV's Finance Minister, who in 1673 commissioned a new garden from André LE NÔTRE. The undulating site presented the possibility of making dramatic water gardens which Le Nôtre proceeded to do, with a spectacular cascade, pools, and fountains. A noble ORANGERY (which survives) was designed by Jules HARDOUIN-MANSART and built in 1685 in the time of Colbert's son, the Marquis de Seignelay, who also added the Grand Canal parallel to Le Nôtre's cascade. After 1755, when the estate was inherited by the Duc de Penthièvre, part of the garden was turned into a *jardin à l'anglaise* (see JARDIN ANGLAIS) but he also added many BOSQUETS to the earlier layout. After the Revolution the estate was sequestrated and the land turned over to agriculture. The chateau survived the Revolution but, after the estate was sold to a private owner in 1798, it was abandoned and eventually demolished. In the 19th century Le Nôtre's layout was substantially reinstated and today much of its broad design but little of its original detail may be appreciated. The cascade has been splendidly rebuilt, with masks by Rodin; the 17th-century octagonal pool and

Grand Canal are in place; and the beautiful Pavillon de l'Aurore (c.1672, possibly by Claude Perrault, with paintings by Charles Le Brun) is intact. In 1932 the handsome Pavillon de Hanovre (1760, by Jean-Michel Chevotet), originally in the Duc de Richelieu's Paris garden, was brought here and erected at the meeting point of three vistas against the west wall of the garden.   PT

Scheemakers, Peter

(1691–1781), sculptor born in Antwerp who worked in Germany, Rome, and England where he spent most of his working life. He carved many monuments, often using Portland stone, including that of Shakespeare in Westminster Abbey (1740), and many of his works were made for gardens. Most of his statues were inspired by ancient originals and survive at COTTESBROOKE HALL, ROUSHAM (a dramatic *Lion Attacking a Horse*), and STOWE. John Davis in the book cited below criticizes the 'stiff formality' found in Scheemakers's busts. Scheemakers also worked in lead.   PT

JOHN DAVIS, *Antique Garden Ornament* (1991).

Schinkel, Karl Friedrich

(1781–1841), German architect and city planner who always aimed to integrate landscape and architecture, rather than to create buildings as self-contained monuments, by means of a modern interpretation of classical forms. He worked closely with LENNÉ, designing a People's Hall and Rotunda for his *Volksgarten* at Magdeburg (1824), and at KLEIN-GLIENICKE. Lenné's work at the TIERGARTEN, Berlin (for which Schinkel designed a Corinthian tea house in the Schlosspark Bellevue, 1824), was very strongly influenced by Schinkel's 1835 plan for the section of the Tiergarten where it meets the Brandenburg Gate.

In the narrower sense of landscape design Schinkel's opportunities were limited. His proposal for revitalizing the Große Stern, Tiergarten, by providing a circle of low, clipped hedges was not implemented. His greatest opportunity came at Charlottenhof (SANSSOUCI), Potsdam, where in his Römische Bäder (1834–6) he succeeded by ingenious changes of level in creating the impression of the picturesque grouping of Italian vernacular architecture, which he had often sketched on his first visit to Italy (1803–5). On a grid plan he made clever and unexpected use of open and closed spaces, and changes of level to create a minor masterpiece. The hippodrome form which he used here (and also in his 1835 plan for the Tiergarten) was derived from the gardens of PLINY THE YOUNGER's Tuscan Villa. It was to become a favourite form with later park designers (especially Gustav MEYER).   PG

Schlaun, Johann Conrad

(1695–1773), German master of works. After training as engineer and architect he studied in Würzburg, Rome, and Paris. He served under Prince Elector and Archbishop Clemens August of Cologne, working 1720–1 with B. Neumann (1687–1753). From 1723 to 1735 he extended the palace and made new gardens in Nordkirchen (island garden with GLORIETTE, orangery, pheasant house). Between 1725 and 1728 he rebuilt Schloss AUGUSTUSBURG. From 1729 in Münster he worked on the fortifications, promenade, royal palace and garden, St Clemens church, hospital, and gardens. His style combined brick and cut stone and traditional Dutch architectural influences with elements of French classicism and Roman high baroque. He also designed summer houses, pheasantries, orangeries (Velen, Eggermühlen), and gardens (Haus Rüschhaus, Nienberge, Schloss Herzford, Lingen, Haus Beck, Kirchhellen). His 1735–44 design of Clemenswerth hunting lodge near Sögel, with cloister garden, park, and water features, is regarded as probably the finest *Jagdsternschloss* in Europe.   MR

Schleißheim ⊛

near Munich, Germany. In 1597 the Bavarian Duke Wilhelm V acquired the isolated holdings of Schleißheim north of Munich and withdrew here to live a life of pious contemplation. In 1616–23 Elector Maximilian I built the 'Old Palace' and added a small Renaissance garden. It was under Elector Max Emanuel that Schleißheim became a residence of major importance: he enlarged the country seat of his ancestors, transforming it into a magnificent palace and garden complex. First, between 1684 and 1689, the Bavarian court architect Henrico Zuccalli built the hunting lodge and garden palace of Lustheim about 1 km/0.6 mile east of the Old Palace. The extensive network of canals in the Schleißheim grounds, which links with the Isar, Amper, and Wurm rivers, was completed at the same time. The New Palace, located directly opposite the Old Palace, was planned over a long period and finally begun in 1701; after a considerable break in the building activity it was recommenced in 1715 under the supervision of Joseph Effner. The gardens that stretch between Lustheim and the New Palace, which are bordered by canals and include an extensive BOSQUET area, were begun in 1684 by Henrico Zuccalli. From 1715 to 1726 Dominique GIRARD produced a more modern design, while retaining Zuccalli's basic concept. In front of the palace a magnificent parterre was created with a lower central section, ornamental flower beds, sculptures, and various water features, with a cascade taking pride of place. The central

axis between the cascade and Lustheim was originally used for the game of pall-mall; the present canal was built in the last quarter of the 18th century. Max Emanuel spent many years outside his country: in Brussels from 1692 to 1701 as governor of the Spanish Netherlands and in France from 1705 to 1715 after his defeat in the Spanish War of Succession. Dutch and French influences were thus incorporated in the design of Schleißheim. From 1865 to 1868, after a long period of neglect, the gardens were renovated by Carl von Effner on the basis of the historic documents available at the time. Today Schleißheim, with an area of 78 hectares/193 acres, is one of the few baroque garden complexes in Germany that has survived with very little change.

RH

Schlosshof (Schloss Hof) ⊛

Lower Austria. Along with BELVEDERE in Vienna and the garden in Obensiebenbrunn, the seven-terrace grounds of Schlosshof are among the most important works commissioned by Prince Eugene of Savoy, who pursued his passion for hunting here in the plain of the river March. Between 1725 and 1732 the troika already known for its work at BELVEDERE—architect Johann Lukas von HILDEBRANDT, master *fontainier* Dominique GIRARD, and court master gardener Anton Zinner—created a garden microcosm dedicated to the prestige of their Prince. Stables, a coach house, and a large dairy, with two orangeries and garden parterres, framed and enhanced this country house in the classical spirit of an Italian villa. The main garden, richly ornamented with cascades, flights of steps, fountains, statues, and *parterres à pièces coupées pour les fleurs* (flower parterres), was enclosed in splendid fortifications; the extravagantly imposing wrought-iron gates are particularly noteworthy. After the death of Prince Eugene in 1736 the palace complex passed to his niece Victoria, who staged many glittering celebrations here before selling it to the Austrian imperial house. The buildings were given an extra storey by architect Franz Anton Hillebrandt and made into a residence for Empress Maria Theresa. Three Canaletto paintings of 1760 show that the gardens were still maintained very intensively at this time. After 1780 interest in the baroque garden waned, and by the early 19th century only the principal structures, with simple lawn parterres, were extant. In the late 19th century Schlosshof was given over to the imperial riding and coaching institute, and most of its sculptures were transported to other royal gardens or sold privately. Since the late 1990s there have been moves to reconstruct the important terraces with baroque beds, following the methodological example of HAMPTON COURT.   GH

Schmidt, J. Palle

(b. 1923), Danish landscape architect. Schmidt worked with Aksel Andersen, who took over G. N. BRANDT's commitments in 1945, and Schmidt succeeded Georg BOYE from 1972 to 1993 as professor at the Landscape Institute at the Royal Veterinary and Agricultural University. Schmidt has designed green spaces at many large social housing developments, low atrium houses, terraced houses, as well as flats. His main intention has been to create diverse and dynamic plantings, as at the developments Bredalsparken in Hvidovre (1949–55), Carlsro (1951–58), Vesterbo in Værløse (1954–60), and terraced houses in Fredensborg. He has designed more than 600 private gardens with well-composed plantings, as in the water garden at Trongård Practice School, Kgs. Lyngby (1958–60), and at Herning Northern Cemetery (1967–70). Working with motorways Schmidt creates strong plant volumes with hedges, forests, and other tree plantings.   AL

Schönbrunn ⊛

Vienna, Austria. Between 1688 and 1690 Johann Bernhard Fischer von ERLACH, commissioned by the Emperor Leopold I, made designs for a monumental palace—larger than Versailles—on the top of Schönbrunn Hill and in the early 1690s designed a revised version. The construction of the palace started in 1696, but already in the previous year the French designer Jean Trehet began to lay out the gardens. In 1743 Archduchess Maria Theresa decided to transform the unfinished palace into her summer residence and her husband Franz Ferdinand (reigned 1740–65) took a particular interest in the garden. He commissioned a team of artists from his native Lorraine, among them the architect Jean Nicolas Jadot, the garden designer Louis Gervais, and the engineer Jean Brequin de Demange. In addition Franz Ferdinand employed the Dutch gardener Adrian von Stekhoven. The gardens were laid out in ROCOCO style with great diagonal alleys and circular pools. Between 1751 and 1752 Jadot designed a circular MENAGERIE. A geometrically structured botanical garden was laid out beside the Dutch Garden designed by Adrian van Stekhoven and his assistant Richard van der Schot. In 1755, a huge orangery, 186 m/610 ft long, was completed. In the late 18th century further additions were made to the garden. The architect Johann Ferdinand Hetzendorf von Hohenberg designed the GLORIETTE (1775) as a crowning belvedere on the hill with terraces and the zigzag paths on the slope. The Neptune Fountain (1780) was built and the Great

Parterre was remodelled with eight compartments and 32 statues aligned on the flanking BOSQUET walls. In the eastern *bosquet* area Hohenberg erected the Obelisk Fountain (1777), the sham RUIN (1778), and probably the circular aviary also dates from that time. In 1773 the sculptor Wilhelm Beyer was commissioned with 32 statues for the Great Parterre.

Between 1828 and 1850 first the geometric Dutch Garden and then the Botanical Garden were transformed into a naturalistic JARDIN ANGLAIS. This in turn was swept away when, in 1880–2, the Great Palm House designed by Franz Xaver Segenschmid was erected on the site of the former Dutch Garden and a historicizing ornamental garden by Adolf VETTER was laid out around it, replacing the landscape garden. In 1904 the Sun Dial House, a *Jugendstil* glass house designed by Alfons Custodis, was constructed west of the Great Palm House. From 1869 to 1886 the garden director Adolf Vetter carried out a substantial reinstatement of the baroque gardens by replanting and trimming of trees and hedges. About 1896 the garden director Anton UMLAUFT redecorated the eight beds of the Great Parterre with neo-baroque ornaments, which still exist today in slightly modified forms.

BH/GH

Schönbusch ⊛

Aschaffenburg, Bavaria, Germany, is one of the earliest landscape gardens in the German-speaking world. The core of the garden is an old game park, the hunting ground of the Mainz electors. In 1775, one year after Friedrich Carl Joseph von Erthal (1719–1802) had become Elector and Archbishop of Mainz, he ordered the game park to be converted into a landscape garden. Erthal's 'First Minister of State', Wilhelm Friedrich von Sickingen (1739–1818), was placed in charge of the project; he supervised the conversion work until 1779 and was frequently at loggerheads with the architect and the gardeners over questions of design. In this period the straight canal, various avenues, the Lower Lake, and the 'mountains' on the shore of the Lower Lake were completed. From 1780 the young SCHWETZINGEN garden designer Friedrich Ludwig SCKELL was entrusted with the further landscaping of Schönbusch. During his apprenticeship years abroad Sckell had also been to England and visited many of the famous English landscape gardens. In 1777 he had laid out part of the Schwetzingen Palace garden in the English landscape style, and was widely praised for his achievement. In Schönbusch Sckell designed the whole north section of the park with its spacious areas of water and meadows, and the

Große Wiesental (Large Meadowed Valley) which still runs through Schönbusch from north to south. By opening up the wooded areas on the edge of the park, Sckell created vistas of the surrounding countryside and thus made the park appear larger than it really was. After its somewhat awkward beginnings under Sickingen, in Sckell's hands Schönbusch became a fully-fledged landscape park. All the park buildings were designed by the Portuguese-born architect Emanuel Joseph von Herigoyen (1746–1817). He also constructed several miniature architectural features which reflect the ideas of the Enlightenment, such as a small Temple of Friendship and a Philosopher's House. With the little village in the southern section of the park, a sentimental rural setting was created which had more in common with the picturesque features of VERSAILLES than the spirit of English landscape gardens. Schönbusch was used not just by the Elector but also by the citizens of the nearby town of Aschaffenburg as a place of entertainment and recreation. In the 18th century there was already a restaurateur catering to the bodily needs of the visitors in the building erected between 1781 and 1783 at the entrance of the park. There were also numerous recreational facilities for the entertainment of the public, as well as a ballroom and of course the boats on the two lakes. After 1814 the Aschaffenburg territory of the Mainz prince electors was absorbed into the kingdom of Bavaria. At the beginning of the 20th century Schönbusch Park became the property of the Free State of Bavaria.

JA

Schreberanlage ⊛

(Schreber layout), Leipzig, Germany, which was the first of its kind in the world, is situated to the west of the city centre. It was initiated by the local educationalist Dr Ernst Innocenz Hauschild (1808–66), who founded the association in May 1864 in memory of Dr Daniel Gottlob Moritz Schreber (1808–61) with the intention to create playgrounds for the physical exercise of adolescents. One year later, in May 1865, the first playground, called Schreberplatz, opened, which was at that time situated in the JOHANNA-PARK, and in 1876 it moved to its present site. At first the Schreberplatz was a simple meadow. In 1868 the teacher and co-initiator Karl Gesell (1800–79) suggested using the site partly to lay out small allotments to teach children gardening. Only one year later these became allotments for the whole family and subsequently the allotments were fenced in and arbours were built. That is the way in which the *Schrebergärten* developed. The central meadow, surrounded by trees and provided with play and gymnastic equipment, was the imaginative and creative centre of the park. Today the eastern part of the meadow has been restored in the historical style with reconstructed historical play equipment, whereas the western part is now occupied by newer allotments. In 1896 the Schreberverein house (architect Carl Fischer) was built. Since 1996 it has housed the German Allotment Museum, which shows numerous exhibits of the German KLEINGARTENWESEN. The owner of the site, which is used by the Dr Schreber Club, is the city of Leipzig.   KF

Schrebergärten. See SCHREBERANLAGE.

Schwartz, Martha

(b. 1950), American landscape architect whose primary focus is on urban projects. Her approach to landscape architecture is informed by a desire to raise the discipline to the level of fine art. This has led to some highly innovative public spaces, identified by a minimalist use of geometric shapes and pure colour in hardscape and a similarly restricted plant palette. While committed to improving American attitudes to landscape and conservation, and criticizing the mind-numbing blandness of urban sprawl, Schwartz is not above using visual jokes to spread her message, as with the notorious 'Bagel Garden' (Boston, 1979), which used rows of outsized synthetic bagels as ground cover. A 1973 graduate (BFA, cum laude) of the University of Michigan, Schwartz holds a master of landscape architecture, 1974-6, and MLA 1977 from the University of Michigan. She is an adjunct professor of landscape architecture at the Harvard University Graduate School of Design, and has an international design practice including projects such as the Exchange Place in Manchester, England, and Swiss Re Headquarters in Munich, Germany.   EC

MARTHA SCHWARTZ and TIM RICHARDSON (eds.), *The Vanguard Landscapes and Gardens of Martha Schwartz* (2004).

Schwerin Castle and Gardens ⊛

Schwerin, Mecklenburg-Pomerania, Germany, owe their unique character to the incorporation of water as a design element. The park's baroque *pièce de résistance* was created by the French architect Jean Laurent Legeay (1710-c.1786), who started work in 1746, and integrated already existing canals into his plan. A cross-shaped canal is flanked by evenly spaced groves of trees on both sides. Lining the canal are fourteen baroque sculptures, copies made in the 1950s and modelled after statues from the workshop of Balthasar Permoser (1651-1732). The baroque axis that begins at the castle is opened by an 1893 equestrian statue of

Frederic Franz II, Grand Duke of Mecklenburg-Schwerin, on a parterre lawn. Starting in 1840, the park was extended and redesigned (about 14 hectares/34.6 acres in size). Peter Joseph LENNÉ, who provided the plans for this project, respected the original geometric matrix. One of the park's new constructions was the Greenhouse Garden, a landscape garden containing a collection of dendrological treasures. Lenné also created the Burggarten that immediately surrounds the castle, which is located on an island. Now the seat of the Landtag, Mecklenburg-Pomerania's state parliament, the castle owes its present architectural form to Georg Adolph Demmler, who created this neo-Renaissance building between 1846 and 1857, assisted by Friedrich August Stüler and Gottfried Semper. From the Burggarten with its animated relief, the surrounding lake can be seen from several terraces and viewpoints. The garden, designed in a mixed style, has a grotto, fountains, fine trees, and an orangery, grouped around a half-open courtyard. In recent years the Burggarten has been completely restored.   PFi

BIRGID HOLZ, *Parks und Gärten der Schlösser Güstrow, Schwerin und Ludwigslust* (n.d.). NEIDHARDT KRAUß and EGON FISCHER, *Schlösser, Gutshäuser und Parks in Mecklenburg-Vorpommern* (2002).

Schwetzingen ⊛

Baden-Württemberg, Germany, was in the 18th century the summer residence of the Palatine court. The central part of the Schloss was originally a medieval moated castle which was rebuilt and extended after it had been destroyed in the Thirty Years War (1618-48). The redesigning of the Schloss was above all the work of Karl Theodor who became Elector of the Palatinate in 1743. He commissioned the famous theatre architect Alessandro Galli Bibiena (1687-c.1769) who, together with the architect Nicolas de Pigage (1723-96), built the two circular buildings which gave the court gardener J. Ludwig Petri the inspiration for the circular parterre. On the west the parterre was bounded by two curved pergolas constructed of trellises. A broad axis connects the Schloss with the town and at the same time leads through the garden into the surrounding countryside. A large rectangular pond was placed at right angles at the end of the baroque garden. The cross-shaped arrangement of the avenues of limes emphasizes the garden's highly original circular design. BOSQUETS lay beyond the avenues.

The garden contained a great deal of statuary and many fountains (such as the Stag Fountain) as well as various buildings, such as the Orangery by Pigage which has a parterre

enclosed by a ditch, and the rococo theatre of 1752, also by Pigage, which stands behind the northern building. It is worth mentioning here that the court orchestra in nearby Mannheim was regarded as one of the finest in Germany and that the Mannheim School exerted a very definite influence on the music of the time. Pigage was also responsible for the once beautifully furnished bathhouse which stands in the *bosquet*. Next to the bathhouse is a delightful waterwork representing water-spouting birds, presumed to have originated from Lunéville; immediately adjacent are aviaries full of live birds.

The 'Court and Pleasure Gardener' Friedrich Ludwig von SCKELL redesigned the outer areas of the garden in the English landscape style from 1776. The rectangular pond became a 'natural' lake. The design of buildings for the new park was again given to the architect and director of gardening, Pigage, and he built the Waldbotanik Temple, the Roman aqueduct, the Temple of Mercury, and the Turkish mosque which had its own garden.

Work on the garden was practically complete when Sckell went to Munich in 1804 after the Elector Karl Theodor had transferred his residence from Mannheim to Munich in 1778 upon succeeding to the throne of Bavaria. The parterre was reconstructed in 1974 to the original design by Petri.   UD

Sckell, Friedrich Ludwig von

(1750-1823), the first great German landscape designer to have been influenced by the English landscape style. He studied in England, where he was rather eclectically influenced by BROWN and CHAMBERS. In his first period, from 1776 to 1804, he was employed at SCHWETZINGEN by Karl Theodor, and worked for many neighbouring princes. He also laid out the fortifications of Mannheim as a public promenade. During this period he began to reject the pre-romantic sentimental style in favour of neoclassicism. His second period began with his assumption of full responsibility for the ENGLISCHER GARTEN, Munich, where he had worked since 1789. Here he aimed to lay out a *Volksgarten* (see PUBLIC PARKS AND GARDENS), although he was more influenced by the narrowly stylistic aspects of HIRSCHFELD's conception. His memorandum of 1807 makes it clear that he had long disapproved of exotic buildings and sentimental monuments, and that a *Volksgarten* must take the middle course between princely magnificence and a park. His other major work during this period was NYMPHENBURG.   PG

Scotland. See BRITISH ISLES.

Scotney Castle ⊛

Lamberhurst, Kent, England, has a garden dating from the early 19th century strongly influenced by theories of the PICTURESQUE landscape which were then distinctly old fashioned, indeed around 40 years after their time. Between 1837 and 1844 Edward Hussey commissioned a new castle here designed by Anthony Salvin (1799–1881). The site for the new castle, chosen with the advice of William Sawrey GILPIN, was a promontory above the quarry from which the stone for it was taken. From this position it commanded views down precipitous slopes to the picturesque partly medieval moated castle below. The 17th-century additions to the old castle were removed to increase its pictorial presence. The rocky slopes between the castles were planted up to form a cataract of trees and shrubs framing the old castle. Close to the new castle a viewing terrace was built from which views of the new picturesque landscape might best be displayed. The style of planting looked forward to the wild gardening of William ROBINSON but the careful scenic picture making owes more to the earlier tradition of the landscape park. Among substantial cedars, cypresses, oaks, and pines (much damaged in the 1987 storm) are azaleas, thickets of *Kalmia latifolia*, magnolias, and Japanese maples. In the forecourt of the old castle is a herb garden designed by Lanning ROPER and, on a shady spit of land jutting out into the moat, a bronze reclining figure by Henry Moore (1898–1986). The estate was left to the NATIONAL TRUST in 1970 in the will of the distinguished garden historian Christopher Hussey (1899–1970). PT

Scott Arboretum ⊛

Swarthmore, Pennsylvania, USA, is located on 300 hectares/741 acres of the Swarthmore College campus. It was established in 1929 as a living memorial to alumnus Arthur Hoyt Scott, who believed gardens could significantly improve the quality of life in an industrial society. The plantings provide a collective catalogue of plants appropriate for garden use in this region, by virtue of their ornamental qualities, resistance to disease, and ease of maintenance. There are two types of plantings: theme gardens and collections. The theme gardens, such as one of fragrant plants, one of winter interest, and one of gold and purple foliage plants, inspire combinations and individual garden uses of plant types. The collections, including roses, hollies, pines, lilacs, tree peonies, and butterfly bush (*Buddleja*) allow close comparisons of varieties and relatives. One of the most novel arboretum plantings, initiated by its first director in 1931, is a botanical evolutionary sequence—from the simplest plants (ginkgo, yew, and pine families) to the most complex (composites) in a counter-clockwise spiral around the campus. A discerning botanical eye can pick out remnants of this spiral, now tucked among other plants and structures. The Scott Arboretum is *overlaid* onto the college, not a discrete precinct, and serves to enliven courtyards and connections among the buildings of the college. The pleasure and subconscious horticultural enrichment thus provided give full complement to the academic virtues of a living study collection. This model seems to foster a much less 'institutional' campus, and a richer learning and living environment. PC

sculpture garden.

The garden devoted to sculptures, which became fashionable in the 20th century, has ancient antecedents. The Belvedere Court in the VATICAN was designed by BRAMANTE and completed in 1523 to display Pope Julius' collection of antique statuary. Almost exactly 100 years later Inigo Jones designed a courtyard at Arundel House (London) to display the Earl of Arundel's collection of classical statues. However, it is in the 20th century, with the great development of museums and many private collectors, that we see the flourishing of sculpture gardens. Some of these are on interesting old sites, such as the National Gallery of Art Sculpture Garden in Washington, DC, which was opened in 1999 with landscaping by the Olin Partnership. The site, on the Mall, is part of land set aside in Pierre L'Enfant's design for Washington (1791) for which A. J. DOWNING made proposals in 1851 which have influenced its appearance to this day. Washington is also home to the Hirshhorn Sculpture Garden, part of the Smithsonian Institution, with a fine collection of largely 20th-century work. Sculptures more often than not are shown to greater advantage in the open spaces of a garden, against a background of planting, than they are in the confinement of a museum building. At the Yorkshire Sculpture Park in England (founded in 1977) a permanent collection of sculptures by Henry Moore is superbly displayed in an undulating and wild parklike setting. The park has an area of 202 hectares/500 acres, some of it parkland laid out in the 18th century, and has ample room for a good permanent collection as well as substantial visiting exhibitions. The KRÖLLER MÜLLER MUSEUM sculpture garden in the Netherlands (founded in 1961), with an area of 25 hectares/62 acres in the Hoge Veluwe National Park, has plenty of space to display large pieces which greatly benefit from the setting. Sculpture gardens attached to the houses of artists often have especially strong atmosphere. The little leafy garden of Barbara Hepworth's studio in St Ives (Cornwall) was used by her to display her work. It survives today, much as she left it, and her studio, with her tools and overall, has the appearance of being only momentarily abandoned. Rodin's great early 18th-century house in Paris, the Hôtel Biron, where he went to live in 1908, has a garden which was restored in 1993 to evoke its original 18th-century appearance in much simplified form. Now opened to the public under the name Musée Rodin it has a symmetrical arrangement of long strips of lawn, simple ALLÉES and PARTERRES, and a circular *bassin* (formal pool) which makes an excellent setting for some of Rodin's best-known works, among them *Le Penseur*, *Les Bourgeois de Calais*, and his portrait figure of Balzac. Collectors of sculpture in the late 20th century often seized upon the garden as the most sympathetic setting for their collections. On the island of Mallorca the collector Dom Bartolomeo March in the 1960s asked Russell PAGE to design such a garden for him at his estate of Sa Torre Cega. On the rocky hilltop site the works of Anthony Caro, Eduardo Chillida, Dode Caedro, Henry Moore, and many others have been skilfully accommodated in diverse and appropriate settings. Russell Page went on, in 1981, to design another notable garden of this kind, the Donald M. KENDALL Sculpture Gardens in the grounds of the PepsiCo Corporation. Dealers in sculpture have seen the value of displaying their stock in the context of a garden. In England an outstanding example of this sort of sculpture garden is Sculpture at Goodwood (West Sussex) in which fine examples of works by living artists are disposed with great skill in a woodland setting. Roche Court (Wiltshire) has an attractive garden which is another good example of a dealer's alfresco premises. In France the Fondation Maeght (Alpes-Maritimes) was founded by the dealer Aimé Maeght in 1964 as a museum of modern art, with a garden to display 20th-century sculptures and a maze designed by Miró. The traditional materials of sculptures, such as bronze, weather very well but stone, in particular marble, in many climates will certainly need winter protection. Sculptors in the 21st century often use mixed media, some of it unconventional, whose ability to survive the elements may be unknown. PT

Seal Harbor ⊛

(Abby Aldrich Rockefeller Garden), Mount Desert Island, Maine, USA, is set on the rocky coast. It harmoniously fuses a rectangular, two-tier exuberant English-style flower border with a naturalistic Asian-like landscape punctuated

by centuries-old oriental sculptures. Laid out on a north–south axis in a wooded location away from the original 100-room house (now demolished), the garden designed by Beatrix FARRAND was inspired by a trip Abby (1894–1948) and John Davison Rockefeller Jr. (1874–1960) took to China in 1921. The building and planting of the garden did not begin, however, until 1927, continuing until 1934 with the installation of sunken annual and perennial beds and lawns, stone retaining walls, intriguing oriental gates, pools, pagoda, a Spirit Walk, and Chinese memorial stele (a sandstone sculpture some 1,400 years old), all enclosed by a rosy-coloured stucco wall crowned by yellow-glazed tiles salvaged from the Forbidden City. Incongruous as this 6-hectare/15-acre East-West amalgamation may seem, it both delights and astonishes, in part because the distinctly different areas remain hidden from each other. Entering from the grand South Gate, one steps onto a long, straight, powdered-stone path, the serene Spirit Walk, flanked by eight 2-m/7-ft stone 17th-century Korean tomb guards which stand at attention in waves of indigenous ground cover, including bunchberry dogwood (*Cornus canadensis*), bearberry (*Arctostaphylos uva-ursi*), and haircap moss (*Polytrichum juniperinum*). A right-angle turn east leads through a double wall to the sunken garden and vibrant borders in which any languishing flower is replaced immediately. Privately owned by David Rockefeller (b. 1915) today, the garden is overseen by his daughter Neva Goodwin and open to the public only rarely by appointment.
HSS

seat.
Serious gardeners have no need for seats for they never have time to sit down in their gardens. The garden seat, so often extremely uncomfortable, is usually best thought of as part of the decor rather than as a place of recuperation. The turf seat, supposedly so common in medieval gardens, could rarely have been of much use in an English climate. Seats are only occasionally found in 17th-century gardens. At VERSAILLES the seats in the BOSQUET of the Allées des Saisons were simple slabs of stone with no back and no armrests, supported on three plain feet. At HAM HOUSE a painting of the WILDERNESS by Henry Danckerts of *c.*1675 shows ornate rococo seats with carved backs. William KENT in the late 1730s at ROUSHAM designed practical and elegant alcove seats with a protective roof and, for his beautiful arcade, Praeneste, exquisitely designed seats, each placed before an arch to display the view and until recently still *in situ*. A painting of CLAREMONT of *c.*1760 by an unknown artist shows sturdy carved wooden benches, one with

a canopy, disposed on a turf amphitheatre. In the early 19th century elegant wrought-iron seats were made by many English makers. The Coalbrookdale iron foundry, established in Shropshire in 1709, was by the middle of the 19th century producing vast quantities of cast-iron garden seats (much cheaper and more durable than wrought iron) and many kinds of garden ornaments—2,000 tons a week at its peak. J. B. Waring's *Masterpieces of Industrial Art and Sculpture in the International Exhibition, 1862* (1862) describes Coalbrookdale's 'cleverly-designed garden-seats, ornamented with natural foliage, olive, fern, passion flower, &c.'. Some of these, specially those with a pattern of ferns, are fine ornaments and originals fetch very high prices at auction. Garden seats today are usually of period character; modern design has made little impact. A rare exception is the English firm of Gaze Burvill which makes handsome modern designs in oak.   PT

Seattle parks ⊕
Seattle, Washington, USA, were designed between 1903 and 1910 by John Charles Olmsted (1852–1920) of the Olmsted Brothers, and are one of the best-surviving 20th-century examples of Olmstedian design principles. The system is centred around a 40-km/24-mile long linked system of parkways and parks on the western side of Lake Washington connecting city, state, and federal properties, such as the Washington Park Arboretum, designed in 1936, the University of Washington campus, Woodland Park Zoo, and terminating in Fort Lawton, now Discovery Park overlooking Puget Sound. The spaces of this seamless system were designed to take full advantage of views over numerous bodies of water and the distant mountains. Olmsted adapted the Olmstedian picturesque design mode to reflect regional character. 'The monotony and gloominess' of the native firs was relieved by a facer planting of smaller and decorative trees and shrubs creating solid walls of vegetation; Volunteer Park and Leschi Park are fine surviving examples. The system was later enlarged by the addition of three innovative new parks. Freeway Park, designed in 1976, is an ambitious roof garden skilfully planted to hide the multi-lane freeway below. A waterfall within a canyon of battered and textured concrete walls creates 'white noise' to muffle the sound. At Gasworks Park, designed in 1976, an abandoned gasplant was remodelled to accommodate large numbers of park users in spaces that combine sculptural industrial fragments with bold landforms. The Woodland Park Zoo Long Range Master Plan (1976) created bioclimatic zones in which animals live outside in simulations of their natural habitat.   DCS

Sefton Park ⊕
Liverpool, England, is a public park designed by Édouard ANDRÉ and Lewis Hornblower (*c.*1823–1879) who in 1867 won a public competition for its design. The park, covering an area of 108 hectares/267 acres, opened in 1872 and was the first in England to be influenced by the ideas that André had evolved in his designs for Paris parks. The park was enclosed in curving drives and the paths within were also curved, following great circles or sweeping ellipses, and concealed from each other by planting or mounding. Larger open areas, screened by trees, were planned for different sports and more intimate spaces for walking or sitting. Vistas, with varied eyecatchers, were carefully planned to enrich the scene. A series of streams and pools runs north and south across the park with, in the Dell, a pool and cascade edged in rockwork. In 1896 a great tiered palm house was completed to the designs of Mackenzie & Moncur of Edinburgh. It is sited in a position of prominence on top of a mound which was originally planned for a BANDSTAND. Damaged in the blitz in 1941 it was restored but fell into decay to be triumphantly restored in 2001 at a cost of £2.5 million. Like many other English public parks Sefton Park fell into neglect after the Second World War but has in recent years been much restored.   PT

Seligenstadt Abbey.
See EHEMALIGE ABTEI SELIGENSTADT.

Seneffe, Château de ⊕
Seneffe, Hainaut, Belgium. A fine arcaded *cour d'honneur* (see ATTRE, CHÂTEAU D'), with statues and urns alternating in a series of niches, leads to the chateau built between 1763 and 1768—a brilliant example of the work of the architect Laurent Benôit Dewez (1731–1812) for Julien Depestre, a banker. The classical garden with a main axis over 1 km/0.6 mile long leading to a triangular pool was modified in 1780 in the English style. A landscape park was created and embellished with a neoclassical theatre, with a domed bay designed by Charles de Wailly (1729–98) and an ICEHOUSE. There is also an ORANGERY, possibly the largest in Belgium, from the same date. At the beginning of the 20th century, a rose garden was added (now disappeared) and in 1972 a neglected POTAGER and orchard to the side of the chateau were transformed into the Garden of the Three Terraces, a formal garden designed by René Pechère. The first terrace with a central circular pool is surrounded by pierced hedges of hornbeam and yew, creating a space for exhibitions and performances. Against the walls of the second terrace flowering shrubs are grown between buttresses of yew. In the centre a symmetrical box parterre has on either side

three square beds with hornbeam-enclosed 'rooms' at each end. Double curved steps lead to the lowest level. On either side of the central path are QUINCUNXES of limes. At the end the wall has been lowered to take advantage of a rural view.   BA

Sentō Gosho ⊛

Kyoto city, Japan, is an aristocratic villa garden created in several stages during the Edo period (1600–1868). Sentō (literally 'hermit's cave') is a poetic appellation for the villa of a retired emperor; Gosho means imperial palace. The site of the Sentō Gosho is just south-east of the imperial palace in Kyoto. The development of the property as we know it today began in 1629 when Emperor Gomizunoo abdicated. The shogun (chief military lord) Tokugawa Iemitsu (1604–51), being responsible for providing for the imperial family, undertook the reconstruction of the existing property. The Emperor occupied the southern portion of the site and the Empress Dowager, Tōfukumonin, occupied the northern section, known as the Join Gosho or Ōmiya Gosho. The present form of the garden, with northern and southern sections divided by a central buffer zone, reflects this initial use. The wall that originally divided the two sides, however, as well as most of the halls and pavilions that used to face onto the garden, are no longer extant. Both sides feature a central pond with wooded strolling paths leading around them, the whole covering almost 5 hectares/12 acres. The restrained rockwork, found only on certain sections of the pond edge, and the elegantly simple design of the ground plan are indicative of the 'modern' taste of the design. The hand of Kobori Enshū, a Minister of Construction who took particular interest in gardens, can be surmised in several sections of the garden. Later generations of retired emperors continued to work on the garden, adding its most striking feature—a 100-m/328-ft long, 10-m/35-ft wide curved beach covered with uniformly fist-sized, smooth, black stones—which was created around 1815. The stones were a gift to Emperor Kōkaku from Ōkubo Tadamasa, lord of Odawara (present-day Kanagawa prefecture), who was supervisor of affairs for the royal family at that time and, accordingly, in charge of projects at the Gosho.   MPK

serpentine wall. See CRINKLE-CRANKLE WALL.

Serralves, Parque de ⊛

Porto, Portugal, a public park with an area of 18 hectares/44 acres laid out in the 1930s by the French modernist landscape architect Jacques Gréber (1882–1962). The cultural centre of the Casa de Serralves, designed by Charles Siclis (1860–1942), is the focal point of Gréber's layout. The pink-washed modernist building faces down a slope where Gréber designed a dazzling water garden following a 500-m/1,640-ft vista pointing towards the river Douro. Cascades, pools, and fountains descend the slope, with TOPIARY shapes of spheres and drums, and ivy clipped tightly against walls. The climax of the vista—a return to nature—is an irregular lake shrouded in trees with an island. This is an outstanding garden of its date, attractive in itself but also harmoniously linking architecture and landscape. Avenues, of horse chestnuts or of *Liquidambar styraciflua*, form main thoroughfares in the park and trees line curving paths interspersed with serene open spaces. A handsome new building of minimalist white stucco, designed by Alvaro Siza (b. 1933), housing a museum of contemporary art, was opened in 2000. Between this new building and the water garden is a very large formal rose garden with beds of largely modern roses edged in box and backed by a pergola. The climate of northern Portugal is particularly favourable for the cultivation of roses and this is said to be the largest rose garden in the country.   PT

Serre de la Madone.
See MADONE, SERRE DE LA.

Sezincote ⊛

near Moreton-in-Marsh, Gloucestershire, England, has a house designed in Indian style by Samuel Pepys Cockerell (1753–1827) for his brother Charles Cockerell. Curving away from one end of the house S. P. Cockerell designed an orangery in Mughal style of irresistible splendour and oddity. Humphry REPTON advised on Sezincote but this probably referred only to the house. The grounds as we see them today are largely the creation of the Kleinwort family in the 20th century. They asked Graham Stuart THOMAS to design the Islam-inspired formal garden leading up to the orangery with a rill, octagonal pool, four-part arrangement of paths, and walks of Irish yews (*Taxus baccata* 'Fastigiata'). North of the house the stream garden (or Thornery as it is known) is overlooked by an orientalist bridge designed by Thomas Daniell (1749–1840) capped with Brahmin bulls. Here are ornamental trees and shrubs, among them *Acer griseum*, *Cercidiphyllum japonicum*, *Cornus kousa* var. *chinensis*, and *Parrotia persica*. The banks of the stream, and of a pool, are planted with moisture-loving perennials—astilbes, Himalayan primulas, hostas, irises, and rodgersias. The pool, known as the Temple Pool, has a Coade stone figure of Souriya in an ornate shrine. Fine trees, beeches (*Fagus sylvatica*), English oaks (*Quercus robur*), as well as exotic conifers fill the enclosing woodland to form a very English backdrop to a rare orientalist scene.   PT

Shah-Goli ⊛

Tabriz, Iran, is by tradition dated to the late 18th century but may well have been constructed earlier—some suggest even in the 14th century—and then restored and the high terraces added in the Qajar period. Situated to the south-east of Tabriz, its main feature is a huge artificial lake, 210 m/700 ft square, of which the northern side was built up, making the lake appear to float over the valley. A causeway leads out to an octagonal pavilion (today a restaurant), which was once crowned with a dome. A spring feeds the lake from the west hillside, a cascade descending in five terraces, flanked by tall poplar trees and willows. Romantic in high summer when surrounded by verdant trees, the garden disappoints in winter when the suburbs of Tabriz are visible in the surrounding orchards. Shah-Goli means the Royal Pond.

PHo

Shāh Jahān

(1592–1666), 5th Mughal Emperor (1628–58), first travelled with his father JAHĀNGĪR to Kashmir, and later made his own contributions to the gardens at SHALAMAR there. For a time he was in rebellion against his father, but in due course succeeded to the throne. He married Mumtaz Mahal, the niece of Nūr Jahān, Jahāngīr's Persian Empress, and his greatest work, the TAJ MAHAL, was her memorial.

Shāh Jahān's reign saw a vast extension of luxury of every kind; his palaces were a setting for court life and ceremonial, and his jewels were world renowned. Designers and craftsmen of every kind were welcomed to his court, from both Europe and Asia. Persian character returned to his buildings and gardens, and quality and design were superb. White marble, with inlays of precious and semi-precious stones (*pietra dura*), was widely used, and the representation of flowers in both inlays and carvings reached an astonishing realism. His palaces and gardens at the RED FORT, Delhi, and the fort at Agra, the SHALAMAR BAGH, Lahore, and the Taj Mahal, show that his real genius for building lay in the level sites of the Indian plains. An exception was the CHASMA SHAHI garden on the slopes above Lake Dal, Kashmir. There were many other minor works, such as the Black Pavilion in the Shalamar Bagh, Srinagar, additions to Lahore Fort, and pavilions at Ajmer.

Towards the end of his life, however, Shāh Jahān's health and character declined, and he was deposed by his son AURANGZĪB, and imprisoned in the fort at Agra, where he remained until his death. His reign saw the zenith of Mughal building, and with his successor there began a slow decline.   SMH

shakkei,

(literally, 'borrowed scenery') is a Japanese term for a gardening technique that incorporates a distant scene as an integral part of a garden. The word first appears in the Chinese gardening manual *Yuan ye* (1631), which was brought to Japan during the Edo period (1600–1868). The author of the manual revels in the beauties of the natural world and describes incorporating them into gardens in five ways: distant, near, above, below, and seasonally. The modern definition of *shakkei* is not precise and what actually constitutes a *shakkei* garden is a matter of dispute. The strict definition maintains that the garden would lose its value if the 'borrowed' view were not incorporated.

A *shakkei* design requires a foreground, middle ground, and background. The foreground is the garden in question; the background is the distant scene, usually a mountain but, at times, a built structure such as a temple roof or pagoda, or a large tree. The design of the middle ground—usually a hedge, fence, wall, or grove of trees—is the key to a successful *shakkei*. Properly designed, the middle-ground element frames the background scene and cuts out any unwanted views that lie between the garden and the distant scene. This framing of the distant view draws it forward, making it seem larger than normal and incorporating it as part of the garden in a painterly way. Some well-known gardens associated with *shakkei* are TENRYŪJI, Nishihonganji, ENTSŪJI, SHUGAKUIN RIKYŪ Detached Palace, and MURINAN. See also BORROWED LANDSCAPE; JIE JING.   MPK

Shalamar Bagh ⊛

Kashmir. Also known in the Mughal period as Farah-Baksh (Bestower of Joy), Shalamar (Abode of Love) is an ancient Hindu name. The garden was commissioned by JAHĀNGĪR (1605–27) and completed by SHĀH JAHĀN (1628–58). It nestles in the foothills on the northern shores of Lake Dal and is connected to the lake by a 400-m/1,300-ft long canal lined with poplars. Today a tarmac road leads directly to the entrance, though the magical experience of a leisurely approach by boat is still possible. The plan of the garden is articulated in three terraces, two of which are CHAHAR BAGHS of equal size, like the homonymous garden in Lahore. A wide canal flows through the entire length of the garden. In the upper *chahar bagh*, where the harem was situated, a transverse canal of the same width intersects the first to create a pool, at the centre of which is a black marble pavilion. Today it is much altered,

and so in order to have an idea of its original appearance we should look to Shāh Jahān's *baradari* (pavilion) on the shores of Lake Ana Sagar in Ajmer. In the lower *chahar bagh*, the Emperor's residence, there was a Diwan-i Khass, or Private Audience Hall. The third, smaller, garden was open to the public. The great central canal, lined with poplars, is an imitation of the natural torrent that was diverted into the garden, as is demonstrated by the different levels, the distance between them increasing as one descends, and by the many small fountains. All the waterfalls are decorated with *chini khanas* (see AMBER) in which lights were placed behind the sheets of falling water. There is a pavilion floating on the water and a pair of matching pavilions, one on either side. The pavilion nearest the lake functioned as a Diwan-i Amm, or Public Audience Hall, where the Emperor sat on a black marble throne above the water that flowed through the pavilion and cascaded into the pool below. The garden was once filled with fruit trees (apple, peach, and almond), though now all that is left is the ancient monumental plane trees.   AP

S. CROWE and S. HAYWOOD, *The Gardens of Mughul India* (1972).

Shalamar Bagh ⊛

Lahore, Punjab, Pakistan, is a royal garden founded by the Emperor Shāh Jahān in 1641, situated 5.5 km/3.5 miles from the city. Surrounded by a continuous wall, its layout consists of a sequence of three terraces like the garden in Kashmir of the same name. The garden was approached from the lower level, open to the public. The intermediate terrace was the private garden of the Emperor, while the top terrace was reserved for women. The main tank on the intermediate terrace sits between two CHAHAR BAGHS and becomes the focal point of the whole composition, studded with water spouts and with a central platform for rest. At one time the *chahar baghs* were subdivided with secondary canals and walkways, forming sixteen plots in all, like the Royal Paradise Carpet of Shah Abbas of Persia. Water, the connecting thread of the garden narration, runs into the 6-m/20-ft wide central canal, down into the great tank on an inclined plane called the *mahepusht* (fish skin), and then into a special room called Chini Khana, decorated with illuminated niches. The current landscape, with its plantings arranged freely in the quadrants, is thickly arranged like a grove in the high terrace and sparser in the lower one, and does not represent the original condition. John Joshua Ketelaar, who visited it in 1712, noted how tall cypresses ran parallel to the paths, while different fruit trees were planted in various quadrants.   AP

S. KAUSAR, M. BRAND, and J. L. WESCOAT, *Shalamar Garden, Lahore: landscape, form and meaning* (1990).

sharawadgi

is a term that first appears in print in William TEMPLE's *Upon the Gardens of Epicurus; or, Of Gardening, in the Year 1685* (1690). Temple wrote that the Chinese preferred an irregular or informal style of planting 'without any Order or Disposition of Parts' and where this is achieved 'they say the *Sharawadgi* is fine'. However, no one has ever found any Chinese word corresponding to *sharawadgi* and the matter remained a puzzle until Ciaran Murray wrote an article, '*Sharawadgi* resolved', in *Garden History* (Vol. 26: No. 2, 1998). Here it was revealed that the word is in fact Japanese—*sorowaji*—denoting asymmetry. Murray quotes from the descriptions of Japanese gardens written by Englebert KAEMPFER who visited the gardens of Kyoto in the late 17th century. Kaempfer noted 'a steep hill planted with trees and bushes in an irregular but agreeable manner' and 'a row of small hills made in imitation of nature'. It was through the Dutch East India Company that Kaempfer was able to visit Japan; Temple, too, had connections with the Dutch as a diplomat assigned to the Netherlands and could easily have met people who had seen Japanese gardens.   PT

Sheffield Park ⊛

Uckfield, East Sussex, England, is a spectacular Gothic house designed by James Wyatt (1746–1813) for the Earl de la Warr in the 1770s. Capability BROWN and Humphry REPTON both did designs, in 1776 and 1789 respectively, for the low ground below the house but it is not known in detail what they did. In this position today is a series of three substantial lakes whose margins were planted by A. G. Soames, who bought the estate in 1909. Substantial trees were planted close to the banks of the lakes interspersed with smaller ornamental trees and flowering shrubs. Virginia Woolf, who lived not far away, caught the essence of the effect when she wrote in 1937, 'rhododendrons . . . massed upon the banks and when the wind passes over the real flowers the water flowers shake and break into each other'. Apart from the dramatic lakeside planting there is much planting of smaller ornamentals chiefly in the hinterland where paths wind through woodland, both exotic and native. Swathes of bluebells (*Hyacinthoides non-scripta*) and of *Narcissus pseudonarcissus* are seen as well as spectacular drifts of such exotics as *Gentiana sino-ornata*. Most of the bold effects are on the lakeside but it is the more intimate planting in the wooded hinterland that is in many ways more beautiful. Since 1954 the gardens, but not the house, have been owned by the NATIONAL TRUST.   PT

shellwork.

The use of shells, native or exotic, to decorate interiors of garden buildings, especially watery places like GROTTOES and NYMPHAEUMS, dates from the 17th century. The nymphaeum at Château de Wideville (Yvelines, France) designed in 1635 by Tommaso FRANCINI is one of the finest surviving examples of its period. In the 18th century shellwork was often used to decorate the interiors of picturesque buildings. At Goldney House (Bristol, England) a three-chambered grotto, made between 1737 and 1764, is partly decorated with exotic shells, fossils, and decorative minerals. At Goodwood House (West Sussex, England) the 2nd Duchess of Richmond, helped by her daughters, in the 1740s made an especially fine shell house with intricate patterns of exotic shells. In this period shellwork was so popular in Ireland as to constitute a craze. At Curraghmore (County Wexford, Ireland) a beautiful surviving grotto has a shellwork interior and bears the inscription 'In two hundred & sixty one days these shells were put up by the proper hands of the Rt. Hon. Cath^{ne} Countess of Tyrone 1754'. Later in the 18th century shellwork is found in ornamental buildings in French picturesque gardens. The Chaumière des Coquillages (Shell Cottage) at RAMBOUILLET was built for the Princesse de Lamballe and retains its architectural interior of infinitely delicate neoclassical patterns of shellwork. In the late 20th century there was a minor renaissance in the use of shellwork of which Blot Kerr-Wilson's exquisite summer house (c.1998) with inventive and finely laid patterns for the Ballymaloe Cookery School garden (Cork, Ireland) is an exceptional example.   PT

Shenstone, William

(1714–63), English poet, garden maker, and garden theorist. From 1745 onwards he made the picturesque garden and FERME ORNÉE at The LEASOWES which was, for a short time, one of the most visited and talked-about 18th-century gardens. It was scattered with ornamental buildings most of which bore inscriptions evoking, sometimes a little optimistically, the spirit of place. Despite this literary bent and the intricate artificiality of his own garden he wrote to Lady Luxborough in 1749, 'Taste in Gardens etc: has little more to do than *collect* the Beauties of Nature into a compass proper for its own observation . . . The necessity of smoothing or brushing the Robe of Nature may proceed entirely from the same Cause.' He also believed that the rural landscape was 'never perfect without the addition of some kind of building'.

The second volume of *The Works in Verse and Prose, of William Shenstone, Esq* (1764–9) contains his 'Unconnected Thoughts on Gardening' in which he defined 'landskip, or picturesque-gardening' as that which pleases 'the imagination by scenes of grandeur, beauty, or variety'. Shenstone was the first person to use the term 'landscape gardening'.   PT

Shepherd, Thomas

(d. 1834), the first professional nurseryman and landscape gardener to work in Australia. An advocate of the principles of landscape design fashionable in the late 18th century, Shepherd emigrated to New South Wales in 1826. He established a nursery at Chippendale, Sydney, in 1827, hybridizing and selling many exotic plants, including camellias and fruit trees. He did not find this profitable, although William McArthur and Alexander MACLEAY were supportive, providing him with young trees for budding and grafting. Shepherd became influential, lecturing on horticulture and landscape at the recently established Mechanics' Institute in Sydney. He died prematurely but his lectures were published in 1835 and 1836 as *Lectures on the Horticulture of New South Wales* and *Lectures on Landscape Gardening in Australia*. They remain the first works published on gardening that relate to Australian conditions. They include descriptions of Lyndhurst at Glebe and ELIZABETH BAY HOUSE, Alexander Macleay's splendid garden. These descriptions were subsequently included in LOUDON's *Encyclopaedia of Gardening* (1840 edn.). Garden historians stress Shepherd's importance because he understood the grander attitudes to garden design, the first professional in Australia to do so. However, Shepherd's influence on the young colony's estates, either through his landscape designs or his books, is difficult to measure as no actual work can be attributed to him.   CMR

Sheringham Hall ✤

Sheringham, Norfolk, England, has a landscape designed by Humphry REPTON, his last work and completed only after his death in 1818, of which he wrote, 'This may be considered my most favourite work.' The site is especially beautiful, a combe on the north coast of Norfolk running northwards towards the sea. Repton's client was Abbot Upcher, for whom a Red Book of proposals was produced in 1812. The existing farmhouse was replaced on a different site by a smart new villa by Repton working in collaboration with his son John Adey Repton. The Red Book, as Stephen Daniels points out in his *Humphry Repton* (1999), contained suggestions for the 'social and

scenic management of the entire estate'. The proposed view from the dining-room window displayed in the Red Book shows a discreet trellis fence shrouded in rough hedging with cattle grazing in a field, beyond which is a ploughed field (Repton usually disapproved of arable farming in the landscape) and rolling wooded country with a temple rising among trees on the brow of the hill. The temple was designed as a possible place of refreshment for visitors come to admire the grounds. Stephen Daniels emphasizes that Repton wanted the house to command views of the busyness of the estate. Both Upcher and Repton died before the house and landscape were completed. Repton's new drive curved towards the house from the north but the proposed temple, immediately east of the drive was not built. It was eventually built in 1975, based on Repton's design but on a different site, well west of the drive, and commissioned by Abbot Upcher's descendant Thomas Upcher. The estate belongs today to the NATIONAL TRUST and what the visitor may see only partly reflects Repton's intentions. A walk through beautiful woodland takes the visitor across a field to the temple. From this point the house is seen against woodland in the combe below and in the distance a glimmer of sea.   PT

Shizilin ✤

Suzhou, Jiangsu province, China, though by no means the best, is perhaps the most famous of the celebrated city gardens of SUZHOU. Commissioned by a Buddhist monk, Tian Ru, in memory of his teacher, and built in 1336 during the Yuan dynasty, it originally formed the northernmost section of the Temple of Bodhi Orthodoxy, in the north-west district of the city. This was already sometimes known as the Lion Grove Temple with several levels of meaning hidden behind the name: for example, one interpretation is that the teacher, Zhong Feng, once lived in retreat by the so-called Lion Cliff at Tianmu mountain; another that over half the garden is given over to an extended false mountain (*jiashan*) of rocks often thought to resemble lions.

The whole garden (long since separated from the temple by a wall) now covers about 0.8 hectare/2 acres. Entering from a tree-lined street, the visitor finds himself in a high, whitewashed enclosure. Wide steps lead to a covered entrance gate and an elegant courtyard surrounded by finely carved balustrades. From here, narrow corridors zigzag past grand halls into further courtyards which gradually become less formal. A rock in one corner assumes the shape of a prancing lion then, as the visitor passes, seems only a rock again; windows (*louchuang*—see CHINA) start to take on playful shapes, of scrolls or pomegranates. As usual in these complex gardens, there are several ways to go, all of them eventually leading to the irregularly shaped pool and the great rockery and various garden buildings that surround it. One corner of the pond is not very successfully taken up with a 20th-century concrete pavilion in the shape of a stone boat (*fang*—see CHINA). A more elegant feature is the long *lang* (see CHINA), enlivened with windows and calligraphic stones let into the walls, which runs irregularly round much of the boundary wall. The pavilion on the north bank of the pool contains a fine wooden *bian* (see CHINA) with its name, Zhen Qu (the Pavilion of Genuine Delight), carved on it in the calligraphy of the Qianlong emperor. Both he and his grandfather Kangxi visited the garden several times during their southern tours and the gardens they subsequently commissioned at the imperial resort at Chengde (see BISHU SHANZHUANG), north of the Great Wall, and at YUANMING YUAN near Beijing were both influenced by the Stone Lion Grove.

The garden's most notable feature is its rockery. According to records, more than ten well-known artists were commissioned to work on its design and one of them, Ni Zan (perhaps the greatest painter of the Yuan period), left a scroll of it in his inimitably austere style. Little remains today of the garden he recorded. From a distance, the eye wanders restlessly over the strange rocks and hollows reflected in the slaty gleam of the lake. But close up the 'mountain' (*jiashan*) is a labyrinth with grottoes and interior caverns. Tiny paths wind up through it to give sudden glimpses, through sharp fissures or from its top, of the lake, the garden, or other visitors as they cross on different levels. It is an evocation of the mountains of the Chinese Immortals, strange, flamboyant, and removed from ordinary life.   G-ZW/MK

Shōmyōji ⊛

Yokohama, Japan, is a temple of the Shingon Risshū sect of Buddhism located in the Kanazawa district of Yokohama city. The garden, which covers roughly 6 hectares/15 acres, is of historic importance as an example of a Pure Land style garden (see JAPAN) from the Kamakura period (1185-1333). The property was first developed as an estate by the shogun Hōjō Sanetoki (1224-76). In 1260, on the seventh anniversary of his mother's death, he built a Buddha hall and named it Shōmyōji. Shōmyō, which literally means, 'Praising the Name', refers to the practice of *nenbutsu*, whereby the name of Buddha is called repeatedly. In 1276 he enshrined the statue of Miroku *bosatsu* (the Future Buddha, Maitreya) that became the temple's primary deity. Sanetoki's

descendant Sadaaki (d. 1333) brought the garden to its completion in 1323 at which time a commemorative painting of the temple was made, the Kekkaizu (Map of the Sacred World). Many of the details of the garden found in the painting, such as the pond shape and certain rocks, are still extant. Others, such as the bridges that lead to the main hall, were restored after archaeological work in the early 1980s, and still others, such as the many subsidiary halls that surrounded the main hall, are no longer extant. The design of the garden—from entry gate across the pond by bridges to the main hall—symbolized passage from the profane world to the heavenly realm of Miroku.   MPK

Shotover Park ⊛

near Oxford, Oxfordshire, England, stands on the site of the medieval royal forest of Shotover. A new house was built from 1715 for Colonel James Tyrrell who laid out formal gardens which largely survive. The Long Canal is 300 m/1,000 ft long and vistas lead to fine buildings, among them a remarkably early Gothic revival temple (*c*.1718) and two buildings by William KENT—an obelisk and an octagonal temple—both built before 1733. Kent may possibly have had a hand in laying out the grounds. Tyrrell was a friend of Colonel Dormer of ROUSHAM, not far away in Oxfordshire, and would have been familiar with Charles BRIDGEMAN's and William Kent's work there.   PT

shows and festivals

of one kind or another, varying enormously in scope and purpose, are a vital part of the world of gardening. In England the annual village show, usually held in late summer or autumn, is a grass-roots celebration of the pleasures of gardening. These shows, usually organized by the local horticultural society, are competitive. Exhibitors submit different categories of fruit, vegetables, ornamental plants, flower arrangements, bouquets, corsages, and so forth. Various of the household skills—baking, brewing, and so forth—are also represented. The judging of the exhibits is taken seriously and successful exhibitors recognize the importance of understanding the criteria that underlie the judges' decisions. The principles are spelled out in a handbook published by the ROYAL HORTICULTURAL SOCIETY which many village shows regard as the definitive word on the subject. In the case of fruit and vegetables it is the appearance that counts, as well as the ability to submit a flawlessly perfect matched set. In the case of vegetables the size may be of the essence although here the criteria vary. The largest parsnip, for example, can be as large as it wants but the dwarf bean should not be too small.

These village shows are no older than the 19th century and many were started in the 20th century. They remain attractive community events as well as forums at which gardeners, and others, can meet and test their skills.

The public flower show is also of 19th-century origin. The Horticultural Society of London (later the Royal Horticultural Society) in 1822 started regular flower shows (or floral fêtes, as they were called), thus starting a tradition which has continued for almost 200 years. Of similar antiquity is the Philadelphia Flower Show, which was founded in 1829, the first of its kind in the USA. It was started by a group of members of the Philadelphia Horticultural Society, itself the oldest such society in the USA, founded in 1827. It has occupied various sites in its history but today uses the facilities of the Pennsylvania Convention Center, in which it fills 13 hectares/33 acres of covered space, making it the largest indoor flower show in the world. It attracts over 275,000 visitors each year and presents a wide range of displays, talks, and demonstrations. It is a selling show, with 140 vendors. Several other large annual shows, all in the spring, are found in the USA. On the west coast San Francisco Flower and Garden Show and Northwest Flower and Garden Show (in Seattle); in the mid-west Chicago Flower Show and Cincinnati Flower Show; the largest in the south-east is the Southeastern Flower Show in Atlanta.

In Europe shows take strikingly different forms. In Belgium the Floralies in Ghent, started in the late 19th century, have had a spasmodic history. They were interrupted by the two world wars but since 1950 have taken place, in the month of April, every five years. Flanders has an extraordinarily ancient history of floriculture—the Sunday market in Antwerp, dating back to the Middle Ages, still sells a vast range of flowers, plants, and seeds. The Journées des Plantes, held twice yearly, in spring and autumn, at COURSON is a uniquely French institution. With something of the atmosphere of a private party, taking place in the grounds of a splendid chateau, it has excellent exhibits by nurseries, lectures by garden writers, and a generally celebratory air. The Festival International des Jardins at CHAUMONT-SUR-LOIRE exhibits a stirringly heterogeneous range of new gardens, specially designed for the show and displayed from spring to autumn. The Netherlands, not surprisingly, has the best bulb show. KEUKENHOF, since 1949, has displayed an extraordinary range, especially of tulips (including many new cultivars), in the attractively wooded 19th-century grounds of a country house. The Floriade is an ingenious form of show, unique to the Netherlands, held every ten years, on a different site. Grounds are laid out to receive the show and are left intact when the show has been dismantled to become a public amenity. Germany, which makes something of a speciality of mammoth trade fairs devoted to books, cars, printing, textiles, and other subjects, organizes what must be the largest horticultural show in the world. The biennial Bundesgartenschau, a national garden festival known as BUGA, was first held in Hamburg in 1953. It is on a scale unimaginable in any other country—the 2005 BUGA took place in Munich on a site of 190 hectares/469 acres and the organizers planned for an attendance of 4,000,000 visitors.

In England the best-known show is the Chelsea Flower Show, held each year in May in the grounds of the 17th-century Royal Hospital. Despite the antiquity of its setting it is of relatively recent origin; the first show took place only in 1913. It was originally called the Great Spring Flower Show. The Chelsea Flower Show today is still much valued by gardeners but it has acquired an unexpected additional allure. Partly because of the royal patronage (the Queen, sometimes with members of her family, visits each year on the day before the show opens to the public), Chelsea (as it is universally known) is an event on the social calendar like events such as rowing at Henley and horse racing at Ascot. It is not a selling show but it does, in fairly cramped quarters, manage to display an exceptionally wide range of things of interest to gardeners. Nurseries are a major attraction and display gardens, both of which compete for medals which are much valued. Garden machinery, glasshouses, garden furniture, and ornaments are also exhibited. Media coverage is intense, with daily television programmes, and articles in the national and horticultural press. In 2004 the Chelsea Flower Show had 157,000 visitors—an uncomfortably large number for such a small site. The ROYAL HORTICULTURAL SOCIETY has in recent years founded two other annual shows—at HAMPTON COURT and at Tatton Park (Cheshire). These, with an attendance of around 185,000 and 113,000 respectively, are deliberately more populist and one of their particular attractions is that they are both selling shows. There are many regional flower shows in Britain but none commands the interest of the three Royal Horticultural Society shows.   PT

shrubbery.
The word has a group of sometimes unhelpfully vague connotations. It seems to have been first used, according to the *Oxford English Dictionary*, in 1748, meaning a planting of shrubs. Shrubs, of course, existed long before the 18th century and some of them were certainly found in gardens. However, from the 18th century

deep into the 20th century, the introduction of exotic shrubs transformed the repertory of flowering plants available to gardeners, and the style of gardening responded to new possibilities. Garden historians have traditionally viewed the 18th century in England as overwhelmed by the landscape park, which had no use for flowering plants. More recently this view has been emphatically changed. John Harvey's *Early Nurserymen* (1974) showed in great detail how the nursery trade in England flourished in the 18th century—as Harvey wrote, 'the nursery trade exploded soon after the beginning of the 18th century'. Mark Laird's *The Flowering of the Landscape Garden* (1999), drawing on his own research and that of many others, spells out in great detail precisely how people were using the great range of plants available from nurseries—many of them went to embellish shrubberies, some of them designed by landscapers such as Capability BROWN. J. C. LOUDON's *Encyclopaedia of Gardening* (1822) defined the shrubbery or shrub garden as a 'scene for the display of shrubs valued for their beauty or fragrance, combining such trees as are considered chiefly ornamental, and some herbaceous flowers'. Later in the 19th century, with the growth of suburban gardening, the shrubbery came to acquire a new meaning—it was used in the front garden to shield the view from passers-by, often with such evergreens as the spotty evergreen *Aucuba japonica*, newly introduced from Japan in the 1850s. Today, the shrubbery has become virtually extinct and shrubs have found a new home in mixed borders.   PT

Shrubland Park ⊛
near Ipswich, Suffolk, England, although going back at least to the 16th century when there was a deer park here, has gardens that are chiefly 19th century. A grand house was built in the 1770s to the designs of James PAINE, and in 1789 Humphry REPTON produced a Red Book of suggestions, one of his earliest, which recommends a path running 'along the natural Terrace under spreading branches of the venerable Chestnut Trees'. Exactly such a walk survives, the Brownslow Terrace, as do magnificent old sweet chestnuts (*Castanea sativa*). In the early 19th century house and garden were altered by John Gandy-Deering (1787–1850) and Donald BEATON and the whole was transformed by Charles BARRY, who remodelled the house and in the 1850s designed a sequence of balustraded Italianate terraces flowing down the slope to the west of the house. They are linked by the Descent, a steep flight of stairs embellished with architectural ornament. Aligned with the Descent, at the lowest point, is a circular pool with fountain and an airy

open loggia. Parterre-like bedding schemes surround the pool. A cross-axis, the Green Terrace, dating from the early 19th century links, to the south, a circular arrangement of beds, the Fountain Garden and the heated Conservatory Wall which originally overlooked an elaborate pattern of 30 beds. It was described in 1867 as 'a perfect blaze of bloom . . . one of the richest scenes in this paradise of beauty'.
PT

shrubs.
A shrub is defined as 'a perennial plant having several woody stems growing from the same root'. Which is fine as far as it goes, but it is as well to remember that the exact line between a shrub and a tree is a distinctly fuzzy one. The quality of 'shrubness' is not necessarily a fixed state: some shrubs have the capacity to turn into trees in time, while natural trees can become shrubs by the skilful use of secateurs and pruning saw. Nevertheless, generally speaking, shrubs are multi-stemmed and rarely grow more than 6 m/20 ft naturally, and often very much less. Indeed, it is possible to buy dwarf shrubs, such as some hebes, which only grow a few inches tall and wide, and stay that way. What defines a shrub is simply its persistent woodiness, which differentiates it from a herbaceous perennial which dies down to a perennating crown in winter. The word 'sub-shrub' is used for shrublets, which are either low-growing, woody shrubs or ones with woody bases but soft stems. Climbers are shrubs which have a natural tendency to grow upwards, sometimes for considerable distances, but, with the exception of annual climbers such as morning glory or canary creeper, they are still shrubs because they have woody bases. Clematis and jasmine are examples of shrubby climbers.

Shrubs are, on the whole, long-lived, which makes garden planning rather less chancy than it might otherwise be. They can, therefore, be used to provide permanent structural elements, especially if they are evergreen, as well as acting as natural supports for more fragile climbers, such as clematis. They can also, of course, be grown for their flowers, scent, leaf colour (especially, though not exclusively, in spring and autumn), fruits, or even bark and stems in winter. Their versatility has ensured an enduring popularity over several centuries although, in recent years, a growing impatience amongst amateur gardeners with the perceived time they take to mature has affected their fortunes.

History
In the past, things were different. In the 16th and 17th centuries, shrubs, essentially those

from Europe and Asia Minor, formed an important element of any garden, especially but not exclusively if they had medicinal or culinary qualities. Lavender was a good example. In the early 18th century, evergreens, native or otherwise, such as phillyrea, box, bay, laurel, cherry laurel, holly, and laurustinus, together with the few deciduous shrubs available, like lilac, were popular with garden owners for creating 'wildernesses'. In the same century, professional plant explorers began to leave these shores—sent out usually by nurseries or by scientific institutions, like the ROYAL BOTANIC GARDENS, KEW—to bring back exotic plants, especially hardy shrubs and trees, from wherever was possible in the temperate world. The pace of this accelerated in the 19th century. The introduction and cultivation of a number of important genera of ornamental shrubs—rhododendron, camellia, viburnum, cotoneaster, and rose—soon had a profound effect on the look of the British garden. Their impact was particularly deeply felt because the native British shrub flora was deficient in evergreens or plants with very large flowers. The 19th-century introductions coincided with a time of rapidly increasing prosperity in Great Britain, and the burgeoning of a manufacturing middle class avid for novelties and specialities, but not hamstrung by owning estates with 17th-century parterres or 18th-century landscape parks.

Despite the magnificence of the plant material available to them, nurserymen and amateur collectors set to work to improve on nature. A great deal of hybridization took place, much of which could not possibly have happened in the wild. A good example of this was the crossing of the Japanese camellia, *Camellia japonica*, with the Chinese species, *C. saluenensis*, by J. C. Williams of CAERHAYS about 1925 to produce *C. × williamsii* and its many cultivars. A great deal of time was devoted by gardeners to seeing what would survive and thrive in the various soil and climatic conditions obtaining in British gardens. In particular (although not exclusively) those areas with a mild climate and acid soils, such as western Scotland, Cornwall, Surrey, and Sussex, were discovered to be suitable for calcifuge genera, such as rhododendron, pieris, magnolia, and camellia. Colourful miniature versions of Himalayan gorges appeared wherever conditions suited and money was little object. However, in humbler gardens, and on alkaline soils, shrubs also had an enormous impact. Forsythia, ribes, philadelphus, and viburnum became widely popular. Shrubberies with a mixture of deciduous and evergreens were a feature of many a rectory or villa garden. The introduction of many shrubs which turned

out after cultivation to be slightly frost tender, such as ceanothus, abutilon, and *Fuchsia magellanica*, gave impetus to the fashion for putting shrubs against walls, in order to create a favourable microclimate where they could survive or grow especially freely. Support for the shrub was forthcoming in the gardening periodicals, which multiplied in the second half of the 19th century. Gertrude JEKYLL, in particular, steered public opinion away from growing shrubs exclusively together and towards putting them in 'mixed' borders which would also include herbaceous perennials, bulbs, and even annuals. This kind of border making was later endorsed by Christopher LLOYD, Graham Stuart THOMAS, and other influential 20th-century writers. Shrubs, from then on, were to be important, rather than exclusive, components of garden plantings.

Modern gardens
Many shrubs grown these days in gardens are not species, but cultivated selections and hybrids. In the past 30 years, there has been emphasis on the selection of mutant forms, rather than on breeding, with variegated forms and coloured-foliage versions of common shrubs eagerly sought by nurserymen keen to catch the attention of a fickle public. There are, for example, at least ten different cultivars of *Spiraea japonica* presently on the market, which are either golden or golden-variegated in leaf colour. At the same time, as a result of increased anxiety about the loss of biodiversity, British native shrubs (hawthorn, blackthorn, elder, dogwood, guelder rose, and dog rose) have made something of a comeback, having been thoroughly put in the shade by exotic imports since the 18th century. There is now quite a lively demand from gardeners for native plants for hedges or as specimens to suit host-specific insects and give shelter and food for birds.

Cultivation
Almost all shrubs sold these days are grown in containers, or containerized for sale. They can, therefore, be planted at most times of the year, except during droughts or severe winter conditions, although spring and autumn are the best seasons. Shrubs repay good soil preparation, as well as an annual mulch in spring to slow evaporation, hinder weed growth, and provide a certain amount of soil conditioning. They should be so placed that they have space to expand to their 'natural' limits, or much pruning will be necessary in later years. If planted in exposed positions, evergreen shrubs should be protected from wind initially, using semi-permeable windbreak material, and frost-tender shrubs should be protected in winter. Most shrubs need pruning

at some time of their lives, either because they have been planted too close to other plants, or because the flowering can be enhanced by doing so. Shrubs divide into two main groups: those which flower on 'wood' made the season before, and those which flower on this season's 'wood'. The former flower in the first half of the year, generally speaking, and the latter after midsummer. Large-flowered clematis often produce both sorts of growth, and must be pruned accordingly, to ensure that the early flowers are not cut off. Shrubs are propagated in a number of ways. Species can be increased by seed, although this is often rather slow. It is more usual to take cuttings or to graft the scion onto a stock of a related species. Layering is also possible with plants which have branches which grow close to ground level, such as rhododendrons and viburnums.

The use of shrubs in the modern garden
The range of shrub characteristics is immense: they can have evergreen foliage, which may be glossy or matt, variegated or entirely green, and sometimes with thick hairs ('indumentum') on the undersides. Deciduous foliage is even more various, sometimes changing dramatically through the growing season. A shrub's habit may be domed, arching, horizontal, or stiffly erect. The flowers are often scented, and may be almost insignificant or immensely striking and showy. The fact that shrubs have rather fallen out of fashion in recent years has less to do with their cost (for they compare quite favourably with herbaceous perennials) but because they are thought to be slow to mature and to fill the allocated space, in comparison with perennials, bulbs, and annuals at least. Yet they can add beautiful incidents to the garden, disguise ugly walls, act as structures for climbing plants, make clippable hedging, provide backcloths to enhance foreground plantings, create understoreys in woodland plantings, and ground cover anywhere. They also make fine specimens for pots, and provide localized shelter and shade for plants, as well as food and shelter for wildlife. They are truly invaluable in the modern garden.   UB

Shugakuin Rikyū (Shugakuin Detached Palace) ⊛
Kyoto, Japan, was built as a country villa by Emperor Gomizunoo (1596–1680). In 1629, reacting to edicts from the Tokugawa *bakufu* (military government) restricting aristocratic rights, the Emperor abdicated and took up residence in the SENTŌ GOSHO. After a decade of working on that estate, he began a quest for land to build the perfect country villa, emphasizing the need for clear running water and a majestic view. From the early 1640s the

Emperor searched for land in the north and north-west, building several temporary villas such as Nagatani-dono and Hataeda-dono (see ENTSŪJI). In 1655, he found his ideal spot when visiting the Enshōji temple in the north-east of Kyoto, removed the existing temple to a site in Nara, and began construction of Shugakuin Rikyū, named after a Heian-period (794–1185) temple of the same name that had occupied the site. The garden and architecture were strongly influenced by Emperor Gomizunoo's passion for the arts of flower arranging and the tea ceremony, revealed in the subtlety of the design, especially the rock placement, water use, and plantings. The villa, which covers some 5 hectares/12 acres, is divided into three sections— lower, middle, and upper—separated by rice fields that are still maintained as part of the grounds. The lower tea house is set in an intimate pond garden crossed by meandering paths, while the upper tea house commands one of the grandest views of any Japanese garden, looking over a large pond and massive clipped-hedge embankment to a distant view of layered mountain ranges.

Whereas Gomizunoo built the upper and lower tea houses as part of his original plan, some features are more recent. The distinctive, roofed bridge in the upper pond was donated in 1824 by the Kyoto administrator of court and nobles, Naitō Nobuatsu (1778–1825), and the middle tea house—which was originally the private villa of the Emperor's daughter Akenomiya, and then became a temple, Rinkyūji, after the Emperor's death—was only incorporated as part of the Rikyū in the Meiji period (1868–1912).   MPK

Shute House ⊛

near Shaftesbury, Dorset, England, is an 18th-century house bought in 1968 by Michael and Lady Anne Tree. The Trees asked Sir Geoffrey JELLICOE to plan a new garden which gently evolved—Jellicoe thought of it as 'a laboratory of ideas'. The site here is a watery one and water plays a major part in the garden design with spring-fed pools supplying it to more formal features. A stepped rill of Persian character descends a gentle slope of very un-Persian turf. The rill breaks out into pools of different geometric shapes with a bubbling fountain at the centre of each and the flow of the falls is broken by copper shapes which Jellicoe believed could be designed to produce harmonic chords. They certainly make a pretty splashing but specialist musical opinion suggests that it is impossible to create true chords by this means. To one side is a water garden of wholly different atmosphere where a broad canal, overlooked by classical busts at its head, has a walk of arum lilies (*Zantedeschia aethiopica*) on one side

and a formal grove of holm oak (*Quercus ilex*) on the other which break out from time to time into wooden viewing platforms. A bench in the woods nearby, on the banks of a natural pool, gives views of the canal with its classical character and, linked at right angles, an irregular pool of romantic flavour. Behind the ilex grove is a formal garden of fruit and flowers with six large square beds hedged in box. Since 1993 the garden has been finely restored by new owners.   PT

Sichtungsgarten,

a garden designed for the study of perennial plants under specific conditions of climate, hydrography, and soil. An important reason for maintaining such gardens is the interest in investigating the hardiness of plants and their resistance to diseases and pests. In addition these gardens take an interest in the cultivation of new hybrids and cultivars of plant species with particular qualities of foliage, shape, and colour of blossom. The Arbeitskreis Staudensichtung (*Staudensichtung* means Study Group), reorganized in 1997, has thirteen affiliated *Sichtungsgärten* in Germany (Bernburg, Düsseldorf, Erfurt, Hanover, Heidelberg, Höxter, Hohenheim, Marquardt, Nürtingen, Osnabrück, QUEDLINBURG, Weihenstephan, and Weinheim) and two in Switzerland (Wädenswil and Oeschberg) which organize the scientific study of perennials in Germany. One of its tasks is the definition of plant species and their exact naming. The results of these examinations are evaluated by the Staatliche Forschungsanstalt für Gartenbau (Governmental Research Institute for Horticulture) in Weihenstephan. The final evaluation assesses six different grades of quality ranging from 'excellent' to 'of little garden value'.

The history of the *Sichtungsgarten* dates back to the end of the 1920s. The garden architect and horticulturist Carl Camillo Schneider (1876–1951) founded in 1930 the Arbeitsgemeinschaft für Deutsche Gartenkultur, which had the goal of assessing perennials along the lines of the plant trials carried out at WISLEY in England. The movement was strongly supported by the Potsdam horticulturist Karl FOERSTER. By 1932 it had already installed about 70 different sites for the systematic examination of perennials such as gladioli, dahlias, and delphiniums and published from 1930 onwards a yearbook to inform the public of its results (*Jahrbuch der Arbeitsgemeinschaft für Deutsche Gartenkultur*). One of the first *Sichtungsgärten* was opened at the Reichsgartenschau Stuttgart in 1939. Other *Sichtungsgärten* in this period were Düsseldorf (specializing in dahlias), Uetersen (specializing in roses), and the garden of the

Freundschaftsinsel in Potsdam. Others were established as parts of botanical gardens such as BREMEN RHODODENDRONPARK, Berggarten Hannover, and PALMENGARTEN Frankfurt am Main. The idea of the *Sichtungsgarten* was taken up after the Second World War by the plant cultivator Richard Hansen, who founded the Sichtungsgarten Weihenstephan in 1948. In 1952 he also presided over the Arbeitsgemeinschaft Selektion und Züchtung der Blütenstauden, a forerunner of the Arbeitskreis Staudensichtung.   US

Siebold, Philipp Franz von

(1796–1866), German doctor and plant collector. Siebold was physician to the Dutch East India Company in 1826 stationed at Deshima, the tiny walled island in Nagasaki Harbour, Japan. Foreigners' movements were restricted, but as an eye surgeon specializing in cataracts Siebold was able to travel, which allowed him to collect plants and seeds, propagating them on the island. Siebold acquired maps during his travels, and having spent a year in prison was expelled in 1830 for espionage. However he took his collection of plants including *Hosta plantaginea* and *H. sieboldiana*, hydrangeas, *Corylopsis spicata*, and *Fatsia japonica*. Siebold established his collection in Ghent, and then later at Leiden where he specialized in Japanese plants. In collaboration with the botany professor at Munich J. G. Zuccarini (1797–1848), he wrote *Flora Japonica*. Siebold returned to Japan for three years in 1859 making new discoveries and returning with *Spiraea thunbergii*.   MC-C

Singraven ⊛

Denekamp, Overijssel, the Netherlands, is situated in a loop of the river Dinkel. This provided the location for a mid 17th-century house, near a 14th-century house. The early history of the estate and its gardens however is scanty till the late 19th century. The architect L. H. Eberson working on the house from 1868 to 1872 implemented a classical façade, and at the same time the forecourt was altered into a lawn, and a main avenue, the Singraver Allee, was laid out. Further alterations at this time included a deer enclosure with lake and island. From 1921 the architect Andries de Maaker restored the house to a 17th-century character, adding gate lodges and from 1934 to 1938 being assisted by the landscape architect Leonard A. SPRINGER, who redesigned parts of the immediate surroundings, particularly with additional planting. One of the main additions of this period was the ARBORETUM.   JW

Sintra, Palácio Nacional de ⊛

Sintra, near Lisbon, Portugal, a 9th-century

Muslim fortress (still known as the Castelo de Mouros) which was taken from the Muslims by Afonso I in 1147. It became a palace of the royal family in the 15th century and some of the rooms are superbly ornamented with AZULEJOS. A series of small terraced gardens of varied date, on slivers of ground, cling to the slopes below the palace ramparts. A shady courtyard has an ornamental stone column, a twisted pattern of organic shapes, crowned with crouching figures and eager dogs—this could date from the time of Manuel I in the early 16th century when the palace was enlarged. Pots of clivias and hydrangeas decorate the scene and a terracotta lion sprawls on a low wall above a bench inlaid with *azulejos* of vine leaves in low relief with a cistern of water behind. A staircase leads up through a vaulted passage to a flagstoned patio with a narrow rectangular pool decorated with old *azulejos* and a stone lion dribbling water. The walls have a dado of green and white *azulejos*. A narrow path leads to a little parterre with an irregular pattern of box-edged beds, a tightly clipped *Arbutus unedo*, a cone of holly, hydrangeas, and waves of forget-me-nots. A yellow Banksian rose cascades on the wall above. The views of the Sintra hills from the palace are magnificent.   PT

Siroko, Villa (Villa Schirokko) ⊕

Sostanj, Slovenia. The villa lies to the west of the town of Sostanj in the north-eastern province of Styria. The villa and the garden were created between 1935 and 1938 by Malvina, the wife of industrialist Herbert Woschnagg, a graduate of the Academy of Fine Arts in Vienna. Provincial landscaping and architectural traditions were reflected in the villa with combined modernist and eclectic elements in a natural forest surrounding. The villa is situated on a wooded hill and is characterized by local stone and leaded windows of various shapes. The façade is shrouded with Virginia creeper and wisteria and thus romantically included in the landscape. The garden consists of a rectangular terrace with low stone walls, stairways, a water basin with a bronze sculpture of a faun, and a semicircular clearing in woodland. The villa is surrounded by straight paths paved with green tuff (the local stone) which lead over a low parapet wall, now with organic shapes of stepping stones, to a wooded slope with scattered groups of ferns. A courtyard at the front of the house is continued to the north with an elevated area featuring a rectangular water basin and a wrought-iron fence. The stairway leading to the pool is symmetrically planted with arbor vitae, hornbeams, and a rambling rose archway. Lawns to the north and south of the villa are edged with woodland which is lined with paths. The vegetation around the villa includes hydrangeas as the main planting together with exotic trees and shrubs whose striking shapes make a sculptural addition to the garden's composition.   AK

Sissinghurst Castle ⊕

near Cranbrook, Kent, England, is the scattered remains of a great Elizabethan house bought in a derelict state by Harold Nicolson and Vita SACKVILLE-WEST in 1930. Already experienced gardeners, they embarked on a garden here before the buildings were habitable. They had worked with Edwin LUTYENS on their previous garden (Long Barn, also in Kent) and they knew Lawrence JOHNSTON of HIDCOTE. They made the best of existing enclosures and of the wonderfully romantic 16th-century brick buildings, adding good structural planting of yew or box hedges and pleached limes. Old shrub, and occasionally species, roses were big and beautiful enough for the setting, and lavish herbaceous perennials filled borders and blurred edges. Although profusely planted the garden is never claustrophobic. The white garden gives way to a long cool passage of yew hedges and the boisterous cottage garden leads to a serene orchard, with *Cyclamen coum* and *Anemone nemorosa* in the grass, and a boundary of an L-shaped moat. Because much of the character of Sissinghurst style has now seeped into general taste it is hard to appreciate the originality of the garden. Although often accused of snobbery Harold Nicolson and Vita Sackville-West showed nothing of the sort in their gardening. Their taste was intrepid and they seemed impervious to 'good taste'. Harold Nicolson loved dahlias when few smart gardeners did, and planted them in their 'cottage' garden, still one of the most attractive features. Vita Sackville-West thought nothing of buying a packet of mixed annuals in Woolworth's, sowing them, and bemoaning the garishly unsuccessful results in her column in *The Observer*. Since the NATIONAL TRUST took over in 1968 the garden has changed in atmosphere—lawns are more crisply stripy and Irish yews are wired and sharply clipped. But the original layout of the garden is intact and shows how, even with slightly modified planting, it provides the framework, and a sequence of enclosures, for a marvellous garden. The present team of gardeners—six for 4 hectares/10 acres—maintains it superbly.   PT

Sítio Roberto Burle Marx (formerly Santo Antônio da Bica) ⊕

Rio de Janeiro state, Brazil, is located in Barra de Guaratiba, 55 km/31 miles from the centre of Rio de Janeiro. This country house was Roberto BURLE MARX's principal research laboratory, work on which began in 1949. The estate is a horticultural centre housing one of the world's most important collections of Brazilian and tropical plants, gathered for research, acclimatization, and reproduction exclusively for the purposes of landscaping—in marked contrast to the aims of botanical gardens in general. Located in a mountainous area with remnants of Atlantic rain forest, the land was previously an agricultural property that had fallen into disuse and disrepair. The estate's characteristics suggest guidelines for its occupation and use in three principal sectors, although Burle Marx had not made any master plan. The parts closest to the entrance were allocated to nurseries for sub-woodland and epiphytic species. In the central area, the main house and the 18th-century chapel were restored and surrounded by more elaborate gardens. The remaining areas were reserved for the main collection of plants, with specimens grouped according to their botanical families, biological needs, and to landscaping criteria. In the 1980s, the collection numbered around 750 species of the Araceae family—500 *Philodendra* and 250 *Anthuria*; 200 of the Bromeliaceae family; 120 of the Musaceae family; 200 of the Orchidaceae family; 130 of the Marantaceae family; 95 of the Velozziaceae family; in addition to a no less abundant number of Apocinaceae, Begoniaceae, and palm species. At the time, the whole collection amounted to 3,500 species, including both those from Brazil and other tropical regions.   GMD

GUILHERME MAZZA DOURADO, 'Utopia verde' (Green Utopia), in Domenico Luciani (ed.), *Luoghi: forma e vita di giardini e di paesaggi* (2001).

FLÁVIO L. MOTTA, *Roberto Burle Marx e a nova visão da paisagem* (1986).

Sitwell, Sir George

(1860–1943), English landowner, author, and garden maker of RENISHAW. He made an assiduous study of Italian Renaissance gardens from the early 1890s onwards—visiting over 200 gardens throughout Italy. He distilled his garden philosophy in one of the best books on garden design, *On the Making of Gardens* (1909), which was also influential in encouraging the study and admiration of Italian gardens about which he wrote very perceptively. Above all he used his knowledge to lay out a new garden at Renishaw—a dazzling vision of Renaissance Tuscany overlooking the industrial wasteland of southern Derbyshire. He yearned for a return to Renaissance purity, and wrote of the baroque garden designer André LE NÔTRE that he 'stole the formulas of garden-making from Rome and Florence, but left the poetry behind'.   PT

SACHEVERELL SITWELL, OSBERT SITWELL, SIR GEORGE SITWELL, and RERESBY SITWELL, *Hortus Sitwellianus* (1984).

Sloane, Sir Hans

(1660–1753), physician, philanthropist, and plant collector. Sloane studied botany and medicine in London, then in Paris under Joseph Pitton de TOURNEFORT. In 1687 he was appointed physician to the governor of Jamaica, Christopher Monck, Duke of Albermarle (1653–88). Following the death of the Duke, Sloane returned, with a collection of 800 plants, which were distributed to, among others, John Ray (1627–1705). Building up a fashionable medical practice, with Queen Anne amongst his patients, and marrying a wealthy widow, enabled him to become a generous benefactor. The causes he espoused flourish to this day: the Royal Society, of which he was president from 1727 to 1741; the Apothecaries' Society, to whom he leased, and then gave, the site of the CHELSEA PHYSIC GARDEN; and the British Museum, built on the site of his house, of which his entire collection of books, manuscripts, and 'curiosities' formed the nucleus.   MC-C

Slot Zeist. See ZEIST, SLOT.

Slovenia,

a state in southern Central Europe, by the northern Adriatic Sea, with predominantly mountainous terrain and a climate ranging from sub-Mediterranean near the coast to moderately continental with sub-Pannonian influences to the east, and to Alpine in the north. The vegetation is exceptionally varied with over 3,200 species and subspecies, eight endemic, and *c.*100 rare species, distributed throughout the country. Due to its position, Slovenia was at the crossroads of interests, primarily those of Austria and Italy, and exposed to political and cultural influences which are reflected in the arts. The main styles in garden art have left considerable traces. Gardens were developed primarily by foreign aristocracy between the 16th and 18th centuries in the provinces of Carniola and Styria. The culture was deeply marked by the Austro-Hungarian Empire (1868–1914) whose influence was strong until the Second World War. The second half of the 20th century saw Slovenia as part of socialist Yugoslavia with a pronounced decay in the state of historic gardens.

The first records of gardens date from the 15th century but only fragments survive. Gardens were inside castle walls and on sloping terraces, with ornamental plants (for example roses) and culinary and medicinal herbs. Some surviving monasteries show traces of medieval gardens. Gardens in the 16th and 17th centuries are much more substantially documented. Numerous manors with gardens are depicted in two albums of copper engravings (1681, 1689) by Georg Matthäus Vischer (1628–96) and Johann Weichard Valvasor (1641–93). Among these are Begunje (Katzenstein), Lisicje, near Ljubljana (Gayerau), Turjak Gardens in Ljubljana, Borl (Anckenstein), and Slovenska Bistrica (Windisch Feistritz). Valvasor's descriptions of exotic plants and garden layouts (*Die Ehre dess Herzogthums Krain*, 1689) testify to a tradition of highly developed garden design and the introduction of exotic plants. Almost nothing of these gardens survives.

In the 18th century Slovenia was strongly influenced by the baroque. Some important ensembles were created in Styria such as DORNAVA, and Radovljica in Carniola. Only some fragments are preserved. The first private botanical gardens were created as a mixture of English style, baroque, and classicistic elements with outstanding collections of exotics. Baron J. K. Erberg (1771–1843) at Dol pri Ljubljani (Lusthal) made a collection of 7,000 species. Another private garden with a fine collection was that of Baron Sigismundus Zois (1747–1819), a cultivated man of the Enlightenment,

---

Slovenia: the 17th-century garden of Slovenska Bistrica (Windisch Feistritz) engraved by Georg Matthäus Vischer in 1681.

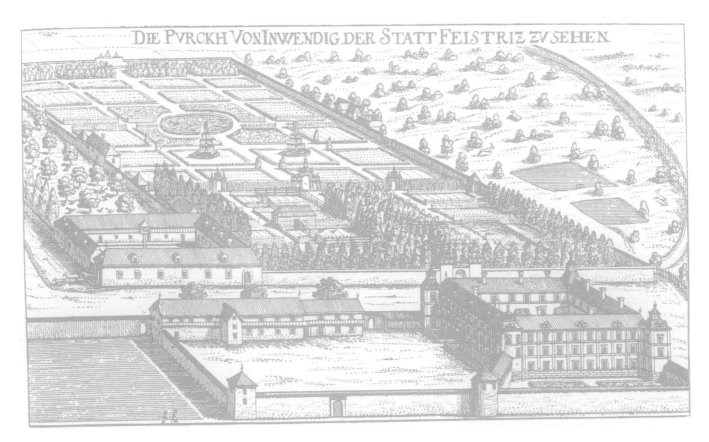

DIE PVRCKH VON INWENDIG DER STATT FEISTRIZ ZV SEHEN

whose Zois Gardens in Ljubljana became the first public gardens. The botanist Karel Zois (1756–99) in Brdo pri Kranju (Egg) cultivated a garden of alpine flora. The first Slovenian botanical book, *Flora Carniolica*, was published in 1760.

Public gardens appeared in the early 19th century under the influence of landscape painting, botanical science, and Enlightenment ideas. Romantic style prevailed with the use of picturesque landscape scenery, promenades, and avenues in classical manner. For the Botanical Garden in Ljubljana, founded in 1810, there was an influx of foreign plants and trees via Trieste and by railway from Vienna from 1847. In public gardens geometric floral ornaments and carpet bedding dominated planting schemes from the 1850s. Among them were Viltus (Wildhaus) in Styria, the gardens of spas at Rogaska Slatina, Rimske Toplice, Bled, TIVOLI PARK in Ljubljana, and the city park in MARIBOR. Several 19th-century private estates, manors, and villas had parks planted with exotic trees.

In the 20th century the strong tradition of the 19th century continued to be felt. There was a spirit of eclecticism and the influence of the ARTS AND CRAFTS movement. This was seen in gardens for private houses, public buildings, and in city squares. Between the wars Secessionism (art nouveau) and modernism prevailed, influencing the work of such outstanding architects as Joze PLEČNIK, in particular the Ljubljana Riverside, and the Ferrari Villa by Max Fabiani. The 1960s were characterized by public parks and residential areas in the spirit of the GARDEN CITY. Additions to historical parks were designed, for example the extension of the Three Ponds in Maribor City Park and the children's playground in Tivoli Park. Forest cemeteries were designed in Novo Mesto and Nova Gorica. The last decades were characterized by postmodern trends in garden and landscape design. Several competition projects for urban open spaces and improvements of degraded landscape outside towns were prepared, but few completed.

Landscape architecture came under foreign influence, in particular that of the Germans and Czechs, and was subsequently developed by Slovenes educated in gardening schools in Lednice and Vienna. The first professional landscape architect, Ciril Jeglic (1897–1988), who worked on VOLCJI POTOK, helped establish several gardening schools. The graduate course in landscape architecture at Ljubljana University was founded in 1972 by Dusan Ogrin (b. 1929). The profession is active in design, planning, and landscape and garden conservation. Two societies are of influence in Slovenia—the Slovene Association of Landscape Architects and the Union of Horticultural Societies of Slovenia.

Historic gardens are protected by the Cultural Heritage Protection Act (1999). Restoration has been organized by the National Institute for the Protection of the Cultural Heritage for the last fifteen years, funded by the Ministry of Culture. Documents on historical gardens are kept in several institutions, the central being the Archive of the Republic of Slovenia in Ljubljana. AK

Smith, Augustus John

(1804–72), English landowner who in 1834 bought a 99-year lease of the Isles of Scilly and started to make at TRESCO ABBEY a garden which was an intrepid pioneer in its day and remains, in the hands of his descendants, one of the most remarkable gardens in the British Isles. Smith was as original a landlord as he was a gardener, stimulating the enfeebled economy of the islands, introducing compulsory education (long before it existed on the mainland), and playing the role of an energetic paternalistic landlord that was not always appreciated by his tenants. PT

Soborsin. See SĂVÂRŞIN.

soil improvement.

The soil provides plants with nutrients, oxygen, and water as well as anchoring the plant. Soils from different locations will vary enormously depending on a number of factors; the parent material on which they develop, their position in the landscape, type of vegetation, climatic variations, and man's inputs. The complex mixture of mineral and organic components which develop cause soils to vary in acidity and alkalinity, the amount of nutrient release and retention, the drainage characteristics, and the ability of the soil to retain water and resist drought.

Plants are adapted to specific habitats and the current interest in growing indigenous species may mean that little soil modification is required. More usually gardeners wish to exhibit variety, from the edible to the decorative, including species that have originated from varying global environments, and thus soil improvement may be necessary. Often the need is to improve the soil in a general way, to alleviate difficult native characteristics and increase fertility. This is achieved by cultivation and the addition of organic matter and fertilizer. More radical changes are needed to produce strikingly different conditions such as a freely draining alpine garden on poorly drained soil, or an acid rhododendron garden on alkaline soil.

Different plant types thrive within a specific pH range, as illustrated by the simple classification of plant groups into calcifuges (lime haters) and calcicoles (lime lovers). Vegetables generally prefer a higher pH value than shrubs and fruit, and calcifuges will not tolerate neutral or alkaline soil. Lime (calcium carbonate) is used to reduce soil acidity and increase soil pH. The correct application rate requires knowledge of the existing soil pH, the target pH being aimed for, and the soil texture. The lime slowly dissolves in the soil neutralizing soil acidity. It is more difficult to reduce the soil pH (increase acidity). Sulphur will slowly acidify soil by means of microbial activity, but this takes several months and is best applied to bare ground to avoid root scorch. The rate applied must be assessed according to the soil texture and the pH required. This method will not work on soils containing particles of calcium carbonate, referred to as 'free lime'. Here the only option is to replace the soil with an acid substrate made from materials like acid topsoil, composted pine-bark, or composted bracken. Traditionally sphagnum peat was used, but environmental concerns about the loss of peat-bog habitats make its use undesirable.

Nutrients, essential for healthy plant growth, can be supplied by means of organic manures or artificially produced fertilizers. Productive areas, where edible crops are removed, require replenishment to maintain soil fertility. Other areas will need lighter maintenance dressings. Fertilizers are usually soluble and immediately available for plant growth. The concentrations of the nutrients they contain are displayed on the product and will usually include nitrogen, potassium, phosphorus, and sometimes magnesium and micronutrients. Organic manure is a mixture of soluble nutrients and insoluble organic materials. The organic components are mineralized by soil microbes and slowly release soluble forms of nutrients that can then be absorbed by roots. Animal-based manures and spent mushroom compost are rich in nutrients, particularly nitrogen, and are suitable where large nutrient inputs are needed.

Good soil structure is essential for regulating water and air and promoting root growth. Cultivation is used to rectify soil compaction and prepare a tilth for seeding or planting. Bulky organic materials are excellent for ameliorating the physical properties of soil and encouraging soil health by increasing microbial activity and diversity. Materials include those mentioned above together with garden compost, and composted green waste, bark, and seaweed. They benefit both extremes of soil type; the heavy clays prone to wetness and light sandy soils liable to drought. Organic matter bonds chemically with the clay particles to improve soil structure, opening up larger pores and improving drainage and aeration essential for root growth. Forming raised beds also increases the amount of well-drained soil available for root growth above a wet zone. Where drainage problems are severe, installing a trench drainage system containing perforated plastic pipes with gravel backfill may be the only way to remove ponded water and drain waterlogged soil.

Applying organic material to sandy soil will improve the water holding and nutrient holding ability of the soil. Large and frequent applications are necessary to maintain these benefits, as even large dressings are readily oxidized and lost. Organic material applied to the surface as a mulch can also protect the surface structure of soils liable to cap, modify extremes of temperature, and conserve water.

CMK

Solar de Mateus. See MATEUS, CASA.

Somerleyton Hall ✤
Somerleyton, near Lowestoft, Suffolk, England, had a notable garden in the 17th century when it was owned by the Wentworth family. At this time (shown in an estate map of 1652) there was a WILDERNESS with serpentine walks, a geometric Great Garden, a terraced walk with banqueting houses, an orchard, and a 53-hectare/131-acre deer park. Little is known of the garden subsequently until 1844 when the estate was bought by Sir Samuel Morton Peto (the father of Harold PETO). He rebuilt the 17th-century house in neo-Jacobean style and laid out new gardens with much advice from W. A. NESFIELD. West of the house there is today a simplified version of an elaborate parterre designed by Nesfield with yew topiary, urns, and shaped rose beds and views over parkland with the remains of an 18th-century lime avenue. North of the house are open lawns and excellent trees, among them a huge Wellingtonia (*Sequoiandendron giganteum*) and cedar of Lebanon which must antedate the 19th-century garden. A walled kitchen garden has fine vine houses (possibly by PAXTON) and mixed borders forming its central axis. Outside the walls is a magnificent yew maze designed by Nesfield (*c*.1855) with a CHINOISERIE pavilion on a mound at its centre.   PT

Sophievka ✤
Uman, Ukraine (156 hectares/385 acres), was laid out in the 1790s and early 19th century on the steep and rocky sides of the river Kamenka on the estate of the Polish magnate Count Potocki (1751–1805). Potocki's wife Sophia (1760–1818)

was born in Turkey to Greek parents of modest means, but her beauty and charm had enabled her to move in high society across Europe. She had been presented to Catherine the Great, had toured Russia with the Prince de LIGNE, and had visited Nieborow and ARKADIA as the guest of Countess Helen Radziwill. She wished to achieve a park even more beautiful than Arkadia. Like Arkadia Sophievka is rooted in classical mythology with a Temple of Diana, a Temple of Flora, a Grotto of Venus, a Terrace of the Muses, a Cretan Labyrinth, Elysian Fields, the Athenian School, the river Styx, and statues of Apollo, Venus, Mercury, Euripides, and Cupid. A tall granite OBELISK bears the message 'Love to Sophia' in Latin and Greek. The principal architect of the park was Ludovic Metsel (1764–1848), a Polish artillery officer who used explosives to deal with granite in reshaping the landscape. The underground river Styx, along which visitors to Sophievka were ferried, was part of the exceptional water system created by Metsel, which also featured an impressively realistic and spectacular waterfall and two large artificial lakes with associated springs and cascades. The winding walks along the thickly planted shores afford pleasant views, and the path to the upper lake is so contrived that the mirror surface of the lake reveals itself most unexpectedly and effectively.

PH

Sørensen, C. Th.
(1893–1979), Danish landscape architect. After an apprenticeship at a manor house in Jutland he worked with landscape architect Erik Erstad Jørgensen (1871–1945) and some years with G. N. BRANDT, whom he succeeded as assistant professor in landscape architecture at the Royal Danish Academy of Fine Arts, School of Architecture, and from 1954 to 1963 as professor. He was strongly influenced by Brandt and outstanding landscape gardeners such as J. K. Jørgensen (1864–1930), former head gardener at the Danish Royal Horticultural Society's garden. Sørensen developed his own sculptural style using geometrical, defined forms by precisely pruned hedges, as in NÆRUM ALLOTMENT GARDENS. This preoccupation with geometric forms, especially the circle, is apparent in much of his work. His idea of Musical Gardens—carefully coordinated hedged enclosures in the shape of triangle, square, polygon, circle, and oval—was first conceived in 1954. This idea was later realized, in 1983, as the Geometric Gardens at HERNING ART MUSEUM. Other famous works include his open-air theatres, the park at Århus UNIVERSITY, the Hans Christian Andersen Gardens in Odense (1943), with Peter Wad (1887–1944), and Vitus Bering Park, Horsens (1954). Sørensen's

influence was far reaching and he carried out over 2,000 commissions, from small gardens to motorways, and the Kongenshus Memorial Park, near Viborg (1945–53). He received both national and international awards. In 1931 he wrote *Parkpolitik i sogn og købstad* (Park Politics in Parish and Borough), a book still relevant today. Its most important contribution was the idea of adventure playgrounds which later spread through Europe and America. Sørensen's idea of the 'skrammellegeplads' (adventure playgrounds) was not realized until 1943, in Emdrup near Copenhagen, and 1956 in the public housing development of Tingbjerg. Sørensen often travelled in Europe studying historical English, French, or Italian gardens and meeting colleagues such as Pietro PORCINAI. He wrote many articles and was the author of important books such as the comprehensive historical survey of gardens: *Europas havekunst* (Europe's Garden Art) (1959), *The Origin of Garden Art* (1963), and *39 haveplaner* (39 Garden Plans) (1966). His last book *Haver: tanker, arbejder* (Gardens: Thoughts and Works) (1975) is an autobiography.   AL

South Africa.
South African gardens were until the closing decades of the 20th century greatly influenced by two factors: the climate and the country's colonial heritage. South Africa is, with the exception of KwaZulu-Natal in the east, largely a hot and fairly dry region. The highveld and the KwaZulu-Natal have summer rainfall and the Western Cape winter rainfall, with rain, possible though sparse, all year round in the Eastern Cape. The Karoo region and the Namaqualand area of the Northern Cape are arid and in parts semi-desert. Of particular note is the 'Cape Floral Kingdom' in the Western Cape. Here is to be found the fynbos vegetation which includes the proteas and the famous Cape ericas.

Colonialism resulted in the introduction of exotic species of plants, though in the Dutch period (1652–1795) it is difficult to speak of a distinctive garden design. Many of the settlements of the eastern parts of the Colony of the Cape of Good Hope were along an unsettled frontier, so gardening was not widespread. Further west the great Dutch estates had kitchen gardens, orchards, and avenues of trees, rather than the formally laid out parterres and terraces of contemporary Europe. That said, the Dutch did install professional horticulturalists or botanists in their Company Garden (see OLD COMPANY GARDEN, THE) in the centre of Cape Town. And during the Dutch period some eminent plant hunters, such as Anders Sparrman (1748–1820), Karl THUNBERG, and Francis MASSON, collected at the Cape and dispatched specimens to Europe. The Cape plants, especially the heaths, became fashionable in Europe as can be judged by the fact that by 1802, 80% of the plates in *Curtis's Botanical Magazine* were of Cape species.

In the 19th century greater stability in most of the Cape outside a military zone in the east meant that the Victorian flower garden made its appearance in such settlements as Wynberg, Graaff-Reinet, and Grahamstown. In the colony of Natal, Pietermaritzburg became famous for its azaleas, and at the coast the Victorian traveller Marianne North wrote in 1882 of the gardens on Durban's Berea ridge being filled with blue *Ipomoea, Bignonia, Tecoma, Thunbergia,* hibiscus, cycads, and *Stangeria.* While most of the plants in these domestic gardens were foreign imports the indigenous flora was being avidly collected as a plant hunting craze swept parts of colonial society. But these finds were rarely introduced into local gardens, instead being dispatched in WARDIAN CASES to Kew Gardens and other overseas botanic gardens.

Early parks
Within a hundred years of its foundation the Old Company Garden in Cape Town had been transformed from a provisions station into a fine park, which at times was in the hands of a botanist. The arrival of the British and a growth in prosperity in the 19th century led to a proliferation of parks, many of which, to attract a colonial government subsidy, termed themselves 'botanic gardens'. In fact there were botanic gardens in the Cape in Cape Town (founded in 1848), Grahamstown (1850), King William's Town (1865), Graaff-Reinet (1872), and Queenstown (1877). In Natal Durban had a thriving botanic gardens, founded in 1849, which acted as the colony's agricultural research station, and the Pietermaritzburg Botanic Gardens, like those on Mauritius, Hong Kong, and at Melbourne, greatly assisted afforestation in the region. Up in the Transvaal Republic a small botanic garden was established in 1874, but the vagaries of the mining republic soon reduced it to what it is today—Burgers Park. These colonial botanic gardens were not universally welcomed. Because they each received only a small government grant and had to sell plants to the public to augment their income, they were regarded as competitors by the rapidly growing nursery trade. One nurseryman in Natal complained that this state-subsidized competition was an outrage in 'a civilised Christian, English colony'.

Public parks were laid out in the colonial era in many towns; some such as Joubert Park in Johannesburg, St George's Park in Port Elizabeth (complete with conservatory),

and the Town Garden in Durban were very attractively laid out with bandstands, fountains, and serpentine paths. Durban's Mitchell Park had a fully-fledged zoological gardens attached, a smaller version of which still survives. Historically interesting parks which have survived today are the Old Company Garden in Cape Town as well as the Old Fort Garden in Durban. Interesting examples for the garden archaeologist are the old botanic gardens in Humansdorp and King William's Town, the former now in ruins and the latter in disrepair.

Botanical nationalism
After the Anglo-Boer War many of the mining magnates built great mansions for themselves with fine gardens, the best surviving example being BRENTHURST in Johannesburg. Still, however, exotic plants dominated public and private gardens, with variegated-leafed shrubs, roses, and azaleas holding pride of place with the ubiquitous araucaria dominating the skyline of many settlements and defining the boundaries of many farmsteads, even acting as navigation beacons for passing ships on the treacherous south-east coastline. But change was coming. In 1913 the National Botanic Garden at KIRSTENBOSCH was established. It was to be an indigenous garden only. It struggled for many years but was kept afloat thanks to the efforts of its early directors—'gentlemen in English tweeds'. By the 1920s there was rivalry from the highveld with the setting up in 1923 of the National Herbarium. Eventually in 1946 a Pretoria National Botanic Garden was commenced, in the grounds of which was built the Botanical Research Institute. The divide between Afrikaner nationalism and English liberalism now extended even into the field of botany. Only in the 1980s did the two sections of South African botany merge to form the National Botanical Institute. Today the NBI has control of the Compton Herbarium in Cape Town (600,000 specimens) and the National Herbarium in Pretoria (1.2 million specimens). In addition NBI controls the following eight National Botanical Gardens, which specialize in growing and carrying on research into South Africa's indigenous flora: Kirstenbosch, Karoo Desert, Worcester (1921), on 155 hectares/ 383 acres, Harold Porter, Betty's Bay (1950), on 200 hectares/494 acres, Free State, Bloemfontein (1967), on 74 hectares/182 acres, WITWATERSRAND, Pretoria (1946), on 76 hectares/ 187 acres, LOWVELD, and Natal, Pietermaritzburg (1874), on 52 hectares/128 acres.

Only some 10 per cent of these botanic gardens are landscaped, most of the land being maintained in as natural a state as possible. Two fine municipal botanic gardens which are

international in their representation of flora, but which also grow indigenous plants, are the Durban Botanic Gardens and the Johannesburg Botanic Gardens at Emmarentia. Stellenbosch University also has a scientific botanic garden.

The pioneering work of Kirstenbosch, alongside the proselytizing work of the Botanical Society of South Africa, eventually led to a movement to promote the growing of indigenous plants in public and private gardens. Government gardens such as Groote Schuur or the State President's Garden in Pretoria are good examples of the former. While exotics are still grown in private gardens, the indigenous plant craze has steadily won ground over the last twenty years. This is in part due to the efforts of writers and broadcasters such as Sima Eliovson, Keith Kirsten, Kristo Pienaar, and Una der Spuy. Today South Africa can offer the visitor a wide variety of gardens, mostly in an informal layout, but with a plethora of colourful or dramatically shaped plants. These range from Kirstenbosch or one of the wine estates, such as Bellingham or Twee Jongegezellen, to the lush subtropical splendour of Amanzimyama at Tongaat north of Durban.   DPMcC

Southcote, Philip
(1698–1758), English landowner and garden theorist who made the first FERME ORNÉE at WOBURN FARM from 1734 onwards. Southcote was a friend of several of the gardening cognoscenti of his day, among them Alexander POPE, Joseph Spence (1699–1768), and the 8th Lord Petre of Thorndon Hall (Essex). Southcote's garden does not survive but many of his ideas do, recorded in Joseph Spence's *Observations, Anecdotes, and Characters of Books and Men* (written in the 1750s but not published until 1820; enlarged edn. 1966). Here Southcote emphasizes the importance of 'Perspective, prospect, distancing, and attracting' and spells out the ways of achieving these effects in the landscape. 'In gardening', he believed, 'the *principal view* is to be observed as the *principal object* is in a picture.' Southcote held lively opinions about the colour of evergreens, the correct positioning of woodland and water, the placing of ornaments, and much else of relevance to landscape design.   PT

Southern University Denmark in Odense ⊛
Denmark. The university, built from 1969 by architects Knud Holscher (b. 1930) with Krohn & Hartvig Rasmussen and landscape architect Jørgen VESTERHOLT, is situated in a rural area south-east of Odense. The building complex was placed in the centre, between three existing woods, with access by a single main drive. One

storey higher is a central promenade, providing access to auditoriums and offices. Large areas were terraced, covered in turf with outer edges terminating in a low grass bank. The fringe of the existing forest created a valuable framework, but new woodland of oak, beech, and ash was planted, too. The university's concentrated, urban form has given rise to 31 courtyards, most of them on a concrete base. Their design is austere, with areas paved with large concrete flagstones, solitary trees such as sycamore or plane in low ground cover, and climbers such as clematis and honeysuckle.

AL

Spain.

Diversity, topographically and culturally, is at the heart of the character of Spain. The Pyrenees, forming the boundary with France, are the most formidable mountain range in Spain, with several peaks exceeding 3,500 m/ 11,482 ft. In the south the two ranges of the Sierra Nevada and the Sierra Morena have as their highest peak Mount Mulhacen, 3,500 m/ 11,483 ft. One of the most influential topographical features is the great central plain, the *meseta*, which covers a vast area—over half the total land mass of Spain—with an average height of 610 m/2,000 ft. The climate and rainfall vary strongly. On the Atlantic coast there is an average winter temperature of 9 °C/ 48 °F and a summer temperature of 18 °C/65 °F with an annual rainfall of 960 mm/38 in. The *meseta* has an average winter temperature of 4 °C/40 °F and a summer temperature of 24 °C/ 75 °F and average annual rainfall is 380 mm/ 15 in. The Mediterranean coast has an average winter temperature of 11 °C/52 °F and a summer temperature of 23 °C/73 °F and an average rainfall of between 250 mm/10 in and 600 mm/24 in (the Sierra Nevada and the Sierra Morena have a much higher rainfall than regions closer to the coast). The Balearic Islands and the Canary Islands have climates similar to the Mediterranean but the latter are a little warmer. This range of climates and of topography provides habitats for an immense range of flowering plants of which there are around 8,000 species. The Canary Islands have around 470 native species but have an unusually high number of endemics, some of them now very rare such as *Dracaena tamarandae* of which only around 50 survive in the wild.

Early history

It is the Mediterranean coast that has been the greatest influence on the history of Spain. Its strategic position and the fertility of the land along the Guadalquivir river in the south made it especially attractive. It was this that drew Greeks and Phoenicians to its shores and, most importantly, the Romans. The town of Mérida in Estremadura was one of the 22 major *coloniae* founded by the Emperor Augustus in Spain. Magnificent archaeological remains tell much about the sophistication of Roman life in Spain. Here were typical Roman houses with central courtyard gardens with a pool and surrounded by a peristyle. Surviving mosaics show grapevines and grapes being crushed under foot, fluttering birds, and potted plants. In terms of agriculture the Spanish colonies were of great importance to Rome with quantities of olive oil and wine flooding back. PLINY THE ELDER, who lived in Spain, gives much information about plants there in his *Naturalis Historia*. He saw many fruit trees—apples, figs, pears, plums, and pomegranates and such nut trees as almonds and pistachios. Among ornamentals he saw box, broom, juniper, roses, and yew and among culinary or medicinal herbs he describes aloe, camomile, mint, oregano, and thyme. The Romans were masters of the skill of irrigation—their aqueducts, cisterns, and ducts were so well engineered that, hundreds of years later, they were often preserved by the Muslims, themselves experts in the watery arts. It is in this, possibly more than any other influence, that Spanish gardening owes most to the Romans. The later, more profound, garden culture of the Muslims has made a much greater contribution to the character of Spanish gardens. By the 5th century AD the Roman presence in Spain was much weakened (as it was in most of the western Roman Empire) and the last stronghold, Tarragona, succumbed to the Visigoths in 470. The Visigoths, who were never numerous in Spain, were content to take over the existing Roman settlements as well as their system of administration. In some cases villas were destroyed but in others they were taken over by the Visigoths, who also built new ones in the Roman tradition. Nothing, however, is known of gardens in their time in Spain. But from what is known about Visigothic culture—new churches built, coins minted, fine sculptures created—it must be assumed that gardens were cultivated.

The Arab invasion in 711 was a decisive event in Spanish history. The people responsible are often referred to as Moors—that is, from Mauretania in north Africa. The first invaders, Berbers under Arabic leadership, were indeed from Mauretania. However, the culture that developed was dominated by ideas that came from the highly developed world of Muslims in the Near East. The Ummayad dynasty, for example, who established the amirate of Córdoba in 756 and later established the caliphate in the 10th century under which they ruled the whole of the Iberian peninsula under Muslim control, came from Syria. It is more reasonable to refer to Muslims or Islam, for this was the chief source of the culture, rather than to Moors. It is not known how many Christians converted to Islam but the profound influence of Arabic on the Spanish language and on place names remains as evidence of the Islamic culture in Spain—there are even instances of Christian tombs having inscriptions in Arabic. Resistance to the Muslim presence was continuous and the *Reconquista* (Reconquest) gathered pace after the collapse of the caliphate of Córdoba in the 11th century. By the late 13th century the whole of Spain was in Christian hands except for Granada which finally succumbed in 1492. Throughout the period of the Muslim presence one of its chief preoccupations was defending the territories that had been colonized. It is significant that the great centres of Islamic culture were the cities of Córdoba, Granada, Seville, and Toledo which it was possible to defend. Agriculture and horticulture were central to the culture. What is known about the palace city of MADINAT AL-ZAHRA attests to its sophistication. The far more complete monuments of the ALHAMBRA in Granada, the Real ALCÁZAR in Seville, the ▶

Colour plates

The Victorian garden at **Forest Lodge**, South Australia

The Temple of Vesta (early 19th century) at **La Garenne-Lemot**, France

New-style naturalistic planting in **Thijsse Park**, the Netherlands

Wild subtropical planting in the water garden at **La Mortella**, Ischia, Italy

Exotic planting at the **Sítio Roberto Burle Marx** in Barra de Guaratiba, Brazil

Palacio de GALIANA in Toledo, and the Alcázar in Córdoba give an eloquent account of the marvels of Islamic garden culture in Spain. But it is the countless surviving fragments, or hints of a layout, of Islamic gardens—cisterns, fountains, rills, patios—found in so many gardens that show the extent of Islamic garden culture. It is a culture, moreover, that has persisted in its influence. After the Reconquest was complete Muslim craftsmen continued to work in Spain. The style of buildings they created are known as *mudéjar* and garden enclosures in this style produced such marvels as the Casa de PILATOS and the Palacio de las DUEÑAS, both in Seville. Many learned books on agriculture were written by Muslims in Spain and some give details of ornamental planting. Ibn Bassal's *Diwan al-filaha*, dating from the late 11th century, describes such ornamental plants as chrysanthemums, lilies, lily of the valley, narcissus, pinks, roses, and violets. He also gives details of the size of beds and the spacing of plants. However, there is no detailed account of a garden dating from the Muslim period, and archaeology has yielded little information apart from irrigation systems which survive intact in many Andalusian gardens. A garden legacy from the Muslims is the use of coloured tiles, AZULEJOS. It should be emphasized that no surviving Islamic garden layout in Spain has authentic planting—insufficient knowledge exists for an authentic recreation. The diversity and tenacity of the Muslim tradition in garden making may be studied in the *carmenes* of Granada. The word *carmen* has something of the meaning of the Italian villa, signifying a house and garden considered as a unit. In the old quarter of Granada, the Albaicín, a sloping site facing across the river Darro towards the Alhambra, many *carmenes*, of different periods, may still be seen. Most of them are private houses but their gardens may often be glimpsed through gateways. If you look across to the Albaicín from the Alhambra it is plain how many houses possess gardens. The 16th-century Casa Morisca del Chapiz has a patio with double height loggia of Islamic character overlooking a long narrow pool edged with box hedges and with an orange tree at each end (when first seen by the author in 1988 a donkey was tethered to the loggia). The nearby premises of the office of the archives of the city of Granada, the Palacio de los Cordova, has a small patio with a pebble mosaic of interlocking squares, a fountain, and pomegranate tree. How many other countries have office buildings whose entrance leads through so charming a garden? In Córdoba, too, the Palacio de VIANA, with its astonishing array of patios, of every period from the 16th to the 20th century, shows

how deeply embedded is the Islamic tradition in garden making.

Monastery gardens certainly existed in medieval Spain but almost nothing is known of them except in the most general terms. In other parts of Europe such gardens were important in the Middle Ages, especially for medicinal herbs. In Spain, however, much of that role was played by Islamic gardens. Many cloisters of medieval churches have gardens today—such as the cathedral in Barcelona, the monastery of Gudalupe, and the monastery of Santa María de Poblet—but all are modern. The history of medieval Christian gardens is dramatically overshadowed by that of Islamic gardens which have left far more traces.

The 16th to 18th century
Very little survives of the period of the Renaissance—one of the best sources of information is the occasional topographical painting. In a sense, the Renaissance had already taken place in Spain with the flourishing of Islamic culture in the Middle Ages. The study of plants, greatly fostered under the Muslims, continued, in particular in those universities whose medical faculty required the study of medicinal herbs. A botanic garden was founded for this purpose in 1567 at the University of VALENCIA and still exists on a new site to which it moved in 1802. A pretty example of a Renaissance pleasure garden was Philip II's late 16th-century Casa de CAMPO with its pattern of square parterres and central fountain. However, one façade of the house had a very Italianate loggia overlooking the garden—nothing survives of this today. Philip II had a garden of greater importance at ARANJUEZ, made from the mid 16th century. With its neat pattern of beds this was closer to Low Countries garden style than to the Italian Renaissance. In the 16th-century garden of the monastery of San Lorenzo in the ESCORIAL a similar pattern of square beds was filled with flowery planting. Another of Philip II's palaces close to Madrid, Valsaín (which does not survive), is seen in an anonymous 17th-century painting in the Instituto Valencia de Don Juan in Madrid. It shows an elaborate palace, in the style of the Escorial, with a very large enclosed parterre with eighteen square beds overlooked by a loggia. The garden at BUEN RETIRO, started for Philip V in the early 17th century, shows a blending of Italian Renaissance influence and baroque exuberance.

Philip V's palace of La GRANJA, built from 1721, has a garden of powerfully baroque character marked by spectacular fountains, cascades, and pools. It is tempting to see this as a Spanish VERSAILLES but in all truth it is not quite like anywhere else. There may be some French

influence in the ornaments (on which French craftsmen worked) but the setting, with open views to wild country, and the dramatically undulating site were not the kind of environment which would have pleased LE NÔTRE. An event of great importance in the 18th century was the foundation of the ROYAL BOTANIC GARDEN in Madrid which played a particularly important role in studying and introducing plants from Latin America (including, most notably from the gardening point of view, the dahlia). There was much botanical activity in this period. The plant collecting of Hipólito RUIZ LOPEZ and José Antonio Pavón y Jimenez (1754–1840) in Chile and Peru revealed the plant riches of those countries and resulted in the publication of *Flora Peruviana* (1792–1802). José Celestino Mutis (1732–1808) (after whom the genus *Mutisia* is named) from 1783 explored the botany of Colombia where he recognized the importance of cinchona, the tree from which quinine is extracted. The influx of new plants also prompted the foundation of gardens dedicated to their cultivation such as the Jardín de Aclimatación de la OROTAVA founded in 1788. The 18th century garden of the Palacio Cuzco at Viznar near Granada shows a characteristic eclecticism. The enclosed garden is overlooked by a cloistered terrace whose walls are painted with scenes from the life of Don Quixote and the garden walls with *trompe l'œil* architectural detail. At the centre of a pattern of clipped box hedges is a tiered fountain fed by a cistern at the upper level, a screen of plane trees gives shade, and a raised terrace is surfaced with pebbles. Here, with a touch of the Renaissance, a definite flavour of Islamic gardens, and an emphatically Spanish sense of atmosphere, we see a garden of timeless attraction. A distinctive local form of garden is seen in an estate like the Pazo de OCA in Galicia. The wet, mild climate here is favourable for growing trees and shrubs which are seen here in the context of a wonderfully decorative formal water garden. In the late 18th century the influence of the picturesque garden tradition is seen at El Capricho de OSUNA.

The 19th century and beyond
The 19th century was a rich period in Spanish gardens. The garden at NARVÁEZ shows an intermingling of formal devices, such as parterres, with a free layout with no dominating axis. The Carmen de los MARTIRES, on a grander scale, is in the same tradition, intermingling classicism and Romanticism—a grand tiered fountain pool juxtaposed to a picturesque lake. At MONFORTE in Valencia an intricate garden was laid out in the mid 19th century with a mount, ornate parterres, pools and fountains, and lavish planting.

The 20th century was one of particular interest for Spanish gardens. It got off to a dazzling start with the extraordinary Park GÜELL—a public park of exceptional originality and charm. The figure of J. C. N. FORESTIER was influential in this period. His distinguished public spaces at MONTJUICH in Barcelona and the Parque MARÍA LUISA in Seville showed how skilful he was in translating his French experience into a very different context. He relished the use of water and the brilliant colours of *azulejos* and devised an attractive neo-Arabic style. He also made private gardens which acknowledged the Islamic tradition. The terraced garden he laid out in 1912 for the Casa del Rey Moro (the House of the Moorish King) on a narrow terrace in Ronda is a masterpiece. In a very different tradition is the Carmen de la Fundación Rodríguez ACOSTA, on the slopes of the Alhambra hill in Granada. Here is a powerfully architectural design in which flowers are superfluous which uses a pared-down modernist language to make brilliant use of a precipitous site.

At Santa María de la Nieves near Toledo an admirable garden was made from 1985 by the Uruguyan garden designer Leandro Silva Delgado (b. 1930), who created a new layout among the beautiful remains of a 15th-century monastery. He replanted ancient olive trees to form an entrance drive and created water gardens of Muslim refinement—a water staircase and an extraordinary water maze edged in PALISSADES of Italian cypresses. At the end of the 20th century there appeared one of the most interesting garden designers of his time, Fernando CARUNCHO whose strong and wholly original work allies Renaissance discipline with inventive planting on a grand scale.

Valuable books on Spanish garden history appeared in the late 20th century. *Jardines de España* by Marquesa de Casa Valdés (1973; translated as *The Gardens of Spain*, 1987) was the first substantial, highly illustrated book on its subject. Later scholarly books have included Consuelo M. Correcher's *The Gardens of Spain* (1993) and *Jardines artísticos de España* by Carmen Añón Feliú, Monica Luengo Añón, and Ana Luengo Añón (1995). However, much remains to be done and the documentation of Spain's historic gardens is sparse. Nor has garden archaeology been pursued with vigour. At Madinat al-Zahra, one of the most important garden sites in Europe, archaeological investigation has been carried out spasmodically since the early 20th century—but only 10 per cent of its area had been excavated by 2001.

The curious traveller in Spain today will glimpse all sorts of attractive private gardens.

Apart from the historic gardens, however, few are open to the public. There is not a highly developed garden visiting culture. Such gardens as there are that do open to the public are exceptionally rewarding to non-Spanish visitors, partly because they are so unfamiliar and so little publicized. If a garden such as the Pazo de Oca were in England it would be far better known and would receive a much greater number of visitors, possibly to its detriment. Spanish gardens have a strongly individual and attractive character yet, apart from the Alhambra (which is among the most visited gardens in Europe), they do not receive the attention they deserve.   PT

Späth Arboretum ✿

Berlin, Germany, was laid out in 1879, designed by Berlin's city gardening director Gustav MEYER for the nursery owner Franz Späth. The 3.5-hectare/9-acre site was intended for trying out newly imported tree species, the breeding of new varieties, the preservation of mother trees, and the display of new exotics. In the style of a 19th-century landscape park the arboretum was part of an axial view from the Späth family's residence to the pond at the other end of the estate. It consisted of 60 subdivisions including a rose garden and, from 1928, a rock garden. By 1930 the collection had some 4,500 tree species (today 1,200), which the nursery's dendrological branch under Gerd Krüssmann had been cataloguing and labelling from 1891 onward. In 1961 responsibility for the arboretum was transferred to the Institute for Special Botany at Humboldt University, which immediately began to carry out necessary work on the tree population: the rock garden was redesigned in 1963, the rose garden in 1963 and again in 1971, and a new sunken garden for dwarf trees laid out in 1973. As well as some of Späth's important introductions like the *Juniperus chinensis pfitzeriana* (1899), the original layout is still intact with the original path network, the pond with its little island, and structural plantings of trees. Preservation and development work is based on Späth's original concept. The arboretum is used as a research and teaching facility and, since 1966, also serves science-oriented educational and PR purposes. The arboretum was awarded the honorary medal of the International Dendrological Society in 1998.   USc

sphinx.

The Egyptian sphinx, like the OBELISK, was much admired by Romans when they discovered Egypt. A sphinx in the Ashmolean Museum (Oxford), part of the Arundel collection and formerly displayed in the OXFORD BOTANIC GARDEN, is thought to be

of Roman origin. As a garden ornament the earliest sphinx seems to have been the 16th-century example in the Sacro Bosco at BOMARZO with an inscription questioning the garden's ornaments—'for trickery or art?' Sphinxes appear in VERSAILLES in 1670 as part of the setting for the Bassin de Latone. At CHISWICK HOUSE a pair of fine Portland stone sphinxes of *c*.1725 survive as does a lead example by John CHEERE. Similar sphinxes, attributed to Cheere, survive at Castle Hill (Devon), Hopetoun House (Lothian), and at the Piccadilly entrance to Green Park (London). Sphinxes were popular throughout the 18th century, made by craftsmen such as Cheere, and later in the century there were Coade stone sphinxes. In the 20th century a rare pair of lead sphinxes was made by W. Ward Willis in 1930 for the Water Terraces at BLENHEIM PALACE with portrait heads of the 9th Duke of Marlborough's second wife.   PT

JOHN DAVIS, *Antique Garden Ornament* (1991).

spirit of place. See PLACE, THE SPIRIT OF.

Springer, Leonard A.

(1855–1940), Dutch garden architect and dendrologist. Leonard Springer, son of the well-known painter Cornelis Springer, trained at the horticultural college Linnaeus from 1871 to 1875. He increased his plant knowledge while working at the nursery of Halverhout & Co. near Amsterdam, for whom he designed his first gardens. Leaving in 1878 he set up as a freelance garden architect designing parks, cemeteries, gardens, and settings for public buildings, as well as housing developments, primarily in landscape style, but later also in the mixed style. He was a prolific author, greatly interested in garden history, and in 1936 produced a bibliography of garden design. Between 1906 and 1924 he was much assisted by his nephew Gerard Bleeker (1882–1956). He was founder member of the Bond van Nederlandsche Tuinarchitecten (Society for Dutch Garden Architects) in 1922, where he acted as its first vice-chairman, and in 1924 of the Nederlandsche Dendrologische Vereeniging (Dutch Dendrological Society).   JW

Steele, Fletcher

(1885–1971), American landscape architect. After attending the Harvard School of Landscape Architecture from 1907 to 1909 he travelled extensively in Europe. Later he was influenced by Le Corbusier and the modern movement in architecture, and more specifically by the work of the contemporary French garden designers VERA, Legrain, and GUEVREKIAN, particularly in their use of the broken axis, manipulation of levels, and use of mirrors and perspective. Their influence may be seen in his own work, notably in his redesign of a neoclassical garden at NAUMKEAG, Stockbridge, Massachusetts, on which he worked from 1925 to the late 1930s. In the Blue Steps (of concrete painted light blue), rising in sweeps over small cascades through a birch wood which he created, selecting trees of various sizes, he has successfully reinterpreted Renaissance forms in terms of the modern concern for values of space, form, texture, and colour. Such concerns are expressed in his writing including *New Pioneering in Garden Design* (1930), *Landscape Design of the Future* (1932), and *Modern Garden Design* (1936).   MLL

ROBIN KARSON, *Fletcher Steele, Landscape Architect* (1989).

Stirling Castle ⊕
Stirlingshire, Scotland, goes back to the 12th century when a chapel was built here and the King's Park was enclosed to the west of the castle. Here, clearly visible far below the castle ramparts, are the earthworks of a great formal garden. Such a garden was made and was in place by 1633 for a visit by Charles I, and a painting by Johannes Vorsterman (*c.* late 1670s) shows such a garden enclosed in walls and profusely ornamented with statuary. Daniel Defoe visited Stirling in the early 18th century and noted 'the Figures of the Walks and Grass plots are plainly to be seen. They seem . . . very old fashioned, but might be thought fine for those times.' There is no other mention or depiction of the garden until 1882 when the Ordnance Survey *Gazetteer* describes 'an octagonal earthen mound with terraces and a depressed centre known as the King's Knot'. No one knows if this is a 19th-century version of the 17th-century garden or its true remains. If the latter, it is the oldest surviving garden layout in Scotland. Either way, it is a marvellous sight from one of the finest castles in the British Isles.   PT

Stockholm park system ⊕
During the late 1930s a new development was initiated in the Stockholm parks by director of parks Oswald Almqvist (1884–1950) and fulfilled by his successor Holger BLOM. The Stockholm park system is in part a coherent system of physically linked parks but above all it represents an ideology, which would later be named the Stockholm School of Park Design. By their design, the Stockholm parks broke away from the predominant park tradition of the late 19th century which advocated formality, a network of curving paths, and massive exotic plantings in GARDENESQUE style. As a new aesthetic point of departure the characteristics of the local, natural landscape around Lake Mälaren were reinterpreted as

designed landscapes in the heart of the city. Indigenous plants, free-form ponds, and exposed rock outcrops were among the design features. In this way, the new parks reacted against the late 19th-century stroll garden destined for a see-and-be-seen-life for the bourgeoisie. The new parks had a strong political impetus and followed as a reaction to industrialism. They directed themselves towards a more informal, everyday park life for multiple use by all kinds of citizens. Social use was emphasized, in such features as the no-charge staffed playground for children, which was introduced during the period. The parks became arenas for the democratization of high culture and the Stockholm Park Theatre was started as well as a programme aimed to use the parks as places for public art. The parks thus became part of the social welfare system for which Sweden became generally famous. The Stockholm parks from the era were also given a strategic role in urban planning, so that they were constructed to form green networks through the city, structuring and connecting city districts. They gave Sweden a world reputation at the time for being the country with the most progressive park policy in the world, which was proudly displayed at the IFLA (International Federation of Landscape Architects) congress in Stockholm 1952. One of the more renowned examples is Norr Mälarstrand (1941–3), designed by Erik GLEMME. The Stockholm park system as a phenomenon belongs to the modernist movement, when traditional values were questioned and re-evaluated.   TA

Stonecrop Gardens ⊕
Cold Spring, New York, USA, occupies a rocky hilltop 335 m/1,100 ft above sea level in the picturesque highlands of the Hudson river. It began in 1958 when Francis H. CABOT and his wife Anne built a summer house and started to garden. A mail-order alpine nursery was soon added. In addition to creating a place of singular beauty, the Cabots' goal had long been to inspire fellow gardeners. It was thus determined that Stonecrop Gardens and a school of practical horticulture be opened, benefiting amateurs and professionals alike. To advance both aims, Caroline Burgess was hired as director in the 1980s. Trained at BARNSLEY HOUSE and KEW, she was in charge of the garden when it opened to the public in 1992. The school quickly followed. Today, Stonecrop consists of 4.8 hectares/12 acres of display gardens surrounded by over 20 hectares/50 acres of fields and woodlands. The extraordinary diversity of plants in the collection is matched only by the range of tone and mood created throughout the site. There are woodland and

water gardens, a grass garden, raised alpine stone beds, a cliff rock garden, an order bed (see BOTANIC GARDEN), and an enclosed flower garden prominently featuring half-hardy plants. A conservatory and numerous speciality display houses showcase further horticultural rarities. Offering a two-year course and shorter internships that are arguably unique in the USA, the school aims to train passionate, technically adept horticulturists who understand the work of garden making within its broad cultural context.   KK

Store Vejleådalen Parkbelt ⊕
Albertslund, Denmark. In the 1960s, a broad team of architects, with the NØRGÅRDS, created a new town, Albertslund, with a succession of recreational areas, atrium gardens, squares, a canal, and parks leading to the open landscape. The valley of Store Vejleådalen stretches from the Vestskov forest to Køge Bay Coastal Park, and the dense urban quarter of Albertslund Syd creates a clear and distinct border to the open landscape. Between 1963 and 1979 the valley was emphasized with expanses of grass, meadows, and lakes, creating areas for sports facilities and the enormous Lake Herstedvester for bathing. Forest plantings, frequently dominated by oak, were made on the upper slopes of the valley, visually strengthening the bowl form. In Kongsholm Park, the excess soil was used to create a 30-m/100-ft high hill shaped like a truncated cone, with belts of pine. From the 1,500-m/5,000-ft long and 8-m/28-ft wide canal the water is led to terraced pools and from there to two large lakes, each of *c.*14 hectares/35 acres, placed on either side of the motorway.   AL

Stourhead ⊕
Stourton, Wiltshire, England, has a Palladian villa designed by Colen CAMPBELL and built for a banker, Henry HOARE, in the 1720s. In 1741 Henry Hoare II inherited the estate and made a garden which has become one of the most admired and most photographed in England. He dammed the river Stour, which flows through a valley at a little distance from the house, and formed an irregular lake (remarkably resembling a map of England) and started to embellish its banks with ornamental buildings. In this he had the help of the architect Henry Flitcroft (1697–1769), who designed many of the buildings and may have had a hand in laying out the grounds. A circuit walk girdles the lake with, close to its banks, Flitcroft's Temple of Flora (originally the Temple of Ceres, 1744–5) on the eastern bank and Pantheon (originally the Temple of Hercules, 1754–6) on the south-west bank. His Temple of Apollo (*c.*1765) was built on higher ground above the south-eastern bank of the

lake. Also built at this time (*c.*1748) was a GROTTO on the west bank, with a river god and a nymph. A window in the grotto frames views across the lake to the Temple of Flora. In 1765 the 14th-century Gothic Bristol High Cross was erected to the east of the lake and, much later, on the facing bank the Gothic Watch Cottage, Gothicized as an afterthought in 1806.

The recommended anti-clockwise circuit starts with the Temple of Flora and its warning from Virgil's *Aeneid* 'Procul, o procul este, profani' ('Be gone, be gone, you who are uninitiated'), the words that greeted Aeneas's approach to the entrance of the Underworld. There have been attempts to interpret the iconography of the garden in terms of Aeneas's wanderings but no rigorous programme of that sort seems to have been carried out. Although most of the original ingredients remain intact at Stourhead the atmosphere of the landscape has been radically altered by the style, and quantity, of later plantings. The 19th-century and 20th-century plantings of rhododendrons introduce a jolly, colourful air which is at odds with the Arcadian essence of the place. The garden, too, has become a notable collection of trees with many distinguished exotics dating largely from the 19th and 20th centuries. The banks of the lake, and many of the buildings, are now often enshrouded in dense planting of trees and shrubs. Coplestone Warre BAMPFYLDE's drawing of *c.*1780 shows the lake from an unencumbered sweep of turf on its southern bank. Elsewhere the banks of the lake are ornamented with occasional shapely clumps and, to the east, the Temple of Apollo stands at the head of an unplanted slope of turf with trees behind and flanking the temple. To the north-east the Temple of Flora is embowered in trees, much as it is today. So what we see today is different from the landscape admired by 18th-century cognoscenti but it is no less enchanting. Since 1946 the estate has been owned by the NATIONAL TRUST.   PT

Stowe ⊛

Buckingham, Buckinghamshire, England, belonged to the Temple family (later viscounts Cobham) in the 16th century, but its fame starts in 1713 when Sir Richard Temple commissioned a new garden from Charles BRIDGEMAN, and later in the century several of the finest garden designers and architects of the day worked here. Bridgeman's landscape is seen in an engraved plan of 1739 with the garden proper, largely south of the house, enclosed in a five-sided HA-HA which breaks out into occasional bastions. Within it a central axis leads to an octagonal pool, with cross-axes, other pools, and

serpentine walks. Beyond the garden to the north-east, linked by a long avenue, is a vast pattern of avenues piercing woods which have winding paths and clearings. By this time Bridgeman's garden had already changed with the advent of William KENT in the 1730s. By 1735 he had created the Elysian Fields where a stream flows through a shallow wooded valley separating two temples. Kent's Temple of British Worthies (1735) is a graceful curved stone screen with niches containing busts of those whom Lord Cobham particularly admired—among them King Alfred, Elizabeth I, Milton, Newton, and Shakespeare. On the other side of the stream, on rising ground, the Temple of Ancient Virtues (1736) contained statues by Peter SCHEEMAKERS of Homer, Socrates, Epaminondas, and Lycurgus, the greatest poet, philosopher, general, and lawyer of the classical world. Bridgeman's Octagon Pool became an informal lake and its easterly neck was embellished in 1738 by a Palladian Bridge attributed to James Gibbs (1682–1754). Nearby is a curious Chinese kiosk, dating from 1738 and possibly by Kent. To its north Hawkwell Field, with something of the FERME ORNÉE, was laid out in around 1740. It is overlooked by two buildings by Gibbs—the classical Queen's Temple (*c.*1742) and an extraordinary Gothic Temple (1741). Cattle or sheep grazed in the pasture, and still do. In 1741 Capability BROWN became, in effect, head gardener, remaining here until 1751. It is not possible to ascribe parts of the garden to him with certainty but the Grecian Valley dates from his time. The monuments and ornaments embody an iconography reflecting Lord Cobham's, and his descendants', Whiggish beliefs. The gardens became famous in their time, much visited by garden connoisseurs and the fashionable. In 1744 Benton Seeley published *A Description of the Gardens of Lord Viscount Cobham at Stow in Buckinghamshire*, the first substantial garden guide ever published in England. By the time Prince PÜCKLER-MUSKAU saw them, in 1826, he found them 'overloaded with temples and buildings'. The estate subsequently languished and was sold up in 1921, with many irreplaceable garden ornaments going to other gardens.

A central awkwardness at Stowe is the fact that the house, a school since 1923, is in separate ownership from the gardens, which have belonged to the NATIONAL TRUST since 1989. The original garden took the house as its starting point but today there is little connection between house and garden. The garden today is less a sublime unity than a sequence of charming and sometimes very beautiful interludes (the interlude of a golf course in the landscape is not charming). As a document in

English garden history Stowe is of the first importance; as a pleasurable landscape it has many attractions.   PT

JOHN MARTIN ROBINSON, *Temples of Delight: Stowe Landscape Gardens* (1990).

stroll garden. See JAPAN.

Strong, Sir Roy

(b. 1935), English art historian, historian, author, gardener, and garden designer who was director of the National Portrait Gallery and of the Victoria and Albert Museum. With his wife Julia Trevelyan Oman he made a garden of subtle originality and much charm at The LASKETT. Of his many books *The Renaissance Garden in England* (1979) and *The Artist and the Garden* (2000) are among the very few works of garden history also read by historians. His *Royal Gardens* (1992) gathered together much out-of-the-way information and remains the most useful book on the subject. As a promoter of the pleasures of gardening his influence is less quantifiable but no less real.   PT

Strybing Arboretum.

See GOLDEN GATE PARK.

Studley Royal ⊛

Fountains, North Yorkshire, England, was made, from 1716, by John AISLABIE. In the fine wooded valley of the river Skell he laid out a great landscape garden which was at first formal and at last dashingly picturesque. The earliest part of the garden is a water parterre in which a canal runs alongside a circular pool (the Moon Pond) and flanking crescent ponds. The surrounding lawn of turf is ornamented with statues and overlooked by the Temple of Piety, a later addition of 1742. On the wooded heights above is the Gothic Octagon Tower (1728 but Gothicized ten years later) and, on the other side of the valley, a banqueting house (1728–32) by Colen CAMPBELL. Further along the valley the river is dammed to form a giant sweeping half-moon pond. High above it, shrouded in woods, is Anne Boleyn's Seat, from which is visible a surprise view round the curve of the valley—the ruins of the great Cistercian Fountains Abbey. John Aislabie had thought of this as the visual climax to his garden but it only became part of the estate after his death when his son William bought it in 1768. Since 1983 the estate has been owned by the NATIONAL TRUST, whose visitors' centre leads visitors on exactly the wrong route—starting with the garden's climax, the abbey, and ending with John Aislabie's water parterre. It remains, however, one of the loveliest of all 18th-century gardens.

PT

Stupinigi, Palazzina di Caccia ⊕

Nichelino, near Turin, Piedmont, Italy. By the early 18th century French baroque influence began to alter classical Italian design. Built by the architect Filippo Juvara (1678–1736) between 1729 and 1734, as a hunting lodge for Amadeo II of Savoy, the Palazzina looks out over a magnificent park designed by the French architect Bernard and his son from 1740. They established a pattern of radiating rides leading out from under the windows through fields into the distant woodland.   PHo

Sturefors ⊕

Östergötland, Sweden, is situated south of the city of Linköping. Carl Piper, although imprisoned in Russia at the time, had the manor house and garden built 1699–1705, designed by Nicodemus TESSIN the younger. The gardens were laid out in a French-inspired formal manner with a central axis, avenues of lime, PARTERRE de broderie, fountains, and an orangery. In 1766 Carl Fredrik Adelcrantz (1716–96) redesigned the parterres, with the broderies and fountains replaced by shaped turf. In the 1770s the owner, Nils-Adam Bielke, wanted an English landscape garden. The results of a plan 1774 by Fredrik Adolf Ulrik Cronstedt (1744–1829) and later ideas in the 1780s, presumably by Fredrik Magnus PIPER, are still visible. A small-scale landscape garden was created outside the formal garden, with paths leading through clumps of trees, past views towards the manor house, ornamental garden buildings, and monuments. A rotunda designed by Cronstedt stands at the end of the central axis. A pond in the central axis, narrowing at the end furthest from the house, creates the illusion of an elongated perspective. In connection to the central pond an island with a circle of oak trees (Quercus robur f. fastigiata Group), form a presumed imitation of Île des Peupliers at ERMENONVILLE. At the far end of the landscape garden a Chinese pavilion reflects the exotic, oriental garden taste of that time. Sturefors is considered one of the best-preserved Swedish manor houses and gardens of the 18th century.

AJ

Suan Pakkad ⊕

Bangkok, Thailand. The garden at Suan Pakkad Palace was started in 1952 by Prince and Princess Chumbhot with the re-erection of some old Thai buildings to make a suite of reception rooms and to house their large collection of art and artefacts dating from the 2nd millennium BC to the 19th century AD. The main pavilion is built on a substructure of cylindrical concrete columns in place of the original teak, and on the garden side they rise straight out of a curved pool—with water lilies, thalias, cannas, spathiphyllums, and weeping willows—which seems to become part of the teak-floored banqueting room which appears to float upon it. Across a wide lawn and backing on to the quiet klong (navigable waterway) which bounds the garden is the famous Siamese Lacquer Pavilion, on massive teak columns, which once stood on the riverside at Bang Kling near Ayudhya. Another pool, seen through the framework of branches of a large and sculptural frangipani (Plumeria rubra var. acutifolia), separates the area of the garden open to the public from the private residence. Suan Pakkad has many rare and unusual plants including a Phyllocladus, a fine specimen of white Erythrina indica from Hawaii, and a striking group of royal palms (Roystonea regia). There are many influences at Suan Pakkad and the stones set as sculpture among informal planting have an echo of Japan, but with the water treatment and the informality of the klong it is essentially Siamese at a highly sensitive level.   MLL

Suan Sampran (The Rose Garden) ⊕

Nakorn Pathom, Thailand, is far more than a rose garden, remarkable though the growing of roses is in this part of the world; it is more in fact a public pleasure garden comparable with many in other countries. It has something of the Copenhagen TIVOLI about it though quieter and more restful, but contains 'something for all the family'. As it is only c.40 km/25 miles from Bangkok families of all nations flock to it at the weekend. Suan Sampran was created by Khunying Walee Yuvabul, wife of a former mayor of Bangkok, and Khunying Urai Leuamrung, on a tract of land surrounded by a belt of casuarinas, and bordered by a quiet unpolluted river in the late 1960s. It offers a fine lake for water sports, a quieter lake with skilfully sited weekend 'chalets', and a wide range of amenities, as well as a nursery garden which specializes in roses and other more tropical plants for sale. Floating restaurants with canopies are moored along the river bank, among willows and callistemon. Both hard surfaces and ground cover are well detailed with stone flags set within broad-leafed Malaysia grass (Axonopus compressus) and areas of Sansevieria hahnii among gnarled tree roots. Casuarina hedges are cut in sculptural shapes and shady walks connect the varied compartments.   MLL

Sui Yuan,

Nanjing (formerly Nanking), Jiangsu province, China, was a garden located at the foot of a range of hills in the city of NANJING and originally owned by Sui Hede, a high official in charge of the imperial fabric industry at the time of the Kangxi Emperor of the Qing. The fame of this garden dates from the 18th century when it was bought and renovated by a well-known poet and playwright, Yuan Mei (1716–98). Although it was destroyed during the Taiping rebellion (1851–64), contemporary paintings and descriptions emphasize its close relationship to the site, laid out around a small lake in a natural valley and so well protected by hills and steep cliffs that it had no need of walls, only a gateway. Literally translated, Sui Yuan means the 'to go along with garden': while views were 'borrowed' (JIE JING) from the scenery round about, its various buildings and trees were placed to look as if they had appeared spontaneously among the contours of the hills. Undulating lang (see CHINA) made it possible to walk to most of the different set pieces even in wet weather, and causeways connected by bridges made such good use of reflections that the whole atmosphere was said to resemble gardens by the famous West Lake of HANGZHOU. Although a number of fine single stones were set up as sculptural pieces in the paved courtyards, Sui Yuan, unlike almost all other Chinese gardens, had no great rockery: with an abundance of natural rocks all around, it had no need of one.   C-ZC/MK

Suizenji Park ⊕

Kumamoto prefecture, Japan, also known as Jōjuen, is an Edo-period (1600–1868) STROLL GARDEN covering approximately 6 hectares/15 acres. The garden was initiated by Hosokawa Tadatoshi (1586–1641), when he was assigned control of Higo province (present-day Kumamoto prefecture) in 1632. Upon moving to his new post, Tadatoshi invited the head priest of Rakanji, a Buddhist temple in his former home province of Ogura (present-day Fukuoka prefecture), to join him and together they founded Suizenji temple. Soon after, Tadatoshi had the temple removed to an adjoining property and used the land to build a villa variously called Jōjuen and Suizenji no Ochaya (the Suizenji Tea House). The initial garden design is thought to have been done under the guidance of tea masters affiliated with the Hosokawa family. Work continued after Tadatoshi's death in 1641 and was largely complete by the time of the third lord Hosokawa Tsunatoshi (1641–1712). An aspect of Edo-period culture that strongly influenced this garden was the system of 'alternate attendance' (sankin kotai) by which provincial lords were required to travel to the capital, Edo (present-day Tokyo), every two years. Landscape scenes along that route, especially along the highway between Edo and Kyoto known as the Tōkaidō, were used as motifs in the design of the garden. The most famous of these is Mount Fuji, the upsweeping form of which was recreated as a lawn-covered earth mound. These strikingly sculptural earthworks, the relative openness of the garden, and its prolific use of natural spring water in streams and ponds, are some salient features of the garden.   MPK

Summer Garden ✿

St Petersburg, Russia, Peter the Great's first garden in St Petersburg, was begun in 1703 and is still the city's most important open space. The present area is 11 hectares/27 acres, but it was once much larger and included what are now the Field of Mars, the Mikhailovsky Garden, and the Engineers' Castle. Among those who worked here were the architects Ivan Matveyev, Mikhail Zemtsov, Le Blond, and RASTRELLI, and the master gardeners Jan Roosen and Ilya Surmin. Peter himself was also directly involved in planning the garden. The early layout reflected the Dutch gardens, which Peter had visited and admired, and the great French gardens, which, at that time, he knew only from books and engravings. Lines of trees were rigorously clipped into smooth green walls or into green tunnels, and single trees were shaped into balls, cubes, and pyramids. There were pavilions, a grotto, and many fountains, fed by the river Fontanka, hence its name. In the 1720s Zemtsov laid out a labyrinth with fountains which incorporated gilded statues illustrating *Aesop's Fables*, a theme which Peter later introduced to the park at PETERHOF. Peter arranged for trees to be brought from various parts of Russia as well as from Western Europe, and for statues to be purchased in Italy. In 1736 there were more than 200 statues, and, though the number is down to about 90, it is still an important collection. The splendid wrought-iron railings by Yuri Felten (1730–1801) are another outstanding feature.   PH

sundial.

The origins of the sundial are unknown but they are exceedingly ancient. In the Bible the Book of Isaiah has the words 'Behold, I will bring again the shadow of the degrees, which is gone down in the sundial of Ahaz' (38: 8). But long before the writing of the Book of Isaiah standing stones, such as those at Stonehenge (*c*.2500 BC), seem to have been disposed in relation to the position of the sun. On European churches vertical wall-mounted sundials are found in the early Middle Ages. At St Gregory's minster, Kirkdale, in Yorkshire, is a Saxon dial dating from around 1055 with an Anglo-Saxon inscription reading 'This is day's Sun marker at every tide'. In gardens they appear in England from the early 16th century. Henry VIII's accounts contain the entry 'Also paid to Bryse Auguston, of Westminster, clockmaker, for making 20 brazen dials for the

King's new garden', which would have been for HAMPTON COURT. The earliest surviving garden sundial known in England was found at Acton Court near Bristol. It is dated 1520 and bears the initials N.K. for Nicholas Kratzer, who was horologist to Henry VIII. The owner of Acton Court, William Poyntz, was a courtier to the King. In Scotland the earliest known sundial, made in 1592, is in the garden at Fingask Castle (Perthshire) although it was made originally for Holyroodhouse (Edinburgh). The 17th century was a great period for sundials in Scotland and many remarkable examples survive in gardens, the most distinctive of which are multifaceted upright structures. The different facets would incorporate moon dials and dials to read the time late on summer evenings in this northern latitude. An example at PITMEDDEN made in 1675 has 24 faces. The example at the centre of DRUMMOND CASTLE garden designed *c*.1630 by John Mylne III (1611–67) is one of the most elaborate of all sundials. A square pedestal with sixteen faces supports a polyhedron with 24 faces which in turn is crowned with an obelisk with 28 faces. John Mylne was also the maker of a surviving polyhedral dial at Holyroodhouse dating from 1633, one of whose gnomons is the nose of a grotesque mask.

In the 18th century, with clocks and watches far more common, the need for sundials diminished but they remained popular garden ornaments. The 19th century was a great period for dialling, with countless pedestal-mounted horizontal dials used in gardens, with all kinds of mottoes. Mrs Alfred Gatty's *The Book of Sun-Dials* (1888), containing hundreds of suitable inscriptions, went through three editions. These, very often in Latin, range from the banal *Tempus fugit* (time flies) to the more intricate *Sine sole sileo* (without the sun I am silent) and the sentimental *Horas non numero nisi serenas* (I count only serene times). In the late 20th century in Britain there was a minor renaissance in dialling. Ian Hamilton FINLAY made a fine vertical dial for the ROYAL BOTANIC GARDEN, EDINBURGH. Some outstanding examples came from the Cambridge workshop of the lettering designer and carver David Kindersley (1915–95).   PT

WINTHROP W. DOLAN, *A Choice of Sundials* (1975).

sunken (sunk) garden.

The idea of garden beds sunk to a lower level than the surrounding ground was found in Islamic gardens in Spain but it is in the ARTS AND CRAFTS gardens of England that they became particularly common. The arrangement, with walks at the upper level, displayed the planted patterns below to particular advantage. The garden that the architect Robert Weir Schultz (1860–1951)

designed for himself *c*.1900 at Hartley Wintney (Hampshire) had a sunken garden surrounded by box hedges, elaborate topiary, and lavishly planted raised beds. The intricately shaped sunken rose garden designed by Edwin LUTYENS *c*.1912 for FOLLY FARM has semicircular flights of steps giving access to the beds below. A very similar arrangement on a much grander scale was designed by Lutyens for the Plat at HESTERCOMBE, a rectangular sunken garden with terrace walks on three sides, a raised pergola on the fourth, and semicircular steps leading down in each corner. One of the most extraordinary sunken gardens is that which may still be seen at Heywood (County Laois, Ireland) designed by Lutyens *c*.1906. It is oval, with a series of terraces and beds descending to an oval pool with a giant fountain vase at its centre.   PT

Sutton Place,

near Guildford, Surrey, England, is a great early Tudor mansion built for Sir Richard Weston and completed *c*.1530. It had walled formal gardens by the end of the 17th century and in the early 20th century, when the estate was owned by the newspaper magnate Lord Northcliffe, Gertrude JEKYLL advised on planting. From 1980, after the estate was bought by Stanley J. Seeger, Sir Geoffrey JELLICOE was commissioned to make a new garden. It was his intention to make a garden which expresses, as he wrote in his *Sutton Place* (1983), 'the modern mind, was sympathetic to the ethos of the place, which comprehends the past, the present and the future'. Jellicoe made a great serpentine lake (like an amoeba) in the park and deployed a dazzling array of gardens about the house. Difficult stepping stones give access to the walled Paradise Garden with snaking paths and arbours of jasmine and roses. A Ben Nicholson white marble wall is reflected in a pool set in turf in a hedged enclosure. In the Moss Garden a plane tree rises from a circle of moss echoed by a circle of lawn, the whole overlooked by a gazebo. In the Swimming Pool Garden a sunken pool has stepping stones leading to a raft inspired by shapes in a Miró painting. A row of noble but preposterously large vases, almost as high as the adjacent wall, in the Magritte Avenue gives a disoriented sense of scale. This was one of Jellicoe's largest private commissions and the garden gives the impression of his gleefully seizing the possibilities.   PT

Suzhou,

Jiangsu province, China, is an ancient city of whitewashed houses, willow avenues, temples, and bridges. This 'Venice of the East' lies on a network of canals west of Shanghai and some 19 km/11 miles from Lake Tai, in the south of Jiangsu province. A garden was recorded in the area in the 4th century but the town itself was built up by He Lu as his capital in the 6th century. During the Five Dynasties period (907-60) the Wu and Yue kingdoms around it suffered little from the fighting and became the richest provinces in China. From 852 to 932 the ruler of the area, Qian Liu, put his son in charge of Suzhou where he led the local gentry in building gardens—including his general, Sun, who made a villa on the site where the CANGLANGTING now stands.

During the Yuan period (1279-1368), a number of officials who refused to serve under a foreign dynasty retired to the city, and in the Ming and Qing, still more built gardens in their retirement. Surrounded by rich agricultural lands 'of fish and rice' and a prosperous silk industry, Suzhou became not only wealthy but a great centre of art and scholarship—and the city from whence came more successful candidates in the imperial examinations than any other in China. After achieving political appointments and amassing (usually) large fortunes, many of these men retired to Suzhou to build gardens. Ideally situated with plentiful water, pleasant hills beyond the town, a genial climate, the finest garden stones (Taihu rocks) nearby, and excellent communications by canal for importing others, Suzhou also offered them a pool of skilled garden craftsmen. Though many villas were damaged during the Taiping rebellion (1851-64) some 100 were recorded in the 1950s, and nine of the largest have been restored and opened to the public: Canglangting; ZHUOZHENG YUAN; WANGSHI YUAN; LIU YUAN and Xiyuan si; YI YUAN; OU YUAN; SHIZILIN and HUANXIU VILLA.

An old and much quoted saying goes 'Above is Heaven, below are HANGZHOU and Suzhou.'
MK

Sweden

from a garden historic perspective is not a distinct conception. The country is 1,600 km/960 miles long, 500 km/300 miles wide, and extends from latitude 55.5° N up to 69° N. The border between north and middle Europe crosses the province of Skåne in the south and the Arctic Circle cuts across the country (66.6° N) in the north. The country is marked by the proximity of the Atlantic and the impact of the Gulf Stream and western winds, which gives a general humid-temperate climate. The natural setting—great distances, vast woodlands, a net of waterways—together with very few people, has determined the way in which the Swedish garden has developed. It is in the wrestling between the natural (mountains, woods, and lakes) and cultural landscapes (meadows, fields,

and pastures) on one hand, and imported gardeners, architects, styles, and plants, that Swedish garden art and landscape architecture has acquired its characteristic form. The indigenous Swedish flora comprises about 2,000-2,500 species. In gardens, however, more than 10,000 species and perhaps as many as 30,000 taxa have been introduced.

Sweden was totally covered in the last inland ice age. During early neolithic times (4000-3300 BC) the first great landscape monuments were raised by man—large stone graves with dolmens and chambered barrows. During the Iron Age (AD 400-550) hillforts, partly natural fortifications on hilltops, were a feature of the landscape. The largest Swedish ship barrow, Ales stenar (67 m/220 ft long with 59 standing stones), dating from the Viking Age, is situated in Kåseberga on the south shore. What was Sweden's oldest garden, where was it situated, and what did it look like? This question is partly etymological. The Swedish word for garden today is *trädgård*, a collective name comprising all earlier yards with a garden-like content. But originally *trä(d)gård* only meant a fenced-off yard with trees, most often fruit trees but also coppiced trees. The word *trädgård* has in its turn evolved from the prehistoric *trægarÞer* and is more than 1,000 years old, formed of the nouns *träd* (tree) and *gård* (yard). The oldest traditional gardens are best considered as small fenced fruit and kitchen gardens in a square or rectangular shape. Such gardens, planted with cabbages, onions, and *Angelica*, are archaeologically known from Birka and later in medieval laws. Another kind of 'garden' is older, though. This is the forest meadow (*lövängen*) and the Scandinavian field culture of coppicing, haymaking, and the cultivation of trees and shrubs bearing fruit, berries, or nuts. The forest meadow culture dates back to the drastic climate change around 500 BC, when the cattle had to be stalled during winter. The meadows, multifunctional and aesthetically arranged, became the quintessence of early designed landscape, still existing, and with a rich meadow flora as a by-product.

The Middle Ages and the Reformation

Medieval garden history (1050-1550) is intimately linked to the establishment of the monastic system. About twenty Cistercian monasteries were founded during the second part of the 12th century. The gardens of the convent of Saint Birgitta in Vadstena (1346) were partly laid out by Johan Päterson, commissioned by Birgitta herself. Together with Sister Botilda at Vårfruberga (14th century) they are the first gardeners in Sweden known by name. The first deer park in Sweden was probably Dalby hage, in connection with

the church of Dalby (1060) in Skåne. Approximately 120 different garden plants were introduced in the medieval period.

The Reformation was a drawn-out process in Sweden, lasting almost the whole of the 16th century. Cultural influences mainly came from the Netherlands and Germany. It was around the castles—in Uppsala, Svartsjö, Gripsholm, Stockholm (KUNGSTRÄDGÅRDEN), Linköping, Strängnäs, and Kalmar—of King Gustav Vasa and his sons that new gardens were laid out, with help from gardeners, architects, and artists from abroad. The oldest garden plan in Sweden is of c.1572, drawn by the Italian architect Fransiscus Pahr, showing a herb garden on a turf bastion. The most prominent Nordic Renaissance garden was laid out around the Danish astronomer Tycho Brahe's (1546-1601) castle URANIBORG on the island of Ven.

The 17th and 18th centuries

During the 17th century Sweden took its position as one of Europe's great powers. A period of intensive building started after the peace treaty of 1648 ending the Thirty Years War. In the field of garden art Sweden advanced from the very periphery to an almost leading position towards the end of the century. In 1648 the French gardener André MOLLET arrived in the country, at the court of Queen Christina. He brought the new, baroque, ideas to Sweden manifested in his trilingual treatise *Lustgård* (*Le Jardin de plaisir*, 1651). His work at KUNGSTRÄDGÅRDEN and Humlegården in Stockholm and at Uppsala Castle does not survive. The garden designer Simon de La Vallée (1590-1642) already in the years 1637-42 had been working on private estates at Ekolsund, Fiholm, Rosersberg, and Örbyhus. His son Jean de La VALLÉE returned after his grand tour to meet his most important client, the Chancellor Count Magnus Gabriel de La Gardie (1622-86), himself an educated and distinguished amateur garden architect and a great commissioner of building projects. Together they worked at Ekolsund, Wenngarn, and Karlberg and Jean de La Vallée also worked on other notable gardens at Läckö and Jakobsdal (ULRIKSDAL). Nicodemus TESSIN Sr. closely followed the style of André LE NÔTRE. With the palaces and gardens of Strömsholm and DROTTNINGHOLM, from 1662 onwards, the French formal garden style became predominant in the country. The Le Nôtre style and the overwhelming power of the central axis reached its perfection with the work of Nicodemus TESSIN Jr.. Returning from his grand tour in 1681 he was put in charge of the building of Drottningholm Palace and gardens as well as of other royal estates like Strömsholm and Ekolsund. Tessin also worked at such private estates as Steninge and

Rosersberg in Uppland, STUREFORS in Östergötland, and Krageholm in Skåne. Johan HÅRLEMAN, one of the most versatile Swedish garden designers of the baroque period, worked both in parallel and together with Tessin Jr. Hårleman's work at Noor Manor in Uppland is a full-scale miniature example of the Le Nôtre style, in detail as well as in its overall design. From the late 16th to the 17th century plants were mostly imported from the Netherlands, and shipments even from England are known. The architecture and garden art in Sweden during the late 17th century are well documented, though slightly flattered, in the extensive volume of engravings *Suecia Antiqua et Hodierna* (1661-1716), carried out by the fortification officer Erik Dahlbergh (1625-1703).

The 18th-century owners of large estates generally moderated their building and garden ambitions. The Swedish ironworks—Forsmark, Leufsta, Söderfors, and Österbybruk in Uppland—were, in a sense, the heirs of the early 18th-century aesthetic and socially conscious art of planning and design. Master of works Carl HÅRLEMAN, son of Johan Hårleman, took a leading position during the first half of the 18th century in Swedish building and garden art, introducing the ROCOCO in his designs. He remained faithful to the French formal garden but often replaced the PARTERRES *en broderie* with *parterres à l'anglaise*—small lawns with elegant contours. He also gave the kitchen garden a central position in the master plan and allowed meadows and groves to spread out in the immediate surroundings. Svartsjö, Ängsö, Stola, Österbybruk, Ulriksdal, and Övedskloster (Skåne) are some of his designs. Carl Fredrik Adelcrantz (1716-96) carried this tradition further in gardens at Stora Ek, at the China Palace (Kina slott) in Drottningholm, and at Sparreholm. GUNNEBO in Västergötland, by Carl Wilhelm Carlberg (1746-1814), is one of the 18th century's most complete Italian-inspired neoclassical rural villas. Thorough restoration works have been carried out here since 1995. In the middle of the 18th century botany enjoyed a spectacular flowering in Sweden through the influence of Carl LINNAEUS and his followers. A steady flood of new plants from almost all corners of the world came to Sweden, in particular to the restored and expanded botanical gardens in UPPSALA and LUND, both designed by Carl Hårleman.

The Scanian nobleman Adolf Fredrik Barnekow (1744-87) drew the first plan suggesting an English park in Sweden in 1771 for Örtofta Manor. The English park in Sweden was mainly introduced by gardening noblemen—two famous examples are Värnanäs and Olivehult. The parks, of strongly varying size and quality, were usually added to existing formal gardens. The most brilliant garden designer of the period was Fredrik Magnus PIPER. Greatly influenced by the English parks of STOURHEAD and PAINSHILL, he was commissioned in 1780 by King Gustav III (1746-92) to reconstruct the gardens at Drottningholm and HAGA. The King himself, as the most prominent of all Swedish gardening noblemen, took an active part, and produced plans and sketches, especially for Ekolsund and Drottningholm. In the 1790s Piper was engaged at Bjärka Säby and Godegård manors in Östergötland, Listonhill at Djurgården in Stockhom, and Wrangelsro in Halland. In his reconstruction of Kungsträdgården in Stockholm Piper adapted the park to the surrounding right-angled city environment in a geometrical pattern. This is also predominant in Piper's design for the new cemeteries outside the city centres, after the edict of 1805 by King Gustav IV Adolf forbidding burial in churches.

The 19th century and beyond
In the 1790s the first county agricultural societies (*hushållningssällskap*) for promoting rural gardening in Sweden were established. In 1811 the Royal Swedish Academy of Agriculture and Forestry (KSLA) was instituted. In 1832 the Swedish Horticultural Society was founded in Stockholm, with a garden of its own at Drottninggatan. Through the parcelling-out reforms (1807 and 1827), under which farmland was grouped more efficiently, the necessary conditions for gardening for many people were also created. In the elementary education statute of 1842 it was provided that all schools should teach horticulture and gardening, and school gardens were gradually established all over the country continuing far into the 20th century. Academic horticultural education is mainly a 19th-century phenomenon. The Royal Swedish Academy of Sciences, founded in 1739, initiated a horticultural programme at Hortus Bergianus in Stockholm as early as 1791. KSLA's horticultural school at Experimentalfältet started in 1832, as did the Swedish Horticultural Society horticultural scheme. In 1876 a horticultural school was instituted at Alnarp. From the mid 19th century both theoretical and practical garden books for the general public were issued, for example those of the German gardener Daniel Müller (1812-57), and the pomologist Olof Eneroth (1825-81), a true pioneer of Swedish horticulture of the time.

From 1855 the larger railways were built and in 1862 the garden department of the Swedish State Railways (SJ) was established, with a planting scheme of its own, employing gardeners and nurseries. Olof Eneroth became the first garden director. SJ's activities became an important pioneer effort in spreading garden culture throughout the whole of the country, even in the very north. SJ's ambitions were presented at the garden exhibition in London 1928. The garden director from 1938, Gösta Reuterswärd (1892-1980), continued this tradition by creating station gardens and railway parks. The first county chief gardener was employed in the north, by the county agricultural society of Västernorrland in 1861. One of the more prominent was Bengt Kjellsson (1848-1912), employed by the county of Malmöhus in 1876.

The 19th century saw few true garden architects. Knut Forsberg (1827-95) could be considered the heir of Piper's ideas. In 1851 he won a prize for his designs for the Bois de Boulogne in Paris (see PARIS PARKS AND GARDENS). Other grounds by his hand are Berzelii Park in Stockholm, Nääs Manor in Bohuslän, and Gerstorp in Östergötland. His characteristic style follows the 'German style', a recreated central axis with perspectives and a certain symmetry near the buildings but with naturalistically laid out plantings further away. The first public city parks came during the 1860s with a peak from the 1880s and to the end of the century. The inspiration came from both England and Germany. Kungsparken (1869) and Slottsparken (1898) in Malmö are among the best known. In Malmö the first people's park, on the initiative of the labour movement, was opened in 1893, followed by parks in Lund and Helsingborg (1895). In 1898 the people's park in Eskilstuna was inaugurated, an important park among the mid-Sweden parks. Already in 1796 the mining councillor Detlof Heijkensköld in Hällefors, Västmanland, laid out the first park for the people, Krokbornsparken. In 1895 the first allotment gardens were constructed close to Pildammarna in Malmö. The towns of Lund and Landskrona were provided with allotment gardens in 1901 and 1904 respectively. In 1921 the Society of Garden Architects of Sweden was founded, which did much to promote the profession. In 1971 followed the establishment of the Swedish Association of Landscape Architects, since 2002 a part of the Swedish Association of Architects. Many of the great 20th-century Swedish garden and landscape figures, and garden designers, were connected with these organizations and also with the Swedish Society for Dendrology and Park Culture, founded in 1920. Among the early 20th century's most prominent designers was Rudolf ABELIN, the man behind the gardens of Norrviken. Women pioneers in Swedish garden architecture were Ruth Brandberg (1875-1944), a Swedish Gertrude JEKYLL introducing an English-inspired ARTS AND CRAFTS gardening style, and Ester Claesson (1884-1931), giving the garden architect an identity of her own, with a status similar to that of artists, architects, and gardeners. Sven A. HERMELIN became in many ways Claesson's heir. He worked as a modern landscape architect, author, debater, and lecturer, influencing garden architecture in Sweden, in particular younger landscape architects, for half a century. His work comprises traditional restorations (Strömsholm and Hässelby manors), new parks for factories and environmental designs (Marabouparken and in Bjuv), nature and cultural landscape commissions, and conservation and recreation schemes (Lötsjön). Another pioneer in the field of garden conservation and restoration, mainly at manors and palaces, especially Drottningholm, was Walter BAUER.

Still active today, and internationally recognized, are the garden architects and professors Per FRIBERG, Gunnar MARTINSSON, and Sven-Ingvar ANDERSSON, all of whom were employed by Sven Hermelin. Today a new generation of landscape architects have built on their foundations, and hold positions as professors in universities, as municipal gardeners, and as advisers to county planning departments dealing with matters of urban and landscape planning, nature conservation, and cultural heritage. The Act on historical monuments of 1989 (SFS 1988:950) now gives the possibility of protecting gardens, parks, avenues, and designed landscapes as cultural monuments, and also demands a maintenance programme and plan. The Forum for Garden History Research, an interdisciplinary body of researchers and professionals who pursue garden historical research within various fields, was founded in 1995. Courses in landscape architecture/landscape planning (five years) are given at SLU, (Swedish University of Agricultural Sciences), at Ultuna (Uppsala), and at Alnarp (Lund); of horticulture (five years), landscape engineers, and garden engineers (three years) at Alnarp.

The public interest in gardens, especially garden design, garden history, and the historic plant material, is high and still growing in Sweden. The tradition of local garden societies is strong. The number of garden exhibitions is increasing and publication, in newsletters, magazines, and on the net, is booming.   KL

THORBJÖRN ANDERSSON, TOVE JONSTOIJ, and KJELL LUNDQUIST (eds.), *Svensk trädgårdskonst under fyrahundra år* (2000).

Sweden, James van.
See OEHME, VAN SWEDEN, & ASSOCIATES.

Swiss garden.
In the early 19th century in England there was a taste for Switzerland fostered by visits to the Alps. In 1840 a public house in the shape of a Swiss cottage, built to the designs of P. F. Robinson (1776-1858) in north London at a busy intersection, became so well known as to give its name to that part of London. Robinson's *Village Architecture* (1830) influenced the fashion for chalet architecture, with overhanging eaves and first-floor verandas. At Queen Victoria's OSBORNE HOUSE a chalet was brought from Switzerland in 1850 and erected in the garden as a holiday home for the royal children. It had a vegetable garden which Prince Albert encouraged his children to cultivate, paying them the market rate for vegetables. Garden buildings in the Swiss style were often given an 'Alpine' setting of conifers. In Central European gardens in the 18th and 19th centuries the *Schweitzerei* was a 'Swiss' dairy of ornamental character with something of the spirit of the FERME ORNÉE.   PT

Swiss Garden, The ⊛
Old Warden, Bedfordshire, England, the only surviving garden in England in the Swiss taste. It was made in the 1820s and 1830s for the 3rd Lord Ongley as, it was rumoured, a love nest for his Swiss mistress. It survives in excellent state and has been well restored. In an area of 3.6 hectares/9 acres, well wooded with mature conifers, it has a picturesque flavour unlike any other garden. A cottage, rising among cedars on the brow of a hillock, has a thickly thatched, deeply overhanging roof supported by columns of unbarked wood. A path winds about the wooded banks of ponds with picturesque ornaments and buildings, not all of them Swiss—an Indian pavilion has stained-glass windows. A rare and beautiful building is the grotto fernery dating from the 1830s. The walls of the fernery chamber are encrusted with tufa and Pulhamite planted with ferns, giving a grotto effect, and the whole is illuminated by a graceful glazed dome of cast iron (a very early date for such a structure). It is said that Lord Ongley encouraged women in the estate village to wear Swiss costume to enhance the Swissness of the place.   PT

Swiss Re Center for Global Dialogue,
Rüschlikon, Canton of Zurich, Switzerland, built in the 1920s as an upper-middle-class country house and redesigned between 1996 and 2000 by architects Meili & Peter in association with landscape architects Kienast Vogt. On a north-facing hillside overlooking Lake Zurich, in the middle of a park, stands Villa Bodmer, a country house built in 1926-7 for industrialist Carl Martin Leonhard Bodmer by architects Sinner and Beyeler in the style of an 18th-century Bernese castle. An avenue of lime trees still leads downhill from the main road into the *cour d'honneur* (see ATTRE, CHÂTEAU D'), enclosed in conifers, in front of the gateway to the neo-baroque villa. Construction of a modern seminar centre with a guest house by Zurich architects Meili & Peter made it necessary to alter and in some cases redesign the park, which has a stock of precious trees. The new design is characterized by respect for the historical park concept, which combined formal French design elements with English landscape features. A curving path leads from the newly designed main entrance to the seminar centre, over a pine-covered hill, past a sculpture by Sol Le Witt (b. 1928), and down to the architectural part of the park. Its extensive, almost square lawn in front of the old villa, enclosed on three sides by imposing trees, still constitutes the garden-architectural heart of the grounds. A large fountain pool, once the central visual focus at the end of the lawn, has disappeared with the passage of time but in its place there now stands a minimalist stone sculpture by Ulrich Rückriem (b. 1938). Two box parterres, formerly planted with roses, have been redesigned in differentiated green tones and organic patterns. They flank the villa and form a prelude to the two long reflecting pools by the old chestnut ALLÉES. From the viewing terrace on the edge of the slope, or from the tea pavilion a little lower down, one has an impressive view over extensive planted areas of flowering shrubs across the lake to the mountains.   UW

Switzer, Stephen
(c.1683-1745), English author, garden designer, and nurseryman. Specializing in water gardens, he described himself as a 'hydrostatician'. G. W. Johnson's *History of English Gardening* (1829) described him as one of the 'Classic Authors of Gardening' and a 'sound practical Horticulturist'. He was also a seedsman 'At the Flower-pot over against the Court of Common Pleas in Westminster Hall; or at his garden at Millbank, Westminster'. An early advocate of naturalistic gardening and of opening views of the surrounding landscape—'If the Beauties of Nature were not corrupted by Art, Gardens would be much more valuable'—he recommended in his *Ichnographia Rustica* (1718) that 'all the adjacent Country be laid open to View, and the eye should not be bounded with high Walls'. He worked on the gardens at BLENHEIM PALACE (1705-10), Kensington Palace (London, 1704-5), Leeswood Hall (Clwyd, c.1724-6), Marston House (Somerset, 1724-5), Cirencester Park (Gloucestershire), and Nostell Priory (North Yorkshire, c.1730-40) and possibly at CASTLE HOWARD, CLAREMONT, DUNCOMBE PARK, and ERDDIG. A delightful

surviving water garden, at Ebberston Hall (North Yorkshire), has been attributed to Switzer. J. C. LOUDON in his *Encyclopaedia of Gardening* (1822) wrote that 'New Liston, Dalkeith House, Hopeton [i.e. Hopetoun] House and various other places near Edinburgh, are also in Switzer's style.' A prolific author, his best-known books are *Iconographia Rustica* (incorporating his earlier *The Nobleman, Gentleman and Gardener's Recreation*, 1715) and *Introduction to a General System of Hydrostaticks and Hydraulicks, Philosophical and Practical* (1729).
PT

Switzerland.

'If ever Nature created a land that unites the astonishing number and diversity of its heroic objects with the exquisite pleasure of its vistas, then it is Switzerland. It seems as if Nature had here, so to speak, wished to be quite original,' was the judgement of German garden theorist C. C. L. HIRSCHFELD in his *Theorie der Gartenkunst* (1779). Within just 41,284 sq. km/ 15,940 sq. miles Switzerland has a remarkable variety of landscapes to offer, from the high glaciers of the Central Alps to the almost Mediterranean regions in the southern Alps of Ticino. With around 3,000 species the range and diversity of Swiss flora is immense, due to the country's striking regional and local variations in soil, habitat, climate, and altitude; even adjacent Alpine valleys can be very different. Only one endemic exists, the *Ladiner Hungerblümchen* (*Draba ladina*), found in high Alpine locations. Around a quarter of the country is woodland: beech and oak dominate middle and lowland areas, while at higher altitudes fir and spruce colonize damp locations and pine and larch the drier places. Mediterranean flora is found mainly on south-facing Alpine slopes and in the Rhône valley; even palms flourish on the banks of Lake Maggiore in Ticino. Alpine meadows and pastures above the treeline are particularly rich in wildflowers. Among the best-known Swiss alpines is edelweiss (*Leontopodium alpinum*), which normally, but not exclusively, grows in exposed locations between 1,700 and 3,400 m/5,577 and 11,154 ft above sea level.

That the country is not numbered among the classic garden landscapes of Europe is partly due to its mountainous terrain, very resistant to cultivation, and also that the political conditions for the creation of great royal gardens never existed; the country, today a confederation of states, was for centuries politically fragmented, preventing the rise of central political structures and a homogeneous culture. Nevertheless, Switzerland today is an influential financial and technological centre

and the setting for internationally regarded, exemplary landscape architecture.

Ancient and medieval periods
Like most of northern Europe, the dominant influence on the emergence of a garden culture in Switzerland was Roman colonization, especially in the climatically favoured Mittelland region. Little is known about the design of Roman villa gardens, but impressions of how a peristyle garden may have looked may be gathered at the reconstructed Roman house in Augst in the Canton of Aargau and the Gutshof Seeb manor house near Zurich. Abbeys were the centres of culture and gardening wisdom throughout the Middle Ages. The island of Reichenau in Lake Constance with its abbey, founded in 724, was one nucleus of European civilization in the Carolingian period; here the ST GALL cathedral plan was drawn up in 816, an idealized plan providing a prototype for the whole of Europe with four types of garden: cloister, graveyard with orchard, vegetable garden, and herb garden. Many monastic gardens have vanished, but the Swiss farmhouse gardens united the traditions of the herb garden with the forms of the French garden PARTERRE. In well-preserved farmhouse gardens in Emmental, central Switzerland, one can still find remarkable examples of 'Kräuterbarock' (herb baroque), a typical Swiss garden form, with flower or vegetable beds enclosed in box hedges. Medieval Swiss towns were relatively small and there were no royal courts, so garden culture remained limited to kitchen gardens. Castle and public gardens were modest and derived from the monastic tradition. Significant public green space was to be found towards the end of the Middle Ages only in the more important towns such as Basle and Zurich. The sylvan Petersplatz in Basle (*c*.1435) and the Lindenhof in Zurich (*c*.1500), a festival ground on the site of a Roman fortress, have been retained to this day as open spaces exerting a shaping influence on the townscape.

Renaissance
The Renaissance influence on Swiss gardens was particularly noticeable in the natural sciences during the first half of the sixteenth century. Konrad von Gessner (1516–65), a Zurich physician and naturalist, devoted himself to the systematic collection of plants and in 1559 published his influential treatise *Horti Germaniae*, describing all the species of plants occurring in German gardens. The Lucerne city chronicler and apothecary Renward Cysat (1545–1614) and the Basle physician and scholar Felix Platter (1536–1614) also devoted themselves to such studies and to the establishment of botanical gardens. The garden arts of the High

Renaissance in Switzerland were furthered by officers returning from service in the French armies and taking French Renaissance gardens as models for their own country estates. The family seats of the Innerschweiz are a variation on them, developing a characteristic type of garden on a hillside site with an enclosing wall and corner pavilions. A few examples, such as the Ital-Reding-Haus (1609) in Schwyz or the garden of Schloss Altishofen (1575–77), have survived.

Baroque
Close trading and military links meant that the effects of French absolutism swiftly became apparent in Switzerland during the 17th and 18th centuries. Solothurn, the seat of the French ambassador to the Swiss confederation, played a particular part in this (see VIGIER, VILLA), but French influence on the garden arts also extended to Berne and Basle. The owners of the more important gardens in Basle were prosperous merchants who created some of the largest baroque gardens in Switzerland in this region close to France (see WENKENPARK). The French influence was naturally stronger in francophone Switzerland than in the German-speaking cantons, and fine baroque gardens were established there, such as the grounds of Schloss Crans (1764–7), Grande Rochette (1729), or Petite Rochette (1746), characteristically laid out overlooking a lakeside in hillside vineyard settings. The small-scale landscape and the lack of royal clients, however, meant that no extensive baroque grounds comparable with VERSAILLES were created. The eighteenth century saw the creation of important green spaces in the towns, both through the conversion of fortifications to tree-lined promenades and through the construction of public gardens on the edges of towns, viewpoints, or parade grounds. Examples are the Promenade des Bastions in Geneva (1726) or the Heiternplatz in Zofingen (1747). These simply designed areas, usually planted with trees, are derived unchanged from baroque patterns, although from about the mid 18th century the English garden style had long since begun to spread across Europe; Hirschfeld criticized the backwardness of Switzerland in this respect in his *Theorie der Gartenkunst*.

Classicism and Romanticism
Through the Enlightenment, the rise of the middle class and the beginnings of the Industrial Revolution, a new conception of nature arose in Europe, along with a new garden style, partly promoted by influential natural philosophers. As early as 1729 the Bernese poet, physician, and naturalist Albrecht von Haller (1708–77) composed the didactic poem 'Die Alpen' in praise of the joys of a

simple rural life. Jean-Jacques ROUSSEAU discovered these joys in his homeland around Lake Geneva and described them in *Julie, ou La Nouvelle Héloïse* (1761). The poetry of Salomon Gessner (1730–88) of Zurich was also devoted to the sensitive portrayal of nature and prepared the ground for the new garden style.

The most impressive Swiss example of an English-style landscape garden is the EREMITAGE in Arlesheim near Basle, but country house gardens were laid out in this style all over Switzerland (such as Villa Belvoir in Zurich, and Villa Mon Repos in Lausanne). To some extent existing baroque gardens, such as the 18th-century Bäumlihof in Basle, were remodelled on English examples. The landscape style also dominated in the growing number of public grounds such as promenades, quays, or the areas of former city walls, as in Basle, Solothurn, and Winterthur; only farm gardens retained the strict geometry of the baroque style. The spread of the landscape garden was accompanied by a growing interest in botany, leading to the construction of palm houses in Basle, Geneva, and Zurich, and to an increase in the propagation, and introduction of exotic plants. Knowledge of botany, propagation, and garden design distinguished the *Kunstgärtner* (artist-gardeners); among the first in Switzerland were Theodor Froebel (1810–93), his son Otto (1844–1906), and Evariste Mertens (1846–1907).

Alpine gardens

'If one wishes to see a proper park, one need only spend four weeks wandering in Switzerland,' wrote Johann Wolfgang von Goethe in 1797 after rambling in Gotthard. This view was important for the infant Alpine tourism and the rise of the alpine garden. All over Europe, alpine flora were introduced to private gardens and parks. The first Swiss alpine garden was laid out by Theodor Froebel in 1836–8 in the old Zurich botanical garden. Later the Geneva botanist Henry Correvon (1854–1939) introduced cultivated alpine plants to garden culture, was instrumental in establishing the characteristic rock and rocaille garden, and promoted the conservation of alpine flora. The rampant expansion of Europe's industrial cities stimulated an interest in nature and, from around 1820, in Alpine tourism. Swiss mountain regions thus became a subject for conservation and a kind of relic of the past, epitomized by the complete reconstruction in about 1870 of the Rütli—scene of the oath of the Everlasting League in 1291—as a picturesque landscape.

20th century

Critical attitudes to 19th-century urbanization went hand in hand with a rejection of traditional landscape garden architecture. In Switzerland after 1913 the Schweitzerische Werkbund (SWB) promoted the reform movement and the development of an architectural garden style that has survived in only a few examples, notably the garden of the Kantonale Gartenbauschule OESCHBERG laid out in 1920 by Albert Baumann (1891–1976). In 1925 the Bund Schweizerischer Gartengestalter (Association of Swiss Garden Designers, BSG, today the BDLA) was founded to represent the interests of the profession. In the mid 1920s the rise of the domestic garden style (*Wohngartenstil*) heralded a return to landscape garden design, which in the course of the 1930s developed into the traditional-conservative homeland style (*Heimatstil*). Modernism was, on the other hand, rejected in this period on political and ideological grounds. After the Second World War there emerged not only the discipline of scientifically based landscape planning, but also a new functionally and aesthetically determined school of garden design intended to encourage post-war social renewal. The dawn of a new age in garden architecture is chronicled in such books as *Neues Planen und Gestalten* (1953) by Albert Baumann, Gustav AMMANN's *Blühende Gärten* (1955), and Ernst Baumann's (1907–92) *Neue Gärten* (1955). The new development manifested itself clearly at the first Swiss gardening exhibition, G|59, in Zurich in 1959, most notably in the avant-garde 'Garten des Poeten' by Ernst Cramer (1898–1980). Stronger international contacts with Scandinavia, Brazil, America, and Japan led to an enrichment of the design repertory in Swiss gardens.

After the enormous economic growth of the 1960s and in the face of worldwide environmental disasters, ecologically oriented landscape planning and architecture came to the fore in the early 1970s. The first specialist degree courses in landscape architecture were introduced, in Lullier near Geneva and in Rapperswil. The Solothurn biologist Urs Schwarz (b. 1928) published *Der Naturgarten* (1971), a polemic for the ecological garden movement that found practical expression at the second Swiss garden exhibition, Grün 80 in Basle. New projects in a 'close to nature' style such as the extensive IRCHEL PARK campus of the University of Zurich, executed 1978–86 by Atelier Stern & Partner, provoked controversy about the relationship between ecology and design. The 1980s and 1990s witnessed the ascendancy of architectural interpretations of landscape design over the diktat of nature, led by the influential Zurich landscape architect and professor at the Swiss Federal Institute of Technology (ETH) Dieter Kienast (1945–98) with his numerous international projects and publications. Ecological principles have since then been more strongly integrated, but ecology is no longer the panacea and nature no longer the sole designer. Concurrently more attention is once again being paid to the history of garden art in Switzerland, with the foundation in 1982 of the *Archiv für Schweizer Landschaftsarchitektur*. Published research into garden art, the shift in practice to more design, and high-quality projects by young Swiss landscape architects are currently bringing Switzerland's landscape architecture into the centre of international interest.   UW

Sydney,

Australia, the country's oldest city, was founded in 1788 in a setting of magnificent natural splendour, the expansive harbour of Port Jackson. The city's skyline is dominated by two icons of 20th-century engineering splendour, the Sydney Harbour Bridge and the Opera House. Set alongside and straddling the harbour's dazzling waters, their unmistakable silhouettes reduce any surrounding plantings to a minor role. Today, in the urban environment of contemporary Sydney, little remains of the original pattern of native vegetation.

From the early 19th century, early settlers of power and influence sought picturesque yet pragmatic settings for their splendid private homes, such as ELIZABETH BAY HOUSE and VAUCLUSE HOUSE, appropriating the harbour views of long, rocky promontories and sandy coves. It is a quest that remains a continuing passion for well-to-do Sydney residents. Honey-coloured sandstone walls and terraces in fashionable locations embrace expensively landscaped gardens that always pay homage to the expansive view. In a few notable exceptions, such as Marion and Walter Burley Griffin's development of Castlecrag (1920–35), flat-roofed houses 'subordinate to the landscape' were built to exploit harbour views through the shapely trunks of *Angophora costata*, and in the 1970s the regreening of Lane Cove North 'brought the bush back to the city'. However, in the past decade, extensive housing development in Sydney's south and west has ignored the wisdom of these and other models, causing residential water consumption to rise dramatically, a dangerous trend for a city experiencing critical water shortages.

The city's major public gardens and open spaces include the Royal Botanic Gardens and adjacent Domain. Established in 1816, the gardens are the oldest in Australia; the 30-hectare/75-acre site is remarkable for its unparalleled combination of landscape, history, and plant science. The grounds of en-Laye. Furthermore, in some cases where the lie of the land would have lent itself to terracing the opportunity was not taken. At Sprotborough (Yorkshire) the house faced directly towards a slope plummeting down to the river Don, but instead of a flight of terraces there was a tame parterre and a viewing platform. In Wales, however, an exceptional terraced garden was made at Llanerch Hall (Denbighshire) before 1662 by Mutton Davies who had visited Italy. A delightful painting of it made in 1662, now in the Yale Center for British Art, shows an enchanting sequence of five terraces ornamented with TOPIARY, elaborate stairs, pavilions, and a fountain descending to a circular pool with Neptune rising on a rock. Only traces of the garden survive today. Another remarkable Welsh garden, not far from Llanerch, dates from the same period and has a rare surviving terraced garden of the 17th century. The medieval POWIS CASTLE has a terraced garden, 180 m/600 ft wide, disposed on a south-facing slope below the castle walls, built in the 1660s and probably designed by William Winde (d. 1722). Strongly architectural in character, the terraces have balustrades, urns, an orangery, and an arcade like an Italian *sala terrena*. In British 19th-century historicizing gardens (such as DRUMMOND CASTLE and SHRUBLAND PARK) terraces are often found. Terracing was attractive to ARTS AND CRAFTS designers but usually on a modest scale. An exception is C. E. Mallows's (1864–1915) design for Tirley Garth (Cheshire), where a series of terraced compartments embraces a rose garden, tennis lawns, and a kitchen garden. A rare, and delightful, example of art deco garden influence is seen in the great terraced garden made between the wars at PORT LYMPNE.   PT

Tessin, Nicodemus the elder

(1615–81), German fortifications engineer who went to Sweden in 1636, where he practised as an architect. He started work on the royal palace of Drottningholm in Stockholm, levelling and laying out the parterre garden between 1664 and 1667; his work was completed by his son.

PRJ

Tessin, Nicodemus the younger

(1654–1728), Swedish architect, who travelled widely in Europe for a number of years from 1674. When he was in England, Christopher Wren suggested to Charles II that he ought to secure Tessin to work for him. Tessin wrote, drew, and collected drawings on such a prolific scale that the Tessin Collection at the National Museum in Stockholm contains almost a more comprehensive assembly of material on French architecture and gardens of the period than is to be found in France.

DROTTNINGHOLM, dubbed the 'Versailles of the North', was his magnum opus. The garden reflects 300 years of garden history—baroque, rococo, the English park style, Romanticism, with a touch of 1880s formalism—but the main composition is totally Tessin's. The parterre was after a pattern from VAUX-LE-VICOMTE, and there are other similarities—the MENAGERIE was a copy of LE VAU's plans for one at VERSAILLES. During the 1690s there were problems with defective earthworks and differential settlement, when the parterre was relaid by J. HÅRLEMAN. Many of the sculptures at Drottningholm were plundered from FREDERIKSBORG CASTLE in Denmark and Wallenstein's palace in Prague; Tessin used these for a composition in the fine Hercules Fountain which can still be seen today. Apart from the groves, which were bordered by eight rows of lime trees and have been replaced by grass lawns, all the main features of Tessin's plan from 1723 were restored in the 1950s and 1960s: the parterres, the containing walls, the basins with fountains, the plateaux with bordering hedges and topiary, etc. The superb cascades have been freely adapted by Ivar Tengbom using Tessin's model.

Tessin made proposals for the Louvre and Versailles, which were shown to Louis XIV by his associate G. J. Adelcrantz (1668–1739). At Versailles he suggested a grand Apollo temple as a view point for the large canal. He managed to design and build a castle at Roissy for the Comte d'Avaux in 1696. In Sweden he designed gardens for manor houses, such as Steninge, STUREFORS, Krageholm, Rosersberg, and Stora Wäsby. Unfortunately his plans for FREDERIKSBERG and CLAUSHOLM were never realized.   PRJ

Tête d'Or, Parc de la ⊕

Lyon, Rhône, France, laid out in 1856 by the brothers Denis and Eugène BÜHLER. The site, with an area of 111 hectares/274 acres, is in the heart of Lyon with the river Rhône sweeping about its northern boundary. The Bühlers floated a great sinuous lake—with an area of 17 hectares/40 acres—in the upper part of the park which today is edged with winding walks and veiled with trees. The site is almost entirely flat and the Bühlers saw that carefully planned groups of trees, with vistas of the lake, were the best way of animating the scene. The rich alluvial soil here has caused the trees to flourish and many are now fine mature specimens. The park also contains a Botanic Garden, founded on a different site in 1793, with an outstanding plant collection of over 8,000 hardy taxa and over 5,000 tender taxa cultivated under glass. Some of the glasshouses are handsome 19th-century buildings of which the best were

designed in the 1880s by the engineer Domenget. Lyon was a great centre of rose breeding and there is a fine collection here. Over 130 species roses show the raw materials from which the breeders could draw and there is an exceptional collection of over 350 varieties of old cultivars. Many of these come from one of the best Lyonnais rose breeders, Pernet-Ducher, a hybrid of two older firms founded in 1881. Among their best-known cultivars are 'Madame Caroline Testout' (1890), 'Château de Clos-Vougeot' (1908), and 'Lawrence Johnston' (1920). A fruticetum contains 350 varieties of fruit trees and there is a collection of 300 cultivars of peony. The park has magnificent entrance gates, designed by Charles Messon in 1900, and splendid bedding schemes in the tradition of MOSAÏCULTURE—a term invented by J. Chrétien who was a gardener here. The Parc de la Tête d'Or is one of the finest and most enjoyable public parks in France. It is a well conceived landscape in the tradition of the 18th-century English landscape park which makes it a marvellous place in which to walk or to sit in the shade of a noble tree. It is furthermore enriched with excellent collections of plants, hardy and tender, giving it a character of particular interest to gardeners.   PT

Thabor, Parc du ⊕

Rennes, Ille-et-Vilaine, France, a public park occupying a hilly site in the centre of the city. The heart of the park was in the 17th century the garden of a Benedictine abbey of Saint-Melaine which named the place Thabor after the mountain in Palestine. It was opened to the public in the 18th century (to men only) and was acquired by the city of Rennes in 1802, making it one of the earliest municipal parks in France. In 1865 it was landscaped by Denis BÜHLER, who contrived a distinguished mixture of open landscape—with lawns and groups of trees—and formal design in the French style. The entrance on the rue Marthenot is very imposing, with a monumental staircase leading to a stone amphitheatre and a glistening cascade in the shade of old conifers. The undulating site covers an area of 10 hectares/25 acres. A grand ORANGERY with arched windows overlooks banked bedding schemes and an elaborate formal garden of scalloped pools, fountains, potted palms, and statuary. In the shade of trees is a picturesque 19th-century octagonal tiered DOVECOTE and AVIARY of a vaguely oriental character. The ground floor is a spacious aviary and the upper part, rising like a tower, houses white doves. The aviary is the work of the architect Jean-Baptiste Marthenot who also designed a music pavilion and the noble wrought-iron entrance gates to the park. Many good trees remain from 19th-century   ▶

plantings, among them cork oaks (*Quercus suber*) and free-standing specimens of *Magnolia grandiflora*.   PT

Thailand

is a country rich in vegetation both indigenous and introduced. It is divided into four natural regions, ranging from the mountainous north to the long southern peninsula; the most populous is the central plain, or Chao Phraya river basin, where the capital of Bangkok is located. The climate is monsoonal, marked by a pronounced rainy season from May to September and a relatively dry season for the rest of the year.

Thanks to the fertility and more or less non-stop growth, gardens of one sort or another have always been a feature of the country. Traditionally, for most people these were predominantly practical, with fruit trees, a variety of culinary herbs, and others that could be used in traditional medicines, with a few ornamental specimens in pots. Only in the royal palaces (and, to a lesser extent, Buddhist temples) did a tradition of ornamental gardens evolve. These were inspired by Chinese influences and consisted of formally clipped

Colour plates

An elegant statue amid superbly trained roses on trelliswork at the **Roseraie de l'Haÿ-les-Roses**, France

The Torre de las Damas and the Partal Palace in the **Alhambra**, Spain

The artificial ruin of the High Priest's House in the 18th-century picturesque garden of **Arkadia**, Poland

The Villa Pia in the **Vatican Gardens**, Rome, Italy, built in the 1560s as a retreat for Pope Pius IV

shrubs, lotus pools, and small artificial mountains. The best examples of these to be seen today are at Bangkok's Grand Palace and the courtyards of nearby Wat Po, the Temple of the Reclining Buddha.

For many years, Thailand lacked a real botanical garden of the sort established by the British in Singapore and the Dutch in Indonesia. This need was at least partially realized with the establishment of the Queen Sirikit Botanical Gardens outside the northern city of Chiang Mai in the late 1990s, where a wide variety of ornamental and commercial plants, as well as a herbarium, can be seen in a well-landscaped setting.

More contemporary international garden designs emerged in the 1950s. They were launched primarily by amateurs, especially those of means who had travelled or studied abroad and acquired a taste for such Western concepts as lawns and mixed beds to enhance their often spacious private gardens. Pioneers in this movement included the late M. R. Pimsai Amranand, whose *Gardening in Bangkok* (1970; revised by William Warren in 1996) is an invaluable source of reference, and the late Princess Chumbhot, who created SUAN PAKKAD in Bangkok and the country estate of WANG TAKRAI, both now open to the public. William Warren has also written *The Tropical Garden* and *Thai Garden Style*, both of which include numerous private and public Thai gardens not only in Bangkok but also in other parts of the country.

Catering to this growing interest, Thai plant dealers have been extremely active in introducing new tropical species from elsewhere in the region as well as from such places as Hawaii, Australia, and South America; particular favourites in recent years have been heliconias, palms, and plumerias. They have also developed countless hybrids of such ornamentals as *Aglaonema*, *Codiaeum*, *Diffenbachia*, and orchids. There are numerous markets around Bangkok, the most varied being Chatuchak, which is devoted to plants on Wednesday and Thursday; in Chiang Mai, the large Kamthieng Plant Market is open daily and offers both tropical and subtropical species.

Some of the most imaginative contemporary Thai gardens can be seen at various hotels and resorts, which are far more spacious than the average home and offer greater scope for horticultural imagination. Bill Bensely, an American-born landscape designer, has created several of these, including the Four Seasons Hotel (formerly the Regent) in Bangkok; Marriott resorts and spas in Bangkok, Hua Hin, and Phuket; and the Four Seasons (formerly Regent) Resort in Chiang Mai, where part of the garden consists of working rice fields. Surasak

Hutasewee, an inventive Thai designer, limits himself to private gardens with a jungle-like atmosphere, among them the latest planting of the JAMES THOMPSON House in Bangkok, now a public museum, and another consisting largely of palms and members of the Cycadaceae family.

Probably the most interesting and extensive public garden in the country is the Nong Nootch Garden in Pattaya, on the Gulf of Thailand, which has assembled an enormous collection of palms, heliconias, gingers, and other specimens collected from all over the tropical world in a large, beautifully landscaped area.

Other gardens of interest in Bangkok include those of the M. R. Kukrit Pramoj now open to the public; the NAI LERT PARK HOTEL (formerly the Hilton); the LURSAK GARDEN; the Prasart Museum, the Australian Embassy, and the BRITISH EMBASSY. Among those outside the capital are the Villa Royale, former residence of M. L. Tri Devakul overlooking the Anadaman Sea, and Trisara, a recently opened resort, both on the island of Phuket; and, near Chiang Mai, the Pong Yang Garden Village, the alpine-like garden of Chare Chutaharatkul, and the new Mandarin Oriental Dhara Dhevi which opened at the end of 2004.   MLL/WLW

Thays, Charles

(1864–1934), French landscaper, botanist, horticulturist, architect, and city planner who practised in Argentina. In France he worked as principal assistant to Édouard ANDRÉ who recommended him to come to Argentina in 1889 for a year's work; but he stayed for the rest of his life. The most important Argentinian landscaper, he designed about 100 public promenades and many private gardens and parks. His work also took him to other South American countries including Uruguay, Chile, and Brazil. He produced a feasibility study for Argentina's first National Parks, introduced 'garden city' urban planning, cultivated *Ilex paraguariensis* (from which the local drink, 'yerba mate', is made), planted 100,000 trees in Buenos Aires streets; laid out central parks for the towns of Córdoba, Mendoza, and Mar del Plata; and in Buenos Aires the Botanical Garden, Major Plaza, and Congress Square. He followed André's style, combining the romantic English informality with the French formal garden, the use of open and closed curved roads, diagonal axes, multiple points of view, lakes with islands, ornamental buildings, sculptures, and monuments. He studied the local flora and used such plants as *Chorisia insignis*, the yellow jacaranda *Tipuana tipu* (syn. *T. speciosa*), and *Tabebuia impetiginosa*, which became widely used. He received numerous

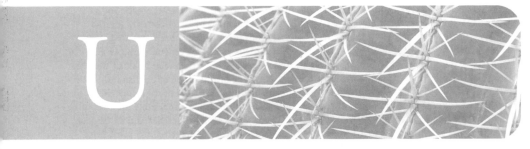

U

pastiche', and concentrated upon a clear marking of the central axis with an arcade of clipped limes. Walter BAUER carried out later restoration work.   KL

umbrella,

or umbrello, a form of small garden building to give protection from the rain. Some resembled an umbrella, with a pillar supporting a curved segmented roof, and others were tentlike dismountable pavilions. Fashionable in late Georgian and Regency gardens, designs for them are illustrated in J. B. Papworth's (1775-1847) *Hints on Ornamental Gardening* (1823).   PT

Umlauft, Anton

(1858-1919), Austrian garden director, son of the head gardener of Duke Nostitz in Bohemia. He entered the service of the Imperial Court Gardens in SCHÖNBRUNN as an assistant in 1877. Due to his special skills in plant cultivation he rose to the post of the inspector for the garden and park in Schönbrunn in 1889 and in 1896 became director of all imperial gardens throughout the Austro-Hungarian Empire. He raised them to a remarkable level of cultivation and, cooperating with exotic plant collections all over the world, built up a collection of over 8,000 varieties. Preferring formal layouts with lavish plantings, he also used the style of the landscape garden. His most important extant works are the landscape park in front of Schönbrunn—the 'Vorpark'—and the large PARTERRE in Schönbrunn. Moreover he redesigned parts of other imperial gardens such as the BELVEDERE (Austria) and the gardens at BUDA ROYAL CASTLE (Hungary). He also laid out numerous private gardens for example in Halbthurn, Eckartsau (Austria), and the parterre in Eszterháza (Hungary) (see FERTŐD). In 1908 Umlauft was, in addition, appointed garden adviser to the court in Vienna. With this he achieved a higher position than any Austrian gardener before him.   JM

United States National Arboretum ⊛

Washington, DC, USA, established by an Act of Congress in 1927. Initially 76.5 hectares/189 acres, the arboretum has grown to 180 hectares/444 acres with 15.2 km/9.5 miles of roadway. As the principal research arm of the US Department of Agriculture, the arboretum maintains a library, HERBARIUM, plant introduction programme, and sponsors national and international cooperative programmes. It constitutes one of the country's most outstanding collections of woody plants as well as the world's most complete living collection of boxwood (*Buxus* spp.). Opened to the public in 1959, the arboretum is   ▶

Ukraine

The climate is generally continental with severe winters, and large areas suffer from the winds from the east and the south-east, but the coastal strip in the Crimea by the Black Sea enjoys near Mediterranean conditions with the temperature rarely falling below 0 °C/32 °F. The average July temperature in Kiev is 19 °C/67 °F and in Yalta 24 °F/75 °C. There is a large area of steppe with fertile black earth and areas of mixed forest and oak and beech forests. The flora by the Black Sea is much richer than elsewhere.

Since the Ukraine was for many years part of the Russian Empire, the gardens have much in common with those of Russia. While SOPHIEVKA and ALUPKA stand out from the rest there are others of considerable merit. At Trostianets (44 kms/27 miles south of Sumy), I. M. Skorpadski, after acquiring the property in 1830, created a park of 175 hectares/432 acres, which he surrounded by single-species groves and mixed woodland on a previously treeless landscape. The resulting favourable conditions made possible the introduction of exotics, and by the end of the century there were more than 600 species of trees and shrubs.

While there was a estate at Sokirentsy (5 km/3 miles off the Romny to Priluki road) in the 18th century, the present palace dates from the 1820s. In the romantic, picturesque park ancient oaks are supported by birch, limes, white poplars, hornbeams, maples, larch, pines, and chestnuts. An eight-columned rotunda on an artificial mound looks out across a lake, and there are summer houses, pools, and bridges.

The palace at Kachanovka in Chernigovshchina dates from the 1770s but was repeatedly altered. The park (exceeding 500 hectares/1,235 acres), created out of natural woodland, now has about 50 species, but mainly maple, lime, oak, chestnut, and birch. A labyrinth of intercrossing paths, on different levels with bridges and romantic ruins, offers vistas to the lakes. The Glinka Pavilion

celebrates the composer, a frequent visitor in the mid 19th century.

At Livadia (2 km/1.25 miles west of Yalta) the White Palace (1910-11) is early Italian Renaissance in style with two courtyards, one Moorish, the other Florentine. The layout is formal near the palace, with straight walks, clipped hedges, and pavilions. Further from the palace the large park, dating from the 1830s, is landscaped in the English style.

Massandra (2 km/1.25 miles east of Yalta), like Alupka, belonged to Count M. S. Vorontsov and was also laid out by Karl Kebach. It was later acquired by the Tsar. There are many fine trees in the park including an avenue of palms.

The NIKITSKY BOTANIC GARDEN is outstanding and there are two impressive botanic gardens in Kiev and others in Odessa and Lvov.   PH

Ulriksdal ⊛

Uppland, Sweden, is a royal pleasure park with clear surviving traces, like a patchwork, of various styles from the mid 17th century. The park and gardens cover an area of 65 hectares/160 acres. The palace was built in 1644 and the oldest gardens, a knot, a GIARDINO SEGRETO, a kitchen garden, a mount, and a deer park, date from c.1650. Another garden, by Hans Georg Kraus from Augsburg, comprised a grotto, labyrinth, BOSQUET, flower beds, and an arbour. The separate gardens were united about a central axis in the 1660s with fountains, sculptures by Jean Baptiste Dieussart, and a temple-like folly (Mons Mariae) by Jean de la VALLÉE and the owner, the Chancellor Count Magnus Gabriel de La Gardie (1622-86). After a period of slight deterioration, the garden was altered by Carl HÅRLEMAN. The parterre became fully symmetrical and the former kitchen garden was turned into a *bosquet*. An English park was added in the beginning of the 19th century. The parterre was planted with specimen exotic trees throughout the century. The last visible overlay dates from the 1930s when garden architect Gösta Reuterswärd (1892-1980) restored the pleasure grounds. His solution has been called a 'neo-baroque

thronged every May when thousands of azaleas bloom on Mount Hamilton. Other popular gardens include the Asian Collections where the floras of China, Japan, and Korea comprise a dramatic landscape on a bank of the Anacostia river. Straddling a stream, Fern Valley is home to a collection of south-eastern coastal plain flora, as well as a prairie. The National Bonsai and Penjing Museum was begun when a superb collection of 53 bonsai was presented as a 200th birthday gift to the United States from the Nippon Bonsai Association. It has since grown with the acquisition of American bonsai and Chinese penjing. The National Herb Garden, 1 hectare/2.5 acres, contains ten theme gardens housing over 900 taxa of herbs. Twenty-two columns, once a part of the east portico of the US Capitol, were rescued from oblivion by Mrs George Garrett and sited in 1988 as garden sculpture on a prominent knoll by Russell PAGE.
CO

United States of America.

From the Arctic tundra of northern Alaska to the subtropical tip of Florida, not forgetting the tropical islands of the offshore state Hawaii, the United States contains almost every possible

Colour plates

The early 17th-century Italianate garden at **Hellbrunn**, Salzburg, Austria

Subtropical planting at **Tresco Abbey gardens**, England

The 18th-century **Pineapple** in the kitchen garden at Dunmore, Scotland

Borders and yew topiary in the 18th-century walled garden at **Crathes Castle**, Scotland

The early 19th-century garden at **Frederiksberg**, Copenhagen, Denmark

variation of climate, soil, and topography in its 9,631,418 sq. km/3,794,083 sq. miles. All that seem to be missing are equatorial jungles and truly arid deserts. Combinations of elevation, soil composition, proximity to large bodies of water, and exposure to currents of wind and water create multiple microclimates, and such curiosities as the fact that the highest recorded temperature for both Alaska and Hawaii is 37.7 °C /100 °F. The United States department of agriculture's Plant Hardiness Zone Map, as revised in 1990, divides the country into eleven zones with subzones based on average annual minimum temperatures. The American Horticultural Society's Plant Heat Zone Map divides the country into twelve zones based on the average number of days each region experiences temperatures over 30 °C/86 °F.

When Europeans first set foot on the area covered by the contiguous 48 states, they were struck by its vegetation and soon began sending plants and seeds back to their homelands. At the same time they could not resist importing plants to which they were accustomed. So began the transformation of the country's flora. Many imports—some deliberate, some hitch-hiking weeds—escaped cultivation and became naturalized. By the 17th century it had become difficult to tell exotic from indigenous. One example: northerners thought peach trees were indigenous—they were not, they had been brought to Florida and Mexico by Spanish settlers. The Indians liked them and carried them north.

The pursuit of new and unusual species brought to North America plant hunters like John TRADESCANT THE YOUNGER, Mark CATESBY, and David DOUGLAS from Great Britain, André MICHAUX from France, Frederick Pursh (1774–1820) from Germany, and Pehr Kalm (1715–79) from Sweden. Very soon American explorers, botanists, and curious amateurs joined the search, among them John BARTRAM and his son William, Cadwalader Colden (1688–1776) and his daughter Jane (1724–66), the Lewis and Clark Expedition (1804–6), John Torrey (1796–1875), and Asa Gray (1810–88). The search continues: more than 1,100 new species have been reported in the last twenty years. Pursh attempted to compile a continent-wide flora in 1814, which was instantly out of date. The same fate befell Torrey and Gray's *Flora of North America* (1838–40). Thereafter botanists confined themselves to compiling regional floras. Now plant taxonomists from botanic gardens, museums, and universities in the United States and Canada are producing a *Flora of North America*, of which eight volumes of the projected 30 have been published along with a simultaneous database and a website. It will cover all of the vascular plants and bryophytes (mosses and

liverworts) on the continent north of the Mexican border. According to the editorial committee, there are about 17,000 species of native and naturalized flowering plants, ferns, and gymnosperms (conifers, cycads, ephedras) in the contiguous United States and Alaska. Hawaii has no gymnosperms but more than 1,800 species of flowering plants, documented in the *Manual of the Flowering Plants of Hawaii* (Wagner et al., 1999). *Hawaii's Ferns and Fern Allies* (Daniel Palmer, 2002) lists more than 200 species.

Pre-Columbian and colonial gardens
It is just possible that what we would call today landscape architecture or even LAND ART preceded gardening and gardens. On the earliest Native American sites so far discovered, Watson Brake (c.3200 BC) and the more extensively studied Poverty Point (c.1750 BC) in Louisiana, the land was shaped into terraces and truncated pyramids or mounds, one topped on the latter site by a bird effigy. So far archaeologists have not found signs of plant cultivation. Given the luxuriant vegetation in that part of the Mississippi valley, plant cultivation may not have been a requirement for these civilizations. Maize, which needs it, was only introduced from Mexico around AD 200. Mound-building cultures appear to have risen and fallen up and down the valley for about 5,000 years, and some remnants still exist, among them Emerald Mound in Mississippi, Serpent Mound in Ohio, Monks Mound at Cahokia in Illinois. In 1759 William Bartram saw and described a magnificent one with its ceremonial landscape in Florida. It vanished under European ploughs within fifteen years. Another Indian culture, which apparently flourished around AD 900 and had disappeared by the time Europeans arrived, created geometrically patterned ridged fields across Michigan, Wisconsin, and Illinois. The designs were at agricultural scale but elaborate enough to suggest aesthetic intention. Quite different were the Indian gardens encountered by European settlers along the east coast. In these gardens, 'the three sisters'—maize, beans, and squash—were all planted together, a practice we now recognize as ecologically and horticulturally sound. The settlers found it messy. While they embraced the three sisters, they sent maize to the ploughed fields, and organized their gardens as they had in their homelands.

The Spanish in Florida and the south-west, the Dutch in New York, the English in New England, the French in Louisiana, all created walled or fenced gardens divided by paths into rectangular beds, usually raised, for plants that needed protection or special care. These early gardens were above all practical, dedicated to the fruits, vegetables, and herbs needed for household or monastic sustenance. Flowering ornamentals like roses found their place because they had medicinal value. The choice of plants has changed over time but this basic vernacular design, one rooted in antiquity, has never vanished from the American garden maker's repertory. It went west with the pioneers and reappears in western patios and eastern backyards, by itself or as a component of a larger estate garden.

It did not take the European settlers long to amass money and land. By the last quarter of the 17th century estate gardens were being built in east coast colonies. Descriptions are sketchy, but indicate that basic four-square layouts were elaborated into simple PARTERRES as in the 1661 Castello Plan of New York City, or enlarged as in the remains of the 1680 garden at Bacon's Castle in Virginia. Elements of baroque or architectural garden design—axial layouts, terraces, ALLÉES, and canals—may have been added that early. By the early 18th century they were in place, adjusted to the realities of colonial life. It is highly doubtful that colonists tried to create the elaborate fountains or topiary work shown in European garden design manuals. Land was cheap, labour dear, and skilled labour almost non-existent through most of the nation's history. MIDDLETON PLACE is the earliest surviving architectural garden, but contemporary accounts of Governor Spotswood's estate in Virginia, Colonel Malbone's in Rhode Island, John Hancock's in Boston, and William Penn's Pennsbury among others mention various features of the style. These gardens represent an early manifestation of the way Americans would treat new ideas in landscape design. The new did not drive out the old, it simply added another set of elements to the garden maker's vocabulary. In 1736 Hancock, for example, built terraces and ordered yews to 'frame up', but he also ordered fruit trees, stating that his garden was to be profitable as well as pleasurable. The enclosed garden would continue to find a place in the pleasure grounds: it was necessary to protect plants from two- and four-footed predators, and no one thought of hiding it. Nor did it disappear when Americans started experimenting with the newly fashionable English naturalistic or landscape garden in the last part of the 18th century. George Washington's MOUNT VERNON offers a good example of the way Americans integrated walled gardens into their blend of ideas selected from both landscape and architectural styles.

The architectural style had its greatest impact on town planning. Early cities and villages had rather higgledy-piggledy layouts, with streets and lots mostly determined by topography and water features, except in the Spanish settlements, which were ordered according to the 1573 Laws of the Indies in a grid running from a central square. What Europeans found different were the trees lining New York streets and the Boston Commons, and the placement of houses in the middle of town lots. In the late 17th century Governor Francis Nicholson successively laid out Annapolis and WILLIAMSBURG according to baroque planning formulas, as Pierre L'Enfant would Washington, DC more than a century later. But the future belonged to the grid. The gridiron plans of early cities like New Haven, Philadelphia, and Savannah included provisions for open space, as did the suggestions of the grid-friendly Thomas JEFFERSON. In the hands of later developers and land speculators these spaces vanished.

Gardening in the new republic
The grid may have dominated civic design at the beginning of the 19th century, but the naturalistic garden was coming into fashion for domestic grounds, much simplified and adjusted to the needs and resources of the middle class. Lacking the custom of primogeniture, restless Americans tended to build suburban villas rather than estates, which even in the colonial period had never been large by European standards. Still, two elements of the baroque style, also simplified, remained popular. Roads and paths flanked by *allées* of trees marked entrances to villas and farmsteads alike, and wherever possible, city or country, houses were placed on high ground terraced down to roads or rivers.

The population more than quadrupled between 1800 and 1850, and by 1850 the United States stretched from coast to coast. As pioneers, native born and immigrant alike, moved into new territory, they needed help. Local expertise scarcely existed on the frontier; European books and journals had limited application to American conditions. The horticultural press filled the gap. Throughout the century a stream of experience-based horticultural books and magazines as well as almanacs and newspapers offered advice on cultivation and garden design, news of plant introductions, announcements of improved tools, adaptations of European fashions, and descriptions of gardens in the United States and abroad. Magazines engaged in a continual dialogue with a literate public, and foreign observers like Alexis de Tocqueville (1805-59) were astonished that householders at the edge of the frontier were as up to the minute as those in the older seaboard communities.

Seedsmen, including the Shakers, who had invented the seed packet in the late 18th century, and nurserymen, such as Bernard MCMAHON, author of the 1806 *American Gardener's Calendar*, were the prime movers. Between 1828 and 1836 they produced popular books like *A Short Treatise on Horticulture* by William Prince, *New American Gardener* by Thomas Fessenden (1771-1835), *The American Flower Garden Directory* by Thomas Hibbert (1783-1833), and William Buist (1805-80); and magazines, especially *The American Gardener's Magazine* (later *The Magazine of Horticulture*) founded by Charles Mason Hovey (1810-87). Like these predecessors, Andrew Jackson DOWNING—writer, editor, designer, and the most famous horticultural and architectural taste maker of the mid 19th century—began as a nurseryman. By 1860, according to the US census, there were 40 magazines and newspapers devoted to farming and gardening; probably as many had started and failed. Nurserymen also expanded their range with more and more sophisticated catalogues—the first one with colour illustrations appeared in 1853—and followed the population westward. That same year a transplanted Massachusetts nurseryman, Colonel James Lafayette Warren (1805-96), produced California's first nursery catalogue.

The year 1853 also saw the opening of Japan to western trade by Commodore Perry—by 1861 Japanese plants were arriving in American nurseries—and the creation of the first planned suburb, Llewellyn Park in New Jersey, a major step in the ongoing suburbanization of the United States. True, suburbs had grown up informally around cities from the late 17th century on; but Llewellyn Park introduced new design and social elements. Its plan organized streets and house lots to retain as much as possible of the dramatic site's topography and vegetation, as well as placing the whole community under a covenant that restricted lot size, barred industrial use, and bound members to contribute to the upkeep of roads and common lands. Although controversial, such restrictive covenants continue to mark planned developments and suburbs.

Mid century designers could lay out suburbs like Llewellyn Park or OLMSTED and Vaux's Riverside (1868) in Illinois in the spirit of the picturesque landscape because recent herd or fence laws forced owners to control cattle, sheep, and pigs rather than letting them run free. In addition, improved transportation, especially the proliferation of railways, made it cheaper for households to buy rather than grow fruits and vegetables. Horticultural writers who preferred the landscape or 'modern' style immediately denounced fences and walls and promoted a simple landscape of turf and trees as the best choice for homeowners who lacked time for or interest in gardening. Thus the iconic affluent American suburb of curving tree-lined streets and broad open front lawns was born. Even in towns and cities fences came down and hedges vanished, their shrubs eventually huddling against houses as foundation planting.

Many of the same nurserymen and horticultural journalists joined dedicated amateurs to found horticultural societies as another means of sharing knowledge and improving plants and gardening techniques. They established libraries, held symposia, organized exhibitions, and gave prizes. The number of horticultural societies grew from five early in the century—New York (1818-37, refounded in 1900 and still thriving); Philadelphia (founded 1827); Geneva (1828-36) and Albany (1829-c.1840), New York; Boston (founded 1829)—to about 40 in 1852. And in some states, like California, agricultural societies devoted much of their attention to horticulture. The men who founded the societies and wrote the magazine articles were also promoters of civic betterment: street tree planting, turfing of town commons, and village improvement societies were favourite causes. General Henry A. S. Dearborn (1783-1851) was a founder of both the Massachusetts Horticultural Society, and of the MOUNT AUBURN CEMETERY. Downing's editorials can claim credit for instigating the creation of Central Park (see NEW YORK CITY PARKS AND GARDENS). Both the garden cemetery and the naturalistically landscaped city park were quickly copied across the country, and Central Park's popularity accelerated the spread of the naturalistic style.

The mid 19th century also saw the beginnings of the conservation and historic preservation movements. Henry David Thoreau (1817-1862) proclaimed that 'in Wildness is the Preservation of the World' (Concord Lyceum Lecture, 1851), and seven years later called for setting aside large national wilderness preserves. In 1853 Ann Pamela Cunningham (1816-75) founded the Mount Vernon Ladies' Association, the oldest national historic preservation organization in the country. By 1858 the association's national campaign had raised enough money from private sources—including schoolchildren's pennies—to buy Mount Vernon from Washington's heirs who could no longer maintain it. The ongoing restoration and maintenance of the house and landscape still depends solely on private funding, a model followed by many later such organizations.

Gardens, preservation, horticulture from the Civil War to the Second World War

If the Civil War (1861-5) caused a brief slowing of garden and park creation, momentum soon returned. The US government pioneered a new field in landscape design by reserving large areas of scenic or scientific interest for public enjoyment, which required expert design and construction of roads and shelters. The first step was the deeding in 1864 to California of the Yosemite valley and the Mariposa Big Tree Grove for public recreational use for all time. Then in 1872 Yellowstone became the first of the National Parks. In 1916 the National Park Service was created to administer what are now 384 parks, monuments, and historic sites including Yosemite.

The federal government also took a hand in horticultural education with the passage of the Morrill Act in 1862, which gave to the states lands for the establishment of colleges offering programmes in agriculture, engineering, and home economics. This mandate was broadly interpreted to include all forms of horticulture. In 1887 the Hatch Act expanded the role of land-grant colleges by funding research and experiment stations, and in 1914 the Smith-Lever Act established the Cooperative Extension System, a partnership between land-grant colleges and universities and the department of agriculture designed to bring research findings and improved practices to local communities. Gardeners who needed soil tested or plant diseases identified soon came to rely on their county extension agent.

The horticultural press had expanded the design vocabulary: CARPET BEDDING, specimen planting, FABRIQUES from the French picturesque garden, ROCK GARDENS, fanciful parterres of boxwood-edged hearts and crescents, not to mention exciting new plants and trees. Most homeowners settled for one or two of these ornaments—perhaps a cone of ribbon bedding on the lawn or a rustic summer house. But some in their enthusiasm tried to cram it all into a 0.8-hectare/2-acre lot. The Victorian garden could be as overstuffed as the Victorian house. Except for a few private estates, the highly labour-intensive craft of bedding out was practised on a large scale primarily in public parks, where it continues to flourish, a perennial crowd pleaser, as installations at LONGWOOD GARDENS and Walt Disney World demonstrate.

Most gardens would continue to be created by their owners aided by books, magazines, and local nurserymen, but this era saw the rise of the professional garden and landscape designer. Downing, himself considered a pioneer, praised André PARMENTIER as the first notable practitioner. Olmsted and Vaux gave the profession its name, landscape architecture. In establishing it simultaneously as an artistic and socially beneficial endeavour, they were aided by *Garden and Forest* (1888-98), the magazine conducted by Charles Sprague SARGENT, and by the critical writing of Mariana Griswold van Rensselaer (1851-1934), particularly her 1893 book *Art Out-of-Doors*. Olmsted and contemporaries like Robert Morris Copeland (1830-74), Jacob Weidenmann (1829-93), and H. W. S. Cleveland (1814-1900) designed parks, cemeteries, suburbs, college campuses, and private estates across the country. From their work and that of the next generation—among them Olmsted's sons John Charles (1852-1920) and F. L. Jr. (1870-1957); Warren Manning (1860-1938); Samuel Parsons (1844-1923); and Beatrix FARRAND; all founding members in 1899 of the American Society of Landscape Architects—evolved an approach to the design of large-scale landscapes which would dominate the profession until the mid 20th century. It would also dominate the teaching in the graduate schools of landscape design at universities nationwide that followed Harvard's establishment of the first in 1900.

The overall layout was naturalistic, but allowed room for structured spaces, when appropriate. Architecturally designed entrance plazas or gardens around public buildings were often inserted in parks. Any number of different gardens in different styles might surround an estate's mansion, but the rest of the grounds were laid out in an abstraction of natural forms. At BILTMORE, Olmsted planted the entrance road to resemble a native forest, but gave the French Renaissance-inspired palace suitably architectural immediate surroundings, then created more and more informal spaces leading down the hillside.

The tycoons who commissioned the estates and the landscape architects who designed them could and did adjust this programme to their own interests and styles. FILOLI, DUMBARTON OAKS, WINTERHUR, and VAL VERDE are just a few that suggest the varied effects that could be achieved. More architecturally formulaic were the estates designed by architects trained at the École des Beaux-Arts in Paris. Its approach was eclectic, blending details from many traditions but emphasizing hardscape to the neglect of horticulture.

The men who built great fortunes were also great travellers, and when they saw something they liked they brought it home, or tried to. Italy was a favourite destination. Italian artefacts—sculptures, urns, well-heads, balustrades—were appealing, and RENAISSANCE GARDENS, softened by age and neglect, seemed both romantic and well suited to the hilly character of much of the American countryside. Some essays in the style were quite incongruous, but designers like Charles PLATT who understood the underlying principles created successful Italianate landscapes, GWINN for example, adjusted to the climate and the way Americans liked to live. So high fashion were Italian gardens that even estates that eschewed the artefacts or allusions tended to have Italian plans. It did not take long before suburban gardeners were trying to scale these down for 0.4-hectare/1-acre lots. Such gardens had structure, and seemed to some more interesting than the old four-square colonial layout, which was making a comeback.

The 1876 Centennial Exhibition in Philadelphia gave a push to the nascent Colonial Revival movement, like the ARTS AND CRAFTS movement, of which it can be considered an American branch, a reaction against industrial commercialism and Victorian clutter. In the eastern United States, the Colonial Revival brought back the picket-fenced vernacular garden, shorn of its vegetables and fruits, its raised beds overflowing with flowers, and edged in boxwood, as they never had been in the 17th and 18th centuries. Arthur Shurcliff (1870-1957), landscape architect for the restoration of Colonial WILLIAMSBURG, was a member of the Boston Society of Arts and Crafts, and the summer place he and his wife, both accomplished woodworkers, built was far more Craftsman than Colonial. But for Williamsburg's gardens he relied on archaeological research that uncovered paths, foundations, postholes, but not planting design. For that he studied gardens in New England and Virginia that he thought were 18th century, but which, we now know, were Victorian interpretations created around 1848. Thus his gardens were too manicured, too ornamental, and overfilled with boxwood.

Colonial Revival flower gardens often appeared in the garden collections on large estates even in California. But the west had its own Spanish Colonial or Mission Revival, which blended the patio, originally a work space and corral, and the *huerta*—a walled or fenced vegetable, fruit, and flower garden—into a romantic flower-filled PATIO. These patios were intended as rooms for living outdoors, a reasonable goal given the California climate and one that captured the nation's imagination.

Since a major tenet of Arts and Crafts thinking was fidelity to the local environment and to local materials, it encouraged distinctively regional approaches to landscape design. In the more recently settled middle west, the native woods and grasslands became the inspiration for landscape architects like Jens JENSEN, Ossian Cole Simonds (1855-1932), Alfred Caldwell (1903-98), and architects like Frank Lloyd Wright (1867-1959), collectively known as the Prairie School. They campaigned for the use of indigenous plants although they were quite capable of using hardy exotics, if that was what the situation called for, and while they habitually stylized the local environment in their landscapes, they would give clients structured flower gardens if wanted.

Gertrude JEKYLL's ideas on planting design and the use of colour were eagerly studied by American gardeners like Mrs Francis King (1863-1948), who knew Jekyll and promoted them in her popular books and articles, and by landscape architects, particularly the group of talented women like Ellen Shipman (1869-1950), Marian Coffin (1876-1957), and Martha Brookes Hutcheson (1871-1959) who followed in Beatrix Farrand's footsteps during what is called 'The Country Place Era' around the turn of the century.

More additions to the American design vocabulary came from the JAPANESE GARDEN, introduced by a very simple tea house garden at the Centennial Exhibition. By the end of the 1880s books and magazines had illustrated and explained the principles; more elaborate versions at the Columbian Exposition of 1893 in Chicago and later World's Fairs had given Americans a chance to study live examples. The artefacts—bridges, lanterns, gates, and tea houses—instantly became fashionable, and a Japanese garden became a must-have for the estates of garden styles collectors. Many even brought over Japanese garden makers to insure authenticity.

More horticulturally minded estate owners focused on building plant collections. Some of these eventually became public arboreta, like the MORRIS and the MORTON, or botanic gardens like the HUNTINGTON and the MISSOURI. Even when botanic gardens and arboreta were founded under the aegis of colleges, universities, or municipal governments, they were generally instigated by pressure plus donations or legacies from private individuals. The ARNOLD ARBORETUM of Harvard University is a case in point, and today more than ever, both the founding and funding of public gardens depend on private donations.

The exertions of private individuals also propelled an increasing number of preservation organizations. The Association for the Preservation of Virginia Antiquities, the oldest (1889) statewide preservation group, has gardens among its 34 properties but focuses on historic buildings and sites. More influential as a model, the Trustees of Reservations was established by the Massachusetts Legislature in 1891 with prodding from Charles Eliot (1859-97), a partner in the Olmsted firm, and a host of distinguished citizens. Empowered by the state to hold land free of taxes for the public to enjoy, the non-profit corporation governed by a board of voluntary trustees accepts and cares for properties donated by private citizens, but only if accompanied by a substantial endowment. Most of today's 94 reservations are natural landscapes but among them are some estates and designed gardens, the most famous of which is Naumkeag. In 1892 a band of California citizens devoted to wilderness and environmental preservation founded the Sierra Club, now a worldwide organization. The Society for the Preservation of New England Antiquities, founded in 1910, owns 35 properties—houses, gardens, and working farms dating from the 17th to the 20th centuries—in five states as well as museum collections of furniture and artefacts, both humble and high style, and archives of great importance.

Occasional financial panics might temporarily halt landscape projects, but neither the income tax nor the First World War reduced the quantity. The period was one of increasing prosperity, and interest in gardening increased right along with it. Garden clubs organized by educated, well-to-do, and energetic women provided an outlet for talents barred by social pressure from participation in business or politics. The Athens Georgia club of 1891 is often cited as the first, but recently garden historians have identified clubs with similar agendas dating from as early as 1869. Individual clubs soon gathered into umbrella organizations like the GARDEN CLUB OF AMERICA founded in 1913, the Women's National Farm and Garden Association organized in 1914 to help with the war effort, the Garden Club of Virginia in 1928, and the National Garden Clubs, Inc. in 1929. Garden clubs are not often given proper credit for their impact on garden design. They gave scholarships; fostered civic beautification; promoted native plant conservation; created archives; raised money for the restoration of historic gardens; and sponsored state and national legislation like the Billboard Control Amendment.

The turn of the 20th century saw a new outpouring of magazines concerned with design. *Country Life in America*, *Garden Magazine*, *House Beautiful*, *House & Garden* took a less intellectual approach than *Garden and Forest* and were lavishly illustrated with photographs. In the beginning they faithfully reported trends from all across the country, but over time concentrated on the east coast and Europe with some notice of California but little of the country in between, probably because most were based in eastern cities. This bias in coverage tended to sap the development of what had been promising regional styles, but they did give their readers a look at new ideas coming from Europe, for example, Fletcher STEELE's articles on modern art and garden design as practised in France in the 1920s.

The stock market crash of 1929 and the ensuing Depression limited but did not completely halt private estate creation. Established landscape designers usually had enough work, but newcomers to the profession found most demand for their services in government agencies like the Tennessee Valley Authority, Civilian Conservation Corps, and the National Park Service. Up until this time, few gardeners with small properties had hired professional designers, although the latter had offered advice in books and magazines. The situation changed in the 1930s, and the change started in California.

Drawing on the patio tradition, the real demands of 20th-century living, and the modernist ideals of functionality, simplicity, and ease of maintenance, Thomas CHURCH, followed by several younger landscape architects, began to unite house and garden as complementary spaces for living, while respecting the native landscape around them. Church's ideas received widespread coverage in magazines, particularly *Sunset*, a venerable magazine retooled in 1929 as the *Magazine of Western Living*. Although he loved plants himself, he suggested that more paving and plants in pots better suited the state's Mediterranean climate with its hot, dry summers. Most of his gardens were rather small: even owners of large ranches did not want to care for more than a modest space.

In 1938 three landscape architecture students at Harvard rebelled against the prevailing Beaux-Arts teaching with its focus on the past, and the out-of-date notion that landscape design could be only axial and architectural or else a stylization of natural forms. Modern painters, sculptors, and architects had shown that there were many more ways to shape space: why couldn't landscape architects do the same? James Rose (1913–91), Garrett ECKBO, and Dan KILEY were thrown out of graduate school but found a forum in the architectural press for their belief that gardens and landscapes should reflect 20th-century reality. Most of their writing dealt with public landscapes, but in practice their ideas were first expressed in small suburban gardens. The entrance of the United States into the Second World War put a stop to the possibility of larger projects

The gardening world of the late 20th century

Ornamental gardening as a whole was little practised during the war: most home gardeners took to growing vegetables. The Victory Gardens of the Second World War were the seedlings from which the present thriving community garden movement grew (see ALLOTMENT). The oldest working community garden, the Richard Parker Victory Garden, was established in Boston in 1942. Today's community gardens, estimated to number 10,000, include whatever the neighbourhood activists who clean up vacant lots to create them want: trees and grass, fruits, flowers, vegetables, play spaces, sitting spaces. To educate and raise funds for community gardeners—and defend them from developers—almost every major city has volunteer associations with colourful names such as New York's Green Guerillas, San Francisco's SLUG, Chicago's SOUL, St Louis's Gateway Greening, Seattle Tilth, and Philadelphia Green.

The end of the Second World War saw the triumph of the California-inspired suburban garden. Returning servicemen passing through the state were taken with its relaxed, open-air way of life. Some returned to live there; others tried to recreate the activity-oriented paved patios, backyard swimming pools, and barbecues in the suburban developments mass produced across the country by builders, who usually scraped sites flat in the name of speed and cost. 'Easy maintenance', 'no-care', became goals for both house and garden in the 1950s and 1960s, abetted by the popular press. Chemical companies promoted fertilizers and pesticides (see PEST CONTROL) as time and labour savers: enter the industrial lawn. Since flowering plants take caring, they were banished to pots or small beds. Fortunately, enough gardening enthusiasts remained to keep nurseries and seed companies going, although diminished in number.

By the 1970s Americans again became hungry for green. The ongoing renewal of gardening's popularity began with herbs and vegetables as more and more people travelled abroad, then could not find in supermarkets the ingredients for recipes they had liked. They had also been impressed by European gardens so it did not take long for the appeal of flowers to rekindle. Interest in gardening grew so fast that county extension offices were overwhelmed with requests for information. Officials from the Washington State University Cooperative Extension came up with a plan in 1972 to give volunteers, to be called master gardeners, extensive horticultural training in return for which they would help provide the public with information. Today master gardeners in all 50 states answer garden questions, teach classes

for adults and children, write articles, and build demonstration gardens among many community-service projects.

With this ever-expanding market, nurseries, new and long established alike, expanded in three directions. Some went wholesale and focused their efforts on hybridizing or developing new methods for mass plant production. Others joined with or turned into garden centres and concentrated on selling quantities of popular plants. Still others devoted themselves to specialities, selling primarily by mail-order catalogue, and now by website.

The California-style backyard garden encountered predictable problems in regions where the climate did not permit year-round outdoor living. Yet gardens were created in the 1950s and 1960s demonstrating that given a sensitive designer and an enlightened homeowner such features as swimming pools and tennis courts could be inserted into a design so that they did not obtrude in seasons when they were unusable.

Landscape architects were rarely called on to create large private estates. What demanded their services were college campuses, office parks, new towns and suburban developments, airports, urban plazas, rooftop gardens, vest pocket parks, and playgrounds. Taking lessons from modern artists, they made free use for both public and private commissions of the ideas gathered into the American design vocabulary. Geometric elements like *allées*, TOPIARY, and QUINCUNXES could be balanced asymmetrically in a scheme; pastoral landscapes like A. E. Bye's (1919–2001) Gainsway Farms could display crisp zigzag paths and HA-HA walls. New materials— aluminum, stainless steel, concrete, fibreglass— might find a place, or familiar ones be used in unfamiliar ways. New sources of inspiration were quickly explored, for example, the land art of Michael Heizer (b. 1944), Walter De Maria (b. 1935), and Robert Smithson (1938–73).

Along with explosive economic and population growth, the post-war period saw a proliferation of historic preservation and conservation initiatives, which shows no sign of abating. In 1949, Congress created the National Trust for Historic Preservation—first partly government funded, now totally member supported—and in 1966 the National Register of Historic Places maintained by the National Park Service. The former seeks to save buildings, gardens, farms, districts, sites, important for their intrinsic significance, quality, or links to important historical figures or events. The latter documents, defines criteria, and provides a wide variety of bibliographic and practical preservation help.

Recent years have seen the founding of more tightly focused non-profit member-supported associations like the Alliance for Historic Landscape Preservation, the GARDEN CONSERVANCY, and the Cultural Landscape Foundation.

On a parallel track American landscape and garden history has become a fast-growing academic field. With his exploration of cultural landscapes in the journal *Landscape,* which he produced and edited from 1951 to 1968, and in his books and teaching John Brinckerhoff Jackson (1909–96) inspired many young historians. In 1971 the Center for Studies in Landscape Architecture at Dumbarton Oaks was founded. Scholars today can access local historical and garden history societies, libraries too numerous to list, and search the Library of Congress, the Archives of American Gardens at the Smithsonian Institution, and the CATALOG of Landscape Records in the United States in the Archives of the New York Botanical Garden.

New kinds of organizations—land trusts, conservancies, legal advocacy groups—work with property owners and governmental bodies to save and restore natural ecosystems as scientists learn more and more about their efficiency in cleaning air and water. The Land Trust Alliance, a consortium of 1,300 national, state, and local groups, organizes the sharing of expertise and problems, and develops and refines new tools like conservation easements, which help concerned property owners preserve undeveloped land, farms, or ranches by donating development rights in return for tax advantages.

These extend the early conservation movement. The major shift in attitude is the growing realization that the choices of each gardener, each landscape designer have a tremendous collective impact on the health of the natural environment. Wake-up calls were Rachel Carson's (1907–64) *The Silent Spring* (1962), documenting the devastating effects of pesticides, and Ian McHarg's (1930–96) *Design with Nature* (1969), a blueprint for ecologically sound planning. The water-guzzling 'toxic lawn' came under siege. In the early 1970s gardeners like Lorrie Otto (b. 1919) who made a prairie lawn of her Wisconsin yard, landscape architects like Darrel Morrison (b. 1937), native plant societies, and specialized seedsmen pioneered wildflower meadow planting. Botanists try to discourage the sale and planting of invasive species that destroy native ecosystems. The xeriscape movement, founded in Colorado in 1981, encourages gardeners to choose plants based on water availability, and the National Gardening Association estimates that one in ten gardeners follow organic methods (see ORGANIC GARDENING).

The responsibilities of individual stewardship offer challenges to garden makers, amateur and professional alike. An ecologically sound plant palette need not be limited to indigenous flora, but contemporary landscape architects like Laurie Olin (b. 1938), Michael Van Valkenburgh (b. 1951), and Steve Martino (b. 1946) have shown that exciting, even highly structured gardens can be made with native plants. The gardener's motto for the 21st century might be 'From stewardship comes art'.   DMO

University of British Columbia Botanic Garden.

See BRITISH COLUMBIA, UNIVERSITY OF, BOTANICAL GARDEN.

University of California Campus, Los Angeles Campus ⊛

Westwood, Los Angeles, California, USA, was developed between 1925 and the present, and is one of the best-planted campuses in the country. Brick northern Italian Romanesque-style buildings shaped the original cross-axial Beaux-Arts plan. After the 1950s this style was supplanted by modernism, resulting in a collection of structures singularly lacking in architectural distinction. Bad architecture was saved by the distinguished landscape designs of Ralph D. Cornell (1890–1972), whose achievements are memorialized in a large stand of eucalyptus trees near the art building. In the early 1960s Cornell was given complete control over the treatment of the spaces between building façades. Roads were planted as formal ALLÉES of trees and the numerous courtyards used the broad range of subtropical shrubs and trees that be can be grown in this region. Throughout the campus Cornell used numerous specimens of the extremely sculptural native sycamore trees (*Platanus racemosa*). The finest space on the campus is the Franklin D. Murphy Sculpture Garden, where the gently contoured lawn is planted with a grove of *Jacaranda mimosifolia*. A very distinguished sculpture collection is displayed on small concrete sitting areas and on broad terraces linked by a tunnel-like *allée* of *Erythrina caffra* trees. The court of the geography building accommodates a collection of tall palm trees. The 3-hectare/7-acre Mildred Matthias Botanic Garden contains a densely planted ravine, the only surviving remnant of a formerly prominent feature of the campus. Here are 60-m/200-ft tall stands of *Eucalyptus grandis*, unusually tall dawn redwoods, and a collection of plants from montane tropical forests.   DCS

Uppsala University Botanic Garden ⊛

Uppland, Sweden, is the country's oldest botanic garden, founded in 1655 by the polymath professor of medicine Olof Rudbeck the elder (1630–1702). In 1685 the garden comprised 1,873 taxa, and was one of the largest in Europe. In 1741 Carl LINNAEUS became the head of the decayed garden and transformed it into one of the world's most famous gardens by plantings disposed according to his sexual system. Carl HÅRLEMAN designed the ORANGERY and grounds. The garden was reconstructed in the 1920s based on Linnaeus' plan of 1745 and is today called Linneträdgården. In 1787 King Gustav III, persuaded by Linnaeus' successor Carl Peter THUNBERG, donated the formal garden of Uppsala Castle, designed in 1750 by Carl Hårleman, to the university. In 1807 the new garden was inaugurated, and all plants were moved in from the old garden. Olof Tempelman (1745–1816) designed a new orangery, Linneanum (1787). The garden has been extended several times and was restored according to Hårleman's original plan in 1974. The garden comprises about 13,000 species and receives about 100,000 visitors a year. Three plants survive from Linnaeus' time, bay laurel (*Laurus nobilis*), *Adhatoda vasica*, and *Cereus hildmannianus*.   KL

Upton Grey Manor House.

See MANOR HOUSE, THE.

Uraniborg ⊛

Scania, Sweden, is situated on the highest point of the island of Ven in the sound (Öresund) between Sweden and Denmark. The grounds constitute Scandinavia's most distinguished early Renaissance structure with respect to composition and symmetry (castle, gardens, borders), forms (squares, circles, cross), and other expressions of Renaissance landscape ideas (ponds, paper mill, aviary). Uraniborg comprised a two-storey red brick castle (1576–81), partly by Hans van Stenwinkel (1545–1601), and an astronomical observatory, chemical laboratory, and dwellings, all built for the famous Danish astronomer Tycho Brahe (1546–1601), owner of the island from 1576, and his assistants and students. There were an inner and outer garden (1581–97) and a defence wall 5 m/16 ft high with four semicircular bastions with summer houses. The internal layout was in the form of a cross, with the castle standing in a circular space at the centre, with a well built below it. A herb garden was laid out in a pattern of beds shaped into triangles, stars, and circles, and beyond them a formal orchard lined the walls. The principal layout had similarities with the botanical garden of Padua (1545) and the castle resembled Andrea PALLADIO's Villa Rotonda. The grounds were demolished in the beginning of the 17th century, providing material for a royal estate. Part of the garden has been reconstructed by Professor Sven-Ingvar ANDERSSON as 'a planted hypothesis' and was inaugurated in 1992, and is the subject of a continuing programme of conservation, especially concerning the plant material of the 16th century.   KL

KJELL LUNDQUIST, 'The plant material in the Renaissance garden of Tycho Brahe at Uraniborg (1581-1597) on the island of Ven—a restoration project in progress', *Museologia Scientifica* (1998). JOHANNA ERLANDSON (ed.), *Tycho Brahe—Stjärnornas herre* (1996).

US Ambassador's Residence,

Buenos Aires, Argentina. This was originally the home of Mr and Mrs Bosch-Alvear, from the grandest Argentinian social class, who built their palace in 1910-18 to the designs of the French architect René Sergent (1865-1927). Sergent designed several great houses in the country but never visited it. He used to call upon Achille DUCHÊNE to design gardens based on his primary sketches. He did so, but in this case, Charles THAYS made a third version—the one that was built. The complex, with an entrance *cour d'honneur* (see ATTRE, CHÂTEAU D') and a French formal garden at the back, became a French architectural landmark in Argentina, both as an imposing residence and as a teaching model for students. The Sergent-Duchêne proposal was symmetrical with three identical PARTERRES *de broderie*, a fountain, and a double staircase connecting the terrace with the garden. The garden built by Thays on a symmetrical basis had a single staircase, a large *parterre de broderie* with four smaller ones, and an iron TREILLAGE for climbing roses. Over the years, the garden lost its shape and in 1998 Thays Landscapers restored it to its original state—the first scientific garden restoration in Argentina. Although it is a small garden, it is a vivid example of neoclassical French style in South America.   SLB

Utens, Giusto

(1558-1609), Italian artist of Flemish origin who, between 1599 and 1602, painted a series of 'lunettes' (semicircular paintings) of notable estates in the countryside surrounding Florence. Apart from being delightful paintings they are especially valuable to garden historians. They show much of the detail of gardens such as the BOBOLI GARDENS, PRATOLINO, and the Villa MEDICI (Castello). Fourteen lunettes survive and are now preserved in Florence at the Museo di Firenze Com'era.   PT

V

Vácrátót Botanical Garden ⊛

near Vác, Pest county, Hungary. The estate at Vácrátót was purchased in 1870 by Count Sándor Vigyázó who two years later set about a complete transformation of the existing landscape garden. The park of around 30 hectares/75 acres, redesigned by Vilmos JÁMBOR and built with the assistance of head gardener Henrik Band, became one of the most magnificent gardens in Hungary. The Count spent a large proportion of his income on the garden: a lake was dug, a mound built from the ensuing earth, which was made more scenic with valleys made with huge slabs of rock, GROTTOES, and a large waterfall, as well as spectacular views. This late example of a picturesque garden was ornamented with a BELVEDERE, a watermill and a mock RUIN, all built between 1870 and the end of the century. The construction of the garden, however, continued right up to 1910. It is Jámbor's work and the owner's interest that resulted in the park's varied and rich exotic collections of trees and underplanting. The garden was left by its founder to the Hungarian Academy of Sciences, which took it over after the death of his son in 1928. The academy's Ecological and Botanical Research Institute has operated here since 1952, and in 1953-4 a taxonomic collection was created, and the floral inventory of the partially restored park is consciously being enriched. Experiments and hybridization take place in new greenhouses. Fifteen thousand taxa can be found in the park today.   GA

Valencia Botanic Garden ⊛

Valencia, Spain, was founded in 1567 as a garden of medicinal plants. In 1802 it moved to its present site and became a garden serving the needs of the university's botany department. More recently the garden has been well restored and has become, in addition to its botanical role, a public park of much charm displaying some outstanding plants. Glasshouses built in 1861 protect collections of tropical palms, carnivorous plants, tropical orchids, and bromeliads. A handsome *umbráculo* (shade-

house) beautifully built of cast iron, has a collection of ferns. Most of the plants, however, are displayed in the open. The garden is finely laid out in a grid of spacious beds often edged in clipped myrtle with paths of fine gravel. A wide-ranging collection of succulents, some of them of very large size, is of special interest. Some plants are grouped by family and particularly well displayed. That of Solanaceae, for example, is gathered together in hedged beds and watered with runnels edged in tiles of Islamic character. Throughout the garden are notable specimens of plants. An enormous old *Yucca arizonica* holds its own alongside a venerable Turkey oak (*Quercus cerris*). There is an attractive display of plants of the Rocalla de Vicarianzes—drylands plants of the Valencia region.   PT

Valentien, Otto

(1897-1987), German garden architect and garden writer. After training as a gardener and studies at the Horticultural College in Berlin-Dahlem (1919-21) Valentien found employment at famous German garden design firms as well as at municipal garden departments. From 1925 he was responsible for the design office of the nursery Ludwig SPÄTH in Berlin, later working for the Frankfurt garden department where he planned the green belt of the river Nidda as a kind of people's park and nature reservation (1928). In 1929 he established a design office in Stuttgart and executed a broad range of different projects (e.g. the garden for the Villa Scheufelen, 1936). He had a strong interest in contemporary art and was aware of the importance of gardens for people with low income. He favoured the architectonic garden with softened lines and his gardens show a great interest in the qualities of individual plants and include crazy paving as well as dry wall planting. He was also a prolific writer (e.g. *Zeitgemäße Wohngärten*, 1932; *Gärten, Beispiele und Anleitungen zur Gestaltung*, 1938; *Neue Gärten*, 1949). In 1957 he settled as a painter in Thumen near Lindau.   US

CHARLOTTE REITSAM, 'Otto Valentien', *Garten + Landschaft*, Vol. 108: No. 10 (1998).

Valentine Garden,

Santa Barbara, California, USA, was created in 1984 on a site of 1.62 hectares/4 acres, and constitutes an outstanding example of creative water conservation. This compactly planned garden designed by Isabelle GREENE lies at the base of the Santa Ynez Mountains. Its design provides a strong contrast to the large expanses of blank white wall of the abstracted pueblo-style house. It is approached through a formal motor court with tiered retaining walls planted with lemons, rosemary, and hollyhocks. Bounding two sides of the house is a walled dry garden with a symbolic 'river' of grey granite chips which originates in a small pool planted with papyrus near the front door. The river terminates in an austere composition of pots at a balustrade, commanding a broad panoramic view of the Pacific ocean and the garden one storey below. Enclosed by low walls this rectangular space was designed to be seen both from above and at ground level, and is tilted slightly upward to counter feelings of vertigo. Inspired by Indonesian rice paddies, its flowing ribbon-like planting beds are retained by low battered concrete walls. Ribbons of water are suggested by *Senecio kleinia*, and sedums, aloes, *Echeveria elegans*, *Artemisia stellerana*, blue zoysia grass, blue penstemon grass, and yuccas. Differing levels of irrigation were achieved through using a drip irrigation system, and rivers of broken slate and decomposed granite paths further reduce areas requiring irrigation. At one corner is an L-shaped pergola of copper columns and beams supporting a giant honeysuckle vine (*Lonicera hildebrandtiana*).

DCS

Valkenberg ⊛

Breda, Noord-Brabant, the Netherlands, was the original medieval estate of the earls of Nassau, becoming Orange-Nassau through inheritance of the principality of Orange in 1544. This is the estate where King Charles II of England resided in 1660 and where in 1667 the peace treaty of the second Anglo-Dutch War was negotiated. At that stage the gardens consisted of an enclosure with seventeen compartments or 'parcken' with arbours on three sides, a separate bower garden, a fishpond and a cruciform BOSQUET with two circular walks and a rose garden. The central compartment contained a SUNDIAL created from box TOPIARY. These gardens dated from the era of Frederik Hendrik (*c*.1640), but may have contained earlier features. Remarkably, despite various proposals, there was never a whole-scale reshaping of the gardens, although the detail in the compartments was replaced with PARTERRES *de broderie* by William III, who also probably removed the majority of the bowers. In the early 19th century the gardens were poorly maintained with the historic structure disappearing, while they were opened to the public in 1812. In 1882 Breda became the official owner of the park, which was redesigned as a landscape park by Lieven Rosseels (1843–1921), to provide a pleasant walk for residents and visitors. This layout was first partially modified by J. T. P. BIJHOUWER in 1952, and in 1995 a new remodelling was made by Michiel van Gessel of Bureau B+B. This renovation aimed to provide for a wide range of requirements, generally upgrading the park (6.5 hectares/16 acres), while respecting the archaeology. A modern re-creation of one of the seventeen parterres serves to bring the historic layout to life, with a copy of an original Hercules in its centre.   JW

VANESSA BEZEMER-SELLERS, *Courtly Gardens in Holland 1600–1650: The House of Orange and the Hortus Batavus* (2001).

WIET KERKHOVEN, 'Het Valkenberg te Breda: vernieuwing van een binnenstadspark', *Groen*, Vol. 52: No. 1 (1996).

Vallée, Jean de la

(1623–96). French architect and garden designer, Born in Paris, who followed his father, the architect Simon de la Vallée (1590–1642), to Holland and then to Stockholm, Sweden, in 1637. After his father's death he travelled through Europe to study garden art and architecture. Back in Sweden by 1650, his work was influenced by French architecture and garden design as well as by late Renaissance Italian villas. His most important works are considered to be the city palaces, villas, and the gardens owned by the nobleman and chancellor Magnus Gabriel de La Gardie (1622–86). De la Vallée made a General Plan for Ekolsund in the 1650s based on drawings by his father contemporary with the design of for VAUX-LE-VICOMTE. The plans include similar monumental features including the main canal, at right angles to the chief vista. Nothing remains of de la Vallée's proposals for the gardens at Jakobsdal (ULRIKSDAL) and Karlberg, both owned by de La Gardie and situated near Stockholm, but de la Vallée's plans and drawings are well documented. At the de La Gardie estate of Venngarn the main features from 1661 remain today, resembling an Italian villa in the late Renaissance period.   AJ

CLAES ELLEHAG, *Jean de la Vallée: kunglig arkitekt* (2003).

Valmarana, 'Ai Nani', Villa ⊛

Vicenza, Veneto, Italy. Built for the jurist Giovanni Maria Bertolo between 1665 and 1670, the small palace is renowned both for the dwarfs which decorate the walled courtyard and for the frescoes completed by Giambattista Tiepolo (1696–1770) and his sons in 1757, portraying the poetic works of the *Iliad* and *Aeneid*, *Orlando furioso*, and *Gerusalemme liberata*. The statues of the dwarfs (*nani*) are supposedly guardians of a dwarf princess who killed herself for love after seeing a beautiful but unattainable prince.   PHo

Val Verde Garden ⊛

Santa Barbara, California, USA, was developed between 1927 and 1948 on a 7-hectare/17-acre site, and is considered one of the finest Mediterranean-style gardens in the country. The large courtyard house was designed in 1915 by Bertram Grosvenor Goodhue (1869–1924) in a version of colonial Mexican architecture, acompanied by a formal garden, incorporating plants from a former international plant and seed collecting business. The formal terraces below the house contrasted with an almost jungle-like profusion of plants. Between 1927 and 1948 Wright Ludington, a distinguished art collector, worked closely with Lockwood de Forest Jnr. (1896–1949) to transform the estate into a formal Mediterranean garden whose abstract qualities are almost modernist. Formal gardens, often with water, and a detached gallery and atrium building housed a distinguished collection of Greek and Roman statues. A new formal motor court was developed, together with additional service buildings and a fountain modelled after the one outside the Villa Medici, Rome (see MEDICI FAMILY). A long curving walk beneath arching oak trees and traversing the lip of a ravine was treated as an abstract composition with an embedded collection of medieval and Renaissance plaques. In the mid-1930s the terraces were given greater geometric clarity with low clipped hedges, and the upper walk was flanked by massive square columns, evoking a ruin. Reflecting pools, floodlit at night, were added on the cross-axis of the house, terminated by statues. In the late 1940s the house and all the structures were painted with several layers of paint to create the effect of an time-worn villa. The Pool House and the surrounding area were sold in 1946. The classical sculpture was removed in 1956.   DCS

Vanbrugh, Sir John

(1664–1726), English architect, landscape designer, playwright, and soldier of Flemish extraction. His career as a playwright gave way to that of architect when in 1699 he was asked to design CASTLE HOWARD for the Earl of Carlisle. Here he showed his understanding of landscape—both the role of the house in its setting as well as the possibilities for animating the landscape with ornamental buildings. In all his work there is a distinctive baroque sense of drama. In 1702 he became Comptroller of His Majesty's Works which he remained, except for a brief hiccup in 1713, until his death. In 1704 he secured his most important commission, to design BLENHEIM PALACE. Here he revealed an original taste for ruins in the landscape by trying, unsuccessfully, to persuade the Duchess of Marlborough to retain in the grounds the picturesque ruins of medieval Woodstock Manor. At Blenheim, in the walls of the kitchen garden garnished with giant bastions, he showed his fondness for the military style—he also built a wall at Castle Howard with bastions and traces of them are still visible in the grounds of Seaton Delaval (Northumberland). The last was Vanbrugh's last house, only completed in 1729 after his death, which was set at the centre of a raised platform of ground with bastions in each corner ornamented with a statue. The house, built for an admiral, overlooks the coast at Whitley Bay, so perhaps Vanbrugh had a fort in mind. At CLAREMONT Vanbrugh's castellated Belvedere (1715–20) certainly has something of a fortress air. There were bulwark-like walls at STOWE where Vanbrugh worked from 1719 but they could have been the work of BRIDGEMAN. Sir Joshua Reynolds thought that Vanbrugh 'was a Poet as well as an Architect . . . an Architect who composed like a Painter'.   PT

CHRISTOPHER RIDGWAY and ROBERT WILLIAMS (eds.), *Sir John Vanbrugh and Landscape Architecture in Baroque England 1690–1730* (2000).

van Buuren Museum, Gardens of ⊛

Uccle, Brussels, Belgium. The gardens of the David and Alice van Buuren Museum complement the art deco house. An art deco rose garden which pre-dated the building was designed by Jules Buyssens in 1924. He also designed a picturesque landscape garden, with exotic trees laid out round a lawn. A labyrinth and the Jardin du Cœur were designed by René Pechère between 1968 and 1970. The labyrinth is made up of 1,300 yews planted to created seven green rooms. Sculptures by Andre Willequet illustrate verses of the Song of Songs. The Jardin du Cœur, a parterre of twelve small heart-shaped beds surrounded by a yew cloister, is a memorial to David van Buuren, a private place for reflection. There is also a garden of modern roses on what was a tennis court, also designed by Pechère, and another court has been transformed into a BOULINGRIN.   BA

van Campen, Jacob.

See CAMPEN, JACOB VAN.

5,413 ft long and its east–west axis, pointed towards the setting sun, was important for the sun imagery which pervaded the garden. Ornamental ships were an important feature of the Grand Canal, being specially made in the arsenals of Dunkirk, Marseille, Rouen, and Venice. In addition, in 1774, a shipyard was established with Venetian craftsmen at the head of the canal—*La Petite Venise*—so that ships could be made on the spot. The southern arm of the Grand Canal led to Louis Le Vau's MENAGERIE, built like a miniature chateau *c*.1663. In its day this was one of the great features of the garden, especially when visitors could be brought here in extravagantly decorated boats on the waters of the canal. Today almost nothing remains of the menagerie except the ruins of ancillary pavilions. Another remarkable building, which lasted an even shorter time, was the Grotto of Thetis. Built between 1664 and 1668 it was designed by Louis Le Vau and Claude Perrault, a three-arched stone pavilion with relief carvings (some of which depicted Apollo) and wrought-iron grills with a pattern of gilt sunbursts. The interior was sumptuous, with arched niches inlaid with exotic animals worked in coral, shells, minerals, and glass. The niches contained carvings of Apollo being bathed by nymphs and sleeping with Thetis. A reservoir concealed in the roof caused water to flow down the interior walls and provided power for water organs—by this date a rather old-fashioned feature. The grotto was short-lived—it was demolished in 1684 to make way for a northern extension of the chateau. The Bosquet des Sources (*bosquet* of the springs) was laid out by Le Nôtre in 1679, a striking and unusual arrangement of winding walks and rills, quite different in character from the other *bosquets*.

Water featured in many parts of the garden and its supply became a vexing problem and remains so to this day, when the fountains at Versailles play only occasionally on Sundays. There was no natural fall to bring water to the gardens and an extraordinary device was built to pump water from the Seine—the Machine de Marly. Fourteen huge waterwheels, each 12 m/ 39 ft in diameter, powered over 200 pumps which took water from the river to a height of 162 m/531 ft where it was gathered in reservoirs and taken by channels and aqueducts to the gardens of Versailles and also of MARLY. The water supply was never sufficient to make all the fountains at Versailles play simultaneously. On grand occasions, when notable visitors were received, a team of skilfully choreographed garden boys, communicating with whistles, turned taps on and off so that visitors were always presented with fountains in action.

Potager du Roi

The King's vegetable garden, with an area of 9 hectares/22 acres, was laid out by Jean-Baptiste de La QUINTINIE between 1678 and 1683. Protected by high walls, it has a rectilinear layout planned with as much care as any of the purely ornamental parts of the garden. Its essential layout survives intact today and it is still used to cultivate a wide range of fruit and vegetables. The centre—*le grand carré* (the great square)—is slightly sunken with a circular pool in the middle with a single water jet. This was originally surrounded by a regular pattern of beds of culinary herbs, each bed outlined with ornamental trees. The King took a particular interest in the *potager* which, horticulturally, was one of the most up-to-date parts of the garden. Walled subdivisions (which for the most part do not do not survive) gave protection both for tender crops and to help in the raising of early crops. From 1685 the glass factory at Saint-Gobain supplied glass for glasshouses and protective lights so that lettuces could be grown as early as January and strawberries and asparagus (of which there were 6,000 plants) in March. Wood-burning stoves were used to heat glasshouses and fresh manure was used to provide warmth for hotbeds. Seven hundred fig trees, planted in *caisses de Versailles*, were given their own protection so that the garden could supply figs—the King's favourite fruit—for six months of the year. Much fruit was espaliered against the walls—some of the internal walls were angled to give the best exposure to sunlight.

Trianon

In 1668 a village named Trianon, standing just beyond the point where the northern arm of the Grand Canal was to end, was bought by the King. The village was destroyed to make way for a private retreat where the King could entertain his mistress, Madame de Montespan. In 1670 Louis Le Vau designed an exotic pavilion, the Trianon de Porcelaine, so named because it was decorated with brilliantly coloured glazed tiles. It lasted a very short time, being replaced in 1687 by the building that survives today—Jules Hardouin-Mansart's Trianon de Marbre, a long, low, columned building of green and pink marble. An engraving by Perelle shows that the first Trianon had an elaborate garden, the work of Michel II LE BOUTEUX, with spectacular fountains, several *parterres de broderie*, and a PATTE D'OIE in the woods to the east. Bouteux's essential layout was retained although much detail was lost when new gardens were laid out for the second Trianon, with a second *bosquet des sources*, with winding rills among trees and islands covered in turf. A parterre of flowers west of

the house was in the 17th century filled with exotic flowering plants, brought annually from the Jardin des Plantes in Toulon. The parterres used immense numbers of bulbs—40,500 tulips, 27,000 narcissi, and 13,500 hyacinths—planted in rows and intermingled with herbaceous perennials. Jean Cotelle's painting of 1693 gives a vivid idea of their flowery profusion.

Petit Trianon and Hameau

In the time of Louis XV, who reigned from 1715 to 1774, the land to the north-east of the Trianon was developed. A new menagerie was built *c*.1750, to the designs of Ange-Jacques Gabriel (1698–1782), not for exotic creatures like the old one, but for different breeds of farm animals. It overlooked a kitchen garden and nearby was an elegant pavilion, the Pavillon Français, also designed by Gabriel and completed in 1750, overlooking its own gardens. From 1762 Gabriel's masterpiece, the Petit Trianon, an exquisite classical miniature chateau, was built for Madame de Pompadour. Louis XV also established a botanic garden here with advice from the botanist Bernard de Jussieu who arranged order beds (see BOTANIC GARDEN) disposed according to his own system of classification. A little later on this site a new, picturesque garden was laid out to the designs of Richard Mique (1728–94) for Marie-Antoinette from 1774. Sandy paths wound through shrubberies and there was a flowery meadow. Overlooking a lake, and alongside dramatic rocks and a grotto, Mique built the Belvedere (1778/9), a beautifully detailed octagonal pavilion with an interior finely painted with fruit, birds, and swags of flowers. Mique also designed a famous rotunda, the Temple of Love, completed in 1778. The Hameau (Hamlet) was laid out from 1783 with a lake on whose bank is a collection of more or less rustic buildings modelled on those that might have been seen in a Normandy village. Five of the eleven houses in the Hameau were reserved for the use of the Queen and her friends. The Maison de la Reine had a dining room with panelling painted to resemble marble and a drawing room with white panelling and tapestries. A dairy, also finely decorated, was another of the buildings reserved for the Queen's use, in which the estate's dairy products could be tasted. Other buildings in the Hameau were inhabited by farm labourers and there was a fully productive farm at a little distance from the Hameau. The story that the Queen liked to frolic here with her friends dressed as milkmaids seems to be merely a legend. Each house in the Hameau had its own garden and pots of plants— hyacinths, wallflowers, stocks, or geraniums— on balconies and external staircases.   ▶

Versailles today

The logistics of laying out, planting, and maintaining a designed landscape of the size and complexity of Versailles in the 17th century have no parallel in any modern garden. With 95 hectares/235 acres of pleasure garden, 1,700 hectares/4,200 acres of ornamental park, and a further 6,000 hectares/14,820 acres of hunting park, the whole domaine was enclosed in walls (43 km/26 miles long). In its heyday there were nine *jardiniers en chef* (head gardeners) responsible, sometimes jointly, for major parts of the pleasure garden and the kitchen garden. Under them were vast numbers of general gardeners, specialist flower gardeners, kitchen gardeners, *terrassiers* (who looked after the sanding of paths), nurserymen, craftsmen to look after trellises (and other specialist craftsmen), and many journeymen labourers brought in for particular works (in November and December 1700, for example, 287 labourers were recruited to construct a new garden for the Trianon). In the book by Dominique Garrigues cited below are published some of the garden accounts for payments made in the single year of 1687. These included 50 spades and 56 pickaxes for the Trianon; the cost of 260

journeys made by Jean de La Quintinie to collect fruit and vegetables for the *potager*; the supply of quantities of manure; 55,000 seedlings of alders and 3,700 seedlings of ash; 2,700 hyacinths, 12,500 tulips, 7,100 irises, 13,900 crocuses, 150 double colchicums, 1,800 fritillaries, and 300 narcissi; and many orange trees and myrtles in *caisses de Versailles*, 20,000 narcissi from England, and numbers of such flowering plants as antirrhinums, campanulas, candytuft, cornflowers, jasmines, pasque flowers, pinks, marguerites, primroses, tuberoses (*Polianthes tuberosa*), and violets.

The Versailles we see today is plainly quite different from that known to Louis XIV. The chateau no longer houses 2,000 people, as it did in his day, and the fêtes are now superseded by public *son et lumière*. The gardens today have the status of a much-enjoyed public park. The passage of time has caused great changes—all the trees were replanted at the end of the 18th century (the resulting devastation memorably painted by Hubert ROBERT) and at the end of the 19th century. In the great millennium storm of December 1999 10,000 trees were destroyed. One thing that has not changed is the problematic water supply—the fountains flow only on Sundays. The garden is still rich in marvellous works of art, constituting the finest collection of garden ornaments in the world. The broad layout—the chief parterres, the Grand Canal, the Bassin de Latone, the Bassin d'Apollon, the orangery with its garden, and some of the *bosquets* are still in place. The overwhelming change is that much intricacy of detail has been lost. Some elaborate yew topiary (of which 17th-century drawings survive) has been reinstated to line the walk from the Parterre d'Eau to the Parterre de Latone. But in the 17th century there was much experimental topiary made of cypress, fir, holly, and pine. Much of the topiary today consists of simple shapes of clipped yew none of which is earlier than the 19th century. The *bosquets* were far more numerous and far richer in ornament than they are today. Jean Cotelle's painting of the Bosquet du Théâtre de l'Eau (1693) shows cascades, soaring water jets, rocaille work, trellises, and tall topiary pyramids against a background of billowing trees. The octagonal Bosquet d'Encelade was enclosed in a BERCEAU scented with honeysuckle and jasmine and decorated with several entrances framed in trellis-work. Today only the central pool with its fountain and the figure of the giant Encelade crushed under rocks hurled down from Mount Olympus remains. However, the *bosquet* of the Salle de Bal, damaged in the 1999 storm, has been finely restored—one of Le Nôtre's last designs, in the form of an amphitheatre with seats and an immense cascade with elaborate

rocaille work. No expense has been spared: the huge lead urns and *torchères* have been meticulously regilded (their original purpose was to reflect the light for evening balls). Another encouraging development was the reinstatement of the Bosquet des Trois Fontaines—demolished in the 18th century but put back into place in 2004 with much financial help from the American Friends of Versailles. Seventeenth-century illustrations of the gardens show flawlessly clipped PALISSADES often with niches to accommodate ornaments. These smooth *palissades* were characteristically backed by freely growing trees to emphasize how nature was mastered. This was one of the recurrent effects in the garden and nowhere today can it be seen precisely as it was. Lastly, what has become of the great number and range of plants which the records show flowed into the garden in the 17th century? The planting of ornamentals today is very sparse and there is little sense of the festive floriferousness of the past. Versailles in the 17th century was an exceptional example of a very large, intricately patterned garden of its time. There were many others but none on quite so grand a scale. No such garden of the period has been reinstated in convincingly authentic detail and if it were its upkeep would be prohibitive. One can experience 17th-century Versailles only by studying its remains, reading about it, and looking at contemporary illustrations.   PT

DOMINIQUE GARRIGUES, *Jardins et jardiniers de Versailles au grand siècle* (2001).
PIERRE-ANDRÉ LABLAUDE, *The Gardens of Versailles* (1995).
KENNETH WOODBRIDGE, *Princely Gardens* (1986).

vertugadin.

A French word meaning a kind of cushion worn by women on top of their dress to make them more shapely. In gardening, from the 17th century, it meant a sloping lawn or a lawn banked into an amphitheatre. See also BOULINGRIN; LAWN.   PT

Vesterholt, Inge (b. 1928) and **Jørgen** (1927–99), Danish landscape architects who specialized in large landscape projects such as motorways, the gravel pit Hedeland, the geometrical landforms of the Great Belt Link (1987–1999), and the Øresund Link (1995–2000) with its artificial peninsula at Kastrup and artificial island, Peberholmen, best seen from the air when taking off or landing at Copenhagen Airport. Other works include ODENSE UNIVERSITY and Galgebakken (1973). The latter is a housing development with courtyard or terraced houses with richly planted lanes with fruit trees and pergolas planted with climbing plants. Play areas are

Colour plates

The **Peter Newton Garden** in California, USA

The first terrace at the **Villa Lante**, Italy

Statue by Claude Poirier (1656–1729) of the nymph Arethusa above a cascade at **Courances**, France

Baroque parterres and fountain pool at **Drottningholm**, Uppland, Sweden

A chinoiserie pavilion in the Jardín del Principe at **Aranjuez**, Madrid, Spain

enclosed in willows and children may play anywhere.   AL

Vetter, Adolf

(1815–91), Austrian garden inspector in Vienna, a descendant of a German gardening family, director of the gardens of the Count Harrach in Bruck an der Leitha (Austria) from 1855. Due to his special knowledge of regeneration of decrepit citrus trees, he was appointed as garden inspector of the imperial garden of SCHÖNBRUNN in 1865. There he managed to restore the run-down baroque garden in an exemplary way. As an early exponent of the formal style, Vetter designed the layout for the garden at the large Conservatory in Schönbrunn with sunken parterres and evergreen topiary in 1883. Also his gardens of the imperial Hermesvilla (near Vienna) and of the Maria Theresien-Platz show the same style. The latter, his most important work, is located between the Museum of Art and the Museum of Natural History in Vienna and is one of the few extant formal garden squares of European historicism.   JM

Viana, Palacio de (Rejas de Don Gome) ✿

Córdoba, Andalusia, Spain, a largely 16th-century house built for the Viana family and owned in recent times by the Marqués de Viana but today the property of a bank, the Caja Provincial de Ahorros. It possesses a sequence of thirteen PATIO gardens of different flavours but all of great charm. They are instructive, too, for deploying the whole range of patio garden styles that are characteristic of Córdoba. Every kind of paving and surface materials is seen—bricks, pebbles, gravel, or sand—and varied planting. The reception patio, a fine cloistered space, is inlaid with an intricate regular pattern of dark and light pebbles. It is shaded by a central date palm and the entrance is garlanded with the West Indian *Cestrum nocturnum* whose flowers give off their scent at night. The Chapel Patio, also with cloisters, is surfaced with finely raked gravel and has plantings of old orange trees in simple circular beds and pots of ferns in the shade. The modern gate patio is paved in chequerboard dark and light pebbles. Water, in the form of pools, fountains, and canals, is everywhere. In the Patio of the Cats is a large sink for washing clothes and the enclosing walls are decorated with ivy, bougainvillea, and hanging flowerpots filled with pelargoniums. The Patio of the Grilles—with views out into the street—has a central fountain pool, paving of squares of pebbles, pots of *Senecio cineraria*, and, trained against the wall, bergamot orange (*Citrus bergamia*) with exceptionally scented flowers. An unenclosed garden has views over the rooftops of the city. A

parterre of venerable box hedges encloses a fountain pool surrounded by orange trees, date palms, and oleanders. A large and unusual evergreen oak *Quercus ilex* var. *ballota* casts its shade. The interior of the house, with many beautiful rooms, may also be visited. Of particular garden interest is an excellent collection of AZULEJOS ranging in date from the 13th to the 19th century.   PT

Vicobello, Villa ✿

Siena, Tuscany, Italy. Redesigned as a country house for the Chigi banking family by the great Sienese architect Baldassare Peruzzi (1481–1536) after his return from Rome in 1527, Vicobello lies at the top of a slope looking towards the walls of Siena. Peruzzi's balanced proportions and manipulation of space hold the design, based on a series of descending terraces, together. The main lemon garden lies to the south side of the square villa through a handsome gateway, its focal point a grove of tall cypresses sheltering an elegant niche. Lemons in pots sit in box-edged beds of grass in front of the big *stanzone* (shelter for overwintering citrus plants). Below the villa, terraces fall down the slope, linked by attractive splayed brick steps, the third terrace added in the 18th century dominated by a giant *Ginkgo biloba*. The Chigi coat of arms, a mound of money bags (or small hills), is carved in stone on the second terrace. To the north of the villa a shady wood of ilex and bay laurel provides a modern access, avoiding the attractive courtyard behind the house. Although the garden needs extensive restoration, Peruzzi's manipulation of garden spaces can still be admired.   PHo

Viczay Park. See HÉDERVÁR.

Vienna, Ringstraße parks,

Austria.The Ringstraße is a grand boulevard with four-row ALLÉES, linking parks, and monumental buildings, initiated by Emperor Franz Joseph I after the demolition of the late medieval city walls on the site of the earth ramparts, and gradually constructed from 1857.

Burggarten
Originally the Kaisergarten of medieval origin, it had its heyday under Emperor Ferdinand I (1521–64) with numerous built structures, which do not survive, and garden features in the present city area between Michaelerplatz and the former Josefsplatz. In 1809 the Augustinerschanze defences were demolished by Napoleon and a new garden created between 1817 and 1819 for the imperial family by architect Ludwig von Remy and court gardener Franz ANTOINE the elder. A large glasshouse by Remy was remodelled as a winter garden around 1840,

demolished around 1900, and rebuilt in 1902–6 by architect Friedrich Ohmann in *Jugendstil*. The years 1847–8 saw the first, and from 1863 the second, landscaping of the Biedermeier garden in English style, with rare and exotic trees, by court gardener Franz ANTOINE the younger. In 1909 the approach to the Neue Hofburg in Burggarten was remodelled by architect Ludwig Baumann.

Maria Theresien Park
Between the two royal museums (today the Naturhistorisches Museum and Kunsthistorisches Museum) as part of Gottfried Semper's planned Kaiserforum, this garden was laid out in 1884–8 by court gardener Adolf VETTER with a French parterre arrangement and topiary, framed in pine trees with magnificent fountains and statues (Vetter was the saviour of SCHÖNBRUNN baroque gardens and the most important exponent of neo-baroque garden art in Vienna). At the centre of the park stands the imposing monument to Empress Maria Theresa, designed by sculptor Anton Dominik von Fernkorn in 1863 and erected 1874–88.

Rathauspark
This park was executed in 1870–3 at the instigation of Mayor Cajetan Felder as an additional recreational area to the Stadtpark in a mixed landscape and geometrical style by city gardener Rudolf Siebeck; it contains numerous monuments, rare trees, and fountains.

Stadtpark
The Stadtpark was laid out from 1860 on the initiative of Viennese citizens to design sketches in the English style by painter Josef Selleny, executed with alterations by city gardener Rudolf Siebeck, and extended with a children's park on the opposite bank of the Wienfluss in 1863. The *casino* building and an artificial lake, with numerous monuments (notably that to Johann Strauss, erected 1904–21) and rare trees, determine its overall appearance along the Ringstraße.The Wienflussportal with its stairs, pavilions, and sculptures, designed and executed in 1903–6 by architects Friedrich Ohmann and Josef Hackhofer, is among the most important *Jugendstil* structures in Vienna.

Volksgarten
On the site of the Burgbastei bastion built by Emperor Franz I, blown up in 1809 by French troops and still state property, the Volksgarten was designed by architect Ludwig von Remy and court gardener Franz Antoine the elder. and laid out between 1817 and 1823. At the centre of the grounds stands the Theseustempel (1819–23) with Antonio Canova's Theseus groups and underground vaulted chambers for a collection of antiquities. The original Lombardy poplars

(in imitation of cypresses) were replaced with chestnut trees after 1860. The Cortisches coffee house by Pietro Nobile was built in 1820-3. The garden's geometrical arrangements of paths were modelled on Napoleonic gardens in Italy such as the Giardino del Popolo in Rome. In 1863-5 a neo-baroque garden alongside the Ringstraße was created by court gardener Franz Antoine the younger with the Grillparzer monument erected in 1877-89 (an important urban prospect to the Burgtheater and Naturhistorisches Museum). In 1903-7 one of the most important *Jugendstil* gardens in Vienna, designed by architect Friedrich Ohmann, was laid out alongside Löwelstraße with a monument to Empress Elisabeth.   GH

Vienna Belvedere. See BELVEDERE.

Vigeland Park ⊗
Oslo, Norway, is a sculpture park of 32 hectares/ 79 acres, laid out *c.*1931-50 after a plan by the sculptor Gustav Vigeland (1869-1943) in a geometric layout. The park contains *c.*200 sculptures in bronze, granite, and wrought iron, all by Vigeland. The main theme is the human being from childhood to old age and the cycle of life. The sculptures are mostly placed along the main east-west axis, 850 m/ 2,790 ft long. From the east the main entrance leads to a bridge across the Frogner dam, a large fountain surrounded by a flagstone labyrinth, the Monolith plateau at the top of a terraced hill, and finally *The Wheel of Life*. The Monolith is a 17-m/55-ft stone column of human sculptures. Between the dam and the fountain a parterre is planted with modern roses. A north-south transverse axis crosses the main axis at the fountain, its north end completed in 1988 with a large figure group called *The Clan*. All axes are lined with sycamores (*Acer pseudoplatanus*) and between these avenues are large lawns, used extensively for recreation all year round. The Vigeland Park was built within the grounds of the Frogner estate where today the main building houses Oslo City Museum, surrounded by a 19th-century landscape park and the remains of an 18th-century formal garden.   ME

Vigier, Villa ⊗
Canton of Solothurn, Switzerland. The Villa Vigier has a garden designed in 1648 in Renaissance style and redesigned in the 18th century as a baroque garden which is today among the best-preserved examples of its kind in Switzerland. The reign of Louis XIV in France had its consequences for building in Solothurn, the seat of the French ambassador to Switzerland; a series of town palaces and summer residences were built in the city

and the surrounding area from the mid 17th century until around 1720, among them the 'Sommerhaus von Vigier' built in 1648, probably by Philipp Wallier, a captain in French service, on the edge of the Renaissance city with the picturesque Jura Mountains in the background. The garden, then enclosed with arcades and walls with corner towers, originally followed the example of the French Renaissance garden with a sunken parterre as known before LE NÔTRE. It was, unlike the preferred terraced gardens of the Renaissance, symmetrically laid out on a level site and surrounded by high walls. After several changes of ownership the house and garden were acquired in 1777 by the treasurer of the French Embassy in Switzerland, François Louis Anzillon, Sieur de Berville. He redesigned the interior of the building and remodelled the garden in the baroque style. The 17th-century corner towers were replaced by sitting places in the eastern corner of the garden raised on a small mount to give views over the wall of the picturesque landscape and back to the house. The garden was bordered on the west side by a shady ALLÉE of lime trees. The *broderie* ornamentation in the small PARTERRE has long since disappeared, but the lawn areas are still enclosed by low clipped box hedges in their original geometrical forms. Clipped yews, over 200 years old, which appear on a plan dated 1763, are still the finest feature of the garden, surrounding a modest fountain on the main axis of the garden leading to the gate.   UW

Vignola, Jacopo (Giacomo) **Barozzi da** (1507-1573), Italian architect, painter, and architectural theorist. In 1550 Vignola settled permanently in Rome, where he worked as an architect for the papacy and for the Farnese family. In the early 1550s he worked on Villa GIULIA, which was conceived by Vasari in consultation with Michelangelo. Vignola was responsible for the construction of the villa, to which he planned to add two wings and a lozenge-shaped garden court. This plan was not realized, because in 1552 Bartolomeo AMMANATI was commissioned to redesign much of the court and NYMPHÄEUM, so the rectangular court and the nymphaeum are the work of Ammanati. Vignola's only contribution to the garden was the hydraulics for the fountains.

Vignola's finest gardens are at Villa FARNESE in Caprarola. The building is pentagonal, and gardens project from the two sides at the rear. Some 400 m/1,300 ft beyond the summer garden Vignola placed an exquisite GIARDINO SEGRETO which is reached by a ramp divided by a *catena d'acqua* (literally 'water chain', an ornamental cascade); the garden around the CASINO was memorably declared by Vasari to have been born rather than built.

Vignola is known to have visited the Villa Gambara (now Villa LANTE), Bagnaia, in 1568, and the similarity of features such as the sculpted *catena d'acqua* that runs along the axis of this magnificent garden to the one at Caprarola has rightly led to the garden being attributed to Vignola.   GC

Villandry, Château de ⊗
Villandry, Indre-et-Loire, France, was built shortly after 1532 when the estate was acquired by Jean Breton. The gardens here were famous in the 16th century but an 18th-century owner, the Marquis de Castellane, thought them old fashioned and put in their place an English-style park. The chateau overlooks the river Cher, upstream from the point where it flows into the Loire. In the early 20th century the estate was bought by Dr Joachim Carvallo who restored the chateau to its Renaissance appearance and set about making an appropriate garden. In the absence of any information about the appearance of the original garden Dr Carvallo took his inspiration from the engravings of 16th-century gardens by Jacques Androuet DU CERCEAU. The gently sloping ground was terraced and at the lowest level Carvallo laid out what has become the most famous feature of the garden—the ornamental POTAGER. The space was divided into nine squares each of which was further divided into an intricate pattern of beds edged with dwarf box. In these beds are grown two seasonal crops of vegetables—for spring and summer. The logistics of planting these two annual arrangements are fearsome but the result, superbly executed, is enchanting. In addition to the vegetables, many of which are chosen for their ornamental qualities, are seasonal plantings of annuals or biennials around the perimeter of each square. At each corner of the squares is a trellis-work BERCEAU veiled with climbing roses. Above the *potager* other gardens are deployed, rich in yew topiary, jets of water, shaped box hedges, and patterned beds of flowers. The garden at Villandry has an area of 5 hectares/12 acres and provides a magnificent and appropriate setting for the house. It may not be authentic in its details (many of the plants grown were unknown in the 16th century) but in its spirit it is wholly convincing and a delight to see.   PT

Villa Royale,
Kata Beach, Phuket, Thailand. Formerly a private estate owned by M. L. Tri Devakul, a prominent Thai architect, this was recently converted into a luxurious boutique hotel. It consists of assorted structures on a rocky terraced hill overlooking the Andaman Sea, linked by gardens planted with both native

and introduced specimens. The landscape is the creation of several designers over the years, most importantly the owner himself with advice from William Warren and Reimund Reisenger. Reisenger, a young German, was mainly responsible for collecting numerous native plants able to withstand the strong, salty winds that sweep in during the monsoon months between July and October with disastrous effect on more tender specimens. Another way of meeting this challenge is a glass-windowed loggia connecting several of the buildings that can be closed to protect an inner garden during storms and by planting a screen of salt-resistant trees and shrubs in more exposed areas. Such trees include sea almond (*Terminalia catappa*), ironwood (*Casuarina equistefolia*), and *Barringtonia asiatica*, all native to Phuket, while among the lower plants are sea hibiscus (*Hibiscus tiliaceus*), sea lettuce (*Scaevola*), coconut palms, wild crinum lilies, and several varieties of *Pandanus*. Some areas of the garden have lawns, in contrast to the otherwise dense planting on every level, and there is a formal series of pools extending down the hillside from what is now the lobby of the resort. Among plants used are *Asplenium* (bird's nest fern), *Anthurium*, *Costus*, *Alpinia*, and *Alocasia*, many of which came from forests on the island. The sea is visible from almost every point in the garden, sometimes as a glimpse of blue through the greenery, sometimes as a sweeping panorama.   WLW

Villette, Parc de la.
See PARIS PARKS AND GARDENS.

Vilmorin family,
French dynasty of nurserymen and seedsmen. The Vilmorin business had its beginnings in the 17th century when Nicaise Le Febvre (c.1610–1669), apothecary at the Jardin du Roi, had a nursery and apothecary's shop in Paris. At the invitation of Charles II he moved to London but the business continued under Pierre Geoffroy (d. 1728). His daughter married Pierre d'Andrieux (d. 1780), seedsman and botanist to Louis XV, who inherited the business, and it was their daughter Adelaide who married Philippe Victoire de Vilmorin (1746–1804). Philippe became a partner in the firm, with a shop on the quai de la Mégisserie (which survives) and nurseries in the rue d'Orillon and later in the rue de Reuilly. A broadsheet of 1769 and a catalogue of 1771 offered an impressive range of plants for sale.

In 1804 on the death of Philippe Victoire the business was continued by his son André de Vilmorin (1776–1862) who remained as head of the firm for nearly 40 years; then in 1843 the grandson of the founder, Pierre Louis François

(1816–60), took over. Pierre was a botanist, plant breeder, and geneticist, and set up an experimental farm at Verrières-le-Buisson 15 km/9 miles south of Paris. His son Charles Philippe Henry (1843–99) had similar qualifications and in 1882 he received the Légion d'Honneur for his scientific work. Known throughout the gardening world, he was later awarded the Veitch Memorial Medal of the ROYAL HORTICULTURAL SOCIETY. Henry's brother Auguste Louis Maurice (1849–1918) was a dendrologist and sylviculturist who founded the *Fruticetum Vilmorinianum*, later becoming the Arboretum National des BARRES, where many of the Chinese plants collected by Père Paul Farges (1844–1912) were grown. The nursery and experimentation continued under Maurice's son Jacques de Vilmorin (1882–1933), his cousin Joseph Marie Phillipe (1872–1917), and then Philippe's son Roger Marie Vincent Philippe (1905–80), who throughout his life was deeply involved in plant nomenclature, becoming president of the International Code of Botanical Nomenclature in 1954. For 47 years, until 1962, he directed the nursery, and on his retirement was engaged with M. Guinochet in a new *Flore de France*. The horticultural achievements of the family have earned it a worldwide reputation.   MC-C

Virgil
(Publius Vergilius Maro) (70–19 BC), Roman poet and gentleman farmer. The *Georgics*, regarded by many as Virgil's most polished work, is a poem of 2,188 lines on farming; as a literary masterpiece, it is more noted for its charm of expression than for its practical advice on husbandry. The four books into which the poem is divided treat of the cultivation of crops; trees, including the olive, and the vine; farm animals; and beekeeping. The references to gardens are incidental, and appropriately occur in Book 4. Violet beds are mentioned, also garden plots, guarded by Priapus, the god of fertility, that woo bees with the fragrance of their yellow flowers. Also mentioned are the twice-blooming rose beds of Paestum, the late-flowering narcissus, the shoot of curled acanthus, ivy, and myrtle. The garden of an old man of Corycus is described; his land was too poor for grazing or for growing the vine, but planted in flowers and trees, it was a haven for bees. Bordered with white lilies and verbena and poppy, it also contained hyacinths and roses and a great variety of trees set in rows.   WFJ

Virginia Water ✿
Egham, Surrey, England, lies at the southern extremity of the royal estate of Windsor Great Park (see WINDSOR CASTLE). It was boggy scrub land whose drainage was a problem from the

17th century. In the 1750s a great lake was formed under the supervision of the Duke of Cumberland which provided both a drainage pool and an ornament at the heart of a landscape which, once the land was drained, could be planted with fine trees, among them ash, beech, elm, oak, and sweet chestnut. A cascade, grotto, belvedere, and Palladian bridge were designed by the architect Henry Flitcroft (1697–1769). A Chinese tea house was built on an island in the lake, linked to the mainland by a CHINOISERIE bridge, and a Chinese junk sailed in the water—none of this survives. In around 1825 a magnificent chinoiserie fishing lodge was built, designed by Jeffry Wyatville (1766–1840); it was rebuilt in 1867–8 but demolished in the 20th century. In 1826, on the banks of the lake, were disposed the ruins of the Temple of Augustus from the Roman city of Leptis Magna. With excellent mature trees, and planned walks about the lake, this is one of the most enjoyable of the royal gardens.   PT

JANE ROBERTS, *Royal Landscape* (1997).

Vizcaya ✿
Miami, Florida, USA, an Italian Renaissance-style villa overlooking Biscayne Bay, was built in 1912–16 as a winter escape from Chicago for James Deering (1884–1925), heir to the International Harvester fortune. Originally a 73-hectare/180-acre estate with a dairy, citrus groves, and greenhouses (all under reconstruction), the property comprises 11 hectares/28 acres today, 5 hectares/12 acres of which are formal gardens. Deering hired École des Beaux-Arts-educated architect F. Burrall Hoffman Jr. (1884–1980) to design the white stucco mansion. Colombian-born landscape architect Diego Suarez (1888–1974), who trained under Arthur Acton in Florence, laid out the multi-levelled gardens, completed in 1922, using elements of 16th-century Italian gardens including spitting fountains and water stairways, and 17th-century French gardens including intricate parterres and ornately pruned trees. Borrowing from the styles and treasures of old Europe, the New York artist Paul Chalfin (1874–1959) oversaw all aesthetic decisions, interior and exterior. The collaboration of talents made for a sensational success. Grand limestone terraces extend east from the villa to stairs descending to an urn-adorned boat landing at the water's edge, and continue around to the south façade. The main garden fans south following a strong central axis, a grassy elevated island planted with an ALLÉE of podocarpus and flanked by pools and rows of sculpted live oaks (*Quercus virginiana*), which ascends to a baroque CASINO on an artificial mount. Geometrically laid paths intersect intricate parterres of

clipped Florida jasmine interplanted with pink pentas. Paths lead east to exquisite ancillary gardens: a maze, a theatre, and a secret garden.   HSS

Voisins, Château de,

Saint-Hilarion, Yvelines, France, was built in 1902 on the site of a 14th-century chateau by Comte Édouard de Fels in the style of Ange-Jacques Gabriel (1698–1782). Fels commissioned a new garden in keeping with the chateau from Henri DUCHÊNE. Instead of being based on an existing layout, or recreating a known design, Duchêne at Voisins was creating a classical revivalist garden based on what he knew of 18th-century French gardens. This he did on the grand scale with terracing, canals, long ALLÉES, and immense parterres. In all this his client collaborated. De Fels gave him suggestions for the design of the parterres, in particular one which 'resembles a huge tapis de la Savonnerie thrown on the ground of an outside salon'. Despite the inspiration of the past, Duchêne's design has a distinctly 20th-century flavour with a touch of chilly totalitarianism about it.
PT

Volcji Potok ⊛

Radomlje, Slovenia. Located at the foot of a wooded hill, the ARBORETUM comprises 82 hectares/203 acres with exceptionally varied natural habitats. Its manor, dating from the 17th century, was destroyed in the Second World War. The arboretum was established in 1885 by Ferdinand Souvan, a wholesale merchant from Ljubljana, and expanded by his son, architect Leon Souvan. He created a symmetrical box parterre with a surrounding frame of exotic conifers. This early garden has been developed since 1949 and was expanded by Ciril Jeglic (1897–1981), in both form and content, from 1955. The romantic tradition is reflected in the names of the parts connected with winding walks—White Magnolia Lake, Red Maple Lake, Fir Dale Lake, The Three Oaks, and the Islet. The collection of 2,500 taxa of woody plants is among the richest in Central Europe, with fine groups of conifers, maples, lime trees, birches, Japanese maples, and shrubs such as magnolias, viburnums, rhododendrons, and azaleas. Annual flower shows and social events take place in the arboretum and there is a nursery for the sale of plants.   AK

Volkspark Altona ⊛

Hamburg-Altona, Germany. In the last decades of the 19th century, the Prussian city of Altona (today a part of Hamburg) expanded rapidly. Parallel to developments in nearby Hamburg the administration of Altona decided to build a new *Volkspark* (people's park). Ferdinand Tutenberg (1847–1956), the first director of the green spaces department of Altona, soon developed a plan for a new park and work began in 1914. During the First World War little work could be done and the park was not completed until 1933. One of its most important elements is the old forest with beautiful trees and footpaths. To the west of the park a large cemetery was built and north of the park a sizeable arena. Today the park covers about 380 hectares/929 acres. The dahlia garden is especially attractive to visitors—the oldest existing dahlia garden in Europe, it displays more than 440 varieties. The Schulgarten, of 25 hectares/62 acres, is located on the eastern side. This garden, for the schoolchildren of Altona, is a beautiful flower garden with perennials, roses, and a small pavilion. Nearby, the Schleswig-Holstein-Garden was built to commemorate the Danish history of Altona. From the 1930s the sport arenas were gradually transformed into modern stadiums and arenas. The Volkspark, the largest park of Hamburg, also has areas for wildlife, sport, and leisure activities.   HG

Vondelpark ⊛

Amsterdam, Noord-Holland, the Netherlands, was named after Joost van den Vondel, the 17th-century poet whose statue was positioned in the first Dutch people's park in 1867. The issue of a park had been discussed in Amsterdam since the early 19th century, but there was a great reluctance to finance this from general resources. This is why in 1864 a 'society for the layout of a ride and promenading park' raised funds by private subscription and commissioned the landscape architects J. D. Zocher Jr. and L. P. Zocher (see ZOCHER family) to prepare designs. The park was laid out as and when resources became available, with the first section opening in 1865 and completion of successive parts in 1867, 1872, and 1877. While all designed in landscape style these stages of development can still be distinguished as different character areas. The first sections contained meadows with cows and there was a farm with a dairy, where milk was sold. There was also a BANDSTAND and an entertainment pavilion. The park remained in private hands, but with increasing maintenance costs was handed over to the council in 1953, since when it has been subjected to a number of restorations to deal with sinking ground levels and an increasingly high water table. Although there are few trees over 40 years of age, the historic structure of the park has been reasonably well maintained and was reviewed in 2000 by landscape architect Michiel van Gessel.   JW

GERRY ANDELA, 'The public park in the Netherlands', *Journal of Garden History*, Vol. 1: No. 4 (1981).

J. GADET, *Het Vondelpark: enig stadspark in Nederland* (1991).

Voorst, De ⊛

Eefde, Gelderland, the Netherlands, built by Arnold Joost van Keppel, Earl of Albemarle, one of William III's aides, between 1695 and 1697. Designed with the involvement of Jacob ROMAN and Daniel MAROT, the proposals for the gardens are well known through the engravings of the latter. It consisted of a large symmetrical formal baroque garden with parterres, forecourt, and avenue, the arrangement of the house and gardens bearing much resemblance to that of Het LOO. This layout was first altered around 1780, with the introduction of serpentine walks, with further features being altered to provide a less formal appearance. In the early 20th century both Leonard SPRINGER and Hugo POORTMAN provided designs to enhance the informal characteristics. The house was gutted by fire in 1943, but was restored externally between 1957 and 1960. The area of 104 hectares/257 acres still shows late 17th-century formal features, while seemingly natural informality of later overlays determines the character of the site, which is now managed by the Gelderland Trust.   JW

Voort, Pieter de La Court van der.
See COURT VAN DER VOORT, PIETER DE LA.

Vries, Hans Vredeman de

(1527–1606), Dutch artist, architect, and garden designer who was influential in the design of late Renaissance mannerist gardens (see RENAISSANCE GARDENS). His book *Hortorum Viridariorumque Elegantes et Multi Plicis Formae* (1583) was a pioneer garden pattern book whose illustrations determined the design of many European gardens in the late 16th and early 17th centuries. His gardens were rectilinear arrangements of hedges enclosing parterres with much use of tunnel BERCEAUX, fountains, elaborate TOPIARY, MAZES, and narrow *platesbandes* (see BORDER).   PT

W

Waddesdon Manor ⊛

near Aylesbury, Buckinghamshire, England, was completed in 1889 to the designs of Hippolyte Destailleur for Baron Ferdinand de Rothschild. Built like a Renaissance chateau on the Loire it stands on the top of a hill with magnificent views of the vale of Aylesbury. As the house was being built the grounds were landscaped by Élie Lainé who devised a pattern of carriage drives sweeping about the hill, the chief of which arrived at a rond-point (a circular space from which paths radiate) from which an avenue of oaks leads to the entrance of the house. The rond-point is ornamented with a marble group of Triton and frolicking Nereids by Giuliano Mozani (d. 1735). Mature trees were planted to give the grounds an instant air of maturity and south of the house a great terrace was laid out with a parterre planted out each year with bedding plants (50,000 of which were required to complete the scheme). At the centre of the terrace, now finely restored, is a pool with a fountain decorated with figures of Pluto and Proserpine, also by Mozani. Traditional bedding schemes are still put into place each year, and for the millennium the artist John Hubbard was commissioned to lay out a new bedding design which he did in flowing drifts of colour. Since 1957 Waddesdon and its gardens have belonged to the NATIONAL TRUST but the Rothschild family remains intimately involved with its fortunes.   PT

  BRENT ELLIOTT, *Waddesdon Manor: The Garden* (1994).

Wakehurst Place ⊛

near Hayward's Heath, West Sussex, England, is a 16th-century house which in the early 20th century was bought by Gerald Loder, of a distinguished gardening family with a particular interest in rhododendrons. Since 1965 it has been owned by the NATIONAL TRUST which leases it to the ROYAL BOTANIC GARDENS, KEW. With 69 hectares/170 acres of acid soil, in attractively undulating country, Wakehurst serves as a rural outpost for Kew specializing in trees and shrubs. National Collections are

held here of *Betula*, *Hypericum*, *Nothofagus*, and *Skimmia*. In addition to these there are very large numbers of other trees and flowering shrubs (particularly rhododendrons) and fine underplanting (especially of bulbs). Plants are grouped by genus, by habitat, or by geographic region. A collection of British natives is arranged by habitat—grassland, wetland, and woodland. Plants are arranged naturalistically so that the visitor may take a walk 'through the temperate woodlands of the world'. A more recent initiative is the Millennium Seed Bank which preserves frozen seeds in an underground vault. By 2010 24,000 different species should be stored here.   PT

Walenburg ⊛

Langbroek, Utrecht, the Netherlands, was leased in 1965 by the architect E. A. Canneman and his wife who rebuilt the 13th-century tower house and gate lodge. Inspired by their many visits to England they also transformed the moated gardens into a four-part layout divided by high beech hedges with a roundel in the centre. The layout and planting clearly reveals the influence of SISSINGHURST and borders contain the mixture of colour coordinated perennials and shrubs that has made it so famous. Following the death of Elias Canneman (1905–87) and later Lysbeth Canneman-Philipse (1909–87) the Dutch Gardens Trust maintained it for a while, but the estate has now been returned to the van Lynden van Sandenburg family, who live in it once again.   JW

  E. A. CANNEMAN, *Walenburg huis en hof* (1984).
  — 'The garden of Walenburg', *RHS Journal* (Apr. 1973).
  JOHN CORNFORTH, 'Walenburg, Holland: the home of Mr and Mrs E. A. Canneman', *Country Life*, Vol. 158: No. 4077 (21 Aug. 1975).

Wales. See BRITISH ISLES.

Wallich, Nathaniel

(1786–1854), Danish botanist and physician born in Copenhagen. Wallich was an

Anglophile and spent time in England, coming to the notice of Sir Joseph BANKS. In 1807 he joined the Danish East India Company as surgeon at Serampore. Six years later it was transferred to the British, and Wallich, on Banks's recommendation, was appointed superintendent of the East India Company's CALCUTTA BOTANIC GARDEN, a post he held for 26 years. Wallich botanized in the East Indies, the Himalayas, Nepal, and Burma, often using native collectors, sending vast numbers of specimens to Sir Joseph Banks in appreciation of his early patronage. Among Wallich's publications was *Plantae Asiaticae Rariories* (1830–32), hailed as a 'new glory to the British nation'. Wallich retired to England, where he was a Fellow of both the Linnean Society (1818) and the Royal Society (1829). The genus *Wallichia* consisting of three Himalayan palms was named in his honour.
MC-C

Walling, Edna

(1895–1973), acknowledged as Australia's most significant and prolific landscape designer. English born, she spent her early years in Devon, arriving in Australia *c.*1914. Her first works are English inspired, particularly by the writings of Gertrude JEKYLL. Walling's early garden designs show Jekyll's influence— the harmonious synthesis of formal and natural—in her strong architectural structure of stone walls and steps, terraces, balustrades, and pergolas. In her planting she used climbing, spreading, and self-seeding plants, bringing a naturalistic style and softening the formal landscaping. For three decades, from the 1920s to the 1950s, Walling designed many gardens of this kind, chiefly in Victoria, for well-to-do clients. Enduring examples of her work include Durrol and Mawarra in the hills outside Melbourne, and Ardgarten and Boortkoi in Victoria's Western District; Markdale and Kildrummie in New South Wales. Her work encompassed sophisticated town gardens for large city mansions, pastoral properties, and simple cottage gardens. At Mooroolbark, near Melbourne, Walling bought land in the 1920s, built herself a stone cottage, added more houses and gardens, and created Bickleigh Vale estate, a peaceful landscape of rustic simplicity, which remains today. Walling's own extensive writings over twenty years in *Australian Home Beautiful* magazine and her books—*Gardens in Australia* (1943), *Cottage and Garden* (1947), *A Gardener's Log* (1948), and *The Australian Roadside* (1952)—introduced and fostered a new interest and taste in garden design in Australia. Many have also come to share Walling's pioneering enthusiasm for the Australian flora and her environmental concerns, which stimulated others to explore this field.   CMR

Walpole, Horace, 4th Earl of Orford

(1717–97), English connoisseur and author, prince of dilettantes and notable instigator of fashion, in particular for the Gothic style of which his own house, Strawberry Hill (Twickenham), was a much-revered model. He was the author of *The History of the Modern Taste in Gardening* (1780) which sings the praises of William KENT and Capability BROWN and urges gardens to be 'set free from . . . prim regularity'. It is in this essay that he famously wrote of Kent: 'He leaped the fence, and saw that all nature was a garden.' Proponent of the naturalistic landscape park, enemy of arid formality, and devotee of heady romanticism, his own garden at Strawberry Hill, inspired by the fashion for the FERME ORNÉE, filled him with delight: 'I am just come out of the garden in the most oriental of all evenings, and from breathing odours beyond those of Araby. The acacias . . . are covered with blossoms, the honeysuckles dangle from every tree in festoons, the syringas are thickets of sweets.' Although he loved the Gothic he did not love gloom and thought it 'comic to set aside a quarter of one's garden to be melancholy in'. His journal and letters give often acute, sometimes ecstatically breathless, accounts of visits to the great gardens of his day. Of houses he was occasionally crisply dismissive—'vast rooms, no taste' was his opinion of Hardwick Hall (Derbyshire). His novel *The Castle of Otranto* (1764) extended his taste for the Gothic into the realms of literature and spawned many imitations.   PT

TIMOTHY MOWL, *Horace Walpole: The Great Outsider* (1996).

Wang Chuan Villa,

Shaanxi province, China, a country estate at the entrance to the valley of Wang Chuan, south-west of Lan Tian county in Shaanxi province, is perhaps the most famous private domain in Chinese history. It belonged to the Tang-dynasty poet and painter Wang Wei (699–759) who, retiring there from the then capital some 50 km/30 miles away, recorded it in poetry and painting on a long (and often copied) handscroll.

The valley was what the Chinese call a 'suddenly-opened-up space' with partially flat, partially undulating ground, a stream, a lake, and an island surrounded by layers of steeply folded hills. Along the rocky shore Wang Wei described twenty views, usually focusing on or seen from a different lodge or summer house. Some of these were double-storeyed halls, with upturned eaves above open balconies; others

like the Cottage in Bamboo Forest or Apricot-Veined Cottage reflected an ideal of rustic simplicity. Flowering fruit trees, willows, and *wutong*, Chinese parasol trees (*Firmiana simplex*), grew around them, making each a little green cell of its own, while stiff pine trees grew thickly on the hills behind. The villa itself lay to the south near the Lu Yuan, or Deer-Park Temple, a rambling series of rooms, pavilions, and halls connected by bridges, winding paths, and *lang* (see CHINA) walkways. Wang Wei's great scroll made sure of his garden's continuing fame, but it was his own character, as poet, musician, painter, calligrapher, and man, that ensures its place in Chinese culture.   G-ZW/MK

Wangshi Yuan ⊛

Jiangsu province, China, situated in 0·6 hectare/1.5 acres in the south-eastern district of SUZHOU, has been the site of a garden since the 12th century. Among the smallest of the famous gardens restored in this city, like them it is hidden away behind high white-plastered walls. Three large, dark, and formal halls, symmetrically placed one behind the other with living accommodation above and tiny, open courts between them, occupy the south-east corner of the site, and the garden—informal, intricate, sparkling, and lively—gains much from this juxtaposition.

Originally built in 1140 by Shi Zhengzhi, a cultivated scholar-official, the garden surrounded his library, the Studio of Ten Thousand Scrolls, and he called it Yuyin (Fisherman's Retreat) to suggest his love of simple pleasures. After him, the garden slips into obscurity until it reappears in records of 1760 undergoing formidable rebuilding by the second of its great designers, Song Zenghuan. A vice-director of imperial entertainment at the court of Qianlong, Song gave the garden the name it still has today, Wang Shi, after his own pen name meaning Master of the Fishing Nets—a nice allusion to the original garden.

Again neglected (by the late 18th century only the pond remained), the Wangshi Yuan was rescued by Qu Yuancun who had it rebuilt by local craftsmen to his own design. He chose many of the names (such as 'A Branch Beyond the Bamboo' and 'Washing Cap-String Pavilion') which, with their allusive literary references, are part of the pleasures offered by the garden. Since then, successive owners have elaborated a composition of more than ten tiny, enclosed gardens and over a dozen different halls and pavilions around the central pond.

Though two doorways connect it directly with the house, the garden has its own small entrance off a narrow alleyway between houses along busy Youyi Street. Its simple door leads onto a plain corridor open to the sky between

white walls. At the end, a sharp right-angled turn reveals a small rectangular courtyard, a fine water-modelled Taihu rock (the rock most highly prized for artificial 'mountains') standing among other stones and shrubs, and full-length pivoting windows which open into a hall. From here there are several ways to go, for the garden is a composition of courtyards fitted together as intricately as a Chinese puzzle. At the beginning they act as a kind of layering, gradually separating the visitor from the world of the city outside. The culmination of this process is the little rocky-bordered lake—the enclosing courtyards opening at last onto what seems by comparison far wider than its 350-sq.-m/1,144-sq.-ft area, with trees and shrubs half hiding many different buildings scattered irregularly around the water's edge.

On the bank opposite the house, raised on rocky stilts above the water, its swooping eaves and trellised seats reflected below, is the Pavilion of the Moon Appearing and the Breeze Arriving. As the focal point of the garden, its function is partly to lure the visitor to explore further, since to reach it he has had to choose to go either left or right around the lake. Either way, he will be diverted from his path by many unexpected delights: to the left the Barrier of Clouds Hall with its glassy interior hidden from the lake by a high rocky bank; the little Lute Garden with its secret courtyard beyond a bamboo grove; the nursery garden with its rows of seasonal flowers in pots, and the Washing Cap-String Pavilion, its terrace overlooking the pool. To the right, a covered walkway zigzags to some smaller garden courts, and thence to the garden's most formal building, the Hall for Viewing the Pines and Seeing a Painting, set back from the lake with its windows opening out onto a low bank still nurturing a group of aged cypress and *Podocarpus*. Beyond this lies the peaceful, rocky-bordered courtyard of the Late Spring Studio, used as a model for the Astor Court garden in the Metropolitan Museum of New York. In a second, smaller studio, tucked into the most westerly corner of this court, a well-known painter Zhang Daqian worked in the 1930s. Although in this garden each individual building, and the house and its small yards, are all strictly rectangular, the different parts do not fit together perfectly and leftover slivers of space are planted with bamboo and rocks to bring light and air into even the smaller rooms. Wangshi Yuan is one of the most intricate and subtle of Suzhou's old gardens—exceptional in the grace of its swoop-eaved porches, in the balance of high and low, open and enclosed spaces, and in the fine quality of its building and decoration, well restored and preserved. Usually the garden most liked by foreigners, it still retains the feeling of a place long and deeply loved.   MK

Wang Takrai,

Nakorn Nayoke, Thailand. The Pool of Takrai is named after the culinary plant *Cymbopogon citratus*, popularly known as lemon grass and, in Thai, as *ta-krai*. This country park created by Princess Chumbhot is in the foothills of the Kao Yai Range north-east of Bangkok, near the famous waterfalls at Salika and Nangrong. There are wide areas of grass (*Zoysia matrella*), and precipitous mountain streams feed a great pool within a grove of enormous madeua trees (*Ficus glomerata*). A collection of native Thai plants and many annuals from temperate climates have been allowed to naturalize. Among the most impressive trees are the erythrinas (including a group of *E. christa-galli*), *Bombax malabaricum*, and various cassias and jacarandas, tabebuias, phyllocladus, and cochlospermums.   MLL/WLW

Ward, Frank Kingdon

(1885–1958), plant collector. After attending Cambridge, Ward went to Shanghai as a schoolmaster but almost immediately set off into the interior on the first of many plant hunting expeditions during which he showed a flair for finding and selecting choice plants for gardens. For the next 50 years he travelled constantly throughout China, Burma, Tibet, and Thailand, and his introductions included rhododendrons, primulas, meconopsis, especially *Meconopsis betonicifolia*, gentians, and lilies. Ward was a prolific and vivid writer, describing all his travels in such books as *Land of the Blue Poppy* (1913), *In Farthest Burma* (1921), and *Plant Hunting on the Edge of the World* (1930); he had outstanding photographic skills, and was a knowledgeable geologist. During the Second World War he organized a jungle-survival school for the army. In 1932 Ward received the RHS Victoria Medal of Honour and in 1934 the Veitch Memorial Medal.   MC-C

Wardian Case.

Nathaniel Bagshaw Ward (1791–1868) was an English physician, botanist, and inventor. His most influential invention was the Wardian Case which was a sealed glass case for transporting plants which allowed the constant recycling of water by absorption and transpiration. This allowed plants to survive unscathed the very long sea journeys from their native countries and was in use by the 1830s. Sir William Hooker (see HOOKER, SIR JOSEPH DALTON), the director of KEW, said that in the fifteen years 1836–51 the Wardian Case has 'been the means . . . of introducing more new and valuable plants to our gardens than were

imported during the preceding century'. It was also used by Kew from the 1850s to distribute useful plants to the colonies and thus played a key role in one of the most important of Kew's activities. In the single year of 1851 useful plants were sent to British Honduras, India, Jamaica, New Zealand, Sierra Leone, Tasmania, and Trinidad. Without the Wardian Case the long-distance gathering and distribution of plants would have been impossible and in many cases it had a profound effect on the world economy. In 1876, for example, Brazilian rubber (*Hevea brasiliensis*) arrived at Kew and was sent out to Malaya (part of modern Malaysia) where by 1909 40,000,000 trees were planted and the Malayan rubber industry was founded. Nathaniel Ward described his invention in *On the Growth of Plants in Closely Glazed Cases* (1842). His name is commemorated in the genus of South American mosses *Wardia*.
PT

Warmelo ⊗

Diepenheim, Overijssel, the Netherlands, was originally a late medieval estate, which from 1633 to 1872 was owned by the Sloet family. Although the house was demolished in 1874 and the present house built, the structure of the gardens had been determined by this stage. On this double moated site part of the outer moat has been filled in to provide a more immediate connection with the landscape park. The new house reused the base of the demolished building as the terrace wall for the gardens. From the late 1920s the landscape architect Hugo POORTMAN made proposals; the area between the moats, including the 'French' formal garden, two rose gardens, and the well garden just outside, all date from this era, as well as the landscape park. The last is dominated by a large lake, while the French garden has sculpted hedges and shaped yew trees, and the well garden has Egyptian style features. During the occupation of Princess Armgard von Lippe Biesterfeld between 1952 and 1971 a rhododendron garden with many conifers was added, designed by Tjaard Koning (1916–92) in 1958.   JW

Warwick Castle ⊗

Warwick, Warwickshire, England, dates from the 11th century although most of the extant castle is 14th century. Its position, on a hill high above a loop of the river Avon, gave rise to marvellous possibilities of landscape design. There were terraced formal gardens here in the 16th century which remained in place until the early 18th century. From 1750 Capability BROWN laid out a new landscape for Lord Brooke (later 1st Earl of Warwick) which is seen in a painting by Canaletto of 1753. Horace WALPOLE saw the

first stage in 1751 and wrote 'little Brooke . . . has submitted to let his garden and park be natural'. The site of the formal garden was shrouded with clumps of trees and a path winds up the Norman mound. Brown also opened out views of the river, with a lawn sweeping down the hill to its banks. At the head of this slope a great orangery was built before 1788 to house the Roman Warwick Vase. In 1868 Robert MARNOCK laid out a lily pool at the centre of a dazzling yew parterre. Marnock also designed a formal but romantic rose garden, destroyed in the 1930s but handsomely reinstated when the plans were discovered in the 1980s. Today, run as a tourist attraction, the gardens are impeccably kept and, with their fine 18th- and 19th-century features, they give great pleasure.   PT

Washington Park Arboretum ⊗

Seattle, Washington, USA, was designed by James Dawson (1874–1941) of the Olmsted Brothers firm, and was founded in the 1930s with funds and labour from the Works Progress Administration, which provided relief during the Depression. Covering 93 hectares/230 acres in the heart of the city, and encompassing collections of *Rhododendron*, *Cornus*, *Malus*, *Ilex*, *Magnolia*, *Camellia*, *Sorbus*, *Quercus*, and *Acer*, the arboretum also has miles of trails for walking and birdwatching, several ponds, and wetlands. The University of Washington's Center for Urban Horticulture manages the collections and offers public education programmes. Plant sales held in spring and autumn offer plants from the region's 50 largest nurseries. The Winter Garden is a most popular attraction, with colour from late November until late March. Cedars and firs provide the backdrop for stewartias and paperbark maples (*Acer griseum*) with ornamental winter bark, flowering *Hamamelis*, and redtwig and yellowtwig dogwoods (*Cornus stolonifera* 'Kelseyi' and *C.s.* 'Flaviramea'). Among the winter-flowering shrubs are *Erica*, *Chimonanthus*, *Sarcococca*, *Viburnum* × *bodnantense* 'Dawn', *Mahonia* 'Arthur Menzies', *Camellia sasanqua*, and *Daphne odora* 'Aureo-marginata'. Spring highlights the arboretum's flowering cherries, rhododendrons, and azaleas, including a tree-sized specimen of *Rhododendron sutchuenense*. Ninety Japanese maples, including *Acer palmatum* 'Beni-schichihenge', *A. palmatum* 'Ukigumo', *A. palmatum* 'Seiryu', and *A. japonicum* 'Aconitifolium', provide autumn colour, and comprise the largest such collection in the United States. A New Zealand Exhibit, a gift from Seattle's sister city, Christchurch, imitates a subalpine tussock grassland, with a trail wandering through a small mountain pass framed by large granite boulders.   BBA

waterfall. See CASCADE.

water in the garden.
'Water is of as much use in a landscape, as Blood is in a body,' wrote William GILPIN in *A Dialogue upon the Gardens at Stowe* (1748). There is no garden without water. Plants cannot live without it and evolution has shown astonishing ingenuity in creating plants in drylands which store water to allow survival in the arid months. As an ornamental ingredient of gardens water has elicited the greatest inventiveness in designers who, from the earliest gardens known right up to the delightful computer-controlled fountains of the 21st century, have shown their relish for its beauty and versatility. In Persian gardens, from Cyrus the Great's garden at PASARGADAE made after 550 BC, water was celebrated as essential to life and an object of beauty. The CHAHAR BAGH, the garden divided into four by rills meeting at a central pool, which so strongly influenced Islamic gardens, proved to be one of the longest-lived ways of laying out a garden. From Persia it spread both to Mughal India and westwards with Islam where it may still be seen in the ALHAMBRA. Here the water is used in expansive pools or arranged like a *chahar bagh* in an intimate patio. In the Alhambra such moving water as there is moves gently, in trickles or burbling in gentle eruptions. In the GENERALIFE the famous Patio de la Acequia (Water Patio) was originally a quadripartite arrangement of rills and flower beds. Its present arrangement, so familiar in countless photographs, of overarching water spouts is a 19th-century addition. Islamic gardens also made an ornament of the essentially practical matter of irrigation, laying out subtle patterns of rills to water formal orange groves, as may still be seen in the Patio de los NARANJOS at Córdoba. In the atmospheric remains of the extraordinary Islamic garden palace of 10th-century MADINAT AL-ZAHRA the remains of great pools may still be seen. These were used to reflect light into buildings shaded by overhanging roofs. In Spanish and Portuguese gardens water has been used skilfully in gardens since the Islamic period, in gardens of Versailles-like splendour, such as La GRANJA, but universally in much more modest gardens. In the garden of the delightful PAZO DE OCA, a 17th-century manor house, water is used purely ornamentally but also an out-of-doors laundry, like an elegant pavilion, adds to the decorative scheme. In the same way the CISTERNS so often found in Portuguese gardens are given decorative purpose. At the Palácio FRONTEIRA in Lisbon such a water tank is made the centrepiece of the garden, with flanking pavilions, and staircases leading to a terrace walk about the cistern—the whole brilliantly decorated with tiles. A rare example of 20th-century use of water on the grand scale is at the Parque de SERRALVES where Jacques Gréber (1882–1962) laid out a brilliant sequence of pools, channels, and fountains for an international modern-style garden of the 1930s.

In Chinese and Japanese gardens water is used with the greatest refinement. In Chinese gardens mountains and water were the vital ingredients, sometimes in the form of water-worn rocks rising like mountains from swirling raked sand. Water was almost invariably treated in this naturalistic way. In Japanese gardens cascades, pools, and streams are also invariably treated in a naturalistic fashion and the movement of water was the subject of a whole aesthetic. A typology of moving water spelt out the different effects from water rippling gently over pebbles to a torrential downpour in a stepped cascade. The sound of a periodic drip of water from a balanced bamboo tube into a small container is a quintessential Japanese garden sound. In Zen temple gardens raked fine sand is used to evoke the flow of water. In Buddhist gardens water had symbolic value, water's journey from the mountains to the sea symbolizing the journey of a human's life.

In Italian Renaissance gardens water is a perennial theme. The science of hydraulics was closely studied by Renaissance scholars and its ornamental possibilties well understood. Agostino Ramelli's *Le diverse e artificiose machine* (Diverse Ingenious Machines) (1588) was ostensibly a textbook but it also shows how water may be harnessed to provide power for twittering birds, moving figures, and GIOCHI D'ACQUA. At PRATOLINO John EVELYN in 1645 described 'a large walke, at the sides whereof several slender streams of water gush out of pipes concealed underneath, that interchangeably fall into each others channells, making a lofty and perfect arch, so that a man on horseback may ride under it and not receive one drop of wet'. The *giochi d'acqua*, the water tricks that delighted visitors, were often found in GROTTOES. In Italian Renaissance gardens water is intricately interwoven into the garden's layout and the river gods who presided over water's most important source were frequently evoked in garden statues. At the Villa d'ESTE (Tivoli) water achieved its apotheosis in the sequence of fountains, cascades, and pools animating a sequence of terraces on a steep slope.

In France the use of water in gardens was strongly influenced by the Italian connection which flourished after Catherine de Médicis married the Duke of Orléans (later Henri II) in 1533. When the new gardens were laid out at SAINT GERMAIN-EN-LAYE in the late 16th century the Florentine Alessandro FRANCINI was in charge of the elaborate water features of the new terraced gardens. Francini had worked on several Tuscan gardens, including Pratolino, and came to live permanently in France in 1600. He became *intendant général des eaux et fontaines* to the King, putting him in charge of all garden waterworks and grottoes. In this role he was, from 1613, in charge of the water for Marie de Médicis's new gardens at the Palais du Luxembourg (see PARIS PARKS AND GARDENS) for which he built a GROTTO, the Fontaine des Médicis. To supply water for the Luxembourg gardens there was built an aqueduct from Rungis 11.5 km/7 miles to the south. The role of *fontainier* was so important at the Luxembourg gardens that an elegant house was built to accommodate him close to the Observatoire which may still be seen today. The water supply for the Luxembourg gardens also supplied all public water to the left bank of Paris and remained its chief source until the 1860s. In the latter part of the 17th century André LE NÔTRE used water on a spectacular scale, often using canals as major structural ingredients in the landscape at CHANTILLY, DAMPIERRE, and VERSAILLES. Le Nôtre also relished a fountain but at Versailles there was a perennial problem about water supply. Even today the great fountains play only on occasional days.

In the Low Countries, where managing water is a matter of survival, canals often served to drain the land and moated houses are a commonplace. Canals were used inventively in 17th-century gardens of the Netherlands, with examples at CLINGENDAEL, Heemstede (Utrecht), ZORGVLIET, and, most spectacularly, at ZEIST where a very elaborate pattern of canals and moats formed the garden's framework. Fountains were also used in Netherlands gardens of this period but there was frequently the problem of finding a sufficient fall of land to create enough pressure to power a substantial water jet. At Het LOO the great King's Fountain, a single jet 14 m/45 ft high, was powered by water brought from higher ground 10 km/6 miles away.

In England a group of early 17th-century gardens of Renaissance influence in which water played a major part is associated with Salomon de CAUS—at Greenwich (London), HATFIELD, Richmond Palace (Surrey), and at WILTON. Canal gardens influenced by the Low Countries appeared in England towards the end of the 17th century of which WESTBURY COURT is a rare survival. The gardens depicted in *Britannia Illustrata* (1707) show the importance of water in late 17th-century English layouts. Formal pools, elaborate fountains, and canals were an essential part of the garden vocabulary of such designers as George LONDON and Henry WISE as well as those, like Charles BRIDGEMAN, who came to the fore early in the 18th century. In Wales a remarkable water garden was made by Humphrey Mackworth at the GNOLL near Swansea. A copper smelter, he came here in the late 17th century drawn by the plentiful supply of water power. He was also aware of the beauty of water, creating a great formal cascade in the 1720s and, a little later, an extraordinary naturalistic cascade at the head of a wooded valley, with a fall of 60 m/200 ft—one of the earliest known naturalistic cascades. Both cascades survive, as do traces of Mackworth's romantic woodland garden. In the landscape garden water was a *sine qua non*. In Capability BROWN's case the serpentine lake in the middle distance became almost a cliché and cascades and waterside grottoes were also frequently used in landscape gardens. Some of the most interesting 18th-century British gardens were drawn to the special possibilities of a riverine setting. At Corby Castle (Cumbria) from 1707 Thomas Howard laid out a garden by the river Eden whose rocky banks he animated with grottoes, a statue of Polyphemus, and temples linked by a planned walk. Howard made an explicit connection with Milton's description of the Garden of Eden in *Paradise Lost*—the 'steep wilderness; whose hairie sides | With thicket overgrown, grottesque and wilde'. He used the setting for a performance of his own masque, *Sensuality Subdued*, inspired by Milton's *Comus*.

The more explicitly picturesque gardens of the later 18th century were particularly drawn to the flowing water of rivers. At PIERCEFIELD, Richard Payne KNIGHT's Downton Castle (Shropshire), and Thomas Johnes's HAFOD the picturesque scenery of the river was the essential attribute of the landscape. At Hackfall Wood (North Yorkshire) the beauties of the river Ure so inspired William AISLABIE that he made a picturesque landscape park on its banks even though there was no house here. In the 19th and 20th centuries water assumed a new role in woodland gardens. Here the moist banks of streams and pools provided the conditions for the herbaceous perennials that are so ornamental in a woodland setting—ferns, *Gunnera manicata*, Himalayan poppies, irises and primulas, and *Lysichiton americanus*. The chapter on 'Brook-side, Water and Bog Gardens' in William Robinson's *The Wild Garden* (1870) inspired countless gardeners to make naturalistic water gardens. Gertrude Jekyll's *Wall and Water Gardens* (1901) argues that it is in 'smaller ponds and pools . . . that most pleasure in true water-gardening may be had'. She emphasizes the wealth of native plants suitable for planting in such gardens. In the late 20th century water was seen, also, as a vital part

of the larger ecology and desirable for that reason.

In the late 20th and early 21st centuries water remains a most expressive and versatile medium in gardens. Isabelle GREENE for a dry garden in southern California, the VALENTINE GARDEN, in a notably dry climate wittily made a flowing stream of slabs of stone to unify a small garden. At SHUTE HOUSE, a distinctly watery garden, Geoffrey JELLICOE brilliantly deployed water's various possibilities, formal and informal, moving and still. For the garden of St Catherine's College, Oxford, Arne JACOBSEN *c.*1962 created visual unity with a long slender canal linking the college buildings with their landscape. Penelope HOBHOUSE was inspired by Italian Renaissance gardens for the new garden she designed at Walmer Castle (Kent) completed in 1995 to celebrate the 95th birthday of Queen Elizabeth the Queen Mother. Its centrepiece is a canal-like lily pool overlooked by an arcaded loggia. Computer-controlled fountains in public places like the Parc André Citroën (Paris) and Somerset House (London) are beautiful and delight visitors. The spectacular cascade designed by Jacques WIRTZ and his son Peter for Alnwick Castle (Northumberland), which is also computer controlled, vividly shows the continuing life of an old garden feature. Wirtz, from Flanders, was brought up with water and very few of his gardens are without it. See also CANAL; CASCADE; CISTERNS AND WATER TANKS; GIOCHI D'ACQUA.   PT

Wave Hill ⊛

Riverdale, New York, USA, was built as a country retreat by William Lewis Morris in 1843. The property overlooks the Hudson river to a backdrop of the cliffs of the Palisades, opposite. A series of succeeding owners expanded the residence and added gardens and greenhouses. Notable residents include Theodore Roosevelt's family (1870–1), Mark Twain (1901–3), Arturo Toscanini (1943–5), and the British delegation to the United Nations (1950s). The Perkins-Freeman family, last private owners of the property, presented the estate to the city of New York in 1960. Wave Hill, Inc., a non-profit corporation, has since expanded the mission, programmes, and facilities to accommodate a public audience. The romantic landscape of Wave Hill encompasses 11 hectares/28 acres of woodlands, lawns, and gardens, along with two historic mansions, a series of glasshouses, and other garden structures. The landscape vision of the current composition of gardens and greenhouses is credited to the former director of horticulture, Marco Polo Stufano, who came to an overgrown Wave Hill in 1967. Stufano combined a respect for historic

gardens with a passion for plants and oversaw the revival and expansion of an exceptional series of gardens and collections there. The central garden, called the Old-Fashioned Flower Garden, was redesigned by John Nally (d. 1988) in an existing large rectangular garden along one of the greenhouses, in 1985. It contains a luxuriant massing of annuals and perennials, with a great range of scale. Striking colour and textural combinations, always in experimental flux, are characteristic of this garden. New introductions and the reinvention of garden plantings are now an established component of Wave Hill's horticultural mission.

The Conservatory, Greenhouses, and the Alpine House displays also give evidence of the collecting passion (Wave Hill has its own import permit) of the gardens' stewards. Extraordinary combinations of exotic specimens are a feast to the eye and the botanical heart. Shrub borders and scattered specimen trees and shrubs punctuate the landscape and separate some of the more formal gardens. The Wild Garden, a free-ranging collection of wild exotic and indigenous plants, holds more to the ROBINSONIAN vision of a wild garden than to the current fashion for indigenous collections. Other gardens include a Herb Garden, a Monocot Garden, an Aquatic Garden, a Pergola Garden, a Dry Garden, and woodland collections. Wave Hill also houses several cultural programmes within its environs. Concert series and other performing arts are staged regularly here. Art exhibits, historic landscape exhibitions, and outdoor sculpture installations are popular, and regular workshops in horticulture and the arts are offered to the public. Lying a half-hour from the heart of New York city, it combines the richness of a botanic garden with the intimate experiences of private gardens. Wave Hill presents a remarkable contrast of senses and sensibilities, and is a model for the possibilities of modest properties and urban spaces. It is one of America's best examples of hybrid design vigour.   PC

Weald and Downland Museum ⊛

near Chichester, West Sussex, England, opened to the public in 1970. It is a collection of vernacular buildings from the Weald and Downland areas of south-east England ranging from the 13th to the 19th century and disposed in the open air in a magnificent valley setting. For several of the houses appropriate VERNACULAR GARDENS have been laid out, using period plants and giving a vivid notion of their garden settings. The 15th-century Bayleaf farmhouse, for example, has an area of

managed woodland, an orchard, and a wattle-fenced kitchen garden showing the range of vegetables cultivated in the late Middle Ages with a few flowering ornamentals among them. A 17th-century cottage, by contrast, shows the greater range of vegetables grown by that time. An early 19th-century Toll Cottage has a dazzling little cottage garden, packed with flowers and enclosed in a white picket fence.
PT

Weimar Belvedere. See BELVEDERE.

Weldam, Kasteel ⚘
Goor, Overijssel, the Netherlands, a 14th-century castle that probably reached its present form with the rebuilding in 1645. The structure of the gardens, laid out in a typical Dutch classicist manner on a double moated site, probably also dates from this time. In 1879 when the van Aldenburg Bentinck-van Heeckeren van Wassenaar family became the new occupiers, they made large-scale alterations, consulting Édouard ANDRÉ whose plans were executed in 1885/6. He slightly changed the original configuration of the garden, filling in a moat and reinforcing the symmetry. The neo-baroque garden included PARTERRES *de broderie*, a maze, and a spectacular beech bower. André left the execution of the design to his pupil Hugo POORTMAN, who continued to work at Weldam from 1887 until 1915 while also taking on other design commissions. It is this late 19th-century layout that survives and determines the character today, though it has been slightly modified in order to simplify maintenance. JW

Wellington Botanic Garden ⚘
Wellington, New Zealand, encompasses a hillside adjacent to the centre of the city where there are mature plantings and an outstanding rose garden. The garden is best known perhaps for its offshoot, Otari-Wilton's Bush, a city-owned reserve on the outskirts devoted solely to the culture of New Zealand's native plants—this country's premier native plant collection. It comprises 5 hectares/12 acres of plant collections and 90 hectares/222 acres of native forest, parts of which were the last extensive remnants of the original forest in the area. Otari has been vested as a city reserve since 1906. In 1926 it was named the Otari Open-Air Native Plant Museum and Dr Leonard Cockayne, a leading botanist of the time, was appointed director. Under his guidance the plant collection began in earnest. Detailed records of plant accessions have been kept since then and currently there are 3,530 of these from within the territories of New Zealand. Many kilometres of tracks through regenerating

forest are designed to provide an insight into a unique forest community. The garden displays both species and cultivars and a large rock garden provides a habitat for alpine plants. A wide range of collections is cultivated—carmichaelia, clematis, coprosma, cordyline, divaricate, and dracophylum are among these. The last, commonly called grass trees, are seldom seen in gardens and are represented in a forest glade underplanted with a mass of the spectacular *Myosotidium hortensia* from the outlying Chatham Islands. GSC

Wenkenpark ⚘
Riehen, Canton of Basle, Switzerland, originally took shape in the 18th century as a prestigious baroque garden, was redesigned several times in the course of its history, and, with its reconstructions and renovations, is today one of the finest gardens in the Basle region. From 1720 in and around Basle, gardens in the style of LE NÔTRE began to be built by prosperous merchants and industrialists who were making their fortunes in the trade and manufacture that flourished close to the border. The level countryside around Basle was also conducive to the creation of large gardens. In 1736 Johann Heinrich Zäslin purchased the Wenkenhof in Riehen, distinguished by its beautiful hillside setting with a view over the countryside. Zäslin had a single-storey pleasure house erected, separated from an older residential building by a courtyard, on the model of the Trianon de Porcelaine at VERSAILLES, containing only rooms for balls and banquets and facing a splendid garden. The creators of the gently terraced baroque garden, with its parterres and ALLÉES, central fountain and statues, figures and urns, are not known. In 1801 Johann Jakob Bischof-Merian acquired the whole Wenkenhof estate, had another storey added to the summer residence, and commissioned architect Achilles Huber (1776–1860) to transform the French garden into an English-style landscape park in the new style. In 1917 Fanny and Alexander Clavel-Respringer purchased the property and in the same year a survey by garden architects Gebrüder Mertens showed that considerable parts of the garden had been Anglicized but that the old geometric forms were still recognizable. Since reconstruction of the French garden by Gebrüder Mertens, which left the English-style north-eastern park untouched, Wenkenhof today, with its architectural turf parterre, newly planted lime *allée*, various historic statues around the building, park with splendid clipped trees, pond, vast lawns, and the section created in the 1950s with a view of the city, is regarded as one of the finest gardens in the Basle region.
UW

Westbury Court ⚘
Westbury-on-Severn, Gloucestershire, England, is a rare survival. It is a garden of small size, 1.6 hectares/4 acres, one of a group of gardens by the river Severn showing a Dutch influence. It was made by Maynard Colchester from 1696, a walled garden with two parallel canals, one of which is T-shaped, and an elegant pavilion at the head of the other. Each canal is precisely aligned with a CLAIRE VOIE in the eastern wall of the garden which runs parallel to the river. In one corner a secret walled garden has a pretty gazebo. In 1967 the decaying remains of Westbury were acquired by the NATIONAL TRUST which carried out a pioneer feat of restoration that is historically accurate and has resulted in a delightful garden. They were able to draw on KIP engravings in Atkyns's *Ancient and Present State of Glostershire* (1712), showing the garden in great detail, and on Colchester's accounts which survive in the Gloucestershire Record Office. Yew hedges, crowned with lollipops of holly, were made to flank the canals, the pavilion was rebuilt, and a pair of little parterres, with period plantings, was laid out to one side of the canal. Espaliered apples, pears, and plums—all cultivars dating from before 1700, were planted against the walls. The secret walled garden was restored with a pattern of box-edged beds largely planted with period plants except for a few 19th-century rose cultivars. When the National Trust embarked on the work at Westbury the idea of accurate historical restoration of a garden was quite new. The result is a triumphant success. PT

Westonbirt Arboretum ⚘
near Tetbury, Gloucestershire, England, was created by the Holford family who came to live here in the 17th century. In 1823 they started to build a neo-Elizabethan mansion and to make a new garden. From 1829 Robert Holford planted trees radiating out northwards from the new house and his son Sir William Holford followed in his footsteps. The house, and its fine early 19th-century gardens, now belongs to a school and the garden is occasionally open to the public. Some 243 hectares/600 acres of land to the north, including parts of Holford's original plantings, now belongs to the Forestry Commission and is the finest collection of trees and shrubs in the British Isles. Over 3,000 taxa are represented here, with additions constantly made. A National Collection of cultivars of Japanese maples (*Acer* cvs.) has over 170 examples, and there are fine collections of every genus of woody plant hardy in a temperate climate. Holford's Ride, the central of the original avenues, is a distinguished feature at the heart of the arboretum with its soaring incense cedars (*Calocedrus decurrens*) and

Wellingtonias (*Sequoiadendron giganteum*) dating from the Holfords' time. Glades and groups of trees, sometimes finely chosen for colour, are disposed about Holford's Ride. In Silk Wood, the newer part of the arboretum, the planting is wilder but no less filled with treasures, with collections of hickories, limes, maples, oaks, poplars, and walnuts. Throughout the garden are excellent shrubs with notable collections of magnolias (nineteen species), rhododendrons (61 species), and viburnums (34 species). The arboretum has many exceptional specimens of trees—over 100 of which are champion trees, the largest known examples of their species in the country.　PT

Westpark ⊛

Munich, Germany, was created between 1978 and 1983 for the Internationale Gartenbauausstellung, IGA 83 (International Garden Show). It covers an area of about 74 hectares/183 acres (60 hectares for Westpark and 14 hectares for the adjacent park of Mollgelände). The area was originally flat, separated by two motorways, and consisting of former agricultural fields and industrial estates. The layout was based on the designs of the landscape architect Peter Kluska in cooperation with landscape architects Gottfried and Anton Hansjakob (who were responsible for the Mollgelände) and Eckhard Brülle as artistic director of the garden show. They proposed a landscape in the shape of an extended valley with streams, lakes, large meadows, curved pathways and luxuriant vegetation, partly consisting of fully grown trees (about 6,000 trees between twenty and 60 years old were transplanted) as well as beds for perennials and gardens of special environments. The park gives the appearance of a romantic landscape, separated from its noisy environment by high earth mounds. The concept of IGA included the layout of so-called *Nationengärten*, 23 gardens in all, each of which represented a different national garden culture, such as China and Japan. Special emphasis was given to a large garden for bedding and sun-loving perennials designed by the landscape architect Gerhard Teutsch from Munich. This garden, in the shape of a spiral, consists of several themes for the arrangement of perennials, emphasizing colour, the use of wild species as well as of perennials for rock gardens, and environments such as steppes. After IGA 83 closed, both parks were opened to the public as Westpark and Mollpark.　US

Gottfried Hansjakob, 'In Mollgelände Dauergrün und Ausstellung getrennt', *Garten + Landschaft*, Vol. 93: No. 4 (1983).
Peter Kluska, 'Der Westpark', *G + L*, 93: 4 (1983).

Gerhard Teutsch, 'Beet und Sonnenstauden', *G + L*, 93: 4 (1983).

West Wycombe Park ⊛

West Wycombe, Buckinghamshire, England, was built in the early 18th century for Sir Francis Dashwood. By 1752, when a painting of the garden by William Hannan was made, there was a picturesque landscape garden arranged about a lake with a rockwork cascade with a river god, an allée leading up to the house, an ornamental sailing boat, a chinoiserie bridge, and a tent on an island. This was possibly the work of Maurice-Louis Jolivet who signed a survey in 1752. Later in the century, *c*.1788, Nicholas Revett (1720–1804) designed a fine pillared Music Temple on the banks of the island. The garden today, owned by the national trust since 1943, retains much of its 18th-century character with some 20th-century additions. West of the lake, on a broad grassy walk, a column surmounted by a figure of Britannia was erected to celebrate the Queen's 60th birthday. Quinlan Terry (b. 1931) designed a domed Temple of Venus (1982) to replace a lost building designed by Jolivet. Terry also refashioned the old cascade, now ornamented with recumbent nymphs, and combined it with a bridge of the east side of the lake. The grounds are well wooded, with many open vistas showing views of the house and of ornamental buildings and monuments. The most remarkable monument, to the north beyond and high above the Oxford road, is an astonishing 18th-century mausoleum containing Dashwood memorials. Of a gigantic size, it is hexagonal and open to the sky, its flint walls bristling with urns.　PT

Whately, Thomas

(d. 1772), English politician, economist, and garden writer. His anonymously published book *Observations on Modern Gardening* (1770) was the most wide-ranging and eloquent account of mid 18th-century English garden taste. Its opening words are 'Gardening, in the perfection to which it has been lately brought in England, is entitled to a place of considerable rank among the liberal arts.' His book deals with the principles of using different garden ingredients and describes particular examples of their use in several notable gardens of his time. The book was influential both as a primer of garden design but also, especially to foreign visitors, as a checklist of gardens worth visiting. Thomas Jefferson used it on his tour of English gardens in 1786. It went through several printings in the late 18th century (five by 1793) and in the early 19th century and was soon translated into French and German. J. C. Loudon described Whately as 'the first and best

of all the writers on this [i.e. the landscape] style'. Among the gardens he described are Blenheim, Claremont, The Leasowes, Painshill, Stowe, and Woburn Farm.　PT

White, Revd Gilbert

(1720–93), English author, gardener, natural historian, and parson. His book *The Natural History and Antiquities of Selborne* (1789) has sold more copies than any other book on natural history and, after the Bible, Shakespeare's plays, and *The Pilgrim's Progress*, is the largest seller in the history of English publishing. He gardened at Wakes, in Selborne (Hampshire), and kept a gardening journal published as *Garden Kalendar 1751–71* (1975) which records his epic struggle in the kitchen garden, especially to grow melons. His garden at Selborne survives, restored and well cared for. Here you may see the English wildflowers he loved, his ha-ha, the zigzag walk he made to a beautiful beechwood, 18th-century cultivars of fruit, a pool with native moisture-loving plants, and much else dating from White's time. Above all, the view from behind his house, looking across fields to the ancient beechwood, remains much as it must have been in his time.　PT

White, Thomas the elder (1736–1811) and Thomas the younger

(*c*.1764–1831), English garden designers working in the north of England and in Scotland. Thomas White the elder had worked in the 1760s in association with Capability Brown from whom he gradually separated himself and set up his own business practising in the Brownian manner. White was a great planter of trees, sometimes proposing quantities that embarassed his clients. The Society of Arts awarded medals for tree planting with a view to providing timber for the navy and for industrial purposes. White repeatedly won such medals with lavish plantings of trees in his own Nottinghamshire estate, and caused some of his clients to win them too. He became the major landscape designer in Scotland where he advised or executed plans for many estates. Among them were commissions at Arniston House, Castle Fraser (Aberdeenshire), Mount Stuart, and Scone Palace (Perthshire). Thomas White the younger practised exclusively in Scotland. J. C Loudon, who may have been influenced by professional jealousy, criticized the Whites in particular for their lack of imagination and for their insensitivity to good existing features of the landscape. They would, it was alleged, destroy avenues and old woodland and plant banal forms in the Brownian style—'a clump, a belt, and a simple tree'. A. A. Tait in his *The Landscape Garden in Scotland: 1735–1835* (1980), which contains

much valuable information about the Whites, disagrees. He finds a much 'looser and freer style, particularly in planting' and complexity in their layouts, in particular of viewpoints.
PT

Wiepking-Jürgensmann, Heinrich Friedrich

(1891–1973), outstanding German landscape architect in the first half of the 20th century. Before the First World War he designed gardens in various countries in Europe, such as Russia, Bohemia, and Italy. Early on, Wiepking had shown his National Socialist orientation and in 1934 he succeeded Erwin BARTH in the chair in garden design at the Agricultural University Berlin. Following National Socialist expansion politics, especially in Poland and the Soviet Union, Wiepking envisioned a 'spring of life for the German landscape and garden designer which exceeds all which even the hottest hearts amongst us have ever dreamed of'. Wiepking actively promoted anti-Semitic, racist, and National Socialist thinking in landscape architecture. His book *Die Landschaftsfibel* (Landscape Primer) appeared in 1942. How closely Wiepking was connected to the sites of the Holocaust is demonstrated by a diploma thesis on the greening of Auschwitz, a rural site in Poland where one of the largest National Socialist concentration camps was established, which he issued to one of his students in 1943. In spite of his clear National Socialist orientation Wiepking managed in 1946 to establish, together with others, the Higher School for Horticulture in Osnabrück, Germany, and the College for Horticulture and Land Culture in Hanover, Germany. In the latter he was given a position as acting chair for land maintenance, landscape, and garden design from 1948 to 1949 and as chair from 1949 to 1959. In 1966 Wiepking received an honorary Ph.D. from the University of Lisbon, Portugal, where one of his students from the Nazi period had a teaching position.   GG

Wiersse, De ⚜

Vorden, Gelderland, the Netherlands, one of the best-maintained estates in the country. As a late medieval castle it was moated and positioned near a river. The main structure of the gardens was determined by the end of the 17th century, since when it has been in the same family, often passing through the female line. The current character, however, was largely determined in the early 20th century. The house was restored and enlarged in 1912 by Victor de Stuers, who allowed his daughter Alice (1895–1988) to take charge of the gardens which she ultimately extended to 16 hectares/29 acres and the park to 32 hectares/79 acres. She started in

1912 with a formal rose garden, and a sunken garden followed in 1913. In 1918 she married W. E. Gatacre (1878–1959) and they worked on the garden together. Gatacre provided a good understanding of design and had an excellent eye for detail, while Alice was particularly interested in planting. By 1928 the historic drive had been re-established and extended, the park planted, and the old pleasure grounds converted into a wild garden, with extensive planting of rhododendrons and bulbs. When labour was reduced after the Second World War, the gardens were gradually simplified. However, from the late 1970s onwards there was a renewed impetus from the present owners, Peter and Laura Gatacre. Advised by employees and friends and assisted by government grants they have revived the gardens and continue to develop and maintain them.   JW

> LAURA GATACRE, 'An English gardener in a Dutch historic garden', *Garden History*, Vol. 30: No. 2 (2002).

Wilanów ⚜

Warsaw, Poland, was the residence of the Polish King John III Sobieski (1629–96), built by Agostino Locci between 1677 and 1679 as a modest manor house and remodelled into a baroque palace between 1681 and 1683 with a further extension later in the century. The garden, put into place at the same time as the palace, was laid out on two terraces. The upper terrace assumed the form of an Italian garden with beds bordered by boxwood, decorated with fountains and gilt sculptures of figures from mythology, while on the lower terrace a French garden with flower parterres was arranged after 1686. To one side the composition was closed with tall lime hedges beyond which is a lake. The spacious *cour d'honneur* (see ATTRE, CHÂTEAU D') was originally flanked by orchards. The King himself planted a number of trees, as he enjoyed gardening, which allowed him to rest from his daily duties.

After the King's death Wilanów changed hands. In the 18th century the estate became the property of August Czartoryski and his daughter Izabela Lubomirska. At this time, in imitation of VERSAILLES, three avenues in the PATTE D'OIE form were marked out in front of the *cour d'honneur* and a new garden was added on the north side with tall hornbeam hedges and flower parterres. About 1784 the first informal garden here was designed by Szymon Bogumił ZUG (1733–1807) on the site of the manor farm. In 1799 Wilanów passed into the hands of Lubomirska's daughter Aleksandra and her husband Stanisław Kostka Potocki (1755–1821), an eminent politician, writer, and collector, who translated J. J. Winckelmann's *History of Ancient Art* into Polish. The garden

was considerably enlarged. While the baroque gardens at the rear of the palace were preserved, the southern part was turned into a landscape park and a further large park added on the northern side. It stretches along the shoreline of Lake Wilanowskie, where an artificial island was raised and a number of park buildings and sculptures were erected. In 1855–6 Bolesław Podczaszyński designed a neo-Renaissance Italian quadripartite garden at the southern side of the palace. After the Second World War Wilanów became a museum and under Gerard CIOŁEK's supervision the garden was restored. Full reconstruction of the baroque layout was carried out only in the eastern part, on the basis of archaeological exploration and paintings by Bernardo Bellotto.   WB

wilderness.

The wilderness was a feature of English, and Scottish, gardens of the 17th and the beginning of the 18th century. Close in spirit to the French BOSQUET or the Italian BOSCO but with its own character, in essence it is a formal planting of hedges sometimes with informal ingredients. J. C. LOUDON's *Encyclopaedia of Gardening* (1822) says that a wilderness is the same as a labyrinth, which he describes as 'a convoluted, plicated, or otherwise rendered intricate, disposition of walks, separated by hedges or shrubbery, sometimes called a wilderness'. Its best contemporary description is Scottish and contained in a curious survival, a manuscript of Thomas Hamilton, the 6th Earl of Haddington (1680–1735), 'Some directions about raising forest trees', written between 1732 and 1735 but only discovered in 1949 and published in 1953. Hamilton lived at Tyninghame House (East Lothian) and in his manuscript he wrote of 'a little of a wilderness' which was a feature 'not . . . long introduced into this country'. He described 'straight views . . . terminating in as fine a prospect as could be had'. He also specified that there were 'serpentine walks that run through the whole, hedged like the straight walks, and the angles planted with a variety of different trees'. He was plainly not writing about his own garden for he ends with the planting he would carry out 'were I to plant a wilderness' in which he lists flowering trees and shrubs and 'a kind of willow that hath a bark of bright yellow' (which must have been *Salix alba* subsp. *vitellina*, known in gardens since at least 1632). At HAMPTON COURT in the first years of the 18th century a wilderness was laid out by George LONDON and Henry WISE to the north of the palace. It is shown in great detail in the painting by Leonard KNYFF of *c.*1702 which still hangs at Hampton Court Palace. It was a geometric design of hedges of box, yew, and holly with a bold, cross-shaped pattern of broad walks meeting an a central circular space. Further patterns of walks, straight or serpentine, were superimposed, embellished from time to time with tiered shapes of TOPIARY. Two mazes were incorporated into the wilderness, one laid out as two half-circles and a second as a triangular lozenge. The second is the only part of the wilderness to survive and it is the oldest hedge maze in Britain. Only traces of wildernesses of this period survive but the NATIONAL TRUST has reinstated two to give a vivid idea of their original appearance. At the 17th-century HAM HOUSE the wilderness was reconstructed on the basis of a late 17th-century plan. A rectangle is enclosed in hornbeam hedges and divided into patterns of straight and curved walks. The turf compartments enclosed are ornamented with round pavilions capped with dashing conical roofs and the grass is planted with wood anemones, cowslips, narcissi, ox-eye daisies, primroses, and ragged robin (*Lychnis flos-cuculi*). At Hanbury Hall (Worcestershire) George London *c.*1700 laid out formal gardens for Thomas Vernon. The National Trust has reinstated them, including a wilderness with straight lines of mixed plants—among them holly, sweet bay, *Phillyrea angustifolia*—enclosing areas of lawn planted with such flowering trees as cherries, Judas trees, and laburnum.   PT

wild garden.

The idea of the wild garden has its origins in the 19th century, in particular when it was made into a polemic in William ROBINSON's *The Wild Garden* (1870). Robinson wanted to attack the fashion for tender bedding plants and to sing the praises of hardy plants, naturalized in appropriate settings—appropriate both aesthetically and in terms of cultivation. He used in his own wild garden 'things that take care of themselves in the soil of the place'. Wild plants, he thought, would not only grow better in wild places but look better too. He was particularly concerned with the 'outer parts of pleasure grounds', with the 'fields, woods and copses . . . and in neglected places in almost every kind of garden'. The spirit of this is not far from that of the FERME ORNÉE but Robinson would have regarded that as artificial and rather silly. He evoked irresistible images of 'the winter Aconite flowering under a grove of naked trees in February' and 'the Blue Apennine Anemone staining an English wood blue before the coming of our bluebells'. He himself grew a very wide range of bulbs—crocus, erythroniums, fritillaries, narcissi, scillas, and tulips—in hay meadows and they may still be seen in his garden at Gravetye Manor (Surrey). In fact much of the planting he recommended was already being practised in the Cornish WOODLAND GARDENS where such English

natives as wood anemones (*Anemone nemorosa*), wild garlic (*Allium ursinum*), and bluebells (*Hyacinthoides non-scripta*) were regarded as a splendid background for the exotic Asiatic flowering shrubs—camellias, magnolias, and rhododendrons—which were the focus of such gardens. In other woodland gardens, particularly in Scotland, naturalistic plantings of herbaceous plants were often of flowering exotics, in particular of Asiatic primulas and of Himalayan poppies (*Meconopsis* spp.). It was a corollary to wild gardening that wild species as opposed to garden forms should always be preferred, for aesthetic as well as practical reasons. Too many cultivars look preposterously artificial in a wild setting and the species, always coming true from seed, are the only plants capable of naturalizing. It is a further advantage that some species, for example roses, are far more resistant to disease than garden forms. Breeding plants in the pursuit of one or more attributes tends to breed out all sorts of other, less superficial, qualities like resistance to disease. In the late 19th century in England there was a fashion for species roses. Robinson recommended them— 'our native wild roses deserve a place in fence or hedgerow, or rough banks if convenient'. Gertrude JEKYLL was also an advocate of wild planting and in her *Roses for English Gardens* (1902) she devotes a chapter to species roses and she certainly used them in garden designs— in the wild garden at the MANOR HOUSE (Upton Grey), for example. At SISSINGHURST CASTLE Vita SACKVILLE-WEST used the wildest roses, such as *Rosa moyesi*, in the context of mixed borders, adding a dimension of wild structure.

Styles of wild gardening have made their mark in many countries through the work of notable garden designers. Roberto BURLE MARX's bold sweeps of a single species of native plants are characteristic of the way he worked. Jens JENSEN's love of native North American plants and his way of disposing them to evoke the natural planting of the prairie was an approach to wild gardening suitable for vast spaces. He carefully studied the way plants arranged themselves in the wild and sought to evoke this atmosphere in his designs. In England Beth CHATTO's emphasis on plants' habitats, and her experiments in establishing naturalistic communities of plants have been deeply influential on British garden style in recent times. Jacques WIRTZ approached the use of ornamental grasses with inventiveness— sometimes using it in the context of patterned formality and sometimes to form bold, sweeping banks to enliven the landscape. In France Gilles CLÉMENT has, like William Robinson, also been interested in 'neglected

places', being inspired by the patterns of natural plant communities as they colonize fallow land. James van Sweden and Wolfgang Oehme (see OEHME, VAN SWEDEN, & ASSOCIATES) in North America use native or exotic plants in great swathes to form strong ingredients of their landscaping.

The ethos of wild gardening was developed in Britain at a time when many middle-class people had large gardens and the style of planting was seized upon as an attractive and appropriate way of animating odd corners of their usually extensive grounds. However, much of this planting is also quite appropriate for small gardens and has become a very common, and attractive, feature of countless modest gardens. Patches of *Cyclamen hederifolium*, beautiful in flower and leaf, thickets of *Iris unguicularis* whose exquisite flowers defy the worst winter weather, golden pools of aconites (*Eranthis hyemalis*) about the trunk of a tree, *Rosa canina* scrambling through a hedge, clumps of snowdrops running along a hedgerow, yellow Welsh poppies (*Meconopsis cambrica*) glowing in the half-shade of a shrub or tree—all these plants are at their best in the context of a wild, naturalistic style of planting rather than cooped up in a formal border. The fact that many naturalistic plantings look after themselves is also an attraction to gardeners. In the late 20th and early 21st centuries this style of wild planting was also seen to be in tune with the spirit of ecological stewardship. It is associated with the desire to make one's garden into a place of rich biological diversity and of harmony. See also NATURALISTIC PLANTING; WOODLAND GARDEN.   PT

Wilhelma Gardens ⊛

Stuttgart-Bad Cannstatt, Germany. At the edge of a landscape park laid out from 1823 to 1840 (Rosensteinpark), King Wilhelm I of Württemberg created a complex of buildings and gardens in a Moorish oriental style which he called the Wilhelma. Between 1839 and 1854 the architect Karl Ludwig von Zanth produced a theatre, a bathing house (Moorish Country House), a banqueting hall, and terraces with a viewing pavilion (Belvedere), connected by roofed passages and hothouses. These glasshouses with their cast-iron frames were the most modern of their kind in Germany and contained numerous exotic plants such as azaleas, camellias, palms, banksia, melaleuca, and *Victoria regia*. The gardens were aligned with the axes of the buildings, decorated with fountains and sculptures and planted with select trees (ginkgo, gleditsia, gymnocladus, paulownia, magnolias, and conifers). The Wilhelma is an unusual example of 19th-century German eclecticism.

In the Second World War the complex was badly damaged by bombs. The historic buildings were reconstructed in the 1950s and 1960s, most of them in a simplified form, and at the same time the whole property was turned into a zoo. Today the Wilhelma is one of the most important zoos in the world and the only combination of zoo and botanical gardens in Germany. Among the remaining plant treasures the old magnolias in the inner garden and the small woodland area planted in 1865 with 40 redwoods (*Sequoiadendron giganteum*) in the conifer valley are of particular interest. Today the restored 19th-century glasshouses have a comprehensive stock of plants, some of it old, consisting of azaleas, camellias, and fuchsias as well as orchids, ferns, succulents, and useful plants from the tropics. In the historic Winter Garden a rural scene with exotic vegetation has been created to give an idea of the way it would have looked in the 1860s. The original splendour of the oriental architecture can still be seen in the Damascene Hall, built in 1863–4 and reconstructed in its original form in 1992. In January 2000 a new tropical rainforest house (Amazon House) was opened on the north-eastern edge of the Wilhelma.   RH

Wilhelmshöhe Schlosspark

Kassel, Hesse, Germany. The origins of the park at Wilhelmshöhe, which today has an area of 240 hectares/593 acres, can be traced back to the 12th century. Under Landgrave Karl (1670–1730) a magnificent work took shape between 1701 and 1714 and immediately attracted admiring descriptions as one of the finest gardens in Europe. Impressed by the Renaissance and baroque gardens of Italy, in 1701 Karl commissioned the Italian Giovanni Francesco Guerniero with the planning and construction of the gigantic grounds on the eastern slopes of the Habichtswald forest. Only the vast octagonal palace with its statue of Hercules and the upper third of the cascade, however, were completed; after the Landgrave's death the estate, named Karlsberg after him, was unchanged for decades.

From 1763 till 1785, under Friedrich II (reigned 1760–85), a labyrinthine array of diverse 'natural' scenery with sweeping pathways and numerous structures took shape to plans by court master gardener August Daniel Schwarzkopf, who left the original baroque concept untouched. From this Anglo-Chinese period the Mulang Chinese Village, Egyptian Pyramid, Sibylline Grotto, Temple to Mercury, and the Hermitage of Socrates are extant. Originally there were several hermitages, simple wooden huts, each dedicated to a philosopher whose writings were displayed for the edification of walkers through the valley. The Chinese Village, built 1782–5 by Simon Louis du Ry, with shepherds' houses, a milking parlour, the Bagatelle lodge, and pagoda, was set in an idealized pastoral landscape. Further landscaping was carried out under Landgrave Wilhelm IX (after 1803 Elector Wilhelm I (reigned 1785–1821)). Making use of the natural topography, under Schwarzkopf's direction an idealized landscape was gradually created along the axis of a baroque cascade. Architects Heinrich Christoph Jussow, du Ry, and water engineer Karl Friedrich Steinhofer added the waterfall, devil's bridge, aqueduct, cascade watercourses, and the lake. The Neuer Wasserfall (New Waterfall) (1826), was built by Steinhofer in imitation of natural waterfalls, quarried from basalt. The Roseninsel (Rose Island) was laid out in 1789–95 at the inflow to the lake with the rose collection begun under Friedrich II and transplanted to the island. These works, and the Löwenburg built from 1793 as a medieval castle, expressed the ideals of the romantic landscape garden.

The palace and park have borne the name Wilhelmshöhe since 1798 when the gable end of the three-winged palace rebuilt in 1763 was so inscribed. In 1822 Wilhelm II (reigned 1821–31) had the Pflanzenhaus (Plant House) erected, one of the first glasshouses with a cast-iron frame built in Germany, designed by Johann Conrad Bromeis. Three glasshouses display tender exotics, tropical plants, and an exceptional collection of camellias. The aesthetic unity of the grounds in the spirit of an English-style landscape garden must rank as the greatest achievement of court gardener Wilhelm Hentze. The baroque waterworks and the naturalistic waterfalls, aqueducts, and watercourse of the landscape garden are a great attraction for the numerous visitors.   BM

Wilhelmsthal Schlosspark

Calden, Hesse, Germany, lies to the north-west of WILHELMSHÖHE. The palace was built after 1743 by Landgrave Wilhelm VIII (1682–1760) to plans by the architect François Cuvilliers (1695–1768) at the same time as the geometric garden. The pentagonal grounds with their three-winged palace and labyrinthine rococo park were linked with the surrounding countryside by ALLÉES fanning out to the east. Under Wilhelm IX (1785–1821), who became Elector Wilhelm I in 1803, the park was reshaped between 1796 and 1813 as a landscape garden by court gardeners Daniel August Schwarzkopf and Karl and Wilhelm Hentze. Sinuous paths, sweeping lawns, and informal groups of trees were woven in the gently undulating grounds in a unique park landscape. Parts of the baroque axes were, however, retained: the central axis leads westwards from the palace across a circular BOULINGRIN lawn and out to the Tiergarten. The south-eastern axis with its canal, grotto (1744–5, probably designed by Cuvilliers), figures, and basins was completed in 1756. In 1962 it was reinstated piece by piece in the area around the grotto, the only building to survive from the ROCOCO GARDEN, and the canal, and today it conveys an impression of the original magnificence. A duck pond (*Ententeich*) was originally flanked by Chinese pavilions but these were demolished in 1800. The palace with its simple but elegant façade and precious interiors is one of the most important works of European rococo art.   BM

Williamsburg

Virginia, USA, was capital of the colony of Virginia from 1699 to 1781. Laid out along a spine of the grand avenue Duke of Gloucester Street, with the Capitol on the eastern terminus and the College of William and Mary (founded in 1693) at the western end, it covered about 2.6 sq. km/1 mile. Colonial Williamsburg was a lively capital, and the venerable college was the seat of learning for many influential Americans, including Thomas JEFFERSON. With a resident population of about 3,000, when the capital was moved to Richmond, Virginia, in 1780, it became a quiet college town. By the early part of the 20th century, Williamsburg had only 3,500 residents, and much of the colonial architecture and structure had been lost. The passionate plea for restoration came from Revd W. A. R. Goodwin, rector of the surviving Bruton Parish Church. He inspired industrialist John D. Rockefeller Jr., in 1926, to sponsor the research, design, land acquisitions, and construction necessary to reconstruct the core of Colonial Williamsburg. A team of architects, landscape architects, and engineers was established to lay out and oversee this unprecedented restoration. This undertaking spanned more than ten years, and set new standards in landscape and architectural archaeology and research (see ARCHAEOLOGY OF GARDENS). Highways were diverted, streets and open spaces restored to their original material appearance, and more than 450 existing later buildings were removed, 66 colonial buildings were restored, and 84 buildings were reproduced on their colonial foundations.

Landscape architect Arthur A. Shurcliff directed the landscape and city planning restoration efforts. The gardens of Williamsburg reflect the status and style of their affiliated residences. From the Governor's Palace, with its extensive grounds and garden features including a maze, a mount, a canal and fish pond, a bowling green, and grand formal gardens, to the simple dooryard gardens of more modest residences, there is a continuum to the style and the plant palette that knits the community together. The overriding stylistic influence is Dutch-English, deriving from the influence of William and Mary in England, with enclosed geometric gardens (invoking HORTUS CONCLUSUS in the New World). These may be the best-preserved examples of this style of gardening, with most English counterparts having been superseded by later fashions. The plantings are an interesting mix of English colonial plants and indigenous American plants, with a few exotics that were directly imported into Virginia. The tree structure of this landscape is formed with native *Carpinus caroliniana*, *Catalpa bignonioides*, *Fagus americana*, *Platanus occidentalis*, and *Quercus virginiana*. Box, *Buxus sempervirens*, is the dominant hedge material, but native *Ilex vomitoria* and *Ilex opaca* are also used. The ornamental and domestic gardens offer much to explore. The re-creation (a more modern term) of the colonial core of the city continues, and Colonial Williamsburg is administered as a period museum, with interpretative and working staff in period costume. Standards of 'correctness' for restorations and reconstructions have evolved since this project began, yet Williamsburg stands as a remarkable evocation of the past, well worth visiting.   PC

Williams-Ellis, Sir Clough

(1883–1978), Welsh architect, author, and garden designer. His garden designs have a taste for the theatrical, decorative, and architectural but often show a refined sense of place. His best surviving work is the two gardens he made in Wales, for his family house at Plas BRONDANW from 1908 onwards and, nearby at PORTMEIRION, his fantasy Mediterranean village with lively landscaping created from 1925. Other gardens where he worked include Cornwell Manor (Oxfordshire), Dalton Hall (Cumbria), Hatton Lodge (Shropshire), and Nantclwyd Hall (Clwyd). His book *England and the Octopus* (1928) is an eloquent and pioneering *cri de cœur* against uncontrolled development of cities, villages, and green space. Because he was charming and eccentric he was too quickly assumed to be merely a dilettante. His own garden at Plas Brondanw, however, is one of the best of its time and his deeply felt writings are remarkably prophetic.   PT

Willmott, Ellen Ann

(1858–1934), English gardener and plantswoman who gardened at Warley Place (Essex) which in the 17th century had belonged to John EVELYN. In the garden's heyday she employed 85 gardeners and grew 100,000 different plants,

one of the greatest plant collections in the world. As Dr W. T. Stearn wrote: 'For certain genera, such as *Epimedium*, *Hedera*, *Iris*, *Narcissus* and *Rosa*, she acquired almost every variety that cash or persuasion could obtain.' She also gardened in France at Tresserve (Haute-Savoie), and on the Italian Riviera at Boccanegra close to Ventimiglia. She supported E. H. WILSON's early plant hunting expeditions (*Ceratostigma willmottianum*, *Lilium davidii* var. *willmottiae*, and *Rosa willmottiae* are Wilson introductions named after her). Her two-volume 25-part book *The Genus Rosa* (1910–14), with illustrations by Alfred Parsons, was a publishing catastrophe. The pretty but spiky and invasive biennial *Eryngium giganteum* is known as 'Miss Willmott's ghost' because of her supposed habit of surreptitiously distributing its seed in gardens she was visiting. She wrote of herself, 'Plants and gardens come before anything else during the day, and after dark I read and write about them.' She received the Victoria Medal of Honour in the first year it was awarded, 1897—the only other woman to receive it in the same year was Gertrude JEKYLL who described her as 'the greatest of the living woman gardeners'. Of her garden at Warley Place only traces survive from her time—some sweet chestnuts (*Castanea sativa*) and a colony of *Crocus vernus* subsp. *albiflorus* which may even date from Evelyn's time.   PT

Wilson, Ernest Henry

(1876–1930), plant collector and writer. Wilson was born at Chipping Campden in Gloucestershire and early on showed great aptitude for botanical study. After training at the BIRMINGHAM BOTANICAL GARDENS, in 1897 he went to the ROYAL BOTANIC GARDENS, KEW. Two years later, at the request of the VEITCH NURSERY, Wilson was recommended to undertake an expedition to central China to collect seeds and plants, particularly of the handkerchief or dove tree (*Davidia involucrata*) which he found, after assistance from Augustine HENRY. He made a return journey on behalf of Veitch in 1903, before undertaking work for the ARNOLD ARBORETUM. Wilson consequently moved to the United States and twice more visited China, in 1906 and 1910, followed by travels throughout Japan in 1914 and 1917, and for three years from 1919, the Antipodes, India, and Africa. Wilson was made assistant director of the Arnold Arboretum in 1919, holding the post until 1927 when he was appointed its keeper. From then until his death in a car accident he hardly travelled. Wilson's prolific writings illustrate his work, beginning with *A Naturalist in Western China* (1913), but his finest literary achievement is considered to be *Lilies of Eastern Asia* (1925). As early as 1906 he

received the Royal Horticultural Society's Veitch Memorial Medal, and was later honoured by the Victoria Medal of Honour. Wilson is credited with introducing about 1,000 new plants into cultivation; some of his best known include *Magnolia wilsonii*, *Berberis wilsonii*, *Clematis armandii*, and *Acer griseum*.

MC-C

Wilton House ✾

near Salisbury, Wiltshire, England, was built from 1543 for William Herbert (later 1st Earl of Pembroke). There was an elaborate Jacobean garden here of which an account survives written in 1623 by John Taylor who described 'walks, hedges and arbours . . . all manner of most delicate fruit trees'. He noted 'three arbours standing in a triangle, having each a recourse to a greater arbour in the midst', and the garden was rich in symbolism—'divine and moral rememberances'. From 1635 Isaac de CAUS started work on remodelling the house for Philip Herbert, 4th Earl of Pembroke. De Caus also designed a new garden, and wrote an illustrated description of it, *Le Jardin de Wilton* (*c.*1645). A bird's-eye view of the garden drawn by him shows three pairs of formal ▶

gardens, identical on each side of a broad central walk which runs up to an arcaded LOGGIA (which had a GROTTO behind). The first pair of gardens had a series of PARTERRES *de broderie* and the remaining gardens had formal groves, statues, and tunnel arbours—with the river Nadder winding its way across the centre. In the grotto sea monsters spouted water and there were figures of Venus and Cupid, tritons, and river gods. Celia Fiennes saw it *c*.1685 and heard the 'melody of Nightingerlls and all sorts of birds' and described 'figures at each corner of the room that can weep water on the beholders'. Roy Strong in *The Renaissance Garden in England* (1979) called this garden 'the greatest of English Renaissance gardens'. It was largely destroyed when a noble Palladian bridge was built across the river in 1737—only some of the statues and parts of the loggia and grotto survive.   PT

Wimbledon House,

Wimbledon, London, England, was built from 1588 for Sir Thomas Cecil (later 1st Earl of Exeter). A plan of house and garden dated 1609 by the architect Robert Smythson (*c*.1535–1614) shows gardens to one side of the house and,

much more extensively, behind it. Some of these are quadripartite arrangements of beds in square enclosures, others are rectangular and marked for special purposes ('A great Orcharde'). There is no unifying central axis, nor are the gardens firmly related to the house. The gardens were remodelled by André MOLLET for Charles I's Queen, Henrietta Maria, in 1642. John EVELYN found it 'a delicious place for prospect' and he was consulted about how to 'contrive the garden after the modern'. Charles BRIDGEMAN made a new garden for the Duchess of Marlborough in 1731 and Capability BROWN made a plan in 1764 for Viscount Spencer for a great lake and tree planting in the park. Sir Joseph PAXTON designed new formal gardens in the 1840s. Few estates have been worked on by such a distinguished list of garden designers with, in the end, so little to show for it. Nothing remains of the Tudor Wimbledon House which survived until the early 18th century and was succeeded by more than one house. The grounds are now part of Wimbledon Park and have found more recent fame—they are largely taken up with sports facilities, most notably the All England Tennis Club. Brown's

noble lake may still be seen and some good trees look as though they date from his time.   PT

Wimpole Hall ✿

Arrington, Cambridgeshire, England, had a deer park in the early 14th century, and from the 17th century, when the present house was largely built, the gardens were laid out, often by notable garden designers, reflecting the changing fashions of their time. The most notable gardens were those laid out in the late 17th century, probably by George LONDON and Henry WISE, which are shown in a KIP engraving in *Britannia Illustrata* (1707)—a pattern of immensely intricate formal gardens behind the house and the whole estate pinned down in the landscape by avenues. In the 1720s Charles BRIDGEMAN added further avenues which were removed when Capability BROWN worked on the park from 1767. By the end of the 18th century Wimpole Hall was standing at the

---

The 17th-century garden at **Wimpole Hall** in an engraving by Johannes Kip from *Britannia Illustrata* (1707).

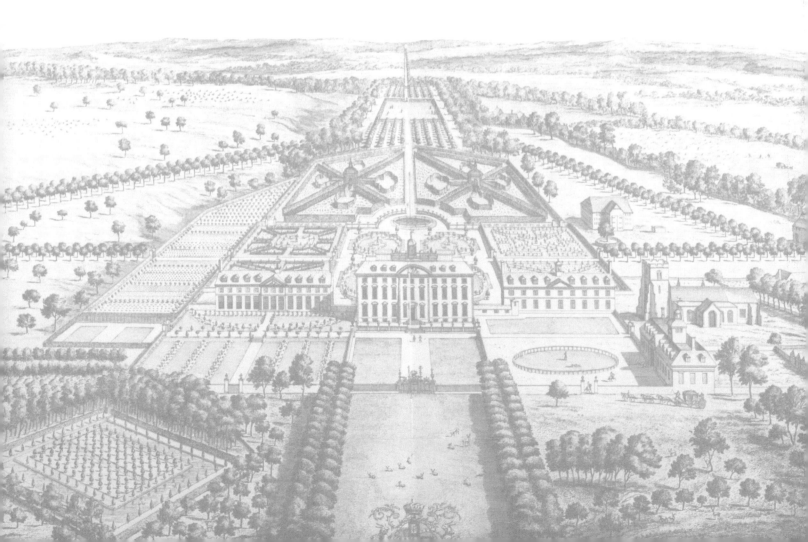

centre of a landscape park. Contrary to what is usually said about Brown obliterating all formality he left a great double avenue of elms (possibly the one seen in the Kip engraving) which remained in place until the 1970s when it was killed by Dutch elm disease. After the NATIONAL TRUST acquired the estate in 1976 the avenue was replanted with limes. From 1801 REPTON worked at Wimpole, making a flower garden north of the house enclosed in railings with a CLAIRE VOIE centred on mock ruins in the park designed by Sanderson MILLER, all of which may still be seen.   PT

Windsor Castle ⊛

Windsor, Berkshire, England, was built in the 11th century by William the Conqueror close to the site of a Saxon royal hunting lodge. There were gardens here as early as the 12th century when 'the King's herbary' is mentioned within the castle's curtain walls and the 'King's Garden' outside the walls had a vineyard by the mid 12th century and 'a fair shrubbery' after 1246. An engraving by Hollar of c.1672 shows the King's Garden to the south of the castle as a patchwork of enclosed gardens with a cluster of small houses. By the early 18th century a KIP engraving shows this area greatly expanded and a very large enclosed formal garden in place with, to its east, the Broad Walk and an avenue leading south into the Little Park. Other gardens are also seen attached to houses, some of which were substantial, below the castle walls. On the north side of the castle, running down to a loop in the river, Henry WISE c.1712 laid out the Maestricht Garden with a central canal and a rectilinear pattern of radiating ALLÉES in a wilderness. Under George III in the 1780s the garden was turned into farmland. In the 1820s Sir Jeffry Wyatville (1766–1840) made new terraced gardens with bedding schemes by William AITON on the site of the King's Garden. A rose garden replaced it in the 1950s but statuary and topiary of golden yew preserve the 19th-century flavour.   PT

JANE ROBERTS, *Royal Landscape: The Gardens and Parks of Windsor* (1997).

Winterthur ⊛

Delaware, USA, is home to a pre-eminent collection of American decorative arts as well as a 24-hectare/60-acre naturalistic garden set in rolling landscape of extraordinary beauty. It is the result of the dual passions of Henry Francis du Pont (1880–1969) who lived at Winterthur his entire life and devoted his energies to amassing the finest American antiques as well as planting his woods and fields with masses of wildflowers, bulbs, and shrubs that would guarantee a succession of interest and bloom throughout the year. He opened the

resulting museum, library, and garden to the public in 1951.

The original property was a working farm of 182 hectares/450 acres purchased by H. F. du Pont's great grandfather at the beginning of the 19th century. When Henry du Pont inherited Winterthur in 1927, he continued to manage the farm, developing perhaps the finest Holstein dairy herd in America. He also nurtured his land, sculpting the hills, planting the streams, and, nearer his house, creating a series of naturalistic gardens as the understorey to his majestic woodland of white oak (*Quercus alba*), tulip poplar (*Liriodendron tulipifera*), and American beech (*Fagus grandiflora*).

In 1929, H. F. du Pont extended his house in order to display his burgeoning collection of 17th- and 18th-century American interiors, and simultaneously called on his friend, landscape architect Marian Coffin (1876–1957), to redesign the surrounding landscape. Coffin's designs are atypical of Winterthur as a whole, being formal and axial in nature. A terraced Italianate staircase, edged with boxwood, descends from the awkward east façade of the house to a stone terrace and walled reflecting pool, flanked by two garden houses. An old summer house and a lattice-work doorway mark the main axis in an iris garden she designed, now the Peony Garden. Years later, after Winterthur was open to the public, Coffin defined the formal outlines for the large circular Sundial Garden which she and du Pont then planted with fragrant April-flowering shrubs and trees.

The garden at Winterthur today is more renowned for its naturalistic sweeps of spring blooms, and its remarkable specimen trees. In early spring the display begins on the March Bank under towering beech and oak with thousands of snowdrops, glory-of the-snow (*Chionodoxa lucilliae*), and *Crocus tomasinianus*. Later, Italian windflowers (*Anemone apennina*) in white and palest blue carpet the ground along with Virginia bluebells (*Mertensia virginica*), spring phlox (*P. divaricata*), and bellworts (*Uvularia grandiflora*). Influenced by the writings of William ROBINSON, du Pont started planting this first naturalistic garden area in 1902 when he was still in his early twenties. The Winterhazel Walk, planted with species of *Corylopsis* and Korean rhododendron (*R. mucronulatum*), is a haze of pale yellow and warm lavender in April. The eight-acre Azalea Wood is in its glory in May, when the native dogwoods (*Cornus florida*) bloom under a canopy of oak and tulip trees with hundreds of pastel-colored Kurume hybrid azaleas and coral *Rhododendron kaempferi*. White trillium, Italian windflowers, Spanish scilla (*Endymion hispanicus*), and ferns carpet the ground. Oak Hill is most memorable in autumn when the

hillside beneath a crimson-leafed sour gum tree (*Nyssa sylvatica*) is covered with lavender colchicums. Groupings of red-fruited tea viburnums (*V. setigerum*) and purple beautyberries (*Callicarpa dichotoma*) echo the colour nearby.

Henry F. du Pont had a deep respect as well as love for his native woodland and rolling meadows. Instead of imposing his designs on them, he celebrated the natural landscape with appropriate plantings. By designating a theme based on a particular plant genus or season of bloom for each garden area, he established restraint in his choice of plants, creating memorable garden pictures.   PD

Wirtz, Jacques

(b. 1924), Flemish garden designer and landscape architect who founded the garden design partnership Wirtz International. He has achieved a very large and diverse body of work, latterly in partnership with his sons Martin and Peter. Most of their work has been in Belgium but they have also designed gardens, for private or corporate clients, in the USA, France, Spain, Portugal, Germany, and the Netherlands. There is no Wirtz formula but there is a very strong identity and the demands of the site are always paramount. He uses hedges with virtuoso skill, either as essential framework or as a way of emphasizing some natural feature. Yew, hornbeam, beech, and box form the repertory of plants on which he has played countless variations. He was a pioneer experimenter in the use of GRASSES not merely as incidental ornaments in the flower garden but as vital structure. He has used them in sweeping raised banks to make a soft contrast for a bold modern office or as an intermediate planting between the sharp formality of an intricate garden and the agricultural landscape that lies beside it. As a profoundly knowledgeable plantsman he has designed countless flower gardens, often in the form of a parterre and usually hidden away from the main axes of the garden to provide a thrilling surprise. Most of his work has been for private clients but good examples of it may be seen at the Carrousel Garden for the Tuileries (Paris), the COGELS PARK (near Antwerp), Canary Wharf (London), and at Alnwick Castle (Northumberland).   PT

PATRICK TAYLOR, *The Wirtz Gardens* (2003).

Wise, Henry

(1653–1738), English nurseryman, garden designer and royal gardener to Queen Anne. In around 1688 he became the sole partner, with George LONDON, in the Brompton Park Nursery which designed gardens, supervised their construction, and supplied plants. This comprehensive service was at this time entirely novel and it proved very successful. After London's death in 1714 Wise left the Brompton Park Nursery but continued to design on his own account. Only a few gardens are known to have been designed by Henry Wise acting alone: WINDSOR CASTLE (Berkshire, 1699 onwards); Bulstrode (Buckinghamshire, possibly with Claude DESGOTS, c.1700); and BLENHEIM PALACE (Oxfordshire, c.1704-15). Among those designed in collaboration with George London are: CHATSWORTH, Chelsea Hospital (London 1688-95), Kensington Park (1689-1712), Stonyhurst (Lancashire, 1696), MELBOURNE, Badminton (Gloucestershire, c.1698), HAMPTON COURT, Staunton Harold (Leicestershire, c.1700), St James's Park (London, 1702), and a garden for Maréchal Tallard (Nottingham, c.1705). Despite Wise's great success—he died a rich man—his work does not seem to have had a strong identity. He seems to have been the complete professional, providing his clients with the smart formal gardens, devoid of any alarming originality, which they desired.   PT

DAVID GREEN, *Gardener to Queen Anne* (1956).

Wisley Garden ⊕

near Woking, Surrey, England, is the ROYAL HORTICULTURAL SOCIETY's largest garden—97 hectares/240 acres of display gardens, glasshouses, plant centre, and educational and research facilities. It has its origins in a private wild garden owned by G. F. Wilson, a friend of Gertrude JEKYLL's who described his garden in her *Wood and Garden* (1904)—'a garden which I take to be about the most instructive it is possible to see'. It was given to the RHS in 1903 as 'an Experimental garden . . . [for] the Encouragement and the Improvement of Scientific and Practical Horticulture'. Today it fulfils this role, giving instruction and pleasure to hundreds of thousands of visitors every year. The layout of the gardens has been fairly haphazard after a strong start with a handsome ARTS AND CRAFTS laboratory building put up in 1914 to the designs of Imrie and Angell. It overlooks a great lily pool with a loggia at the other end. Formal gardens were laid out here by Sir Geoffrey JELLICOE and Lanning ROPER. An early, and admirable, feature is a great rock garden (1911) built by James PULHAM & Sons and maintained today in full Edwardian splendour. There are passages of good later design—a flowery and formal Country Garden designed by Penelope HOBHOUSE in 1999 and bold sweeping borders of swathes of herbaceous perennials by Piet Oudolf (b. 1945) in 2000. But it is as an exceptional collection of plants and as a display ground of the best horticultural skills that Wisley has its chief value. Regular trials of different groups of plants, ornamental and edible, are made and displayed in Portsmouth Field. With Wilson's garden as a nucleus the wild garden now has many trees, flowering shrubs, and great expanses of naturalized bulbs—National Collections of crocus and snowdrops are held here and there are admirable displays of narcissi. A National Collection of heathers has over 1,000 species and cultivars, and, more recondite, a collection of rhubarb has 95 species and cultivars.   PT

Witley Court ⊕

Great Witley, near Worcester, Worcestershire, England, is all that remains of a spectacular Victorian garden laid out by W. A. NESFIELD (he called it his 'monster work') in the 1850s. Two great fountain pools survive, a pair of mysteriously orientalist pavilions, and the vague outlines of the great garden—poignant and full of atmosphere. Woodland, with some good flowering shrubs, has been used to display a collection of late 20th-century sculpture—the Jerwood Sculpture Park. Since 1972 the estate has belonged to English Heritage and it is well cared for.   PT

Witwatersrand National Botanical Garden ⊕

near Roodepoort/Krugersdorp, South Africa. The 300-hectare/740-acre garden is part of the National Botanical Institute's network of botanic gardens which grow and conserve the indigenous flora of South Africa. Though the Witwatersrand garden was founded only in 1982, this area has been a tourist beauty spot for over a century. Some 20 hectares/49 acres have been landscaped. Interesting specimens of *Protea*, *Aloe*, stinkwood (*Celtis africana*), grassland flowers, and larger bulbs such as *Clivia* may be found. The natural vegetation of the garden is rocky highveld grassland, and as this name suggests there is much attractive savannah grassland. There are densely wooded streams and kloofs or gorges where riverine forest can be found. The jewel of the garden, however, is the magnificent Witpoortjie waterfall, which makes a spectacular centrepiece for visitors. The garden has an education centre, a restaurant, a small nursery where indigenous plants may be purchased, and a well-stocked visitors' shop. Environmental education programmes for school learners are provided, and the garden has a small herbarium and library. The fauna of the garden includes wild jackal and various small buck. The number of bird species is about 230 and the garden is particularly famous for its breeding black eagles.   DPMcC

Woburn Abbey ⊕

Woburn, Bedfordshire, England, has belonged to the Russell family (dukes of Bedford) since 1547. In the early 17th century Isaac de CAUS made a magnificent GROTTO ornamented with shell- and rockwork and decorated with dolphins, mermaids, and figures of Cupid and Neptune. It remains in fine condition, a very rare and enchanting survival of the Renaissance. A map of 1661 shows formal enclosed gardens west of the house, and early in the 18th century George LONDON made a new approach with a circular pool. Henry Holland (1745-1806) built a polygonal CHINOISERIE dairy in 1788 and laid out pleasure grounds about it. In 1804 Humphry REPTON produced a Red Book of recommendations which, among much else, recommended doing away with Holland's scheme. The first words of the Red Book are 'I must condemn what Mr Holland has done at Woburn, as a Landscape Gardener'. Although this was one of Repton's largest commissions very little of it remains. The chinoiserie dairy may be seen and, at the centre of a maze, a chinoiserie pavilion, designed by Sir William CHAMBERS in 1757 but only built here in 1833. Woburn was a pioneer in opening to the public and providing appropriate entertainments. A safari park was established but there is plenty of room for it, for the whole park has an area of 1,200 hectares/2,964 acres and there are still herds of deer.   PT

Woburn Farm,

Surrey, England, was the FERME ORNÉE laid out by Philip SOUTHCOTE from 1735. It was visited in 1757 by Richard Pococke, the travelling Irish cleric: 'This is the first improvement of the Farm kind, & is esteem'd the most elegant, in England.' Pococke describes walks round meadows, 'a poultry house . . . in the form of a temple' and walks 'adorn'd . . . with spots & beds of flowering shrubs & other flowers'. Thomas WHATELY gave the garden great publicity in his *Observations on Modern Gardening* (1770). He describes an estate of 61 hectares/150 acres of which 14 hectares/35 acres 'are adorned to the highest degree'. Whately admired the variety of this landscape, the drawing in of external views (of Windsor Castle and St Ann's Hill), the scented climbers entwined in hedges lining winding walks, the finely disposed groves and clumps, and even 'the lowing of the herds, the bleating of the sheep, and the tinklings of the bell-wether'. Whately leaves no doubt that this was a skilfully designed landscape of high artistry, not a merely frivolous joke.   PT

Wollerton Old Hall ⊕

near Market Drayton, Shropshire, England, is an excellent example of the continuing vitality of the HIDCOTE/SISSINGHURST tradition in English gardening. The 16th-century house was bought by John and Lesley Jenkins in 1984.

The house overlooks a walled garden to one side and the entrance yard, with glasshouses and nursery, on the other. The walled garden, to the east of the house, is divided into several enclosures and leads at its eastern extremity to the Croft Garden, a wilder place of distinguished trees and shrubs about a winding walk. The whole area is 1.2 hectares/3 acres of which the walled garden, occupying less than half the area, is the most intricately planned and planted. The strength of the design comes from long and logical axes, the sudden revelation of hidden enclosures, and variety of atmosphere. A walk of Irish yews is underplanted with English roses. A rill garden is paved with finely laid stone of distinct ARTS AND CRAFTS character. It leads to a rose-swathed summer house which itself stands at the head of an axis leading along a deep herbaceous border to the concealed four-part well garden with pale and mysterious planting. A calm lime ALLÉE is underplanted with *Viola labradorica* and leads into a late summer garden of quite different character ruled by dramatic shapes and explosive colours of crocosmias, dahlias, ligularias, lobelias, rudbeckias, and salvias. The garden is packed with interest but never seems claustrophobic.   PT

Woodland Cemetery ⊗

Davos Platz, Canton of Graubünden, Switzerland, was built in 1919–21 by the architect Rudolf Gaberel (1882–1963) and is impressive in its unpretentious, simple beauty and charming rural setting. The idea of the *Waldfriedhof* (woodland cemetery) originated in Germany and was taken up in Switzerland in the early 20th century as the old graveyards in many towns and cities became full. It is an extension of the park cemetery, which since the 19th century had pursued the idea of integrating graves in an idealized Arcadian landscape. Among the most remarkable woodland cemeteries in Switzerland, along with Schaffhausen from the 1920s, is that at Davos Platz, built when the old cemetery had become too small. Rather remote from the city, on a small plateau above the river, a larch wood (*Larix decidua*) was chosen as a setting for the new cemetery, which is oval in shape and enclosed by a simple drystone wall. One enters through a gateway of massive ashlar and the large oval burial field is divided by a longitudinal and several lateral axes. The graves are closely spaced, while in the rest of the grounds there is a more open arrangement. Planning and construction emphasized, in contrast to the more usual ostentation of the time, the virtues of modesty and simplicity. The dimensions of gravestones, crosses, and plants are regulated, polished granite and marble

blocks are prohibited, and there are no surrounding walls to the graves, all of which lends the grounds a uniformity of character. Many simple crosses of larch, to be found in numerous Graubünden cemeteries, mark the final resting place of the deceased. Nearby is the Jewish cemetery, opened in 1931, which contains a grave with the ashes and mortal remains of victims from Buchenwald concentration camp.
    UW

woodland garden.

The idea of the woodland garden has its origins in the 19th century when newly introduced flowering shrubs, in particular rhododendrons, were changing British gardens. The fashion grew of planting these, and other Asiatic flowering shrubs like camellias and magnolias, in naturalistic woodland, with occasional clearings to provide greater light for those plants needing it. Thus, the appearance of the garden had much less to do with abstract aesthetics than with the problem of providing a congenial habitat. The gardens that were made in this tradition are among the most attractive and interesting in Britain and remain curiously under-appreciated. The most attractive sites were those that had acid soil, high rainfall, and a benign coastal microclimate, especially those parts affected by the North Atlantic Drift of the Gulf Stream. Thus the south coast of Cornwall, the north-west coast of Wales, and the west coast of Ireland and Scotland were the most favoured areas. There are exceptions to this, such as KNIGHTSHAYES COURT far from the sea in Devon, Holker Hall and Muncaster Castle in Cumbria, and Howick Hall close to the Northumberland coast. The earliest gardens were in Cornwall where Glendurgan was started in the 1830s and TREBAH in 1842, and in Scotland INVEREWE was started in 1862. The explosion of interest in woodland gardening, however, took place in the late 19th and early 20th centuries prompted by the new plants introduced in this time, particularly from China by E. H. WILSON, George FORREST (who introduced more than 300 new species of rhododendron), and Frank Kingdon WARD. J. C. Williams's CAERHAYS CASTLE is one of the great woodland gardens of this period. He was a sponsor of plant collecting expeditions and one of E. H. Wilson's finest plants, *Rhododendron williamsianum*, is named after him.

The style of planting within these gardens is often called naturalistic, but nature does not dispose hundreds of different species in a small area. Furthermore, the plants grown in woodland gardens come from many different countries and would not be found growing together in the wild. Several woodland gardens in Britain take advantage of precipitous sites—

such as BODNANT, CRARAE, Glendurgan, and Trebah. Paths along the upper contours of such gardens give fine views of plantings below. On a flat site whole plants of large size, such as a full-grown *Rhododendron arboreum*, can only be fully displayed in a clearing. A modest degree of wild dishevelment seems best to suit woodland gardens. At Penjerrick (Cornwall), which has a remarkable collection of mature exotics, the density of planting is such as to give the impression of exploring a Himalayan jungle. The woodland garden is not a fashionable style among modern gardeners. Perhaps the impetus of floods of newly discovered flowering shrubs is needed to stimulate a new generation of woodland gardeners.   PT

Woods, Richard

(1716–93), English landscape designer, surveyor, and architect who from the 1750s designed parks and pleasure grounds for several English estates, with particular concentrations in Yorkshire (in his early career) and Essex (at the end of his career). Woods was a Catholic and worked on the grounds of such Catholics as the Arundells of Wardour Castle (Wiltshire), the Giffards at Chillington (Staffordshire), Edward Weld of Lulworth (Dorset), and Lord Petre at Thorndon Hall (Essex). He practised in a generally BROWNIAN fashion but had a particular fondness for more intimate flowery walks, and almost all his commissions included the laying out of pleasure grounds. One of Woods's most attractive designs was for the Elysium at Audley End (1780) in which Placido Columbani (b. *c.*1744) also had a hand. Here was a flowery pleasure ground with winding walks and a cascade whose layout, if not the original detailed planting, survives. Of his architecture very little survives—there are the ruins of a Gothic temple at Wardour, and a bridge and a windowless pinery at Cannon Hall (Yorkshire). Fiona Cowell remarks that he was especially skilful in laying out grounds of modest size and quotes J. C. LOUDON's opinion of Cusworth (Yorkshire)—'the grounds are everything that could be desired in a moderate space'.   PT

FIONA COWELL, 'Richard Woods (?1716–1793): a preliminary account', Parts I, II, and III, *Garden History*, Vol. 14: No. 2 (1986), Vol. 15: No. 1 (1987), Vol. 15: No. 2 (1987).

Woolmers ⊗

Tasmania, Australia, is one of a select number of fine 19th-century Tasmanian gardens in which the layout and detailing survives largely intact. The site was granted to Thomas Archer in 1817 and the first house, completed by 1819, was almost certainly complemented by a simple cottage garden. Thomas's second son William, an architect, returned from Britain in the 1840s;

at this time, an extension in the newly fashionable Italianate style was added to the existing homestead, although no definitive date has yet been detected. Situated on high ground above the Macquarie river, the garden is enclosed by high walls and hedging, punctuated with impressive gateways. The centrepiece of the garden is the lawn with its pond and cast-iron fountain, encircled by a gravelled carriageway. Two cross-axes, centred about the carriage loop and fountain, give the garden its strong structure. One is formed by the drive and related gateways; the second by paths, porches, and archways linking the house, stables, and orchard. Australian garden historians have noted that the design at Woolmers appears to have been heavily influenced by J. C. LOUDON's *The Suburban Gardener and Villa Companion* (1838). Recently, the National Rose Garden of Australia has been established at Woolmers, displaying examples of the recognized rose groups from historic to modern hybrids. The plan of the garden, alongside the river, is formal and symmetrical, acknowledging the 19th-century context of the surrounding estate.   CMR

World Heritage Site.

Since 1972 UNESCO has designated certain places as World Heritage Sites. The Convention on World Heritage Sites, undertaking to protect them, has been signed by 170 countries. The sites may be natural or man-made; the latter, designated Cultural Sites, are defined as 'a masterpiece of human creative genius' and are chosen with advice from ICOMOS (INTERNATIONAL COUNCIL ON MONUMENTS AND SITES). The World Heritage Fund may grant funding, or give advice, to aid the conservation of a designated site. Many gardens, almost entirely from Old World countries, are World Heritage Sites, with very few surprises among them. They include the palace and gardens of VERSAILLES, the ALHAMBRA and GENERALIFE, MONTICELLO, DROTTNINGHOLM, the DESSAU-WÖRLITZ GARTENREICH, STUDLEY ROYAL, the Villa d'ESTE (Tivoli), and the Palace and Gardens of SCHÖNBRUNN. UNESCO also includes a list of endangered sites which, in 2004, contained no garden sites. In some cases it may be thought that increased publicity is an unwelcome burden, bringing even greater numbers of visitors to sites which are already overvisited. In the case of natural sites the most effective way of ensuring their survival is to exclude visitors totally. But that is the sort of paradox which the philosophy of conservation seems scarcely to have addressed.   PT

Wörlitz. See DESSAU-WÖRLITZ GARTENREICH.

Wrest Park ✬

Silsoe, Bedfordshire, England, has a history going back to the 13th century when the de

The 17th-century garden at **Wrest Park** in an engraving by Johannes Kip from *Britannia Illustrata* (1707).

Grey family (later earls of Kent) came to live here. By the end of the 18th century, in the time of the 11th Earl, there was a great garden here with mazes, parterres, and a large canal cutting across parkland to the south of the house—all this is seen in a KIP engraving in *Britannia Illustrata* (1707). Shortly after this garden was laid out Thomas ARCHER built a dashing domed pavilion (*c.*1710) as an eyecatcher at the southern end of the canal. Between 1758 and 1760 Capability BROWN worked on the landscape. Horace WALPOLE saw the garden in 1764 which he found 'very ugly in the old fashioned manner with high hedges and canals . . . a frightful Temple designed by Mr Archer'. He added that 'Mr Brown has much corrected this garden'. Today there is little in the garden that suggests the work of Brown. Nothing remains of the 17th-century garden except the canal. The house was rebuilt in 1830 in 18th-century French style and gardens to match were laid out—still in place, with bedding schemes. A pattern of formal rides, probably of the early 18th century, is still visible on either side of the canal. A winding stream marks the eastern boundary of the garden, crossed by a CHINOISERIE bridge and with a chinoiserie pavilion on its bank.

PT

Wright, Thomas

(1711–86), English astronomer, architect, and garden designer known as 'the Wizard of Durham'. His only surviving landscape design is Stoke Park (near Bristol, 1740s), a landscape park whose novel feature was a series of formal woodland clearings which Wright called 'saloons', with a seat or an ornamental building, and planted with flowering exotics of which many were bought in 1750–1. George Mason in his *Essay on Design in Gardening* (1795) wrote: 'Stoke gave me more than anything I had seen the idea of what might be done by the internal arrangement of a wood.' It is difficult to attribute many works to Wright with certainty. Among Wright's surviving garden buildings are: the HERMITAGE at Badminton (Gloucestershire, 1747); (possibly) the Shepherd's Monument at Shugborough (Staffordshire, after 1755); (probably) the GROTTO at Hampton Court House (Middlesex, 1750s); (possibly) the MENAGERIE at Horton (Northamptonshire, *c.*1760); Codger Castle (1769) at Rothley (Northumberland); and, possibly, the grotto and park at Forcett Hall (North Yorkshire). In Ireland he possibly designed the Barbican Gate and Lord Limerick's Follies for Tollymore (County Down) although the former was not built until 1777 by which time Wright had left Ireland. An incomplete Gothic/rustic grotto at Belvedere (County Westmeath, *c.*1760) seems to be copied from a Wright engraving. He published two volumes of engravings: *Six Original Designs for Arbours* (1755) and *Six Original Designs of Grottoes* (1758)—the first, and only, volumes of a proposed *Universal Architecture*.

PT

Würzburg Court Garden ⊗

Würzburg, Bavaria, Germany. After the Residenz was completed, it was during the reign of the Würzburg Prince Bishop Adam Friedrich von Seinsheim (from 1755 to 1779) that work began on the Würzburg Court Garden. For this project, Seinsheim appointed the Bohemian garden designer J. P. MAYER as his new court gardener. Mayer skilfully divided the complex area, which rose steeply towards the bastion, into individual, symmetrical, and self-contained garden sections. In this way he created three sections of equal size, the east garden, the south garden, and the nursery. Mayer filled all the sections with clipped fruit trees, hedges, espaliers, tub plants, and pergolas. The east garden was developed as an extension of the central Residenz axis and begins with a large circular parterre. A cascade was originally planned for the terraces that rise behind it to the tip of the bastion, but this was never built. By contrast with the east garden, the south garden is laid out on level ground. Today the eight large yew trees grouped in the centre around a circular pool and clipped into cone form are the distinguishing feature of this garden. The sculptures in the Court Garden are from the workshop of the court sculptor Johann Peter Wagner (1730-1809). The garden is also famous for its elaborate wrought-iron garden gates, made in the workshop of the court locksmith and ornamental metalworker Johann Georg Oegg. For several years now, the flower beds framing the parterres of the east and south gardens have been planted in their original design, and in 2001, in the reconstructed kitchen garden below the orangery, fruit trees were planted which were to be clipped according to historic methods. On the town side, in front of the geometrical garden sections, is a small landscape garden dating from the early 19th century.   JA

Xiequ Yuan

Beijing, China, is situated on the eastern side of Wan Shou Shan hill in YIHE YUAN (the Summer Palace). This walled garden-within-a-garden was started in the latter half of the 18th century on the orders of the Qianlong Emperor; it was originally known as Hui Shan Yuan, since it was planned and built after the style of the JI CHENG garden in Hui Shan, Wuxi, which had pleased Qianlong on his southern tours. It is a garden of pavilions and open walkways centred on an irregular reflecting pool. A large artificial hill laid with Taihu rocks (the rock most highly prized for artificial 'mountains') hides a cascade called Yuqinxia (the Gorge of Jade Music), named after the Stream of Octave in the Wuxi garden. During reconstruction at the end of the 19th century, the Hanyuantang was added on the western shore of the pond and, flanked by two wings of covered corridors connecting the buildings on both sides of the pond, became the garden's main hall. The bridge cutting across the south-east corner of the water is called Zhi yu, meaning Understanding the Fishes, after the anecdote from an ancient work of philosophy in which Zhuangzh, looking down from a bridge, remarks on the happiness of the fish below. 'You are not a fish, so how can you tell?' answers Huizi. 'You are not me,' says the philosopher, 'so can you be sure I don't understand the pleasure of fishes?'   D-HL/MK

Xing Qing Palace,

Shaanxi province, China. The construction of this Tang-dynasty palace began in 714. Covering 135 hectares/333 acres within the city wall in the north-eastern part of Chang'an (Xi'an), where Emperor Xuanzong and his brothers lived before he came to the throne in 713, its main gate differed from the usual layout of most imperial palaces in facing west instead of south. In front of the complex of halls and courts lay an 18-hectare/44-acre oblong lake, the Dragon Pool, surrounded by pavilions and flower gardens. Emperor Xuanzong's famous concubine Yang Guifei once accompanied him to a pavilion in the garden to see the peonies, an occasion described by the Tang poet Li Bai (Li Po) as 'the mutual appreciation of the world's fairest flower and rarest beauty'.   D-HL/MK

Y

Yalta, Nikitsky Botanic Garden of.

See NIKITSKY BOTANIC GARDEN.

Yangzhou

(formerly Yangchow), Jiangsu province, China. Recorded from the Han dynasty (206 BC–AD 220) and long famous in China for its culture and charm, Yangzhou grew prosperous because of both its position on the left bank of the Grand Canal at its junction with the Changjiang (Yangtze river), and its long association with the salt trade. In the Song dynasty it was already well known for its rock gardens, and under the Qing was famous for its peonies. The painter and garden designer Shi Tao made many gardens around the city and today several small but interesting gardens, also laid out under the Qing, remain along the shores of the Narrow West Lake, Shouxi Hu, an elongated serpentine pool crossed by a decorative bridge surmounted by five pavilions, which was built in 1775. Within the city, two interesting but currently somewhat run-down gardens, HE YUAN and GE YUAN, are open to the public.   MK

Yelagin Island ✪

in the estuary of the river Neva, St Petersburg, owes its name to I. P. Yelagin, who built a house there in 1785 with a remarkable formal garden and landscaping beyond. There was an attractive orangery and several conservatories where exotic flowering and fruiting plants were grown, among them pineapples, peaches, and grapes. There was also a winter garden with singing and ornamental birds, statues, and rare plants. In 1817 Yelagin Island was acquired by Alexander I for his mother, the Empress Maria Fedorovna, as a place to stay when visiting the city from PAVLOVSK. The classical palace was built for her by Carlo Rossi (1775–1849), who also built the stables and kitchen, both appearing as impressive park buildings with nothing to indicate their actual function. The windows were all within inner courts, and the semicircular façade of the kitchen has, where windows would have been, niches with statues of ancient gods and heroes. Joseph Busch (1760–

1838), whose father John BUSCH worked for Catherine the Great at TSARSKOE SELO, was engaged to take charge of the gardens and the landscape. The Empress, a keen plantswoman, had a private garden by the palace where many rare plants were grown, and there were orangeries and hothouses. The island was greatly enhanced by Busch's landscaping. What had been a large formal parterre in front of the palace became a meadow. A series of picturesque pools was formed, which solved a drainage problem, and many trees were planted, mainly oak, lime, ash, birch, and sycamore.

PH

yew.

There are several species of the genus *Taxus*, of which the best known for garden purposes is *Taxus baccata*, common yew. All species are evergreen and have a very wide distribution. The western, or Pacific, yew, *T. brevifolia*, is found from southern Alaska to California. *T. chinensis* is found only in China; *T. cuspidata*, the Japanese yew, is also found in Siberia. Common yew is found in North Africa, Central Asia, Scandinavia, and elsewhere in Europe as far west as Spain and the British Isles. It is genetically very variable and many cultivars are known. The Irish yew, *T. baccata* 'Fastigiata', was found in Northern Ireland at Florence Court in County Fermanagh in the late 18th century. It is female and will not breed true when fertilized by a male of the type. All existing examples are descended by vegetative propagation from the Florence Court yew, the original of which still survives. Gold-leafed forms (*T. baccata* Aurea Group) are very variable and have been known since the 17th century, but they were greatly popularized in Britain in the 19th century by William BARRON at ELVASTON CASTLE where by 1849 there were 1,000 plants of it, many of which survive. Prostrate forms, such as the West Felton yew, *T. baccata* 'Dovastoniana', are also known. This striking form was discovered *c.*1776 by John Dovaston and old, wide-spreading specimens have tremendous character.

As a garden plant it is common yew that is most valuable. It is an anciently revered tree, producing a remarkably hard and durable wood. The oldest known wooden implement in the world is a 250,000-year-old yew spear found at Clacton in Essex. One of the most extraordinary wild groups of yews may be seen in England at Kingley Bottom (more politely known as Kingley Vale) in West Sussex—it is said to be the largest yew forest in Europe. The site here goes back to the Bronze Age but the oldest yews are only about 500 years old. As yews go these are mere children—the living remains of a yew in Perthshire, the Fortingall Yew, are reckoned to be between 2,000 and 9,000 years old. Like many old yews, this is found in a churchyard, in this case one with druidic associations. This is not the only yew surviving in a churchyard from pre-Christian times; another exceptional example, at Tandridge church in Surrey, is probably over 2000 years old. No one knows why yews are found in churchyards but the Christian association of immortality and its lustrous evergreen foliage seems most likely—and Romans used yew fronds at burials. Perhaps early Christian churches were built close to ancient yews. Robert Turner (b. 1626), in his *Botanologia* (1664) thought the yew 'attracts and imbibes putrefaction and gross oleaginous vapours' which could be valuable in a graveyard. Sometimes yews were plainly planted in churchyards for purely ornamental purposes. At St Mary's church, Painswick (Gloucestershire), 99 splendidly clipped yews, planted *c.*1792, crowd the churchyard.

The common yew was used in Italian Renaissance gardens in the BOSCO. In French, Dutch, and English gardens of the 17th century it was an essential ingredient of parterres and of PALISSADES. LOUDON's *Encyclopaedia of Gardening* (1822) says it is 'one of the best hedge plants for gardens, topiary work &c. and for this purpose was much employed when the geometric style of gardening prevailed'. He also says that it is 'increased only by seeds'. In the 19th century, particularly in historicizing gardens and in the reinstatement of historic layouts such as those by Achille DUCHÊNE, yew was an essential garden plant. It remained so, for both topiary and hedging, in the architectural gardens of the ARTS AND CRAFTS designers. For hedges and topiary in European gardens it has remained one of the most important plants. As a hedge its lustrous dark colour is both ornamental in its own right as well as providing an unbeatable background for borders. In the past yew hedges were usually propagated from seed, and hedges thus exhibited much variation in colour. Today it is far commoner to have plants raised from cuttings which gives hedges complete uniformity of colour. In recent times yew has been criticized as a hedging plant because it grew too slowly. It does grow more slowly than Leyland cypress (× *Cupressocyparis leylandii*) but in reasonable conditions will easily exceed 30 cm/1 ft per annum. Above all, it makes a hedge of much greater distinction than Leyland cypress which in many gardens quickly outstays its welcome and becomes an embarassment rather than an ornament. Its popularity among nurserymen probably owed more to its ease of propagation than to its intrinsic merits. An intriguing discovery in the late 20th century was the value of taxol, an extract of yew foliage, in the treatment of cancer. See also HEDGE; TOPIARY.   PT

Yihe Yuan ⊛

near Beijing, Hebei province, China, is a walled imperial retreat widely known as the Summer Palace. Over 1,000 years ago the hill in this great garden, while still in its natural state, was called Weng Shan, the Jar Hill, and water from several springs converged on its slopes to form the small Weng Shan lake. During the Ming dynasty (1368–1644), dykes were made for paddy fields and lotus and other aquatic plants were grown in the lake until gradually the well-tended fields came to resemble the countryside south of the Changjiang (Yangtze river) known in China as Jiangnan. In the early 18th century, the Kangxi Emperor of the Qing started to reside here occasionally, and in 1750, the Qianlong Emperor began relandscaping the entire area. The lake was dredged and enlarged, dykes built to divide it, and the hill remade. Two years later, as the garden began to take shape, a new name was chosen for it, Qingyi Yuan or the Garden of Clear Ripples. Weng Shan became Wanshou Shan or Longevity Hill, and the lake Kunming Hu. Construction continued for fourteen years and, of all the pleasure grounds he had built in and around the Western Hills, this became the Emperor's favourite: 'Where in all Yan shan is the mind so free?' he wrote in a poem, 'Peerless sight, the wind and moon over Lake Kunming.'

In 1860 Qingyi Yuan was burnt down by the combined forces of Britain and France and only a few structures in stone and bronze survived. But six years later, the Empress Dowager Cixi diverted funds allocated for establishing a national navy to its rebuilding. After nine years of construction it was finally given the name it still has today, Yihe Yuan, or Garden of Happy Harmony, to honour her wish for the conservation of peace. Despite minor changes to its many buildings, it was virtually a reproduction of the old park and represented a high point in the development of Chinese landscape gardening. In 1900 after the Boxer

rebellion, it was again destroyed by an allied force of eight countries, then renovated once more in 1903. Finally, in 1961, restored yet again, it was listed as a Key National Place of Historic and Cultural Importance.

The estate falls into two parts: to the north, Wanshou Shan hill falls steeply to the irregular ribbon of the narrow 'back lake' behind it; and Kunming lake, which occupies three-quarters of the total 300 hectares/741 acres, stretches out in front of it to the south. None of this, however, is visible from the main entrance in the east, which leads into two large courtyards enclosed by red walls and dominated by Cixi's throne hall. A complex of palace courts, including a large open theatre in a courtyard, stretches from here along the northern shore of the lake towards the hill, but if the visitor avoids these and instead walks past some low mounds to the left, he will find himself, as if by chance, facing the whole horizontal expanse of Kunming lake, with the outlines of the Western Hills lying beyond it like a screen. To the left the seventeen-arch marble bridge of Qianlong draws the eye across the water to the rocky South Lake Island with its Dragon King Temple. To the right a series of buildings, their yellow roof tiles gleaming against the hillside like a waterfall, rise steeply up the slope of Wanshou Shan to the massive octagonal Tower of the Fragrance of the Buddha (where the Emperor and Empress attended religious services) and the Hall of Dispelling the Cloud, which dominate the summit.

Along both sides of this steep axis various smaller buildings build up to the main halls, enhancing by contrast the solemnity, grandeur, and compactness of the central complex. Along the whole length of the shore there runs an unbroken white marble balustrade, curving out into the lake to emphasize the central axis. And behind it, dividing the narrow space before the steep rise of the hill, is the famous covered gallery 1,728 m/5,669 ft long with its 273 bays brilliantly coloured with little vignettes of garden scenes and flowers painted beneath the eaves.

The back lake and hill area embrace all the places to the north of Longevity Hill, a large part of which is taken up by its steep northern slope. Except for a specially designed lamasery (lama monastery) with terraces and a pagoda in Tibetan style in the centre of the slope, the buildings here were sparsely laid out and, since most were reduced to ashes by the foreign invaders, only broken walls and ruins remain to give an idea of what they were like. The so-called back lake is actually a long watercourse winding for about 1,000 m/3,280 ft along the northern foot of the hill. The north bank was piled up with mud dug from this excavation, creating

the expectation of a contrasting expanse of open land beyond. The middle part of the lake is relatively narrow. In Qianlong's time rows of make-believe shops simulating a riverside street in SUZHOU were lined up along the bank and, though these have long since disappeared, the name remains. North-east of this there is the XIEQU YUAN, a garden-within-a-garden, built during the reign of the Qianlong Emperor, in imitation of the JICHANG YUAN in Wuxi.

It is, however, the great expanse of the front lake that makes the garden. Here the monotony of the surface is broken by the flowing lines and pavilion bridges of Xidi, the West Dyke, which divides it into three unequal spaces. The largest of these is the eastern lake, focused on South Lake Island and its seventeen-arch bridge with, beyond, a group of small islands that take their names from the legendary homes of the Immortals: Penglai, Fangzhang, and Yingzhou. The Xidi was built after the fashion of a famous dyke built by the poet Su Dongpo in HANGZHOU, where weeping willows line the water's edge in the manner of waterside villages south of the Changjiang (formerly Yangtze river). Here the panorama of the lake 'borrows' scenes (JIE JING) of the Jade Fountain Hill and the whole sweep of the Western Hills beyond the garden walls.   G-ZW/MK

Yildiz Park ⊛

near Dolmabahce Sarayi, Turkey. Originally known as Ciragan, these gardens, which now cover some 35 hectares/70 acres and lie to the north of Dolmabahce Sarayi, were bestowed by Sultan Murat IV (1574–95) on his daughter Kaya Sultan. Later they reverted to the imperial family. Sultan Ahmet III (1703–30) gave the gardens to his son-in-law, who hosted the Sultan and his court to the flamboyant spring fêtes of the Lale Devi, the Tulip Period. The original private entrance for the Sultan from Ciragan Palace by triumphal arch over the public road still remains. Anna Bowman noted, 'Beneath the boughs of trees in Yildiz interminable stretches of geraniums, begonias and stranger petalled flowers bordered the carriage road. The Turk in his landscape gardening, as in his art, has known how to take the best of that which he has found elsewhere, and has known, also, how best to adapt such foreign features to his own needs' (*In the Palaces of the Sultan*, 1904). The estate is now a public park entered through a Tuscan gateway opposite the Ciragan Palace (now a hotel), with numerous paths exploring an extensive wooded valley on both sides of a steep ravine through which a stream once cascaded over waterfalls into two lakes. The Tent KIOSK with its small lake and island, and the fine Malta Kiosk which offers views to the Bosporus, have been restored by the Turkish Touring and Automobile Club (TTOK) and converted into cafés. The park also houses a mock castellated building built as a porcelain factory. The wooded areas have been allowed to revert to nature.

Two Ottoman residences were built immediately outside the park boundary: Sale Kosku, a grand residence comprising two timber houses brought from the Ukraine and re-erected for Kaiser Wilhelm II to use during his visit to Istanbul to sign a treaty with Sultan Abdul Hamit II in 1895. The 2-hectare/4-acre garden beneath a wide terrace is laid out with a stream leading to a waterfall. The rocks and bridge balustrades are of reinforced concrete with a rustic timber finish, the inspiration of the adjoining garden at Yildiz Sarayi. An elaborate Ottoman glasshouse remains behind the aviary, now converted to offices. Adjacent to but separated by a high wall from the park is Yildiz Sarayi, the Palace of the Star, commenced by Sultan Mahmut II (1808–39) originally in the upper gardens of the park. Sultan Abdul Hamit II (1876–1909) preferred this secluded wooded site to the exposed location of Dolmabahce Sarayi. Here he designed a garden of 4 hectares/10 acres, laying out a canal in the shape of his signature in Arabic, with landing stages for small sailing boats and thickly planted with specimen trees. Beneath the palace is a stone grotto and in the grounds are rustic rose arbours, three rock terraces, and rustic balustrades with tree trunks severed at waist height to serve as ashtrays for the inveterate chain-smoking Sultan. All these are built in reinforced concrete with imitation rustic timber and stone finish. The canal banks are supported by exposed tree roots, also in concrete. An elegant two-storey timber kiosk built alongside the garden wall affords fine views to the Bosporus and the Princes Islands.

LJD

Yi Yuan ⊛

Jiangsu province, China, built between 1862 and 1908 by Gu Wenbin, a high official of the Qing dynasty, is the most recent of the famous old city gardens in SUZHOU. Typically, Gu chose a site which, in its eastern section, had been occupied since the Ming dynasty (1368–1644) by the house of a Minister of Government Affairs, Wu Kuan. The western part, however, was an addition designed by his son Gu Cheng, with several well-known artists of the time, including the painter Ren Bonian, as his advisers.

For historians its chief interest lies in the way these men have borrowed themes and motifs from more ancient Suzhou gardens. Its double *lang* (see CHINA) or covered walkway was

probably inspired by the one at CANGLANGTING; its artificial 'mountain' by the great rockery at HUANXIU VILLA; its rock-bordered lotus pond by the WANGSHI YUAN; its boat-shaped pavilion by the one called Fragrant Land at ZHUOZHENG YUAN. In each case, the borrowing is subtle, more adaptation than direct copy, and the whole garden so skilfully developed in the comparatively small area (*c*.0.6 hectare/1.5 acres) that Yi Yuan is often said to offer the best of all the gardens in the region south of the Changjiang (formerly Yangtze river).

The entrance is by way of a pleasant wide courtyard with high, whitewashed walls and a floor worked in a flower design of soft pink and grey pebbles. The garden divides roughly into an eastern part, composed mostly of buildings and small courtyards intricately related, and a western part arranged around the hills and ponds. This also is divided into two parts hidden from each other by the steep and rocky outlines of a large artificial hill (*jiashan*) built up with hidden grottoes below and slivers of stalagmites standing, like stone needle points, among the Taihu rocks (the rock most highly prized for artificial 'mountains') and shrubs above. The whole makes what the Chinese call a fine 'facing view' for the Lotus Root Fragrance Pavilion on the opposite bank. From here, the pond runs westwards through a steep bottleneck, then expands to the north-west, where the Painting Boat Studio, a double-storeyed *fang* (see CHINA) or stone-boat pavilion, looms over the water. Still further west lies another small enclosure of the type the Chinese call a garden-within-a-garden, separated from the rest by a *lang* (see CHINA) and containing within it the Hall of Pure Dew.

C-ZC/MK

Yoch, Florence

(1890–1972), American designer of gardens and film sets practising in California. Influenced by English ARTS AND CRAFTS gardens and by her studies of Italian Renaissance gardens she designed strongly architectural gardens, sometimes for prominent Hollywood figures such as David Selznick, the producer of *Gone with the Wind* for which she also designed the sets. In 1925 she established her office in Pasadena in partnership with Lucile Council (d. 1964). In all she designed around 250 gardens of which half were for clients in Pasadena and the rest largely in Monterey and Santa Barbara. A meticulous craftswoman—often designing garden furniture and buildings for her layouts—she also became knowledgeable about plants. The garden at Il Brolino (Santa Barbara) she designed in 1922 for Mary Stewart with terraces, parterre, pool garden, and pergola also took advantage of the grand views of the Santa Ynez mountains.

PT

JAMES Y. YOCH, *Landscaping the American Dream* (1989).

Yuanming Yuan,

Hebei province, China, located in the north-west outskirts of Beijing, is only about 0.5 km/ 0.3 mile east of YIHE YUAN; the ruins of this great imperial park are also known as the Old Summer Palace. It was once joined to the Changchun Yuan, or Garden of Everlasting Spring, and Wanchun Yuan, or Garden of Ten Thousand Springs, and all three were collectively known as Yuan Ming Yuan, or Garden of Perfect Brightness. Regrettably, this masterpiece of classic Chinese gardening was destroyed and looted in October 1860 by the combined forces of Britain and France, but its ruins, landscaped extensively with trees since 1956, draw an increasing number of visitors today.

The predecessor of Yuanming Yuan was a private garden owned by a relative of the Ming emperors. In 1707, the Emperor Kangxi of the Qing dynasty gave it to his fourth son Yin Zhen, who, when he came to the throne as the Emperor Yongzheng in 1723, ordered it to be expanded into an imperial garden and gave inscriptions for the creation of 28 separate scenes. During the reign of the Emperor Qianlong (1736–95), another twelve scenes were added and later Changchun Yuan and Wanchun Yuan, forming a triple layout, were built to the east and south-east. The total area of the three gardens with a circumference together of *c*.10 km/6 miles was 350 hectares/ 864 acres, of which Yuanming Yuan covered 200 hectares/494 acres. The terrain was rather flat with water flowing through it from the Jade Fountain of the Western Hills. The hills and mounds were all man-made and among them the water surfaces, sometimes in large sheets—as the Fu Hai or Sea of Felicity covering some 500 sq. m/1,640 sq. ft in the centre of the three gardens—sometimes irregularly shaped, and sometimes in tortuous brooks or wide canals, altogether occupied over a third of the total area.

Yuanming Yuan is celebrated for the many smaller gardens, each with its own characteristic features, contained within it, so that it has long been called the garden of 10,000 gardens. There were some 150 specific scenes, among them 40 dominant ones celebrated in poems by the Qing emperors and painted by many artists (some of these are now in the Bibliothèque Nationale, Paris). In most of these architecture played an important role. In the south were palace halls for holding court and attending to state affairs, and also buildings for living, some enclosing tiny gardens. Other gardens contained various structures within them, some built in a rustic style and others lavishly. Many of the scenes were modelled after famous sites south of the Changjiang (Yangtze river): Three Deeps Reflecting the Moon, the Autumn Moon over the Quiet Lake, Winding Courtyard with Wind-Blown Lotus, and Sunset Behind the Thunder-Peak Pagoda were all borrowed from HANGZHOU, while SUZHOU was represented by SHIZILIN, and Haining by ANLAN YUAN. A great library, Wenyuange, where the Siku Quanshu or 'Four Vaults of Classics' were once stored, was built after the design of Tianyige in Ningbo, Zhejiang province; temples for worshipping the Buddha and commemorating the sages, halls for attending ceremonies and for stage performances, mountain villages and mock-up shopping streets, and facsimiles of the mythical island homes of the Chinese Immortals were all constructed in Yuanming Yuan. To the north of Changchun Yuan once stood a group of peculiar structures, known as Xiyanglou. Unique in China when they were built for the Qianlong Emperor, they were designed in a Western style under the supervision of Père Giuseppe Castiglione and his Jesuit and other colleagues serving in the imperial court. Ruins and contemporary etchings show that these marble buildings (which included fountains and a water clock), though fundamentally baroque in style, were—as in the glazed tiles which top the walls and roofs—also distinctly Chinese in many of their details.   G-ZW/MK

Yuan ye

is a three-volume treatise of 'Garden Making and Landscape Architecture' (literally Garden Tempering), which was completed in 1634 by JI CHENG (Chi Cheng), a prominent Ming-dynasty landscape designer. It is the most famous and comprehensive work on the subject in Chinese. The first volume has chapters on construction, selecting and investigating sites, placing garden buildings and artificial hills, and on their design and that of lattice-work grids for doors, windows, and ceilings. The second concentrates entirely on balustrades. The third consists of six chapters: on doors and windows, on walls, pavings, the construction of artificial hills, the selection of rocks, and on 'borrowing' views (see JIE JING). The first four and last three chapters give detailed descriptions on both theory and practice, and are considered to contain the essence of Ji Cheng's message.

Evocative descriptions suggest moods and inspire themes for a garden rather than presenting specific or logical arguments, for the author insists that 'though there are principles (in gardening) there are no rules'. For a city garden he advises a secluded site, ideally with a distant view of mountains: 'let the swallows fly in with the wind. The petals of the flowers hover like snowflakes . . . let your feelings dwell among hills and valleys; there you may feel removed from all the unrest of this world.' For Ji Cheng gardening is based on illusion, and what must be captured is the 'life-spirit' both of the particular place and of nature itself—even within the confines of a city.   C-ZC/MK

Yuhua Yuan ⊛

Beijing, China, is a rectangular garden, some 130 m × 90 m/426 ft × 295 ft, covering c.3 hectares/7 acres within the dusty red walls of the imperial city and immediately south of its northern gate. In fact the garden is the last in the vast processional sequence of gates, halls, and courtyards that lead north from Tiananmen Square to Coal Hill (JING SHAN). Coming after the culmination of this sequence of the triple halls of state on their marble terraces, it is a deliberate anticlimax, a place where the emperors could relax after the awesome formalities of court ceremony. On first acquaintance, however, it suggests only a very controlled loosening of decorum since the plan is meticulously symmetrical, the trees in rows, the flowers (peonies in late spring, chrysanthemums in autumn) in beds, and the ground paved: but within this formal framework there are many unexpected effects.

Originally laid out during the Ming dynasty in the 15th century, the garden now owes much to Qing rebuilding. Its main hall on the central axis is the Qinandian, the Hall of Divine Tranquillity, enclosed in its own red walls and with green bamboos planted nearby. In front of them, a collection of rare and strangely shaped stones has been set up on carved marble plinths. Pebble pictures (luanshi pudi) in traditional designs of flowers, pavilions, and trees—mixed ingenuously with a bicyclist or a 1920s motor car—have been worked into the pathways. Three 'false mountains' (jiashan) of water-modelled stone make it possible to climb up above the pavilions; but it is in its junipers (Juniperus chinensis), planted in the mid 14th century under the Ming, that the magic of the garden lies. The bark of these extraordinary specimens seems to swirl round the knots and contours of their ancient trunks like water in a turbulent stream, while above the enclosing walls and imperial yellow roofs, twisted branches braced with huge wooden props hold up a feathery canopy of needles, swaying freely against the brilliant northern sky.   G-ZW/MK

Yu Yuan ⊛

Shanghai, China. A provincial governor of Sichuan, Pan Yunduan, built this complex garden in his home city of Shanghai between 1559 and 1577 for his father Pan En: its name means 'to please the old parent'. The garden, then one of the most famous in the region south of the Changjiang (Yangtze river), covered c.5 hectares/12 acres, but in 1760 part of it was bought, renovated, and renamed Xi Yuan (the West Garden), since its neighbour NEI YUAN was then named Dong Yuan, or East Garden. From the first half of the 19th century it was used by some craft and merchant guilds, and a market gradually emerged in its south-western part. The large tea house reached by a rather crudely designed zigzag bridge, now outside the garden, is supposed to have inspired the English 'willow-pattern' plate design in the 19th century. It was seriously damaged both in 1855 when the government put down the uprising of the Dagger Society, which used the garden's Dianchun Hall as its headquarters, and again in 1862 when it was used as a military camp during the Taiping rebellion. From 1956 it was restored by a grant from the People's Government; however, although the Nei Yuan was included in it, it occupies today only about half of its original site. In 1982 it was named a Key National Place of Historic and Cultural Significance.

The garden falls into three main parts. In the first, the main feature is a large artificial hill of yellow rock (huangshi), with the elegant Ming-dynasty Cuixiutang, or Hall of the Assemblage of Grace, below it to the east and, on its top, the Wangjiang or Viewing the River Pavilion which 'borrows' views (JIE JING) of the Huang Pu river from beyond the eastern wall. This rocky hill, designed and laid out by Zhang Nanyang, a late Ming-dynasty master of the art of rockery, is the biggest to have survived in China. At the end of the Qing dynasty a realistically modelled dragon's head was added to the undulating wall which surrounds this rockery and three similar heads cap the ends of other walls in the garden. Although these are rather amusing, connoisseurs of gardens find them somewhat jarring—the additions of guild merchants lacking the subtle refinement of China's scholarly tradition. South of the rockery, a waterfall once fell into the deep pool that lies between it and the large and elaborately finished Yanshantang, or Hall of Looking Up to the Mount, with small, sculptured elephants standing on its roof. Other lively figures—of soldiers on horseback and monsters spitting out roof beams—which prance across several of the Yu Yuan's deep roofs, are, like the dragon heads, additions by the guild merchants. In the same idiom but in keeping with scholarly ideals are the very finely crafted brick reliefs let into many of the walls. Two streams flow out of the pond, one north-eastwards back to the rocky hill, the other eastwards, beside a double, zigzag lang (see CHINA) and through a half-moon opening to a pool in front of the Wanhualou, or Storeyed Pavilion of Ten Thousand Flowers. Beyond the next dragon wall, the garden is densely composed with a number of pavilions set on rockeries, and halls, including a sheltered stage with the Dianchun Hall facing it to accommodate the audience. At the less intensely designed southern end of the garden, through a gateway surrounded by two more dragon heads, a magnificent standing rock over 5 m/16 ft high named Exquisite Jade is said to have been earmarked, during the Song dynasty, for the imperial garden GENYUE. Beyond it, enclosed by rocks and walls, lies the Nei Yuan.

D-HL/MK

Zagreb Public Gardens ⊛

Zagreb, Croatia, are known as the 'green horseshoe' or 'Lenuci horseshoe' (Milan Lenuci (1849–1924) was the chief town planner of Zagreb 1882–1912). Seven public gardens and a botanic garden were arranged in the shape of a horseshoe. Public gardens developed gradually from the 1870s until the 1930s as a part of the urban development of Zagreb at the end of the 19th century. The idea of a whole horseshoe appeared first on the urban plan of Zagreb in 1887. This was a grandiose achievement of historicist culture in Croatia, in some way comparable with the RINGSTRAßE in Vienna. Each of the public gardens is rectangular in plan and enclosed with two-storey residential housing. Each is associated with a particular building—Music Pavilion (1891), Academy of Science and Art (1877, designed by Friedrich von Schmidt), Pavilion of Art (1895, designed by Floris Korb and Kalman Giergl), Railway Station (1891, designed by Ferenc Pfaff), Hotel Esplanade (1922, designed by Dionis Sunko), National and University Library (1911, designed by Rudolf Lubynski), and Croatian National Theatre (1894, designed by Hermann Helmer and Ferdinand Fellner). Each garden is distinct in its design with historicist plantings of flowers, shrubs and trees, sculptures, and fountains. The south-western part of the 'green horseshoe' is a botanic garden laid out in geometric style in 1889, designed by Professor Antun Heinz and Viteslav Durhanek.
MOŠ/BBOŠ

MLADEN OBAD ŠĆITAROCI and BOJANA BOJANIĆ OBAD ŠĆITAROCI, 'Zagreb', *Centropa—A Journal of Central European Architecture and Related Arts*, Vol. I: No. 1 (2001).

Zeist, Slot ⊛

Zeist, Utrecht, the Netherlands, originally a medieval castle, acquired by Willem Adriaan Count van Nassau-Odijk, a cousin of William III, in 1677. The old castle was demolished and rebuilding was only completed by 1686. The main building was the last part to be finished, while the gardens had been completed by 1682. Like the house they were probably designed by Jacob ROMAN and consisted of a Dutch classical layout of moated gardens, with in this case the shape of the plan determined by the hippodrome which formed the site of the main parterre. It was surrounded by a bower; on either side of the house were a bowling green and an oval pond surrounded by orangery plants. The layout continued beyond the garden with the main avenue extending over 5 km/3 miles. Near the castle there were orchards and BOSQUETS, while in front there was a further garden for orangery plants. In 1745 the estate was bought by the Amsterdam merchant Cornelis Schellinger, who offered it for the use of the Herrnhutters, an evangelical fraternity. They continued to maintain the layout whilst occupying a Broeder and Zuster plein (Brother and Sister Square) which were added on either side of the main avenue in front of the castle. After several changes of ownership it was acquired in 1830 by Jan Elias Huydecooper who employed J. D. ZOCHER Jr. to modernize the gardens. They were changed to the landscape style, with a new network of paths and vistas, while the canal system was naturalized. From 1960 to 1968 the castle, which is now in council ownership, was restored and at the same time the area immediately surrounding the house reinstated to Zocher's layout, which still contains elements of the 17th-century layout, including a famous garden pavilion.   JW

GERVASE JACKSON-STOPS, 'Slot Zeist, Netherlands-II: the property of the council of Zeist', *Country Life* (2 Sept. 1976).
IRMIN VISSER, *Het Slot te Zeist* (1986).

Zen gardens. See JAPAN.

Zhang Lian

(b. 1587), also known as Zhang Nanyuan, like many other Chinese garden designers and rock artists, studied painting in his youth and his work showed his grasp of the principles of composition in traditional landscape painting. Born in Huating, now Songjiang county, Shanghai, he worked for some 50 years in the late Ming and early Qing dynasties south of the Changjiang (Yangtze river), where many gardens were made under his direction. According to records, his famous works included Fu Shui Shan Zhuang, or Villa of Whisking Water in Changshu, and White Sand with Green Bamboos and Precipice of River Village in Yangzhou, but none still exists. His son ZHANG RAN also became a well-known garden designer.   D-HL/MK

Zhang Nanyang

(b. 1517), known also as Woshi Shanren or the Hermit who Reclines on Rocks, was a master of the art of piling artificial hills and was responsible for the large rockery in YU YUAN, the most famous old garden in his native city of Shanghai, China. As a boy he learned painting from his father (they were not related to the other Zhang family of rock artists) and his rockeries, which characteristically have no earth visible anywhere, owe much to his grasp of the principles of composition in Chinese landscape painting.   C-ZC/MK

Zhang Ran

was a 17th-century Chinese artist, skilled in building artificial hills during the Qing dynasty; he was the son of another well-known garden designer ZHANG LIAN. Responsible for Ying Tai in Nanhai, the Jing Ming Yuan on Jade Spring Hill in the western suburbs of Beijing, and CHANGCHUN YUAN, he worked in the service of the imperial court, Beijing, for more than 30 years, and was famous for his ingenious handling of water surfaces and his natural-looking rockeries.   C-ZC/MK

Zhonghai and Nanhai,

Beijing, China. Among the citizens of Beijing, the names of these two great water gardens in the centre of their city are usually run together as Zhongnanhai, Central (and) Southern Sea. In fact, they are a southerly continuation of the lake and park of BEIHAI, the Northern Sea, which, until Yuan Shikai separated them in 1912 to make his Imperial Palace, were together called the Three Seas. When first dug out in the late 12th and early 13th centuries under the Jin and Yuan dynasties, the lake of Zhonghai was, with Beihai, part of the Taiyi (Pool of Heavenly Water). Nanhai was built later, under the Ming, but today, while Beihai is a public park, only part of Zhongnanhai is open to the public. The total area of both parks is some 100 hectares/247 acres, most of it water. The lake in Zhonghai is long and narrow, running from north to south, its shores densely planted with trees which surround, among others, the Ten Thousand Good Deeds Hall and the Thousand

Z

Sage Hall enclosed in flower-planted courtyards. A mid lake Pavilion of Water and Cloud, reflected in the water to the east, balances the Ziguangge or Tower of Propitious Omens to the west. A dyke, some 100 m/328 ft wide, divides the two lakes, and where this joins the western shore, some 30 courtyards are grouped around the Jurentang or Hall of Living Benevolence, and Huairentang or Hall of Cherishing Benevolence. Huge blue-green pines, cypresses, willows, yulan magnolias (*Magnolia denudata*), and crab apples are planted among them. The lake of Nanhai is roughly circular. On the small island, Ying Tai, lying off its northern shore, the Guangxu Emperor was imprisoned after 1898 by his aunt, the formidable Empress Dowager Cixi, for his attempt at constitutional reform.　G-ZW/MK

Zhuozheng Yuan ⊛

Jiangsu province, China, the largest of the old private gardens in SUZHOU, was first built between 1506 and 1521 during the Ming dynasty by a court examiner, Wang Xianchen, on his retirement. Its name is variously translated as the humble, foolish, or unsuccessful politician's garden. Wen Chengming, one of the Four Great Painters of the Ming, lived here for a time and left a record of it in two albums of poetry and drawings. It is regarded as the 'quintessence of a water-garden'—more than half of it is taken up by a complex arrangement of irregular and interconnecting pools. In fact, it is almost a water labyrinth, with large reflective areas divided by islands in the northern part and long fingers of water winding south under bridges into secret backwaters. Though its buildings are grand and their workmanship fine, it is said to have the atmosphere of the water villages in that prosperous and lovely area south of the Changjiang (Yangtze river) known in China as Jiangnan ('south of the Yangtze'). The most important building is the formal Hall of Distant Fragrance, standing back from the south bank of the lake in the centre of this part of the garden. Northwards, it looks across water to two mounded green islands, embellished with the Pavilion of Fragrant Snow and Glorious Clouds and a little gazebo called Waiting for the Frost.

In the north-west corner, a peninsula planted with flowering shrubs is encircled by roofed and open walkways which zigzag along the edge of the water. In the south-west, a further series leads to a group of secluded rooms and tiny, planted enclosures culminating in the Blue Waves Water Courtyard overlooking a shadowy pool. The south-east section is separated from the water by a hill and an undulating grey wall enclosing courtyards which, with their fine proportions and delicate pebble-patterned floorings, are some of the most appealing in the garden. To the north, on the easternmost shore of the lake, stands the unusual Bamboo Quiet Resort, a square pavilion with a large circular moon door cut in each wall to frame the view.

All these buildings are arranged according to the principles of 'facing views' (*duijing*) and 'borrowing views' (JIE JING) so that, as the visitor moves through the garden, the views compose and recompose themselves around him, sometimes formally and sometimes in the distance as if by chance.

Of the other two sections of the garden, the western is the most interesting: a garden in its own right, it was originally built by a family named Zhang at the end of the Qing dynasty and named Bu Yuan. It, too, is a water garden, forming a happy imitation of the Zhuozheng garden's theme. Its most notable feature is the Thirty-Six Mandarin Duck Hall, a large square building with blue glass panes. Beyond it, the pool winds round and elongates into a rocky channel giving the illusion of a stream disappearing out of sight behind a distant summer house, though in fact it stops at the garden wall.

By comparison, the eastern section is much less densely arranged, with only three or four pavilions and one large hall spread out along paths that meander among irregularly planted trees, low hills, and waterways.

Now classified as a Key National Place of Historical and Cultural Importance, only the middle section of Zhuozheng Yuan corresponds to the original site.　C-ZC/MK

Zocher family,

a German dynasty of gardeners that settled in the Netherlands. J. D. Zocher Sr. (1763–1817) was born in Saxony from a gardener's family that moved to the Netherlands *c*.1780. Here he worked for the landscape gardener and architect J. G. MICHAEL, who also originated in Germany, and in 1788 married his daughter Maria Christina. From 1789 he registered as an independent architect and in 1801 started a nursery in Haarlem. His appointment as the court architect for King Louis Napoleon in 1807 assured work at the royal properties at Huis ten Bosch, Soestdijk, Ameliswerd, Utrecht, and Paviljoen Welgelegen. Despite being discredited after the departure of Louis Napoleon in 1810, his popularity as a designer in the landscape style assured further private commissions, but he died prematurely whilst working on Soestdijk. His nursery and practice were taken over by his son J. D. Zocher Jr. (1791–1870). He had trained as an artist and *c*.1808 won the Prix de Paris, which enabled him to study at the École des Beaux-Arts in Paris. Here he won the Prix de Rome, allowing him to undertake further studies in Rome, returning to the Netherlands *c*.1815. He took over his father's commission at Soestdijk and commenced a successful career in both architecture and garden design, being specifically known for his neoclassical buildings in open landscape-style settings. His later much maligned architecture was celebrated at the time and he was a respected member of influential organizations in the Netherlands, but he was also elected as a member of the RIBA in England in 1838, the year of its inception. His oeuvre included a large number of parks and gardens with country houses as well as garden buildings, general cemeteries in Haarlem, Heemstede, and Alkmaar, and the VONDELPARK, Amsterdam. J. D. Zocher Jr.'s son L. P. Zocher (1820–1915) was largely trained by his father, the two going into partnership in 1849. Louis Paul travelled widely and was a great entrepreneur; from 1875 his tree and bulb nursery at Rozenhagen was managed for him by J. J. Kerbert who continued it till 1918. In his designs L. P. Zocher remained faithful to the landscape style, introducing formal elements in his late work, as in the Vondelpark.　JW

Zorgvliet,

The Hague, Zuid-Holland, the Netherlands, is probably best known as the official residence of the Dutch Prime Minister, the Catshuis. It is named after the original owner, the city adviser and poet Jacob Cats, who bought the estate in 1643. This consisted of a range of dunes, which he began to reclaim and cultivate in 1652, and where he built a single-storey house designed by Lodewijk Huygens. In his estate poem *Ouderdom, buytenleven en hofgedachten, op Sorghvliet* (1656), which idealized country life in the manner of the ancient Roman authors, Cats provides a detailed description of his achievements which he was only to enjoy for four more years. In 1675 the estate was bought by Hans Willem BENTINCK, later superintendent of gardens to King William III, who became Earl of Portland. The house, parterres, bower, and semicircular orangery were positioned eccentrically in the design, which had the Mount of Parnassus and maze as dominant features, surrounded by extensive plantations and orchards. During the late 18th century Willem Bentinck altered the estate in landscape style. After being extended by adding adjoining estates in the first half of the 19th century, the estate was partly sold off in sections for housing, while the remainder was surrounded by a wall in 1920. The Dutch state bought this section in 1955 and in 1961 the house became the official residence of the Prime Minister. Access to the grounds, which were renovated in 2002–3 following designs by Anneke Nauta and Ank Bleeker with planting by Jaqueline van der Kloet, has recently been discontinued.   JW

Vanessa Bezemer-Seller, 'The Bentinck garden at Sorgvliet', in J. D. Hunt, *The Dutch Garden in the Seventeenth Century* (1990).

Zug, Szymon Bogumił

(1733-1807), the most influential and energetic propagandist of the English picturesque garden among the Polish neoclassical architects of the 1770s and 1780s. Born in Merseburg in Saxony, he worked there and visited Italy before coming to Poland in 1756. His first important garden, at Solec on the outskirts of Warsaw, was begun in 1772, for one of the relatives of King Stanisław August Poniatowski; others employed him at Książęce (1776) and Góra (1779). His best suburban garden was probably (for all of them have disappeared) either Powązki, laid out in the mid-1770s for Izabela Czartoryska (see PUŁAWY) or Mokotów ('Mon Coteau') of 1774. The former was based on a series of views radiating from a group of cottages; the latter was a long rectangle divided by a wood which hid from the house the lake with its islands and bridges and (in Zug's words) 'un aspect vraiement champêtre'. In 1778 he began the still well-preserved garden at ARKADIA. In the mid-1780s he contributed an account of the beginnings of Polish picturesque gardening to the French edition (1779-85, vol. v) of HIRSCHFELD's *Théorie de l'art des jardins*.

Zug's town architecture is notable for its classical clarity—notably the cylindrical Lutheran church of 1777 in Warsaw. In his garden buildings, however, he popularized the new eclecticism; he built villas with asymmetrical turrets and imitations of rustic watermills, and experimented not only with 'Gothic' structures but also with the inflation of an architectural detail (such as a capital) into part of a building. The passage of time has made his garden plans hard to evaluate, but Arkadia at least has preserved an evocative melancholy. It is odd that a designer who emphasized so much the importance of true English models should apparently have relied entirely on his patrons' descriptions of them.   DBK

Zürichhorn ⊗

Canton of Zurich, Switzerland, has been continually developed since the middle of the 19th century into one of the liveliest open spaces in Zurich. This park and lakeside promenade, together with the adjacent open spaces of Utoquai to the north and Tiefenbrunnen bathing beach to the south, constitute the liveliest and most popular open-air amenity in the city of Zurich. The varied design is the result of over a 100 years of development. The mouth of the Wildbach river, flowing from the hills into Lake Zurich and shaping the topography here, had long remained untouched, an idyllic landscape with magnificent trees. In 1879-81 the watercourse was altered to prevent flooding and diverted southwards into the lake. In 1887 it was decided to extend the quay from Seefeldquai to the Zürichhorn in order to create a recreational space, and in the following years, to plans by artist-gardeners Otto Froebel (1844-1906) and Evariste Mertens (1846-1907), an extensive

The mount—the green hill of Parnassus—at **Zorgvliet** illustrated in an etching by J. van de Avelen (early 1690s).

park landscape was created enclosed by the existing backdrop of trees. Several major exhibitions on this site have left their traces, such as the duck pond and Fischstube restaurant dating from the Swiss national exhibition of 1939. Garden architects Ernst Baumann (1907–92) and Willi Neukom (1917–83) created a picturesque lakeside walk of large sandstone paving stones and coarse pebbles, offering inviting and informal access to the lake, for the first Swiss garden exhibition in 1959, and it later provided the model for many other landscape architecture projects at home and abroad. Architecture, art, garden, and landscape are interwoven at Zürichhorn into a varied scene with many attractions—the Villa Egli (1902) with its park, the Heidi-Weber-Haus by Le Corbusier, and an elaborate Chinese garden (1993). Masterpieces of the modern visual arts, including the large *Sheep Piece* sculpture by Henry Moore and Jean Tinguely's *Heureka*, are placed as striking discoveries during a stroll along the promenade.   UW

Colour plates

The 18th-century nymphaeum on Roman foundations in the **Jardins de la Fontaine**, Nîmes, France

The water garden at **El Retiro**, Spain

The great water tank and tiled terrace walk at the **Palácio Fronteira**, Portugal

The 19th-century cascade in the woodland garden of the **Mata Nacional de Buçaco**, Portugal

Clouds of purple *Geranium palmatum* and a stone bench on the terrace at **Cothay Manor**, England

Select Bibliography

General

Michel Baridon, *Les Jardins: paysagistes–jardiniers–poètes* (1998).

Marie Luise Gothein, *A History of Garden Art* (1928).

John Harvey, *Mediaeval Gardens* (1981).

Penelope Hobhouse, *The Story of Gardening* (2002).

— and Patrick Taylor (eds.), *The Gardens of Europe* (1990).

John Dixon Hunt, *Greater Perfections: The Practice of Garden History* (2000).

— *The Picturesque Garden in Europe* (2002).

Sir Geoffrey Jellicoe and Susan Jellicoe (consultant eds.), Patrick Goode and Michael Lancaster (executive eds.), *The Oxford Companion to Gardens* (1986).

Monique Mosser and Georges Teyssot, *The History of Garden Design: The Western Tradition from the Renaissance to the Present Day* (1990).

Russell Page, *The Education of a Gardener* (1962).

Simon Schama, *Landscape and Memory* (1995).

Candice A. Shoemaker (ed.), *Chicago Botanic Garden Encyclopedia of Gardens* (2001).

Christopher Thacker, *The History of Gardens* (1979).

British Isles

BIBLIOGRAPHIES

Ray Desmond, *Bibliography of British Gardens* (1984).

— *Dictionary of British and Irish Botanists and Horticulturalists* (1994).

Blanche Henrey, *British Botanical and Horticultural Literature before 1800* (3 vols., 1975).

PERIODICALS

Country Life, appearing weekly since 1897, has published a very large number of articles on gardens and gardening illustrated with photographs. The publishers produce an invaluable cumulative index.

Garden History (the journal of the Garden History Society) was founded in 1972 and appears twice a year. Earlier issues were British in emphasis but later ones are more international.

Studies in the History of Gardens and Designed Landscapes (formerly *Journal of Garden History*) was founded in 1980 and appears quarterly. It publishes scholarly articles with an international emphasis.

Hortus, founded in 1987, appears four times a year. It publishes a wide range of often finely written articles mostly on British subjects.

GENERAL

Mavis Batey and David Lambert, *The English Garden Tour* (1990).

Ann Bermingham, *Landscape and Ideology: The English Rustic Tradition, 1740–1860* (1986).

Tim Buxbaum, *Scottish Garden Buildings* (1989).

E. Cox, *A History of Gardening in Scotland* (1935).

Brent Elliott, *Victorian Gardens* (1986).

John Harris, *The Artist and the Country House* (1979).

Wendy Hitchmough, *Arts and Crafts Gardens* (1997).

James Howley, *The Follies and Garden Buildings of Ireland* (1993).

John Dixon Hunt and Peter Willis (eds.), *The Genius of the Place: The English Landscape Garden 1620–1820* (1975).

David Jacques, *Georgian Gardens* (1983).

Barbara Jones, *Follies & Grottoes* (1953; rev. edn. 1974).

Leonard Knyff and Johannes Kip, *Britannia Illustrata* (1707; repr. 1984).

Stephen Lacey, *Gardens of the National Trust* (1996).

Mark Laird, *The Flowering of the Landscape Garden: English Pleasure Grounds 1720–1800* (1999).

Todd Longstaffe-Gowan, *The London Town Garden 1740–1840* (2001).

Edward Malins, *English Landscaping and Literature 1660–1840* (1966).

— and Patrick Bowe, *Irish Gardens and Demesnes from 1830* (1980).

— and the Knight of Glin, *Lost Demesnes: Irish Landscape Gardening, 1660–1845* (1976).

David Ottewill, *The Edwardian Garden* (1989).

Charles Quest-Ritson, *The English Garden: A Social History* (2001).

Roy Strong, *The Renaissance Garden in England* (1979).

A. A. Tait, *The Landscape Garden in Scotland 1735–1835* (1980).

Judith B. Tankard, *Gardens of the Arts and Crafts Movement* (2004).

Patrick Taylor, *The Gardens of Britain & Ireland* (2003).

Christopher Thacker, *The Genius of Gardening: The History of Gardens in Britain and Ireland* (1994).

John Verney, *The Gardens of Scotland* (n.d., c.1977).

Tom Williamson, *Polite Landscapes: Gardens and Society in Eighteenth-Century England* (1995).

ARCHAEOLOGY

A. E. Brown (ed.), *Garden Archaeology*, Council for British Archaeology Research Report, No. 78 (1991).

David Jaques (ed.), *The Techniques and Uses of Garden Archaeology*, *Journal of Garden History*, Vol. 17: No. 1 (1997).

Christopher Taylor, *The Archaeology of Gardens* (1983).

— 'Medieval ornamental landscapes', *Landscapes*, Vol. 1: No. 1 (2000).

GARDEN DESIGNERS

Charles Bridgeman

Peter Willis, *Charles Bridgeman and the English Landscape Garden* (2nd edn. 2002).

Capability Brown

Dorothy Stroud, *Capability Brown* (1975).

'Lancelot Brown (1716-1783) and the landscape park', special issue of *Garden History*, Vol. 29: No. 1 (2001).

Ian Hamilton Finlay

Yves Abrioux, *Ian Hamilton Finlay, a Visual Primer* (1985; rev. edn. 1994).

Gertrude Jekyll

Richard Bisgrove, *The Gardens of Gertrude Jekyll* (1992).

Jane Brown, *Gardens of a Golden Afternoon: The Story of a Partnership: Edwin Lutyens & Gertrude Jekyll* (1982).

Judith B. Tankard and Martin A. Wood, *Gertrude Jekyll at Munstead Wood* (1996).

Michael Tooley and Primrose Arnander (eds.), *Gertrude Jekyll: Essays on the Life of a Working Amateur* (1995).

William Kent

John Dixon Hunt, *William Kent: Landscape Garden Designer* (1987).

John Claudius Loudon

Melanie Louise Simo, *Loudon and the Landscape: From Country Seat to Metropolis* (1988).

Edwin Lutyens

Jane Brown, *Gardens of a Golden Afternoon: The Story of a Partnership: Edwin Lutyens & Gertrude Jekyll* (1982).

Sir Joseph Paxton

Kate Coquhoun, *A Thing in Disguise: The Visionary Life of Joseph Paxton* (2003).

Alexander Pope

Mavis Batey, *Alexander Pope: The Poet and the Landscape* (1999).

Humphry Repton

Stephen Daniels, *Humphry Repton: Landscape Gardening and the Geography of Georgian England* (1999).

Dorothy Stroud, *Humphry Repton* (1962).

Vita Sackville-West

Jane Brown, *Vita's Other World: A Garden Biography of V. Sackville-West* (1985).

John Tradescant (father and son)

Prudence Leith-Ross, *The John Tradescants: Gardeners to the Rose and Lily Queen* (1984).

Sir John Vanbrugh

Christopher Ridgway and Robert Williams (eds.), *Sir John Vanbrugh and Landscape Architecture in Baroque England 1690–1730* (2000).

INDIVIDUAL GARDENS

Chris Crowder, *The Garden at Levens* (2005).

Ray Desmond, *Kew: The History of the Royal Botanic Gardens* (1995).

The Duchess of Devonshire, *The Garden at Chatsworth* (1999).

Peter Hayden, *Biddulph Grange: A Victorian Garden Rediscovered* (1989).

Todd Longstaffe-Gowan, *The Gardens at Hampton Court Palace* (2005).

Jane Roberts, *Royal Landscape: The Gardens and Parks of Windsor* (1997).

John Martin Robinson, *Temples of Delight: Stowe Landscape Gardens* (1990).

Jessie Sheeler, *Little Sparta: The Garden of Ian Hamilton Finlay* (2003).

Sue Snell, *The Gardens at Hatfield* (2005).

Australia

Guidebook to Australia's Open Garden Scheme Guidebook, published annually.

Australian Garden History: Journal of the Australian Garden History Society (five issues per annum).

GENERAL

Marylyn Abbott, *Gardening with Light and Colour* (1999).

Richard Aitken and Michael Looker, *The Oxford Companion to Australian Gardens* (2002).

Judith Baskin and Trisha Dixon, *Australia's Timeless Gardens* (1996).

Clive Blazey, *The Australian Vegetable Garden* (1999).
—— *The Australian Flower Garden* (2001).

Beatrice Bligh, *Cherish the Earth: The Story of Gardening in Australia* (1973).

Scott Carlin, *Elizabeth Bay House: A History & Guide* (2000).

Victor Crittenden, *Yesterday's Gardens: A History and Bibliography of Australian Gardening Books* (2nd edn. 2002).

Peter Cuffley, *Cottage Gardens in Australia* (1983).

Trisha Dixon and Jennie Churchill, *The Vision of Edna Walling* (1998).

Louise Earwaker and Neil Robertson, *The Open Garden: Australian Gardens and their Gardeners* (2000).

Rodger Elliot and David Jones, *Encyclopaedia of Australian Plants*, vols. i–viii (1990–2002).

Gordon Ford, *The Natural Australian Garden* (1999).

Helen Hewson, *Australia: 300 Years of Botanical Illustration* (1999).

Susan Irvine, *Rose Gardens of Australia* (1997).

Betty Maloney and Jean Walker, *Designing Bush Gardens* (1966).

Howard Tanner, *Converting the Wilderness: The Art of Gardening in Colonial Australia* (1979).
—— and Jane Begg, *The Great Gardens of Australia* (1976).

Paul Thompson, *Australian Planting Design* (2002).

Edna Walling, *Gardens in Australia* (1943).
—— *Cottage and Garden in Australia* (1947).

Peter Watts and Margaret Barrett (eds.), *Historic Gardens of Victoria: A Reconnaissance* (1983).

Georgina Whitehead (ed.), *Planting the Nation* (2001).

Austria

Maria Auböck and Gisa Ruland, *Paradiesträume* (1998).

Eva Berger, *Historische Gärten Österreichs: Garten- und Parkanlagen von der Renaissance bis um 1930* (2003).

Robert R. Bigler, *Schloss Hellbrunn* (1996).

Monika Frenzel, *Gartenkunst in Tirol* (1998).

Géza Hajós, *Romantische Gärten der Aufklärung* (1989).

Sepp Kratochwill, *Wiener Stadtlandschaften* (1999).

Maximilian Ludwigstorff and Gerhard Trumler, *Parks & Gärten in Niederösterreich* (2001).

Österreichische Gesellschaft für historische Gärten/Géza Hajós, *Historische Gärten in Österreich/Vergessene Gesamtkunstwerke* (1993).

Jana Gräfin Revedin, *Gärten in Kärnten* (1996).

Robert Rotenberg, *Landscape and Power in Vienna* (1995).

Belgium

Christine de Groote. *Le Guide de jardins de Belgique* (1995).

Jan Balis, *Hortus Belgicus*, catalogue of an exhibition at the Bibliothèque Albert I (Aug.–Sept. 1962).

Laurence Baudoux-Rousseau and Charles Givry-Deloisin (eds.), *Le Jardin dans les anciens Pay-Bas* (2003).

Jardins Ouverts a.s.b.l./Open Tuinen v.z.w. *Jardins ouverts*. Annually: Belgian Open Gardens Scheme.

René Pechère. *Parcs et jardins de Belgique* (1976).

Jean de Séjournet, *Jardins en Belgique* (1989).

Patrick Taylor, *The Wirtz Gardens* (2003).

Brazil

João Barbosa Rodrigues, *Hortus Fluminensis ou breve noticia sobre as plantas cultivadas no Jardim Botanico do Rio de Janeiro* (Hortus Fluminensis or a Short Essay on the Plants Cultivated in the Botanical Gardens of Rio de Janeiro) (1894).

Hugo Segawa, *Ao amor do público: jardins no Brasil* (For the Love of the Public: Gardens in Brazil) (1996).

Canada

Edwinna von Baeyer, *Rhetoric and Roses: A History of Canadian Gardening* (1984).
—— and Pleasance Crawford (eds.), *Garden Voices: Two Centuries of Canadian Garden Writing* (1995).
——, Mark Laird, and Linda Dicaire, *Rideau Hall Landscape Conservation Study* (1991).

Francis H. Cabot, *A Greater Perfection* (2001).

Marjorie Harris, *Botanica North America: The Illustrated Guide to our Native Plants, their Botany, History, and the Way They Have Shaped our World* (2003).

Carol Martin, *A History of Canadian Gardening* (2000).

Denmark

Sven Hansen, *Eksempler på landskabs- og havekunst* (Examples of Landscape and Garden Architecture) (1980).

Steen Høyer and Sven-Ingvar Andersson, *C. Th. Sørensen—Landscape Modernist* (2001).

Annemarie Lund, *Danmarks Havekunst III* (2002).
—— *Guide to Danish Landscape Architecture 1000–2003* (new edn. 2003).

Carsten Thau and Kjell Vindum, *Arne Jacobsen* (2001).

Egypt

Jean-Claude Hugonot, *Le Jardin dans l'Égypte ancienne* (1989).

Lise Manniche, *An Ancient Egyptian Herbal* (1989).

Alix Wilkinson, *The Garden in Ancient Egypt* (1998).

Finland

C. J. Gardberg and Kaj Dahl, *Finlands herrgårdar* (1989).

Maunu Häyrynen, *Maisemapuistosta reformipuistoon. Helsingin kaupunkipuistot ja puistopolitiikka 1880-luvulta 1930-luvulle* (From Scenic Parks to Reform Parks: Public Parks and the Park Policy of Helsinki from the 1880s to the 1930s) (1994).

— et al. (eds.), *Hortus Fennicus, Suomen puutarhataide* (2001).

Leena Iisakkila, *Maisema-arkkitehti ajan virrassa* (2000).

Pekka Leskinen, Hanna Keskinen, and Terhi Lohela (eds.), *Suomi Viherrakentaa 2001* (Finnish Landscape Architecture 2001) (2001).

Maire Mattinen et al. (eds.), *Monuments and Sites: Finland* (1999).

Gabriel Nikander (ed.), *Herrgårdar i Finland*, i–ii (1928).

Paul Olsson, *Trädgårdskonst i Finland* (1946).

Maj-Lis Rosenbröijer and Anna-Liisa Ahmavaara, *Pihoja ja puutarhoja* (1968).

Eeva Ruoff, *Vanhoja suomalaisia puutarhoja* (2001).

Pirjo Uino, *Villa Gullrandas trädgårdsarkitektur* (1980).

France

BIBLIOGRAPHY

Ernest de Ganay, *Bibliographie de l'art des jardins* (1989).

GENERAL

William Howard Adams, *The French Garden 1500–1800* (1979).

Marie-Blanche d'Arneville, *Parcs et jardins sous le Premier Empire* (1981).

Michel Baridon, *Les Jardins: paysagistes–jardiniers–poètes* (1998).

Jacques Benoist-Méchin, *L'Homme et ses jardins* (1975).

Michel Conan, *Dictionnaire historique de l'art des jardins* (n.d., c.2000).

Bernd H. Dams and Andrew Zega, *Pleasure Pavilions and Follies in the Gardens of the Ancien Régime* (1995).

Eleanor P. DeLorme, *Garden Pavilions and the 18th Century French Court* (1996).

Dorothée Imbert, *The Modernist Garden in France* (1993).

Jardiner à Paris au temps des rois (2003).

Elizabeth B. MacDougall and F. Hamilton Hazlehurst (eds.), *The French Formal Garden* (1974).

Michel Racine, *Jardins en France* (2004).

Dora Wiebenson, *The Picturesque Garden in France* (1978).

Kenneth Woodbridge, *Princely Gardens: The Origins and Development of the French Formal Style* (1986).

REGIONS AND INDIVIDUAL GARDENS

Béatrice de Andia, Gabrielle Joudiou, and Pierre Wittmer (eds.), *Cent Jardins à Paris et en Île-de-France* (1992).

Valentine de Ganay and Laurent Le Bon, *Courances* (2003).

Nicole Garnier, *André Le Nôtre (1613–1700) et les jardins de Chantilly*, exhibition catalogue (2000).

Dominique Garrigues, *Jardins et jardiniers de Versailles au Grand Siècle* (2001).

Dominique Jarrassé, *L'Art des jardins parisiens* (2002).

Diana Ketcham, *Le Désert de Retz* (1994).

Pierre-André Lablaude, *Les Jardins de Versailles* (1995); trans. as *The Gardens of Versailles* (1995).

Louis XIV, *Manière de montrer les jardins de Versailles* (1992).

Gérard Mabille, Louis Benech, and Stéphane Castelluccio, *Vues des jardins de Marly: le roi jardinier* (1998).

Jean-Marie Pérouse de Monclos, *Vaux-le-Vicomte* (1997).

Marie-Claude Pascal, *Jardins historiques de Dijon* (1996).

Michel Racine, Ernest J. P. Boursier-Mougenot, and Françoise Binet, *The Gardens of Provence and the French Riviera* (1987).

Marie-Françoise Valéry, *Gardens in Normandy* (1995).

Emmanuel de Waresquiel, *Kerdalo, un jardin d'exception* (1995).

INDIVIDUAL GARDEN DESIGNERS

André Le Nôtre

Michael Baridon and Aurélia Rostaing et al., *Le Nôtre, un inconnu illustre* (papers of international conference at Chantilly and Versailles held in 2000) (2003).

Gisèle Caumont, *La Main du jardinier, l'œuvre du graveur—Le Nôtre et les jardins disparus de son temps*, exhibition catalogue (2000).

Ernest de Ganay, *André Le Nostre 1613–1700* (1962).

F. Hamilton Hazlehurst, *Gardens of Illusion; The Genius of André Le Nostre* (1980).

Thierry Mariage, *L'Univers de Le Nostre: les origines de l'aménagment du territoire* (1995); trans. as *The World of André le Nôtre* (1998).

Henri and Achille Duchêne

Claire Frange et al., *Le Style Duchêne: Henri & Achille Duchêne, architectes paysagistes, 1841–1947* (1998).

Dorothée Imbert, *The Modernist Garden in France* (1993).

J. C. N. Forestier

Dorothée Imbert, *The Modernist Garden in France* (1993).

André Mollet

Michel Conan, postface in André Mollet, *Le Jardin de plaisir* (facsimile, 1981).

Hubert Robert

Jean de Cayeux, *Hubert Robin et les jardins* (1987).

Germany

GENERAL

Gartenlust und Stadtbaukunst: Friedrich Ludwig von Sckell 1750–1823, exhibition catalogue from the Bayerischen Akademie der Schönen Kunste (2000).

Gert Gröning, 'Teutonic Myth, Rubble, and Recovery: Landscape Architecture in Germany, 1940–1960', in *The Architecture of Landscape, 1940–1960* (2002).

— and Uwe Schneider, *Die Heide in Park und Garten: Zur Geschichte und Bedeutung des Heidemotivs in der Gartenkultur* (1999).

— — (eds.), *Gartenkultur und nationale Identität: Strategien nationaler und regionaler Identitätsstiftung in der deutschen Gartenkultur* (2001).

— and Joachim Wolschke-Bulmahn, *Grüne Biographien: Biographisches Handbuch zur Landschaftsarchitektur des 20. Jahrhunderts in Deutschland* (1997).

— — *1913–1988: 75 Jahre Bund Deutscher Landschafts-Architekten BDLA* (1988).

— — *DGGL Deutsche Gesellschaft für Gartenkunst und Landschaftspflege e.V.: Ein Rückblick auf 100 Jahre DGGL* (1987).

Institut für Denkmalpflege der DDR (ed.), *Hermann Ludwig Heinrich Fürst von Pückler Muskau, Gartenkunst und Denkmalpflege* (1989).

GARDEN SHOWS

Gustav Allinger, *Das Hohelied von Gartenkunst und Gartenbau: 150 Jahre Gartenbau-Ausstellungen in Deutschland* (1963).

THE LANDSCAPE GARDEN

Adrian von Buttlar, *Der Landschaftsgarten: Gartenkunst des Klassizismus und der Romantik* (1989).

Heidi Ebbinghaus, *Der Landschaftsgarten: Natur und Phantasie in der deutschen Literatur des 18. und frühen 19. Jahrhunderts* (1997).

Siegmar Gerndt, *Idealisierte Natur: Die literarische Kontroverse um den Landschaftsgarten des 18. und frühen 19. Jahrhunderts in Deutschland* (1981).

Marcus Köhler, *Frühe Landschaftsgärten in Rußland und Deutschland: Johann Busch als Mentor eines neuen Stils* (2003).

HISTORIC GARDENS

Adrian von Buttlar and Margita M. Meyer (eds.), *Historische Gärten in Schleswig-Holstein* (1996).

Die Gärten der Herzöge von Württemberg im 18. Jahrhundert. Ausstellungskatalog (1981).

Ursula Gräfin zu Dohna, *Die Gärten Friedrich des Großen und seiner Geschwister* (2000).

Andrea von Dülmen, *Das irdische Paradies: Bürgerliche Gartenkultur der Goethezeit* (1999).

Günther Franz (ed.), *Geschichte des deutschen Gartenbaues* (1984).

Generaldirektion der Stiftung Schlösser and Gärten Potsdam-Sansouci (ed.), *Potsdamer Schlösser und Gärten, Bau- und Gartenkunst vom 17. bis 20. Jahrhundert* (1993).

Stefan Gugenhan, *Die Landesherrlichen Gärten zu Stuttgart im 16. und 17. Jahrhundert* (1997).

Harri Günther (ed.), *Gärten der Goethezeit* (1993).

Sylvia Habermann, *Bayreuther Gartenkunst: Die Gärten der Markgrafen von Kulmbach im 17. und 18. Jahrhundert* (1982).

Wilfried Hansmann, *Gartenkunst der Renaissance und des Barock* (1983).

Dieter Hennebo (ed.), *Gartendenkmalpflege: Grundlagen der Erhaltung historischer Gärten und Grünanlagen* (1985).

—— and Alfred Hoffmann, *Geschichte der deutschen Gartenkunst*, 3 vols. (1962–3).

Frank P. Hesse, Sylvia Borgmann, and Jörg Haspel (eds.), *'Was nützet mir ein schöner Garten . . .': Historische Parks und Gärten in Hamburg* (1990).

Heimatbund Niedersachsen (ed.), *Historische Gärten in Niedersachsen: Katalog zur Landesausstellung* (2000).

Bernd Modrow, *Gartenkunst in Hessen: Historische Gärten und Parkanlagen* (1998).

Helmut-Eberhard Paulus (ed.), *Paradiese der Gartenkunst in Sachsen. Historische Gartenanlagen der Stiftung Thüringer Schlösser und Gärten* (2003).

Michael Rohde and Rainer Schomann (eds.), *Historische Gärten heute: Zum 80. Geburtstag von Professor Dr. Dieter Hennebo* (2003).

Anna-Franziska von Schweinitz, *Die landesherrlichen Gärten in Schaumburg-Lippe von 1647–1918* (2000).

Stiftung Preußische Schlösser and Gärten Berlin-Brandenburg (ed.), *Preußisch Grün: Hofgärtner in Brandenburg-Preußen* (2004).

Vereinigung der Landesdenkmalpfleger in der Bundesrepublik Deutschland und Landesdenkmalamt Berlin (ed.), *Historische Gärten. Eine Standortbestimmung* (2003).

Folkwin Wendland, *Berlins Gärten und Parke. Von der Gründung der Stadt bis zum ausgehenden neunzehnten Jahrhundert* (1979).

Clemens Alexander Wimmer, *Bäume und Sträucher in historischen Gärten: Gehölzverwendung in Geschichte und Denkmalpflege* (2001).

—— and Iris Lauterbach, *Bibliographie der deutschen Gartenbücher 1471–1750* (2003).

GARDEN DESIGNERS

Claudia Gröschel, *Wilhelm Hentze: Ein Gartenkünstler des 19. Jahrhunderts* (dissertation, Universität Basel, 1996).

Marketa Haist, 'Achtundzwanzig Männer brauchen einen neuen Anzug: Die internationalen Gärten auf der Internationalen Gartenbauausstellung 1963 in Hamburg', *Die Gartenkunst*, Vol. 8: No. 2 (1996).

Joachim W. Jacobs, 'Bauhaus und Außenraumplanung', *Die Gartenkunst*, Vol. 6: No. 1 (1994).

Institut für Grünplanung and Gartenarchitektur, Universität Hannover (ed.), *StadtLandschaf–Tagungsbericht 1999* (1999).

Ursula Kellner, *Heinrich Friedrich Wiepking (1891–1973): Leben, Lehre und Werk* (dissertation, Universität Hannover, 1998).

Rüdiger Kirsten, *Die sozialistische Entwicklung der Landschaftsarchitektur in der Deutschen Demokratischen Republik: Ideen, Projekte, Personen. Unter besonderer Berücksichtigung des Wirkens von Reinhold Lingner* (dissertation, Hochschule für Architektur und Bauwesen Weimar, 1989).

Claus Lange, 'Wechselflor in Düsseldorfer Anlagen: Ein Blick auf die Zeit von 1955–1970', *Die Gartenkunst*, Vol. 13: No. 2 (2001).

Peter Joseph Lenné, *Gartenkunst im 19. Jahrhundert. Beiträge zur Lenné-Forschung* (1992).

—— *Volkspark und Arkadien* (1989).

—— *Katalog der Zeichnungen* (1993).

Ursula Poblotzki, *Menschenbilder in der Landespflege 1945–1970* (1992).

Michael Rohde, *Von Muskau bis Konstantinopel: Eduard Petzold ein europäischer Gartenkünstler 1815–1891* (1998).

Anke Schekahn, *Spurensuche 1700–1933: Frauen in der Disziplingeschichte der Freiraum- und Landschaftsplanung* (2000).

Uwe Schneider, *Hermann Muthesius und die Reformdiskussion in der Gartenarchitektur des frühen 20. Jahrhunderts* (2000).

Hans Stimmann (ed.), *Neue Gartenkunst/New Garden Design in Berlin* (2001).

Jörg Wacker, *Georg Potente (1876–1945), Pläne und Zeichnungen* (2003).

Werner Wenzel, *Die Gärten des Lothar Franz von Schönborn (1655–1729)* (dissertation, Universität Frankfurt a.M., 1970).

Joachim Wolschke-Bulmahn and Peter Fibich, *Vom Sonnenrund zur Beispiellandschaft: Entwicklungslinien der Landschaftsarchitektur in Deutschland, dargestellt am Werk von Georg Pniower (1896–1960)* (2004).

INDIVIDUAL GARDENS

An exhaustive list of literature on garden history (including individual gardens) in Germany, Austria, and Switzerland may be obtained from the homepage of the journal *Die Gartenkunst*; this list was compiled as an annual bibliography by Clemens Alexander Wimmer with help of colleagues and covers the years from 1990 to 2002. **www.die-gartenkunst.de/home/ index_home.html**.

www.garden-cult.de (annotated bibliography of garden articles from historical garden journals).

PLANT HUNTING

Kej Hielscher and Renate Hücking, *Pflanzenjäger: In fernen Welten auf der Suche nach dem Paradies* (2002).

GERMAN GARDEN HISTORICAL PERIODICALS

Die Gartenkunst (two issues per year).

Stadt und Grün (twelve issues per year; not all carry garden historical contributions).

Ancient Greece

Maureen Carroll, *Earthly Paradises. Ancient Gardens in History and Archaeology* (2003).

Maureen Carroll-Spillecke, *Κῆπος. Der antike griechische Garten* (1989).

—— 'The Gardens of Greece from Homeric to Roman Times', *Journal of Garden History*, Vol. 12: No. 2 (1992).

Hungary

BIBLIOGRAPHY

Gábor Alföldy, 'Az 1790 és 1919 közötti magyarországi kertművészet válogatott bibliográfiája' (Selected Bibliography of Hungarian Garden Design Literature from 1790 to 1919). In: János Stirling and János Géczi (eds.), *Régi magyar kertek* (Old Hungarian Gardens) (1999).

GENERAL

Kristóf Fatsar, 'Magyarországi barokk kertművészet a képi források alapján' (Hungarian Baroque Garden Design in the Light of Pictorial Sources) (dissertation, St István University, Budapest, 2001) (manuscript).

Géza Galavics, *Magyarországi angolkertek* (English Gardens in Hungary) (2001).

—— (ed.), *Történeti kertek: Kertművészet és művemlékvédelem* (Historic Gardens in and around Hungary) (2000).

Imre Ormos, *A kerttervezés története és gyakorlata* (The History and Practice of Garden Design) (1955).

Raymund Rapaics, *Magyar kertek* (Hungarian Gardens) (1940).

János Stirling, *Magyar reneszánsz kertművészet a XVI–XVII. században* (Hungarian Renaissance Garden Design in the 16th and 17th Centuries) (1996).

Anna Zádor, 'The English Garden in Hungary', in Nikolaus Pevsner (ed.), *The Picturesque Garden and its Influence outside the British Isles* (1974).

INDIVIDUAL GARDENS

Gábor Alföldy, 'A királyi Várkert az újkorban' ('The Royal Palace Gardens in Modern Times';

Budapest Royal Castle Gardens), *Tanulmányok Budapest Múltjából*, Vol. 29 (2001), 267–92.

—— 'A Royal Phoenix in Hungary' (Budapest Royal Castle Gardens), *Historic Gardens Review*, No. 14 (2005), 16–19.

—— *A dégi Festetics-kastélypark* (Festetics Park at Dég) (in preparation).

—— 'Apponyi Antal hőgyészi kastélyparkja' ('Antal Apponyi's Palace Gardens at Hőgyész'), *Művészettörténeti Értesítő*, Vol. 50: Nos. 1–2 (2001), 57–83.

—— 'A Brief History of Festetics Park at Keszthely', in Gábor Alföldy (ed.), *Principal Gardens of Hungary* (2001).

'Ein Deutsche Landschaftsgarten' ('A German Landscape Garden'; Orczy Gardens), in Johann Leibitzer, *Die Landschaftsgärtnerei* (1836).

'Englischer Landschaftsgarten auf einer Insel' ('An English Landscape Garden on an Island'; Margitsziget), in Johann Leibitzer, *Die Landschaftsgärtnerei* (1836).

Miklós Galántai, 'A vácrátóti botanikus kert története' (The history of the Botanical Garden at Vácrátót), *Dunakanyar*, Vol. 1 (1985), 33–7, Vol. 2 (1985), 33–7.

Géza Galavics, 'Eszterháza 18. századi ábrázolásai' (18th Century Depictions of Eszterháza/Fertőd), *Ars Hungarica*, Vol. 1 (2000), 37–71.

—— 'Pictorial Representation of the Gardens of Hungary—Part I. 17th Century', in *Történeti kertek—kertművészet és műemlékvédelem* (Historic Gardens in and around Hungary; Archbishop's Garden in Bratislava) (2000).

Mária Hornyák, 'A Brunszvik család martonvásári angolkertjének története a források tükrében' (The history of the Brunszvik family's English garden at Martonvásár in the light of the sources), *Művészettörténeti Értesítő*, Vol. 41 (1992), 87–99.

Henry Ernest Milner, *The Art and Practice of Landscape Gardening* [Keszthely] (1890).

Mihály Mőcsényi, 'The Epochs of Eszterháza' [Fertőd], in Gábor Alföldy (ed.), *Principal Gardens of Hungary* (2001).

Jan Mokre, 'Karl Ritter—Ein sächsischer Gärtner in Wien' (Karl Ritter—A Saxon gardener in Vienna; Tata), *Die Gartenkunst*, Vol. 10: No. 2 (1998), 229–42.

Dorothee Nehring, 'Das Stadtwäldchen in Pest' (Városliget City Park), in D. Nehring, *Stadtparkanlagen in der ersten Hälfte des 19. Jahrhunderts* (1979).

Károly Örsi, 'Der Schlosspark von Alcsút (Alcsútdoboz)' (The Country House Park at Alcsút (Alcsútdoboz)), *Die Gartenkunst*, Vol. 1 (1992), 55–67.

—— *Nagycenk–Kastélypark* (1981).

—— 'Graf Esterházys Landschaftsgarten in Tata' (Count Esterházy's landscape garden at Tata), *Garten und Landschaft*, Vol. 7 (1984), 44–8.

Bernhard Petri, 'Der Naturgarten des Herrn Baron Ladislaus Ortzy bei Pest' (Orczy Gardens), *Becker's Taschenbuch für Gartenfreunde* (1797).

—— 'Beschreibung des Naturgartens des Herrn Grafen von Viczay zu Hedervar' [Hédervár (Viczay Park)], *Becker's Taschenbuch für Gartenfreunde* (1798).

Szaniszló Priszter, *A budapesti egyetemi botanikus kert 1771–1971* (The University Botanical Gardens in Budapest 1771–1971) (Budapest, 1971).

József Sisa, 'Die Margaretheninsel in Budapest, als sie noch Palatin-Insel hieß.' ('Margaret Island when it was called Palatine Island'; Margitsziget), *Die Gartenkunst*, Vol. 1 (1992), 67–78.

—— 'Survival of an Urban Park' (Városliget City Park), *Historic Gardens Review* (Summer 1998).

—— 'A csákvári Esterházy-kastély parkja' ('The Esterházy Palace Gardens at Csákvár'), *Művészettörténeti Értesítő*, Vol. 46: Nos. 1–2 (1997), 147–9.

—— *A dégi Festetics-kastély* (The Festetics Mansion at Dég) (2005).

János Stirling, 'Lippai György esztergomi érsek pozsonyi kertje' (Archbishop György Lippay's garden in Pozsony; Archbishop's Garden in Bratislava), in *Magyar reneszánsz kertművészet a XVI–XVII. században* (Hungarian Renaissance Gardens in the 16th–17th Centuries) (1996), 89–102.

Éva Szikra, 'The Restoration of Hungarian Landscape Gardens: Hédervár, Dénesfa, Iszkaszentgyörgy', in *Történeti kertek–Kertművészet és Műemlékvédelem* (Historic Gardens in and around Hungary) (2000).

Indian subcontinent

MUGHAL GARDENS

S. Crowe and S. Haywood, *The Gardens of Mughul India* (1972).

B. Gascoigne, *The Great Moghuls* (1971).

Marg. A Magazine of the Arts, Vol. 26 (1972).

E. B. Moynihan, *Paradise as a Garden in Persia and Mughal India* (1979).

—— (ed.), *The Moonlight Garden* (2000).

A. Petruccioli, *Il giardino come anticipazione della città: storie parallele*, in *Il giardino Islamico: Architettura, natura, paesaggio* (1993).

—— 'Gardens and Urban Design', in *The Mughal Garden: Interpretation, Conservation and Implications. Lahore* (1996).

C. M. Villiers Stuart, *Gardens of the Great Mughals* (1913).

Iran

Sheila S. Blair and Jonathan Bloom, *The Art and Architecture of Islam 1250–1800* (1994).

Sir John Chardin, *Voyages de chevalier Chardon en Perse, et autre lieux de l'Orient* (1711).

Penelope Hobhouse, *Gardens of Persia* (2003).

Mehdi Khansari, M. Reza Moghtader, and Minouch Yavari, *The Persian Garden* (1998).

E. B. MacDougall and R. Ettinghausen (eds.), *The Islamic Garden* (1976).

—— and Donald Wilber, *Persian Gardens and Garden Pavilions* (1962).

Keith McLaghan, *The Neglected Garden: Politics & Ecology of Agriculture in Iran* (1988).

George Michell (ed.), *Architecture of the Islamic World* (1978).

Elizabeth Moynihan, *Paradise as a Garden in Persia and Mughal India* (1979).

A. Upham Pope, *A Survey of Persian Art* (1939).

—— *Persian Architecture* (1965).

Dr Alexander Smith, 'Gardens of Persia', *Journal of Landscape Design* (Nov. 1995).

Sir Percy Sykes, *A History of Persia*, vols. i and ii (1921).

—— *Ten Thousand Miles in Persia* (1902).

Italy

David R. Coffin, *The Villa in the Life of Renaissance Rome* (1979).

—— *Gardens and Gardening in Papal Rome* (1991).

Terry Comito, *The Idea of the Garden in the Renaissance* (1979).

Dumbarton Oaks, *The Italian Garden* (1972).

Penelope Hobhouse, *Plants in Garden History* (1992).

—— *Gardens of Italy* (1998).

—— *The Story of Gardening* (2002).

John Dixon Hunt, *Garden and Grove* (1986).

Sir Geoffrey Jellicoe and Susan Jellicoe (consultant eds.), Patrick Goode and Michael Lancaster (executive eds.), *The Oxford Companion to Gardens* (1986).

Claudia Lazzaro, *The Italian Renaissance Garden* (1990).

Georgina Masson, *Italian Gardens* (1961).

Monique Mosser and Georges Teyssot (eds.), *The History of Garden Design* (1991).

Japan

Francois Berthier, *Reading Zen in the Rocks: The Japanese Dry Landscape Garden* (Jardin du Ryoanji), trans. Graham Parkes (2000).

Josiah Conder, *Landscape Gardening in Japan* (repr. 1981).

Teiji Itoh, *Space and Illusion in the Japanese Garden* (Shakkei to Tsuboniwa), trans. Ralph Friedrich and Masajiro Shimamura (1973).

—— *The Gardens of Japan* (1984).

Marc P. Keane, *Japanese Garden Design* (1996).

Loraine E. Kuck, *The World of the Japanese Garden: From Chinese Origins to Modern Landscape Art* (1980).

Wybe Kuitert, *Themes in the History of Japanese Garden Art* (2002).

Akira Naito, *Katsura: A Princely Retreat*, trans. Charles S. Terry (1997).

Samuel Newsom, *A Thousand Years of Japanese Gardens* (1957).

Gunter Nitschke, *Japanese Gardens: Right Angle and Natural Form (Gartenarchitektur in Japan)*, trans. Karen Williams (1993).

David A. Slawson, *Secret Teachings in the Art of Japanese Gardens: Design Principles, Aesthetic Values* (1987).

Jiro Takei and Marc Keane, *Sakuteiki: Visions of the Japanese Garden: A Modern Translation of Japan's Gardening Classic* (2001).

Toshiro Inaji, *The Garden as Architecture: Form and Spirit in the Gardens of Japan, China, and Korea*, trans. Pamela Virgilio (1998).

Mesopotamia

Stephanie Dalley, 'Nineveh, Babylon and the Hanging Gardens: Cuneiform and Classical Sources reconciled', *Iraq*, Vol. 56 (1994), 45–58.

—— 'More about the Hanging Gardens', in L. Al-Gailani-Werr, J. Curtis, H. Martin, A. McMahon, and J. Reade (eds.), *Of Pots and Plans: Studies in honour of David Oates*, 67–73 (2002).

Netherlands

SPECIAL COLLECTIONS OF WAGENINGEN UR LIBRARY (http://library.wur.nl/speccol/about.html) provides a complete bibliography of garden history and gardens in the Netherlands, as well as an index of nursery catalogues from 1830 onwards (http://library.wur.nl/speccol/nursery_catalogues/index.html).

The database Tuin http://library.wur.nl/tuin/, provides an index to Dutch gardens and landscape architects.

GENERAL

Anna G. Bienfait, *Oude Hollandsche tuinen* 2 vols. (1943).

J. T. P. Bijhouwer, *Nederlandse tuinen en buitenplaatsen* (1943).

—— *Nederlandse Boerenerven* (1943).

Elisabeth Cremers, Fred Kraaij, and Clemens Steenbergen, *Bolwerken als stadparken: Nederlandse stadswandelingen in de 19e en 20e eeuw* (1981).

Gerritjan Deunk, *20th Century Garden and Landscape Architecture in the Netherlands* (2001).

John Dixon Hunt (ed.), *The Anglo-Dutch Garden in the Age of William and Mary/De Gouden Eeuw van de Hollandse Tuinkunst*, a special double issue of *Journal of Garden History*, Vol. 8: Nos. 2–3 (1988).

—— *The Dutch Garden in the Seventeenth Century* (1990).

David Jacques and Arend Jan van der Horst, *The Gardens of William and Mary* (1988).

Erik de Jong, *Nature and Art: Dutch Garden and Landscape Architecture, 1650–1740* (2000).

—— and Marleen Domenicus-van Soest, *Aardse Paradijzen*, 2 vols. (1996, 1999).

Marianne van Lier and Willy Leufgen, *Oasegids: Natuurrijke parken en tuinen* (2003).

Hans Lörzing, *Van Bosplan tot Floriade* (1992).

R. L. P. Mulder-Radetzky, *Tuinen van de Friese Adel* (1992).

Carla S. Oldenburger-Ebbers, Anne Mieke Backer, and Eric Bloc, *Gids voor Nederlandse tuin- en landschapsarchitectuur*, 4 vols. (1995, 1996, 1998, 2000).

Maurits van Rooijen, *De Groene Stad: een historische studie over de groenvoorziening in de Nederlandse stad* (1984).

Vanessa Bezemer Sellers, *Courtly Gardens in Holland 1600-1650: The House of Orange and the Hortus Batavus* (2001).

Kitty de Smit and Arend Jan van Der Horst, *Stadstuinen in Nederland* (undated).

Meto J. Vroom, *Ontwerpen van Nederlandse tuin- en landschapsarchitecten in de periode na 1945/ Environments Designed by Dutch Landscape Architects since 1945* (1992).

—— and J. H. A Meeus, *Learning from Rotterdam: Investigating the Process of Urban Park Design* (1990).

H. W. M. van der Wijck, *De Nederlandse Buitenplaats: aspecten van ontwikkeling, bescherming en herstel* (1982).

Jan Woudstra (ed.), *Garden History*, Vol 30: No. 2; special issue devoted to Netherlands garden history (2002).

Bonica Zijlstra, *Nederlandse tuinarchitectuur 1850–1940: Waard om beschermd te worden!* (1986).

INDIVIDUAL GARDENS

The following contain detailed bibliographies referring to individual gardens. The first up to 1980 and the second from 1980 to 2000.

Erik de Jong, special Dutch issue of the *Journal of Garden History*, Vol. 1: No. 4 (1981).

Carla S. Oldenburger-Ebbers, Anne Mieke Backer, and Eric Bloc, *Gids voor Nederlandse tuin- en landschapsarchitectuur* (vol. 4, 2000).

New Zealand

Matthew Bradbury, *A History of the Garden in New Zealand* (1995).

Denis Friar and Jillian Friar, *Friars' Guide to NZ Gardens Open to Visit* (2002).

David R. Given, *Rare and Endangered Plants in New Zealand* (1981).

Helen Leach, *One Thousand Years of Gardening in New Zealand* (1984).

Philip Simpson, *Dancing Leaves: The Story of New Zealand's Cabbage Tree* (2000).

Poland

Wojciech Bałus, *Krakau zwischen Traditionen und Wegen in die Moderne. Zur Geschichte der Architektur und der öffentlichen Grünanlagen im 19. Jahrhundert* (2003).

Janusz Bogdanowski, *Polskie ogrody ozdobne. Historia i problemy rewaloryzacji* (2000).

Gerard Ciołek, *Ogrody polskie*, ed. Janusz Bogdanowski (1987).

Izabela Czartoryska, *Myśli różne o sposobach zakładania ogrodów* (1805).

Wojciech Fijałkowski, *Wilanów* (1972).

Marek Kwiatkowski, *Szymon Bogumił Zug, architekt polskiego oświecenia* (1971).

Longin Majdecki (ed.), *Rejestr ogrodów polskich*, vols. i–vii (1964-9).

Anna Mitkowska and Marek Siewniak, *Tesaurus sztuki ogrodowej* (1998).

Włodzimierz Piwkowski, *Arkadia Heleny Radziwiłłowej: studium historyczne* (1998).

Wacław Sierakowski, *Postać ogrodów, która do dwóch zmysłów smaku w owocach i powonienia w kwiatach szczególnie ściąga się* (1792).

Małgorzata Szafrańska, *Ogród polski w XIX wieku: antologia tekstów* (1998).

Władysław Tatarkiewicz, *Łazienki warszawskie* (1968).

Portugal

William Beckford, *Diário de William Beckford em Portugal e Espanha* (1983).

Helder Carita and Homem Cardoso, *Portuguese Gardens* (1990).

Maria Inês Ferro, *Queluz: The Palace and Gardens* (1997).

Monte Palace: A Tropical Garden (1999).

Paulo Pereira and José Martins Carneiro, *Pena Palace* (1999).

Ruínas de Conimbriga (1999).

Barbara Segall, *Gardens of Spain and Portugal* (1999).

Romania

GENERAL

Marcus Rica, *Parcuri şi grădini din România* (Parks and Gardens in Romania) (1957).

INDIVIDUAL GARDENS

József Biró, *A bonczhidai Bánffy-kastély* (Bánffy Palace at Bonchida) (1935).

—— *A gernyeszegi Teleki-kastély* (Teleki House at Gernyeszeg, Gorneşti) (1938).

Anna Ecsedy, *Huszadik századi szerzemények a magyarországi kertek barokk szoboranyagában: Schmidt Miksa kertdekorációs tevékenysége a 'gernyeszegi sorozat' kapcsán* (20th-Century Collecting of 18th-Century Statuary in Hungarian Gardens: The Work of Max Schmidt through the 'Series of Gernyeszeg'; Gorneşti) (dissertation, St István University, 2003).

—— 'Wandernde Statuen: Vorstudien zur Geschichte der Gartenplastik in Ungarn und Österreich im 18. Jahrhundert und in der Zeit des Historismus' [Gorneşti], *Acta Historiae Artium* (2005; in preparation).

Albert Fekete, *Kolozsvári kertek* (Gardens of Cluj) (2004).

Narcis Dorin Ion, *Castele, palaste și conace din România* [Săvârșin], vol. i (2002).

Marcus Rica, *Parcuri și grădini din România* (Parks and Gardens in Romania; Bucharest City Parks) (1957).

Ancient Rome

Maureen Carroll, *Earthly Paradises: Ancient Gardens in History and Archaeology* (2003).

Linda Farrar, *Ancient Roman Gardens* (1998).

Katherine L. Gleason, 'Porticus Pompeiana: A New Perspective on the First Public Park of Ancient Rome', *Journal of Garden History*, Vol. 14: No. 1 (1994).

Wilhelmina F. Jashemski, *The Gardens of Pompeii, Herculaneum and the Villas Destroyed by Vesuvius* (1979).

—— 'Roman Gardens in Tunisia: Preliminary Excavations in the House of Bacchus and Ariadne and in the East Temple at Thuburbo Maius', *American Journal of Archaeology*, Vol. 99 (1995).

—— and Eugenia S. P. Ricotti, 'Preliminary Excavations in the Gardens of Hadrian's Villa: The Canopus Area and the Piazza d'Oro', *American Journal of Archaeology*, Vol. 96 (1992).

Elisabeth B. Macdougall (ed.), *Ancient Roman Villa Gardens* (1987).

—— and Wilhelmina F. Jashemski (eds.), *Ancient Roman Gardens* (1981).

F. Villedieu (ed.), *Il giardino dei Cesari* (2001).

Robert J. Zeepvat, 'Roman Gardens in Britain', in Alan E. Brown (ed.), *Garden Archaeology* (1991).

Russia

Peter Hayden, *Russian Parks and Gardens* (2005), also in French, *Jardins de Russie* (2005).

Dimitri Shvidkovsky, *The Empress and the Architect: British Architecture and Gardens at the Court of Catherine the Great* (1996).

Slovakia

GENERAL

Geyza Steinhübel, *Slovenské parky a záhrady* (Slovakian parks and gardens) (1990).

Veronika Vágenknechtová, 'Történeti kertek Szlovákiában' (Historic gardens in the Slovak Republic), in Géza Galavics (ed.), *Történeti kertek: kertművészet és műemlékvédelem* [*Historic Gardens in and around Hungary*] (2000), 59–68, 258–9.

INDIVIDUAL GARDENS

Géza Galavics, *Magyarországi angolkertek* (Landscape Gardens in Hungary; Dolná Krupá, Brunswick Park) (1999).

Martin Kriak, *Prírodný Park v Betliari* [Betliar, Andrássy Park] (1982).

József Sisa, 'Landscape Gardening in Hungary and its English Connections' [Betliar, Andrássy Park], *Acta Historiae Artium*, Vol. 35 (1990-2), 193–206.

—— *Alois Pichl (1782–1856) építész Magyarországon* (Alois Pichl (1782–1856) Architect in Hungary; Topoľčianky) (1989).

Geyza Steinhübel, *Slovenské parky a záhrady* (Slovakian Parks and Gardens; Jasov Monastery Garden) (1990).

—— *Slovenské parky a záhrady* (Slovakian Parks and Gardens; Topoľčianky) (1990).

Jana Šulcová, *Tri kapitoly zo stavebných dejín kaštieľa v Dolnej Krupej* [Dolná Krupá, Brunswick Park] (1996), 161–214.

Ivo Tábor and Radek Pavlačka, *Arboretum Mlyňany* (1992).

Anna Zádor, 'A Hungarian Landscape Garden around 1800' [Hodkovce, Csáky Gardens], *New Hungarian Quarterly* No. 100 (1985), 116–22.

Spain

Carmen Añón Feliú, Monica Luengo Añón, and Ana Luengo Añón, *Jardines artísticos de España* (1995).

Marquesa de Casa Valdes, *Jardines de España* (1973); trans. as *Spanish Gardens* (1987).

Guy Cooper and Gordon Taylor, *Mirrors of Paradise: The Gardens of Fernando Caruncho* (2000).

Consuelo Correcher, *The Gardens of Spain* (1993).

Richard Ettinghausen (ed.), *The Islamic Garden* (1976).

Robert Irwin, *The Alhambra* (2004).

Eduardo Mencos, *Hidden Gardens of Spain* (2004).

A. Fairchild Ruggles, *Gardens, Landscape, and Vision in the Palaces of Islamic Spain* (2000).

Barbara Segall, *Gardens of Spain & Portugal* (1999).

C. N. Villiers-Stuart, *Spanish Gardens: Their History, Types and Features* (1929).

Sweden

Torbjörn Andersson, Tove Jonstoij, and Kjell Lundquist (eds.), *Svensk trädgårdskonst under fyrahundra år* (2000).

Walter Bauer, *Parker, trädgårdar, landskap: förnya och bevara* (1990).

Byggnadsstyrelsen, *Drottningholms lindar-restaurering av träd i slottsmiljö* (1992).

Sten Karling, *Trädgårdskonstens historia i Sverige intill Le Nôtrestilens genombrott* (1931).

Göran Lindahl, 'Nicodemus Tessin d.ä. (1615-1681)', *Svensk Trädgårdskonst under fyrahundra år* (2000).

—— 'Nicodemus Tessin d.y. (1654-1728)', *Svensk Trädgårdskonst under fyrahundra år* (2000).

Catharina Nolin, *Drottningholms slottspark: historik och vägledning* (2000).

Lars Nyberg, 'André Mollet (1600-1665)', *Svensk Trädgårdskonst under fyrahundra år* (2000).

Magnus Olausson, *Den Engelska parken under gustaviansk tid* (1993).

Nils G. Wollin, *Drottningholms lustträdgård och park* (1927).

—— 'Kungsträdgården i Stockholm', *S:t Eriks årsbok* (1923-4).

Switzerland

Gustav Ammann, *Blühende Gärten. Landscape Gardens. Jardins en fleurs* (1955).

Archiv für Schweizer Gartenarchitektur und Landschaftsplanung (ed.), *Vom Landschaftsgarten zur Gartenlandschaft* (1996).

Albert Baumann, *Neues Planen und Gestalten für Haus und Garten* (1953).

BSLA Regionalgruppe Zürich (ed.), *Gute Gärten–Gestaltete Freiräume in der Region Zürich* (1995).

Mercedes Daguerre, *Birkhäuser Architekturführer Schweiz. 20. Jahrhundert* (1997).

Anne Hansen and Men Kräuchi, *Zürichs grüne Inseln . . . unterwegs in 75 Gärten und Parks* (1997).

Albert Hauser, *Bauerngärten in der Schweiz* (1976).

Hans-Rudolf Heyer, *Historische Gärten der Schweiz. Die Entwicklung vom Mittelalter bis zur Gegenwart* (1980).

Dieter Kienast, *Kienast Gärten, Gardens* (1997).

—— *Kienast Vogt–Aussenräume. Open Spaces* (2000).

—— *Kienast Vogt–Parks und Friedhöfe. Parks and Cemeteries* (2002).

Anna Meseure, Martin Tschanz, and Wilfried Wang (eds.), *Architektur im 20. Jahrhundert. Schweiz* (1998).

Urs Schwarz, *Der Naturgarten* (1980).

Johannes Schweizer, *Kirchhof und Friedhof* (1980).

Stichting Kunstboek (ed.), *Switzerland. Landschafts- und Gartenarchitekten und ihre Kreationen. Paysagistes et architectes de jardins et leurs créations* (1999).

Udo Weilacher, *Visionäre Gärten. Die modernen Landschaften von Ernst Cramer* (2001).

—— *Visionary Gardens. Modern Landscapes by Ernst Cramer* (2001).

—— and Peter Wullschleger, *Landschaftsarchitekturführer Schweiz* (2002).

JOURNALS

Anthos. Zeitschrift für Landschaftsarchitektur. Une revue pour le paysage.

Turkey

John Freely, *Istanbul—Blue Guide* (1997).

TBMM Milli Saraylar Daire Baskanligi, *Aynalikavak Kasri* (1994).

—— *Beylerbey Sarayi* (1994).

—— *Dolmabahce Sarayi* (1994).

Nurhan Atasoy, *A Garden for the Sultan: Gardens and Flowers in the Ottoman Culture* (2002).

Ekrem Hakki Ayverdi, 'Album of Tulip Paintings for Ahmet III (c.1725)', *Christies Sale Catalogue* (May 1998).

Pierre Belon, *Les Observations singulaires et choses Mémorables* (1555).

Anna Bowman, *In the Palaces of the Sultan* (1904).

Lord Broughton, *A Journey through Albania to Constantinople* (1813).

Evliya Celebi, *Narrative of Travels in Europe in the 17th Century* (1834–50).

Peter H. Davis, *The Flora of Turkey*, vols. i–ix (1965), vol. x supplement (1988).

Joseph Grelot, *A Late Voyage to Constantinople* (1683).

John Harvey, 'Turkey as a Source of Garden Plants', *Garden History*, Vol. 4: No. 3 (1976).

Hayrettin Karaca, 'The Karaca Arboretum, Turkey', *International Dendrology Society Yearbook* (2002).

Antoine Ignace Melling, *Voyages pittoresque de Constantinople et des rives du Bosphore* (1819).

Aubrey de la Montray, *Travels though Europe, Asia and Africa* (1730).

Julia Pardoe, *The Beauties of the Bosphorus* (1864).

John Ray, *Collection of Curious Travels and Voyages* (1698).

N. Stravroulakis, 'The Flora of Ottoman Gardens', *Mediterranean Garden* (1997–8).

Robert Withers, *A Description of the Grand Signior's Seraglio or Turkish Emperor's Court* (1650).

USA
GENERAL

Charles Birnbaum and Robin Karson (eds.), *Pioneers of American Landscape Design* (2000).

Felice Frankel and Jory Johnson, *Modern Landscape Architecture: Redefining the Garden* (1991).

The Garden Conservancy, *Open Days Directory*. Published yearly.

Mac Griswold and Eleanor Weller, *The Golden Age of American Gardens* (1991).

U. P. Hedrick, *A History of Horticulture in America to 1860* (1950); with addendum by Elizabeth Woodburn (1988).

Mary Zuazua Jenkins, *National Geographic Guide to America's Public Gardens* (1998).

Denise Otis, *Grounds for Pleasure: Four Centuries of the American Garden* (2002).

Elizabeth Barlow Rogers, *Landscape Design: A Cultural and Architectural History* (2001).

Marc Treib, *Modern Landscape Architecture: A Critical Review* (1993).

Peter Walker and Melanie Simo, *Invisible Gardens* (1994).

REGIONS AND INDIVIDUAL GARDENS

Paul Bennett, *Garden Lover's Guide to the Northeast* (1999).

—— *Garden Lover's Guide to the South* (2000).

—— *Garden Lover's Guide to the Midwest* (2000).

Nancy Bernier and Susan Lowry, *The Garden Guide: New York City* (2002).

Jon Emerson and Suzanne Turner, 'A Plan for the Preservation, Management, and Interpretation of Bayou Bend Gardens' (1994).

Alan Emmet, *So Fine a Prospect* (1996).

Eric Homberger, *The Historical Atlas of New York City* (1994).

Kenneth T. Jackson (ed.), *The Encyclopedia of New York City* (1995).

Kathleen McCormick, *Garden Lover's Guide to the West* (2000).

A. J. Meek and Suzanne Turner, *The Gardens of Louisiana: Places of Work and Wonder* (1997).

New York City Parks & Recreation, *A Timeline of New York City Park History* (1986).

Victoria Padilla, *Southern California Gardens: An Illustrated History* (repr. 1994).

Susan Davis Price, *Minnesota Gardens: An Illustrated History* (1995).

Elizabeth Barlow Rogers, *Rebuilding Central Park: A Management and Restoration Plan* (1987).

—— *Landscape Design: A Cultural and Architectural History* (2001).

Barbara Wells Sarudy, *Gardens and Gardening in the Chesapeake 1700–1805* (1998).

N. Phelps Stokes, *The Iconography of Manhattan Island, 1489–1909* (1915–28).

David C. Streatfield, *California Gardens: Creating a New Eden* (1994).

Judith M. D. Taylor and Harry Butterfield, *Tangible Memories: Californians and their Gardens 1800–1850* (2003).

Marc Treib, *The Donnell and Eckbo Gardens: Modern Californian Masterworks* (2005).

INDIVIDUAL GARDEN DESIGNERS
Thomas Church

Thomas Church, *Gardens are for People* (1955).

Marc Treib, *Thomas Church, Landscape Architect: Making a Modern Californian Landscape* (2004).

A. J. Downing

Judith K. Major, *To Live in the New World: A. J. Downing and American Landscape Gardening* (1997).

Garrett Eckbo

Garrett Eckbo, *The Art of Home Landscaping* (1956).

Marc Treib and Dorothée Imbert, *Garrett Eckbo: Modern Landscapes for Living* (1997).

Beatrix Farrand

Jane Brown, *Beatrix: The Gardening Life of Beatrix Jones Farrand 1872–1959* (1995).

Diane Kostial McGuire (ed.), *Beatrix Farrand's Plant Book for Dumbarton Oaks* (1980).

Eleanor McPeck, Diana Balmori, and Diane Kostial McGuire (eds.), *Beatrix Farrand's American Landscapes, her Gardens and Campuses* (1985).

Cynthia Zaitzevsky, *Long Island Landscapes and the Women Who Designed Them* (2004).

Dan Kiley

Dan Kiley and Jane Amidon, *Dan Kiley: The Complete Works of America's Master Landscape Architect* (2003).

Frederick Law Olmsted

C. E. Beveridge and P. Rocheleau, *Frederick Law Olmsted: Designing the American Landscape* (1995).

Lee Hall, *Olmsted's America* (1995).

Martha Schwartz

Tim Richardson (ed.), *The Vanguard Landscapes and Designs of Martha Schwartz* (2004).

Fletcher Steele

Robin Karson, *Fletcher Steele, Landscape Architect* (1989).

Select Index

Picture Acknowledgements

The Publishers are grateful to the following for their permission to reproduce the illustrations. Although every effort has been made to contact copyright holders, it has not been possible in every case and we apologise for any that have been omitted. Should the copyright holders wish to contact us after publication, we would be happy to include an acknowledgement in subsequent reprints.

Colour plates

Between pages 18 and 19
Royal Botanic Gardens, Melbourne
© Patrick Taylor
© Patrick Taylor
© Jerry Harpur

Between pages 34 and 35
© Patrick Taylor
Peter Hayden
© Patrick Taylor
© Patrick Taylor

Between pages 66 and 67
© Jerry Harpur
Top and bottom: © Patrick Taylor
© Patrick Taylor
Peter Hayden

Between pages 82 and 83
©Schutze/Rodemann/Bildarchiv Monheim
© Patrick Taylor
© Patrick Taylor
Andrew Lawson

Between pages 114 and 115
Sofia Brignone, sofiabrignone@wanadoo.fr
    66, rue St Sabin 75011 Paris
Peter Hayden
Peter Hayden
© Patrick Taylor

Between pages 130 and 131
Photo: Gabor Alfoldy
Peter Hayden
© Patrick Taylor
Peter Hayden

Between pages 162 and 163
© Patrick Taylor
Top and bottom: © Patrick Taylor
© Patrick Taylor
Peter Hayden

Between pages 178 and 179
© Jerry Harpur
© Patrick Taylor
Top and bottom: © Patrick Taylor
Top and bottom: © Barbara Opitz/Bildarchiv
    Monheim

Between pages 210 and 211
Dennis Finnin/American Museum of Natural
    History Library
© Patrick Taylor
Courtesy of the Chicago Botanic Garden,
    Photographer: William Biderbost
Monticello/Thomas Jefferson Foundation, Inc

Between pages 226 and 227
Clive Nichols
© Patrick Taylor
Top: Picture 1.9 Fernando Caruncho Studio/
    Photo: Dieter Zoern
Bottom: Picture 7.4 Fernando Caruncho Studio/
    Photo: Laurence Toussaint
Peter Hayden

Between pages 258 and 259
© Patrick Taylor
© Patrick Taylor
Peter Hayden
Top: Sofia Brignone, sofiabrignone@wanadoo.fr
    66, rue St Sabin 75011 Paris
Bottom: © Patrick Taylor

Between pages 274 and 275
© Jerry Harpur
GardenWorld Images/Françoise Davis
© Florian Monheim/Bildarchiv Monheim
Top and bottom: Volčji Potok Arboretum

Between pages 306 and 307
Photo: Carol Betsch
© Luca Tettoni
Axel Griesinger
SANBI- Kirstenbosch Garden (South African
    National Biodiversity Institute)
    Photographer: Jeanette Loedolff

Between pages 322 and 323
All: © Patrick Taylor

Between pages 354 and 355
Peter Hayden
© Patrick Taylor
Courtesy of the Chicago Botanic Garden,
    Photographer: William Biderbost
© Patrick Taylor

Between pages 370 and 371
Peter Hayden
Peter Hayden
© Patrick Taylor
GardenWorld Images/Françoise Davis

Between pages 402 and 403
Andrew Lawson
Top and bottom: © Patrick Taylor
© Patrick Taylor
Andrew Lawson

Between pages 418 and 419
Peter Hayden
Top and bottom: © Patrick Taylor
© Patrick Taylor
GardenWorld Images/Françoise Davis

Between pages 450 and 451
© Jerry Harpur
Top: © Patrick Taylor
Bottom: Sofia Brignone,
    sofiabrignone@wanadoo.fr
    66, rue St Sabin 75011 Paris
Axel Griesinger
© John Feltwell/Garden Matters

Between pages 466 and 467
© Patrick Taylor
© Patrick Taylor
Peter Hayden
Axel Griesinger

Between pages 482 and 483
Schlossverwaltung Hellbrunn, Photographer:
    Foto Sulzer
© Patrick Taylor
© Patrick Taylor
Top: © Patrick Taylor
Bottom: Axel Griesinger

Between pages 498 and 499
© George Waters
Top and bottom: © Patrick Taylor
Peter Hayden
© Marcus Bassler/Bildarchiv Monheim

Between pages 514 and 515
© Jerry Harpur
GardenWorld Images/Françoise Davis
Peter Hayden
© Patrick Taylor

Between pages 530 and 531
All: © Patrick Taylor

Engravings
9   From J. C. Loudon, *An Encyclopedia of Gardening* (London, 1834)
30   © Stephanie Dalley
51   From H. Inigo Triggs, *The Art of Garden Design in Italy* (London, 1906)
59   From A. J. Dezallier d'Argenville, *La Théorie et la pratique du jardinage* (1709)
89   Bibliothèque nationale de France, Paris
99   From *Britannia Illustrata* (1707)
110 From Fleming & Gore, *The English Garden* (Michael Joseph, 1979)
116 From Marie-Claude Pascal's *Jardins Historiques de Dijon* (1996)
133 From Georges Le Rouge, *Détails de nouveaux jardins à la mode (Jardins anglo-chinois)* (Cahier XIII, Paris, 1785)
160 Photo: Gabor Alfoldy
164 From Crispin Van De Passe, *Hortus Floridus* (1615)
167 Bibliothèque nationale de France, Paris
201 From *Britannia Illustrata* (1707)
213 Photo: Gabor Alfoldy
222 From Thomas Hill's *The Gardener's Labyrinth* (1577)
225 Hanover Technical University Library, Haupt Collection
230 *Hypnerotomachia Poliphili*, published by Thames & Hudson, London and New York
261 Photo: Gabor Alfoldy
276 Dumbarton Oaks, Research Library and Collection, Washington, DC
298 Photo: Gabor Alfoldy
300 Shelf mark 457.a.4 (2). By permission of the British Library
303 Dumbarton Oaks, Research Library and Collection, Washington, DC
304 From A. J. Dezallier d'Argenville, *The Theory and Practice of Gardening* (1712)

307 Photo: RMN/ © Gerard Blot
334 From *Britannia Illustrata* (1707)
345 Bibliothèque nationale de France, Paris
353 Photo: Gabor Alfoldy
360 From A. J. Dezallier·d'Argenville, *La Théorie et la pratique du jardinage* (1709)
362 Bibliothèque nationale de France, Paris
367 From A. J. Dezallier d'Argenville's *The Theory and Practice of Gardening* (1712)
369 From Georges Le Rouge, *Détails de nouveaux jardins à la mode (Jardins anglo-chinois)*, Cahier XIII, Paris, 1785
374 Bibliothèque nationale de France, Paris
398 From Georges Le Rouge, *Détails de nouveaux jardins à la mode (Jardins anglo-chinois)*, Cahier XIII, Paris, 1785
403 Photo: K. Woodbridge
413 From Thomas Wright, *Six original designs for arbours* (1755)
416 From Georges Le Rouge, *Détails de nouveaux jardins à la mode (Jardins anglo-chinois)*, Cahier XIII, Paris, 1785
423 From Fleming and Gore, *The English Garden* (Michael Joseph, 1979)
428 Bibliothèque nationale de France, Paris
446 Central Library Celje, Local History Department
471 From Thomas Hill, *The Gardeners Labyrinth* (1577)
493 Bibliothèque nationale de France, Paris
497 Bibliothèque nationale de France, Paris
515 From *Britannia Illustrata* (1707)
519 From *Britannia Illustrata* (1707)
529 Artificial Mount Parnassus, engraved by Johannes Van den Aveele (d.1727) (engraving), Visscher, Nicolas (1618–1709) (after)/Victoria & Albert Museum, London, UK/Bridgeman Art Library

Picture research: Helen Nash/Carrie Hickman

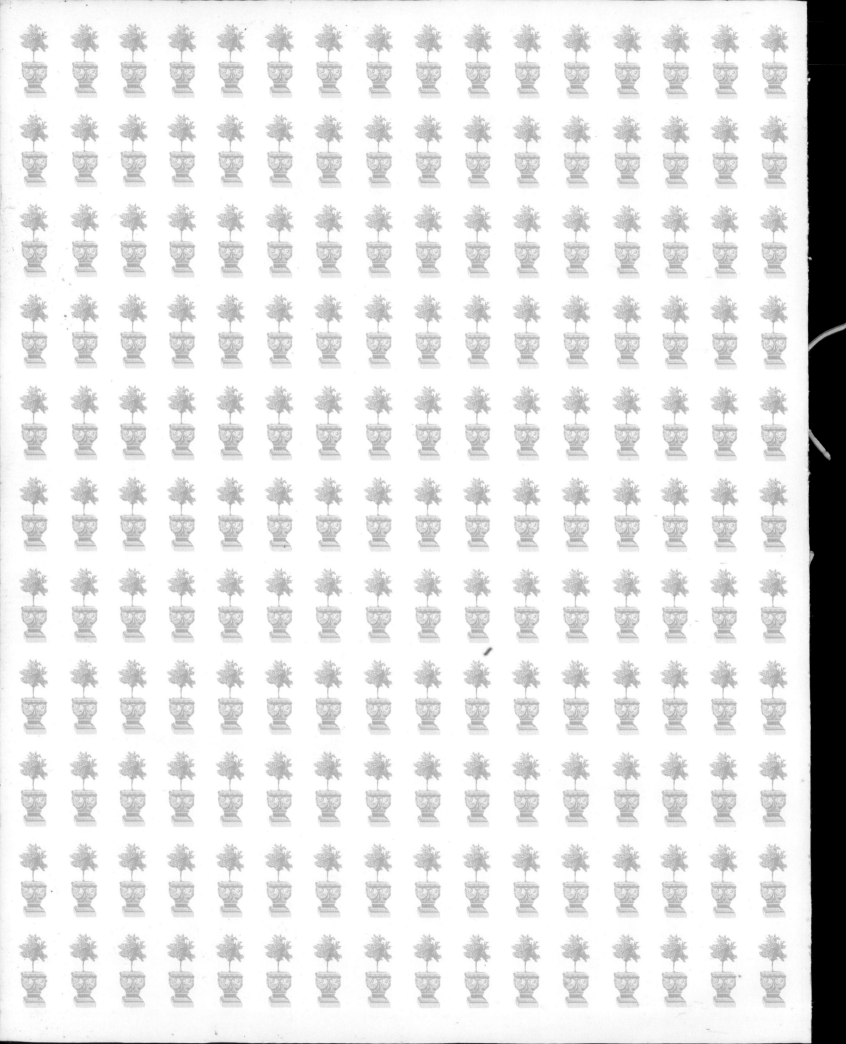